Frommer's®

England 2011

by Darwin Porter & Danforth Prince

WILEY
Wiley Publishing, Inc.

Published by:

WILEY PUBLISHING, INC.

111 River St.

Hoboken, NJ 07030-5774

ISBN 978-0-470-61538-6 (paper); ISBN 978-0-470-90250-9 (ebk); ISBN 978-0-470-64176-7 (ebk); ISBN 978-0-470-40722-6 (ebk)

Editor: Leslie Shen *with* Ian Skinnari

Production Editor: Erin Amick

Cartographer: Andrew Murphy

Photo Editor: Richard Fox

Production by Wiley Indianapolis Composition Services

Front cover photo: Dockey Woods, Ashridge Estate, Buckinghamshire © John Woodworth / Alamy Images.

Back cover photo: White Cliffs of Dover, Kent © Peter de Clercq / Alamy Images.

For information on our other products and services or to obtain technical support, please contact our Customer Care Department within the U.S. at 877/762-2974, outside the U.S. at 317/572-3993 or fax 317/572-4002.

Wiley also publishes its books in a variety of electronic formats. Some content that appears in print may not be available in electronic formats.

Manufactured in the United States of America

5   4   3   2   1

CONTENTS

LIST OF MAPS

HOW TO CONTACT US

In researching this book, we discovered many wonderful places—hotels, restaurants, shops, and more. We're sure you'll find others. Please tell us about them, so we can share the information with your fellow travelers in upcoming editions. If you were disappointed with a recommendation, we'd love to know that, too. Please write to:

Frommer's England 2011
Wiley Publishing, Inc. • 111 River St. • Hoboken, NJ 07030-5774
frommersfeedback@wiley.com

AN ADDITIONAL NOTE

Please be advised that travel information is subject to change at any time—and this is especially true of prices. We therefore suggest that you write or call ahead for confirmation when making your travel plans. The authors, editors, and publisher cannot be held responsible for the experiences of readers while traveling. Your safety is important to us, however, so we encourage you to stay alert and be aware of your surroundings. Keep a close eye on cameras, purses, and wallets, all favorite targets of thieves and pickpockets.

ABOUT THE AUTHORS

As a team of veteran travel writers, **Darwin Porter** and **Danforth Prince** have produced numerous titles for Frommer's which have included, France, Italy the Caribbean, Spain, and Germany.

Porter wrote the first ever Frommer's guide to Paris and the first ever Frommer's guide to a single European country—back then it was called England on $5 a Day. He has lived, on occasion, in London and has traveled England extensively since he left college. In 1982, he was joined by Danforth Prince, who was previously employed by the Paris bureau of the *New York Times*. Today he is the president of Blood Moon Productions and other media-related firms.

Porter is also a film critic, columnist, broadcaster and Hollywood biographer.

FROMMER'S STAR RATINGS, ICONS & ABBREVIATIONS

Every hotel, restaurant, and attraction listing in this guide has been ranked for quality, value, service, amenities, and special features using a **star-rating system.** In country, state, and regional guides, we also rate towns and regions to help you narrow down your choices and budget your time accordingly. Hotels and restaurants are rated on a scale of zero (recommended) to three stars (exceptional). Attractions, shopping, nightlife, towns, and regions are rated according to the following scale: zero stars (recommended), one star (highly recommended), two stars (very highly recommended), and three stars (must-see).

In addition to the star-rating system, we also use seven feature icons that point you to the great deals, in-the-know advice, and unique experiences that separate travelers from tourists. Throughout the book, look for:

special finds—those places only insiders know about

fun facts—details that make travelers more informed and their trips more fun

kids—best bets for kids and advice for the whole family

special moments—those experiences that memories are made of

overrated—places or experiences not worth your time or money

insider tips—great ways to save time and money

great values—where to get the best deals

The following **abbreviations** are used for credit cards:

AE	American Express	DISC	Discover	V	Visa
DC	Diners Club	MC	MasterCard		

TRAVEL RESOURCES AT FROMMERS.COM

Frommer's travel resources don't end with this guide. Frommer's website, **www.frommers. com**, has travel information on more than 4,000 destinations. We update features regularly, giving you access to the most current trip-planning information and the best airfare, lodging, and car-rental bargains. You can also listen to podcasts, connect with other Frommers. com members through our active-reader forums, share your travel photos, read blogs from guidebook editors and fellow travelers, and much more.

THE BEST OF ENGLAND & WALES

Planning a trip to England presents a bewildering array of options. We've scoured the country in search of the best places and experiences; in this chapter, we share our very personal and opinionated selections to help you get started.

THE best TRAVEL EXPERIENCES

- **Going to the Theater:** The torch passed from Shakespeare still burns brightly. London's theater scene is acknowledged as the finest in the world, with two major subsidized companies: the Royal Shakespeare Company, performing at Stratford-upon-Avon and at the Barbican in London; and the Royal National Theatre, on the South Bank in London. Fringe theater offers surprisingly good and often innovative productions staged in venues ranging from church cellars to the upstairs rooms of pubs.
- **Pub-Crawling:** The pursuit of the pint takes on cultural significance in England. Ornate taps fill tankards and mugs in pubs that serve as the social heart of every village and town. Quaint signs for such names as the Red Lion, the White Swan, and the Royal Oak dot the landscape and beckon you in, not only for the pint but also for the conviviality—and perhaps even the entertainment or the food.
- **Motoring through the Cotswolds:** If *driving* involves a determined trip from one place to another, *motoring* is wandering at random. And there's no better place for it than the Cotswolds, less than 161km (100 miles) west of London, its rolling hills and pasturelands peppered with ivy-covered inns and honey-colored stone cottages. See chapter 13.
- **Punting on the Cam:** This is Cantabrigian English for gliding along in a flat-bottom boat with a long pole pushed into the River Cam's shallow bed. You bypass the weeping willows along the banks, watch the strolling students along the graveled walkways, and take in the picture-postcard vistas of green lawns along the water's edge. See p. 531.

- **Touring Stately Homes:** England has hundreds of mansions open to visitors, some centuries old, and we tell you about dozens of them. The homes are often surrounded by beautiful gardens; when the owners got fanciful, they added splashing fountains and miniature pagodas or temples.

- **Shopping for Antiques:** Whatever treasure you're looking for, you can find it in England. We're talking Steiff teddy bears, a blunderbuss, an 1890 tin-plate toy train, an egg cup allegedly used by Queen Victoria, a first-edition English print from 1700, or the definitive Henry Harper grandfather clock. No one polishes up their antiques and curios quite as brightly as English dealers. From auction houses to quaint shops, from flea markets to country fairs, England, particularly Victorian England, is for sale.

- **Cruising on Lake Windermere:** Inspired by the lyric poetry of Wordsworth, you can board a boat at Windermere or Bowness and sail England's most famous lake. You'll see the Lake District's scenery, with its tilled valleys lying in the shadow of forbidding peaks, as it was meant to be viewed—from the water. A great jaunt is the round-trip from Bowness to Ambleside, at the head of the lake, and back around to the village of Lakeside, at the southern tip. See chapter 18.

THE best OF LITERARY ENGLAND

- **Dr. Johnson's House** (London; ✆ 020/7353-3745; www.drjohnsonshouse. org): The backwater at 17 Gough Sq., situated on the north side of Fleet Street, was Samuel Johnson's home from 1748 to 1759. It was here that he worked on his *Rambler* essays and his dictionary, and here that his beloved wife, "Tetty," died in 1752. See p. 196.

- **Keats House** (London; ✆ 020/7332-3868): Most of the poet's brief life was spent in London, where he was born in 1795 in a livery stable run by his father. He moved to Hampstead in 1817 and met his fiancée, Fanny Brawne, there. In this house, he coughed blood into his handkerchief. "That drop of blood is my death warrant," he said. "I must die." He left for Rome in 1820 and died there a year later. See p. 200.

- **Jane Austen Country** (Hampshire): The author of *Pride and Prejudice* and *Sense and Sensibility* wrote of rural delights and a civilized society—set mainly in her beloved Hampshire. In 1809, she moved with her mother to Chawton, 80km (50 miles) south of Bath, where she lived until 1817. Her house is now a museum. Her novels *Persuasion* and *Northanger Abbey* are associated with the city of Bath, where she visited frequently in her youth and lived from 1801 to 1806. In her final year, she moved to 8 College St., in Winchester. She is buried in Winchester Cathedral. See chapter 9.

- **Stratford-upon-Avon** (Warwickshire): The folks who live in touristy Stratford gleefully peddle Shakespeare's literary legacy, including his birthplace, where the son of a glover was born on April 23, 1564. Anne Hathaway's Cottage, in the hamlet of Shottery, is also popular; Shakespeare married Hathaway when he was only 18 years old. See "Stratford-upon-Avon," in chapter 14.

- **Sherwood Forest** (Nottinghamshire, East Midlands): You won't find Errol Flynn in Technicolor-green tights gallivanting through a forest of mighty oaks with his band of merry men. Although most of the forest has been open grassland since the 14th century, it lives on in legend, literature, and lore as the most famous woodland in the world. At the Sherwood Forest Visitor Centre at Edwinstowe, the world of Friar Tuck and Little John lives on. See "Nottinghamshire: Robin Hood Country," in chapter 16.

o **Grasmere** (Cumbria, Lake District): William Wordsworth lived here with his sister, Dorothy, who commented on the "domestic slip of mountain" behind their home, Dove Cottage. The cottage itself is now part of the Wordsworth Museum, displaying manuscripts and memorabilia. The poet also lived for a time at nearby Rydal Mount, just north of Ambleside (one of his descendants still owns the property), where you can see gardens landscaped by the poet. Throughout the region, you'll find the landscapes that inspired this giant of English Romanticism, including the shores of Ullswater, where Wordsworth saw his famous "host of golden daffodils." See "Grasmere," in chapter 18.

o **Haworth** (West Yorkshire): Second only to Stratford-upon-Avon as a major literary pilgrimage site is Haworth, the home of the Brontë Parsonage Museum. Here the famous Brontë sisters lived and spun their web of romance. Emily wrote *Wuthering Heights,* Charlotte wrote *Jane Eyre* and *Villette,* and even Anne wrote two novels, *The Tenant of Wildfell Hall* and *Agnes Grey,* though neither measures up to her sisters' works. See "Haworth: Home of the Brontës," in chapter 19.

THE best OF LEGENDARY ENGLAND

o **Stonehenge** (near Salisbury, Wiltshire): The most celebrated prehistoric monument in Europe, Stonehenge is some 5,000 years old, but its original purpose remains a mystery. The romantic theory that Stonehenge was constructed by the Druids, however, is nonsense: It was completed before the Druids reached Britain in the 3rd century B.C., but the legend persists. See p. 373.

o **Glastonbury Abbey** (Somerset): One of the great abbeys of England and once a center of culture and learning, Glastonbury quickly fell into ruins following the Dissolution of the Monasteries. One story about the abbey says that Jesus came here as a child with Joseph of Arimathea. According to another legend, King Arthur was buried at Glastonbury, the site of the fabled Avalon. See p. 395.

o **Tintagel** (Cornwall): On the windswept Cornish coast, the castle of Tintagel is said to be the birthplace of King Arthur. The castle was actually built much later than the Arthurian legend, around 1150. But who wants to stand in the way of a good story? No one in Cornwall, that's for sure. Tintagel merrily touts the King Arthur legend—in town, you can order an Excaliburger! See "Tintagel Castle: King Arthur's Legendary Lair," in chapter 12.

THE best OF ANCIENT & ROMAN ENGLAND

o **Roman Painted House** (Dover, Kent): Called Britain's "buried Pompeii," this 1,800-year-old structure has exceptionally well-preserved walls and an under-floor heating system used by the Romans. It's best known for its unique Bacchic murals. See p. 291.

- **Avebury** (west of Marlborough, Wiltshire): Although not as famous as Stonehenge, this is one of Europe's leading prehistoric monuments. Located east of Bath, its circle of more than 100 stones—some of them weighing in at 50 tons—is arrayed on an 11-hectare (28-acre) site. See p. 374.

- **Roman Baths** (Bath, Somerset): Dedicated to the goddess Sulis Minerva, the baths were founded in A.D. 75. Among the finest Roman remains in the country, they're still fed by Britain's most famous hot spring. The site of the Temple of Sulis Minerva is excavated and open for viewing. See p. 384.

- **Corinium Museum** (Cirencester, Gloucestershire, the Cotswolds): This museum contains one of the best collections of archaeological remains from the Roman occupation of Britain. You'll see Roman mosaics that have remained in Britain, along with such provincial sculpture as figures of Minerva and Mercury. See p. 465.

- **Hadrian's Wall** (near Hexham, Northumberland): A World Heritage Site, this wall—now in ruins—was ordered built by Hadrian, the Roman emperor, in A.D. 122 to hold back barbarian invasions from the north. Marking the far northern border of the Roman Empire, the wall stretched 118km (73 miles) from Wallsend, or Wall's End, north of Newcastle upon Tyne in the east to Bowness-on-Solway beyond Carlisle in the west. A milecastle (small fort) was added at every mile along the wall. A highlight is Vindolanda, the last of eight successive Roman forts built on a site adjacent to the wall. See "Hexham, Hadrian's Wall & the Pennine Way," in chapter 19.

THE best OF NORMAN & MEDIEVAL ENGLAND

- **Rye** (East Sussex): Near the English Channel, this port—one of England's best preserved towns—was a smuggling center for centuries. Louis Jennings once wrote, "Nothing more recent than a Cavalier's Cloak, Hat, and Ruffles should be seen on the streets of Rye." See "The Ancient Seaport of Rye," in chapter 8.

- **Battle Abbey** (East Sussex): At this site of the famous Battle of Hastings (fought on Oct 14, 1066), the Normans defeated King Harold's English army. William the Conqueror built a great commemorative abbey here; the high altar of its church was erected over the spot where Harold fell in battle. The abbey was destroyed during the Dissolution of the Monasteries (1538–39). Some ruins and buildings remain, about which Tennyson wrote, "O Garden, blossoming out of English blood." See p. 298.

- **Hastings Castle** (East Sussex): Now in ruins, this was the first of the Norman castles erected in England (ca. 1067). The fortress was unfortified in 1216. An audiovisual presentation of the castle's history includes the famous battle of 1066. See p. 298.

- **Dunster Castle** (Somerset): This castle was built on the site of a Norman castle granted to William de Mohun of Normandy by William the Conqueror shortly after his conquest of England. A 13th-century gateway remains from the original fortress. The Luttrell family held possession of the castle and its lands from 1376 until 1976, when the National Trust took it over. See p. 401.

- **Warwick Castle** (Warwickshire): This is the finest medieval castle in England, lying on a cliff overlooking the River Avon. Its most powerful commander in the

1400s was the earl of Warwick, who, during the War of the Roses, was called the "Kingmaker." One of the best collections of medieval armor and weapons in Europe is behind its walls. See p. 499.

o **Fountains Abbey & Studley Royal** (near Ripon, North Yorkshire): These ruins evoke monastic life in medieval England. In 1132, Cistercian monks constructed "a place remote from all the earth." You can explore the ruins as well as the Studley Royal, whose lavish 18th-century landscaping is one of the few surviving examples of a Georgian green garden. See p. 670.

o **Conwy Castle** (North Wales): Edward I ordered this masterpiece built after he subdued the last native prince of Wales. Visitors today can tour the royal apartment where Edward brought his queen, Eleanor. The castle's eight towers command the estuary of the River Conwy. See p. 748.

THE best OF TUDOR & GEORGIAN ENGLAND

o **Hampton Court Palace** (outside London): The most magnificent of the grand residences and royal palaces lining the River Thames west of central London, Hampton Court was built in grand style for Cardinal Wolsey—until Henry VIII snatched it away. Henry added the great hall in 1532, forcing laborers to toil 24 hours a day in shifts. The sheer size of the palace is amazing, and on its grounds is the world's first indoor tennis court. See p. 201.

o **Bath** (Somerset): Much magnificent 18th-century architecture remains exactly as Jane Austen saw it, despite repeated World War II bombings. At one time, Bath was the most fashionable spa in Britain. Architect John Wood (1704–54), among others, helped create a city of harmony and beauty, with landscaped terraces, famous crescents such as the Royal Crescent, and Palladian villas. See "Bath: Britain's Most Historic Spa Town," in chapter 10.

o **Kenilworth Castle** (Warwickshire): This castle was the setting for Sir Walter Scott's novel *Kenilworth,* first published in 1862, which recounts the supposed murder of Amy Robsart, wife of Robert Dudley, earl of Leicester. Elizabeth I had presented Kenilworth Castle to her favorite earl in 1563. The castle was destroyed after the civil war and is now in ruins. See p. 501.

THE best OF VICTORIAN ENGLAND

o **Palace of Westminster (Houses of Parliament)** (London): No government building in England symbolizes the Victorian age like the Palace of Westminster, which houses Parliament. Replacing a palace destroyed by fire in 1834, it cost £2 million to build, a princely sum at the time. The building was completed in 1860 and turned out to be Gothic fantasy, its facade decorated with monarchs ranging from William the Conqueror to Queen Victoria. See p. 172.

o **Albert Memorial** (London): If any statue symbolizes an era, it's this flamboyant tribute to Victoria's consort, her beloved Albert (1819–61), in Kensington Gardens. The epitome of Victorian excess, the statue depicts Albert holding a catalog of the Great Exhibition and overlooking the Royal Albert Hall, his last legacy. The

4m-high (14-ft.) statue went into place in 1876 and was instantly described as an "outsize reliquary casket." See p. 178.

- **Osborne House** (Isle of Wight): This was the most cherished residence of Queen Victoria and Prince Albert. Constructed at Queen Victoria's own expense, it is imbued with her spirit. The rooms are a perfect period piece of Victoriana, with all their artifacts and stuffy chairs—a cozy clutter best evoked by her sitting room. Grief-stricken at the death of Albert in 1861, the queen requested that the house be kept as it was upon the death of her husband. See p. 353.
- **Manchester** (the Northwest): A major inland port since 1894, Manchester long had a reputation as a blackened, foggy, and forbidding city, grim and dowdy, the worst of the Midlands. But it has since been cleaned up, and today the center is filled with masterpieces of sturdy, solid Victorian architecture, including homes built for the great industrial barons of the 19th century. See "Manchester: Gateway to the North," in chapter 17.
- **National Railway Museum** (York, North Yorkshire): The first national museum to be built outside of London is devoted to the locomotive, which changed the face of Victorian England. Set in an original steam-locomotive depot, the museum is filled with railway memorabilia, more than 40 full-size locomotives, and the century-old Royal Saloon, in which Queen Victoria rode until her death. See p. 656.

THE best MUSEUMS

- **British Museum** (London): When Sir Hans Sloane died in 1753, he bequeathed to England his vast collection of art and antiquities for only £20,000, forming the nucleus of a collection that would one day embrace everything from the Rosetta Stone to the hotly contested Elgin Marbles (Greece wants them back). It's all here—and much, much more—in one of the world's great museums. See p. 174.
- **Tate Britain** (London): Sir Henry Tate, a sugar producer, started the 10,000-piece collection with only 70 paintings. The Tate was considerably enlarged when J. M. W. Turner bequeathed some 300 oils and 19,000 watercolors to England upon his death. The **Tate Modern,** a repository of avant-garde modern art, is across the river. See p. 175.
- **National Gallery** (London): One of the world's greatest collections of Western art dazzles the eye. Artists ranging from da Vinci to Rembrandt to Picasso are represented here. The gallery is especially rich in works by Renaissance artists. See p. 177.
- **American Museum in Britain** (Claverton, near Bath, Somerset): Housed in a neoclassical country house, this collection presents 2 centuries of American life and styles—including George Washington's mother's recipe for gingerbread. See p. 383.
- **Fitzwilliam Museum** (Cambridge, East Anglia): Although London dominates this list, some outstanding regional museums exist, including this gem near King's College. Exhibits range from paintings by Titian and Renoir to Chinese, Egyptian, and Greek antiquities. See p. 533.
- **Walker Art Gallery** (Liverpool, the Northwest): One of the finest collections of European and British paintings in Britain, this gallery deserves to be better known. A nearly complete study of British paintings is displayed here, from Tudor

days to the present. The gallery also owns an outstanding collection of pre-Raphaelites. See p. 609.

o **National Museum Cardiff** (Cardiff, South Wales): This museum, Wales's finest, presents the panorama of the history of this little country from prehistoric times until the present. Its collection of 18th-century porcelain is one of the finest in the world. See p. 701.

THE best CATHEDRALS

o **Westminster Abbey** (London): One of the world's greatest Anglo-French Gothic buildings has witnessed a parade of English history—from the crowning of William the Conqueror on Christmas Day 1066 to the funeral of Princess Diana in 1997. With few exceptions, the kings and queens of England have all been crowned here, and many are buried here as well. See p. 171.

o **Canterbury Cathedral** (Canterbury, Kent): The object of countless pilgrimages, as described in Chaucer's *Canterbury Tales,* this cathedral was rebuilt twice after being destroyed by fires in 1067 and 1174. Thomas à Becket, the archbishop of Canterbury, was murdered here, and his shrine was an important site for pilgrims until the Reformation. See p. 285.

o **Winchester Cathedral** (Winchester, Hampshire): Construction of the cathedral that dominates this ancient city and capital of old Wessex began in 1079. In time, Winchester Cathedral became England's longest medieval cathedral, noted for its 12-bay nave. Many famous people are buried here, including Jane Austen. See p. 336.

o **Salisbury Cathedral** (Salisbury, Wiltshire): The most stylistically unified of England's cathedrals, this edifice was built in the mid–13th century. Its landmark spire—its most striking feature—was completed in 1325. The cathedral epitomizes the Early English style of architecture. See p. 371.

o **York Minster** (York, North Yorkshire): The largest Gothic cathedral north of the Alps is also among the grandest, with incredible stained-glass windows. Its unusual octagonal Chapter House has a late-15th-century choir screen by William Hyndeley. See p. 657.

o **Durham Cathedral** (Durham): Built between 1095 and 1133, this cathedral exemplifies Norman architecture on a broad scale. Its nave, a structure of almost majestic power, is its most notable feature. See p. 683.

o **Llandaff Cathedral** (Cardiff, South Wales): Begun under the Normans, this cathedral outside Cardiff makes a dramatic impression. Its west front is one of the best works of medieval art in Wales. That didn't prevent Cromwell's armies from using the edifice as a beer hall, though. See p. 700.

THE best CASTLES, PALACES & HISTORIC HOMES

o **Windsor Castle** (Windsor, Berkshire): The largest inhabited stronghold in the world and England's largest castle, Windsor Castle has been a royal abode since William the Conqueror constructed a motte and bailey on the site 4 years after conquering England. Severely damaged by fire in 1992, the castle has been mainly restored. Its major attraction is the great Perpendicular Chapel of St.

George's, begun by Edward IV. The chancel is known for its three-tiered stalls, with its misericords (ledges used for support) and ornate carvings. See p. 239.

- **Blenheim Palace** (Woodstock, Oxfordshire): England's answer to Versailles, this extravagant baroque palace was the home of the 11th duke of Marlborough and the birthplace of Sir Winston Churchill. The structure was designed by Sir John Vanbrugh, of Castle Howard fame. Sarah, the duchess of Marlborough, battled the architects and builders from the beginning, wanting "a clean sweet house and garden, be it ever so small." That she didn't get—the structure measures 255m (850 ft.) from end to end. Capability Brown designed the gardens. See p. 268.

- **Hatfield House** (near St. Albans, Hertfordshire): Hatfield was the childhood home of Elizabeth I, who was under an oak tree here when she learned she had become queen of England. Hatfield remains one of England's largest and finest country houses, with antiques, tapestries, paintings, and even the red silk stockings Elizabeth I wore. See p. 274.

- **Woburn Abbey** (Woburn, Bedfordshire): A Cistercian abbey for 4 centuries, Woburn Abbey has been visited by everyone from Queen Victoria to Marilyn Monroe. You'll see Queen Victoria's bedroom as well as the Canaletto Room, with its 21 perspectives of Venice. The grounds, more popular than the house, include the Woburn Safari Park, the best zoological collection in England after the London Zoo. See p. 277.

- **Hever Castle & Gardens** (Edenbridge, Kent): This was the childhood home of Anne Boleyn, second wife of Henry VIII and mother of Queen Elizabeth I. In 1903, William Waldorf Astor, an American multimillionaire and Anglophile, bought the castle, restored it, and landscaped the grounds. From the outside, it still looks as it did in Tudor times, with a moat and drawbridge protecting the castle. See p. 302.

- **Knole** (near Tunbridge, Kent): Begun in 1456 by the archbishop of Canterbury, Knole is celebrated for its 365 rooms (one for each day of the year), its 52 staircases (for each week of the year), and its seven courts (for each day of the week). One of England's largest private houses and set in a 404-hectare (1,000-acre) deer park, Knole is a splendid example of Tudor architecture. See p. 303.

- **Penshurst Place** (near Tunbridge, Kent): One of England's most outstanding country homes, this mansion was the former residence of Elizabethan poet Sir Philip Sidney (1554–86). In its day, the house attracted literati such as Ben Jonson. The original 1346 hall has seen the subsequent addition of Tudor, Jacobean, and neo-Gothic wings. See p. 304.

- **Beaulieu Abbey & Palace House** (Beaulieu, in the New Forest, Hampshire): Home of the first Lord Montagu, the Palace House blends monastic Gothic architecture from the Middle Ages with Victorian trappings. Yet many visitors consider the National Motor Museum, also on the premises and with a collection of more than 250 antique automobiles, more fascinating than the house. See p. 348.

THE best GARDENS

- **Royal Botanic Gardens, Kew** (near London): A delight in any season, everything blooms in profusion in this 121-hectare (300-acre) garden, from delicate exotics to commonplace flowers and shrubs. An easy trip from London, Kew

Gardens, as it's known, possesses the largest herbarium on earth. Famed landscape architect Capability Brown helped lay out part of the grounds. See p. 202.

o **Sissinghurst Castle Garden** (near Maidstone, Kent): A notorious literary couple, Vita Sackville-West and Harold Nicolson, created this garden. Its flamboyant parentage, unusual landscaping (the grounds were laid between the surviving parts of an Elizabethan mansion), and location just 34km (21 miles) northeast of Cranbrook make it the most intriguing garden on London's doorstep. Overrun by tourists in summer, it's best in autumn, when the colors peak. See p. 304.

o **Wisley Garden** (Wisley, Kent): Wisley Garden sprawls across 101 hectares (250 acres) filled with an abundance of flowers and shrubs. Maintained by the Royal Horticultural Society, it ranges from alpinelike meadows to summer carpets of flowers. In early summer, the gardens are brilliant with flowering rhododendrons. The landscaped orchid house alone is worth the trip here. See p. 307.

THE best LONDON EXPERIENCES

o **Wandering through Covent Garden:** George Bernard Shaw got his inspiration for *Pygmalion* here, where the character of Eliza Doolittle sold violets to wealthy operagoers. The old fruit-and-vegetable market, with its Cockney cauliflower peddlers and butchers in blood-soaked aprons, is long gone. But what's left is just as interesting: Today's Covent Garden is London's best example of urban renewal. An antiques market is in the piazza on Monday, a crafts market Tuesday through Saturday. See p. 107 and p. 215.

o **Enjoying a Traditional Afternoon Tea:** Nothing is more typically British, and it's a great way to spend an afternoon. We suggest our favorite places for tea on p. 165.

o **Viewing the Turners at the Tate:** Upon his death in 1851, J. M. W. Turner bequeathed his personal collection of 19,000 watercolors and some 300 paintings to the people of Britain. He wanted his finished works, some 100 paintings, displayed under one roof. Today at the Tate, you get not only Turner but also glimpses of the Thames through the museum's windows. How appropriate—the artist lived and died on its banks, in Chelsea, and painted the river in its many changing moods. See p. 175.

o **Rowing on the Serpentine:** When the weather is right, we like to head to this 17-hectare (41-acre) artificial lake, dating from 1730 and located in Hyde Park. A stream was dammed to create the lake, whose name derives from its winding, snakelike shape. At the Boathouse, you can rent a boat by the hour. With the right companion, it's one of the most idyllic ways to spend a sunny London afternoon. See p. 198.

o **Cruising London's Waterways:** In addition to the Thames, London is riddled with an antique canal system, complete with towpaths, bridges, and wharves. Replaced by the railroad, the system was forgotten until rediscovered by a new generation. An urban renewal effort has restored the system, with bridges painted and repaired, and towpaths cleaned up. See p. 207.

o **Watching the Sunset at Waterloo Bridge:** Waterloo Bridge is the best place in London to watch the sun set over Westminster. From here, you can also see the last rays of sunlight bounce off the city spires in the East End.

○ **Spending an Evening at a West End Theater:** London is the theater capital of the world. The live stage offers a unique combination of variety, accessibility, and economy—and a look at next year's Broadway hit. Coverage of the London theater scene begins on p. 217.

○ **Crawling the London Pubs:** With some 5,000 pubs within the city limits, enough traditional ones remain, especially in central London. Make a crawl worthwhile by fortifying yourself with a ploughman's lunch or a plate of shepherd's pie. Our favorites include **Grenadier** (p. 229), **Salisbury** (p. 231), and the **Red Lion** (p. 232).

THE best OF MODERN BRITAIN

○ **Tate Modern** (London): A Bankside Power Station in Southwark was transformed into a vast collection of modern art, even 21st-century avant-garde works. Favorite artists are showcased here, including painters ranging from Matisse to Andy Warhol, Salvador Dalí to Picasso and Francis Bacon. In addition to the permanent collection, there are first-rate changing exhibitions. See p. 176.

○ **London Eye** (London): Taking a ride in a "pod," you can see for 40km (25 miles) on a clear day. It's London viewed as a bird might see it. For nearly half an hour, you hover over the city in slow-motion flight. See p. 197.

○ **Eden Project** (near St. Austell, Cornwall): Lying 48km (30 miles) west of Plymouth in breezy Cornwall, this geodesic dome shelters some of the world's most exotic plants, including those rare species that grow in the Amazon. The gardens spread over 51 hectares (125 acres) in a former clay quarry. Locals refer to the attraction as the "Garden of Eden." See p. 437.

○ **National Space Centre** (Leicester, East Midlands): Crowned by a futuristic rocket tower, this is Britain's only attraction dedicated to space science and astronomy. Visitors are taken through eight themed galleries, where they see space rockets, satellites, and capsules. Many attractions are hands-on. See p. 565.

○ **Castlefield** (Manchester, the Northwest): This historic core has been designated an urban heritage park, inviting exploration. In a feat of gentrification, city authorities are turning this once-blighted area of warehouses and canals into a thriving community full of restaurants, bars, museums, and art galleries. The first railway station in the world, dating from 1830, has been converted into the Museum of Science & Industry. See "Exploring Castlefield" (p. 596).

THE most charming VILLAGES

○ **Clovelly** (Devon): It is said that the little community of Clovelly has been featured on more calendars than any other village in England. Starting at a great height, the village cascades down to the harborfront along narrow, cobblestone High Street. You park your car at the top and make the trip on foot. Supplies are carried down by donkeys. See p. 428.

- **Painswick** (Gloucestershire, the Cotswolds): Deep in the heart of the Cotswolds, this old wool town is remarkably well preserved, its ancient buildings still guarding the narrow streets blanketed by antique cottages of honey-colored stone. The church is known for its 99 yew trees. According to legend, the devil won't let the 100th yew tree grow. To the north of the town, the Painswick Rococo Garden is visited by people from all over the world. See p. 465.
- **Bibury** (Gloucestershire, the Cotswolds): For sheer charm and quaintness, the old town of Bibury rivals Painswick for the title of most picturesque village in England. Sitting idyllically on the River Coln, Bibury is known for its Arlington Row, a charming cluster of 17th-century weavers' cottages that are remarkably preserved. See p. 471.
- **Betws-y-Coed** (North Wales): Deep in the heart of the national park of Snowdonia, this oddly named village lies in a tree-lined valley of the River Conwy. Its antique church, tumbling rivers, and waterfalls are set against a backdrop of mountain scenery. The town, which is also known for its eight bridges, makes an ideal center for exploring the attractions of North Wales. See p. 734.

THE best WALKS & HIKES

- **The South Downs Way:** Beginning in the cathedral city of Winchester, in Hampshire, the South Downs Way, one of the most scenic hikes in the south of England, goes all the way to the town of Eastbourne, in East Sussex. The distance across the bucolic terrain is 159km (99 miles). A bridleway forms the trail across these chalk uplands as you traverse miles of woodland. A highlight is the cliffs of the Seven Sisters. On the Web, check out **www.nationaltrail.co.uk/south downs**. Bookstores in Winchester sell copies of *A Guide to South Downs Way,* by Miles Jebb (Constable Press), and the even more detailed *South Downs Way,* by Paul Millmore (Aurum Press).
- **The New Forest:** Requisitioned by William the Conqueror as a game reserve in 1079, the 375-sq.-km (145-sq.-mile) New Forest isn't very new. Today, the New Forest is one of southern England's best rural playgrounds, attracting eight million annual visitors. You can ramble its carefully laid-out trails at leisure, or else take a guided scenic walk offered by the **Forestry Commission** (⟨ **023/8028-6840;** www.forestry.gov.uk/newforest). Our favorite is the **Arboretum Sensory Trail,** stretching for .8km (.5 mile). See p. 346.
- **Dartmoor National Park:** Rich in legend and lore, this national park northeast of Plymouth is home to gorges, fields of purple heather, and the Dartmoor pony. The park is crisscrossed with about 805km (500 miles) of walking and hiking trails, along with bridle paths. To get the scenic most out of this area, join one of the guided walks offered by the **Dartmoor National Park Authority** (p. 415), ranging from an easy 1½-hour jaunt to 6 long hours of trekking.
- **The Cotswolds Way:** One of the great hiking rambles of England is the Cotswolds Way, a 167km (104-mile) trail that cuts through some of England's most beautiful scenery in the bucolic Cotswolds. Laid out as late as 1968, the ramble goes from the town of Chipping Campden, in the north, all the way to the spa city of Bath. The trail is clearly signposted at every intersection en route. The hike takes from 7 to 8 days, but, of course, you can stop at any point. Go to **www. nationaltrail.co.uk/Cotswold** for more information.

○ **The Great Cotswold Ramble:** One of the most memorable walks in England is between the two idyllic villages of Upper and Lower Slaughter—and it's only 1.6km (1 mile). A well-worn footpath, Warden's Way, meanders beside the edge of the swift-flowing River Eye. You pass quaint cottages, antique houses, stately trees, footbridges, and old millponds. You can also extend the walk another 2.5km (1.5 miles) to romantic Bourton-on-the-Water. See p. 478.

○ **Peak District National Park:** A district of moors, dales, green valleys, water-falls, and steep hills, the Peak District National Park is the scenic highlight of the East Midlands, covering some 1,404 sq. km (542 sq. miles). The national park visitor centers will supply you with details for hiking through this rugged terrain. The most evocative walk is the **Monsal Trail,** lying between Buxton and Bakewell—two towns that make the best centers for touring the park. Coverage of Peak District National Park begins on p. 567.

THE best HISTORIC LUXURY HOTELS

○ **Brown's Hotel** (London; ✆ 020/7493-6020; www.brownshotel.com): All Chippendale and chintz, Brown's was launched by the former manservant to Lord Byron in 1837, and it has been going strong ever since. Today, it occupies 14 historic houses just off Berkeley Square and coddles its well-heeled guests in luxury. See p. 120.

○ **Chewton Glen Hotel & Spa** (New Milton, Hampshire; ✆ 800/398-4534 in the U.S., or 01425/275341; www.chewtonglen.com): This hotel is the best place to stay in southwest England. Service, taste, and quality are its hallmarks. The health club has a stunning design with a centerpiece swimming pool, and the property includes 28 hectares (70 acres) of manicured grounds. Guest rooms feature period furniture, and the restaurant turns out meals prepared with first-rate ingredients. See p. 346.

○ **Sharrow Bay Country House Hotel** (Ullswater, Cumbria, Lake District; ✆ 01768/486301; www.sharrowbay.co.uk): This gem is known as much for its cuisine as for its accommodations. The location alone would justify checking in: a 4.8-hectare (12-acre) site, with several gardens, in a national park on bucolic Lake Ullswater, beneath Barton Fell. The lakeside dining room offers panoramic views of the water, and you can always find something delectable on the menu. See p. 646.

○ **Bodysgallen Hall** (Llandudno, North Wales; ✆ 01492/584466; www.bodys gallen.com): One of Wales's greatest country-house hotels, this 17th-century mansion lies on 81 hectares (200 acres) of gardens and parkland. Even though an antique, it oozes with modern comforts while retaining its charms in elegantly furnished suites. See p. 749.

THE best MODERATELY PRICED HOTELS

○ **Fielding Hotel** (London; ✆ 020/7836-8305; www.thefieldinghotel.co.uk): Named after the novelist Henry Fielding, of *Tom Jones* fame, this hotel is one of the most eccentric in London. You'll either love it or hate it. Most guests appreciate its cramped, quirky, quaint aura, and its location at Covent Garden is unbeatable. Everything is old-fashioned and traditional, but if you complain that the bedrooms are too small, Smokey, the African gray parrot, will tell you off! See p. 130.

o **Sanctuary House Hotel** (London; ✆ 020/7799-4044; www.fullershotels. com): In a historic building close to Westminster Abbey, a brewery has converted an old building into a traditional English inn with a pub downstairs. It's like something you might find in the countryside of England, but instead it's in the historic heart of London. The place is a bit nostalgic, like the food served—all the old favorites such as roast beef, Welsh lamb, and Dover sole. See p. 131.

o **Hoxton Hotel** (London; ✆ 020/7550-1000; www.hoxtonhotels.com): In the increasingly gentrified Shoreditch neighborhood, near London's financial district, this hotel is dedicated to keeping the prices low. As such, it offers one of the best deals in town in comfortable, modern bedrooms. See p. 133.

o **ABode Canterbury** (Canterbury, Kent; ✆ 01227/766266; www.abodehotels. co.uk): Since Victoria's day, there has been a hotel standing on this spot, but today it's better than ever. In fact, it's the best in town, although prices remain affordable. See p. 282.

o **Mermaid Inn** (Rye, East Sussex; ✆ 01797/223065; www.mermaidinn.com): England's most famous smugglers' inn, the Mermaid sheltered Elizabeth I on her visit to Rye in 1573. At the time of the queen's visit, the inn had already been operating for 150 years. Still going strong, it leans heavily on English romance— old-world furnishings, some four-poster beds, and even a secret staircase. From its doorstep, the cobblestone streets of ancient Rye await exploration. See p. 293.

o **Powder Mills Hotel** (Battle, East Sussex; ✆ 01424/775511; www.powder millshotel.com): Near the famous battlefield at Battle Abbey, this Georgian house stands on 61 hectares (150 acres). The historic property that once catered to luminaries such as the duke of Wellington has been successfully converted to receive paying guests, housing them in style and comfort—all at an affordable price. See p. 297.

o **Apsley House Hotel** (Bath, Somerset; ✆ 01225/336966; www.apsley-house. co.uk): Away from the city center, this 1830 house was supposedly constructed for the duke of Wellington. Its owners have restored it and created a period house of character with an ambience of subdued elegance. See p. 378.

o **Ravenwood Hall** (Bury St. Edmunds, Suffolk; ✆ 01359/270345; www.raven woodhall.co.uk): Deep in the heart of East Anglia, this was once called Tudor Hall. Today, it stands in a 2.7-hectare (7-acre) park and gardens and boasts an outdoor pool and tennis courts. Sleep in a four-poster bed and immerse yourself in old England after enjoying a good dinner and a toasty "warm-up" at the fireplace. See p. 541.

o **Mount Royale Hotel** (York, North Yorkshire; ✆ 01904/628856; www.mount royale.co.uk): Two generations of the Oxtaby family have run this guesthouse, which was converted from a private home dating from 1833. A neighboring house from the same era has been incorporated into the hotel. See p. 653.

THE best B&BS

- **Jenkins Hotel** (London; ☎ 020/7387-2067; www.jenkinshotel.demon.co.uk): Hailed by one London publication as one of the 10 best hotel values in town, the Jenkins was featured on the PBS series *Poirot*. Those seeking decent accommodations in Bloomsbury, at an affordable price, have made their way to this address in Cartwright Gardens ever since Maggie Jenkins opened the place in the 1920s. Rooms are small but well furnished, and some of the original Georgian charm remains. See p. 128.

- **New England Hotel** (London; ☎ 020/7834-1595; www.newenglandhotel. com): If you want a location near Victoria Station, this is one of your best bets, in a restored 19th-century town house that's one of the most welcoming in the area. See p. 131.

- **White Vine House** (Rye, East Sussex; ☎ 01797/224748; www.whitevinehouse. co.uk): In the romantic old seaport of Rye, this B&B has won many awards for the beauty of its garden and the quality of its restoration. The former 1568 sea captain's house was but a derelict shell when restored in 1987. The creeper-clad cottage offers inviting bedrooms with both modern comforts and antiques. See p. 294.

- **The Beadles** (Salisbury, Wiltshire; ☎ 01980/862922; www.staywiththe beadles.com): This modernized Georgian house, with antique furnishings and a view of the cathedral, is a standout. It lies 11km (7 miles) from Salisbury in a well-manicured garden with tastefully furnished bedrooms. See p. 368.

- **Fir Trees Guest House** (Windermere, Cumbria, Lake District; ☎ 01539/ 442272; www.fir-trees.co.uk): This attractive and inviting guesthouse lies near Lake Windermere, so beloved by poets such as Wordsworth. A warm welcome greets you as you're ushered to one of the comfortably furnished bedrooms in this antiques-filled Victorian house that was successfully converted to receive guests. See p. 629.

- **Big Sleep Hotel** (Cardiff, South Wales; ☎ 029/2063-6363; www.thebigsleep hotel.com): In the capital of Wales, this B&B—hailed by *Condé Nast Traveller* as one of the "coolest places to stay"—has been converted from a 1960s office tower. Offering affordable prices and chic minimalism, the hotel is owned in part by actor John Malkovich. See p. 696.

THE best RESTAURANTS

- **Le Gavroche** (London; ☎ 020/7408-0881; www.le-gavroche.co.uk): Long known for its top-rate French cuisine, this stellar restaurant has risen to the top once more following a bit of a slump in the 1990s. Come here for a grand meal and skip the trip to Paris (we don't really mean that). The menu options are a delight, with such tantalizing dishes as a cassoulet of snails with herb-seasoned frogs' legs. Naturally, the wine cellar is among London's finest. See p. 142.

- **The Square** (London; ☎ 020/7495-7100; www.squarerestaurant.org): One of the great London restaurants to have emerged in the 21st century, this gourmet citadel is the domain of master chef Philip Howard, whose Continental cuisine has dazzled the food critics of London. Howard is justifiably praised for his magic in the kitchen and for his use of stunningly fresh ingredients, which he deftly concocts into masterpieces. See p. 142.

- **Pied à Terre** (London; ✆ 020/7636-1178; www.pied-a-terre.co.uk): Chef Shane Osborn lures some of the most cultivated palates in London to this bastion of French cuisine, the best dining choice in Bloomsbury when you're visiting the British Museum. A classical technique is combined with modern inventiveness, and the well-crafted dishes have both flair and flavor. See p. 151.

- **Le Manoir aux Quat' Saisons** (Great Milton, near Oxford, Oxfordshire; ✆ 800/237-1236 in the U.S., or 01844/278881; www.manoir.com): The country-house hotel and restaurant of self-taught chef Raymond Blanc have brought him his own TV series, cookbooks, and a school of cuisine. A new lightness, inspired mainly by Japan and the Mediterranean, is more evident in the celebrated chef's creations, and more meatless dishes appear on the seasonal menu. But the intensely French loyalties remain: sweetbread-stuffed pigs' trotters, kidneys, foie gras, and even veal tongue. See p. 258.

- **Moody Goose** (Bath, Somerset; ✆ 01761/416784; www.moodygoose.co.uk): The spa city of Bath offers some of the finest dining in the West Country, and this English restaurant is the market leader. A most refined cuisine is served here in an elegant Georgian setting. The kitchen is known for its passion for fresh ingredients, and everything is cooked to order and to perfection. See p. 380.

- **Le Champignon Sauvage** (Cheltenham, Gloucestershire, the Cotswolds; ✆ 01242/573449; www.lechampignonsauvage.co.uk): David Everitt-Matthias has awakened the sleepy taste buds of Cheltenham. Thoroughly versed in the French classics, he also adds more modern and lighter touches to his table d'hôte menus, the finest at this old spa. Some dishes reach into the traditional English repertoire, including stuffed leg of wild rabbit served with black pudding and turnip sauerkraut. His desserts are acclaimed as the most luscious in England. See p. 469.

THE best PUBS

- **Grenadier** (London; ✆ 020/7235-3074): Arguably London's most famous pub, and reputedly haunted, the Grenadier was once frequented by the duke of Wellington's officers on leave from fighting Napoleon. It pours the best Bloody Marys in town, and filet of beef Wellington is always a specialty. See p. 229.

- **Salisbury** (London; ✆ 020/7836-5863): Glittering cut-glass mirrors, old-fashioned banquettes, and lighting fixtures of veiled bronze girls in flowing togas re-create the Victorian gin-parlor atmosphere in the heart of the West End. Theatergoers drop in for homemade meat pie or a salad buffet before curtain. See p. 231.

- **Ship Inn** (Exeter, Devon; ✆ 01392/272040): Frequented by Sir Francis Drake and Sir Walter Raleigh, this pub near Exeter Cathedral is the most celebrated in Devon. It still provides tankards of real ale, the same drink swilled by the likes of Sir John Hawkins. You can also eat here; portions are large, as in Elizabethan times. See p. 407.

- **Cott Inn** (Dartington, near Totnes, Devon; ✆ 01803/863777; www.greene kinginns.co.uk/devon/inn_02/index.htm): Constructed in 1320 and believed to be the second-oldest inn in England, the Cott is a low, rambling, two-story building of stone, cob, and plaster under a thatched roof. A gathering place for the locals of Dartington, it's a good place for a drink on a windy night, as log fires keep the lounge and bar snug. See p. 419.

- **Punch Bowl Inn** (Lanreath, near Looe, Cornwall; ⓒ **01503/220778;** www. thefamouspunchbowlinn.co.uk): Licensed since 1620 as a pub, this was a former rendezvous for smugglers. High-backed settees and fireplaces evoke the atmosphere of old England. Sample drinks in one of the kitchens—among the few "kitchens" in England licensed as bars. See p. 436.

- **Turk's Head** (Penzance, Cornwall; ⓒ **01736/363093;** www.turkshead penzance.co.uk): Dating from 1233, this durable local favorite is filled with artifacts and timeworn beams. Drinkers take their lagers into a summer garden or retreat inside to the snug chambers when the wind blows cold. See p. 441.

- **Lamb Inn** (Burford, the Cotswolds; ⓒ **01993/823155;** www.cotswold-inns-hotels.co.uk): This is our favorite place for a lager in all the Cotswolds. In a mellow old house from 1430, with thick stones and mullioned and leaded windows, it's a good place to spend the night, have a traditional English meal, or quaff a beer. Snacks are served in the timeworn bars and lounges or in a garden in summer. See p. 474.

ENGLAND & WALES IN DEPTH

E ngland was attracting visitors—most of them, especially the Romans and Vikings, unwanted—long before William the Conqueror and his invading Normans crossed the Channel.

That invasion continues today, with millions of foreign visitors winging or boating in to see what all the excitement is about. They are joined by thousands upon thousands of poor immigrants, who have decided that their hope for a good life lies in these great islands whose people once conquered a global empire—two-fifths of the world—on which the sun has long ago set.

The charismatic Princess Di is still a cherished memory. The Beatles are half gone or else paying off crushing divorce settlements. The queen herself is still presiding with grace over a dysfunctional family. In her post-Di humiliation, she's even had her privacy invaded with an intrusive movie and resorted to opening the doors of Buckingham Palace every August to raise extra funds from those willing to pay the hefty entrance fee.

That legendary stiff British upper lip isn't so stiff anymore. You get that impression if you visit an English pub, some 5,000 of them in London alone. In some pubs you'll wonder where those famous English manners went, especially if you encounter lager louts ruling the night after too many pints. Some of the clichés remain, though. The English still consume, on a daily basis, oceans of fish, served with their soggy chips. However, with the influx of immigrants in the past decades, almost an equal number of curry dishes are devoured as well.

As Victoria and her quaint morals lie sleeping in her grave outside Windsor, London—and England in general—have become cutting edge in music, fashion, culture, art, and even architecture, the latter much too daringly avant-garde for the likes of tradition-minded Prince Charles.

The fading English aristocracy, to pay the tax man, is even opening its castles and manor houses to overnight visitors. So far, the queen isn't running a B&B at Windsor Castle yet, but many dukes or duchesses are sharing their royal abodes with hordes of tourist invaders.

As you tour this England with its 60 million people, you'll encounter "Brit ego." The people have a lot to be proud of, along with some shameful scars in their colonization. They did give the world the Magna Carta, and almost everything viewed as "Western," even law. They spearheaded the Industrial Revolution and won nearly all their foreign wars in spite of their country's small size.

Before Tony Blair was sent packing from 10 Downing Street, he said, "We Brits are now living in the post–Industrial Age, and we may not quite have reinvented ourselves. But we're doing so every day, and I'm sure our future generations will have many marvelous surprises to spring upon the world."

ENGLAND TODAY

The England you'll encounter today has moved from the prim and proper Victorianism of the mid–19th century and is now an exciting land of change and experiment, being forever altered by the massive arrival of immigrants from around the globe.

It's not a big country, but 2,500 eventful years have left their mark. Traveling in England is like experiencing a living, illustrated history book, one that encompasses the ancient mystery of Stonehenge, Hadrian's Wall from the Roman Empire, grand cathedrals, and the lofty spires of village churches.

Monuments aside, the highly individualistic people who inhabit England today are an attraction unto themselves. Known for their privacy and reserve, they have endless tolerance for eccentricity.

As a long-term cultural shift, Britain's class system seems to be waning. The average visitor will hardly know that it even exists. Yet the number of titles has grown from some 115 peers (nobles) some 2 centuries ago to almost 2,000 titles today. The explosion in titles derives from the policy of elevating to the peerage anyone who

DATELINE

54 B.C. Julius Caesar invades England.

A.D. 43 Romans conquer England.

410 Jutes, Angles, and Saxons form small kingdoms in England.

500–1066 Anglo-Saxon kingdoms fight off Viking warriors.

1066 William, duke of Normandy, invades England, defeats Harold II at the Battle of Hastings.

1154 The Plantagenets launch their rule (which lasts until 1399) with the crowning of Henry II.

1215 King John signs the Magna Carta at Runnymede.

1337 Hundred Years' War between France and England begins.

1485 Battle of Boswoth Field ends the Wars of the Roses between the houses of York and Lancaster; Henry VII launches the Tudor dynasty.

1534 Henry VIII brings the Reformation to England and dissolves the monasteries.

2
England Today
ENGLAND & WALES IN DEPTH

18

The Bulldog & a Question of Character

The fact that the English have adopted the bulldog as their symbol gives you a clue to their character, at least according to George Orwell, author of *1984* and *Animal Farm*. In 1947, he wrote that millions of Brits "willingly accept as their national emblem the bulldog, an animal noted for its obstinacy, ugliness, and impenetrable stupidity." Orwell, both a socialist and a critic of socialism, had no kind feelings toward his fellow citizens.

Countless others have attempted to characterize the English, including the writer Arthur Koestler, who described an average Englishman as an "attractive hybrid between an ostrich and a lion: keeping his head in the sand for as long as possible, but when forced to confront reality, capable of heroic deeds."

The Brits have always baffled the Americans, perhaps ever since the latter ceased being Brits and became Americans. Writer Paul Gallico noted: "No one can be as calculatedly rude as the British, which amazes Americans, who do not understand studied insult and can only offer abuse as a substitute."

continues in a major way to contribute "to the well-being of Britain"—the late Lord Laurence Olivier, for example.

Britain is the only country in the world that has granted titles to members of labor unions. At the bottom of the rung are knights and ladies (dames) whose titles come from their achievements, perhaps in politics or the arts. Such a title of "Dame Elizabeth" was bestowed on Elizabeth Taylor.

Of course, members of the House of Lords still must come from the peers of the realm; otherwise, a politician is "banished" to the House of Commons. As a political issue, there are those who want to abolish the House of Lords. The argument goes that the very nature of Britain's legislative process is deeply rooted in the class system. But to get rid of Britain's aristocracy would necessitate a radical change in Parliament.

1558	The accession of Elizabeth I ushers in an era of exploration and a renaissance in science and learning.
1588	Spanish Armada defeated.
1603	James VI of Scotland becomes James I of England, thus uniting the crowns of England and Scotland.
1620	Pilgrims sail from Plymouth on the *Mayflower* to found a colony in the New World.
1629	Charles I dissolves Parliament, ruling alone.
1642–49	Civil War between Royalists and Parliamentarians; the Parliamentarians win.
1649	Charles I beheaded, and England is a republic.
1653	Oliver Cromwell becomes Lord Protector.
1660	Charles II restored to the throne with limited power.
1665–66	Great Plague and Great Fire decimate London.
1688	James II, a Catholic, is deposed, and William and Mary come to the throne, signing a bill of rights.

continues

One BBC commentator said, "The royals don't rule anymore, but they provide us with amusement, which is the only reason we keep them around." Dishing the dirt on the royals lures millions of tabloid readers daily. Times sure have changed: Contrast today's situation to the prolonged press silence on the courtship of King Edward VIII and American divorcée Wallis Warfield Simpson in the 1930s.

The very existence of the monarchy still is a hot political issue to press in a London pub. As Labor's "shadow minister," Jack Straw, longtime critic of the monarchy, said that he would like to see "the type of monarch they have in Norway, or perhaps Sweden. Let the royals shop for groceries like the rest of us. It would signal a classless British society." Even Prince Charles has admitted "that a lot of people need to be taken off the royal payroll and the monarchy scaled back if it is to survive."

Nothing is changing in England today more than demographics. The 2001 census listed a population just under 50 million, with slightly more females than males. The mean age of England's population is around 39 years, and some 90% of its people were born in the British Isles. Life expectancy for males is 77, for females 81. England's ethnic minorities make up some 15.3% of the population, with Asians forming the largest number of residents.

LOOKING BACK AT ENGLAND

FROM MURKY BEGINNINGS TO ROMAN OCCUPATION Britain was probably split off from the continent of Europe some 8 millennia ago by the continental drift and other natural forces. The early inhabitants, the Iberians, were later to be identified with stories of fairies, brownies, and "little people." These are the people whose ingenuity and enterprise are believed to have created **Stonehenge** (p. 373), but despite that great and mysterious monument, little is known about them.

They were replaced by the iron-wielding Celts, whose massive invasions around 500 B.C. drove the Iberians back to the Scottish Highlands and Welsh mountains, where some of their descendants still live today.

1727	George I, the first of the Hanoverians, assumes the throne.
1756–63	In the Seven Years' War, Britain wins Canada from France.
1775–83	Britain loses its American colonies.
1795–1815	The Napoleonic Wars lead, finally, to the Battle of Waterloo and the defeat of Napoleon.
1837	Queen Victoria begins her reign as Britain reaches the zenith of its empire.
1901	Victoria dies, and Edward VII becomes king.
1914–18	England enters World War I and emerges victorious on the Allied side.
1936	Edward VIII abdicates to marry an American divorcée.
1939–45	In World War II, Britain stands alone against Hitler from the fall of France in 1940 until the U.S. enters the war in 1941. Dunkirk is evacuated in 1940; bombs rattle London during the Blitz.
1945	Germany surrenders. Churchill is defeated; the Labour government introduces the welfare state and begins to dismantle the empire.

King Arthur & the Knights of the Round Table

England's preeminent myth is, of course, the Arthurian legend of Camelot and the Round Table. So compelling was this legend that medieval writers treated it as a tale of chivalry, even though the real Arthur, if he lived, probably did so around the time of the Roman or Saxon invasions. Despite its universal adoption throughout Europe, the legend initially developed and blossomed in Wales and southern England. The story was polished and given a literary form for the first time by Geoffrey of Monmouth around 1135. Combining Celtic myth and Christian and classical symbolism (usually without crediting his sources), Geoffrey forged a fictional history of Britain whose form, shape, and elevated values were centered on the mythical King Arthur. Dozens of other storytellers embellished the written and oral versions of the tale. The resulting stew pot described the birth of Arthur, the exploits of the king and his knights, the establishment of a knightly fellowship of the Round Table, and the search for the Holy Grail, the cup Jesus drank from at the Last Supper. This idyllic and noble kingdom was shattered by the adultery of Arthur's queen, Guinevere, with his favorite knight, Lancelot, and the malice of Mordred, Arthur's illegitimate son.

To visit King Arthur's legendary lair, head to **Tintagel Castle (p. 455)**, in Cornwall.

In 54 B.C., Julius Caesar invaded England, but the Romans did not become established there until A.D. 43. They went as far as Caledonia (now Scotland), where they gave up, leaving that land to "the painted ones," or the warring Picts. **Hadrian's Wall** (p. 687), built by the emperor across the north of England, marked the northernmost reaches of the Roman Empire. During almost 4 centuries of occupation, the Romans built roads, villas, towns, walls, and fortresses; they farmed the land and introduced first their pagan religions, then Christianity. Agriculture and trade flourished.

1952	Queen Elizabeth II ascends the throne.
1973	Britain joins the European Union.
1979	Margaret Thatcher becomes prime minister.
1982	Britain defeats Argentina in the Falklands War.
1990	Thatcher is ousted; John Major becomes prime minister.
1991	Britain fights with Allies to defeat Iraq.
1992	Royals are jolted by fire at Windsor Castle and marital troubles of their two sons.

Britain joins the European Single Market. Deep recession signals the end of the booming 1980s.

1994 England is linked to the Continent by rail via the Channel Tunnel, or Chunnel. Tony Blair elected Labour Party leader.

1996 The IRA breaks a 17-month cease-fire with a truck bomb at the Docklands that claims two lives. Charles and Di divorce. The government concedes a possible link between mad-cow disease and a fatal brain ailment afflicting humans; British beef imports face banishment globally.

continues

FROM ANGLO-SAXON RULE TO THE NORMAN CONQUEST   When the Roman legions withdrew, around A.D. 410, they left the country open to waves of invasions by Jutes, Angles, and Saxons, who established themselves in small kingdoms throughout the former Roman colony. From the 8th through the 11th century, the Anglo-Saxons contended with Danish raiders for control of the land.

By the time of the Norman Conquest, the Saxon kingdoms were united under an elected king, Edward the Confessor. His successor was to rule less than a year before the Norman invasion.

The date 1066 is familiar to every English schoolchild. It marked an epic event, the only successful military invasion of Britain in history, and one of England's great turning points: King Harold, the last Anglo-Saxon king, was defeated at the Battle of Hastings, and William of Normandy was crowned William I. To wander those ancient battlefields, visit **Hastings** and **Battle** (p. 298).

One of William's first acts was to order a survey of the land he had conquered, assessing all property in the nation for tax purposes. This survey was called the Domesday Book, or "Book of Doom," as some pegged it. The resulting document was completed around 1086 and has been a fertile sourcebook for British historians ever since.

Norman rule had an enormous impact on English society. All high offices were held by Normans, and the Norman barons were given great grants of lands; they built Norman-style castles and strongholds throughout the country. French was the language of the court for centuries—few people realize that heroes such as Richard the Lionheart probably spoke little or no English.

FROM THE RULE OF HENRY II TO THE MAGNA CARTA   In 1154, Henry II, the first of the Plantagenets, was crowned (reigning until 1189). This remarkable character in English history ruled a vast empire—not only most of Britain but also Normandy, Anjou, Brittany, and Aquitaine in France.

Henry was a man of powerful physique, both charming and terrifying. He reformed the courts and introduced the system of common law, which still operates in moderated form in England today and also influenced the American legal system. But

1997 London swings again. The Labour Party ends 18 years of Conservative rule with a landslide election victory. The tragic death of Diana, Princess of Wales, prompts worldwide outpouring of grief.	**2002** Queen Elizabeth, the Queen Mother, dies at age 101.
	2005 Suicide bomb attacks devastate London.
1998 Prime Minister Tony Blair launches "New Britain"—young, stylish, and informal.	**2007** Tony Blair steps down; Gordon Brown becomes prime minister.
1999 England rushes toward the 21st century with the Millennium Dome at Greenwich.	**2009** England suffers economic slowdown.
2000 London presides over millennium celebration; gays allowed to serve openly in the military.	**2010** Labour Party continues its decline. Conservative David Cameron sweeps to victory and becomes prime minister in a coalition with his rivals, the Liberal Democrats.

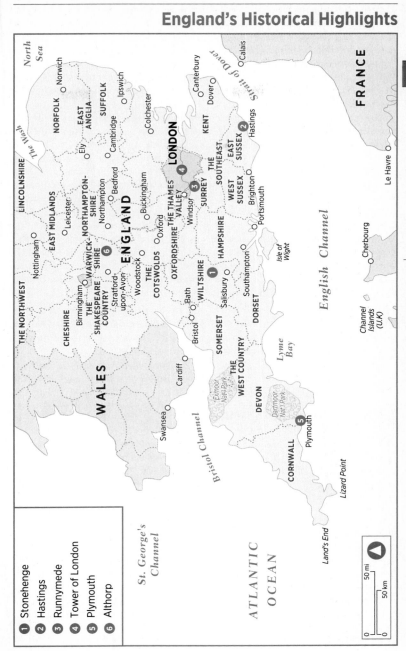

- 1 Stonehenge
- 2 Hastings
- 3 Runnymede
- 4 Tower of London
- 5 Plymouth
- 6 Althorp

North Sea
North West
The Wash
LINCOLNSHIRE
NORFOLK
Norwich
EAST ANGLIA
SUFFOLK
Ipswich
Ely
Cambridge
Colchester
EAST MIDLANDS
Nottingham
Leicester
NORTHAMPTON-SHIRE
Northampton
Bedford
Buckingham
ENGLAND
Oxford
THE THAMES VALLEY
Windsor
LONDON
Canterbury
Calais
Dover
Strait of Dover
KENT
THE SOUTHEAST
EAST SUSSEX
Hastings
SURREY
WEST SUSSEX
Brighton
Portsmouth
OXFORDSHIRE
Woodstock
THE COTSWOLDS
Stratford-upon-Avon
WARWICK-SHIRE
THE SHAKESPEARE COUNTRY
Birmingham
THE NORTHWEST
CHESHIRE
WILTSHIRE
HAMPSHIRE
Salisbury
Southampton
Isle of Wight
Bath
Bristol
SOMERSET
DORSET
Lyme Bay
English Channel
Cherbourg
Le Havre
FRANCE
Channel Islands (U.K)
Cardiff
Swansea
WALES
Bristol Channel
THE WEST COUNTRY
DEVON
Exmoor Nat'l Park
Dartmoor Nat'l Park
CORNWALL
Plymouth
Lizard Point
Land's End
St. George's Channel
ATLANTIC OCEAN
50 mi
50 km

Henry is best remembered for ordering the infamous murder of Thomas à Becket, archbishop of Canterbury. Henry, at odds with his archbishop, exclaimed, "Who will rid me of this turbulent priest?" His knights, overhearing and taking him at his word, murdered Thomas in front of the high altar in **Canterbury Cathedral** (p. 285).

Henry's wife, Eleanor of Aquitaine, the most famous woman of her time, was no less of a colorful character. She accompanied her first husband, Louis VII of France, on the Second Crusade, and it was rumored that she had a romantic affair at that time with the Saracen leader, Saladin. Domestic and political life did not run smoothly, however, and Henry and Eleanor and their sons were often at odds. The pair has been the subject of many plays and films, including *The Lion in Winter, Becket,* and T. S. Eliot's *Murder in the Cathedral.*

Two of their sons were crowned kings of England. Richard the Lionheart actually spent most of his life outside England, on crusades or in France. John was forced by his nobles to sign the Magna Carta at **Runnymede** (p. 242), in 1215—another date well known to English schoolchildren.

The Magna Carta guaranteed that the king was subject to the rule of law and gave certain rights to the king's subjects, beginning a process that eventually led to the development of parliamentary democracy as it is known in Britain today. This process would have enormous influence on the American colonies many years later. The Magna Carta became known as the cornerstone of English liberties, though it only granted liberties to the barons. It took the rebellion of Simon de Montfort, half a century later, to introduce the notion that the common people should also have a voice and representation.

THE BLACK DEATH & THE WARS OF THE ROSES   In 1348, half the population died as the Black Death ravaged England. By the end of the century, the population of Britain had fallen from four million to two million.

England also suffered in the Hundred Years' War, which went on intermittently for more than a century. By 1371, England had lost much of its land on French soil.

The Legend of Robin Hood

Another story that has captured the world's imagination is the legend of Robin Hood, the folk hero of tale and ballad. His slogan, "Take from the rich and give to the poor," fired the imagination of a hardworking, sometimes impoverished English people.

Celebrating their freedom in verdant Sherwood Forest, Robin Hood's eternally youthful band rejoiced in "hearing the twang of the bow of yew and in watching the gray goose shaft as it cleaves the glistening willow wand or brings down the king's proud buck." Life was one long picnic beneath the splendid oaks, with plenty of ale and flavorful venison

poached from the primeval forests of an oppressive king. The clever guerrilla rebellion that "Robin Hood" waged against authority (represented by the haughty, despotic, and overfed sheriff of Nottingham) was punctuated by heroic exploits and a yearning to win justice for the victims of oppression. Later, such historical figures as the Scottish bandit and soldier of fortune Robert MacGregor, known as Rob Roy (1671–1734), were imbued with the heroism and bravado of Robin Hood, and many English reformers drew upon his heroism as they battled the forces of oppression.

To visit **Sherwood Forest,** see p. 577.

Henry V, immortalized by Shakespeare, revived England's claims to France, and his victory at Agincourt was notable for making obsolete the forms of medieval chivalry and warfare.

After Henry's death in 1422, disputes arose among successors to the crown that resulted in a long period of civil strife, the Wars of the Roses, between the Yorkists, who used a white rose as their symbol, and the Lancastrians, with their red rose. The last Yorkist king was Richard III, who got bad press from Shakespeare but is defended to this day as a hero by the people of the city of York. Richard was defeated at **Bosworth Battlefield** (p. 566), and the victory introduced England to the first Tudor, the shrewd and wily Henry VII.

THE TUDORS TAKE THE THRONE   The Tudors were unlike the kings who had ruled before them. They introduced into England a strong central monarchy with far-reaching powers. The system worked well under the first three strong and capable Tudor monarchs, but it began to break down later when the Stuarts came to the throne.

Henry VIII is surely the most notorious Tudor. Imperious and flamboyant, a colossus among English royalty, he slammed shut the door on the Middle Ages and introduced the Renaissance to England. He is best known, of course, for his treatment of his six wives and the unfortunate fates that befell five of them.

When his first wife, Catherine of Aragon, failed to produce a son, and his ambitious mistress, Anne Boleyn, became pregnant, he tried to annul his marriage, but the pope refused and Catherine contested the action. Defying the power of Rome, Henry had his marriage with Catherine declared invalid and secretly married Anne Boleyn in 1533.

The events that followed had profound consequences and introduced the religious controversy that was to dominate English politics for the next 4 centuries. Henry's break with the Roman Catholic Church and the formation of the Church of England, with himself as supreme head, was a turning point in English history. It led eventually to the Dissolution of the Monasteries, civil unrest, and much social dislocation. The confiscation of the church's land and possessions brought untold wealth into the king's coffers, wealth that was distributed to a new aristocracy that supported the monarch. In one sweeping gesture, Henry destroyed the ecclesiastical culture of the Middle Ages. Among those executed for refusing to cooperate with Henry's changes was Sir Thomas More, humanist, international man of letters, and author of *Utopia*.

Anne Boleyn bore Henry a daughter, the future Elizabeth I, but failed to produce a male heir. She was brought to trial on a trumped-up charge of adultery and was beheaded in May 1536; that same year, Henry married Jane Seymour, who died giving birth to Edward VI. For his next wife, he looked farther afield and chose Anne of Cleves from a flattering portrait, but she proved disappointing—he called her the "great Flanders mare." He divorced her the same year and next picked a pretty young woman from his court, Catherine Howard. She was also beheaded on a charge of adultery but, unlike Anne Boleyn, was probably guilty. Finally, he married an older woman, Catherine Parr, in 1543. She survived him.

Henry's heir, sickly Edward VI (reigned 1547–53), did not live long. He died of consumption—or, as rumor has it, overmedication—at age 15. He was succeeded by Mary I (reigned 1553–58), his sister, and the trouble Henry had stirred up with the break with Rome came home to roost for the first time. Mary restored the Roman Catholic faith, and her persecution of the adherents of the Church of England earned her the name of "Bloody Mary." Some 300 Protestants were executed, many burned alive at the stake. She made an unpopular and unhappy marriage to Philip II of Spain; despite her bloody reputation, her life was a sad one.

Elizabeth I (reigned 1558–1603) came next to the throne, ushering in an era of peace and prosperity, exploration, and a renaissance in science and learning. An entire age was named after her: the Elizabethan Age. She was the last great and grand monarch to rule England, and her passion and magnetism were said to match her father's. Through her era marched Drake, Raleigh, Frobisher, Grenville, Shakespeare, Spenser, Byrd, and Hilliard. During her reign, she had to face the appalling precedent of ordering the execution of a fellow sovereign, Mary, Queen of Scots. Her diplomatic skills kept war at bay until 1588, when, at the apogee of her reign, the Spanish Armada was defeated. She will be forever remembered as "Good Queen Bess." To see where she lived as a young girl, you can visit **Hatfield House** (p. 274).

FROM THE RESTORATION TO THE NAPOLEONIC WARS   The reign of Charles II was the beginning of a dreadful decade that saw London decimated by the Great Plague and destroyed by the Great Fire.

His successor, James II, attempted to return the country to Catholicism, an attempt that so frightened the powers that be that Catholics were, for a long time, deprived of their civil rights. James was deposed in the Glorious Revolution of 1688 and succeeded by his daughter Mary (1662–94) and William of Orange (1650–1702). (William of Orange was the grandson of Charles I, the tyrannical king whom Cromwell helped to depose.) This secured a Protestant succession that has continued to this day. These tolerant and levelheaded monarchs signed a bill of rights, establishing the principle that the monarch reigns not by divine right but by the will of Parliament. William outlived his wife, reigning until 1702.

Queen Anne then came to the throne, ruling from 1702 until her own death in 1714. She was the sister of Mary of Orange and was another daughter of James II. The last of the Stuarts, Anne marked her reign with the most significant event, the 1707 Act of Union with Scotland. She outlived all her children, leaving her throne without an heir.

Upon the death of Anne, England looked for a Protestant prince to succeed her and chose George of Hanover, who reigned from 1714 to 1727. Though he spoke only German and spent as little time in England as possible, he was chosen because he was the great-grandson of James I. Beginning with this "distant cousin" to the throne, the reign of George I marked the beginning of the 174-year rule of the Hanoverians, who preceded Victoria.

George I left the running of the government to the English politicians and created the office of prime minister. Under the Hanoverians, the powers of Parliament were extended, and the constitutional monarchy developed into what it is today.

The American colonies were lost under the Hanoverian George III, but other British possessions were expanded: Canada was won from the French in the Seven Years' War (1756–63), British control over India was affirmed, and Captain Cook claimed Australia and New Zealand for England. The British became embroiled in the Napoleonic Wars (1795–1815), achieving two of their greatest victories and acquiring two of their greatest heroes: Nelson at Trafalgar and Wellington at Waterloo.

THE INDUSTRIAL REVOLUTION & THE REIGN OF VICTORIA   The mid-to late 18th century saw the beginnings of the Industrial Revolution. This event changed the lives of the laboring class, created a wealthy middle class, and transformed England from a rural, agricultural society into an urban, industrial economy. England was now a world-class financial and military power. Male suffrage was extended, though women were to continue under a series of civil disabilities for the rest of the century. To see the beginnings of the Industrial Revolution, visit the village of **Ironbridge** (p. 514).

Queen Victoria's reign, from 1837 to 1901, coincided with the height of the Industrial Revolution. When she ascended the throne, the monarchy as an institution was in considerable doubt, but her 64-year reign, the longest tenure in English history, was an incomparable success.

The Victorian era was shaped by the growing power of the bourgeoisie, the queen and her consort's personal moral stance, and the perceived moral responsibilities of managing a vast empire. During this time, the first trade unions were formed, a public school system was developed, and railroads were built.

Victoria never recovered from the death of her German husband, Albert. He died from typhoid fever in 1861, and the queen never remarried. Though she had many children, she found them tiresome but was a pillar of family values nonetheless. One historian said her greatest asset was her relative ordinariness.

Middle-class values ruled Victorian England and were embodied by the queen. The racy England of the past went underground. Our present-day view of England is still influenced by the attitudes of the Victorian era, and we tend to forget that English society in earlier centuries was famous for its rowdiness, sexual license, and spicy scandal.

Victoria's son Edward VII (reigned 1901–10) was a playboy who had waited too long in the wings. He is famous for his mistresses, especially Lillie Langtry, and his love of elaborate dinners. You can actually spend the night at **Langtry Manor** in Bournemouth (p. 355), which the king built for his favorite mistress. During his brief reign, he, too, had an era named after him: the Edwardian age. Under Edward, the country entered the 20th century at the height of its imperial power. At home, the advent of the motorcar and the telephone radically changed social life, and the women's suffrage movement began.

World War I marked the end of an era. It had been assumed that peace, progress, prosperity, empire, and even social improvement would continue indefinitely. But World War I and the troubled decades of social unrest, political uncertainty, and the rise of Nazism and fascism put an end to these expectations.

THE WINDS OF WAR   World War II began in 1939, and soon thereafter Britain found a new and inspiring leader, Winston Churchill. Churchill led the nation during its "finest hour." You can visit Churchill's private home, **Chartwell** in Kent (p. 301), and the underground **Churchill War Rooms** in London (p. 182), where he rode out parts of World War II. From the time the Germans took France, Britain stood alone against Hitler. The evacuation of Dunkirk in 1940, the Blitz of London, and the Battle of Britain were dark hours for the British people, and Churchill is remembered for urging them to hold onto their courage. Once the British forces were joined by their American allies, the tide finally turned, culminating in the D-day invasion of German-occupied Normandy. These bloody events are still remembered by many with pride, and with nostalgia for the era when Britain was still a great world power.

The years following World War II brought many changes to England. Britain began to lose its grip on an empire (India became independent in 1947), and the Labour government, which came into power in 1945, established the welfare state and brought profound social change to Britain.

QUEEN ELIZABETH RULES TO THE PRESENT DAY   Upon the death of the "wartime king," George VI, Elizabeth II ascended the throne in 1953. Her reign has seen the erosion of Britain's once-mighty industrial power and, in recent years, a severe recession.

Political power has seesawed between the Conservative and Labour parties. Margaret Thatcher, who became prime minister in 1979, seriously eroded the welfare state and was ambivalent toward the European Union. Her popularity soared during the successful Falklands War, when Britain seemed to recover some of its military glory for a brief time.

Though the queen has remained steadfast and has punctiliously performed her ceremonial duties, rumors about the royal family abounded, and in the year 1992, which Queen Elizabeth labeled an *annus horribilis,* a devastating fire swept through **Windsor Castle** (p. 239), the marriages of several of her children crumbled, and the queen agreed to pay taxes for the first time. Prince Charles and Princess Diana agreed to a separation, and there were ominous rumblings about the future of the House of Windsor. By 1994 and 1995, Britain's economy was improving after several glum years, but Conservative prime minister John Major, heir to Margaret Thatcher's legacy, was coming under increasing criticism.

The IRA, reputedly enraged at the slow pace of peace talks, relaunched its reign of terror across London in February 1996, planting a massive bomb that ripped through a building in London's Docklands, injuring more than 100 people and killing two. Shattered, too, was the 17-month cease-fire by the IRA, which brought hope that peace was at least possible. Another bomb went off in Manchester in June.

Headlines about the IRA bombing gave way to another big bomb: the end of the marriage of Princess Diana and Prince Charles. The Wedding of the Century had become the Divorce of the Century. The lurid tabloids had been right all along about this unhappy pair. But details of the $26-million divorce settlement didn't satisfy the curious: Scrutiny of Prince Charles's relationship with Camilla Parker Bowles, as well as gossip about Princess Diana's love life, continued in the press.

In 1997, the political limelight now rested on the young Labour leader Tony Blair. From his rock-star acquaintances to his "New Labour" rhetoric, which was chock-full of pop-culture buzzwords, he was a stark contrast to the more staid Major. His media-savvy personality obviously registered with the British electorate. On May 1, 1997, the Labour Party ended 18 years of Conservative rule with a landslide election victory. At age 44, Blair became Britain's youngest prime minister in 185 years, following in the wake of the largest Labour triumph since Winston Churchill was swept out of office at the end of World War II.

Blair's election—which came just at the moment when London was being touted by the international press for its renaissance in art, music, fashion, and dining—had many British entrepreneurs poised and ready to take advantage of what they perceived as enthusiasm for new ideas and ventures. Comparisons to Harold Macmillan and his reign over the Swinging Sixties were inevitable, and insiders agreed that something was in the air.

However, events took a shocking turn in August 1997, when Princess Diana was killed—along with her companion, Harrods heir Dodi Al-Fayed—in a high-speed car crash in Paris. The ancestral home of the late princess at **Althorp** (p. 560) is open to the public.

The "People's Princess" continued to dominate many headlines in 1998 with bizarre conspiracy theories about her death. But the royal family isn't the real force in Britain today.

Meanwhile, Blair led Britain on a program of constitutional reform without parallel in the last century. Critics feared that Blair would one day preside over a "dis-united" Britain, with Scotland breaking away and Northern Ireland forming a self-government.

Of course, the future of the monarchy still remains a hot topic of discussion in Britain. There is little support for doing away with the monarchy in Britain today, in spite of wide criticism of the royal family's behavior in the wake of Diana's death. Apparently, if polls are to be believed, some three-quarters of the British populace want the monarchy to continue. Prince Charles is even making a comeback with the British public and has appeared in public—to the delight of the paparazzi—with his longtime mistress, now wife, Camilla Parker Bowles. At the very least, the monarchy is good for the tourist trade, on which Britain is increasingly dependent. And what would the tabloids do without it?

The big news among royal watchers early in 2002 was the death of Princess Margaret at age 71, followed 7 weeks later by the death of Queen Mother Elizabeth at the age of 101. The most popular royal, the "Queen Mum" was a symbol of courage and dignity, especially during the tumultuous World War II years when London was under bombardment from Nazi Germany. The remains of the Queen Mother were interred alongside her husband in the George VI Memorial Chapel at St. George's at Windsor Castle. The ashes of Princess Margaret were also interred with her parents in the same chapel.

At the dawn of the millennium, major social changes occurred in Britain. No sooner had the year 2000 begun than Britain announced a change of its code of conduct for the military, allowing openly gay men and women to serve in the armed forces. The action followed a European court ruling in the fall of 1999 that forbade Britain to discriminate against homosexuals. This change brings Britain in line with almost all other NATO countries, including France, Canada, and Germany. The United States remains at variance with the trend.

After promising beginnings, the 21st century got off to a bad start in Britain. In the wake of flare-ups of mad-cow disease, the country was swept by a foot-and-mouth-disease epidemic that disrupted the country's agriculture and threatened one of the major sources of British livelihoods, its burgeoning tourist industry. After billions of pounds in tourism were lost, the panic eventually subsided. The government has intervened to take whatever preventive measures it can.

Following the terrorist attacks on New York City and Washington, D.C., on September 11, 2001, Tony Blair and his government joined in a show of support for the United States, condemning the aerial bombardments and loss of life. Not only that, the British joined in the war in Afghanistan against the dreaded Taliban. By 2003, however, Blair's backing of George W. Bush's stance against President Saddam Hussein of Iraq brought his popularity to an all-time low. Britain's involvement in Iraq remains an unpopular cause. In February 2003, an estimated one million protesters, the largest demonstration in the history of London, gathered to oppose military intervention in Iraq.

On the economic front, Britain still shies away from joining the so-called euro umbrella. In June 2003, Tony Blair and Chancellor Gordon Brown declared that abandoning British pound sterling in favor of the euro, prevailing on the Continent, was not right for the country at the time.

England has long endured terrorist attacks from the IRA, but was shaken on the morning of July 7, 2005, when four suicide bombs were detonated on public transportation in London, killing 52 victims. These bombs were the deadliest attacks suffered by the city since the darkest days of World War II.

Following the 2005 election, Blair's population plummeted, and he resigned in May 2007. Succeeding him was Gordon Brown, his chancellor of the exchequer, who became prime minister in June 2007.

In 2008, England, like most of the rest of the world, including the United States, experienced an economic slowdown, with the government at times having to intervene.

Brown's popularity with British voters continued to fall in 2009, when four of his cabinet ministers were forced to resign after using taxpayers' money to finance everything from X-rated movies to velvet-and-wool carpets.

In May 2010, David Cameron, the Conservative Party challenger, defeated Brown and became, at age 43, Britain's youngest prime minister in 2 centuries. Amazingly, he swept into power by forming a new coalition with a rival party, the Liberal Democrats. That's like putting President Obama and Rush Limbaugh in the same political party. The coming together of the two parties is Britain's first coalition government since World War II. In an emotional farewell in front of 10 Downing Street, Brown brought an end to 13 years of rule by the Labour Party.

ENGLAND'S ART & ARCHITECTURE

No single artist, period, or museum defines England's art and architecture. You can see the country's art in everything from medieval illuminated manuscripts to Thomas Gainsborough portraits to Damien Hirst's pickled cows. Its architecture ranges from Roman walls and Norman castles to baroque St. Paul's Cathedral and towering postmodern skyscrapers. This section will help you make sense of it all.

Celtic & Medieval Art (ca. 9th c. B.C.–16th c. A.D.)

Celtic art survived the Roman conquest and medieval Christianity mainly as carved swirls and decorations on the "Celtic crosses" peppering cemeteries. During the medieval period, colorful Celtic images and illustrations decorated the margins of Bibles and Gospels, giving the books the moniker of **illuminated manuscripts.**

The best example of this art is the **Wilton Diptych** at London's National Gallery, the first truly British painting. It was crafted in the late 1390s for King Richard II by an unknown artist. The **Lindisfarne Gospels** at London's British Library is one of the greatest illuminated manuscripts from the 7th century.

Renaissance & Baroque Art (16th–18th c.)

The **Renaissance** hit England late, but its museums contain many Old Master paintings from Italy and Germany. A few foreign Renaissance masters did come to work at the English courts and influenced some local artists, but significant Brits didn't emerge until the baroque.

The **baroque,** a more decorative version of the Renaissance approach, mixes compositional complexity and explosions of dynamic fury, movement, color, and figures with an exaggeration of light and dark, called chiaroscuro, and a kind of super-realism based on using peasants as models. The rococo period is baroque art gone awry; it's frothy and chaotic.

Significant British artists of this period include:

o **Joshua Reynolds (1723–92).** A fussy baroque painter and first president of the Royal Academy of Arts, Reynolds was a firm believer in a painter's duty to celebrate history. Reynolds spent much of his career casting his noble patrons as ancient gods in portrait compositions cribbed from Old Masters. Many of his works are in London's **National Gallery, Tate Britain, Wallace Collection,** and **Dulwich Picture Gallery;** Oxford's **Cathedral Hall;** Liverpool's **Walker Art Gallery;** and Birmingham's **Museum and Art Gallery.**

o **Thomas Gainsborough (1727–88).** Although he was a classical/baroque portraitist like his rival Reynolds, at least Gainsborough could be original. Too bad his tastes ran to rococo pastels, frothy feathered brushwork, and busy compositions. When not immortalizing such noble patrons as Jonathan Buttall (better known as *The Blue Boy*), he painted a collection of landscapes just for himself. His works grace the **Victoria Art Gallery** in Bath (where he first came to fame), London's **National Gallery** and **National Portrait Gallery,** Cambridge's **Fitzwilliam Museum,** Oxford's **Cathedral Hall** and **Ashmolean Museum,** Liverpool's **Walker Art Gallery,** and Birmingham's **Museum and Art Gallery.**

Paintings by the Romantics (Late 18th–19th c.)

The Romantics felt the Gothic Middle Ages was the place to be. They idealized the tales of chivalry and had a deep respect for nature, human rights, and the nobility of peasantry.

Significant British artists of this period include:

o **William Blake (1757–1827).** Romantic archetype Blake snubbed the stuffy Royal Academy of Arts to do his own engraving, prints, illustrations, poetry, and

England's Art & Architecture

CHURCH architecture 101

While each architectural era has its distinctive features, there are some elements, floor plans, and terms common to many. This is particularly true of churches, large numbers of which were built in England and Wales from the Middle Ages through the 18th century.

From the Norman period on, most churches consist of either a single, wide **aisle** or a wide central **nave** flanked by two narrower aisles. The aisles are separated from the nave by a row of **columns,** or square stacks of masonry called **piers,** and connected by arches.

This main nave/aisle assemblage is usually crossed by a perpendicular corridor called a **transept** near the far, east end of the church so that the floor plan looks like a Latin cross (shaped like a crucifix). The shorter, east arm of the nave is called the **chancel;** it often houses the **altar** and stalls of the **choir.** If the far end of the chancel is rounded off, it is called an **apse.**

An **ambulatory** is a curving corridor outside the altar and choir area, separating it from the ring of small **chapels** radiating off the chancel and apse.

It's worth pointing out that very few buildings (especially churches) were built in one particular style. Massive, expensive structures often took centuries to complete, during which time tastes would change and plans would be altered.

Church Floor Plan

painting. His works are filled with melodrama, muscular figures, and sweeping lines. Judge for yourself at London's **Tate Britain** and Manchester's **Whitworth Art Gallery.**

o **J. M. W. Turner (1775–1851).** The "First Impressionist" was a prolific and multitalented artist whose mood-laden, freely brushed watercolor landscapes influenced Monet. The River Thames and London, where he lived and died, were frequent subjects. London's **Tate Britain** displays the largest number of Turner's works.

o **John Constable (1776–1837).** Constable was a great British landscapist whose scenes (especially those of happy, agricultural peasants) grew more idealized with each passing year—while his compositions and brushwork became freer. You'll find his best stuff in London's **National Gallery** and **Victoria and Albert Museum,** and in Liverpool's **Walker Art Gallery.**

o **Pre-Raphaelites (1848–70s).** This "brotherhood" of painters declared that art had gone all wrong with Italian Renaissance painter Raphael (1483–1520) and set about to emulate the Italian painters who preceded him. The works of **Dante**

Gabriel Rossetti, William Hunt, and John Everett Millais most evoke this school. Their symbolically imbued, sweetly idealized, hyper-realistic work depicts scenes from Romantic poetry and Shakespeare as much as from the Bible. You can see pre-Raphaelite art at London's **Tate Britain,** Oxford's **Ashmolean Museum,** Liverpool's **Walker Art Gallery,** and Manchester's **Manchester Art Gallery.**

20th-Century Art

Art of the last century often followed international schools or styles—no major ones truly originated in Britain—and the major British artists listed here tended to move in and out of styles over their careers:

- **Henry Moore (1898–1986).** A sculptor, Moore saw himself as a sort of reincarnation of Michelangelo. The **Henry Moore Institute** in Leeds, where he studied, preserves his drawings and sculpture. You'll also find his work at Cambridge's **Fitzwilliam Museum** and **Clare College.**
- **Francis Bacon (1909–92).** A dark and brooding Expressionist, Bacon presented man's foibles in formats usually reserved for religious subjects, such as the triptych (a set of three panels, often hinged and used as an altarpiece). You can find his works in London, Birmingham, and Manchester's **Whitworth Art Gallery.**
- **David Hockney (b. 1937).** The closest thing to a British Andy Warhol, Hockney employs a less pop-arty style than the famous American—though Hockney does reference modern technologies and culture. His work resides in London and Liverpool.
- **Damien Hirst (b. 1965).** The guy who pickles cows, Hirst is a celebrity artist whose work sets out to shock. He's a past winner of Britain's Turner Prize.

Norman Architecture (1066–1200)

The oldest surviving architectural style in England dates from when the 1066 Norman Conquest brought the Romanesque era to Britain, where it flourished as the **Norman** style.

Churches in this style were large, with wide naves and aisles to accommodate the crowds who came to hear Mass and worship at the altars of various saints. But to support the weight of all that masonry, the walls had to be thick and solid, giving Norman churches a dark, somber, mysterious, and often oppressive feeling.

The best examples of Norman architecture include London's **White Tower** (1078), William the Conqueror's first building in Britain at the Tower of London; **Durham Cathedral** (1093–1488), with a Norman floor plan; and **Ely Cathedral** (1083–1189), with a nave and south transept that are perfectly Norman.

White Tower, London

Gothic Architecture (1150–1550)

The French Gothic style invaded England in the late 12th century, trading rounded arches for pointy ones—an engineering discovery that freed church architecture from the heavy, thick walls of Norman structures and allowed ceilings to soar, walls to thin, and windows to proliferate.

The Gothic proper in Britain can be divided into three overlapping periods or styles: **Early English** (1150–1300), **Decorated** (1250–1370), and **Perpendicular** (1350–1550).

The best example of Early English is **Salisbury Cathedral** (1220–65), unique in Europe for the speed with which it was built. The first to use pointy arches was **Wells Cathedral** (1180–1321), which has 300 statues on its original facade.

The facade, nave, and chapter house of **York Minster** (1220–1480), which preserves the most medieval stained glass in Britain, is Decorated, though the chancel is Perpendicular and the transepts are Early English. **Exeter Cathedral** (1112–1206) has an elaborate Decorated facade and fantastic nave vaulting.

The Perpendicular **King's College Chapel** at Cambridge (1446–1515) has England's most magnificent fan vaulting, along with some fine stained glass. **Henry VII's Chapel** (1503–19) in London's Westminster Abbey is textbook Perpendicular.

Salisbury Cathedral

Renaissance Architecture (1550–1650)

It wasn't until the Elizabethan era that the Brits turned to the **Renaissance** style sweeping the Continent. England's greatest Renaissance architect, **Inigo Jones** (1573–1652), brought back from his Italian travels a fevered imagination full of the exactingly classical theories of **Palladianism,** a style derived from the buildings and publications of **Andrea Palladio** (1508–80). However, most English architects at this time tempered the Renaissance style with a heavy dose of Gothic-like elements.

Jones applied his theories of Palladianism to such edifices as the **Queen's House** (1616–18 and 1629–35) in Greenwich, the **Queen's Chapel** (1623–25) in St. James's Palace in London, and the **Banqueting House** (1619–22) in Whitehall, also in London.

Baroque Architecture (1650–1750)

England's greatest architect was **Christopher Wren** (1632–1723), a scientist and member of Parliament who got the job of rebuilding London after the Great Fire of 1666. He designed 53 replacement churches alone, plus the new St. Paul's Cathedral, which was the crowning achievement of English **baroque** and of Wren himself.

Other proponents of baroque architecture were **John Vanbrugh** (1664–1726) and his mentor and oft-collaborator **Nicholas Hawksmoor** (1661–1736), who sometimes worked in a more Palladian idiom.

Neoclassical & Greek Revival Architecture (1714–1837)

Many 18th-century architects cared little for the baroque period, and during the Georgian era (1714–1830) a restrained, simple **neoclassicism** reigned. This **Greek Revival** style was practiced by architects such as **James "Athenian" Stuart** (1713–88), who wrote a book on antiquities after a trip to Greece, and the somewhat less strict **John Soane** (1773–1837).

Much of the city of **Bath** was made over in the 18th century, most famously by the father-and-son team of **John Wood the Elder** and **John Wood the Younger** (1704–54 and 1728–81, respectively). They were responsible, among others, for the **Royal Crescent** (1767–75), where you can visit one house's interior and even lodge in another.

Royal Crescent, Bath

Victorian Gothic Revival Architecture (1750–1900)

The early Romantic movement swept up others with rosy visions of the past. This imaginary and fairy-tale version of the Middle Ages led to such creative developments as the pre-Raphaelite painters (see "Paintings by the Romantics," above) and Gothic Revival architects, who really got a head of steam under their movement during the eclectic Victorian era.

Gothic "Revival" is a bit misleading, as its practitioners usually applied their favorite Gothic features at random rather than faithfully re-creating a whole structure.

The best example is the **Palace of Westminster (Houses of Parliament)** in London (1835–52). **Charles Barry** (1795–1860) designed the wonderful British

Palace of Westminster, London

Canary Wharf Tower, London

seat of government in a Gothic idiom that, more than most, sticks pretty faithfully to the old Perpendicular period's style. His clock tower, usually called **Big Ben** after its biggest bell, has become an icon of London itself.

20th-Century Architecture

After the World War II Blitz, much of central London had to be rebuilt. Most of the new commercial buildings in the city held to a functional school of architecture aptly named **Brutalism.** It wasn't until the boom of the late 1970s and 1980s that **postmodern** architecture gave British architects a bold, new direction with a skyscraper motif.

Stellar examples of modern architecture include the **Lloyd's building** in the City of London (1978–86), the masterpiece of **Richard Rogers** (b. 1933), and **Canary Wharf Tower (One Canada Square)** (1986), also in London, a complex designed by **César Pelli** (b. 1926).

ENGLAND IN POPULAR CULTURE: BOOKS, FILM & MUSIC

Books

England has produced one of the world's greatest libraries of literature and drama—and not just William Shakespeare. Here is a mere preview of what's out there, at least enough to whet your appetite.

GENERAL & HISTORY   Anthony Sampson's *The Changing Anatomy of Britain* (Random House) still gives great insight into the idiosyncrasies of English society; Winston Churchill's *History of the English-Speaking Peoples* (Dodd Mead) is a tour de force in four volumes; while *The Gathering Storm* (Houghton-Mifflin) captures Europe on the brink of World War II.

My Love Affair with England (Ballantine), by Susan Allan Toth, tells of England's "many-layered past" and includes such tidbits as why English marmalade tastes good only when consumed as part of a real (make that greasy) English breakfast.

Britons: Forging the Nation (1707–1837) (Yale University Press), by Linda Colley, took more than a decade to finish. Colley takes the reader from the date of the Act of Union (formally joining Scotland and Wales to England) to the succession of the adolescent Victoria to the British throne. *Children of the Sun* (Basics Books), by Martin Green, portrays the "decadent" 1920s and the lives of such people as Randolph Churchill, poet Rupert Brooke, the Prince of Wales, and Christopher Isherwood.

In *A Writer's Britain* (Knopf), contemporary English author Margaret Drabble takes readers on a tour of the sacred and haunted literary landscapes of England, places that inspired Hardy, Woolf, Spenser, and Marvell.

Outsiders often paint more penetrating portraits than residents of any culture ever can. In England's case, many have expressed their views of the country over different periods. An early-18th-century portrait is provided by K. P. Moritz in *Journeys of a German in England in 1782* (Holt, Rinehart & Winston), which covers his travels from London to the Midlands. Nathaniel Hawthorne recorded his impressions in *Our Old Home* (1863), as did Ralph Waldo Emerson in *English Traits* (1856). For an ironic portrait of mid-19th-century Victorian British morals, manners, and society, seek out *Taine's Notes on England* (1872). Henry James's comments on England at the turn of the 20th century in *English Hours* (1905) are worth a read. In *A Passage to England* (St. Martin's Press), Nirad Chaudhuri analyzes Britain and the British in a delightful, humorous book—a process continued today by such authors as Salman Rushdie, V. S. Naipaul, and Paul Theroux.

Among the interesting portraits written by natives are Cobbet's *Rural Rides* (1830), depicting early-19th-century England; *In Search of England* (Methuen), by H. V. Morton; and *English Journey* (Harper), by J. B. Priestley. For what's really going on behind that serene Suffolk village scene, read Ronald Blythe's *Akenfield: Portrait of an English Village* (Random House).

ART & ARCHITECTURE   For general reference, there's the huge multivolume *Oxford History of English Art* (Oxford University Press) and also the *Encyclopedia of British Art* (Thames Hudson), by David Bindman. *Painting in Britain 1530–1790* (Penguin), by Ellis Waterhouse, covers British art from the Tudor miniaturists to Gainsborough, Reynolds, and Hogarth, while *English Art, 1870–1940* (Oxford University Press), by Dennis Farr, covers the modern period.

On architecture, for sheer amusing, opinionated entertainment, try John Betjeman's *Ghastly Good Taste: Or, a Depressing Story of the Rise and Fall of English Architecture* (St. Martin's Press). *A History of English Architecture* (Penguin), by Peter Kidson, Peter Murray, and Paul Thompson, covers the subject from Anglo-Saxon to modern times. Nikolaus Pevsner's *The Best Buildings of England: An Anthology* (Viking) and his *Outline of European Architecture* (Penguin) concentrate on the great periods of Tudor, Georgian, and Regency architecture. Mark Girouard has written several books on British architecture, including *The Victorian Country House* (Country Life) and *Life in the English Country House* (Yale University Press), a fascinating social/architectural history from the Middle Ages to the 20th century, with handsome illustrations.

ABOUT LONDON   *London Perceived* (Hogarth), by novelist and literary critic V. S. Pritchett, is a witty portrait of the city's history, art, literature, and life. Virginia Woolf's *The London Scene: Five Essays* (Random House) brilliantly depicts the London of the 1930s. *In Search of London* (Methuen), by H. V. Morton, though written in the 1950s, is filled with anecdotal history and well worth reading.

In *London: The Biography of a City* (Penguin), popular historian Christopher Hibbert paints a lively portrait. For some real 17th-century history, you can't beat the *Diary of Samuel Pepys* (written 1660–69); and for the flavor of the 18th century, try Daniel Defoe's *Tour Thro' London About the Year 1725* (Ayer).

Americans in London (William Morrow), by Brian N. Morton, is a street-by-street guide to clubs, homes, and favorite pubs of more than 250 illustrious Americans who made London a temporary home. George Williams's *Guide to Literary London* (Batsford) charts literary tours through London from Chelsea to Bloomsbury.

The Architect's Guide to London (Reed International), by Renzo Salvadori, documents 100 landmark buildings with photographs and maps. *Nairn's London* (Penguin), by Ian Nairn, is a stimulating discourse on London's buildings. Donald Olsen's *The City as a Work of Art: London, Paris, and Vienna* (Yale University Press) is a well-illustrated text tracing the evolution of these great cities. *London One: The Cities of London and Westminster* and *London Two: South* (Penguin) are works of love by well-known architectural writers Bridget Cherry and Nikolaus Pevsner. David Piper's *The Artist's London* (Oxford University Press) does what the title suggests—captures the city that artists have portrayed. In *Victorian and Edwardian London* (Batsford), John Betjeman expresses his great love of those eras and their great buildings. *Looking Up in London* (Wiley Academy), by Jane Peyton, offers colorful photos of some of London's architectural features.

CLASSIC FICTION & BIOGRAPHY   Among English writers are found some of the greatest exponents of mystery and suspense novels, from which a reader can get a good feel for English life, both urban and rural. Agatha Christie, P. D. James, and Dorothy Sayers are a few of the familiar names, but the great London character, of course, is Sherlock Holmes, created by Arthur Conan Doyle. Any of these writers will give pleasure and insight into your London experience.

England's literary heritage is so vast, it's hard to select particular titles, but here are a few favorites. Master storyteller Charles Dickens re-creates Victorian London in such books as *Oliver Twist, David Copperfield,* and his earlier satirical *Sketches by Boz.*

Edwardian London and the 1920s and 1930s are captured wonderfully in any of Evelyn Waugh's social satires and comedies. Any work from the Bloomsbury Group will also prove enlightening, such as Virginia Woolf's *Mrs. Dalloway,* which peers beneath the surface of the London scene. For a portrait of wartime London, there's Elizabeth Bowen's *The Heat of the Day;* for an American slant on England and London, there's Henry James's *The Awkward Age.*

Among 18th-century figures, there's a great biography of Samuel Johnson by his friend James Boswell, whose *Life of Samuel Johnson* (Modern Library College Editions) was first published in 1791. Antonia Fraser has written several biographies of English monarchs and political figures, including Charles II and Oliver Cromwell. Her most recent is *The Wives of Henry VIII* (Knopf), telling the sad story of the six women foolish enough to marry the Tudor monarch.

Another great Tudor monarch, Elizabeth I, emerges in a fully rounded portrait: *The Virgin Queen, Elizabeth I, Genius of the Golden Age* (Addison-Wesley), by Christopher Hibbert.

Another historian, Anne Somerset, wrote *Elizabeth I* (St. Martin's Press), hailed by some critics as the most "readable and reliable" portrait of England's most revered monarch to have emerged since 1934.

No woman—or man, for that matter—had greater influence on London than did Queen Victoria during her long reign (1837–1901). Sarah Ferguson, the duchess of York (Prince Andrew's former wife, "Fergie"), along with Benita Stoney, a professional researcher, captures the era in *Victoria and Albert: A Family Life at Osborne House* (Prentice Hall). One reviewer said that Fergie writes about "England's 19th-century rulers not as historical figures but as a loving couple and caring parents."

Another point of view is projected in *Victoria: The Young Queen* (Blackwell), by Monica Charlot. This book has been praised for its "fresh information"; it traces the life of Victoria until the death of her husband, Prince Albert, in 1861. Queen Elizabeth II granted Charlot access to the Royal Archives.

In *Elizabeth II, Portrait of a Monarch* (St. Martin's Press), Douglas Keay drew on interviews with Prince Philip and Prince Charles.

Richard Ellman's *Oscar Wilde* (Knopf) also reveals such Victorian-era personalities as Lillie Langtry, Gilbert and Sullivan, and Henry James along the way. Quintessential English playwright Noël Coward and the London he inhabited, along with the likes of Nancy Mitford, Cecil Beaton, John Gielgud, Laurence Olivier, Vivien Leigh, Evelyn Waugh, and Rebecca West, are captured in Cole Lesley's *Remembered Laughter* (Knopf). *The Lives of John Lennon* (William Morrow), by Albert Goldman, traces the life of this most famous of all '60s musicians.

Dickens (Harper Perennial), by Peter Ackroyd, is a study of the painful life of the novelist. It's a massive volume, tracing everything from the reception of his first novel, *The Pickwick Papers*, to his scandalous desertion of his wife.

Other good reads include *Wild Spirit: The Story of Percy Bysshe Shelley* (Hodder & Stoughton), by Margaret Morley, a fictionalized biography of the poet. *Gertrude Jekyll* (Viking), by Sally Festing, paints a portrait of the woman called "the greatest artist in horticulture." *Anthony Trollope* (Knopf), by Victoria Glendinning, is a provocative portrait of the English novelist. *Lawrence and the Women: The Intimate Life of D. H. Lawrence* (HarperCollins), by Elaine Feinstein, examines involvements with the female friends and lovers of this passionately sensitive novelist.

CONTEMPORARY LITERATURE Born to a Jamaican mother and a British father, Zadie Smith is one of the most talented young authors in England today. Published in 2000, her bestselling novel *White Teeth* (Vintage) brought her early acclaim. She followed up with *The Autograph Man* (Vintage, 2002) and *On Beauty* (Penguin, 2005), both of which won prizes for fiction. Her writing is known for its deep penetration of the rainbow-hued races inhabiting Britain today.

The writings of Nick Hornby have earned him the title "European Ambassador of Goodness." An autobiographical work, his first book, *Fever Pitch* (Penguin), was published in 1992 to both success and acclaim. In subsequent novels, he explores sports, music, "and aimless and obsessive personalities." Several of his works have been adapted for film, including *About a Boy*, starring Hugh Grant.

Influenced by the writing of his father, Sir Kingsley Amis, Martin Amis has written some of the best-known works of English modern literature, especially *Money* (Penguin, 1986) and *London Fields* (Vintage, 1989). The *New York Times* called him the undisputed master of "the new unpleasantness." He explores the excesses of the capitalist world, plunging a sword into the heart of grotesque caricatures. His memoir, *Experience* (Vintage), explored his relationship with his father. His 2003 novel *Yellow Dog* (Vintage), although praised by fans, was a disappointment in some quarters.

The English fiction writer Joanne Rowling, writing under the pen name of J. K. Rowling, created the Harry Potter fantasy series, which has sold nearly 400 million copies worldwide and made her an estimated fortune of $1 billion, a first for any author. She was an unemployed single mom when she completed her first novel, *Harry Potter and the Philosopher's Stone* (1997; the American title is *Harry Potter and the Sorcerer's Stone*). In 2007, Rowling released *Harry Potter and the Deathly Hallows*, which she claims will be the last of the series.

Other modern writers include Adam Thorpe, a poet, playwright, and novelist. Although born in Paris, he grew up in India. His first novel, *Ulverton* (Farrar, Straus and Giroux, 1992), a panoramic portrait of English rural history, brought him much acclaim. He continues to write today, publishing *Between Each Breath* in 2007, *The Standing Pool* in 2008, and *Hodd* in 2009 (all published by Random House).

Another acclaimed and often controversial writer is Irvine Welsh, a brilliant storyteller and—unarguably—one of the funniest and "filthiest" writers in Britain. He shot to fame upon the release of his book, *Trainspotting* (W. W. Norton), in 1993.

Film

Some of the greatest stars came from Britain but made their mark in Hollywood, notably Charlie Chaplin, Cary Grant, and violet-eyed Elizabeth Taylor. In spite of its native-born talent, Hollywood even turned to Britain to cast Scarlett O'Hara in the 1939 film *Gone With the Wind*.

Great directors, including that master of suspense, Alfred Hitchcock, also moved from London to Hollywood for greater fame. Lord Laurence Olivier frequently was cast in Hollywood films, as were a long line of Shakespeare-trained actors who followed him—Judi Dench, Maggie Smith, Jeremy Irons, Ian McKellen.

Some British films seem to live on forever, as in the case of *A Hard Day's Night* (1964), which depicts a "typical" day in the life of the Beatles and includes many of their famous songs.

Tame by today's standards, *My Beautiful Laundrette* (1985) was a scandal upon its release. It not only brought actor Daniel Day-Lewis into international renown, but also dealt with homosexuality and interracial relationships.

Born in poverty in Northern Ireland, Kenneth Branagh has brought Shakespeare to mainstream audiences, notably with *Much Ado About Nothing* (1993) and a widely acclaimed *Hamlet* (1996). He's been nominated for four Oscars.

Director/writer Mike Leigh's *Secrets & Lies* (1996) was nominated for five Oscars; it depicts a black woman who traces her birth mother, a lower-class white woman.

The happy team of Merchant and Ivory has turned out a series of films that achieved international fame, including *Maurice* (1987), *A Room with a View* (1985), and *Howards End* (1992).

Still a great favorite with British students, *Withnail & I* (1987) is set in London in 1969, featuring two unemployed and unemployable actors who go for an idyllic (yeah, right) holiday in the countryside.

Two films depicting unusual stories from the blue-collar ghettos of the north of England have been much honored: *Billy Elliot* (2000), in which Jamie Bell plays a talented young boy who wants to be a ballet dancer, and *The Full Monty* (1997), in which six unemployed steelworker blokes form a male striptease act.

Four Weddings and a Funeral (1994), a comedy-drama about a group of British friends, stars Hugh Grant giving his most charming performance to date.

24 Hour Party People (2002) is a tale of music, sex, drugs, and larger-than-life characters, plus the birth of one of the most famous dance clubs in the world. The music and dance heritage of Manchester from the late '70s to the early '90s is depicted.

Guy Ritchie is a director-actor-producer-writer who achieved some fame with releases such as *Lock, Stock and Two Smoking Barrels* (1998) and *Snatch* (2000), the latter starring Brad Pitt. He's had a run of bad luck in recent years, including when he cast his then-wife, Madonna, in *Swept Away* (2002). The public was hardly swept away; nor were the critics. But Ritchie is still a young man and might redeem his early promise, although *Revolver* (2005) waited 2 years to find a distributor and then opened and closed overnight.

No films have ever equaled the success of the Harry Potter franchise, a series based on the novels of J. K. Rowling. Kicked off in 2001 with *Harry Potter and the Sorcerer's Stone,* the series continues to break box-office records. Many Potter fans visit film sites such as including Alnwick Castle and Christ Church College in Oxford, and even Fort William in the Scottish Highlands. The latest in the series is *Harry Potter and the Half-Blood Prince* (2009).

One of the most-viewed British films of 2008 was actually a BBC television mini-series, *Sense & Sensibility,* based on the Jane Austin novel. The cast and settings were more wonderful than the screenplay.

Music

The music performed at Elizabeth I's court, including compositions by Thomas Morley (ca. 1557–1602), have been recorded by the Deller Consort; one of their titles is *Now Is the Month of Maying: Madrigal Masterpieces.*

England's Renaissance church music is best exemplified by English composer William Byrd (1543–1623); listen to his *Cantiones sacrae: 1575,* performed by the Choir of New College, Oxford, and recorded in the New College Chapel for London Records.

Henry Purcell's *Dido and Aeneas* is widely available in several performances. For an example of Purcell's orchestral music, listen to *The Virtuoso Trumpet,* performed by trumpeter Maurice André, who is accompanied by the Academy of St. Martin in the Fields, with Sir Neville Mariner conducting.

John Gay's *The Beggar's Opera,* first performed in 1728, is available in a recording by Britain's National Philharmonic Orchestra and the London Opera Chorus for Polygram Records.

The works of the beloved British team of Sir Arthur Sullivan (composer) and Sir W. S. Gilbert (librettist) are widely available. *The Mikado,* performed by the Pro Arte Orchestra and the Glyndebourne Festival Chorus, with Sir Malcolm Sargent conducting, is available on CD.

The compositions of Sir Edward Elgar can be heard on the British Philharmonic Orchestra's recording of the *Pomp and Circumstance* marches, conducted by Andrew Davis.

Two fine recordings of England's modern master, Ralph Vaughan Williams, are his *Symphony no. 3* ("Pastoral"), performed by the London Symphony Orchestra; and his *Sea Symphony,* performed by the London Symphony Orchestra and Chorus, with conductor André Previn.

Benjamin Britten's *Ceremony of Carols,* performed by the Choir of St. John's College, Cambridge, and his *Variations for a String Orchestra,* performed by the London Philharmonic Orchestra, with Roger Best on viola, are both fine examples of this preeminent British composer.

Richard Thompson, who performs on *Amnesia,* has been reviewed as one of the most unusual and iconoclastic of modern British folk performers. He uses guitar, mandolin, and hammer dulcimer in his melodies, and his lyrics showcase political and social satire as well as soulfully nostalgic ballads.

Of course, nothing in British musical history has equaled the popular enthusiasm that greeted the British revolution of the 1960s. Aided by improvements in acoustical technology and the changing sociology of Britain, music was suddenly the passionate interest of millions of youthful Brits, setting the scene for a cultural invasion of American shores that hadn't been seen since the 18th century.

It began with the Beatles, of course—John, Paul, George, and Ringo, who won the hearts of every schoolgirl in America when they appeared on the *Ed Sullivan Show* in February 1964. They seemed to be in the vanguard of every cultural and musical movement, and as the 1960s progressed, the Beatles didn't simply capitalize on their success or the musical styles that had originally made them popular. Their music evolved with the times and helped shape the cultural and political texture of their era.

The Beatles were only the first of many British bands that found fertile ground and a receptive audience overseas. They were soon followed by the Rolling Stones, the Who, and David Bowie.

Past Masters is a two-volume retrospective collection of Beatles music. Equally important is their milestone album *Sgt. Pepper's Lonely Hearts Club Band,* which was a musical watershed when it was released in 1967.

The Rolling Stones's *Flashpoint* is a textbook study of the spirit of rock 'n' roll, with a guest performance by Eric Clapton on a track entitled "Little Red Rooster." Another Rolling Stone great is *Exile on Main Street.*

Britain birthed David Bowie, Gary Glitter, the Sex Pistols, the Clash, and Faces. These icons were followed by the neo-Brit brats Oasis, with brothers Liam and Noel Gallagher selling millions of records. Along came Blur, Cast, and Ocean Colour Scene, acknowledging the influence of the Beatles and the Stones. The cities that gave birth to these talents—London, Liverpool, and Manchester—have an ever-changing but always exciting music scene today.

Prince Harry fell hard for the Spice Girls, an English pop group formed in 1994, but David Beckham made off with Posh.

One of the biggest names today is the Grammy Award–winning Amy Winehouse, mistress of soul, vocal jazz, R&B, and doo-wop. Her personal troubles and beehive hairstyle continue to make tabloid headlines.

Way down the musical scale in pecking order are the London group called the Rakes—"skinny as rakes"—shooting to fame in 2005 with post–punk rock music. From Leeds, the indie-rock band Pigeon Detectives were voted "the band most likely to leap to the main stage in 2007." From Brighton come the Kooks, indie and pop rockers who released their second album, *Konk,* in the spring of 2008.

Bloc Party, another London group singing indie, rock, and post-punk revival, made "Album of the Year" in 2005 with their debut, *Silent Alarm.* Yet another post-punk revival group, Franz Ferdinand, originated in Glasgow as an indie favorite. The band's second album, *You Could Have It So Much Better,* topped the charts in the U.K. The alternative rock group Coldplay achieved worldwide fame for their hit single "Yellow," followed by the success of their debut album, *Parachutes.*

EATING & DRINKING IN ENGLAND

The late British humorist George Mikes wrote that "the Continentals have good food; the English have good table manners." But the British no longer deserve their reputation for soggy cabbage and tasteless dishes. Contemporary London—and the country as a whole—boasts fine restaurants and sophisticated cuisine.

The buzzword for British cuisine today is *magpie,* meaning borrowing ideas from global travels, taking them home, and improving on the original. If you want to see what Britain is eating today, just drop in at Harvey Nichol's Fifth Floor, in London's Knightsbridge, for its dazzling display of produce from all over the globe.

A pundit once noted that to dine out in London now requires a knowledge of foreign languages. Increasingly, that is true for the rest of England and, to a lesser degree, Wales. Foreign-cuisine restaurants, especially Indian and Chinese, seem to flourish in almost every village.

All major towns and most definitely all English cities have their immigrant communities, bringing with them the food of their native lands. In addition to Chinese, Thai and Indonesian restaurants are popping up more and more. Spanish tapas bars are all the rage, and Japanese cuisine is going over big time with the Brits who flock to sushi places.

For decades now, French and Italian restaurants have been the dining rooms of choice for those who like to dine out. The ranks of British gastronomic restaurants continue to grow, and now even small towns seem to have at least one gastronomic shrine.

TAXES & tipping

All restaurants and cafes are required to display the prices of their food and drink in a place visible from outside. Charges for service, as well as any minimums or cover charges, must also be made clear. The prices shown must include the 17.5% VAT, the so-called "value-added" tax. Most restaurants add a 15% service charge to your bill, but check to make sure. If nothing has been added, leave a 10% to 15% tip. It is by no means considered rude to tip, so feel free to leave something extra if service was good.

Be aware that many of the trendiest, most innovative restaurants are mind-blowingly expensive, especially in London. We've pointed out some innovative but affordable choices in this book, but if you're really trying to save on dining costs, you'll no doubt find yourself falling back on the traditional pub favorites—or better still, turning to an increasingly good selection of ethnic restaurants.

WHAT YOU'LL FIND ON THE MENU IN ENGLAND   Of course, many who visit England want to sample the local cuisine. English cooking has been ridiculed for years (those long-boiled Brussels sprouts, for example), but the food is better than ever these days. The country has wonderful produce, from its Cotswold lamb to its Scottish salmon. You don't always have to dine foreign for a true gastronomic experience. English chefs, many of whom have trained on the Continent, have returned to put more flavor and flair in their native recipes.

On any pub menu, you're likely to encounter such dishes as the **Cornish pasty** (*past*-ee) and **shepherd's pie.** The first, traditionally made from Sunday-meal leftovers and taken by West Country fishermen for Monday lunch, consists of chopped potatoes, carrots, and onions mixed with seasoning and put into a pastry envelope. The second is a deep dish of chopped cooked beef mixed with onions and seasoning, covered with a layer of mashed potatoes, and served hot. Another version is **cottage pie,** which is minced beef covered with potatoes and also served hot. Of course, these beef dishes are subject to availability. In addition to a pasty, Cornwall also gives us **Stargazy pie**—a deep-dish fish pie with a crisp crust covering a creamy concoction of freshly caught herring and vegetables.

The most common pub meal, though, is the **ploughman's lunch,** traditional farmworkers' fare, consisting of a good chunk of local cheese, a hunk of homemade crusty white or brown bread, some butter, and a pickled onion or two, washed down with ale. You'll now find such variations as pâté and chutney occasionally replacing the onions and cheese. Or you might find **Lancashire hot pot,** a stew of mutton, potatoes, kidneys, and onions (sometimes carrots). This concoction was originally put into a deep dish and set on the edge of the stove to cook slowly while the workers spent the day at the local mill.

Among the best-known traditional English meals is **roast beef** and **Yorkshire pudding** (the pudding is made with a flour base and cooked under the roast, allowing the fat from the meat to drop onto it). The beef could easily be a large sirloin (rolled loin), which, so the story goes, was named by James I when he was a guest at Houghton Tower, Lancashire. "Arise, Sir Loin," he cried, as he knighted the leg of beef before him with his dagger. Another dish that makes use of a flour base is **toad-in-the-hole,** in which sausages are cooked in batter. Game, especially **pheasant** and **grouse,** is also a staple on British tables.

On any menu, you'll find fresh **seafood:** cod, haddock, herring, plaice, and Dover sole, the aristocrat of flatfish. Cod and haddock are used in making British **fish and chips** (the chips are fried potatoes or thick french fries), which the true Briton covers with salt and vinegar. Every region of England has its seafood specialties. If you like **oysters,** try some of the famous Colchester variety. On the west coast, you'll find a not-to-be-missed delicacy: **Morecambe Bay shrimp.** In Ely, lying in the marshy fen district of East Anglia, it might be fenland **eel pie** with a twiggy seaweed as your green vegetable. **Samphire** also grows here in the salt marshes and along the Norfolk Coast. It's pickled in May and June and appears as a delicacy on many summer menus.

The **East End of London** has quite a few intriguing old dishes, among them tripe and onions. In winter, the Cheshire Cheese tavern on Fleet Street offers a beefsteak, kidney, mushroom, and game pudding in a suet case; in summer, there's a pastry case. East Enders can still be seen on Sunday at the Jellied Eel stall by Petticoat Lane, eating eel, cockles (small clams), mussels, whelks, and winkles—all with a touch of vinegar.

The British call desserts **sweets,** though some people still refer to any dessert as **pudding.** The most famous English dessert is **trifle,** consisting of sponge cake soaked in brandy or sherry, coated with fruit or jam, and topped with cream custard. A **fool,** such as gooseberry fool, is a light cream dessert whipped up from seasonal fruits. Regional sweets include the northern **flitting dumpling** (dates, walnuts, and syrup mixed with other ingredients and made into a pudding that is easily sliced and carried along when you're "flitting" from place to place). Similarly, **hasty pudding,** a Newcastle dish, is supposed to have been invented by people in a hurry to avoid the bailiff. It consists of stale bread to which some dried fruit and milk are added before it is put into the oven.

Cheese is traditionally served after dessert as a savory. There are many regional cheeses, the best known being cheddar, a good, solid, mature cheese. Others are the semismooth Caerphilly, from a beautiful part of Wales, and Stilton, a blue-veined crumbly cheese that's often enjoyed with a glass of port.

A TASTE OF WALES   The food served in Wales is often indistinguishable from that in England, but there are a number of specialties you should try that you won't find elsewhere.

The **leek** is one of the national emblems of Wales and is used in a number of dishes. The selection of the leek for this national honor is lost in the dim past, although it is associated with St. David, patron saint of Wales. Today, the leek is worn on St. David's Day, March 1, a national holiday.

Among dishes in which the leek is used is *cawl mamgu,* a rich soup or stew. The most commonly used recipe calls for lamb or mutton, turnips (the Welsh call them Swedes), carrots, potatoes, parsnips, onions, and leeks. The **leek pasty,** usually made in the shape of a little leek, is a popular appetizer or side dish.

The potato became a dietary staple of Wales in the 18th century. **Anglesey** eggs feature potatoes and leeks as well as cheese. **Punchnep** is a combination of potatoes and turnips served with heavy cream. *Teisen nionod,* or onion cake, is a tasty slow-baked potato-and-onion dish.

Most people are familiar with **Welsh rarebit** (or rabbit, if you prefer), but another cheese dish you should try that is not found elsewhere is **Glamorgan sausage,** a meatless concoction of onion, cheese, bread crumbs, and seasonings, shaped like sausages, dipped in bread crumbs, and fried. Another good dish, **skirettes,** is sort of a mashed-potato pancake with a difference. The difference is supplied by grated walnuts, prawns, hard-boiled eggs, onion, cheddar cheese, and spices. It's all given a bread-crumb coating and baked or deep-fried.

Faggots used to be made of meat fragments left over after pig slaughter, wrapped in membrane that covers the pig's abdominal organs, and shaped like sausages. Today, it's all a little more palatable sounding, being made of liver, bacon, onions, bread crumbs, and sage, then cooked and served cold.

Rabbit, chicken, turkey, duckling, game, even pheasant appear on the menus, and a rabbit casserole is offered in some restaurants as a Taste of Wales, so popular is the meat. Special dishes include a **poacher's pie** (containing beef, rabbit, chicken, and game) and **Welsh salt duck,** which rivals any offered on Asian menus.

Predominant on the list of what to eat while in Wales are freshwater fish and seafood. **Trout** and **salmon** prevail among the products of rivers and lakes, tumbling practically from the fisherman's creel to your plate, with a little detour through the kitchen. Perhaps you'll get to taste a rare salmon, *gwyniad,* which is found only in Bala Lake. Baked trout with bacon is a favorite.

From the ocean and coastal waters come crabs, lobsters, sewin (sea trout), crayfish, mackerel, herring, Pollack, bass, hake, ling, whiting, and flatfish, as well as cockles, limpets, scallops, and mussels. The Romans were great cockle eaters, as revealed by huge mounds of the shells found in excavating the sites occupied by the long-ago conquerors. You may enjoy the **cockle-and-bacon pie** offered on some menus, or **Gower scallops and bacon.** Also popular are mussel stew and mussel-and-queenie (scallop) **cawl,** which is like a bouillabaisse.

The Welsh word for bread is *bara.* At least once, you should try **laverbread (*bara lawr*),** which has probably been part of the Welsh diet since prehistoric times. It's made of laver weed, a parchmentlike seaweed, which is boiled and mixed with oatmeal, shaped into laverbread cakes, and fried like pancakes. It's full of vitamins and minerals. You'll find it on all Taste of Wales menus, so take a nibble at least. *Bara ceirch,* a flat oatcake, is rolled very thin and cooked on a griddle. A rich currant bread, *bara brith,* is found all over the country, although the ingredients may vary. It's baked in a loaf, and some cooks use raisins and candied citrus peel along with the currants.

Perhaps you'll get a chance to sample **Welsh cakes** made with currants. You may want to buy some at Dylan Thomas's boathouse at Laugharne and munch them with your tea as you look across the wide estuary where the poet had much the same view as his Iron Age predecessors. **Oat biscuits** are another treat, much like the oatmeal cookies you may have had back home. Desserts (*puddings* they're called here, whatever their form) seem to be mainly **fruit crumbles**—blackberry, apple, what have you—topped with custard and/or thick cream.

ENGLISH BREAKFASTS & AFTERNOON TEA   The country is famous for its enormous **English breakfast** of bacon, eggs, grilled tomato, and fried bread. Some places have replaced this cholesterol festival with a continental breakfast, but you'll still find the traditional morning meal available.

Kipper, or smoked herring, is also a popular breakfast dish. The finest come from the Isle of Man, Whitby, or Loch Fyne, in Scotland. The herrings are split open, placed over oak chips, and slowly cooked to produce a nice pale-brown smoked fish.

Many people still enjoy **afternoon tea,** which may consist of a simple cup of tea or a formal tea, and starts with tiny crustless sandwiches filled with cucumber or watercress. It then proceeds through **scones** and **crumpets** with jam or clotted cream (a thick cream), and is followed by cakes and tarts—all accompanied by a proper pot of tea. The tea at Brown's, in London, is quintessentially English, whereas the Ritz's tea is an elaborate affair, complete with orchestra and dancing.

In the country, tea shops abound, and in Devon, Cornwall, and the West Country, you'll find the best **cream teas,** with scones spread with jam and thick, clotted

Devonshire cream. It's a delicious treat, indeed. People in Britain drink an average of four cups of tea a day, though many younger people prefer coffee.

WHAT TO WASH IT ALL DOWN WITH   English pubs serve a variety of cocktails, but their stock in trade is beer: brown beer, or **bitter;** blond beer, or **lager;** and very dark beer, or **stout.** The standard English draft beer is much stronger than American beer and is served "with the chill off," because it doesn't taste good cold. Lager is always chilled, whereas stout can be served either way. Beer is always served straight from the tap, in two sizes: half pint (10 oz.) and pint (20 oz.). (Note that a British imperial pint is 20 oz., whereas an American pint is 16 oz.)

One of the most significant changes in English drinking habits has been the popularity of **wine bars,** and you will find many to try, including some that turn into discos late at night. Britain isn't known for its wine, though it does produce some medium-sweet fruity whites. Its **cider,** though, is famous—and mighty potent in contrast to the American variety.

Whisky (spelled without the *e*) refers to Scotch. Canadian and Irish whiskey (spelled with the *e*) are also available, but only the very best stocked bars have American bourbon and rye.

While you're in England, you may want to try the very English drink called **Pimm's,** a mixture developed by James Pimm, owner of a popular London oyster house in the 1840s. Though it can be consumed on the rocks, it's usually served as a Pimm's Cup—a drink that will have any number and variety of ingredients, depending on which part of the world (or empire) you're in. Here, just for fun, is a typical recipe: Take a very tall glass and fill it with ice. Add a thin slice of lemon (or orange), a cucumber spike (or a curl of cucumber rind), and 2 ounces of Pimm's liquor. Then finish with a splash of either lemon or club soda, 7-Up, or Tom Collins mix.

The English tend to drink everything at a warmer temperature than Americans are used to. So if you like ice in your soda, be sure to ask for lots of it, or you're likely to end up with a measly, quickly melting cube or two.

PLANNING YOUR TRIP TO ENGLAND & WALES

Of almost any destination in the world, flying into England, if your documents are in order, is one of the most effortless undertakings in global travel. There are no shots to get, no particular safety precautions, no unusual aspects of planning a trip. With your passport, airline ticket, and enough money, you just go. In general, if you're not bringing any illegal item into the British Isles, Customs officials are courteous and will speed you on your way into their country.

Of course, before you lift off the ground in your native country, you can do some advance preparation, as will be detailed in this chapter. That could mean checking to see if your passport is up to date (or obtaining one if you don't already possess one), or taking care of your health needs before you go, including medication. In the case of London, you might want to make reservations at some highly acclaimed restaurants or even buy tickets in advance to hit plays in the West End.

In the pages that follow, you'll find everything you need to know about the practicalities of planning your trip in advance: finding the best airfare, deciding when to go, figuring out British currency, and more.

For additional help in planning your trip and for more on-the-ground resources in England and Wales, please turn to "Fast Facts," on p. 754.

WHEN TO GO

The Weather

Yes, it rains, but you'll rarely get a true downpour—it's heaviest in November (2½ in. on average). British temperatures can range from 30° to 110°F (−1° to 43°C), but they rarely drop below 35°F (2°C) or go above 78°F (26°C). Evenings are cool, even in summer. Note that the British, who consider chilliness to be wholesome, like to keep the thermostats below the typical American comfort level. Hotels have central heating systems, which are usually kept just above the goose bump (in Britspeak, "goose pimple") margin.

London's Average Daytime Temperatures & Rainfall

	JAN	FEB	MAR	APR	MAY	JUNE	JULY	AUG	SEPT	OCT	NOV	DEC
Temp. (°F)	40	40	44	49	55	61	64	64	59	52	46	42
Temp. (°C)	4	4	7	9	13	16	18	18	15	11	8	6
Rainfall (in.)	2.1	1.6	1.5	1.5	1.8	1.8	2.2	2.3	1.9	2.2	2.5	1.9

Cardiff's Average Daytime Temperatures & Rainfall

	JAN	FEB	MAR	APR	MAY	JUNE	JULY	AUG	SEPT	OCT	NOV	DEC
Temp. (°F)	40	40	43	46	52	57	61	61	57	52	44	42
Temp. (°C)	4	4	6	8	11	14	16	16	14	11	7	6
Rainfall (in.)	4.2	3.0	2.9	2.5	2.7	2.6	3.1	4.0	3.8	4.6	4.3	4.6

When You'll Find Bargains

In short, spring offers the countryside at its greenest, autumn brings the bright colors of the northern moorlands, and summer's warmer weather gives rise to the many outdoor music and theater festivals. But winter offers savings across the board and a chance to see Britons going about their everyday lives largely unhindered by tourist invasions.

The cheapest time to travel to Britain is during the off-season: from November 1 to December 12 and from December 25 to March 14. In the last few years, the airlines have offered irresistible fares during these periods. And no matter when you travel, keep in mind that weekday flights are cheaper than weekend fares (often by 10% or more).

Rates generally increase between March 14 and June 5, and then hit their peak in high travel seasons between June 6 and September 30 and December 13 and 24. July and August are also when most Britons take their holidays, so besides higher prices, you'll have to deal with crowds and limited availability of accommodations.

You can avoid crowds by planning trips for November or January to March. Sure, it may be rainy and cold—but England doesn't shut down when the tourists leave! In fact, the winter season includes some of London's best theater, opera, ballet, and classical music offerings, and gives visitors a more honest view of English life. Additionally, many hotel prices drop by 20%, and cheaper accommodations offer weekly rates (unheard of during peak travel times). By arriving after the winter holidays, you can also take advantage of post-Christmas sales to buy woolens, china, crystal, silver, fashion clothing, handicrafts, and curios.

England & Wales Calendar of Events

For an exhaustive list of events beyond those listed here, check http://events.frommers.com, where you'll find a searchable, up-to-the-minute roster of what's happening in cities all over the world.

JANUARY

London Boat Show. This is the largest boat show in Europe, held at the ExCeL center in Docklands. For information, call ✆ **0870/906-3769** or visit www.londonboatshow.com. Mid-January.

Charles I Commemoration, London. To mark the anniversary of the execution of King Charles I "in the name of freedom and democracy," hundreds of cavaliers march through central London in 17th-century dress, and prayers are said at Whitehall's Banqueting House. Last Sunday in January.

FEBRUARY

Chinese New Year, London. The famous Lion Dancers in Soho perform free on the nearest Sunday to Chinese New Year. Call the London Chinatown Chinese Association at ✆ **020/7851-6686** or visit www.london chinatown.org. Late January or early February (based on the lunar calendar).

Jorvik Festival, York. This 2-week festival celebrates the historic cathedral city's role as a Viking outpost. For information, call ✆ **01904/543400** or visit www.jorvik-viking-centre.co.uk. Mid-February.

MARCH

St. David's Day Parade, Cardiff. The capital of Wales comes to a standstill on Wales's national day, honoring its patron saint with the country's showiest and most fun-filled parade. Contact the Wales Tourist Board, Cardiff Tourist Information Centre, the Old Library, the Hayes, Cardiff (✆ **029/2087-2087;** www.stdavidsday.org). March 1.

Crufts Dog Show, Birmingham. The English, they say, love their pets more than their offspring. Crufts offers an opportunity to observe the nation's pet lovers doting on 23,000 dogs, representing 209 breeds. It's held at the National Exhibition Centre. Tickets can be purchased at the door. For information, call ✆ **0844/463-3980** or visit www.crufts.org.uk. Early March.

APRIL

John Smith's Grand National, outside Liverpool. England's premier steeplechase event takes place on a 6.5km (4-mile) course at **Aintree Racecourse,** Aintree (✆ **0151/522-2911;** www.aintree.co.uk). Early April.

Easter Parade, London. A memorable parade of brightly colored floats and marching bands occurs around Battersea Park. Easter Monday.

The Shakespeare Season, Stratford-upon-Avon. The Royal Shakespeare Company begins its annual season, presenting works by the Bard in his hometown, at the **Royal Shakespeare Theatre,** Waterside (✆ **01789/403444;** www.rsc.org.uk). Tickets are available at the box office or through such agents as Keith Prowse (✆ **800/669-8687;** www.keithprowse.com). April to October.

Glyndebourne Festival Opera. One of England's major cultural events, this festival is centered at the 1,200-seat Glyndebourne Opera House in East Sussex, some 87km (54 miles) south of London. Tickets cost anywhere from £10 to £200. For information, contact the Glyndebourne Festival, Lewes, East Sussex BN8 5UU (✆ **01273/815000;** www.glyndebourne.com). Mid-April to late August.

Chichester Festival Theatre. Some great classic and modern plays are presented at this West Sussex theater. For tickets and information, contact the Chichester Festival Theatre, Oaklands Park, Chichester, West Sussex PO19 6AP (✆ **01243/784437;** www.cft.org.uk). Mid-April to October.

Virgin London Marathon. More than 30,000 competitors run from Greenwich Park to Buckingham Palace; call ✆ **020/7902-0200** or visit www.virginlondonmarathon.com for information. If you'd like to take the challenge, call in May or June for an application. Mid- or late April.

MAY

Brighton Festival. England's largest arts festival features some 400 different cultural events. For information, call ✆ **01273/709-709** or visit www.brightonfestival.org. Most of May.

Royal Windsor Horse Show. The country's major show-jumping presentation, held at the Home Park in Windsor, Berkshire, is attended by the queen herself. For information, call ✆ **0871/230-5568** or see www.royal-windsor-horse-show.co.uk. Mid-May.

Bath International Music Festival. One of Europe's most prestigious international festivals of music and the arts features as many as 1,000 performers at various venues in Bath. For information, contact the Bath Festivals Box Office, 2 Church St., Abbey Green, Bath BA1 1NL (✆ **01225/463362;** www.bathfestivals.org.uk). Mid-May to early June.

Chelsea Flower Show, London. The best of British gardening, with plants and flowers of the season, is displayed at the Royal Hospital Chelsea. For information, contact the Chelsea Show Ticket Office, Shows Department, Royal Horticultural Society, 80 Vincent Sq., London SW1P 2PE (✆ **0845/260-5000;** www.rhs.org.uk). Late May.

JUNE

Royal Academy Summer Exhibition, London. The Royal Academy of Arts, founded in 1768, has for some 2 centuries held Summer Exhibitions of living painters at its home in Burlington House, Piccadilly. For information, call ✆ **020/7300-8000** or visit www.royalacademy.org.uk. Early June to mid-August.

Derby Stakes, Epsom. This famous horse-racing event (the "Darby," as it's called here) is held at Epsom Downs, in Surrey. Men wear top hats; women, including the queen, put on silly millinery creations. For more details, call ✆ **0844/579-3004** or check out www.epsomderby.co.uk. First week of June.

Trooping the Colour, London. This is the queen's official birthday parade, a quintessential British event, with exquisite pageantry and pomp as she inspects her regiments and takes their salute, while they parade their colors before her at the Horse Guards Parade, Whitehall. Tickets for the parade and two reviews, held on preceding Saturdays, are free and allocated by ballot. Applicants must write between January 1 and the end of February, enclosing a self-addressed, stamped envelope or International Reply Coupon to the Ticket Office, HQ Household Division, Horse Guards, Whitehall, London SW1X 6AA. The ballot is held in mid-March, and only successful applicants are informed in April. Call ✆ **020/7414-2479** or visit www.trooping-the-colour.co.uk

for more details. Held on a day designated in June (not necessarily the queen's actual birthday).

Aldeburgh Festival. The composer Benjamin Britten launched this 2-week festival in his coastal town of Suffolk back in 1948. For more details on the events and for the year-round program, call ✆ **01728/687110** or visit www.aldeburgh.co.uk. Mid- to late June.

Royal Ascot Week, Berkshire. Though Ascot Racecourse is open year-round for guided tours, events, exhibitions, and conferences, there are 25 race days throughout the year, with the feature races being the Royal Meeting, held over several days in June. Besides the Royal Meeting in June, key race days include King George Day (formerly known as Diamond Day) in late July and the Ascot Festival in late September. For information, contact **Ascot Racecourse,** Ascot, Berkshire SL5 7JX (✆ **0870/727-1234;** www.ascot. co.uk).

Shakespeare under the Stars, London. The Bard's works are performed at the **Open Air Theatre,** Inner Circle, Regent's Park, NW1. Take the Tube to Baker Street. Performances are Monday to Saturday at 8pm, plus Wednesday, Thursday, and Saturday matinees at 2:30pm. For information, call ✆ **0844/826-4242** or visit www.openair theatre.org. June to mid-September.

City of London Festival. This annual arts festival is held in venues throughout the City of London's square-mile area. For information, call ✆ **020/7583-3585** or visit www. colf.org. Late June to mid-July.

Exeter Summer Festival. The town of Exeter, in Devon, hosts more than 150 events celebrating classical music, ranging from concerts and opera to lectures. Festival dates and offerings vary from year to year; more information is available by contacting the Exeter Festival Office (✆ **01392/265200;** www.exeter.gov.uk/festival). Late June to mid-July.

The Championships, Wimbledon, London. Ever since players took to the grass courts at Wimbledon in 1877, this tournament has attracted quite a crowd, and there's still an excited hush and a certain thrill at Centre Court. Savor the strawberries and cream that are part of the experience. Early bookings for the world's most famous tennis tournament are strongly advised. Acquiring tickets and overnight lodgings can be difficult to arrange independently. Two outfits that book both hotel accommodations and tickets to the event are **Steve Furgal's International Tennis Tours,** 11305 Rancho Bernardo Rd., Ste. 108, San Diego, CA 92127 (✆ **800/258-3664** or 858/675-3555; www.tours4tennis.com); and **Championship Tennis Tours,** 13951 N. Scottsdale Rd., Ste. 133, Scottsdale, AZ 85254 (✆ **800/468-3664** or 480/429-7700; www.tennistours.com). Tickets for Centre and Number One courts are obtainable through a lottery. From August to December, write to **All England Lawn Tennis Club,** P.O. Box 98, Church Road, Wimbledon, London SW19 5AE (✆ **020/8944-1066;** www.wimbledon.org). Outside court tickets are available daily, but be prepared to wait in line. Late June to early July.

Ludlow Festival. This is one of England's major arts festivals, complete with an open-air Shakespeare performance within the Inner Bailey of Ludlow Castle. Concerts, lectures, readings, exhibitions, and workshops round out the offerings. From March onward, a schedule can be obtained by sending a self-addressed, stamped envelope to the Ludlow Festival Box Office, Castle Square, Ludlow, Shropshire SY8 1AY (✆ **01584/872150;** www.ludlowfestival. co.uk). Late June to early July.

Cardiff Festival. In venues across the Welsh capital, this festival features pop, jazz, theater, street performances, amusement parks, opera, comedies, and children's events. Most events are free and take place in public and open-air places. For more information, call ✆ **029/2087-2087** or visit www.cardiff-festival.com. Late June through August.

Kenwood House Picnic Concerts, London. These summer concerts on the north side of Hampstead Heath have continued a British tradition of outdoor performances for more than 50 years. Fireworks displays and laser shows enliven the premier musical performances. The audience catches the music as it drifts across the lake from the performance shell. For more information, call ✆ **0870/890-0146** or visit www.picnic concerts.com. Every Saturday from late June through August.

JULY

Henley Royal Regatta. This international rowing competition in Oxfordshire is the premier event on the English social calendar. For more information, call ✆ **01491/572153** or visit www.hrr.co.uk. Early July.

The Proms, London. A night at "the Proms"—the annual Henry Wood Promenade Concerts at Royal Albert Hall—attracts music aficionados from around the world. Staged almost daily (except for a few Sun), these traditional concerts were launched in 1895 and are the principal summer engagements for the BBC Symphony Orchestra. Cheering and clapping, Union Jacks on parade, banners and balloons—it's great summer fun. Check out www.bbc.co.uk/proms for more details. Mid-July to mid-September.

MusicFest Aberystwyth. This is a pageant of cultural and sporting events in Aberystwyth, the cultural center of the western section of middle Wales. For more information, contact Aberystwyth Arts Centre, Penglais, Aberystwyth SY23 3DE (✆ **01970/623232;** www.aberystwythartscentre.co.uk). End of July.

AUGUST

Cowes Week, off the Isle of Wight. For details about this yachting festival, call ✆ **01983/295744** or visit www.skandia cowesweek.co.uk. Early August.

Pontardawe Festival. The little Welsh village of Pontardawe, lying 13km (8 miles) north of Swansea, attracts some of the world's leading folk and rock musicians for its annual summer concert series. For more information, call ☎ **01792/830200** or see www.pontardawefestival.com. Mid-August.

Notting Hill Carnival, Ladbroke Grove, London. Notting Hill is the setting for one of the largest annual street festivals in Europe, attracting more than half a million people. There's live reggae and soul music, plus great Caribbean food. For information, call ☎ **020/7727-0072** or visit www.notting hillcarnival.biz. Two days in late August.

International Beatle Week Festival, Liverpool. Tens of thousands of fans gather to celebrate the music of the Fab Four. There's an entire series of concerts by international cover bands, plus tributes, auctions, and tours. It's organized by Cavern City Tours (☎ **0151/236-9091;** www.beatlesfestival. co.uk), which offers festival packages that include accommodations and tickets to tours and events. Late August.

SEPTEMBER

Land Rover Burghley Horse Trials, Lincolnshire. This annual event is staged on the grounds of the largest Elizabethan house in England, Burghley House, in Stamford (☎ **01780/752131;** www.burghley-horse. co.uk). Early September.

Raising of the Thames Barrier, Unity Way, London. Once a year, usually in September, a full test is done on this miracle of modern engineering; all 10 massive steel gates are raised against the low and high tides. For exact date and time, call ☎ **020/8854-8888** or go to www.greenwich.gov.uk.

Horse of the Year Show, Birmingham. Riders fly from every continent to join in this festive display of horsemanship (much appreciated by the queen). The British press calls it an "equine extravaganza." It's held at the National Exhibition Centre. For information, call ☎ **01582/711-411** or see www.hoys. co.uk. Late September to early October.

Ascot Festival, Berkshire. This is Britain's greatest horse-racing weekend, providing the grand finale to the summer season at Ascot. The 3-day "meeting" combines some of the most valuable racing of the year with other entertainment. A highlight of the festival is the £250,000 Watership Down Stud Sales race, restricted to 2-year-old fillies. Other racing highlights include the Queen Elizabeth II Stakes, with the winning horse crowned champion miler in Europe. For information, contact **Ascot Racecourse,** Ascot, Berkshire SL5 7JX (☎ **0870/727-1234;** www.ascot.co.uk). Last weekend in September.

OCTOBER

Quit Rents Ceremony, London. The origins of this ceremony go back so far they have been forgotten. The city solicitor pays the queen's remembrancer (medieval term for collector of the queen's rents) token rents for properties long ago leased—in many cases no longer standing. It's all for fun, show, and tradition. For example, the solicitor will pay the remembrancer two faggots of wood, a billhook, and a hatchet for land in Shropshire; or else 61 nails and six horseshoes for a long-gone forge in the Strand. The ceremony is held at the Royal Courts of Justice. For information, call ☎ **020/7947-6000** or visit www.hmcourts-service.gov. uk. Early October.

Cheltenham Literature Festival. This event features readings, book exhibitions, and theatrical performances—all in the famed spa town of Gloucestershire, in the Cotswolds. For details, call ☎ **01242/774400** or visit www.cheltenhamfestivals.co.uk. Early to mid-October.

Opening of Parliament, London. Ever since the 17th century, when the English beheaded Charles I, British monarchs have been denied the right to enter the House of Commons. Instead, the monarch opens Parliament in the House of Lords, reading an official speech that is in fact written by the government. Queen Elizabeth II rides from Buckingham Palace to Westminster in a royal coach accompanied by the Yeoman of the Guard and the Household Cavalry. The public galleries are open on a first-come, first-served basis. Call ☎ **020/7219-3107** or go to www.parliament.uk. Late October to mid-November.

London to Brighton Veteran Car Run. This race begins in London's Hyde Park and ends in the seaside resort of Brighton, in East Sussex. For more details, call (C) **01462/742-818** or see www.vccofgb.co.uk. First Sunday in November.

Guy Fawkes Night, throughout England. This British celebration commemorates the anniversary of the Gunpowder Plot, on November 5, 1605, an attempt to blow up King James I and Parliament. Huge organized bonfires are lit throughout London, and Guy Fawkes, the plot's most famous conspirator, is burned in effigy. Check *Time* *Out* or www.gunpowder-plot.org for locations. Early November.

Lord Mayor's Show, the City of London. The queen has to ask permission to enter the square mile in London called the City of London—and the right of refusal has been jealously guarded by London merchants since the 17th century. Suffice it to say that the lord mayor is a powerful character, and the procession from the Guildhall to the Royal Courts is appropriately impressive. You can watch the procession from the street; the banquet is by invitation only. For details, call (C) **020/7222-4345** or visit www.lordmayor show.org. Second Saturday in November.

ENTRY REQUIREMENTS

Passports

All U.S. citizens, Canadians, Australians, New Zealanders, and South Africans must have a passport with at least 2 months' validity remaining. No visa is required. A passport will allow you to stay in the country for up to 6 months. The immigration officer will also want proof of your intention to return to your point of origin (usually a round-trip ticket) and of visible means of support while you're in Britain. If you're planning to fly from the United States or Canada to the United Kingdom and then on to a country that requires a visa (India, for example), you should secure that visa before you arrive in Britain.

For information on how to get a passport, go to "Passports" under "Fast Facts: England & Wales" (p. 756).

Customs

WHAT YOU CAN BRING INTO BRITAIN

Non-E.U. nationals 18 years and older can bring in, free of duty, 200 cigarettes, 100 cigarillos, 50 cigars, or 250 grams of smoking tobacco. This amount is doubled if you live outside Europe. You can also bring in 2 liters of wine and either 1 liter of alcohol more than 22% by volume or 2 liters of wine less than 22% by volume. In addition, you can bring in 60cc (2 oz.) of perfume and a quarter liter (250ml) of eau de toilette. Visitors 15 and older may also bring in other goods totaling £145; the allowance for those 14 and younger is £73. (Customs officials tend to be lenient about general merchandise, realizing the limits are unrealistically low.)

You can't bring your pet for a visit to Britain. Six months' quarantine is required before it is allowed in. An illegally imported animal may be destroyed.

WHAT YOU CAN TAKE HOME FROM BRITAIN

For information on what you're allowed to bring home, contact the relevant agency:

U.S. Citizens: U.S. Customs & Border Protection (CBP), 1300 Pennsylvania Ave. NW, Washington, DC 20229 ((C) **877/287-8667;** www.cbp.gov).

Canadian Citizens: Canada Border Services Agency (© **800/461-9999** in Canada, or 204/983-3500; www.cbsa-asfc.gc.ca).

Australian Citizens: Australian Customs Service (© **1300/363-263**; www.customs.gov.au).

New Zealand Citizens: New Zealand Customs Service, The Customhouse, 17–21 Whitmore St., Box 2218, Wellington (© **04/473-6099** or 0800/428-786; www.customs.govt.nz).

Medical Requirements

Unless you're arriving from an area known to be suffering from an epidemic, particularly cholera or yellow fever, inoculations or vaccinations are not required for entry into the U.K.

For more information about health concerns, refer to "Health," later in this chapter.

GETTING THERE & GETTING AROUND

Getting to England & Wales

BY PLANE

The major airport for arrivals from North America is **Heathrow** (LHR), outside London. This is the hub for most airlines, including British Airways and American carriers, and has the best transportation links to London. **Gatwick** (LGW) is the second major airport outside London, receiving many flights from elsewhere in Europe.

Chances are you will not land at London's minor airports, certainly not if you're making a transatlantic crossing; however, you might land at one of these airports if you're winging in from the Continent. They include **London City** (LCY), **London Stansted** (STN), **London Luton** (LTN), and **London Southend** (SEN).

If you plan to skip London altogether, you might have a direct flight into one of the two leading regional airports of England, **Manchester** (MAN) and **Birmingham** (BHX).

Chances are you will not use one of the small airports in Wales, since most visitors there arrive by rail or car. However, there are airports in the capital of **Cardiff** (CWL) and in the second city of **Swansea** (SWS).

British Airways (© **800/247-9297**; www.britishairways.com) offers flights from 19 U.S. cities to Heathrow and Gatwick airports, as well as many others to Manchester. Nearly every flight is nonstop. With more add-on options than any other airline, BA can make a visit to Britain cheaper than you may have expected. Ask about packages that include both airfare and discounted hotel accommodations.

Known for consistently offering excellent fares, **Virgin Atlantic Airways** (© **800/821-5438**; www.virgin-atlantic.com) flies daily to either Heathrow or Gatwick from Boston, Newark, New York's JFK, Los Angeles, San Francisco, Washington's Dulles, Miami, Orlando, and Las Vegas.

American Airlines (© **800/433-7300**; www.aa.com) offers daily flights to Heathrow from half a dozen U.S. gateways—New York's JFK, Chicago, Boston, Miami, Los Angeles, and Dallas.

Depending on the day and season, **Delta Air Lines** (✆ **800/221-1212;** www.delta.com) runs either one or two daily nonstop flights between Atlanta and Gatwick. Delta also offers nonstop daily service from Cincinnati.

Continental Airlines (✆ **800/231-0856;** www.continental.com) has daily flights to London from Cleveland, Houston, Newark, Orlando, and San Francisco.

Northwest Airlines (✆ **800/225-2525** or 800/447-4747; www.nwa.com) flies nonstop from Minneapolis and Detroit to Gatwick.

United Airlines (✆ **800/864-8331;** www.united.com) flies nonstop from New York's JFK and Chicago to Heathrow two or three times daily, depending on the season. United also offers nonstop service from Dulles Airport, near Washington, D.C.; Newark; Los Angeles; and San Francisco.

For travelers departing from Canada, **Air Canada** (✆ **888/247-2262;** www.aircanada.com) flies daily to London's Heathrow nonstop from Vancouver, Montreal, and Toronto. There are also frequent direct flights from Calgary, Ottawa, and St. John's. **British Airways** (✆ **800/247-9297**) has direct flights from Toronto, Montreal, and Vancouver.

For travelers departing from Australia, **British Airways** (✆ **1300/767-177**) has flights to London from Sydney, Melbourne, Perth, and Brisbane. **Qantas** (✆ **612/131313;** www.qantas.com) offers direct flights to London's Heathrow from Sydney and Melbourne. Some flights have the bonus of free stopovers in Bangkok or Singapore.

Departing from New Zealand, **Air New Zealand** (✆ **800/262-1234** in the U.S., or 0800/737-000 in New Zealand; www.airnewzealand.co.nz) has direct daily flights to London from Auckland.

Short flights from Dublin to London are available through **British Airways** (✆ **800/247-9297**), with four flights daily into London's Gatwick airport; **Aer Lingus** (✆ **800/IRISH-AIR** [474-7424]; www.aerlingus.com), which flies into Heathrow; **Ryanair** (✆ **353-1-812-1676;** www.ryanair.com); and **British Midland** (✆ **0870/6070555;** www.flybmi.com).

For a list of which airlines travel to England and Wales, see "Airline, Hotel & Car-Rental Websites," p. 758.

BY CAR

Your valid driver's license and at least 1 year of driving experience are required to drive personal or rented cars in England.

If you plan to transport a rented car between Britain and France, check in advance with the car-rental company about license and insurance requirements and additional drop-off charges before you begin.

The English Channel is crisscrossed with "drive-on, drive-off" car-ferry services, with many operating from Boulogne and Calais in France. From either of those ports, Sealink ferries will carry you, your luggage, and, if you like, your car. The most popular point of arrival along the English coast is Folkestone.

Taking a car beneath the Channel is more complicated and more expensive. Since the opening of the Channel Tunnel (commonly called the "Chunnel"), most passengers have opted to ride the train alone, without being accompanied by their car. The Eurostar trains, discussed below, carry passengers only; **Eurotunnel** trains carry freight cars, trucks, and passenger cars.

The cost of moving a car on Eurotunnel varies according to the season and day of the week. Frankly, it's a lot cheaper to transport your car across by conventional ferryboat, but if you insist, here's what you'll need to know: You'll negotiate both British and French Customs as part of one combined process, usually on the English side of the Channel. You can remain within your vehicle even after you drive it onto a flatbed railway car during the 35-minute crossing. (For 19 min. of this crossing, you'll actually be underwater; if you want, you can leave the confines of your car and ride within a brightly lit, air-conditioned passenger car.) When the trip is over, you simply drive off the flatbed railway car and toward your destination. Total travel time between the French and English highway system is about 1 hour. As a means of speeding the flow of perishable goods across the Channel, the car and truck service usually operates 24 hours a day, at intervals that vary from every 15 minutes to once an hour, depending on the time of day. Neither BritRail nor any of the agencies dealing with reservations for passenger trains through the Chunnel will reserve space for your car in advance, and considering the frequency of the traffic on the Chunnel, they're usually not necessary. For information about Eurotunnel car-rail service after you reach England, call ℂ **0844/335-3535** or go to **www.eurotunnel.com**.

Duty-free stores, restaurants, and service stations are available to travelers on both sides of the Channel. A bilingual staff is on hand to assist travelers at both the British and French terminals.

BY TRAIN

Britain's isolation from the rest of Europe led to the development of an independent railway network with different rules and regulations from those observed on the Continent. That's all changing now, but one big difference that may affect you still remains: If you're traveling to Britain from the Continent, *your Eurailpass will not be valid when you get here.*

In 1994, Queen Elizabeth of England and President Francois Mitterrand of France officially opened the Channel Tunnel, or Chunnel, and the Eurostar express passenger train began twice-daily service between London and both Paris and Brussels. In 2003, the completion of a new section of high-speed rail in England, the **Channel Tunnel Rail Link,** shaved 20 minutes off the trip between London and Paris, reducing it to just 2 hours and 35 minutes (or 2 hr., 20 min. to Brussels). This extension allows Eurostar trains to go at the rate of 482kmph (300 mph). One of the great engineering feats of all time, the tunnel is the first link between Britain and the Continent since the Ice Age.

So if you're coming to London from say, Rome, your Eurailpass will get you as far as the Chunnel. At that point, you can cross the English Channel aboard the Eurostar, and you'll receive a discount on your ticket. Once in England, you must use a separate BritRail pass or purchase a direct ticket to continue on to your destination.

Rail Europe (ℂ **888/382-7245;** www.raileurope.com) sells direct-service tickets on the Eurostar between Paris or Brussels and London. A one-way fare between Paris and London costs $271 to $363 in second class and $184 to $501 in first class.

In London, make reservations for **Eurostar** by calling ℂ **08705/186-186;** in the United States, call ℂ **800/EUROSTAR** (800/387-6782; www.eurostar.com). Eurostar trains arrive and depart from London's St. Pancras International (replacing Waterloo Station), Paris's Gare du Nord, and Brussels's Central Station.

BY BUS

Bus connections to Britain from the Continent are generally not comfortable, though some lines are more convenient than others. One line with a relatively good reputation is **Eurolines,** 52 Grosvenor Gardens, SW1W 0AU (℗ **0871/781-81-81;** www.nationalexpress.com). It books passage on buses traveling twice a day between London and Paris (9 hr.); three times a day from Amsterdam (12 hr.); three times a week from Munich (24 hr.); and three times a week from Stockholm (44 hr.). On longer routes, which use alternating drivers, the bus proceeds almost without interruption, taking only occasional breaks for meals.

BY BOAT

P&O Ferries (℗ **08716/645645;** www.poferries.com) operates car and passenger ferries between Dover and Calais, France (25 sailings a day; 75 min. each way).

Getting Around

MAPS   Upon arriving in London, you should arm yourself with a detailed street map if you plan to do a lot of walking. London is a maze of narrow streets and "villages" within a vast city, and many addresses are obscure and hard to find.

If you plan to motor through England, arm yourself with a road atlas, especially one of the large-format ones produced by AA, RAC, Collins, and Ordnance Survey. Virtually every motorway gas (petrol) station in England stocks one or more of the big road atlases.

At **www.multimap.com,** you can access detailed street maps of the whole United Kingdom—just key in the location or even just the postal code, and a map of the area with the location circled will appear. For directions to specific places in London, consult **www.streetmap.co.uk**.

BY CAR

There's no doubt about it, the best way to explore England's little villages and off-the-beaten-path attractions is by car. It's also the most expensive, far more so than the train or bus. For budget-saving suggestions, see below.

Because cars in Britain travel on the left side of the road, steering wheels are positioned on the "wrong" side of the vehicle. Remember that most rental cars are manual, so be prepared to shift with your left hand; you'll pay more for an automatic (make sure to request one when you reserve).

Speed limits are generally 50 to 60kmph (30–40 mph) in heavily populated areas, or 110kmph (70 mph) on motorways or "dual carriageways," as the English call divided highways with a central median.

In England you drive on the left and pass on the right. Road signs are clear and international symbols are used. It's a good idea to get a copy of the *British Highway Code,* available from almost any gas (petrol) station or newsstand in Britain.

Warning: Pedestrian crossings are marked by striped lines (zebra striping) on the road; flashing lights near the curb indicate that drivers must stop and yield the right of way if a pedestrian has stepped out into the zebra zone to cross the street.

GETTING THE BEST DEAL ON YOUR RENTAL CAR   The British car-rental market is among the most competitive in Europe. Nevertheless, car rentals are expensive, unless you avail yourself of one of the promotional deals that are frequently offered by British Airways and others. It's always cheaper to arrange a car in advance through one of the big chains such as Hertz or Avis. You might also look into a fly/drive deal.

Car-rental rates vary even more than airline fares. The price you pay depends on the size of the car, where and when you pick it up and drop it off, length of the rental period, where and how far you drive it, whether you purchase insurance, and a host of other factors. It's cheaper to rent a car with a stick shift; if you can't drive a stick shift, you can rent a vehicle with automatic drive, but invariably you'll pay more for this convenience.

The best car-rental deals are made in the off-season, as thousands upon thousands of potential motorists descend on Britain to drive its clogged highways and country lanes in fair weather.

For booking rental cars online, the best deals are usually found at rental-car company websites, although all the major online travel agencies also offer rental-car reservations services. Priceline and Hotwire work well for rental cars, too; the only "mystery" is which major rental company you get, and for most travelers the difference between Hertz, Avis, and Budget is negligible.

Virtually every kind of car imaginable is for rent in England, including an old Rolls-Royce discarded by the queen or a small little budget number from Japan that seats two uncomfortably.

Keep in mind that most companies will only rent to persons 23 years and older. Many agencies will not rent to people age 70 or older.

Rentals are available through **Avis** (📞 800/331-1212; www.avis.com), **Budget** (📞 800/527-0700; www.budget.com), and **Hertz** (📞 800/654-3001; www.hertz.com). **Kemwel Drive Europe** (📞 877/820-0668; www.kemwel.com) is among the cheapest and most reliable of the rental agencies. **AutoEurope** (📞 888/223-5555 in the U.S., or 0800/223-5555 in London; www.autoeurope.com) acts as a wholesale company for rental agencies in Europe. For additional listings of the major car-rental agencies in England or Wales, see "Airline, Hotel & Car-Rental Websites" (p. 758).

When booking your rental car, a few key questions could save you hundreds of dollars:

○ Are weekend rates lower than weekday rates? Ask if the rate is the same for pickup Friday morning, for instance, as it is for Thursday night.

○ Is a weekly rate cheaper than the daily rate? If you need to keep the car for 4 days, it may be cheaper to keep it for 5, even if you don't need it for that long.

○ Does the agency assess a drop-off charge if you do not return the car to the same location where you picked it up? Is it cheaper to pick up the car at the airport compared to a downtown location?

○ Are special promotional rates available? If you see an advertised price in your local newspaper, be sure to ask for that specific rate; otherwise you may be charged the standard cost. The terms change constantly, and phone operators may not volunteer information.

○ Are discounts available for members of AARP, AAA, frequent-flier programs, or trade unions? If you belong to any of these organizations, you are probably entitled to discounts of up to 30%.

○ What is the cost of adding an additional driver's name to the contract?

○ How many free miles are included in the price? Free mileage is often negotiable, depending on the length of your rental.

○ How much does the rental company charge to refill your gas tank if you return with the tank less than full? Though most rental companies claim these prices are "competitive," fuel is almost always cheaper in town. Try to allow enough time to refuel the car yourself before returning it.

When you reserve a car, make sure you find out the total price, including the 17.5% value-added tax (VAT).

SMART INSURANCE TIPS   Before you drive off in a rental car, be sure you're insured. Hasty assumption about your personal auto insurance or a rental agency's additional coverage could end up costing you tens of thousands of dollars—even if you are involved in an accident that was clearly the fault of another driver.

U.S. drivers who already have their own car insurance are usually covered within the United States for loss of or damage to a rental car and liability in case of injury to any other party involved in an accident. But coverage probably doesn't extend outside the United States. Be sure to find out whether you are covered in England, whether your policy extends to all persons who will be driving the rental car, how much liability is covered in case an outside party is injured in an accident, and whether the type of vehicle you are renting is included under your contract. (Rental trucks, sport utility vehicles, and luxury vehicles, such as the Jaguar, may not be covered.)

Most **major credit cards** provide some degree of coverage as well—provided they are used to pay for the rental. Terms vary widely, however, so be sure to call your credit card company directly before you rent. But though they will cover damage to or theft of your rental, *credit cards will not cover liability* or the cost of injury to an outside party and/or damage to an outside party's vehicle.

Bear in mind that each credit card company has its own peculiarities. American Express, for instance, does not cover vehicles valued at over $50,000 when new, such as luxury vehicles or vehicles built on a truck chassis. Most American Express Optima cards do not provide any insurance at all. MasterCard does not provide coverage for loss, theft, or fire damage, and only covers collision if the rental period does not exceed 15 days. Call your own credit card company for details.

If you do not hold an insurance policy valid outside the United States, you may want to seriously consider purchasing additional liability insurance from your car-rental company. Be sure to check the terms, however. Some rental agencies only cover liability if the renter is not at fault.

BREAKDOWNS   Membership in one of the two major auto clubs can be helpful: the **Automobile Association (AA),** at Norfolk House, Priestly Road, Basingstoke, Hampshire RG24 9NY (℃ **0870/5444-444;** www.theaa.com), or the **Royal Automobile Club (RAC),** 8 Surrey St., Norwich ℃ **01922/727-313;** www.rac.co.uk). You can join these clubs through your car-rental agent. (Members of AAA in the U.S. can enjoy reciprocity overseas.)

Roadside emergency telephone boxes can be found about every mile along the motorways. If you don't see one, walk down the road for a bit to the blue-and-white marker with an arrow that points to the nearest box. The 24-hour number to call for the AA is ℃ **0800/887-766;** for the RAC, it's ℃ **0800/82-82-82.** In addition, you can call a police traffic unit that will contact either of the auto clubs on your behalf.

Even if you're not a member, you can call these organizations, though a substantial fee will be involved for nonmembers.

Getting There & Getting Around

PLANNING YOUR TRIP TO ENGLAND & WALES

GASOLINE   There are plenty of gas ("petrol") stations in England and Wales, especially around cities and big towns and most definitely along the motorways. In remote areas, however, they're often few and far between, and many are closed on Sunday. If you're planning a lot of Sunday driving in remote parts, always make sure your tank is full on Saturday.

Note that gasoline costs more in Britain than in North America, and to encourage energy saving, the government has imposed a 25% tax on gas.

PARKING   In overcrowded cities, such as London, parking has become a nightmare, and it costs a fortune. Touring English cities by car, especially London, is not recommended. Use public transportation instead. Even in small villages, parking can be a problem, especially in summer. There are only so many spaces.

In general, long- or short-stay car parks are cheaper than using city or town meters, which usually limit you to 2 hours. When you see a yellow line along the edge of a road, that means parking is restricted; refer to the nearest sign to read the conditions. A double yellow line indicates that parking is forbidden at all times.

BY TRAIN

Eurailpasses are not valid in Great Britain, but there are several special passes for train travel outside London. For railroad information, go to Rail Travel information centers in the main London railway stations (Waterloo, Kings Cross, Euston, and Paddington).

You can download faxable order forms or order online from BritRail at **www. britainontrack.com**, or else call ✆ **888/667-9734.**

TRAVEL PASSES   BritRail passes allow unlimited travel in England, Scotland, and Wales on any British Rail scheduled train over the whole of the network during the validity of the pass without restrictions. If you're traveling beyond London anywhere in the United Kingdom and plan to hop on and off the train, consider purchasing a **BritRail Consecutive Pass.** These passes allow you to travel for a consecutive number of days for a flat rate. In first class, adults pay $379 for 4 days, $535 for 8 days, $799 for 15 days, $1,015 for 22 days, and $1,195 for 1 month. In second class, fares are $249 for 4 days, $359 for 8 days, $535 for 15 days, $675 for 22 days, and $795 for 1 month. Seniors (60 and older) qualify for discounts in first-class travel and pay $319 for 4 days, $455 for 8 days, $679 for 15 days, $859 for 22 days, and $1,015 for 1 month. Passengers 25 and younger qualify for a **Youth Pass.** In second class, rates are $199 for 4 days, $285 for 8 days, $425 for 15 days, $539 for 22 days, and $635 for 1 month. One child (age 14 and younger) can travel free with each adult or senior pass when the **BritRail Family Pass** is requested while buying the adult pass. Additional children pay half the regular adult fare.

A more versatile pass is the **BritRail FlexiPass,** allowing you to travel when you want during a 2-month period of time. In first class, it costs $465 for 4 days, $679 for 8 days, and $1,025 for 15 days of travel. In second class, it costs $315 for 4 days, $459 for 8 days, and $689 for 15 days of travel.

For more information on rail passes and on rail vacation packages in England and the U.K., contact **BritRail** (✆ **866/BRIT-RAIL** [274-8724] in the U.S. and Canada; www.britrail.com).

England & Wales

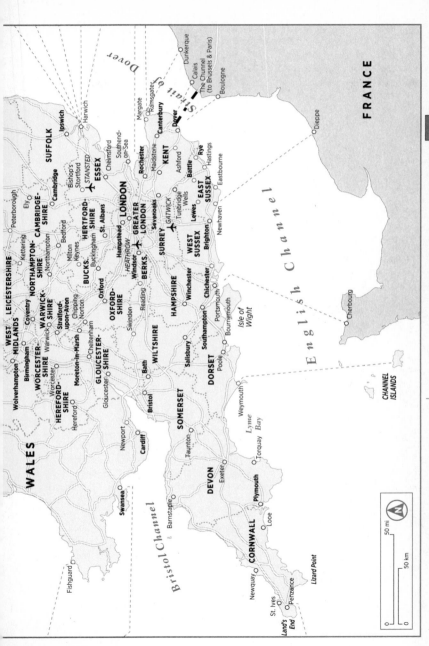

Train Travel from London to Principal Cities

TO	STATION	TYPICAL NO. OF TRAINS PER DAY	MILES	TRAVEL TIME
Bath	Paddington	25	107	1 hr. 11 min.
Birmingham	Euston/Paddington	35	113	1 hr. 37 min.
Bristol	Paddington	46	119	1 hr. 26 min.
Cardiff	Paddington	24	148	2 hr.
Carlisle	Euston	10	299	3 hr. 40 min.
Chester	Euston	16	179	2 hr. 36 min.
Exeter	Paddington	17	174	1 hr. 55 min.
Leeds	Kings Cross	19	185	2 hr. 12 min.
Liverpool	Euston	14	193	2 hr. 34 min.
Manchester	Euston	16	180	2 hr. 27 min.
Newcastle	Kings Cross	26	268	2 hr. 50 min.
Penzance	Paddington	9	305	5 hr.
Plymouth	Paddington	14	226	2 hr. 35 min.
York	Kings Cross	27	188	1 hr. 57 min.

Travelers who arrive from France by boat and pick up a BritRail train at Dover arrive at **St. Pancras Station,** in the center of London. Those journeying south by rail from Edinburgh arrive at **Kings Cross Station,** on the edge of central London.

If you plan to explore Wales at length, a **Freedom of Wales Flexi Pass** allows you to discover that small country by bus and rail. The pass also offers 20% discounts on narrow-gauge railways. The pass costs £74 and grants 4 days of rail travel and 8 days of bus travel. You can also inquire about passes granting more extended travel time. For information, see **www.walesflexipass.co.uk** or contact **Arriva Trains Wales,** St. Mary's House, Penarth Road, Cardiff CF10 5DJ (© **0845/6061-660;** www.arrivatrainswales.co.uk).

BY BUS

In Britain, a long-distance touring bus is called a "coach," whereas "buses" are taken for local transportation. An efficient and frequent express motorcoach network—run by National Express and other independent operators—links most of Britain's towns and cities. Destinations off the main route can be easily reached by transferring to a local bus at a stop on the route. Tickets are relatively cheap, often half the price of rail fare; it's usually cheaper to purchase a round-trip ("return") ticket rather than two one-way fares separately.

Victoria Coach Station, Buckingham Palace Road (© **020/7730-3466**), is the departure point for most large coach operators. The coach station is located just 2 blocks from the Victoria rail station. For 24-hour information, call © **020/7222-1234** or visit www.tfl.gov.uk. For cash purchases, get here at least 30 minutes before the coach's departure time.

National Express (© **0871/781-81-81;** www.nationalexpress.com) runs long-distance coaches that are equipped with reclining seats, toilets, and nonsmoking areas. You can obtain details about all coach services by calling the company between 8am and 10pm daily. The National Express ticket office at Victoria Station is open from 6am to 11pm daily.

For journeys within a 56km (35-mile) radius of London, try **Green Line** (© **0844/801-7261**; www.greenline.co.uk), which operates routes called Country Bus Lines that circle the periphery of London. Though they do not usually go directly into the center of the capital, they hook up with the routes of the Green Line coaches and red buses that do.

To the delight of frugal travelers, a new no-frills coach service has been introduced in England. **Megabus** (© **08705/505050**, 10p per min.; www.megabus.com) charges the lowest fares in the country—only £1 to £5 for a single journey on any route. From London, popular stops include Oxford, Brighton, and the old port of Plymouth. The network uses double-decker buses that once rolled through the streets of Hong Kong. Reserve online at the company's website, which levies a booking charge of less than a U.S. dollar.

In Wales, 65 independent bus operators serve the little country. Public transport guides for local areas are available at tourist offices. One of the most important is **Arriva Buses Wales** (© **0844/800-4411**; www.arriva.co.uk), serving North Wales. The area around Cardiff is covered by **Cardiff Bus** (© **029/2066-6444**; www.cardiffbus.com).

BY PLANE

British Airways (© **800/AIRWAYS** [247-9297]; www.ba.com) flies to more than 20 cities outside London, including Manchester. To get to the heart of England quickly, many visitors fly BA to Manchester, which is served by a dozen flights per day from London's Heathrow and seven flights per day from London's Gatwick.

MONEY & COSTS

THE VALUE OF THE BRITISH POUND VS. OTHER POPULAR CURRENCIES

UK£	US$	Can$	Euro (€)	Aus$	NZ$
£1	$1.60	C$1.70	€1.15	A$1.80	NZ$2.25

London is becoming one of the most expensive cities on the planet, far more expensive than New York (Brits now view the Big Apple as a bargain basement). It's not as expensive as Tokyo or Oslo, but even an average hotel rate can be £100 or more—in many cases, much, much more.

You'll avoid lines at airport ATMs by exchanging at least some money—just enough to cover airport incidentals and transportation to your hotel—before you leave home (though don't expect the exchange rate to be ideal). You can exchange money at your local American Express or Thomas Cook office or at your bank. American Express also dispenses traveler's checks and foreign currency via www.americanexpress.com or © **800/528-4800,** but it will charge a $15 order fee and additional shipping costs.

Frommer's lists exact prices in the local currency. The currency conversions quoted above were correct at press time. However, rates fluctuate, so before departing, consult a currency-exchange website such as **www.oanda.com/convert/ classic** to check up-to-the-minute rates.

Pounds & Pence

Britain's decimal monetary system is based on the pound (£), which is made up of 100 pence (written as "p"). Pounds are also called **quid** by Britons. There are £1 and £2 coins, as well as coins of 50p, 20p, 10p, 5p, 2p, and 1p. Bank notes come in denominations of £5, £10, £20, and £50.

ATMs

ATMs, sometimes referred to as "cash machines" or "cashpoints," are widely available in Britain, certainly in all cities and bigger towns, and even at a bank or two in smaller places. But don't always count on it. If you're venturing into rural England, it's always good to have pounds in your pocket.

The **Cirrus** (© 800/424-7787; www.mastercard.com) and **PLUS** (www.visa. com) networks span the globe; look at the back of your bank card to see which network you're on, and then call or check online for ATM locations at your destination. Be sure you know your personal identification number (PIN) and daily withdrawal limit before you depart.

There are some problems involved in the use of ATMs. For example, if you make a mistake and punch your secret code incorrectly into the machine three times, that machine will swallow your card on the assumption that it is being fraudulently used.

Users with alphabetical rather than numerical PINs may be thrown off by the lack of letters on English cash machines. And if your PIN is longer than four digits, check with your bank to see if you can use the first four digits; if not, you will have to get a new number for use in Britain.

To get a cash advance by using a credit card at an ATM, ask for a PIN from your credit card company, such as Visa, before leaving your home country.

Note: Remember that many banks impose a fee every time you use a card at another bank's ATM, and that fee can be higher for international transactions (up to $5 or more) than for domestic ones (where they're rarely more than $2). In addition, the bank from which you withdraw cash may charge its own fee. For international withdrawal fees, ask your bank.

Credit Cards

Credit cards are another safe way to carry money, but their use has become somewhat more difficult, especially in England (see below). They provide a convenient record of all your expenses, and they generally offer relatively good exchange rates. You can usually withdraw cash advances from your credit cards at banks or ATMs, provided you know your PIN. Keep in mind that you'll pay interest from the moment of your withdrawal, even if you pay your monthly bills on time. Also, note that many banks now assess a 1% to 3% "transaction fee" on *all* charges you incur abroad (whether you're using the local currency or your native currency).

There is almost no difference in the acceptance of a debit card or a standard credit card.

Unfortunately, some establishments in Britain might not accept your credit card unless you have a computer chip imbedded in it. The reason? To cut down on credit card fraud. More and more places in England are moving from the old magnetic-strip credit card to the new system of "Chip and PIN." With these microchip-equipped cards, you must enter a four-digit PIN on a keypad when making a transaction.

With the changeover in technology, some retailers have falsely concluded that they can no longer take swipe cards, or can't take signature cards that don't have PINs. For the time being, both the new and old cards are used in shops, hotels, and restaurants regardless of whether they have the old credit card machines or the new Chip and PIN machines installed. Expect a lot of confusion when you arrive in England.

Traveler's Checks

You can buy traveler's checks at most banks, and they are widely accepted in England, although frankly merchants prefer cash. Because of difficulties with credit cards (see above) or ATMs that can reject your card for no apparent reason, travelers are once again buying traveler's checks for security in case something goes wrong with their plastic. They are offered in denominations of $20, $50, $100, $500, and sometimes $1,000. Generally, you'll pay a service charge ranging from 1% to 4%.

WHAT THINGS COST IN ENGLAND	UK£
Taxi from Heathrow to central London	50.00–80.00
Underground from Heathrow to central London	4.00
Park & Ride bus into Oxford center	2.50
Double room at the Bath Priory in Bath (expensive)	185.00
Double room at Grasmere House Hotel in Salisbury (moderate)	106.00
Double room at Park View Hotel in Exeter (inexpensive)	65.00
Lunch for one at Gilbey's Bar & Restaurant in Windsor (moderate)	16.50
Lunch for one at the Red Lion in Southampton (inexpensive)	12.00
Dinner for one at Le Manoir aux Quat' Saisons in Oxford (very expensive)	95.00
Dinner for one at Pied à Terre in London (expensive)	58.00
Dinner for one at Mr. Thomas's Chop House in Manchester (moderate)	22.00
Dinner for one at Dojo Noodle Bar in Cambridge (inexpensive)	10.00
Pint of Beer	3.00–4.00
Coca-Cola (large)	2.50
Admission to British Museum in London	Free
Movie ticket	6.00–9.00

The most popular traveler's checks are offered by **American Express** (℃ **800/528-4800,** or 800/221-7282 for cardholders—this number accepts collect calls, offers service in several foreign languages, and exempts AmEx gold and platinum cardholders from the 1% fee) and **Visa** (℃ **800/222-4357**). Members of AAA can obtain Visa checks for a $9.95 fee (for checks up to $1,500) at most AAA offices or by calling ℃ **866/339-3378.** For information on **MasterCard** traveler's checks, call ℃ **800/223-9920.**

American Express, Thomas Cook, Visa, and MasterCard offer **foreign-currency traveler's checks,** which are useful if you're traveling within one foreign country or to the euro zone; they're accepted at locations where dollar checks may not be.

If you carry traveler's checks, keep a record of their serial numbers separate from your checks in the event that they are stolen or lost—you'll get your refund faster.

Tips on Shopping

When shopping for the best buys in England, note that British goods, even products from Wales and Scotland, may offer sensational buys even when sold in England. You will also find Irish stores and Irish departments in some stores often selling merchandise at the same good value you'd find on a shopping trip to Ireland itself. Many French brands are actually less expensive in the United Kingdom than in France!

THE BEST BUYS OF BRITAIN

When bargain hunting, focus on those goods that are manufactured in England and are liable to cost much more when exported. These include anything from the Body Shop to Doc Martens; many woolens and some cashmeres; most English brands of bone china; and antiques, used silver, and rare books.

ANTIQUES   Whether you're looking for museum-quality antiques or simply fun junk, England has the stores, the resources, the stalls, and the markets. You can shop the fanciest of upmarket shops—mostly in London, Bath, and the Cotswolds—or browse through antiques shows, markets, fairs, buildings, centers, arcades, warehouses, jumble fairs, fetes, and car-boot sales throughout the country. (A car-boot sale is the British version of a yard sale. Participants set up tables at an abandoned parking lot or airfield to sell their goods.)

Actually, prices are better once you get outside of London. Entire towns and areas in Britain are known to be treasure troves for those seeking anything from architectural salvage to a piece of the Holy Grail. Whereas the Cotswolds and Bath are known as charming places to shop for antiques, there are warehouses in Suffolk, Merseyside, and in the Greater Manchester (Yorkshire and Lancashire) area that aren't glamorous, but offer dealers and those in the know the best buys. Serious shoppers can head directly to the Manchester area, get a car or van, and just start shopping. The best hunting grounds are Boughton (right outside Chester), Liverpool, Prestwich, and Stockport. Harrogate and nearby Knaresborough are known for antiques, but they offer a far more upscale scene, with prices competitive with those in the Cotswolds.

AROMATHERAPY   The British must have invented aromatherapy—just about every store sells gels, creams, lotions, or potions made with the right herbs and essential oils to cure whatever ails you, including jet lag. Whether it works or not is secondary to the fact that most of the British brands are half the U.S. price when bought on home soil. The **Body Shop** becomes the best store in the world at prices like these. Check out drugstore brands as well: **Boots the Chemist** sells Body Shop knockoffs, as well as its own line (sold in another part of the store) of healing foot gels. Both of these are national brands available all over the United Kingdom.

BASIC BRIT GEAR   Don't assume any bargains on woolens, cashmeres, tweeds, and the like—often British quality is much higher than similar and less expensive goods available in the United States. If you want the best and expect it to last forever, however, you can't beat British-made, especially in gear that has been fine-tuned over the last century for the weather and outdoor lifestyle: from wax coats (**Barbour** is the leading status brand) to raincoats to guns (and English roses). While we can hardly put **Doc Martens** in the traditional Brit category, these shoes do cost a lot less in Britain than in America.

BEAUTY PRODUCTS   Dime-store brands of makeup cost less than they do in the United States. The French line **Bourjois** (made in the same factories that produce Chanel makeup) is cheaper in London than in Paris. **Boots** makes its own Chanel knockoff line, called **No. 7.**

BONE CHINA   Savings actually depend on the brand, but can be as much as 50% off United States prices. The trick is that shipping and U.S. duties may wipe out any savings; know what you're doing before you buy—and how you plan to get it back. Don't forget factory outlets that sell seconds.

DESIGNER THIS & THAT   Designer clothing from any of the international makers may cost less in London than in the United States or Paris, but know your prices. Often the only difference is the VAT refund, which at 15% to 17.5% is substantial. This game is also highly dependent on the value of the dollar.

While you won't get a VAT refund on used designer clothing, London has the best prices on used Chanel (and similar) clothing of any major shopping city.

ROYAL SOUVENIRS   Forget about investing in Diana memorabilia; word is that it won't appreciate significantly because there was so much of it. Still, royal collectibles range from cheap kitsch bought in street markets to serious pieces (from coronations long past) found in specialists' shops. If you're buying new for investment purposes, it must be kept in mint condition.

TAPESTRY & KNITTING   For some reason, the English call needlepoint "tapestry." It's a passion, perhaps the seasonal flip side to gardening. Tapestry kits by the famous English designers, and Welsh queen of needles Elizabeth Bradley, cost a fraction of their U.S. prices when purchased anywhere in England or Wales.

Whereas England is famous for its sweaters (jumpers), what it should be famous for are the sweater kits: do-it-yourself jobs from major designers that come with yarn, instructions, and a photo. English knitter-designers are cult heroes in Britain and do everything but knit autographs.

HEALTH
Staying Healthy

Traveling to England doesn't pose any health risk. The tap water is safe to drink, the milk is pasteurized, and health services are good. The crisis regarding mad-cow disease is long over, as is the foot-and-mouth disease epidemic.

England has some of the greatest medical services in the world. And, get this, all the doctors speak English. It is easy to get over-the-counter medicine, and general equivalents of common prescription drugs are available throughout the British Isles.

What to Do if You Get Sick Away from Home

If you need a doctor, your hotel can recommend one, or you can contact your embassy or consulate. Outside London, dial ℂ **100** and ask the operator for the local police, who will give you the name, address, and telephone number of a doctor in your area.

Note: U.S. visitors who become ill while they're in Britain are eligible only for free *emergency* care. For other treatment, including follow-up care, you'll be asked to pay.

Bring your insurance ID card with you when you travel. In most cases, your existing health plan will provide the coverage you need. But double-check; you may want to buy **travel medical insurance** instead. (See "Insurance" under "Fast Facts: England & Wales," p. 755.)

If you suffer from a chronic illness, consult your doctor before your departure. For conditions such as epilepsy, diabetes, or heart problems, wear a **MedicAlert Identification Tag** (ℂ **888/633-4298** or 209/668-3333; www.medicalert.org), which will immediately alert doctors to your condition and give them access to your records through MedicAlert's 24-hour hot line.

Pack **prescription medications** in your carry-on luggage and carry prescription medications in their original containers, with pharmacy labels—otherwise they won't make it through airport security. Also bring along copies of your prescriptions, in case you lose your pills or run out. Don't forget an extra pair of contact lenses or prescription glasses. Carry the generic name of prescription medicines, in case a local pharmacist is unfamiliar with the brand name.

We list additional **emergency numbers** in "Fast Facts," p. 755.

SAFETY

Like all big cities, London has its share of crime, but in general it is one of the safer destinations in Europe. Pickpockets are a major concern, though violent crime is relatively rare, especially in the heart of London, which hasn't seen a Jack the Ripper in a long time. Even so, it is not wise to go walking in parks at night. In London, take all the precautions a prudent traveler would in going anywhere, be it Los Angeles, Paris, or New York. Conceal your wallet or else hold onto your purse, and don't flaunt jewelry or cash. In other words, do as your mother told you.

The same precautions prevail in larger cities such as Birmingham, Leeds, and Manchester. However, in rural Britain you are relatively safe, though if you watch a lot of murder mysteries on TV or read about them in paperbacks, there seem to be a lot of murders going on. Nonetheless, Britain is one of the safer destinations of the world, but the sensible precautions you would heed anywhere prevail, of course.

Motorists should know that sleeping in your car is not only potentially dangerous but also illegal in the U.K., and there are always perils linked to hitchhiking, which is not recommended.

Any unrest or protest demonstrations around London's Trafalgar Square should not concern the usual visitor, who is advised to stay out of the area during any demonstrations.

Local law-enforcement officials in Britain have a long history of being fair and impartial to foreign visitors. Unlike Germany and parts of America, England seems to practice great tolerance. There is little racial, ethnic, or religious discrimination, including that of sexual orientation.

Women traveling alone encounter less aggressive or so-called macho behavior than they will find in such countries as Spain and Italy. Of course, discretion is always advised—that is, don't get in a car with three lager louts at 2 o'clock in the morning.

SPECIALIZED TRAVEL RESOURCES

In addition to the destination-specific resources listed below, please visit Frommers. com for additional specialized travel resources.

Gay & Lesbian Travelers

Britain has one of the most active gay and lesbian scenes in the world, centered mainly in London, much less so in Cardiff. Gay bars, restaurants, and centers are also found in all large English cities, notably Bath, Birmingham, Manchester, and especially Brighton.

London Lesbian & Gay Switchboard (✆ 020/7837-7324; www.llgs.org.uk) is open 24 hours a day, providing advice in general as well as information about gay-related activities in London.

London's best gay-oriented bookstore is **Gay's the Word,** 66 Marchmont St., WC1 (✆ 020/7278-7654; http://freespace.virgin.net/gays.theword; Tube: Russell Sq.), the largest such store in Britain. The friendly and helpful staff will offer advice about the ever-changing scene in London. It's open Monday to Saturday from 10am to 6:30pm and Sunday from 2 to 6pm.

At Gay's the Word and other gay-friendly venues, you can find a number of publications, many free, including the popular *Boyz, Pink Paper* (with a good lesbian section), and *9X,* filled with data about new clubs and whatever else is hot on the scene.

The **International Gay & Lesbian Travel Association** (**IGLTA;** ✆ 800/448-8550 or 954/630-1637; www.iglta.org), the trade association for the gay and lesbian travel industry, offers an online directory of gay- and lesbian-friendly travel businesses.

Many agencies offer tours and travel itineraries specifically for gay and lesbian travelers. **Above and Beyond Tours** (✆ 800/397-2681; www.abovebeyondtours. com) is a gay and lesbian tour operator. **Now, Voyager** (✆ 800/255-6951; www. nowvoyager.com) is a well-known San Francisco–based gay-owned and -operated travel service. **Gay.com Travel** (✆ 415/834-6500; www.gay.com/travel) is an excellent source for travel.

The following travel guides are available at many bookstores, or you can order them from any online bookseller: *Spartacus International Gay Guide* (Bruno Gmünder Verlag; www.spartacusworld.com); *Odysseus: The International Gay Travel Planner* (Odysseus Enterprises, Ltd.); and the *Damron* guides (www. damron.com), with separate annual books for gay men and lesbians.

Travelers with Disabilities

Many hotels, museums, restaurants, and sightseeing attractions in London have wheelchair ramps, though less so in rural England. Persons with disabilities are often granted special discounts—called "concessions" in Britain—at attractions and, in some cases, nightclubs. Free information and advice is available from **Holiday Care Service,** Hawkins Suite, Enham Place, Andover SP11 6JS (© **0845/124-9971;** fax 01539/735-567; www.holidaycare.org.uk).

Many bookstores in London carry *Access in London* (www.accessinlondon.org), a publication listing facilities for persons with disabilities, among other things.

The transport system, cinemas, and theaters are still largely off-limits, but **Transport for London** publishes a leaflet called *Access to the Underground,* which gives details of elevators and ramps at individual Tube stations; call © **020/7222-1234** or visit www.tfl.gov.uk.

London Black Cab (© **0845/108-3000;** www.londonblackcab.com) vehicles are perfectly suited for those in wheelchairs; the roomy interiors have plenty of room for maneuvering.

London's most visible organization for information about access to theaters, cinemas, galleries, museums, and restaurants is **Artsline,** 54 Chalton St., London NW1 1HS (© **020/7388-2227;** fax 020/7383-2653; www.artsline.org.uk). It offers free information about wheelchair access, theaters with hearing aids, tourist attractions, and cinemas. Artsline mails information to North America, but it's more helpful to call once you arrive in London; the line is staffed Monday to Friday from 9:30am to 5:30pm.

Many travel agencies offer customized tours and itineraries for travelers with disabilities. **Flying Wheels Travel** (© **877/451-5006** or 507/451-5005; www.flying wheelstravel.com) offers escorted tours and cruises that emphasize sports and private tours in minivans with lifts. **Access-Able Travel Source** (www.access-able.com) offers extensive access information and advice for traveling around the world with disabilities. **Accessible Journeys** (© **800/846-4537** or 610/521-0339; www.disabilitytravel.com) caters specifically to slow walkers and wheelchair travelers and their families and friends.

Organizations that offer assistance to travelers with disabilities include **MossRehab** (© **215/663-6000;** www.mossresourcenet.org/travel.htm), which provides a library of accessible-travel resources online; the **American Foundation for the Blind** (AFB; © **800/232-5463** or 212/502-7600; www.afb.org), a referral resource for the blind or visually impaired that includes information on traveling with Seeing Eye dogs; and **SATH** (Society for Accessible Travel & Hospitality; © **212/447-7284;** www.sath.org), which offers a wealth of travel resources for all types of disabilities and informed recommendations on destinations, access guides, travel agents, tour operators, vehicle rentals, and companion services.

Air Ambulance Card (© **877/424-7633;** www.airambulancecard.com) allows you to preselect top-notch hospitals in case of an emergency.

The "Accessible Travel" link at **Mobility-Advisor.com** (www.mobility-advisor.com) offers a variety of travel resources to persons with disabilities.

Check out the quarterly magazine *Emerging Horizons* (www.emerginghorizons.com), published by SATH.

Information for travelers with disabilities going to Wales is available from **Disability Wales,** Bridge House, Caerphilly Business Park, Van Road, Caerphilly CF83 3GW (*©* **029/2088-7325;** www.disabilitywales.org). The staff can tell you about suitable facilities in accommodations, restaurants, cafes, pubs, public restrooms, and attractions.

Family Travel

If you have enough trouble getting your kids out of the house in the morning, dragging them thousands of miles away may seem like an insurmountable challenge. But family travel can be immensely rewarding, giving you new ways of seeing the world through smaller pairs of eyes.

On airlines, you must request a special menu for children at least 24 hours in advance. If baby food is required, however, bring your own and ask a flight attendant to warm it to the right temperature.

Arrange ahead of time for such necessities as a crib, a bottle warmer, and a car seat (in England, small children aren't allowed to ride in the front seat).

If you're staying with friends in London, you can rent baby equipment from **Chelsea Baby Hire,** 31 Osborne House, 414 Wimbledon Park Rd., SW19 6PW (*©* **020/8789-9673;** www.chelseababyhire.com).

London Black Cab (*©* **0208/789-9673;** www.londonblackcab.com) is a lifesaver for families; the vehicles' roomy interior allows a stroller to be lifted right into the cab without unstrapping the baby.

For babysitting referrals, ask your hotel's concierge.

Before you go, have your children check out **www.kidslovelondon.com**, a site created to give kids the lowdown on attractions and events geared toward them.

Recommended family-travel websites include **Family Travel Forum** (www.familytravelforum.com), a comprehensive site that offers customized trip planning; **Family Travel Network** (www.familytravelnetwork.com), an award-winning site that offers travel features, deals, and tips; **Traveling Internationally with Your Kids** (www.travelwithyourkids.com), a comprehensive site offering sound advice for long-distance and international travel with children; and **Family Travel Files** (www.thefamilytravelfiles.com), which offers an online magazine and a directory of off-the-beaten-path tours and tour operators for families.

Some Frommer's guides were written specifically for families, including *Frommer's London with Kids, Frommer's Devon & Cornwall with Your Family,* and *Frommer's Wales with Your Family.*

To locate accommodations, restaurants, and attractions that are particularly kid-friendly, refer to the "Kids" icon throughout this guide.

Senior Travel

Be advised that in Britain you often have to be a member of an association to get senior discounts. Public-transportation discounts, for example, are available only to holders of British Pension books (given to retired seniors living on a government pension). However, many attractions do offer discounts for seniors (women 60 or older and men 65 or older). Even if discounts aren't posted, ask if they're available.

If you're older than 60, you're eligible for special 10% discounts on **British Airways** through its Privileged Traveler program. You also qualify for reduced restrictions on APEX cancellations. Discounts are granted for BA tours and for intra-Britain air tickets booked in North America. **BritRail** offers seniors discounted rates on first-class rail passes around Britain (see "Getting There & Getting Around," earlier in this chapter).

Don't be shy about asking for discounts, but do carry some kind of identification that shows your date of birth. Also, mention you're a senior when you make your reservations. Many hotels offer senior discounts. In most cities, people older than 60 qualify for reduced admission to theaters, museums, and other attractions, as well as discounted fares on public transportation.

Members of **AARP,** 601 E St. NW, Washington, DC 20049 (© **888/687-2277;** www.aarp.org), get discounts on hotels, airfares, and car rentals. AARP offers members a wide range of benefits, including *AARP The Magazine* and a monthly newsletter. Anyone older than 50 can join.

Many reliable agencies and organizations target the 50-plus market. **Road Scholar** (© **800/454-5768;** www.roadscholar.org), formerly known as Elderhostel, arranges worldwide study programs mostly for those ages 50 and older.

Recommended publications offering travel resources and discounts for seniors include the quarterly magazine *Travel 50 & Beyond* (www.travel50andbeyond. com) and *Unbelievably Good Deals and Great Adventures That You Absolutely Can't Get Unless You're Over 50* (McGraw-Hill), by Joann Rattner Heilman.

Student Travel

If you plan to travel outside the U.S., you'd be wise to arm yourself with an **International Student Identity Card (ISIC),** which offers substantial savings on rail passes, plane tickets, and entrance fees. It also provides you with basic health and life insurance and a 24-hour help line. The card is available for $22 from **STA Travel** (© **800/781-4040;** www.statravel.com), the biggest student travel agency in the world. If you're no longer a student but are still 25 or younger, you can get an **International Youth Travel Card (IYTC)** for the same price from the same people, entitling you to some discounts (but not on museum admissions).

Travel CUTS (© **800/592-2887;** www.travelcuts.com) offers similar services for Canadians and U.S. residents alike. Irish students should turn to **USIT** (© **01/602-1906;** www.usit.ie).

The **International Student House,** 229 Great Portland St., W1W 5PN (© **020/7631-8300;** www.ish.org.uk), lies at the foot of Regent's Park in London, across from the Tube stop for Great Portland Street. It's a beehive of activity, with discos and film showings, and also rents institutional, blandly furnished rooms. Laundry facilities are available and a key deposit is charged. Reserve way in advance.

The **University of London Student Union,** Malet Street, WC1 (© **020/7664-2000;** www.ulu.co.uk; Tube: Goodge St. or Russell Sq.), is the best place to go to learn about student activities in the greater London area. The student union has a swimming pool, fitness center, gymnasium, general store, sports shop, ticket agency, banks, bars, inexpensive restaurants, venues for live events, an office of STA Travel, and many other facilities. It's open Monday to Thursday 8:30am to 11pm, Friday 8:30am to 1pm, Saturday 9am to 2pm, and Sunday 9:30am to 10:30pm. Bulletin boards provide a rundown on events; some you may be able to attend, others may be "closed door."

Single Travelers

Many people prefer traveling alone, and for independent travelers, solo journeys offer infinite opportunities to make friends and meet locals. Unfortunately, if you like resorts, tours, or cruises, you're likely to get hit with a "single supplement" to the base price. Single travelers can avoid these supplements, of course, by agreeing to room with other single travelers on the trip. An even better idea is to find a compatible roommate before you go, from one of the many roommate locator agencies.

Travel Buddies Singles Travel Club (© 800/998-9099; www.travelbuddies worldwide.com), based in Canada, runs small, intimate, single-friendly group trips and will match you with a roommate free of charge, saving you the cost of single supplements. **TravelChums** (www.travelchums.com) is an Internet-only travel-companion matching service with elements of an online personals–type site, hosted by the respected New York–based Shaw Guides travel service.

Many reputable tour companies offer singles-only trips. **Singles Travel International** (© 877/765-6874; www.singlestravelintl.com) offers singles-only trips to London. **Backroads** (© 800/462-2848; www.backroads.com) offers more than 160 active trips to 30 destinations worldwide, including England.

SUSTAINABLE TOURISM

England is a land of beautiful landscapes beloved by painters such as Thomas Gainsborough and John Constable. Hikers find it one of the most rewarding terrains in Europe. So it only makes sense that long before most of the world became concerned with ecotourism, England took strides to maintain its "greenness."

More than three dozen districts of England have been designated as areas of natural beauty; in addition, England boasts 10 national parks, 12 national trails, and a protected coastline that stretches for miles and miles, including around the entire peninsula of Cornwall. Visitors in search of green spaces can choose from rolling hills, moorland, vast parks such as that in Derbyshire, and even huge "green lungs" in such city centers as London. For more information about these areas from Yorkshire to the West Country, go to **www.enjoyengland.com** or call © 020/7678-1400.

If you'd like to explore the national parks, the best source of information is the **Association of National Park Authorities,** 126 Bute St., Cardiff CF10 5L3, in Wales (© 029/2049-9966; www.nationalparks.co.uk). This organization provides information for both Wales and England, from the Yorkshire Dales to Snowdonia in the north of Wales.

Rambler's Right of Way

One of the most sustainable ways to explore England is on foot, and doing so was made easier in 2000, when the country passed the **Rights of Way Act,** granting countryside ramblers access to open land even if it is held by a private owner. Of course, all walkers must leave the land as they find it, including carrying out all trash and personal belongings.

A trio of national parks in Wales covers around 20% of the land mass of this tiny country. With the addition of the South Downs and the New Forest, designated for preservation in 2011, 10% of the land mass in England and Wales combined will be part of the national park system.

Park officials can offer advice on hiking and camping, and will also steer you to festivals or special events being staged.

The **Great Outdoor Recreation Page** (www.gorp.com) offers the best and most up-to-date information on camping and otherwise getting the most out of the English countryside.

Before you go to England, check out **Leave No Trace Center for Outdoor Ethics,** P.O. Box 997, Boulder, CO 80306 (www.lnt.org). It has drawn up a code for outdoor travelers to protect unspoiled landscapes, such as those found in the English countryside.

The **Green Tourism Business Scheme** (www.green-business.co.uk) lists numerous eco-friendly farmhouses, B&Bs, and lodges throughout England and Wales; many have received awards for their environmentally sensitive accommodations.

Another source for environmentally sensitive hotels is **It's a Green Green World** (www.itsagreengreenworld.com). It previews green accommodations throughout England, ranging from an organic farmhouse B&B dating from the 19th century in the east of England to an eco-friendly manor house on the north Norfolk coastline. Visitors can even rent English "eco cottages" that are powered by the wind and sun.

Those who want to further reduce the size of their carbon footprint can travel through England on bike. For details on cycling through England, contact the U.K.'s **National Cyclists Organization** at its national headquarters at CTC, Parklands, Railton Road, Guildford, Surrey GU2 9JX (© **0844/736-8450;** www.ctc.org.uk). Membership is £36.

If you don't want to explore green England on your own, you can take part in an eco-friendly tour. Ranging from canoeing to kayaking, mountain climbing to archaeological digs, the best clearinghouse for organized adventure trips is **Specialty Travel Index,** P.O. Box 458, San Anselmo, CA 94979 (© **888/624-4030;** www.specialtytravel.com).

The true green traveler, one who wants to leave England's environment better than he or she found it, might want to contact **Volunteering England** (© **0845/305-6979;** www.volunteering.org.uk), the best source for volunteer projects. Outdoorsy types will be especially interested in the group's efforts to save both the landscapes and the wildlife of North England, an area facing depopulation of certain species and in serious danger of forest erosion.

Before you commit to a volunteer program, it's important to make sure any money you give is truly going back to the local community and that the work you'll be doing will be a good fit for you. **Volunteer International** (www.volunteerinternational.org) has a helpful list of questions to ask to determine the intentions and nature of a volunteer program in England.

Tourism Concern (www.tourismconcern.org.uk) works to reduce social and environmental problems linked to tourism in the U.K.

The **Association of Independent Tour Operators** (www.aito.co.uk) is a group of specialist operators leading the field in making U.K. holidays sustainable.

Finally, the **Association of British Travel Agents** (**ABTA**; www.abta.com) acts as a focal point for the U.K. travel industry and is one of the leading groups spearheading responsible tourism in Britain.

SPECIAL-INTEREST TRIPS & ESCORTED GENERAL-INTEREST TOURS

Biking

Brits have rediscovered the bicycle: A **National Cycle Network** ★★ covers about 16,000km (10,000 miles) throughout the country, running from Dover in southeast England to Inverness in the Highlands. Call ℂ **0845/113-0065** for more information. Go to **www.sustrans.org.uk** for route maps.

Most routes cross old railway lines, canal towpaths, and riversides. Among the more popular routes are the **C2C (Coast to Coast or Sea to Sea) Cycle Route,** a 225km (140-mile) path linking the Irish Sea with the North Sea across the Pennine Hills and into the northern Lake District and the Durham Dales. The **Essex Cycle Route** covers 402km (250 miles) of countryside, going through some of England's most charming villages. The **Devon Coast to Coast Route**—our favorite—runs for 145km (90 miles) in southwest England, skirting the edge of Dartmoor. The **West Country Way** links the Cornish coast to Bath and Bristol for 399km (248 miles). And the **Severn & Thames Cycle Route** links two of Britain's major rivers for 161km (100 miles).

For a free copy of *Britain for Cyclists,* with information on these routes, call the **British Tourist Authority** (ℂ **800/462-2748** in the U.S., or 888/847-4885 in Canada) or contact the **Cyclists Touring Club,** Parklands, Railton Road, Guildford, Surrey GU2 9JX (ℂ **0870/873-0060,** or 01544/370666 in Wales; www.ctc.org.uk), which can suggest routes and provide information. Memberships cost £36 a year.

A leader in biking tours since 1974, **Euro-Bike & Walking Tours** ★, P.O. Box 81025, Billings, MT 59108 (ℂ **800/575-1540** in the U.S. and Canada; www.eurobike.com), is currently the best outfitter.

Fishing

Fly-fishing was born here, and it's an art form. Local fishing guides are available to lead you to English waters that are well stocked with trout, perch, grayling, sea bream, Atlantic salmon, and such lesser known species as rudd and roach.

To learn about fishing vacations, contact **Angling Direct Holidays,** the Homestead, Thurgarton Road, Aldborough, Norfolk NR11 2NY (ℂ **01603/407596;** www.anglingdirectholidays.com).

If you prefer to go it alone without a guide, contact the **Salmon & Trout Association,** Fishmonger's Hall, London Bridge, London EC4R 9EL (ℂ **020/7283-5838;** www.salmon-trout.org), for information about British fishing regulations.

An excellent guide to fishing is *Where to Fly Fish in Britain & Ireland,* available on Amazon.com.

Golf

Though the sport originated in Scotland, golf has been around in Britain since Edward VII first began stamping over the greens of such courses as Royal Lytham & St. Annes, in England's Northwest, and Royal St. Georges, near London.

The unyielding reality is that golf in Britain remains a clubby sport where some of the most prestigious courses are usually reserved exclusively for members. Rules at most British golf courses tend to be stricter in matters of dress code and protocol than their equivalents in the United States.

If your heart is still set on enjoying a round or two on the emerald-colored turf of Britain, **Golf International** ★, 14 E. 38th St., New York, NY 10016 (© **800/833-1389** or 212/986-9176; www.golfinternational.com), can open doors for you. Golf packages are arranged for anywhere from 7 to 14 days and can include as much or as little golf, on as many different courses, as a participant wants.

Worthy competitors that operate on a less comprehensive scale than Golf International include **Adventures in Golf,** 22 Greeley St., Ste. 7, Merrimack, NH 03054 (© **877/424-7320** or 603/424-7320; www.adventures-in-golf.com); and **Jerry Quinlan's Celtic Golf,** 1129 Rte. 9 South, Cape May Courthouse, NJ 08210 (© **800/535-6148** or 609/465-0600; www.celticgolf.com). Each of the tours is customized and usually includes lodging in anything from simple guest-houses to five-star deluxe manor houses.

Hiking, Walking & Rambling

England and Wales alone have some 161,000km (100,000 miles) of trails and footpaths. The **Ramblers' Association,** Camelford House, 87–90 Albert Embankment, 2nd Floor, London SE1 7TW (© **020/7339-8500,** or 029/2064-4308 in Wales; www.ramblers.org.uk), has several books and maps on hiking and walking in Great Britain. Prices range from free to £15.

Wilderness Travel, Inc., 1102 Ninth St., Berkeley, CA 94710 (© **800/368-2794** or 510/558-2488; www.wildernesstravel.com), specializes in treks and inn-to-inn hiking tours.

English Lakeland Ramblers ★, 15404 Beachview Dr., Montclair, VA 22025 (© **800/724-8801** or 703/680-4276; www.ramblers.com), offers 7- or 8-day walking tours for the average active person. On its Lake District tour, you'll stay and have your meals in a charming 17th-century country inn near Ambleside and Windermere. A minibus takes hikers and sightseers daily to trails and sightseeing points. Experts tell you about the area's culture and history and highlight its natural wonders. There are also tours of the Cotswolds, as well as inn-to-inn tours and privately guided tours.

Another contender is **Country Walkers,** P.O. Box 180, Waterbury, VT 05676 (© **800/464-9255** or 802/244-1387; www.countrywalkers.com). This company's "walking vacations" last 7 days in either the Cotswolds region or the Lake District.

To explore the mountain activities of Wales's Snowdonia National Park, contact Bob Postings at **Pathfinder,** Clynnog Fawr, Tan-yr-allt, Caernarfon, Gwynedd LL54

5NS, in North Wales (☎ **01286/660202;** www.pathfindersnowdonia.co.uk). Bob and his skilled team specialize in walking the summits, rock climbing, kayaking, and rafting, among other activities.

One of the best outfitters for walks through the West Country and the Cotswolds is **Walking Holidays** ★ (☎ **01761/233807;** www.bathwestwalks.com). On these guided tours, you take in such attractions as the Wiltshire Downs and the Mendip Hills, as well as the coastal scenery of Exmoor.

To read about the vast hiking possibilities of Britain, you can order from Amazon. com a copy of *Stilwell's National Trail Companion* (Stilwell Publishing, 2001), by Tim Stilwell. It's the ultimate where-to-stay guide for walkers and also documents an extensive national system of 48 hiking trails through Britain.

Horseback Riding

Horseback riding is one of the reasons many visitors head to England, a country of great equestrians, in the first place.

A number of American companies offer horseback-riding package tours of Britain. **Equitour** ★, P.O. Box 807, Dubois, WY 82513 (☎ **800/545-0019** or 307/455-3363; www.ridingtours.com), is one such firm, specializing in package tours for riding enthusiasts who want to experience the horsey traditions of the land of foxes and hounds. Two types of tours can be arranged: stationary tours, with instruction in jumping and dressage during a 7-day period at a stable beside the Bristol Channel or on the fields of Dartmoor, and "progressive" tours in Wales, with a 7-day trek. Most riders, eager to experience as wide a view of England as possible, opt for the latter, spending nights at different B&Bs or inns and lodging their mount at nearby stables. Accommodations are simple, and prices are kept deliberately low.

Eastern Trekking Associates, P.O. Box 357, Thomson, GA 30824 (☎ **888/836-6152** or 706/541-2450), leads small groups of around six riders each on tours of the Exmoor region, arguably the most beautiful district of England. Horseback-riding trips are also arranged in Wales.

Literary Tours

Devotees of English literature and bookworms in general can explore England as it was seen and observed by famous writers, not just Shakespeare, but also the Brontë sisters, who lived in Yorkshire, or Beatrix Potter and Wordsworth, who wrote of the glorious landscapes of the Lake District.

The best such escorted tours are offered by **Lynott Tours,** 205 Mineola Blvd., Ste. 1B, Mineola, NY 11501 (☎ **800/221-2474;** www.lynotttours.com). Accommodations, breakfasts, dinners, afternoon tea, and a full-time guide are included in these jaunts. The most popular tours include "Much Ado About Shakespeare," "Literary Cotswolds," and "The Brontës Literature and Countryside" tour of the dramatic moors of Northeast England.

The **British Connection** (☎ **404/373-1420;** www.thebritishconnection.com) offers literary tours with a focus on Shakespeare, Jane Austen, Agatha Christie, and even British mystery writers. It also arranges garden tours and various history and archaeological tours, including one that grants private access to Stonehenge.

University Study Programs

You can study British literature at renowned universities such as Oxford and Cambridge during the week and then take weekend excursions to the countryside of Shakespeare, Austen, Dickens, and Hardy. While doing your coursework, you can live in dormitories with other students and dine in elaborate halls or the more intimate Fellows' clubs. Study programs in England are not limited to the liberal arts, or to high school or college students. Some programs are designed specifically for teachers and seniors. For more information, contact the organizations listed below.

Affiliated with Richmond College in London, the **American Institute for Foreign Study,** River Plaza, 9 W. Broad St., Stamford, CT 06902 (© **866/906-2437** or 203/399-5000; www.aifs.com), offers 4 weeks or more of traveling programs for high school students, as well as internships and academic programs for college students. There are also programs leading to the British equivalent of an MBA.

The **Institute of International Education (IIE),** U.S. Student Programs Division, 809 United Nations Plaza, New York, NY 10017 (© **212/883-8200;** www.iie.org), administers a variety of academic, training, and grant programs for the U.S. Information Agency (USIA), including Fulbright grants. It is especially helpful in arranging enrollment for U.S. students in summer school programs.

Worldwide Classrooms, P.O. Box 1166, Milwaukee, WI 53201 (© **414/224-3476;** www.worldwide.edu), produces an extensive listing of schools offering study-abroad programs in England.

Escorted General-Interest Tours

Escorted tours are structured group tours, with a group leader. The price usually includes everything from airfare to hotels, meals, tours, admission costs, and local transportation.

Abercrombie & Kent (© **800/554-7016;** www.abercrombiekent.com) offers extremely upscale escorted tours that are loaded with luxury. They're the best in the business.

Martin Randall Travel (© **800/988-6168;** www.martinrandall.com) offers cultural tours led by expert lecturers in the fields of archaeology, architecture, art, history, music, and so on. Its tours focus on everything from English country houses and gardens to Hadrian's Wall to the Welsh National Opera in Cardiff. It also organizes all-inclusive classical music holidays centered around international festivals.

Other contenders in the upscale package-tour business include **Maupintour** (© **800/255-4266;** www.maupintour.com) and **Tauck World Discovery** (© **800/788-7885;** www.tauck.com).

But not all escorted tours are so pricey. Older British folks make up a large portion of the clientele of one of the United Kingdom's largest tour operators, **Wallace Arnold Worldchoice** (© **0845/365-6747;** www.waworldchoice.com). Most of the company's tours last between 5 and 10 days, include lodgings (at solid but not particularly extravagant hotels) and most meals, and are reasonably priced.

U.S.-based **Trafalgar Tours** (© **866/544-4434;** www.trafalgartours.com) offers more affordable packages, with lodgings in unpretentious but comfortable hotels. It's one of Europe's largest tour operators. There may not be a lot of frills, but you can find 7-day itineraries priced from $1,075 per person, double occupancy, without airfare, that include stopovers in Stratford-upon-Avon and Bath; also available are

8-day packages at first-class hotels in London, starting at $899 per person, double occupancy.

One of Trafalgar's leading competitors, known for roughly equivalent moderately priced tours through Britain, is **Globus & Cosmos Tours** (℃ **866/755-8581;** www.globusandcosmos.com).

Despite the fact that escorted tours require big deposits and predetermine hotels, restaurants, and itineraries, many people derive security and peace of mind from the structure they offer. Escorted tours—whether they're navigated by bus, motorcoach, train, or boat—let travelers sit back and enjoy the trip without having to drive or worry about details. They take you to the maximum number of sights in the minimum amount of time with the least amount of hassle. They're particularly convenient for people with limited mobility, and they can be a great way to make new friends.

On the downside, you'll have little opportunity for serendipitous interactions with locals. The tours can be jam-packed with activities, leaving little room for individual sightseeing, whim, or adventure—plus they often focus on the heavily touristed sites, so you miss out on many a lesser-known gem.

For more information on escorted general-interest tours, including questions to ask before booking your trip, see www.frommers.com/planning.

STAYING CONNECTED

Telephones

To call England from North America, dial **011** (international code), **44** (Britain's country code), the local area code (usually three or four digits and found in every phone number we've given in this book), and the local phone number. The local area codes found throughout this book all begin with "0"; you drop the "0" if you're calling from outside Britain, but you need to dial it along with the area code if you're calling from within Britain. For calls within the same city or town, the local number is all you need.

For **directory assistance** in London, dial ℃ **142;** for the rest of Britain, ℃ **192.**

Within the U.K., despite the growing prevalence of mobile phones, you'll still find at least three kinds of **public pay phones:** those relatively old-fashioned models that accept only coins; those accepting only prepaid phone cards; and those accepting both phone cards and credit cards. *Note:* The "old-fashioned" phone boxes with the royal coat of arms and the bright red coat of paint tend to be maintained by British Telecom and fall into the latter of these three categories. Telephones that accept such credit cards as Access/MasterCard, Visa, American Express, and Diners Club tend to be most common at airports and large railway stations.

In a "confrontation" with a coin-operated phone, insert your (British) coins before dialing, with the understanding that the minimum charge these days even for calls placed to destinations within the same neighborhood will begin at 30p—more, pro-rated per call, than equivalent calls paid for with a phone card.

Phone cards are issued throughout the U.K. by a wide variety of corporate issuers, and with a wide variety of denominations that begin at £2.50 and go up to as much as £50 or higher. Each is reusable until the card's total value has been electronically depleted. Phone cards are sold in post offices, newsstands, and within large retail supermarkets, including branches of Tesco and Sainsbury's.

To make an **international call** from Britain, dial the international access code **(00),** then the country code, then the area code, and finally the local number. Or call through one of the following long-distance access codes: **AT&T USA Direct** (✆ 1800/CALL-ATT [225-5288]), **Canada Direct** (✆ 0800/890016), **Australia** (✆ 0800/890061), and **New Zealand** (✆ 0800/890064). Common country codes are: U.S. and Canada, **1;** Australia, **61;** New Zealand, **64;** and South Africa, **27.**

To make a **collect call,** or if you need an international operator, dial ✆ **155.**

Caller beware: Some hotels routinely add outrageous surcharges onto phone calls made from your room. Inquire before you call! It may be a lot cheaper to use your own calling-card number or to find a pay phone.

Cellphones

The three letters that define much of the world's wireless capabilities are GSM (Global System for Mobiles), a big, seamless network that makes for easy cross-border cellphone use throughout England and dozens of other countries worldwide. In general, reception is good. But you'll need a SIM (Subscriber Identity Module) card specific to England that gives you a local phone number and plugs you into a regional network. In the U.S., T-Mobile, AT&T Wireless, and Cingular use this quasi-universal system; in Canada, Microcell and some Rogers customers are GSM; and all Europeans and most Australians use GSM. Unfortunately, per-minute charges can be high. Calls to the U.S. average 70p per minute.

For many, **renting a phone** is a good idea. While you can rent a phone from any number of overseas sites, including kiosks at airports and car-rental agencies, we suggest renting one before you leave home. North Americans can contact **InTouch USA** (✆ **800/872-7626** or 703/222-7161; www.intouchglobal.com) or **RoadPost** (✆ **888/290-1616** or 905/272-5665; www.roadpost.com). InTouch will also, for free, advise you on whether your existing phone will work overseas.

Depending on your business obligations in the U.K., your lifestyle, and your phone habits, **buying a phone** might be economically attractive, as the U.K. is one of the most cellphone-permeated societies in the world and local competition is fierce. Once you arrive, stop by a local mobile-phone shop (T-Mobile, Virgin, Vodafone, and British Telecom all maintain their respective outlets) and compare the cheapest packages. Buying a no-frills phone might cost as little as £30, and in some cases, depending on the promotion of the moment, might carry as much as £10 of prepaid minutes. From abroad, researching the wide array of options is a daunting task, but as a means of getting started in your search, go to www.britishtelecom.com.

Voice over Internet Protocol (VoIP)

If you have Web access while traveling, consider a broadband-based phone service—in technical terms, **Voice over Internet Protocol,** or **VoIP**—such as **Skype** (www.myskyp.com) or **Vonage** (www.vonage.com), which allow you to make free international calls from your laptop or in a cybercafe. Neither service requires the people you're calling to also have that service (though there are fees if they do not). Check the websites for details.

Internet & E-mail
WITH YOUR OWN COMPUTER
More and more hotels, cafes, and retailers in England are signing on as Wi-Fi (wireless fidelity) "hot spots." **T-Mobile Hotspot** (www.t-mobile.com/hotspot or www.t-mobile.co.uk) offers wireless connections at coffee shops nationwide. **Boingo** (www.boingo.com) has networks in airports and high-class hotel lobbies. **iPass** providers (see below) also give you access to a few hundred wireless hotel lobby setups. To locate other hot spots that provide free wireless networks in cities in England, go to **www.jiwire.com**.

For dial-up access, most business-class hotels offer dataports for laptop modems, and a few thousand hotels in England now offer free high-speed Internet access. In addition, major Internet service providers (ISPs) have **local access numbers** around the world, allowing you to go online by placing a local call. The **iPass** network also has dial-up numbers around the world. You'll have to sign up with an iPass provider, who will then tell you how to set up your computer for your destination(s). For a list of iPass providers, go to www.ipass.com and click on "Individuals Buy Now." One solid provider is **i2roam** (© **866/811-6209** or 920/233-5863; www.i2roam.com).

Wherever you go, bring a **connection kit** of the right power and phone adapters, a spare phone cord, and a spare Ethernet network cable—or find out whether your hotel supplies them to guests.

WITHOUT YOUR OWN COMPUTER
To find cybercafes, check **www.cybercaptive.com** and **www.cybercafe.com**. Cybercafes are located in all large U.K. cities, especially London, where they can be found on almost every business street. **easyInternetcafe** (© **020/7241-9000;** www.easyinternetcafe.com) has several Great Britain locations.

Aside from formal cybercafes, most **youth hostels** and **public libraries** have Internet access. Avoid **hotel business centers** unless you're willing to pay exorbitant rates.

Internet kiosks appear within the public areas of every large and medium-size airport in the U.K. These usually provide basic Web access for a per-minute fee. More conveniently, if you have access to the business-class lounges of most airlines, including British Airways, Delta, American, Continental, and most of their competitors, free Internet stations are standard features within any of them.

TIPS ON ACCOMMODATIONS
Reserve your accommodations as far in advance as possible, even in the so-called slow months from November to April. Travel to London peaks between May and October, and during that period, it's hard to come by a moderate or inexpensive hotel room. Sometimes you can get better rates by calling the hotel directly. Ask for the type of room you want. If you're sensitive to noise, for example, request a room that's quieter, perhaps in the rear so you won't hear traffic noise out front. Remember that in the older hotels and inns, guest rooms tend to be small and each room is different, often with varied plumbing. If you need a bathtub, ask for one, or else you might end up with a small shower cubicle.

Classifications

Unlike some countries, England has no rigid hotel classification system. The tourist board grades hotels by stars. Hotels are judged on standards, quality, and hospitality, and are rated "approved," "commended," "highly commended," and "deluxe." Five stars (deluxe) is the highest rating. A classification of "listed" refers to accommodations that are, for the most part, very modest.

All establishments from two stars upward are required to have 100% en suite (private bathroom) facilities. In a one-star hotel, buildings are required to have hot and cold running water in all rooms, but in "listed" hotels, hot and cold running water in rooms is not mandatory. Star ratings are posted outside the buildings. However, the system is voluntary, and many hotels do not participate.

Many hotels, especially older ones, still lack private bathrooms for all rooms. However, most have hot and cold running water, and many have modern wings with all the amenities (and older sections that are less up-to-date). When making reservations, always ask what section of the hotel you'll be staying in.

All hotels once included in the room price a full English breakfast of bacon and eggs, but today that is true of only some hotels. A continental breakfast is commonly included, usually comprising just tea or coffee and toast.

Bed & Breakfasts

In towns, cities, and villages throughout Britain, homeowners take in paying guests; watch for the familiar bed-and-breakfast (B&B) signs. Generally, these are modest family homes, but sometimes they may be built like small hotels, with as many as 15 rooms. If they're that big, they are more properly classified as guesthouses. B&Bs are the cheapest places you can stay in England and still be comfortable.

Reservations for bed-and-breakfast accommodations in London can be made by writing (not calling) the **Britain and London Visitor Centre (BLVC),** 1 Lower Regent St., London SW1Y 4XT. Once in London, you can also visit its office (Tube: Piccadilly Circus).

In addition, Susan Opperman and Rosemary Lumb run **Bed & Breakfast Nationwide,** P.O. Box 2100, Clacton-on-Sea, Essex CO16 9BW (✆ **01255/831235;** fax 01255/831437; www.bedandbreakfastnationwide.com), an agency specializing in privately owned bed-and-breakfasts all over Great Britain. Host homes range from small cottages to large manor houses, as well as working farms, and the prices vary accordingly. One thing you can be sure of is that owners have been specially selected for their wish to entertain visitors from overseas. Remember that these are private homes, so hotel-type services are not available. You will, however, be assured of a warm welcome, a comfortable bed, a hearty breakfast, and a glimpse of British life. Write for a free brochure.

Farmhouses

In many parts of the country, farmhouses have one, two, even four rooms set aside for paying guests, who usually arrive in the summer months. Farmhouses don't have the facilities of most guesthouses, but they do offer a rustic appeal and charm, especially for motorists, as they tend to lie off the beaten path. Prices are generally lower than those at bed-and-breakfasts or guesthouses, and sometimes you're offered good country home cooking (at an extra charge) if you make arrangements in advance.

Farm Stay UK, National Agricultural Centre, Stoneleigh Park, Warwickshire CV8 2LG (*©* **024/7669-6909;** www.farmstayuk.co.uk) publishes an annual directory (£4.50) that includes 1,000 farms and bed-and-breakfasts throughout the United Kingdom. The listings include quality ratings, the number of bedrooms, nearby attractions and activities, prices, and line drawings of each property. Also listed are any special details, such as rooms with four-poster beds or activities on the grounds (fishing, for example). Many farms are geared toward children, who can participate in light chores—gathering eggs or just tagging along—for an authentic farm experience. The approximate prices range from £30 to £75 a night and include an English breakfast and usually private facilities. (The higher prices are for stays at mansions and manor houses.)

Another option is self-catering accommodations, which are usually cottages or converted barns that cost from £200 per week and include dishwashers and central heating. Each property is inspected annually not only by the Farm Holiday Bureau, but also by the English Tourist Board. The majority of the properties, with the exception of those located in the mountains, are open year-round.

For apartment, farmhouse, or cottage stays of 2 weeks or more, **Untours** (*©* **888/868-6871;** www.untours.com) provides exceptional lodgings for reasonable prices, which include air/ground transportation, cooking facilities, and on-call support from a local resident. Best of all, Untours donates most profits to provide low-interest loans to underprivileged entrepreneurs around the world (see website for details).

National Trust Properties

The **National Trust Holiday Cottages,** Holiday Booking Office, P.O. Box 536, Melksham, Wiltshire SN12 8SX (*©* **0844/800-2070;** www.nationaltrustcottages. co.uk), is Britain's leading conservation organization. In addition to the many castles, forests, and gardens it maintains, the National Trust owns nearly 350 houses and cottages in some of the most beautiful parts of England, Wales, and Northern Ireland. Some of these properties are in remote and rural locations, some have incomparable views of the coastline, and others stand in the hearts of villages and ancient cities. Most of these comfortable self-catering holiday accommodations are available for rental throughout the year. Many can be booked for midweek or weekend breaks on short notice, particularly in autumn and winter. National Trust properties can sleep from 2 to 12 guests.

Though anyone can book rentals in National Trust properties, it's worth mentioning the trust's U.S. affiliate, the **Royal Oak Foundation,** 26 Broadway, Ste. 950, New York, NY 10004 (*©* **800/913-6565** or 212/480-2889; www.royal-oak.org), which publishes a full-color 400-page booklet that describes all National Trust holiday rental properties, their facilities, and prices. Copies cost $12 for nonmembers. Individual annual memberships are $55, and family memberships are $90. Benefits include free admission to all National Trust sites and properties open to the public, plus discounts on air travel, train tickets, and reservations at cottages and houses owned by the National Trust.

Holiday Cottages & Villages

Throughout Britain, fully furnished studios, houses, cottages, "flats" (apartments), and even trailers suitable for families or groups can be rented by the month. From October to March, rents are sometimes reduced by 50%.

The British Tourist Authority and most tourist offices have lists available. The BTA's free *Apartments in London and Holiday Homes* lists rental agencies such as **At Home Abroad, Inc.,** 163 Third Ave., Box 319, New York, NY 10003 (© **212/421-9165;** fax 212/228-4860; www.athomeabroadinc.com). Interested parties should write or fax a description of their needs; At Home Abroad will send listings at no charge.

Cottages 4 You (© **0870/078-2100;** www.cottages4you.co.uk) represents about 9,000 rental properties in the United Kingdom. It has everything from thatch-roofed cottages to castles.

Barclay International Group (BIG), 6800 Jericho Turnpike 212W, Syosset, NY 11791 (© **800/845-6636** or 516/364-0064; www.barclayweb.com), specializes in short-term apartment (flat) rentals in London and cottages in the English countryside. These rentals can be appropriate for families, groups of friends, or business-people traveling together and are sometimes less expensive than equivalent stays in hotels. Apartments, available for stays as short as 1 night (though the company prefers that guests stay a minimum of 3 nights and charges a premium if your stay is shorter), are usually more luxurious than you'd imagine. Since they're furnished with kitchens, they offer a low-cost alternative to restaurant meals. For extended stays in the English countryside, BIG has country cottages in such areas as the Cotswolds, the Lake District, and Oxford, as well as farther afield in Scotland and Wales. The company can also arrange tickets for sightseeing attractions, BritRail passes, and various other extras.

At the cheaper end of the spectrum, there's **Hoseasons Holidays,** Lowestoft, NR32 2LW (© **0844/847-1356;** www.hoseasons.co.uk), a reservations agent based in Suffolk (East Anglia). It arranges stopovers in at least 400 vacation villages throughout Britain. Though many are isolated in bucolic regions far from any of the sites covered within this guide, others lie within an hour's drive of Stratford-upon-Avon. Don't expect luxury or convenience: Vacation villages in England usually consist of a motley assortment of trailers, noninsulated bungalows, and/or mobile homes perched on cement blocks. They're intended as frugal escapes for claustrophobic urbanites with children. Such a place may not meet your expectations for a vacation in the English countryside (and a minimum stay of 3 nights is usually required), but it's hard to beat the rate.

Chain Hotels

Many American chains, such as Best Western, Hilton, Sheraton, and Travelodge, are found throughout Britain. In addition, Britain has a number of leading chains with which North American travelers are generally not familiar. **Thistle Hotels** (© **020/7138-0000;** www.thistle.com) is a well-regarded chain of moderate to upscale full-service hotels that caters to business and leisure travelers alike. An exclusive chain of government-rated three-crown hotels is called **Malmaison** (© **0845/365-4247;** www.malmaison.com); there's not a bad hotel on their list.

BRITAIN BANS PUBLIC smoking

Some 4 centuries ago King James I denounced tobacco, calling it "loathsome to the eye, hateful to the nose, harmful to the brain, and dangerous to the lungs."

Britain has now heard his words, banning smoking in most public places, including **hotels, restaurants,** and **pubs** that serve food. Antismoking activists welcomed the proposal, but criticized the government for letting smokers continue lighting up in some pubs and bars.

Still, it's a big step for a country that has long had a love-hate affair with tobacco, and whose smoky pubs are at the heart of the nation's social life.

Since the law was enacted, many hotels have opted to become 100% nonsmoking, even in the bedrooms, while others—at their discretion—have set aside a few of their rooms for smokers. Always ask before booking if you want a room in which you can smoke.

Premier Inn (✆ **0870/242-8000;** www.premierinn.com) is a chain of modern, moderately priced accommodations across the U.K., each featuring a licensed restaurant.

House Swapping

The market leader in home exchanges is **HomeLink International,** 2937 NW9 Terrace, Fort Lauderdale, FL 33311 (✆ **800/638-3841** or 954/566-2687; www.homelink.org), which costs $110 to join. This is the oldest, largest, and best home-exchange holiday organization in the world.

A competitor is **Intervac U.S. & International,** 30 Corte San Fernando, Tiburon, CA 94920 (✆ **800/756-HOME** [4663]; www.intervacus.com). To hook up with this outfitter, you pay $65 annually. Intervac is adept at securing a list of home exchanges throughout Great Britain.

Youth Hostels

Youth Hostels Association (England and Wales) operates a network of 230 hostels in major cities, in the countryside, and along the coast. You can contact the Customer Services Department, YHA, Trevelyan House, Dimple Road, Matlock, Derbyshire DE4 3YH (✆ **01629/592-600;** www.yha.org.uk), for a free map with locations of each youth hostel and full details, including prices.

SUGGESTED ENGLAND ITINERARIES

Vacations are getting shorter, and a "lean-and-mean" schedule is called for if you want to experience the best of any country in a relatively short span of time. If you're a time-pressed traveler, as most of us are, with only 1 or 2 weeks for England, you may find the first two itineraries helpful. But before planning your schedule, take a moment to review each of England's unique regions.

4

THE REGIONS IN BRIEF

England is a part of the United Kingdom, which is made up of England, Wales, Scotland, and Northern Ireland. Only 130,347 sq. km (50,327 sq. miles)—about the same size as New York State—England has an amazing amount of rural land and natural wilderness and an astonishing regional, physical, and cultural diversity. See the "England and Wales" map in the insert at the beginning of this book for the regions outlined below.

England

LONDON   Some seven million Londoners live in this mammoth metropolis, a parcel of land that's more than 1,577 sq. km (609 sq. miles) in size. The City of London proper is merely 2.5 sq. km (1 sq. mile), but the rest of the city is made up of separate villages, boroughs, and corporations. London's neighborhoods and outlying areas are described in chapter 5.

THE THAMES VALLEY· England's most famous river runs westward from Kew to its source in the Cotswolds. A land of meadows, woodlands, attractive villages, small market towns, and rolling hillsides, this is one of England's most scenic areas. Highlights include **Windsor Castle** (Elizabeth II's favorite residence) and nearby **Eton College,** founded by a young Henry VI in 1440. **Henley,** site of the Royal Regatta, remains our favorite Thames-side town; and at the university city of **Oxford,** you can tour the colleges.

THE SOUTHEAST (KENT, SURREY & SUSSEX)   This is the land of Charles Lamb, Virginia Woolf, Sir Winston Churchill, and Henry James. It's where you'll find some of the nation's biggest attractions: **Brighton, Canterbury, Dover,** and dozens of country homes and castles—not only **Hever** and **Leeds castles,** but also **Chartwell,** the more modest abode where Churchill lived. In small villages, such as Rye and Winchelsea in Sussex, you discover the charm of the region. Almost all of the Sussex shoreline is built up, and seaside towns, such as Eastbourne and Hastings, are often tacky. In fact, though the area's major attraction is **Canterbury Cathedral,** the **Royal Pavilion at Brighton** rates as an outstanding, extravagant folly. Tea shops, antiques stores, pubs, and small inns abound in the area. Surrey is essentially a commuter suburb of London and is easily reached for day trips.

HAMPSHIRE & WILTSHIRE   Southwest of London, these counties possess two of England's greatest **cathedrals,** Winchester and Salisbury, and one of Europe's most significant prehistoric monuments, **Stonehenge.** Hampshire is bordered on its western side by the woodlands and heaths of **New Forest.** The towns of **Portsmouth** and **Southampton** loom large in naval heritage. You may also want to take a ferry over to the **Isle of Wight,** once Queen Victoria's preferred vacation retreat. In Wiltshire, you encounter the beginning of the **West Country,** with its scenic beauty and monuments. Here you'll find Wilton House, the 17th-century home of the earls of Pembroke, and Old Sarum, the remains of what is believed to have been an Iron Age fortification.

THE SOUTHWEST (DORSET, SOMERSET, DEVON & CORNWALL)   These four counties are the great vacation centers and retirement havens of England. Dorset, associated with Thomas Hardy, is a land of rolling downs, rocky headlands, well-kept villages, and rich farmlands. Somerset—the Somerset of King Arthur and Camelot—offers such magical towns as **Glastonbury.** Devon has both **Exmoor** and **Dartmoor national parks,** and its northern and southern coastlines are peppered with famous resorts such as Lyme Regis and villages such as Clovelly. In Cornwall, you're never more than 32km (20 miles) from the rugged coastline, which ends at **Land's End.** Among the cities worth visiting in these counties are **Bath,** with its impressive Roman baths and Georgian architecture; **Plymouth,** the departure point of the *Mayflower;* and **Wells,** the site of a great cathedral.

THE COTSWOLDS   A wonderful region to tour, this is a pastoral land of honey-colored limestone villages where rural England unfolds before you like a storybook. In the Middle Ages, wool made the Cotswolders prosperous, but now they put out the welcome mat for visitors, with famously lovely inns and pubs. Start at Burford, the traditional gateway to the region, continuing on to Bourton-on-the-Water, Lower and Upper Slaughter, and Stow-on-the-Wold. **Cirencester** is the uncrowned capital of the south Cotswolds, and **Cheltenham** is still an elegant Regency spa. Our two favorite villages are **Painswick,** with its minute cottages, and **Bibury,** with Arlington Row, its cluster of former weavers' cottages.

STRATFORD & WARWICK   This region encompasses both Shakespeare country and the Midlands. The Midlands was the birthplace of the Industrial Revolution, which made Britain the first industrialized country in the world. Its foremost tourist town is **Stratford-upon-Avon,** but also drawing visitors are **Warwick Castle,** one of England's great castles, and the ruins of **Kenilworth Castle.** The city of **Coventry,** heavily bombed in World War II, is visited mainly for its outstanding modern cathedral.

BIRMINGHAM & THE WEST MIDLANDS   The area known as the West Midlands embraces the so-called "Black Country." **Birmingham,** nicknamed "Brum," is Britain's largest city after London. This sprawling metropolis is still characterized by its overpass jungles and tacky suburbs, as well as its great piles of Victorian architecture. Urban renewal is underway, however. The English marshes cut through the old counties of **Shropshire** and **Herefordshire.** The **Ironbridge Gorge** was at the heart of the Industrial Revolution, and the famous **Potteries** are in Staffordshire.

EAST ANGLIA (ESSEX, CAMBRIDGESHIRE, NORFOLK & SUFFOLK)
East Anglia, a semicircular geographic bulge northeast of London, is the name applied to these four very flat counties. The land of John Constable is still filled with the landscapes he painted. The **Fens**—that broad expanse of fertile, black soil lying north of Cambridge—remains our favorite district. Go there to see **Ely Cathedral. Cambridge,** with its colleges and river, is the chief attraction. The most important museum is the **Fitzwilliam** in Cambridge, but visitors also flock to East Anglia for the scenery and its solitary beauty—fens, salt marshes, and villages of thatched cottages.

THE EAST MIDLANDS (DERBYSHIRE, LEICESTERSHIRE, LINCOLN-SHIRE, NORTHAMPTONSHIRE & NOTTINGHAMSHIRE)   This area encompasses some of the worst of industrial England, yet there is still great natural beauty to be found, as well as stately homes. These include **Chatsworth** in Derbyshire, the seat of the dukes of Devonshire; **Sulgrave Manor** in Northamptonshire, the ancestral home of George Washington; and **Althorp House,** also in Northamptonshire, the childhood home of Diana, Princess of Wales. **Lincoln** has one of England's great cathedrals, rebuilt in the 13th and 14th centuries. **Nottingham** recalls Robin Hood, though the deforested Sherwood Forest is obviously not what it was in the outlaw's heyday.

THE NORTHWEST   Stretching from Liverpool to the Scottish border, northwest England can be a rustic delight if you steer clear of its industrial pockets. Most people come here to follow in the footsteps of such Romantic poets as Wordsworth, who wrote of the beauty of the Lake District (see below). But **Chester, Manchester,** and **Liverpool** merit stopovers along the way. The resort of **Blackpool** is big, brash, and a bit tawdry, drawing the working class of the Midlands for Coney Island–style fun by the sea. In contrast, the Roman city of Chester is a well-preserved medieval town, known for its encircling wall. And Liverpool is culturally alive and always intriguing, if only to see where the Beatles came from; it also has a branch of London's Tate Gallery.

THE LAKE DISTRICT   The literary Lakeland evokes memories of the Wordsworths, Samuel Taylor Coleridge, John Ruskin, and Beatrix Potter, among others. **Windermere** is the best location for touring the area, but there are many other charming towns as well, including **Grasmere** and **Ambleside.** The Lake District contains some of England's most dramatic scenery.

YORKSHIRE & NORTHUMBRIA   Yorkshire will be familiar to fans of the Brontës and James Herriot. **York,** with its immense cathedral and medieval streets, is the city to visit, though more and more visitors are calling on **Leeds** and **Bradford** as well. Northumbria comprises **Northumberland, Cleveland, Durham,** and **Tyne and Wear** (the area around **Newcastle**). The whole area echoes the ancient border battles between the Scots and English. **Hadrian's Wall,** built by the Romans, is a highlight. The **cathedral** at Durham is one of Britain's finest examples of Norman church architecture, and **Fountains Abbey** is among the country's greatest ecclesiastical ruins. Country homes abound; here you find **Harewood House** and **Castle Howard.**

Wales

CARDIFF & SOUTH WALES   The capital of Wales, **Cardiff** is a large seaport on the tidal estuary of the River Taff. As the center of the small landmass that is Wales, Cardiff admittedly can't compare very well with London or Edinburgh, but it's a charmer in its own right. Newly restored, the capital invites with such attractions as the treasure trove of the **National Museum of Wales,** along with **Cardiff Castle** and all its rich architectural detail. If time remains, dip into **South Wales,** which isn't all remnants of the Industrial Revolution—in fact, it's filled with beauty spots, such as the **Brecon Beacons National Park.** West of Cardiff is the city of **Swansea,** opening onto Swansea Bay. This is Dylan Thomas country.

NORTH WALES   Even more rewarding in scenery than South Wales, North Wales is a land of mountain peaks, spectacular estuaries, and rugged cliffs brooding over secluded coves, little rivers, valleys, and lakes. Its great towns and villages include **Betws-y-Coed, Llandudno,** and **Conwy,** along with such historic castles as **Harlech, Caernarfon,** and especially **Conwy Castle,** ordered built by Edward I and a masterpiece of medieval architecture. In this region, **Snowdonia National Park** covers 2,176 sq. km (840 sq. miles) of North Wales' coastal areas and rugged hills.

ENGLAND IN 1 WEEK

Use the following itinerary to make the most out of a week in England, but feel free to drop a place or two to save a day to relax. One week provides enough time, although barely. Allow a day or two to introduce yourself to some of the attractions of London, such as the **Tower of London** or the **British Museum.** On Day 3 you can head for **Windsor Castle,** and on Days 4 and 5 you can call on the Bard at **Stratford-upon-Avon,** with a side trip to **Warwick Castle.** Finally, you can make a quick day trip to **Oxford** on Day 6, finishing your final day in England with a jaunt to **Blenheim Palace** and a trip down the Thames to **Hampton Court Palace.**

Days 1 & 2: Arrival in London ★★★

Take a flight that arrives in London as early as possible on Day 1. Check into your hotel and enjoy an old-fashioned English breakfast. You might even find yourself skipping lunch.

Take the Tube to **Westminster Abbey** (p. 171), the shrine of the nation where most of England's queens and kings have been crowned and where they are also buried. Check out the fan-vaulted Henry VII's Chapel (one of the loveliest in all of Europe), the shrine to Edward the Confessor, and, for a final look, Poets' Corner, where the literati are buried. After your visit (allow 1½ hr.), stroll by the **Houses of Parliament** and that landmark clock of London, **"Big Ben"** (p. 172).

Continue walking north along **Whitehall,** bypassing **10 Downing Street,** the official residence of the prime minister, and ending at **Trafalgar Square,** the hub of London and its most famous square. See p. 181.

On the north side of the square stands the **National Gallery** (p. 177), where you will be able to see some of the highlights in 1½ hours. Directly north of the square, you enter the precincts of **Covent Garden** (p. 153), with dozens of places for lunch.

Then take the Tube to Charing Cross Station. Armed with a good map, walk along the **Mall** all the way to **Buckingham Palace** (p. 175). If it's late summer, you might even be able to visit the palace when the queen is away.

After a look, head east for the one big attraction of the afternoon, the **Tower of London** (p. 167). The much-photographed Beefeaters conduct hour-long guided tours.

On Day 2, take the Tube to Russell Square for your descent on the **British Museum** (p. 174). This is the mammoth home of one of the world's greatest treasure troves—much of it plundered from other parts of the globe when Britannia ruled the waves. The most exciting of these treasures are the Elgin Marbles, taken from Greece, and the Rosetta Stone, taken from Egypt. You'll need at least 2 hours for the most cursory of visits.

After the British Museum, head to the **City,** the financial district of London lying in the East End. An evocative and atmospheric luncheon stopover is **Bow Wine Vaults,** at 10 Bow Churchyard, EC4 (p. 230).

Fortified for the afternoon, head for **St. Paul's Cathedral** (p. 178), the masterpiece of architect Sir Christopher Wren. At the top you'll be rewarded with one of the most panoramic of all London views.

On the south side of the Thames, pay a visit to the **Tate Modern** (p. 176), housing the greatest collection of 20th-century art in Britain. Allow at least 1½ hours for the most cursory of visits.

Head for **Westminster Bridge** (Tube: Westminster), the embarkation point for a ride on the **London Eye** (p. 197), the world's largest observation wheel. On a clear day, it provides you with a panoramic sweep of 40km (25 miles). It's the most popular ride in London.

Day 3: A Side Trip to Windsor Castle ★★★

Having sampled the charms of London in just 2 days, make Day 3 different by heading north of London to visit **Windsor Castle** (p. 239), which the queen prefers as a royal residence even to Buckingham Palace itself. In just half an hour, a fast train from London will deliver you to the royal town of Windsor, site of England's most legendary castle. If you skipped the Changing of the Guard ceremony at Buckingham Palace, you can see an even more exciting pageant take place here from April to July, Monday to Saturday at 11am (off-season

Suggested England Itineraries

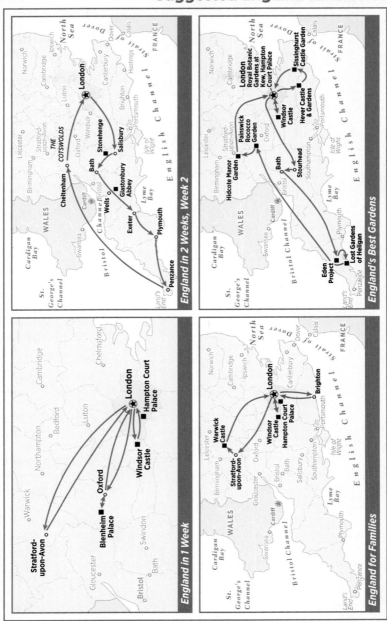

England in 2 Weeks, Week 2

England's Best Gardens

England in 1 Week

England for Families

hours differ slightly—see p. 240 for details). Wander through such attractions as **St. George's Chapel,** where some British monarchs are entombed; and visit the **Jubilee Gardens,** spread over .8 hectare (2 acres). You'll need at least 2 hours to explore the castle.

Head back to London, arriving at Waterloo or Paddington station, where you can take the Tube to **Hyde Park** (Tube: Marble Arch). Strolling through this "green lung of London," take in the miniature lake, the Serpentine, and listen to protesters at Speakers' Corner demanding the overthrow of the government.

Afterwards, head for the heart of Mayfair, **Grosvenor Square,** before window-shopping along **Oxford Street** or **New** and **Old Bond streets.** End up at the **Burlington Arcade** (p. 209) and have tea at the world's most famous grocery store, **Fortnum & Mason** (p. 210). After tea, walk east into **Piccadilly Circus** (p. 105), the hub of London.

Days 4 & 5: Stratford-upon-Avon ★★

From London's Paddington Station, you can be in **Stratford-upon-Avon** in just 2 hours. After checking into a hotel here for 2 nights, you can begin your tour of the Shakespeare properties, first stopping in at the **Shakespeare Birthplace Trust** (p. 493) and purchasing a global ticket.

After lunch in Stratford, try to visit at least three of the Shakespeare-related properties in the afternoon, including **Shakespeare's Birthplace** (p. 495); **Holy Trinity Church** (p. 494), where he is buried; and **Hall's Croft** (p. 493), where his daughter Susanna lived.

That night, have dinner and a pint at the **Black Swan,** nicknamed the **Dirty Duck** (p. 492).

On the morning of Day 5, continue your exploration of the Shakespeare properties by visiting **Anne Hathaway's Cottage** (p. 493) and **Mary Arden's House (Glebe Farm) & Palmer's Farm** (p. 494).

After lunch in Stratford, head in the afternoon to **Warwick Castle** (p. 499), England's greatest medieval castle, lying only 13km (8 miles) northeast of Stratford. Trains run frequently throughout the day between Stratford and the city of Warwick. You can go on a 2-hour tour before the castle closes at 6pm in summer.

Return to Stratford for the night. Instead of going to the **Royal Shakespeare Theatre** on this visit, see what's on at its auxiliary space, the **Swan Theatre,** since it presents somewhat more unconventional productions but with actors just as skilled as those who perform in the main theater.

Day 6: Oxford & Its University ★★

Return to London and then transfer to another fast train leaving from Paddington Station, reaching **Oxford** in 1½ hours. Five trains run to Oxford every hour.

For atmosphere and affordable food, have lunch at the **Turf Tavern** (p. 266), following in the footsteps of everybody from Elizabeth Taylor to Bill Clinton.

After lunch, we recommend a 2-hour **walking tour** that departs from the **Oxford Tourist Information Centre** (p. 254). This is the best orientation for the highlights of this university city. To crown the afternoon, climb **Carfax Tower** (p. 262) for a panoramic view of the "city of dreaming spires." If there's still time in the afternoon, engage in that popular local pastime: **punting the River Cherwell** (p. 263).

Day 7: Blenheim Palace ★★★ & Hampton Court Palace ★★★

If you move fast enough, you can see two of England's greatest palaces—each one different—before the day's end. From Oxford, trains depart every 12 minutes to Woodstock, home of **Blenheim Palace** (p. 268), called England's answer to Versailles. The ancestral seat of the dukes of Marlborough, it was also the birthplace of Sir Winston Churchill. After a tour of the palace, lasting 1½ hours, return to Oxford and take a fast train back to London, where you can check into a hotel.

There will still be time in the afternoon to visit **Hampton Court Palace** (p. 201), the 16th-century palace once lived in by the lusty Henry VIII ("the marrying kind"). Frequent trains depart London for the 21km (13-mile) journey. Allow yourself a minimum of 3 hours to explore this magnificent palace and its great gardens.

ENGLAND IN 2 WEEKS

Two parts of England are always special treats for us to visit: the **West Country** (Wiltshire, Somerset, Devon, and Cornwall) and the scenic villages of the **Cotswolds.** The highlights of both of these destinations can be reached by public transportation, but schedules and connections can be difficult, consuming precious vacation time. So for your second week in England, we recommend that you rent a car. Because England is such a small island nation, distances from one major attraction to another are relatively short. Of course, if you've already spent 1 week in England, you will have already "conquered" the touristy highlights—**London, Oxford, Stratford-upon-Avon,** and the country's three great palaces: **Windsor Castle, Blenheim Palace,** and **Hampton Court Palace.**

Days 1–7

Follow the "England in 1 Week" itinerary as outlined above.

Day 8: Salisbury ★★ & Stonehenge ★★★

The drive from London to the cathedral city of **Salisbury** (coverage begins on p. 366) is only 145km (90 miles) to the southwest. You can easily arrive in time to check into a hotel for the night and visit **Salisbury Cathedral** (p. 371), whose architectural framework may already be familiar to you because of the John Constable paintings. Allow 1½ hours to visit its interior and wander about the cathedral complex.

If you're ready for a busy afternoon, you can head first for **Wilton House** (p. 372), ancestral home of the earls of Pembroke, where General Eisenhower lived as he plotted the D-day landings on the beaches of Normandy in 1944. Allow 1½ hours for a visit, including a stroll through the rose and water gardens and a riverside walk.

You'll still have time to descend on ancient **Stonehenge** (p. 373), which will take 1½ hours to see. Lying 14km (9 miles) north of Salisbury, this colossal circle of stones is, of course, one of the world's greatest prehistoric monuments, though still a mystery to archaeologists. It dates from 3000 B.C.

Day 9: The Spa Town of Bath ★★★

In a trail blazed before you by the likes of Queen Anne and Jane Austen, **Bath** is the grandest and most elegant city of the West Country, lying 185km (115 miles) west of London. Northwest of Salisbury, a distance of 67km (41 miles), Bath can be easily reached in a morning's drive.

After checking into a hotel and having lunch in Bath, you can view some of its grand squares, such as the **Circus** (p. 382), dating from 1754, and take in **Bath Abbey** (p. 383) and the **Roman Baths & Pump Room** (p. 384), all in an afternoon. That evening, try to catch a performance at **Theatre Royal Bath** (p. 384).

Day 10: Wells ★★, Glastonbury Abbey ★★ & Exeter ★★

A busy day indeed. Leave Bath in the morning and drive 34km (21 miles) southwest to the city of **Wells,** where you can visit its famous **cathedral** (p. 394), dating from the 12th century. The structure is noted for its vast and intricate inverted arches added in 1338. Allow less than an hour for your visit.

Continue 9.5km (6 miles) to the southwest to visit historic **Glastonbury Abbey** (p. 395, the famous abbey ruins and legendary retreat of King Arthur and Queen Guinevere. Allow 45 minutes.

Arrive in **Exeter,** the capital of Devon, and check into a hotel. Exeter lies 151km (94 miles) southwest of Bath. If time remains, visit its **cathedral** (p. 407) dating from 1112.

Day 11: Plymouth & the *Mayflower* ★★

In the morning, drive to **Powderham Castle** (p. 408), the seats of the earls of Devon and a site used in Merchant Ivory's *The Remains of the Day,* starring Anthony Hopkins and Emma Thompson. The location is 13km (8 miles) to the south.

After a visit, continue southwest following the southern coastline of Devon, heading for a luncheon stopover in the port of **Dartmouth,** 56km (35 miles) southeast of Exeter. This is the ancient seaport home of the Royal Naval College.

Continue for the night to the historic seaport of **Plymouth,** a distance of 390km (242 miles) southwest of London. If you arrive in time, you can visit the spot where the *Mayflower* sailed to the New World and walk along the **Barbican** (p. 424), with its maze of narrow streets and old houses.

Either in the late afternoon or in the early morning of the next day, visit the **National Marine Aquarium** (p. 427), the best in Britain.

Day 12: Penzance ★ on the Cornish Coast

A good part of the day will be consumed driving along the southern Devon and Cornish coasts, one of the most historic of England, until you arrive in the city of **Penzance** (p. 439), a distance of 451km (280 miles) southwest of London. Check into a hotel for the night in Penzance.

Spend 2 hours visiting the **Castle on St. Michael's Mount** (p. 442) and try to catch a performance that evening at the **Minack Theatre** (p. 442).

Day 13: Cheltenham ★

In the morning, cut inland and take the A30 northeast toward the Cotswolds, until you reach the scenic village of **Painswick** (p. 465), where you can break for lunch and pay a visit to the **Rococo Garden** (p. 467).

In the afternoon, continue northeast into **Cheltenham,** where you can book into a hotel for the night. Try to catch a performance that evening at the **Everyman Theatre** (p. 470). But before dinner and the theater, walk through the historic core of Cheltenham, especially along its **Promenade,** one of the most beautiful thoroughfares in England.

Day 14: A Drive through the Cotswolds ★★★

For your final day in England, arm yourself with a good map and set out to explore the most beautiful villages in the Cotswolds. Coverage of these towns and villages is found in chapter 13.

From Cheltenham, and by doing some crisscrossing here and there, you can take in the best of the Cotswolds. Scenic highlights of your day will include **Upper** and **Lower Slaughter, Bourton-on-the-Water, Bibury, Burford,** and **Stow-on-the-Wold.**

ENGLAND FOR FAMILIES

England offers many attractions that kids enjoy. Perhaps your main concern with having children along is pacing yourself with museum time. Our suggestion is to explore **London** for 2 days with family in tow, then spend a good part of the third day wandering around **Windsor Castle** and the little Thames town, followed by a fourth day in **Brighton** with some fun on the beach. On Days 5 and 6, head for **Stratford-upon-Avon** and **Warwick Castle,** concluding with a final day in London and a side trip to **Hampton Court Palace.**

Days 1 & 2: Arrival in London ★★★

Your kid has probably been held captive on a long plane ride and will be eager for exercise. After a fortifying English breakfast, head for a stroll of an hour or two in **Hyde Park** (p. 198), which is a great way to "find your legs" in a new city. You can walk around the Serpentine lake, created in the 1730s, and even take a boat out if you wish.

Follow this by booking the 1½-hour-long **Original London Sightseeing Tour** (p. 207), on a traditional double-decker bus (kids pay reduced prices, and ages 4 and under ride free). This will give you a thorough overview of London. Some tours feature the **Changing of the Guard** at Buckingham Palace, great English pomp and circumstance that thrills all ages.

After the tour, head for the **London Eye** (p. 197), the world's largest observation wheel, which will take you for a grand sweep in the skies of London in a "pod." Kids love this, and so do adults.

In the afternoon, stroll by the **Houses of Parliament** and **Big Ben** (p. 172), perhaps more for yourself than for the kids, and call at **Westminster Abbey** (p. 171). This is such an awesome sight that even if your kids aren't that interested in churches, they will find much to behold here.

Later, take a ferry ride down the Thames to the **Tower of London** (p. 187), a sure kid-pleaser, hooking up with one of the red-coated Beefeater tours.

On Day 2, descend on the **British Museum** (p. 174) when it opens. Even if your kid is not a museum buff, there is wonder here and at times utter fascination, especially in the Egyptian rooms with all those scary mummies.

After lunch in Bloomsbury, head for **Madame Tussauds** (p. 190), where you'll encounter wax effigies of everybody from Mel Gibson to Saddam Hussein. Very young children may be disturbed by some of the "blood-and-gore" exhibitions.

To finish off the afternoon, head for the **London Zoo** (p. 199). A total of 8,000 animals, some of the rarest species on earth, wander about the 15-hectare (36-acre) site of fascination.

End your day with a fun-filled stroll through **Battersea Park** (p. 199), where there is, among other attractions, a little zoo just for children.

Day 3: A Side Trip to Windsor Castle ★★★

Having sampled the charms of London in just 2 days, you can launch Day 3 by heading out of town to nearby **Windsor Castle** (p. 239). In just half an hour, a train from London will deliver you to Windsor Castle. If you missed the Changing of the Guard ceremony in London, you can see an even more exciting pageant take place here from April to July, Monday through Saturday at 11am (winter hours differ—see p. 240 for details).

The highlight of Windsor Castle for younger children is a perfect miniature **Queen Mary's Dolls' House** (p. 239), accurate to the minutest detail—even royal toilets that flush in all five bathrooms.

After lunch, stroll through **Eton College** (p. 240), the most famous public school in England (it would be called private in the United States), wandering the same grounds as Prince William.

For a final attraction, head for **LEGOLAND** (p. 241), a 61-hectare (150-acre) theme park outside Windsor, with everything from puppet theaters to "knight-and-dragon" castles. Return to London on a fast train for the night.

Day 4: A Side Trip to Brighton ★★

On Day 4, while still based in London, take one of the fast trains from Victoria Station, which will put you in "London by the Sea," as **Brighton** is called, in 55 minutes.

Even children adore the **Royal Pavilion at Brighton** (p. 320). This faux Indian mogul's palace is like something Disney might have created. Allow 2 hours for a visit.

After a tour and time out for lunch, enjoy the seaside amusements on the boardwalk and even the pebbly beaches if the weather is fair. The **Palace Pier** is filled with video arcades, games, and souvenir stands. Before leaving Brighton, stroll the maze of narrow alleyways in the Old Town, called the **Lanes** (p. 321). Return to London for the night.

Days 5 & 6: Stratford-upon-Avon ★★ & Warwick Castle ★★★

Check out of your London hotel and take a train from Paddington Station, reaching the town of **Stratford-upon-Avon** in 2 hours. Check into one of the family-friendly B&Bs for 2 nights.

Few children will want to see plays by the Bard, but many of the sights associated with Shakespeare have appeal for all ages. Of most interest to children—all of which can be seen in 1 day—are **Anne Hathaway's Cottage** (p. 493), **Mary Arden's House (Glebe Farm) & Palmer's Farm** (p. 494), and **Shakespeare's Birthplace** (p. 495).

On Day 6, head north for 13km (8 miles) to the finest medieval castle in England, **Warwick Castle** (p. 499). Surrounded by gardens, this 17th-century castle has fairy-tale aspects for most children—and interests grown-ups, too. You can see fascinating exhibits such as the dungeon and torture chamber (a little frightening for particularly young kids) and a Victorian rose garden and water garden. Family tickets are sold. Have lunch in Warwick and return to Stratford in the afternoon.

If you get back to Stratford in time, you might need a diversion from all the Shakespeareana. Children delight in the **Stratford Butterfly Farm,** Swan's Nest Lane (✆ **01789/299-288;** www.butterflyfarm.co.uk), containing Europe's largest display of butterflies, with a mock rainforest as well. It is open April through September, daily from 10am to 6pm, with slightly earlier closing times the rest of the year. Admission is £6 adults, £5 children.

After another overnight in Stratford, return to London in the morning for your final day in England.

Day 7: A Side Trip to Hampton Court Palace ★★★

On Day 7, leave your London hotel and take a train from Waterloo Station to **Hampton Court Palace** (p. 201), on the north side of the Thames, 21km (13 miles) west of London. You'll reach it in about half an hour. Allow at least 3 hours for an unhurried visit, nearly 1 hour of which you can spend wandering through the beautiful gardens. Enjoy lunch at the complex.

From April to September, you can take a boat back into London, a 4-hour journey that will bring you to Westminster Pier.

If time remains, use your final hours in London to take the kids to the **Natural History Museum** (p. 192). For children, the highlight of this exhibit is the display of 14 complete dinosaur skeletons, with such re-creations as a full-size robotic dinosaur lunching on a freshly killed Tenontosaurus.

ENGLAND'S BEST GARDENS IN 1 WEEK

Reaching these gardens by public transportation is possible in most cases, but rather awkward. The only way to see all of them in a single week is with a rental car. However, you'll only need to rent a car for the last 4 days of the itinerary. The other gardens in and around London can be reached by public transportation. Note that this tour should be considered only from May to August, when English gardens are at their best.

Day 1: Arrival in London ★★★

Pay a morning visit to **Kensington Gardens** (p. 198). Adjacent to Hyde Park, these gardens are very different. At one time, they were reserved for royal owners such as George III. In 1841, young Queen Victoria opened them to "respectably dressed people—but no soldiers, sailors, or servants."

The 111-hectare (274-acre) park is filled with hawthorns, weeping willows, maples, ash, swamp white oaks, and red oaks. The ideal place for lunch in the gardens is the **Orangery** (p. 166). This is also an idyllic place for afternoon tea.

Spend the rest of the afternoon on a romp through **Regent's Park** (p. 198). With its gardens, lake, and zoo, this is like the estate of an English country gentleman covering 191 hectares (472 acres). The park was once a hunting ground for Henry VIII.

Day 2: Royal Botanic Gardens, Kew ★★★

Spend Day 2 in the world-famous **Kew Gardens** (p. 202), as they're usually called. Set on 121 hectares (300 acres), the gardens include pavilions, lakes, greenhouses, and flower-bordered walks. Reached by Tube or boat, these former royal pleasure gardens can easily occupy the good part of your day.

Originally planted in 1759 by the mother of King George III, Kew once employed Capability Brown, England's most famous landscaper, to shape and enlarge the gardens. Captain Cook sent men off around the world to collect rare specimens. The Palm House, for example, contains every known variety of palm, including the African cycad.

Day 3: Windsor Castle ★★★ & Hampton Court Palace ★★★

Get an early start by taking a 30-minute train ride from London's Waterloo or Paddington station, which will put you in Windsor, site of **Windsor Castle** (p. 239). Visit **St. George's Chapel,** the highlight of the tour, before exploring the **Jubilee Gardens** around the castle (p. 238). In a romantic setting with white rambling roses, among other species, you can wander for at least 30 minutes, taking in the beauty.

If you have a car, consider driving to **Windsor Great Park** (p. 241), 8km (5 miles) from Windsor along A30. This 14-hectare (35-acre) garden is one of the most spectacular in Europe. Allow at least an hour, maybe more, to visit this park.

Return to London and take the train from Waterloo Station to **Hampton Court Palace** (p. 201), 21km (31 miles) west of the city. The ideal time to visit is in early July, when the **Hampton Court Palace Flower Show** (✆ 020/8781-9500; www.rhs.org.uk/Shows-Events) is held on the grounds. Wend your way through the famous maze—and get lost—before heading back to London.

Day 4: Hever Castle & Gardens ★★ & Sissinghurst Castle Garden ★★

On Day 4, leave London in a rental car, heading for **Hever Castle & Gardens** (p. 302), where Henry VIII wooed Anne Boleyn. Most celebrated and beautiful is the much-photographed Italian Garden, filled with statuary and sculpture dating from Roman days to the Renaissance. Other highlights here include a rose garden and a Tudor herb garden. Allow at least 1½ hours for a visit.

After lunch, spend the afternoon visiting **Sissinghurst Castle Garden** (p. 304). This is the far point of the day's tour, taking you 85km (53 miles) southeast of London. These are among the most romantic gardens in England and can be overrun with visitors. Highlights include the white garden with its white or silver foliage, the spring garden that bursts into bloom with enough daffodils to please Wordsworth, and the alluring wild garden in the orchard.

Return to London for the night.

Day 5: West to Stourhead ★★★

In the county of Wiltshire in the West Country, the gardens of **Stourhead** (p. 398) are the most celebrated example of English landscape gardening in the country. Although a "garden for all seasons," Stourhead is best visited in May and June, when its masses of rhododendrons are at their fullest bloom. Built around a 1721 Palladian villa and set on 40 hectares (100 acres), Stourhead is a wonder to behold. It comes complete with rare trees, miles of flowering shrubs, a beautiful lake, classical temples, and grottoes.

Consider basing yourself in the historic spa town of **Bath** (p. 374) for the night.

Day 6: Eden Project ★★ & the Lost Gardens of Heligan ★★

From your overnight stopover in Bath, you can drive to the southwest into Cornwall for a look at two of England's most bizarre and mysterious gardens: the Eden Project and Heligan.

Visit the **Eden Project** (p. 437) first, lying at Bodelva, St. Austell, a 48km (30-mile) journey west of the city of Plymouth in Devon. This geodesic dome exhibits the world's major plant systems in microcosm, a former china clay pit boasting more than 70,000 plants.

After lunch in the area, continue the short distance south for a visit to the **Lost Gardens of Heligan** (p. 438). This site spreads across 32 hectares (80 acres) near the fishing village of Mevagissey. Once part of a 404-hectare (1,000-acre) Victorian estate, the gardens slumbered for 70 years as they were gradually buried by wild, unchecked overgrowth in Cornwall's subtropical climate.

After a day of fascination, head to **St. Mawes** (p. 437) or to one of the fishing villages, such as **Looe** (p. 434) or **Polperro** (p. 434), for the night. These villages lie west of Plymouth.

Day 7: Painswick Rococo Garden ★

Get an early start in the morning and drive northeast to the towns of the Cotswolds (covered in chapter 13).

The enchanting village of **Painswick** is arguably the most beautiful in England. A rare English garden in that it's a throwback to the 1720s style of flamboyant gardens that flourished then, **Painswick Rococo Garden** (p. 467) lies .8km (½ mile) north of Painswick. Today, it has been restored to its original glory.

After visiting the gardens, lunch in Painswick and spend the night in one of the Cotswolds towns before returning to London the next morning.

SETTLING INTO LONDON

Europe's largest city is like a great wheel, with **Piccadilly Circus** at the hub and dozens of communities branching out from it. In Britspeak, Circus means a circular area at an intersection of streets, not a Barnum & Bailey spectacular under the tent. London is such a conglomeration of neighborhoods, each with its own personality, first-time visitors may be confused until they get the hang of it. You'll probably spend most of your time in the **West End,** where many attractions are located, and in the historic part of London known as the **City,** which includes the Tower of London. This chapter will help you get your bearings.

ORIENTATION

Arriving

BY PLANE

LONDON HEATHROW AIRPORT   West of London in Hounslow, Heathrow (℮ **0844/335-1801;** www.baa.co.uk and www.heathrow airport.com) is one of the world's busiest airports. It has four terminals, each relatively self-contained. Terminal 4, the most modern, handles the long-haul and transatlantic operations of British Airways. Most transatlantic flights on U.S.-based airlines arrive at Terminal 3. Terminals 1 and 2 receive the intra-European flights of several European airlines.

To get from Heathrow to the center of London, it takes 45 to 50 minutes via the **Underground (Tube)** and costs £4 to make the 24km (15-mile) trip. For more information about Tube or bus connections, call ℮ **020/7222-1234** or go to **www.tfl.gov.uk**.

The British Airport Authority now operates the **Heathrow Express** (℮ **0845/600-1515;** www.heathrowexpress.com), a 161kmph (100-mph) train service running every 15 minutes daily from 5:10am until 11:40pm between Heathrow and Paddington Station in the center of London. Trips cost £18 one-way in economy class, rising to £26 one-way in first class. Children 14 and younger pay £9 in economy, £13 in first class. (You can save £1.50 by booking online or by phone.) Tickets are sold at self-service machines at Heathrow Airport; if you purchase them on the train, you'll pay a surcharge of up to £5. The trip takes 15 minutes each way between Paddington and terminals 1, 2, and 3, and 23 minutes from Terminal 4. The trains have special areas for wheelchairs. From Paddington, you can connect to other trains and the Underground, or you can hail a taxi.

If you take a **taxi** to central London, the fare is likely to range from £50 to £80.

LONDON GATWICK AIRPORT While Heathrow still dominates, more and more scheduled flights land at relatively remote Gatwick ($\copyright$ **0844/335-1802;** www.gatwickairport.com), located some 40km (25 miles) south of London in West Sussex, but only a 30-minute train ride away.

From Gatwick, the fastest way to get to London is via the **Gatwick Express** ($\copyright$ **0845/850-1530;** www.gatwickexpress.com). These trains depart approximately every 15 minutes daily between 4:35am and 1:35am. The one-way fare between Gatwick and Victoria Station in central London is £17 for adults and £8.45 for children. The travel time each way is 30 minutes Monday to Saturday, 35 minutes on Sunday. It is cheaper to purchase a day travel card for £7, which is good for travel into London on the Southern route and on the Tube for the rest of the day.

A **taxi** from Gatwick to central London costs from £77 to £100. Fares vary according to a printed price list that defines the price from Gatwick to whichever neighborhood of London you're traveling to. Meters in this case don't apply because Gatwick lies outside the Metropolitan Police District. For further transportation information, call $\copyright$ **020/7222-1234.**

LONDON CITY AIRPORT Some business travelers prefer London City Airport ($\copyright$ **020/7646-0088;** www.londoncityairport.com) because of its convenient location, 5km (3 miles) east of the business centers of Canary Wharf, the Docklands, and the ExCeL convention center. If you have business within these districts, London City Airport is a better arrival point than equivalent flights into Heathrow, Gatwick, or Stansted. Accepting flights from 23 cities throughout western Europe and Scandinavia, City Airport serves airlines that include British Airways, Cirrus Airlines, Luxair, KLM, CityJet, OLT, Lufthansa, Scot Airways, Air France, Eastern Airways (not to be confused with the now-defunct, U.S.-based Eastern Airlines), SAS, Darwin Airlines, Swiss International Airlines, and VLM.

Trains on the **Docklands Light Railway** ($\copyright$ **020/7222-1234;** www.tfl.gov.uk/dlr) make runs at 10-minute intervals from City Airport to the Underground station known as "Bank" (short for Bank of England), in the heart of London's financial district, which is known locally as "the City." One-way passage costs £4 for adults and £1 for children 15 and younger.

As a final means of getting from the airport to central London, consider boarding **London Bus no. 473 or 474,** with frequent runs between the airport and various points in East London, including the Plaistow Tube (Underground) station. From here, you can make connections to virtually any other point in London.

LONDON STANSTED AIRPORT Located some 80km (50 miles) northeast of London's West End, Stansted, in Essex ($\copyright$ **0844/335-1803;** www.baa.com), handles mostly flights to and from the European continent.

To get to central London from Stansted, your best bet is the **Stansted Express** (℃ **0845/850-0150;** www.stanstedexpress.co.uk) to Liverpool Street Station, a 45-minute ride. These trains run every 15 minutes from 6am to 11:45pm (every 30 min. in the early mornings on weekends). It costs £18 for a standard ticket and £27 for first class.

By bus, you can take the **Airbus A6** (℃ **0870/580-8080**), which runs regular departures 24 hours a day to many central London locations; it costs £11.

If you prefer the relative privacy of a **taxi,** you'll pay dearly for the privilege. A ride to London's West End will cost £85 to £120. Expect the trip to take around 75 minutes during normal traffic conditions, but beware of Friday afternoons, when dense traffic may double your travel time. Our advice: Stick to the Express.

BY TRAIN

Each of London's train stations is connected to the city's vast bus and Underground network, and each has phones, restaurants, pubs, luggage storage areas, and Transport for London Travel Information Centres.

St. Pancras International (www.stpancras.com) is the London hub for Eurostar, replacing Waterloo Station as the arrival point from the Continent. Restored and opened in 2007, it is the point where the high-speed Eurostar pulls into London, connecting England with Belgium and France through the Channel Tunnel.

The station boasts Europe's longest champagne bar, a daily farmers' market, all the Wi-Fi you'll ever need, plus dozens of boutiques—and some of the world's fastest trains. It is also served by six underground Tubes, including Victoria, Northern, Piccadilly, Circle, Hammersmith & City, and Metropolitan, as well as seven other rail companies. With such a vast network of transport, you can head virtually anywhere in greater London.

BY CAR

Once you arrive on the English side of the Channel, the M20 takes you directly into London. *Remember to drive on the left.* Two roadways encircle London: The A406 and A205 form the inner beltway; the M25 rings the city farther out. Determine which part of the city you want to enter and follow signposts.

We suggest you confine driving in London to the bare minimum, which means arriving and parking. Due to parking problems and heavy traffic, getting around London by car is not a viable option. Once you're here, leave your car in a garage and rely on public transportation or taxis. Before arrival in London, call your hotel and inquire if it has a garage (and what the charges are), or ask the staff to give you the name and address of a garage nearby.

Visitor Information

Visit London, the official tourism organization for London, operates the **Britain and London Visitor Centre (BLVC),** 1 Lower Regent St., London SW1Y 4XT (℃ **8701/566-366;** www.visitlondon.com; Tube: Piccadilly Circus), which can help you with almost anything, from the most superficial to the most serious. Located within a 10-minute walk from Piccadilly Circus, it deals chiefly with booking accommodations in all price categories through an on-site travel agency (www.lastminute.com), which can also book transit on British Rail or with bus carriers throughout the U.K. There's a kiosk for procuring theater or group tour tickets, a bookshop loaded with titles dealing with travel in the British Isles, a souvenir shop, and a staff that's pleasant, helpful, and friendly. It's open year-round, Monday 9:30am to 6:30pm, Tuesday through Friday 9am to 6:30pm, and Sunday 9am to 5pm. Between October and May, Saturday hours are 10am to 4pm, and between June and September, Saturday hours are 9am to 5pm.

A roughly equivalent organization that was conceived to help foreign visitors with their inquiries about London is the **London Information Centre,** at Leicester Square, W1 (*©* **020/7292-2333;** www.londoninformationcentre.com; Tube: Leicester Sq.). The London Information Centre is a privately owned, commercially driven organization that may have a vested interest in steering you toward a particular venue.

Another option for help navigating the logistics of one of the world's biggest cities is calling *©* **0800/LONDON** (566366), available daily from 8am to midnight. The sales staff at this number can provide city information and book sometimes discounted rates for London hotels, theaters, sightseeing tours, and airport transfers.

London's Neighborhoods in Brief

THE WEST END NEIGHBORHOODS

Mayfair Bounded by Piccadilly, Hyde Park, and Oxford and Regent streets, this is the most elegant, fashionable section of London, filled with luxury hotels, Georgian town houses, and swank shops. Grosvenor Square (pronounced *Grov*-nor) is nicknamed "Little America," home to the American embassy and a statue of Franklin D. Roosevelt; Berkeley Square (*Bark*-ley) was made famous by the song "A Nightingale Sang in Berkeley Square." At least once you'll want to dip into this exclusive section. One curiosity of Mayfair is **Shepherd Market,** a tiny village of pubs, two-story inns, book and food stalls, and restaurants, sandwiched among Mayfair's greatness. Mayfair is London's toniest address for hotels, as the prices indicate. If you stay here, you'll be in the very heart of London, with all the great shops on Bond Street and the Cork Street galleries near at hand. Even if you don't lodge here, come for long walks of discovery.

Marylebone First-timers to London head to Marylebone (*Mar*-le-bone) to explore Madame Tussauds or walk along Baker Street in the make-believe footsteps of Sherlock Holmes. The streets form a near-perfect grid, with major ones running north–south from Regent's Park toward Oxford Street. Marylebone Lane and High Street retain some of their former village

atmosphere, but this is otherwise a now rather anonymous area. At Regent's Park, you can visit Queen Mary's Gardens or, in summer, see Shakespeare performed in an open-air theater. In addition to exploring, you can also lodge here at often half the price you'd pay in Mayfair.

St. James's Often called "Royal London," St. James's is home to Elizabeth II, who lives at the neighborhood's most famous address, Buckingham Palace. The neighborhood begins at Piccadilly Circus and moves southwest, incorporating Pall Mall, the Mall, St. James's Park, and Green Park; it's "frightfully convenient," as the English say, enclosing many of London's leading department stores. One must-see is Fortnum & Mason, at 181 Piccadilly, the world's most luxurious grocery store. Other than the queen, Prince Charles and the duchess of Cornwall are residents, too. The district is even more courtly and graceful than Mayfair.

Piccadilly Circus & Leicester Square Piccadilly Circus is the very center of London—its gaudy living room. The circus isn't Times Square yet, but its traffic, neon, and jostling crowds do nothing to make it fashionable. If you want a little more grandeur, retreat to the Regency promenade of exclusive shops, the Burlington Arcade, designed in 1819.

A bit tawdrier is Leicester Square, a center of theaters, restaurants, movie palaces, and nightlife. Once a chic address, it changed forever in the Victorian era when four towering entertainment halls were opened (even Queen Victoria saw a circus here). In time, the old palaces changed from stage to screen; three still show films. The district is known more for fun and amusement than for hotels.

Soho These densely packed streets in the heart of the West End are famous for a gloriously cosmopolitan mix of people and trades. A decade ago, much was heard about the decline of Soho, when the thriving sex industry threatened to engulf it. That destruction has now largely been halted. Respectable businesses have returned, and chic restaurants and shops prosper; it's now the heart of London's expanding gay colony. But Soho wouldn't be Soho without a few sex shops and porn theaters. Surprisingly, it has a few of the most posh and expensive hotels in London, attracting fashionistas and movie stars who want to be right in the heart of the theater district.

Soho starts at Piccadilly Circus and spreads out, basically bordered by Regent Street, Oxford Street, Charing Cross Road, and the theaters of Shaftesbury Avenue. Carnaby Street, a block from Regent Street, was the center of the universe in the swinging '60s and appears to be rising again. Across Shaftesbury Avenue, a busy street lined with theaters, is London's **Chinatown,** centered on Gerrard Street: small, authentic, and packed with excellent restaurants. But Soho's heart—with marvelous French and Italian delicatessens, fine butchers, fish stores, and wine merchants—is farther north, on Brewer, Old Compton, and Berwick streets; Berwick is also a wonderful open-air fresh-food market. To the north of Old Compton Street, Dean, Frith, and Greek streets have fine little restaurants, pubs, and clubs. The British movie industry is centered at Wardour Street.

Bloomsbury This district, a world in itself, lies northeast of Piccadilly Circus, beyond Soho. It is, among other things, the academic heart of London; you'll find the University of London, several other colleges, and many bookstores. Despite its student population, this neighborhood is fairly staid. Its reputation has been fanned by such writers as Virginia Woolf, who lived within its bounds and became one of the unofficial leaders of a group of artists and writers known as the Bloomsbury Group.

The heart of Bloomsbury is **Russell Square,** and the streets jutting off from the square are lined with hotels and B&Bs. Most visitors come to the neighborhood to visit the British Museum, one of the world's greatest repositories of treasures. The British Telecom Tower (1964), on Cleveland Street, is a familiar landmark. If you're hotel shopping, not just sightseeing, Bloomsbury is a solid, respectable address and lined with moderately priced and affordable small hotels that have none of the glamour of such places as Mayfair or Chelsea.

Nearby is **Fitzrovia,** bounded by Great Portland, Oxford, and Gower streets. Goodge Street, with its many shops and pubs, forms the heart of the "village." Once a major haunt of artists and writers—this was the stamping ground of Ezra Pound and George Orwell, among others—the bottom end of Fitzrovia is a virtual extension of Soho, with a cluster of Greek restaurants.

Kings Cross Long a seedy area in the heart of London, Kings Cross is facing a massive regeneration program. Millions of pounds are going into its decaying infrastructure. The area is still far from chic, but was given renewed importance with the arrival of Eurostar, the Channel Tunnel Rail Link coming into St. Pancras instead of Waterloo. Because of this change in venue, it's estimated that some 50 million passengers will pass through Kings Cross annually. Six Tubes now convene underneath Kings Cross station, and it is the number-one connection hub enabling visitors to get to and from Gatwick and Heathrow airports.

St. Pancras Alongside Kings Cross, St. Pancras International is the new transport hub for Eurostar, bringing renewed life to this once-decaying part of London. The station is to London what Penn Station was to New York, the finest architectural icon of the Age of Steam. British poet John Betjeman called the 1868 structure, with its gargoyles and Gothic Revival towers, "too beautiful and too romantic to survive."

Today, the glamorous and vastly restored station is a dazzling entry point into Britain for those passengers arriving on Eurostar from the Continent. Stay tuned for hotel, shopping, and restaurant developments to blossom around the station. For more information, contact ✆ **020/ 7843-4250** (www.stpancras.com).

Holborn The old borough of Holborn, abutting the City of London to the west, takes in the heart of legal London—the city's barristers, solicitors, and law clerks call it home. A 14-year-old Dickens was once employed as a solicitor's clerk at Lincoln's Inn Fields. Old Bailey has stood for English justice through the years (Fagin went to the gallows from this site in *Oliver Twist*). Everything here seems steeped in history. Even as you're quenching your thirst with a half pint of bitter at the Viaduct Tavern (126 Newgate St.; Tube: St. Paul's), you learn the pub was built near the notorious Newgate Prison (which specialized in death by pressing) and was named after Holborn Viaduct, the world's first overpass.

Covent Garden & the Strand The flower, fruit, and "veg" market is long gone, but memories of Professor Higgins and Eliza Doolittle linger on. Covent Garden now contains the city's liveliest group of restaurants, pubs, and cafes outside of Soho, as well as some of the city's hippest shops—including the world's only Dr. Martens superstore. The restored marketplace, with its glass and iron roofs, has been called a "magnificent example of urban recycling." Covent Garden is traditionally London's theater area, and Inigo Jones's St. Paul's

Covent Garden is known as the actors' church. The Theatre Royal Drury Lane was where Charles II's mistress Nell Gwynne made her debut in 1665. Some of London's most posh and daring contemporary—but also superexpensive—hotels have opened in "the garden" in recent years.

Beginning at Trafalgar Square, the Strand runs east into Fleet Street and borders Covent Garden to the south. Flanked with theaters, shops, hotels, and restaurants, it runs parallel to the River Thames; to walk it is to follow the footsteps of Mark Twain, Henry Fielding, James Boswell, William Thackeray, and Sir Walter Raleigh. The Savoy Theatre helped make Gilbert and Sullivan household names.

Westminster The seat of the British government since the days of Edward the Confessor and dominated by the Houses of Parliament and Westminster Abbey, this area runs along the Thames to the east of St. James's Park. **Trafalgar Square,** at the area's northern end and one of the city's major landmarks, remains a testament to England's victory over Napoleon in 1805, and the paintings in the National Gallery will restore your soul. Whitehall is the main thoroughfare, linking Trafalgar Square with Parliament Square. You can visit Churchill's Cabinet War Rooms; 10 Downing Street, the world's most famous street address, home to Britain's prime minister; and Westminster Abbey, one of the world's great Gothic churches.

Westminster encompasses **Victoria,** an area that takes its unofficial name from bustling Victoria Station, known as the "gateway to the Continent." As a hotel district, many affordable and often budget hotels cluster around Victoria Station. These are not the quietest or the most glamorous hotels in London, but they are serviceable, affordable, and convenient without any of the grandeur or poshness of Belgravia, Chelsea, or Mayfair. Westminster also has a few first-class hotels in rather staid palaces for those willing to spend more pounds.

5

SETTLING INTO LONDON

London's Neighborhoods in Brief

The City of London When Londoners speak of "the City," they don't mean all of London; they mean the original 2.5 sq. km (1 sq. mile) that's now the British version of Wall Street. The buildings of this district are known all over the world: the Bank of England, the London Stock Exchange, and Lloyd's of London. This was the origin of Londinium, as it was called by its Roman conquerors. Despite its age, the City doesn't easily reveal its past; much of it has been swept away by the Great Fire of 1666, the German bombs of 1940, the IRA bombs of the early 1990s, and the zeal of modern developers. Still, it retains its medieval character; one of its landmarks is St. Paul's Cathedral, the masterpiece of Sir Christopher Wren, which stood virtually alone among the rubble after the Blitz. Since the millennium, many very expensive hotels have opened in the City, catering to those who need to be near the financial center. Otherwise, the City is far too removed from the heart of London for the visitor more intent on sightseeing.

London's journalistic hub since William Caxton printed the first book in English, **Fleet Street** has been abandoned by all of the London tabloids for the Docklands development across the river.

The City of London still prefers to function on its own, separate from the rest of the city; in keeping with its independence, it maintains its own Information Centre, at St. Paul's Churchyard, EC4 (☎ **020/7332-1456**). It's open daily from 9:30am to 5:30pm.

Docklands In the last 2 decades, this area—bordered roughly by Tower Bridge to the west and London City Airport and the Royal Docks to the east—has witnessed an ambitious redevelopment. Thames-side warehouses have been converted to Manhattan-style lofts, and the neighborhood has attracted many businesses, including most of the Fleet Street newspapers, as well as museums, entertainment complexes, shops, and an ever-growing list of restaurants.

Canary Wharf, on the Isle of Dogs, is the heart of Docklands; a 240m-high (800-ft.) tower designed by César Pelli, the tallest building in the United Kingdom, dominates this huge 29-hectare (72-acre) site. The piazza is lined with shops and restaurants. On the south side of the river at Surrey Docks, the Victorian warehouses of **Butler's Wharf** have been converted by Sir Terence Conran into offices, workshops, houses, shops, and restaurants; Butler's Wharf is also home to the Design Museum.

To get to Docklands, take the Underground to Bank and pick up the Docklands Light Railway (☎ **020/7222-1234;** www.tfl.gov.uk/dlr), which operates Monday to Friday 5:30am to 1am, Saturday 5am to 1am, and Sunday 6:40am to midnight.

The East End Traditionally one of London's poorest districts, it was nearly bombed out of existence by the Nazis. Hitler, in the words of one commentator at the time, created "instant urban renewal." The East End extends from the City Walls east, encompassing Stepney, Bow, Poplar, West Ham, Canning Town, and other districts. The East End has always been filled with legend and lore. It's the home of the Cockney, London's most colorful characters. To be a true Cockney, it's said that you must have been born "within the sound of Bow Bells," a reference to the church St. Mary-le-Bow, rebuilt by Sir Christopher Wren in 1670. Many immigrants to London have found a home here.

South Bank Although not officially a district like Mayfair, South Bank is the setting today for the South Bank Arts Centre, now the largest arts center in western Europe and still growing. Reached by Waterloo Bridge, it lies across the Thames from the Victoria Embankment. Culture buffs flock to its galleries and halls, including the National Theatre, Queen Elizabeth Hall, Royal Festival Hall, and Hayward Gallery. It's also the setting of the National Film Theatre. Neighborhoods nearby are Elephant & Castle and **Southwark,** home to the grand Southwark Cathedral. To get here, take the Tube to London Bridge.

CENTRAL LONDON BEYOND THE WEST END

Knightsbridge One of London's most fashionable neighborhoods, Knightsbridge is a top residential and shopping district, just south of Hyde Park. Harrods, on Brompton Road, is its chief attraction. Right nearby, Beauchamp Place (*Beech*-am) is a Regency-era, boutique-lined shopping street with a scattering of fashionable restaurants. Knightsbridge, former stamping ground of Princess Di, is one of the great and central locations of London, with several pricey hotels. For the serious shopper, there could be no more idyllic address in London.

Belgravia South of Knightsbridge, this area has long been the aristocratic quarter of London, rivaling Mayfair in grandness. Although it reached the pinnacle of its prestige during the reign of Queen Victoria, it remains a chic address; the duke and duchess of Westminster, one of England's richest families, still live at Eaton Square. Its centerpiece is Belgrave Square, built between 1825 and 1835. When the town houses were built, the aristocrats followed—the duke of Connaught, the earl of Essex, even Queen Victoria's mother, the duchess of Kent. Chopin, on holiday in 1837, was appropriately impressed: "And the English! And the houses! And the palaces! And the pomp, and the carriages! Everything from soap to the razors is extraordinary." It's better for walking and exploring than for living. There are few hotels in the district and not a lot to do at night. We prefer livelier Chelsea for our address.

Chelsea This stylish Thames-side district lies south of Belgravia. It begins at Sloane Square, where flower sellers hustle their flamboyant blooms year-round. The area has been a favorite of writers and artists, including such names as Oscar Wilde, George Eliot, James Whistler, J. M. W. Turner, Henry James, and Thomas Carlyle. Mick Jagger and Margaret Thatcher have been more recent residents, and the late Princess Diana and the "Sloane Rangers" of the 1980s gave it even more fame.

Its major boulevard is **King's Road,** where Mary Quant launched the miniskirt in the '60s and where the English punk look began. King's Road runs the entire length of Chelsea; it's at its liveliest on Saturday. The hip-hop of King's Road isn't typical of otherwise upmarket Chelsea, an elegant village filled with town houses and little mews dwellings that only successful stockbrokers and solicitors can afford to occupy. Although a hike from the center, Chelsea is sprinkled with a few discreet hotels of charm and grace. It has one major drawback: There are few Tube connections, but plenty of buses.

On the Chelsea/Fulham border is Chelsea Harbour, a luxury development of apartments and restaurants with a private marina. You can spot its tall tower from far away; the golden ball on top moves up and down to indicate tide level.

Kensington This Royal Borough lies west of Kensington Gardens and Hyde Park and is traversed by two of London's major shopping streets, Kensington High Street and Kensington Church Street. Since 1689, when asthmatic William III fled Whitehall Palace for Nottingham House (where the air was fresher), the district has enjoyed royal associations. In time, Nottingham House became Kensington Palace, and the royals grabbed a chunk of Hyde Park to plant their roses. Queen Victoria was born here. "KP," as the royals say, was the home of Princess Diana and her two young princes for a time. Kensington Gardens is now open to the public.

Southeast of Kensington Gardens and Earl's Court, primarily residential **South Kensington** is often called "museumland" because it's dominated by a complex of museums and colleges—set upon land bought with the proceeds from Prince Albert's Great Exhibition, held in Hyde Park in 1851—that include the Natural History Museum, Victoria and Albert Museum, and Science Museum; nearby is Royal Albert Hall. South Kensington is also home to some fashionable restaurants and town-house hotels. One of the district's chief curiosities is the Albert Memorial; for sheer excess, the Victorian monument is unequaled in the world.

Both Kensington and South Kensington, though away from the center, have some of the choicest hotels in London, although they are priced rather high. These beautiful, urban neighborhoods free you from some of the horrendous congestion of such districts as Piccadilly Circus. Many streets are quiet at night, and much of a neighborhood feel remains.

Earl's Court Earl's Court lies below Kensington, bordering the western half of Chelsea. For decades a staid residential district, Earl's Court now attracts a new and younger crowd (often gay), particularly at night, to its pubs, wine bars, and coffeehouses. It's a popular base for budget travelers (particularly Australians), thanks to its wealth of B&Bs and budget hotels, and to its convenient access to central London: A 15-minute Tube ride takes you into the heart of Piccadilly, via either the District or Piccadilly lines.

Once regarded as the boondocks, nearby **West Brompton** is seen today as an extension of central London. It lies directly south of Earl's Court (take the Tube to West Brompton) and directly southeast of West Kensington. It also has many good restaurants, pubs, and taverns, as well as some budget hotels.

Notting Hill Increasingly fashionable Notting Hill is bounded on the south by Bayswater Road and on the east by Kensington. Hemmed in on the north by West Way and on the west by the Shepherd's Bush ramp leading to the M40, it has many turn-of-the-20th-century mansions and small houses sitting on quiet, leafy streets, plus a growing number of hot restaurants and clubs. Gentrified in recent years, it's becoming an extension of central London. This is one of the hippest and hottest districts of London and has a few scattered and select hotels of charm and grace. If you're staid, stay in St. James's or Mayfair, but if you're Nicole Kidman, you can hang out here.

On the north end, across Notting Hill, west of Bayswater, is the increasingly hip neighborhood known as **Notting Hill Gate;** its Portobello Road is home to one of London's most famous street markets. The area Tube stops are Notting Hill Gate, Holland Park, and Ladbroke Grove.

Nearby **Holland Park** is a stylish residential neighborhood visited chiefly by the chic guests of Halcyon Hotel, one of the grandest of London's small hotels.

Paddington & Bayswater Centering on Paddington Station, north of Kensington Gardens and Hyde Park, Paddington is one of the major centers in London, attracting budget travelers who fill up the B&Bs in Sussex Gardens and Norfolk Square. After the first railway was introduced in London in 1836, it was followed by a circle of sprawling railway termini, including Paddington Station, which spurred the growth of this middle-class area, now blighted in parts.

Just south of Paddington, north of Hyde Park, and abutting more fashionable Notting Hill to the west, is **Bayswater,** a sort of unofficial area filled with a large number of B&Bs attracting budget travelers. Inspired by Marylebone and elegant Mayfair, a relatively prosperous set of Victorian merchants built homes for their families in this area. These districts are for the frugal hotel shopper unconcerned about a chic address.

FARTHER AFIELD

Greenwich Some 6.5km (4 miles) from the city, Greenwich—ground zero for use in the reckoning of terrestrial longitudes—enjoyed its heyday under the Tudors. Henry VIII and both of his daughters, Mary I and Elizabeth I, were born here. Greenwich Palace, Henry's favorite, is long gone, though; today's visitors come to this lovely port village for nautical sights along the Thames, including the 1869 tea clipper *Cutty Sark.*

Hampstead This residential suburb of north London, beloved by Keats and Hogarth, is a favorite spot for weekending Londoners. Notables from Sigmund Freud to John Le Carré have lived here, and it remains one of the most desirable districts in the greater London area to call home. Its centerpiece is Hampstead Heath, nearly 323 hectares (800 acres) of rolling meadows and woodlands with panoramic views; it maintains its rural atmosphere though engulfed by cityscapes on all sides. The hilltop village is filled with cafes, tearooms, and restaurants, as well as pubs galore, some with historic pedigrees.

Highgate With Hampstead, Highgate in north London is another choice residential area, particularly on or near Pond Square and along Highgate High Street. It was long a desirable place to live. Londoners used to flock to its taverns and pubs for "exercise and harmless merriment"; some still do. Today, most visitors come to see moody Highgate Cemetery, London's most famous cemetery, the final resting place of such famous figures as Karl Marx and George Eliot.

GETTING AROUND

Remember that cars drive on the left and vehicles have the right of way in London over pedestrians. Wherever you walk, always look both ways before stepping off a curb.

By Public Transportation

The London Underground and the city's buses operate on the same system of six fare zones. The fare zones radiate in rings from the central zone 1, which is where most visitors spend the majority of their time. Zone 1 covers the area from Liverpool Street in the east to Notting Hill in the west, and from Waterloo in the south to Baker Street, Euston, and Kings Cross in the north. To travel beyond zone 1, you need a multizone ticket. Note that all single one-way, round-trip, and 1-day pass tickets are valid only on the day of purchase. Tube and bus maps should be available at any Underground station. You can download them before your trip from the excellent Transport for London (TfL) website at **www.tfl.gov.uk/tfl**.

TfL also runs **Travel Information Centres** at several major Tube stations (Kings Cross, Liverpool Street, and Piccadilly Circus), at the rail stations at Euston and Victoria, and at Heathrow Airport's Terminal 123 Tube station. Most of them are open daily from at least 9am to 5pm. A 24-hour public-transportation information service is also available at ✆ **020/7222-1234.**

DISCOUNT PASSES If you plan to use public transportation a lot, investigate the range of fare discounts available. **Travelcards** offer unlimited use of buses, Underground, Docklands Light Railway, and National Rail services in greater London for any period ranging from a day to a year. Travelcards are available from Underground ticket offices, TfL Travel Information Centres, main post offices in the London area, many newsagents, and some newsstands. Children 10 and younger generally travel free on the Tube and buses when accompanied by an adult.

The **1-Day Travelcard** allows you to go anywhere throughout greater London. For travel within zones 1 and 2, the cost is £7.20 for adults, £3.60 for children 5 to 15. The **Off-Peak 1-Day Travelcard,** which is valid after 9:30am on weekdays, is even cheaper. For two zones, the cost is £5.60 for adults and £2 for children 5 to 15. The **1-Week Travelcard** for zones 1 and 2 costs £26 for adults and £13 for children 5 to 15.

Central London

King's Cross
Station

King's Cross
St. Pancras

Upper St.

Angel

Pentonville Rd.

FINSBURY

City Rd.

New North Rd.

Stoke Newington Rd.

SHOREDITCH

BETHNAL
GREEN

Hackney Rd.

Old St.

Old St.

Leonard St.

Commercial St.

ST.
PANCRAS

Coram's
Fields

Russell Sq.

Gray's Inn Rd.

Amwell St.

Percy St.

Rosebery Ave.

St. John St.

Goswell Rd.

City Rd.

City Rd.

CLERKENWELL

ST.
LUKE'S

Whitecross St.

Burnhill Row

City Road

Sun St.

St. Paul St.

Old St.

Liverpool St.
Station

Liverpool
St.

Bishopsgate

Middlesex St.

Houndsditch

Chancery
Lane

Holborn

HOLBORN

High Holborn

Lincoln's Inn
Fields

Farringdon

Barbican

The Barbican
Centre

London Wall

Gresham St.

Moorgate

Moorgate

London Wall

Old Broad St.

Camomile

Aldgate

Fenchurch
Station

COVENT
GARDEN

Covent
Garden

Covent
Garden
Market

THE
STRAND

Strand

Fleet St.

The
Temple

Temple

Law
Courts

Newgate St.

Ludgate Hill

St. Paul's
Cathedral

St. Paul's

Cheapside

Bank of
England

Threadneedle St.

Bank

THE
CITY

Mansion House

Leadenhall St.

Charing Cross
Station

Charing
Cross

Embankment

Thames

Blackfriars

Blackfriars
Station

Queen Victoria St.

Cannon St.

Cannon St.
Station

Monument

Lower Thames St.

Tower Hill

DLR

SOUTH
BANK

Waterloo
Bridge

Blackfriars
Bridge

Millennium
Bridge

Globe
Theatre

BANKSIDE

Southwark
Bridge

London
Bridge

London
Bridge
Station

Tower of
London

H.M.S.
Belfast

Tower
Bridge

Waterloo
East

Waterloo

Waterloo
Station

Southwark

SOUTHWARK

Union Street

Southwark

St. Thomas St.

Snowsfields

Bermondsey St.

Druid St.

Tower Bridge Rd.

Westminster

Houses of
Parliament

Westminster
Bridge

Lambeth
North

Borough

THE
BOROUGH

Long Lane

Lambeth
Palace

Lambeth Rd.

George's Rd.

Borough Rd.

London Rd.

Newington Causeway

NEWINGTON

Great Dover St.

Grange Rd.

Lambeth
Bridge

Imperial War
Museum

Elephant
& Castle

New Kent Rd.

Old Kent Rd.

LAMBETH

ELEPHANT
& CASTLE

Kennington Lane

Kennington

Walworth Rd.

WALWORTH

Vauxhall
Bridge

0   1/2 mi

0   500 m

Consider purchasing the **Oyster card** (www.oystercard.com), a travel discount card that's all the rage. You can prepay for single fares, which cost considerably less than a paper ticket—usually about half the price. Oysters are valid on the Tube, DLR, tram, and National Rail services within your chosen zones and across the entire London bus network. For 24-hour information, call the Oyster hot line at ℂ **0871/2301100.** The card has a daily price cap, meaning you never pay more than £7.20 regardless of how many trips you make in 1 day. You can buy an Oyster card at any ticket office.

THE UNDERGROUND

The Underground, or Tube, is the fastest and easiest way to get around. All Tube stations are clearly marked with a red circle and blue crossbar. Routes are conveniently color-coded.

If you have British coins or a credit card, you can get your ticket at a vending machine. Otherwise, buy it at the ticket office. You can transfer as many times as you like as long as you stay in the Underground. Children 4 and younger travel free if accompanied by an adult.

Slide your ticket into the slot at the gate and pick it up as it comes through on the other side, and hold on to it—it must be presented when you exit the station at your destination. If you're caught without a valid ticket, you'll be fined £20 on the spot. If you owe extra money, you'll be asked to pay the difference by the attendant at the exit. The Tube runs roughly from 5am to 12:30am Monday to Saturday and 7:30am to 10:30pm Sunday. Outside those hours, you must take a taxi or night bus to your destination. For information on the London Tube system, call the **London Underground** at ℂ **020/7222-1234,** but expect to stay on hold for a good while before a live person comes on the line. Information is also available online at **www.tfl.gov.uk.**

The Jubilee Line Extension has been extended eastward to serve the growing suburbs of the southeast and the Docklands area. This east–west axis helps ease traffic on some of London's most hard-pressed Underground lines. The line also makes it much easier to reach Greenwich.

BY BUS

The comparably priced bus system is almost as good as the Underground and gives you better views of the city. To find out about current routes, pick up a free bus map at one of Transport for London's Travel Information Centres, listed above. You can also obtain a map at **www.tfl.gov.uk**.

As with the Underground, fares vary according to distance traveled. Generally, bus fares are £1.20 to £3.80. If you want your stop called out, simply ask the conductor or driver. To speed up bus travel, passengers have to purchase tickets before boarding; drivers no longer collect fares on board. Some 300 roadside ticket machines serve stops in central London—in other words, it's "pay as you board." You'll need the exact fare, however, as ticket machines don't make change.

Buses generally run 24 hours a day. A few night buses have special routes, running once an hour or so; most pass through Trafalgar Square. Keep in mind that night buses are often so crowded (especially on weekends) that they are unable to pick up passengers after a few stops. If you find yourself waiting a long time, you may want to take a taxi instead. Call the 24-hour **hot line** (ℂ **020/7222-1234**) for bus schedule and fare information.

By Taxi

London cabs are among the most comfortable in the world. You can pick one up by either heading for a cab rank or hailing one in the street. (The taxi is available if the yellow taxi sign on the roof is lit.) To **call a taxi,** phone ℭ **0871/871-8710.**

The meter starts at £2.20, increasing in increments of £2 per mile thereafter, based on distance or time. Surcharges are imposed after 8pm and on weekends and public holidays. All these tariffs include VAT; plan to tip 10% to 15%.

If you call for a cab, the meter starts running when the taxi receives instructions from the dispatcher, so you could find that the meter already reads a few pounds more than the initial drop of £2.20 when you step inside.

Minicabs are also available, and they're often useful when regular taxis are scarce or when the Tube stops running. These cabs are meterless, so you must negotiate the fare in advance. Unlike regular cabs, minicabs are forbidden by law to cruise for fares. They operate from sidewalk kiosks, such as those around Leicester Square. If you need to call one, try **Brunswick Chauffeurs/Abbey Cars** (ℭ **020/8969-2555**) in west London or **Newham Minicars** (ℭ **020/8472-1400**) in south London. Minicab kiosks can be found near many Tube or British Rail stops, especially in outlying areas.

If you have a complaint about taxi service or if you leave something in a cab, contact the **Public Carriage Office,** 15 Penton St., N1 9PU (ℭ **0845/602-7000** or 020/7222-1234; Tube: Angel Station). If it's a complaint, you must have the cab number, which is displayed in the passenger compartment.

By Car

Don't drive in congested London. It's easy to get around without a car; traffic and parking are nightmares; and, to top it off, you have to drive on the left side of the road. It all adds up to a big headache. Another disincentive is that you will have to pay a Congestion Charge of £8 to drive in most of central London between 7am and 6pm Monday to Friday. Larger gas-guzzling cars are charged £25.

By Bicycle

To avoid heavy and potentially dangerous traffic in central London, bikers should stick to the designated paths along the streets.

One of the most popular bike-rental shops is **On Your Bike,** 52–54 Tooley St., London Bridge, SE1 (ℭ **020/7378-6669;** www.onyourbike.com; Tube: London Bridge), open Monday to Friday 7:30am to 7pm, Saturday 10am to 6pm, and Sunday 11am to 5pm. The first-class mountain bikes, with high seats and low-slung handlebars, cost £12 for the first day and £8 for each day thereafter, or £35 per week, and require a 1 pence deposit on a credit card, so they will have your credit card number.

[FastFACTS] LONDON

American Express The main office is at the American Express Travel Service at 78 Brompton Rd., Knightsbridge SW (ℭ **020/7761-7905**; Tube: Knightsbridge).

Area Code London's area code is **020.** Within the city limits, you don't need to dial it; use only the eight-digit number. If you're calling London from home before your trip, the country code for England is **44,** which precedes the London area code. When you're calling London from outside Britain, drop the "0" in front of the local area code.

Babysitters If your hotel can't recommend a sitter, call **Sitters** (✆ **0800/38-900-38** or 1202/713-911; www.sitters.co.uk). Call or check the website for rates and membership information.

Dentist For dental emergencies, call **Eastman Dental Hospital** (✆ **020/7915-1000;** www.ucl.ac.uk/eastman; Tube: Kings Cross).

Doctor Call ✆ **999** in a medical emergency. Some hotels have physicians on call for emergencies. For nonemergencies, try **Medical Express,** 117A Harley St., W1 (✆ **020/7499-1991;** www.medicalexpressclinic.com; Tube: Regent's Park). A private British clinic, it's not part of the free British medical establishment. The clinic is open Monday to Friday 9am to 6pm and Saturday 10am to 2pm.

Emergencies In London, for police, fire, or an ambulance, dial ✆ **999.**

Hospitals Royal Free Hospital, Pond Street (✆ **020/7794-0500;** Tube:

Belsize Park), and **University College Hospital,** 235–250 Euston Rd., NW1 (✆ **0845/46-47;** Tube: Great Portland St.), offer emergency care, 24 hours a day, with the first treatment free under the National Health Service. Many other London hospitals also have accident and emergency departments.

Internet Access If you've brought your laptop, the quest for access will be easier, as many hotels have Wi-Fi; rates run from £10 to £20 a day, although £12 is probably the average. Countless Internet cafes and coin-operated kiosks can be found around town. Libraries are reserved for residents, so you can't rely on them. The most common Internet-cafe chain is **easyInternetcafe** (www.easyinternetcafe.com), with 15 locations around town, including the basement of the following West End Burger Kings: 46 Regent St., W1 (Tube: Piccadilly Circus); 358 Oxford St., W1 (Tube: Bond St.); 9–16 Tottenham Court Rd., W1 (Tube: Tottenham Court Rd.); and east of Trafalgar Square at 456–459 Strand, WC2 (Tube: Charing Cross).

Maps If you plan to explore London in any depth, you'll need a detailed street map with an index, not one of those superficial overviews given away at many hotels and tourist offices. The best ones are published by Falk and are available at most newsstands and nearly all bookstores. And no Londoner is without a **London A to Z** (www.a-zmaps.co.uk), the ultimate street-by-street reference, available at bookstores and newsstands everywhere.

Police In an emergency, dial ✆ **999** (no coins are needed).

Post Office The main post office is at 24–28 William IV St., WC2 (✆ **020/7484-9307;** Tube: Charing Cross). Hours for stamps and postal services are Monday to Friday 8:30am to 6:30pm and Saturday 9am to 5:30pm. Other post office branches are open Monday to Friday 9am to 5:30pm and Saturday 9am to 12:30pm. Many branches are closed for an hour at lunch.

Telephone For **directory assistance** for London, dial ✆ **118212** for a full range of services; for the rest of Britain, dial ✆ **118118.** See also "Area Code," above.

WHERE TO STAY

Since the 21st century began, more than 10,000 hotel rooms have opened to the public in London. The downside is that most of these hotels are in districts far from the city center and are of the no-frills budget-chain variety. In spite of these bandbox modern horrors sprouting up, some hoteliers wisely decided to adapt former public or institutional buildings rather than start from scratch.

London boasts some of the most famous hotels in the world—temples of luxury such as Claridge's, the Dorchester, and the Ritz. The problem is that London has too many of these high-priced hotels (and many cheap budget options) and not enough moderately priced options.

Even at the luxury level, you may be surprised at what you don't get. Many of the stately Victorian and Edwardian gems are so steeped in tradition that they lack some of the modern conveniences that come standard in other luxury hotels around the world. Some have modernized with a vengeance, but others retain amenities from the Boer War era. However, the cutting-edge hotels are not necessarily superior; they frequently lack the personal service and spaciousness that characterize the grand old hotels.

It's also harder to get a hotel room, particularly an inexpensive one, during July and August. Inexpensive hotels are also tight in June, September, and October. If you arrive without a reservation, begin looking for a room as early in the day as possible. Many West End hotels have vacancies, even in peak season, between 9 and 11am, but by noon they are often booked.

If you're looking for budget options, don't despair. London has some good-value places in the lower price ranges, and we've included the best of these. An affordable option is a bed-and-breakfast, which you can book with the help of the following reliable services. The reputable **London Bed & Breakfast Agency Ltd.** (© **020/7586-2768;** fax 020/7586-6567; www.londonbb.com) offers inexpensive accommodations in selected private homes for £26 to £90 per person per night, based on double occupancy (although some accommodations will cost a lot more). **London Bed & Breakfast** (© **800/872-2632** in the U.S.; fax 619/531-1686; www.londonbandb.com) offers B&B accommodations in private family residences or unhosted apartments. Homes are inspected for quality and comfort, amenities, and convenience.

Instead of B&Bs, some savvy visitors prefer long-term options, including self-catering accommodations or else vacation or apartment rentals. One of the best establishments for arranging this type of rental is **Coach House London Rentals** ★★, 2 Tunly Rd., London SW17 7QJ (© **020/8133-8332;** fax 020/8181-6152; www.rentals.chslondon.com). The agency represents more than 75 properties, ranging from modest flats for couples to spacious homes that can sleep up to 12. The minimum length of a stay is 5 nights, and a car can be sent to the airport to pick you up.

For the upmarket traveler, the aptly named **Uptown Reservations,** 8 Kelso Place, London W8 5QD (© **020/7937-2001;** fax 020/7937-6660; www.uptownres.co.uk), features attractive, comfortably furnished accommodations in elegant private homes in swanky districts of the city. A substantial breakfast is included in the price, and you share your digs with the hosts themselves, many of whom are artists, diplomats, businesspeople, or, in some rare cases, lords of the realm who need extra money.

Amazing discounts, seemingly unavailable elsewhere, are offered by **VisitHotels.com,** 37B New Cavendish St., London W1G 8JR (www.visithotels.com). Sometimes discounts on a room can range up to 70%.

Where to Stay in London

ST. JOHN'S WOOD

HAMPSTEAD

CAMDEN

EUSTON

St. John's
Wood

Maida Vale

MAIDA
VALE

MAIDA VALE

WARWICK
AVENUE

NOTTING
HILL

BAYSWATER

BAYSWATER

QUEENSWAY

Prince Albert Rd.

Delancey St.

London
Zoo

REGENT'S PARK

Boating
Lake

Wellington Rd.

Grove End Rd.

Albany St.

Hampstead Rd.

Eversholt St.

EUSTON
STATION

Euston
Station

Park Rd.

GREAT
PORTLAND
ST.

EUSTON
SQUARE

Lisson Grove

St. John's Wood Rd.

MARYLEBONE

BAKER STREET

REGENT'S PARK

Regent's
Park
Crescent

Euston Rd.

Tottenham

WARREN ST.

BLOOMS-
BURY

Clifton Gdns.

Edgware Rd.

LISSON
GROVE

EDGWARE ROAD

Marylebone Rd.

High St.

Portland Pl.

Gt. Portland St.

Gower St.

Bedford Sq.

GOODGE ST.

1

3

MARYLEBONE

5

Goodge St.

6

7

2

WESTWAY A40 (M)

ROYAL OAK

PADDINGTON

PADDINGTON
STATION

Bishop's Bridge Rd.

Eastbourne Ter.

Praed St.

Seymour Pl.

Gloucester Pl.

Baker St.

11

4

9

8

10

Wigmore St.

Regent St.

New Bond St.

OXFORD
CIRCUS

Oxford St.

TOTTENHAM
COURT ROAD

19

20

SOHO

22

14

Leinster Gdns.

Queensway

Craven Rd.

Sussex Gdns.

12

13

16

17

MARBLE
ARCH

Bayswater Rd.

Seymour St.

Cumberland
Gate

Oxford St.

BOND ST.

Brook St.

Grosvenor
Sq.

Grosvenor St.

Bond St.

18

Savile Row

THE
WEST END

21

PICCADILLY
CIRCUS

Shaftesbury Ave.

15

QUEENSWAY

LANCASTER
GATE

HYDE PARK

West Carriage Dr.

Park Ln.

Park Ln.

Berkeley
Sq.

MAYFAIR

24

GREEN PARK

23

25

St. James's St.

26

Jermyn St.

Pall Mall

The Mall

Round
Pond

KENSINGTON
GARDENS

Broad Walk

Serpentine Rd.

The Serpentine

HYDE PARK
CORNER

27

Piccadilly

GREEN
PARK

ST. JAMES'S

ST. JAMES'S
PARK

Kensington
Palace

Kensington Gore Rd.

South Carriage Dr.

Knightsbridge

28

Constitution Hill

Grosvenor Pl.

Buckingham
Palace

ST. JAMES'S
PARK

Walk

29

KENSINGTON

Gloucester Rd.

Exhibition Rd.

KNIGHTS-
BRIDGE

KNIGHTSBRIDGE

Victoria
and Albert
Museum

Harrods

Brompton Rd.

Beau-
champ
Pl.

Sloane St.

31

32

Belgrave
Sq.

Buckingham Gate

30

Buckingham Palace Rd.

Victoria St.

VICTORIA
STATION

VICTORIA

Horseferry Rd.

Cromwell Rd.

36

35

SOUTH
KENSINGTON

Pelham St.

Pont St.

34

BROMPTON

Sloane
Sq.

BELGRAVIA

Eaton Sq.

Eccleston
St.

33

Victoria St.

Vauxhall Bridge Rd.

37

38

EARL'S COURT

39

Drayton Gdns.

Sydney St.

SOUTH
KENSINGTON

Sloane Ave.

King's Rd.

40

41

SLOANE
SQUARE

Lwr. Sloane St.

Pimlico Rd.

Chelsea
Bridge
Rd.

Ebury
Bridge
Rd.

42

Warwick
Way

Belgrave Rd.

PIMLICO

PIMLICO

WEST
BROMPTON

Old Brompton Rd.

Redcliffe Gdns.

Fulham Rd.

Edith Grove

Beaufort St.

CHELSEA

Royal Hospital Rd.

Oakley St.

Chelsea Embankment

Chelsea
Bridge

Queenstown Rd.

Grosvenor
Bridge

Grosvenor Rd.

Nine Elms Ln.

HAMMERSMITH

Cheyne
Walk

Albert
Bridge

Battersea
Bridge

Thames

BATTERSEA PARK

The Academy **2**
Andaz Liverpool Street **54**
base2stay **38**
B&B Belgravia **33**
Bermondsey
  Square Hotel **60**
Best Western
  Mornington Hotel **16**
Brown's Hotel **23**
Charing Cross Hotel **59**
City Inn Westminster **61**
Claridge's **18**
Courthouse Doubletree
  by Hilton **19**
Covent Garden Hotel **56**
Crescent Hotel **46**
Dean Street Townhouse **21**
Diplomat Hotel **34**
The Dorchester **24**
Draycott Hotel **41**
Dukes Hotel **26**
Durrants Hotel **3**
easyHotel **36**

Edward Lear Hotel **10**
Elysee Hotel **13**
Fielding Hotel **55**
41 Hotel **30**
Gate Hotel **15**
Grange Blooms Hotel **52**
Hallam Hotel **1**
Harlingford Hotel **45**
Hart House Hotel **9**
Haymarket Hotel **58**
Hazlitt's **22**
Hoxton Hotel **49**
Jenkins Hotel **47**
Jesmond Dene Hotel **44**
Knightsbridge Green Hotel **28**
Knightsbridge Hotel **32**
The Langham **5**
London Elizabeth Hotel **17**
Malmaison London **51**
myhotel Bloomsbury **7**
New England Hotel **42**
Parkcity Hotel **35**
Park Plaza Sherlock Holmes **4**

Pavilion Hotel **11**
Portobello Hotel **14**
The Ritz **25**
The Rockwell **37**
The Rookery **50**
Rough Luxe Hotel **43**
Ruskin Hotel **53**
St. Martins Lane **57**
Sanctuary
  House Hotel **29**
Sanderson **6**
San Domenico House **40**
Sheraton Park
  Lane Hotel **27**
Soho Hotel **20**
Stafford London
  by Kempinski **26**
Sumner Hotel **8**
30 Pavilion Road **31**
Tudor Court Hotel **12**
Twenty Nevern
  Square Hotel **39**
The Zetter **48**

5

SETTLING INTO LONDON | Where to Stay

119

A NOTE ABOUT PRICES Unless otherwise noted, published prices are rack rates for double rooms with a private bathroom. Many include breakfast (usually continental) and a 10% to 15% service charge. The British government also imposes a VAT (value-added tax) that adds 17.5% to your bill. This is not included in the prices quoted in the guide. Always ask for a better rate, particularly at the first-class and deluxe hotels (B&Bs generally charge a fixed rate). Parking rates are per night.

RATE REGULATIONS All hotels, motels, inns, and guesthouses in Britain with four bedrooms or more (including self-catering accommodations) must display notices listing minimum and maximum overnight charges in a prominent place in the reception area or at the entrance, and prices must include any service charge and may include VAT. It must be made clear whether these items are included; if VAT isn't included, then it must be shown separately. If meals are included, this must be stated. If prices aren't standard for all rooms, then only the lowest and highest prices need be given.

Mayfair
VERY EXPENSIVE

Brown's Hotel ★★ Nearly every year a hotel sprouts up trying to evoke an English-country-house ambience with Chippendale and chintz; this quintessential town-house hotel watches such competitors come and go, always coming out on top. Brown's was founded by James Brown, a former manservant to Lord Byron, who knew the tastes of well-bred gentlemen and wanted to create a dignified, clublike place for them. He opened its doors in 1837, the same year Queen Victoria took the throne. Today, Brown's occupies 14 historic houses just off Berkeley Square. Its guest rooms, completely renovated, vary considerably in decor, but all show restrained taste; even the wash basins are antiques. Accommodations range in size from small to extra spacious; some suites have four-poster beds.

30 Albemarle St., London W1S 4BP. © **020/7493-6020.** Fax 020/7493-9381. www.brownshotel.com. 117 units. £475–£645 double; £885–£3,200 suite. AE, DC, MC, V. Off-site parking £50. Tube: Green Park. **Amenities:** Restaurant; bar; concierge; health club & spa; room service. *In room:* A/C, TV/DVD, hair dryer, Internet (£15), minibar, MP3 docking station.

Claridge's ★★★ This once-fading 1812 beauty has experienced a rebirth, and its staid image has changed. *Dynasty* diva Joan Collins may have staged her latest marriage here, but now Kate Moss is spotted in the hip bar, Elizabeth Hurley strolls through the lobby, and Gordon Ramsay—Britain's most talked-about and controversial chef (and also the best)—is loud-mouthing it in the kitchen. If you want to live in the total lap of luxury, at an even tonier address than the Connaught and the Dorchester, make it Claridge's. Much of the Art Deco style of the 1930s remains, although there are other distinctive styles as well, ranging from modern to neoclassical. The hotel's strong sense of tradition and old-fashioned "Britishness" are also intact, in spite of the gloss and the hip clientele. Afternoon tea at Claridge's remains a quintessentially English tradition. The accommodations here are the most diverse in London, ranging from the costly and stunning Brook Penthouse—complete with a personal butler—to the less expensive, so-called "superior" queen rooms with queen-size beds.

Brook St., London W1A 2JQ. ⓒ **020/7629-8860.** Fax 020/7499-2210. www.claridges.co.uk. 203 units. £299–£400 double; £650–£3,950 suite. AE, DC, MC, V. Parking £50. Tube: Bond St. **Amenities:** 3 restaurants; 2 bars; babysitting; concierge; health club & spa; room service. *In room:* A/C, TV/DVD/VCR, hair dryer, minibar, Wi-Fi (free).

The Dorchester ★★★   One of London's best hotels, it has all the elegance of the Connaught, but without the upper-crust attitude that can verge on snobbery. Few hotels have the time-honored experience of "the Dorch," which has maintained a tradition of fine comfort and cuisine since it opened in 1931. Breaking from the neoclassical, the most ambitious architects of the era designed a building of reinforced concrete clothed in terrazzo slabs. Inside, the Dorchester boasts guest rooms outfitted with Irish linen sheets on comfortable beds, all the electronic gadgetry you'd expect, and double- and triple-glazed windows to keep out noise, along with plump armchairs, cherrywood furnishings, and, in many cases, four-poster beds piled high with pillows.

53 Park Lane, London W1A 2HJ. ⓒ **800/727-9820** in the U.S., or 020/7629-8888. Fax 020/9629-8080. www.thedorchester.com. 244 units. £295–£565 double; £720–£3,800 suite. AE, DC, MC, V. Parking £45. Tube: Hyde Park Corner or Marble Arch. **Amenities:** 3 restaurants (including Alain Ducasse, p. 139); bar; babysitting; concierge; health club & spa; room service. *In room:* A/C, TV/DVD, CD player, fax, hair dryer, Internet (£20); minibar.

EXPENSIVE

Sheraton Park Lane Hotel ★★   Since 1924, this has been the most traditional of the Park Lane mansions, even more so than the Dorchester. The hotel was sold in 1996 to the Sheraton group, which continues to upgrade it but maintains its quintessential British style. Its Silver Entrance remains an Art Deco marvel that has been used as a backdrop in many films, including the classic BBC miniseries *Brideshead Revisited*. Overlooking Green Park, the hotel offers luxurious accommodations that are a good deal—well, at least for pricey Park Lane. The rooms have all benefited from impressive refurbishment. In the more deluxe rooms, you get better views. The most tranquil units open onto a street in the rear; those rooms opening onto the court are dark. Many suites have marble fireplaces and original marble bathrooms.

Piccadilly, London W1J 7BX. ⓒ **800/325-3535** in the U.S., or 020/7499-6321. Fax 020/7499-1965. www.starwoodhotels.com or www.sheratonparklane.com. 302 units. £189–£299 double; £264–£349 suite. AE, DC, MC, V. Parking £45. Tube: Hyde Park Corner or Green Park. **Amenities:** 2 restaurants; bar; concierge; state-of-the-art health club; room service. *In room:* A/C (in some), TV/DVD, movie library, hair dryer, Wi-Fi (£18).

Marylebone

VERY EXPENSIVE

The Langham ★★   After it was bombed in World War II, this well-located hotel languished as dusty office space for the BBC until the early 1990s, when it was painstakingly restored. The Langham's public rooms reflect the power and majesty of the British Empire at its apex. Guest rooms are somewhat less opulent but are still attractively furnished and comfortable, featuring French Provincial furniture and red oak trim. The hotel is within easy reach of Mayfair and Soho restaurants and theaters, as well as shopping on Oxford and Regent streets. Plus, Regent's Park is just blocks away.

1C Portland Place, London W1B 1JA. © **800/223-6800** or 020/7636-1000. Fax 020/7323-2340. www.london.langhamhotels.co.uk. 425 units. £350–£470 double; from £470 suite; £490–£795 club room. AE, DC, MC, V. Tube: Oxford Circus. **Amenities:** 2 restaurants; 3 bars (including Artesian, p. 228); concierge; health club & spa; indoor pool; room service. *In room:* A/C, TV/DVD, hair dryer, minibar, Wi-Fi (£20).

EXPENSIVE

Durrants Hotel ★   This historic hotel off Manchester Square (established in 1789), with its Georgian-detailed facade, is snug, cozy, and traditional—almost like a poor man's Brown's (p. 120). We find it to be one of the most quintessentially English of all London hotels—you could invite the queen to Durrants for tea. Over the 100 years that they have owned the hotel, the Miller family has incorporated several neighboring houses into the original structure. A walk through the pine-and-mahogany-paneled public rooms is like stepping back in time: You'll even find an 18th-century letter-writing room. The guest rooms are rather bland except for elaborate cove moldings and comfortable furnishings, including good beds. Some are air-conditioned, and some are, alas, small. Bathrooms are tiny, with tub/shower combinations.

26–32 George St., London W1H 5BJ. © **020/7935-8131.** Fax 020/7487-3510. www.durrantshotel.co.uk. 92 units. £250 double; £265 family room for 3; £295–£425 suite. AE, MC, V. Tube: Bond St. or Baker St. **Amenities:** Restaurant; bar; babysitting; concierge; room service. *In room:* A/C (in most), TV, hair dryer, Wi-Fi (£10).

Park Plaza Sherlock Holmes   It's not located at that legendary address, 221B Baker St., but it's nearby. The converted boutique hotel was once part of Bedford College for Women and later the YWCA. Former tenants wouldn't know the place today. Modern portraits of the world's most famous detective are on display, but the decor is contemporary. Bedrooms come in a wide range of sizes and styles, ranked superior, executive, or studio. Most preferred, at least by us, is a trio of loft suites. Guests gather in Sherlock's Bar & Grill for good British beer and food.

108 Baker St., London W1U 6LJ. © **888/201-1803** or 020/7486-6161. Fax 020/7958-5211. www.parkplazasherlockholmes.com. 119 units. £109–£144 double; £139–£485 studio or loft suite. AE, MC, V. Tube: Baker St. **Amenities:** Restaurant; bar; concierge; health club & spa. *In room:* A/C, TV, hair dryer, minibar, Wi-Fi (£15).

MODERATE

Hallam Hotel   This heavily ornamented stone-and-brick Victorian—one of the few on the street to escape the Blitz—is just a 5-minute stroll from Oxford Circus. It's the property of brothers Grant and David Baker, who maintain it well. The hotel is warm and friendly, and the central location that you get for these prices can't be beat. The guest rooms are comfortably furnished with good beds. Several of the twin-bedded rooms are quite spacious and have adequate closet space.

12 Hallam St., Portland Place, London W1N 5LF. © **020/7580-1166.** Fax 020/7323-4527. www.hallamhotel.com. 25 units. £105–£120 double. Rates include English breakfast. AE, DC, MC, V. Tube: Oxford Circus. **Amenities:** Bar. *In room:* TV, hair dryer, minibar, Wi-Fi (£5).

Hart House Hotel ★ ☺   Hart House is a long-enduring favorite with Frommer's readers. In the heart of the West End, this well-preserved historic building—one of a group of Georgian mansions occupied by exiled French nobles during the French Revolution—lies within easy walking distance of many theaters. The rooms are spick-and-span, each one with a different character. They're decorated with a combination of furnishings, ranging from Portobello antique to modern. Favorites include no. 7, a triple with a big bathroom and shower, and no. 11, on the top floor, for a brightly lit aerie. Housekeeping rates high marks here, and each bedroom is comfortably appointed with chairs, an armoire, a desk, and a large chest of drawers. Hart House has long been known as a good, safe place for traveling families. Many of its rooms are triples, and larger families can avail themselves of special family accommodations with connecting rooms.

51 Gloucester Place, Portman Sq., London W1U 8JF. ✆ **020/7935-2288.** Fax 020/7935-8516. www. harthouse.co.uk. 15 units. £110–£150 double; £130–£175 triple; £155–£185 quad. Rates include English breakfast. MC, V. Tube: Marble Arch or Baker St. **Amenities:** Babysitting. *In room:* TV, hair dryer, Wi-Fi (£5).

Sumner Hotel ★ 🛍 The Sumner, part of an 1820s Georgian terrace, has blossomed into one of the finest boutique town-house hotels in central London. It retains much of the original architectural allure from its days as a private Georgian residence. All accommodations are designer-decorated and luxuriously appointed. The standard rooms are midsize and attractively furnished, but you can also rent deluxe rooms with artwork and better furnishings. There's an elegant sitting room with a working fireplace and timber flooring.

54 Upper Berkeley St., Marble Arch, London W1H 7QR. ✆ **020/7723-2244.** Fax 087/0705-8767. www. thesumner.com. 20 units. £135–£170 double. Rates include buffet breakfast. AE, MC, V. Tube: Marble Arch. *In room:* A/C, TV, fridge, hair dryer, Wi-Fi (free).

INEXPENSIVE

Edward Lear Hotel This popular hotel, situated a block from Marble Arch, is made all the more desirable by the bouquets of fresh flowers in its public rooms. It occupies a pair of brick town houses dating from 1780. The western house was the London home of 19th-century artist and poet Edward Lear, famous for his nonsense verse; his illustrated limericks adorn the walls of one of the sitting rooms. Steep stairs lead up to cozy rooms, which range from spacious to broom-closet size. They're looking better than ever following a wholesale renovation in 2007. If you're looking for classiness, know that the bacon on your plate comes from the same butcher used by the queen. One major drawback to the hotel: This is a very noisy part of town. Rear rooms are quieter.

28–30 Seymour St., London W1H 7JB. ✆ **020/7402-5401.** Fax 020/7706-3766. www.edlear.com. 32 units, 18 w/bathroom. £68–£85 double without bathroom; £94–£117 double w/bathroom; £94–£117 triple without bathroom; £124–£150 triple w/bathroom (shower only). Rates include English breakfast and tax. AE, MC, V. Tube: Marble Arch. *In room:* TV, Wi-Fi (free).

St. James's

VERY EXPENSIVE

The Ritz ★★★ Built in French Renaissance style and opened by César Ritz in 1906, this hotel overlooking Green Park is synonymous with luxury. Gold-leafed molding, marble columns, and potted palms abound, and a gold-leafed statue, *La Source,* adorns the fountain of the oval-shaped Palm Court. After a major restoration, the hotel is better than ever: New carpeting and air-conditioning have been installed in the guest rooms, and an overall polishing has recaptured much of the Ritz's original splendor. Still, this Ritz lags far behind the much grander one in Paris (with which it is not affiliated). The Belle Epoque guest rooms, each with its own character, are spacious and comfortable. Many have marble fireplaces, elaborate gilded plasterwork, and a decor of soft pastel hues. A few rooms have their original brass beds and marble fireplaces. Corner rooms are grander and more spacious.

150 Piccadilly, London W1J 9BR. © **877/748-9536** in the U.S., or 020/7493-8181. Fax 020/7493-2687. www.theritzlondon.com. 135 units. £270–£600 double; £520–£4,500 suite. Children 15 and younger stay free in parent's room. AE, DC, MC, V. Parking £56. Tube: Green Park. **Amenities:** 2 restaurants (including the Palm Court); bar; babysitting; concierge; health club & spa; room service. *In room:* A/C, TV/DVD, fax, hair dryer, Internet (£25).

EXPENSIVE

Dukes Hotel ★★★   Dukes provides elegance without ostentation in what was presumably someone's *Upstairs, Downstairs* town house. Along with its nearest competitors, the Stafford and 22 Jermyn Street, it caters to those looking for charm, style, and tradition in a hotel. It stands in a quiet courtyard off St. James's Place; turn-of-the-20th-century gas lamps help put you into the proper mood before entering the front door. Each well-furnished guest room is decorated in the style of a particular English period, ranging from Regency to Edwardian. It's a lot cozier, more intimate, and even more clubbish than the Stafford; Dukes is also more tranquil because it's set in its own gas-lit alley.

35 St. James's Place, London SW1A 1NY. © **800/381-4702** in the U.S., or 020/7491-4840. Fax 020/7493-1264. www.campbellgrayhotels.com. 90 units. £235–£365 double; £450–£1,125 suite. AE, DC, MC, V. Parking £55. Tube: Green Park. **Amenities:** Restaurant; bar; babysitting; concierge; health club & spa; room service. *In room:* A/C, TV/DVD, hair dryer, minibar, MP3 docking station, Wi-Fi (free).

Stafford London by Kempinski ★★★   Famous for its American Bar, its St. James's address, and the warmth of its Edwardian decor, the Stafford, now managed by the Kempinski group, competes well with Dukes for a tasteful, discerning clientele. Although this was a former stables with rooms upstairs for the horsemen of the Royal Guard, you can bet that no 18th-century horse ever slept with the electronic safes, stereo systems, and quality furnishings (mostly antique reproductions) that these rooms feature. Much has been done to retain the style of these rooms, including preservation of the original A-beams on the upper floors. Many singles contain queen-size beds, and some of the deluxe units offer four-posters that will make you feel like Henry VIII. Units on the top floor are small. In 2007, 26 junior and master suites were added in the Stafford Mews, each filled with antiques and luxury facilities.

16–18 St. James's Place, London SW1A 1NJ. © **800/525-4800** in the U.S., or 020/7493-0111. Fax 020/7493-7121. www.kempinski.com. 107 units. £235–£440 double; £640–£1,390 suite. AE, DC, MC, V. No parking. Tube: Green Park. **Amenities:** Restaurant; bar; babysitting; concierge; exercise room; room service. *In room:* A/C, TV/DVD, CD player, hair dryer, Wi-Fi (free).

Trafalgar Square
EXPENSIVE

Charing Cross Hotel ★   When it was built of massive sandstone blocks in 1865, architects marveled at its location directly above the fourth largest railway station in London, Charing Cross, and the way it comprises two separate wings interconnected by an enclosed aerial bridge spanning a pedestrian walkway, Villiers Street, below. After a massive renovation by the Guoman Hotels group, it launched itself as a serious contender in an attraction-packed and highly competitive neighborhood, the Strand and Trafalgar Square. Whereas the public areas retain their high-ceilinged Victorian flair, bedrooms are sleekly contemporary, with pricing that varies according to their size and their view (vistas over the Strand command the highest prices). There's a well-managed on-site restaurant, the Terrace on the Strand, focusing on Continental cuisine, and an international staff well versed in the needs of travelers.

The Strand, London WC2N 5HX. ✆ **0871/376-9012.** Fax 0871/376-9112. www.guoman.com. 239 units. £129–£239 double; £229–£269 junior suite. AE, DC, MC, V. Tube: Charing Cross. **Amenities:** Restaurant; bar; concierge; exercise room. *In room:* A/C, TV, minibar, Wi-Fi (£10).

Soho

EXPENSIVE

Courthouse Doubletree by Hilton ★★ Guests from Oscar Wilde to Mick Jagger have passed through the doors of this historic former courthouse. In a spectacular reclamation of an existing structure, the hotel retains many aspects of its landmark building, including original Robert Adams fireplaces. A bar has been installed inside three of the original prison cells. The judges' bench, witness stand, and dock still occupy center stage in Silk, the hotel's deluxe dining room. The location is among the best in London, just off Regent Street, opposite Carnaby Street and the department store Liberty's. Bedrooms are midsize to spacious, each comfortably and tastefully decorated, with 13 suites. The best rooms are in the new wing that was built on the site of a former police station. Our favorite retreat here is the roof terrace, where light meals and cocktails are served.

19-21 Great Marlborough St., London W1F 7HL. ✆ **800/426-3135** in the U.S., or 020/7297-5555. Fax 020/7297-5566. www.courthouse-hotel.com. 112 units. £169–£311 double; £314–£426 suite. AE, DC, MC, V. Tube: Oxford Circus. **Amenities:** 2 restaurants; bar; concierge; health club & spa; indoor pool; room service. *In room:* A/C, TV/DVD, hair dryer, minibar, Wi-Fi (£15).

Dean Street Townhouse ★ 🏠 Deep in the heart of Soho, this boutique hotel in a restored four-story Georgian townhouse is an offbeat oddity. Formerly the home of the Gargoyle Club, it has been converted to receive paying guests, and its Georgian architecture has been more or less preserved. Do not check in here if you're a movie star with lots of luggage. Accommodations range from "broom cupboard" to tiny, small, medium, and bigger. Rooms have four-poster beds, hand-painted wallpaper, and other retro-chic touches. Bathrooms are fitted with rainforest showers and stocked with goodies from the famous Cowshed Spa. An all-day dining room features a weekly changing menu of seasonal British food.

69-71 Dean St., London W1D 3SE. ✆ **020/7434-1775.** www.deanstreettownhouse.com. 39 units. £90–£160 standard double; £220–£270 larger double. AE, MC, V. Tube: Oxford Circus. **Amenities:** Restaurant; bar. *In room:* TV/DVD, hair dryer, minibar, Wi-Fi (free).

Haymarket Hotel ★★★ This is a chic upmarket choice for those who want to avoid the grandes dames. Next to the historic Haymarket Theatre, the hotel is ideal for theatergoers. Like all Firmdale hotels, it makes a bold statement with colors of turquoise, fuchsia, mango, and acid green. Although completely modernized and perhaps the most sophisticated small hotel of London, many satisfying proportions of the original 19th-century John Nash architecture remain. Original works of art and antiques are used, and the bedrooms are sumptuously elegant with fine linens and the latest amenities. There's even an indoor pool lounge.

1 Suffolk Place, London SW1Y 4BP. ☎ **020/7470-4000.** Fax 020/7470-4004. www.firmdale.com. 50 units. £250–£330 double; £400–460£ junior suite; £1,750–£2,250 suite. AE, DC, MC, V. Tube: Tottenham Court Rd. **Amenities:** Restaurant; bar; concierge; exercise room; indoor pool; room service. *In room:* A/C, TV/DVD, CD player, hair dryer, Wi-Fi (£20).

Hazlitt's ★★ 🛏 This gem, housed in three historic homes on Soho Square, is one of London's best small hotels. Built in 1718, the hotel is named for William Hazlitt, who founded the Unitarian Church in Boston and wrote four volumes on the life of his hero, Napoleon. The hotel is a favorite with artists, actors, and models. It's eclectic and filled with odds and ends picked up around the country at estate auctions. Some find its Georgian decor a bit spartan, but the 2,000 original prints hanging on the walls brighten it considerably. Some of the floors dip and sway, and there's no elevator, but it's all part of the charm. Hazlitt's has just as much character as the Fielding Hotel (p. 130) but is a lot more comfortable. Some rooms are a bit small, but most are spacious, all with state-of-the-art appointments. Many units have four-poster beds. Accommodations in the back are quieter but perhaps too dark.

6 Frith St., London W1D 3JA. ☎ **020/7434-1771.** Fax 020/7439-1524. www.hazlittshotel.com. 23 units. £159–£295 double; £450–£700 suite. AE, DC, MC, V. Tube: Leicester Sq. or Tottenham Court Rd. **Amenities:** Babysitting; concierge; room service. *In room:* A/C, TV, hair dryer, minibar, Wi-Fi (free).

Sanderson ★★★ Ian Schrager, the king of New York hip, has brought Manhattan's Tenth Avenue to London. For his latest London hotel, Schrager secured the help of talented partners Philippe Starck and Andra Andrei to create an "ethereal, transparent urban spa," in which walls are replaced by glass and sheer layers of curtains. The hotel, located in a former corporate building near Oxford Street, north of Soho, has a lush bamboo-filled roof garden, a large courtyard, and a spa. That's not all—Alain Ducasse, arguably the world's greatest chef, directs its restaurant. The accommodations are cutting edge. Your bed is likely to be an Italian silver-leaf sleigh attended by spidery polished stainless-steel night tables and draped with a fringed pashmina shawl. Although the transformation of this building into a hotel has been remarkable, the dreary grid facade of aluminum squares and glass remains.

50 Berners St., London W1T 3NG. ☎ **800/697-1791** or 020/7300-1400. Fax 020/7300-1401. www.sandersonlondon.com. 150 units. £215–£650 double; £700–£2,800 suite. AE, DC, MC, V. Tube: Oxford Circus or Tottenham Court Rd. **Amenities:** Restaurant; 2 bars; babysitting; concierge; health club & spa. *In room:* A/C, TV/DVD, CD player, hair dryer, minibar, Wi-Fi (£15).

Soho Hotel ★★★ British hoteliers Kit and Tim Kemp have come up with a stunner here. A former parking garage in the heart of bustling Soho, it's now our favorite nest in London. When it's time to check out, we never want to leave. At night, you get a cocoonlike feeling entering this luxury lair in a cul-de-sac off Dean Street. The theaters of Shaftesbury are only a block or two away, as is the Ivy restaurant. All of the extremely spacious bedrooms are individually designed in granite and oak. There are four penthouses on the fifth floor, with tree-lined terraces opening onto panoramic sweeps of London. All the famous Kemp touches can be found, from boldly striped furnishings to deep bathtubs for a late-night soak. The glitterati, mostly actors and filmmakers, can be seen hanging out at the bar.

4 Richmond Mews, London W1D 3DH. ☎ **020/7559-3000.** Fax 020/7559-3003. www.firmdale.com. 91 units. £290–£360 double; £400–£2,750 suite. AE, MC, V. Tube: Oxford Circus or Piccadilly Circus. **Amenities:** Restaurant; bar; concierge; exercise room; room service. *In room:* A/C, TV/DVD, CD player, hair dryer, Wi-Fi (£20).

Bloomsbury

EXPENSIVE

The Academy ★   The Academy is in the heart of London's publishing district. If you look out your window, you can see where Virginia Woolf and other members of the Bloomsbury Group passed by every day. Many original architectural details were preserved when these three 1776 Georgian row houses were joined. Grace notes include glass panels, colonnades, and intricate plasterwork on the facade. The hotel was substantially upgraded in the 1990s, with a bathroom added to every bedroom (whether there was space or not). With overstuffed armchairs and half-canopied beds, accommodations sometimes evoke English-country-house living, but that of the poorer relations. Guests who have been here before always request rooms opening on the garden in back and not those in front with ducted fresh air (though the front units have double-glazing to cut down on the noise). *Warning:* If you have a problem with stairs, know that no elevators rise to the four floors.

21 Gower St., London WC1E 6HG. © **020/7631-4115.** Fax 020/7636-3442. www.theetoncollection.com. 49 units. £235 double; £353 suite. AE, DC, MC, V. Tube: Tottenham Court Rd., Goodge St., or Russell Sq. **Amenities:** Bar; room service. *In room:* A/C, TV, CD player, hair dryer, minibar, Wi-Fi (free).

Grange Blooms Hotel ★   This restored 18th-century town house has a pedigree: It stands in what were formerly the grounds of Montague House (now the British Museum). Even though it's in the heart of London, the house has a country-home atmosphere, complete with fireplace, period art, and copies of *Country Life* in the magazine rack. Guests take morning coffee in a walled garden overlooking the British Museum. In summer, light meals are served. The small- to medium-size bedrooms are individually designed with traditional elegance, in beautifully muted tones.

7 Montague St., London WC1B 5BP. © **020/7323-1717.** Fax 020/7636-6498. www.grangehotels.com. 26 units. £75–£180 double. AE, DC, MC, V. Tube: Russell Sq. **Amenities:** Restaurant; bar; room service. *In room:* TV, hair dryer, Internet (£10), minibar.

myhotel Bloomsbury ★ 🎒   Creating shock waves among staid Bloomsbury hoteliers, myhotel is a London row house on the outside with an Asian *moderne*–style interior. It is designed according to principles of feng shui—the ancient Chinese art of placement that utilizes the flow of energy in a space. For instance, the guest rooms have mirrors, but they're positioned so you don't see yourself when you first wake up—feng shui rule number one (probably a good rule, feng shui or no feng shui). All rooms are havens of comfort, taste, and tranquillity, with excellent sleep-inducing beds. Tipping is discouraged, and each guest is assigned a personal assistant responsible for his or her happiness. Aimed at today's young, hip traveler, myhotel lies within a short walk of Covent Garden and the British Museum.

11–13 Bayley St., Bedford Sq., London WC1B 3HD. © **020/7667-6000.** Fax 020/7667-6044. www. myhotels.co.uk. 78 units. £148–£279 double; £566–£805 suite. AE, DC, MC, V. Tube: Tottenham Court Rd. or Goodge St. **Amenities:** Restaurant; bar; babysitting; exercise room; room service. *In room:* A/C, TV, hair dryer, Wi-Fi (free).

MODERATE

Harlingford Hotel 🗝   This hotel comprises three town houses built in the 1820s and joined around 1900 with a bewildering array of staircases and meandering hallways. Set in the heart of Bloomsbury, it's run by folks who seem genuinely concerned about the welfare of their guests, unlike the management at many of the neighboring hotel rivals. (They even distribute little mincemeat pies to their guests during the Christmas holidays.) Double-glazed windows cut down on the street noise, and all rooms are inviting. The most comfortable units are on the second and third levels, but expect to climb some steep English stairs (there's no elevator). Avoid the rooms on ground level, as they are darker and have less security.

61–63 Cartwright Gardens, London WC1H 9EL. ✆ **020/7387-1551.** Fax 020/7387-4616. www.harlingford hotel.com. 43 units. £110 double; £125 triple; £135 quad. Rates include English breakfast. AE, MC, V. Tube: Russell Sq., Kings Cross, or Euston. **Amenities:** Use of tennis courts in Cartwright Gardens. *In room:* TV, hair dryer, Wi-Fi (free).

INEXPENSIVE

Crescent Hotel   Although Ruskin and Shelley no longer pass by, the Crescent still stands in the heart of academic London. The private square is owned by the City Guild of Skinners (who are furriers, as you might have guessed) and guarded by the University of London, whose student residential halls are across the street. Guests have access to the gardens and private tennis courts belonging to the City Guild of Skinners. The hotel owners view the Crescent as an extension of their home and welcome you to its comfortably elegant Georgian surroundings, which date from 1810. Some guests have been returning for 4 decades. Bedrooms range from small singles with shared bathrooms to more spacious twin and double rooms with private bathrooms.

49–50 Cartwright Gardens, London WC1H 9EL. ✆ **020/7387-1515.** Fax 020/7383-2054. www.crescent hoteloflondon.com. 27 units, 18 w/bathroom (some w/shower only, some w/tub and shower). £51 single w/shared bathroom; £102 double w/bathroom; £126 family room. Rates include English breakfast. MC, V. Tube: Russell Sq., Kings Cross, or Euston. **Amenities:** Babysitting; use of tennis courts in Cartwright Gardens. *In room:* TV, Wi-Fi (£6).

Jenkins Hotel ★ ✦   Followers of the Agatha Christie TV series *Poirot* will recognize this Cartwright Gardens residence—it was featured on the show. The antiques are gone and the rooms are small, but some of the original charm of the Georgian house remains—enough so that the London *Mail on Sunday* proclaimed it one of the 10 best hotel values in the city. All rooms have been redecorated in traditional Georgian style, and many have been completely refurbished. The location is great, near the British Museum, theaters, and antiquarian bookshops. There are some drawbacks: no lift and no reception or sitting room. Nonetheless, this is a place where you can settle in and feel at home.

45 Cartwright Gardens, London WC1H 9EH. ✆ **020/7387-2067.** Fax 020/7383-3139. www.jenkins hotel.demon.co.uk. 14 units. £95 double; £110 triple. Rates include English breakfast. MC, V. Tube: Russell Sq., Kings Cross, or Euston. **Amenities:** Use of tennis courts in Cartwright Gardens. *In room:* TV, fridge, hair dryer, Wi-Fi (free).

Ruskin Hotel   Although the hotel is named for author John Ruskin, the ghosts of other literary legends who lived nearby haunt you: Mary Shelley plotting her novel *Frankenstein,* and James Barrie fantasizing about *Peter Pan.* This hotel has been managed for 2 decades by a hardworking family and enjoys a repeat clientele. Management keeps the place spick-and-span, though you shouldn't expect a decorator's flair. The furnishings, though well polished, are a bit worn. Double-glazing in the front blots out the noise, but we prefer the cozily old-fashioned chambers in the rear, as they open onto a park. Sorry, no elevator. *Note:* Prices here are kept low because only a half-dozen rooms have private bathrooms.

23–24 Montague St., London WC1B 5BH. © **020/7636-7388.** Fax 020/7323-1662. 33 units, 6 w/bathroom. £75 double without bathroom, £85 double w/bathroom; £98 triple without bathroom, £115 triple w/bathroom. Rates include English breakfast. AE, DC, MC, V. Tube: Russell Sq., Holborn, or Tottenham Court Rd. *In room:* Hair dryer.

Kings Cross

MODERATE

Rough Luxe Hotel ★ 🎁 Just minutes from St. Pancras International station, this small boutique hotel was salvaged from the remains of one of the area's many nondescript guesthouses. Set in a row of Georgian townhouses, the decor is almost industrial, like the interior of a warehouse art gallery. Decades of wallpaper and paint were peeled away, leaving distressed walls of hand-painted mosaic wallpaper and plaster of yesterday. Many of the antiques were purchased at an auction of the Savoy Hotel's throwaways. Modern art is displayed throughout, including artist Daniel Baker's controversial *This Is Shit*. No two bedrooms are alike. Three units come with private bathroom, with glass-enclosed showers and rainforest shower heads.

1 Birkenhead St., London WC1H 8BA. © **020/7837-5338.** www.roughluxe.co.uk. 9 units, 3 w/bathroom. £155 double without bathroom; £210 double w/bathroom; £280 suite. Rates include continental breakfast. AE, MC, V. Tube: Kings Cross. **Amenities:** Breakfast room. *In room:* TV (retro '80s sets with static), hair dryer.

INEXPENSIVE

Jesmond Dene Hotel Well-maintained and cozy bedrooms are found at this well-run B&B in the rapidly gentrifying area of Kings Cross. For those who plan to use this terminus, this is a good, convenient choice for transportation, including Eurostar to Paris. All of the small bedrooms here are comfortable, tasteful, and refurbished.

27 Argyle St., London WC1H 8EP. © **020/7837-4654.** Fax 020/7833-1633. www.jesmonddenehotel. co.uk. 23 rooms, 20 w/private bathroom. £65 double without bathroom, £90 double w/bathroom; £120 triple; £135 quad. AE, DC, MC, V. Tube: Kings Cross. **Amenities:** Breakfast room. *In room:* TV, Wi-Fi (free).

Covent Garden

EXPENSIVE

Covent Garden Hotel ★★★ This former hospital building lay neglected for years until it was reconfigured in 1996 by hot hoteliers Tim and Kit Kemp—whose flair for interior design is legendary—into one of London's most charming boutique hotels, in one of the West End's hippest shopping neighborhoods. *Travel + Leisure* called this hotel one of the 25 hottest places to stay in the *world*. It remains so. Behind a bottle-green facade reminiscent of a 19th-century storefront, the hotel has a welcoming lobby outfitted with elaborate inlaid furniture and elegant draperies, plus a charming restaurant. Upstairs, accessible via a dramatic stone staircase, the soundproof bedrooms are furnished in English style with Asian fabrics, many adorned with hand-embroidered designs. The hotel has a decorative trademark— each room has a clothier's mannequin.

10 Monmouth St., London WC2H 9HB. © **800/553-6674** in the U.S., or 020/7806-1000. Fax 020/7806-1100. www.firmdale.com. 58 units. £240–£340 double; £395–£1,195 suite. AE, DC, MC, V. Tube: Covent Garden or Leicester Sq. **Amenities:** Restaurant; bar; babysitting; concierge; exercise room; room service. *In room:* A/C, TV/DVD, movie library, CD player, hair dryer, minibar, Wi-Fi (£20).

St. Martins Lane ★★★ Ian Schrager transformed this 1960s office building into a chic and cutting-edge Covent Garden enclave. This was the first hotel Schrager designed outside the United States, after a string of successes from New York to West Hollywood. The mix of hip, irreverent design and a sense of cool have been imported across the pond. Whimsical touches abound—for example, a string of daisies replaces DO NOT DISTURB signs. Rooms are all white, but you can use the full-spectrum lighting to make them any color. Floor-to-ceiling windows in every unit offer a panoramic view of London.

45 St. Martin's Lane, London WC2N 4HX. ✆ **800/697-1791** in the U.S., or 020/7300-5500. Fax 020/7300-5501. www.stmartinslane.com. 204 units. £215–£330 double; £380–£550 suite. AE, DC, MC, V. Tube: Covent Garden or Leicester Sq. **Amenities:** Restaurant; 2 bars; babysitting; concierge; exercise room; room service. *In room:* A/C, TV/DVD, movie library, hair dryer, minibar, Wi-Fi (£15).

MODERATE
Fielding Hotel ★ 🛍 One of London's more eccentric hotels, this rickety walk-up is cramped, quirky, and quaint, and an enduring favorite of some. Luring media types, the hotel is named after novelist Henry Fielding of *Tom Jones* fame, who lived in Broad Court. It lies on a pedestrian street still lined with 19th-century gas lamps. The Royal Opera House is across the street, and the pubs, shops, and restaurants of lively Covent Garden are just beyond the front door. Rooms are small but charmingly old-fashioned and traditional. Some units are redecorated or at least "touched up" every year, though floors dip and sway, and the furnishings and fabrics, though clean, have known better times. With a location like this, in the heart of London, the Fielding keeps guests coming back; in fact, some love the hotel's claustrophobic charm. Children 12 and younger are not welcome; occasionally the staff makes adult patrons feel the same.

4 Broad Court, Bow St., London WC2B 5QZ. ✆ **020/7836-8305.** Fax 020/7497-0064. www.thefielding hotel.co.uk. 24 units. £115–£170 double. AE, DC, MC, V. Tube: Covent Garden. *In room:* TV, Wi-Fi (free).

Westminster/Victoria
EXPENSIVE
41 Hotel ★★★ 🛍 This relatively unknown but well-placed gem offers the intimate atmosphere of a private club combined with a high level of personal service. Completely self-contained, it occupies the fifth (top) floor of the building whose lower floors contain the Rubens at the Palace hotel. It's best suited to couples or those traveling alone—especially women. Public areas feature an abundance of mahogany, antiques, fresh flowers, and rich fabrics. Guests can read, relax, or watch TV in the library-style lounge, where a complimentary continental breakfast and afternoon snacks are served each day. Bedrooms are individually sized, but all feature elegant black-and-white color schemes and magnificent beds with Egyptian-cotton linens.

41 Buckingham Palace Rd., London SW1W OPS. ✆ **877/955-1515** in the U.S. or Canada, or 020/7300-0041. Fax 020/7300-0141. www.41hotel.com. 30 units. £274–£295 double; £525–£725 suite. Rates include continental breakfast, afternoon snacks, and evening canapés. AE, DC, MC, V. Tube: Victoria. **Amenities:** Bar; babysitting; concierge; room service. *In room:* A/C, TV/DVD, CD player, hair dryer, Internet (free), MP3 docking station.

MODERATE
City Inn Westminster ★ Next door to the Tate Britain and Parliament, this purpose-built inn with a vast array of rooms is at the nexus of elite London. The

River Thames and London Eye are within a short walk. The lobby is graced with stone, oak, and leather chairs, and the on-site restaurant specializes in game and salmon, as befits the hotel's Scottish ownership. The best accommodations are the 67 City Club rooms or the 16 suites, but all units are comfortable, with a fresh, light, and contemporary design. They're also soundproof, with 18 inches of concrete between each unit. Try, if possible, for a room opening onto the Thames or else views of Parliament. You can drink and dine in the City Café restaurant and bar, with its alfresco terrace, and the stylish Millbank Lounge bar is a popular rendezvous point at night. Business clients predominate during the week, but on weekends rates are often slashed to bargain prices (ask about this when booking).

30 John Islip St., London SW1P 4DD. ✆ **020/7630-1000.** Fax 020/7233-7575. www.cityinn.com. 460 units. £119–£159 double; £139–£179 City Club room; £219–£259 suite. AE, DC, MC, V. Tube: Pimlico or Westminster. **Amenities:** Restaurant; 2 bars; concierge; exercise room; room service. *In room:* A/C, TV/ DVD, CD player, hair dryer, minibar, Wi-Fi (free).

New England Hotel   A family-run business for nearly 25 years, this hotel shut down at the millennium for a complete overhaul. Today, it's better than ever and charges an affordable price. Located on a corner in the Pimlico area, which forms part of the City of Westminster, its elegant 19th-century exterior conceals a completely bright and modern interior. The hotel is neat and clean and one of the most welcoming in the area—it justly prides itself on its clientele of "repeats." It's also one of the few hotels in the area with an elevator.

20 St. George's Dr., London SW1V 4BN. ✆ **020/7834-1595.** Fax 020/7834-9000. www.newengland hotel.com. 20 units. £85–£99 double; £129–£139 triple; £139–£149 quad. Rates include continental breakfast. MC, V. Tube: Victoria. *In room:* TV, hair dryer, Wi-Fi (£3 per hr.).

Sanctuary House Hotel ★   Only in the new London, where hotels are bursting into bloom like daffodils, would you find a hotel so close to Westminster Abbey. And a pub hotel, no less, with rooms on the upper floors above the tavern. The building was converted by Fuller, Smith & Turner, a traditional brewery in Britain. Accommodations have a rustic feel, but with first-rate beds. Downstairs, a pub/restaurant, part of the Sanctuary, offers old-style British meals that have ignored changing culinary fashions. The food is excellent if you appreciate the roast beef, Welsh lamb, and Dover sole that pleased the palates of Churchill and his contemporaries. Naturally, there's always plenty of brew on tap.

33 Tothill St., London SW1H 9LA. ✆ **020/7799-4044.** Fax 020/7799-3657. www.fullershotels.com. 34 units. £139–£195 double. AE, DC, MC, V. Tube: St. James's Park. **Amenities:** Restaurant; pub; room service. *In room:* A/C, TV, hair dryer, Wi-Fi (£11 per day).

The City of London & Environs
EXPENSIVE

Andaz Liverpool Street ★★   In 2007, a branch of the Hyatt group (Andaz) transformed one of the East End's most venerable hotels into a glossy and very upscale monument to relaxed chic. Strategically positioned at the junction of two trendy, arts-conscious neighborhoods (Shoreditch and Hoxton) and the financial district, it manages to gracefully incorporate respect for the cutting-edge arts with allegiance to old-fashioned British pomp and circumstance. The original hotel dates from 1884, when it was designed by architect Charles Barry, best known for his work on the Houses of Parliament. The hotel's exterior is abloom in all its Victorian glory, complete with a stained-glass dome. Inside, the bedrooms are supremely comfortable, with state-of-the-art bathrooms and color schemes of dark red and white.

40 Liverpool St., London EC2M 7QN. © **800/228-9000** or 020/7961-1234. Fax 020/7961-1235. www. hyatt.com or www.london.liverpoolstreet.andaz.hyatt.com. 267 units. £125–£360 double; £250–£460 suite. AE, DC, MC, V. Tube: Liverpool St. **Amenities:** 4 restaurants; 5 bars; concierge; state-of-the-art health club; room service. *In room:* A/C, TV/DVD, CD player, hair dryer, minibar, MP3 docking station, Wi-Fi (free).

Malmaison London ★★   Who could imagine that this used to be a dreary nursing home? Talk about recycling. The Victorian mansion block overlooks a green cobbled square and is the first London showcase for the U.K.-only hotel chain that is known for opening up winning hotels with clever contemporary designs, state-of-the-art facilities, and, as always, a chic little brasserie serving French classics. On the southern rim of once dreary, now trendy Clerkenwell, in East London, Malmaison is awash in dark teakwood; tall, glowing floor lamps; a highly polished European staff; tasteful fabrics in neutral shades; and a portrait and bust in the lobby of Napoleon and Josephine, who spent many a "wanton night" at the original Château Malmaison outside Paris. The dark-wood guest rooms are individually designed and larger than average for central London.

18–21 Charterhouse Sq., London EC1M 6AH. © **020/7012-3700.** Fax 020/7012-3702. www.malmaison-london.com. 97 units. £225–£295 double; £315–£520 suite. AE, MC, V. Tube: Barbican or Farringdon. **Amenities:** Restaurant; bar; concierge; exercise room; room service. *In room:* A/C, TV/DVD, CD player, CD library, minibar, Wi-Fi (free for 30 min., then £10 per day).

The Rookery ★ 🛏   When this hotel opened in the late 1990s, it salvaged the last three remaining then-derelict antique houses in Clerkenwell, a neighborhood midway between the West End and the City of London. The result is a setting that's permeated with a sense of Johnson and Boswell's London, an oasis of intentionally crooked and creaky floors, labyrinthine hallways, and antique accessories and furnishings that manage to be simultaneously fun and functional. Bedrooms are charming and quirky, furnished with carved 18th- and 19th-century bed frames and lace or silk draperies. Bathrooms contain Edwardian-era fittings, including claw-foot bathtubs. Overall, this place is quirky, eccentric, and abundantly laden with a sense of the antique.

12 Peter's Lane, Cowcross St., London EC1M 6DS. © **020/7336-0931.** Fax 020/7336-0932. www. rookeryhotel.com. 33 units. £126–£185 double; £178–£354 suite. AE, DC, MC, V. Tube: Farringdon. **Amenities:** Breakfast room; concierge; room service. *In room:* A/C, TV, minibar, Wi-Fi (free).

The Zetter ★★★   Heaven will be a letdown after this. Imagine hall vending machines dispensing champagne, or espresso makers providing complimentary coffee on every floor. This converted Victorian warehouse between the financial district and the West End features seven rooftop studios with patios and panoramic views of the London skyline, among other lures, including a sky-lit atrium flooding its core with natural light. Many of the features and "scars" of the original structure were retained, as tradition was blended with a chic, urban modernity. Bedrooms, ranging from small to midsize, are spread across five floors. These accommodations open onto balconies that circle the atrium. Unplastered brick walls reach up to "floating" ceilings and customized wallpaper panels. Secondhand furnishings are set beside classic modern pieces. The designers have achieved their goal of "a great bed, a great shower, and state-of-the-art in-room technology."

St. John's Sq., 86–88 Clerkenwell Rd., London EC1M 5RJ. ☎ **020/7324-4444.** Fax 020/7324-4445. www.thezetter.com. 59 units. Mon–Thurs £180–£360 double; Fri–Sun £153–£360 double. AE, DC, MC, V. Tube: Farringdon. **Amenities:** Restaurant; bar; concierge; room service. *In room:* A/C, TV/DVD, CD player, Internet (free), MP3 docking station.

INEXPENSIVE

Hoxton Hotel ★ 🍴 Custom-built in 2006 in the Shoreditch neighborhood near London's financial district, the Hoxton has a stated aim of avoiding hotel rip-offs. It's come up with many innovative policies—for example, instead of getting gouged if you make a phone call from your room, you are charged only 5p a minute for calls to Canada and the United States, and you'll find "supermarket prices" at the mini-market in the lobby. The main investor and figurehead, Sinclair Beecham, founder of Britain's popular Pret A Manger fast-food chain, bases his price structure on policies in effect at budget airlines, offering frequent promotions to the rates noted below. Everything is simplified here: The "Lite Pret" breakfast—a bag containing freshly squeezed orange juice, granola, yogurt, and a banana—is hung on your doorknob. Bedrooms are functional and rather small but tastefully furnished, each with either one queen-size or two twin beds.

81 Great Eastern St., London EC2A 3HU. ☎ **020/7550-1000.** Fax 020/7550-1090. www.hoxtonhotels. com. 205 units. £49–£189 double. Rates include Lite Pret breakfast. AE, DC, MC, V. Tube: Old St. **Amenities:** Grill; bar; access to nearby gym (£7). *In room:* TV, fridge, hair dryer, Wi-Fi (free).

Southwark

MODERATE

Bermondsey Square Hotel ★ 🎒 Time was when no one would think of staying in Bermondsey, in southeast London. But the times are changing, and galleries, boutiques, bars, and restaurants are opening. This property, the first boutique hotel in the area, is part of the neighborhood's renaissance. Overlooking one of London's largest antiques markets, the cool spot caters to both foodies, drawn to its Alfie's Bar & Kitchen, and fashionistas, attracted to its designer chic bedrooms. Rooms on the penthouse floor are named for hit songs from the '60s, including "Lucy" and "Jude." A rooftop terrace is a special feature of the Bermondsey.

Bermondsey Sq., Tower Bridge Rd., London SE1 3UN. ☎ **0870/111-25-25.** www.bermondseysquare hotel.co.uk. 79 units. £129 standard double; £350 deluxe double; £500 junior suite. AE, MC, V. Tube: London Bridge, then bus no. 78. **Amenities:** Restaurant; bar; concierge; room service. *In room:* A/C, TV/ DVD, hair dryer, minibar, MP3 docking station, Wi-Fi (free).

Knightsbridge

EXPENSIVE

Knightsbridge Green Hotel ★ Repeat guests from around the world view this dignified 1890s structure as their home away from home. In 1966, when it was converted into a hotel, the developers kept its wide baseboards, cove moldings, high ceilings, and spacious proportions. Even without kitchens, the well-furnished suites come close to apartment-style living. Most units are spacious, with adequate storage space. Bedrooms are decorated with custom-made colors and are often individualized—one has a romantic sleigh bed. This is a solid choice for lodging, just around the corner from Harrods.

159 Knightsbridge, London SW1X 7PD. ☎ **020/7584-6274.** Fax 020/7225-1635. www.thekghotel.co.uk. 28 units. £225 double; £300–£350 suite. AE, DC, MC, V. Tube: Knightsbridge. **Amenities:** Room service. *In room:* A/C, TV, hair dryer, Wi-Fi (free).

Knightsbridge Hotel ★★ 🌶   The Knightsbridge Hotel attracts visitors from all over the world seeking a small, comfortable hotel in a high-rent district. It's fabulously located, sandwiched between fashionable Beauchamp Place and Harrods, with many of the city's top theaters and museums close at hand. Built in the early 1800s as a private town house, this place sits on a tranquil, tree-lined square, free from traffic. Hoteliers Kit and Tim Kemp, celebrated for their upmarket boutique hotels, have gone slightly more affordable with their revamp of this hotel in the heart of the shopping district. All the Kemp "cult classics" are found here, including such luxe touches as granite-and-oak bathrooms, the Kemps' famed honor bar, and Frette linens. Most bedrooms are spacious and furnished with traditional English fabrics. The best units are nos. 311 and 312 at the rear, each with a pitched ceiling and a small sitting area.

10 Beaufort Gardens, London SW3 1PT. © **020/7584-6300.** Fax 020/7584-6355. www.firmdale.com. 44 units. £220–£310 double; £360–£625 suite. AE, DC, MC, V. Tube: Knightsbridge. **Amenities:** Self-service bar; babysitting; room service. *In room:* TV/DVD, CD player, hair dryer, minibar, Wi-Fi (£20).

MODERATE

30 Pavilion Road ★ 🎒   Searcy, one of London's best catering firms, operates this recycled surprise: an old pumping station that has been turned into a hotel, located just a hop, skip, and a jump from Harrods and the boutiques of Sloane Street. At this Knightsbridge oasis, you press a buzzer and are admitted to a freight elevator that carries you to the third floor. Upstairs, you'll encounter handsomely furnished rooms with antiques, tasteful fabrics, comfortable beds (some with canopies), and often a sitting alcove. Some of the tubs are placed right in the room instead of in a separate area. Check out the rooftop garden.

30 Pavilion Rd., London SW1X 0HJ. © **020/7584-4921.** Fax 020/7823-8694. www.30pavilionroad. co.uk. 10 units. £180 double; £200 suite. Rates include continental breakfast. AE, DC, MC, V. Tube: Knightsbridge. **Amenities:** Room service; babysitting. *In room:* A/C, TV, Wi-Fi (free).

Belgravia

MODERATE

B+B Belgravia ★★   In its first year of operation (2005), this elegant town house won a top Gold Award as the best B&B in London. It richly deserves it. Design, service, quality, and comfort are tops. The prices are also reasonable, the atmosphere stylish, and the location grand: just a 5-minute walk from Victoria Station. The good-size bedrooms are luxuriously furnished. The lounge offers comfy sofas, an open fire on nippy nights, a DVD library, a laptop for guests' use, and tea and coffee 24 hours a day. The full English breakfast in the morning is one of the finest in the area.

64–66 Ebury St., Belgravia, London SW1W 9QD. © **020/7259-8570.** Fax 020/7259-8591. www.bb-belgravia.com. 17 units. £120–£130 double; £150–£160 family room. Rates include English breakfast. AE, MC, V. Tube: Victoria Station. **Amenities:** Breakfast room. *In room:* TV, Wi-Fi (free).

Diplomat Hotel ★ 🎒   Part of the Diplomat's charm is that it is a small and reasonably priced hotel located in an otherwise prohibitively expensive neighborhood. Only minutes from Harrods, it was built in 1882 as a private residence by noted architect Thomas Cubbitt. The registration desk is framed by the sweep of a partially gilded circular staircase; above it, cherubs gaze down from a Regency-era chandelier. The staff is helpful, well mannered, and discreet. The high-ceilinged guest rooms are tastefully done in Victorian style. They're a bit small and usually furnished with twin beds. You get good—not grand—comfort here.

2 Chesham St., London SW1X 8DT. ℰ **020/7235-1544.** Fax 020/7259-6153. www.thediplomathotel. co.uk. 26 units. £115–£170 double. Rates include English buffet breakfast. AE, DC, MC, V. Tube: Sloane Sq. or Knightsbridge. **Amenities:** Snack bar; babysitting. *In room:* TV, hair dryer, Wi-Fi (free).

Chelsea

EXPENSIVE

Draycott Hotel ★★★   Everything about this place, radically upgraded into a government five-star rating, reeks of British gentility, style, and charm. Past clients are greeted like old friends by a staff that manages to be both hip and cordial. The Draycott took its present-day form when a third brick-fronted town house was added to a pair of interconnected town houses that had been functioning as a five-star hotel since the 1980s. That—coupled with tons of money spent on English antiques, rich draperies, and an upgrade of those expensive infrastructures you'll never see, including security—has transformed this place into a gem. Bedrooms are outfitted uniquely, each with haute English style and plenty of fashion chic. As a special feature, the hotel serves complimentary drinks—tea at 4pm, champagne at 6pm, and hot chocolate at 9:30pm.

26 Cadogan Gardens, London SW3 2RP. ℰ **800/747-4942** or 020/7730-6466. Fax 020/7730-0236. www.draycotthotel.com. 35 units. £260–£315 double; £385 suite. AE, DC, MC, V. Tube: Sloane Sq. **Amenities:** Bar; access to nearby health club & spa; room service. *In room:* A/C, TV/DVD, CD player, minibar, Wi-Fi (free).

San Domenico House ★★   This "toff" (dandy) address, a redbrick Victorian-era town house that has been tastefully renovated in recent years, is located in Chelsea near Sloane Square. It combines valuable 19th-century antiques with modern comforts. Our favorite spot here is the rooftop terrace; with views opening onto Chelsea, it's ideal for a relaxing breakfast or drink. Bedrooms come in varying sizes, ranging from small to spacious, but all are opulently furnished with flouncy draperies, tasteful fabrics, and sumptuous beds. Many rooms have draped four-poster or canopied beds.

29 Draycott Place, London SW3 2SH. ℰ **800/324-9960** in the U.S., or 020/7581-5757. Fax 020/7584-1348. www.sandomenicohouse.com. 15 units. £235–£255 double; £295–£360 suite. AE, DC, MC, V. Tube: Sloane Sq. **Amenities:** Airport transfers; babysitting; room service; Wi-Fi (free in lobby). *In room:* A/C, TV, hair dryer, Internet (£9), minibar.

Kensington

EXPENSIVE

Parkcity Hotel ★   Close to the shopping districts of Kensington and Knightsbridge, this is a very successful restoration of a Victorian structure that has been thoroughly modernized with a striking design. Contemporary furnishings grace both the public and private areas. The town-house–style hotel is rated four stars by the government because its facilities range from a business center to a gym. Gourmet Italian food is featured at Lessandro, Ruby's Cocktail Bar is a sophisticated rendezvous spot, and an alfresco dining terrace is open in summer.

18–30 Lexham Gardens, London W8 5JE. ℰ **020/7341-7090.** Fax 020/7835-0189. www.theparkcity. com. 62 units. £109–£450. AE, MC, V. Tube: Gloucester Rd. **Amenities:** Restaurant; bar; concierge; exercise room; room service. *In room:* A/C, TV/DVD, Internet (£6.50), minibar.

The Rockwell ★★★ 🎒 One of London's latest hotels proves that high style doesn't always come with a high price tag. This independently owned bastion of deluxe comfort occupies a converted Georgian manse in South Kensington. Accommodations are tricked out with oak furnishings (including bespoke solid-oak cupboards and desks) and Neisha Crosland wallpaper, all crafted to combine traditional English aesthetics with modern design. Rooms are bright and airy with large windows and simple lines. The beds are large and inviting and dressed with the finest of Egyptian cotton, feather pillows, and Merino wool blankets. We prefer the garden units with their own private patios. The trendy One-Eight-One bistro features a menu based on English fare with a contemporary twist. Yes, it serves lavender ice cream.

181 Cromwell Rd., London SW5 0SF. ☎ **020/7244-2000.** Fax 020/7244-2001. www.therockwell.com. 40 units. £160–£180 double; £200 suite. AE, DC, MC, V. Tube: Earl's Court or Gloucester Rd. **Amenities:** Restaurant; bar; access to nearby gym; room service. *In room:* A/C, TV, Internet (free), minibar.

INEXPENSIVE

base2stay 🍴 Down in Kensington a new concept in hotels has emerged, offering great value by providing what guests really need and use—minus the frills. What you get are stylish, comfortably furnished accommodations with small kitchenettes. The cheapest units contain bunk beds for two, and suites can be made by way of interconnecting rooms. Living may be stripped to the basics, but this is no hostel, as there is a 24-hour reception service as well as daily maid service.

25 Courtfield Gardens, London SW5 0PG. ☎ **800/511-9821** in the U.S., or 020/7244-2255. www.base2stay.com. 67 units. £93–£103 bunk beds for 2; £105–£161 double; £199 deluxe unit for 4. AE, MC, V. Tube: Earl's Court. **Amenities:** Wi-Fi (free). *In room:* A/C, TV, kitchenette.

easyHotel 🍴 This hotel runs on the principle that guests would rather have smaller hotel rooms and pay less. If you're claustrophobic, it's definitely not for you. The rooms are 6 to 7 sq. m (65–75 sq. ft.), with most of the space taken up by standard double beds. If you can get a room with a window, do so—it makes a big difference. Just off Cromwell Road between South Kensington and Earl's Court, easyHotel offers all double rooms with cramped bathrooms containing a shower. There are flatscreen TVs in every unit, but a £5 fee is assessed to use the set. One staff member is permanently on-site, but no services are offered. Housekeeping costs an optional £10 per day, there is no elevator, and checkout time is 10am. Instead of by phone, all bookings are taken and confirmed by credit card through its website.

14 Lexham Gardens, London W8 5JE. ☎ **020/7706-9911.** www.easyhotel.com. 34 units. £30–£50 double. MC, V. Tube: South Kensington or Earl's Court. *In room:* A/C, TV, Wi-Fi (£10).

Earl's Court

INEXPENSIVE

Twenty Nevern Square Hotel Many of the affordable hotels around Earl's Court are seedy, but not this restored hotel, a stately redbrick Victorian house with a distinctly Asian feel, from the lounge's porcelain vases and ornate bird cages to the heavy silk draperies. The most elegant of the accommodations is the Pasha Suite, which has luxurious silk draperies printed with a peacock design. Some of the smaller rooms are made to feel even smaller by the heavy furniture, most of which was shipped in from Indonesia. Several rooms feature private terraces; most of these are at the lower end of the price scale.

20 Nevern Sq., Earl's Court, London SW5 9PD. © **020/7565-9555.** Fax 020/7565-9444. www.20nevernsquare.com. 20 units. £79–£109 double; £135–£159 suite. AE, MC, V. Tube: Earl's Court. **Amenities:** Bar; cafe; access to nearby gym; room service. *In room:* TV, CD player, hair dryer, Wi-Fi (free).

Notting Hill

MODERATE

Portobello Hotel ★   On an elegant Victorian terrace near Portobello Road, two 1850s-era town houses have been combined to form a quirky property that has its devotees. We remember these rooms when they looked better, but they still have plenty of character. Who knows what will show up in what nook? Perhaps a Chippendale, a claw-foot tub, or a round bed tucked under a gauze canopy. Try for no. 16, with a full-tester bed facing the garden. Some of the cheaper rooms are so tiny that they're basically garrets, but others have been combined into large doubles. An elevator goes to the third floor; after that, it's the stairs. Since windows are not double-glazed, request a room in the quiet rear. Some units are air-conditioned. Service is erratic at best, but this is still a good choice.

22 Stanley Gardens, London W11 2NG. © **020/7727-2777.** Fax 020/7792-9641. www.portobello-hotel. co.uk. 24 units. £190–£225 double; £265–£630 suite. Rates include continental breakfast. AE, MC, V. Tube: Notting Hill Gate or Holland Park. **Amenities:** Restaurant; bar; room service. *In room:* A/C (in some), TV, hair dryer, Internet (free), minibar.

INEXPENSIVE

Gate Hotel   This antiques-hunters' favorite is the only hotel along the length of Portobello Road—and because of rigid zoning restrictions, it will probably remain the only one for years to come. It was built in the 1820s as housing for farmhands at the now-defunct Portobello Farms and has functioned as a hotel since 1932. It has two cramped but cozy bedrooms on each of its three floors. Be prepared for some *very* steep English stairs. Rooms are color coordinated, with a bit of style, and come with such extras as full-length mirrors and built-in wardrobes. Housekeeping is excellent. Especially intriguing are the wall paintings that show the original Portobello Market: Every character looks straight from a Dickens novel. The on-site manager can direct you to the attractions of Notting Hill Gate and nearby Kensington Gardens, both within a 5-minute walk.

6 Portobello Rd., London W11 3DG. © **020/7221-0707.** Fax 020/7221-9128. www.gatehotel.co.uk. 7 units. £80–£100 double; £105–£125 triple. Rates include continental breakfast (served in room). AE, MC, V. Tube: Notting Hill Gate or Holland Park. **Amenities:** Room service. *In room:* TV, hair dryer, minibar, Wi-Fi (£5).

Paddington & Bayswater

MODERATE

Best Western Mornington Hotel ★   Affiliated with Best Western, the Mornington brings a touch of northern European hospitality to the center of London. Just north of Hyde Park and Kensington Gardens, the hotel has a Victorian exterior and a Scandinavian-inspired decor. The area isn't London's most fashionable, but it's close to Hyde Park and convenient to Marble Arch, Oxford Street shopping, and the ethnic restaurants of Queensway. Renovated guest rooms are tasteful and comfortable. Every year we get our annual Christmas card from "the gang," as we refer to the hotel staff—and what a helpful crew they are.

12 Lancaster Gate, London W2 3LG. ℭ **800/633-6548** in the U.S., or 020/7262-7361. Fax 020/7706-1028. www.bw-morningtonhotel.co.uk. 66 units. £89–£145 double. Rates include Scandinavian and English breakfast. AE, DC, MC, V. Parking £25. Tube: Lancaster Gate. **Amenities:** Bar. *In room:* TV, Wi-Fi (free).

London Elizabeth Hotel ★   This elegant Victorian town house is ideally situated, overlooking Hyde Park. Amid the buzz and excitement of central London, the hotel's atmosphere is an oasis of charm and refinement. Even before the hotel's recent £3-million restoration, it oozed character. Individually decorated rooms range from executive to deluxe and remind us of staying in an English country house. Deluxe rooms are fully air-conditioned, and some contain four-poster beds. Executive units usually contain one double or twin bed. Some rooms have special features such as Victorian antique fireplaces. Suites are pictures of grand comfort and luxury—the Conservatory Suite boasts its own veranda, part of the house's original 1850 conservatory.

Lancaster Terrace, Hyde Park, London W2 3PF. ℭ **800/721-5566** in the U.S., or 020/7402-6641. Fax 020/7224-8900. www.londonelizabethhotel.co.uk. 49 units. £165–£190 double; £275 suite. AE, DC, MC, V. Parking £12. Tube: Lancaster Gate or Paddington. **Amenities:** Restaurant; bar; room service. *In room:* A/C (in some), TV, hair dryer, minibar, Wi-Fi (free).

Pavilion Hotel ★ 🎒   Until the early 1990s, this was a rather ordinary-looking B&B. Then a team of entrepreneurs with ties to the fashion industry took over and redecorated the rooms with sometimes wacky themes, turning it into an idiosyncratic little hotel. The result is a theatrical and often outrageous decor that's appreciated by the many fashion models and music-industry folks who regularly make this their temporary home in London. Rooms are, regrettably, rather small, but each has a distinctive style. Examples include a kitschy 1970s room ("Honky-Tonk Afro"), an Asian bordello–themed room ("Enter the Dragon"), and even rooms with 19th-century ancestral themes. One Edwardian-style room, a gem of emerald brocade and velvet, is called "Green with Envy."

34-36 Sussex Gardens, London W2 1UL. ℭ **020/7262-0905.** Fax 020/7262-1324. www.pavilionhotel uk.com. 30 units. £100 double; £120 triple. Rates include continental breakfast. AE, MC, V. Parking £10. Tube: Edgeware Rd. *In room:* TV, Wi-Fi (free).

INEXPENSIVE

Elysee Hotel   Finding an inexpensive hotel in central London grows harder by the year. However, this affordable choice is a good bet for the frugal traveler, facing Hyde Park and lying on Craven Terrace; it's famous for its Mitre Pub, the location of two Woody Allen movies. Privately owned and renovated, it offers comfortable but very basic bedrooms. For those who can pay more, we recommend the more spacious and better furnished standard rooms. Guests can unwind in the refurbished lounge and bar. Single, double, twin, and family rooms (sleeping up to six) are available.

25-26 Craven Terrace, London W2 3EL. ℭ **020/7402-7633.** Fax 020/7402-4193. www.hotelelysee. co.uk. 55 units. £73–£89 double; £110–£125 triple; £129–£150 quad. MC, V. Parking nearby £15. Tube: Lancaster Gate. **Amenities:** Bar. *In room:* TV, hair dryer, Wi-Fi (free).

Tudor Court Hotel   Originally built in the 1850s and much restored and altered, this Victorian structure is now a boutique hotel of tranquillity and comfort, lying only a 3-minute walk from Paddington Station. It is a standout in a section of less desirable hotels. Bedrooms are midsize, completely restored, and comfortably furnished, with a choice of single, double (or twin), triple, and family rooms available. Rooms without bathrooms have a wash basin, with facilities right outside the door. The hotel's maintenance and affordable price make this one a winner—that, plus a helpful staff.

10–12 Norfolk Sq., London W2 1RS. ☎ **020/7723-6553.** Fax 020/7723-0727. www.tudorcourtpaddington. co.uk. 36 units. £89 double w/bathroom; £78 double without bathroom, £108 triple w/bathroom. Rates include English breakfast. AE, DC, MC, V. Limited street parking. Tube: Paddington. **Amenities:** Breakfast room. *In room:* TV, Wi-Fi (in rooms w/bathroom; free).

WHERE TO DINE

London is one of the great food capitals of the world. Both its veteran and upstart chefs have fanned out around the globe for culinary inspiration, returning with innovative dishes, flavors, and ideas that London diners have never seen before—or at least not at such unprecedented rates. These chefs are pioneering a new style of modern English cooking, which is forever changing yet comfortingly familiar in many ways. They've committed to centering their dishes on local ingredients from field, stream, and air, and have become daringly innovative with traditional recipes—too much so in the view of some critics, who don't like fresh mango over their blood pudding.

Traditional English cooking has made a comeback, too. The dishes that English mums have been forever feeding their reluctant families are fashionable again. Yes, we're talking English soul food: bangers and mash, Norfolk dumplings, nursery puddings, cottage pie—the works. This may be a rebellion against the excessive minimalism of the nouvelle cuisine that ran rampant through London in the 1980s, but who knows? Maybe it's just plain old nostalgia. Pigs' noses with parsley-and-onion sauce may not be your idea of cutting-edge cuisine, but Simpson's-in-the-Strand (p. 153) is serving it for breakfast.

If you want a lavish meal, London is a good place to eat it. Some of the world's top restaurants call the city home. For those who don't want to break the bank, we include many affordable restaurants where you can dine well. You'll find that London's food revolution has infiltrated every level of the dining scene—even the lowly pub has entered London's culinary sweepstakes. Believe the unthinkable: At certain pubs, you can now dine better than in many restaurants. In some, standard pub grub has given way to modern English and Mediterranean-style fare; in others, oyster bars have taken hold.

Mayfair

VERY EXPENSIVE

Alain Ducasse at the Dorchester ★★ FRENCH In 2007, the maestro of upper-strata French cuisine reached across the Channel and planted a bulkhead in England with the establishment of this ultrachic corner of gastronomy. Outfitted in tones of pastels and grays, it's rather startlingly arranged around a circular central table for six, which is surrounded with a translucent silk curtain and illuminated with a "waterfall" of illuminated fiber-optic cables. Collectively, it seems to conceal the patrons in a gauzy cloud. What, pray, does someone order in an environment this

Where to Dine in London

Acorn House Restaurant **50**	Galvin Bistrot de Luxe **9**	Prince Bonaparte **11**
Admiral Codrington **38**	Georgian Restaurant **34**	Prism **64**
Alain Ducasse at	Gordon Ramsay **49**	Quaglino's **40**
the Dorchester **25**	Hakkasan **19**	Racine **37**
Amaya **35**	Hush **15**	Randall & Aubin **18**
Arbutus **6**	The Ivy **20**	Rex Whistler
Assaggi **32**	Jenny Lo's Teahouse **41**	Restaurant **72**
Aubergine **47**	J. Sheekey **60**	Richoux **33**
Automat **27**	L'Anima **19**	Rules **59**
Amaya **35**	Le Café Anglais **10**	St. James's Restaurant & the
Belgo Centraal **57**	Le Cercle **42**	Fountain Restaurant **28**
Bengal Clipper **68**	Le Gavroche **23**	Salt Yard **3**
Bibendum Restaurant	Le Metro **36**	Scott's **24**
& Oyster Bar **39**	Leon **8**	Shampers **17**
Black & Blue **32**	Maze **14**	Shepherd's Restaurant **71**
Bob Bob Ricard **7**	The Narrow **66**	Simpson's-in-
Bountiful Cow **53**	National Dining Rooms **70**	the-Strand **61**
Butlers Wharf Chop House **67**	Nobu London **30**	The Square **22**
Café Spice Namasté **65**	Odin's **1**	Suze in Mayfair **13**
Cantina Vinopolis **63**	The Orangery **31**	Tamarind **26**
Chelsea Ram **43**	Orrery **1**	Texture **12**
Cinnamon Kitchen **55**	OSatsuma **19**	Tom Aikens **45**
Clarke's **32**	Oxo Tower Restaurant **62**	Tom's Kitchen **46**
Club Gascon **54**	Pied á Terre **4**	Villandry **2**
Cork & Bottle Wine Bar **58**	The Pig's Ear **48**	Wagamama **52**
The Cow **11**	Porters English	Wild Honey **16**
Criterion **21**	Restaurant **29**	Ye Olde Cheshire
The Enterprise **44**	Portrait Restaurant **69**	Cheese **56**
Fung Shing **21**		

rarified? Consider prawns wrapped in a hot and spicy cocoon of seaweed; steamed crayfish with hearts of artichoke, served in a potato and truffle shell; steamed halibut with yogurt, spicy condiments, and beans; or a filet of beef Rossini style, with seared foie gras, root veggies, and Perigueux sauce. Can you expect to see the maestro himself whipping up sauces in the kitchen? It's unlikely, since he's farmed out many of the day-to-day operations to his long-term disciple, Jocelyn Herland. Nonetheless, he keeps a tight rein on the place from other parts of his empire.

In the Dorchester hotel (lobby level), Park Lane, W1. © **020/7629-8866.** www.alainducasse-dorchester. com. Reservations required 2 weeks in advance. Set-price menus £75 for 3 courses, £95 for 4 courses, £115 for 7 courses. AE, DC, MC, V. Tues–Fri noon–2pm; Tues–Sat 6:30–10pm. Tube: Green Park, Hyde Park Corner, or Marble Arch.

Le Gavroche ★★★ FRENCH   Although challengers come and go, this luxurious "gastro-temple" remains the number-one choice in London for classical French cuisine. It may have fallen off briefly in the early 1990s, but it's fighting its way back to stellar ranks. There's always something special coming out of the kitchen of Michel Roux, Jr., the son of the chef who founded the restaurant in 1966. The service is faultless, and the ambience formally chic without being stuffy. The menu changes constantly, depending on the fresh produce that's available and the current inspiration of the chef. But it always remains classically French, though not of the "essentially old-fashioned bourgeois repertoire" that some critics suggest. Signature dishes, honed over years of unswerving practice, include the town's grandest cheese soufflé (Soufflé Suissesse); warm foie gras with crispy cinnamon-flavored crepes; and Scottish filet of beef with port-wine sauce and truffled macaroni. Depending on availability, game is often served as well. Truly Gallic choices are the cassoulet of snails with frog thighs or the mousseline of lobster in a champagne sauce.

43 Upper Brook St., W1. © **020/7408-0881.** Fax 020/7491-4387. www.le-gavroche.co.uk. Reservations required as far in advance as possible. Main courses £30–£60; fixed-price lunch £48; *Le Menu Exceptional* £95 without wine, £150 with wine. AE, MC, V. Mon–Fri noon–2pm; Mon–Sat 6:30–11pm. Tube: Marble Arch.

The Square ★★★ FRENCH   Hip, chic, casual, sleek, and modern, the Square still doesn't scare Le Gavroche as a competitor for first place on London's dining circuit, but it is certainly a stop to make on a serious London gastronomic tour. Chef Philip Howard delivers the goods at this excellent restaurant, where you get creative, personalized cuisine in a cosseting atmosphere with abstract modern art on the walls. The chef has a magic touch, crafting such concoctions as a starter of terrine of partridge with smoked foie gras and pear with cider jelly, or else a lasagna of Cornish crab with a champagne foam. For a main course, we urge you to try the peppered aged rib-eye of Ayrshire beef with smoked shallots, Tuscan snails, and a red-wine sauce, or else the roast saddle of hare with port-glazed endive. The fish dishes, such as steamed turbot with buttered langoustine claws and poached oysters, are always fresh, and Bresse pigeon is as good as it is in its hometown in France.

6–10 Bruton St., W1. © **020/7495-7100.** www.squarerestaurant.org. Reservations required. Fixed-price lunch £60–£75, dinner £100. AE, DC, MC, V. Mon–Fri noon–3pm; Mon–Sat 6:30–10:45pm; Sun 6:30–10pm. Tube: Bond St. or Green Park.

EXPENSIVE

Hush CONTINENTAL   It's charming, it's trendy, and it's a retreat with lots of attractive people and not a tourist in sight. Hush is one of a number of outdoor restaurants in a cul-de-sac. On a summer day, the terrace outside seats up to 60 and offers some of London's best alfresco dining. On the ground floor, expect a chic decor with a combination of light-wood tables and limestone floors, warmed up with touches of spice tones. The well-chosen menu features traditional brasserie food—in this case, such items as smoked haddock fishcakes, lobster and chips with garlic butter, and most definitely the Hush Hamburger, which some critics have hailed as the best in London. Start with Andalusian gazpacho or a meze platter (a selection of Greek hors d'oeuvres). Classic dishes include sautéed calves' liver or Toulouse sausages with creamed potatoes and a mustard sauce. The desserts are hard to resist, especially the champagne jelly with mixed berries or the lemon cheesecake with raspberries.

8 Lancashire Court, Brook St., W1. © **020/7659-1500.** www.hush.co.uk. Reservations recommended. Fixed-price menus £35–£55. Brasserie main courses £9–£24. AE, DC, MC, V. Restaurant daily noon–3pm and 6:30–11pm. Brasserie Mon–Fri 7:30am–11pm; Sat noon–11pm; Sun noon–4pm. Bar daily 11am–midnight. Tube: Bond St.

Maze ★★ INTERNATIONAL   Gordon Ramsay may be the leading chef of London, but our nomination for the most promising chef is Jason Atherton, a one-time protégé of Ramsay. Atherton learned his master's secrets and has plenty of creative culinary imagination of his own. His combinations may sound a bit bizarre, but the resulting flavors and ingredients taste sublime. He's a chef who appeals to "grazers" (that is, those diners who prefer a series of small plates or tapas to a traditional main course). In a New York–inspired interior by the American architect David Rockwell, Atherton enthralls with dish after dish, which reflect the changing seasons. Take his starters: Orkney scallops roasted with spices and served with a peppered golden raisin purée, or else foie gras marinated in pinot noir. For a main, we'd recommend the roasted partridge with plum preserves or the roast Scottish filet of beef with Landes foie gras and an ox-cheek cottage pie.

10–13 Grosvenor Sq., W1. © **020/7107-0000.** www.gordonramsay.com. Reservations required. Fixed-price lunch £29–£43; main dishes (small platters) £12–£14. AE, DC, MC, V. Daily noon–2:30pm and 6–10:30pm. Tube: Bond St.

Nobu London ★★ JAPANESE/SOUTH AMERICAN   London's innovative restaurant, a celebrity haunt, owes much to its founders, actor Robert De Niro and chef Nobu Matsuhisa. Those on the see-and-be-seen circuit don't seem to mind the high prices that go with these incredibly fresh dishes. The kitchen staff is brilliant and as finely tuned as their New York counterparts. The sushi chefs create gastronomic pyrotechnics. Elaborate preparations lead to perfectly balanced flavors. Where else can you find an excellent sea urchin tempura? Salmon tartare with caviar is a brilliant appetizer, followed by a perfectly done filet of sea bass in a sour bean paste and then soft-shell crab rolls. The squid pasta is sublime, as is the incredibly popular sukiyaki. Cold sake arrives in a green bamboo pitcher.

In the Metropolitan Hotel, 19 Old Park Lane, W1. © **020/7447-4747.** www.noburestaurants.com. Reservations required 1 month in advance. Main courses £11–£33; sushi and sashimi £3–£8.25 per piece; fixed-price lunch £26, dinner £11–£33. AE, DC, MC, V. Mon–Fri noon–2:15pm and 6–10:15pm; Sat 12:30–2:30pm and 6–11pm; Sun 12:30–2:30pm and 6–9:30pm. Tube: Hyde Park Corner.

Scott's ★★ SEAFOOD   In business after a long slumber, Scott's has regained its position as one of London's great seafood restaurants. Opened as an oyster warehouse in 1851 by a young fishmonger, John Scott, the restaurant first earned its fame at its Haymarket site, where it resided until 1968. Now filled with cosmopolitan glitter in Mayfair, it doesn't rest on its long-ago fame but has made its reputation anew. Once a favorite of Ian Fleming, creator of the James Bond character, it was the setting in the '50s and '60s where he discovered the dry martini—"shaken, not stirred." Scott's is dear to the seafood lover's heart, from its market-fresh Dover sole to "cockles and mussels." Always ask about the fresh catch of the day, or else order filet of halibut with chervil butter or Scottish lobster thermidor. For meat eaters, there's rib steak or braised pork cheeks.

20 Mount St., W1. ℂ **020/7495-7309.** www.scotts-restaurant.com. Reservations required. Main courses £16–£40. AE, DC, MC, V. Mon–Sat noon–10:30pm; Sun noon–10pm. Tube: Green Park or Bond St.

Tamarind ★ INDIAN   In favor with critics as well as the lunchtime business crowd, Tamarind is the most popular Indian restaurant in Mayfair. The basement dining room has gold pillars and a tandoor window so that you can watch the chefs pull their flavorful dishes from the ovens. Chef Alfred Prasad leads a culinary brigade from Delhi that selects the best, freshest ingredients in the markets each day. The kitchen prides itself on nouvelle dishes but also excels at traditional Indian fare. The monkfish marinated in saffron and yogurt is delectable, and the mixed kabob platter, with all the kabobs cooked in a charcoal-fired tandoor, is extraordinary—these chefs are the kings of kabobs. Your best bet for a curry? Opt for the prawns in a five-spice mixture. Vegetarians will find refuge here, especially if they go for the *dal Bukhari,* a black-lentil specialty of northwest India.

20–22 Queen St., W1. ℂ **020/7629-3561.** www.tamarindrestaurant.com. Reservations required. Main courses £13–£26; fixed-price dinner £56; fixed-price 2- or 3-course lunch £15–£25. AE, DC, DISC, MC, V. Sun–Fri noon–2:45pm; Mon–Sat 6–11:30pm; Sun 6:30–10:30pm. Tube: Green Park.

MODERATE

Wild Honey ★ EUROPEAN   In the gilded environs of Mayfair, chef Anthony Demetre rules in the oak-paneled former digs of a gentleman's club. Those gents never ate food like what's served now. The chef is at the top of his form, treating fresh local products with loving care as he fashions them into temptations for your palate. The menu specializes in game, but other dishes are equally fine, including English snails scattered over a thick pancake, or line-caught cod with Cornish cockles. Another specialty is buttery Scottish Buccleuch beef. Roast Norfolk hare appears with caramelized endive; the wild duck with Armagnac sauce. Finish with the namesake "Wild Honey" ice cream with the actual honeycomb.

12 St. George St., W1. ℂ **020/7758-9160.** www.wildhoneyrestaurant.co.uk. Reservations required. Main courses £14–£27. AE, MC, V. Mon–Sat noon–2:30pm and 6–11pm; Sun noon–3pm and 6–10:30pm. Tube: Oxford Circus, Bond St., Green Park, or Piccadilly Circus.

INEXPENSIVE

Automat AMERICAN   The famous faces who flocked to this "American brasserie" when it opened aren't seen too much anymore, but a clientele of Yankees patronizes the modern precincts, enjoying everything from macaroni and cheese to a soft-shell po' boy sandwich with fries. Some of the best U.S. beef in London is also offered, including New York strip sirloin. London food critics have called it "Mayfair's slice of the Big Apple," after digging into the crab cakes with guacamole or the chili con carne. Salad is a wedge of iceberg lettuce with blue-cheese dressing. Perhaps the most popular item on the menu is the Automat Hamburger with fries.

33 Dover St., W1. ✆ **020/7499-3033.** www.automat-london.com. Reservations recommended. Main courses £8–£28. AE, DC, MC, V. Mon–Fri 7–11am and noon–3pm; Sat–Sun 11am–4pm; Mon–Sat 6pm–midnight. Tube: Green Park.

Leon ★ 🍴 MEDITERRANEAN Its biggest fans call it "gourmet fast food." While gourmet it is not, this is a great place to just sit and eat without being rushed during a day of shopping on Oxford Street. It does what its nearby competitors don't do: It produces fresh, wholesome food at affordable prices. Everything is freshly cooked, and that means certain dishes may be variable, but we find ourselves returning in spite of a flaw here and there. Everything on the menu is fresh, often organic. The salads, chicken nuggets, and hearty stews are all good. The nuggets are made with succulent breast meat and doused in a creamy yogurt-and-garlic sauce. Even the chili con carne is different: It's a bowl of spicy, tender minced beef with black kidney beans, served with fluffy organic brown rice speckled with pumpkin, sunflower, and sesame seeds, and accompanied by a tasty cabbage and beet slaw. Your drink of choice might be a ginger and carrot juice. Save room for the chocolate brownie "zinged" up with orange zest and swaddled in sinful scoops of ice cream made from Jersey cream. Leon is also the best place in the area for breakfast—don't miss the organic porridge.

35 Great Marlborough St., W1. ✆ **020/7437-5280.** www.leonrestaurants.co.uk. Reservations not required. Breakfast items from £2.30; main courses £5–£7. AE, MC, V. Mon–Fri 8am–10:30pm; Sat 9:30am–10:30pm; Sun 10:30am–6:30pm. Tube: Oxford Circus.

Suze in Mayfair PACIFIC RIM The owners of this wine bar attach equal importance to their food and to their impressive wine list. On the ground floor, you can enjoy fine wines along with a well-chosen selection of bar food. Upon arrival, a basket of homemade bread, along with olives, goat cheese, salami, and roasted peppers, is placed before you. The menu has been upgraded and made more sophisticated and appealing. Consider starting with the timbale of plum tomato and peppercorn mousse with an avocado salad, or else New Zealand green shell mussels with lime leaf, coriander, and ginger broth. For a main, we'd suggest fresh Australian fish with chips and a salad, or perhaps the New Zealand lamb filet with a vegetable medley.

41 N. Audley St. (btw. Upper Brook and Oxford Sts.), W1. ✆ **020/7491-3237.** www.suzeinmayfair.com. Reservations recommended. Main courses £11–£32. AE, MC, V. Mon–Sat noon–11pm. Tube: Bond St.

Marylebone

EXPENSIVE

Odin's ★ INTERNATIONAL Set adjacent to its slightly less expensive twin, Langan's Bistro, Odin's features ample space between tables and an eclectic decor that includes evocative paintings and Art Deco accessories. As other restaurants nearby have come and gone, the cookery here remains solid and reliable. The standard of fresh ingredients and well-prepared dishes is always maintained. The menu changes with the seasons: Typical fare may include forest mushrooms in brioche, braised leeks glazed with mustard and tomato sauce, roast duck with applesauce and sage-and-onion stuffing, or roast filet of sea bass with a juniper cream sauce.

27 Devonshire St., W1. ✆ **020/7935-7296.** www.langansrestaurants.co.uk. Reservations required. Fixed-price meal £33 for 2 courses, £37 for 3 courses. AE, DC, MC, V. Mon–Fri noon–2:30pm; Mon–Sat 6:30–11pm. Tube: Regent's Park.

Orrery ★★ FRENCH/INTERNATIONAL   On the second floor of the Conran Shop in Marylebone is one of London's classic French restaurants, featuring ingredients imported from France. Sea bass from the shores of Montpellier, olive oil from Maussane-les-Alpilles, mushrooms from the fields of Calais, and poultry from Bresse—they all turn up on a highly refined menu that changes seasonally to take advantage of the best produce. Our favorites among the first-rate dishes are the Bresse pigeon, served with savoy cabbage and mushroom ravioli, and the duckling with an endive tatin and *cèpe* (flap mushrooms) sauce. Everything has a brilliant, often whimsical touch, as evoked by the sautéed leeks in pumpkin oil. We ended with a cheese plate featuring a Banton goat cheese so fresh that it oozed onto the plate. On summer evenings, you can sit on a fourth-floor terrace while drinking and ordering light fare from the bar menu.

In the Conran Shop, 55 Marylebone High St., W1. ✆ **020/7616-8000.** www.orreryrestaurant.co.uk. Reservations required. Fixed-price 3-course lunch £29; fixed-price dinner £44 for 2 courses, £50 for 3 courses. AE, DC, MC, V. Daily noon–2:30pm and 6:30–10pm. Tube: Baker St.

Texture ★★ EUROPEAN   This extraordinary restaurant treats us to the sensuous flavors of a talented chef, Iceland-born Agnar Sverrisson, who worked for the celebrated Raymond Blanc at Le Manoir Aux Quat' Saisons outside Oxford. He is assisted by French-born Xaviar Rousset, acclaimed as the U.K.'s best sommelier. Their 60-seat restaurant and 30-seat champagne bar are the toast of London foodies. The chef's Icelandic roots are evident in such good-tasting signature dishes as lamb from Skagafjördur and Icelandic cod. Another specialty is chargrilled Anjou pigeon with a red-wine sauce and "bacon popcorn." Vegetables change with the season—in autumn, wild mushrooms, hazelnuts, and Umbrian black truffles dominate.

34 Portman St., W1. ✆ **020/7224-0028.** www.texture-restaurant.co.uk. Reservations required. Main courses £22–£29; fixed-price lunch £19 for 2 courses, £22 for 3 courses; tasting menu £59; fish tasting menu £53. AE, MC, V. Tues–Sat noon–2:30pm and 6:30–11pm. Tube: Marble Arch.

MODERATE

Galvin Bistrot de Luxe ★ FRENCH   Evoking the fabled bistros of Paris, this Gallic-inspired restaurant has brought foodies to what was once a gastro wasteland along Baker Street. Chris and Jeff Galvin, two brothers, provide straightforward French cuisine at a decent price (at least for London). The French classics appear in full-flavored combinations using the finest of seasonal ingredients. In an unpretentious setting, you can dine on a superb *soupe de poisons* (fish soup) or a classic endive salad with Roquefort, pear, and walnuts. That old-fashioned starter, salad of poached lamb's tongue with sauce ravigote, also appears on the menu. For robust eaters, there is an array of such dishes as roasted veal brains in *beurre noisette,* part of a platter that also includes roast rump of veal and melt-in-the-mouth braised veal cheeks.

66 Baker St., W1. ✆ **020/7935-4007.** www.galvinrestaurants.com. Reservations required. Main courses £13–£20; fixed-price menu £18. AE, MC, V. Daily noon–2:30pm; Mon–Wed 6–10:30pm; Thurs–Sat 6–11pm; Sun 6–9:30pm. Tube: Baker St.

Villandry ★ CONTINENTAL/INTERNATIONAL   Food lovers and gourmands flock to this food store, delicatessen, and restaurant, where racks of the world's finest meats, cheeses, and produce are displayed and changed virtually every hour. The best of the merchandise is whimsically transformed into the restaurant's menu choices. The setting is an oversize Edwardian-style storefront north of Oxford Circus. The inside is a kind of minimalist temple dedicated to the glories of fresh produce and esoteric foodstuffs. Ingredients here change so frequently that the menu is rewritten twice a day—during our latest visit, it proposed such perfectly crafted dishes as breast of duck, served with fresh spinach and a gratin of baby onions, and pan-fried turbot with deep-fried celery, artichoke hearts, and hollandaise sauce.

170 Great Portland St., W1. © **020/7631-3131.** www.villandry.com. Reservations recommended. Main courses £15–£23. AE, MC, V. Restaurant Mon–Sat noon–3pm and 6–10:30pm; Sun 11:30am–4pm. Food store Mon–Sat 8am–10pm; Sun 10am–4pm. Tube: Great Portland St.

St. James's
MODERATE

Quaglino's ★ CONTINENTAL Come here for fun, not culinary subtlety and finesse, and be prepared to wear your best duds. In 1993, noted restaurateur and designer Sir Terence Conran brought this restaurant—first established in 1929 by Giovanni Quaglino—into the postmodern age with a vital new decor. Menu items have been criticized for their quick preparation and standard format, but considering that on some nights up to 800 people might show up, the marvel is that this place functions as well as it does. That's not to say there isn't an occasional delay. The menu changes often, but your choice of appetizer might include wild mushroom and truffle soup or a goat-cheese tart with caramelized onions. For a main, you can settle for an old favorite—haddock and chips—or go for the whole roasted sea bass with braised fennel. The oyster selection is one of the best in central London. Although some diners shy away from organ meats these days, the English still order calves' liver with bacon here. Desserts are mostly favorites such as apple and blackberry crumble or sticky toffee pudding with walnut ice cream. *Note:* A mezzanine with bar features live jazz every night and Sunday at lunch.

16 Bury St., SW1. © **020/7930-6767.** www.quaglinos.co.uk. Reservations recommended. Main courses £14–£55; fixed-price menu (available only for lunch and pretheater dinner from 5:30–6:30pm) £15 for 2 courses, £20 for 3 courses. AE, DC, MC, V. Daily noon–3pm; Mon–Thurs 5:30pm–midnight; Fri–Sat 5:30pm–1am; Sun 5:30–11pm. Tube: Green Park.

Trafalgar Square
MODERATE

National Dining Rooms ENGLISH In the National Gallery, this dining choice lies over the foyer of the Sainsbury Wing, providing a panoramic view of fabled Trafalgar Square. Classic dishes using market-fresh ingredients go into starters such as warm watercress mousse with braised pearl onions or smoked mackerel pâté with apple and chicory. Try main dishes such as monkfish, mullet, and mussel stew or else baked lemon chicken with Savoy cabbage and creamed potatoes. The cheese selection from Great Britain is amazing in its variety, everything from traditionally aged Stilton to soft goat cheese from the Cotswolds. Finish off with one of the freshly baked cakes, such as layered chocolate or walnut and banana.

There is a **National Café** offshoot, in the basement of the main building, that makes a good choice for sandwiches, pastas, soups, and pastries.

In the National Gallery, Trafalgar Sq., WC2. © **020/7747-2525.** www.peytonandbyrne.com. 2-course menu £23; 3-course menu £26. AE, MC, V. Thurs–Tues 10am–5:30pm; Wed 10am–8:45pm. Tube: Charing Cross.

Portrait Restaurant ★ MODERN ENGLISH   This rooftop restaurant is a sought-after dining ticket on the fifth floor of the National Portrait Gallery's Ondaatje Wing. Along with the view (Nelson's Column, the London Eye, Big Ben, and the like), you get superb meals. Patrons usually go for lunch, not knowing that the kitchen is also open on Thursday and Friday nights. The chefs aren't afraid of simple preparations, mainly because they are assured of the excellence of their products. In spring, there's nothing finer than the green English asparagus. All of the main courses are filled with flavor. The high quality of the produce really shines through in such dishes as roast breast of guinea fowl with truffles and wild mushrooms, or pan-fried filet of Scotch salmon with bacon-and-onion potato cakes. For your "pudding," nothing beats the steamed chestnut and honey pudding with toffee and pecan sauce. The wine list features some organic choices.

In the National Portrait Gallery, St. Martin's Place, WC2. ℂ **020/7312-2490.** www.searcys.co.uk/national portraitgallery/101/restaurant. Reservations recommended. 2-course meal £15, 3-course meal £19. AE, MC, V. Daily 11:45am–2:45pm; Thurs–Fri 5:30–8:30pm. Tube: Leicester Sq. or Charing Cross.

Piccadilly Circus & Leicester Square
EXPENSIVE

Fung Shing ★★ CANTONESE   In a city where the competition is stiff, Fung Shing emerges as London's finest Cantonese restaurant. Firmly established as a culinary landmark, it dazzles with classic and nouvelle Cantonese dishes. Look for the seasonal specials. Some of the dishes may be a bit experimental—notably stir-fried fresh milk with scrambled egg white—but you'll feel right at home with the soft-shell crab sautéed in a light batter and served with tiny rings of red-hot chili and deep-fried garlic. Chinese gourmets come here for the fried intestines; you may prefer the hotpot of stewed duck with yam. The spicy sea bass and the stir-fried crispy chicken are worthy choices, too. There are more than 150 dishes from which to choose, and most are moderate in price.

15 Lisle St., WC2. ℂ **020/7437-1539.** www.fungshing.co.uk. Reservations required. Main courses £8–£26. AE, DC, MC, V. Daily noon–11:30pm. Tube: Leicester Sq.

The Ivy ★★ MODERN ENGLISH/INTERNATIONAL   Effervescent and sophisticated, the Ivy is the dining choice of visiting theatrical luminaries and has been intimately associated with the theater district ever since it opened in 1911. With its ersatz 1930s look and tiny bar near the entrance, this fun spot hums with the energy of London's glamour scene. The kitchen has a solid appreciation for fresh ingredients and a talent for preparation. Some appetizers may be a bit much, like wild rabbit salad with black pudding, whereas others are more appealing, such as Bang Bang chicken. The crispy duck and watercress salad is another favorite. For years, the 14-ounce Dover sole has been enjoyed by celebrities and wannabes alike. Mains feature a chargrilled fish of the day, and carnivores take to the sautéed veal kidneys or the escalope of veal Holstein. The Ivy Hamburger continues to appear on the menu. Desserts are familiar, including chocolate pudding soufflé or rhubarb sponge pudding with custard.

1–5 West St., WC2. ℂ **020/7836-4751.** www.the-ivy.co.uk. Reservations required. Main courses £8–£40; Sat–Sun fixed-price lunch £29. AE, DC, MC, V. Mon–Sat noon–3pm; Sun noon–3:30pm; daily 5:30pm–midnight (last order). Tube: Leicester Sq.

J. Sheekey ★ SEAFOOD   English culinary tradition lives on at this fish joint, long a favorite of West End actors. The jellied eels that delighted Laurence Olivier and Vivien Leigh are still here, along with an array of fresh oysters from the coasts of Ireland and Brittany, plus that Victorian favorite, fried whitebait. Sheekey's fish pie remains on the menu, as does Dover sole. The old "mushy" peas still appear, but the chefs also offer the likes of steamed organic sea beet. Opt for the traditional dishes or specials based on the fresh catch of the day. The double chocolate pudding soufflé is a delight, and many favorite puddings remain.

28–32 St. Martin's Court, WC2. ✆ **020/7240-2565.** www.j-sheekey.co.uk. Reservations recommended. Main courses £13–£40. AE, DC, MC, V. Mon–Sat noon–3pm and 5:30pm–midnight; Sun noon–3:30pm and 6pm–midnight. Tube: Leicester Sq.

MODERATE

Cork & Bottle Wine Bar ★★ 🍷 INTERNATIONAL   Don Hewitson, a connoisseur of fine wines for more than 30 years, presides over this trove of blissful fermentation. The ever-changing wine list features an excellent selection of Beaujolais Crus from Alsace, 30 selections from Australia, 30 champagnes, and a good selection of California labels. If you want something to nibble, the most successful dish is a raised cheese-and-ham pie, with a cream cheese–like filling and crisp, well-buttered pastry—not your typical quiche. There's also chicken and apple salad, black pudding, Mediterranean prawns with garlic and asparagus, lamb in ale, and a Thai chicken-wings platter.

44–46 Cranbourn St., WC2. ✆ **020/7734-7807.** www.corkandbottle.net. Reservations not accepted after 6:30pm. Fixed-price menu £11–£14; main courses £8–£16. AE, DC, MC, V. Mon–Sat 11am–midnight; Sun noon–11pm. Tube: Leicester Sq.

Soho

MODERATE

Arbutus ★ 🍷 BRITISH/CONTINENTAL   This Soho eatery was the brainchild of Anthony Demetre and Will Smith, who have operated other Michelin-starred restaurants elsewhere. They now bring their quality cooking and service to the heart of Soho in rather unpretentious surroundings. They don't please all diners, but not for lack of effort. Sometimes they use parts of the pig not seen since the days of Henry VIII—pig's head, for example, which may be too rich for diners who'd prefer the wintery beef daube in a dark but flavorful sauce. Ever had a squid and mackerel burger? It's an oddity but won't put McDonald's out of business. Other winning dishes include smoked eel risotto, Welsh breast of lamb, and pork rillettes with a celeriac rémoulade. A traditional bouillabaisse also scores points (it's made with regular fish, not shellfish).

63–64 Frith St., W1. ✆ **020/7734-4545.** www.arbutusrestaurant.co.uk. Reservations required. Main courses £15–£20; 3-course lunch £17; pre- and post-theater fixed-price menu £19. AE, DC, MC, V. Mon–Sat noon–2:30pm and 5–11pm; Sun noon–3pm and 5:30–10:30pm. Tube: Tottenham Court Rd.

Bob Bob Ricard ENGLISH   From the early morning to the wee hours (a rarity in London), this eatery serves a sophisticated but old-fashioned version of English comfort food. How many places in London can you find a prune milkshake on the menu? You can start with quail eggs and go on to poached Loch Duart salmon. Sir Winston Churchill, should he return, might delight in the pork cheeks braised in port or the 28-day aged Aberdeenshire beef cutlet. For dessert, we'd opt for the piña colada soufflé flavored with 7-year-old Havana rum. At tea time, crumpets and tea cakes are served. Why not a spread of rose-petal jelly on your crumpet? For some diners, the decor evokes Liberace's living room.

1 Upper James St., W1. ☎ **020/3145-1000.** www.bobbobricard.com. Reservations not needed. English breakfast £14; main dishes £13–£29. MC, V. Mon–Fri 7am–1am; Sat 10am–3am; Sun 10am–midnight. Tube: Piccadilly Circus.

Criterion ★ FRENCH/MODERN ENGLISH   Designed by Thomas Verity in the 1870s, this palatial neo-Byzantine mirrored marble hall is a glamorous backdrop for a superb cuisine, served under a golden ceiling, with theatrical peacock-blue draperies. The menu is wide-ranging, offering everything from Paris brasserie food to "nouvelle-classical," a combination of classic French cooking techniques with some of the lighter, more experimental leanings of modern French cuisine. The food is excellent, though it falls short of sublime. Start with beef carpaccio in a mustard dressing or else spaghetti with clams and chili peppers, to be followed by such fish as wild sea bass with a shellfish fondue or else roast suckling pig in applesauce.

224 Piccadilly, W1. ☎ **020/7930-0488.** www.criterionrestaurant.com. Main courses £16–£26; 2- to 3-course lunch special £17–£20. AE, MC, V. Mon–Sat noon–2:30pm and 5:30–11:30pm; Sun noon–3:30pm and 5:30–10:30pm. Tube: Piccadilly Circus.

Hakkasan ★ 🍴CHINESE   Asian mystique and pastiche are found in this offbeat restaurant in a seedy alley off Tottenham Court Road. This is another London venture created by Alan Yau, who became a citywide dining legend because of his Wagamama noodle bars. Come here for great dim sum and tantalizing cocktails. Feast on such dishes as *har gau* (steamed prawn dumplings) and strips of tender barbecued pork. The spring roll is refreshing with the addition of fried mango and a delicate prawn-and-scallop filling. Steamed scallop *shumai* (dumplings) with tobiko caviar are fresh and meltingly soft. Desserts in most of London's Chinese restaurants are hardly memorable, but the offerings here are an exception to that rule, especially the layered banana sponge with chocolate cream.

8 Hanway Place, W1. ☎ **020/7927-7000.** www.hakkasan.com. Reservations recommended. Main courses £10–£68. AE, MC, V. Lunch Mon–Fri noon–3pm, Sat noon–5pm; dinner Mon–Sat 6–11:30pm, Sun 6–11pm. Tube: Tottenham Court Rd.

Randall & Aubin ★ 🍴SEAFOOD   Past the sex boutiques of Soho you stumble upon this real discovery, whose consultant is TV chef Ed Baines, an ex-Armani model who turned this butcher shop into a hip champagne-and-oyster bar. The impressive shellfish display of the night's goodies is the "bait" used to lure you inside. Chances are you won't be disappointed. Loch Fyne oysters, lobster with chips, pan-fried fresh scallops—the parade of seafood we've sampled here, in each case, has been genuinely excellent. The *soupe de poisson* (fish soup) is the best in Soho, or else you might want to start with delightful Japanese-style fish cakes or fresh Cornish crab. Yes, they still have Sevruga caviar for Lotto winners. For the rare meat-only eater, there is a limited array of dishes such as a perfectly roasted chicken on the spit that has been flavored with fresh herbs. The lemon tart with crème fraîche rounds out a perfect meal.

16 Brewer St., W1. ☎ **020/7287-4447.** www.randallandaubin.com. Reservations not accepted. Main courses £10–£29. AE, DC, MC, V. Daily 10am–11pm. Tube: Piccadilly Circus or Leicester Sq.

INEXPENSIVE

OSatsuma JAPANESE   This funky Japanese canteen is all the rage in London. The clean lines, stark white walls, and long wooden tables suggest an upmarket youth hostel. But patrons come for good food at reasonable prices. The restaurant is ideal for a pretheater visit. Your meal comes in a lacquered bento box on a matching tray. Try the chicken teriyaki or fresh chunks of tuna and salmon. The dumplings are excellent, as is the miso soup. A specialty is the large bowl of seafood ramen, with noodles swimming in a well-seasoned broth studded with mussels, scallops, and prawns. Tofu steaks are a delight, as are udon noodles with wok-fried chicken and fresh vegetables. You can finish with deep-fried tempura ice cream.

56 Wardour St., W1. ✆ **020/7437-8338.** www.osatsuma.com. Reservations not accepted. Main courses £6–£16. AE, DC, MC, V. Mon–Tues noon–11pm; Wed–Thurs noon–11:30pm; Fri–Sat noon–midnight; Sun noon–10:30pm. Tube: Piccadilly Circus or Leicester Sq.

Shampers CONTINENTAL   This is a favorite of West End wine-bar aficionados. In addition to the street-level wine bar serving snacks, there's a more formal basement-level restaurant. In either venue, you can order such main dishes as grilled calves' liver with bacon, chips, and salad; pan-fried prawns with ginger, garlic, and chili; and platters of cheeses. Salads are popular, including the spicy chicken salad or the grilled eggplant salad with tomato, avocado, buffalo mozzarella, and pesto. The platter of Irish mussels cooked in a cream-and-tarragon sauce is everybody's favorite. The restaurant is now open in the evening, but the wine bar also serves an extensive menu, offering fresh squid, tuna steak, pan-fried tiger prawns, free-range chicken, and other tasty specialties. There is also a daily specials menu.

4 Kingly St. (btw. Carnaby and Regent sts.), W1. ✆ **020/7437-1692.** www.shampers.net. Reservations recommended. Main courses £9–£15. AE, DC, MC, V. Restaurant and wine bar Mon–Sat noon–11pm. Closed Dec 24–Jan 2. Tube: Oxford Circus or Piccadilly Circus.

Bloomsbury

EXPENSIVE

Pied à Terre ★★★ FRENCH   A meticulously rendered French cuisine is served at the most acclaimed restaurant in Bloomsbury. The interior is stylish, with intimate tables; we prefer those in the rear. Chef Shane Osborn cleverly combines a classical technique with his own modern inventiveness in the kitchen, demonstrating a flair for flavorful "marriage" of ingredients. Try his seared and poached foie gras with borlotti beans or the steamed halibut with a tomato fondue. Black leg chicken breast from Landes arrives with a garlic purée, or else you can order kid goat with caramelized endive and roasted shallots, or certainly the roasted Devonshire loin of venison with a quince purée and walnuts. New- and old-world wines are on the *carte*.

34 Charlotte St., W1. ✆ **020/7636-1178.** www.pied-a-terre.co.uk. Set-price 2-course lunch £24; 2-course pretheater dinner £40, 2-course dinner £58, 3-course dinner £72, 10-course tasting menu £87, 10-course vegetarian tasting menu £77. Mon–Fri 12:15–2:30pm; Mon–Sat 6:15–11pm. Tube: Goodge St.

INEXPENSIVE

Salt Yard ★ SPANISH/ITALIAN   Calling itself a "charcuterie bar and restaurant," this is a fashionable choice with a bustling downstairs. The chefs here specialize in affordable plates of tasty Spanish and Italian dishes that are often shared. This joint is far superior to most tapas houses. How many places do you know that serve truffle-laced honey? Its Serrano ham, 18 months in "curing," is arguably the finest in London. Braised beef cheek comes with broad beans, the fresh squid arrives with aioli, and zucchini flowers are stuffed with Monte Enebro cheese and drizzled with honey. Bar snacks are also served.

54 Goodge St., W1. ☎ **020/7637-0657.** www.saltyard.co.uk. Tapas £3.50–£8; charcuterie platters £7.60–£13. AE, MC, V. Mon–Fri noon–11pm (3–6pm bar menu only); Sat 5–11pm. Tube: Goodge St.

Wagamama JAPANESE   This noodle joint, in a basement just off New Oxford Street, is noisy and overcrowded, and you'll have to wait in line for a table. It calls itself a "nondestination food station" and caters to some 1,200 customers a day. Many dishes are built around ramen noodles paired with your choice of chicken, beef, or salmon. Try the tasty *gyoza,* light dumplings filled with vegetables or chicken. Vegetarian dishes are available, but skip the so-called Korean-style dishes.

4 Streatham St., WC1. ☎ **020/7323-9223.** www.wagamama.com. Reservations not accepted. Main courses £7–£11. AE, MC, V. Mon–Sat noon–11pm; Sun noon–10pm. Tube: Tottenham Court Rd.

Kings Cross

MODERATE

Acorn House Restaurant ★ 🍴 BRITISH   Near St. Pancras station, this is one of the most eco-friendly restaurants in London, with chefs who are dedicated to healthy eating from fresh seasonal menus. At weekday lunches, you face a large display of plates and trays filled with fresh vegetables, cured meats, fish, chilled salads, ripe fruits, and homemade breads and desserts—all laid out on a counter for your selection. A hot menu can be cooked to order as well. Soups, takeout sandwiches, and salads to go are also available. Dinner is more formal, with a larger and more structured menu, including four seasonal starters, three "midcourses," and four main dishes such as duck confit with braised bok choy or basil-scented sea bream with pancetta.

69 Swinton St., WC1. ☎ **020/7812-1842.** www.acornhouserestaurant.com. Reservations recommended. Main courses £13–£18; fixed-price menus £29–£40. MC, V. Mon–Fri noon–3pm and 6–10pm; Sat 6–9:30pm. Tube: Kings Cross.

Holborn

MODERATE

Bountiful Cow ★★ STEAK   This 1960s pub in Holborn, between the City of London and the West End, has been turned into a "public house" devoted to top beef. The owner, Roxy Beaujolais, is the author of the classic pub cookbook *Home from the Inn Contented.* It's harder to find better steaks and burgers in the Holborn district, or even far beyond. All of the steaks come from select beef hung for at least 2 weeks. Five cuts of beefsteak are featured on the menu: onglet or flank steak, rib-eye, sirloin, filet, and T-bone. These steaks are tender and full of flavor. You can select from such sauces as béarnaise or green peppercorn. Vegetarian dishes and daily market specials are also served. You can down cask-conditioned ales, such as Adams, taking in such poster art as Barbara Stanwyck and Ronald Reagan in *Cattle Queen of Montana.*

51 Eagle St., WC1. ☎ **020/7404-0200.** www.thebountifulcow.co.uk. Reservations required. Main courses £9.50–£21. AE, MC, V. Mon–Sat 11am–11pm; Sun noon–8pm. Tube: Holborn.

Covent Garden & the Strand

EXPENSIVE

Rules ★ TRADITIONAL ENGLISH   If you're looking for the most quintessentially British restaurant in town, eat here. London's oldest restaurant was established in 1798 as an oyster bar; today, the antler-filled Edwardian dining rooms exude nostalgia. You can order such classics as Irish or Scottish oysters, jugged hare, and mussels. Game and fish dishes are offered from mid-August to February or March, including wild Scottish salmon, wild sea trout, wild Highland red deer, and game birds such as grouse, snipe, partridge, pheasant, and woodcock. As a finale, the "great puddings" continue to impress.

35 Maiden Lane, WC2. ✆ **020/7836-5314.** www.rules.co.uk. Reservations recommended. Main courses £17-£28. AE, DC, MC, V. Mon-Sat noon-11:30pm; Sun noon-10:30pm. Tube: Covent Garden.

Simpson's-in-the-Strand ★★ ☺ TRADITIONAL & MODERN ENGLISH   Simpson's is more of an institution than a restaurant. Long a family favorite with lots of large tables, it has been in business since 1828, and as a result of a recent £2-million renovation, it's now better than ever, with its Adam paneling, crystal, and an army of grandly formal waiters serving traditional English fare. The owners object to the word "menu" here—"too French." It's called "bill of fare" instead. Men and women can now dine together, though before 1904, such an "outrage" was forbidden. Through the years, the dress code has become more relaxed—in other words, Elizabeth Taylor in trousers would no longer be barred from entering. Famous diners of yesterday include everyone from Charles Dickens to Charles Chaplin, and the restaurant is often used as a setting for films, including Alfred Hitchcock's *Sabotage*. Most diners agree that Simpson's serves the best roasts in London, an array that includes roast sirloin of beef; roast saddle of mutton with red-currant jelly; roast Aylesbury duckling; and steak, kidney, and mushroom pie.

100 Strand (next to the Savoy Hotel), WC2. ✆ **020/7836-9112.** www.simpsonsinthestrand.co.uk. Reservations required. Main courses £16-£33; 3-course fixed-price pretheater dinner £30; 2-course meal £25; breakfast items £12-£21. AE, DC, MC, V. Mon-Fri 7:15-10:30am; Mon-Sat 12:15-2:45pm and 5:45-10:45pm; Sun noon-2:45pm and 5:45-9pm. Tube: Charing Cross or Embankment.

MODERATE

Belgo Centraal BELGIAN   Chaos reigns supreme in this cavernous basement, where mussels *marinières* with fries, plus 100 Belgian beers, are the raison d'être. Take a freight elevator past the busy kitchen and into a converted cellar, divided into two large eating areas. One section is a beer hall seating about 250; the menu here is the same as in the restaurant, but you don't need reservations. The restaurant side has three nightly seatings: 5:30, 7:30, and 10pm. Although heaps of fresh mussels are the big attraction, you can also opt for fresh Scottish salmon, roast chicken, a perfectly done steak, or one of the vegetarian specialties. Gargantuan plates of wild boar sausages arrive with *stoemp*—Belgian mashed spuds and cabbage. Belgian stews, called *waterzooï*, are also served.

50 Earlham St., WC2. ✆ **020/7813-2233.** www.belgo-restaurants.co.uk. Reservations required in restaurant. Main courses £11-£13. AE, DC, MC, V. Mon-Thurs noon-11pm; Fri-Sat noon-11:30pm; Sun noon-10:30pm. Closed Dec 25. Tube: Covent Garden.

Porters English Restaurant ★★ ☺ TRADITIONAL ENGLISH   The seventh earl of Bradford serves "real English food at affordable prices." He succeeds notably—and not just because Lady Bradford turned over her carefully guarded recipe for banana-and-ginger steamed pudding. This comfortable two-storied restaurant is family friendly, informal, and lively. It specializes in classic English pies, including fish, lamb and apricot, and, of course, bangers and mash. The overwhelming favorite is steak, Guinness, and mushroom pie. Main courses are so generous—and accompanied by vegetables and side dishes—that you hardly need appetizers. The owners have also added grilled English fare to the menu, including sirloin and lamb steaks and marinated chicken. To finish, Porters is famous for its mouthwatering puddings. Where else can you find a good spotted dick these days? It's a steamed syrup sponge cake with sultanas (raisins). Another favorite is a dark-chocolate-chip pudding made with steamed chocolate sponge, chocolate chips, and chocolate custard. Even the ice cream is homemade. The bar does quite a few exotic cocktails, as well as beer, wine, and English mead. A traditional English tea is served from 2:30 to 5:30pm.

17 Henrietta St., WC2. ✆ **020/7836-6466.** www.porters.uk.com. Reservations recommended. Main courses £11–£19; fixed-price lunch and pretheater menu £12; fixed-price dinner menu £23. AE, MC, V. Mon–Sat noon–11:30pm; Sun noon–10:30pm. Tube: Covent Garden or Leicester Sq.

Westminster/Victoria

EXPENSIVE

Shepherd's Restaurant TRADITIONAL ENGLISH   Some observers claim that many of the inner workings of the English government operate from the precincts of this conservative, likable restaurant. Set in the shadow of Westminster's Clock Tower, it enjoys a regular clientele of barristers, members of Parliament, and their constituents from far-flung districts. So synchronized is this place to the goings-on at Parliament that a Division Bell rings in the dining room, calling MPs back to the House of Commons when it's time to vote. Even the decor is designed to make them feel at home, with leather banquettes, sober 19th-century accessories, and a worthy collection of European portraits and landscapes. The menu reflects years of English culinary tradition, and dishes are prepared intelligently, with fresh ingredients. In addition to the classic roast, you'll find a cream-based mussel stew, hot salmon-and-potato salad with dill dressing, salmon and prawn fish cakes in spinach sauce, and roast leg of lamb with mint sauce.

Marsham Court, Marsham St. (at Page St.), SW1. ✆ **020/7834-9552.** www.langansrestaurants.co.uk. Reservations recommended. Fixed-price menu £33 for 2 courses, £37 for 3 courses. AE, DC, MC, V. Mon–Fri noon–3pm and 6–11pm (last order at 11pm). Tube: Pimlico or St. James's.

MODERATE

Rex Whistler Restaurant ★★ 🍴 MODERN ENGLISH   The Tate Britain's restaurant is particularly attractive to wine fanciers, offering what may be the best bargains for superior wines anywhere in Britain. Bordeaux and burgundies are in abundance, and the management keeps the markup between 40% and 65%, rather than the 100% to 200% added in most restaurants. In fact, the prices here are lower than they are in most wine shops. Wine begins at £15 per bottle or £4 per glass. Oenophiles frequently come for lunch, when the restaurant offers an English menu that changes about every month. Dishes might include fish of the day fresh from the Newlyn boats in Cornwall, roast partridge with bread sauce, and Welsh lamb with caramelized sweetbreads. One critic found the staff and diners as traditional "as a Gainsborough landscape." Access to the restaurant is through the museum's main entrance on Millbank.

In the Tate Britain, Millbank, SW1. © **020/7887-8825.** www.tate.org.uk. Reservations recommended. Fixed-price menu £16 for 2 courses, £20 for 3 courses; breakfast items from £4; afternoon tea £7.25. AE, DC, MC, V. Mon–Fri 11:30am–3pm; Sat–Sun 10am–3pm; daily 3:30–5pm for afternoon tea. Tube: Pimlico. Bus: 77 or 88.

INEXPENSIVE

Jenny Lo's Teahouse CANTONESE/SZECHUAN   London's noodle dives don't get much better than this. Before its decline, Ken Lo's Memories of China offered the best Chinese dining in London. The late Ken Lo, whose grandfather was the Chinese ambassador to the court of St. James, made his reputation as a cookbook author. Jenny Lo is Ken's daughter, and her father taught her many of his culinary secrets. Now Belgravia matrons and young professionals come here for perfectly prepared, reasonably priced fare. Ken Lo cookbooks contribute to the dining-room decor of black refectory tables set with paper napkins and chopsticks. Opt for such fare as a vermicelli rice noodle dish (a large plate of noodles topped with grilled chicken breast and Chinese mushrooms) or white noodles with minced pork. Rounding out the menu are stuffed Peking dumplings, chili-garnished spicy prawns, and wonton soup with slithery dumplings. The black-bean seafood noodle dish is a delight, as is the chili-beef soup.

14 Eccleston St., SW1 9LT. © **020/7259-0399.** www.jennylo.co.uk. Reservations not accepted. Main courses £7–£8.50. No credit cards. Mon–Fri noon–3pm; Mon–Sat 6–10pm. Tube: Victoria.

The City of London
EXPENSIVE

L'Anima ★★ ITALIAN   The name of this restaurant means "soul" in Italian, and that's what Francesco Mazzei puts into his creative cuisine. When his restaurant opened in 2009, several organizations voted it best newcomer of the year, and his standards seem even higher as each year goes by. Many of the dishes are native to his homeland in the south of Italy, especially Calabria, Puglia, and Sicily. From the starters, such as octopus with cannellini, to the homemade soups, risottos, and pastas, his cuisine reaches the summit. So do his main courses, including sea-salt-crusted sea bass, Sicilian rabbit, and especially spit-roasted leg of lamb or slow-roasted black pig belly in a cantarata sauce. Finish off with one of the luscious desserts, like the cappuccino tiramisu.

1 Snowden St., Broadgate West, EC2. © **020/7422-7000.** www.lanima.co.uk. Main courses £12–£32; set lunch £24 for 2 courses, £27 for 3 courses. AE, DC, MC, V. Mon–Fri 11:45am–1am; Sat 5:30–11pm. Tube: Liverpool St.

Prism ★★ MODERN ENGLISH   This restaurant attracts London's movers and shakers, at least those with demanding palates. In the former Bank of New York, Harvey Nichols—known for his chic department store in Knightsbridge—took this 1920s neo-Grecian hall and installed Mies van der Rohe chairs in chrome and lipstick-red leather. In this setting, traditional English dishes from the north are given a light touch—try the tempura of Whitby cod or cream of Jerusalem artichoke soup with roasted scallops and truffle oil. For a first course, opt for a salad composed of flecks of Parmesan cheese seasoning savoy cabbage and Parma ham. The menu reveals the chef has traveled a bit—note such dishes as Moroccan-spiced chicken livers served with a lemon-and-parsley couscous.

147 Leadenhall St., EC3. ✆ **020/7256-3875.** www.harveynichols.com. Reservations required. Main courses £13–£37. AE, DC, DISC, MC, V. Mon–Fri 11:30am–3pm and 6–10pm. Tube: Bank or Monument.

MODERATE

Café Spice Namasté ★★ INDIAN This is our favorite Indian restaurant in London, where the competition is stiff. It's cheerfully housed in a landmark Victorian hall near Tower Bridge, just east of the Tower of London. The Parsi chef, Cyrus Todiwala, is a former resident of Goa (a Portuguese territory absorbed by India long ago), where he learned many of his culinary secrets. His southern and northern Indian dishes often show a strong Portuguese influence. Chicken and lamb are prepared a number of ways, from mild to spicy hot. As a novelty, Todiwala occasionally even offers a menu of emu dishes; when marinated, the meat is rich and spicy and evocative of lamb. Emu is not the only dining oddity here. Ever have ostrich gizzard kabob, alligator tikka, or minced moose, bison, or blue boar? Many patrons journey here just for the complex chicken curry known as *xacutti*.

16 Prescot St., E1. ✆ **020/7488-9242.** www.cafespice.co.uk. Reservations required. Main courses £5–£19. AE, DC, MC, V. Mon–Fri noon–3pm and 6:15–10:30pm; Sat 6:30–10:30pm. Tube: Tower Hill.

Cinnamon Kitchen ★ INDIAN In a bright, airy space converted from a historic East India Company spice warehouse, this restaurant near Liverpool Street has been compared to a New York steakhouse in atmosphere. But the food is strictly from India, showcasing first-rate ingredients. The standard of refined cuisine makes this one of the best Indian restaurants of London, and the waitstaff is top of the line, too. You can pop in throughout the day for a spicy breakfast or brunch and stick around for lunch or dinner from the Indian grill and tandoor bar. There is also an all-weather alfresco terrace. The list of starters—one of the best in the City—includes duck with sesame and tamarind glaze. This could be followed by such mains as black leg chicken with fresh fenugreek or tandoori king prawns with kedgeree. The sides are especially good, including a selection of three Indian breads.

9 Devonshire Sq., EC21. ✆ **020/7626-5000.** www.cinnamon-kitchen.com. Reservations recommended. Main courses £8–£20; set menus £15 for 2 courses, £18 for 3 courses. AE, MC, V. Mon–Fri 11am–midnight; Sat 6pm–midnight. Tube: Liverpool St.

Club Gascon ★★ 🍴 FRENCH This slice of southwestern France serves such tasty treats as foie gras, Armagnac, and duck confit. Chef Pascal Aussignac is all the rage in London, ever since he opened his bistro next to the meat market in Smithfield. He dedicates the place to his favorite ingredient: foie gras. Foie gras appears in at least nine different incarnations, and most of the first-class ingredients are imported from France. His menu is uniquely divided into these categories: the Salt Route, Ocean, and Kitchen Garden. The best way to dine here is to arrive in a party of four or five and share the small dishes, each harmoniously balanced and full of flavor, and each accompanied by a carefully selected glass of wine. After a foie gras pigout, proceed to such main courses as a heavenly quail served with pear and rosemary honey. A cassoulet of morels and truffles transforms a plain but perfectly cooked steak.

57 West Smithfield, EC1. ✆ **020/7796-0600.** www.clubgascon.com. Reservations required. Main courses £13–£22. AE, MC, V. Mon–Fri noon–2pm and 7–10pm; Sat 7–10:30pm. Tube: Barbican.

INEXPENSIVE

Ye Olde Cheshire Cheese ☺ TRADITIONAL ENGLISH   The foundation of this carefully preserved building was laid in the 13th century, and it holds the most famous of the old City of London chophouses and pubs. Established in 1667, it claims to be the spot where Dr. Samuel Johnson (who lived nearby) entertained admirers with his acerbic wit. Charles Dickens and other literary lions also patronized the place. Later, many of the ink-stained journalists and scandalmongers of 19th- and early-20th-century Fleet Street made it their watering hole. You'll find five bars and two dining rooms here. The house specialties include Ye Famous Pudding (steak, kidney, mushrooms, and game) and Scottish roast beef with Yorkshire pudding and horseradish sauce. Sandwiches, salads, and favorites such as steak-and-kidney pie are also available, as are dishes such as Dover sole. The Cheshire is the best and safest venue to introduce your children to an English pub.

Wine Office Court, 145 Fleet St., EC4. ✆ **020/7353-6170.** Main courses £8–£12. AE, DC, MC, V. Meals Mon–Fri noon–10pm; Sat noon–2:30pm and 6–9:30pm; Sun noon–2:30pm. Drinks and bar snacks Mon–Sat 11am–11pm; Sun noon–6pm. Tube: St. Paul's or Blackfriars.

Docklands

EXPENSIVE

Butlers Wharf Chop House ★ TRADITIONAL ENGLISH   Of the four restaurants housed in Butler's Wharf, this one is the closest to Tower Bridge. It was modeled after a large boathouse, with banquettes, lots of exposed wood, flowers, candles, and windows overlooking Tower Bridge and the Thames. Dishes are largely adaptations of English recipes, such as fish and chips with mushy peas, steak-and-kidney pudding with oysters, and roast pork loin with applesauce. The bar features several English wines, plus a half-dozen French clarets by the jug.

36E Shad Thames, Butler's Wharf, SE1. ✆ **020/7403-3403.** www.chophouse.co.uk. Reservations recommended. Main courses £14–£20; fixed-price lunch £25 for 2 courses, £28 for 3 courses. AE, DC, MC, V. Mon–Fri noon–3pm; Sat–Sun noon–4pm; Mon–Sat 6–11pm (until 10pm May–Oct); Sun 6–10pm. Tube: Tower Hill or London Bridge.

MODERATE

Bengal Clipper ★ INDIAN   This former spice warehouse by the Thames serves what it calls "India's most remarkable dishes." The likable and often animated restaurant is outfitted with cream-colored walls, tall columns, and modern artwork inspired by the Moghul Dynasty's depictions of royal figures, soaring trees, and well-trained elephants. Seven windows afford sweeping views over the industrialized Thames-side neighborhood, and live piano music plays in the background. The cuisine includes many vegetarian choices derived from the former Portuguese colony of Goa and the once-English colony of Bengal. There is a zestiness and spice to the food, but it's never overpowering. A tasty specialty is stuffed *murgh masala*, a tender breast of chicken with potatoes, onions, and apricots. The duckling (off the bone) comes in a tangy sauce with a citrus bite. One of the finest dishes we tasted in northern India is served here and has lost nothing in the transfer: marinated lamb simmered in cream with cashew nuts.

11-12 Cardamom Bldgs., Shad Thames, Butler's Wharf, SE1. ✆ **020/7357-9001.** www.bengalclipper. co.uk. Reservations recommended. Main courses £8–£14; set menu £15 (available July–Apr); Sun lunch buffet £10. AE, DC, MC, V. Mon–Sat noon–2:30pm and 6–11:30pm; Sun noon–4pm and 6–11pm. Tube: Tower Hill.

South Bank

MODERATE

Cantina Vinopolis ★ 🏛 CONTINENTAL   Not far from the re-created Globe Theatre of Shakespeare's heyday, this place has been called a "Walk-Through Wine Atlas." In the revitalized Bankside area, south of the Thames near Southwark Cathedral, this bricked, walled, and high-vaulted brasserie was converted from long-abandoned Victorian railway arches. Inside, you can visit both the Vinopolis Wine Gallery and the Cantina Restaurant. Although many come here just to drink wine, the food is prepared with quality ingredients (very fresh), and the menu is sensibly priced. Start with a bit of heaven such as the pea and ham soup. Pan-fried snapper, with crushed new potatoes and salsa verde, won us over. A rump of lamb was tender and perfectly flavored and served with a polenta cake. Many of the dishes have the good country taste of a trattoria you'd find in southern Italy. Naturally, the wine list is the biggest in the U.K.

1 Bank End, SE1. ✆ **0870/899-8856.** www.cantinavinopolis.com. Reservations required. Main courses £13–£23; 2-course menu £26, 3-course menu £30. AE, DC, MC, V. Mon–Wed 6–11:30pm; Thurs noon–3pm and 6–10:30pm; Fri–Sat noon–10:30pm; Sun noon–4pm. Tube: London Bridge.

Oxo Tower Restaurant ★ INTERNATIONAL   In the South Bank complex, on the eighth floor of the Art Deco Oxo Tower Wharf, you'll find this dining sensation operated by the department store Harvey Nichols. Down the street from the rebuilt Globe Theatre, this 140-seat restaurant could be visited for its view alone, but the food is also stellar. In a chic 1930s-style decor, you'll enjoy a sweeping view of St. Paul's Cathedral and the City of London, all the way to the Houses of Parliament. The cuisine is rich and prepared with finesse. Menu items change based on the season and the market. Count on a modern interpretation of British cookery, as well as the English classics. The fish is incredibly fresh here. The whole sea bass for two is delectable, as is the roast rump of lamb with split pea, mint purée, and balsamic vinegar sauce. We were also impressed with the roast filet of plaice with olive oil and truffle cabbage cream.

22 Barge House St., SE1. ✆ **020/7803-3888.** www.harveynichols.com. Fixed-price 3-course lunch £23–£29; dinner main courses £20–£32. AE, DC, MC, V. Mon–Sat noon–2:30pm and 6–11pm; Sun noon–3pm and 6:30–10pm. Tube: Blackfriars or Waterloo.

Knightsbridge

EXPENSIVE

Amaya ★ INDIAN   This chic restaurant, a hot dining ticket, is credited with introducing the small-plates concept to Indian food. Dishes are shared, hopefully with a party of friends. This is no mere curry house, but rather an ambitious restaurant with skilled chefs standing over grills and tandoor ovens in an eye-catching open kitchen. After devouring the rock oysters in a ginger-studded coconut sauce, we knew we were in for a special meal. Our table shared grilled baby eggplant sprinkled with mango powder; chicken tikka, one of the signature dishes; fork-tender lamb chops; and beautifully spiced lobster. Vegetarians will delight in the tandoor-cooked broccoli in a yogurt sauce or the artichoke biryani (basmati rice cooked with spices) baked in a pastry-sealed pot. For dessert, try the fresh pomegranate granita, which is sugar-free.

Halkin Arcade, Motcomb St., SW1. © **020/7823-1166.** www.amaya.biz. Reservations required. Main courses £10–£36; set-price lunch £16–£25; set-price dinner £45. AE, DC, MC, V. Mon–Sat 12:30–2:15pm and 6:30–11:30pm; Sun 12:45–2:45pm and 6–10:30pm. Tube: Knightsbridge.

MODERATE

Racine FRENCH   The chef, Henry Harris, may be as English as they get, but the cuisine at this bustling French brasserie puts you across the Channel in Paris. Francophiles flock to this bistro with wooden floors, dark-leather banquettes, and black-and-white-clad waiters. Seasonal dishes are featured on the ever-changing menu composed by Harris, who serves what he loves to cook and eat. That means such bistro favorites as rabbit in mustard sauce or salad lyonnaise, even *ris de veau* (sweetbreads) with wild mushrooms or sauerkraut Alsacienne. A veal head is served in the classic sauce ravigote. Expect true, robust flavors and a minimum of pretension.

239 Brompton Rd., SW3. © **020/7584-4477.** www.racine-restaurant.com. Main courses £15–£26; set-price lunch £15 for 2 courses, £18 for 3 courses. MC, V. Daily noon–3pm and 6–10:30pm. Tube: Knightsbridge or South Kensington.

INEXPENSIVE

Le Metro INTERNATIONAL   Located just around the corner from Harrods, Le Metro draws a fashionable crowd to its basement precincts. The place serves good, solid, reliable food prepared with flair. The menu changes frequently. As your starting point, you might choose the homemade soup of the day with freshly baked bread or the twice-baked cheese soufflé with an arugula salad. For a main, opt for such dishes as salmon fish cakes with horseradish mayonnaise or else pork, leek, and herb sausages with red-onion gravy.

In the Levin hotel, 28 Basil St., SW3. © **020/7589-6286.** www.thelevinhotel.co.uk. Main courses £10–£16; 2-course lunch £15; breakfast items £3.50–£6.50. AE, DC, MC, V. Daily noon–10pm. Tube: Knightsbridge.

Chelsea

VERY EXPENSIVE

Aubergine ★★ FRENCH   "Eggplant" is luring savvy diners down to the lower reaches of Chelsea. Although popular with celebrities, the restaurant remains unpretentious and refuses to pander to the whims of the rich and famous. (Madonna was once refused a late-night booking!) Every dish here is satisfyingly flavorful, from warm salad of truffled vegetables with asparagus purée to roasted monkfish served with crushed new potatoes, roasted leeks, and red-wine sauce. Starters continue to charm and delight, ranging from ravioli of crab with mussels, chili, ginger, and coriander *nage* to terrine of foie gras with confit of duck and pears poached in port. Also resting on your Villeroy & Boch eggplant plate might be mallard with a celeriac fondant, assiette of lamb with a thyme-scented jus, or the stunning tranche of sea bass with bouillabaisse potatoes. There are only 14 tables, so bookings are imperative.

11 Park Walk, SW10. © **020/7352-3449.** www.atozrestaurants.com/auberginechelsea. Reservations required and accepted as many as 4–8 weeks in advance. Fixed-price 3-course lunch £29, fixed-price 3-course dinner £68; 8-course menu gourmand £85, or £145 with wine. AE, DC, MC, V. Tues–Sat noon–2:30pm and 7–11pm. Tube: South Kensington.

Gordon Ramsay ★★★ 🍴 FRENCH   One of the city's most innovative and talented chefs is Gordon Ramsay. All of London is rushing to sample his wares, which means he has had to turn away some big names. The queen hasn't been denied a table yet, but that's only because she hasn't called. Every dish from the kitchen is gratifying, reflecting subtlety and delicacy without any sacrifice to the food's natural essence. Try, for example, Ramsay's celebrated cappuccino of white beans with grated truffles. His appetizers are likely to dazzle: salad of crispy pigs' trotters with calves' sweetbreads, fried quail eggs and a cream vinaigrette, or foie gras three ways—sautéed with quince, *mi-cuit* with an Earl Grey consommé, or pressed with truffle peelings. From here, you can grandly proceed to the main courses, including oven-roasted pigeon from Anjou wrapped in Parma ham with foie gras, or perhaps pan-fried filets of John Dory with crab and caviar.

68 Royal Hospital Rd., SW3. ✆ **020/7352-4441.** www.gordonramsay.com. Reservations essential and accepted 4 or more weeks in advance. Fixed-price 3-course lunch £45, 3-course dinner £90, 7-course dinner £120. AE, DC, MC, V. Mon–Fri noon–2:30pm and 6:30–11pm. Tube: Sloane Sq.

EXPENSIVE

Le Cercle ★★ FRENCH   The owners of Club Gascon have come up with another winner in this chic subterranean dining room, a sort of Chelsea speakeasy. At last, Sloane Street has a restaurant that is to food what the boulevard has long been to fashion. Service may not be the most efficient, and the noise level is at times deafening, but the food is amazing, served among an occasional famous face and a lot of lesser mortals. The French-styled dishes come in tapas-size portions. The menu is divided into seven sections according to principal ingredients. The waitstaff suggests three portions of these small plates before choosing one of the delectable desserts. Our favorite dish is the tuna carpaccio with crispy pork cubes. The milk-fed Pyrenean lamb is meltingly tender. The chefs turn out one of the most succulent cuts of beef in London—it appears as *onglet* on the menu. Also memorable are the duck and fig combo and the chestnut risotto. For dessert, the chocolate fondant may arguably be the best in London. It's served with vanilla and pepper (you heard right) ice cream. As for the cheese selection, one habitué described it to us as "top dog."

1 Wilbraham Place, SW1. ✆ **020/7901-9999.** www.lecercle.co.uk. Reservations required. Fixed-price lunch (Tues–Sat noon–3pm) £15–£20; small plates £5–£25. AE, MC, V. Tues–Sat noon–3pm and 6–11pm. Tube: Sloane Sq.

Tom's Kitchen ★ BRITISH   Down in Chelsea, a former pub has been stylishly converted into this chic restaurant, attracting a loyal following of the local smart set. Now a bright, bustling brasserie, with an open kitchen in back, it's a dream come true for Tom Aikens, who is assisted by his twin brother, Rob. Stop in for breakfast if you crave brioche French toast with caramelized apples, cinnamon ice cream, and maple syrup. Or else make a lunchtime rendezvous to tuck into Tom's seductive fish and chips.

27 Cale St., SW3. ✆ **020/7349-0202.** www.tomskitchen.co.uk. Reservations required. Main courses £14–£30. AE, MC, V. Mon–Fri 7–10am, noon–3pm, and 6–11pm; Sat–Sun 6–11pm. Tube: Sloane Sq. or South Kensington.

INEXPENSIVE

Chelsea Ram ENGLISH   A short distance from the King's Road, this much-frequented establishment, one of the best gastropubs in the area, features a daily changing menu. Look for the specials posted on a blackboard. The pub has a cozy atmosphere with its wooden floors, contemporary art, and lots of books in shelves lining the walls. We prefer the haddock and salmon fishcakes, though the chef often gets fancy with such offerings as roast pheasant breast flavored with fresh thyme leaves. Pork and leek sausages come with herbed mashed potatoes and onion gravy—how English can you get? For dessert, how about an apple and berry crumble with thick "double cream"?

32 Burnaby St., SW10. ℰ **020/7351-4008.** Reservations not needed. Main dishes £8–£12. MC, V. Mon–Sat noon–3pm and 6–10pm; Sun noon–4pm. MC, V. Tube: Fulham Broadway or Earl's Court.

The Pig's Ear ★ 🍴 ENGLISH   The staff is still talking about the surprise visit of Prince William; he may be heir to one of the world's most fabled fortunes, but at the end of the evening here, he split the bill among his friends, paying only his fair share at this, one of the best gastropubs in Chelsea. It might be called the Pig's Ear, but it's really the silk purse when it comes to food. Start with such dishes as Jerusalem artichoke soup with truffle oil, or else the chicken livers flavored with sherry vinegar. Other options include seared tuna with black olives and chicory or foie gras ballantine with onion marmalade. Filet of sea bass appears with beet and baby leeks, a roast wood pigeon is stuffed with garlic-laced portobello mushrooms, and, in honor of its namesake, the chefs also deep-fry pigs' ears. The atmosphere is friendly and unpretentious in both the ground-floor pub area and the wood-paneled restaurant upstairs.

35 Old Church St., SW3. ℰ **020/7352-2908.** www.thepigsear.info. Reservations required in restaurant. Main courses £12–£15. AE, DC, MC, V. Mon–Sat noon–11pm; Sun noon–10:30pm. Tube: Sloane Sq.

Kensington & South Kensington

VERY EXPENSIVE

Tom Aikens ★★★ CONTINENTAL   The amazingly skilled Tom Aikens is one of the truly top-flight Gallic chefs of London. Aikens certainly was trained well, working in Paris under Joël Robuchon during the time he was proclaimed France's greatest chef. Aikens also ran London's prestigious Pied à Terre (p. 151). Here, in elegant surroundings in chic South Kensington, the food is basically a modern interpretation of high French cuisine, with a great deal of flourish and some very elaborately worked dishes. Regardless of the contrast in ingredients, main courses show harmony and cohesion, as exemplified by the poached sea bass with saffron risotto and a bouillabaisse sauce. Everything sounds like an unlikely combination, but the end result is most satisfying. The menu's most voluptuous side is evoked by braised suckling pig with roasted fresh almonds, apple purée, and pork lasagna.

43 Elystan St., SW3. ℰ **020/7584-2003.** www.tomaikens.co.uk. Reservations required. Fixed-price lunch £23 for 2 courses, £29 for 3 courses; dinner main courses £25–£40; tasting menu £80, or £140 with wine pairings. AE, DC, MC, V. Tues–Fri noon–2:30pm; Mon–Sat 6:45–11pm. Tube: South Kensington.

EXPENSIVE

Bibendum Restaurant & Oyster Bar ★ FRENCH/MEDITERRANEAN   In trendy Brompton Cross, this still-fashionable restaurant occupies two floors of a garage that's now an Art Deco masterpiece. Though its heyday came in the early 1990s, the white-tiled room with stained-glass windows, lots of sunlight, and a chic clientele is still an extremely pleasant place. The eclectic cuisine, known for its freshness and simplicity, is based on what's available seasonally. Dishes might include roast pigeon with celeriac purée and apple sauté, rabbit with artichoke and parsley sauce, or grilled lamb cutlets with a delicate sauce. Some of the best dishes are for splitting between two people, like the Bresse chicken flavored with fresh tarragon and the grilled veal chops with truffle butter.

Simpler meals and cocktails are available in the **Oyster Bar,** on the building's street level. The bar-style menu stresses fresh shellfish presented in the traditional French style, on ice-covered platters adorned with strands of seaweed.

Michelin House, 81 Fulham Rd., SW3. ℭ **020/7581-5817.** www.bibendum.co.uk. Reservations required in Bibendum; not accepted in Oyster Bar. Main courses £17–£46; fixed-price lunch £25 for 2 courses, £30 for 3 courses; cold seafood platter in Oyster Bar £30. AE, DC, MC, V. Bibendum Mon–Fri noon–2:30pm and 7–11pm; Sat 12:30–3pm and 7–11pm; Sun 12:30–3pm and 7–10:30pm. Oyster Bar daily noon–11pm. Tube: South Kensington.

Clarke's ★ MODERN ENGLISH   Sally Clarke is one of the finest chefs in London, and this is one of the hottest restaurants around. *Still.* She opened it in the Thatcher era, and it's still going strong. Everything is bright and modern here, with wood floors, discreet lighting, and additional space in the basement where tables are more spacious and private. The menu, which changes daily, emphasizes chargrilled foods with herbs and seasonal veggies. You might begin with an appetizer salad of blood orange with red onions, watercress, and black olive–anchovy toast; then follow that with roasted breast of chicken with black truffle, crisp polenta, and arugula.

124 Kensington Church St., W8. ℭ **020/7221-9225.** www.sallyclarke.com. Reservations recommended. Main courses £15–£18 lunch, £18–£20 dinner; fixed-price 3-course dinner £40; Sun 3-course brunch £32. AE, DC, MC, V. Sun–Fri 12:30–2pm; Sat noon–2:30pm; Mon–Sat 6:30–10pm. Tube: High St. Kensington or Notting Hill Gate.

MODERATE

Admiral Codrington ★ 🏠 CONTINENTAL/MODERN ENGLISH   Once a lowly pub, this stylish bar and restaurant is now all the rage. The exterior has been maintained, but the old "Cod," as it is affectionately known, has emerged to offer plush dining, with a revitalized decor by Nina Campbell and a glass roof that rolls back on sunny days. The bartenders still offer a traditional pint, but the sophisticated menu features such delectable fare as grilled calves' liver and crispy bacon, pan-fried rib-eye with a truffled horseradish cream, or charbroiled tuna with eggplant caviar and a red-pepper vinaigrette.

17 Mossop St., SW3. ℭ **020/7581-0005.** www.theadmiralcodrington.co.uk. Reservations recommended. Main courses £10–£20. AE, MC, V. Mon–Thurs 11:30am–midnight; Fri–Sat 11:30am–1am; Sun noon–10:30pm. Lunch served Mon–Fri until 2:30pm, Sat until 3:30pm, Sun until 4pm; dinner served Mon–Sat 6:30–11pm, Sun 7–10:30pm. Tube: South Kensington.

Black & Blue ★ STEAK/ENGLISH   The atmosphere is marvelously informal, the prices affordable, and the steaks of high quality, each from a traditionally reared, grass-fed Scottish cow. Take your pick—Scottish sirloin, rib-eye, T-bone. We especially like the *côte de boeuf,* a hefty rib of beef for two to share. The sauces served with the steaks are divine. Burgers, chargrilled chicken, and fish dishes are also on offer on the changing menu, even freshly made salads and platters for the vegetarian.

215–217 Kensington Church St., W8. ℭ **020/7727-0004.** www.blackandbluerestaurants.com. Reservations required. Main courses £9–£26. MC, V. Sun–Thurs noon–11pm; Fri–Sat noon–11:30pm. Tube: Notting Hill Gate.

The Enterprise EUROPEAN/TRADITIONAL ENGLISH   The Enterprise's proximity to Harrods attracts regulars and out-of-town shoppers alike. Although the joint swarms with singles at night, during the day it feeds "ladies who lunch." With

Déclassé or not, Britain's national dish of fish and chips was called "the good companions" by Sir Winston Churchill. Introduced to London by Murano Jews, this dish has been Britain's fast food since the mid-19th century. Those slightly limp chips (fries to Americans) burst open with flavor with a squirt of malt vinegar, and each dish is accompanied by a "wally," in chippy vernacular (that's a pickled gherkin to the rest of you). Britons consume some 300 million fish-and-chips meals per year. The staunchest of devotees claim that the fish has to be cooked in beef drippings, but there has been much disagreement on that point in recent years.

We always head for **Rock & Sole Plaice,** 47 Endell St., WC2 (✆ **0871/426-3380;** Tube: Covent Garden), for our fish-and-chips fix. This is London's oldest chippy, having existed under one name or another since 1871. Fish here is cooked in a puffy, ale-colored batter. The cooks here prefer to fry the fish, such as sweet, delicate lemon sole, in clean peanut oil instead of beef drippings. Count on spending £10 to £15 for a meal, served Monday to Saturday 11:30am to 10:30pm and Sunday noon to 10pm.

Another authentic choice is the **Golden Hind,** 73 Marylebone Lane (✆ **0871/3327-803;** Tube: Bond St.), tucked away on a side street since 1914. Fresh fish arrives daily from the port of Grimsby on the western coast. Locals claim that "haddock is for heroes, cod for zeroes," so haddock is the way to go here. It's concealed in a thin batter (not overpuffed like most chippies). A dinner ranges from £5 to £11; hours are Monday to Friday noon to 3pm and Monday to Saturday 6 to 10pm.

banquettes, white linen, and fresh flowers, you won't mistake it for a lowly boozer. The kitchen serves respectable traditional English fare as well as European favorites. Featured dishes include fried salmon cakes with buttered spinach, golden calamari, and grilled steak with fries and salad. The juicy, properly aged, flavorful entrecôte slice of beef is about the best you can find in London.

35 Walton St., SW3. ✆ **020/7584-3148.** www.theenterprise.co.uk. Reservations accepted for Mon–Fri lunch only. Main courses £8–£18. AE, MC, V. Mon–Fri noon–3pm and 6–10:30pm; Sat–Sun noon–3:30pm and 6–10pm (Sat until 10:30pm). Tube: South Kensington or Knightsbridge.

Notting Hill & Bayswater
MODERATE
Assaggi ★ 🎁 ITALIAN   You wouldn't think of heading to the second floor of a very ordinary pub in Bayswater for fine Italian cuisine, but we urge you to do so in this case to sample chef Nino Sassu's take on Italian classics, especially those from the south. Serious London foodies have discovered this low-key venue and flock here for food prepared with flair and passion, using market-fresh and top-quality ingredients. The chef sets out to prove that straightforward dishes can often be the best when simply handled. Grilled Mediterranean vegetables in virgin olive oil and fresh herbs are always a winning appetizer, followed by such mains as grilled sea bass or filet of pork with black truffles. The menu is short but long on flavor, especially if you try such dishes as butter-and-sage ravioli, tender calf's liver, or panna cotta.

39 Chepstow Place, W2. © **020/7792-9033.** Reservations required. Main courses £19–£28. AE, MC, V. Mon–Sat 12:30–2:30pm and 7:30–11pm. Tube: Bayswater.

The Cow ★ 🍴 MODERN ENGLISH   You don't have to be a young fashion victim to enjoy the superb cuisine served here (although many of the diners are). This increasingly hip Notting Hill watering hole looks like an Irish pub, but the accents you'll hear are "trustafarian" rather than street-smart Dublin. With a pint of Fuller's or London Pride, you can linger over the modern European menu, which changes daily but is likely to include ox tongue poached in milk, mussels in curry and cream, or a mixed grill of lamb chops, calf's liver, and sweetbreads. The seafood selections are delectable. The Cow Special—a half-dozen Irish rock oysters with a pint of Guinness or a glass of wine for £11—is the star of the show. A raw bar downstairs serves other fresh seafood choices.

89 Westbourne Park Rd., W2. © **020/7221-5400.** www.thecowlondon.co.uk. Reservations required. Main courses £10–£19. MC, V. Daily noon–midnight. Tube: Westbourne Park.

Le Café Anglais ★★ BRITISH   This exciting restaurant evokes the spirit of an Art Deco Parisian brasserie, but fundamentally the cookery is firmly rooted in Britain. The extensive menu looks like dinner on the Titanic, but you won't sink regardless of what you order. To get into the spirit, start perhaps with a fresh elderflower cordial for an aperitif and then dazzle your palate with starters, everything from kipper pâté to mackerel teriyaki or salsify fritters. Chef Rowley Leigh is one of the founders of contemporary British cookery and author of a food column for the *Financial Times*. He specializes in the most tantalizing rotisserie dishes in London—saddle of roebuck, English partridge, wild duck, whatever. Ever had roast hare with chili and pumpkin? The setting is in an offbeat location in West London, adjoining Notting Hill, on the second floor of the Whiteleys shopping center.

8 Porchester Gardens, W2. © **020/7221-1415.** www.lecafeanglais.co.uk. Reservations required. Main courses £14–£25; fixed-price lunch £17–£20; set dinner £20–£25. AE, MC, V. Daily noon–3:30pm; Mon–Thurs 6–11pm; Fri–Sat 6–11:30pm; Sun 6:30–10:15pm. Tube: Bayswater or Queensway.

INEXPENSIVE

Prince Bonaparte INTERNATIONAL   This offbeat restaurant serves great pub grub in what used to be a grungy boozer before Notting Hill Gate became fashionable. Now pretty young things show up, spilling onto the sidewalk when the evenings are warm. The pub is filled with mismatched furniture; CDs of jazz and lazy blues fill the air, competing with the babble. It may seem at first that the staff doesn't have its act together, but once the food arrives, you won't care—the dishes served here are very good. The menu roams the world for inspiration: Moroccan chicken with couscous is as good, or even better, than any you'll find in Marrakech, and the seafood risotto is delicious.

80 Chepstow Rd., W2. © **020/7313-9491.** www.theprincebonapartew2.co.uk. Main courses £12–£22. AE, MC, V. Mon–Sat noon–10:30pm. Tube: Notting Hill Gate or Westbourne Park.

Limehouse

INEXPENSIVE

The Narrow ★ 🍴 MODERN BRITISH   London's most celebrated chef, Gordon Ramsay, has launched an East End gastropub standing on a bend of the Thames in the Limehouse district. Warmed by open fires, the restaurant and pub are chicly decorated in nautical navy and white. The menu is a modernized version of a nostalgic English kitchen—for example, such delights "on toast" as soft herring roes or deviled lamb's kidneys. In how many places today can you find braised Gloucester pig cheeks with mashed "neeps" (turnips)? Other tempting mains include a whole baked gilthead bream with fennel and watercress and a Hereford sirloin with portobello mushrooms and anchovy butter. For dessert, there's a good version of the famous Bakewell Tart.

44 Narrow St., E14. © **020/7592-7950.** www.gordonramsay.com. Reservations required in restaurant. Main courses £12–£16; bar snacks £3.50–£11. AE, MC, V. Mon–Fri 11:30am–3pm and 6–10:30pm; Sat noon–10pm; Sun noon–9pm. Tube: Limehouse.

Richmond

MODERATE

Petersham Nurseries Café ★★★ 🍴 INTERNATIONAL South of the Thames in Richmond, Surrey, an easy commute from central London, you'll find the domain of "restless Aussie" chef Skye Gyngell, the hottest dining reservation in London. She may remain in that lofty position for years to come, because there's no one quite like her. She became known as a chef when she wrote two best-selling cookbooks, *A Year in My Kitchen* and *My Favourite Ingredients*. Her restaurant is simplicity itself, even though she's a media darling (she's even fed Madonna). "I just love to cook—that's all." That's not all. She's modest but supremely talented. Her dishes may be "unfussy," but they are utterly captivating, ranging from a tomatoey chowder of clams and monkfish to a rabbit cooked with duck fat, verjuice, and mustard. Sitting on the alfresco summer terrace and eating her homemade rhubarb ice cream is about as good as it gets. There is no alcohol here—just jugs of homemade lemon cordial.

Church Lane (off Petersham Rd.), Richmond, TW10. © **020/8605-3527.** www.petershamnurseries. com. Reservations required (as far in advance as possible). 2 courses for £28, 3 courses for £30. AE, DC, MC, V. Wed–Sun noon–2:30pm. Tube: Richmond.

AFTERNOON TEA

Everyone should indulge in a formal afternoon tea at least once while in London. This relaxing, drawn-out, civilized affair usually consists of three courses, all elegantly served on delicate china: first, dainty finger sandwiches (with the crusts cut off, of course); then fresh-baked scones served with jam and deliciously decadent clotted cream (the rich, thick cream is also known as Devonshire cream); and lastly, an array of bite-size sweets. All the while, an indulgent server keeps the pot of your choice fresh at hand. Sometimes ports or aperitif are on offer for your final course. It's a quintessential English experience; below are a few of our favorite places to indulge.

Mayfair

St. James's Restaurant & the Fountain Restaurant   This pair of tea salons

functions as a culinary showplace for London's most prestigious grocery store, Fortnum & Mason. The more formal of the two, St. James's, on the store's fourth floor, is a pale-green-and-beige homage to formal Edwardian taste. More rapid and less formal is the Fountain Restaurant, on the street level, where a sense of tradition and manners is very much a part of the dining experience, but in a less opulent setting.

There is no longer an "official" afternoon tea at the Fountain, but you can order pots of tea plus food from an a la carte menu that includes sandwiches, scones, and the like.

In Fortnum & Mason, 181 Piccadilly, W1. ✆ **020/7973-4140** for the Fountain; **020/7734-8040,** ext. 2241, for St. James's. www.fortnumandmason.com. St. James's afternoon tea £32–£38. Fountain menu items £13–£32. AE, DC, MC, V. St. James's Mon-Sat noon–6:30pm; Sun noon–4:30pm. Fountain Mon-Sat 7:30–11am, noon–3pm, and 6–11pm; Sun 11am–3pm and tea 3–5:30pm. Tube: Piccadilly Circus.

Knightsbridge

Georgian Restaurant   For as long as anyone can remember, tea at Harrods has been a distinctive feature of Europe's most famous department store. A flood of visitors is gracefully herded into a high-volume but elegant room on the fourth floor. Many come here for the ritual of the tea service, as staff members haul silver pots and trolleys laden with pastries and sandwiches through the cavernous dining hall.

In Harrods, 87-135 Brompton Rd., SW1. ✆ **020/7225-6800.** www.harrods.com. Reservations recommended. High tea £24 per person, or £33 per person with Harrods champagne. AE, DC, MC, V. Daily 3:30–5:30pm (last order). Tube: Knightsbridge.

Richoux   There's an old-fashioned atmosphere at Richoux, established in the 1920s. You can order four hot scones with strawberry jam and whipped cream or choose from a selection of pastries. Of course, tea is obligatory; always specify lemon or cream, one lump or two. A full menu, with fresh salads, sandwiches, and burgers, is served all day.

There are three other locations, all open Monday to Friday from 8am to 11pm and Saturday from 8am to 11:30pm: 172 Piccadilly, at the bottom of Bond Street (✆ **020/ 7493-2204;** Tube: Piccadilly Circus or Green Park); 41A S. Audley St. (✆ **020/ 7629-5228;** Tube: Green Park or Hyde Park Corner); and 3 Circus Rd. (✆ **020/7483- 4001;** Tube: St. John's Wood).

86 Brompton Rd. (opposite Harrods), SW3. ✆ **020/7584-8300.** www.richoux.co.uk. Full tea £9.25–£30. AE, MC, V. Mon-Sat 8am–9pm; Sun 10am–9pm. Tube: Knightsbridge.

Kensington

The Orangery ★ 📖   In its way, the Orangery is the most amazing place for afternoon tea in the world. Set 46m (150 ft.) north of Kensington Palace, it occupies a long, narrow garden pavilion built in 1704 by Queen Anne. In homage to her original intentions, rows of potted orange trees bask in sunlight from soaring windows, and tea is served amid Corinthian columns, ruddy-colored bricks, and a pair of Grinling Gibbons wood carvings. There are even some urns and statuary that the royal family imported from Windsor Castle. The menu includes soups and sandwiches, served with a salad and a portion of kettle chips. The array of different teas is served with high style, accompanied by fresh scones with clotted cream and jam, plus Belgian chocolate cake.

In Kensington Gardens, W8. ✆ **020/7376-0239.** www.digbytrout.co.uk and www.hrp.org.uk/Kensington Palace. Reservations not accepted. Pot of tea £1.95–£5; cakes and puddings £3.50–£8.75; afternoon tea £13–£35; champagne tea £22. MC, V. Daily 3–5pm. Tube: High St. Kensington or Queensway.

EXPLORING LONDON

London is more eclectic and electric than it's been in years. Some even think it has surpassed New York for sheer energy, outrageous fashion, trendy restaurants, and a nightlife that's second to none.

But the cool youth culture that grabs headlines is not all there is to London today. What makes the city so fascinating is its cultural diversity. It seems that half the world is flocking here, not just from the far-flung former colonies of the once-great British Empire, but also from Algeria, Argentina, China, and Senegal. With their talent and new ideas, these transplants are transforming a city once maligned as drab and stuffy. In London today, where everything's changing, only the queen appears the same. (After she's gone, even the House of Windsor may be in for a shake-up.)

Though London is more open and dynamic than it has been since 1969, problems exist here, as elsewhere, that all the happening restaurants and pricey boutiques in the world can't obliterate. The gulf between rich and poor continues to widen, and violent crime, once relatively rare, is on the rise.

In this chapter, we can explore only a fraction of what's exciting in London. We went in search of what's creating the hottest buzz in shopping and nightlife, but we also provide plenty of detail about London's time-tested treasures: ancient monuments, literary shrines, walking tours, Parliament debates, royal castles, waxworks, palaces, cathedrals, and royal parks.

THE TOP ATTRACTIONS

As a rule, and unless otherwise stated in the listings below, children's prices at London attractions apply to those ages 16 and younger. You must be 60 years of age or older to obtain available senior discounts at some attractions. For students to get available discounted admissions, they must have a valid student ID card.

Tower of London ★★★ ☺   This ancient fortress continues to pack in the crowds with its macabre associations with the legendary figures imprisoned and/or executed here. There are more spooks here per square foot than in any other building in the whole of haunted Britain. Headless bodies, bodiless heads, phantom soldiers, icy blasts, clanking chains—

| 0 | 1 mi |
| 0 | 1 km |

✝ Church
ⓘ Information
⊖ Tube stop
Note: not all Tube stations are featured on this map

Apsley House (Wellington Museum) 17
Battersea Park 12
Benjamin Franklin House 33
Big Ben 25
British Library 41
British Museum 40
Buckingham Palace 16
Carlyle's House 11
Charles Dickens Museum 42
Churchill War Rooms 30
City Hall 55
Clarence House 18
Courtauld Gallery 38
Dr. Johnson's House 44
Green Park 19
Guildhall Art Gallery 46
Hayward Gallery 28
Horse Guards Building 31
Household Cavalry Museum 31
Hyde Park 5

Jewel Tower 24
Kensington Gardens 6
Kensington Palace 7
London Aquarium 26
London Dungeon 54
London Eye 27
London Transport Museum 34
London Zoo 1
Madame Tussauds 3
Museum of London 45
National Army Museum 13
National Gallery 35
National Portrait Gallery 36
Natural History Museum 10
Old Bailey 48
Palaces of Westminster (Houses of Parliament) 22
Queen's Gallery 16
Regent's Park 2
Saatchi Gallery 14
St. Bride's Church 49

St. Etheldreda's Church 43
St. James's Park 2
St. Martin-in-the-Fields 37
St. Paul's Cathedral 47
Science Museum 8
Shakespeare's Globe Theatre & Exhibition 51
Sir John Soane's Museum 39
Tate Britain 21
Tate Modern 50
Tower Bridge 53
Tower of London 52
Trafalgar Square 32
V&A Museum of Childhood 56
Victoria and Albert Museum 9
Wallace Collection 4
Westminster Abbey 23
Westminster Cathedral 15
Whitehall 29

you name them, the Tower's got them. Centuries after the last head rolled on Tower Hill, a shivery atmosphere of impending doom still lingers over the Tower's mighty walls. Plan on spending a lot of time here.

The Tower is actually an intricately patterned compound of structures built throughout the ages for varying purposes, mostly as expressions of royal power. The oldest is the **White Tower,** begun by William the Conqueror in 1078 to keep London's native Saxon population in check. Later rulers added other towers, more walls, and fortified gates, until the buildings became like a small town within a city. Until the reign of James I (beginning in 1603), the Tower was also one of the royal residences. But above all, it was a prison for distinguished captives.

Every stone of the Tower tells a story—usually a gory one. In the **Bloody Tower,** according to Shakespeare, Richard III's henchmen murdered the two little princes (the sons of Edward IV). On the walls of the **Beauchamp Tower,** you can still read the last messages scratched by despairing prisoners. Through **Traitors' Gate** passed such ill-fated, romantic figures as Robert Devereux, the second earl of Essex and a favorite of Elizabeth I. A plaque marks the eerie place at **Tower Green** where two wives of Henry VIII, Anne Boleyn and Catherine Howard, plus Sir Thomas More and the 4-day queen, Lady Jane Grey, all lost their lives.

The Tower, besides being a royal palace, a fortress, and a prison, was also an armory, a treasury, a menagerie, and, in 1675, an astronomical observatory. Reopened in 1999, the White Tower holds the **Armouries,** which date from the reign of Henry VIII, as well as a display of instruments of torture and execution that recall some of the most ghastly moments in the Tower's history. In the Jewel House, you'll find the Tower's greatest attraction, the **Crown Jewels.** Here, some of the world's most precious stones are set into robes, swords, scepters, and crowns. The Imperial State Crown is the most famous crown on earth; made for Victoria in 1837, it's worn today by Queen Elizabeth II when she opens Parliament. Studded with some 3,000 jewels (principally diamonds), it includes the Black Prince's Ruby, worn by Henry V at Agincourt. The 530-carat Star of Africa, a cut diamond on the Royal Scepter with Cross, would make Harry Winston turn over in his grave. You'll have to stand in long lines to catch just a glimpse of the jewels as you and hundreds of others roll by on moving sidewalks, but the wait is worth it.

The presumed **prison cell** of Sir Thomas More is open to the public. More left this cell in 1535 to face his executioner after he'd fallen out with King Henry VIII over the monarch's desire to divorce Catherine of Aragon, the first of his six wives. More is believed to have lived in the lower part of the Bell Tower during the last 14 months of his life, although some historians doubt this claim.

A **palace** inhabited by King Edward I in the late 1200s stands above Traitors' Gate. It's the only surviving medieval palace in Britain. Guides at the palace are dressed in period costumes, and reproductions of furniture and fittings, including Edward's throne, evoke the era, along with burning incense and candles.

With the opening of a visitor center and the restoration of the Tower's 13th-century wharf, the attraction is more user-friendly than ever before. To the west of the Tower is **Tower Hill Square,** designed by Stanton Williams, with a series of pavilions housing ticketing facilities, a gift shop, and a cafeteria.

Oh, yes—don't forget to look for the ravens. Six of them (plus two spares) are all registered as official Tower residents. According to legend, the Tower of London and the kingdom will stand as long as those ominous black birds remain, so to be on the safe side, one of the wings of each raven is clipped.

One-hour **guided tours** of the entire compound are given by the Yeoman Warders (also known as Beefeaters) daily every half-hour, starting at 9:30am, from the Middle Tower near the main entrance. The last guided walk starts about 3:30pm in summer, 2:30pm in winter—weather permitting, of course.

You can also attend the nightly **Ceremony of the Keys,** the ceremonial locking up of the Tower by the Yeoman Warders. For free tickets, write to the Ceremony of the Keys Office, Waterloo Block, Tower of London, London EC3N 4AB, and request a specific date, but also list alternate dates. At least 2 to 3 months' notice is required. Accompany all requests with a stamped, self-addressed envelope (British stamps only) or two international reply coupons. With ticket in hand, a Yeoman Warder will admit you at 9:35pm. Frankly, we don't think it's worth the trouble to see this rather cheesy ceremony, but we know some who disagree with us.

Tower Hill, EC3. © **0844/482-7777.** www.hrp.org.uk. Admission £17 adults, £15 students and seniors, £9.50 children 5-15, £47 family ticket, free for children 4 and younger. Mar-Oct Tues-Sat 9am-5:30pm, Sun-Mon 10am-5:30pm; Nov-Feb Tues-Sat 9am-4:30pm, Sun-Mon 10am-4:30pm. Tube: Tower Hill.

Westminster Abbey ★★★   With its identical square towers and superb archways, this Early English Gothic abbey is one of the greatest examples of ecclesiastical architecture on earth. But it's far more than that: It's the shrine of a nation, the symbol of everything Britain has stood for and stands for, and the place in which most of its rulers were crowned and where many lie buried.

Nearly every figure in English history has left his or her mark on Westminster Abbey. Edward the Confessor founded the Benedictine abbey in 1065 on this spot overlooking Parliament Square. The first king crowned in the abbey may have been Harold, in January 1066, but the man who defeated him at the Battle of Hastings later that year, William the Conqueror, had the first recorded coronation in the abbey on Christmas Day in that year. The coronation tradition has continued to the present day, although Edward V and Edward VIII were never crowned. The essentially Early English Gothic structure existing today owes more to Henry III's plans than to those of any other sovereign, although many architects, including Wren, have contributed to the abbey.

Built on the site of the ancient Lady Chapel in the early 16th century, the **Henry VIII Chapel** is one of the loveliest in Europe, with its fan vaulting, Knights of Bath banners, and Torrigiani-designed tomb for the king himself, near which hangs a 15th-century Vivarini painting, *Madonna and Child.* Also here, ironically buried in the same tomb, are Catholic Mary I and Protestant Elizabeth I (whose archrival, Mary, Queen of Scots, is entombed on the other side of the Henry VII Chapel). In one end of the chapel, you can stand on Cromwell's memorial stone and view the **Royal Air Force Chapel** and its Battle of Britain memorial window, unveiled in 1947 to honor the Royal Air Force.

You can also visit the most hallowed spot in the abbey, the **Shrine of Edward the Confessor** (canonized in the 12th c.). Near the tomb of Henry V is the Coronation Chair, made at the command of Edward I in 1300 to display the mystical Stone of Scone (which some think is the sacred stone mentioned in Genesis and known as Jacob's Pillar). Scottish kings were once crowned on the stone (it has since been returned to Scotland).

When you enter the transept on the south side and see a statue of the Bard, with one arm resting on a stack of books, you've arrived at **Poets' Corner.** Shakespeare himself is buried at Stratford-upon-Avon, but resting here are Chaucer, Samuel Johnson, Tennyson, Browning, and Dickens; there's even an American, Henry Wadsworth Longfellow, as well as monuments to just about everybody: Milton, Keats, Shelley, Henry James, T. S. Eliot, George Eliot, and others. The most stylized monument is Sir Jacob Epstein's sculptured bust of William Blake. More recent tablets commemorate Dylan Thomas and Lord Laurence Olivier.

Statesmen and men of science—Disraeli, Newton, Charles Darwin—are also interred in the abbey or honored by monuments. Near the west door is the 1965 memorial to Sir Winston Churchill. In the vicinity of this memorial is the **Tomb of the Unknown Warrior,** commemorating the British dead of World War I.

Although most of the abbey's statuary commemorates notable figures of the historic past, 10 new statues were unveiled in 1998. Placed in the Gothic niches above the West Front door, these statues honor 10 modern-day martyrs drawn from every continent and religious denomination. Designed by Tim Crawley and carved under his general direction from French Richemont limestone, the sculptures include Elizabeth of Russia, Janani Luwum, and Martin Luther King, Jr., representatives of those who have sacrificed their lives for their beliefs.

Off the Cloisters, the **College Garden** is the oldest garden in England, under cultivation for more than 900 years. Established in the 11th century as the abbey's first infirmary garden, this was once a magnificent source of fruits, vegetables, and medicinal herbs. Five of the trees in the garden were planted in 1850 and continue to thrive today. High walls surround the garden, flowering trees dot the lawns, and park benches provide comfort where you can hardly hear the roar of passing traffic. The garden is open April through September, Tuesday to Thursday 10am to 6pm, and October through March, Tuesday to Thursday 10am to 4pm.

Insider's tip: Far removed from the pomp and glory is the **Abbey Treasure Museum,** which displays a real bag of oddities in the undercroft, or crypt, part of the monastic buildings erected between 1066 and 1100. You'll find royal effigies that were used instead of the real corpses for lying-in-state ceremonies because they smelled better. You'll see the almost lifelike effigy of Admiral Nelson (his mistress arranged his hair) and even that of Edward III, his lip warped by the cerebral hemorrhage that felled him. Other oddities include Henry V's funeral armor, a unique corset from Elizabeth I's effigy, and the Essex Ring that Elizabeth I gave to her favorite (Robert Devereux, Earl of Essex) when she was feeling good about him.

On Sundays, the abbey is open for services only and all are welcome. The rest of the church is open unless a service is being conducted. For times of services, phone the **Chapter Office** (© 020/7222-5152).

Broad Sanctuary, SW1. © **020/7222-5152.** www.westminster-abbey.org. Admission £15 adults, £12 students and seniors, £6 children 11–18, £32 family ticket, free for children 10 and younger. Mon–Tues and Thurs–Fri 9:30am–4:30pm; Wed 9:30am–6pm; Sat 9:30am–2:30pm. Tube: Westminster or St. James's Park.

Palace of Westminster (Houses of Parliament) & Big Ben ★★ The Houses of Parliament, along with their trademark clock tower, are the ultimate symbols of London. They're the strongholds of Britain's democracy, the assemblies that effectively trimmed the sails of royal power. Both the House of Commons and the House of Lords are in the former royal Palace of Westminster, which was the king's residence until Henry VIII moved to Whitehall. The current Gothic Revival buildings date from 1840 and were designed by Charles Barry. (The earlier buildings were destroyed by fire in 1834.) Assisting Barry was Augustus Welby Pugin, who designed the paneled ceilings, tiled floors, stained glass, clocks, fireplaces, umbrella stands, and even the inkwells. There are more than 1,000 rooms and 3km (1¾ miles) of corridors. The clock tower at the eastern end houses the world's most famous timepiece. **"Big Ben"** refers not to the clock tower itself, but to the largest bell in the chime, which weighs close to 14 tons and is named for the first commissioner of works, Sir Benjamin Hall.

You may observe debates for free from the **Strangers' Galleries** in both houses. Sessions usually begin in mid-October and run to the end of July, with recesses at Christmas and Easter. The chances of getting into the House of Lords when it's in session are generally better than for the more popular House of Commons. Although we can't promise you the oratory of a Charles James Fox or a William Pitt the Elder, the debates in the House of Commons are often lively and controversial (seats are at a premium during crises).

For years, London tabloids have portrayed members of the House of Lords as a bunch of "Monty Pythonesque upper-class twits," with one foreign secretary calling the House of Lords "medieval lumber." Today, the House of Lords is being shaken up as lords lose their inherited posts. Panels are studying what to do with this largely useless house, its members often descendants of royal mistresses and ancient landowners.

Those who'd like to book **guided tours** can do so, but it takes a bit of work. Both houses are open to the general public for guided tours only for a limited season in July and August. The palace is open Monday, Tuesday, Friday, and Saturday from 9:15am to 4:30pm during those times. All tour tickets cost £15 for adults; £10 for seniors, students, and children 15 and younger; and £32 for a family ticket. Children 3 and younger may enter free. For advance tickets, call *©* **0844/847-1672** or go to www.ticketmaster.co.uk/housesofparliament.

If you arrive just to attend a session, these are free, but you will need a card of introduction. Foreign and Commonwealth visitors should apply to their embassy or High Commission in the U.K. for a card of introduction, which will normally permit entry during the early afternoon. Embassies and High Commissions may issue no more than four cards on any day, so visitors from certain countries may find cards are booked for several weeks ahead. Please note that such cards do not guarantee entry. Quite often, it will not be possible to admit their bearers until *after* Prime Minister's Questions. British embassies abroad do not issue such cards. With your card of introduction in hand, you line up at Stephen's Gate, heading to your left for the entrance into the Commons or to the right for the Lords. The London daily newspapers announce sessions of Parliament.

Insider's tip: The hottest ticket and the most exciting time to visit is during **Prime Minister's Questions (PMQs)** on Wednesdays. It lasts only from noon to 12:30pm, but must seem like hours to David Cameron, who is on the hot seat. It's not quite as thrilling as it was back when Margaret Thatcher exchanged barbs with the MPs (Members of Parliament), but still worth a viewing.

Across the street is the **Jewel Tower** ★, Abingdon Street (*©* **020/7222-2219;** www.english-heritage.org.uk), one of only two surviving buildings from the medieval Palace of Westminster. It was constructed in 1365 as a place where Edward III could stash his treasure trove. The tower hosts an exhibition on the history of Parliament and makes for a great introduction to the inner workings of the British government. The video presentation on the top floor is especially informative. A touch-screen computer allows visitors to take a virtual tour of both houses of Parliament. The tower is open daily, April to October 10am to 5pm and November to March 10am to 4pm. Admission is £3.20 for adults, £2.60 for students and seniors, and £1.60 for children.

Westminster Palace, Old Palace Yard, SW1. House of Commons © **020/7219-4272;** House of Lords © **020/7219-3107.** www.parliament.uk. Free admission. Mid-Oct to Aug Mon–Tues 9am–noon; Wed 9–9:20am; Fri 3:30–5pm. Both houses are open for guided tours by advance arrangement (see above). Join line at St. Stephen's entrance. Tube: Westminster.

British Museum ★★★   Set in scholarly Bloomsbury, this immense museum grew out of a private collection of manuscripts purchased in 1753 with the proceeds of a lottery. It grew and grew, fed by legacies, discoveries, and purchases, until it became one of the most comprehensive collections of art and artifacts in the world. It's impossible to take in this museum in a day.

The overall storehouse splits basically into the national collections of antiquities; prints and drawings; coins, medals, and bank notes; and ethnography. Even on a cursory first visit, be sure to see the Asian collections (the finest assembly of Islamic pottery outside the Islamic world), the Chinese porcelain, the Indian sculpture, and the prehistoric and Romano-British collections. Special treasures you might want to seek out on your first visit include the **Rosetta Stone,** in the Egyptian Room, whose discovery led to the deciphering of hieroglyphics; the **Elgin Marbles,** a series of pediments, metopes, and friezes from the Parthenon in Athens, in the Duveen Gallery; and the legendary **Black Obelisk,** dating from around 860 B.C., in the Nimrud Gallery. Other treasures include the contents of Egyptian royal tombs (including mummies); fabulous arrays of 2,000-year-old jewelry, cosmetics, weapons, furniture, and tools; Babylonian astronomical instruments; and winged lion statues (in the Assyrian Transept) that guarded Ashurnasirpal's palace at Nimrud. The exhibits change throughout the year, so if your heart is set on seeing a specific treasure, call to make sure it's on display.

Insider's tip: If you're a first-time visitor, of course you will want to concentrate on some of the fabled treasures previewed above. But what we do is duck into the British Museum several times on our visits to London, even if we have only an hour or two, to see the less heralded but equally fascinating exhibits. We recommend wandering rooms 33 and 34, and 91 to 94, to take in the glory of Asia, covering Taoism, Confucianism, and Buddhism. The Chinese collection is particularly strong. Sculpture from India is as fine as anything at the Victoria and Albert. The ethnography collection is increasingly beefed up, especially the Mexican Gallery in room 33C, which traces that country's art from the 2nd millennium B.C. to the 16th century A.D. A gallery for the North American collection is also open nearby. Another section of the museum is devoted to the **Sainsbury African Galleries** ★, one of the finest collections of African art and artifacts in the world, featuring changing displays selected from more than 200,000 objects. Finally, the museum has opened a new Money Gallery in room 68, tracing the story of money. You'll learn that around 2000 B.C. in Mesopotamia, money was grain and that printed money came into being in the 10th century in China.

For information on the British Library, see p. 186.

Great Russell St., WC1. © **020/7323-8299.** www.britishmuseum.org. Free admission. Sat–Wed 10am–5:30pm; Thurs–Fri 10am–8:30pm. Tube: Holborn, Tottenham Court Rd., Goodge St., or Russell Sq.

Buckingham Palace ★★ ☺ This massive, graceful building is the official residence of the queen. The redbrick palace was built as a country house for the notoriously rakish duke of Buckingham. In 1762, King George III, who needed room for his 15 children, bought it. It didn't become the official royal residence, though, until Queen Victoria took the throne; she preferred it to St. James's Palace. From George III's time, the building was continuously expanded and remodeled, faced with Portland stone, and twice bombed (during the Blitz). Located in a 16-hectare (40-acre) garden, it's 108m (354 ft.) long and contains 600 rooms. You can tell whether the queen is at home by checking to see if the Royal Standard is flying from the mast outside.

For most of the year, you can't visit the palace without an official invitation. Since 1993, though, much of it has been open for tours during an 8-week period in August and September, when the royal family is usually vacationing outside London. Elizabeth II agreed to allow visitors to tour the State Room, the Grand Staircase, the Throne Room, and other areas designed by John Nash for George IV, as well as the Picture Gallery, which displays masterpieces by Van Dyck, Rembrandt, Rubens, and others. You have to buy a timed-entrance ticket the same day you tour the palace. Tickets go on sale at 9am, but rather than lining up at sunrise with all the other tourists—this is one of London's most popular attractions—call to book with a credit card and give yourself a few more hours of sleep.

Buckingham Palace's most famous spectacle is the vastly overrated **Changing of the Guard** (daily May–July and on alternating days the rest of the year). The new guard, marching behind a band, comes from either the Wellington or Chelsea barracks and takes over from the old guard in the forecourt of the palace. The ceremony begins at 11:30am, although it's frequently canceled because of bad weather, state events, and other harder-to-fathom reasons. We like the Changing of the Guard at Horse Guards (p. 184) better because you can actually see the men marching and you don't have to battle such tourist hordes. However, few first-time visitors can resist the Buckingham Palace Changing of the Guard. If that's you, arrive as early as 10:30am and claim territorial rights to a space in front of the palace. If you're not firmly anchored here, you'll miss much of the ceremony.

At end of the Mall (on the road running from Trafalgar Sq.). © **020/7766-7300.** www.royalcollection.org.uk. Palace tours £17 adults, £16 seniors 61 and older and students, £9.75 children 5–16, £45 family ticket, free for children 4 and younger; Changing of the Guard free. Palace July 27–Sept 29 (dates can vary), plus additional dates may be added; daily 9:45am–6pm. Changing of the Guard May–July daily 11:30am; on alternating days the rest of the year at 11am. Tube: St. James's Park, Green Park, or Victoria.

Tate Britain ★★★ Fronting the Thames near Vauxhall Bridge in Pimlico, the Tate looks like a smaller and more graceful relation of the British Museum. The most prestigious gallery in Britain, it houses the national collections, covering British art from the 16th century to the present day, as well as an array of international works. In the spring of 2000, the Tate moved the bulk of its 20th- and 21st-century art to the **Tate Modern** (see below). This split helped to open more display space at the Tate Britain, but the collection here is still much too large to be displayed all at once, so the works on view change from time to time.

The older works include some of the best of Gainsborough, Reynolds, Stubbs, Blake, and Constable. William Hogarth is well represented, particularly by his satirical *O, the Roast Beef of Old England* (known as *The Gate of Calais*). You'll find the illustrations of William Blake, the incomparable mystical poet, including such works as *The Book of Job, The Divine Comedy,* and *Paradise Lost.* The collection of works by J. M. W. Turner is the Tate's largest such collection by a single artist—Turner himself willed most of his paintings and watercolors to the nation.

Also on display are the works of many major 19th- and 20th-century painters, including Paul Nash, Matisse, Dalí, Modigliani, Munch, Bonnard, and Picasso. Truly remarkable are the several enormous abstract canvases by Mark Rothko, the group of paintings and sculptures by Giacometti, and the paintings by one of England's best-known modern artists, Francis Bacon. Sculptures by Henry Moore and Barbara Hepworth are also occasionally displayed.

Insider's tip: After you've seen the grand art, don't hasten away. Drop into the **Tate Britain Shop** for some of the best art books and postcards in London. The shop sells whimsical T-shirts with art masterpieces on them, those ubiquitous Tate Gallery canvas bags seen all over London, and the town's best art posters (all make great souvenirs). Invite your friends for tea at the Tate Britain Café, with its excellent cakes and pastries, or lunch at the **Rex Whistler Restaurant** (p. 154), where you'll get to enjoy good food, Rex Whistler art, and the best and most reasonably priced wine list in London.

Millbank, SW1. © **020/7887-8008.** www.tate.org.uk. Free admission; special exhibitions sometimes incur a charge of £5–£15. Daily 10:30am–5:50pm. Tube: Pimlico.

Tate Modern ★★★   In a transformed Bankside Power Station in Southwark, this museum, which opened in 2000, draws some two million visitors a year to see the greatest collection of international 20th-century art in Britain. How would we rate the collection? At the same level of the Pompidou in Paris, with a slight edge over New York's Guggenheim. Of course, New York's Museum of Modern Art remains in a class of its own. The Tate Modern is also viewer-friendly, with eye-level hangings. All the big painting stars are here, a whole galaxy ranging from Dalí to Duchamp, from Giacometti to Matisse and Mondrian, from Picasso and Pollock to Rothko and Warhol. The Modern is also a gallery of 21st-century art, displaying new and exciting art.

The Tate Modern, which claims it is the most visited modern art museum in the world, unveiled plans for a £400-million extension to be completed in time for the London Olympics of 2012. The extension will resemble glass boxes stacked up arbitrarily to form a 67m (220-ft.) pyramid. This new wing will make Tate Modern comparable in size to the Museum of Modern Art in New York.

The museum makes extensive use of glass for both its exterior and interior, offering panoramic views. Galleries are arranged over three levels and provide different kinds of space for display. Instead of exhibiting art chronologically and by school, the Tate Modern, in a radical break from tradition, takes a thematic approach. This allows displays to cut across movements.

To get here, you can cross the Thames via the **Millennium Bridge,** a pedestrian-only walk from the steps of St. Paul's. Or else you can hop aboard the **Tate to Tate Boat** (© **020/7887-8888**), which takes art lovers on an 18-minute journey across the Thames from the Tate Britain to the Tate Modern, with a stop at the London Eye and the Saatchi Gallery. A ticket costs £5 for adults, £2.50 for children under 16, and £10 for families. Leaving from Millbank Pier, this catamaran is decorated with the trademark colorful dots of that *enfant terrible* artist Damien Hirst.

Bankside, SE1. (C) **020/7887-8888.** www.tate.org.uk. Free admission. Sun–Thurs 10am–6pm; Fri–Sat 10am–10pm. Tube: Southwark or Blackfriars.

National Gallery ★★★ This stately neoclassical building contains an unrivaled collection of Western art spanning 7 centuries—from the late 13th to the early 20th—and covering every great European school. For sheer skill of display and arrangement, it surpasses its counterparts in Paris, New York, Madrid, and Amsterdam.

The largest part of the collection is devoted to the Italians, including the Sienese, Venetian, and Florentine masters. They're now housed in the **Sainsbury Wing,** which was designed by noted Philadelphia architects Robert Venturi and Denise Scott Brown and opened by Queen Elizabeth II in 1991. On display are such works as Leonardo's *Virgin of the Rocks;* Titian's *Bacchus and Ariadne;* Giorgione's *Adoration of the Magi;* and unforgettable canvases by Bellini, Veronese, Botticelli, and Tintoretto. Botticelli's *Venus and Mars* is eternally enchanting. The Sainsbury Wing is also used for large temporary exhibits.

Of the early Gothic works, the Wilton Diptych (French or English school, late 14th c.) is the rarest treasure; it depicts Richard II being introduced to the Madonna and Child by John the Baptist and the Saxon kings, Edmund and Edward the Confessor. Then there are the Spanish giants: El Greco's *Agony in the Garden* and portraits by Goya and Velázquez. The Flemish-Dutch school is represented by Bruegel, Jan van Eyck, Vermeer, Rubens, and de Hooch; the Rembrandts include two of his immortal self-portraits. None of van Eyck's art creates quite the stir that the ***Arnolfini Portrait*** does. You probably studied this painting from 1434 in your Art History 101 class. The stunning work depicts Giovanni di Nicolao Arnolfini and his wife (who is not pregnant as is often thought; she is merely holding up her full-skirted dress in the contemporary fashion). There's also an immense French Impressionist and post-Impressionist collection that includes works by Manet, Monet, Degas, Renoir, and Cézanne. Particularly charming is the peep-show cabinet by Hoogstraten in one of the Dutch rooms: It's like spying through a keyhole.

British and modern art are the specialties of the Tate galleries (see listings above), but the National Gallery does have some fine 18th-century British masterpieces, including works by Hogarth, Gainsborough, Reynolds, Constable, and Turner.

Long written off as a "fake," a painting of Mary, Queen of Scots (1542–87) is on display. The portrait, purchased for less than £100 (today's exchange rate) was acquired by the gallery in 1916 at a Christie's auction. It gathered dust in a warehouse until it was rediscovered and authenticated. The age of the wood, on which the image of Mary was painted, turned out to be from the late 16th century. Today, the work is believed to be one of the only two paintings made in the lifetime or shortly after the death of the queen.

Free **guided tours** of the National Gallery are offered twice daily at 11:30am and 2:30pm, plus Fridays at 7pm. Various audio tours are also available, providing information on paintings of your choice with the mere push of a button (£3.50 for adults, £2.50 for seniors and students, and free for children under 12).

Insider's tip: The National Gallery has a computer information center where you can design your own personal tour map for free. The computer room, located in the Micro Gallery, includes a dozen hands-on workstations. The online system lists 2,200 paintings and has background notes for each work. Using a touch-screen computer, you can design your own personalized tour by selecting a maximum of 10 paintings you would like to view. Once you have made your choices, you print a personal tour map with your selections.

North side of Trafalgar Sq., WC2. *©* **020/7747-2885.** www.nationalgallery.org.uk. Free admission. Daily 10am–6pm (Fri until 9pm). Closed Jan 1 and Dec 24–26. Tube: Charing Cross, Leicester Sq., or Piccadilly.

Kensington Palace ★ ☺   Once the residence of British monarchs, Kensington Palace hasn't been the official home of reigning kings since George II. William III and Mary II acquired it in 1689 as an escape from the damp royal rooms along the Thames. Since the end of the 18th century, the palace has housed various members of the royal family, and the State Apartments are open for tours.

It was here in 1837 that a young Victoria was awakened with the news that her uncle, William IV, had died and she was now the queen of England. You can view a collection of Victoriana, including some of her memorabilia. In the apartments of Queen Mary II is a striking 17th-century writing cabinet inlaid with tortoiseshell. Paintings from the Royal Collection line the walls. A rare 1750 lady's court dress and splendid examples of male court dress from the 18th century are on display in rooms adjacent to the State Apartments, as part of the Royal Ceremonial Dress Collection, which features royal costumes dating as far back as 200 years.

Kensington Palace was the London home of the late Princess Margaret and is the current home of the duke and duchess of Kent. The palace was also the home of Diana, Princess of Wales, and her two sons. (Harry and William now live with their father at St. James's Palace.) The palace is probably best known for the millions of flowers placed in front of it during the days following Diana's death.

Warning: You don't get to see the apartments where Princess Di lived or where both Di and Charles lived until they separated. Many visitors think they'll get to peek at these rooms and are subsequently disappointed. Charles and Di lived on the west side of the palace, still occupied today by minor royals.

The **Kensington Gardens** are open to the public for leisurely strolls through the manicured grounds and around the Round Pond. One of the most famous sights is the controversial Albert Memorial, a lasting tribute not only to Victoria's consort, but also to the questionable taste of the Victorian era. There's a wonderful afternoon tea offered in the **Orangery** (p. 166).

The Broad Walk, Kensington Gardens, W8. *©* **0844/482-7777.** www.hrp.org.uk. Admission £13 adults, £11 seniors and students, £6.25 children 5–15, £34 family ticket, free for children 4 and younger. Mar–Oct daily 10am–6pm; Nov–Feb daily 10am–5pm. Tube: Queensway or Notting Hill Gate; or High St. Kensington on south side.

St. Paul's Cathedral ★★★   During World War II, newsreel footage reaching America showed St. Paul's Cathedral standing virtually alone among the rubble of the City of London, its dome lit by fires caused by bombings all around it. That the cathedral survived at all is a miracle, since it was badly hit twice during the early years of the bombardment of London. But St. Paul's is accustomed to calamity, having been burned down three times and destroyed by invading Norsemen. During the

Great Fire of 1666, the old St. Paul's was razed, making way for a new structure designed by Sir Christopher Wren and built between 1675 and 1710. The cathedral is architectural genius Wren's ultimate masterpiece.

The classical dome of St. Paul's dominates the City's square mile. The golden cross surmounting it is 110m (361 ft.) above the ground; the golden ball on which the cross rests measures 2m (6½ ft.) in diameter, though it looks like a marble from below. In the interior of the dome is the **Whispering Gallery,** an acoustic marvel in which the faintest whisper can be heard clearly on the opposite side. Sit on one side, have your traveling companion sit on the opposite side, and whisper away. You can climb to the top of the dome for a 360-degree view of London. From the Whispering Gallery a second steep climb leads to the **Stone Gallery,** opening onto a panoramic view of London. Another 153 steps take you to the **Inner Golden Gallery,** situated at the top of the inner dome. Here an even more panoramic view of London unfolds.

St. Paul's Churchyard, EC4. © **020/7246-8350.** www.stpauls.co.uk. Cathedral and galleries £13 adults, £12 seniors and students, £4.50 children 6–16, £30 family ticket, free for children 5 and younger; guided tours £3 adults, £2.50 students and seniors, £1 children; recorded tours £4, free for children 5 and younger. Cathedral (excluding galleries) Mon–Sat 8:30am–4pm; galleries Mon–Sat 9:30am–4pm. No sightseeing Sun (services only). Tube: St. Paul's, Mansion House, Cannon St., or Blackfriars.

Clarence House ★★　From 1953 until her death in 2002, the Queen Mother lived at Clarence House in a wing of St. James's Palace. It was constructed between 1825 and 1927 to the designs of John Nash. Today, it is the official residence of the Prince of Wales and is open to the public only during a specified period of the year (see below). The present Queen Elizabeth and the duke of Edinburgh lived here following their marriage in 1947.

After the death of the Queen Mother, the house was refurbished and redecorated, with antiques and art added from the royal collection. Visitors are taken on a guided tour of five of the staterooms, where much of the queen's collection of works of art and furniture is on display, along with pieces added by Prince Charles. The Queen Mother had an impressive collection of 20th-century British art, including works by John Piper, Augustus John, and Graham Sutherland. She also was known for her superb collection of Fabergé and English porcelain and silver, especially pieces from her family collection (the Bowes-Lyon family).

Stable Yard Gate, SW1. © **020/7766-7303.** www.royalcollection.org.uk. Admission £8.50 adults, seniors, and students; £4.50 children 5–16; free for children 4 and younger. Aug–Sept (dates subject to change; call first) daily 10am–5:30pm. Tube: Green Park or St. James's Park.

Victoria and Albert Museum ★★★　The Victoria and Albert is the greatest decorative-arts museum in the world. It's also one of the liveliest and most imaginative museums in London—where else would you find the quintessential "little black dress"—made famous by Coco Chanel—in the permanent collection?

The medieval holdings include such treasures as the Early English Gloucester Candlestick; the Byzantine Veroli Casket, with its ivory panels based on Greek plays; and the Syon Cope, a unique embroidery made in England in the early 14th century. An area devoted to Islamic art houses the Ardabil Carpet from 16th-century Persia.

The V&A boasts the largest collection of Renaissance sculpture outside Italy. A highlight of the 16th-century collection is the marble group *Neptune with Triton* by Bernini. The cartoons by Raphael, which were conceived as designs for tapestries for the Sistine Chapel, are owned by the queen and are on display here. A most unusual, huge, and impressive exhibit is the **Cast Courts,** life-size plaster models of ancient and medieval statuary and architecture.

The museum has the greatest collection of Indian art outside India, plus Chinese and Japanese galleries. In complete contrast are suites of English furniture, metal-work, and ceramics, along with a superb collection of portrait miniatures, including the one Hans Holbein the Younger made of Anne of Cleves for the benefit of Henry VIII, who was again casting around for a suitable wife. The fashion collection includes a representation of corsets through the ages that's sure to make you wince. There's also a remarkable assortment of musical instruments.

The V&A has 15 modern galleries—the **British Galleries ★★★**—telling the story of British design from 1500 to 1900. No other museum in the world houses such a diverse collection of British design and decorative art. From Chippendale to Morris, all of the top British designers are featured in some 3,000 exhibits, ranging from the 5m-high (16-ft.) Melville Bed (1697), with its luxurious wild-silk damask and red-velvet hangings, to 19th-century classics such as furniture by Charles Ren-nie Mackintosh. One of the most prized possessions is the "Great Bed of Ware," mentioned in Shakespeare's *Twelfth Night.* Also on exhibit is the wedding suite of James II.

And don't miss the V&A's most bizarre gallery, **Fakes and Forgeries.** The impos-tors here are amazingly authentic—in fact, we'd judge some of them as better than the Old Masters themselves. The interactive displays hold special interest. Learning about heraldry is far more interesting when you're designing your own coat of arms.

Also on view is a suite of five painting galleries that were originally built in 1850. A trio of these galleries focuses on British landscapes as seen through the eyes of Turner, Constable, and others. Constable's oil sketches were donated by his daugh-ter, Isabel, in 1888. Another gallery showcases the bequest of Constantine Ionides, a Victorian collector, with masters such as Botticelli, Delacroix, Degas, Tintoretto, and Ingres. There's even a piano here designed by the famous Edward Burne-Jones, which once belonged to Ionides's brother.

In 2009, the **Gilbert Collection ★★★**, one of the most important bequests of the decorative arts ever made in England, was moved to a suite of galleries in the V&A. Sir Arthur Gilbert made his gift of gold, silver, mosaics, and gold snuffboxes to the nation in 1996, at which time the value was estimated at £75 million. The collection of some 800 objects in three fields is among the most distinguished in the world. The array of mosaics, from Roman to Florentine examples, is among the most comprehensive ever gathered. The gold and silver collection has exceptional breadth, ranging from the 15th to the 19th centuries, spanning India to South America. It is strong in masterpieces of great 18th-century silversmiths, such as Paul de Lamerie. Such exhibits as the Maharajah pieces, the "Gold Crown," and Catherine the Great's Royal Gates are fabulous. The gallery also displays one of the most representative collections of gold snuffboxes in the world, with some 200 examples. Some of the snuffboxes were owned by Louis XV, Frederick the Great, and Napoleon.

Cromwell Rd., SW7. ℘ **020/7942-2000.** www.vam.ac.uk. Free admission. Temporary exhibitions often £12. Daily 10am–5:45pm (until 10pm every Wed and the last Fri of each month). Tube: South Kensington.

Trafalgar Square   One of the landmark squares of London, Trafalgar Square honors one of England's great military heroes, Horatio Viscount Nelson (1758–1805), who died at the Battle of Trafalgar. Although he suffered from seasickness all his life, he went to sea at the age of 12 and was an admiral at the age of 39. Lord Nelson was a hero of the Battle of Calvi in 1794 where he lost an eye, the Battle of Santa Cruz in 1797 where he lost an arm, and the Battle of Trafalgar in 1805 where he lost his life.

The square today is dominated by a 44m (145-ft.) granite column, the work of E. H. Baily in 1843. The column looks down Whitehall toward the Old Admiralty, where Lord Nelson's body lay in state. The figure of the naval hero towers 5m (17 ft.) high, not bad for a man who stood 1.5m (5 ft., 4 in.) in real life. The capital is of bronze cast from cannons recovered from the wreck of the *Royal George*. Queen Victoria's favorite animal painter, Sir Edward Landseer, added the four lions at the base of the column in 1868. The pools and fountains were not added until 1939, the last work of Sir Edwin Lutyens.

Political demonstrations still take place at the square and around the column, which has the most aggressive pigeons in London. These birds will even land on your head or perform less desirable stunts. Actually, the birds are part of a long feathery tradition, for this site was once used by Edward I (1239–1307) to keep his birds of prey. Called "Longshanks," he came here often before he died of dysentery in 1307. Richard II, who ruled from 1377 to 1399, kept goshawks and falcons here, too. By the time of Henry VII, who ruled from 1485 to 1509, the square was used as the site of the royal stables. Sir Charles Barry, who designed the Houses of Parliament, created the present square in the 1830s.

Trafalgar Square has lately become more user-friendly. A grand staircase has replaced the street between the square and the National Gallery. That's not all: Pedestrian crossings on the other streets enveloping the square make approaching it on foot less risky. Before, you were likely to get run over by a speeding vehicle. Of course, the summer fun of concerts, street entertainment, and open-air cafe-sitting will continue.

To the southeast of the square, at 36 Craven St., stands a house once occupied by Benjamin Franklin, when he was a general of the Philadelphia Academy (1757–74). On the north side of the square rises the National Gallery, constructed in the 1830s. In front of the building is a copy of a statue of George Washington by J. A. Houdon.

Trafalgar Sq., WC2. www.london.gov.uk/trafalgarsquare. Tube: Charing Cross, Leicester Sq., or Piccadilly.

National Portrait Gallery ★★   In a gallery of remarkable and unremarkable portraits (they're collected for their subjects rather than their artistic quality), a few paintings tower over the rest, including Sir Joshua Reynolds's first portrait of Samuel Johnson ("a man of most dreadful appearance"), Nicholas Hilliard's miniature of handsome Sir Walter Raleigh, a full-length portrait of Elizabeth I, and a Holbein cartoon of Henry VIII. There's also a portrait of William Shakespeare (with a gold earring) by an unknown artist that bears the claim of being the "most authentic contemporary likeness" of its subject. One of the most famous pictures in the gallery is the group portrait of the Brontë sisters (Charlotte, Emily, and Anne) by their brother, Bramwell. An idealized portrait of Lord Byron by Thomas Phillips is also on display.

The later-20th-century portraiture includes major works by such artists as Warhol and Hambling. Some of the more flamboyant personalities of the past 2 centuries are on show: T. S. Eliot, Disraeli, Macmillan, Sir Richard Burton (the explorer, not the actor), Elizabeth Taylor, and our two favorites, G. F. Watts's famous portrait of his great actress wife, Ellen Terry, and Vanessa Bell's portrait of her sister Virginia Woolf. A portrait of the late Princess Diana, on the Royal Landing, seems to attract the most viewers.

In 2000, Queen Elizabeth opened the Ondaatje Wing, increasing the gallery's exhibition space by more than half. The splendid Tudor Gallery features portraits of Richard III and Henry VII, Richard's conqueror in the Battle of Bosworth in 1485. There's also a portrait of Shakespeare that the gallery acquired in 1856. Rooms lead through centuries of English monarchs, with literary and artistic figures thrown in. It took a decade, but the top-floor Regency Galleries cover the period from the start of the French Revolution to 1832, with portraits of such luminaries as Napoleon, Admiral Nelson, Jane Austen, and the duke of Wellington. A Balcony Gallery taps into the cult of celebrity, displaying more recent figures whose fame has lasted longer than Warhol's 15 minutes. These include everybody from Mick Jagger to the Baroness Thatcher.

The National Gallery operates an on-site cafe and art bookshop.

St. Martin's Place, WC2. *©* **020/7306-0055.** www.npg.org.uk. Free admission; fee charged for certain temporary exhibitions. Sat–Wed 10am–6pm; Thurs–Fri 10am–9pm. Tube: Charing Cross or Leicester Sq.

Tower Bridge ★★   This is one of the world's most celebrated landmarks and possibly the most photographed and painted bridge on earth. Despite its medieval appearance, Tower Bridge was built in 1894.

In 1993, the Tower Bridge Exhibition opened inside the bridge to commemorate its century-old history; it takes you up the north tower to high-level walkways between the two towers with spectacular views of St. Paul's, the Tower of London, and the Houses of Parliament. You're then led down the south tower and into the bridge's original engine room, containing the Victorian boilers and steam engines that used to raise and lower the bridge for ships to pass. Exhibits in the towers use animatronic characters, video, and computers to illustrate the history of the bridge.

Tower Bridge Rd., SE1. *©* **020/7403-3761.** www.towerbridge.org.uk. Tower Bridge Exhibition £7 adults, £5 students and seniors, £3 children 5–15, £14 family ticket, free for children 4 and younger. Tower Bridge Exhibition Apr–Sept daily 10am–6:30pm; off-season daily 9:30am–6pm. Closed Dec 24–26. Tube: Tower Hill, London Bridge, or Fenchurch St.

MORE ATTRACTIONS

Official London

Whitehall ★, the seat of the British government, grew up on the grounds of Whitehall Palace and was turned into a royal residence by Henry VIII, who snatched it from its former occupant, Cardinal Wolsey. Whitehall extends south from Trafalgar Square to Parliament Square. Along it you'll find the Home Office, the Old Admiralty Building, and the Ministry of Defence.

Visitors today can see the **Churchill War Rooms** ★, formerly known as the Churchill Museum and Cabinet War Rooms. The bombproof bunker rooms are just as they were when abandoned by Winston Churchill and the British government at

Official London: Westminster & Whitehall

0 100 yds
0 100 m

PICCADILLY CIRCUS

St. Martin-in-the-Fields 1

National Portrait Gallery 2

National Gallery 3

Trafalgar Square

CHARING CROSS

Strand

Northumberland Ave.

GREEN PARK

GREEN PARK

Constitution Hill

St. James's Sq.

Pall Mall

Carlton House Terr.

The Mall

Horse Guards Rd.

Whitehall Pl.

Whitehall

Horse Guards Ave.

ST. JAMES'S PARK

Downing St.

King Charles St.

Queen Victoria Memorial

The Spur

St. James's Park Lake

Birdcage Walk

Queen Anne's Gate

Old Queen St.

Gt. George St.

WESTMINSTER

Bridge St.

Parliament Square

Guildhall

Big Ben

BUCKINGHAM PALACE GARDENS

Palace Rd.

Palace St.

Wilfred St.

Castle La.

Petty France

ST. JAMES'S PARK

Tothill St.

Caxton St.

Victoria St.

Broad Sanctuary

Houses of Parliament

Buckingham Palace Rd.

Bres senden Pl.

Stag Pl.

VICTORIA

Victoria Station

Wilton Rd.

Vauxhall Bridge Rd.

Carlisle Pl.

Francis St.

Ambrosden Ave.

Howick Pl.

Victoria St.

Greencoat Pl.

Horseferry Rd.

Great Peter St.

Monck St.

Smith Sq.

Millbank St.

Tube station (T)
Information (i)

Benjamin Franklin House 6
Buckingham Palace 11
Churchill War Rooms 13
Clarence House 10
Horse Guards Building 8
Household Cavalry Museum 8
Jewel Tower 16
London Transport Museum 1
National Gallery 3
National Portrait Gallery 2

Palaces of Westminster (Houses of Parliament) 15
Queen's Gallery 11
St. James's Park 9
St. Martin-in-the-Fields 5
Trafalgar Square 4
Tate Britain 17
Westminster Abbey 14
Westminster Cathedral 12
Whitehall 7

Regent's Park
THE CITY
THE WEST END
Area of Detail
0 1 Mi
0 1 Km

the end of World War II. You can see the Map Room with its huge wall maps, the Atlantic map a mass of pinholes (each hole represents at least one convoy). Next door is Churchill's bedroom-cum-office, which has a bed and a desk with two BBC microphones on it for his famous speech broadcasts that stirred the nation. Between 1945 and 2003, parts of this underground bunker were closed to the public. Today, however, you can view nine more Cabinet War Rooms. You can also see Churchill's private kitchen and dining room as well as Mrs. Churchill's bedroom. There's everything here from a pencil cartoon of Hitler to a mousetrap in the kitchen to the original chamber pots under the beds (they had no flush toilets). The **Transatlantic Telephone Room,** its full title, is little more than a broom closet, but it housed the Bell Telephone Company's special scrambler phone, called *Sigsaly,* and it was where Churchill conferred with Roosevelt. Visitors are provided with a step-by-step personal sound guide, providing a detailed account of each room's function and history.

Also part of the complex is the **Churchill Museum,** the world's first major museum dedicated to the life of Sir Winston Churchill. It explores in various exhibits and photographs the saga of Britain's wartime prime minister. The opening marked the 40th anniversary of the prime minister's death. The museum through its memorabilia introduces the visitors to the private man but also traces his development as a world leader.

The entrance to the Churchill War Rooms is by Clive Steps at the end of King Charles Street, SW1 (✆ **020/7930-6961;** http://cwr.iwm.org.uk; Tube: Westminster or St. James's), off Whitehall near the Westminster Palace Clock Tower (Big Ben). Admission is £15 for adults, £12 for seniors and students, and free for children 15 and younger. The rooms are open daily 9:30am to 6pm.

At the Cenotaph (honoring the dead of both World Wars I and II), look down **Downing Street** to the modest little town house at no. 10, flanked by two bobbies. It is no longer possible to walk down the street because of security reasons; you can only peer through the gates. Walpole was the first prime minister to live here; Churchill was the most famous. But Margaret Thatcher was around longer than any of them.

Nearby, north of Downing Street, is the **Horse Guards building** ★, Whitehall (no phone; Tube: Westminster), now the headquarters of the horse guards of the Household Division and London District. There has been a guard change here since 1649, when the site was the entrance to the old Palace of Whitehall. You can watch the Queen's Life Guard ceremony at 11am Monday through Saturday and 10am on Sunday; for details, go to www.army.mod.uk/events/ceremonial/2355.aspx. You can also see the hourly smaller **Changing of the Guard,** when mounted troopers are changed. And at 4pm, you can watch the evening inspection, when 10 unmounted troopers and two mounted troopers assemble in the courtyard.

Across the street is Inigo Jones's **Banqueting House,** Palace of Whitehall, Horse Guards Avenue (✆ **0844/482-7777;** www.hrp.org.uk; Tube: Westminster or Embankment), site of the execution of Charles I. William and Mary accepted the crown of England here, but they preferred to live at Kensington Palace. The Banqueting House was part of Whitehall Palace, which burned to the ground in 1698, but the ceremonial hall escaped razing. Its most notable feature today is an allegorical ceiling painted by Peter Paul Rubens. Admission to the Banqueting House is £4.80 for adults, £4 for seniors and students, and free for children 15 and younger.

A City of Wine

At **Vinopolis**, 1 Bank End, Park Street, SE1 (📞 **0870/241-4040**; www.vinopolis.co.uk), you can partake of London's largest selection of wine sold by the glass. On the South Bank, this "city of wine" lies under cavernous railway arches created in Victoria's era. The bacchanalian attraction was created in a multimedia format, at the cost of £23 million. You can journey virtually through some of the earth's most prestigious wine regions, driving a Vespa through the Tuscan countryside or taking a "flight" over the vineyards of Australia. The price of entrance includes free tastings of five premium wines, and an on-site shop sells almost any item related to the grape. There's also a good restaurant, Cantina Vinopolis (p. 158). Depending on the ticket and package purchased, admission ranges from £24 to £100. Hours are Thursday through Saturday noon to 10pm, Sunday noon to 6pm (last entrance 2½ hr. before closing).

It's open Monday to Saturday 10am to 5pm (last admission 4:30pm). Banqueting House often closes on short notice, so it's best to call before going.

Legal London

The smallest borough in London, bustling **Holborn** (pronounced *Ho*-burn) is often referred to as Legal London, home of the city's barristers, solicitors, and law clerks. It also embraces the university district of Bloomsbury. Holborn, which houses the ancient **Inns of Courts**—Gray's Inn, Lincoln's Inn, Middle Temple, and Inner Temple—was severely damaged during World War II bombing raids. The razed buildings were replaced with modern offices, but the borough retains pockets from its former days.

At the 60 or more **Law Courts** presently in use on the Strand, all civil and some criminal cases are heard. Designed by G. E. Street, the neo-Gothic buildings (1874–82) have more than 1,000 rooms and 5.5km (3½ miles) of corridors. Sculptures of Christ, King Solomon, and King Alfred grace the front door; Moses is depicted at the back. Admission is free, and courts are open during sessions Monday through Friday from 10am to 4:30pm (Tube: Holborn or Temple). No cameras, tape recorders, video cameras, or cellphones are allowed during sessions.

The court known as the **Old Bailey,** on Newgate Street, EC4 (📞 **020/7248-3277**; www.oldbaileyonline.org), replaced the infamous Newgate Prison, once the scene of public hangings and other forms of "public entertainment." It's fascinating to watch the bewigged barristers presenting their cases to the high court judges. Entry is strictly on a first-arrival basis, and visitors line up outside. Courts 1 to 4, 17, and 18 are entered from Newgate Street, and the balance from Old Bailey (the street). To get here, take the Tube to Temple, Chancery Lane, or St. Paul's. Travel east on Fleet Street, which along the way becomes Ludgate Hill. Cross Ludgate Circus and turn left to the Old Bailey, a domed structure with the figure of Justice standing atop it. Admission is free; children 13 and younger are not admitted, and those ages 14 to 16 must be accompanied by an adult. No cameras, tape recorders, or cellphones are allowed. Hours are Monday to Friday 10am to 1pm and 2 to 5pm. The best time to line up is 9am.

More Museums

Apsley House (Wellington Museum) ★   This was the former town house of Arthur Wellesley, the "Iron Duke" of Wellington, the British general (1769–1852) who defeated Napoleon at the Battle of Waterloo and later became prime minister. It was designed by Robert Adam (1728–92), who pioneered the neoclassical style in Britain, with light, elegant lines unbound by strict classical proportion. Wellington once retreated behind the walls of Apsley House, fearing an attack from Englishmen outraged by his autocratic opposition to reform. In the vestibule is a colossal marble statue of Napoleon by Antonio Canova (1757–1822), the greatest Italian sculptor from the 18th century until today. The statue is nude—ironic, to say the least. It was presented to the duke by King George IV. In addition to the famous *Waterseller of Seville* by Velázquez, the Wellington collection includes works by Correggio, Jan Steen, and Pieter de Hooch.

Insider's tip: Apsley House has some of the finest silver and porcelain pieces in Europe. Grateful to Wellington for saving their thrones, European monarchs endowed him with treasures. Head for the Plate and China Room on the ground floor. The Sèvres Egyptian service was intended as a divorce present from Napoleon to Josephine, but she refused it. Eventually Louis XVII of France presented it to Wellington. The Portuguese Silver Service in the dining room was created between 1812 and 1816; it has been hailed as the single greatest artifact of Portuguese neoclassical silver.

149 Piccadilly, Hyde Park Corner, W1. ✆ **020/7499-5676.** www.english-heritage.org.uk/apsleyhouse. Admission £6 adults, £5.10 seniors and students, £3 children 15 and younger. Apr–Oct Tues–Sun 11am–5pm; Nov–Mar Tues–Sun 11am–4pm. Tube: Hyde Park Corner.

Benjamin Franklin House ★   The only surviving home of Benjamin Franklin in London opened as a museum in 2006. Off Trafalgar Square, the modest four-story brick building was Franklin's home between 1757 and 1775, when he served as a diplomat on behalf of the American colonists. Curators call the house the "first de facto U.S. Embassy." The building was also the site of many of Franklin's scientific experiments. It was here that he invented bifocal glasses and created the glass armonica, an ethereal-sounding musical instrument. (Mozart and Beethoven later created music on this armonica.) Franklin lived here in "serene comfort and affection," often having a full household of friends or relatives. Among other attractions, visitors can view the parlor where Franklin—a great fan of fresh air—sat "air bathing" naked by the open windows. The museum stages a "Historical Experience" every 45 minutes throughout the day. Visitors are taken through the various rooms by actors presenting a re-creation of Franklin's last night in London.

36 Craven St., WC2. ✆ **020/7839-2006.** www.benjaminfranklinhouse.org. Admission £7 adults, free for children 15 and younger. Wed–Sun noon–5pm. Tube: Charing Cross or Embankment.

British Library ★★   In 1996, one of the world's great libraries moved its collection of some 12 million books, manuscripts, and other items from the British Museum to its very own home in St. Pancras. You get modernistic beauty here, rather than the fading glamour and the ghosts of Karl Marx, William Thackeray, and Virginia Woolf of the old library at the British Museum. You are also likely to get the book you want within an hour instead of 3 days. Academics, students, writers, and bookworms from the world over come here. On one visit, we sat next to a student researching the history of pubs.

Sights from Knightsbridge to Kensington

Apsley House
(Wellington Museum) **3**

Carlyle's House **7**

Kensington Gardens **2**

Kensington Palace **1**

National Army Museum **8**

Natural History Museum **5**

Saatchi Gallery **9**

Science Museum **4**

Victoria and Albert Museum **6**

Church ✠
Tube station Φ
Information ⓘ

Regent's Park

THE CITY

THE WEST END

Area of Detail

The bright, roomy interior is far more inviting than the rather dull redbrick exterior suggests (writer Alain de Botton likened the exterior to a supermarket). Still, Colin St. John Wilson, the architect, says he has been delighted by the positive response to his building. The most spectacular room is the Humanities Reading Room, constructed on three levels with daylight filtered through the ceiling.

The fascinating collection includes such items of historic and literary interest as two of the four surviving copies of the Magna Carta (1215), a Gutenberg Bible, Nelson's last letter to Lady Hamilton, and the journals of Captain Cook. Almost every major author—Dickens, Jane Austen, Charlotte Brontë, Keats, and hundreds of others—is represented in the section devoted to English literature. Beneath Roubiliac's 1758 statue of Shakespeare stands a case of documents relating to the Bard, including a mortgage bearing his signature and a copy of the First Folio of 1623. There's also an unrivaled collection of stamps and stamp-related items.

Using headphones set around the room, you can hear thrilling audio snippets such as James Joyce reading a passage from *Finnegans Wake*. Curiosities include the earliest known tape of a birdcall, dating from 1889. Particularly intriguing is an exhibition called "Turning the Pages," where, for example, you can electronically read a complete Leonardo da Vinci notebook by putting your hands on a special computer screen that flips from one page to another. There is a copy of *The Canterbury Tales* from 1410, and even manuscripts of *Beowulf* (ca. 1000). On display are reproductions of illuminated texts, including the *Codex Sinaitticus* and *Codex Alexandrius,* 3rd-century Greek gospels. In the Historical Documents section are letters by everybody from Henry VIII to Napoleon, from Elizabeth I to Churchill. In the music displays, you can seek out original sheet music by Beethoven, Handel, Stravinsky, and Lennon and McCartney. An entire day spent here will only scratch the surface.

Walking tours of the library cost £8 for adults and £7 for seniors, students, and children. They are conducted Monday, Wednesday, and Friday at 3pm, and Saturday at 10:30am and 3pm. Library tours that include a visit to one of the reading rooms take place on Sundays and bank holidays at 10:30am and 3pm (£8 adults, £6.50 for seniors and students). Reservations can be made up to 2 weeks in advance.

96 Euston Rd., NW1. © **020/7412-7676.** www.bl.uk. Free admission. Mon and Wed-Fri 9:30am-6pm; Tues 9:30am-8pm; Sat 9:30am-5pm; Sun 11am-5pm. Tube: Kings Cross/St. Pancras or Euston.

City Hall   On the South Bank of the Thames adjacent to Tower Bridge, the mayor of London and the London Assembly got a new home in 2002. A gleaming, egg-shaped building, this 10-story steel-and-glass structure was dedicated by Her Majesty. The new home for city government has become London's latest—some say, most controversial—landmark. Half of City Hall is open to the public. The views from its rooftop gallery are worth the trek over to the South Bank. An exhibition space highlights changing cultural exhibits, and there is also an on-site cafe.

The Queen's Walk, SE1. © **020/7983-4000.** www.london.gov.uk. Free admission. Visitor information desk Mon-Fri 9am-5pm. Cafe Mon-Fri 8am-8pm. Tube: London Bridge.

Courtauld Gallery   The nucleus of this collection was acquired by Samuel Courtauld, who died in 1947, leaving his collection to the University of London. Today, it houses the biggest collection of Impressionist and post-Impressionist paintings in Britain, with masterpieces by Monet, Manet, Degas, Renoir, Cézanne, van Gogh, and Gauguin. The gallery also has a superb collection of Old Master paintings and drawings, including works by Rubens and Michelangelo; early Italian paintings, ivories, and majolica; the Lee collection of Old Masters; and early-20th-century English, French, and British paintings.

The galleries on the second floor display a series of paintings and sculptures, some 100 pieces of art from the late 19th and 20th centuries, including an outstanding grouping of Fauve paintings along with art by everybody from Matisse to Dufy, as well as a remarkable series of paintings and drawings by Kandinsky. We come here at least once every season to revisit one work in particular: Manet's exquisite *A Bar at the Folies-Bergère* ★. Many of the paintings are displayed without glass, giving the gallery a more intimate feeling than most. This gallery is but one of three major attractions at Somerset House.

Somerset House, Strand, WC2. ✆ **020/7848-2526.** www.courtauld.ac.uk. Admission £5 adults, £4 seniors and students, free for children 17 and younger. Daily 10am–6pm (last admission 5:30pm). Tube: Temple, Covent Garden, Charing Cross, or Holborn.

Guildhall Art Gallery ★　In 1999, Queen Elizabeth opened this £70-million gallery, a continuation of the original gallery, which was launched in 1886 and burned down in a severe air raid in May 1941. Many famous and much-loved pictures, which for years were known only through temporary exhibitions and reproductions, are once again available for the public to see in a permanent setting in the City, though the gallery can display only 250 of the 4,000 treasures it owns at a time. The Corporation of London in the City owns these works and has been collecting them since the 17th century. Since World War II, all paintings acquired by the gallery have concentrated on London subjects. A curiosity is the huge double-height wall built to accommodate Britain's largest independent oil painting, John Singleton Copley's *The Defeat of the Floating Batteries at Gibraltar, September 1782.* The most popular pieces are in the Victorian collection, including such favorites as Millais's *My First Sermon* and *My Second Sermon,* and Landseer's *The First Leap.* There is also a large landscape of Salisbury Cathedral by John Constable. Included in your admission price is entrance to the ruins of the only Roman amphitheater discovered in London—it was unearthed in 1988.

Guildhall Yard, EC2. ✆ **020/7332-3700.** www.cityoflondon.gov.uk. Admission £2.50 adults, £1 seniors and students, free for children 15 and younger; free Fri and after 3:30pm on every other day. Mon–Sat 10am–5pm; Sun noon–4pm. Tube: Bank, St. Paul's, Mansion House, or Moorgate.

Hayward Gallery　Opened by Elizabeth II in 1968, this gallery presents a changing program of major contemporary and historical exhibits. It's part of the Southbank Centre, which also includes the Royal Festival Hall, the Queen Elizabeth Hall, and the Purcell Room. Every exhibition is accompanied by a variety of educational activities, including tours, workshops, lectures, and publications. The gallery closes between exhibitions, so call before crossing the Thames.

In the Southbank Centre, Belvedere Rd., South Bank, SE1. ✆ **0871/6632500.** www.southbankcentre.co.uk. Admission varies, but usually £10 adults, £6.50 students and seniors, free for children 11 and younger; half-price Mon. Hours subject to change, depending on the exhibit, but usually Thurs and Sat-Mon 10am–6pm; Fri 10am–9pm; Tues–Wed 11am–8pm. Tube: Waterloo or Embankment.

Household Cavalry Museum　The queen herself showed up in 2008 to open this museum installed in the Whitehall stables, which are still in use. The Household Cavalry consists of the Life Guards and the Blues and Royals, the oldest and most senior regiments in the British Army. Founded in 1661, on orders of King

Charles II, the cavalry guards Her Majesty on ceremonial occasions. Some of the men in the regiment are also deployed on active service in Afghanistan and Iraq. This is a living museum, where you can see, for example, troopers working with horses in their original stables from the 1700s. The museum also contains regimental collections of arms and militaria.

Horse Guards, Whitehall SW1. (C) **020/7930-3070.** www.householdcavalrymuseum.co.uk. Admission £6 adults; £4 seniors, students, and children 5-16; £15 family ticket. Mar–Sept daily 10am–6pm; Oct–Feb daily 10am–5pm. Tube: Charing Cross, Westminster, or Embankment.

London Transport Museum ★ ☺   After a vast restoration and expansion, this museum has increased its display space by 25%. A collection of nearly 2 centuries of historic vehicles is displayed in a splendid Victorian building that formerly housed the Flower Market at Covent Garden. The museum shows how London's transport system evolved, and a representative collection of road vehicles includes a reconstruction of George Shillibeer's Omnibus of 1829. Also of interest are a steam locomotive that ran the world's first underground railway, a knifeboard bus, London's first trolleybus, and a Feltham tram. The museum's galleries also consider the future of London's transport as well as the past. For the first time, Harry Beck's original 1930s artwork for the world-famous Underground map is now on public display, along with gems from the museum's valuable poster collections, including some by such famous artists as Man Ray.

Covent Garden Piazza, WC2. (C) **020/7379-6344.** www.ltmuseum.co.uk. Admission £10 adults, £8 seniors, £6 students, free for children 15 and younger. Sun–Tues 10am–6:30pm; Wed–Thurs and Sat 10am–7pm; Fri 11am–7pm. Tube: Covent Garden, Leicester Sq., Charing Cross, or Holburn.

Madame Tussauds ✋ ☺   Madame Tussauds is not so much a wax museum as an enclosed amusement park. A weird, moving, sometimes terrifying (to children) collage of exhibitions, panoramas, and stage settings, it manages to be most things to most people, most of the time.

Madame Tussaud attended the court of Versailles and learned her craft in France. She personally took the death masks from the guillotined heads of Louis XVI and Marie Antoinette (which you'll find among the exhibits). She moved her original museum from Paris to England in 1802. Her exhibition has been imitated in every part of the world, but never with the realism and imagination on hand here. Madame herself molded the features of Benjamin Franklin, whom she met in Paris. All the rest—from George Washington to John F. Kennedy and Mary, Queen of Scots, to Sylvester Stallone—have been subjects for the same painstaking (and often breathtaking) replication.

In the well-known Chamber of Horrors—a kind of underground dungeon—are all kinds of instruments of death, along with figures of their victims. The shadowy presence of Jack the Ripper lurks in the gloom as you walk through a Victorian London street. Present-day criminals are portrayed within the confines of prison. The latest attraction to open here is the Spirit of London, a musical ride that depicts 400 years of London's history, using special effects that include audio-animatronic figures that move and speak. Visitors take "time-taxis" that allow them to see and hear "Shakespeare" as he writes and speaks lines, to be received by Queen Elizabeth I, and to experience the Great Fire of 1666 that destroyed London.

We've seen these changing exhibitions so many times over the years that we feel they're a bit cheesy, but we still remember the first time we were taken here as kids. We thought it fascinating back then.

Insider's tip: To avoid the long lines, sometimes more than an hour in summer, call in advance and reserve a ticket for fast pickup at the entrance. If you don't want to bother with that, be aggressive and form a group of nine people waiting in the queue. A group of nine or more can go in almost at once through the "group door." Otherwise, go when the gallery first opens or late in the afternoon when crowds have thinned.

Marylebone Rd., NW1. ℭ **0871/894-3000.** www.madametussauds.com. Admission £22–£41 adults, £18–£30 children 15 and younger; £80–£89 family ticket. ***Note:*** Prices can be higher or lower at different times during the year. Mon–Fri 9:30am–5:30pm; Sat–Sun 9am–6pm. Tube: Baker St.

Museum of London ★★   In the Barbican district near St. Paul's Cathedral, the Museum of London allows visitors to trace the city's history from prehistoric times to the postmodern era through relics, costumes, household effects, maps, and models. Anglo-Saxons, Vikings, Normans—they're all here, displayed on two floors around a central courtyard. The exhibits are arranged so that visitors can begin and end their chronological stroll through 250,000 years at the museum's main entrance; there are quick labels for museum sprinters to read, more extensive ones for those who want to study, and still more detail for scholars. It's an enriching experience for everybody—allow at least an hour for a full (but still quick) visit.

While here, you'll see the death mask of Oliver Cromwell; the Great Fire of London in living color and sound; reconstructed Roman dining rooms with kitchen and utensils; cell doors from Newgate Prison, made famous by Charles Dickens; and an amazing shop counter with pre–World War II prices on the items. But the *pièce de résistance* is the Lord Mayor's coach, built in 1757 and weighing 3 tons. Still used each November in the Lord Mayor's Procession, this gilt-and-red horse-drawn vehicle is like a fairy-tale coach. Also on-site is the World City Gallery, an entire floor whose 2,000 exhibits and artifacts trace life in London between 1789 and 1914, the beginning of World War I.

You can reach the museum, which overlooks London's Roman and medieval walls, by going up to the elevated pedestrian precinct at the corner of London Wall and Aldersgate, 5 minutes from St. Paul's.

150 London Wall, EC2. ℭ **020/7001-9844.** www.museumoflondon.org.uk. Free admission. Mon–Sat 10am–6pm; Sun noon–5:50pm. Tube: St. Paul's, Barbican, or Moorgate.

National Army Museum ★ ☺   The National Army Museum occupies a building adjoining the Royal Hospital, a home for retired soldiers, in Chelsea. Whereas the Imperial War Museum is concerned with wars of the 20th century, the National Army Museum tells the colorful story of British armies from 1485 on. You'll find uniforms worn by British soldiers in every corner of the world, plus weapons and other gear, flags, and medals. Even the skeleton of Napoleon's favorite charger is here. Also on display are Florence Nightingale's jewelry, the telephone switchboard from Hitler's headquarters (captured in 1945), and Orders and Medals of HRH the Duke of Windsor. A more recent gallery, "The Rise of the Redcoats," contains exhibitions detailing the life of the British soldier from 1485 to 1793. Included in the exhibit are displays on the English Civil War and the American War of Independence.

Royal Hospital Rd., SW3. ☏ **020/7730-0717.** www.national-army-museum.ac.uk. Free admission. Daily 10am–5:30pm. Closed Jan 1, Good Friday, 1st Mon in May, and Dec 24–26. Tube: Sloane Sq.

Natural History Museum ★★ ☺   This is the home of the national collections of living and fossil plants, animals, and minerals, with many magnificent specimens on display. The zoological displays are quite wonderful; though not up to the level of the Smithsonian in Washington, D.C., they're definitely worthwhile and exciting exhibits designed to encourage people of all ages to learn about natural history. The Mineral Gallery features marvelous examples of crystals and gemstones. The Meteorite Pavilion exhibits fragments of rock that have crashed into the earth, some from the farthest reaches of the galaxy. What attracts the most attention is the dinosaur exhibit, displaying 14 complete skeletons. In the "Earth Today and Tomorrow" exhibit, visitors are invited to explore the planet's dramatic history from the big bang to its inevitable death.

The latest development here is the **Darwin Centre,** dedicated to the great naturalist Charles Darwin. The center reveals the museum's scientific work with specimens, research, and outreach activities. You're given an insider's look that answers such questions as how specimens are collected today and addresses ethical considerations as well. These are not just specimens in a bottle. You learn, for example, how mosquito DNA helps scientists track down the spread of malaria, or about the alien habitat of the deep sea and the strange animals that inhabit these murky depths. Free behind-the-scenes **guided tours** (for ages 9 and older only) are given daily at various times; you should book immediately upon entering the museum if you're interested.

Cromwell Rd., SW7. ☏ **020/7942-5000.** www.nhm.ac.uk. Free admission. Mon–Sat 10am–5:50pm; Sun 11am–5:50pm. Tube: South Kensington.

Queen's Gallery ★★   The refurbished gallery at Buckingham Palace reopened to the public in 2002, in time for the Golden Jubilee celebration of Queen Elizabeth II. John Nash designed the original building in 1831, but it was destroyed in a Nazi air raid in 1940. Visitors going through the Doric portico entrance will now find three times as much space as before. The gallery is dedicated to changing exhibitions of the wide-ranging treasure trove that forms the Royal Collection. Anticipate special exhibitions of paintings, prints, drawings, watercolors, furniture, porcelain, miniatures, enamels, jewelry, and other works of art. At any given time, expect to see such artistic peaks as Van Dyck's equestrian portrait of Charles I, the world-famous *Lady at the Virginal* by Vermeer, a dazzling array of gold snuff boxes, paintings by Monet from the collection of the late Queen Mother, personal jewelry, and studies by Leonardo da Vinci.

Buckingham Palace, SW1. ☏ **020/7766-7301.** www.royalcollection.org.uk. Admission £5 adults, £4.50 students and seniors, £3 children 5–16, £13 family ticket, free for children 4 and younger. Daily 10am–5:30pm. Tube: Hyde Park Corner, Green Park, or Victoria.

Saatchi Gallery ★★   This world-famous gallery has settled into its latest home, in the former Royal Military Asylum building of 1801. British mega-collector Charles Saatchi is known for shocking the world with his stunningly avant-garde exhibitions. Art lovers define the controversial collector as the vision of the 21st century—or else demand that he be jailed at once and the key thrown away. If you're offended by the revered Madonna (no, not *that* one) with elephant dung, or Damien

Hirst's pickled sharks, then go look at a Rembrandt. This former ad man has been called everything from a "modern-day Medici" to a "Machiavellian mogul." Saatchi's aim is to bring contemporary art to the widest possible audience. He presents works by unseen young artists or by established international artists whose work is rarely if ever exhibited in the U.K. Regardless of what's on display at the time of your visit, it's liable to be controversial.

Duke of York's Headquarters, King's Rd., SW3. 𝒞 **020/7811-3070.** www.saatchi-gallery.co.uk. Free admission. Daily 10am–6pm. Tube: Sloane Sq.

Science Museum ★★★ ☺ This museum traces the development of science and industry and their influence on everyday life. These scientific collections are among the largest, most comprehensive, and most significant anywhere. On display are Stephenson's original rocket and the tiny prototype railroad engine; you can also see Whittle's original jet engine and the *Apollo 10* space module. The King George III Collection of scientific instruments is the highlight of a gallery on science in the 18th century. Health Matters is a permanent gallery on modern medicine. The museum also has two hands-on galleries, as well as working models and video displays.

Insider's tip: A large addition to this museum explores such topics as genetics, digital technology, and artificial intelligence. Four floors of the new Wellcome Wing shelter half a dozen exhibition areas and a 450-seat IMAX theater. One exhibition explores everything from drug use in sports to how engineers observe sea life with robotic submarines. On an upper floor, visitors can learn how DNA was used to identify living relatives of the Bleadon Man, a 2,000-year-old Iron Age Man. On the third floor is the computer that Tim Berners-Lee used to design the World Wide Web outside Geneva, writing the first software for it in 1990.

Note also the marvelous interactive consoles placed strategically in locations throughout the museum. These display special itineraries, including directions for getting to the various galleries for families, teens, adults, and those with special interests.

Exhibition Rd., SW7. 𝒞 **0870/870-4868.** www.sciencemuseum.org.uk. Free admission. Daily 10am–6pm. Closed Dec 24–26. Tube: South Kensington.

Sir John Soane's Museum ★ This is the former home of Sir John Soane (1753–1837), an architect who rebuilt the Bank of England (not the present structure). With his multiple levels, fool-the-eye mirrors, flying arches, and domes, Soane was a master of perspective and a genius of interior space; his picture gallery, for example, is filled with three times the number of paintings a room of similar dimensions would be likely to hold. William Hogarth's satirical series *The Rake's Progress* includes his much-reproduced *Orgy* and *The Election,* a satire on mid-18th-century politics. Soane also filled his house with paintings and classical sculpture. On display is the sarcophagus of Pharaoh Seti I, found in a burial chamber in the Valley of the Kings. Also exhibited are architectural drawings from the collection of 30,000 in the Soane Gallery.

13 Lincoln's Inn Fields, WC2. 𝒞 **020/7440-4263.** www.soane.org. Free admission (donations invited). Tues–Sat 10am–5pm; 1st Tues of each month 6–9pm. Tours given Sat at 11am; £5 tickets distributed at 10:30am, first-come, first-served (group tours by appointment only). Tube: Holborn.

Wallace Collection ★★ 🏛 Located in a palatial setting (the modestly described "town house" of the late Lady Wallace), this collection is a contrasting array of art and armaments. It's evocative of the Frick Museum in New York and the Musée d'Jacque André in Paris. The art collection (mostly French) includes works by Watteau, Boucher, Fragonard, and Greuze, as well as such classics as Frans Hals's *Laughing Cavalier* and Rembrandt's portrait of his son Titus. The paintings of the Dutch, English, Spanish, and Italian schools are outstanding. The collection also contains important 18th-century French decorative art, including furniture from a number of royal palaces, Sèvres porcelain, and gold boxes. The European and Asian armaments, on the ground floor, are works of art in their own right: superb inlaid suits of armor, some obviously for parade rather than battle, with more businesslike swords, halberds, and magnificent Persian scimitars.

Manchester Sq., W1. © **020/7563-9500.** www.wallacecollection.org. Free admission (fee for some exhibits). Daily 10am–5pm. Tube: Bond St. or Baker St.

Literary Landmarks

See the discussion of Hampstead Village, below, for details on the Keats House. See "The Top Attractions" section, earlier in this chapter, for details on Poets' Corner in Westminster Abbey.

Born in London in 1882, the author **Virginia Woolf** lived and worked in **Bloomsbury,** and she wrote many of her works in London. Virginia spent her formative years at 22 Hyde Park Gate, off Kensington High Street, west of Royal Albert Hall. After the death of her father, the family left Kensington for Bloomsbury and settled in the area around the British Museum (upper-class Victorians at that time, however, didn't view Bloomsbury as "respectable"). From 1905, they lived first at 46 Gordon Sq., east of Gower Street and University College. Here the nucleus of the soon-to-be celebrated **Bloomsbury Group** was created, which, in time, would embrace Clive Bell (husband of Virginia's sister Vanessa) and Leonard Woolf, who was to become Virginia's husband. Later, Virginia lived at 29 Fitzroy Sq., west of Tottenham Court Road, in a house once occupied by George Bernard Shaw. During the next 2 decades, Virginia resided at several more addresses in Bloomsbury, including on Brunswick Square, Tavistock Square, and Mecklenburg Square; these homes have either disappeared or been altered beyond recognition. During this time, the Bloomsbury Group reached out to include artists Roger Fry and Duncan Grant, and Virginia became friends with economist Maynard Keynes and author E. M. Forster. At Tavistock Square (1924–39) and at Mecklenburg Square (1939–40), she operated Hogarth Press with Leonard. She published her own early work here, as well as T. S. Eliot's *The Waste Land.* To escape from urban life, Leonard and Virginia purchased Monk's House, in the village of Rodmell between Lewes and Newhaven in Sussex. They lived there until 1941, when Virginia drowned herself in the nearby Ouse. Her ashes were buried in the garden at Monk's House.

Carlyle's House From 1834 to 1881, Thomas Carlyle, author of *The French Revolution,* and Jane Baillie Welsh Carlyle, his noted letter-writing wife, resided in this modest 1708 terraced house. Furnished essentially as it was in Carlyle's day, the house is located about three-quarters of a block from the Thames, near the Chelsea Embankment along King's Road. The most interesting room is the not-so-sound-proof "soundproof" study in the sky-lit attic. It's filled with Carlyle memorabilia—his

What to See & Do in Bloomsbury

British Library **1**

British Museum **2**

Charles Dickens
Museum **4**

Courtauld Gallery **6**

Dr. Johnson's House **7**

Hayward Gallery **10**

National Gallery **5**

London Eye **9**

St. Bride's Church **8**

Shakespeare's
Globe Theatre
& Exhibition **12**

Sir John Soane's
Museum **4**

Tate Modern **11**

Church †
Tube station ⊖

Regent's Park

Area of Detail

THE CITY

THE WEST END

0   1 Mi
0   1 Km

0   1/4 mi
0   1/4 km

books, a letter from Disraeli, personal effects, a writing chair, and even his death mask.

24 Cheyne Row, SW3. ℂ **020/7352-7087.** www.nationaltrust.org.uk/carlyleshouse. Admission £4.90 adults, £2.50 children 6–16, free for children 5 and younger , £12 family ticket. Wed–Sun and bank holidays 2–5pm. Closed Nov–mid-Mar. Tube: Sloane Sq. or South Kensington.

Charles Dickens Museum   Here in Bloomsbury stands the simple abode in which Charles Dickens wrote *Oliver Twist* and finished *The Pickwick Papers* (his American readers actually waited at the dock for the ship that brought in each new installment). The place is almost a shrine: It contains his study, manuscripts, and personal relics, as well as reconstructed interiors. During Christmas week (including Christmas Day), the museum is decorated in the style of Dickens's first Christmas here. The higher Christmas admission prices of £10 for adults and £5 for children include hot mince pies and a few glasses of "Smoking Bishop," Dickens's favorite hot punch, as well as a copy of the museum's guidebook.

48 Doughty St., WC1. ℂ **020/7405-2127.** www.dickensmuseum.com. Admission £6 adults, £4.50 students and seniors, £3 children, £15 family ticket. Mon–Sat 10am–5pm; Sun 11am–5pm. Tube: Russell Sq., Chancery Lane, or Holborn.

Dr. Johnson's House ★★   Samuel Johnson and his copyists compiled a famous dictionary in this Queen Anne house, where the lexicographer, poet, essayist, and fiction writer lived from 1748 to 1759. Although Johnson also lived at Staple Inn in Holborn and at a number of other places, the Gough Square house is the only one of his residences remaining in London. The 17th-century building has been painstakingly restored, and it's well worth a visit.

17 Gough Sq., EC4. ℂ **020/7353-3745.** www.drjohnsonshouse.org. Admission £4.50 adults, £3.50 students and seniors, £1.50 children, £10 family ticket, free for children 10 and younger. Oct–Apr Mon–Sat 11am–5pm; May–Sept Mon–Sat 11am–5:30pm. Tube: Blackfriars, Chancery Lane, Temple, or Holborn. Walk up New Bridge St. and turn left onto Fleet St.; Gough Sq. is tiny and hidden, north of Fleet St.

Shakespeare's Globe Theatre & Exhibition ★   A re-creation of what was probably the most important public theater ever built, it's on the exact site where many of Shakespeare's plays opened. The late American filmmaker Sam Wanamaker worked for some 20 years to raise funds to re-create the theater as it existed in Elizabethan times, thatched roof and all. A fascinating exhibit tells the story of the Globe's construction, using the materials (including goat hair in the plaster), techniques, and craftsmanship of 400 years ago. The new Globe isn't an exact replica: It seats 1,500 patrons, not the 3,000 who regularly squeezed in during the early 1600s, and this thatched roof has been specially treated with a fire retardant. Guided tours are offered throughout the day. See p. 219 for information on attending a play here.

21 New Globe Walk, Bankside, SE1. ℂ **020/7902-1400.** www.shakespeares-globe.org. Admission £11 adults, £8.50 seniors and students, £6.50 children 5–15, £28 family ticket, free for children 4 and younger. Oct–Apr daily 10am–5pm; May–Sept Mon–Sat 9am–12:30pm and 1–5pm; Sun 9–11:30am and noon–5pm. Tube: Mansion House, London Bridge, Southwark, or Blackfriars.

Landmark Churches

Many of the churches listed below offer free **lunchtime concerts;** it's customary to leave a small donation. A full list of churches offering lunchtime concerts is available from the **Britain and London Visitor Centre (BLVC),** 1 Lower Regent St.,

London SW1Y 4XT (© **8701/566-366;** www.visitlondon.com; Tube: Piccadilly Circus).

St. Martin–in-the-Fields ★, overlooking Trafalgar Square, WC2 (© **020/7766-1100;** www2.stmartin-in-the-fields.org; Tube: Charing Cross), is the Royal Parish Church. The first known church on the site dates from the 13th century, but the present classically inspired church, with its famous steeple, dates from 1726. From St. Martin's vantage position in the theater district, it has drawn many actors to its door—none more notable than Nell Gwyn, the mistress of Charles II. On her death in 1687, she was buried in the crypt. Throughout the war, many Londoners rode out uneasy nights in the crypt while Blitz bombs rained down overhead. One bomb, in 1940, blasted out all the windows. Today, the crypt contains a pleasant restaurant, a bookshop, and a gallery. It is home to London's original **Brass Rubbing Centre** (© **020/7766-1122**), which is open Monday to Wednesday 10am to 7pm, Thursday to Saturday 10am to 10pm, and Sunday noon to 7pm.

St. Bride's Church ★, Fleet Street, EC4 (© **020/7427-0133;** www.stbrides. com; Tube: Blackfriars), known as the church of the press, is a remarkable landmark: The current church is the eighth one that has stood here. Its spire has four octagonal tiers capped by an obelisk that's topped off with a ball and vane. This soaring confection (70m/234 ft. tall) reportedly inspired the wedding cakes of a pastry cook who lived on Fleet Street in the late 17th century. The crypts are now a museum.

St. Etheldreda's Church, 14 Ely Place, EC1 (© **020/7405-1061;** www. stetheldreda.com; Tube: Farringdon or Chancery Lane), Britain's oldest Roman Catholic church, lies off Charterhouse Street at Holborn Circus. Built in 1251, it was mentioned by the Bard in both *Richard II* and *Richard III*. One of the survivors of the Great Fire of 1666, the church was built by, and is the property of, the diocese of Ely. The church has a distinguished musical tradition, with 11am Latin Mass on Sunday.

The spectacular brick-and-stone **Westminster Cathedral,** 42 Francis St., SW1 (© **020/7798-9055;** www.westminstercathedral.org.uk; Tube: Victoria), is headquarters of the Roman Catholic church in Britain. Done in high Byzantine style, it's massive; 100 different marbles compose the richly decorated interior. Mosaics emblazon the chapels and the vaulting of the sanctuary. If you climb to the top of the 82m-tall (273-ft.) campanile, you'll be rewarded with a sweeping view over Victoria and Westminster.

Hanging "Around" in London

The world's largest observation wheel, the **London Eye** ★, Jubilee Gardens (© **0870/5000-600;** www.ba-londoneye.com; Tube: Westminster or Waterloo), opened in 2000. It is the fourth-tallest structure in London, offering panoramic views that extend for some 40km (25 miles), if the weather's clear. Passengers are carried in 32 "pods" that make a complete revolution every half-hour. Along the way you'll see some of London's most famous landmarks from a bird's-eye view.

Built out of steel by a European consortium, it was conceived and designed by London architects Julia Barfield and David Marks, who claim inspiration from the Statue of Liberty in New York and the Eiffel Tower in Paris. Some 3.5 million visitors ride the Eye every year.

The Eye lies close to Westminster Bridge (you can hardly miss it). Tickets for the ride are £18 for adults, £14 for seniors and students, and £9.50 for children 4 to 15; you can save 20% by booking your tickets online. Family tickets go for £49; it's free for kids 3 and under. Hours are October to May, daily 10am to 8pm; June and September, daily 10am to 9pm; and July and August, daily 10am to 9:30pm.

LONDON'S PARKS & GARDENS

London has the greatest system of parklands of any large city on the globe. Not as rigidly laid out as the parks of Paris, London's are maintained with a loving care and lavish artistry that puts their American equivalents to shame.

The largest—and one of the world's biggest—is **Hyde Park** ★, W2 (www.royal parks.org.uk/parks/hyde_park). With the adjoining Kensington Gardens, it covers 252 hectares (636 acres) of central London with velvety lawn interspersed with ponds, flower beds, and trees. Hyde Park was once a favorite deer-hunting ground of Henry VIII. Running through the width is a 17-hectare (41-acre) lake known as the Serpentine. Rotten Row, a 2.5km (1½-mile) sand track, is reserved for horseback riding and on Sunday attracts some skilled equestrians.

At the northeastern corner of Hyde Park, near Marble Arch, is **Speakers' Corner** (www.speakerscorner.net), where anyone can speak. The only rules: You can't blaspheme, be obscene, or incite a riot. The tradition actually began in 1855—before the legal right to assembly was guaranteed in 1872—when a mob of 150,000 gathered to attack a proposed Sunday Trading Bill. Orators from all over Britain have been taking advantage of this spot ever since. The corpse of Oliver Cromwell was hung up here in a cage for the public to gape at or throw rotten eggs at. The king wanted to warn others against what might happen to them if they wished to abolish the monarchy.

The lovely **Kensington Gardens,** W2 (www.royalparks.org.uk/parks/kensington_gardens), blending with Hyde Park, border the grounds of Kensington Palace. These gardens are home to the celebrated statue of Peter Pan, with the bronze rabbits that toddlers are always trying to kidnap. The Albert Memorial is also here, and you'll recall the sea of flowers and tributes left here after the death of Diana, Princess of Wales.

East of Hyde Park, across Piccadilly, stretch **Green Park** ★, SW1 (www.royal parks.org.uk/parks/green_park), and **St. James's Park** ★, SW1 (www.royalparks.org.uk/parks/st_james_park), forming an almost-unbroken chain of landscaped beauty. This is an ideal area for picnics, and one that you'll find hard to believe was once a festering piece of swamp near a leper hospital. There is a romantic lake, stocked with a variety of ducks and pelicans, descendants of the pair that the Russian ambassador presented to Charles II in 1662.

Regent's Park ★★★, NW1 (www.royalparks.org.uk/parks/regents_park), covers most of the district by that name, north of Baker Street and Marylebone Road. Designed by 18th-century genius John Nash to surround a palace of the prince regent that never materialized, this is the most classically beautiful of London's parks. The core is a rose garden planted around a small lake alive with waterfowl and spanned by humped Japanese bridges. The open-air theater and London Zoo are here, and, as in all local parks, hundreds of deck chairs are on the lawns for sunbathers. The deck-chair attendants, who collect a small fee, are mostly college students on vacation.

The **London Zoo** ★ (*© 020/7722-3333;* www.zsl.org) is more than 150 years old. Run by the Zoological Society of London, the 15-hectare (36-acre) garden houses some 8,000 animals, including some of the rarest species on earth. It has waned in popularity the last few years, but a recent campaign won the zoo corporate sponsorship that is funding a modernization program. Zoo admission is £17 for adults, £15 for students and seniors, £14 for children 3 to 15, and £55 for a family ticket (two adults and two children or one adult and three children). Hours are March to October, daily 10am to 5:30pm; November to early February, daily 10am to 4pm; and mid-February to the end of February, daily 10am to 4:30pm. Take the Tube to Camden Town or bus no. 274 or C2.

Battersea Park, SW11 (*© 020/8871-7530;* www.batterseapark.org), is a vast patch of woodland, lakes, and lawns on the south bank of the Thames, opposite Chelsea Embankment, between Albert Bridge and Chelsea Bridge. Formerly known as Battersea Fields, the present park was laid out between 1852 and 1858 on an old dueling ground. The park, which measures 1km (⅔ mile) on each of its four sides, has a lake for boating, a fenced-in deer park with wild birds, fields for tennis and football (soccer), and a children's zoo. The architectural highlight is the Peace Pagoda, built of stone and wood. The park, open daily from dawn until dusk, is not well served by public transportation. The nearest Tube is in Chelsea on the right bank (Sloane Sq.); from there it's a brisk 15-minute walk. If you prefer the bus, take no. 137 from the Sloane Square station, exiting at the first stop after the bus crosses the Thames.

SIGHTS ON THE OUTSKIRTS

Hampstead Heath & Village ★

Located about 6.5km (4 miles) north of the center of London, **Hampstead Heath,** a 320-hectare (800-acre) expanse of high heath surrounded entirely by London, is a chain of continuous park, wood, and grassland. On a clear day you can see St. Paul's Cathedral and even the hills of Kent south of the Thames. For years, Londoners have come here to fly kites, sun worship, fish the ponds, swim, picnic, or jog. In good weather, it's also the site of big 1-day fairs. At Kenwood House, in the northern section, is a concert platform devoted to symphony and pop performances on summer evenings. In the northeast corner, in Waterlow Park, ballets, operas, and comedies are staged occasionally at the Grass Theatre in June and July.

When the Underground came to **Hampstead Village** (Tube: Hampstead) in 1907, its attraction as a place to live became widely known, and writers, artists, architects, musicians, and scientists—some from the City—came to join earlier residents. D. H. Lawrence, Rabindranath Tagore, Percy Bysshe Shelley, Robert Louis Stevenson, and Kingsley Amis once lived here; John Le Carré still does.

The Regency and Georgian houses in this village are just 20 minutes by Tube from Piccadilly Circus. Along Flask Walk, a pedestrian mall, is a palatable mix of historic pubs, toyshops, and chic boutiques. The original village, on the side of a hill, still has old roads, alleys, steps, courts, and groves to be strolled through.

Fenton House This National Trust property is on the west side of Hampstead Grove, just north of Hampstead Village. Built in 1693, its paneled rooms contain furniture and pictures; 18th-century English, German, and French porcelain; and an outstanding collection of early keyboard musical instruments.

Windmill Hill, NW3. © **020/7435-3471.** www.nationaltrust.org.uk/fentonhouse. Admission £6 adults, £3 children, £14 family ticket. Mar Sat–Sun 2–5pm; Apr–Oct Sat–Sun 11am–5pm, Wed–Fri 2–5pm. Closed Nov–Feb. Tube: Northern Line to Hampstead.

Freud Museum After Sigmund Freud and his family left Nazi-occupied Vienna as refugees, he lived, worked, and died in this spacious three-story house in northern London. On view are rooms with original furniture, letters, photographs, paintings, and the personal effects of Freud and his daughter Anna. In the study and library, you can see the famous couch and Freud's large collection of Egyptian, Roman, and Asian antiquities.

20 Maresfield Gardens, NW3. © **020/7435-2002.** www.freud.org.uk. Admission £6 adults, £4.30 seniors, £3 students 12–16, free for children 11 and younger. Wed–Sun noon–5pm. Tube: Jubilee Line or Metropolitan Line to Finchley Rd.

Highgate Cemetery A stone's throw east of Hampstead Heath, Highgate Village has a number of 16th- and 17th-century mansions and small cottages, lining three sides of the now-pondless Pond Square. Its most outstanding feature, however, is this beautiful cemetery, laid out around a huge 300-year-old cedar tree and laced with serpentine pathways. The cemetery was so popular and fashionable in the Victorian era that it was extended on the other side of Swain's Lane in 1857. The most famous grave is that of Karl Marx, who died in Hampstead in 1883; his grave, marked by a gargantuan bust, is in the East Cemetery. In the old West Cemetery—accessible only by guided tour, given hourly on weekends—are the graves of scientist Michael Faraday and poet Christina Rossetti.

Swain's Lane, N6. © **020/8340-1834.** www.highgate-cemetery.org. East Cemetery admission £3 adults, £2 students, free for children 15 and younger. West Cemetery admission by guided tour only £7 adults, £3 children 8–16 (no children 7 and younger allowed in West Cemetery). East Cemetery Mar–Oct Mon–Fri 10am–5pm, Sat–Sun 11am–5pm (last admission 4:30pm); Nov–Feb Mon–Fri 10am–4pm, Sat–Sun 11am–4pm (last admission 3:30pm). West Cemetery guided tours Mar–Nov Mon–Fri at 2pm (book in advance by phone); Mar–Oct Sat–Sun hourly 11am–4pm (no advance booking); Nov–Feb Sat–Sun hourly 11am–3pm (no advance booking); Dec–Feb by advance arrangement. Both cemeteries closed at Christmas and during funerals. Tube: Northern Line to Archway; then walk or take bus no. 143, 210, or 271.

Keats House ★★ The poet John Keats lived here for only 2 years, but that was nearly half of his creative life; he died of tuberculosis in Rome in 1821, at the age of 25. In Hampstead, Keats wrote some of his most celebrated odes, including "Ode on a Grecian Urn" and "Ode to a Nightingale." His Regency house possesses the manuscripts of his last sonnet ("Bright star, would I were steadfast as thou art") and a portrait of him on his deathbed in a house on the Spanish Steps in Rome.

Keats Grove, NW3. © **020/7332-3868.** www.keatshouse.cityoflondon.gov.uk. Admission £5 adults, £3 students and seniors, free for children 15 and younger. Tues–Sun 1–5pm. Tube: Northern Line to Hampstead or Belsize Park.

Kenwood House ★★ Kenwood House was built as a gentleman's country home and was later enlarged and decorated by the famous Scottish architect Robert Adam, starting in 1764. The house contains period furniture and paintings by Turner, Frans Hals, Gainsborough, Reynolds, and more.

Hampstead Lane, NW3. ☎ **020/8348-1286.** www.english-heritage.org.uk/kenwoodhouse. Free admission. Apr–Oct daily 11am–5pm; Nov–Mar daily 11am–4pm. Tube: Northern Line to Golders Green or Archway, then bus no. 210.

Hampton Court

Hampton Court Palace ★★★ The 16th-century palace of Cardinal Wolsey can teach us a lesson: Don't try to outdo your boss, particularly if he happens to be Henry VIII. The rich cardinal did just that, and he eventually lost his fortune, power, and prestige, and ended up giving his lavish palace to the Tudor monarch. Henry took over, even outdoing the Wolsey embellishments. The Tudor additions included the Anne Boleyn gateway, with its 16th-century astronomical clock that tells the high-water mark at London Bridge. From Clock Court, you can see one of Henry's major contributions, the aptly named Great Hall, with its hammer-beam ceiling. Also added by Henry were the tiltyard (where jousting competitions were held), a tennis court, and a kitchen.

To judge from the movie *A Man for All Seasons,* Hampton Court had quite a retinue to feed. Cooking was done in the Great Kitchen. Henry cavorted through the various apartments with his wife of the moment—from Anne Boleyn to Catherine Parr (the latter reversed things and lived to bury her erstwhile spouse). Charles I was imprisoned here at one time and managed to temporarily escape his jailers.

Although the palace enjoyed prestige and pomp in Elizabethan days, it owes much of its present look to William and Mary—or rather to Sir Christopher Wren, who designed and had built the Northern or Lion Gates, intended to be the main entrance to the new parts of the palace. The fine wrought-iron screen at the south end of the south gardens was made by Jean Tijou around 1694 for William and Mary. You can parade through the apartments today, filled as they were with porcelain, furniture, paintings, and tapestries. The King's Dressing Room is graced with some of the best art, mainly paintings by Old Masters on loan from Queen Elizabeth II. Finally, be sure to inspect the royal chapel (Wolsey wouldn't recognize it). To confound yourself totally, you may want to get lost in the serpentine shrubbery maze in the garden, also the work of Wren. More and more attention is focusing on improving and upgrading the famous gardens here—the formal gardens are among the last surviving examples of garden methods and designs from several important periods of history.

The 24-hectare (60-acre) gardens—including the Great Vine, King's Privy Garden, Great Fountain Gardens, Tudor and Elizabethan Knot Gardens, Board Walk, Tiltyard, and Wilderness—are open daily year-round from 7am until dusk (but not later than 9pm) and can be visited free except for the Privy Garden. A garden cafe and restaurant are in the Tiltyard Gardens.

Hampton Court, on the north side of the Thames and 21km (13 miles) west of London, is easily accessible. Frequent trains run from Waterloo Station (Network Southeast) to **Hampton Court Station** (☎ **0845/748-4950**). Once at the station, buses will take you the rest of the way to the palace. If you're driving from London, take the A308 to the junction with the A309 on the north side of Kingston Bridge over the Thames.

East Molesey, Surrey. ✆ **0844/482-7777.** www.hrp.org.uk. Palace admission £14 adults, £12 students and seniors, £7 children 5-15, £38 family ticket, free for children 4 and younger; general gardens free admission; south and east formal gardens Apr–Sept £4.60 adults, £4 students and seniors, free for children 14 and younger. Cloisters, courtyards, state apartments, Great Kitchen, cellars, and Hampton Court exhibition Mar–Oct daily 10am–6pm, Nov–Feb daily 10am–4:30pm; gardens year-round daily 7am–dusk (no later than 9pm).

Kew ★★★

Kew Palace ★★   About 15km (9 miles) southwest of central London, Kew is home to one of the best-known botanical gardens in Europe. It's also the site of Kew Palace, former residence of George III and Queen Charlotte. A dark redbrick structure, it is characterized by its Dutch gables. The house was constructed in 1631, and at its rear is the Queen's Garden, in a very formal design and filled with plants thought to have grown here in the 17th century. The interior is very much an elegant country house of the time, fit for a king, but not as regal as Buckingham Palace. You get the feeling that someone could have actually lived here as you wander through the dining room, the breakfast room, and upstairs to the queen's drawing room, where musical evenings were staged. The rooms are wallpapered with designs used at the time. Perhaps the most intriguing exhibits are little possessions once owned by royal occupants here—everything from snuffboxes to Prince Frederick's gambling debts. Allow about 30 minutes to visit the palace.

Royal Botanic Gardens, Kew, Richmond, Surrey. ✆ **0844/482-7777.** www.hrp.org.uk/kewpalace. Admission £5 adults, £4.50 seniors and students, free for children 15 and younger. Early Apr to late Sept Mon 11am–5pm, Tues–Sun 10am–5pm. Tube: District Line to Kew Gardens, on the south bank of the Thames.

Royal Botanic Gardens, Kew ★★★   These world-famous gardens offer thousands of varieties of plants. But Kew Gardens, as they're known, are no mere pleasure gardens—they're essentially a vast scientific research center that happens to be beautiful. The gardens, on a 121-hectare (300-acre) site, encompass lakes, greenhouses, walks, pavilions, and museums, along with examples of the architecture of Sir William Chambers. Among the 50,000 plants are notable collections of ferns, orchids, aquatic plants, cacti, mountain plants, palms, and tropical water lilies. No matter what season you visit, Kew always has something to see, from the first spring flowers through to winter. Gigantic hothouses grow species of shrubs, blooms, and trees from every part of the globe, from the Arctic Circle to tropical rainforests. Attractions include a newly restored Japanese gateway in traditional landscaping, as well as exhibitions that vary with the season. The newest greenhouse, the Princess of Wales Conservatory (beyond the rock garden), encompasses 10 climatic zones, from arid to tropical; it has London's most thrilling collection of miniature orchids. The Marianne North Gallery (1882) is an absolute gem, paneled with 246 different types of wood that the intrepid Victorian artist collected on her world journeys; she also collected 832 paintings of exotic and tropical flora, all displayed on the walls. The visitor center at Victoria Gate houses an exhibit telling the story of Kew, as well as a bookshop.

Kew, Richmond, Surrey. ✆ **020/8332-5655.** www.rbgkew.org.uk. Admission £13 adults, £11 students and seniors, free for children 16 and younger. Apr–Aug Mon–Fri 9:30am–6pm, Sat–Sun 9:30am–7pm; Sept–Oct daily 9:30am–5:30pm; Nov–Jan daily 9:30am–3:45pm; Feb–Mar daily 9:30am–5pm. Tube: District Line to Kew Gardens.

Kew Gardens

To Richmond & Ham House

Thames

London
HEATHROW
KEW GARDENS
Thames

Main Gate

KEW BRIDGE

Queens Garden

Brentford Gate

Broadwalk

Victoria Gate

KEW GARDENS
Silverlink & District Lines

Syon Vista

Pagoda Vista

Lion Gate

12 Lilac Garden
13 Waterlily House
14 Azalea Garden
15 Rhododendron Dell

16 Bamboo Garden
17 Queen Charlotte's Cottage
18 Conservation Area
19 Pagoda
20 Pavilion Restaurant
21 Evolution House
22 Temperate House

1 Victoria Gate Centre
2 Palm House
3 Rose Garden
4 Woodland Garden

5 Princess of Wales Conservatory
6 Rock Garden
7 Grass Garden

8 Aquatic Garden
9 Alpine House
10 White Peaks
11 Kew Palace

Greenwich ★★★

When London overwhelms you, and you'd like to escape for a beautiful, sunny afternoon on the city's outskirts, make it Greenwich. Greenwich Mean Time is the basis of standard time throughout most of the world, and Greenwich has been the zero point used in the reckoning of terrestrial longitudes since 1884. But this lovely village—the center of British seafaring when Britain ruled the seas—is also home of the Royal Naval College, the National Maritime Museum, and the Old Royal Observatory.

ESSENTIALS

GETTING THERE   The fastest way to get to Greenwich is to take the Tube from central London to Waterloo Station, where you can take a fast train to Greenwich Station.

The Tube is for speed, taking only 15 minutes, but if you'd like to travel the 6.5km (4 miles) to Greenwich the way Henry VIII did, you still can. In fact, getting to Greenwich is half the fun. The most appealing way involves boarding any of the frequent ferryboats that cruise along the Thames at intervals that vary from every half-hour (in summer) to every 45 minutes (in winter). Boats that leave from Charing Cross Pier (Tube: Embankment) and Tower Pier (Tube: Tower Hill) are run by **City Cruises** (✆ 020/7740-0400; www.citycruises.com). An adult ticket to Greenwich costs £9 one-way or £12 round-trip. A kid's ticket goes for £4.50 one-way or £6 return.

VISITOR INFORMATION   The **Greenwich Tourist Information Centre** is at 2 Cutty Sark Gardens (✆ 0870/608-2000; www.greenwich.gov.uk); it's open daily from 10am to 5pm. The center conducts **walking tours** of Greenwich's major sights, costing £6 for adults and £5 for students, seniors, and children. These depart daily at 12:15 and 2:15pm and last 1¼ to 1½ hours. Advance reservations aren't required, but you may want to phone ahead to ask about any last-minute schedule changes.

SEEING THE SIGHTS

The **National Maritime Museum, Old Royal Observatory,** and **Queen's House** stand together in a beautiful royal park, high on a hill overlooking the Thames. All three attractions are free to get into and open daily from 10am to 5pm (until 6pm in summer). For more information, call ✆ 020/8858-4422 or visit **www.nmm.ac.uk**.

From the days of early seafarers to 20th-century sea power, the **National Maritime Museum** ★★ illustrates the glory that was Britain at sea. The cannon, relics, ship models, and paintings tell the story of a thousand naval battles and a thousand victories, as well as the price of those battles. Look for some oddities here—everything from the dreaded cat-o'-nine-tails used to flog sailors until 1879 to Nelson's Trafalgar coat, with the fatal bullet hole in the left shoulder clearly visible. In time for the millennium, the museum spent £20 million on a massive expansion that improved visitor facilities and added 16 new galleries devoted to British maritime history.

The **Old Royal Observatory** ★, the original home of Greenwich Mean Time, has the largest refracting telescope in the United Kingdom along with a collection of historic timekeepers and astronomical instruments. You can stand astride the meridian and set your watch precisely by the falling time-ball. Sir Christopher Wren designed the Octagon Room. It was here that the first royal astronomer, Flamsteed, made the 30,000 observations that formed the basis of his *Historia Coelestis Britannica*. Edmond Halley, of the eponymous Halley's Comet, succeeded him. In 1833, the ball on the tower was hung to enable shipmasters to set their chronometers accurately.

Designed by Inigo Jones, the **Queen's House** ★★ (1616) is a fine example of this architect's innovative style. It's most famous for the cantilevered tulip staircase, the first of its kind. Carefully restored, the house contains a collection of royal and marine paintings and other objets d'art.

The **Wernher Collection at Ranger's House** ★★, Chesterfield Walk (© 020/8853-0035; www.english-heritage.org.uk/rangershouse), is a real find and one of the finest and most unusual 19th-century mixed-art collections in the world. Acquired by a German diamond dealer, Sir Julius Wernher, the collection contains some 650 exhibits, some dating as far back as 3 B.C. It's an eclectic mix of everything, including jewelry, bronzes, ivory, antiques, tapestries, porcelain pieces, and classic paintings. Hanging on the walls of the gallery are rare works by such Old Masters as Hans Memling and Filippino Lippi, along with portraits by English painters including Reynolds and Romney. One salon is devoted to the biggest collection of Renaissance jewelry in Britain. Look also for the carved medieval, Byzantine, and Renaissance ivories, along with Limoges enamels and Sèvres porcelain. The most unusual items are enameled skulls and a miniature coffin complete with 3-D skeleton. Don't expect everything to be beautiful—Wernher's taste was often bizarre. Admission is £6 for adults, £5.10 for seniors and students, £3 for children, and free for kids 4 and younger. The attraction is open April through September only, Monday to Wednesday from 11am to 5pm.

Nearby is the **Royal Naval College** ★★, King William Walk, off Romney Road (© 020/8269-4747; www.oldroyalnavalcollege.org). Designed by Sir Christopher Wren in 1696, it occupies 4 blocks named after King Charles, Queen Anne, King William, and Queen Mary. Formerly, Greenwich Palace stood here from 1422 to 1640. It's worth stopping in to see the magnificent Painted Hall, by Thornhill, where the body of Nelson lay in state in 1805, and the Georgian chapel of St. Peter and St. Paul. It's open daily from 10am to 5pm; admission is free.

ESPECIALLY FOR KIDS

The official tourism organization known as Visit London maintains a website—**www.kidslovelondon.com**—that provides a fun and educational guide for planning time in the capital. The site boasts interactive quizzes, up-to-date information on what's hot, and children's reviews of London attractions, with tips on everything from walking with "dinosaurs" to cool places to eat.

London has fun places for children of all ages. In addition to what's listed below, kids love the **Tower of London,** the **Natural History Museum, Madame Tussauds,** the **Science Museum,** and the **National Maritime Museum** in Greenwich, all discussed earlier in this chapter.

Horniman Museum   This century-old museum, set in 6.5 hectares (16 acres) of landscaped gardens, is quirky, funky, and fun. The collection was accumulated by Frederick Horniman, a Victorian tea trader. A full range of events and activities takes place here, including storytelling and art-and-crafts sessions for kids, along with workshops for adults. The museum owns some 350,000 objects ranging from a gigantic, overstuffed walrus to such oddities as oversize model insects. There are also displays of live insects and a small aquarium constructed in waterfall-like tiers. The torture chair thought to have been an original used at the Spanish Inquisition was proven to be a fake, but the instruments are genuine.

100 London Rd., Forest Hill, SE23. (℡) **020/8699-1872.** www.horniman.ac.uk. Free admission except for temporary exhibitions. Museum daily 10:30am–5:30pm; library Wed–Sat 10:30am–5pm, Sun 2–5:30pm; gardens Mon–Sat 7:30am–dusk, Sun 8am–dusk. Tube: London Bridge; then train to Forest Hill.

London Aquarium ★   One of the largest aquariums in Europe, this South Bank attraction boasts 350 species of fish, everything from British freshwater species to sharks that once patrolled the Pacific. Observe the bountiful riches of the coral reefs of the Indian Ocean and what lurks in the murky depths of the Atlantic and Pacific oceans, including an array of eels, sharks, piranhas, rays, jellyfish, and other denizens of the deep. You ford a freshwater stream into a mangrove swamp to reach a tropical rainforest. The seawater, incidentally, is just normal Thames water mixed with 8 tons of salt at a time.

County Hall, Westminster Bridge Rd., South Bank, SE1. (℡) **0871/663-1678.** www.sealife.co.uk. Admission £18 adults, £16 students and seniors, £13 children 3–14, £54 family ticket. Sept–July daily 10am–6pm; Aug daily 10am–7pm. Closed Dec 25. Tube: Waterloo.

London Dungeon   This ghoulish place was designed to chill the blood while reproducing the conditions of the Middle Ages. Set under the arches of London Bridge Station, the dungeon is a series of tableaux more grisly than those at Madame Tussauds. The rumble of trains overhead adds to the atmosphere, and tolling bells bring a constant note of melancholy; dripping water and caged rats make for even more atmosphere. Naturally, it offers a burning at the stake as well as a torture chamber with racking, branding, and fingernail extraction. The special effects here were originally conceived for major film and TV productions. In "Traitor: Boat Ride to Hell," you're sentenced to death (by actors, of course) and taken on a boat ride to meet your fate. If you survive, a Pizza Hut is on-site, and a souvenir shop sells certificates that testify you made it through the works. Added in 2007, "Extremis: Drop Ride to Doom" is a thrill attraction that simulates a hanging (only without those pesky nooses): When the trapdoor opens, you plummet down into the dark. New for 2010 is "Bloody Mary: Killer Queen." Visitors to the dungeon should use discretion with young children.

28–34 Tooley St., SE1. (℡) **020/7403-7221.** www.thedungeons.com. Admission £23 adults, £21 students and seniors, £17 children 5–14, free for children 4 and younger. Nov to early Mar daily 10:30am–5pm; mid-Mar to early Apr daily 9:30am–5:30pm; early Apr to late May daily 10am–5pm; late May to Oct daily 10am–7:30pm. Tube: London Bridge.

V&A Museum of Childhood   This branch of the Victoria and Albert, founded in 1872 as the Bethnal Green Museum, specializes in toys. The variety of dolls alone is staggering; some have such elaborate period costumes that you don't even want to think of the price tags they would carry today. With the dolls come dollhouses, from simple cottages to miniature mansions, complete with fireplaces, grand pianos, kitchen utensils, and carriages. You'll also find optical toys, marionettes, puppets, a considerable exhibit of soldiers and war toys from both World War eras, trains and aircraft, and a display of clothing and furniture relating to the social history of childhood.

Cambridge Heath Rd., E2. © **020/8983-5200.** www.vam.ac.uk/moc. Free admission. Daily 10am–5:45pm. Tube: Central Line to Bethnal Green.

ORGANIZED TOURS

Bus Tours

For the first-timer, the quickest and most economical way to bring the big city into focus is to take a bus tour. One of the most popular is the **Original London Sightseeing Tour,** 17–19 Cockspur St., Trafalgar Square, SW1 (© **020/8877-1722;** www.theoriginaltour.com; Tube: Piccadilly or Charing Cross), which passes by all the major sights in just about 1½ hours. The tour—which uses a traditional double-decker bus with live commentary by a guide—is £25 for adults, £12 for children 5 to 15, and free for kids 4 and younger. A family ticket costs £86. Your ticket, valid for 24 hours, allows you to hop on or off the bus at any point in the tour at no extra charge. Departures are from convenient points within the city; you can choose your departure point when you buy your ticket. Tickets can be purchased on the bus, at the company's Trafalgar Square visitor center, by phone, or at a discount online or from any Transport for London Travel Information Centre or London Tourist Information Centre. Most hotel concierges also sell tickets.

The **Big Bus Company,** 48 Buckingham Palace Rd., SW1 (© **020/7233-9533;** www.bigbus.co.uk), operates a 2-hour tour in summer, departing frequently between 8:30am and 4:30pm daily from Marble Arch by Speakers' Corner, Green Park by the Ritz hotel, and Victoria Station (Buckingham Palace Rd., by the Royal Westminster Hotel). Tours cover the highlights—18 in all—ranging from the Houses of Parliament and Westminster Abbey to the Tower of London and Buckingham Palace (exterior looks only), accompanied by live commentary. The cost is £26 for adults, £10 for children; a family ticket is £62. A 1-hour tour follows the same route but covers only 13 sights. Tickets are valid all day; you can hop on and off the bus as you wish.

Walking Tours

The **Original London Walks,** 87 Messina Ave., P.O. Box 1708, London NW6 4LW (© **020/7624-3978;** www.walks.com), the oldest established walking-tour company in London, is run by an Anglo-American journalist/actor couple, David and Mary Tucker. Their hallmarks are variety, reliability, reasonably sized groups, and—above all—superb guides. The renowned crime historian Donald Rumbelow, the leading authority on Jack the Ripper and author of the classic guidebook *London Walks,* is a regular guide, as are several prominent actors (including classical actor Edward Petherbridge). Walks are scheduled daily and cost £7 for adults, £5 for students and seniors; children 14 and younger go free. Call for a schedule; no reservations are needed.

River Cruises

A trip up or down the river gives you an entirely different view of London. You can see how the city grew along and around the Thames and how many of its landmarks turn their faces toward the water. Several companies operate motor launches from the Westminster piers (Tube: Westminster), offering panoramic views of one of Europe's most historic waterways en route.

Thames River Services, Westminster Pier, Victoria Embankment, SW1 (*©* **020/7930-4097;** www.westminsterpier.co.uk), concerns itself only with down-river traffic from Westminster Pier to such destinations as Greenwich. The most popular excursion departs for Greenwich (a 50-min. ride) at half-hour intervals between 10am and 4pm daily in April, May, September, and October, and between 10am and 5pm from June to August; from November to March, boats depart from Westminster Pier at 40-minute intervals daily from 10:40am to 3:20pm. One-way fares are £9 for adults and £4.50 for children 15 and younger. Round-trip fares are £12 for adults, £6 for children. A family ticket costs £30 round-trip.

Westminster Passenger Service Association (Upriver) Ltd., Westminster Pier, Victoria Embankment, SW1 (*©* **020/7930-2062** or 020/7930-4721; www. wpsa.co.uk), offers the only riverboat service upstream from Westminster Bridge to Kew, Richmond, and Hampton Court, with regular daily sailings from the Monday before Easter until the end of October on traditional riverboats, all with licensed bars. Trip time, one-way, can be as little as 1½ hours to Kew and between 2½ and 4 hours to Hampton Court, depending on the tide. Cruises from Westminster Pier to Hampton Court via Kew Gardens leave daily at 10:30am, 11:15am, and noon. Round-trip tickets are £20 for adults, £13 for seniors, £9.75 for children 4 to 14, and £49 for a family ticket; one child 3 or younger accompanied by an adult goes free.

SHOPPING
The Top Shopping Streets & Neighborhoods

Several key streets offer some of London's best retail stores—or simply one of every-thing—compactly located in a niche or neighborhood so that you can just stroll and shop.

THE WEST END   The West End includes the Mayfair district and is home to the core of London's big-name shopping. Most of the department stores, designer shops, and multiples (chain stores) have their flagships in this area.

The key streets are **Oxford Street** for affordable shopping (start at the Marble Arch Tube station if you're ambitious, or the Bond St. Tube station if you just want to see some of it) and **Regent Street,** which intersects Oxford Street at Oxford Circus (Tube: Oxford Circus).

While there are several London branches of the private-label department store **Marks & Spencer,** its Marble Arch store, on Oxford Street, is the flagship and worth shopping for its high-quality goods. There's a grocery store in the basement and a home-furnishings department upstairs.

Regent Street has fancier shops—more upscale department stores (including the famed **Liberty of London**), as well as specialty dealers—and leads all the way to Piccadilly.

Parallel to Regent Street is **Bond Street.** Divided into New and Old, Bond Street (Tube: Bond St.) also connects Piccadilly with Oxford Street and is synonymous with the luxury trade. Bond Street has had a revival and is the hot address for all the international designers; **Donna Karan** has not one, but two shops here. Many international hotshots have digs surrounding hers, from **Chanel** and **Ferragamo** to **Versace.**

Burlington Arcade (Tube: Piccadilly Circus), the famous glass-roofed, Regency-style passage leading off Piccadilly, looks like a period exhibition and is lined with intriguing shops and boutiques. The small, smart stores specialize in fashion, jewelry, Irish linen, cashmere, and more. If you linger in the arcade until 5:30pm, you can watch the beadles in their black-and-yellow livery and top hats ceremoniously put in place the iron grills that block off the arcade until 9am the next morning, at which time they just as ceremoniously remove them to mark the start of a new business day. Also at 5:30pm, a hand bell, called the Burlington Bell, is sounded, signaling the end of trading.

Just off Regent Street (actually tucked right behind it) is **Carnaby Street** (Tube: Oxford Circus), which is also having a comeback. While it no longer dominates the world of pace-setting fashion as it did in the 1960s, it's still fun for teens who may need cheap souvenirs, a purple wig, or a little something in leather. A convenient branch of **Boots the Chemist** is also here.

For a total contrast, check out **Jermyn Street,** on the far side of Piccadilly, a tiny 2-block-long street devoted to high-end men's haberdashers and toiletries shops; many have been doing business for centuries. Several hold royal warrants, including **Turnbull & Asser,** where HRH Prince Charles has his PJs made.

The West End leads to the theater district and to two more shopping areas: the still-not-ready-for-prime-time **Soho,** where the sex shops are slowly being turned into cutting-edge designer shops, and **Covent Garden,** which is a masterpiece unto itself. The marketplace has eaten up the surrounding neighborhood so that even though the streets run a little higgledy-piggledy and you can easily get lost, it's fun to just wander and shop.

KNIGHTSBRIDGE & CHELSEA This is the second-most famous of London's retail districts and the home of **Harrods** (Tube: Knightsbridge). A small street nearby, **Sloane Street,** is chockablock with designer shops; **Cheval Place,** in the opposite direction, is also lined with designer resale shops.

Walk toward Museum Row, and you'll soon find **Beauchamp Place** (pronounced *Beech*-am; Tube: Knightsbridge). The street is only a block long, but it features the kinds of shops where young British aristos buy their clothing.

Head out at the **Harvey Nichols** end of Knightsbridge, away from Harrods, and shop your way through the designer stores on Sloane Street—**Hermès, Armani, Prada,** and the like. Walk past Sloane Square and you're in an altogether different neighborhood: Chelsea.

King's Road (Tube: Sloane Sq.), the main street of Chelsea, which starts at Sloane Square, will forever remain a symbol of London in the swinging '60s. Today, the street is still frequented by young people, but with fewer Mohawks, "Bovver boots," and Edwardian ball gowns than before. More and more, King's Road is a lineup of markets and "multistores," large or small conglomerations of indoor stands, stalls, and booths in one building or enclosure.

Chelsea doesn't begin and end with King's Road. If you choose to walk the other direction from Harrods, you connect to a part of Chelsea called **Brompton Cross,** another hip and hot area for designer shops, made popular when Michelin House was rehabbed by Sir Terence Conran for the **Conran Shop.**

Also seek out **Walton Street,** a tiny little snake of a street running from Brompton Cross back toward the museums. About 2 blocks of this 3-block street are devoted to fairy-tale shops for m'lady, where you can buy needlepoint, costume jewelry, or aromatherapy from **Jo Malone,** or perhaps meet with your interior designer, who runs a small shop of objets d'art.

Finally, don't forget all those museums right there in the corner of the shopping streets. They all have great gift shops.

KENSINGTON & NOTTING HILL   **Kensington High Street** (Tube: High St. Kensington) is the new hangout of the classier breed of teen who has graduated from Carnaby Street and is ready for street chic. While a few staples of basic British fashion are on this strip, most of the stores feature items that stretch; are very, very short; or are very, very tight.

From Kensington High Street, you can walk up **Kensington Church Street,** which, like Portobello Road, is one of the city's main shopping avenues for antiques. Kensington Church Street dead-ends into the Notting Hill Gate Tube station, which is where you would arrive for shopping on **Portobello Road.** The dealers and the weekend market are 2 blocks beyond.

The Department Stores

Contrary to popular belief, Harrods is not the only department store in London. The British invented the department store, and they have lots of them—mostly in Mayfair, and each with its own customer profile.

Fenwick of Bond Street   Fenwick (the "w" is silent), dating from 1891, is a stylish fashion store that offers an excellent collection of designer women's wear, ranging from moderately priced ready-to-wear items to more expensive designer fashions. A wide range of lingerie in all price ranges is also sold. 63 New Bond St., W1. © **020/7629-9161.** www.fenwick.co.uk. Tube: Bond St.

Fortnum & Mason   The world's most elegant grocery store is a British tradition dating from 1707. This store exemplifies the elegance and style you would expect from an establishment with three royal warrants (meaning they supply goods to the royal family). Enter and be transported to another world of deep-red carpets, crystal chandeliers, spiraling wooden staircases, and unobtrusive, tail-coated assistants.

The grocery department is renowned for its impressive selection of the finest foods from around the world—the best champagne, the most scrumptious Belgian chocolates, and succulent Scottish smoked salmon. Wander through the four floors and inspect the bone china and crystal cut glass, find the perfect gift in the leather or stationery departments, or reflect on the changing history of furniture and ornaments in the antiques department. Fortnum & Mason offers exclusive and specialty ranges for the home, as well as beauty products and fashions for women and men alike. Dining choices include **St. James's Restaurant** and the **Fountain Restaurant** (p. 165). 181 Piccadilly, W1. © **020/7734-8040.** www.fortnumandmason.com. Tube: Piccadilly Circus.

Harrods   An institution as firmly entrenched in English life as Buckingham Palace and the Ascot Races, Harrods is an elaborate emporium, at times as fascinating as a museum. The sheer range, variety, and quality of merchandise are dazzling. If you visit only one store in all of England, make it Harrods, even if you're just looking.

The fifth floor is devoted to sports and leisure, with a wide range of equipment and attire. Toy Kingdom is on the fourth floor, along with children's wear. On the ground floor are Harrods Shop, for logo gifts, and the Egyptian Hall, which sells crystal from Lalique and Baccarat, plus porcelain. You'll also find a men's grooming room, an enormous jewelry department, and a fashion-forward department for younger customers. In the basement, there's a bank, a theater-booking service, and a travel bureau. When you're ready for a break, you have a choice of 28 restaurants and bars. Best of all are the Food Halls, stocked with a huge variety of foods and several cafes. Harrods began in 1849 as a grocer, still the heart of the business. 87–135 Brompton Rd., SW1. ℭ **020/8479-5100.** www.harrods.com. Tube: Knightsbridge.

John Lewis Trends come and go, but this department store remains one of the most traditional outlets in London. Their motto is that they are never knowingly undersold, and they mean that. We've always found great bargains at this store, most recently in a clearance sale of fine earthenware by Royal Stafford. Whatever you're looking for—from mauve Egyptian towels to clothing and jewelry—it's likely to be for sale here. 300 Oxford St., W1. ℭ **020/7629-7711.** www.johnlewis.com. Tube: Oxford Circus.

Liberty This major British department store is celebrated for its Liberty prints: top-echelon, carriage-trade fabrics, often in floral patterns, prized by decorators for adding a sense of English tradition to a room. The front part of the store on Regent Street isn't particularly distinctive, but don't be fooled: Some parts of the place have been restored to Tudor-style splendor that includes half-timbering and lots of interior paneling. Liberty houses six floors of fashion, china, and home furnishings, as well as the famous Liberty prints in fashion fabrics, upholstery fabrics, scarves, ties, luggage, and gifts. 210–220 Regent St., W1. ℭ **020/7734-1234.** www.liberty.co.uk. Tube: Oxford Circus.

Some Classic London Favorites

ANTIQUES See also "The Markets," below. Portobello Road is really the prime hunting ground.

At the **Antiquarius Antiques Centre,** 131–141 King's Rd., SW3 (ℭ **020/7823-3900;** www.antiquarius.co.uk; Tube: Sloane Sq.), more than 120 dealers offer specialized merchandise such as antique and period jewelry, silver, first-edition books, boxes, clocks, prints, and paintings, with an occasional piece of antique furniture. You'll find a lot of items from the 1950s. Open Monday to Saturday 10am to 6pm; closed Sunday.

Alfies Antique Market, 13–25 Church St., NW8 (ℭ **020/7723-6066;** www.alfiesantiques.com; Tube: Marylebone or Edgware Rd.), is the biggest and one of the best-stocked conglomerates of antiques dealers in London, all crammed into the premises of what was built before 1880 as a department store. It contains more than 370 stalls, showrooms, and workshops scattered across 3,250 sq. m (35,000 sq. ft.) of floor space. Open Tuesday to Saturday 10am to 6pm; closed Sunday and Monday. A whole antiques district has grown up around Alfies along Church Street.

ARTS & CRAFTS Hailed by the *Times of London* as "the best place to see contemporary art in north London," **Camden Arts Centre** ★, Arkwright Road, NW3 (ℭ **020/7472-5500;** www.camdenartscentre.org), opened after a multimillion-dollar refurbishment. Today, it invites you to its cafe, bookstore, studios, and exhibition galleries, where the displays are frequently changed.

Gabriel's Wharf, 56 Upper Ground, SE1 (☎ 020/7021-1686; www.coin-street.org; Tube: Blackfriars, Southwark, Waterloo, or Embankment), is a South Bank complex of shops, restaurants, and bars open Tuesday to Sunday from 11am to 6pm (dining and drinking establishments open later). Lying 2 minutes by foot from Oxo Tower Wharf, it is filled with some of the most skilled of London craftspeople, turning out original pieces of sculpture, jewelry, ceramics, art, and fashion. The place is a lot of fun to poke around in—from food to fashion, arts to crafts, it all awaits you here.

BATH & BODY   Branches of the **Body Shop** are seemingly everywhere. Check out the one at 374 Oxford St., W1 (☎ 020/7409-7868; www.thebodyshop.com; Tube: Bond St.). Prices are much lower in the United Kingdom than in the United States.

Boots the Chemist has branches all over Britain. A convenient branch is at 490 Oxford St., W1C (☎ 020/7491-8546; www.boots.com; Tube: Marble Arch). The house brands of beauty products are usually the best, whether the main Boots line (try the cucumber facial scrub), the Boots versions of the Body Shop, or the Boots versions of Chanel makeup (called No. 7).

Drop by **Culpeper the Herbalist,** 8 The Market, Covent Garden, WC2 (☎ 020/7379-6698; www.culpeper.co.uk; Tube: Covent Garden), to stock up on essential oils, or perhaps dream pillows, candles, sachets of letters of the alphabet, and aromatherapy fans.

Floris, 89 Jermyn St., SW1 (☎ 0845/702-3239; www.florislondon.com; Tube: Greek Park), stocks a variety of toilet articles and fragrances in floor-to-ceiling mahogany cabinets, which are architectural curiosities in their own right, dating from the Great Exhibition of 1851.

Lush, 11 The Piazza, Covent Garden (☎ 020/7240-4570; www.lush.co.uk; Tube: Covent Garden), sells the most intriguing handmade cosmetics in London. This outlet is always launching something new, such as the best-selling bubble-gum-pink Rock Star soap or the Creamy Candy Bubble Bar. The selection goes on and on, with all products made of fresh fruit and vegetables, the finest essential oils, and safe synthetics—no animal ingredients.

The Victorian perfumery called **Penhaligon's,** 41 Wellington St., WC2 (☎ 020/7836-2150; www.penhaligons.co.uk; Tube: Covent Garden), offers a large selection of perfumes, after-shaves, soaps, and bath oils for women and men. Gifts include antique-silver scent bottles and leather traveling requisites.

FASHION, PART I: THE TRUE BRIT   Every internationally known designer worth his or her weight in shantung has a boutique in London, but the best buys are on the sturdy English styles that last forever.

The name **Burberry,** 157–167 Regent St., SW1 (☎ 020/7806-1328; www.burberry.com; Tube: Piccadilly Circus), has been synonymous with raincoats ever since Edward VII publicly ordered his valet to "bring my Burberry" when the skies threatened. An impeccably trained staff sells the famous raincoats, along with excellent men's shirts, sportswear, knitwear, and accessories. Raincoats are available in women's sizes and styles as well. Prices are high, but you get quality and prestige.

THE COMEBACK OF carnaby street

What happened to Carnaby Street? A faded echo left over from the swinging '60s? That was true for a long time, but Carnaby is rising again. An influx of talented designers and offbeat shops is popping up not only on Carnaby, but also along its offshoot streets—Newburgh Street, Foubert's Place, Kingly Street, Marlborough Court, and Lowndes Court. Innovative boutiques seem to open each week behind these small Georgian shop fronts.

Among the shops here are such favorites as **Lambretta Clothing,** 29 Carnaby St., W1 (© 020/7437-7078; www.lambrettaclothing.co.uk; Tube: Oxford Circus), which retains the mod lifestyle philosophy and has launched a range of casual wear for men and footwear for men and women. The line has a retro feel, but uses the latest fibers and fabric finishes of today.

Office, 16 Carnaby St. (© 020/7434-2530; www.office.co.uk; Tube: Oxford Circus), sells chic and well-designed footwear for both men and women. Within the store is a section devoted to Poste Mistress, a more upmarket designer line for girls and women. It's more sophisticated—with everything from multistrap to almond-toe shoes—and also more expensive.

Stella McCartney, 30 Bruton St., W1 (© 020/7518-3100; www.stella mccartney.com; Tube: Bond St. or Oxford Circus), is a nearby showcase for the clothing designs of Paul McCartney's daughter. Vegetarians and animal lovers adore her "no leather, no suede, and no fur policy," while fashionistas seek out the chic look of her designs. Male and female clients are shown to a drawing room on the second floor of this glamorous Mayfair town house, where they are presented with some 50 illustrations for trousers, jackets, skirts, and overcoats—all of which are very expensive.

The finest name in men's shirts, **Hilditch & Key,** 37 and 73 Jermyn St., SW1 (© 020/7734-4707; www.hilditchandkey.co.uk; Tube: Piccadilly Circus or Green Park), has been in business since 1899. The two shops on this street offer men's clothing (including a bespoke shirt service) and women's ready-made shirts. Hilditch also has an outstanding tie collection. Shirts go for half-price during the twice-yearly sales. Men fly in from all over the world for them.

Alfred Dunhill at Bourdon House, 2 Davies St., W1 (© 0845/458-0779; www.dunhill.com; Tube: Oxford Circus), is the epitome of London chic and luxury for gents, situated in the 18th-century Mayfair residence of the Duke of Westminster. The store is known for its leather goods and tailored men's wear. It is both a retail shop and a private club, the latter with four suites and a luxury restaurant. It's also the place to go for accessories, gifts, and gadgets.

FASHION, PART II: THE CUTTING EDGE   Currently the most cutting-edge shopping street in London is **Conduit Street,** in Mayfair, W1 (Tube: Oxford Circus). Once known for its dowdy display of international airline offices, it is now London's smartest street for fashion. Trendy shops are opening between Regent Street and the "blue-chip" boutiques of New Bond Street even as we speak. Current stars include **Vivienne Westwood,** 44 Conduit St., W1 (© 020/7924-4747;

www.viviennewestwood.com), who has overcome her punk origins to become the grande dame of English fashion.

Other famous designers with boutiques on Conduit Street include **Krizia,** 25 Conduit St., W1 (© **020/7491-4987;** www.krizia.net); **Yohji Yamamoto,** 14–15 Conduit St., W1 (© **020/7491-4129;** www.yohjiyamamoto.co.jp); and **Issey Miyake,** 52 Conduit St., W1 (© **020/7851-4620;** www.isseymiyake.co.jp).

Despite its name, the **Library,** 268 Brompton Rd., SW3 (© **020/7589-6569;** www.thelibrary1994.com; Tube: South Kensington or Knightsbridge), is a showcase for some of the best of the young designers for men. It's very cutting edge without dipping into the extremities of male fashion. The Library is famous for having introduced Helmut Lang to London, but now features such designers as Fabrizio del Carlo and Kostas Murkudis.

FASHION, PART III: VINTAGE & SECONDHAND CLOTHING A London institution since the 1940s, **Pandora,** 16–22 Cheval Place, SW7 (© **020/7589-5289;** www.pandoradressagency.com; Tube: Knightsbridge), stands in fashionable Knightsbridge, near Harrods. Several times a week, chauffeurs drive up with bundles packed anonymously by the gentry of England. One woman voted best dressed at Ascot several years ago was wearing a secondhand dress acquired here. Prices are generally one-third to one-half the retail value. Outfits are usually no more than two seasons old.

For the best in original street wear from the '50s, '60s, and '70s, **Pop Boutique,** 6 Monmouth St., WC2 (© **020/7497-5262;** www.pop-boutique.com; Tube: Covent Garden), is tops. Right next to the chic Covent Garden Hotel, it has fabulous vintage wear at affordable prices.

Note: There's no value-added tax (VAT) refund on used clothing.

FURNITURE David Linley Furniture, 60 Pimlico Rd., SW1 (© **020/7730-7300;** www.davidlinley.com; Tube: Sloane Sq.), is a showcase for the remarkable furniture of the Viscount Linley, a designer who bears a resemblance to his mother, the late Princess Margaret. He designs pieces of furniture of a complex nature, in terms of both design and structure. For example, one of his designs, the Apsley House Desk, is made of French walnut, with ebony and nickel-plated detailing, and contains secret drawers. The desk is rimmed with a miniature of the neoclassical Apsley House. The director at the Victoria and Albert Museum has predicted that Linley's furnishings and accessories will become the antiques of the future.

HOME DESIGN & HOUSEWARES At the **Conran Shop,** Michelin House, 81 Fulham Rd., SW3 (© **020/7589-7401;** www.conranshop.co.uk; Tube: South Kensington), you'll find high style at reasonable prices from the man who invented it all for Britain: Sir Terence Conran. It's great for gifts, home furnishings, and tabletop knickknacks—or just for gawking.

The **Couverture Shop,** 188 Kensington Park Rd., W11 (Tube: Notting Hill Gate), is an emporium of the unexpected, with original products for both adults and children as well as the home. It's strongest on what it calls "bedroom must-haves," embracing bed linen, throws, cushions, and the like. Vintage finds and designer pieces, often handmade, are also sold.

JEWELRY The flagship store for **Stephen Webster,** 93 Mount St., W1 (© **020/7486-6576;** www.stephenwebster.com; Tube: Bond St.), in the heart of the West End in Mayfair, features glamour with a rock-'n'-roll edge. From "fire earrings" to diamond enamel bracelets, it's all on display here. Funky jewelry is a specialty—for example, to celebrate the opening of an oyster and chop house, the store designed gold-and-enamel lamb-chop pendants.

SHOES   Shoes for both men and women are stocked at **Natural Shoe Store,** 13 Neal St., WC2 (℃ **020/7836-5254;** www.thenaturalshoestore.com; Tube: Covent Garden), which also does repairs for some labels. The selection includes comfort and quality footwear lines, from Birkenstock to the best of the British classics.

TOYS   **Hamleys,** 188–196 Regent St., W1 (℃ **0800/2802-444;** www.hamleys. com; Tube: Oxford Circus), is the finest toy shop in the world—more than 35,000 toys and games on seven floors of fun and magic. A huge selection is offered, including cuddly stuffed animals, dolls, radio-controlled cars, train sets, model kits, board games, outdoor toys, and computer games. A small branch is also at Heathrow Airport.

The Markets

THE WEST END   **Covent Garden Market** ★ (℃ **020/7836-9136;** www. coventgardenlondonuk.com; Tube: Covent Garden), the most famous market in all of England, offers several markets Monday through Saturday from 10am to 6pm—but we think it's most fun to come on Sunday from 11am to 6pm, when more vendors are set up and street entertainment is at its peak. It can be a little confusing until you dive in and explore. **Apple Market** is the bustling market in the courtyard, where traders sell—well, everything. Many of the items are what the English call collectible nostalgia: a wide array of glassware and ceramics, leather goods, toys, clothes, hats, and jewelry. Some of the merchandise is truly unusual. Many items are handmade, with some of the craftspeople selling their own wares—except on Monday, when antiques dealers take over. Some goods are new, some are very old. Out back is **Jubilee Market** (℃ **020/7836-2139**), also an antiques market, which takes place on Monday; the rest of the week, it's sort of a fancy hippie market with cheap clothes and books. Out front there are a few tents of cheap stuff, except on Monday. The indoor market section of Covent Garden Market (in a superbly restored hall) is one of the best shopping venues in London. Specialty shops sell fashions and herbs, gifts and toys, books and dollhouses, cigars, and much more. There are bookshops and branches of famous stores (Hamleys, the Body Shop), and prices are kept moderate.

The thriving neighborhood of Marylebone continues to blossom with chic boutiques, restored Victorian pubs, designer shops, epicurean emporiums, and markets. One of our favorites is the amusingly named **Cabbages & Frocks Market,** in the churchyard of St. Marylebone Parish Church, Marylebone High Street, W1 (℃ **020/7794-1636;** www.cabbageandfrocks.co.uk; Tube: Baker St.). The stalls here will tempt you with an array of clothing from new designers, as well as vintage clothing, along with jewelry, blown glass, and cute duds for kids. The market is open Saturday from 11am to 5pm, at which time it also offers a number of food specialties, ranging from Japanese delicacies to Argentinian steak sandwiches.

St. Martin–in-the-Fields Market (Tube: Charing Cross) is good for teens and hipsters who are interested in imports from India and South America, crafts, and local football (soccer) souvenirs. It's located near Trafalgar Square and Covent

Garden; hours are Monday through Saturday from 11am to 5pm and Sunday from noon to 5pm.

Berwick Street Market (Tube: Oxford Circus or Tottenham Court Rd.) may be the only street market in the world that's flanked by two rows of strip clubs, porno stores, and adult-movie dens. Don't let that put you off. Humming 6 days a week in the scarlet heart of Soho, this array of stalls and booths sells the best and cheapest fruit and vegetables in town. It also hawks ancient records, tapes, books, and old magazines, any of which may turn out to be a collector's item one day. It's open Monday through Saturday from 8am to 5:30pm.

On Sunday mornings along **Bayswater Road,** artists hang their work on the railings along the edge of Hyde Park and Kensington Gardens for more than 1.5km (1 mile). If the weather's right, start at Marble Arch and walk west. You'll see the same thing on the railings of **Green Park** along Piccadilly on Saturday afternoons.

NOTTING HILL **Portobello Market** (Tube: Notting Hill Gate) is a magnet for collectors of virtually anything. It's mainly a Saturday happening, from 6am to 5pm. You needn't be here at the crack of dawn, though; 9am is fine. Once known mainly for fruit and vegetables (still sold here throughout the week), in the past 4 decades Portobello has become synonymous with antiques. But don't take the stallholder's word for it that the fiddle he's holding is a genuine Stradivarius left to him in the will of his Italian great-uncle; it might just as well have been "nicked" from an East End pawnshop.

The market is divided into three major sections. The most crowded is the antiques section, running between Colville Road and Chepstow Villas to the south. (**Warning:** There's a great concentration of pickpockets in this area.) The second section (and the oldest part) is the "fruit and veg" market, lying between Westway and Colville Road. In the third and final section is the flea market, where Londoners sell bric-a-brac and lots of secondhand goods they didn't really want in the first place. But looking around still makes for interesting fun.

Note: Some 90 antiques-and-art shops along Portobello Road are open during the week, when the street market is closed. This is actually a better time for the serious collector to shop because you'll get more attention from dealers, and you won't be distracted by the organ grinder.

SOUTH BANK Open on Fridays only, **New Caledonian Market** is commonly known as the **Bermondsey Market** because of its location on the corner of Long Lane and Bermondsey Street (Tube: London Bridge, and then bus no. 78 or walk down Bermondsey St.). The market is at the extreme east end, beginning at Tower Bridge Road. It's one of Europe's outstanding street markets for the number and quality of the antiques and other goods. The stalls are well known, and many dealers come into London from the country. Prices are generally lower here than at Portobello and the other markets. It gets started at 5am—with the bargains gone by 9am—and closes at noon. Bring a torch (flashlight) if you go in the wee hours.

LONDON AFTER DARK

Weekly publications such as *Time Out* and *Where* carry full entertainment listings, including information on restaurants and nightclubs. You'll also find listings in daily newspapers, notably the *Times* and the *Telegraph*.

The Theater

In London, you'll have a chance to see the world-renowned English theater on its home ground. Matinees are typically on Wednesday—or Thursday at some theaters—and Saturday. Theaters are closed on Sunday. It's impossible to describe all of London's theaters in this space, so below are listed just a few from the treasure trove.

GETTING TICKETS

To see specific shows, especially hits, purchase your tickets in advance. The best method is to buy your tickets from the theater's box office, which you can do over the phone using a credit card. You'll pay the theater price and pick up the tickets at the box office on the day of the show.

You can also go to a ticket agent, especially for discount tickets such as those sold by the **Society of London Theatre,** on the southwest corner of Leicester Square (© 020/7557-6700; www.officiallondontheatre.co.uk), open Monday to Saturday 10am to 7pm and Sunday noon to 3pm. A £2 service fee is charged. You can purchase all tickets here, although the booth specializes in half-price sales for shows that are undersold. These tickets must be purchased in person—not over the phone. For phone or online orders, you have to contact **Ticketmaster** (© 0870/060-2340; www.ticketmaster.co.uk).

For tickets and information before you go, try **Keith Prowse,** 234 W. 44th St., Ste. 1000, New York, NY 10036 (© 800/669-8687 or 212/398-4175; www.keithprowse.com). Its London office (which operates under the name of both Global Tickets and First Call Tickets) is at the **Britain and London Visitor Centre (BLVC),** 1 Lower Regent St., London SW1Y 4XT (© 0870/906-3860; Tube: Piccadilly Circus). The office will mail your tickets, fax a confirmation, or leave your tickets at the appropriate production's box office. Instant confirmations are available for most shows. A booking and handling fee of up to 20% is added to the price of all tickets.

Applause Theatre & Entertainment Service, 311 W. 43rd St., Ste. 601, New York, NY 10036 (© 800/451-9930 or 212/307-7050; fax 212/397-3729; www.applause-tickets.com), can sometimes get you tickets when Prowse can't. In business for some 2 decades, it is a reliable and efficient company.

Another option is **Theatre Direct International (TDI;** © 800/BROADWAY [276-2392] in the U.S. only, or 212/541-8457; www.broadway.com). TDI specializes in providing London fringe-theater tickets but also has tickets to major productions, including those at the Royal National Theatre and the Barbican. The service allows you to arrive in London with your tickets or have them held for you at the box office.

If you're staying at a first-class or deluxe hotel with a concierge, you can also call and arrange tickets before you arrive, putting them on a credit card.

London theater tickets are priced quite reasonably when compared to those in the United States. Prices vary greatly depending on the seat—from £25 to £150. Sometimes gallery seats (the cheapest) are sold only on the day of the performance, so you'll have to head to the box office early in the day and return an hour before the performance to queue up because they're not reserved seats.

Many of the major theaters offer reduced-price tickets on a standby basis to students, but not to the general public. When available, these tickets are sold 30 minutes prior to curtain. Line up early for popular shows, as standby tickets go fast and furious. Of course, you must have a valid student ID.

Warning: Beware of scalpers who hang out in front of theaters with hit shows. Many report that scalpers sell forged tickets, and their prices are outrageous.

THE MAJOR COMPANIES & THEATERS

One of the world's finest theater companies, the **Royal Shakespeare Company** ★★★ performs at various theaters throughout London. Check its website at **www.rsc.org.uk** for current shows and venues or call ✆ **0844/800-1110** Monday to Saturday 9am to 8pm. The theater troupe performs in London during the winter months, naturally specializing in the plays of the Bard. In summer, it tours England and abroad.

Cadogan Hall   Nestled in the heart of Chelsea, this decommissioned church, the first Christian Science church in the world, founded in 1893, has been turned into a concert hall for the Royal Philharmonic Orchestra. Completely restored and massively altered, the building now boasts a 900-seat auditorium and all the acoustics of the 21st century. The box office is open Monday through Saturday from 10am to 7pm and Sunday from 10am to 7pm on performance days only. 5 Sloane Terrace, SW1. ✆ 020/7730-4500. www.cadoganhall.com. Ticket prices vary according to event. Tube: Sloane Sq.

Open Air Theatre   This outdoor theater is in Regent's Park; the setting is idyllic, and both seating and acoustics are excellent. Presentations are mainly of Shakespeare, usually in period costume. Its theater bar, the longest in London, serves both drink and food. In the case of a rained-out performance, tickets are offered for another date. The season runs from June to mid-September, Monday through Saturday at 8pm, plus Wednesday, Thursday, and Saturday matinees at 2:30pm. Inner Circle, Regent's Park, NW1. ✆ 0844/826-4242. www.openairtheatre.org. Tickets £10–£33. Tube: Baker St.

Royal Court Theatre   This theater has always been a leader in producing provocative, cutting-edge new drama. In the 1950s, it staged the plays of the angry young men, notably John Osborne's then-sensational *Look Back in Anger;* earlier it debuted the plays of George Bernard Shaw. The theater is home to the English Stage Company, formed to promote serious stage writing. The box office is open Monday through Saturday from 10am to 6pm. Sloane Sq., SW1. ✆ 020/7565-5000. www.royalcourttheatre.com. Tickets £10–£45; call for the latest information. Tube: Sloane Sq.

Royal National Theatre   Home to one of the world's greatest stage companies, the National Theatre is not one but three theaters—the Olivier, reminiscent of a Greek amphitheater with its open stage; the more traditional Lyttelton; and the Cottesloe, with its flexible stage and seating. The National presents the finest in world theater, from classic drama to award-winning new plays, including comedies, musicals, and shows for young people. A choice of at least six plays is offered at any one time.

It's also a full-time theater center, with an amazing selection of bars, cafes, restaurants, free foyer music and exhibitions, short evening performances, bookshops, backstage tours, riverside walks, and terraces. You can have a three-course meal in Mezzanine, the National's restaurant; enjoy a light meal in the brasserie-style Terrace cafe; or have a snack in one of the coffee bars. The box office is open Monday through Saturday from 10am to 8pm. South Bank, SE1. ☏ **020/7452-3000.** www. nationaltheatre.org.uk. Tickets £10–£50; midweek matinees, Sat matinees, and previews cost less. Tube: Waterloo, Embankment, or Charing Cross.

Shakespeare's Globe Theatre   In May 1997, the new Globe Theatre—a replica of the Elizabethan original, thatched roof and all—staged its first slate of plays (*Henry V* and *A Winter's Tale*) yards away from the site of the 16th-century theater where the Bard originally staged his work.

Productions vary in style and setting; not all are performed in Elizabethan costume. In keeping with the historic setting, no lighting is focused just on the stage, but floodlighting is used during evening performances to replicate daylight in the theater—since Elizabethan performances took place in the afternoon. Theatergoers sit on wooden benches of yore—in thatch-roofed galleries, no less—but these days you can rent a cushion to make yourself more comfortable. About 500 "groundlings" can stand in the uncovered yard around the stage, just as they did when the Bard was here.

From May to September, the company holds performances Tuesday through Saturday at 2 and 7pm. A limited schedule is offered in winter. In any season, the schedule may be affected by weather because this is an outdoor theater. Performances last 2½ to 4 hours, depending on the play.

For details on the exhibition about the painstaking re-creation of the Globe, as well as guided tours of the theater, see p. 196. New Globe Walk, Bankside, SE1. ☏ **020/7902-1400** for box office. www.shakespeares-globe.org. Tickets £5 for groundlings, £15–£35 for gallery seats; exhibition £11 adults, £8.50 seniors and students, £6.50 children 5-15. Tube: Mansion House, London Bridge, Southwark, or Blackfriars.

Theatre Royal Drury Lane   Drury Lane is one of London's oldest and most prestigious theaters, crammed with tradition—not all of it respectable. This, the fourth theater on this site, dates from 1812; the first was built in 1663. Nell Gwynne, the rough-tongued Cockney lass who became Charles II's mistress, used to sell oranges under the long colonnade in front. Nearly every star of London theater has taken the stage here at some time. It has a wide-open repertoire but leans toward musicals, especially long-running hits. Guided tours of the backstage area and the front of the house are given most days at 10:15am, noon, 2:15pm, and 4:45pm. The box office is open Monday through Saturday from 10am to 8pm. Evening performances are held Monday through Saturday at 7:30pm, with matinees on Wednesday and Saturday at 2:30pm. Catherine St., Covent Garden, WC2. No phone. www.theatre-royal.com. Tickets £27–£70. Tube: Covent Garden.

The Rest of the Performing Arts Scene

Currently, London supports five major orchestras—the **London Symphony,** the **Royal Philharmonic,** the **Philharmonia Orchestra,** the **BBC Symphony,** and the **BBC Philharmonic**—and several choirs, plus many smaller chamber groups and historic instrument ensembles. Look for the **London Sinfonietta,** the **English Chamber Orchestra,** and, of course, the **Academy of St. Martin in the Fields.** Performances are held in the Southbank Centre and the Barbican. Smaller recitals are at Wigmore Hall and St. John's Smith Square.

Barbican Centre   The largest art and exhibition center in western Europe, the roomy and comfortable Barbican complex is the perfect setting for enjoying music and theater. Barbican Hall is the permanent home address of the **London Symphony Orchestra,** as well as host to visiting orchestras and performers of all styles, from classical to jazz, folk, and world music.

In addition to its hall and two theaters, the Barbican Centre encompasses the Barbican Art Gallery, the Curve Gallery, and foyer exhibition spaces; Cinemas One and Two, which show recently released mainstream films and film series; the Barbican Library, a general lending library that places a strong emphasis on the arts; the Conservatory, one of London's largest greenhouses; and restaurants, cafes, and bars. The box office is open Monday to Saturday from 9am to 8pm. Silk St., EC2. ℂ **020/7638-8891.** www.barbican.org.uk. Ticket prices vary according to event. Tube: Barbican or Moorgate.

London Coliseum   Built in 1904 as a variety theater and converted into an opera house in 1968, the London Coliseum is the city's largest theater. The 2,358-seat Coliseum still remains the largest proscenium theater in England. For its 100th birthday, the renowned opera house received a multimillion-pound restoration fit for a diva. Today, not only is the Edwardian splendor restored, but there are also roomier foyers, plus a two-story lobby and bar with views of Trafalgar Square.

The London Coliseum is home to one of two national opera companies, the **English National Opera,** and also hosts touring companies. The English National Opera performs a range of works here, from classics to Gilbert and Sullivan to new experimental works. All performances are in English. The company presents a repertory of 18 to 20 productions 5 or 6 nights a week for 10 months of the year; the theater is dark mid-July to mid-September. Although balcony seats are cheaper, many visitors seem to prefer the upper circle or dress circle. The box office is open Monday to Saturday from 10am to 6pm. St. Martin's Lane, WC2. ℂ **0871/911-0200.** www.eno.org. Tickets from £10 balcony, £26–£110 upper or dress circle or stalls; about 100 discount balcony tickets sold on the day of performance from 10am. Tube: Charing Cross or Leicester Sq.

Royal Albert Hall   Opened in 1871 and dedicated to the memory of Victoria's consort, Prince Albert, this circular building holds one of the world's most famous auditoriums. With a seating capacity of 5,200, it's a popular place to hear music by stars. Occasional sporting events (especially boxing) figure strongly here, too.

Since 1941, the hall has hosted the BBC Henry Wood Promenade Concerts, known as "the Proms," an annual series that lasts for 8 weeks between mid-July and mid-September. The Proms, incorporating a medley of rousing, mostly British orchestral music, have been a British tradition since 1895. Although most of the audience occupies reserved seats, true aficionados usually opt for standing room in the orchestra pit, with close-up views of the musicians on stage. Newly commissioned works are often premiered here. The final evening is the most traditional, when the rousing favorites "Jerusalem" or "Land of Hope and Glory" echo through the hall. Check out **www.bbc.co.uk/proms** for more details.

After its 8-year restoration, the Albert Hall now allows tours every 30 minutes, starting at 10:30am Friday through Tuesday and ending at 2:30pm, at a cost of £7.50. Limited to only 15 participants, tours take in such sights as the Queen's Box and the Royal Retiring Room used by royals during intermission. Those on tour are also shown the Royal Albert Hall organ, with its 9,999 pipes. The box office is open daily from 9am to 9pm. Kensington Gore, SW7. ℂ **020/7589-8212.** www.royalalberthall. com. Tickets £5–£150, depending on the event. Tube: South Kensington.

Royal Opera House   The **Royal Ballet** and the **Royal Opera** are at home again in this magnificently restored theater. Opera and ballet aficionados hardly recognize the renovated place, with its spectacular public spaces, including the Floral Hall (a chamber-music venue), a rooftop restaurant, and bars and shops. The entire northeast corner of one of London's most famous public squares has been transformed, finally realizing Inigo Jones's original vision for this colonnaded plaza.

Performances of the Royal Opera are usually sung in the original language, but supertitles are projected. The Royal Ballet, which ranks with top companies such as the Kirov and the Paris Opera Ballet, performs a repertory with a tilt toward the classics, including works by its earlier choreographer-directors Sir Frederick Ashton and Sir Kenneth MacMillan. The box office is open Monday to Saturday from 10am to 8pm. Bow St., Covent Garden, WC2. ✆ **020/7304-4000.** www.royalopera.org. Tickets £6–£200. Tube: Covent Garden.

Sadler's Wells Theatre   This is a premier venue for dance and opera. It occupies the site of a series of theaters, the first built in 1683. In the early 1990s, the turn-of-the-20th-century theater was mostly demolished, and construction began on an innovative new design completed at the end of 1998. The facade has been retained, but the interior has been completely revamped with a stylish cutting-edge design. The new theater offers classical ballet, modern dance of all degrees of "avant-gardeness," and children's theatrical productions, including a Christmas ballet. Performances are usually at 7:30pm. The box office is open Monday to Saturday from 9am to 8:30pm. Rosebery Ave., EC1. ✆ **020/7863-8198.** www.sadlerswells.com. Tickets £10–£70. Tube: Northern Line to Angel.

Southbank Centre   Three of the most acoustically perfect concert halls in the world were erected here between 1951 and 1964: the Royal Festival Hall, the Queen Elizabeth Hall, and the Purcell Room, all located in this complex. Together, the halls present more than 1,200 performances a year, including classical music, ballet, jazz, popular music, and contemporary dance. Also here is the internationally renowned Hayward Gallery (p. 189).

The Southbank Centre, which usually opens daily at 10am, offers an extensive array of things to see and do, including free exhibitions in the foyers and occasional free lunchtime music at 12:30pm. On Friday from 5:15 to 6:45pm, "Commuter Jazz" in the foyer is free. The Poetry Library is open Tuesday to Sunday from 11am to 8pm. Shops display a selection of books, records, and crafts. Food and drink are served at various venues: Head to Skylon (www.skylonrestaurant.co.uk), a new restaurant on Level 3, for modern Continental cuisine with panoramic views of the London skyline. Less formal dining is available at the Riverside Terrace Café on Level 2, where guests dine outdoors in fair weather, watching boat traffic on the Thames. The box office is open daily from 9am to 8pm. Belvedere Rd., South Bank, SE1. Box office ✆ **0844/875-0073.** www.southbankcentre.co.uk. Tickets £8–£80. Tube: Waterloo or Embankment.

Wigmore Hall   An intimate auditorium, Wigmore Hall offers an excellent series of voice recitals, piano and chamber music, early and baroque music, and jazz. A cafe/bar and restaurant are on the premises; a cold supper can be preordered if you are attending a concert. Performances are held nightly in addition to "Sunday Morning Coffee Concerts" at 11:30am and Sunday afternoon concerts at 4pm. The box office is open Monday to Saturday from 10am to 7pm and Sunday from 10:30am to

5pm. 36 Wigmore St., W1. ℂ 020/7935-2141. www.wigmore-hall.org.uk. Tickets £10–£50. Tube: Bond St. or Oxford Circus.

OUTSIDE CENTRAL LONDON

Kenwood House Picnic Concerts   These band and orchestral concerts on the north side of Hampstead Heath have been a British tradition for more than half a century. In recent years, laser shows and fireworks have been added to a repertoire that includes everything from rousing versions of the *1812 Overture* to jazz to operas such as *Carmen*. The final concert of the season always features some of the "Pomp and Circumstance" marches of Sir Edward Elgar. Music drifts across the lake to serenade wine-and-cheese parties on the grass. Concerts take place late June through August, Saturday at 7:30pm. The box office is open Monday to Saturday from 9:30am to 6:30pm. Kenwood, Hampstead Lane, Hampstead Heath, NW3. ℂ 0844/412-2706. www.picnicconcerts.com. Tickets £20 for lawn seats, £35 for reserved deck chairs. Discounts for students, children 12 and younger, and seniors. Tube: Northern Line to Golders Green or Archway, and then bus no. 210, a 30–45-min. jaunt to the north of London.

The Club & Music Scene

COMEDY

The Comedy Store   The Comedy Store is London's showcase for established and rising comic talent. Inspired by comedy clubs in the U.S., the club has given many comics their start, and today a number of them are established TV personalities. Even if their names are unfamiliar, you'll enjoy the spontaneity of live comedy before a British audience. Visitors must be 18 and older; dress is casual. Reserve through **Ticketmaster** (ℂ 0844/847-1637); the club opens 1½ hours before each show. Tuesday through Sunday, doors open at 6:30pm and the show starts at 8pm; on Friday and Saturday, an extra show starts at midnight (doors at 11pm). *Insider's tip:* Go on Tuesday, when the humor is more cutting-edge. 1A Oxendon St., off Piccadilly Circus, SW1. ℂ 0844/847-1728. www.thecomedystore.co.uk. Cover £20–£50. Tube: Leicester Sq. or Piccadilly Circus.

LIVE MUSIC

The Bull & Gate   Outside central London, and smaller, cheaper, and often more animated and less touristy than many of its competitors, the Bull & Gate is the unofficial headquarters of London's pub rock scene. Indie and relatively unknown rock bands are served up in back-to-back handfuls at this somewhat battered Victorian pub. The place attracts a young crowd, mainly in their 20s. If you like spilled beer, this is off-the-beaten-track London at its most authentic. Bands that have played here and later ascended to fame on Europe's club scene include Madness, Blur, and Pulp. There's music nightly from 8pm to midnight. 389 Kentish Town Rd., NW5. ℂ 020/8826-5000. www.bullandgate.co.uk. Cover from £5. Tube: Northern Line to Kentish Town.

O₂ Shepherd's Bush Empire   Located in an old BBC television theater with great acoustics, this is a major venue for big-name pop and rock stars. Announcements appear in the local press. The spot mostly attracts fans in their 20s. There's a seating capacity of 2,000. The box office is open Monday to Friday from noon to 4pm, but you can book 24 hours through **Ticketweb** (ℂ 0870/771-2000).

Shepherd's Bush Green, W12. ✆ **020/8354-3300.** www.O2shepherdsbushempire.co.uk. Ticket prices vary according to show. Tube: Hammersmith & City Line to Shepherd's Bush or Goldhawk Rd.

Roundhouse In a Victorian steam-engine repair shed, the Roadhouse in Camden is once again a cultural venue, presenting live music from emerging young talent, even theater and dance. In days of yore, Jimi Hendrix, Paul McCartney, and the Who performed here. After reopening in 2006, it now attracts young London; it can house up to 3,300 patrons standing. The on-site cafe sells fresh, seasonal food at a reasonable price. Chalk Farm Rd., NW1. ✆ **0844/482-8008.** www.roundhouse.org.uk. Phone bookings Mon–Fri 9am–6pm; Sat 9am–4pm. Prices vary according to event. Tube: Camden Town.

Sound This 700-seat venue in the heart of London has booked the big acts, everybody from Sinéad O'Connor to Puff Daddy to the Spice Girls. It functions as a restaurant and bar every night, with limited live music and a DJ until 11pm; after 11pm, the mood changes, the menu is simplified to include only bar snacks, and the site focuses much more heavily on live music and dancing. The music program is forever changing; call to see what's on at the time of your visit and to reserve tickets. Crowds and age levels vary depending on what act is featured. Reservations are recommended for dinner, but reservations after 11pm are not accepted. The box office is open Monday to Saturday from 10am to 6pm. 1 Leicester Sq., W1. ✆ **020/7287-1010.** www.soundlondon.com. Free admission until 9pm daily; cover £10 9–10pm, £10–£12 10–11pm, £15 from 11pm. Tube: Leicester Sq.

Windmill ★★ It's the music that lures devotees to the back streets of Brixton. This unpretentious club, whose reputation went from zero to great, is now hailed as one of the top-10 music venues in the U.K. Entry is cheap, and so is the beer. The staff is friendly, the atmosphere candlelit. The beer garden overflows with a hip, young crowd of Londoners and foreigners who come to hear everything from the Black Lips to Die! Die! Die! Sounds embrace psycho beats, punk, Goth rock, and music as yet unlabeled. This place is open Monday to Saturday from 8pm to 2am. 22 Blenheim Gardens, SW2. ✆ **020/8671-0700.** www.windmillbrixton.co.uk. Cover £3–£20. Tube: Brixton.

TRADITIONAL ENGLISH MUSIC

Cecil Sharpe House CSH was the focal point of the folk revival in the 1960s, and it continues to treasure and nurture folk music and dance. You'll find a whole range of traditional music and dance here, with different evenings devoted to Irish set dances, English barn dances (similar to American square dances), dances from Louisiana's Cajun country, even reenactments of 18th-century quadrilles. Although many of the regular patrons of this bar and dance club know these arcane dances by heart, they're usually charitable toward quick-learning and agile newcomers who can pick up the steps and the beat quickly. Call to see what's on while you're in town. The box office is open Monday to Friday from 9:30am to 5:30pm. 2 Regent's Park Rd., NW1. ✆ **020/7485-2206.** www.efdss.org. Tickets £5–£30. Tube: Northern Line to Camden Town.

JAZZ & BLUES

100 Club Although less plush and pricey than some jazz clubs, 100 Club is a serious contender on the music front. Its cavalcade of bands includes the best

British jazz musicians and some of their Yankee brethren. Rock, R&B, and blues are also on tap. Serious devotees of jazz from ages 20 to 45 show up here. Open Monday through Thursday and Sunday 7:30 to 11:30pm; Friday noon to 3pm and 8:30pm to 2am; and Saturday 7:30pm to 1am. *Note:* These hours are subject to change. 100 Oxford St., W1. (✆) **020/7636-0933.** www.the100club.co.uk. Cover £6–£30. Club members get a £1 discount Sat nights. Tube: Tottenham Court Rd. or Oxford Circus.

Pizza Express Don't let the name fool you: This restaurant/bar serves some of the best jazz in London by mainstream artists, along with thin-crust Italian pizza. You'll find local bands or visiting groups, often from the U.S. The place draws an equal mix of Londoners and visitors in the 20-to-40 age bracket. Although the club has been enlarged, it's still important to reserve ahead of time. The restaurant is open daily from 11:30am to midnight; jazz plays from 7:30 to 11pm. 10 Dean St., W1. (✆) **020/7734-3220.** www.pizzaexpresslive.com. Cover £15–£35. Tube: Tottenham Court Rd.

Ronnie Scott's Ask about jazz in London, and people immediately think of Ronnie Scott's, the European vanguard for modern jazz. Only the best English and American combos, often fronted by top-notch vocalists, are booked here. In the heart of Soho, Ronnie Scott's is a 10-minute walk from Piccadilly Circus along Shaftesbury Avenue. In the Main Room, you can watch the show from the bar or sit at a table and order dinner. The Downstairs Bar is more intimate; among the regulars at your elbow may be some of the world's most talented musicians. The club is open Monday to Saturday 6pm to 3am, Sunday 6pm to midnight. Reservations are recommended. 47 Frith St., W1. (✆) **020/7439-0747.** www.ronniescotts.co.uk. Tickets £5–£50, depending on the event. Tube: Leicester Sq. or Piccadilly Circus.

606 Club Located in a discreet basement in Chelsea, this jazz supper club, in the boondocks of Fulham, presents live music nightly. Predominantly a venue for modern jazz, its styles range from traditional to contemporary. Local musicians and some very big names play here, whether at planned gigs or informal jam sessions after they finish shows elsewhere in town. Because of license requirements, patrons can order alcohol only with food. Locals show up here along with a trendy crowd from more posh neighborhoods in London. Open Monday to Wednesday 7:30pm to 1am; Thursday to Saturday 8pm to 1:30am; and selected Sundays noon to 4pm and 8pm to midnight. 90 Lots Rd., SW10. (✆) **020/7352-5953.** www.606club.co.uk. Cover Sun–Thurs £8, Fri–Sat £15. Bus: 11, 19, 22, 31, 39, C1, or C3. Tube: Earl's Court.

DANCE, DISCO & ECLECTIC

Bar Rumba Despite its location on Shaftesbury Avenue, this Latin bar and music club could be featured in a book on underground London. A hush-hush address, it leans toward radical jazz-fusion on some nights and phat funk on other occasions. It boasts two full bars and a different theme every night. All the music here is live. On weeknights, you have to be 18 or older; on Saturday and Sunday, nobody under 21 is allowed in. 36 Shaftesbury Ave., W1. (✆) **020/7287-6933.** www.barrumba.co.uk. Cover £4–£20. Free Sat before 10pm. Tube: Piccadilly Circus.

Cargo This watering hole in ultratrendy Hoxton draws a smart urban crowd from their expensive West End flats. Its habitués assure us it's the place to go for a "wicked time" and great live bands. If there are no bands on a particular night, then DJs dominate the club. Music and dancing start at 6pm and the joint is jumping by 9:30pm nightly. It's fun and funky, with two big arched rooms, fantastic acoustics, and a parade of videos. As for the patrons, the bartender characterized it just right: "We get the freaks and the normal people." Open Monday to Thursday noon to 1am, Friday noon to 3am, Saturday 6pm to 3am, and Sunday 1pm to midnight. Kingsland Viaduct, 83 Rivington St., Shoreditch, EC2. ⓒ **020/7739-3440.** www.cargo-london.com. Cover £6–£35, after 10pm. Tube: Liverpool St.

Egg ★ There's a wild party going on here for serious clubbers drawn to the somewhat seedy location across from Kings Cross. Spread over three floors, the warehouse-style joint embraces everything from electro-disco beats to house (its specialty). Egg is a leading contender in London's underground scene, complete with a large garden and balcony terrace. Sexy clubbers—both gay and straight—show up for such events as "Playtime" on Friday nights. Open Friday from 10pm until 6am the next day, and Saturday from 10pm until noon on Sunday. 200 York Way, N7. ⓒ **020/7609-8364.** www.egglondon.net. Tube: Kings Cross.

The End This club is better than ever after its enlargement. You'll find a trio of large dance floors, along with four bars and a chill-out area. Speaker walls will blast you into orbit. The End is the best club in London for live house and garage music, drawing both straight and gay Londoners. From its drinking fountain to its swanky toilets, the club is alluring. Dress for glam and to be seen on the circuit. Some big names in London appear on the weekends. Open Monday and Wednesday 9pm to 3am, Tuesday 6pm to 3am, Thursday 8pm to 3am, Friday 6pm to 3:30am, Saturday 9pm to 3:30am, and Sunday 9pm to 1:30am. 18 W. Central St., WC1. ⓒ **020/7419-9199.** www.endclub.com. Cover £5–£20. Tube: Tottenham Court Rd.

Fabric While other competitors have come and gone, Fabric continues to draw crowds since opening in 1999. Its main allure is that it has a license for 24-hour music and dancing from Thursday to Sunday. This is one of the most famous clubs in the increasingly trendy East London sector. On some crazed nights, at least 2,500 young Londoners and international visitors crowd into this mammoth place. It has a trio of dance floors, bars wherever you look, unisex toilets, chill-out beds, and even a roof terrace. Live acts are presented on Fridays, with DJs reigning on weekends. You'll hear house, garage, soca, reggae, and whatever else is big on the underground scene. Open Thursday and Friday 9:30pm to 5am, Saturday 10pm to 7am. 77A Charterhouse St., EC1. ⓒ **020/7336-8898.** www.fabriclondon.com. Cover £8–£16. Tube: Farringdon.

Ministry of Sound Removed from the city center, this club-of-the-hour remains hot, hot, hot. With a large bar and huge sound system, it blasts garage and house music for the energetic crowds that pack the two dance floors. If music and lights in the rest of the club have gone to your head, you can chill in the lounge. *Note:* The cover is stiff, and bouncers decide who is cool enough to enter, so slip into your most glamorous club gear. Open Friday 10pm to 5am and Saturday 11pm to 7am. Student night is Tuesday 10pm to 4am. 103 Gaunt St., SE1. ⓒ **870/060-0010.** www. ministryofsound.com. Cover £12–£20. Tube: Northern Line to Elephant & Castle.

Notting Hill Arts Club This is one of the hippest nighttime venues in London, with the action taking place in a no-frills basement in increasingly fashionable Notting Hill Gate. Yes, that was Liam Gallagher you spotted dancing with Courtney Love. To justify the name of the club, art exhibitions are sometimes staged here. Most of the clients are under 35 and come from a wide range of backgrounds—from

Madonna to Ziggy Marley wannabes. The music is eclectic, varying from night to night—jazz, salsa, hip-hop, indie, and so on. Open Monday to Friday 6pm to 2am, Saturday 4pm to 2am, and Sunday 4pm to 1am. Bands perform Monday to Thursday, Saturday, and Sunday. 21 Notting Hill Gate, W11. © **020/7460-4459.** www.notting hillartsclub.com. Cover £5–£15. Tube: Notting Hill Gate.

Vibe Bar As more and more of hip London heads east, bypassing even Clerkenwell for Hoxton, Vibe has been put on the map. The *Evening Standard* named it among the top five DJ bars in London. The paper compared it to an "expensively distressed pair of designer jeans." It's a nightspot operated by Truman Brewery. In summer, the action overflows into a courtyard. Patrons check their e-mail, lounge on comfortable couches, and listen to diverse music such as reggae, Latin, jazz, R&B, African, or hip-hop. Hours are Sunday to Thursday 1:30 to 11:30pm, Friday and Saturday 5pm to 1am. 91 Brick Lane, E1. © **020/7426-0491.** www.vibe-bar.co.uk. Cover free to £5, sometimes assessed after 6pm. Tube: Liverpool St.

Zoo Bar The owners spent millions of pounds outfitting this club in the slickest, flashiest, and most psychedelic decor in London. If you're looking for a true Euro nightlife experience, replete with gorgeous au pairs and trendy Europeans, this is it. Zoo Bar upstairs is a menagerie of mosaic animals beneath a glassed-in ceiling dome. Downstairs, the music is intrusive enough to make conversation futile. Clients range in age from 18 to 35; androgyny is the look of choice. Hours are daily from 4pm to 3am. 13–17 Bear St., WC2. © **020/7839-4188.** www.zoobar.co.uk. Cover £2–£15, after 10pm. Tube: Leicester Sq.

The Gay & Lesbian Scene

Time Out has listings on gay and lesbian clubs. Another good place for finding out what's hot and hip is **Prowler Soho,** 5–7 Brewer St., W1 (© **020/7734-4031;** Tube: Piccadilly Circus), the largest gay lifestyle store in London, selling everything from jewelry to CDs and books, fashion, and sex toys. It's open until 10pm Monday to Saturday, Sunday from noon to 8pm. On the Web, **www.gingerbeer.co.uk** is the best site for lesbians to find out what's going on in London, and **G3** (www.g3mag. co.uk) is the magazine that all bona fide lesbians read.

Admiral Duncan Gay men and their friends go here to drink, have a good time, and make a political statement. British tabloids shocked the world in 1999 when they reported that this pub had been bombed, with three people dying in the attack. Within 6 weeks, the pub reopened its doors. We're happy to report that the bar is better than ever, now also attracting nongays showing their support. Open Monday to Thursday noon to 11pm, Friday and Saturday noon to 11:30pm, and Sunday noon to 10:30pm. 54 Old Compton St., W1. © **020/7437-5300.** Tube: Piccadilly Circus or Leicester Sq.

The Box Adjacent to one of Covent Garden's best-known junctions, Seven Dials, this sophisticated Mediterranean-style bar attracts all kinds of men. In the afternoon, it is primarily a restaurant, serving salads, club sandwiches, and soups. Food service ends abruptly at 5pm, after which the place becomes a cheerful, popular rendezvous for London's gay and counterculture crowds. The Box considers itself a "summer bar," throwing open its doors and windows to a cluster of outdoor tables at the slightest hint of sunshine. Open Monday to Saturday 11am to 11:30pm and

Sunday 11am to 11pm. 32–34 Monmouth St. (at Seven Dials), WC2. ℂ **020/7240-5828.** www.boxbar.com. Tube: Leicester Sq.

Candy Bar   This is the most popular lesbian bar in London at the moment. It has an extremely mixed clientele, ranging from butch to femme and young to old. Design is simple, with bright colors and mirrors upstairs and darker, more flirtatious decor downstairs in the bar and club. Men are welcome as long as a woman escorts them. Open Monday to Thursday 5 to 11:30pm, Friday and Saturday 5pm to 2am, and Sunday 5 to 11pm. 4 Carlisle St., W1. ℂ **020/7494-4041.** www.candybarsoho.com. Cover Fri £5, Sat £6. Tube: Tottenham Court Rd.

The Edge   Few bars in London can rival the tolerance, humor, and sexual sophistication found here. The first two floors are done up in decor that, like an English garden, changes with the seasons. Dance music can be found on the crowded, high-energy lower floors. Three menus are offered: a funky daytime menu, a cafe menu, and a late-night menu. Dancers hit the floors starting around 7:30pm. Clientele ranges from flamboyantly gay to hetero pub-crawlers. Open Monday to Saturday noon to 1am and Sunday 2 to 11:30pm. 11 Soho Sq., W1. ℂ **207/439-1313.** www. edgesoho.co.uk. Tube: Tottenham Court Rd.

First Out Café Bar   First Out prides itself on being London's first (est. 1986) all-gay coffee shop. Set in a 19th-century building whose wood panels have been painted the colors of the gay-liberation rainbow, the bar and cafe are not particularly cruisy. Cappuccino and whisky are the preferred libations, and an exclusively vegetarian menu includes curry dishes, potted pies in phyllo pastries, and salads. Don't expect a raucous atmosphere—some people come here with their grandmothers. Look for the bulletin board with leaflets and business cards of gay and gay-friendly entrepreneurs. Open Monday to Saturday 10am to 11pm and Sunday 11am to 10:30pm. 52 St. Giles High St., W1. ℂ **020/7240-8042.** www.firstoutcafebar.com. Tube: Tottenham Court Rd.

Heaven   This club, housed in the vaulted cellars of Charing Cross railway station, is a London landmark. It's one of the biggest and best-established gay venues in Britain. Painted black and reminiscent of an air-raid shelter, the club is divided into at least four areas, connected by a labyrinth of catwalk stairs and hallways. Each room offers a different type of music, from hip-hop to rock. Heaven also has theme nights, which are frequented at different times by gays, lesbians, or a mostly heterosexual crowd. Thursday in particular seems open to anything, but on Saturday it's gays only. Call before you go. Open Monday 10pm to 6:30am, Wednesday 10:30pm to 3am, Friday 11pm to 6am, and Saturday 10:30pm to 5am. Under the Arches, Villiers St., WC2. ℂ **020/7930-2020.** www.heaven-london.com. Cover £12–£20. Tube: Charing Cross or Embankment.

The Bar & Pub Scene
OUR FAVORITE BARS

Absolut Icebar   You might say that this watering hole is the coolest joint in town. The temperature is kept at 5°F (−15°C) year-round, with everything inside made out of crystal-clear ice from the Torne River in Sweden. Make a reservation to chill out for 40 minutes, and you'll be given a silver cape and hood to wear for the experience, accompanied by a vodka cocktail to warm your soul. Open Monday to Thursday 3:30

to 11pm, Friday 2:45pm to 1:10am, Saturday 12:30pm to 1:10am, and Sunday 3 to 11pm. 31–33 Heddon St., W1. 🕾 **020/7478-8910.** www.belowzerolondon.com. Cover Sun–Wed £13; Thurs–Sat £16. Tube: Oxford Circus.

Artesian This lilac-hued lounge in the Langham hotel is a chic rendezvous with pricey cocktails. It boasts more than 50 types of rum, a drink associated more with the Caribbean than London. The bartender's specialty is hot buttered rum: The dark rum is blended with apple cider, spices, and a clove-infused apricot brandy, among other ingredients. Open Monday through Friday 4pm to midnight, Saturday and Sunday around noon to midnight. In the Langham hotel, 1C Portland Place, W1. 🕾 **020/7636-1000.** www.artesian-bar.co.uk. Tube: Oxford Circus.

Axis & the Lobby Bar These bars are found at One Aldwych, one of London's best deluxe hotels. We advise checking out the dramatic visuals in both before selecting your preferred nesting place. The Lobby Bar occupies what was built in 1907 as the grand, high-ceilinged reception area for one of London's premier newspapers. Many under-40 fashionistas frequent the travertine, hardwood, and leather-sheathed bar in the Axis restaurant. The Lobby Bar is open Monday to Saturday 9am to midnight, Sunday 8am to 6:30pm; the Axis bar is open Monday to Saturday 5:45 to 11pm. In the One Aldwych hotel, 1 Aldwych, WC2. 🕾 **020/7300-1000.** www.campbellgrayhotels.com. Tube: Covent Garden.

Bartok ★ 🎒 It's been around for about a decade, but still isn't very well known—though it should be. It's the hippest bar in Camden, specializing in classical music (of all things) and named for the Hungarian composer Béla Bartók. It's been called the ultimate chill-out bar in London, ideal for a romantic evening regardless of your sexual persuasion. Crystal chandeliers and the flicker of candles set the rather decadent, hedonistic mood. Visitors sprawl out on tapestry-covered couches, enjoying actual conversation, the music, the food, the drink, and each other. Open Monday to Thursday 5pm to 3am, Friday 5pm to 4am, Saturday 1pm to 4am, and Sunday 1pm to 3am. 78–79 Chalk Farm Rd. (opposite the Roundhouse), NW1. 🕾 **020/7916-0595.** Tube: Chalk Farm.

Beach Blanket Babylon This Portobello joint is very cruisy. Come here if you're looking for a hot singles bar that attracts a crowd in its 20s and 30s. The decor is a bit wacky, no doubt designed by an aspiring Salvador Dalí who decided to make it a fairy-tale grotto (or was he going for a medieval-dungeon look?). It's close to the Portobello Market. Friday and Saturday nights are the hot, crowded times for bacchanalian revelry. Open daily noon to midnight. 45 Ledbury Rd., W11. 🕾 **020/7229-2907.** www.beachblanket.co.uk. Tube: Notting Hill Gate.

Cantaloupe This bustling pub and restaurant is hailed as the bar that jump-started the increasingly fashionable Shoreditch scene. Businesspeople commuting from their jobs in the City mix with East End trendoids in the early evening at what has been called a "gastropub/preclub bar." The urban beat is courtesy of the house DJ. The restaurant and tapas menus are first-rate. Open Thursday to Saturday noon to midnight, Sunday to Wednesday noon to 11pm. 35 Charlotte Rd., Shoreditch, EC2. 🕾 **020/7729-5566.** www.cantaloupelondon.co.uk. Tube: Old St.

Lab ★ Perhaps the best mixologists in town are found right in the heart of London at this '70s kitsch-inspired cocktail bar, where bartenders will whip you up the best Feijon Flip or Red Hot Chili Pepper around. Come here for the ultimate in intoxication, hanging out in a glam, glossy setting of leather and Formica spread over two floors. A thick cocktail book lies on every table; if you're in London long enough you may want to work your way through all the drinks, from the classics to house specialties. DJs keep the mood relaxed. Open Monday to Saturday 4pm to midnight and Sunday 4 to 10:30pm. 12 Old Compton St., W1. *C* 020/7437-7820. www.lab-townhouse.com. Tube: Leicester Sq.

Match EC1 This epicenter for the fashionable 20s-to-30s set in London has put the *P* in partying in the once-staid Clerkenwell district. Drinkers sit on elegant sofas or retreat to one of the cozy booths for a late snack. The bar claims to be the home of the Cosmopolitan cocktail, which swept across the drinking establishments of New York. The bartenders make some of the best drinks in London, but warn that "there is no such thing as a chocolate martini." Open Monday to Thursday 11am to midnight, Friday 11am to 2am, and Saturday 6pm to 2am. 45–47 Clerkenwell Rd., EC1. *C* 020/7250-4002. www.matchbar.com. Tube: Farringdon.

Phoenix Artist Club What's something so old it's new again? This bar is underneath the Phoenix Theatre, where Laurence Olivier made his stage debut in 1930 and couldn't stop giggling—even though the play was a drama. Live music is featured, but it's the hearty welcome, the good beer, and the friendly patrons from ages 20 to 50 who make the rediscovered theater bar worth a detour. It's open to the general public from 5 to 8pm only—it's "members only" after 8pm, but if it's relatively quiet at that time, the club will also admit nonmembers. 1 Phoenix St. (at Charing Cross Rd.), WC2. *C* 020/7836-1077. www.phoenixartistclub.com. Tube: Tottenham Court Rd. or Leicester Sq.

LONDON'S MOST EVOCATIVE PUBS
Belgravia
Grenadier Tucked away in a mews, the Grenadier is one of London's reputedly haunted pubs, the ghost here being an 18th-century British soldier. Aside from the poltergeist, the basement houses the original bar and skittles alley used by the duke of Wellington's officers. The scarlet front door of the one-time officers' mess is guarded by a scarlet sentry box and shaded by a vine. The bar is nearly always crowded. Lunch and dinner are offered daily—even on Sunday, when it's a tradition to drink Bloody Marys (made from a well-guarded recipe) here. In the stalls along the side, you can order good-tasting fare based on seasonal ingredients. Well-prepared dishes include pork Grenadier, beef Wellington, and a chicken-and-Stilton roulade. Such snacks as fish and chips are available at the bar. 18 Wilton Row, SW1. *C* 020/7235-3074. Tube: Hyde Park Corner.

Bloomsbury
Museum Tavern Across the street from the British Museum, this pub (ca. 1703) retains most of its antique trappings: velvet, oak paneling, and cut glass. It lies right in the center of the University of London area and is popular with writers, publishers, and researchers from the museum. Karl Marx supposedly wrote while dining here. Traditional English food is served: shepherd's pie, sausages cooked in English cider, turkey-and-ham pie, ploughman's lunch, and salads. Several English ales, cold lagers, cider, Guinness, wines, and spirits are available. Food and coffee are served all day. The pub gets crowded at lunchtime. 49 Great Russell St., WC1. *C* 020/7242-8987. www.thespiritgroup.com. Tube: Holborn or Tottenham Court Rd.

The City of London

Bow Wine Vaults   Bow Wine Vaults has existed since long before the wine-bar craze began in the 1970s. One of the most famous in London, the bar attracts cost-conscious diners and drinkers to its vaulted cellars for such traditional fare as deep-fried Camembert, lobster ravioli, and a mixed grill, along with fish. The cocktail bar is popular with the after-work crowd (Mon–Fri 11:30am–11pm). More elegant meals, served in the street-level dining room, include Thai green mussels in curry sauce, escalope of veal Milanese garnished with pasta, and haddock Monte Carlo. Wines from around the world are available; the last time we were here, the wine of the day was a Chilean chardonnay. 10 Bow Churchyard, EC4. ☎ **020/7248-1121.** www.bowwinevaults.com. Tube: Mansion House, Bank, or St. Paul's.

Jamaica Wine House   This was one of the first coffeehouses in England and, reputedly, the Western world. Merchants and sea captains once came here to transact deals over rum and coffee. Nowadays, the two-level house dispenses coffee, beer, ale, lager, and fine wines, among them a variety of ports. The oak-paneled bar is on the street level and attracts crowds of investment bankers. You can order standard but filling dishes such as a ploughman's lunch and toasted sandwiches. St. Michael's Alley, off Cornhill, EC3. ☎ **020/7929-6972.** Tube: Bank.

Covent Garden

Lamb & Flag   Dickens once frequented this pub, and the room has changed little from the days when he prowled the neighborhood. The pub has an amazing and scandalous history. Poet and author Dryden was almost killed by a band of thugs outside its doors in 1679, and the pub gained the nickname the "Bucket of Blood" during the Regency era (1811–20) because of the bare-knuckled prizefights here. Tap beers include Courage Best and Directors, Old Speckled Hen, John Smith's, and Wadworth 6X. 33 Rose St., off Garrick St., WC2. ☎ **020/7497-9504.** Tube: Leicester Sq.

Nags Head   This Nags Head is one of London's most famous Edwardian pubs. In days of yore, patrons had to make their way through a fruit-and-flower market to drink here. Today, the pub is popular with young people. The draft Guinness is very good. Lunch (noon–4pm) is typical pub grub: sandwiches, salads, pork cooked in cider, and garlic prawns. Snacks are available all afternoon. 10 James St., WC2. ☎ **020/7836-4678.** Tube: Covent Garden.

The East End (Wapping)

Prospect of Whitby   One of London's most historic pubs, Prospect was founded in the days of the Tudors, taking its name from a coal barge that made trips between Yorkshire and London. Come here for a tot, a noggin, or whatever it is you drink, and soak up the atmosphere. The pub has got quite a pedigree: Author Charles Dickens and diarist Samuel Pepys used to drop in, and painter Turner came here for weeks at a time studying views of the Thames. In the 17th century, the notorious Hanging Judge Jeffreys used to get drunk here while overseeing hangings at the adjoining Execution Dock. Tables in the courtyard overlook the river. You can order a Morland Old Speckled Hen from a hand-pump or a malt whisky. 57 Wapping Wall, E1. ☎ **020/7481-1095.** Tube: Wapping.

Holborn

Cittie of Yorke   This pub boasts the longest bar in all of Britain, rafters ascending to the heavens, and a long row of immense wine vats, all of which give it the air of a great medieval hall—appropriate because a pub has existed at this location since 1430. Samuel Smith's is on tap. 22 High Holborn, WC1. ℭ **020/7242-7670.** Tube: Holborn or Chancery Lane.

Knightsbridge

Nag's Head   This Nag's Head (not to be confused with the more renowned one at 10 James St.; see above) is on a back street a short walk from the Berkeley hotel. Previously a jail dating from 1780, it's said to be the smallest pub in London. In 1921, it was sold for £12 and 6p. Have a drink up front or wander to the tiny bar in the rear. For food, you might enjoy "real ale sausage" (made with pork and ale), shepherd's pie, or the quiche of the day, all served by the welcoming staff. A cosmopolitan clientele—newspaper people, musicians, and travelers—patronizes this warm, cozy pub. It touts itself as an "independent," or able to serve any "real ale" it chooses because of its lack of affiliation. 53 Kinnerton St., SW1. ℭ **020/7235-1135.** Tube: Hyde Park Corner or Knightsbridge.

Leicester Square

Salisbury   An original gin palace, Salisbury's cut-glass mirrors reflect the faces of English stage stars (and hopefuls) sitting around the curved buffet-style bar. A less prominent place to dine is the old-fashioned wall banquette with its copper-topped tables and Art Nouveau decor. The pub's specialties, home-cooked pies set out in a buffet cabinet with salads, or fish and chips, are quite good and inexpensive. 90 St. Martin's Lane, WC2. ℭ **020/7836-5863.** Tube: Leicester Sq.

Mayfair

Shepherd's Tavern   One of the focal points of the all-pedestrian shopping zone of Shepherd Market, this pub occupies an 18th-century town house amid a warren of narrow, cobble-covered streets behind Park Lane. The street-level bar is cramped but congenial. Many of the regulars recall this tavern's popularity with the pilots of the Battle of Britain. Bar snacks include shepherd's pie and fish and chips. More formal dining is available upstairs in the cozy, cedar-lined Georgian-style restaurant. The classic British menu probably hasn't changed much since the 1950s; you can always get honey-roasted ham or roast beef with Yorkshire pudding. 50 Hertford St., W1. ℭ **020/7499-3017.** Tube: Green Park.

Notting Hill Gate

Ladbroke Arms   Previously honored as London's "dining pub of the year," Ladbroke Arms is that rare pub known for its food. A changing menu includes roast cod filet with lentils and salsa verde, along with aged bone-in rib steak with mustard, peppercorn, and herb-and-garlic butter. With background jazz and rotating art prints, the place strays from the traditional pub environment. It makes for a pleasant stop and a good meal. The excellent Eldridge Pope Royal is on tap, as well as John Smith's, Courage Directors, and several malt whiskies. 54 Ladbroke Rd., W11. ℭ **020/7727-6648.** www.capitalpubcompany.com/the-ladbroke-arms. Tube: Notting Hill Gate or Holland Park.

St. James's

Red Lion   This Victorian pub, with its early 1900s decorations and 150-year-old mirrors, has been compared to Manet's painting *A Bar at the Folies-Bergère* (on display at the Courtauld Gallery). You can order premade sandwiches; on Saturday, homemade fish and chips are served. Wash down your meal with Ind Coope's fine ales or the house's special beer, Burton's, a brew made of spring water from the Midlands town of Burton-on-Trent. 2 Duke of York St. (off Jermyn St.), SW1. (C) **020/7321-0782.** Tube: Piccadilly Circus.

Soho

Dog & Duck   This snug little joint, a Soho landmark, is the most intimate pub in London. A wide mix of ages and persuasions flocks here, usually chatting amiably. Publicans here stock an interesting assortment of English beers, including Tetley's, Fuller London, and Timothy Taylor Landlord. In autumn, customers will ask for Addlestones Cider. The cozy upstairs bar is also open. 18 Bateman St. (at Frith St.), W1. (C) **020/7494-0697.** Tube: Tottenham Court Rd. or Leicester Sq.

Southwark

George   The existing structure was built in 1877 to replace the original pub, which was destroyed in the Great Fire of 1666. That pub's accolades date from 1598, when it was reviewed as a "faire inn for the receipt of travelers." The present pub was built in the typical traditional Victorian style, with stripped oak floors, paneled walls, a curved bar counter, brass ceiling lights, and windows of etched and cut glass. Three huge mirrors decorate the walls. It's still a great place to enjoy Flowers Original, Boddingtons, and London Pride Abbot on tap. 77 Borough High St., SE1. (C) **020/7407-2056.** Tube: Northern Line to London Bridge or Borough.

Trafalgar Square

Sherlock Holmes   The Sherlock Holmes was the gathering spot for the Baker Street Irregulars, a once-mighty clan of lovers of mystery who met to honor the genius of Sir Arthur Conan Doyle's famous fictional character. Upstairs, you'll find a re-creation of the living room at 221B Baker St. and such "Holmesiana" as the serpent from *The Speckled Band* and a faux beast's head from *The Hound of the Baskervilles*. Complete meals with wine are served in the upstairs dining room. Downstairs is mainly for drinking, but there's also a good snack bar with cold meats, salads, cheeses, and wine and ales sold by the glass. 10 Northumberland St., WC2. (C) **020/7930-2644.** www.sherlockholmespub.com. Tube: Charing Cross or Embankment.

THE THAMES VALLEY: ROYAL WINDSOR & REGAL OXFORD

7

T he historic Thames Valley and Chiltern Hills lie so close to London that you can easily reach them by car, train, or Green Line coach. In fact, you can explore this area during the day and return to London in time to see a West End show.

The second-most-visited historic site in England is **Windsor Castle,** 34km (21 miles) west of London. If you base yourself in Windsor, you can spend another day exploring some of the sights on its periphery, including **Eton** (which adjoins Windsor), **Runnymede,** and **Windsor Great Park.**

If your visit coincides with the spring social sporting season, you can head to Ascot or Henley-on-Thames for the famous social sporting events: Ascot and the Royal Regatta.

Some great historic homes and gardens in the area include Woburn Abbey, Hatfield House, Hughenden Manor, Mapledurham House, and Wellington Ducal Estate. If your time is severely limited, the two most important country mansions to visit are **Woburn Abbey** and **Hatfield House.** Woburn Abbey could consume an entire day, whereas you can visit Hatfield in a half-day.

It's not just the historic homes that make the Home Counties intriguing to visit; the land of river valleys and gentle hills makes for wonderful drives. The beech-clad Chilterns are at their most beautiful in spring and autumn. This 64km (40-mile) chalk ridge extends in an arc from the Thames Valley to the old Roman city of St. Albans in Hertfordshire. The whole region is popular for boating holidays on its 322km (200-mile) network of canals.

Oxfordshire is a land of great mansions, old churches of widely varying architectural styles, and rolling farmland. Certainly your main reason for visiting Oxfordshire is to explore the university city of **Oxford,** about an hour's ride from London by car or train. It's not a good day trip, though, as it has too much to see and do. Plan to spend the night; the next morning you can visit Blenheim Palace, England's answer to Versailles.

WINDSOR & ETON ★

34km (21 miles) W of London

Were it not for the castle, Windsor might still be a charming Thames town to visit. But because it is the home of the best-known asset the royal family possesses, it is overrun in summer by tourists who all but obscure the town's charm.

The good news is that after the disastrous fire of 1992, Windsor Castle is restored, though some of the new designs for it have been called a "Gothic shocker" or "ghastly." Actually, in spite of some media criticism, a remarkable activity in restoration went on, as woodcarvers, gilders, and plasterers followed the same techniques their predecessors did in the Middle Ages, when William the Conqueror built the castle. Queen Elizabeth opened the state apartments in November 1997 following a $62-million project that returned most of the ruined part of the castle to its original condition. Windsor Castle remains Britain's second-most-visited historic building, behind the Tower of London, attracting 1.2 million visitors a year.

Essentials

GETTING THERE More than a dozen trains per day make the 30-minute trip from Waterloo or Paddington Station in London (you'll have to transfer at Slough to the Slough-Windsor shuttle train). The cost is £8.50 round-trip. Call ℂ **0845/748-4950** or visit **www.nationalrail.co.uk** for more information.

Green Line coach no. 702 (ℂ **0844/801-7261;** www.greenline.co.uk) takes about 1¼ hours from Victoria Station in London. A same-day round-trip costs between £8 and £11, depending on the time of the day and week. The bus drops you near the parish church, across the street from the castle.

If you're driving from London, take the M4 west.

VISITOR INFORMATION A **Tourist Information Centre** is at Booking Hall, Windsor Royal Shopping Center (ℂ **01753/743900;** www.windsor.gov.uk). It is open May through September, Monday to Saturday 9:30am to 5pm and Sunday 10am to 4pm; and October through April, Monday to Saturday 10am to 5pm and Sunday 11am to 4pm. It also books walking tours for the Oxford guild of guides.

Where to Stay in the Windsor Area

During the Ascot races and Windsor Horse Show, reservations are necessary far in advance. Unlike such towns as Oxford, you will find a not-so-great collection of B&Bs in Windsor. In a pinch, the Tourist Information Centre (see above) will book you into budget accommodations in the area but will charge £5 for doing so, plus a 10% deposit.

Ascot Racecourse **21**
Batchwood Hall Mansion **6**
Blenheim Palace **2**
Buckinghamshire County
   Museum **4**
Cathedral of St. Albans **6**
Cliveden **11**
DeHavilland Aircraft
   Heritage Center **8**
Eton College **17**
Hatfield House **7**
Hughenden Manor **10**
Jubilee Gardens **18**
Mapledurham House **13**
Museum of St. Albans **6**
Oxford University **3**
Queen Mary's Dolls' House **18**
River & Rowing Museum **12**
Roman Theatre **6**

Runnymede **20**
St. George's Chapel **18**
Shaw's Corner **5**
Stratfield Saye House **16**
Verulamium Museum at
   St. Michael's **6**
Waddesdon Manor **1**
West Wycombe Park **9**
Wellington Country Park **14**
Wellington Ducal Estate **15**
Windsor Castle **18**
Windsor Farm Shop **18**
Windsor Great Park **19**
Woburn Abbey **1**

EXPENSIVE

Mercure Castle Windsor ★   In the shadow of Windsor Castle, on the main street, is this solid choice with a dignified Georgian facade. It was originally built in the 15th century to shelter the workers laboring on the town's foundations and royal buildings. The grounds behind the hotel once served as the stable yard for Windsor Castle, but now they contain a modern wing, where the bedrooms are much more sterile than those in the main building. Some rooms have four-poster beds.

18 High St., Windsor, Berkshire SL4 1LJ. ✆ **01753/851577.** Fax 01753/856-930. www.mercure.com. 108 units. £110–£260 double; £180–£330 suite. AE, DC, MC, V. Children 12 and younger stay free in parent's room. **Amenities:** Restaurant; bar; room service. *In room:* A/C, TV/DVD, hair dryer, minibar, Wi-Fi (£14 per 24 hr.).

The Oakley Court ★★   Built beside the Thames (a 20-min. drive from Heathrow) by a Victorian industrialist, the Oakley Court is imbued with a sense of tradition. Today it's affiliated with the Queens Moat Houses hotel chain. The building's jutting gables and bristling turrets have lent themselves to the filming of several classic movies, including *The Rocky Horror Picture Show* and *Dracula.* The hotel is far superior to choices in the heart of Windsor. Although the grandest public areas are in the main house, most rooms are in a trio of well-accessorized modern wings that ramble through the estate's 14 hectares (35 acres) of parks and gardens. Some rooms offer four-poster beds and views of the River Thames.

Windsor Rd., Water Oakley, Windsor, Berkshire SL4 5UR. © **01753/609988.** Fax 01628/637011. www. oakleycourt.com. 118 units. £130–£260 double. AE, DC, MC, V. Take the river road, A308, 5km (3 miles) from Windsor toward Maidenhead. Free parking. **Amenities:** 2 restaurants; bar; babysitting; health club; Jacuzzi; indoor heated pool; room service; sauna; 2 outdoor tennis courts. *In room:* A/C, TV, hair dryer, minibar, Wi-Fi (£15 per 24 hr.).

Runnymede Hotel & Spa ★★   Because of the dearth of top-of-the-line hotels within Windsor itself, more and more guests are seeking out this hotel and spa on the lovely banks of the Thames between Windsor and Staines. A privately owned hotel, the complex lies only 30 minutes by train from London, just off the A30. The spa is one of the finest in the greater London and greater Windsor area, offering personalized exercise programs and healthcare treatments plus a splendid neoclassi-cal-style pool. Bedrooms are fairly spacious and beautifully designed. The contemporary Leftbank restaurant is one of the finest in the area, opening onto the Thames and designed around an aquatic theme, with a trio of aquariums and an open seafood bar.

Windsor Rd., Egham, Surrey TW20 0AG. © **01784/220960.** Fax 01784/436340. www.runnymede hotel.com. 180 units. Mon–Thurs £180–£325 double; Fri–Sun £100–£235 double. Rates include English breakfast. AE, MC, V. Take Rte. A308 out of Windsor, a 15-min. drive. **Amenities:** 2 restaurants (see below); bar; babysitting; exercise room; indoor heated pool; room service; spa; 3 outdoor tennis courts. *In room:* A/C, TV, hair dryer, Wi-Fi (free).

Sir Christopher Wren's House Hotel ★   Designed by Christopher Wren in 1676 as his home, this former town house occupies a prime position on the Thames, just a 3-minute walk from the castle. Wren's oak-paneled former study is equipped with his Empire desk, a fireplace, and shield-back Hepplewhite chairs. The bay-windowed main drawing room opens onto a garden and a riverside flagstone terrace for after-dinner coffee and drinks. Rooms come in a wide range of sizes; some have fine old furniture and a full-canopied bed, while others have a half-canopied bed. Several units overlook the river. Room no. 2, Wren's bedroom, is said to be haunted. In 2008, the hotel opened the finest spa in the county.

Thames St., Windsor, Berkshire SL4 1PX. © **01753/861354.** Fax 01753/860172. www.sirchristopher wren.co.uk. 96 units. £230 double; £320 suite. AE, DC, MC, V. Parking £10. **Amenities:** Restaurant (see below); bar; babysitting; exercise room; room service; spa. *In room:* TV, hair dryer, Wi-Fi (free).

Ye Harte & Garter Hotel   On Castle Hill opposite Windsor Castle is the old Garter Inn. Named for the Knights of the Garter and used as the setting for scenes in Shakespeare's *The Merry Wives of Windsor,* the Garter burned down in the 1800s and was rebuilt as part of one hostelry that included the Harte. From the front rooms, you can watch the guards marching up High Street every morning on their way to change the guard at the castle. The renovated rooms are comfortable and rather functionally furnished, though they vary greatly in size. More expensive are the Windsor rooms, which have front views and Jacuzzis.

31 High St., Windsor, Berkshire SL4 1PH. © **0844/855-9131.** Fax 01753/830527. www.foliohotels.com/ harteandgarter. 79 units. £165–£270 double; £310–£920 suite. AE, DC, MC, V. **Amenities:** 2 restaurants; bar. *In room:* TV, hair dryer, Wi-Fi (free).

MODERATE

Royal Adelaide Hotel   This landmark Georgian building is opposite the famous Long Walk leading to Windsor Castle, 5 minutes away. Named for Queen Adelaide, who visited the premises during her reign—thereby dubbing it "royal"—all its well-furnished rooms have recently been refurbished. Though small, bathrooms have sufficient shelf space and many have tub/shower combinations.

46 King's Rd., Windsor, Berkshire SL4 2AG. ℂ **01753/863916.** Fax 01753/830682. www.theroyaladelaide. com. 42 units. £85–£140 double. Rates include English breakfast. AE, MC, V. **Amenities:** Restaurant; bar; babysitting; room service. *In room:* TV, hair dryer, Wi-Fi (free).

INEXPENSIVE

Langton House 🍴   The best B&B near the castle is run by welcoming hosts, Paul and Sonja Fogg, who have converted a Victorian town house that dates from 1890 when it housed Queen Victoria's government officials. Lying only a 5-minute walk from the castle, the large, double-fronted Victorian house is built of dark red brick. In later life, it was a nursing home before being turned into a B&B, offering comfortably furnished, midsize bedrooms, each with private bathroom equipped with a shower stall.

46 Alma Rd., Windsor, Berkshire S14 3HA. ℂ **01753/858299.** www.langtonhouse.co.uk. 4 units. £93 double. Rates include English breakfast. AE, MC, V. **Amenities:** Wi-Fi (free, in lobby). *In room:* TV, hair dryer.

Where to Dine in Windsor & Eton

Many visitors prefer to dine in Eton; most of the restaurants and fast-food places along the main street of Windsor, in front of the castle, serve dreary food.

You'll find good, cheap food at the **Waterman's Arms,** Brocas Street (ℂ **01753/861-001;** www.watermans-eton.com), just over the bridge to Eton. Founded in 1542, it's a student favorite. Featured are four varieties of fish and chips, including cod, haddock, plaice, and skate. Platters cost £8 to £11. Meat pies and other main dishes are also served. Our favorite is the beef and Guinness. Special English roast dinners, including beef and lamb, are offered on Sunday, costing £8.50 to £15. It's open daily 11:30am to 11:30pm. MasterCard and Visa are accepted.

Al Fassia ★ MOROCCAN   Worthy of comparison to some of the best Moroccan restaurants in London, Al Fassia brings more exotic cuisine to Windsor. It doesn't look too hot on the outside, but once the food is served you will be glad you're here. The menu is a bit pricey but worth it, utilizing top-quality ingredients. Chefs prepare the traditional tagine or couscous with great care, and you can use freshly baked khübz (bread) to mop up the juices or sauce. Most meals begin with a tempting meze selection of olives or cold and cooked salads. Mint tea and sweet pastries are served at the end of the meal.

27 St. Leonards Rd., Windsor. ℂ **01753/855370.** Reservations required. Main courses £15–£38. AE, MC, V. Mon–Sat noon–2pm and 6:30–10:30pm.

Gilbey's Bar & Restaurant MODERN ENGLISH/CONTINENTAL   Just across the bridge from Windsor, this charming place is located on Eton's main street, among the antiques shops. A glassed-in conservatory, furnished with pinewood tables and simple chairs, is out back. A brigade of seven chefs turns out quite good modern English dishes. Begin with one of the well-prepared soups. For a main course, the temptations include slow-braised venison with a chestnut ravioli, or perhaps pan-fried rump steak with an onion and thyme-flavored compote. For dessert, try sticky toffee pudding with butterscotch sauce and a crème fraîche.

82–83 High St., Eton. ℭ **01753/854921.** www.gilbeygroup.com. Reservations recommended. Main courses £15–£22; fixed-price 2-course menu £17; fixed-price 3-course menu £22. AE, MC, V. Sun–Thurs noon–2:30pm and 6–9:30pm; Fri–Sat noon–2:30pm and 6–10:30pm.

Leftbank ★★ MEDITERRANEAN A premier dining choice in the area is at this previously recommended hotel. Expect a first-rate gastronomic experience if you dine here. The finest of local ingredients go into the inspired menus of chef Laurence Curtis. The setting is memorable, too, especially if you begin the evening with an aperitif in the private lounge bar, library, or drawing room. In summer, the terrace overlooking the Thames is the most romantic dining spot around. Sunday lunch is accompanied by a live jazz band.

Runnymede Hotel, Windsor Rd., Egham. ℭ **01784/220960.** Reservations recommended. Main courses £15–£40. AE, DC, MC, V. Mon–Sat 12:30–2:15pm; Sun 12:30–3pm.

Strok's MODERN ENGLISH/CONTINENTAL This restaurant, located near the castle, is Windsor's most elegant, possessing garden terraces, a conservatory, and a dining room designed a bit like a greenhouse. Chef Stephen Boucher selects an individual garnish to complement each well-prepared dish. For starters, try the tower of smoked salmon and asparagus. For a main course, enjoy halibut with a ginger and prawn crust, tiger prawns with crispy wontons and lime cream foam, or breast of guinea fowl with a sweet potato purée and truffle sausage.

Sir Christopher Wren's House Hotel, Thames St., Windsor. ℭ **01753/442422.** Main courses £17–£27. AE, DC, MC, V. Daily 12:30–2:15pm and 6:30–9:45pm.

ON THE OUTSKIRTS

The Fat Duck ★★★ MODERN In the post–nouvelle cuisine era, the self-taught master chef Heston Blumenthal is hailed by many British food critics as running the "hottest and most exciting restaurant in the country." Who said that ice cream can't be made of crab, or that mashed potatoes can't be mixed with lime jelly? The grain-mustard ice cream and the red-cabbage gazpacho were firsts for us—and a delight. Don't become unduly alarmed, however—not all dishes are this experimental. Starters include the likes of goat cheese and roasted pepper with shaved truffle salad or game terrine with parsnips, spring onion spaghetti, and grape jelly. Delectable main dishes include salmon poached in licorice with white truffles, or perhaps filet of beef with pan-fried foie gras, wild mushroom flan, and beet balsamic jus.

1 High St., Bray. ℭ **01628/580333.** www.fatduck.co.uk. Reservations required. Dinner menus £93–£120; set lunch £150 tasting menu. AE, DC, DISC, MC, V. Tues–Sun noon–2pm and 7–9:30pm. Leave the motorway at exit 4. On the roundabout, take the exit to Maidenhead (A404M/M4) and follow the dual carriageway to the roundabout at the M4. Take the 1st left exit to Maidenhead Central. At the 2nd roundabout, take the exit to Bray and Windsor (A308). Continue 1km (½ mile) and turn left at the sign to Bray Village (B3028). After entering the village, continue past the bottleneck; the Fat Duck is on the right adjacent to the Hinds Head Hotel.

Castle Hill Sights

Jubilee Gardens To celebrate Queen Elizabeth's Jubilee, the .8-hectare (2-acre) Jubilee Gardens were installed inside the castle's main entrance. Filled with trees, roses, and flowering shrubs, they were created by Tom Stuart-Smith, a Chelsea Flower Show gold medalist. The gardens are the first established at Windsor Castle since the days of George IV in the 1820s. They extend from the main gates of Windsor to St. George's Gate on Castle Hill. Color is provided by broad swaths of woodland perennials. White rambling roses clothing the old stone walls are particularly romantic.

Same hours and admission as Windsor Castle (see below).

Queen Mary's Dolls' House ☺   A palace in perfect miniature, the Dolls' House was given to Queen Mary in 1923. It was a gift of members of the royal family, including the king, along with contributions made by some 1,500 tradesmen, artists, and authors. The house, designed by Sir Edwin Lutyens, was created on a scale of 1 to 12. It took 3 years to complete. Every item is a miniature masterpiece; each room is exquisitely furnished, and every item is made exactly to scale. Working elevators stop on every floor, and there is running water in all five bathrooms.

Castle Hill. ℂ **01753/831118** for recorded information. Admission is included in entrance to Windsor Castle. Mar–Oct daily 9:45am–5:15pm; Nov–Feb daily 9:45am–4:15pm. As with Windsor Castle, it's best to call ahead to confirm opening times.

St. George's Chapel ★★★   A gem of the Perpendicular style, this chapel shares the distinction with Westminster Abbey of being a pantheon of English monarchs (Victoria is a notable exception). The present St. George's was founded in the late 15th century by Edward IV on the site of the original Chapel of the Order of the Garter (Edward III, 1348). You first enter the nave, which contains the tomb of George V and Queen Mary, designed by Sir William Reid Dick. Off the nave in the Urswick Chapel, the Princess Charlotte memorial provides an ironic touch; if she had survived childbirth in 1817, she, and not her cousin Victoria, would have ruled the British Empire. In the aisle are tombs of George VI and Edward IV. The latest royal burial in this chapel was an urn containing the ashes of the late Princess Margaret. The Edward IV "Quire," with its imaginatively carved 15th-century choir stalls, evokes the pomp and pageantry of medieval days. In the center is a flat tomb, containing the vault of the beheaded Charles I, along with Henry VIII and his third wife, Jane Seymour.

Castle Hill. ℂ **01753/848885.** www.stgeorges-windsor.org. Admission is included in entrance to Windsor Castle. Mon–Sat 10am–4pm, last admission 4pm. Closed for a few days in June and Dec.

Windsor Castle ★★★   William the Conqueror first ordered a castle built on this location, and, since his day, it has been a fateful spot for English sovereigns: King John cooled his heels at Windsor while waiting to put his signature on the Magna Carta at nearby Runnymede; Charles I was imprisoned here before losing his head; Queen Bess did some renovations; Victoria mourned her beloved Albert, who died at the castle in 1861; the royal family rode out much of World War II behind its sheltering walls; and when Queen Elizabeth II is in residence, the royal standard flies. With 1,000 rooms, Windsor is the world's largest inhabited castle.

The apartments display many works of art, armor, three Verrio ceilings, and several 17th-century Gibbons carvings. Several works by Rubens adorn the King's Drawing Room. In the relatively small King's Dressing Room is a Dürer, along with Rembrandt's portrait of his mother and Van Dyck's triple portrait of Charles I.

Of the apartments, the grand reception room, with its Gobelin tapestries, is the most spectacular.

George IV's elegant **Semi-State Chambers** ★★ are open only from the end of September until the end of March. They were created by the king in the 1820s as part of a series of royal apartments designed for his personal use. Seriously damaged by fire in 1992, they have been returned to their former glory, with lovely antiques, paintings, and decorative objects. The Crimson Drawing Room is evocative of the king's flamboyant taste, with its crimson silk damask hangings and sumptuous art.

We recommend that you take a free guided tour of the castle grounds, including the Jubilee Gardens (described above). Guides are very well informed and recapture the rich historical background of the castle.

In our opinion, the Windsor **Changing of the Guard** ★ is a more exciting experience than the London exercises. The guard marches through the town whether or not the court is in residence, stopping traffic as it wheels into the castle to the tunes of a full regimental band; when the queen is not here, a drum-and-pipe band is mustered. From April to July, the ceremony takes place Monday to Saturday at 11am. In winter, the guard is changed every 48 hours Monday to Saturday. It's best to call ℂ **020/7766-7304** for a schedule.

Castle Hill. ℂ **01753/83118.** www.royalcollection.org.uk. Admission £16 adults, £15 students and seniors, £9.50 children 16 and younger, £42 family of 5 (2 adults and 3 children 16 and younger). Mar–Oct daily 9:45am–5:15pm; Nov–Feb daily 9:45am–4:15pm. Last admission 1 hr. before closing. Closed for periods in Apr, June, and Dec, when the royal family is in residence.

Windsor Farm Shop ★ 🎁   Had any of the queen's jars of jam lately, maybe her homemade pork pie, or a bottle of her special brew? If not, head for this outlet, which sells produce from her estates outside Windsor, including pheasants and partridges bagged at royal shoots. The cream, yogurt, ice cream, and milk come from the two Royal Dairy farms. The meat counter is especially awesome, with its cooked hams and massive ribs of beef. The steak-and-ale pies are quite tasty. You can also purchase 15-year-old whisky from Balmoral Castle in Scotland. Stock up on the queen's vittles and head for a picnic in the area.

Datchet Rd., Old Windsor. ℂ **01753/623800.** www.windsorfarmshop.co.uk. Free admission. Mon–Sat 9am–5pm; Sun 10am–4pm.

Nearby Eton College ★★

Eton is home of what is arguably the most famous public school (Americans would call it a private school) in the world. From Windsor Castle's ramparts, you can look down on the river and onto the famous playing fields of Eton.

To get here, take a train from Paddington Station, go by car, or catch the Green Line bus to Windsor. If you go by train, you can walk from the station to the campus. By car, take the M4 to exit 5 to go straight to Eton.

Insider's tip: Parking is likely to be a problem, so we advise turning off the M4 at exit 6 to Windsor; you can park here and take an easy stroll past Windsor Castle and across the Thames Bridge. Follow Eton High Street to the college.

Eton College (ℂ **01753/671000;** www.etoncollege.com) was founded by 18-year-old Henry VI in 1440. Some of England's greatest men, notably the duke of Wellington, have played on these fields. Twenty prime ministers were educated here, as well as such literary figures as George Orwell, Aldous Huxley, Ian Fleming, and Percy Bysshe Shelley, who, during his years at Eton (1804–10), was called "Mad Shelley" or "Shelley the Atheist" by his fellow pupils. Prince William, second in line to the throne, was a student here. If it's open, take a look at the Perpendicular chapel, with its 15th-century paintings and reconstructed fan vaulting.

The history of Eton College, since its inception in 1440, is depicted in the **Museum of Eton Life** (📞 **01753/671000**), located in vaulted wine cellars under College Hall (originally used as a storehouse by the college's masters). The displays, ranging from formal to extremely informal, include a turn-of-the-20th-century boy's room, schoolbooks, and canes used by senior boys to apply punishment.

Admission to the school and museum is by guided tour only. The cost is £6.20 for adults, £5.20 for seniors and children. Eton College is open to the public from approximately March 25 to April 12 and June 20 to September 3 daily from 10:30am to 4:30pm, and April 17 to June 19 and September 4 to October 5 daily from 2 to 4:30pm. *Note:* These dates vary every year and Eton may close for special occasions. It's best to call ahead.

More to Do in & Around Windsor

Windsor is largely Victorian, with lots of brick buildings and a few remnants of Georgian architecture. In and around the castle are two cobblestone streets, Church and Market, which have antiques shops, silversmiths, and pubs. After lunch or tea, you can stroll along the 5km (3-mile) aptly named **Long Walk.**

Savill Garden, Wick Lane, Englefield Green, Egham, and Surrey are all in **Windsor Great Park** ★ (📞 **01753/860222;** www.theroyallandscape.co.uk), which is signposted from Windsor, Egham, and Ascot. Started in 1932, the 14-hectare (35-acre) garden is one of the finest. The display starts in spring with rhododendrons, camellias, and daffodils beneath the trees; then, throughout the summer, spectacular displays of flowers and shrubs are presented in a natural and wild state. It's open daily year-round (except at Christmas) from 10am to 6pm (to 4pm in winter). There is no admission charge, except for the Savill Garden, which costs £8 adults, £7.50 seniors, and £3.75 ages 6 to 16 from March to October; £6 adults, £5.50 seniors, and £2.25 for children from November to February. Family tickets range from £14 to £20, and kids 5 and under go in free. The location is 8km (5 miles) from Windsor along the A30; turn off at Wick Road and follow the signs to the gardens. The nearest rail station is at Egham; you'll need to take a taxi a distance of 5km (3 miles). A self-service restaurant and gift shop are on site.

Adjoining Savill Garden are the **Valley Gardens,** full of shrubs and trees in a series of wooded natural valleys running to the water. It's open daily year-round. There is no admission charge to enter the gardens, but parking is free for only 90 minutes; thereafter it costs £1 per hour, up to a maximum of £5 per day.

On the B3022 Bracknell/Ascot Road, outside Windsor, **LEGOLAND** (📞 **0870/504-0404;** www.legoland.co.uk), a 61-hectare (150-acre) theme park, opened in 1996. Although a bit corny, it's fun for the entire family. Attractions, spread across five main activity centers, include Duplo Gardens, offering a boat ride, puppet theater, and waterworks, plus a Miniland, showing European cities and villages re-created in minute detail from millions of Lego bricks. Enchanted Forest has treasure trails, a castle, and animals created from Lego bricks. Dragon Knight's Castle takes you back to the days of knights and dragons and includes a blazing dragon roller coaster. The park is open daily from 10am to 5pm mid-March to October (until 7pm on school holidays). Admission varies through the season, starting at £38 for adults, £28 for seniors and children 3 to 15.

Only 5km (3 miles) south of Windsor is **Runnymede,** the 75-hectare (188-acre) meadow on the south side of the Thames, in Surrey, where it's believed that King John put his seal on the Great Charter after intense pressure from his feudal barons and lords. Runnymede is also the site of the John F. Kennedy Memorial, an acre of ground given to the United States by the people of Britain. The memorial, a large block of white stone, is clearly signposted and reached after a short walk. The pagoda that shelters it was placed here by the American Bar Association to acknowledge the fact that American law stems from the English system. The historic site, to which there is free access all year, lies beside the Thames, 1km (a half mile) west of the hamlet of Old Windsor on the south side of the A308. If you're driving on the M25, exit at Junction 13. The nearest rail connection is at Egham, 1km (½ mile) away. The train ride from London's Waterloo Station takes about 25 minutes.

Tours of Windsor

The tourist office can put you in touch with a Blue Badge (official) guide to lead you on a **walking tour** of town. The cost depends upon the number of people and the length of the tour. Advance booking is essential.

The best way to see the area around Windsor is from the water. Informative **boat tours** depart from Windsor's main embarkation point along Windsor Promenade, Barry Avenue, for a 40-minute round-trip to Boveney Lock. The cost is £5.20 for adults, £2.60 for children. You can also take a 2-hour tour through the Boveney Lock and up past stately private riverside homes, the Bray Film Studios, Queens Eyot, and Monkey Island for £8.40 for adults, £4.20 for children. Of all the tours offered, we find this one the most scenic, insightful, and evocative. In addition, there's a 45-minute tour from Runnymede on board the *Lucy Fisher,* a replica of a Victorian paddle steamer. It passes Magna Carta Island, among other sights, and costs £5.20 for adults, £2.60 for children. Longer tours between Maidenhead and Hampton Court are also offered. The boats offer light refreshments and have a well-stocked bar; the decks are covered in case of an unexpected shower. Tours are operated by **French Brothers, Ltd.,** Clewer Boathouse, Clewer Court Road, Windsor (© **01753/ 851900;** www.boat-trips.co.uk).

Shopping

For a survey of the best antiques for sale in Windsor, walk through the shops on **High Street, King Edward Court,** and **Peascod Street.**

Windsor Royal Station, the shopping center at the main railway station (© **01753/797070;** www.windsorroyalshopping.co.uk), has a concentration of shops, often with London connections.

A colorful traditional English perfumery, **Woods of Windsor,** 50 High St. (© **01753/868125;** www.woodsofwindsor.co.uk), dates from 1770. It offers soaps, shampoos, scented drawer liners, and hand and body lotions, all prettily packaged in pastel-floral and bright old-fashioned wraps.

If you're not going to Scotland, head for the **Edinburgh Woollen Mill,** 10 Castle Hill (© **01753/855151;** www.ewm.co.uk), with the finest selection of Scottish knitwear and tartans in Windsor. At **Billings & Edmonds,** 132 High St., Eton (© **01753/861348;** www.billingsandedmonds.co.uk), you may think you've blundered into a time warp. This distinctive clothing store supplies school wear, suits made to order, and a complete line of cuff links, shirts, ties, and accessories.

Windsor After Dark

Except for pub life, it's fairly quiet. The major cultural venue is **Theatre Royal,** Thames Street (© **01753/853888;** www.theatreroyalwindsor.co.uk), with a tradition of putting on plays that goes back 2 centuries. This is one of the finest regional theaters in England, often drawing first-rate actors from London's West End. During the 6 weeks preceding Christmas, a series of pantomimes is presented. The box office is open Monday to Saturday from 10am to 8pm (call the phone number above for bookings). Performances are Monday to Saturday at 8pm, with matinees on Thursday at 2:30pm and Saturday at 4:45pm. Tickets cost between £12 and £120.

Side Trips from Windsor

If you have time to spare, you can take any number of fascinating excursions. But if you can squeeze in only one, make it Hughenden Manor (see below).

HUGHENDEN MANOR: DISRAELI CALLED IT HOME

Hughenden Manor ★★   This country manor gives insight into the age of Victoria and acquaints us with a remarkable man: Benjamin Disraeli, one of the most enigmatic figures of 19th-century England. At age 21, "Dizzy" anonymously published his five-volume novel, *Vivian Grey.* In 1839, he married an older widow for her money, though they apparently developed a most harmonious relationship. He entered politics in 1837 and continued writing novels, his later ones meeting with more acclaim.

In 1848, Disraeli acquired Hughenden Manor, a country house that befitted his fast-rising political and social position. He served briefly as prime minister in 1868, but his political fame rests on his stewardship as prime minister from 1874 to 1880. He became friends with Queen Victoria, who, in 1877, paid him the rare honor of a visit. In 1876, Disraeli became earl of Beaconsfield; he died in 1881. Instead of being buried at Westminster Abbey, he preferred the simple little graveyard of Hughenden Church.

Today, Hughenden houses an odd assortment of memorabilia, including a lock of Disraeli's hair, letters from Victoria, and a portrait of Lord Byron.

High Wycombe. © **01494/755565.** www.nationaltrust.org.uk. Admission £7.25 adults, £3.70 children, £18 family ticket; garden only £2.90 adults, £2.10 children. Mar–Oct Wed–Sun 1–5pm. Closed Nov–Feb and Good Friday. From Windsor, take M4 (toward Reading), and then A404 to A40. Continue north of High Wycombe on A4128 for about 2.5km (1½ miles). From London (Heathrow Airport), catch coach A40 (operated by Carousel Buses) to High Wycombe, and then board a Beeline bus (High Wycombe–Aylesbury no. 323 or 324).

WEST WYCOMBE ★

Snuggled in the Chiltern Hills 48km (30 miles) west of London and 24km (15 miles) northwest of Windsor, the village of West Wycombe still has an atmosphere of the early 18th century. The thatched roofs have been replaced by tiles, and some of the buildings have been rebuilt, but the village is still 2 centuries removed from the present day.

From Windsor, take the M4 (toward Reading), and then the A404 to the A40. Signs to follow en route include MAIDENHEAD, MARLOW, and OXFORD. If you previously visited Hughenden Manor, the village of West Wycombe lies immediately to the west. Public transportation is awkward, but the Chiltern Line from London stops at High Wycombe, from which you can catch a bus from the station to West Wycombe or hail a taxi.

A visit to West Wycombe wouldn't be complete without a tour of **West Wycombe Park,** seat of the Dashwood family. Now owned by the National Trust, it's of both historical and architectural interest. The house is one of the best examples of Palladian-style architecture in England. The interior is lavishly decorated with paintings and antiques from the 18th century.

In the mid-18th century, Sir Francis Dashwood began an ambitious building program at West Wycombe. His strong interest in design led Sir Francis to undertake a series of monuments and parks that are still among the finest in the country.

Sir Francis also commissioned the excavation of a cave on the estate to serve as a meeting place for the notorious Hellfire Club, which spent its time partying and drinking. The cave is about 1km (a half mile) long, filled with stalactites and stalagmites, and dotted with statues.

The house and grounds are open April and May, Sunday to Thursday 2 to 6pm; and June through August, Sunday to Thursday 2 to 6:30pm. Admission is £6.90 for adults, £3.50 for children, and £17 for a family ticket. If you wish to visit only the grounds (open Apr–Aug), the cost is £3.50. The caves are open April through October, daily from 11am to 5:30pm; off-season hours are on Saturday and Sunday only, from 11am to 5:30pm. Admission is £5 for adults, £4 for seniors and children. The 30-minute cave tour includes stops for talks about former Hellfire members. For information, call the West Wycombe Estate Office at West Wycombe (© **01494/513569**) or the caves at © **01494/533739** (www.hellfirecaves.co.uk).

Other sights include the **Church of St. Lawrence,** perched on West Wycombe Hill and topped by a huge golden ball. Parts of the church date from the 13th century; its interior was copied from a 3rd-century Syrian sun temple. The view from the hill is worth the trek up. Near the church stands the **Dashwood Mausoleum,** built in a style derived from Constantine's Arch in Rome.

CLIVEDEN: FORMER HOME OF LADY ASTOR

Cliveden ★★   Now a National Trust property, Cliveden, former home of Lady Astor, stands on a constructed terrace of mature gardens high above the Thames. The estate's original mansion and sweeping lawns were created by William Winde in 1666 for the second duke of Buckingham. Later, the father of King George III reared his sons here. After a fire in 1795, Sir Charles Barry, the architect of the Houses of Parliament, converted the house into its present gracefully symmetrical form. A soaring clock tower was added to one side as a later Victorian folly. When the house was sold by the duke of Southerland to the Astors in 1893, Queen Victoria lamented the passage. The house remained part of the Astor legacy, a repository of a notable collection of paintings and antiques, until 1966.

The surrounding **gardens** have a distinguished variety of plantings, ranging from Renaissance-style topiary to meandering forest paths with vistas of statuary and flowering shrubs. Features here include a glade garden, a magnificent parterre, and an amphitheater where "Rule Britannia" was played for the first time. There are 150 hectares (375 acres) of gardens and woodland to explore.

16km (10 miles) northwest of Windsor. © **01628/605069.** www.nationaltrust.org.uk. Admission to house and grounds £8 adults, £4 children, family ticket £20. Grounds mid-Mar to Oct daily 11am–6pm, Nov–Dec 11am–4pm; house Apr–Oct Thurs and Sun 3–5:30pm (3 rooms of the mansion are open to the public, as is the Octagon Temple, with its rich mosaic interior). From Windsor, follow M4 toward Reading to the junction at no. 7 (direction Slough West). At the roundabout, turn left onto A4, signposted MAIDENHEAD. At the next roundabout, turn right, signposted BURNHAM. Follow the road for 4km (2½ miles) to a T junction with B476. The main gates to Cliveden are directly opposite.

Where to Stay & Dine

Cliveden House ★★★   Lady Astor's former estate is one of the most beautiful and luxurious hotels in England. Often acclaimed as "Hotel of the Year" by various rating services in England, this majestic property was home to a prince of Wales and a scattering of dukes before the Astors moved in. It was also a setting for the infamous Profumo scandal of the 1960s, which shook the empire.

Rooms—named for famous guests who've stayed here, including T. E. Lawrence and Charlie Chaplin—are sumptuous, each furnished in impeccable taste. The bathrooms with deep marble tubs are among the finest we've seen in England. Less preferred are recently added rooms in the Clutton Wing. Nothing (except perhaps renting Lady Astor's bedroom itself) is more elegant here than walking down to the river and boarding a hotel boat for a champagne cruise before dinner. In the morning, you can go horseback riding on the 150-hectare (371-acre) estate along the riverbank.

Cliveden, Taplow, Maidenhead, Berkshire SL6 0JF. © **01628/668561.** Fax 01628/661837. www.cliveden house.co.uk. 39 units. £210–£600 double; £540–£1,290 suite; £1,545–£1,745 cottage. Rates include English breakfast. AE, DC, MC, V. **Amenities:** 3 restaurants; bar; babysitting; health club & spa; 2 pools (1 heated indoor, 1 outdoor); room service; outdoor tennis court (lit). *In room:* A/C (in some), TV, hair dryer.

THE COTTAGE WHERE MILTON WROTE *PARADISE LOST*

The modern residential town of **Gerrards Cross** is often called the Beverly Hills of England, as it attracts many wealthy Londoners, among others. To the north of it is **Chalfont St. Giles,** where poet John Milton lived during the Great Plague in 1665. To reach it, take the A355 north from Windsor for 74km (46 miles), bypassing Beaconsfield until you come to the signposted cutoff for Chalfont St. Giles to the east.

Today Chalfont St. Giles is a typical English village, though its history goes back to Roman times. The charm of the village is in its center, with shops, pubs, and cafes clustered around the green and the village pond.

The 16th-century **John Milton's Cottage,** Chalfont St. Giles (© **01494/872313;** www.miltonscottage.org), is the site where the great poet completed *Paradise Lost* and started *Paradise Regained.* Its four rooms contain many relics and exhibits devoted to Milton. It is open March through October, Tuesday to Sunday 10am to 1pm and 2 to 6pm. Admission is £4 for adults and £2 for children 14 and younger.

ASCOT

45km (28 miles) W of London

While following the royal buckhounds through Windsor Forest, Queen Anne decided to have a racecourse on Ascot Heath. The first race meeting at Ascot, which is directly south of Windsor at the southern end of Windsor Great Park, was held in 1711. Since then, the Ascot Racecourse has been a symbol of high society, as pictures of the royal family enjoying the races there, including the queen and Prince Philip, have been flashed around the world. Women should be sure to wear a hat.

Getting There

Trains travel between London's Waterloo and Ascot Station, about a 1-hour trip, roughly every 30 minutes during the day. For rail information, call © **0845/748-4950** or visit **www.nationalrail.co.uk**. Ascot Station is about 10 minutes from the racecourse.

Buses depart frequently from London's Victoria Coach Station. For information, call © **0871/781-81-78** or visit **www.nationalexpress.com**.

If you're driving from Windsor, take the A332 west.

Where to Stay & Dine

The entire town of Ascot and its racecourse don't even appear in budget guides to England. If you're a frugal traveler you can visit just for the day, returning to London or elsewhere for the night. Ascot is known for some superb, but pricey, inns, catering only to the well-heeled horsey set. If you want an affordable room, ask for one of the least expensive accommodations at the Brockenhurst (see below).

Brockenhurst 🗡 A small, tastefully refurbished 1905 Edwardian hotel of charm and distinction, Brockenhurst is conveniently situated near shops and the train station. Bedrooms are generally spacious. Well appointed and maintained rooms are mostly modern, though some contain antiques. Classy and reasonably priced, this is a very good alternative to the pricey Royal Berkshire or Berystede.

Brockenhurst Rd., S. Ascot, Berkshire SL5 9HA. © **01344/621912.** Fax 01344/873252. www.brockenhurst. com. 20 units. £100–£120 double. Rates include continental breakfast. AE, MC, V. Free parking. **Amenities:** Restaurant; bar; babysitting. *In room:* TV, hair dryer, Wi-Fi (free).

Macdonald Berystede Hotel & Spa ★ This hotel just south of Ascot is a Victorian fantasy of medieval towers, steeply pitched roofs, and a landscaped garden. Drawing racegoers and businesspeople, it also caters to conferences (at which time it's best avoided). With their high ceilings and chintz, rooms evoke a private country house. The best units are in the main house and are more spacious and better decorated. Most of the other rooms are in a more modern annex with less character. For optimum sunshine and more space, try to book room no. 360 or 369. A roof terrace has been installed for summer dining.

Bagshot Rd., Sunninghill Ascot, Berkshire SL5 9JH. © **888/892-0038** in the U.S., 0870/400-81111, or 01344/623311. Fax 01344/872301. www.macdonaldhotels.co.uk/berystede. 126 units. £98–£170 double; from £170 suite. AE, DC, MC, V. Free parking. Take A330 2.5km (1½ miles) south of Ascot. **Amenities:** Restaurant; bar; babysitting; exercise room; indoor heated pool; room service; spa. *In room:* A/C, TV, hair dryer, minibar, Wi-Fi (£10 per 24 hr.).

Golf, Goldfinger & Posh Decadence

One of Europe's greatest hotels lies only 30 minutes from London's West End and in close proximity to Ascot and Windsor. It's **Stoke Park Club,** Park Road, Stoke Poges, Buckinghamshire SL2 4PG (✆ **01753/717171;** www. stokeparkclub.com). Golfers from all over the world flock to the 27-hole golf course designed by celebrated architect Harry Shapland Colt. James Bond defeated Goldfinger on its 18th green in 1964. Each bedroom or suite is individually decorated with antiques, paintings, and original prints; all units feature fireplaces; and some have balconies. Double rooms range from £275 to £345 per night, with suites costing from £525. The hotel has three indoor tennis courts, six Wimbledon-standard grass tennis courts, and four all-weather tennis courts; a gym; a spa; a steam room; and an indoor heated pool that incorporates two underwater massage areas with hydroseat Jacuzzis.

Royal Berkshire ★★   This is a prestigious and elegant hotel with a rich history. Built in Queen Anne style in 1705, it housed the Churchill family for many years. The stylish rooms are divided between the main house and an annex. All rooms are spacious with thick carpeting and large, luxe beds. While the annex rooms are exceedingly comfortable and well furnished, they aren't equal to those in the main building. If you want the character of old England, opt for the latter.

London Rd., Sunninghill, Ascot, Berkshire SL5 0PP. ✆ **01344/623322.** Fax 01344/627100. www.ramada jarvis.co.uk. 63 units. £99–£129 double; £159–£220 suite. AE, DC, MC, V. Free parking. Take A322 3km (2 miles) northeast of Ascot. **Amenities:** Restaurant; bar; babysitting; exercise room; indoor heated pool; room service; sauna; 2 outdoor tennis courts. *In room:* TV, fridge, hair dryer.

Ascot Racecourse ★

Ascot Racecourse, High Street (✆ **0870/722-7227;** www.ascot.co.uk), England's largest and most prestigious course, is open throughout the year. The facility hosts 27 days of racing yearly. The highlight of the Ascot social season is the **Royal Meeting** (or **Royal Week**), when many women wear fancy hats and white gloves. Excellent racing also takes place on De Beers Diamond Day (fourth Sat in July) and during the Festival at Ascot (last Fri, Sat, and Sun in Sept), when the prize money usually exceeds £1 million per event.

You can buy tickets for one of three distinctly different observation areas, known as "enclosures." These include the Members Enclosure, which, during the Royal Meeting (5 days in June), is known as the Royal Enclosure. Also available are the Tattersalls Enclosure, largest of the three; and the Silver Ring, which does not enjoy direct access to the paddocks and has traditionally been the site of most of Ascot's budget seating. Except during the Royal Meeting, newcomers can usually secure viewing space in the Members Enclosure, but only if they call ahead to confirm that space is available. General admission prices range from £14 to £66. Children 16 and younger are admitted free (except to the Royal Enclosure) if accompanied by an adult, and there is free supervised day care for children 7 and younger.

Beginning January 1 every year, you can arrange advance bookings for guaranteed seating in the most desirable areas during the most popular races. For tickets, write to the Secretary's Office, Ascot Racecourse, Ascot, Berkshire SL5 7JN, or book online at www.ascot.co.uk. Credit cards are accepted at © 0870/727-1234. Car parking is free except during the Festival Meeting in September.

7 HENLEY-ON-THAMES & THE ROYAL REGATTA

56km (35 miles) W of London

At the eastern edge of Oxfordshire, Henley-on-Thames, a small town and resort on the river at the foothills of the Chilterns, is the headquarters of the **Royal Regatta,** held annually in late June and early July. Henley, which lies on a stretch of the Thames that's known for its calm waters, unobstructed bottom, and predictable currents, is a rower's mecca. The regatta, which dates from the first years of Victoria's reign, is the major competition among international oarsmen and oarswomen, who find it both challenging and entertaining.

The Elizabethan buildings, tearooms, and inns along the town's High Street will live up to your preconception of an English country town. Henley-on-Thames is an excellent stopover en route to Oxford, though its fashionable inns are far from cheap.

Essentials

GETTING THERE   Trains depart from London's Paddington Station but require a change at the junction in Twyford. More than 20 trains make the journey daily; the trip takes about 40 minutes. For information, call © 0845/748-4950 or visit **www.nationalrail.co.uk**.

About 10 buses depart every day from London's Victoria Coach Station for Reading. From Reading, take local bus no. 421 to Henley. These buses depart every hour. For information, call **0870/580-8080** or visit **www.nationalexpress.com**.

If you're driving from London, take the M4 toward Reading to Junction 819, and then head northwest on the A4130.

VISITOR INFORMATION   The **Tourist Information Centre** is at King's Arms Barn, Kings Road (© 01491/578034; www.visithenley-on-thames.co.uk). Hours are Monday to Saturday 10am to 5pm.

An entire book could be written about these government-funded national trails—and indeed one has. It's the *National Trail Guide* (Aurum Press), by David Sharp, and it details every twist and turn of the river.

Where to Stay

It's impossible to find a room during the Royal Regatta, unless you've made reservations months in advance.

Hotel du Vin ★★   This riverside town has been invaded by the Hotel du Vin chain, which has taken a former Brakspears Brewery and imaginatively converted it into a fine example of industrial recycling. What has emerged is the poshest hotel in the area. Each of the beautifully furnished rooms, with solid oak pieces and Shaker simplicity, is named after a vineyard. The decorator ordered that all walls be painted a "toast color" and installed thick wall-to-wall carpeting and "dreamboat beds." Fine Egyptian linens and spectacular power showers in the bathrooms are further allures.

New St., Henley-on-Thames, Oxfordshire RG9 2BP. © **01491/848400.** Fax 01491/848401. www.
hotelduvin.co.uk. 43 units. £150–£195 double; £210–£425 suite. AE, DC, MC, V. Parking £15. **Amenities:**
Restaurant; bar; room service. *In room:* TV, hair dryer, minibar, Wi-Fi (£10 per 24 hr.).

Lenwade Guest House ◈   Built in the early 1900s, this semidetached Victorian
guesthouse is owned and operated by Jacquie and John Williams. Entering from a
small courtyard filled with flowering vines and lush foliage, you'll see a 1.5m (5-ft.)
stained-glass window thought to depict Joan of Arc. Another memorable detail is the
winding staircase with its original handrails. The small to midsize bedrooms are
individually decorated and comfortably furnished.

3 Western Rd., Henley-on-Thames, Oxfordshire RG9 1JL. © **01491/573468.** Fax 01491/411664. www.
w3b-ink.com/lenwade. 4 units. From £70 double. Rates include English breakfast. No credit cards. Free
parking. *In room:* TV, hair dryer, Wi-Fi (free).

Red Lion Hotel ★   This wisteria-covered coaching inn (ca. 1531) near Henley
offers a guest list that reads like a hall of fame: Johnson and Boswell, George IV
(who, it is said, consumed 14 mutton chops one night), and Charles I. You can book
the room in which Princess Grace stayed when her brother Jack was competing in
the Royal Regatta in 1947. Most of the well-furnished rooms overlook the Thames.
Bedrooms are midsize to spacious; the three most expensive units sport four-poster
beds.

Hart St., Henley-on-Thames, Oxfordshire RG9 2AR. © **01491/572161.** Fax 01491/410039. www.redlion
henley.co.uk. 39 units. £165–£195 double. AE, MC, V. Free parking. **Amenities:** Restaurant; bar; babysitting; room service. *In room:* TV, hair dryer, Wi-Fi (free).

Where to Dine

Argyll ENGLISH/SCOTTISH   This very Scottish pub, complete with tartan carpeting and framed prints of Scottish soldiers, is a popular lunch spot with locals. The
homemade meals are the main attraction, featuring hearty portions of steak-and-
kidney pie, shepherd's pie, and other favorites.

15 Market Place. © **01491/573400.** www.theargyllhenley.com. Main courses and platters £8–£13. AE,
MC, V. Sun–Thurs 10am–midnight; Fri–Sat 10am–1am.

The Thames: Liquid History

Stretching for 289km (180 miles),
Thames Path ★★ is one of more than
a dozen government-protected national
trails in England. You can choose any
part of this river for exploration, our
favorite being the "secret" section
between Kelmscott and Oxford.
Between the two towns, you will find
48km (30 miles) of lonely meadow-
lands of grazing sheep and cattle. You'll
come across a stone-built bridge leading to a Thames-side pub with a mellow atmosphere. The Thames Valley has
more than 60 river-bordering marinas
and boatyards. The best deals are
made with **Kris Cruisers**, in Datchet
(© **01753/543930;** www.kriscruisers.
co.uk). The outfitter rents the largest
fleet of fully equipped cruisers on the
Thames, containing between two and
eight berths. From Datchet, you can
travel upstream to Windsor and Eton or
on to such towns as Maidenhead. Heading downstream, you can visit attractions like Runnymede, with its
associations with the Magna Carta.

The Henley Royal Regatta ★★

The Henley Royal Regatta, held the first week in July, is one of the country's premier racing events. For a close-up view from the Stewards' Enclosure, you'll need a guest badge, obtainable only through a member—in other words, you have to know someone in order to get special privileges. Admission to the Regatta Enclosure, however, is open to all. Entry fees are £30 to £100. For information, contact the Secretary, Henley Royal Regatta, Henley-on-Thames, Oxfordshire RG9 2LY (© **01491/ 572153;** www.hrr.co.uk).

During the annual 5-day event, up to 100 races are organized each day, with starts scheduled as frequently as every 5 minutes. This event is open only to all-male crews of up to nine at a time. In late June, rowing events for women are held at the 3-day Henley Women's Regatta.

If you want to float on the waters of the Thames yourself, stop by the town's largest and oldest outfitter, **Hobbs & Sons, Ltd.,** Station Road Boathouse (© **01491/572035;** www.hobbs-of-henley.com), established in 1870. Open April through October daily from 8:30am to 5:30pm, Hobbs has an armada of watercraft, including rowboats that rent for £15 to £20 per hour. Motorboats go for £25 to £50 per hour. Prices include fuel. An on-premises chandlery shop sells virtually anything a boat crew could need, as well as T-shirts and boaters' hats.

A Museum Celebrating the Thames

River & Rowing Museum 🛈 This museum celebrates the Thames and those oarsmen and oarswomen who row upon it. Opened by Queen Elizabeth in 1998, the museum, designed by English architect David Chipperfield, is the finest of its kind in Britain. A short walk south of Henley Bridge, it opens onto the banks of the Thames. The Rowing Gallery follows the saga of rowing from the days of the Greeks. It's all here: models of arctic whaleboats in the 1700s, elaborate Venetian gondolas fit for a doge, and coastal lifeboats that pulled many a victim from the cold waters of the North Sea. In a more modern exhibit, you'll find the boat in which British oarsmen captured the gold medal at the 1996 Olympic Games in Atlanta. The museum reaches out to embrace the saga of the Thames itself, as well as the history of the regatta in Henley.

Mill Meadows. © **01491/415600.** www.rrm.co.uk. Admission £7.50 adults; £5.50 children 4–16; £22 family ticket for 4, £26 for 5, and £28 for 6. May–Aug daily 10am–5:30pm; Sept–Apr daily 10am–5pm.

Side Trips from Henley
A ROMANTIC BOAT TRIP TO A HISTORIC HOME

Mapledurham House 🛈 The Blount family mansion lies beside the Thames in the unspoiled village of Mapledurham. In the house, you'll see Elizabethan ceilings and a great oak staircase, as well as portraits of the two beautiful sisters with whom the poet Alexander Pope, a frequent visitor here, fell in love. The family chapel, built in 1789, is a fine example of modern Gothic architecture. Cream teas with homemade cakes are available at the house. On the grounds, the last working water mill on the Thames still produces flour.

The most romantic way to reach this lovely old house is to take the boat that leaves the promenade next to Caversham Bridge at 2pm on Saturday, Sunday, and bank holidays from Easter to September. The journey upstream takes between 30 and 80 minutes, and the boat leaves Mapledurham again at 5pm for the return trip to Caversham, giving you plenty of time to walk through the house. The round-trip boat ride from Caversham costs £7 for adults and £5 for children. An additional landing fee of £2 adults and £1 for children is charged. You can get further details about the boat from **Thames Rivercruise Ltd.,** Pipers Island, Bridge Street, Caversham Bridge, Reading (ℂ **07900/352-235;** www.thamesrivercruise.co.uk).

Mapledurham. ℂ **01189/723350.** www.mapledurham.co.uk. Admission to house and mill £6.75 adults, £3 children 5–16, free for children 4 and younger. Sat–Sun and bank holidays 2–5:30pm. Closed Oct–Easter. From Henley-on-Thames, head south along A4155 toward Reading; at the junction with A329, head west; Mapledurham is signposted from this road. Or take the boat trip described above.

THE WELLINGTON DUCAL ESTATE

Stratfield Saye House ★   This combined house and country park provides tangible evidence of the fortune of the duke of Wellington and his descendants. The complex's centerpiece is the Stratfield Saye House, the home of the dukes of Wellington since 1817, when the 17th-century house was bought for the Iron Duke to celebrate his victory over Napoleon at the Battle of Waterloo. A grateful Parliament granted a large sum of money for its purchase. Many memories of the first duke remain in the house, including his billiard table, battle spoils, and pictures. The funeral carriage that once rested in St. Paul's Cathedral crypt is on display. In the gardens is the grave of Copenhagen, the charger ridden to battle at Waterloo by the first duke. There are also extensive landscaped grounds, together with a tearoom and gift shop.

If you're looking for greenery and lovely landscaping, you'll find it 5km (3 miles) away, on the opposite side of the A33 highway, at the **Wellington Country Park.**

1.5km (1 mile) west of Reading, beside A33 to Basingstoke. ℂ **01256/882882.** www.stratfield-saye. co.uk. Mon–Fri £7 adults, £6 students and seniors, £4 children; Sat–Sun £9 adults, £8 students, £5 children. Mar 20–24 and July 3–28 daily 11:30am–3:30pm. From Henley, head south along A1455.

Wellington Country Park ★ 🎁   Under the same administration as Stratfield Saye, this favorite place for locals to picnic and stroll has a nice lake and miles of well-maintained walking paths. But a handful of attractions are inside as well: The park contains a riding school, a miniature steam railway, a deer park, and the Thames Valley Time Trail, a walk-through series of exhibits related to the geology of the region and the dinosaurs that once inhabited it.

Riseley, Reading, Berkshire. ℂ **01189/326444.** www.wellington-country-park.co.uk. Admission £6.75 adults, £6.25 seniors, £5.75 children 3–15, free for children 2 and younger. Park and exhibits Feb–Nov daily 9:30am–5:30pm.

MARLOW: RETREAT OF *THE COMPLEAT ANGLER*

This Thames-side town, 56km (35 miles) northwest of London and 13km (8 miles) east of Henley-on-Thames, is a miniature version of the better-known Henley. To reach it from Henley, take Route 4155 and follow the signs. Many prefer its more pastoral look to the larger Henley.

Along this middle reach of the Thames is some of the most beautiful rural scenery in England, a land of green fields and deep woods, of stately mansions and parks. It was in these surroundings that Izaak Walton wrote his immortal work on fishing, *The Compleat Angler,* published in 1655. On the south bank of the river facing Marlow itself stood the inn in which he stayed. That inn still stands and is named after his work.

Where to Stay

Marlow attracts mainly well-heeled fishermen who like to stay at the **Compleat Angler** (see below), a very pricey hotel because of its associations with Izaak Walton. If you're a frugal traveler and find yourself trapped in the area for the night, you can find reasonable but hardly spectacular accommodations at **Glade End,** 2 Little Marlow Rd., Marlow, Buckinghamshire S17 1HD (☎ **01628/471334;** www. gladeend.com), where doubles go for £110 to £125 a night.

Macdonald Compleat Angler Hotel ★★ This hotel of charm and character blends architectural eras, including Queen Anne, Regency, Georgian, and Victorian. It occupies an emerald swath of lawns stretching down to the banks of the Thames. It's had a long and distinguished list of guests, including Percy Shelley and his wife, Mary, along with Dame Nellie Melba (for whom the peach dessert was named), J. M. Barrie (author of *Peter Pan*), and F. Scott Fitzgerald. The hotel is a well-organized and impeccably polite center of English chintz, predictably elegant bars, and very fine dining. Each room is outfitted like a private country home, with antiques or reproductions and plush, comfortable beds. The more expensive rooms look out on the Thames. The finest accommodations are in a modern wing with balconies overlooking the rushing weir. Modern bathrooms with separate showers are offered.

Marlow Bridge, Bisham Rd., Marlow, Buckinghamshire SL7 1RG. ☎ **0844/879-9128.** Fax 01628/486388. www.macdonaldhotels.co.uk/compleatangler. 64 units. £150–£205 double; £252–£450 suite. AE, DC, MC, V. **Amenities:** 2 restaurants; bar; babysitting; room service. *In room:* A/C, TV, hair dryer, minibar.

Where to Dine

The Vanilla Pod ★★ FRENCH/ENGLISH   Michael Macdonald has struck out on his own with this absolutely delightful dining choice. In a tasteful room, known for its fine service, a truly excellent cuisine is offered on a menu that changes monthly to take advantage of the best produce in any season. Starters are memorable, especially the endive tatin with foie gras and citrus sauce, or the carpaccio of beet with goat cheese and aged balsamic vinegar. Delectable main dishes are likely to include steamed sole with a cèpe mousse with white beans, roast pork filet rolled in fennel seed, and roast duck breast with a date purée and woodland mushrooms.

31 West St. ☎ **01628/898101.** www.thevanillapod.co.uk. Reservations required (as far in advance as possible). Set-price 2-course lunch £16, 3-course lunch £20; 3-course dinner £40; 7-course gourmand dinner £50. AE, MC, V. Tues–Sat noon–2pm and 7–10pm. Closed 2 weeks around Easter.

OXFORD: THE CITY OF DREAMING SPIRES ★★

87km (54 miles) NW of London; 87km (54 miles) SE of Coventry

A walk down the long sweep of the High, one of the most striking streets in England; a mug of cider in one of the old student pubs; the sound of May Day dawn when choristers sing in Latin from Magdalen Tower; students in traditional gowns whizzing past on rickety bikes; towers and spires rising majestically; nude swimming at Parson's Pleasure; the roar of a cannon launching the bumping races; a tiny, dusty bookstall, where you can pick up a valuable first edition—romantic Oxford is still here, but to get to it, you have to experience the bustling and crowded city that is also Oxford. You may be surprised by a never-ending stream of polluting buses and

All Souls College **19**	Magdalen College **23**	St. Catherine's College **22**
Balliol College **8**	Mansfield College **4**	St. Hilda's College **33**
Brasenose College **25**	Merton College **32**	St. John's College **7**
Carfax Tower **14**	Modern Art Oxford **26**	St. Peter's College **13**
Christ Church **29**	New College **21**	Sheldonian Theatre **17**
Corpus Christi College **31**	Old Bodleian Library **18**	Somerville College **1**
Exeter College **16**	Oriel College **30**	Town Hall **27**
Harris Manchester College **12**	Pembroke College **28**	Trinity College **9**
Jesus College **15**	The Queen's College **20**	University Museum **3**
Keble College **2**	Regent's Park College **6**	Wadham College **11**
Lincoln College **24**	Rhodes House **10**	Worcester College **5**

the fast-flowing pedestrian traffic. Surrounding the university are suburbs that keep growing, and not in a particularly attractive manner.

At any time of the year, you can enjoy a tour of the colleges. The Oxford Tourist Information Centre (see below) offers guided walking tours daily throughout the year. Just don't mention the other place (Cambridge), and you shouldn't have any trouble. Comparisons between the two universities are inevitable: Oxford is better known for the arts, Cambridge more for the sciences.

The city predates the university—in fact, it was a Saxon town in the early part of the 10th century. By the 12th century, Oxford was growing in reputation as a seat of learning, at the expense of Paris, and the first colleges were founded in the 13th century. The story of Oxford is filled with conflicts too complex and detailed to elaborate upon here. Suffice it to say, the relationship between town and gown wasn't as peaceful as it is today. Riots often flared, and both sides were guilty of abuses. Nowadays, the young people of Oxford take out their aggressiveness in sporting competitions.

Ultimately, the test of a great university lies in the caliber of the people it turns out. Oxford can name-drop a mouthful: Roger Bacon, Sir Walter Raleigh, John Donne, Sir Christopher Wren, Samuel Johnson, William Penn, John Wesley, William Pitt, Matthew Arnold, Lewis Carroll, Harold Macmillan, Graham Greene, A. E. Housman, T. E. Lawrence, and many others. Women were not allowed until 1920, but since then many have graduated from Oxford and gone on to fame—Indira Gandhi and Margaret Thatcher are both alumnae of Somerville College.

Essentials

GETTING THERE   Trains from London's Paddington Station reach Oxford in 1½ hours. Five trains run every hour. A cheap, same-day round-trip ticket costs £28. For information, call ℂ **0845/748-4950** or visit **www.nationalrail.co.uk**.

Stagecoach (ℂ **01865/772250**; www.stagecoachbus.com) operates the Oxford Tube, with buses leaving London at the rate of three to five per hour, costing £14 one-way (£11 for students).

If you're driving, take the M40 west from London and follow the signs. Traffic and parking are a disaster in Oxford. However, there are four large park-and-ride lots on the north, south, east, and west of the city's ring road, all well marked. They're located on the Woodstock road near the Peartree traffic circle, on the Botley road toward Farringdon, on the Abingdon road in the southeast, and on the A40 toward London. Parking is £2 to £2.50 per hour. From 9:30am on and all day Saturday, you pay £2 for a round-trip ticket for a bus ride into the city, which drops you off at St. Aldate's Cornmarket or Queen Street to see the city center. The buses run every 8 to 10 minutes in each direction. There is no service on Sunday. See "Getting Around," below, for more info on buses.

VISITOR INFORMATION   The **Oxford Tourist Information Centre** is at 15–16 Broad St. (ℂ **01865/252200**; www.visitoxford.org). It sells a comprehensive range of maps, brochures, and souvenir items, as well as the famous Oxford University T-shirts. Guided walking tours leave from the center daily (see "Exploring the City," later in this chapter). Hours are Monday to Saturday 9:30am to 5pm, Sunday and bank holidays 10am to 4pm.

GETTING AROUND   The **Oxford Bus Company,** 395 Cowley Rd. (*©* **01865/ 785400;** www.oxfordbus.co.uk), operates green Park-and-Ride buses that leave from four parking lots in the city using north-south or east-west routes. A round-trip ticket costs £2 to £2.50. Its blue Airline buses travel to Heathrow and Gatwick. A one-way ticket from Oxford to Heathrow costs £20 for adults, £10 for children ages 5 to 15; to Gatwick, £25 for adults, £13 for children. The company's red local buses cover 15 routes in all suburbs, with a day pass allowing unlimited travel for £6. Weekly and monthly passes are also available.

The competition, **Stagecoach,** Unit 4, Horsepath, Cowley (*©* **01865/772250;** www.stagecoachbus.com/oxfordshire), uses blue-and-cream minibuses and coaches colored red, blue, and orange. City buses leave from Queen Street in Oxford's city center. The 1-day Dayrider ticket, which allows unlimited travel within Oxford city, costs £3.50.

Where to Stay

Accommodations in Oxford are limited, though motels have sprouted on the outskirts of town—good for those who want modern amenities. If you have a car, you may want to consider country houses or small B&Bs on the outskirts. Bedrooms, albeit expensive ones, are also provided at **Le Manoir aux Quat' Saisons** (p. 258).

The **Oxford Tourist Information Centre** (*©* **01865/252200**) operates a year-round room-booking service for a £5 fee, plus a 10% refundable deposit. If you'd like to seek lodgings on your own, the center has a list of accommodations, maps, and guidebooks.

EXPENSIVE

Macdonald Randolph Hotel ★   Since 1864, the Randolph has overlooked St. Giles, the Ashmolean Museum, and the Cornmarket. The hotel is an example of how historic surroundings can be combined with modern conveniences to make for elegant accommodations. The lounges, though modernized, are cavernous enough for dozens of separate and intimate conversational groupings. The furnishings are traditional. Some rooms are quite large; others are a bit cramped. The double-glazing on the windows appears inadequate to keep out the noise of midtown traffic. We'd opt first for the more stylish and intimate Old Parsonage (see below) before checking in here.

Beaumont St., Oxford, Oxfordshire OX1 2LN. *©* **0844/8799132.** Fax 01865/791678. www.macdonald-hotels.co.uk/Randolph. 151 units. £141–£346 double; £261–£626 suite. AE, DC, MC, V. Parking £25. Bus: 7. **Amenities:** Restaurant; 2 bars; babysitting; concierge; room service; spa. *In room:* TV, CD player, hair dryer.

Malmaison Oxford Castle ★★ 🎁   In a TripAdvisor poll of the top 10 quirkiest hotels in the world, the Malmaison in Oxford made the list. Formerly it was meant for inmates detained at Her Majesty's pleasure, and many aspects of prison life, including barred windows, have been retained. Guest rooms, in a converted Victorian building, are actually remodeled "cells" that flank two sides of a large central atrium, a space that rises three stories and is crisscrossed by narrow walkways like in one of those George Raft prison movies of the '30s. The former inmates never had it so good—great beds, mood lighting, power showers, satellite TV, and serious wines. In spite of its former origins, this is a stylish and comfortable place to stay.

3 Oxford Castle, Oxford OXI 1AY. © **01865/268400.** Fax 01865/3654247. www.malmaison.com. 94 units. £170–£240 double; £255–£505 suite. AE, DC, MC, V. Parking (prebooking required) £20. **Amenities:** Restaurant; bar; exercise room; room service. *In room:* TV/DVD, CD player, minibar, Wi-Fi (£10 per 24 hr.).

Old Bank Hotel ★★ The first hotel created in the center of Oxford in 135 years, the Old Bank opened in 1999 and immediately surpassed the traditional favorite, the Randolph (not reviewed), in both style and amenities. Located on Oxford's main street and surrounded by some of its oldest colleges and sights, the building dates back to the 18th century and was indeed once a bank. The hotel currently features a collection of 20th-century British art handpicked by the owners. Bedrooms are comfortably and elegantly appointed, many opening onto views. A combination of velvet and shantung silk–trimmed linen bedcovers gives the accommodations added style.

92–94 High St., Oxford OX1 4BN. © **01865/799599.** Fax 01865/799598. www.oldbank-hotel.co.uk. 42 units. £230–£270 double; £370 suite. AE, DC, MC, V. Free parking. Bus: 7. **Amenities:** Restaurant; bar; babysitting; room service. *In room:* A/C, TV, CD player, hair dryer.

Old Parsonage Hotel ★★ This extensively renovated hotel, near St. Giles Church and Keble College, looks like an extension of one of the ancient colleges. Originally a 13th-century hospital, it was restored in the early 17th century. In the 20th century, a modern wing was added, and in 1991, it was completely renovated and made into a first-rate hotel. This intimate old property is filled with hidden charms, such as tiny gardens in the courtyard and on the roof terrace. In this tranquil area of Oxford, you'll feel like you're living at one of the colleges yourself. The rooms are individually designed but not large; each opens onto the private gardens.

1 Banbury Rd., Oxford OX2 6NN. © **01865/310210.** Fax 01865/311262. www.oldparsonage-hotel.co.uk. 30 units. £175–£230 double; £240–£260 suite. AE, DC, MC, V. Free parking. Bus: 7. **Amenities:** Restaurant; bar; room service. *In room:* A/C, TV, hair dryer, Internet (free).

MODERATE

Barceló Oxford Hotel This is a good choice if you have a car; it's 3km (2 miles) north of the city center and hidden from traffic at the junction of A40 and A34. It attracts a lot of business travelers, but also visitors, and is a good base for exploring not only Oxford but also the Cotswolds, which are within easy reach. The M40 motorway is just a 13km (8-mile) drive away. Rooms are motel-like, with modern, contemporary furnishings.

Godstow Rd., Wolvercote Roundabout, Oxford, Oxfordshire OX2 8AL. © **01865/489988.** Fax 01865/489952. www.barcelo-hotels.co.uk. 168 units. £109–£213 double. DC, MC, V. Free parking. Bus: 6. **Amenities:** Restaurant; bar; exercise room; indoor heated pool; room service; spa. *In room:* A/C, TV, hair dryer, Wi-Fi (£4 per hr.).

Bath Place Hotel ★★ 📖 Its owners took these 17th-century weavers' cottages and converted them into a small inn of charm and grace, one of the "secret addresses" of Oxford. Bath Place lies on a cobbled alleyway off Holywell Street in the center of Oxford between New College and Hertford College. Flemish weavers built the cottages around a tiny flagstone courtyard. The Turf Tavern, adjacent to the hotel, is the oldest in Oxford. The site has had a notorious history, especially when it was known as the Spotted Cow, as a center for illicit gambling, bear baiting, and cockfighting. Thomas Hardy mentioned the cottages in his novel *Jude the Obscure*.

The address became a hideaway for the married Richard Burton and his mistress, Elizabeth Taylor, when he was acting at the Oxford Playhouse. Completely refurbished to a high standard, the inn today offers comfortable and well-appointed bedrooms.

4–5 Bath Place, Oxford OX1 3SU. © **01865/791812.** Fax 01865/791834. www.bathplace.co.uk. 13 units. £99–£160 double; £165–£200 family suite. Rates include continental buffet or room-service breakfast. AE, DC, MC, V. Free parking. **Amenities:** Room service. *In room:* TV, minibar.

Mercure Eastgate Hotel ★ The Eastgate, built on the site of a 1600s structure, stands within walking distance of Oxford College and the city center. Recently refurbished, it offers modern facilities while somewhat retaining the atmosphere of an English country house. The bedrooms are well worn but still cozy, ranging in size from small to medium.

73 High St., Oxford, Oxfordshire, OX1 4BE. © **1865/248332.** Fax 01865/791681. www.mercure.com. 63 units. £128–£209 double. AE, DC, MC, V. Parking £14. Bus: 3, 4, 7, or 52. **Amenities:** Bar; babysitting; room service. *In room:* A/C, TV, hair dryer, minibar.

Weston Manor ★★ This 5.2-hectare (13-acre) manor has existed since the 11th century; portions of the present building date from the 14th and 16th centuries. The estate is the ancestral home of the earls of Abingdon and Berkshire. It was also an abbey, until Henry VIII abolished the abbeys and assumed ownership of the property. Of course, there are ghosts: Mad Maude, the naughty nun who was burned at the stake for her "indecent and immoral" behavior, returns to haunt the Oak rooms. Most of the bedrooms are spacious and furnished with antiques (often four-poster beds). They're divided between the main house and a former coach house that was skillfully converted. Regardless of location, each bedroom is first-rate and extremely comfortable.

Weston-on-the-Green, Oxfordshire OX25 3QL. © **01869/350621.** Fax 01869/350901. www.weston manor.co.uk. 35 units. £125–£215 double; £205–£240 suite. Rates include English breakfast. AE, MC, V. Free parking. Drive 9.5km (6 miles) north of Oxford on A34. **Amenities:** Restaurant; bar; outdoor pool; room service. *In room:* A/C, TV, hair dryer, Wi-Fi (in some; free).

INEXPENSIVE

Dial House 🍴 Three kilometers (2 miles) east of the heart of Oxford, beside the main highway leading to London, is this country-style house originally built between 1924 and 1927. Graced with mock Tudor half-timbering and a prominent blue-faced sundial (from which it derives its name), it has cozy and recently renovated rooms. The owners, the Morris family, serve only breakfast in their bright dining room.

25 London Rd., Headington, Oxford, Oxfordshire OX3 7RE. © **01865/425100.** Fax 01865/427388. www.dialhouseoxford.co.uk. 8 units. £80–£85 double; £90–£125 family room. Rates include English breakfast. AE, MC, V. Free parking. Bus: 2, 7, 7A, 7B, or 22. *In room:* TV, hair dryer, no phone.

Galaxie Hotel When it was built about a century ago, this redbrick property served as a plush private mansion for a prosperous local family. Today, this little hotel is better than ever, following a refurbishment that added a conservatory lounge. Each of the well-maintained bedrooms is well furnished to a high standard. Although no meals other than breakfast are served, the hotel is within a short walk of no fewer than five restaurants and two pubs. A public bus runs down Banbury Road to the center of Oxford.

180 Banbury Rd., Oxford, Oxfordshire OX2 7BT. © **01865/515688.** Fax 01865/556824. www.galaxie. co.uk. 32 units, 28 with bathroom. £98–£125 double. Rates include English breakfast. MC, V. Limited street parking. *In room:* TV, hair dryer, Wi-Fi (free).

Green Gables Guest House   This hotel was originally the large Edwardian private residence of a local toy manufacturer. Today's hosts, among the best in Oxford, continue to make improvements to the property. Many of the bedrooms are quite large, all in spick-and-span condition. The breakfast room is bright and inviting. Trees screen the house from the main road, and parking for eight cars is available.

326 Abingdon Rd., Oxford, Oxfordshire OX1 4TE. © **01865/725870.** Fax 01865/723115. www.green gables.uk.com. 11 units. £75 double; £90–£100 family room. Rates include English breakfast. AE, MC, V. Free parking. 1.6km (1 mile) south of Oxford on A4144. *In room:* TV.

Victoria House Hotel 🍴   Just minutes from the colleges, this centrally located hotel is one of the best deals for the price in the heart of Oxford, where everything is relatively expensive. You don't get glamour, but you are offered renovated bedrooms in a no-frills atmosphere. Many businesspeople—the ones who aren't on expense accounts—check in here during the week. University students gather in the basement bar, which features a resident DJ on weekends.

29 George St., Oxford OX1 2AY. © **01865/727400.** Fax 01865/727402. www.victoriahouse-hotel.co.uk. 14 units. £85–£95 double. Extra bed £15. AE, DC, MC, V. Parking £10. **Amenities:** Bar. *In room:* TV, hair dryer, Wi-Fi (free).

Where to Dine

VERY EXPENSIVE

Le Manoir aux Quat' Saisons ★★★ MODERN FRENCH   Some 19km (12 miles) southeast of Oxford, Le Manoir aux Quat' Saisons offers the finest cuisine in the Midlands. The gray-and-honey-colored stone manor house, originally built by a Norman nobleman in the early 1300s, has attracted many famous visitors. Today, the restaurant's connection with France has been masterfully revived by the Gallic owner and chef, Raymond Blanc. His reputation for comfort and cuisine attracts guests from as far away as London. The menu changes seasonally to take advantage of the best produce. The best-loved dishes here are smoked haddock soup with sea bass tartare and caviar as a starter, followed by Cornish red mullet with a fricassee of squid. Diners have nothing but praise for the slow-roasted aromatic Cornish turbot, the roast Gressingham duck breast with a confit of yuzu fruit, and the braised Cornish brill with scallops and wild asparagus. For dessert, try a raspberry soufflé with its own sorbet.

Accommodations are also available. Each very pricey room—rates are £460 to £670 for a double, from £815 to £970 for a suite—is decorated with luxurious bed linens, ruffled canopies, and reproduction antiques.

Church Rd., Great Milton, Oxfordshire. © **800/237-1236** in the U.S., or 01844/278881. Fax 01844/278847. www.manoir.com. Reservations required. Main courses £41 lunch or dinner; lunch *menu du jour* £53; 5-course lunch or dinner £95; dinner or Sat-Sun lunch *menu découverte* £125. AE, DC, MC, V. Daily noon–2:30pm and 7–10pm. Take exit 7 off M40 and head along A329 toward Wallingford; look for signs for Great American Milton Manor about 1.6km (1 mile) after.

EXPENSIVE

Cherwell Boathouse Restaurant ★ FRENCH/MODERN ENGLISH   An Oxford landmark on the River Cherwell, this restaurant is owned by Anthony Verdin, who is assisted by a young crew. The cooks change the intriguing menu every 2 weeks to take advantage of the freshest vegetables, fish, and meat. The kitchen is often cited for its "sensible combinations" of ingredients. The success of the main dishes is founded on savory treats such as pork belly with a foie gras terrine, crispy pork cutlets with a Provençal sauce, and confit of duck in a port sauce. A special treat is the grilled gray mullet with ratatouille accompanied by a basil-and-chili sauce. For dessert, indulge in the lemon-and-almond roulade. The style is sophisticated yet understated, with a heavy reliance on quality ingredients whose natural flavors are always preserved. There is a very reasonable, even exciting, wine list.

Bardwell Rd. ℂ **01865/552746.** www.cherwellboathouse.co.uk. Reservations recommended. Main courses £15–£22; fixed-price dinner from £15; Mon–Fri set lunch £19. AE, MC, V. Daily noon–2:30pm and 6–9:30pm. Closed Dec 24–30. Bus: Banbury Rd.

Fishers ★★ SEAFOOD   Both university dons and students who have received a check from home patronize Oxford's best seafood restaurant. Predictably, the interior is decorated with a nautical theme, with porthole windows and red sails fluttering in the breeze. The fish always tastes remarkably fresh, even though Oxford is inland. A long list of starters includes everything from seafood bouillabaisse to deep-fried whitebait. Irish rock oysters are served over crushed ice, and you can also order both hot and cold shellfish platters. Canadian lobster is flown in, but the traditional favorite of students is haddock and chips. Black mussels from the Scottish Highlands, succulent turbot from Wales, and red mullet caught by Cornish fishermen round out the menu.

36–37 St. Clement's St. ℂ **01865/242003.** Reservations required. Main courses £14–£22. MC, V. Mon–Sat noon–2:30pm and 6–10:30pm; Sun 12:30–3pm and 6–10pm.

MODERATE

Brasserie Blanc ★ MODERN BRITISH/FRENCH   Master restaurateur Raymond Blanc took a former piano shop and converted it into a stylish eatery, one of the best in Oxford. The informal brasserie, with its striking modern interior, bustles with diners, ranging from visitors to students. Here you can get a taste of this famous chef's creations without paying the high prices of the swanky Le Manoir aux Quat' Saisons (p. 258). The menu is more straightforward here, featuring highly praised dishes such as slow-cooked beef and onions with a parsnip purée or roast Barbary duck breast with blackberry sauce.

71–72 Walton St. ℂ **01865/510999.** www.brasserieblanc.com. Reservations recommended. Main courses £9–£18. AE, MC, V. Mon–Fri noon–2:45pm and 5:30–10:30pm; Sat noon–11pm; Sun noon–10pm.

Browns 🍴 ENGLISH/CONTINENTAL   Oxford's busiest and most bustling English brasserie suits all groups, from babies to undergraduates to grandmas. A 10-minute walk north of the town center, it occupies the premises of five Victorian shops whose walls were removed to create one large, echoing, and very popular space. A thriving bar trade (where lots of people seem to order Pimm's) makes the place an evening destination in its own right. A young and enthusiastic staff serves traditional English cuisine. Exceptional items prepared with a finely honed technique include a whole baked sea bream with lemon and ginger; monkfish wrapped in prosciutto and served with a sweet pepper confit; and braised pork with black pudding and sage gravy.

5–11 Woodstock Rd. ℂ **01865/511995.** www.browns-restaurants.co.uk. Main courses £8–£19. AE, MC, V. Mon–Wed 9am–11pm; Thurs–Sat 9am–11:30pm; Sun 9am–10:30pm. Bus: 2 or 7.

Oxford: The City of Dreaming Spires

Gee's Restaurant ★ MEDITERRANEAN/INTERNATIONAL   This restaurant, in a spacious Victorian glass conservatory, was converted from what, for 80 years, housed the leading florist of Oxford. Its original features were retained by the owners, also of the Old Parsonage Hotel (p. 256), who have turned it into one of the most nostalgic and delightful establishments in the city. Based on fine ingredients and a skilled preparation, the meals are likely to include smoked eel with horseradish potatoes, lamb sweetbreads with pearl barley, and deep-fried haddock and chips with a warm caper sauce. A good dessert choice is the lemon tart with blackberries.

61 Banbury Rd. ✆ **01865/553540.** www.gees-restaurant.co.uk. Reservations recommended. Main courses £15–£22; fixed-price 2-course menu £22, fixed-price 3-course menu £25; set lunch and pretheater menu £14–£17. AE, MC, V. Mon–Sat noon–2:30pm; Sun noon–3:30pm; daily 6–10:30pm.

INEXPENSIVE

Al-Shami LEBANESE   Bearing the archaic name for the city of Damascus, this Lebanese restaurant contains two separate dining rooms: one with blessings from the Koran stenciled in calligraphic patterns under the coves, the other with pale beige walls and lots of wood paneling. Expect a clientele of local residents and a formally dressed Arabic- and English-speaking staff wearing black trousers, bow ties, and white vests. Many diners don't go beyond the appetizers, which comprise more than 40 delectable hot and cold selections—everything from falafel to a salad made with lamb's brains. Chargrilled chopped lamb, chicken, or fish constitute most of the main-dish selections. Desserts are chosen from the cart, and vegetarian meals are also available.

25 Walton Crescent. ✆ **01865/310066.** www.al-shami.co.uk. Reservations recommended. Main courses £6.20–£12. MC, V. Daily noon–midnight.

The Birch at Woburn ENGLISH/CONTINENTAL   Just outside of Woburn, this family-run establishment offers modern pub dining and does so very well. It makes a good luncheon stopover, featuring an extensive menu as well as an open grill where you can choose from a selection of fresh steaks or fish cooked to order. A fresh soup is made daily, or else you can order such starters as a duck and pistachio rillette or baked goat's cheese with ratatouille and pesto. Specialties include pepper venison steak and seared Gressingham duck breast. From the griddle comes the catch of the day and a succulent aged sirloin.

20 Newport Rd. ✆ **01525/290295.** www.birchwoburn.com. Reservations not needed. Main courses £6.50–£10 lunch, £11–£23 dinner. AE, MC, V. Mon–Sat 11:30am–3pm and 6–11pm; Sun noon–6pm.

The Pub Scene

These places are all good choices for affordable meals, too.

The **Head of the River,** Abingdon Road at Folly Bridge, near the Westgate Centre Mall (✆ **01865/721600**), is operated by the family brewery Fuller, Smith & Turner. It's a lively place offering true traditional ales and lagers, along with good sturdy fare. In summer, guests can sit by the river and rent a punt or a boat with an engine. Twelve rooms, all with bathrooms and overlooking the river, are available for £95 to £120, including breakfast, newspaper, and parking.

At the **Eagle and Child,** 49 Saint Giles St. (✆ **01865/302925**), literary history suffuses the dim, paneled alcoves and promotes a sedate atmosphere. For 25 years, it was frequented by the likes of C. S. Lewis and J. R. R. Tolkien. In fact, *The Chronicles of Narnia* and *The Hobbit* were first read aloud at this pub. Known as the

"Bird and Baby," this hallowed ground still welcomes the local dons. It's a settled, quiet place to read the papers, listen to classical music on CDs, and enjoy good food.

The **King's Arms,** 40 Holywell St. (© **01865/242369**), hosts a mix of students, gays, and professors. One of the best places in town to strike up a conversation, the pub, owned by Young's Brewery, features six of the company's ales along with visiting lagers and bitters that change periodically.

Exploring the City

The best way to get a running commentary on the important sights is to take a 2-hour **walking tour** through the city and the major colleges. They leave daily from the Oxford Tourist Information Centre, 15–16 Broad St. (© **01865/252200;** www. visitoxford.org), at 11am, 1, and 2pm, and cost £7 for adults and £3.75 for children 15 and younger; these tours do not include New College or Christ Church. There are two tours that do include admission to Christ Church; these leave the Tourist Information Centre on Saturday at 10:30am and 1:30pm and cost £7.50 adults, £4 children.

 A Nostalgic Walk

> Our favorite pastime here is to take **Addison's Walk** through the water meadows. The stroll is named after a former Oxford alumnus, Joseph Addison, the 18th-century essayist and playwright noted for his contributions to *The Spectator* and *The Tatler.*

The Tourist Information Centre also offers a **ghost tour** that explores Oxford's ghoulish and gory past. From June to October, it's offered Friday and Saturday evenings at 6:45pm, covering the dark alleyways around the ancient schools. The cost is £6 for adults and £3 for children; tickets are available at the center during the day.

For a good orientation, take a 1-hour, open-top bus tour with **City Sightseeing Oxford** (© **01865/790522;** www.citysightseeingoxford.com), whose office is at the railway station (tours also start from the railway station; other pickup points are Sheldonian Theatre, Gloucester Green Bus Station, and Pembroke College). Buses leave every 10 to 15 minutes daily. Tours run November to February daily from 9:30am to 3:40pm, March daily from 9:30am to 4:40pm, and April to October daily 9:30am to 6:30pm. The cost is £12 for adults, £9.50 for students and seniors, £6 for children 5 to 14 years; a family ticket for two adults and three children is £31. Tickets can be purchased from the driver and are valid for 24 hours.

Exploring Oxford University

Many Americans arriving at Oxford ask, "Where's the campus?" If a local looks amused when answering, it's because Oxford University is in fact made up of 35 colleges sprinkled throughout the town. To tour all of these would be a formidable task. It's best to focus on just a handful of the better-known colleges.

A word of warning: The main business of a university is, of course, to educate— and this function at Oxford has been severely hampered by the number of visitors who disturb the academic work of the university. Thus visiting is restricted to certain hours and to small groups of six or fewer. Furthermore, visitors are not allowed at all in certain areas, but the tourist office will be happy to advise you on which sights of this great institution are open to the public.

WHICH college TO CHOOSE: OXFORD OR CAMBRIDGE?

Not everyone can go to both Oxford and Cambridge, so which should you choose if pressed for time and you can spare only a day outside of London? We'd opt for Cambridge over Oxford because Cambridge more closely lives up to the image of what an English university town is like.

Although central Oxford is dominated by the university, it is also an industrial city known for its motor industry. Its 120,000 permanent residents seem to keep to themselves and go about their lives trying to evade the thousands of tourists descending on their inner core. Of course, Oxford has some of England's greatest architecture, some excellent museums, and great student pubs. On an ideal itinerary, it should not be crossed off the list.

Then there is Cambridge. It's really an agricultural market town, a more tranquil and secluded place, set at the door-

step of the Fens, a vast area just north of the city that's a strange but fascinating terrain of reclaimed marshland and quaking bogs. In addition to its architecture and university, Cambridge allows you to preview the life of East Anglia, which remains one of the country's bucolic landscapes as painted by John Constable.

Unlike the city of Oxford, Cambridge is more compact and can be more easily walked and explored on a rushed day trip. You can go punting on the River Cam; explore "the Backs," that green swath of land straddling the river; and walk the 1km (½-mile) parade of colleges from Magdalene to Peterhouse. Not bad for a day's outing. You may so fall in love with English university towns, you'll decide to stay in England for that extra day so you can take in Oxford after all. See chapter 15 for details on Cambridge.

AN OVERVIEW   For a bird's-eye view of the city and colleges, climb **Carfax Tower** ★, located in the center of town. This structure is distinguished by its clock and figures that strike on the quarter-hour. Carfax Tower is all that remains from St. Martin's Church, where William Shakespeare once stood as godfather for William Davenant, who also became a successful playwright. A church stood on this site from 1032 until 1896. The tower used to be higher, but after 1340 it was lowered, following complaints from the university to Edward III that townspeople threw stones and fired arrows at students during town-and-gown disputes. Admission is £2.10 for adults, £1 for children. The tower is open year-round, except for Christmas Eve to January 1. From April to October, hours are 10am to 5:30pm daily. Off-season hours are 10am to 3pm Monday to Saturday. Children 4 and younger are not admitted. For information, call ✆ **01865/792653.**

CHRIST CHURCH ★★ ☺   Begun by Cardinal Wolsey as Cardinal College in 1525, Christ Church (✆ **01865/276492;** www.chch.ox.ac.uk), known as the House, was founded by Henry VIII in 1546. Facing St. Aldate's Street, Christ Church has the largest quadrangle of any college in Oxford. Tom Tower houses Great Tom, an 18,000-pound bell. It rings at 9:05pm nightly, signaling the closing of the college gates. The 101 times it peals originally signified the number of students in residence at the time the college was founded. Although the student body has

Punting the River Cherwell

Punting on the River Cherwell remains the favorite outdoor pastime in Oxford. At Punt Station, **Cherwell Boathouse,** Bardwell Road (☎ **01865/515978;** www.cherwellboathouse.co.uk), you can rent a punt (a flat-bottomed boat maneuvered by a long pole and a small oar) for £12 to £14 per hour, plus a £60 to £70 deposit. **Magdalen Bridge Boathouse,** Bardwell Road (☎ **01865/202-** 643; www.oxfordpunting.co.uk), charges similar rental rates. Punts are available from mid-March to mid-October, daily from 9:30am until dusk. Hours of operation seem to be rather informal, however, and you're not always guaranteed that someone will be here to rent you a boat, even if the punt itself is available.

grown significantly, Oxford traditions live on forever. There are some portraits in the 16th-century Great Hall, including works by Gainsborough and Reynolds. There's also a separate portrait gallery.

The college chapel was constructed over a period of centuries, beginning in the 12th century. (Incidentally, it's not only the college chapel but also the cathedral of the diocese of Oxford.) The cathedral's most distinguishing features are its Norman pillars and the vaulting of the choir, dating from the 15th century. In the center of the great quadrangle is a statue of Mercury mounted in the middle of a fishpond. This a popular stop for kids of all ages because many scenes from the *Harry Potter* films have been shot here, with the cloisters, quads, and staircases of Christ Church standing in for Hogwarts. The college is open Monday to Saturday 9am to 5pm, Sunday 1 to 5pm, charging £6 for adults or £4.50 for students and seniors (free for kids under 5).

MAGDALEN COLLEGE   Pronounced *Maud*-lin, Magdalen College, High Street (☎ **01865/276000;** www.magd.ox.ac.uk), was founded in 1458 by William of Waynflete, bishop of Winchester and later chancellor of England. Its alumni range from Wolsey to Wilde. Opposite the Botanic Garden, the oldest in England, is the bell tower, where the choristers sing in Latin at dawn on May Day. Charles I, his days numbered, watched the oncoming Roundheads from this tower. Visit the 15th-century chapel, in spite of many of its latter-day trappings. Ask when the hall and other places of special interest are open. The grounds of Magdalen are the most extensive of any Oxford college; there's even a deer park. July through September, it's open daily from noon to 6pm; October through June, daily from 1 to 6pm. Admission is £4 adults; £3 seniors, students, and children.

MERTON COLLEGE ★★   Founded in 1264, Merton College, Merton Street (☎ **01865/276310;** www.merton.ox.ac.uk), is among the three oldest colleges at the university. It stands near Corpus Christi College on Merton Street, the sole survivor of Oxford's medieval cobbled streets. Merton College is noted for its library, built between 1371 and 1379, and said to be the oldest college library in England. Though a tradition once kept some of its most valuable books chained, now only one book is secured in that manner to illustrate that historical custom. One of the library's treasures is an astrolabe (an astronomical instrument used for measuring the altitude of the sun and stars) thought to have belonged to Chaucer. You pay £2 to

7

Often overlooked by the average visitor is an unheralded little gem known as **Christ Church Picture Gallery** (☎ **01865/276-172; www.chch.ox.ac. uk**), entered through the Canterbury Quad. Here you'll come across a stunning collection of Old Masters, mainly from the Dutch, Flemish, and Italian schools, including works by Michelangelo and Leonardo da Vinci. The gallery is open May through September, Monday to Saturday from 10:30am to 5pm, Sunday from 2 to 5pm; October through April, Monday to Saturday from 10:30am to 1pm and daily from 2 to 4:30pm. Admission is £3 for adults, £2 for students and seniors.

visit the ancient library as well as the Max Beerbohm Room (dedicated to the satirical English caricaturist who died in 1956). The library and college are open Monday to Friday 2 to 4pm, Saturday and Sunday 10am to 4pm. It's closed for 1 week at Easter and Christmas and on weekends during the winter. Call ahead for information.

NEW COLLEGE   New College, Holywell Street (☎ **01865/279555;** www.new. ox.ac.uk), was founded in 1379 by William of Wykeham, bishop of Winchester and later lord chancellor of England. His college at Winchester supplied a constant stream of students. The first quadrangle, dating from before the end of the 14th century, was the initial quadrangle built in Oxford and formed the architectural design for the other colleges. In the antechapel is Sir Jacob Epstein's remarkable modern sculpture of Lazarus and a fine El Greco painting of St. James. One of the treasures of the college is a crosier (pastoral staff of a bishop) belonging to the founding father. Don't miss the beautiful garden outside the college, where you can stroll among the remains of the old city wall. It's an evocative, romantic site. The college (entered at New College Lane) can be visited from Easter to October daily between 11am and 5pm, and in the off-season daily between 2 and 4pm. Admission is £2 from Easter to October, free in the off-season.

OLD BODLEIAN LIBRARY ★★   This famed library on Catte Street (☎ **01865/277000;** www.bodley.ox.ac.uk) was launched in 1602, initially funded by Sir Thomas Bodley. It is home to some 50,000 manuscripts and more than five million books. Over the years, the library has expanded from the Old Library complex to other buildings, including the Radcliffe Camera next door. The easiest way to visit the library is by taking a guided tour, which leaves from the Divinity School across the street from the main entrance. In summer, there are four tours Monday through Friday and two on Saturday; in winter, there are two tours per day. Call for specific times.

Shopping

Golden Cross, an arcade of first-class shops and boutiques, lies between Cornmarket Street and the Covered Market, or between High and Market streets. Parts of the colorful gallery date from the 12th century. Many buildings remain from the medieval era, along with some 15th- and 17th-century structures. The market has a reputation as the Covent Garden of Oxford, with live entertainment on Saturday

A Quiet Oasis

The oldest in Great Britain, the **Botanic Garden,** opposite Magdalen (© **01865/286690;** www.botanic-garden.ox.ac.uk), was first planted in 1621 on the site of a Jewish graveyard from the early Middle Ages. Bounded by a curve of the Cherwell, it still stands today and is the best place in Oxford to escape the invading hordes.

The Botanic Garden is open March through October, daily from 9am to 5pm (until 6pm May–Aug); November through February, Monday to Friday from 9am to 4:30pm (last admission 45 min. before closing). Admission is £3 for adults, £2.50 for students, and free for children 11 and younger.

mornings in summer. In the arcade shops is a diverse selection of merchandise, including handmade Belgian chocolates, clothing for women and men, and luxury leather goods.

In its way, **Alice's Shop,** 83 St. Aldate's (© **01865/723793;** www.alicein wonderlandshop.co.uk), played an important role in English literature. Set within a 15th-century building that has housed some kind of shop since 1820, it functioned as a general store (selling brooms, hardware, and the like) during the period that Lewis Carroll, at the time a professor of mathematics at Christ Church College, was composing *Alice in Wonderland.* It is believed to have been the model for important settings within the book. Today, the place is a favorite stopover of Lewis Carroll fans from as far off as Japan, who gobble up commemorative pencils, chess sets, bookmarks, and, in rare cases, original editions of some of Carroll's works.

The **Bodleian Library Shop,** Old School's Quadrangle, Radcliffe Square, Broad Street (© **01865/277091;** www.shop.bodley.ox.ac.uk), specializes in Oxford souvenirs, from books and paperweights to Oxford banners and coffee mugs.

Castell & Son (The Varsity Shop), 13 Broad St. (© **01865/244000;** www. varsityshop.co.uk), is the best outlet in Oxford for clothing emblazoned with the Oxford logo or heraldic symbol. Choices include both whimsical and dead-on-serious neckties, hats, T-shirts, pens, beer and coffee mugs, and cuff links. It's commercialized Oxford, but it's still got a sense of relative dignity and style. A second location is at 109–114 High St. (© **01865/249491**).

Oxford After Dark

THE PERFORMING ARTS

Highly acclaimed orchestras playing in truly lovely settings mark the Music at Oxford series at the **Oxford Playhouse Theatre,** Beaumont Street (© **01865/305305;** www.oxfordplayhouse.com). The autumn season runs from mid-September to December, the winter season from January to April, and the spring–summer season from May to early July. Tickets range from £7 to £50. Classical music is performed by outstanding groups such as the European Union Chamber Orchestra, the Canterbury Musical Society, the Bournemouth Symphony, and the Guild Hall String Ensemble of London. All performances are held in the Sheldonian Theatre, a particularly attractive site, designed by Sir Christopher Wren, with paintings on the ceiling. The box office is open Monday to Saturday from

🎁 pubs WITH A PEDIGREE

Every college town the world over has a fair number of bars, but few can boast local watering holes with such atmosphere and history as Oxford.

A short block from the High, overlooking the north side of Christ Church College, the **Bear Inn,** 6 Alfred St. (✆ **01865/728164**), is an Oxford landmark, built in the 13th century and mentioned time and again in English literature. The Bear brings together a wide variety of people in a relaxed way. You might talk with a raja from India, a university don, or a titled gentleman who's the latest in a line of owners that goes back more than 700 years. Some former owners developed an astonishing habit: clipping neckties. Around the lounge bar you'll see the remains of

thousands of ties, which have been labeled with their owners' names.

Even older than the Bear is the **Turf Tavern,** 7 Bath Place (off Holywell St.; ✆ **01865/243235;** www.theturftavern. co.uk), on a very narrow passageway near the Bodleian Library. The pub is reached via St. Helen's Passage, which stretches between Holywell Street and New College Lane. (You'll probably get lost, but any student worth his or her beer can direct you.) Thomas Hardy used the place as the setting for *Jude the Obscure.* It was "the local" of the future U.S. president Bill Clinton during his student days at Oxford. In warm weather, you can choose a table in any of the three separate gardens that radiate outward from the pub's central core.

9:30am to 6pm (or until half an hour after the start of an evening performance) and on Sunday starting at least 2 hours before a performance.

New Theatre (formerly the Apollo), George Street (✆ **01865/320760;** www. newtheatreoxford.org.uk; or Ticketmaster ✆ **0844/8471585** for bookings), is Oxford's primary theater. Tickets are £15 to £50. A continuous run of comedy, ballet, drama, opera, and even rock contributes to the variety. Both the Welsh National Opera and the Glyndebourne Touring Opera appear here regularly. Advance booking is highly recommended, though some shows may have tickets the week of the performance. The box office is open Monday to Saturday from 10am to 8pm (to 6pm if there is no evening performance).

THE CLUBS: BLUES, JAZZ & CELTIC ROCK

As a sign of the times, **Freud,** 119 Walton St. (✆ **01865/311171;** www.freud living.co.uk), has turned an 18th-century church, stained-glass windows and all, into a jazz and folk club with an expansive array of drink choices. There is no cover. Hours are Tuesday noon to 11pm, Wednesday through Sunday noon to 2am.

OFS, 40 George St. (✆ **01865/297170**), covers all the bases, including live entertainment, a bar, a theater, an art museum, and a science museum called Curiosity, with a light show and other exhibits. Music cover charges begin at 11pm and are £5. Offerings change nightly but include '70s disco, blues, jazz, and local bands. Open daily 9pm to 2am.

The **Jericho Tavern,** 56 Walton St. (✆ **01865/311775;** www.thejericho.co. uk), comprises two levels. Downstairs patrons consume the suds inside, where there's a modern decor, or outside in the beer garden. Upstairs is another area for

For wintertime warmth, braziers are lighted in the courtyard and in the gardens. A food counter set behind a glass case displays the day's fare—salads, soups, sandwiches, and so on. Local ales (including one named Headbanger, with a relatively high alcohol content) are served, as well as a range of wines.

Just outside of town, hidden away some 4km (2½ miles) north of Oxford, the **Trout Inn,** 195 Godstow Rd., Wolvercote (© **01865/510930;** www. thetroutoxford.co.uk), is a private world where you can get ale and beer and standard fare. Have your drink in one of the historic rooms, with their settles (wooden benches), brass, and old prints, or go outside in sunny weather to sit on a stone wall. On the grounds are peacocks, ducks, swans, and herons that live in and around the river and an adjacent weir pool; they'll join you if you're handing out crumbs. Take an arched stone bridge, architecture with wildly pitched roofs and gables, add the Thames River, and you have the Trout. The Smoking Room, the original 12th-century part, complements the inn's relatively "new" 16th-century bars. Hot meals are served all day in the restaurant, with daily specials including salads in summer and grills in winter. On your way there and back, look for the view of Oxford from the bridge. To get here, take bus no. 6A, 6B, or 6C to Wolvercote, and then walk 1km (½ mile); it's also fun to bike here from Oxford. Hours are Monday to Saturday 11am to 11pm, Sunday 11am to 10:30pm.

drinking. Live music is featured Friday and Saturday, when a £5 to £8 cover is imposed. Open Monday through Friday noon to midnight, Saturday and Sunday 10am to midnight.

Thirst, 7–8 Park End St. (© **01865/242044;** www.thirstbar.com), is a popular student hangout with a lounge bar and a small garden. A DJ rules the night. Open Friday through Wednesday 6:30pm to 2am, Thursday 8pm to 2am.

WOODSTOCK & BLENHEIM PALACE

100km (62 miles) NW of London; 13km (8 miles) NW of Oxford

The small country town of Woodstock, birthplace in 1330 of the Black Prince, ill-fated son of King Edward III, lies on the edge of the Cotswolds. Some of the stone houses here were constructed when Woodstock was the site of a royal palace. This palace had so suffered the ravages of time that its remains were demolished when Blenheim Palace was built. Woodstock was once the seat of a flourishing glove industry.

Essentials

GETTING THERE Take the train to Oxford (see "Essentials" in the Oxford section, earlier in this chapter). Bus no. S3 operated by **Stagecoach** (© **01865/772250;** www.stagecoachbus.com) leaves Oxford about every 30 minutes during the day. The trip takes a little more than 30 minutes. If you're driving, take the A44 from Oxford.

VISITOR INFORMATION   The **Tourist Information Centre** is at the Oxfordshire Museum, Park Street (© **01993/813276;** www.oxfordshirecotswolds.org). It's open Monday to Saturday 10am to 5pm year-round.

Where to Stay & Dine

The Feathers ★   Just a short walk from Blenheim Palace, the Feathers dates from the 17th century and has been an inn since the 18th century. The bedrooms in this beautifully furnished hotel are individually decorated; some have draped awnings over the beds. The two lounges feature wood fires. A multitude of stuffed birds (from which the house took its name) adorn the bar; from here you can go into the delightful garden in the courtyard.

Market St., Woodstock, Oxfordshire OX20 1SX. © **01993/812291.** Fax 01993/813158. www.feathers.co.uk. 20 units. £165–£195 double; £235–£275 suite. Rates include English breakfast. AE, DC, MC, V. **Amenities:** Restaurant; bar; babysitting; room service. *In room:* TV, hair dryer, Wi-Fi (free).

Macdonald Bear Hotel ★★   The Bear Hotel is one of the six oldest coaching inns in England, dating from the 13th century. The half-stone structure is located in the center of Woodstock. Richard Burton and Elizabeth Taylor, at the height of their tempestuous romance in the 1960s, stayed in the Marlboro Suite, an attractively decorated sitting room paired with bedroom and bathroom. According to legend, one of the chambers of the hotel is haunted. Rooms come in a variety of sizes and styles, but each offers grand comfort and a mix of modern luxuries with antiques; nine of the rooms contain four-poster beds. Blazing hearth fires are found throughout the hotel when the days and nights are cool.

Park St., Woodstock, Oxfordshire OX20 1SZ. © **0844/879-9143.** Fax 01993/810968. www.macdonald-hotels.co.uk. 54 units. £107–£208 double; £187–£228 suite. AE, DC, MC, V. Free parking. **Amenities:** Restaurant; bar; room service. *In room:* TV, CD player, hair dryer, minibar, Wi-Fi (£10 per hr.).

A Favorite Local Pub

Star Inn, 22 Market Place (© **01993/811373**), has three locally brewed real ales from which to choose: Tetley's, Wadworth's 6X, and Marston's Pedigree. You can enjoy the requisite bar munchies as well as full dinners. The management boasts that its half-shoulder of lamb is the most tender around because of the slow-cooking process.

One of England's Most Magnificent Palaces

Blenheim Palace ★★★ ☺   The extravagantly baroque Blenheim Palace is England's answer to Versailles. Blenheim is the home of the 11th duke of Marlborough, descendant of the first duke John Churchill, once an on-again, off-again favorite of Queen Anne's. In his day (1650–1722), the first duke became the supreme military figure in Europe. Fighting on the Danube near a village named Blenheim, Churchill defeated the forces of Louis XIV, and the lavish palace of Blenheim was built for him as a gift from the queen. It was designed by Sir John Vanbrugh, who was also the architect of Castle Howard; the landscaping was created by Capability Brown. The palace is loaded with riches: antiques, porcelain, oil paintings, tapestries, and chinoiserie. North Americans know Blenheim as the birthplace of Sir Winston Churchill. The room in which he was born is included in the palace tour, as is the Churchill exhibition: four rooms of letters, books, photographs, and other relics.

Today, the former prime minister lies buried in Bladon Churchyard, near the palace.

Insider's tip: **Marlborough Maze,** 540m (1,800 ft.) from the palace, is the largest symbolic hedge maze on earth, with an herb and lavender garden, a butterfly house, and inflatable castles for children. Also, be sure to look for the castle's gift shops, tucked away in an old palace dairy. Here you can purchase a wide range of souvenirs, handicrafts, and even locally made preserves.

Brighton Rd., Woodstock. © **08700/602080.** www.blenheimpalace.com. Admission £18 adults, £15 students and seniors, £10 children 5-15, £48 family ticket, free for children 4 and younger. Daily 10:30am–5:30pm. Last admission 4:45pm. Closed mid-Dec to mid-Feb (except for park).

AYLESBURY

74km (46 miles) NW of London; 35km (22 miles) E of Oxford

Aylesbury has retained much of its ancient charm and character, especially along the narrow Tudor alleyways and in the 17th-century architecture of the houses in the town center. Among the more ancient structures is St. Mary's Church, which dates from the 13th century and features an unusual spirelet. The 15th-century King's Head Public House, a National Trust property, has seen many famous faces in its time, including Henry VIII, who was a frequent guest while he was courting Anne Boleyn.

The market, which has been an integral part of the town since the 13th century, is still a thriving force in Aylesbury life. Markets are held on Wednesday, Friday, and Saturday, plus a flea market on Tuesday. During the 18th and 19th centuries, ducks were the most famous commodity of the Aylesbury market. The pure white ducks were a delicacy for the rich and famous of London and were much desired for their dinner tables. The demand for the Aylesbury duck declined in the 20th century, though not before the breed became threatened with extinction. Today, however, most ducks found on restaurant menus are raised elsewhere, and the threat to the Aylesbury duck has subsided. The ivory fowl are now enjoyed more for their beauty than for their flavor.

Essentials

GETTING THERE   Aylesbury is 1 hour and 12 minutes by train from London's Marylebone Station, or 25 minutes off the M25 via the A41. For information, call © **0845/748-4950** or visit **www.nationalrail.co.uk**.

VISITOR INFORMATION   The **Aylesbury Tourist Information Centre,** Kings Head Passage, off Market Square (© **01296/330559;** www.visit buckinghamshire.org), is open April through October, Monday to Saturday 9:30am to 5pm, and November through March, Monday to Saturday 10am to 4:30pm.

Where to Stay & Dine

Hartwell House ★★★   One of England's great showcase country estates and a member of Relais & Châteaux, Hartwell House lies just 3km (2 miles) southwest of Aylesbury (the nearest rail station) on the A418, and about 32km (20 miles) from Oxford. It stands on 36 hectares (90 acres) of landscaped parkland. As you enter the house, you can enjoy a medley of architectural styles, ranging from the 16th through the 18th centuries. The home was built for the Hampden and Lee families, ancestors of the Confederacy's Gen. Robert E. Lee. Wander from the morning room to the oak-paneled bar, pausing in the library where a former tenant, the exiled Louis XVIII, signed the document returning him to the throne of France. Bedrooms are as regal as the prices. The stellar accommodations—even those recently built in a converted stable block—ooze with comfort, charm, and character.

Oxford Rd., Aylesbury, Buckinghamshire HP17 8NR. ⓒ **01296/747444.** Fax 01296/747450. www.hartwell-house.com. 46 units. £260–£490 double; £490–£650 suite. AE, MC, V. Free parking. **Amenities:** 2 restaurants; bar; exercise room; indoor heated pool; room service; spa; 2 outdoor tennis courts. *In room:* TV, hair dryer, Wi-Fi (£5 per 24 hr.).

West Lodge Hotel   Close to Aylesbury, this Victorian hotel on the A41 outdoes all others in the area with its facilities, the best of which must be its own hot-air balloon. The comfortable bedrooms are furnished with nice extras and private shower-only bathrooms. For dinner, Montgolfier is a French restaurant located across the street and named after the brothers who made the first successful hot-air balloon flight in 1783.

45 London Rd., Aston Clinton, Aylesbury HP22 5HL. ⓒ **01296/630362.** Fax 01296/630151. www.westlodge.co.uk. 9 units. £89–£94 double. Rates include English breakfast. AE, MC, V. **Amenities:** Restaurant; bar; Jacuzzi; room service; sauna. *In room:* TV/DVD, hair dryer, Wi-Fi (free).

Seeing the Sights

Following in the footsteps of the Rothschilds (see Waddesdon Manor, below), many wealthy Victorian merchants built mansions in and around Aylesbury, and many of these half-timbered examples of regal domestic architecture still stand. If you aren't busy spending money at the market, you may want to stroll through the town to see the houses and buildings that line the streets. **Hickman's Almshouses** and the **Prebendal Houses** are structures that date from the 17th century; you can walk by after enjoying tea at St. Mary's Church, which is just down the road.

Buckinghamshire County Museum ☺   This museum is located in two buildings, a house and a grammar school, both dating from the 18th century. The latest addition to the museum is the Roald Dahl Children's Gallery. The author's children's books, especially *Charlie and the Chocolate Factory* and *James and the Giant Peach,* come to life as visitors ride in the Great Glass Elevator or crawl inside the Giant Peach. Even in the main museum, innovative displays, focusing on the cultural heritage of Buckinghamshire, are interactive and touchable. Advance arrangements are necessary for the Children's Gallery because of the large number of school groups that visit.

Church St. ⓒ **01296/331441.** www.buckscc.gov.uk/museum. Free admission to main museum. Children's Gallery £4; free for 2 and younger. Mon–Sat 10am–5pm; Sun 2–5pm.

Waddesdon Manor ★   Built by Baron Ferdinand de Rothschild in the 1870s, the manor features French Renaissance architecture and a variety of French furniture, carpets, and porcelain. Eighteenth-century artwork by several famous English and Dutch painters is exhibited; of course, you can also view the wine cellars. An aviary in the surrounding gardens houses exotic birds. On the premises are a restaurant and a gift shop, both featuring a vast assortment of Rothschild wines.

Bicester Rd. ✆ **01296/653226.** www.waddesdon.org.uk. Admission to house and grounds £2–£15 adults, £2.50–£11 children 5–16, family ticket £14–£18, free for children 4 and younger; grounds only £5.50–£7 adults, £2.75–£3.50 children 5–16, free for children 4 and younger. House Mar–Oct Wed–Fri noon–4pm, Sat–Sun 11am–4pm; grounds and aviary Jan to mid-Mar Sat–Sun 10am–5pm, mid-Mar to Dec Wed–Sun 10am–5pm. Audio guide can be rented at the entrance for £2. Bus: 16 or 17.

Aylesbury After Dark

Hobgoblin, 14 Kingsbury Sq. (✆ **01296/415100**), is a pub housed in a structure from 1742. Among on-tap offerings are house ales, Hobgoblin and Wychwood, as well as John Smith's, and there is also a full bar. Snack food is available, as are such distractions as pool tables, TVs, and video games. Sunday nights are karaoke.

ST. ALBANS ★

43km (27 miles) NW of London; 66km (41 miles) SW of Cambridge

Some 2,000 years old, today's cathedral city of St. Albans was named after a Roman soldier who was the first Christian martyr in England. Medieval pilgrims made the trek to visit the shrine of St. Alban, and visitors today still find the ancient cathedral city and the surrounding countryside inspiring.

Peter Rabbit was created in this county by Beatrix Potter, and George Bernard Shaw found inspiration in the view from his countryside home near Ayot St. Lawrence. As you explore St. Albans and nearby attractions, you'll tread in the footsteps of Queen Elizabeth I and Henry VIII, who passed through before you.

Although today industry has crept in and greater London keeps getting greater and greater, St. Albans is situated at the center of what was known as the "market basket of England." The 1,000-year-old tradition of the street market continues as merchants of every kind set up colorful stalls to display their goods. Held on Wednesday and Saturday, it's one of the largest in the southeast.

Essentials

GETTING THERE   St. Albans is easily reached from London. The rail connection, ThamesLink, takes you from London's King Cross to St. Albans in just 20 minutes. From London's Heathrow, Green Line coach no. 724 also runs to St. Albans frequently. For rail information, call ✆ **0845/748-4950** or visit **www.nationalrail.co.uk**. For bus information, dial ✆ **0870/608-2608** or visit **www.stagecoachbus.com**.

If you're driving, take the M25 Junction 21A or 22; M1 Junctions 6, 7, or 9; and A1 (M) Junction 3.

VISITOR INFORMATION   The **Tourist Information Centre** is at the Town Hall, Market Place (✆ **01727/864511**; www.visiteastofengland.com). Hours are Monday to Saturday 10am to 4:30pm.

Where to Stay

Black Lion Inn   This is the nicest pub hotel in the area as well as one of the best bargains. A former bakery built in 1837, it lies in the most colorful part of town, St. Michael's Village, where bustling coaches from London once arrived. Bedrooms are simple and plain and, although a bit cramped, well maintained. Free Wi-Fi is available in the reception area and bar.

St. Michael's Village, 198 Fishpool St., St. Albans, Hertfordshire AL3 4SB. © **01727/848644.** Fax 01727/859243. www.theblacklioninn.com. 16 units, 14 with bathroom. £65–£70 double; £85 family room. AE, MC, V. **Amenities:** Bar; babysitting; Wi-Fi (free, in lobby). *In room:* TV, hair dryer.

St. Michael's Manor ★★   Set on 2 hectares (5 acres) of beautifully maintained lakeside gardens, the manor dates from 1586. Constructed on medieval fortifications, the hotel stands in award-winning gardens with an abundance of wildlife. It's hard to imagine you're in a city. Rooms are individually decorated with fine antique pieces and come stocked with everything from mineral water to a teddy bear to sleep with. Each unit has a certain charm, with no bad choice among them. The manor also has a superb restaurant, the Terrace Room, with an ornate Victorian conservatory overlooking the floodlit lawns.

St. Michael's Village, Fishpool St., St. Albans, Hertfordshire AL3 4RY. © **01727/864444.** Fax 01727/848909. www.stmichaelsmanor.com. 30 units. £180–£320 double. Special weekend rate £145–£255 double. Rates include English breakfast. AE, MC, V. **Amenities:** Restaurant; bar; room service. *In room:* A/C, TV/DVD, hair dryer.

Sopwell House ★★★   This place is in a neck-to-neck competition with St. Michael's Manor (see above), though Sopwell has more facilities. A private mansion from the days of George III, at one time it belonged to Lord Louis Mountbatten and has seen its share of royal heads. Converted into a hotel of taste, charm, and character, it occupies nearly a dozen acres (nearly 5 hectares) 3km (2 miles) southeast of the city center. Avoid it if it's hosting a conference, but at other times you can enjoy the grace of an English country house. From the drawing room to the library, public rooms are elegant and comfy. Some of the guest rooms are equipped with four-poster beds and have a traditional feel, whereas others are more contemporary. Regardless, the decor is tasteful, rather chic, and handsomely coordinated.

Cottonmill Lane, St. Albans, Hertfordshire AL1 2HQ. © **01727/864477.** Fax 01727/844741. www.sopwellhouse.co.uk. 129 units. £105–£155 double; £165–£195 suite. AE, DC, MC, V. **Amenities:** 2 restaurants; 2 bars; babysitting; exercise room; indoor heated pool; room service; spa. *In room:* A/C (in some rooms), TV, hair dryer, Wi-Fi (free).

Where to Dine

The Restaurant at Sopwell House ★ FRENCH/ENGLISH Consistently serving the best food in the area, this restaurant lies beneath a glass roof that's pierced with a trio of magnolias whose branches gracefully arch into the open air outside. The ambience is light, elegant, upscale, and inviting, partly because of the formal and well-trained staff, and partly because the food is more sophisticated and prepared with more flair than anywhere else in town. Consider starting with an award-winning version of seared scallops with chili-and-lime salsa. Main courses change with chef James Chapman's inspiration, but you might try beef with a truffle mash and a bourguignon sauce or else strips of beef in a black-bean sauce.

The terrace bar is open daily (in summer only) from 11am to 11pm. The food it serves is a lot more down-home and a lot cheaper.

In the Sopwell House Hotel, Cottonmill Lane. © **01727/864477.** Reservations highly recommended. Main courses £12–£28. AE, DC, MC, V. Tues–Fri and Sun 12:30–2pm; Tues–Sat 7–9:30pm.

Exploring the Town

The Tourist Information Centre provides **guided walks** that cost £2 to £6. These include a tour of the ancient Roman city of Verulamium and the Medieval Town, a ghost walk, and a coaching-inn walking tour. In addition to prebooked tours, free public guided walks are available on several Sundays; these depart at 11:15am and 3pm from the Tourist Information Centre. Tours are not always conducted regularly, so it's best to call ahead. Guides are also available, Sunday at 2:30pm at the Verulamium Museum and Roman Theatre, to give short talks on a number of topics concerning the Romans and their time in the area. You can get full details from the Tourist Information Centre (see above).

The **Cathedral of St. Albans** ★, Holywell Hill and High Street (✆ 01727/860780; www.stalbanscathedral.org.uk), is still known as "the Abbey" to locals, though Henry VIII dissolved it as such in 1539. Construction of the cathedral began in 1077; it is one of England's early Norman churches. The bricks, especially visible in the tower, came from Verulamium, an old Roman city located at the foot of the hill. The nave and west front date from 1235.

The new chapter house, the first modern structure built beside a great medieval cathedral in the country, was opened by the queen in 1982. The building houses an information desk, gift shop, and restaurant. There is also a video detailing the history of the cathedral that you can view for free (donations appreciated).

The cathedral and chapter house are generally open daily from 8:30am to 5:45pm. In addition to church services, organ recitals are often open to the public. The church's choir can sometimes be heard rehearsing, if it's not on tour.

Verulamium Museum at St. Michael's ★ (✆ 01727/751810; www.stalbansmuseums.org.uk) stands on the site of the ancient Roman city of the same name. Here you'll view some of the finest Roman mosaics in Britain as well as re-created Roman rooms. Part of the Roman town hall, a hypocaust (an ancient design for heating rooms), and the outline of houses and shops are still visible in the park that surrounds the museum. The museum is open year-round Monday to Saturday 10am to 5:30pm and Sunday 2 to 5:30pm; admission is £3.50 for adults, £2 for seniors and children, and £9 for a family ticket. By car, Verulamium is 15 to 20 minutes from Junction 21A on the M25; it is also accessible from Junction 9 or 6 on the M1; follow the signs for St. Albans and the Roman Verulamium. A train to St. Albans City Station will put you within 3km (2 miles) of the museum.

Just a short distance from Verulamium is the **Roman Theatre** (✆ 01727/835035; www.romantheatre.co.uk). The structure is the only theater of the period that is open to visitors in Britain. You can tour the site daily between 10am and 5pm (4pm in winter). Admission is £2.50 for adults, £2 for students and seniors, and £1.50 for children.

The **Museum of St. Albans,** Hatfield Road (✆ 01727/819340; www.stalbansmuseums.org.uk), details the history of St. Albans from the departure of the Romans to the present day. It's open Monday to Saturday 10am to 5pm and Sunday 2 to 5pm. Admission is free. Located in the city center, it's a 5-minute walk from St. Albans City Station.

Batchwood's 18-hole golf course is one of the finest public courses in the country. The Batchwood Indoor Tennis Centre, which has four indoor courts plus outdoor courts, has professional coaches available for all play levels. Both the golf course and the tennis center are located on the grounds of the **Batchwood Hall Mansion,** on Batchwood Drive (© **01727/856596;** www.batchwoodhall.com).

Shopping

The twice-weekly **street market,** held every Wednesday and Saturday on St. Peters Street, is defined by its frantic pace. In contrast, modern off-street precincts and small specialty shops in St. Albans combine to create a unique, laid-back atmosphere the rest of the week.

The **Past Times Shop,** 33 Market Place (© **01727/812817;** www.pasttimes. com), sells items that cover 12 historic eras. Here you'll find books on historic places, jewelry, clothes, and CDs featuring music from a variety of time periods.

For antiques, visit **By George,** 23 George St. (© **01727/853032**). St. Albans's largest antiques center, the building also houses a tearoom and crafts arcade.

Theater Performances

St. Albans's nightlife centers on theater. The Company of Ten, with its base at the **Abbey Theatre,** Westminster Lodge, Holywell Hill (© **01727/857861;** www. abbeytheatre.org.uk), is one of the leading amateur dramatic companies in Britain. The troupe presents 10 productions each season in either the well-equipped main auditorium or a smaller studio. Performances begin at 8pm; tickets cost from £8 to £10. The box office is open Monday to Saturday 10:30am to 7pm.

Maltings Arts Theatre, in the Maltings Shopping Centre (© **01727/844222;** www.stalbans.gov.uk/mat), presents performances based on literary works ranging from Shakespeare to modern novels. Plays are generally presented only once and begin at 8:30pm on Thursday, Friday, and Saturday (there's a children's show at 3pm). Tickets are £7 to £15. The box office is open Monday to Saturday 11am to 5pm.

Side Trips from St. Albans

DeHavilland Aircraft Heritage Center   This is the oldest aircraft museum in Britain. The hall where De Havilland Aircraft Company developed the "Mosquito," known as the most versatile aircraft of World War II, is no longer open to the public. However, the museum has more than 20 types of aircraft on view, including modern military and civil jets, along with aircraft engines and other memorabilia. Several of the displays are hands-on.

On the grounds of Salisbury Hall, on the south side of the main M25 London–St. Albans Rd. © **01727/822051.** www.dehavillandmuseum.co.uk. Admission £5 adults; £4 seniors, students with ID, and children 5–16; £14 family ticket; free for children 4 and younger. Mar–Oct Tues, Thurs, and Sat 2–5:30pm; Sun and bank holidays 10:30am–5:30pm. Closed Nov–Feb. Take M25 Junction 22 at London Colney 8km (5 miles) south of St. Albans. The museum is on B556.

Hatfield House ★★★   Hatfield was a part of the lives of both Henry VIII and Elizabeth I. In the old palace, begun in 1497, Elizabeth romped and played as a child. Though Henry was married to her mother, Anne Boleyn, at the time of Elizabeth's birth, the marriage was later nullified. (Anne lost her head; Elizabeth, her legitimacy.) Henry stashed away his oldest daughter, Mary Tudor, at Hatfield. But when Mary became queen of England and set about earning the dubious distinction of "Bloody Mary," she found Elizabeth to be a problem and kept her for a while in the Tower of London, eventually letting her return to Hatfield. In 1558, Elizabeth learned of her succession to the throne of England while at Hatfield.

Only the banqueting hall of the original Tudor palace remains; the rest of the house is Jacobean. The brick-and-stone structure that exists today contains antique furniture and many tapestries and paintings, as well as three often-reproduced portraits, including the ermine and rainbow portraits of Elizabeth I. The Great Hall is suitably medieval, complete with a minstrel's gallery. One of the rarest exhibits is a pair of silk stockings, which, it is said, were worn by Elizabeth herself, the first woman in England to don such apparel. The park and the gardens are also worth exploring. Luncheons and teas are available from 11am to 5:30pm in the converted coach house.

Elizabethan banquets are staged with much gaiety and music in the banqueting hall of the Old Palace on Fridays. Guests are invited to drink in an anteroom, then share the long tables for a five-course feast with continuous entertainment from a group of Elizabethan players, minstrels, and jesters. Wine is included in the cost of the meal, but predinner drinks are not. The menu isn't particularly medieval, and you're granted the (modern-day) luxury of knives and forks. The entertainment is a bit cheesy and the banquets are very touristy, but they are packed every night. The cost of the banquet starts at £49. *Warning:* Prices fluctuate frequently. For current prices, reservations, and more information, call either the number listed below or Ⓒ **01707/262055,** or go online to www.hatfield-house.co.uk.

9.5km (6 miles) east of St. Albans on A414. Ⓒ **01707/287010** for information. www.hatfield-house. co.uk. Admission £12 adults, £11 seniors, £6 children 5–15. House daily noon–5pm; park and gardens daily 11am–5:30pm. Closed Oct–Good Friday. From St. Albans, take A414 east and follow the brown signs that lead directly to the estate. By bus, take the university bus from St. Albans City Station. Hatfield House is directly across from Hatfield Station.

Shaw's Corner 🏠 George Bernard Shaw lived here from 1906 to 1950. The utilitarian house, with its harsh brickwork and rather comfortless interior, is practically as he left it at his death. In the hall, for example, his hats are still hanging, as if ready for him to don one. Shaw wrote 6 to 8 hours a day, even when he'd reached his 90s. Evidence of his longtime relationship with the written word is obvious; one of his old typewriters is still in position. Shaw was, of course, famous for his eccentricities, his vegetarianism, and his longevity. And, of course, he was famed for his vast literary output, the most well known of which remains *Pygmalion,* on which the musical *My Fair Lady* was based.

Off Hill Farm Lane, in the village of Ayot St. Lawrence. Ⓒ **01438/820307.** www.nationaltrust.org.uk. Admission £5.50 adults, £2.75 children. Wed–Sun and bank holidays 1–5pm. Closed Nov–early Mar. From St. Albans, take B651 to Wheathampstead. Pass through the village, go right at the roundabout, and take the 1st left turn; 1.5km (1 mile) up on the left is Brides Hall Lane, which leads to the house.

WOBURN ABBEY: ENGLAND'S GREAT GEORGIAN MANOR ★★★

71km (44 miles) N of London

Aside from Windsor Castle, the most visited attraction in the Home Counties is Woburn Abbey, which is so spectacular you should try to visit even if you have to miss all the other historic homes described in this chapter. The great 18th-century

Georgian mansion has been the traditional seat of the dukes of Bedford for more than 3 centuries.

Where to Stay

Bell Hotel & Inn   This 17th-century inn is a mixture of Tudor, Georgian, and Victorian architecture. Its modernized bedrooms are small to midsize, each tastefully and comfortably furnished. The Bell Inn is convenient for touring Woburn Abbey and the safari park. A good, filling English breakfast greets you in the morning.

21 Bedford St., Woburn, Bedfordshire MK17 9QB. © **01525/290280.** Fax 01525/290017. www.bellinn-woburn.com. 24 units. £85–£95 double; £105 4-poster double. Rates include English breakfast. AE, MC, V. **Amenities:** Restaurant; bar; room service. *In room:* TV, hair dryer, Wi-Fi (free).

Inn at Woburn ★   After visiting the abbey, head here for food and lodging at the gates of the estate. This Georgian coaching inn has a checkered history that blends old and new. Tastefully modernized, it preserves a certain mellow charm. Guests are housed in one of several well-furnished and beautifully maintained rooms, which have been refurbished. A more modern block provides "executive bedrooms," which don't have the charm of the older units but are more up-to-date and comfortable.

1 George St., Woburn, Bedfordshire MK17 9PX. © **01525/290441.** Fax 01525/290432. www.theinnat woburn.com. 57 units. £135–£175 double; £190–£220 suite. Children 15 and younger stay free in parent's room. AE, DC, MC, V. **Amenities:** Restaurant; bar; concierge; room service. *In room:* TV, hair dryer, minibar.

Where to Dine

The Black Horse ENGLISH/INTERNATIONAL   Our favorite pub in Woburn opened in 1824 as a coaching inn, and it retains a dark, woodsy interior evocative of that era. It sits behind a stucco-sheathed Georgian facade on the town's main street. Accompanying the ales and lagers at lunchtime are simple pub platters, which include "filled baguettes" (sandwiches on French bread). Steaks, lasagna, a plough-man's lunch of bread and cheese, and spicy soups inspired by Thai recipes are also served. In a separate room you can order more substantial restaurant fare, including free-range chicken breast with wild mushroom sauce, braised oxtail with dumplings, or sweet potato and roasted vegetable croquettes with a tomato chutney.

1 Bedford St. © **01525/290210.** www.blackhorsewoburn.co.uk. Main courses £10–£16. AE, MC, V. Daily noon–3pm and 6–9:45pm.

Magpies Hotel ENGLISH   After your visit to Woburn Abbey (see below), head to the Magpies for food and drink. This is a small, family-run pub housed in a 16th-century former coaching inn near the Woburn Golf Club. The beers of choice are Ruddles Best, Webster's, and Marston's Pedigree. The food is fresh, good, and filling fare, including well-stuffed sandwiches and a ploughman's lunch of bread and cheese. More substantial meals include lamb shank cooked in red wine or sirloin steak in a peppercorn sauce. Another specialty is spicy green chicken curry cooked in coconut milk. There is also a separate room for dining, plus a courtyard with tables where guests can eat and drink outside in fair weather.

18 Bedford St. © **01525/290219.** www.magpieshotel.co.uk. Bar lunches and sandwiches £6.95–£10; main courses £6.75–£13. MC, V. Mon–Fri noon–2pm; Sat noon–2:30pm; Sun 11:30am–2:30pm; daily 6:30–9:30pm.

Touring the Estate

Woburn Abbey ★★★ In the 1950s, the present duke of Bedford opened Woburn Abbey to the public to pay off his debt of millions of pounds in inheritance taxes. In 1974, he turned over the estate to his son and daughter-in-law, the marquess and marchioness of Tavistock, who reluctantly took on the business of running the 75-room mansion. And what a business it is, today drawing hundreds of thousands of visitors a year and employing more than 300 people to staff the shops and grounds.

Its state apartments are rich in furniture, porcelain, tapestries, silver, and a valuable art collection, including paintings by Van Dyck, Holbein, Rembrandt, Gainsborough, and Reynolds. One of the most notable paintings is the Armada Portrait of Elizabeth I. Her hand rests on the globe, as Philip's invincible armada perishes in the background.

Queen Victoria and Prince Albert visited Woburn Abbey in 1841; Victoria's dressing room displays a fine collection of 17th-century paintings from the Netherlands. Among the oddities and treasures at Woburn Abbey are a grotto of shells, a Sèvres dinner service (gift of Louis XV), and a chamber devoted to memorabilia of "the Flying Duchess," the wife of the 11th duke of Bedford, a remarkable woman who disappeared on a solo flight in 1937 (coincidentally, the same year as Amelia Earhart). The duchess was 72 years old at the time.

Today, Woburn Abbey is surrounded by a 1,214-hectare (3,000-acre) deer park, including the famous Père David deer herd, which was originally from China and saved from extinction at Woburn. The **Woburn Safari Park** has lions, tigers, giraffes, camels, monkeys, Przewalski's horses, bongos, and other animals.

1km (½ mile) southeast of the village of Woburn, which is 21km (13 miles) southwest of Bedford. ✆ **01525/292148.** www.woburnabbey.co.uk. Admission £12 adults, £9 seniors, £5 children 3-15. House Apr–Sept daily 11am–5pm (3pm in winter); park daily 10am–4:30pm. In summer, travel agents can book you on organized coach tours out of London. Otherwise, if driving, take M1 north to Junction 12 or 13, where directions are signposted.

Nearby Shopping & Afternoon Tea

In a wonderful old building, **Town Hall Antiques,** Market Place (✆ **01525/290950;** www.townhallantiques.co.uk), is a treasure trove of collectibles and antiques, including Early English porcelain and pieces from the 1940s. Some unusual commemorative items are also sold, such as an array of Victorian, Georgian, and Edwardian memorabilia. There's something here to suit a wide range of pocketbooks, including clocks, Victorian jewelry, brass, copper, "kitchenalia," paintings (originals and reproductions), guns, and swords.

At teatime, head to **Capriocoli,** 15 Market Place (✆ **01525/290464**); it's inside a B&B with low-beamed ceilings that add to its intimacy and charm. A pot of tea with clotted cream and cake is £3.50. Baked goods include scones (chocolate, lemon, and Victoria sponge), Italian pastries, and cake (carrot, coffee, and fruit), as well as daily specials. The tearoom is open Tuesday to Sunday 10am to 5pm, but it's a good idea to call on weekends between January and Easter, as it may be closed if business is slow.

KENT, SURREY & SUSSEX: THE GARDEN OF ENGLAND

8

South and southeast of London are the shires (counties) of Kent, Surrey, and East and West Sussex. Traditionally, this is a playground used by Londoners for quick holiday breaks, often weekend jaunts.

In **Kent,** the major highlight is **Canterbury,** which makes the best base for exploring the area. Another convenient option is **Dover,** Britain's historic gateway to the Continent and famed for its white cliffs. Though Kent is on London's fringe, it's far removed in spirit and scenery. Since the days of the Tudors, cherry blossoms have enlivened the fertile landscape. Orchards and hop fields abound, earning Kent its title, "garden of England"—and in England, that's tough competition. Kent suffered severe destruction during World War II, as it was the alley over which the Luftwaffe flew in its Blitz of London. But despite much devastation, it's still filled with interesting old towns and castles.

In fact, Kent has some of Europe's grandest mansions. If time is limited, seek out the big four: **Knole,** one of the largest private houses of England, a great example of Tudor architecture; **Hever Castle,** dating from the end of the 13th century, a gift from Henry VIII to the "great Flanders mare," Anne of Cleves; **Penshurst Place,** a magnificent English Gothic mansion and one of the outstanding country houses of Britain; and lovely **Leeds Castle,** near Maidstone, dating from A.D. 857. Although it doesn't compare with these grand castles, **Chartwell** also merits a visit because of the man who used to call it home: Sir Winston Churchill. For more advice on how to tour these homes, refer to "Kent's Country Houses, Castles & Gardens," later in this chapter.

With the continuing expansion of London's borders, it's a wonder that the tiny county of **Surrey** hasn't been gobbled up and turned into a sprawling suburb. Yet its countryside remains unspoiled, though many people commute from here to London (only about 45–60 min. away).

If King Harold hadn't loved **Sussex** so much, English history might have been changed forever. Had the brave Saxon waited longer in the

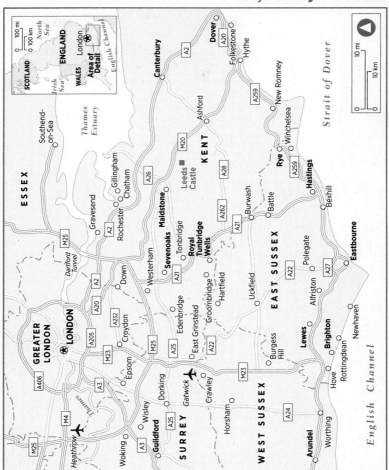

north, he could have marshaled more adequate reinforcements before striking south to meet the Normans. But Duke William's soldiers were ravaging the countryside he knew so well, and Harold rushed down to counter them.

Harold's enthusiasm for Sussex is understandable. The landscape rises and falls like waves. The county is known for its woodlands, from which came the timbers to build England's mighty fleet in days gone by. The shires lie south of London and Surrey, bordering Kent in the east, Hampshire in the west, and opening directly onto the English Channel, where the coast is dotted with seaside towns.

Like other sections in the vulnerable south of England, Sussex was the setting of some of the most significant events in English history. Apart from the Norman landings at **Hastings,** the most life-changing transformation occurred in the 19th century, as middle-class Victorians flocked to the seashore, pumping new spirit into **Brighton** and even old Hastings.

The old towns and villages of Sussex, particularly **Rye** and **Winchelsea,** are far more intriguing than the seaside resorts. No Sussex village is lovelier than **Alfriston** (and the innkeepers know it, too); **Arundel** is noted for its castle; and the cathedral city of **Chichester** is a mecca for theater buffs. The old market town of **Battle** was the setting for the Battle of Hastings in 1066.

Where to base yourself in Sussex? The best option is Brighton, because it has a wide choice of hotels, restaurants, and nightclubs. There's more excitement here at "London by the Sea" than at Hastings. If you're seeking old-English charm and village life, head instead to Alfriston or Rye.

CANTERBURY ★★★

90km (56 miles) SE of London

Under the arch of the ancient West Gate journeyed Chaucer's knight, solicitor, nun, squire, parson, merchant, miller, and others—spinning tales. They were bound for the shrine of Thomas à Becket, archbishop of Canterbury, who was slain by four knights of Henry II on December 29, 1170. (The king later walked barefoot from Harbledown to the tomb of his former friend, where he allowed himself to be flogged in penance.) The shrine was finally torn down in 1538 by Henry VIII, as part of his campaign to destroy the monasteries and graven images. But Canterbury, by then, had already become an attraction.

The medieval Kentish city on the River Stour is the ecclesiastical capital of England. Once completely walled, many traces of its old fortifications remain. Canterbury was inhabited centuries before the birth of Jesus Christ. Although its most famous incident was the murder of Becket, the medieval city witnessed other major events in English history, including Bloody Mary's order to burn nearly 40 victims at the stake. Richard the Lion-Hearted returned this way from crusading, and Charles II passed through on the way to claim his crown.

Canterbury "pilgrims" continue to arrive today, except now they're called daytrippers and they overrun the city and its monuments. Because it lay in the pathways of bombers heading for London during the Nazi Blitz of 1941, historic Canterbury suffered enormous damage to its center. After the war, there was some attempt at restoration, but the city no longer has its wonderful prewar medieval look. Yet there is much still left to intrigue today's visitor, who can easily spend a day here. The city has an active university life—mainly students from Kent—and an enormous number of pubs. Its High Street is filled with shoppers in from the country. We suggest exploring Canterbury in the early morning or the early evening, after the busloads have departed.

Essentials

GETTING THERE   Frequent train service arrives from Victoria, Charing Cross, Waterloo, and London Bridge stations. The journey takes 1½ hours. For rail information, call ℂ **0845/748-4950** or visit **www.nationalrail.co.uk**.

8

North Sea

SCOTLAND

Irish Sea

ENGLAND

London

Canterbury

WALES

English Channel

100 mi

0 100 km

200 yds

0

200 m

i Information

Chaucer Rd.

Tourtel Rd.

A 28

St. Gregory's Rd.

Edgar Rd.

College Rd.

North Holmes Rd.

Canterbury Prison

Longport

St. Augustine's Rd.

Pilgrim's Way

Spring Ln.

St. Martin's Hill

Military Rd.

Union St.

Victoria Row

Northgate

Old Ruttington Ln.

Havelock St.

Monastery St.

Christchurch College

Lower Chantry Ln.

Ivy Ln.

11

New Dover Rd.

A 2050

Cossington Rd.

River Stour

St. Radigund St.

Mill Ln.

Blackfriars

Pound Ln.

North Ln.

The Friars

St. Peter's Ln.

Palace St.

King St.

Sun St.

High St.

Broad St.

Lower Bridge St.

City Walls

The King's School

4

3

Burgate

St. Mary Magdelene's Tower

8

9

10

Parade

Dover St.

St. George's Pl.

13

12

Vernon Pl.

Upper Bridge St.

Bus Station

Oaten Hill

Old Dover Rd.

Landsdown Rd.

14

St. Peter's Grove

Black Griffin Ln.

St. Peter's Place

Greyfriars

6

6

7

i

St. Margaret's St.

Beer Cart Ln.

Rose Ln.

Marlowe Ave.

Stour St.

Castle St.

City Walls

Rhodaus Town

5

Dane John Mound

Pin Hill

Rhodaus Cl.

Whitehall Rd.

Station Rd.

Kirby's Ln.

2

Station Rd.

Canterbury West Station

Gas St.

Canterbury East Station

Gordon Rd.

Tudor Rd.

Winchcap

York Rd.

Rheims Way

Queens Ave.

Rheims Way

London Rd.

St. Dunstan's St.

Orchard St.

St. Dunstan's Ter.

A 2050

1

ATTRACTIONS ●
Canterbury Cathedral **4**
Canterbury Roman
Museum **9**
The Canterbury Tales **7**
Museum of Canterbury **5**
St. Augustine's Abbey **11**

ACCOMMODATIONS ■
ABode Canterbury **6**
Cathedral Gate Hotel **8**
Chaucer Hotel **12**
Ebury Hotel **13**
Falstaff Hotel **2**
Yorke Lodge **1**

DINING ◆
Café Mauresque **10**
Duck Inn **14**
Michael Caines Restaurant
at ABode **6**
Osteria Posillipo **3**

The bus from Victoria Coach Station takes 1½ to 2 hours and leaves every hour. For schedules, call 🕾 **0871/781-81-78** or visit **www.nationalexpress.com**.

If you're driving from London, take the A2, and then the M2. Canterbury is sign-posted all the way. The city center is closed to cars, but it's only a short walk from several parking areas to the cathedral.

VISITOR INFORMATION   A few doors from St. Margaret's Church, the **Canterbury Tourist Information Centre,** 12–13 Sun St. (🕾 **01227/378100;** www. canterbury.co.uk), is generally open Monday to Saturday 9:30am to 5pm (to 4pm off-season).

GETTING AROUND BY BIKE   Using your credit card as a security deposit, you can arrange rentals at **Downland Cycle Hire,** St. Stephens Road (🕾 **01227/ 479643;** www.downlandcycles.co.uk), which charges from £15 per day.

Where to Stay

In spite of all its fame as a tourist destination, Canterbury still lacks a really first-class hotel. What you get isn't bad, but it's not state-of-the-art.

MODERATE

ABode Canterbury ★★   This hotel has been around since the end of Victoria's reign, with a recorded history dating from 1588. But never in its life has it been such a fine bastion of comfort and class, thanks to its takeover by the ABode hotel chain. Lying inside the ancient city walls and within minutes of the cathedral, ABode's location is one of the best in town. All of the bedrooms accent luxury with comfortable, tasteful furnishings. Rooms are amusingly ranked "desirable" (impossible to resist); "enviable" (sinfully self-indulgent), and "fabulous" (the ultimate in ABode luxury). The hotel's Michael Caines Restaurant is Canterbury's finest choice for dining (p. 284).

High St., Canterbury, Kent CT1 2RX. 🕾 **01227/766266.** Fax 01227/784874. www.abodehotels.co.uk. 72 units. £99–£185 double; from £295 suite. AE, DC, MC, V. Parking £5. **Amenities:** Restaurant; bar; babysitting; exercise room; room service. *In room:* TV/DVD, hair dryer, Wi-Fi (free).

Chaucer Hotel ★   Located on a historic street, the Chaucer Hotel is in a Georgian house a few minutes' walk from the cathedral. Comfortably furnished rooms lie at the end of a labyrinth of stairs, narrow hallways, and doors. (The hotel staff carries your luggage and parks your car.) The best rooms, with views over Canterbury rooftops and the cathedral, are nos. 60, 61, and 65. All rooms, however, are named in a wonderfully quirky way that honors former archbishops as well as some of Chaucer's racier pilgrims. Units range from midsize to most spacious, each chamber evoking a country inn. The most elegant room is no. 20, the honeymoon chamber with a Henry VIII–style four-poster bed. If you'd like to share a room with a ghost, book no. 62.

63 Ivy Lane (off Lower Bridge St.), Canterbury, Kent CT1 1TU. 🕾 **01227/464427.** Fax 01227/450397. www.swallow-hotels.com. 42 units. £94–£114 double. AE, MC, V. Free parking. **Amenities:** Restaurant; bar; babysitting; room service. *In room:* A/C, TV, hair dryer, minibar.

Ebury Hotel ★ 🍴   One of the finest small inns in Canterbury, this gabled Victorian house stands on .8 hectares (2 acres) of gardens at the city's edge, easy walking distance from the city center. Built in 1850, it's composed of two separate houses that were joined several years ago; the management also rents flats on a weekly basis. Accommodations are roomy and pleasantly decorated. The rooms, ranging from small to medium, are constantly being refurbished. *Note:* Rooms fill up quickly, so it's important to reserve in advance.

65-67 New Dover Rd., Canterbury, Kent CT1 3DX. ℂ **01227/768433.** Fax 01227/459187. www.ebury-hotel.co.uk. 15 units. £95–£150 double; £125–£155 family room. Rates include English breakfast. AE, MC, V. Free parking. Closed Dec 23 to mid-Jan. Follow the signs to A2, Dover Rd., on left-hand side, south of the city. **Amenities:** Restaurant; bar; Jacuzzi; indoor heated pool; room service. *In room:* TV, hair dryer, Wi-Fi (£5 per 24 hr.).

Falstaff Hotel   Just 360m (1,200 ft.) from the West Station, this classic Canterbury choice, complete with a flagstone-covered courtyard, retains its sense of history. Next to the Westgate Tower, it has a parking lot and easy access to the M2 and the M20. Many of the small, cozy rooms evoke old England with their polished oak tables, leaded-glass windows, and original ceiling beams; most have solid modern furniture. Some units are spacious enough to accommodate small families. Accommodations in the main building are more traditional with wood beams, whereas those in the other two annexes are more contemporary in styling. Public rooms are as cozy as the bedrooms, and you can relax in a comfortable lounge.

8-10 St. Dunstan's St., Canterbury, Kent CT2 8AF. ℂ **01227/462138.** Fax 01227/463525. www.thefalstaffincanterbury.com. 46 units. £75–£130 double. Rates include English breakfast. AE, DC, MC, V. Free parking. **Amenities:** Restaurant; bar; room service. *In room:* TV, hair dryer, Wi-Fi (£5 per 24 hr.).

Yorke Lodge ★ 🍴   Built in 1888, this former private residence has been turned into one of the best stopovers in Canterbury. Lying on the fringe of the city, this large Victorian manse is a government-rated, five-star B&B. Facilities include an elegant breakfast room opening onto a conservatory and sun terrace. Each of the immaculate bedrooms is individually decorated. Resident owners Wayne and Vicky O'Shea are among the most hospitable hosts in town.

50 London Rd., Canterbury, Kent CT2 8LF. ℂ **01227/451242.** www.yorkelodge.com. 8 units. £85–£110 double. MC, V. Free parking. *In room:* TV, hair dryer, Wi-Fi (free).

INEXPENSIVE

Cathedral Gate Hotel   For those who want to stay close to the cathedral and perhaps have a view of it, this is the choice. Built in 1438, adjoining Christchurch Gate and overlooking the Buttermarket, this former hospice was one of the first fashionable teahouses in England in the early 1600s, and the interior reveals many little architectural details of that century. Rooms are modestly furnished, with sloping floors and massive oak beams. You'll sleep better than the former pilgrims who often stopped over here—and sometimes crowded as many as six to eight in a bed.

36 Burgate, Canterbury, Kent CT1 2HA. ℂ **01227/464381.** Fax 01227/462800. www.cathgate.co.uk. 25 units, 12 with bathroom (shower only). £62–£74 double without bathroom, £103 with bathroom. Rates include English breakfast. AE, DC, MC, V. Parking £5 nearby. **Amenities:** Restaurant; bar; room service. *In room:* TV, hair dryer.

Where to Dine

Café Mauresque ★ 🍴 SPANISH/MOROCCAN   A touch of exotica and the aura of the souk are brought to Canterbury with the opening of this cafe/restaurant that not only serves the tastiest sandwiches in town but also offers the best tapas. Sandwiches feature the likes of Serrano lamb and manchego cheese flavored with saffron aioli. You can also order such delights as a salad of barbecued squid stuffed with chorizo, cherry tomatoes, and olives. A *salon de thé,* or tea salon, also operates daily from midday to 5pm, serving a good selection of delicious tarts and homemade cakes along with mint tea or coffee. As to be expected, couscous and tagines are the specialties. One of the most delightful of the tagines is duck with honey-glazed squash, almonds, sultanas, and cinnamon, although the lamb shank with baby eggplant and dates flavored with ginger was almost as delectable. The orange-and-almond cake makes a tasty dessert.

8 Butchery Lane. © **1227/464300.** www.cafemauresque.com. Reservations recommended. Main courses £9.50–£17; tapas £2.95–£4.95; lunch sandwiches £5.95–£6.95. AC, DC, MC, V. Daily 10am–10pm.

Duck Inn ★ 🍴 ENGLISH/MEDITERRANEAN   Once called the Woodsmen Arms, this restaurant is known as the Duck Inn because of its low door. (As you entered, the clientele would shout "Duck!") It's set within a 16th-century building that once belonged to the grandmother of novelist Ian Fleming, author of the James Bond series (he wrote the first draft of *You Only Live Twice* within its garden). From its kitchens emerge a combination of old-fashioned English country fare—steak-and-kidney pudding, cod filets with chips, and Mediterranean food such as mussels in white wine and pesto-flavored pasta. Blackboards list the various, and frequently changing, specials of the day. In summer, the garden offers seating outdoors, but throughout the rest of the year, most visitors prefer the timbered nostalgia-laden interior.

Pett Bottom, near Bridge. © **1227/830354.** Reservations recommended. Main courses £7–£13. AE, DC, MC, V. Tues–Fri noon–3pm and 6–11pm; Sat–Sun noon–11pm. Drive 8km (5 miles) outside Canterbury near the village of Bridge on the road to Dover.

Michael Caines Restaurant at ABode Canterbury ★★★ ENGLISH/CONTINENTAL   At long last, Canterbury has a deluxe restaurant serving a light, elegant cuisine. The beautifully designed restaurant forms the centerpiece of the town's top-ranked hotel. Although modernized, it maintains a classic elegance. The chefs secure the best of local ingredients from the "garden of England," as Kent is called, and their cooking style is not overly adorned so as to mask natural flavors. Their larder also branches out to include Sussex beef and Romney Marsh lamb plus shellfish from Whitstable (especially those delectable oysters). Appetizers include herb-crusted filet of halibut with lyonnaise potatoes or fresh green-bean soup scented with smoked bacon and white truffle oil, followed by such mains as roast partridge with braised chicory and quince puree or slow-cooked organic salmon with dill and a wasabi Greek yogurt.

In the ABode Canterbury hotel, High St. © **1277/826684.** www.abodehotels.co.uk or www.michael caines.com. Reservations required. Main courses £19–£25. AE, DC, MC, V. Mon–Sat noon–2:30pm and 7–10pm; Sun 12:30–2:30pm.

Osteria Posillipo ★ ITALIAN   This trattoria is a bastion of zesty Italian cookery. Some dishes are standard, including the pastas, beef, and veal found on most Italian menus, but the daily specials have a creative flair and are based on the freshest ingredients available that day. Some of the best starters include fresh mussels in white-wine sauce or bruschetta topped with garlic, basil, and fresh tomatoes. Among the tasty mains are mixed seafood and shellfish in a white wine and cherry tomato sauce or chargrilled rib-eye steak with Parmesan shavings and balsamic vinegar.

16 The Borough. © **1227/761471** or 1227/784924. www.posillipo.co.uk. Reservations recommended, especially at lunch. Main courses £8.95–£15. AE, MC, V. Daily noon–3pm and 6–11pm. Closed last 2 weeks in Aug.

Seeing the Sights

Canterbury Cathedral ★★★   The foundation of this splendid cathedral dates from A.D. 597, but the earliest part of the present building is the great Romanesque crypt built around A.D. 1100. The monastic quire erected on top of this at the same time was destroyed by fire in 1174, only 4 years after the murder of Thomas à Becket on a dark December evening in the northwest transept, which is still one of the most famous places of pilgrimage in Europe. The destroyed quire was immediately replaced by a magnificent early Gothic one, the first major expression of that architectural style in England.

Frankly, the exterior of the cathedral is more impressive than the interior, which is surprising since this is the mother church of Anglican Christianity and the seat of the archbishop of Canterbury. The landmark 72m (235-ft.) **Bell Harry Tower ★★**, completed in 1505, is the most distinctive feature of the building. You enter through the ornate **Christ Church Gate ★** from the early 16th century.

Inside, you wander into a stage setting that evokes T. S. Eliot's play *Murder in the Cathedral.* Our favorite architectural fantasies are the fan-vaulted colonnades of the **Great Cloister ★** on the northern flank of the building. From the cloister you can enter the **Chapter House,** with its magnificent web of intricate tracery from the 1300s. This architectural ensemble supports the roof and a wall of stained glass, depicting scenes from Becket's tragic life.

Perpendicular arches support intricate fan vaulting from the 1400s at the crossing of the nave and transepts, creating architectural drama under the Bell Harry Tower. Look for the slender shafts of columns that rise without interruption into the high vault.

The lofty aisles were meant to provoke awe in the Canterbury pilgrim. Abundant light floods in from windows designed to create an air of tranquillity, although that is shattered by the thousands of visitors who descend every day.

The cathedral is noteworthy for its medieval tombs of royal personages, such as King Henry IV and Edward the Black Prince. Prince Edward of England was the eldest son of Edward III and the father of Richard II. Prince Edward was one of England's ablest military commanders during the Hundred Years' War. His nickname was probably derived from the color of his armor, but nobody knows for sure.

To the later Middle Ages belong the great 14th-century nave and the Bell Harry Tower. The cathedral stands on spacious precincts amid the remains of the buildings of the monastery—cloisters, chapter house, and Norman water tower—which have survived intact from Henry VIII's Dissolution.

Becket's shrine was destroyed by the Tudor king, but the site of that tomb is in Trinity Chapel, near the high altar. The saint is said to have worked miracles, and the cathedral has some rare stained glass depicting those feats.

But the most miraculous event is that the windows escaped Henry VIII's agents of destruction as well as Hitler's bombs. The windows were removed as a precaution at the beginning of the war. During the war, a large area of Canterbury was flattened, but the main body of the church was unharmed. However, the cathedral library was damaged during a German air raid in 1942. The replacement windows of the cathedral were blown in, which proved the wisdom of having the medieval glass safely stored away.

Insider's tip: We prefer to visit the cathedral at Evensong, when you can hear beautiful cathedral music played. Performances are Monday to Friday at 4:30pm and Saturday and Sunday at 2:30pm. Admission is free for Evensong, but you must tell the warder at the gate that you'd like to attend a performance; otherwise you'll be charged an entrance fee. You can also rent a 40-minute audio tour—one of the best of any cathedral in England—costing £4 for adults or £3 for students and seniors.

11 The Precincts. © **01227/762862.** www.canterbury-cathedral.org. Admission £7–£7.50 adults; £5.50–£6.50 students, seniors, and children. Guided tours £5 adults, £4 students and children. Easter–Sept 30 Mon–Sat 9am–5pm; Oct 1–Easter Monday–Sat 9am–4:30pm; year-round Sun 12:30–2pm. No guided tours on Sun.

Canterbury Roman Museum This museum is located beneath street level and is constructed around actual archaeological excavations. Interactive computer shows and the actual handling of Roman artifacts bring the past to life for all ages. The Roman town of Durovernum Cantiacorum was established shortly after Emperor Claudius's invasion of the area in A.D. 43 and continued to flourish for nearly 400 years. Visitors can follow the archaeologists' detective work through an excavated Roman house site containing patterned mosaics that were discovered after the wartime bombing. Other exhibits include the reconstruction of a Roman marketplace.

Butchery Lane. © **01227/785575.** www.canterbury.gov.uk. Admission £3 adults; £2 students, seniors, and children; £8 family ticket. Year-round Mon–Sat 10am–5pm; June–Oct Sun 1:30–5pm. Last admission 4pm. Closed Christmas week and Good Friday.

The Canterbury Tales 👆 This is a rather cheesy, yet very popular, commercial attraction. You might give it a try if you're hard up for something to do. Visitors are handed headsets with earphones, which give oral recitations of five of Chaucer's *Canterbury Tales* and the murder of St. Thomas à Becket. Audiovisual aids bring famous characters to life, and stories of jealousy, pride, avarice, and love are recounted. The sideshow re-creates the pilgrimages of Chaucerian England through a series of medieval tableaux that children might find a bit scary (and that older visitors may find a little boring). A tour of all exhibits takes about an hour.

23 St. Margaret's St. (off High St., near the cathedral). © **01227/479227.** www.canterburytales.org.uk. Admission £7.75 adults, £6.75 students and seniors, £5.75 children 5–15, free for children 4 and younger. Mar–June and Sept–Oct daily 10am–5pm; July–Aug daily 9:30am–5pm; Nov–Feb daily.10am–4:30pm.

Museum of Canterbury ☺ Set in the ancient Poor Priests' Hospital with its medieval interiors and soaring oak roofs, the museum features award-winning displays that showcase the best of the city's treasures and lead visitors through crucial moments that have shaped Canterbury's history. State-of-the-art video, computer, and hologram technology transports visitors back in time to such events as the Viking raids and the wartime Blitz. Collections include a huge display of pilgrim badges from medieval souvenir shops. Kids will love the Rupert Bear Gallery, a children's museum centered on a toy bear, Rupert, and his chums. Little ones can do everything from watch Paul McCartney videos to play with toy giant snakes, even attend Rupert's tea party.

Stour St. © **01227/475202.** Admission £3.60 adults; £2.30 students, seniors, and children; £9.20 family ticket. Year-round Mon–Sat 10:30am–5pm; June–Sept Sun 1:30–5pm. Last admission 4pm. Closed Christmas week and Good Friday.

St. Augustine's Abbey ★★ One of the most historic religious centers in the country, only its ruins remain, mostly at ground level. Augustine was buried here. (Augustine is not to be confused with the also-famous St. Augustine of Hippo, who is sometimes known as "Augustine the African.") In an attempt to convert the Saxons, Pope Gregory I sent Augustine to England in 597. Ethelbert, the Saxon King, allowed Augustine and his followers to build a church outside the city walls, and it endured until Henry VIII tore it down. In its day, the abbey church rivaled the cathedral in size, and enough of the ruins remain to conjure the whole of the cloister, church, and refectory.

The ruins are in a grassy field, so the average visitor who doesn't have a particular interest or who doesn't know the history may want to look elsewhere. Adjacent to the remains are the abbey buildings that were converted into a royal palace by Henry VIII and used briefly by several monarchs, including Elizabeth I and Charles I.

Corner of Lower Chantry Lane and Longport Rd. ✆ **01227/767345.** www.english-heritage.org.uk. Admission £4.40 adults, £3.80 students and seniors, £2.30 children. Mar 21–June 30 Wed–Sun 10am–5pm; July–Aug daily 10am–6pm; Sept–Mar 20 Sat–Sun 11am–5pm. Closed Dec 24–26 and Jan 1.

Walking & Boat Tours

Daily guided walking tours are organized by **Canterbury Tourist Guides** (formerly known as the Guild of Guides; ✆ **01227/459779;** www.canterbury-walks.co.uk), costing £6 for adults, £5.50 for students and seniors, £4.25 for children 11 and younger, and £16 for a family ticket. The cold stones of Canterbury take on new life as you take this tour, often conducted by witty and insightful guides. Meet at the Tourist Information Centre, 12–13 Sun St. At press time, tours leave daily at 11am, with an additional 2pm tour offered July through September and during bank and school holidays. Call for the latest details.

From just below the Weavers House, **Canterbury Historic River Tours** (✆ **07790/534744;** www.canterburyrivertours.co.uk) operates 40-minute boat trips with commentary on the history of the buildings you pass. We recommend these boat tours, even if you've taken the walking tour. They can be a lot of fun and they let you see Canterbury from a different perspective—that is, from the water. Prices are £7.50 for adults, £6.50 for seniors and students, £5 for children 12 to 16, and £4.50 for children under 12. Tours leave March through October daily from 10am to 5pm, with departures every 15 to 20 minutes.

Horseback Riding

The **Bursted Manor Riding Centre,** in Pett Bottom (✆ **01227/830568;** www.burstedmanor.co.uk), is open Tuesday to Sunday 9am to 6pm. On Saturday and Sunday, the last lesson is at 5pm. A 1-hour group lesson or hack ride is available for £35. The location is 4.5km (2¾ miles) southeast of Canterbury.

Shopping

Handmade pottery—vases, mugs, and teapots in earth colors of blues, greens, and browns—is sold at **Canterbury Pottery,** 38A Burgate, just before Mercury Lane (✆ **01227/452608;** www.canterburypottery.co.uk). This is sturdy ware that wears well. House-number plates take 2 weeks to complete but can be mailed to your home.

The World of Charles Dickens Lives Again

In the town of Chatham, where Charles Dickens spent part of his childhood, **Dickens World** has opened at Leviathan Way (© 01634/890-421; www.dickens world.co.uk). The town also holds a Dickens Festival every summer to honor the author of *A Christmas Carol*.

At this theme park, the cobbled streets of Victorian England are peopled once again by pickpockets, wenches, rogues, and runaways, but it's all in fun. Visitors will have a chance to see the Ghost of Christmas Past in Ebenezer Scrooge's haunted house, be hectored by a schoolmaster at Dothe-

boxs Hall, and peer into the fetid cells of the notorious Newgate Prison. Expect more than a whiff of kitsch, and know that Dickens purists will be offended.

The location is 56km (35 miles) southwest of London following the A2/M2; exit at Junction 1, 3, or 4. Trains from Victoria Station also go to Chatham Station, where a shuttle bus will take you to the theme park for £1. Open daily 10am to 5pm, the park charges £12 for adults, £10 for seniors, and £7.30 for children 5 to 15.

Put on your tweed jacket and grab your pipe for a trip to the **Chaucer Bookshop,** 6–7 Beer Cart Lane (© 01227/453912; www.chaucer-bookshop.co.uk), which sells first editions (both old and modern), out-of-print books, special leatherbound editions, and a large selection of local history books.

Canterbury After Dark

Gulbenkian Theatre, University of Kent, Giles Lane (© 01227/769075; www.kent.ac.uk/gulbenkian), is open from 11am to 5pm during school terms and 5:30 to 9pm on Saturday and Sunday. It offers a potpourri of jazz and classical productions, dance, drama, comedy, and a mix of new and student productions. The highlight of the theater season occurs at Cricket Week during the first week of August. Tickets cost £1 to £20. The location is too far from the center of Canterbury to walk to—you need to drive or take a taxi.

Marlowe Theatre, the Friars (© 01227/787787; www.marlowetheatre.com), is Canterbury's only commercial playhouse. It's open year-round and offers drama, jazz and classical concerts, along with contemporary dance and classical ballet. Tickets cost £10 to £40. The box office at Marlowe Theatre is open Monday to Saturday 10am to 9pm (Tues from 10:30am), though it closes at 7pm on nonperformance nights. Most shows begin at 7:30pm.

A favorite local pub, **Alberry's Wine Bar,** 38 St. Margaret's St. (© 01227/452378; www.alberrys.co.uk), offers a clubby atmosphere every night with a DJ spinning hiphop, drum and bass, or chart music. The cover is £5 after 9pm Tuesday to Thursday and after 10pm on Friday and Saturday.

A laid-back student hangout, the **Cherry Tree,** 10 White Horse Lane (© 01227/451266), offers a wide selection of beers, including Bass Ale on draft, Cherry Tree ale, three traditional lagers, and four bitters. It's a good spot for casual conversation.

THE WHITE CLIFFS OF DOVER

122km (76 miles) SE of London; 135km (84 miles) NE of Brighton

In Victoria's day, Dover was popular as a seaside resort; today it's known as a port for cross-Channel car and passenger traffic between England and France (notably Calais). Because it was one of England's most vulnerable and easy-to-hit targets during World War II, repeated bombings destroyed much of its harbor. The opening of the Channel Tunnel (Chunnel) in 1994 renewed Dover's importance.

Essentials

GETTING THERE   Frequent trains run from London's Victoria Station or Charing Cross Station, daily from 5am to 10pm. You arrive at Priory Station, off Folkestone Road. During the day, two trains per hour depart from Canterbury East Station heading for Dover. For rail information, call ℂ **0845/748-4950** or visit **www.nationalrail.co.uk**.

Frequent Dover-bound buses leave throughout the day—from 7am to 11:45pm daily—from London's Victoria Coach Station. For schedules, call ℂ **0871/781-81-78** or visit **www.nationalexpress.com**. The local bus station is on Pencester Road (no phone). **Stagecoach** provides daily bus service between Canterbury and Dover.

If you're driving from London, head first to Canterbury (see "Essentials" in section 1), and then continue along the A2 southeast until you reach Dover on the coast.

VISITOR INFORMATION   The **Tourist Information Centre** is on Old Town Gaol Street (ℂ **01304/205108;** www.whitecliffscountry.org.uk). It's open June through August, daily 9am to 5:30pm; the rest of the year, Monday to Friday 9am to 5:30pm, Saturday and Sunday 10am to 4pm.

Where to Stay

East Lee Guest House   This restored Victorian house, the former home of a local artist, William Henry East, who lived here in the 19th century, has been tastefully restored and turned into a welcoming B&B for those arriving from or heading to the Continent. Within walking distance of the town center, the house is often filled with cruise passengers. Your resident hosts, Patricia and Michael Knight, are among the most helpful in the city, and staying here is like living in a private home. Bedrooms are immaculately and cozily furnished. A traditional English breakfast is served in the elegant dining room.

108 Maison Dieu Rd., Dover, Kent CT16 1RT. ℂ **01304/210176.** Fax 01304/206705. www.eastlee.co.uk. 4 units. £60–£65 double. Rates include English breakfast. MC, V. **Amenities:** Breakfast room. *In room:* TV, hair dryer.

Number One Guest House   This terraced Victorian residence, completely restored, is one of the better choices in town for cruise passengers spending a night in Dover. The hosts are used to early departures around here. Established and run by the Reidy family for 25 years, the house is cozily furnished and decorated for the most part in the Victorian style. Bedrooms are well furnished, most comfortably, with antique pine pieces. The location is close to the town center and below Dover Castle.

1 Castle St., Dover, Kent CT16 1HQ. ℂ **01304/202007.** Fax 01304/214078. www.number1guesthouse.co.uk. 4 units. £54–£60 double; £60–£65 triple; £65–£75 family room. MC, V. Parking: £3. **Amenities:** Breakfast room. *In room:* TV, hair dryer.

Ramada Dover   Situated 5km (3 miles) north of Dover's center, within a semi-industrial maze of superhighways and greenbelts, the property was originally custom-built as a motel in the 1970s. Bedrooms are carefully positioned so that most of them overlook lawns (and a view of the motorway), fields, and a children's playground next door. Each room is functional and comfortable.

Singledge Lane, Whitfield, Dover, Kent CT16 3LF. © **01304/821230.** Fax 01304/825576. www.ramada dover.co.uk. 68 units. £59 double; £89–£143 suite. AE, MC, V. Free parking. Located adjacent to the Whitfield exit of the A2 motorway. **Amenities:** Restaurant; bar; babysitting; exercise room; room service. *In room:* TV, hair dryer, minibar, Wi-Fi (free).

Wallett's Court ★ 🎁   Surrounded by fields and gardens in a tiny hamlet 2.5km (1½ miles) east of Dover, this is our preferred stopover in the area. The setting, near cliff tops overlooking the English Channel, is savored by bird-watchers and hill climbers. Rebuilt in the Tudor style in the 1400s, the property rests on a foundation dating from the time of the Norman Conquest of England. In 1975, it was in seriously dilapidated condition until members of the Oakley family bought and restored it. Each carefully restored bedroom features a different decorative theme, with the more expensive ones containing four-poster beds. Some lie within a barn that's been comfortably converted into living quarters. Richly accessorized, each has a vivid Edwardian country-house motif and lots of mementos.

West Cliffe, St. Margaret's at Cliffe, Dover, Kent CT15 6EW. © **01304/852424.** Fax 01304/853430. www.wallettscourthotel.com. 16 units. £129–£169 double; £199 suite. Rates include English breakfast. AE, DC, MC, V. Closed Dec 24–27. Follow A258 for 2.5km (1½ miles) east from the center of Dover (signposted DEAL). Wallett's Court is signposted off A258. **Amenities:** Restaurant (see Wallett's Court review, below); bar; babysitting; health club and spa; indoor heated pool; room service. *In room:* TV/DVD, CD player, hair dryer, Wi-Fi (free).

Where to Dine

Wallett's Court ★ ENGLISH/INTERNATIONAL   One of the most appealing restaurants in the area lies within a half-timbered Jacobean-era manor house, grandly restored over 15 years. Within a dining room that's exemplary for its sense of history, you can enjoy dishes that change with the season—spring lamb, lobster and Dover sole in summer, or game in the autumn and winter months. For starters, try the caramelized Rye Bay scallops and medallions of wild rabbit with bay leaf (flavored with orange and cardamom), or else seared yellowfin tuna carpaccio with red chard, mango, lime, and chili. Some of the most delicious mains include a traditional roast turkey stuffed with white pudding and served with cranberry jus, or else Kentish pheasant breast stuffed with black pudding and served with roast parsnips and sweet potatoes.

In Wallett's Court hotel, West Cliffe, St. Margaret's at Cliffe. © **01304/852424.** Reservations recommended. Fixed-price 3-course menu £25–£40. AE, DC, MC, V. Tues–Sat 7–9pm; Sun noon–2pm and 7–9pm. Closed 1 week at Christmas.

Exploring Dover

Your best view of the famous **white cliffs** ★★★ is when arriving at Dover by ferry or hovercraft from Calais. Otherwise, walk out to the end of the Prince of Wales pier, the largest of the town's western docks. From here, the cliffs loom above you. Or drive 8km (5 miles) east to the pebble-covered beaches of the fishing hamlet of Deal. A local fisher may take you on an informal boat ride.

Deal Castle ★   Deal Castle is .5km (¼ mile) south of the Deal town center, 8km (5 miles) from Dover. A defensive fort built around 1540, it's the most spectacular example of the low, squat forts constructed by Henry VIII. Its 119 gun positions made it the most powerful of his defense forts. Centered on a circular keep surrounded by two rings of semicircle bastions, the castle was protected by an outer moat. The entrance was approached by a drawbridge with an iron gate. The castle was damaged by bombs during World War II but has since been restored to its earlier form. The admission price includes an audio tour.

On the seafront. ℂ **01304/372762.** www.english-heritage.co.uk. Admission £4.30 adults, £3.70 seniors, £2.20 children. Daily 10am–6pm. Closed Oct–Mar.

Dover Castle ★★★   Rising nearly 120m (400 ft.) above the port is one of the oldest and best-known castles in England. Its keep was built at the command of Becket's fair-weather friend, Henry II, in the 12th century. The ancient castle was called back to active duty as late as World War II. The Pharos on the grounds is a lighthouse built by the Romans in the first half of the 1st century. The Romans first landed at nearby Deal in 54 B.C., but after 6 months they departed and didn't return until nearly 100 years later, in A.D. 43, when they stayed and occupied the country for 400 years. The castle houses a military museum and a film center, plus "Live and Let's Spy," an exhibition of World War II spying equipment. Audio tours of the castle are included in the admission price.

Castle Hill. ℂ **01304/211067.** www.english-heritage.co.uk. Admission £14 adults, £12 students and seniors, £7 children 5–15, free for children 4 and younger. Apr–Oct daily 10am–6pm; Nov–Mar daily 10am–4pm.

Roman Painted House ★★   This 1,800-year-old Roman structure, called Britain's "buried Pompeii," has exceptionally well-preserved walls and an under-floor heating system. It's famous for its unique Bacchic murals. Brass-rubbing is also offered. You'll find it in the town center near Market Square.

New St. ℂ **01304/203279.** www.theromanpaintedhouse.co.uk. Admission £3 adults, £2 seniors and children 16 and younger. Early to mid-Apr Tues–Sat 10am–5pm; late Apr to May Tues and Sat 10am–5pm; June to mid-Sept Tues–Sat 10am–5pm; Oct–Mar by prior arrangement only..

Secret War Time Tunnels ★ 📖   These secret tunnels, used during the evacuation of Dunkirk in 1940 and the Battle of Britain, can now be explored on a 40-minute guided tour. The tunnels were originally excavated to house cannons to be used (if necessary) against an invasion by Napoleon. Some 60m (200 ft.) below ground, they were the headquarters of Operation Dynamo, when more than 300,000 troops from Dunkirk were evacuated. On once forbidden ground to all but those with the strongest security clearance, you can stand in the very room where Ramsey issued orders; experience the trauma of life in an underground operating theater; and look out over the English Channel from the hidden, cliff-top balcony, just as Churchill did during the Battle of Britain.

Dover Castle, Castle Hill. ℂ **01304/211067.** Admission included in Dover Castle price (see above). Last tour leaves 1 hr. before castle closing time.

THE ANCIENT SEAPORT OF RYE ★★

100km (62 miles) SE of London

"Nothing more recent than a Cavalier's Cloak, Hat, and Ruffles should be seen on the streets of Rye," said Louis Jennings. This ancient town, formerly an island, flourished in the 13th century. In its early days, Rye was a smuggling center, its residents sneaking in contraband from the marshes to stash away in little nooks.

But the sea receded from Rye, leaving it perched like a giant whale out of water, 3km (2 miles) from the Channel. Attacked several times by French fleets, Rye was practically razed in 1377. But it rebuilt successfully, in full Elizabethan panoply. When Queen Elizabeth I visited in 1573, she was so impressed that she bestowed upon the town the distinction of Royal Rye. This has long been considered a special place and, over the years, has attracted famous people such as the novelist Henry James.

Its narrow cobblestone streets twist and turn like a labyrinth, and jumbled along them are buildings whose sagging roofs and crooked chimneys indicate the town's medieval origins. Rye overflows with sites of architectural interest.

Neighboring Winchelsea has also witnessed the water's ebb. Its history traces back to Edward I and includes many dramatic moments, such as sacking by the French. In the words of one 19th-century writer, Winchelsea is "a sunny dream of centuries ago." The finest sight of this dignified residential town is a badly damaged 14th-century church with a number of remarkable tombs.

Essentials

GETTING THERE   From London, the Southeastern Line offers trains south from Charing Cross or Cannon Street Station, with a change at Ashford, before continuing on to Rye. You can also go via Tunbridge Wells with a change in Hastings. Trains run every hour during the day, arriving at the Rye Rail Station off Cinque Ports Street. The trip takes 1½ to 2 hours. Call ✆ **0845/748-4950** or visit **www.national rail.co.uk** for schedules and information.

You'll need to take the train to get to Rye, but once there you'll find buses departing every hour on the hour for many destinations, including Hastings. Various bus schedules are posted on signs in the parking lot. For information on bus connections in the surrounding area, call ✆ **0870/608-2608.**

If you're driving from London, take the M25, M26, and M20 east to Maidstone, going southeast along the A20 to Ashford. At Ashford, continue south on the A2070.

VISITOR INFORMATION   The **Rye Tourist Information Centre** is at 4–5 Lion St. (✆ **01797/226696**; www.visitrye.co.uk), open April to September daily 10am to 5pm, October to March daily 10am to 4pm. The **Rye Heritage Centre,** on the Strand Quay (✆ **01797/226696**; www.ryeheritage.co.uk), houses a sound-and-light show depicting more than 700 years of Rye history. Adults pay £3.50, students and seniors £2.50, and children 15 and under £1.50.

Where to Stay

The George ★   This coaching inn enjoys a long history dating from 1575. In the 18th century, it drew a diverse clientele: some traveling by horse-drawn carriage, others by boat between London and France. The half-timbered architecture charms visitors like no other small inn in the region (except the Mermaid, which has an even more antique atmosphere; see below). Some of the timbers may be from the wreck of an English ship broken up in Rye Harbour after the defeat of the Spanish Armada. Bedrooms have been refurbished and modernized, each individually designed with custom furniture and Italian linens.

High St., Rye, East Sussex TN31 7JT. ✆ **01797/222114.** Fax 01797/224065. www.thegeorgeinrye.com. 24 units. £125–£175 double; £225 suite. Rates include English breakfast. AE, DC, MC, V. **Amenities:** Restaurant; bar; babysitting; room service. *In room:* TV/DVD, hair dryer.

Hope Anchor Hotel   At the end of a cobblestone street, on a hill dominating the town, stands this 17th-century hostelry, which enjoys panoramic views of the surrounding countryside and overlooks the Strand Quay, where impressive yachts can be seen at their moorings. Oak beams and open fires in winter make this a most inviting place to spend a few days. Bedrooms are comfortable, ranging from small to midsize; two feature four-poster beds and have been refurbished. The most expensive unit is the Admiral Apartment, which is luxurious and spacious with a large drawing room and deluxe bathroom.

Watchbell St., Rye, East Sussex TN31 7HA. ✆ **01797/222216.** Fax 01797/223796. www.thehopeanchor. co.uk. 15 units. £90–£150 double; £160–£210 family room. Rates include English breakfast. AE, MC, V. Free parking. **Amenities:** Restaurant; bar; babysitting; room service. *In room:* TV, hair dryer, Wi-Fi (in most; free).

Jeake's House ★ 📖   Down a cobblestone lane, you come upon this house, which dates in part from the 1600s. It was once a wool store and later a meeting place for Baptists. The beautifully furnished and traditionally styled bedrooms open onto a view of the historic town, with its red rooftops. Each room is named after an artistic figure or member of the literati who visited Rye, ranging from Conrad Aiken to Radclyffe Hall, the notorious author of *The Well of Lonelilness*. Aiken, the American poet and Pulitzer Prize winner, actually owned Jeake's House in 1924.

Mermaid St., Rye, East Sussex TN31 7ET. ✆ **01797/222828.** Fax 01797/222623. www.jeakeshouse.com. 11 units. £52–£79 double. Rates include English breakfast. MC, V. **Amenities:** Breakfast room. *In room:* TV, hair dryer.

Mermaid Inn ★★   The Mermaid Inn is one of the most famous of the old smugglers' inns of England, known to that band of cutthroats, the real-life Hawkhurst Gang, as well as to Russell Thorndike's fictional character Dr. Syn. (One of the rooms, in fact, is called Dr. Syn's Bedchamber: It's connected to the bar by a secret staircase, stowed away in the thickness of the wall.) This place, with its Elizabethan associations and traditional touches, remains one of the most romantic old-world inns in Sussex. The accommodations vary considerably in shape and size, some quite large, others a bit cramped, as befits a building of this age. Comfort is the keynote, regardless of room assignment. Six units are spacious enough for a small family; five units have four-poster beds; and the most sought-after rooms are in the building overlooking the cobblestone street.

Mermaid St. (btw. West St. and the Strand), Rye, East Sussex TN31 7EY. © **01797/223065.** Fax 01797/225069. www.mermaidinn.com. 31 units. £80–£105 per person double with breakfast, £110–£135 per person double with breakfast and dinner. AE, DC, MC, V. Free parking. **Amenities:** Restaurant; bar; babysitting; room service. *In room:* TV, hair dryer, Wi-Fi (in some; free).

White Vine House ★ 🏨   The winner of several awards for the beauty of its small front garden and the quality of its restoration, this charming house dates from 1568. Restored from an almost derelict shell in 1987 and recently refurbished by its owners, the creeper-clad inn carefully maintains the Georgian detailing of the formal public rooms and the Tudor-style wall and ceiling beams of the bedrooms. The restored bedrooms are light and airy, furnished mostly in white and cream with period pieces. In 2005, the oak panels in the restaurant and bar were restored for the first time since the inn was built.

High St., Rye, East Sussex TN31 7JF. © **01797/224748.** Fax 01797/223599. www.whitevinehouse.co.uk. 7 units. £130–£170 double; £150–£190 family room. Rates include English breakfast. AE, DC, MC, V. Free parking. **Amenities:** Restaurant; bar. *In room:* TV/DVD, CD player, MP3 docking station, Wi-Fi (free).

Where to Dine

Our preferred spot for teatime is the **Swan Cottage Tea Rooms,** 41 The Mint, High Street (© **01797/222423**), dating from 1420 and situated on the main street. This black-and-white half-timbered building is one of the most historic in town. We gravitate to the room in the rear with its big brick fireplace. Delectable pastries and freshly made cakes await you, along with a selection of teas, including Darjeeling, Earl Grey, Pure Assam, and others. Hours are Monday to Friday 10:30am to 4pm, Saturday and Sunday 10:30am to 5pm.

Flushing Inn ★ SEAFOOD/ENGLISH   The best restaurant in Rye, this 16th-century inn has preserved the finest of the past, including a wall-size fresco dating from 1544 that depicts a menagerie of birds and heraldic beasts. A rear dining room overlooks a flower garden. A special feature is the Sea Food Lounge Bar, where sandwiches and plates of seafood are available. Start off with the fresh crab rolled into smoked salmon, followed by such mains as lobster in a seafood sauce or Tudor-style sirloin steak with a cream and sherry sauce.

4 Market St. © **01797/223292.** www.theflushinginn.com. Reservations recommended. Fixed-price lunch £20, fixed-price dinner £27–£38; seafood main courses £28–£37. DC, MC, V. Wed–Sun noon–1:45pm and 7–8:45pm. Closed 1st 2 weeks in Jan and 1st 2 weeks in June.

Landgate Bistro MODERN ENGLISH   People come from miles around to dine in this pair of interconnected Georgian shops whose exteriors are covered with "mathematical tiles" (18th-c. simulated brick, applied over stucco facades to save money). Inside, Martin Peacock and Nilla Westin make everything from scratch, including their sourdough bread and ice cream, using local ingredients whenever possible. The bistro has the largest list of starters in town, delectable items such as a leek and Roquefort tart or turbot and salt-cod cakes. The fresh fish brought in by the local fleet—especially the Dover sole—is the most popular item on the menu. You might try such dishes as a whole Dover sole, a sage-stuffed leg of guinea fowl with wholegrain mustard, or a loin of venison with wine-braised red cabbage and potatoes gratin.

5-6 Landgate. © **01797/222829.** www.landgatebistro.co.uk. Reservations required on Sat–Sun. Main courses £8.50–£13 lunch, £13–£17 dinner. AE, DC, MC, V. Wed–Fri 7–10pm; Sat noon–3pm and 7–10pm; Sun noon–3pm.

Exploring the Area

In Rye, the old town's entrance is **Land Gate,** where a single lane of traffic passes between massive, 12m-high (40-ft.) stone towers. The top of the gate has holes through which boiling oil used to be poured on unwelcome visitors, such as French raiding parties.

Rye has had potteries for centuries, and today is no exception, with a number of outlets in town. The best is **Rye Pottery,** Wishward Street (✆ **01797/223038;** www.ryepottery.co.uk). The town also abounds in antiques and collectibles shops and new and used bookstores.

Lamb House Henry James lived at Lamb House from 1898 to 1916. Many James mementos are scattered throughout the house, which is set in a walled garden. Its previous owner joined the gold rush in North America but perished in the Klondike, and James was able to buy the freehold for a modest £2,000. Some of his well-known books were written here. In *English Hours,* James wrote: "There is not much room in the pavilion, but there is room for the hard-pressed table and tilted chair—there is room for a novelist and his friends."

West St. (at the top of Mermaid St.). ✆ **01580/762334.** www.nationaltrust.org.uk. Admission £4 adults, £2.10 children. Thurs and Sat 2–6pm. Closed Dec–Mar.

Rye Castle Museum This stone fortification was constructed around 1250 by King Henry III to defend the coast against attack by the French. For 300 years it was the town jail, but has long since been converted into a museum that documents the town history. In 1996, the medieval Ypres Tower was restored.

3 East St. ✆ **01797/226728.** www.ryemuseum.co.uk. East St. site (main site) admission £2.50 adults, £2 students and seniors, free for children 15 and younger; Ypres Tower £2.95 adults, £2.50 students and seniors, free for children 15 and younger; combined ticket to both sites £5 adults, £4 students and seniors. East St. site Sat–Sun and holidays 10:30am–5pm; Ypres Tower daily 10:30am–5pm.

St. Mary's Parish Church One notable historical site is the mid-12th-century church with its 16th-century clock flanked by two gilded cherubs (known as Quarter Boys because of their striking of the bells on the quarter-hour). The church is often referred to as the "Cathedral of East Sussex" because of its expansive size and ornate beauty. If you're brave, you can climb a set of wooden stairs and ladders to the bell tower of the church for an impressive view.

Church Sq. ✆ **01797/224935.** www.stmaryskirk.com. Admission to tower £2 adults, £1 children. Free admission to church; contributions appreciated. June–Aug daily 9am–6pm; off-season daily 9am–4pm.

Smallhythe Place 🏠 On the outskirts of Winchelsea, this was for 30 years the country house of Dame Ellen Terry, the English actress acclaimed for her Shakespearean roles, who had a long theatrical association with Sir Henry Irving; she died in the house in 1928. This timber-framed structure, known as a "continuous-jetty house," was built in the first half of the 16th century and is filled with Terry memorabilia—playbills, props, makeup, and a striking display of costumes. An Elizabethan barn, adapted as a theater in 1929, is open for viewing on most days.

Smallhythe (on B2082 near Tenterden, about 9.5km/6 miles north of Rye). ✆ **01580/762334.** Admission £5.80 adults, £3.15 children, £15 family ticket. Mar 1–9 Sat–Sun 11am–5pm; Mar 10–Oct 26 Mon–Wed and Sat–Sun 11am–5pm. Take bus no. 312 from Tenterden or Rye.

1066 & ALL THAT: HASTINGS ★★★ & BATTLE ★★

Hastings: 72km (45 miles) SW of Dover; 101km (63 miles) SE of London. Battle: 55km (34 miles) NE of Brighton; 88km (55 miles) SE of London

The world has seen bigger skirmishes, but few are as well remembered as the Battle of Hastings in 1066. When William, duke of Normandy, landed on the Sussex coast and lured King Harold (already fighting Vikings in Yorkshire) south to defeat, the destiny of the English-speaking people was changed forever.

The actual battle occurred at what is now Battle Abbey (13km/8 miles away), but the Norman duke used Hastings as his base of operations. You can visit the abbey, have a cup of tea in Battle's main square, and then be off, as the rich countryside of Sussex is much more intriguing than this sleepy market town.

Present-day Hastings is a little seedy and run-down. If you're seeking an English seaside resort, head for Brighton instead.

Essentials

GETTING THERE   Daily trains run hourly from London's Charing Cross Station to Hastings. The trip takes 1½ to 2 hours. The train station at Battle is a stop on the London-Hastings rail link. For rail information, call ☎ **0845/748-4950** or visit **www.nationalrail.co.uk**.

Hastings is linked by bus to Maidstone, Folkestone, and Eastbourne, which has direct service with scheduled departures. **National Express** operates regular daily service from London's Victoria Coach Station. If you're in Rye or Hastings in summer, several frequent buses run to Battle. For bus information and schedules, call ☎ **0871/781-81-78** or visit **www.nationalexpress.com**.

If you're driving from the M25 ring road around London, head southeast to the coast and Hastings on the A21. To get to Battle, cut south to Sevenoaks and continue along the A21 to Battle via the A2100.

VISITOR INFORMATION   The **Hastings Tourist Information Centre** is at Queen's Square, Priory Meadow (☎ **01424/451111**; www.visit1066country.com). It's open Monday to Friday 8:30am to 6:15pm, Saturday 9am to 5pm, and Sunday 10:30am to 4pm.

The **Battle Tourist Information Centre** is at Battle Abbey Gatehouse (☎ **01424/776789**; www.visit1066country.com). It's open April to September, daily 10am to 6pm, and October to March, daily 10am to 4pm.

Where to Stay

IN HASTINGS

Bannatyne Spa Hotel ★   This hotel has a cozy country-house aura and is more intimate and hospitable than the Best Western Royal Victoria (reviewed below). Originally the private estate of General Murray, former governor of Quebec, the building was destroyed by fire in 1923 and rebuilt in the old style. It's surrounded by beautiful gardens; the Italian-style grounds in the rear feature statuary and flowering shrubbery. Rooms range from midsize to large, some fitted with elegant four-poster beds.

Battle Rd. (A2100), Hastings, East Sussex TN38 8EA. © **01424/851222.** Fax 01424/852465. www. bannatyne.co.uk. 25 units. £95–£130 double; £150–£170 suite. Rates include English breakfast. AE, DC, MC, V. Head 5.5km (3½ miles) northwest of Hastings, to the junction of A2100 and B2159. **Amenities:** Restaurant; bar; golf course (9 holes); state-of-the-art health club & spa; room service; outdoor tennis court (lit). *In room:* TV, hair dryer, Wi-Fi (free).

Best Western Royal Victoria ★   This seafront hotel, constructed in 1828, offers the most impressive architecture in town and the best accommodations in Hastings or St. Leonards. It has welcomed many famous visitors, including its name-sake, Queen Victoria herself. Many of the elegant and comfortably appointed rooms have separate lounge areas and views of the English Channel and Beachy Head. Some of the bedrooms are extremely large; all look as if Laura Ashley traipsed through, as evoked by dozens of half-tester beds in English chintz. Some units are large enough for families, and a number of them are duplexes.

Marina, St. Leonards, Hastings, East Sussex TN38 0BD. © **800/780-7234** in the U.S., or 01424/445544. Fax 01424/721995. www.royalvichotel.co.uk. 52 units. £135–£150 double. Children 15 and younger stay free in parent's room. Rates include English breakfast. AE, DC, MC, V. Free parking. **Amenities:** Restaurant; 3 bars; room service. *In room:* TV, hair dryer, Wi-Fi (free).

Eagle House Hotel ★   One of the best hotels in the area, this three-story man-sion, originally built in 1860 as a palatial private home, lies in a residential section about a 10-minute walk from the beaches (it's adjacent to St. Leonards Shopping Centre). The well-furnished bedrooms come in various shapes and sizes.

12 Pevensey Rd., St. Leonards, East Sussex TN38 0JZ. © **01424/430535.** Fax 01424/437771. www. eaglehousehotel.co.uk. 18 units. £65 double. Rates include English breakfast. DC, MC, V. **Amenities:** Restaurant; bar; room service. *In room:* TV, hair dryer.

Parkside House   A 15-minute walk north of Hastings's center, in a neighborhood of legally protected architecture and wildlife, this bed-and-breakfast hotel dates from 1880, when it was built of brick and slate. Views from many of the windows overlook a private garden and a duck pond in Alexander Park, a greenbelt that's said to be the largest municipal park in southeast England. Brian Kent, the owner, offers comfortable and well-maintained small- to medium-size bedrooms. Guests have access to the hotel's modest inventory of recorded films.

59 Lower Park Rd., Hastings, East Sussex TN34 2LD. © **01424/433096.** Fax 01424/421431. 5 units. £55 double. Rates include English breakfast. AE, MC, V. *In room:* TV, hair dryer.

IN BATTLE
Powder Mills Hotel ★ 📖   Near Battle Abbey and adjacent to the fabled battle-field of 1066, this restored Georgian house sits on 81 hectares (200 acres). On site was a thriving gunpowder industry, which operated for 2 centuries beginning in 1676. The name of the hotel honors that long-ago tradition. Privately owned by Douglas and Julie Cowpland, the property has attracted such distinguished guests as the duke of Wellington. It's also said to be haunted by a lady dressed in white. Bedrooms are spacious and tastefully furnished, mostly with antiques and various period pieces. Some rooms offer four-poster beds. Grace notes include log fires on winter evenings, a drawing room, a music room, and the Orangery Restaurant, with its colonial-style wicker seating.

Powdermill Lane, Battle, East Sussex TN33 0SP. © **01424/775511.** Fax 01424/774540. www.powdermills hotel.com. 40 units. £115–£170 double; £165–£350 suite. Rates include English breakfast. AE, DC, MC, V. **Amenities:** Restaurant; bar; babysitting; outdoor pool; room service. *In room:* TV, Wi-Fi (free).

Exploring the Historic Sites

Battle Abbey ★ ☺   King Harold, last of the Saxon kings, fought bravely here, not only for his kingdom but also for his life. As legend has it, he was killed by an arrow through the eye, and his body was dismembered. To commemorate the victory, William the Conqueror founded Battle Abbey; some of the construction stone was shipped from his lands at Caen in northern France.

During the Dissolution of the Monasteries from 1538 to 1539 by King Henry VIII, the church of the abbey was largely destroyed. Some buildings and ruins, however, remain in what Tennyson called "O Garden, blossoming out of English blood." The principal building still standing is the Abbot's House, which is leased to a private school for boys and girls and is open to the general public only during summer holidays. Of architectural interest is the gatehouse, which has octagonal towers and stands at the top of Market Square. All the north Precinct Mall is still standing, and one of the most interesting sights of the ruins is the ancient Dorter Range, where the monks once slept.

The town of Battle flourished around the abbey. Although it has remained a medieval market town, many of the old half-timbered buildings have regrettably lost much of their original character because of stucco plastering carried out by past generations.

This is a great place for the kids, who will enjoy a themed play area. A daily activity sheet is distributed at the gate. You can relax with a picnic or stroll the parkland that once formed the monastery grounds.

At the south end of Battle High St. (a 5-min. walk from the train station). 📞 **01424/773792.** £7 adults, £6 students and seniors, £3.50 children, £18 family ticket. Apr–Sept daily 10am–6pm; Oct–Mar daily 10am–4pm.

Hastings Castle ★★   In ruins now, the first of the Norman castles built in England sprouted on a western hill overlooking Hastings, around 1067. The fortress was unfortified by King John in 1216 and was later used as a church. Owned by the Pelham dynasty from the latter 16th century to modern times, the ruins have been turned over to Hastings. There is now an audiovisual presentation of the castle's history, including the famous battle of 1066. From the mount, you'll have a good view of the coast and promenade.

Castle Hill Rd., West Hill. 📞 **01424/444412.** Admission £3.75 adults, £3.10 seniors, £2.70 children, £12 family ticket. Easter–Sept daily 10am–5pm; Oct–Easter Sat daily 11am–3pm. Take the West Hill Cliff Railway from George St. to the castle for £1.60 adults, £1 children.

ROYAL TUNBRIDGE WELLS

58km (36 miles) SE of London; 53km (33 miles) NE of Brighton

Dudley Lord North, courtier to James I, is credited with the accidental discovery in 1606 of the mineral spring that led to the creation of a fashionable resort, Royal Tunbridge Wells. Over the years, "Chalybeate Spring" became known for its curative properties, the answer for everything from too many days of wine and roses to failing sexual prowess. It's still possible to take the waters today.

The spa resort reached its peak in the mid-18th century under the foppish patronage of Beau Nash (1674–1761), a dandy and final arbiter on how to act, what to say, and even what to wear (for example, he got men to remove their boots in favor of stockings). Tunbridge Wells continued to enjoy a prime spa reputation up through the reign of Queen Victoria, who used to vacation here as a child, and in 1909 Tunbridge Wells received its Royal status.

Today, the spa is long past its zenith. But the town is still a pleasant place to stay, and can be used as a base for exploring the many historic homes in Kent (see "Kent's Country Houses, Castles & Gardens," below); it's very easy, for example, to tour Sissinghurst and Chartwell from here.

The most remarkable feature of the town itself is the **Pantiles** ★, a colonnaded walkway for shoppers, tea drinkers, and diners, built near the wells. If you walk around town, you'll see many other interesting and charming spots. Entertainment is presented at the **Assembly Hall** (www.assemblyhalltheatre.co.uk) and **Trinity Arts Centre** (www.trinitytheatre.net).

Essentials

GETTING THERE   During the day, two to three trains per hour leave London's Charing Cross Station bound for Hastings, going via the town center of Royal Tunbridge Wells. The trip takes 50 minutes. For rail information, call ✆ **0845/748-4950** or visit **www.nationalrail.co.uk**.

If you're driving, after reaching the ring road around London, continue east along the M25, cutting southeast at the exit for the A21 to Hastings.

VISITOR INFORMATION   The **Tourist Information Centre,** Old Fish Market, the Pantiles (✆ **01892/515675;** www.visittunbridgewells.com), provides a full accommodations list and offers a reservations service. The office is open Monday to Saturday 9am to 5pm and Sunday 10am to 4pm (to 5pm May–Aug).

Where to Stay

Hotel du Vin ★★   The spa's finest lodging is part of a chain of boutique and luxury hotels, which took over this historic town's architectural landmark, a sandstone mansion built as a private residence in 1762. Without destroying its classic architecture, the new owners turned it into a hotel with exquisitely decorated bedrooms, featuring lots of elegant touches such as antiques and memorabilia. On a summer day, the best place to relax with a book is on the garden terrace, with views across Calverley Park. For a romantic weekend, the staff is always able to manage a bottle of champagne, chocolate-coated strawberries, and a red rose.

Crescent Rd., Royal Tunbridge Wells, Kent TN1 2LY. ✆ **01892/526455.** Fax 01892/512044. www.hotelduvin.com. 34 units. £149–£190 double; £215 junior suite; £230 suite. AE, DC, MC, V. **Amenities:** Restaurant; bar; room service. *In room:* A/C, TV, hair dryer, minibar, Wi-Fi (free).

Spa Hotel ★ ☺   Standing on 6 hectares (15 acres), this building dates from 1766. Once a private home, it was converted to a hotel in 1880 and remains the town's top lodging choice. The kind of old-fashioned place where guests check in for long stays, its bedrooms are of various sizes and shapes, as was typical in the 19th century. They're individually furnished, some with four-poster beds, and many with panoramic vistas. The hotel offers a few activities for kids, including a special pony-riding paddock.

Mt. Ephraim, Royal Tunbridge Wells, Kent TN4 8XJ. ✆ **800/528-1234** in the U.S., or 01892/520331. Fax 01892/510575. www.spahotel.co.uk. 70 units. £150 double; £220 suite. AE, DC, MC, V. Free parking. From the Pantiles, take Major Yorke Rd. **Amenities:** Restaurant; bar; babysitting; health club & spa; indoor heated pool; room service; outdoor tennis court (lit). *In room:* TV, hair dryer, Wi-Fi (free).

Where to Dine

Thackeray's ENGLISH/FRENCH   You'll get a bit of history to accompany the finest food in town, as this 1660 house was once inhabited by novelist William Makepeace Thackeray, who wrote *Tunbridge Toys* here. Owner/chef Richard Phillips has created an elegant atmosphere, backed by attentive service, for his specialties. Care goes into all his dishes, and many have flair. Flavors and textures are beautifully balanced in such choices as butter-poached lobster with saffron linguine or medallions of roast monkfish with Parma ham. For starters, try the venison carpaccio with beet or the layers of oak-smoked salmon with young spinach and a lime crème fraîche.

85 London Rd. (at Mt. Ephraim Rd.). © **01892/511921.** www.thackerays-restaurant.co.uk. Reservations required. Main courses £20–£32; fixed-price 2-course lunch £17, fixed-price 3-course lunch £19. AE, MC, V. Tues–Sun noon–2:30pm and 6:30–10:30pm.

KENT'S COUNTRY HOUSES, CASTLES & GARDENS

Many of England's finest country houses, castles, and gardens are in Kent, where you'll find the palace of **Knole,** a premier example of English Tudor or half-timbered architecture; **Hever Castle,** the childhood home of Anne Boleyn and later the home of William Waldorf Astor; **Leeds Castle,** a spectacular castle with ties to America; and **Penshurst Place,** a stately home that was a literary salon of sorts during the first half of the 17th century. Kent also has a bevy of homes that once belonged to famous men but have since been turned into intriguing museums, such as **Chartwell,** where Sir Winston Churchill lived for many years, and **Down House,** where Charles Darwin wrote *On the Origin of Species,* and where you can now amble down the same path the naturalist trod every evening.

It would take at least a week to see all of these historic properties—more time than most visitors have. When you make your choices, consider that Knole, Hever, Leeds, Penshurst, and Chartwell are the most deserving of your attention.

We have found the guided tours to some of Kent's more popular stately homes too rushed and too expensive to recommend. Each attraction can be toured far more reasonably on your own. Because public transportation into and around Kent can be awkward, we advise driving from London, especially if you plan to visit more than one place in a day. Accordingly, this section is organized as you may drive it from London. However, if it's possible to get to an attraction via public transportation, we include that information in the individual listings below.

Leeds Castle: "The Loveliest in the World" ★★★

Once described by Lord Conway as the loveliest castle in the world, **Leeds Castle** (© **01622/765400;** www.leeds-castle.com) dates from A.D. 857. Originally constructed of wood, it was rebuilt in 1119 in its present stone structure on two small islands in the middle of the lake; it was an almost impregnable fortress before the importation of gunpowder. Henry VIII converted it into a royal palace.

The castle has strong ties to America through the sixth Lord Fairfax, who, as well as owning the castle, owned 2 million hectares (5 million acres) in Virginia and was a close friend and mentor of the young George Washington. The last private owner, the Hon. Lady Baillie, who restored the castle with a superb collection of fine art, furniture, and tapestries, bequeathed it to the Leeds Castle Foundation. Since then, the royal apartments, known as Les Chambres de la Reine (the queen's chambers), in the Gloriette, the oldest part of the castle, have been open to the public. The Gloriette, the last stronghold against attack, dates from Norman and Plantagenet times, with later additions by Henry VIII.

Within the surrounding parkland is a wildwood garden and duckery where rare swans, geese, and ducks abound. This is the best place for country walks in this part of England. The redesigned **Aviary** contains a superb collection of birds, including parakeets and cockatoos. Dog lovers will enjoy the **Dog Collar Museum** at the gatehouse, with a unique collection of collars dating from the Middle Ages. A 9-hole **golf course** is open to the public. The **Culpepper Garden** is a delightful English-country flower garden. Beyond are the castle greenhouses, with the maze centered on a beautiful underground grotto and the vineyard recorded in William the Conqueror's survey document, the Domesday Book (1086), which is once again producing Leeds Castle English white wine.

Snacks, salads, cream teas, and hot meals are offered daily at a number of places on the estate, including **Fairfax Hall,** a restored 17th-century tithe barn, and the **Terrace Restaurant,** which provides a full range of hot and cold meals.

From March 21 to September, the park is open daily 10am to 5pm, the castle 10:30am to 6pm; off-season, the park is open daily 10am to 3pm, the castle 10:30am to 4pm. The castle and grounds are closed on the last Saturday in June and the first Saturday in July before open-air concerts. Admission to the castle and grounds is £17 for adults, £14 for students and seniors, and £9.50 for children 4 to 15. Car parking is free, with a free ride on a fully accessible minibus available for those who cannot manage the 1km (½-mile) or so walk from the parking area to the castle.

The best way to get here from London is via coaches operated by **National Express** (© **0871/781-81-78;** www.nationalexpress.com), departing from Victoria Coach Station at 9am and arriving at the castle at 10:35am, costing £13 for adults, £6.25 for children. Seats must be booked in advance. Trains run frequently from London's Victoria Station to Maidstone, 58km (36 miles) to the southeast. If you're driving from London's ring road, continue east along the M26 and the M20. The castle is 6.5km (4 miles) east of Maidstone at the junction of the A20 and the M20 London-Folkestone roads.

Other Kent Attractions

Chartwell ★   Sir Winston Churchill's home from 1922 until his death, though not as grand as his birthplace (Blenheim Palace; p. 268), Chartwell has preserved its rooms as the Conservative politician left them—maps, documents, photographs, pictures, personal mementos, and all. Two rooms display gifts that the prime minister received from people all over the world. A selection of many of his well-known uniforms includes his famous "siren-suits" and hats. Many of Churchill's paintings are displayed in a garden studio. You can see the garden walls that the prime minister built with his own hands and the pond where he sat to feed the Golden Orfe. A restaurant on the grounds serves food on days when the house is open.

Near the town of Edenbridge. © **01732/868381.** www.nationaltrust.org.uk. Admission to house, garden, and studio £11 adults, £5.60 children, £28 family ticket. Mar 17–June and Sept–Oct Wed–Sun 11am–5pm; July–Aug Tues–Sun 11am–5pm. If driving from London, head east on M25, taking the exit to Westerham. Drive 3km (2 miles) south of Westerham on B2026 and follow the signs.

Down House   Here stands the final residence of the famous naturalist Charles Darwin. In 1842, upon moving in, he wrote, "House ugly, looks neither old nor new." Nevertheless, he lived there "in happy contentment" until his death in 1882. The drawing room, dining room, billiard room, and old study have been restored to the way they were when Darwin was working on his famous, and still controversial, book *On the Origin of Species,* first published in 1859. The garden retains its original landscaping and a glass house, beyond which lies the Sand Walk or "Thinking Path," where Darwin took his daily solitary walk.

On Luxted Rd., in Downe. Ⓒ **01689/859119.** www.english-heritage.org.uk. Admission £9.30 adults, £7.90 students and seniors, £4.70 children, family ticket £23. Apr–June and Sept–Oct Wed–Sun 11am–5pm; Nov 1 to Dec 20, Feb and Mar Wed–Sun 11am–4pm; July–Aug daily 11am–5pm. Closed Dec 21–Jan 31. From Westerham, get on A233 and drive 9km (5½ miles) south of Bromley to the village of Downe. Down House is .5km (¼ mile) southeast of the village. From London's Victoria Station, take a train (available daily) to Bromley South, and then go to Downe by bus no. 146 (Mon–Sat only) or to Orpington by bus no. R2.

Groombridge Place Gardens   These formal gardens, with a vineyard and woodland walks, date from the 17th century. Part of the complex includes an Enchanted Forest, an ancient woodland in which the artist Ivan Hicks designed a series of "interactive" gardens, using natural objects, native wildflowers, mirrors, and glass to create a mysterious, surreal ambience. The White Rose Garden is compared favorably to that at fabled Sissinghurst. The English Knot Garden is based on paneling in the drawing room of an English country house. In the Fern Valley, huge Jurassic plants are as old as time.

At the center is Groombridge Place, built on the site of a 12th-century castle and one of the most beautiful moated manor houses in England. Sir Christopher Wren, or so it is believed, helped with the architecture. The palace was built in 1662 by one of the courtiers to King Charles II, Philip Packer. Sir Arthur Conan Doyle was a regular visitor to the house to take part in séances, and the manor was the setting for the Sherlock Holmes mystery *The Valley of Fear.*

The gardens are often visited after an exploration of Knole, near Sevenoaks. After leaving Sevenoaks, you can take A21 southeast until you reach the junction of A26 south. Follow this route until you see the signposted cutoff heading west to the little village of Groombridge and its gardens.

Groombridge. Ⓒ **08192/861444.** www.groombridge.co.uk. Admission £8.95 adults, £7.45 seniors and children 3–12, £30 family ticket. Last 2 Sat–Sun of Mar and daily Apr–Nov 3 10am–5:30pm.

Hever Castle & Gardens ★★   Hever Castle dates from 1270, when the massive gatehouse, the outer walls, and the moat were first constructed. Some 200 years later, the Bullen (or Boleyn) family added a comfortable Tudor dwelling house inside the walls. Hever Castle was the childhood home of Anne Boleyn, the second wife of Henry VIII and mother of Queen Elizabeth I.

In 1903, William Waldorf Astor acquired the estate and invested time, money, and imagination in restoring the castle, building the Tudor Village, and creating the gardens and lakes. The Astor family's contribution to Hever's rich history can be appreciated through the castle's collections of furniture, paintings, and objets d'art, as well as the quality of its workmanship, particularly in the woodcarving and plasterwork.

The gardens are ablaze with color throughout most of the year. The spectacular Italian Garden contains statuary and sculpture dating from Roman to Renaissance times. The formal gardens include a walled Rose Garden, fine topiary work, and a maze. There's also a 14-hectare (35-acre) lake and many streams, cascades, and fountains.

Hever, near Edenbridge. ✆ **01732/865224.** www.hevercastle.co.uk. Admission to castle and gardens £13 adults, £11 students and seniors, £7 children 5-14, £33 family ticket, free for children 4 and younger. Gardens daily 11am–5pm; castle daily noon–5pm; closes at 4pm Mar, 3pm Nov–Dec 23 (castle only in Dec). Closed Jan–Feb. Follow the signs northwest of Royal Tunbridge Wells; it's 5km (3 miles) southeast of Edenbridge, midway btw. Sevenoaks and East Grinstead, and 30 min. from exit 6 of M25.

Ightham Mote ★   Dating from 1320, Ightham Mote was extensively remodeled in the early 16th century, and the work is still going on. The chapel, with its painted ceiling, timbered outer wall, and ornate chimneys, reflects the Tudor period. You'll cross a stone bridge over a moat to its central courtyard. From the Great Hall, known for its magnificent windows, a Jacobean staircase leads to the old chapel on the first floor, where you go through the solarium, which has an oriel window, to the Tudor chapel.

Unlike many other ancient houses in England that have been occupied by the same family for centuries, Ightham Mote passed from owner to owner, with each family leaving its mark on the place. When the last private owner, an American who was responsible for much of the restoration, died, he bequeathed the house to the National Trust, which chose to keep the Robinson Library laid out as it was in a 1960 edition of *Homes & Gardens*.

Mote Rd., Ivy Hatch. ✆ **01732/810378.** www.nationaltrust.org.uk. Admission £10 adults, £5 children, £25 family ticket. Sun–Mon and Thurs–Fri 11am–5pm. Closed Dec–Mar. Drive 9.5km (6 miles) east of Sevenoaks on A25 to the small village of Ivy Hatch; the estate is 4km (2½ miles) south of Ightham; it's also signposted from A227.

Knole ★★   Begun in the mid-15th century by Thomas Bourchier, archbishop of Canterbury, and set in a 404-hectare (1,000-acre) deer park, Knole is one of the largest private houses in England and is one of the finest examples of pure English Tudor–style architecture.

Henry VIII liberated the former archbishop's palace from the church in 1537. He spent considerable sums of money on Knole, but history records only one visit (in 1541) after extracting the place from the reluctant Archbishop Cranmer. It was a royal palace until Queen Elizabeth I granted it to Thomas Sackville, first earl of Dorset, whose descendants have lived here ever since. (Virginia Woolf, often a guest of the Sackvilles, used Knole as the setting for her novel *Orlando*.)

The house covers 2.8 hectares (7 acres) and has 365 rooms, 52 staircases, and seven courts. The elaborate paneling and plasterwork provide a background for the 17th- and 18th-century tapestries and rugs, Elizabethan and Jacobean furniture, and collection of family portraits. If you want to see a bed that's to die for, check out the state bed of James II in the King's Bedroom.

8km (5 miles) north of Tunbridge, at the Tunbridge end of the town of Sevenoaks. ✆ **01732/462100.** www.nationaltrust.org.uk. Admission to house £9.50 adults, £4.75 children, £24 family ticket; gardens £5 adults, £2.50 children. House mid-Mar to Oct Wed–Sun noon–4pm, gardens every Wed of the month late Mar–late Oct 11am–4pm (last admission 3:30pm); park daily to pedestrians and cars only during house hours. To reach Knole from Chartwell, drive north to Westerham, pick up A25, and head east for 13km (8 miles). Frequent train service is available from London (about every 30 min.) to Sevenoaks; then take the connecting hourly bus service or a taxi, or walk the remaining 2.5km (1½ miles) to Knole.

Penshurst Place ★★ ☺ Stately Penshurst Place is one of Britain's outstanding country houses, as well as one of England's greatest defended manor houses, standing in a peaceful rural setting that has changed little over the centuries. In 1338, Sir John de Pulteney, four times lord mayor of London, built the manor house whose Great Hall still forms the heart of Penshurst. The boy king, Edward VI, presented the house to Sir William Sidney, and it has remained in that family ever since. In the first half of the 17th century, Penshurst was known as a center of literature and attracted such personages as Ben Jonson, who was inspired by the estate to write one of his greatest poems.

The Nether Gallery, below the Long Gallery with its suite of ebony-and-ivory furniture from Goa, houses the Sidney family collection of armor. You can also see the splendid state dining room. In the Stable Wing is a toy museum, with playthings from past generations. On the grounds are nature and farm trails plus an adventure playground for children.

9.5km (6 miles) west of Tunbridge. ✆ **01892/870307.** www.penshurstplace.co.uk. Admission to house and grounds £9.50 adults, £6 children 5–16, £25 family ticket; grounds only £7.50 adults, £5.50 children 5–16, £22 family ticket; free for children 4 and younger. Daily house noon–4pm, grounds 10:30am–6pm (Sat–Sun only in Mar). Closed Nov–Feb. From M25 Junction follow A21 to Tunbridge, leaving at the Tunbridge (north) exit; then follow the brown tourist signs. The nearest mainline station is Tunbridge.

Sissinghurst Castle Garden ★★ These spectacular gardens, which are situated between surviving parts of an Elizabethan mansion, were created by one of England's most famous and dedicated gardeners, Bloomsbury writer Vita Sackville-West, and her husband, Harold Nicolson. In spring, the garden is resplendent with flowering bulbs and daffodils in the orchard. The white garden reaches its peak in June. The large herb garden, a skillful montage that reflects Sackville-West's profound plant knowledge, has something to show all summer long, and the cottage garden, with its flowering bulbs, is at its finest in the fall. It is also possible to visit the library and study of Sackville-West from April to October 15, Monday, Tuesday, and Friday noon to 5:30pm and Saturday and Sunday 10am to 5:30pm. Meals are available in the Granary Restaurant. The garden area is flat, so it is wheelchair accessible; note, however, that only two wheelchairs are allowed at a time.

Sissinghurst, near Cranbrook. ✆ **01580/710700.** www.nationaltrust.org.uk/sissinghurst. Admission £9.50 adults, £4.70 children, £24 family ticket. Mid-Mar to Oct Mon–Tues and Fri–Sun 11am–6:30pm. The garden is 85km (53 miles) southeast of London and 24km (15 miles) south of Maidstone. It's most often approached from Leeds Castle, which is 6.5km (4 miles) east of Maidstone at the junction of A20 and M20 London-Folkestone roads. From this junction, head south on B2163 and A274 through Headcorn. Follow the signposts to Sissinghurst.

Squerryes Court Built in 1681, this manor house has been owned by the Warde family for the last 250 years. At one time, British General James Wolfe, who commanded forces in the bombardment of Quebec, lived here with his family. The house still contains pictures and relics of General Wolfe's family. The Warde family has restored the formal gardens, dotting banks surrounding the lake with spring bulbs, herbaceous borders, and old roses to retain its beauty year-round, and returned rooms to their original uses. You can enjoy the fine collection of Old Master paintings from the Italian, 17th-century Dutch, and 18th-century English schools, along with antiques, porcelain, and tapestries, all acquired or commissioned by the family in the 18th century. General Wolfe received his commission on the grounds of the house—the spot is marked by a cenotaph.

1km (½ mile) west of the center of Westerham (10 min. from exit 6 or exit 5 on M25). © **01959/562345.** www.squerryes.co.uk. Admission to house and garden £7 adults, £6 students and seniors, £4 children 15 and younger, £14 family ticket; garden only £4.50 adults, £4 seniors, £2.50 children 15 and younger, £9 family ticket. Apr 1–Sept 30 Wed, Sun, and bank holiday Mon house 1–5:30pm, grounds 11:30am–5:30pm (last admission 4:30pm). Take A25 just west of Westerham and follow the signs.

HISTORIC MANSIONS & GARDENS IN DORKING & GUILDFORD

Dorking, birthplace of Lord Laurence Olivier, lies on the Mole River at the foot of the North Downs. Within easy reach are some of the most scenic spots in the county, including Silent Pool, Box Hill, and Leith Hill.

The guildhall in Guildford, a country town on the Wey River, has an ornamental projecting clock that dates from 1683. Charles Dickens claimed that the High Street, which slopes to the river, was one of the most beautiful in England.

Essentials

GETTING THERE   Frequent daily train service to Dorking takes 45 minutes from London's Victoria Station or Waterloo Station. The train to Guildford departs London's Waterloo Station and takes 40 minutes. For information, call © **0845/748-4950** or visit **www.nationalrail.co.uk**.

National Express (© **0871/781-81-78;** www.nationalexpress.com) operates buses from London's Victoria Coach Station daily, with a stopover at Guildford on its runs from London to Portsmouth. It's usually more convenient to take the train.

If you're driving to Dorking from London, take the A24 south. If you're driving to Guildford from London, head south along the A3.

VISITOR INFORMATION   The **Guildford Tourist Information Centre** is at 14 Tunsgate (© **01483/444333;** www.guildford.gov.uk). It's open October to April, Monday to Saturday 9:30am to 5pm; May to September, Monday to Saturday 9am to 5:30pm and Sunday 10am to 4:30pm.

Where to Stay & Dine

IN DORKING

Mercure Burford Bridge Hotel ★   This inn is the best in Dorking, offering stylish living in a rural town. At the foot of beautiful Box Hill, the hotel has many historical associations. Keats completed "Endymion" here in 1817; Wordsworth and Robert Louis Stevenson also visited the hotel. You get the best of both the old and the new, including a tithe barn (ca. 1600). All guest rooms are refurbished. The grounds include a flowered patio and fountain that are particularly enjoyable in summer.

Box Hill, Dorking, Surrey RH5 6BX. © **01306/884561.** Fax 01306/887821. www.mercure.com. 57 units. £125–£171 double. AE, DC, MC, V. Free parking. Take A24 2.5km (1½ miles) north of Dorking. **Amenities:** Restaurant; bar; concierge; outdoor pool; room service. *In room:* TV, hair dryer, Wi-Fi (free).

Mercure White Horse Hotel   Just 16km (10 miles) from Gatwick Airport, this inn is supposed to have been the home of the "Marquis of Granby" in *The Pickwick Papers*. Dickens was known to have frequented the bar parlor. Bedrooms have been refurbished, and all are comfortable and well maintained; a few have four-poster beds. Some units are in a rather sterile modern annex. The inn's restaurant offers a moderately priced table d'hôte dinner. The hotel also has a rose garden and can arrange a temporary membership in a nearby sports club with its own swimming pool.

High St., Dorking, Surrey, RH4 1BE. ☎ **800/225-5843** in the U.S. and Canada, or 01306/881138. Fax 01306/880386. www.mercure.com. 78 units. £84–£125 double. AE, DC, MC, V. **Amenities:** Restaurant; bar; room service. *In room:* TV, hair dryer, Wi-Fi (free).

IN GUILDFORD

Holiday Inn Guildford   Though part of a chain, the feeling of heritage at this hotel is conveyed by its natural red-elm joinery, marble floors, and landscaped grounds. Business and leisure travelers alike fill the attractively decorated bedrooms, which are generally midsize and incorporate both living and sleeping areas. The latest addition to the hotel contains a series of modern rooms that are better appointed and more spacious than the older units.

Egerton Rd., Guildford, Surrey GU2 7XZ. ☎ **0870/400-9036.** Fax 01483/457256. www.ichotelsgroup. com. 168 units. £85–£265 double. AE, DC, MC, V. Free parking. Head about 3km (2 miles) southwest of the center of Guildford, just off A3. **Amenities:** Restaurant; bar; babysitting; exercise room; indoor heated pool; room service; Wi-Fi (£15 per day). *In room:* TV, hair dryer.

Where to Share a Pint

The **White House,** 8 High St. (☎ **01483/302006**), is a riverside pub with a conservatory overlooking a lovely waterside garden. Pub grub is available at lunch and dinner; sandwiches are offered all day. You can wash it down with traditional London ales aged in barrels.

Seeing the Sights

Loseley House ★   This beautiful and historic Elizabethan mansion visited by Queen Elizabeth I, James I, and Queen Mary has been featured on TV and in numerous films. Its works of art include paneling from Henry VIII's Nonsuch Palace, period furniture, a unique carved chalk chimney piece, magnificent ceilings, and cushions made by Queen Elizabeth I. Lunches and teas are served in the Courtyard Tearoom daily from 11am to 5pm; there's also a restaurant that serves more substantial meals.

Loseley Park (4km/2½ miles southwest of Guildford). ☎ **01483/304440.** www.loseley-park.com. Admission to house and gardens £8 adults, £7 students and seniors, £4 children; gardens only £4.50 adults, £4 students and seniors, £2.25 children. House May–Aug Tues–Thurs and Sun 1–5pm; gardens May–Sept Tues–Sun 11am–5pm.

Polesden Lacey   Built in 1824, this former Regency villa houses the Greville collection of antiques, paintings, and tapestries. In the early part of the 20th century, it was enlarged to become a comfortable Edwardian country house, home of celebrated hostess Mrs. Ronald Greville, who frequently entertained royalty from 1906 to 1939. The estate has 560 hectares (1,400 acres). Stroll the 18th-century garden, lined with herbaceous borders and featuring a rose garden and beech trees.

Signposted from Great Bookham, off A246 Leatherhead-Guildford Rd. ℭ **01372/452048.** www. nationaltrust.org.uk. Admission to grounds £6.70 adults, £3.50 children, £17 family ticket; admission to house £11 adults, £5.50 children, £27 family ticket. Grounds daily Mar–Oct 10am–5pm, Nov–Feb daily 10am–4pm; house mid-Mar to Oct Wed–Sun and bank holidays 11am–5pm.

Wisley Garden ★★ Every season, this 101-hectare (250-acre) garden, one of the great gardens of England, has a profusion of flowers and shrubs, ranging from the alpine meadow carpeted with wild daffodils in spring, to Battleston Hill brilliant with rhododendrons in early summer, to the heather garden's colorful foliage in fall, and a riot of exotic plants in the greenhouses in winter. Model gardens and a landscaped orchid house can also be visited. Mid-2007 saw the opening of the massive Glasshouse, which shelters endangered and delicate plants from three climatic zones. This greenhouse looks onto a manicured artificial lake. The garden is also the site of a laboratory where botanists, plant pathologists, and entomologists experiment and assist amateur gardeners. A large gift shop stocks a variety of gardening books.

Wisley (near Ripley, just off M25, Junction 10, on A3 London-Portsmouth Rd.). ℭ **01483/224234.** www.rhs.org.uk. Admission £9.50 adults, £3 children 6–16, free for children 5 and younger. Mar–Oct Mon–Fri 10am–6pm, Sat–Sun 9am–6pm; Nov–Feb Mon–Fri 10am–4:30pm, Sat–Sun 9am–4:30pm (last admission 1 hr. before closing).

CHICHESTER

50km (31 miles) W of Brighton; 111km (69 miles) SW of London

Chichester might have been just a market town if the Chichester Festival Theatre had not been born there. One of the oldest Roman cities in England, Chichester draws a crowd from all over for its theater. Though it lacks other attractions, the town is a good base for exploring a history-rich part of southern England.

Essentials

GETTING THERE Trains depart for Chichester from London's Victoria Station once every hour during the day. The trip takes 1½ hours. However, if you visit Chichester to attend the theater, plan to stay over—the last train back to London is at 9pm. For rail information, call ℭ **0845/748-4950** or visit **www.nationalrail. co.uk**.

Buses leave from London's Victoria Coach Station once a day. For schedules, call ℭ **0871/781-81-78** or visit **www.nationalexpress.com**.

If you're driving from London's Ring Road, head south on the A3, turning onto the A286 for Chichester.

VISITOR INFORMATION The **Tourist Information Centre,** 29A South St. (ℭ **01243/775888;** www.visitchichester.org), is open October to March, Monday 10:15am to 5:15pm and Tuesday to Saturday 9:15am to 5:15pm; and April to September, Monday to Saturday 9:15am to 5:15pm and Sunday 10:30am to 3pm.

Where to Stay in the Area

Millstream Hotel The Millstream, built in the 1700s to provide food and lodging for travelers through Sussex from other parts of England, is 8km (5 miles) south of Chichester. The property is in the hamlet of Bosham, with its beautiful harbor.

Behind a facade of weathered yellow bricks, the hotel exudes a sense of history. The rooms, modern in style, have been redecorated and upgraded.

Bosham Lane (at Moreton Rd.), Chichester, West Sussex PO18 8HL. ℂ **01243/573234.** Fax 01243/573459. www.millstream-hotel.co.uk. 35 units. £145–£165 double; £169–£215 suite. Rates include English breakfast. AE, DC, MC, V. Bus: Bosham bus from Chichester. Take the road to the village of Bosham and its harbor, off A27. **Amenities:** Restaurant; bar; babysitting; room service. *In room:* TV, hair dryer, minibar, Wi-Fi (free).

Ship Hotel   A classic Georgian building, the Ship is only a few minutes' walk from Chichester Cathedral, Chichester Festival Theatre, and many fine antiques shops. Built as a private house in 1790 for Admiral Sir George Murray, it retains an air of elegance and comfort, made all the more so by a wholesale renovation in 2007. A grand staircase leads from its main entrance to the bedrooms, which are named after historic ships. Some rooms have four-poster beds; others are specially designated for families.

57 North St., Chichester, West Sussex PO19 1NH. ℂ **01243/778000.** Fax 01243/788000. www.the shiphotel.net. 36 units. £95–£175 double; from £120 family room. Rates include English breakfast. AE, DC, MC, V. Free parking. **Amenities:** Restaurant; bar; room service. *In room:* TV, hair dryer.

Spread Eagle Hotel & Spa ★★ 🛍   This 1430 inn, and the market town of Midhurst, are so steeped in history that the room you sleep in and the pavement you walk on each probably have a thousand tales to tell. Curiosities include the White Room, where smugglers allegedly made a secret passage, and the Queen's Room, from which Elizabeth I watched the revelry on the square during her 1591 visit. The rooms here are medieval in character, with beams, small mullioned windows, and unexpected corners. The most elegant have four-poster antique beds, fireplaces, and 500-year-old wall paneling. The eagle in the lounge is the actual one from the back of Hermann Göring's chair in the Reichstag. It was acquired for its apt illustration of the hotel's name.

South St., Midhurst, West Sussex GU29 9NH. ℂ **01730/816911.** Fax 01730/815668. www.hshotels.co.uk. 39 units. £120–£305 double; £320–£350 suite. Rates include English breakfast. AE, DC, MC, V. Free parking. Midhurst bus from Chichester. **Amenities:** Restaurant; bar; exercise room; indoor heated pool; spa. *In room:* TV, hair dryer.

Where to Dine in the Area

If you're on the run and don't want a formal meal, drop in at the **George & Dragon,** 51 North St. (ℂ **01243/785660;** www.georgeanddragoninn.co.uk), in the heart of the city. It's a family-run bar and restaurant with a traditional feel.

Comme Ça ★ FRENCH   This is the best French restaurant in town—in fact, the best restaurant, period. The unpretentious decor blends old Victorian and Edwardian prints with objets d'art. The theme continues in the garden room leading through French doors to an enclosed patio and garden. In summer, you'll want to dine out here, although in winter, a log fire in the inglenook fireplace welcomes you to the bar. Try delights of the field or river. Only the finest-quality ingredients are used. All menus have vegetarian dishes, and special dietary requirements can also be accommodated. Starters—including pan-fried tiger prawns flambéed with cognac and served in a phyllo basket with a brochette of apple crisps, or seared scallops in spicy shrimp butter—have harmonious pairings of flavors. Well-crafted main dishes include free-range roasted guinea fowl with Madeira jus and French lentils, or else seared filet of wild sea bass with lemon, olive oil, and herbed potatoes with warm chorizo and a red-pepper vinaigrette.

67 Broyle Rd. (a 10-min. walk from the town center). © **01243/788724.** www.commeca.co.uk. Reservations required. Main courses £16–£24; fixed-price 2-course lunch £21, fixed-price 3-course lunch £24. AE, DC, MC, V. Wed–Sun 11:30am–2pm; Tues–Sat 6–10pm.

The Dining Room at Purchase's ★ MODERN BRITISH/FRENCH This restaurant in a Georgian house ranks with Comme Ça as the best dining choice in Chichester. Each of these restaurants has its devotees among serious foodies. The Purchase's is owned by the country's oldest wine merchant and has one of the finest cellars in Sussex. In an elegant setting in the center, you can dine in a place run by the same family since 1780. There is a conservatory and a charming courtyard garden for summer seating. The cuisine here brashly takes tradition in hand, and then turns it on its head with its inventive yet harmonious medley of dishes. Try, for example, pan-fried partridge breast with a wild mushroom and chestnut sauce or saddle of venison with beet and sweet potato gratin. The restaurant does not allow children under 14.

31 North St. © **01243/537352.** www.thediningroom.biz. Reservations required. Main courses £13–£30. Fixed-price 2-course menu £15, 3-course menu £20. AE, MC, V. Mon–Sat noon–3pm and 7:30–9:30pm.

Chichester Festival Theatre ★

Only a 5-minute walk from the Chichester Cathedral and the old Market Cross, the 1,400-seat theater, with its apron stage, stands on the edge of Oaklands Park. It opened in 1962, and its first director was none other than Lord Laurence Olivier. Its reputation has grown steadily, pumping new vigor and life into the former walled city, although originally many irate locals felt the city money could have been better spent on a swimming pool instead of a theater.

The Chichester Festival Theatre and the Minerva Studio Theatre are managed by the same board of governors but show different programs and different plays. The **Chichester Festival Theatre,** built in the 1960s, offers plays and musicals during its summer season (mid-Apr to Oct); the winter and spring months feature orchestras, jazz, opera, theater, ballet, and a Christmas show for the entire family. The **Minerva Studio Theatre,** built in the late 1980s, is a multifunctional cultural center that includes a theater plus dining and drinking facilities.

Theater reservations made over the phone will be held for a maximum of 4 days (© **01243/781312** for the box office, or 01243/784437 for general info; www.cft. org.uk). Festival ticket prices range from £10 to £55.

A Racetrack

One of the most famous sports-car race courses in the world, **Goodwood Motor Circuit** (© **01243/755000;** www.goodwood.co.uk) reopened in 1998, near Chichester, and was restored to its look of 50 years ago. The course became dangerous for faster cars and was retired as an active track in the 1960s, as the 4km (2½-mile) circuit was never modernized. Now that's part of its charm, offering a chance to relive the days when courageous drivers raced Jaguars or Ferraris on tracks enveloped by cornfields and hay bales. Today, the course is used for special exhibition races featuring historic sports cars from the '50s and '60s. To get here, take the A3 to Milford, the A283 to Petwork, and then the A285 to Halnaker, following the signposts from there. Call to see if any exhibitions are being staged during your visit to the area.

Other Attractions

Fishbourne Roman Palace   This is what remains of the largest Roman residence yet discovered in Britain. Built around A.D. 75 in villa style, it has many mosaic-floored rooms and even an under-floor heating system. The gardens have been restored to their original 1st-century plan. The story of the site is told both by an audiovisual program and by text in the museum. Guided tours are offered twice a day—you can see what an archaeological dig in 1996 unearthed. In 2006, the attraction underwent a multimillion-dollar redevelopment; it now offers a state-of-the-art computer graphic reconstruction of the palace. Roman artifacts are on display in the Discovery Centre.

North of A259, off Salthill Rd. (signposted from Fishbourne; 2.5km/1½ miles from Chichester). ✆ **01243/785859.** www.sussexpast.co.uk. Admission £7.60 adults, £6.80 students and seniors, £4 children, £21 family ticket. Jan Sat–Sun 10am–4pm; Feb daily 10am–4pm; Mar–July and Sept–Oct daily 10am–5pm; Aug daily 10am–6pm; Nov–Dec 10am–4pm (not always open during this time; call first). Buses stop regularly at the bottom of Salthill Rd., and the museum is within a 10-min. walk of British Rail's station at Fishbourne.

Weald & Downland Open Air Museum   In the beautiful Sussex countryside, historic buildings, saved from destruction, are reconstructed on a 20-hectare (49-acre) downland site. The structures show the development of traditional building from medieval times to the 19th century, in the weald and downland area of southeast England. Exhibits include a Tudor market hall, a working water mill producing stone-ground flour, a blacksmith's forge, plumbers' and carpenters' workshops, a toll cottage, a charcoal burner's camp, and a 19th-century village school. A "new" reception area with shops and offices is set in Longport House, a 16th-century building rescued from the site of the Channel Tunnel.

At Singleton, 9.5km (6 miles) north of Chichester on A286 (the London Rd.). ✆ **01243/811363.** www.wealddown.co.uk. Admission £9 adults, £8.15 seniors, £4.80 students and children 5–15, £25 family ticket. Apr–Oct daily 10:30am–6pm; Nov–Dec 22 daily 10:30am–4pm; Jan 3–Feb 18 Wed and Sat–Sun 10:30am–4pm; Feb 19–Mar daily 10:30am–4pm. Bus no. 60 from Chichester.

ARUNDEL CASTLE ★★

34km (21 miles) W of Brighton; 93km (58 miles) SW of London

The small town of Arundel in West Sussex nestles at the foot of one of England's most spectacular castles. Without the castle, it would be just another English market town. The town was once an Arun River port, and its residents enjoyed the prosperity of considerable trade and commerce. Today, however, the harbor traffic has been replaced with buses filled with tourists.

Essentials

GETTING THERE   Trains leave hourly during the day from London's Victoria Station. The trip takes 1¼ hours. For rail information, call ✆ **0845/748-4950** or visit **www.nationalrail.co.uk**.

Most bus connections are through Littlehampton, opening onto the English Channel west of Brighton. From Littlehampton, you can leave the coastal road by taking bus no. 700 (run by **Stagecoach Coastline**), which runs between Little-hampton and Arundel every 30 minutes between 7am and 7pm. If you're dependent on public transportation, the Tourist Information Centre (see below) keeps an update on the possibilities.

If you're driving from London, follow the signs to Gatwick Airport; from there, head south toward the coast along the A29.

VISITOR INFORMATION   The **Tourist Information Centre,** 1–3 Crown Yard Mews, River Rd. (✆ **01903/882268;** www.sussexbythesea.com), is open April to October, Monday to Saturday 10am to 5pm (to 6pm July–Aug), Sunday 10am to 4pm; off-season hours are daily 10am to 3pm.

Where to Stay in the Area

Amberley Castle ★★ 🏨   The best place for food and lodging is this Relais & Châteaux member near the village of Amberley, where Joy and Martin Cummings offer accommodations in a 14th-century castle with sections dating from the 12th century. Elizabeth I held the lease on this castle from 1588 to 1603, and Cromwell's forces attacked it during the civil war. Charles II visited the castle on two occasions. Each of the sumptuous rooms is named after a castle in Sussex. They're the ultimate in English-country-house luxury; you can choose from four-poster, twin four-poster, or brass double beds. All rooms also have a video library.

Amberley, near Arundel, West Sussex BN18 9LT. ✆ **01798/831992.** Fax 01798/831998. www.amberley castle.co.uk. 19 units. £190–£520 double. Rates include English breakfast. AE, DC, MC, V. Free parking. Take B2139 north of Arundel; the hotel is 2.5km (1½ miles) southwest of Amberley. **Amenities:** Restaurant (see Queen's Room review, below); golf course (18 holes); room service; outdoor tennis court. *In room:* TV, hair dryer, minibar.

Hilton Avisford Park ★   This is not your usual Hilton. Set in 36 hectares (89 acres) of gardens and lovely parkland, it opens onto England's South Downs. Once it was the home of Baronet Montagu, admiral and friend of Lord Nelson. Now successfully converted into a hotel, it is completely modernized but still keeps some of the allure of its original construction. Bedrooms come in a range of styles, sizes, and designs, and are handsomely laid out. The hotel is also the best equipped in the area, especially if sports are part of your vacation. The Cedar Restaurant is a first-class dining choice.

Yapton Lane, Walberton, Arundel, West Sussex BN18 0LS. ✆ **01243/558300.** Fax 01243/552485. www. arundel.hilton.com. 139 units. £84–£192 double; £164–£247 suite. Rates include English breakfast. AE, DC, MC, V. Free parking. Located 4.8km (3 miles) west of Arundel on B2132 (off A27). **Amenities:** Restaurant; bar; babysitting; exercise room; golf course (18 holes); indoor heated pool; room service; outdoor tennis court; Wi-Fi (£ 3 per 24 hr.). *In room:* TV, fridge, hair dryer.

Norfolk Arms   A former coaching inn, the Norfolk Arms is on the main street just a short walk from the castle. It's the best place to stay if you want to be in the market town itself. The lounges and dining room are in the typical English-country-inn style. The hotel has been restored, with many modern amenities blending with the old architecture. Bedrooms are handsomely maintained and furnished, each with personal touches. Rooms vary considerably in size, from small to spacious. Some units lie in a separate modern wing overlooking the courtyard. Four bedrooms are large enough for small families.

22 High St., Arundel, West Sussex BN18 9AD. ℰ **01903/882101.** Fax 01903/884275. www.norfolkarms hotel.com. 34 units. £139–£149 double. Children 13 and younger stay free in parent's room. Rates include English breakfast. AE, DC, MC, V. Free parking. **Amenities:** Restaurant; 2 bars; room service. *In room:* TV, hair dryer, Wi-Fi (£10 per 24 hr.).

Where to Dine in the Area

China Palace BEIJING/SZECHUAN   The most prominent Chinese restaurant in the region, it has an elaborately carved 17th-century ceiling imported by a former owner from a palace in Italy. Interior decorations include the artfully draped sails from a Chinese junk. It's located across the road from the crenellated fortifications surrounding Arundel's castle. The Beijing and Szechuan cuisine includes such classic dishes as Peking duck, king prawns kung pao, and lobster with fresh ginger and spring onions.

67 High St. ℰ **01903/883702.** Reservations recommended Sat–Sun. Main courses £8–£13; fixed-price 3-course dinner for 2 £40–£42. AE, MC, V. Daily noon–2:15pm and 6pm–midnight.

Queen's Room Restaurant ★★ ENGLISH/CONTINENTAL   No contest: The best cuisine around Arundel is served at the Amberley Castle hotel (see above). The chef has raided England's culinary past for inspiration but gives his dishes modern interpretations. We especially admire his use of natural ingredients from the area—wild Southdown rabbit, lavender, lemon thyme, and nettles. The offerings change frequently, though the special menu of the day is always alluring. For starters, enjoy such delights as seared foie gras or roast Anjou quail, followed by well-crafted mains such as filet of Scottish beef with baby vegetables, a cutlet of Cornish lamb with a shallot puree, or Cornish red mullet with an anchovy flavoring. The staff is attentive and friendly, yet warmly informal, and there's a well-chosen wine list.

In the Amberley Castle hotel, Amberley, near Arundel. ℰ **01798/831992.** www.amberleycastle.co.uk. Reservations required. Fixed-price 2-course lunch £25, 3-course lunch £30; dinner £80. AE, DC, MC, V. Daily noon–2pm and 7–9pm.

Seeing the Sights

Arundel Castle ★★   The ancestral home of the dukes of Norfolk, Arundel Castle is a much-restored mansion of considerable importance. Its legend is associated with some of the great families of England—the Fitzalans and the powerful Howards of Norfolk. This castle received worldwide exposure when it was chosen as the backdrop for *The Madness of King George* (it was "pretending" to be Windsor Castle in the film).

Arundel Castle has suffered destruction over the years, particularly during the civil war, when Cromwell's troops stormed its walls, perhaps in retaliation for the sizable contribution to Charles I made by the 14th earl of Arundel (Thomas Howard). In the early 18th century, the castle had to be virtually rebuilt, and in late Victorian times it was remodeled and extensively restored again. Today, it's filled with a valuable collection of antiques, along with an assortment of paintings by Old Masters such as Van Dyck and Gainsborough. The latest attraction is the first-time opening of the Gate House. In various rooms you can see exhibits of the civil war that was fought at the castle between 1642 and 1645. Costumed mannequins and an audio presentation bring this former era to life.

Surrounding the castle, in the center off High Street, is a 445-hectare (1,100-acre) park whose scenic highlight is Swanbourne Lake.

Mill Rd. ℂ **01903/883136.** www.arundelcastle.org. Admission £7.50–£16 adults, £7.50–£14 students and seniors, £7.50 children 5–16, £36–£39 family ticket, free for children 4 and younger. Tues–Sun noon–5pm (last admission 4pm). Closed Nov–Mar.

Arundel Cathedral   The Roman Catholic Cathedral of Our Lady and St. Philip Howard stands at the highest point in town. A. J. Hansom, inventor of the Hansom taxi, built it for the 15th duke of Norfolk. However, it was not consecrated as a cathedral until 1965. The interior includes the shrine of St. Philip Howard, featuring Sussex wrought-iron work.

London Rd. ℂ **01903/882297.** www.arundelcathedral.org. Free admission; donations appreciated. Daily 9:30am–dusk. From the town center, continue west from High St.

BRIGHTON: LONDON BY THE SEA ★★

84km (52 miles) S of London

Brighton was one of the first of the great seaside resorts of Europe. The prince of Wales (later George IV), the original swinger who was to shape so much of its destiny, arrived in 1783; his presence and patronage gave it immediate status.

Fashionable dandies from London, including Beau Brummell, turned up. The construction business boomed as Brighton blossomed with charming and attractive town houses and well-planned squares and crescents. From the prince regent's title came the voguish word *Regency*, which was to characterize an era, but more specifically refers to the period between 1811 and 1820. Under Victoria, and despite the fact that she cut off her presence, Brighton continued to flourish.

But as the English began to discover more glamorous spots on the Continent, Brighton lost much of its old *joie de vivre*. People started to call it "tatty," and it began to feature the usual run of funfair-type English seaside amusements. Because of its boardwalk and pier world, it still has a Coney Island–type of ambience, although much of its historic core has been gentrified. Vacationers flock here on day trains for a rowdy time spent at "London-by-the-Sea," and this clientele still makes Brighton a bit tawdry.

As Betty Kemp, publican, said, "But that's all right, ducky. We've always been a place where Londoners can slip off for some hanky-panky. Now, who would ever want to change that state of affairs? Brighton will always be the goal of the off-the-record weekender."

A huge number of Londoners have moved in (some of whom now commute), and the invasion has made Brighton increasingly lighthearted and sophisticated today. It also attracts a fair number of gay vacationers, and a beach east of town has been set aside for nude bathers (Britain's first such venture).

Essentials

GETTING THERE   Fast trains (41 a day) leave from Victoria or London Bridge Station, making the trip in 55 minutes. For rail information, call ℂ **0845/748-4950** or visit **www.nationalrail.co.uk**.

Buses from London's Victoria Coach Station take about 2 hours.

If you're driving, the M23 (signposted from central London) leads to the A23, which takes you into Brighton.

VISITOR INFORMATION At the **Tourist Information Centre,** 4–5 Pavilion Buildings (© **0906/711-2255** in the U.K., 50p per min.; www.visitbrighton.com), next to the Royal Pavilion shop, you can book hotel rooms, reserve tickets for National Express coaches, and pick up a list of current events. It's open Monday to Saturday 10am to 5pm; from March to October, there are also Sunday hours from 10am to 4pm.

GETTING AROUND Brighton & Hove Bus and Coach Company (© **01273/886200;** www.buses.co.uk) runs frequent and efficient service in both Brighton and Hove. Local fares are only £1.50 to £2.20. Free maps of the company's routes are available at the Tourist Information Centre (see above).

SPECIAL EVENTS If you're here in May, the international **Brighton Festival** (© **01273/709709;** www.brightonfestival.org), the largest arts festival in England, features drama, literature, visual art, dance, and concerts ranging from classical to rock. A festival program is available annually in February for those who want to plan ahead.

Where to Stay

Gay travelers should refer to "Brighton's Gay Scene," later in this section, for a selection of gay-friendly accommodations.

VERY EXPENSIVE

The Grand ★★★ Opening onto the seafront promenade, Brighton's premier hotel was originally constructed in 1864 and entertained some of the most eminent Victorians and Edwardians. This landmark was massively damaged in a 1984 terrorist attack directed at Margaret Thatcher and other key figures in the British government. Mrs. Thatcher narrowly escaped, though several of her colleagues were killed; entire sections of the hotel looked as if they had been hit by an air raid. Today, the hotel is the most elegant Georgian re-creation in town.

Guests enter via a glassed-in conservatory and register in a grandiose public room. The rooms, of a very high standard, are generally spacious with many extras, including hospitality trays and PlayStations. The sea-view units have minibars and new beds; the deluxe units offer separate sitting rooms and views of the English Channel. "Romantic rooms" offer double whirlpool tubs. All standard rooms have been refurbished with new bathrooms.

97-99 King's Rd., Brighton, East Sussex BN1 2FW. © **01273/224300.** Fax 01273/224321. www.grand brighton.co.uk. 200 units. £110–£390 double; from £310 suite. Rates include English breakfast. AE, DC, MC, V. Parking £25. Bus: 1, 2, or 3. **Amenities:** Restaurant; bar; babysitting; concierge; exercise room; indoor heated pool; room service; spa. *In room:* TV, hair dryer, minibar.

EXPENSIVE

Hilton Brighton Metropole ★ Originally built in 1889, with a handful of its rooms housed in a postwar addition, the Brighton Metropole is the largest hotel in Brighton and one of the city's top three or four picks (though not as grand as the Grand or Thistle Brighton). This property, with a central seafront location, often hosts big conferences. The refurbished rooms are comfortable and generous in size,

ACCOMMODATIONS ■
Barceló Brighton
  Old Ship Hotel **7**
Blanch House **17**
Court Craven Guest House **20**
Coward's Guest House **21**
The Grand **6**
Hilton Brighton Metropole **5**
Legends Hotel **18**
Nineteen **14**
Paskins Hotel **19**
Regency Hotel **2**
Thistle Brighton **8**
Topps Hotel **3**

ATTRACTIONS ●
Brighton Museum &
  Art Gallery **13**
The Royal Pavilion
  at Brighton **12**
DINING ◆
Bill's Produce Store **11**
China Garden **1**
Due South **4**
English's of Brighton **9**
Location 3 **7**

Mock Turtle Tea Shop **15**
The Restaurant at Drakes **16**
Terre à Terre **10**

with roomy sitting areas. The spacious bathrooms include faux marble vanities and tub/shower combos. Each unit has a PlayStation game console.

106 King's Rd., Brighton, East Sussex BN1 2FU. ✆ **01273/775432.** Fax 01273/207764. www.hilton.co. uk. 334 units. £79–£157 double; £229–£244 suite. AE, DC, MC, V. Parking £16. Bus: 1, 2, or 3. **Amenities:** Restaurant; 2 bars; babysitting; concierge; exercise room; indoor heated pool; room service; spa. *In room:* TV, hair dryer.

Thistle Brighton ★★ This relatively modern hotel is one of the finest in the south of England, topped in Brighton only by the Grand. Rising from the seafront promenade, just minutes from the Royal Pavilion, it has been luxuriously designed for maximum comfort. Rooms tend to be large but are often blandly decorated in a sort of international modern style. Each is exceptionally comfortable, with small sitting areas and long desks.

King's Rd., Brighton, East Sussex BN1 2GS. ✆ **0871/3769041.** Fax 0871/3769141. www.thistle.com. 208 units. £99–£190 double; £299–£499 suite. Children 16 and younger stay free in parent's room. AE, DC, MC, V. Parking £23. Bus: 1, 2, or 3. **Amenities:** 2 restaurants; bar; babysitting; concierge; health club & spa; indoor heated pool; room service. *In room:* A/C, TV, hair dryer, minibar, Wi-Fi (£6 per 24 hr.).

MODERATE

Barceló Brighton Old Ship Hotel ★ First used as an inn in 1559, this sea-bordering hotel, a favorite among conference groups, is the largest and best of Brighton's midpriced choices. The place is proud of its pedigree and was once the site of royal gatherings and society balls. Most of its structure dates from the 1880s; despite many subsequent modernizations, it retains a sense of its late Victorian origins. Although it's Brighton's oldest hotel, it has managed to stay abreast of the times in comfort. The east wing has the most smartly furnished rooms. Accommodations come in various sizes and shapes, but most of them are light and airy, and decorated in vibrant colors to reflect the nautical location. Suites, with separate lounge area and dining table, open onto panoramic views of the promenade and the sea. Prices drop if you stay for more than 1 night.

31–38 King's Rd., Brighton, East Sussex BN1 1NR. © **01273/329001.** Fax 01273/820718. www.barcelo-hotels.co.uk. 152 units. £79–£199 double; £289–£370 suite. Children 11 and younger stay free in parent's room. Rates include English breakfast. AE, DC, MC, V. Parking £20. Bus: 1, 2, or 3. **Amenities:** Restaurant (Location 3, p. 319); bar; babysitting; concierge; room service. *In room:* TV, hair dryer, Wi-Fi (free).

Blanch House ★ 👜 Is it a hotel or is it theater? Only 2 blocks from the sea, this small hotel in a restored Georgian building is known for its very theatrical theme rooms, ranging from Moroccan to Snowstorm to our favorite, the Decadence Suite. For those who got off on the movie of the same name, there is always Boogie Nights. Rooms have queen- or king-size beds. The bar is one of the hippest in Brighton, where the competition is severe, and the on-site restaurant is a gastronomic delight, with such offerings as seared pigeon breast with grilled salsify and butternut squash, or a fresh pea-and-mint risotto with honeyed parsnip "pearls."

17 Atlingworth St., Brighton, East Sussex BN2 1PL. © **01273/603504.** Fax 01273/689813. www.blanch house.co.uk. 12 units. £99–£169 double; £190–£230 suite. AE, DC, MC, V. Parking £10. **Amenities:** Restaurant; bar. *In room:* TV/DVD, hair dryer.

Nineteen ★ 👜 Only a block from the beach, this rather stunning urban hotel lies close to the Brighton Pier. It's located in Kemp Town, a rapidly gentrified and up-and-coming section of Brighton. The hotel is an oasis of pure white, punctuated by works from contemporary local artists, slatted silver window blinds, and glass-brick platform beds illuminated by blue lighting. That same subtle blue lighting bathes the rooms in a lovely glow. Everything is as modern as tomorrow, including state-of-the-art bathrooms with tub and shower. Guests are invited to make their own snacks in the cellar kitchen.

19 Broad St., Brighton, East Sussex BN2 1TJ. © **01273/675529.** Fax 01273/675531. www.hotelnineteen. co.uk. 8 units. £125–£250 double. Rates include English breakfast. 2-night minimum Sat–Sun. AE, MC, V. Parking £8. **Amenities:** Bar; concierge; room service. *In room:* TV/DVD, CD player, hair dryer, Wi-Fi (free).

INEXPENSIVE

Paskins Hotel This well-run eco-friendly hotel is 2 blocks from the sea and a short walk from the Palace Pier and Royal Pavilion. Bedrooms are individually decorated with contemporary styling. Bathrooms, compact but tidily maintained, have shower stalls. Recent upgrading has made this one of the more charming B&Bs in Brighton. Rates vary depending on plumbing and furnishings; the most expensive units are fitted with four-poster beds. A friendly, informal atmosphere prevails; the freshly cooked award-winning English breakfast (vegetarians are specially catered to), served in a cozy room, is one of the best in town.

18–19 Charlotte St., Brighton, East Sussex BN2 1AG. ☏ **01273/601203.** Fax 01273/621973. www.paskins. co.uk. 19 units, 16 with shower. £65–£80 double without shower, £95 with shower; £110–£140 double with four-poster bed. Rates include English breakfast. AE, MC, V. Parking £5. Bus: 7. **Amenities:** Room service; Wi-Fi (free, in lobby). *In room:* TV, hair dryer.

Regency Hotel   A block from the sea, this typical 1820 Regency town house, once the home of Jane, dowager duchess of Marlborough and great-grandmother of Sir Winston Churchill, is a skillfully converted family-managed hotel with a licensed bar and modern comforts. Many rooms enjoy window views across the square and out to the sea. Accommodations come in a variety of shapes and sizes, but each is well furnished with such extras as bedside radios. The Regency Suite has a half-tester bed (1840) and antique furniture, along with a huge bow window dressed with ceiling-to-floor swagged curtains and a balcony facing the sea and West Pier. The Regency is only a few minutes' walk from the Conference Center and an hour by train or car from Gatwick Airport.

28 Regency Sq., Brighton, East Sussex BN1 2FH. ☏ **01273/202690.** Fax 01273/220438. www.regency hotelbrighton.com. 14 units (shower only). £65–£75 double; £90–£180 Regency Suite. Rates include English breakfast. AE, DC, MC, V. Parking £13. Bus: 1, 2, 3, 5, or 6. **Amenities:** Breakfast room; bar; room service. *In room:* TV, hair dryer, Wi-Fi (free).

Topps Hotel   This cream-colored hotel enjoys a diagonal view of the water from its position beside the sloping lawn of Regency Square, a half-block from the sea. Each room is differently shaped and individually furnished. Except for the singles, most units have fireplaces. Try for a room with a four-poster bed and private balcony opening to a view of the sea.

16–18 Regency Sq., Brighton, East Sussex BN1 2FG. ☏ **01273/770988.** Fax 01273/746912. www. toppshotel.com. 14 units. £90–£175 double. Rates include English breakfast. AE, DC, MC, V. Parking £12. Bus: 1, 2, 3, 5, or 6. **Amenities:** Room service. *In room:* TV, hair dryer, minibar.

IN NEARBY HOVE

The Claremont ★ 🎒   In neighboring Hove, this chic boutique hotel in a restored Victorian house is close to the heart of Brighton and just off the seafront. Tall windows and high ceilings are the remaining 1890s architectural features. Bedrooms are for the most part traditionally decorated with modern touches and spotlessly maintained.

Second Ave., Hove, East Sussex BN3 2LL. ☏ **01273/735-161.** Fax 01273/736836. www.theclaremont.eu. 11 units. £130–£185 double. MC, V. Parking £5. *In room:* TV/DVD, hair dryer, Wi-Fi (free).

Park Inn Brighton   Near the seafront in Hove, 3.2km (2 miles) west of Brighton, the Park Inn (formerly Lansdowne Place) is just a few blocks from the resort's bronze statue of Queen Victoria. Going up marble steps, you register within view of 18th-century antiques. The large, high-ceilinged public rooms are adorned with deeply comfortable chairs and chandeliers. Bedrooms offer tall windows and stylish furniture. Most units are midsize with walnut furnishings and well-appointed bathrooms (with bidets, marble basins, and even heated towel racks).

Lansdowne Place, Hove, Brighton, East Sussex BN3 1HQ. ☏ **01273/736266.** Fax 01273/729802. www. lansdowneplace.co.uk. 84 units. £74–£130 double; £175–£295 suite. AE, DC, MC, V. Parking £15. Bus: 2 or 5. **Amenities:** Restaurant; bar; babysitting; exercise room; room service; spa. *In room:* TV, hair dryer.

Where to Dine

The **Mock Turtle Tea Shop,** 4 Pool Valley (✆ **01273/327380**), is a small but busy tearoom that has many locals stopping by to gossip and take their tea. It offers a variety of cakes, flapjacks, tea breads, and light, fluffy scones with homemade preserves. Everything is made fresh daily. The most popular item is the scone with strawberry preserves or whipped cream.

MODERATE

China Garden BEIJING/CANTONESE   The menu at the China Garden is large and satisfying. It may not be ready for London, and it's certainly pricey, but it's the brightest in town, with many classic dishes deftly handled by the kitchen staff. Dim sum (a popular luncheon choice) is offered only until 4pm. Try crispy sliced Szechuan-style pork or Peking roast duck with pancakes. We've found that some of the most savory dishes on the menu include delectable soft-shell crab, spicy barbecue spareribs, and a superb salt-and-pepper squid. The location is only 3 blocks from the sea.

88 Preston St. (in the town center off Western Rd.). ✆ **01273/325124.** www.chinagarden.name. Reservations recommended. Main courses £7.80–£36. AE, DC, MC, V. Daily noon–11:30pm. Closed Dec 25–26.

Due South ★ MODERN BRITISH   This restaurant has the best green credentials in Sussex. Its chefs seek the very best "organic, free-range, and biodynamic" ingredients they can find, most of their foodstuffs coming from a 56km (35-mile) radius of Brighton Beach. That means that fresh fish and shellfish are their strong points. True to their green philosophy, they keep the decor rather simple—wooden furniture and floors. The location is under one of the arches of the Brighton Promenade close to the beach.

The cooking is straightforward and honest, as evoked by such starters as beet soufflé or pan-roasted quail with wilted greens. Classic, well-prepared mains include pan-fried guinea fowl breast with chestnuts or pan-seared loin of venison with celeriac and a truffle purée. The selection of fresh oysters is the best in town. "Puds" are sometimes startlingly original—ever had a Jerusalem artichoke and thyme crème brûlée?

139 King's Road Arches. ✆ **01273/821218.** www.duesouth.co.uk. Reservations recommended. Main courses £16–£28. AE, MC, V. Daily noon–4pm and 6–10pm.

English's of Brighton SEAFOOD   This popular seafood restaurant occupies a trio of very old fishermen's cottages a block from the sea. Owned and operated by the same family since the end of World War II, it sits in the center of town, near Brighton's bus station. The food is solid and reliable—and fresh. Quality ingredients go into creating such starters as classic English potted shrimp or smoked Scottish salmon. Fresh seafood such as Dover sole and lobster dominate the main courses. Chefs often dress up the fish with intriguing seasonings, as in the pan-fried scallops with sesame seeds and mild chili peppers. English seafood platters are also served. The upstairs dining area incorporates murals depicting Edwardian dinner and theater scenes. In summer, guests can dine alfresco on the terrace.

28 East St. ✆ **01273/327980.** www.englishs.co.uk. Reservations recommended. Main courses £13–£30. AE, DC, MC, V. Mon–Sat noon–10pm; Sun 12:30–9:30pm.

Location 3 ENGLISH   A longtime favorite, this restaurant in the Old Ship Hotel, in the center of town, enjoys an ideal location on the waterfront. When possible, locally caught fish is on the menu. Come here to savor such dishes as mussels in a fennel-and-black-pepper cream sauce, or grilled cod steak with a homemade tomato sauce. A meat specialty is roast rump of Southdown lamb with confit potatoes. The wine list is excellent. Stop in the adjoining pub for a before- or after-dinner drink.

In the Barceló Brighton Old Ship Hotel, King's Rd. ℭ **01273/329001.** Reservations recommended. Main courses £11–£16. AE, DC, MC, V. Daily noon–2pm and 6–9pm. Bus: 1, 2, or 3.

The Restaurant at Drakes ★ MODERN BRITISH/FRENCH   Arguably the best restaurant in Brighton, this basement eatery presents a harmoniously balanced choice of contemporary British dining with French twists. Food is presented with skill and assurance by a well-trained staff in intimate surroundings. Soothing neutral tones predominate in this softly lit, tranquil atmosphere. Starters are startling but tasty, as evoked by the pan-fried lamb sweetbreads and kidneys with duck-fried croutons. For a main, dig into such delights as saddle of venison with garlic potato cakes or rabbit wrapped in pancetta and prunes with a carrot purée.

In the Drakes hotel, 44 Marine Parade. ℭ **01273/696934.** www.therestaurantatdrakes.co.uk. Reservations required. Fixed-price 2-course dinner £28; 3-course dinner £37. AE, MC, V. Daily 12:30–2pm and 7–9:45pm.

INEXPENSIVE

Bill's Produce Store ★ 🎁 MODERN BRITISH   The Bill in the name of this eatery is Bill Collison, who takes great care to support local farmers, preferring them for his supply of varied fruit and vegetables. In what used to be the Brighton bus depot, he has created this successful fresh produce store, deli, and modern dining room that evokes a food market. Start your morning here with such breakfast offerings as crumpets with blackberry butter or buttermilk pancakes. As the day progresses, the menu offers such temptations as steamed Cornish mussels in beer or a charcuterie plate that features Bill's meats with grilled breads. One of the most tantalizing offerings is a Thai spiced pumpkin and coconut curry. You can drop in all day long to sample his market-fresh offerings backed up by a selection of organic wines.

The Depot, 100 North St. ℭ **01273/692894.** www.billsproducestore.co.uk. Reservations recommended after 5pm. Main courses £8.95–£16. AE, MC, V. Mon–Sat 8am–8pm; Sun 10am–4pm.

Terre à Terre ★★ 🎁 VEGETARIAN/VEGAN   The finest vegetarian restaurant on the south coast of England, this is a truly outstanding choice even if you're a carnivore. Guests dine in a trio of spacious rooms in vivid colors, and everything has a bustling brasserie aura. The cooks roam the world for inspiration for their delectable dishes. Sushi, couscous, pizza—it's all here, and does it ever taste good, especially the selection of tapas. To give you an idea of what to expect, good appetizers include goat-cheese crostini with onions and pumpkin confit and a green olive mash, or the lentils cooked in wine with mixed greens. For a main course, vegetable soufflés are often featured, as are potatoes mousseline or stuffed deep-fried green olives. Breads are Italian, and the house wine is organic French. Children's meals are available. The location is 1½ blocks from the sea.

71 East St. ℭ **01273/729051.** www.terreaterre.co.uk. Reservations recommended. Main courses £12–£15. AE, DC, MC, V. Tues–Fri noon–10:30pm; Sat noon–11pm; Sun noon–10pm.

The Royal Pavilion

The Royal Pavilion at Brighton ★★★   Among royal residences in Europe, the Royal Pavilion at Brighton, a John Nash version of an Indian mogul's palace, is unique. Ornate and exotic, it has been subjected over the years to the most devastating wit of English satirists and pundits, but today we can examine it more objectively as one of the most outstanding examples of the Asian tendencies of England's Romantic Movement.

Originally a farmhouse, a neoclassical villa was built on the site in 1787 by Henry Holland, but it no more resembled its present appearance than a caterpillar does a butterfly. By the time Nash had transformed it from a simple classical villa into an Asian fantasy, the prince regent had become King George IV, and the king and one of his mistresses, Lady Conyngham, lived in the palace until 1827.

A decade passed before Victoria, then queen, arrived in Brighton. Though she was to bring Albert and the children on a number of occasions, the monarch and Brighton just didn't mix. The very air of the resort seemed too flippant for her. By 1845, Victoria began packing, and the royal furniture was carted off. Its royal owners gone, the Pavilion was in serious peril of being torn down when, by a narrow vote, Brightonians agreed to purchase it. Gradually it was restored to its former splendor, enhanced in no small part by the return of much of its original furniture, including many items on loan from the queen. A new exhibit tours the Royal Pavilion Gardens.

Of exceptional interest is the domed **Banqueting Room,** with a chandelier of bronze dragons supporting lilylike glass globes. In the **Great Kitchen,** with its old revolving spits, is a collection of Wellington's pots and pans from his town house at Hyde Park Corner. In the **State Apartments,** particularly the domed salon, dragons wink at you, serpents entwine, and lacquered doors shine. The **Music Room,** with its scalloped ceiling, is a fantasy of water lilies, flying dragons, reptilian paintings, bamboo, silk, and satin.

In the first-floor gallery, look for Nash's views of the Pavilion in its elegant heyday. Other attractions include **Queen Victoria's Apartments,** beautifully re-created, and the impressively restored **South Galleries,** breakfast rooms for George IV's guests. Refreshments are available in the **Queen Adelaide Tea Room,** which has a balcony overlooking the Royal Pavilion Gardens.

ⓒ **01273/290900.** www.royalpavilion.org.uk. Admission £9.50 adults, £7.50 students and seniors, £5.40 children 5–15, £24 family ticket, free for children 4 and younger. Apr–Sept daily 9:30am–5:45pm; Oct–Mar daily 10am–5:30pm. Closed Dec 25–26.

Other Attractions

Brighton Museum & Art Gallery ★★   After a £10-million redevelopment, one of the great cultural attractions in the southeast of England has opened. Set in Victorian buildings opposite the Royal Pavilion, the museum is devoted to an eclectic collection of world art and artifacts, ranging from Salvador Dalí's "Mae West's Lips Sofa" to costumes worn at King George IV's coronation in 1821. Employing all the latest interpretive techniques, the museum is one of the most user-friendly outside London. The central gallery displays 20th-century decorative art, including furniture by Philippe Starck, works by Lalique and Bugatti, and a host of other luminaries. You'll see everything from Henry Willett's collection of 2,000 pieces of innovative porcelain to Shiro Kuramata's "How High the Moon Chair" from 1986 (it was inspired by the Duke Ellington jazz standard). The Fashion & Style Gallery draws upon Brighton's extensive collections of period costumes. In the museum's World Art Collection, you'll find some 15,000 objects from the Americas, Africa, Asia, and the Pacific, ranging from Vietnamese water puppets to a black basalt George Washington bust by Wedgwood.

Royal Pavilion Gardens. (℘ **03000/290900.** www.brighton.virtualmuseum.info. Free admission. Tues-Sun 10am–5pm.

Shopping

Mall rats head for **Churchill Square,** Brighton's spacious shopping center, which is home to major chain stores. The shopping center runs from Western Road to North Street (about 3km/2 miles long) and offers many inexpensive shops and stalls, with great buys on everything from antiques to woolens. On Saturdays, there are many more antiques vendors and sidewalk stalls. The mall is open Monday to Wednesday 9am to 6pm, Friday and Saturday 9am to 7pm, and Sunday 11am to 5pm.

Regent Arcade, which is located between East Street, Bartholomew Square, and Market Street, sells artwork, jewelry, and other gift items, as well as high-fashion clothing.

Everyone raves about the shopping on the **Lanes.** The Lanes are a close-knit section of alleyways off North Street in Brighton's Old Town; many of the present shops were formerly fishers' cottages. The shopping is mostly for tourists, and while you may fall for a few photo ops, you'll find that the nearby **North Laine**—between the Lanes and the train station—is the area for up-and-coming talent and for alternative retail. Just wander along a street called Kensington Gardens to get the whole effect. Innumerable shops in the Lanes carry antique books and jewelry, and many boutiques are found in converted backyards on Duke Lane just off Ship Street. In the center of the Lanes is Brighton Square, which is ideal for relaxing or people-watching near the fountain on one of the benches or from a cafe-bar.

Bargain hunters head for the **Kemptown Flea Market,** 31A Upper James St., held Monday to Saturday 9:30am to 5:30pm and Sunday 10:30am to 5pm. A more famous **flea market** is held in the parking lot of the train station, but only on Sunday from 6am to 2pm.

Framework, 26 Kensington Gardens (℘ **01273/818585**), has old photographs of the local area, illustrations, prints, and a complete framing service.

Brighton also abounds in specialty shops. The latest British designers for women are showcased at a fashionable store, **Pussy,** 3A Kensington Gardens (℘ **01273/604861**). One of our favorite gift shops is the **Pavilion Shop,** 4–5 Pavilion Buildings (℘ **01273/292798**), next to the Royal Pavilion. Here you can purchase home furnishings in the style of design schools ranging from Regency to Victorian. Books, jams, needlepoint kits, notebooks, pencils, stencil kits, and other souvenirs are also available.

Brighton After Dark

Brighton offers lots of entertainment options. You can find out what's happening by looking for *What's On,* a single sheet of weekly events posted throughout the town.

Offering drama year-round is the **Theatre Royal,** New Road (© **08700/606650**), with pre-London shows. Bigger concerts are held at **Brighton Centre,** King's Road (© **01273/290131;** www.brightoncentre.co.uk), a 5,000-seat facility featuring mainly pop-music shows.

Nightclubs also abound. Cover charges range from free admission (most often on early or midweek nights) to £10, so call ahead to find out about covers and updated schedules, which often vary from week to week or season to season.

Audio, 10 Marine Parade (© **01273/606906;** www.audiobrighton.com), home to both gay and straight clientele, has one floor for dancing and offers different music styles on different nights of the week on the second floor.

The hot, hot club is **Oceana Brighton,** West Street (© **0845/2968590**), a new multiroom complex and the first nightclub in the area to offer an early-evening bar. There are three different venues under one roof: the Deep Bar, the New York Disco, and the Reykjavik Icehouse. There's disco dancing on Europe's largest illuminated dance floor. Expect to pay a cover of £10, but this could vary depending on the night.

For a change of pace, **Casablanca,** Middle Street (© **01273/321817;** www.casablancajazzclub.com), features jazz with an international flavor.

Pubs are a good place to kick off an evening, especially the **Colonnade Bar,** New Road (© **01273/328728**), serving drinks for over 100 years. It gets a lot of theater business because of its proximity to the Theatre Royal. **Cricketers,** Black Lion Street (© **01273/329472;** www.goldenliongroup.co.uk), is worth a stop because it's Brighton's oldest pub, parts of which date from 1549. Drinking lures patrons to **Fortune of War,** 157 King's Rd. (© **01273/205065**).

Brighton's Gay Scene

After London, Brighton has the most active gay scene in England. Aside from vacationers, it's home to gay retirees and executives who commute into central London by train. The town has always had a reputation for tolerance and humor, and according to the jaded owners of some of the town's 20 or so gay bars, more drag queens live within the local Regency town houses than virtually anywhere else in England.

But the gay scene here is a lot less glittery than in London. And don't assume that the south of England is as chic as the south of France. Its international reputation is growing, but despite that, gay Brighton remains thoroughly English and, at times, even a bit dowdy.

GAY-FRIENDLY PLACES TO STAY

Court Craven Guest House   This three-story hotel isn't particularly exciting and doesn't have many facilities, but it's the cheapest option we recommend, and it has an atmosphere of casual permissiveness. It's proud of a clientele that's almost 100% gay and mostly male. Breakfasts are served communally, with all the traditional English accompaniments. The bedrooms are rather bare-bones: You stay here for the camaraderie—not grand comfort.

2 Atlingworth St., Brighton BN2 1PL. © **01273/696005.** www.courtcraven.co.uk. 12 units (shower only). Mon–Thurs £50–£65 double; Fri–Sun £60–£70 double. Rates include English breakfast. 2-night minimum Sat–Sun. MC, V. **Amenities:** Bar. *In room:* TV.

Coward's Guest House   Originally built in 1807, this five-story, Regency-era house is extremely well maintained. Inside, Jerry and his partner, Cyril (a cousin of the late playwright and bon vivant Noël Coward), welcome only gay men, of all degrees of flamboyance. Don't expect any frills in the conservative, standard rooms, such as those you might find in any modern hotel in England. It offers very few extras, though a number of gay bars and watering holes lie nearby.

12 Upper Rock Gardens, Brighton BN2 1QE. ℂ **01273/692677.** www.cowardsbrighton.co.uk. 6 units. £70–£80 double. Rates include full English breakfast. 2-night minimum Sat–Sun. AE, MC, V. *In room:* TV, fridge.

Legends Hotel Hands-down, this is the largest, busiest, and most fun gay hotel in Brighton. First, it's a bona fide hotel, not a B&B like most of Brighton's other gay-friendly lodgings. Unlike many of its competitors, it welcomes women, though very few of them tend to be comfortable here. Because of the high jinks and raucousness that can float up from the bars below, rooms can be noisy but are nonetheless comfortable, clean, and unfrilly. All units have well-kept bathrooms with shower units. In addition to these rooms, the few luxury boutique doubles are more spacious and furnished more stylishly, with upgraded bathrooms. The staff is happy to camp it up for you before your arrival (adding balloons, champagne, flowers, and streamers), for a fee.

31-32 Marine Parade, Brighton BN2 1TR. ℂ **01273/624462.** Fax 01273/624575. www.legendsbrighton. com. 40 units. £75–£100 double. Rates include English breakfast. 2-night minimum Sat–Sun. AE, DC, MC, V. Nearby parking £10. **Amenities:** 2 bars. *In room:* TV, hair dryer.

GAY NIGHTLIFE

A complete up-to-date roster of the local gay bars is available in any copy of *G-Scene* magazine (ℂ **01273/722457;** www.gscene.com), distributed free in gay hotels and bars throughout the south of England. See also "Brighton After Dark," above, for a few popular dance clubs.

   Doctor Brighton's Bar, 16 King's Rd. (ℂ **01273/328765;** www.doctorbrightons. co.uk), is the largest and most consistently reliable choice. The staff expends great energy on welcoming all members of the gay community. In their words, "We get everyone from 18-year-old designer queens to 50-year-old leather queens, and they, along with all their friends and relatives, are welcome." Originally built around 1750, with a checkered past that includes stints as a smuggler's haven and an abortion clinic, it also has more history and more of the feel of an old-time Victorian pub than any of its competitors. It's open Monday to Thursday 2pm to midnight, Friday 2pm to 1am, Saturday 1pm to 1am, and Sunday 1 to 11pm. With no real lesbian bar in town, gay women tend to congregate at Doctor Brighton's, too.

   Two of the town's busiest and most flamboyant gay bars lie within the Legends Hotel (see above). The one with the longer hours is **Legends Bar,** a pubby, clubby spot with a view of the sea that's open to the public daily from 11am to 11pm and to residents of the Legends Hotel and their guests until 3:30am. Legends Bar features cross-dressing cabarets, with tweedy-looking English matrons and diaphanous Edwardian vamps portrayed with loads of tongue-in-cheek satire and humor. The **Basement Club** is a cellar-level denim-and-leather joint, open daily 11pm to 3:30am.

   The **Marlborough,** 4 Princes St. (ℂ **01273/570028**), has been a staple on the scene for years. Set across from the Royal Pavilion, this Victorian-style pub has a cabaret theater on its second floor. It remains popular with the gay and, to a lesser degree, straight communities. A changing roster of lesbian performance art and both gay and straight cabaret is presented in the second-floor theater.

A SIDE TRIP TO kipling's HOMETOWN

"Heaven looked after it in the dissolute times of mid-Victorian restoration and caused the vicar to send his bailiff to live in it for 40 years, and he lived in peaceful filth and left everything as he found it," wrote **Rudyard Kipling.**

He was writing of **Bateman's** ★ (📞 01435/882302; www.nationaltrust. org.uk), the 17th-century ironmaster's house in the village of Burwash, on the A265, the Lewes-Etchingham road, some 43km (27 miles) northeast of Brighton, close to the border with Kent.

Born in Bombay, India, in 1865, Kipling loved the countryside of Sussex, and the book that best expressed his feelings for the shire is *Puck of Pook's Hill,* written in 1906. The following year he won the Nobel Prize for literature. He lived at Bateman's from 1902 until his death in 1936. His widow died 3 years later, leaving the house to the National Trust.

Kipling is known mainly for his adventure stories, such as *The Jungle Book* (1894) and *Captains Courageous* (1897). He is also remembered for his tales about India, including *Kim* (1901). He lived in the United States after his marriage to Caroline Balestier in 1892. But by 1896, he had returned to the south of England, occupying a house at Rottingdean, a little village on the Sussex Downs, 6.5km (4 miles) east of Brighton. Here he wrote the famous line: "What should they know of England who only England know?"

In a steam-driven motorcar, Kipling and Caroline set out to explore Sussex, of which they were especially fond. Though the population of Rottingdean was only that of a small village, they decided at some point that it had become too crowded. In their motorcar one day, they spotted Bateman's, their final home. "It is a good and peaceable place standing in terraced lawns nigh to a walled garden of old red brick, and two fat-headed oasthouses with red-brick stomachs, and an aged silver-grey dovecot on top," Kipling wrote.

The Burwash city fathers invited Kipling to unveil a memorial to the slain of World War I, and he agreed. It's in the center of town at the church. Kipling said that visitors should "remember the sacrifice." Both the church and an inn across the way appear in the section of *Puck of Pook's Hill* called "Hal o' the Draft." The famous writer and son of Anglo-Indian parents died in London and was given an impressive funeral before being buried in Poets' Corner at Westminster Abbey.

The interior of Bateman's is filled with Asian rugs, antique bronzes, and other mementos the writer collected in India and elsewhere. Kipling's library is quite interesting. The house and gardens are open mid-March through October, Saturday to Wednesday 11am to 5pm. Admission is £7.45 for adults, £4.10 for children, and £19 for a family ticket.

ALFRISTON ★★ & LEWES ★

97km (60 miles) S of London

Nestled on the Cuckmere River, Alfriston is one of the most beautiful villages of England. It lies northeast of Seaford on the English Channel, near the resort of Eastbourne and the modern port of Newhaven. During the day, Alfriston is overrun by coach tours (it's that lovely and that popular). The High Street, with its old market cross, looks just like what you would always imagine a traditional English village to be. Some of the old houses still have hidden chambers where smugglers stored their loot (alas, the loot is gone). There are also several old inns.

About a dozen miles away along the A27 toward Brighton is the rather somber market town of Lewes. Thomas Paine lived at Bull House on High Street in what is now a restaurant. Because the home of the Glyndebourne Opera is only 8km (5 miles) to the east, it's hard to find a place to stay, even in Lewes, during the renowned annual opera festival.

Essentials

GETTING THERE Every day, two trains per hour leave from London's Victoria Station for Lewes. The trip is 1¼ hours. For rail information, call ℰ **0845/748-4950** or visit **www.nationalrail.co.uk**. Alfriston has no rail service.

Buses run daily from London's Victoria Coach Station to Lewes, though the 3-hour trip has so many stops that it's better to take the train. Call ℰ **0871/781-81-78** or visit **www.nationalexpress.com** for schedules.

Bus no. 125 runs from Lewes to Alfriston every 90 minutes. It's operated by **Countryliner** (ℰ **01444/506919;** www.countryliner-coaches.co.uk). For bus information and schedules in the area, call ℰ **0871/200-2233.** The bus station at Lewes is on East Gate Street in the center of town.

If you're driving, head east along the M25, the London Ring Road, and cut south on the A26 via East Grinstead to Lewes. Once at Lewes, follow the A27 east to the signposted turnoff for the village of Alfriston.

VISITOR INFORMATION The **Tourist Information Centre** is in Lewes at 187 High St. (ℰ **01273/483448;** www.enjoysussex.info). In season, from Easter until the end of October, hours are Monday to Friday 9am to 5pm, Saturday 9:30am to 5:30pm, and Sunday 10am to 2pm. Off-season hours are Monday to Friday 9am to 5pm, Saturday 10am to 2pm.

Where to Stay

IN ALFRISTON

Dean's Place Hotel Dean's Place offers English-country-house living at a reasonable price. The property dates from the 1300s, though it has been much improved and architecturally altered over the years. Set in beautifully landscaped gardens, it is a cliché of English country charm with creeper-covered walls. Bedrooms come in a variety of sizes, all comfortably appointed with firm beds. The staff is polite and helpful. The location is convenient for trips to Lewes and Brighton, among other places.

Seaford Rd., Polgate, East Sussex BN26 5TW. ℰ **01323/870248.** Fax 01323/870918. www.deansplace hotel.co.uk. 36 units. £115–£170 double. Rates include English breakfast. AE, MC, V. On the 2nd round-about after Lewes, take the 3rd exit for Alfriston and Drusilla's Zoo. Pass through Alfriston to the south side. The hotel is on the left side of the road. **Amenities:** Restaurant; bar; outdoor heated pool; room service. *In room:* TV/DVD, hair dryer.

George Inn The George dates from 1397, making it one of the oldest inns in the country. It was once a rendezvous for smugglers. The midsize bedrooms are inviting and comfortable; two of them have four-poster beds. All rooms have neatly kept bathrooms equipped with a tub. The George, however, is better known for its good food. A garden is in back, but most guests head for the restaurant with its Windsor chairs and beamed ceiling.

High St., Alfriston, East Sussex BN26 5SY. 📞 **01323/870319.** Fax 01323/871384. www.thegeorge-alfriston.com. 6 units. £90–£130 double. 2-night minimum Sat–Sun. Rates include English breakfast. MC, V. **Amenities:** Restaurant; bar. *In room:* A/C, TV/DVD, hair dryer, no phone.

Riverdale House   Set on a hill overlooking the town, this small B&B is one of the finest in the area. A restored Victorian home, it offers handsomely furnished bedrooms in various sizes. Each comes with a small but tidy private bathroom with shower. Most rooms open onto lovely countryside views, including a well-kept garden in front. Riverdale also has a large conservatory where guests socialize or enjoy the reading material.

Seaford Rd., Alfriston, East Sussex BN26 5TR. 📞 **01323/871038.** www.riverdalehouse.co.uk. 4 units. £80–£105 double; £130–£140 suite. Rates include English breakfast. MC, V. *In room:* TV/DVD.

The Star ★   This inn—the premier place to stay in Alfriston—occupies a building dating from 1450, though it was originally founded in the 1200s to house pilgrims en route to Chichester and the shrine of St. Richard. Located in the center of the village, its carved front remains unchanged. The lounges are on several levels, a forest of old timbers. Bedrooms vary in size and style, but each one in the main building is well maintained with an old-world aura. We infinitely prefer these rooms, which have far more character even though they've been altered and renovated over the years. Out back is a more sterile motel wing with studio units.

High St., Alfriston, East Sussex BN26 5TA. 📞 **01323/870495.** Fax 01323/870922. www.thestaralfriston. co.uk. 37 units. £115–£160 double. Rates include English breakfast. AE, DC, MC, V. Free parking. **Amenities:** Restaurant; bar; babysitting; room service. *In room:* TV, hair dryer, Wi-Fi (free).

IN LEWES

Lewes is blessed with a number of affordable B&Bs, the largest concentration of recommendable ones found along Gundreda Road. The best of these include **Two Chimneys Bed & Breakfast,** 25 Gundreda Rd., Lewes BN7 1PT (📞 **01273/476079;** www.visitlewesbedandbreakfast.co.uk), which charges £75 double.

Crown Inn   Built around 1760, this is one of the oldest inns in Lewes, a 30-minute ride from Gatwick and 60 minutes from London. Located opposite the town's war memorial, it stands at a traffic circle on the main street. The hotel is considerably refurbished, though still a bit creaky. Pub lunches and dinner are served daily in a Victorian conservatory.

191 High St., Lewes, East Sussex BN7 2NA. 📞 **01273/480670.** Fax 01273/480679. www.crowninnlewes. co.uk. 8 units, 7 with bathroom. £60 double without bathroom, £70 w/bathroom; £80 family room. Rates include English breakfast. MC, V. **Amenities:** Bar. *In room:* TV, hair dryer.

The Shelleys ★   The earl of Dorset owned this 1526 manor house before it was sold to the Shelley family, wealthy Sussex landowners (and relatives of the poet Percy Bysshe Shelley). Radical changes were made to the architecture in the 18th century. A complete refurbishment has turned the hotel into a luxurious two-restaurant country-house retreat. There are traditional details throughout, such as the family coat of arms in the central hall. The standards of the management are reflected in the fine antiques, bowls of flowers, paintings and prints, well-kept gardens, and, most important, helpful staff. The bedrooms are personal, individually furnished, usually spacious, and most comfortable.

136 High St., Lewes, East Sussex BN7 1XS. © **01273/472361.** Fax 01273/483152. www.the-shelleys.co.uk. 19 units. £115–£260 double. Children 5 and younger stay free in parent's room. AE, DC, MC, V. **Amenities:** Restaurant; bar; babysitting; room service. *In room:* TV, hair dryer, minibar.

Where to Dine
IN ALFRISTON

Around teatime, head for the **Tudor House,** on Alfriston's High Street (© **01323/870891;** www.tudorhouse-restaurant.co.uk). The well-lit interior has two tearooms that provide a calm setting for afternoon tea. Cheese, ham-and-cheese, and egg-salad sandwiches and muffins, Danish, scones, and cakes are served. Afternoon tea costs £4.50 to £7, sandwiches £4 to £6, and cakes and pastries from £2.50. It's open daily 10:30am to 4:30pm, Wednesday to Saturday 7 to 9pm.

IN LEWES

The Juggs ENGLISH   In a romantic setting in the South Downs, this old pub serves good food and plenty of beer and ale in the satellite village of Kingston, 4.8km (3 miles) southeast of Lewes. A tile-coated 1400s cottage, it is said to be named for a woman called "Juggs," who walked from Brighton with baskets of fresh fish for sale in the countryside. You can still order fresh fish here along with such English specialties as steak-and-kidney pudding and roasts. Look for daily specials as well. For dessert, why not have the homemade chocolate brownie with chocolate fudge sauce?

The Street, Kingston. © **01273/472523.** Reservations not needed. Main courses £9–£18. MC, V. Mon-Sat 11am–11pm; Sun noon–10pm.

Pailin ☺ THAI   Spicy-hot Thai food has come to Lewes, though some of the fiery dishes have been toned down for English taste buds. Begin perhaps with the lemon chicken soup with lemon grass, followed by a crab-and-prawn hot pot. A special favorite with locals is the barbecued marinated chicken, which is served with a spicy but delectable sweet-and-sour plum sauce. Vegetarian meals are available, and children are welcome and given small portions at reduced prices.

20 Station St. © **01273/473906.** Reservations not needed. Main courses £7–£8.50. AE, DC, MC, V. Tues–Sat noon–3pm and 6–10:30pm. Closed Nov 5 and Dec 25–26.

Glyndebourne Festival Opera ★

In 1934, a group of local opera enthusiasts established an opera company based in the hamlet of Glyndebourne, which is 2.5km (1½ miles) east of Lewes and 8km (5 miles) northwest of Alfriston. (See listings under either of these towns for a selection of places to overnight if you'd like to stay in the area after the performances and not take the train back to London.) The festival has been running ever since and is now one of the best regional opera companies in Britain.

In 1994, the original auditorium was demolished, and a dramatically modern glass, brick, and steel structure, designed by noted English architect Michael Hopkins, was built adjacent to some remaining (mostly ornamental) vestiges of the original building. The new auditorium is known for its acoustics.

Operas are presented only between mid-April and late August, and productions tend to be of unusual works. For information, contact the **Glyndebourne Festival,** Glyndebourne, Lewes, East Sussex BN8 5UW (© **01273/815000;** www.glyndebourne.com). You can call the box office at © **01273/813813.** Ticket prices range from £10 to £150. You can usually get last-minute tickets because of cancellations by season-ticket holders. If you want to see a specific show, however, it's a good idea to purchase tickets several months in advance. Credit card orders (Visa and MasterCard) are accepted, and for an additional postage charge, you can have tickets delivered to you. Dress is formal: Many Londoners show up in black tie, which is requested but not required.

To get to the theater from Lewes, take the A26 to the B2192, following the signs to Glynde and Glyndebourne. From Alfriston, follow the hamlet's main street north of town in the direction of the A27, then turn left following signs first to Glynde, and then to Glyndebourne. There are also trains from London that are specially scheduled to deliver operagoers to Glyndebourne, and then take them home after the picnic and the performances.

Exploring the Two Towns

Anne of Cleves House This half-timbered house was part of Anne of Cleves's divorce settlement from Henry VIII, but Anne never lived in the house and there's no proof that she ever visited Lewes. Today, it's a museum of local history, cared for by the Sussex Archaeological Society. The museum has a furnished bedroom and kitchen and displays of furniture, local history of the Wealden iron industry, and other crafts.

52 Southover High St., Lewes. © **01273/474610.** Admission £4.20 adults, £3.70 students and seniors, £2.10 children. Mar–Oct Tues–Thurs 10am–5pm; Sun–Mon 11am–5pm. Bus: 123.

Barbican House Museum Lewes, of course, matured in the shadow of its Norman castle. Adjacent to the castle is this museum, where a 20-minute audiovisual show is available by advance request. Audio tours of the castle are also available.

169 High St., Lewes. © **01273/486290.** www.sussexpast.co.uk. Joint admission ticket to both castle and museum £6 adults, £5.40 students and seniors, £3 children, £16 family ticket. Both sites Tues–Sat 10am–5:30pm; Sun–Mon 11am–5:30pm. The castle closes at dusk in the winter. Closed Dec 25–26. Bus: 27, 28, 121, 122, 166, 728, or 729.

Drusilla's Park ☺ This fascinating but not-too-large park has a flamingo lake, Japanese garden, and unusual breeds of some domestic animals, among other attractions. The park is perfect for families with children. Check out the newly converted £85,000 bat house, where a family of 20 Rodrigues fruit bats (also called mega bats) has taken up residence. With a wingspan of about 1m (3 ft.) and rich golden brown fur, they are one of the rarest and most beautiful bat species in the world.

About 1.5km (1 mile) outside Alfriston, off A27. © **01323/874100.** www.drusillas.co.uk. Admission £11–£14, free for children 1 and younger. Daily 10am–5pm (to 4pm in winter). Closed Dec 24–26.

A Side Trip from Lewes: Virginia Woolf's Home ★ & the Bluebell Railway

This is gorgeous countryside for walks. If you want some direction in your ramblings, consider the rustic properties below. The most scenic walk you can take is the 4.8km (3-mile) trek south of Lewes (it's signposted) to the village of Rodmell. If you take this walk to call on the former home of Virginia Woolf, you'll be following a trail blazed by other walkers, each a part of the Bloomsbury Group, whose roster included T. S. Eliot, Aldous Huxley, Bertrand Russell, and E. M. Forster.

The small downland village of **Rodmell** lies midway between Lewes and the port of Newhaven on C7. It has a 12th-century church, a working farm, and a tiny Victorian school still in use. Take Southdown bus no. 123 from the Lewes rail station if you prefer not to walk.

Rodmell is best known for **Monk's House** (✆ **01323/870001;** www.national trust.co.uk), a National Trust property that was bought by Virginia and Leonard Woolf in 1919, and served as their home until his death in 1969. Much of the house was furnished and decorated by Virginia's sister, Vanessa Bell, and the artist Duncan Grant. The house has limited visiting hours: from April to October, and then only on Wednesday and Saturday from 2 to 5:30pm. Admission is £4 for adults, £2 for children, and free for kids 4 and younger. A family ticket costs £10.

The trail of Virginia Woolf also leads to **Charleston Farmhouse** (✆ **01323/811265;** www.charleston.org.uk), located along the A27 at Charleston, near Firle, 9.5km (6 miles) east of Lewes. This house is the former country residence of Vanessa Bell and the artist Duncan Grant, the glittering faces of the artistically influential Bloomsbury Group early in the 20th century. Preserved much as they left it, the property is filled with mementos and is open to guided tours on most days. Opening times are April through June and September through October, Wednesday to Saturday 1 to 6pm and Sunday 11am to 5:30pm; July and August, Wednesday to Saturday noon to 6pm and Sunday 1 to 5:30pm. Admission is £9 for adults, £5.50 for children, and £23 for a family ticket. On Sundays, no tours are offered, but visitors are free to explore the house on their own. The trust that runs the property also displays changing exhibitions and sponsors an annual literary and arts festival.

The all-steam **Bluebell Railway** (✆ **01825/720825;** www.bluebell-railway. co.uk) starts at Sheffield Park Station near Uckfield in East Sussex, on A275 between East Grinstead and Lewes. The name is taken from the spring flowers that grow alongside the track, running from Sheffield Park to Kingscote. It's a delight for railway buffs, with locomotives dating from the 1870s through the 1950s, when British Railways ended steam operations. You can visit locomotive sheds and a small museum, and then later patronize the bookshop or have lunch in a large buffet, bar, and restaurant complex. The round-trip takes 1½ hours as the train wanders through a typical English countryside. It costs £13 for adults and £6.25 for children 3 to 16, with a family ticket going for £35. Trains run daily from April to September, and on Saturday and Sunday only during the rest of the year.

HAMPSHIRE & DORSET: AUSTEN & HARDY COUNTRY

9

ampshire and Dorset are two counties jealously guarded as special rural treasures. Everybody knows of Southampton and Bournemouth, but less familiar is the hilly countryside farther inland, which is best previewed in Hampshire's New Forest. And in Dorset, you can discover tiny villages and thatched cottages, untouched by the industrial invasion, at Chideock and Charmouth.

Jane Austen wrote about the firmly middle-class inhabitants of **Hampshire** in her six novels, including *Pride and Prejudice* and *Sense and Sensibility,* which earned her a permanent place among the pantheon of 19th-century writers and unexpected popularity among 1990s film directors and producers. You can visit her grave in **Winchester Cathedral** and the house where she lived, **Chawton Cottage.**

Hampshire encompasses the **South Downs,** the **Isle of Wight** (Victoria's favorite retreat), and the naval city of **Portsmouth.** More than 36,421 hectares (90,000 acres) of the **New Forest** were preserved by William the Conqueror as a private hunting ground; this vast woodland and heath remains ideal for walking and exploring. In this chapter, we concentrate primarily on two major areas: **Southampton,** for convenience, and **Winchester,** for history.

To the west, the county of **Dorset** is Thomas Hardy country. Born in Dorset in 1840, the celebrated writer disguised the county of his birth as "Wessex" in his novels. "The last of the great Victorians," as he was called, died in 1928 at age 88. His tomb occupies a position of honor in Westminster Abbey.

Hampshire & Dorset

HAMPSHIRE & DORSET: AUSTEN & HARDY COUNTRY

9

One of England's smallest shires, Dorset is a southwestern county that borders the English Channel. It encompasses the old seaport of **Poole** in the east and **Lyme Regis** (known to Jane Austen) in the west. It's known for its cows, and Dorset butter is served at many an afternoon tea. This is mainly a land of farms and pastures, with plenty of sandy heaths and chalky downs.

The most prominent tourist center of Dorset is the Victorian seaside resort of **Bournemouth.** If you decide not to stay here, you can try a number of Dorset's other seaports, villages, and country towns; we mostly stick to the areas along the impressive coastline.

You'll find the largest number of hotels, but not the greatest charm, at Bournemouth. If you're interested in things maritime, opt for Portsmouth, the premier port of the south and home of HMS *Victory,* Nelson's flagship. For history buffs and Austen fans, Winchester, the ancient capital of England, with a cathedral built by William the Conqueror, makes a good base for exploring the countryside.

The best beaches are at Bournemouth, set among pines with sandy beaches and fine coastal views; and **Chesil Beach,** a 32km-long (20-mile) bank of shingle running from Abbottsbury to the Isle of Portland—great for beachcombing. However, the most natural spectacle is New Forest itself, 375 sq. km (145 sq. miles) of heath and woodland, once the hunting ground of Norman kings.

WINCHESTER ★★

116km (72 miles) SW of London; 19km (12 miles) N of Southampton

The most historic city in all of Hampshire, Winchester is big on legends because it's associated with King Arthur and the Knights of the Round Table.

The city is also linked with King Alfred, who is honored today by a statue. Alfred the Great, born in 849, was crowned king in 871, ruling until his death in 899. He is called "the Great," because he defended Anglo-Saxon England against Viking raids, formulated a code of laws, and fostered a rebirth of religious and scholarly activity.

Of course, Winchester is a mecca for Jane Austen fans. You can visit her grave in Winchester Cathedral (Emma Thompson did, while working on her adapted screenplay of *Sense and Sensibility*), as well as Chawton Cottage, Jane Austen's house, which is 24km (15 miles) east of Winchester.

Its past glory but a memory, Winchester is essentially a market town today, lying on the downs along the Itchen River.

Essentials

GETTING THERE   Frequent daily train service runs from London's Waterloo Station to Winchester. The trip takes 1 hour. For rail information, call ✆ **0845/748-4950** or visit **www.nationalrail.co.uk**. Arrivals are at Winchester Station, Station Hill, northwest of the city center.

National Express coaches make regular daily departures for Winchester from London's Victoria Coach Station. The trip takes 2 hours. Call ✆ **0871/781-81-78** or visit **www.nationalexpress.com** for schedules and information.

If you're driving from Southampton, head north on the A335; from London, take the M3 motorway southwest.

VISITOR INFORMATION The **Tourist Information Centre,** on Winchester High Street (📞 **01962/840500;** www.visitwinchester.co.uk), is open October through April, Monday to Saturday 10am to 5pm; and May through September, Monday to Saturday 9:30am to 5:30pm and Sunday 11am to 4pm. Guided walking tours, which depart from this tourist center, are conducted for £4 per person. Departure times vary; check with the center once you're in town.

Where to Stay

Lainston House ★★★ The beauty of this restored William and Mary redbrick manor house strikes visitors as they approach via a long, curving, tree-lined drive. It's situated on 25 hectares (63 acres) of rolling land and linked with the name Lainston in the Domesday Book. Elegance is key inside the stately main house, where panoramically big suites are located. Other rooms, less spacious but also comfortable and harmoniously furnished, are in a nearby 1990 annex. The better units have large dressing areas and walk-in closets. The latest block of beautifully appointed rooms is a series of six converted stables.

Sparsholt, Winchester, Hampshire SO21 2LT. © **01962/776088.** Fax 01962/776672. www.lainston house.com. 50 units. £125–£330 double; £210–£785 suite. MC, V. Free parking. Take B3420 2.5km (1½ miles) northwest of Winchester. **Amenities:** Restaurant; bar; babysitting; exercise room; room service; 2 outdoor tennis courts. *In room:* TV, hair dryer, Jacuzzi (in some), Wi-Fi (free).

Winchester Royal   This fine hotel is a comfortable choice. Built at the end of the 16th century as a private house, it was used by Belgian nuns as a convent for 50 years before being turned into a hotel, quickly becoming the center of the city's social life. Only a few minutes' walk from the cathedral, it still enjoys a secluded position. A modern extension overlooks gardens, and all bedrooms have traditional English styling. Rooms in the main house are more traditional than those in the modern wing, but each unit is well appointed.

St. Peter St., Winchester, Hampshire SO23 8BS. © **01962/840840.** Fax 01962/841582. www.the winchesterroyalhotel.co.uk. 75 units. £90–£130 double. Rates include English breakfast. AE, DC, MC, V. Free parking. **Amenities:** 2 restaurants; bar; babysitting; room service. *In room:* TV, hair dryer, Wi-Fi (£6 per hr.).

Wykeham Arms ★ 🏚   Our longtime favorite in Winchester, the Wykeham Arms lies behind a 200-year-old brick facade in the historic center of town, near the cathedral. Rooms are traditionally furnished with antiques or reproductions and decorated with such touches as fresh flowers and baskets of potpourri. Most bedrooms are a bit small but attractively appointed. Six rooms were added in a 16th-century building that faces the original hotel. The annex has the most luxurious and spacious accommodations, containing well-equipped large modern bathrooms, each with tub and shower. A large suite with cozy fire-warmed sitting room and upstairs bedroom is also available. Overlooking the Winchester College Chapel, these annex rooms have the same amenities as the original rooms. ***Note:*** The hotel does not accept children 13 or younger.

75 Kingsgate St., Winchester, Hampshire SO23 9PE. © **01962/853834.** Fax 01962/854411. www.fullers hotels.com. 14 units. £115 double in original building; £130 double in annex; £150 suite. Rates include English breakfast. AE, DC, MC, V. Free parking. **Amenities:** Restaurant; bar. *In room:* TV, hair dryer, minibar, Wi-Fi (free).

Where to Dine

Hotel du Vin & Bistro ★ 🍴 ENGLISH/CONTINENTAL   This inn offers both food and lodging, bringing a touch of chic to Winchester. It's a town-house hotel that dates from 1715 and has a walled garden. Gerard Basset and Robin Hutson learned their lessons well at exclusive Chewton Glen (p. 346) before embarking on their own enterprise. The chef delivers some of the finest food in Winchester today. The bistro fare is excellent and a good value, with a menu that always features regional ingredients: Try the filet of sea bass with a crayfish velouté, or the roast pheasant with wild mushroom jus. Basset has the finest wine list in the county.

You can stay overnight in one of 24 double rooms decorated with a wine theme. The comfortable rooms have good beds, antiques, TVs, and state-of-the-art bathrooms. Rates are £140 to £225.

14 Southgate St. © **01962/841414.** Fax 01962/842458. www.hotelduvin.com. Reservations recommended. Main courses £15–£20. AE, DC, MC, V. Mon–Fri noon–1:45pm; Sat 12:30–1:45pm; Sun 12:30–2:15pm; Sun–Thurs 7–9:30pm; Fri–Sat 7–10:30pm.

Old Chesil Rectory ★★★ FRENCH   One of the finest restaurants in Hampshire, this 15th-century building, restored over the years, is aglow with half-timbered architecture and whitewashed panels. White candles, white flowers, and white table linens create a lovely mood for dining. The chef turns out refined versions of classic French dishes, made lighter for more modern and discerning palates. The menu is adjusted seasonally to take advantage of regional produce. Full of brawny flavor and heady perfumes, starters range from house-cured salmon with a sweet dill dressing to a tart of creamed leeks with goat cheese. Main-dish temptations are likely to include roast rump of lamb with braised red cabbage and a potato fondant, or else braised Hampshire beef with a horseradish potato puree and seasonal greens.

1 Chesil St. ⓒ **01962/851555.** www.chesilrectory.co.uk. Reservations required. Main courses £12–£18; fixed-price 2-course lunch £15, 3-course lunch £20. DC, MC, V. Wed–Sat noon–3pm; Tues–Sat 7–10pm.

Exploring the Area

Winchester and its surrounding countryside lend themselves to walks. Space is too tight here to document the many possibilities, but the Tourist Information Centre (see above) has a helpful free pamphlet, *The Winchester Walk,* that details various walking tours.

Castle Great Hall ★   This is the only part that remains of the castle first erected in Winchester by the Normans. Dating from the 1200s, it is one of the finest examples of a medieval hall in England, with its timber roof supported on columns of Purbeck marble. The first fortress here was erected by William the Conqueror after he'd subdued England. Henry III rebuilt a castle on its foundation. It was once a royal seat, and the English Parliament met here for the first time in 1246. The castle played a part in English history, including the trial of Sir Walter Raleigh, who was condemned to death here in 1603 for conspiring against King James I. See an exhibition on the history of the castle and walk through tranquil Queen Eleanor's Medieval Garden.

Castle Hill. ⓒ **01962/846476.** www.hants.gov.uk/greathall. Free admission. Mid-Feb to Oct daily 10am–5pm; Nov to early Feb daily 10am–4pm.

Chawton Cottage ★   At Chawton you can see where Jane Austen spent the last 7½ years of her life, her most productive period. In the unpretentious but pleasant cottage is the table on which she penned new versions of three of her books and wrote three more, including *Emma.* You can also see examples of Austen's needlework and jewelry, the rector's George III mahogany bookcase, and a silhouette likeness of the Reverend Austen presenting his son to the Knights. It was in this cottage that Jane Austen became ill in 1816 with what would have been diagnosed by the middle of the 19th century as Addison's disease. She died in July 1817.

The grounds feature an attractive garden, where you can picnic, and an old bake house with Austen's donkey cart. A bookshop stocks new and secondhand books.

Chawton, 1.5km (1 mile) southwest of Alton off A31 and B3006, 24km (15 miles) east of Winchester. ⓒ **01420/83262.** www.jane-austens-house-museum.org.uk. Admission £7 adults, £6 students and seniors, £2 children 6–16. June–Aug daily 10am–5pm; Sept–Dec and Mar–May daily 10:30am–4:30pm. Closed Dec 25–26 and Jan–Feb.

Hospital of St. Cross ★★   Founded in 1132, the hospital is the oldest charitable institution in England. It was established by Henri du Blois, grandson of William the

Conqueror, as a link for social care and to supply life's necessities to the local poor and famished travelers. It continues the tradition of providing refreshments to visitors today. Simply stop at the Porter's Lodge for a Wayfarer's Dole, and you'll receive some bread and ale. In the inner courtyard of the hospital, you can see the Brethren's houses from 1450, the refectory, and a church, which is a fine example of medieval architecture (ca. 1250). Inside the church is a lectern from 1510. In the south chapel is a triptych created in the 1530s. The English lyric poet John Keats has associations with this hospital: He spent 3 months here in 1818 attending his brother, Tom, who was seriously ill with tuberculosis.

After your visit to this complex, you can head east to St. Catherine's Hill, rising 78m (255 ft.), where you can enjoy a vista of the town and country and see the ruins of an Iron Age fort and a medieval chapel. On a clear day, you can see the hamlet of Chilcomb and its small early Norman church to the northeast.

St. Cross Rd. Ⓒ **01962/852888.** www.stcross.f2s.com. Admission £3 adults, £2.50 students and seniors, £1 children under 13. Apr–Oct Mon–Sat 9:30am–5pm, Sun 1–5pm; off-season Mon–Sat 10:30am–3:30pm.

Winchester Cathedral ★★★ This is one of the great churches of England. The present building, the longest medieval cathedral in Britain, dates from 1079, and its Norman heritage is still in evidence. When a Saxon church stood on this spot, St. Swithun, bishop of Winchester and tutor to young King Alfred, suggested modestly that he be buried outside. Following his subsequent indoor burial, it rained for 40 days. The legend lives on: Just ask a resident of Winchester what will happen if it rains on St. Swithun's Day, July 15, and you'll get a prediction of rain for 40 days.

The Perpendicular nave, with its two aisles, is the architectural highlight of the building. The elaborately carved choir stalls from 1308 are England's oldest. The cathedral is graced with a series of beautiful ornamental screens dating from the late 15th century. Other architectural highlights include the Lady Chapel, rebuilt by Elizabeth of York at the dawn of the 16th century after her son was baptized in the cathedral. Jane Austen is buried here; her grave is marked with a commemorative plaque. In addition, chests contain the bones of many Saxon kings and the remains of the Viking conqueror Canute and his wife, Emma. The son of William the Conqueror, William Rufus (who reigned as William II), is also buried at the cathedral.

The library houses Bishop Morley's 17th-century book collection, and an exhibition room contains the 12th-century Winchester Bible. The Triforium shows sculpture, woodwork, and metalwork from 11 centuries and affords magnificent views over the rest of the cathedral.

The Close. Ⓒ **01962/857200.** www.winchester-cathedral.org.uk. Admission to cathedral £6 adults, £4.80 seniors, £3.50 students, free for children 15 and younger; admission to library and Triforium Gallery £1 adults. Free guided tours year-round 10am–3pm hourly. Crypt is often flooded during winter, but part may be seen from a viewing platform. Cathedral Mon–Sat 8:30am–6pm; Sun 8:30am–5:30pm. Library and Triforium Gallery Apr–Oct Mon 1:30–4pm, Tues–Sat 11am–1pm and 1:30–4pm; Nov–Mar Wed and Sat 11am–3:30pm (Jan–Feb Sat only).

Winchester College ★ Winchester College was founded by William of Wykeham, bishop of Winchester and chancellor to Richard II, and was first occupied in 1394. Its buildings have been in continuous use for more than 600 years, making it the oldest continuously open school in England. The structures vary from Victorian Tudor Gothic to the more modern trimmings of the New Hall, designed in 1961.

The Chapel Hall, kitchens, and the Founder's Cloister date from the 14th century. In the 17th century, buildings were added on the south side, including a schoolroom constructed between 1683 and 1687. Exploration of the college is possible only by guided tour, lasting an hour and covering the Chamber Court, the 14th-century Gothic chapel, and the College Hall, among other sights.

73 Kingsgate St. © **01962/621209.** www.winchestercollege.co.uk. Admission £4 adults, £3.50 students and seniors. Guided tours Tues and Thurs 10:45am and noon; Mon, Wed, and Fri–Sat 10:45am, noon, 2:15, and 3:30pm; Sun 2:15 and 3:30pm.

Shopping

Fill up those empty suitcases at **Cadogan,** 30–31 The Square (© **01962/877399;** www.cadoganandcompany.co.uk), which carries an upscale and stylish selection of British clothing for men and women alike. For a unique piece of jewelry created by one of today's most acclaimed designers, stop by **Carol Darby Jewellery,** 23 Little Minster St. (© **01962/867671**). The oldest book dealer in town is **P&G Wells,** 11 College St. (© **01962/852016;** www.bookwells.co.uk), with both new releases and secondhand fiction and nonfiction.

Winchester After Dark

The place to go is the **Porthouse,** Upper Brook Street (© **01962/869397;** www.porthousenightclub.com), a pub-cum-nightclub, sprawling across three floors. Different nights have different themes, from funk to pop. After 9pm, you'll pay a cover of £2 to £5, depending on the night.

PORTSMOUTH ★ & SOUTHSEA

121km (75 miles) SW of London; 31km (19 miles) SE of Southampton

Virginia, New Hampshire, and Ohio may each have a Portsmouth, but the forerunner of them all is the old port and naval base on the Hampshire coast, seat of the British Navy for 500 years. German bombers in World War II leveled the city, hitting about 90% of its buildings. But the seaport was rebuilt admirably and now aggressively promotes its military attractions. It draws visitors interested in the nautical history of England as well as World War II buffs.

Its maritime associations are known around the world. From Sally Port, the most interesting district in the Old Town, countless naval heroes have embarked to fight England's battles, including on June 6, 1944, when Allied troops set sail to invade occupied France.

Southsea, adjoining Portsmouth, is a popular seaside resort with fine sands, lush gardens, bright lights, and a host of vacation attractions. Many historic monuments are located along the stretches of open space, where you can walk on the Clarence Esplanade, look out on the Solent Channel, and view the busy shipping activities of Portsmouth Harbour.

Essentials

GETTING THERE Trains from London's Waterloo Station stop at Portsmouth and Southsea Station frequently throughout the day. The trip takes 2 hours. Call © **0845/748-4950** or visit **www.nationalrail.co.uk**.

National Express (𝒞 **0871/781-81-78;** www.nationalexpress.com) operates buses out of London's Victoria Coach Station that make the run to Portsmouth and Southsea every 2 hours during the day. The trip takes 2 hours and 45 minutes.

If you're driving from London's Ring Road, head south on the A3.

VISITOR INFORMATION   The **Tourist Information Centre,** at the Hard, in Portsmouth (𝒞 **023/9282-6722;** www.visitportsmouth.co.uk), is open daily 9:30am to 5:15pm.

Where to Stay

Best Western Royal Beach Hotel   The balconied Victorian facade of this hotel, directly east of Southside Common, rises above the boulevard running beside the sea. Restored by its owners, the hotel's interior decor ranges from contemporary to full-curtained traditional, depending on the room. Each of the bedrooms has been renovated with built-in furniture.

South Parade, Southsea, Portsmouth, Hampshire PO4 0RN. 𝒞 **023/9273-1281.** Fax 023/9281-7572. www.royalbeachhotel.co.uk. 126 units. £75–£125 double; £185–£225 suite. Rates include English breakfast. Children 5 and younger stay free in parent's room. AE, DC, MC, V. Free parking. **Amenities:** Restaurant; bar; room service. *In room:* TV, hair dryer, Wi-Fi (free).

Westfield Hall ★ 📷   In the resort of Southsea, two early-20th-century homes near the water have been turned into a hotel with a certain charm and character. One of the most inviting and most comfortable of the little family-run hotels in the area, this highly commendable establishment offers a warm welcome and beautifully maintained, comfortably furnished bedrooms. Many units are graced by large bay windows. Guests enjoy the use of three lounges.

65 Festing Rd., Southsea, Portsmouth, Hampshire PO4 0NQ. 𝒞 **023/9282-6971.** Fax 023/9287-0200. www.whhotel.info. 26 units. £68–£146 double. Rates include English breakfast. AE, DC, MC, V. Free parking. **Amenities:** Restaurant; bar. *In room:* TV, hair dryer, Wi-Fi (free).

IN NEARBY WICKHAM

Old House Hotel ★ 📷   A handsome early Georgian (1715) structure, the Old House is surrounded by low, medieval timber structures around the square. The hotel has undergone a classic refurbishment, giving it the look of a proud English country house. The paneled rooms on the ground and first floors of the hotel contrast with the beamed bedrooms on the upper floors, once the servants' quarters. All bedrooms have period furniture, many of the pieces original antiques, and warm, comfortable beds. Four of the units are called "Garden Suites," although they are rooms, not suites. These are located in an annex and are more spacious than rooms in the main building. Although modern, these so-called suites do have some period furniture.

The Square, Wickham, Fareham, Hampshire PO17 5JG. 𝒞 **01329/833049.** Fax 01329/833672. www.oldhousehotel.co.uk. 12 units. £90–£165 double. Rates include continental breakfast. AE, MC, V. Free parking. Bus no. 69 from Fareham. Head 14km (9 miles) west from Portsmouth on M27; exit at no. 10. The village is 3km (2 miles) north of the junction of B2177 and A32. **Amenities:** Restaurant; bar. *In room:* TV, hair dryer, Wi-Fi (free).

Where to Dine

Bistro Montparnasse ★ ENGLISH/FRENCH   Serving the best food in the area, this bistro offers a welcoming atmosphere. Fresh produce is delicately prepared

Portsmouth & Southsea

HM NAVAL BASE

Victory Gate

Ferry to Gosport

Ferry to Ryde

Queen St.

University of Portsmouth

Market Way

Alfred Rd.

Anglesey Rd.

Kent St.

The Hard St.

Park Rd.

Burnaby Rd.

RN Sports Centre

Ferry Terminal

Gunwharf Rd.

George Rd.

Cambridge Rd.

Hants Terr.

St. Paul's Rd.

Museum Rd.

St. James Rd.

Somers Rd.

Winston

Churchill Ave.

King's Rd.

Broad St.

St. Thomas St.

High St.

Square Tower

Round Tower

Penny St.

Pembroke Rd.

Castle Rd.

Ferry to Fishbourne

Amusement Park

Pier Rd.

Southsea Terr.

Duisburg Way

Hovercraft Terminal

0   1/4 mi
0   1/4 km

Scotland / England map inset:
0   100 mi
0   100 km
SCOTLAND
North Sea
Irish Sea
ENGLAND
WALES
London
Portsmouth
English Channel

Charles Dickens' Birthplace Museum **1**
HMS *Victory* **3**
Mary Rose **2**
Mary Rose Museum **5**
Royal Naval Museum **4**
Royal Navy Submarine Museum **6**
Spinnaker Tower **7**

in the well-rounded selection of dishes here. The cooking is familiar fare but well executed. Homemade breads and fresh fish, caught locally, are specialties. Especially recommended are the breast of duck and roast leg of duck with orange and honey flavors, the filet of sea bass with creamed sweet corn and a wild mushroom mousseline, and the rosemary and ricotta gnocchi with pine nuts.

103 Palmerston Rd., Southsea. ✆ **023/9281-6754.** www.bistromontparnasse.co.uk. Reservations recommended. Main courses £14–£20; fixed-price 2-course dinner £29, 3-course dinner £34. AE, MC, V. Tues–Sat 11:45am–2pm and 7–9:30pm. Southsea bus. Follow signs to the D-Day Museum, and at the museum turn left and go to the next intersection; the restaurant is on the right.

Maritime Attractions in Portsmouth

You can buy a combination ticket that includes admission to several attractions: the HMS *Victory,* the HMS *Warrior 1860,* the Mary Rose Museum, and the Royal Naval Museum. It costs £18 for adults, £16 for seniors, £14 for children 5 to 15, and £51 for a family ticket. Individual attraction tickets are £13 for adults, £11 for seniors, £8.50 for children 5 to 15, and £33 for a family ticket. Stop by the visitor center of the **Portsmouth Historic Dockyard** (✆ **023/9272-8060**), or buy tickets online at **www.historicdockyard.co.uk**. The center is open April through October, daily 10am to 6pm; and November through March, daily 10am to 5:30pm.

HMS *Victory* ★★★ Of major interest is Lord Nelson's flagship, a 104-gun, first-rate ship that is the oldest commissioned warship in the world, launched May 7, 1765. It earned its fame on October 21, 1805, in the Battle of Trafalgar, when the English scored a victory over the combined Spanish and French fleets. It was in this battle that Lord Nelson lost his life. The flagship, after being taken to Gibraltar for repairs, returned to Portsmouth with Nelson's body on board (he was later buried at St. Paul's in London).

1-7 College Rd., Portsmouth Naval Base. © **023/9283-9766.** www.historicdockyard.co.uk. See above for admission prices. Apr–Oct daily 10am–6pm; Nov–Mar daily 10am–5:30pm. Last admission 1½ hr. before closing. Closed Dec 24–26. Use the entrance to the Portsmouth Naval Base through Victory Gate and follow the signs.

Mary Rose Museum ★ The *Mary Rose,* flagship of the fleet of King Henry VIII's wooden men-of-war, sank in the Solent Channel in 1545 in full view of the king. In 1982, Prince Charles watched the *Mary Rose* break the water's surface after more than 4 centuries on the ocean floor, not exactly in shipshape condition, but surprisingly well preserved nonetheless. The hull and more than 20,000 items brought up by divers constitute one of England's major archaeological discoveries. On display are the almost-complete equipment of the ship's barber-surgeon, with cabin saws, knives, ointments, and plaster all ready for use; long bows and arrows, some still in shooting order; carpenters' tools; leather jackets; and some fine lace and silk.

Note: The hull of the *Mary Rose* is closed to the public until 2012 while a new £35-million museum is constructed around the vessel. However, the Mary Rose Museum will remain open throughout the construction.

College Rd., Portsmouth Naval Base. © **023/9283-9766.** www.historicdockyard.co.uk. See above for admission prices. Apr–Oct daily 10am–6pm; Nov–Mar daily 10am–5:30pm. Last admission 1½ hr. before closing. Closed Dec 24–26. Use the entrance to the Portsmouth Naval Base through Victory Gate and follow the signs.

Royal Naval Museum ★ The Royal Naval Museum is next to Nelson's flagship, HMS *Victory,* and the *Mary Rose,* in the heart of Portsmouth's historic naval dockyard. The only museum in Britain devoted exclusively to the general history of the Royal Navy, it houses relics of Nelson and his associates, together with unique collections of ship models, naval ceramics, figureheads, medals, uniforms, weapons, and other memorabilia. Special displays focus on "The Rise of the Royal Navy" and "HMS *Victory* and the Campaign of Trafalgar."

In the dockyard, Portsmouth Naval Base. © **023/9272-7562.** www.historicdockyard.co.uk. www.royalnavalmuseum.org. See above for admission prices. Apr–Oct daily 10am–6pm; Nov–Mar daily 10am–5:30pm. Last admission 1½ hr. before closing. Closed Dec 24–26. Use the entrance to the Portsmouth Naval Base through Victory Gate and follow the signs.

Royal Navy Submarine Museum Cross Portsmouth Harbour via one of the ferries that bustles back and forth all day to Gosport. Some departures go directly from the station pontoon to HMS *Alliance* for a visit to the submarine museum, which traces the history of underwater warfare and life from the earliest days to the present nuclear age. Within the refurbished historical and nuclear galleries, the principal exhibit is HMS *Alliance;* after a brief audiovisual presentation, visitors are guided through the boat by ex-submariners.

Haslar Jetty Rd., Gosport. ✆ **023/9252-9217.** www.rnsubmus.co.uk. Admission £9 adults, £6 children and seniors, £25 family ticket. Apr–Oct daily 10am–5:30pm; Nov–Mar daily 10am–4:30pm. Last tour 1 hr. before closing. Closed Dec 24–26 and Jan 1. Bus: 19. Ferry: From the Hard, in Portsmouth, to Gosport.

Spinnaker Tower ★★   Towering over the historic Portsmouth Harbour, this 170m (558-ft.) tower has become one of the biggest attractions of southern England. On a clear day, you can see for 37km (23 miles) in three directions. Glide to the top in a panoramic lift or else take a high-speed internal lift. The panoramic elevator reaches the top in 90 seconds, the internal elevator in 30 seconds. Sightseers experience the thrill of "walking on air," or daring to cross the largest glass floor in Europe. On the top deck, Crow's Nest, visitors are exposed to the elements. In addition to the open-air view, there is a trio of glass-enclosed viewing decks. At the on-site **Tower Café & Bar,** you can order and enjoy coffee, cakes, and sandwiches while soaking up the view.

Gunwharf Quays. ✆ **023/9285-7520.** www.spinnakertower.co.uk. Admission £7 adults, £6.20 students and seniors, £5.50 children 3–15, free for children 2 and younger. Children 15 and younger must be accompanied by an adult. Daily 10am–6pm.

More Attractions

Charles Dickens' Birthplace   The 1804 small terrace house, in which the famous novelist was born in 1812 and lived for a short time, has been restored and furnished to illustrate the middle-class taste of the southwestern counties of the early 19th century. It is recommended that you call in advance to see if the museum is indeed open.

393 Old Commercial Rd. (near the center, off Mile End Rd./M275 and off Kingston Rd.), Portsmouth. ✆ **023/9282-7261.** www.charlesdickensbirthplace.co.uk. Admission £3.50 adults, £3 seniors, £2.50 children, £9.50 family ticket, free for children 12 and younger. Daily 10am–5:30pm. Closed Oct to mid-May.

D-Day Museum   Next door to Southsea Castle, this museum, devoted to the Normandy landings, displays the Overlord Embroidery, which shows the complete story of Operation Overlord. The appliquéd embroidery, believed to be the largest of its kind (82m/272 ft. long and 1m/3 ft. high), was designed by Sandra Lawrence and took 20 women of the Royal School of Needlework 5 years to complete. A special audiovisual program includes displays such as reconstructions of various stages of the mission. You'll see a Sherman tank in working order, jeeps, field guns, and even a DUKW (popularly called a "Duck"), an extremely useful amphibious truck that operates on both land and sea.

Clarence Esplanade (on the seafront), Southsea. ✆ **023/9282-7261.** www.ddaymuseum.co.uk. Admission £6 adults, £5 seniors, £4.20 students and children, £16 family ticket, free for children 4 and younger. Apr–Sept daily 10am–5:30pm; Oct–Mar 10am–5pm. Closed Dec 24–26.

Portchester Castle   On a spit of land on the northern side of Portsmouth Harbour are the remains of this castle, plus a Norman church. Built in the late 12th century by King Henry II, the castle is set inside the **Roman walls** ★ of a 3rd-century fort built as a defense against Saxon pirates, when this was the northwestern frontier of the declining Roman Empire. This is the most complete set of Roman walls remaining in northern Europe. However, the castle itself is long gone. But the central tower remains, and from it you can take in a panoramic view of the harbor and the rocky coast.

On the south side of Portchester off A27 (btw. Portsmouth and Southampton, near Fareham). ℂ **023/9237-8291.** www.english-heritage.org.uk. Admission £4.50 adults, £3.80 seniors, £2.30 children 5-15, free for children 4 and younger. Mar 21-Sept daily 10am-6pm; Oct-Mar 20 daily 10am-4pm.

Southsea Castle   A fortress built of stones from Beaulieu Abbey in 1545 as part of King Henry VIII's coastal defense plan, the castle is now a museum. Exhibits trace the development of Portsmouth as a military stronghold, as well as the naval history and the archaeology of the area. The castle is in the center of Southsea near the D-Day Museum.

Clarence Esplanade, Southsea. ℂ **023/9282-7261.** www.southseacastle.co.uk. Admission £3.50 adults, £3 seniors, £2.50 students and children ages 13-18, £9.50 family ticket, free for children 12 and younger. Daily 10am-5:30pm. Closed Oct-Mar.

Shopping

In quay-side Portsmouth, you might turn into a shopaholic. All the big-name outlets are found along **Commercial Road,** especially in the mall called **Cascades Arcade.** It's best to go Thursday, Friday, or Saturday when a historic market takes place here. At the least, it's worth a browse. Still, we prefer to gravitate to the waterside development, **Gunwharf Quays,** with nearly 100 designer outlet shops.

SOUTHAMPTON

140km (87 miles) SW of London; 259km (161 miles) E of Plymouth

For many North Americans, England's number-one passenger port is the gateway to Britain. Southampton is a city of sterile wide boulevards, parks, and dreary shopping centers. During World War II, some 31.5 million men set out from here (in World War I, more than twice that number), and Southampton was repeatedly bombed, destroying its old character. Today, the rather shoddy downtown section represents what happens when a city's architectural focus is timeliness rather than grace, with more to see on the city's outskirts than in the city itself. If you're spending time in Southampton, you may want to explore some of the nearby sights of Hampshire (New Forest, Winchester, the Isle of Wight), along with Bournemouth, in neighboring Dorset.

Its supremacy as a port dates from Saxon times, when the Danish conqueror Canute was proclaimed king here in 1017. Southampton was especially important to the Normans and helped them keep in touch with their homeland. Its denizens were responsible for bringing in the bubonic plague, which wiped out a quarter of the English population in the mid-14th century. On the Western Esplanade is a memorial tower to the Pilgrims, who set out on their voyage to the New World from Southampton on August 15, 1620. Both the *Mayflower* and the *Speedwell* sailed from here but were forced by storm damages to put in at Plymouth, where the *Speedwell* was abandoned.

In the spring of 1912, the "unsinkable" White Star liner, the 46,000-ton *Titanic,* sailed from Southampton on its maiden voyage. Shortly before midnight on April 14, while steaming at 22 knots, the great ship collided with an iceberg and sank to the bottom of the icy Atlantic. The sinking of the *Titanic,* subject of the Oscar-winning box-office smash of 1997, was one of the greatest disasters in maritime history, as 1,513 people perished.

Southampton

Essentials

GETTING THERE   Trains depart from London's Waterloo Station several times daily. The trip takes a little more than an hour. For information, call ✆ **0845/748-4950** or visit **www.nationalrail.co.uk**.

National Express (✆ **0871/781-81-78**; www.nationalexpress.com) operates hourly departures from London's Victoria Coach Station. The trip takes 2½ hours.

If you're driving, take the M3 southwest from London.

VISITOR INFORMATION   The **Tourist Information Centre,** 9 Civic Centre Rd. (✆ **023/8083-3333**; www.visit-southampton.co.uk), is open Monday to Saturday 9:30am to 5pm, Sunday and bank holidays 10am to 3:30pm.

Where to Stay

Finding a place to stay right in Southampton isn't as important as it used to be. Very few ships arrive these days, and accommodations outside the city are generally better.

Map labels (within image):

Mayflower Theatre · Art Gallery · Southampton Central Station · Civic Centre Guild Hall · Southampton Institute · East Park · East Park Terrace · Havelock Rd. · Western Esplanade · Civic Centre Rd. · New Rd. · Marlands Shopping Centre · Palmerston Rd. · North Front · Winton St. · South Front · Kingsway Highway · St. Mary St. · Post Office · Grove · James St. · Coleman St. · Southampton College · St. Mary's Church · Portland Terrace · Portland St. · Above Bar St. · Hoglands Park · Hanover Buildings · Houndwell Pl. · Dept. Store · East Street Shopping Centre · Chapel · Central Hall · Bargate St. · East St. · Post Office · Marsh Ln. · Castle Way · Queensway · Orchard Ln. · King St. · West Quay Retail Park · Tudor House Museum · Bugle St. · High St. · Bernard St. · Briton St. · Customs House · Queen's Park · West Quay Rd. · Mayflower Park · French St. · Platform Rd. · Town Quay · Museum of Archaeology · Test · Royal Pier

Inset map: SCOTLAND · North Sea · Irish Sea · ENGLAND · WALES · London · Southampton · English Channel · 0 100 mi · 0 100 km

ATTRACTIONS ●
Southampton Maritime Museum **3**

ACCOMMODATIONS ■
De Vere Grand Harbour Hotel **2**
Holiday Inn Southampton **1**

DINING ◆
Red Lion **5**
White Star Tavern **4**

De Vere Grand Harbour Hotel ★★ If you must stay in town and you can afford it, this is the most comfortable place to be. Completed in 1994, the five-story structure, sheathed in granite and possessing a dramatically tilted glass facade, is the most exciting hotel to open in Southampton since World War II. The brightly painted bedrooms range from midsize to spacious, each with a pair of armchairs, traditional polished wood pieces, and snug beds. Most of the bathrooms are outfitted with luxurious tubs, separate walk-in showers, and granite vanities. Some rooms offer balconies; some have waterfront views; and around 30 units have air-conditioning.

West Quay Rd., Southampton, Hampshire SO15 1AG. ℭ **023/8063-3033.** Fax 023/8063-3066. www. devere-hotels.com. 173 units. £99–£159 double; £259–£349 suite. Rates include English breakfast. AE, DC, MC, V. Free parking. **Amenities:** Restaurant; bar; babysitting; exercise room; indoor heated pool; room service; spa. *In room:* TV, CD player (in some); hair dryer, minibar, Wi-Fi (free).

Holiday Inn Southampton This 10-floor high-rise across from Mayflower Park was built near the new docks to overlook the harbor; it's only 5 minutes away from the city center. Rooms are standard but generally spacious, with built-in furniture and picture-window walls. They've recently been refurbished and upgraded to ensure a pleasant stay. It's not big on extras, but what you get is adequate for the price.

Herbert Walker Ave., Southampton, Hampshire SO15 1HJ. ℭ **888/465-4329** or 0870/400-9073. Fax 023/8033-2510. www.ichotelsgroup.com. 132 units. £90–£171 double. AE, DC, MC, V. Free parking. **Amenities:** Restaurant; bar; exercise room; indoor heated pool; room service. *In room:* A/C, TV, hair dryer.

Jurys Inn Southampton ★ 🖋 After the De Vere Grand Harbour, this contemporary hotel close to the city center is our second choice. Overlooking East Park and the central train station, it's convenient to the town's attractions. It is also the largest hotel in Southampton, with ample-sized accommodations, furnished in a modern way with comfortable beds and immaculate bathrooms. Rooms can be rented to just one traveler or to as many as three adults or a family of two adults and two children. The hotel operates a stylish bar and a good, affordable restaurant, where succulent steaks and Atlantic salmon are specialties.

1 Charlotte Place, Southampton, Hampshire SO14 0TB. ℭ **023/8037-1111.** fax 023/8037-1100. http:// southamptonhotels.jurysinns.com. 270 units. £65 double. Rates include breakfast. AE, DC, MC, V. **Amenities:** Restaurant; bar; coffee shop; room service. *In room:* TV, hair dryer, Internet (£10 per day).

Where to Dine

Red Lion ★ ENGLISH One of the few architectural jewels to have survived World War II, the Red Lion traces its roots to the 13th century (as a Norman cellar), but its Henry V Court Room, with high ceilings and rafters, is from Tudor times. The room was the scene of the trial of the earl of Cambridge and his accomplices, Thomas Grey and Lord Scrope, who were condemned to death for plotting against the life of the king in 1415. Today, the Court Room is adorned with coats of arms of the noblemen who were peers of the condemned trio. The Red Lion is a fascinating place for a drink and a chat. Typical pub snacks are served in the bar, whereas in the somewhat more formal restaurant section, the well-seasoned specialties include an array of steaks (including sirloin), stews, roasts, and fish platters. Try the rib-eye steak with crushed black peppercorns, the steak-and-kidney pudding, cod and chips, or even a barbecued chicken breast.

You can also rent a comfortable double room here for £50 a night.

55 High St. ℂ **023/8033-3595.** Reservations not needed. Main courses £6–£18; pub snacks £2–£7. MC, V. Mon–Sat 11am–11pm; Sun noon–10:30pm. Bus: 1, 2, 6, or 8.

White Star Tavern ENGLISH   This former seafarers' hotel has been stylishly revived and turned into a bar-cum-restaurant where you can dine on "bar bites" or full-course meals. At this gastropub, the cooking is classic English, featuring even such pub classics as wild boar and apple sausage or beer-battered fish. Other menu items include whole grilled lemon sole with anchovy butter, pan-fried sea bream with Scottish mussels, and local wood pigeon breast with roast chicory and Serrano ham in a sherry vinegar emulsion. For dessert, try a classic Bakewell tart with cherry ice cream or a selection of local cheese with fruity preserves.

If you'd like to stay overnight, you'll find comfortably furnished rooms costing from £89 to £149 double.

28 Oxford St. ℂ **023/80821990.** www.whitestartavern.co.uk. Reservations not needed. Main courses £5–£18 lunch, £11–£18 dinner. AE, MC, V. Mon–Thurs noon–2:30pm and 6–9:30pm; Fri–Sat 11am–3pm and 6–10pm; Sun noon–8pm.

Exploring Southampton

Ocean Village and the town quay on Southampton's waterfront are bustling with activity and are filled with pubs, restaurants, and entertainment possibilities.

West Quay Retail Park, the first phase of Southampton's £250-million Esplanade development, has become a major hub for shoppers from the surrounding areas. For a vast array of shops, you can try the **Town Quay** (ℂ **023/8022-8353**) or **Southampton Market** (no phone), but there may be little here to interest the international traveler.

Better shopping on the outskirts can be found at the **Whitchurch Silk Mill,** 28 Winchester St., Whitchurch (ℂ **01256/892065;** www.whitchurchsilkmill.org.uk). Admission is £4 for adults, £3.50 for students and seniors, £2.25 for children 4 to 16, and £9.25 for a family ticket. Visitors flock to this working mill, located in colorful surroundings on the River Test. The gift shop sells silk on the roll, ties, scarves, handkerchiefs, jewelry, and souvenirs. Hours are Tuesday through Sunday 10:30am to 5pm.

Southampton Maritime Museum   This museum is housed in an impressive 14th-century stone warehouse with a magnificent timber ceiling. Its exhibits trace the history of Southampton, including a model of the docks as they looked at their peak in the 1930s. Also displayed are artifacts from some of the great ocean liners whose home port was Southampton.

The most famous of these liners was the fabled *Titanic,* which was partially built in Southampton and sailed from this port on its fateful, fatal voyage. James Cameron's box-office smash has increased traffic to the relatively small *Titanic* exhibit at the museum. It features photographs of the crew (many of whom were from Southampton) and passengers, as well as letters from passengers, Capt. Edward Smith's sword, and a video with a dated interview with the fallen captain plus modern interviews with survivors.

The Wool House, Town Quay. ℂ **023/8063-5904.** Admission £2.50 adults, £1.50 seniors, £5.50 family ticket, free for children 6 and younger. Mon–Fri 10am–4pm; Sat–Sun 11am–4pm.

THE NEW FOREST ★★

153km (95 miles) SW of London; 16km (10 miles) W of Southampton

Encompassing 37,231 hectares (92,000 acres), the New Forest is a large tract created by William the Conqueror, who laid out the limits of this then-private hunting preserve. Successful poachers faced the executioner if they were caught, and those who hunted but missed had their hands severed. Henry VIII loved to hunt deer in the New Forest, but he also saw an opportunity to build up the British naval fleet by supplying oak and other hard timbers to the boatyards at Buckler's Hard on the Beaulieu River.

Today, you can visit the old shipyards and the Maritime Museum at Buckler's Hard (see below), with its fine models of men-of-war, pictures of the old yard, and dioramas showing the building of these ships, their construction, and their launching. Away from the main roads, where signs warn of wild ponies and deer, you'll find a private world of peace and quiet.

Essentials

GETTING THERE   By train, go to Southampton, where you can make rail connections to a few centers in the New Forest. Where the train leaves off, you can make bus connections to all towns and many villages. Southampton and Lymington have the best bus connections to New Forest's villages.

If you're driving, head west from Southampton on the A35.

VISITOR INFORMATION   The **New Forest Visitor Information Centre,** Main Car Park, Lyndhurst (ℂ **023/8028-2269;** www.thenewforest.co.uk), is open daily from 10am to 5pm.

Where to Stay

VERY EXPENSIVE

Chewton Glen Hotel & Spa ★★★   A gracious country house on the fringe of the New Forest National Park, Chewton Glen, within easy reach of Southampton and Bournemouth, is the finest place to stay in southwest England (with princely rates to match). In the old house, a magnificent staircase leads to well-furnished double rooms opening onto views of the spacious grounds. In the new wing, ground-level rooms have French doors opening onto your own private patio. Accommodations vary widely and come in different shapes, sizes, and period styles. Attic rooms and all newly refurbished rooms contain air-conditioners. The best accommodations are the Croquet Lawn Rooms, which open onto the greens and have big private balconies or terraces.

Christchurch Rd., New Milton, Hampshire BH25 6QS. ℂ **800/398-4534** in the U.S., or 01425/275341. Fax 01425/272310. www.chewtonglen.com. 58 units. £329–£595 double; £534–£1,411 suite. AE, DC, MC, V. After leaving the village of Walkford, follow signs off A35 (New Milton–Christchurch Rd.), through parkland. **Amenities:** Restaurant; bar; bikes; golf course (9 holes); health club & spa; 2 heated pools (1 indoor, 1 outdoor); room service; 4 lit tennis courts (2 indoor, 2 outdoor). *In room:* A/C (in some), TV, hair dryer, minibar, Wi-Fi (free).

EXPENSIVE

Balmer Lawn Hotel ★ ☺   This hotel lies about a 10-minute walk from Brockenhurst's center in a woodland location. Built as a private home during the 17th century, it was later enlarged into an imposing hunting lodge. During World War II, it was a military hospital. (In the past decade, many overnight guests have spotted the ghost of one of the white-coated doctors with his stethoscope, roaming the hotel's first floor.) The hotel has pleasant and humorous staff (who refer to the ghost as "Dr. Eric"). Accommodations come in all shapes and sizes, including three family rooms; each bedroom has its own individual character. Request a room with a view of the forest.

Lyndhurst Rd., Brockenhurst, Hampshire SO42 7ZB. ℂ **01590/623116.** Fax 01590/623864. www.balmer lawnhotel.com. 54 units. £155–£275 double; £270–£350 family room. Rates include English breakfast. Children 16 and younger stay free in parent's room. AE, DC, MC, V. Free parking. Take A337 (Lyndhurst-Lymington Rd.) about 1km (½ mile) outside Brockenhurst. **Amenities:** Restaurant; bar; bikes; exercise room; 2 heated pools (1 indoor, 1 outdoor); room service; small spa; tennis court (outdoor); Wi-Fi (free, in lobby). *In room:* TV, hair dryer.

Careys Manor & SenSpa ★★   This manor house dates from Charles II, who used to come here when it was a hunting lodge. Greatly expanded in 1888, the building became a country hotel in the 1930s. Much improved in recent years, the old house is still filled with character, possessing mellow, timeworn paneling and a carved oak staircase. Most bedrooms, whether in the restored main building or in the garden wing, have balconies. Six rooms contain an old-fashioned four-poster bed, but whether your room does or not, it will still have a firm bed offering cozy comfort. The spa is one of the best in the West Country, offering 16 luxurious treatment rooms and everything from a mud room to an ozone pool.

Lyndhurst Rd., Brockenhurst, Hampshire SO42 7RH. ℂ **01590/623551.** Fax 01590/622799. www. careysmanor.com. 79 units. £178–£278 double; £318–£378 suite. Rates include English breakfast. 2-night minimum Sat–Sun. AE, DC, MC, V. Free parking. From the town center, head toward Lyndhurst on A337. No children under 10. **Amenities:** 2 restaurants; bar; health club & state-of-the-art spa; room service. *In room:* TV, hair dryer, Wi-Fi (free).

Montagu Arms Hotel ★★   This hotel has an interesting history: It was built in the 1700s to supply food and drink to the laborers who hauled salt from the nearby marshes to other parts of England. The garden walls were constructed with stones salvaged from Beaulieu Abbey after it was demolished by Henry VIII. The hexagonal column supporting a fountain in the hotel's central courtyard is one of six salvaged, according to legend, from the ruined abbey's nave. Bedrooms are individually decorated in an English-country-house tradition, come in a range of shapes and sizes, and have extras including a trouser press and a writing desk. Many units contain a traditional four-poster bed.

Palace Lane, Beaulieu, Hampshire SO42 7ZL. ℂ **01590/612324.** Fax 01590/612188. www.montaguarms hotel.co.uk. 22 units. £90–£110 per person double; £145–£210 per person suite. Rates include English breakfast. Extra person £35. AE, DC, MC, V. **Amenities:** 2 restaurants; 2 bars; room service. *In room:* TV, hair dryer.

MODERATE

Best Western Crown Hotel   Though the present building is only 100 years old, a hostelry has been here on the main street of the New Forest village of Lyndhurst for centuries. For generations, it has been a favorite of visitors to the New Forest, who delight in its gardens, where afternoon tea is served, and its roaring fireplace in winter. Bedrooms are most inviting, each furnished in the classic tradition of an English country house, many featuring four-poster beds. Some rooms are more modern, with padded headboards and fine furnishings. A few of the superior rooms can accommodate families.

9 High St., Lyndhurst, Hampshire SO43 7NF. ✆ **023/8028-2922.** Fax 023/8028-2751. www.crown hotel-lyndhurst.co.uk. 38 units. £87–£129 double; £109–£155 suite. Rates include English breakfast. Children 15 and younger stay free in parent's room. AE, DC, MC, V. Bus: 56 or 56A. Exit M27 at Junction 1 and drive 5km (3 miles) due south. **Amenities:** Restaurant; bar; babysitting; room service. *In room:* TV, hair dryer, Wi-Fi (free).

Lyndhurst Park Hotel   This large Georgian country house lies on 2 hectares (5 acres) of beautiful gardens. Located at the edge of town where Lyndhurst meets the New Forest, this hotel often attracts conferences. Much of the property remains characteristically rustic, though filled with modern comforts. Bedrooms are medium in size and extremely well kept, often with brass headboards crowning the fine English beds.

High St., Lyndhurst, Hampshire SO43 7NL. ✆ **0808/144-9494** or 023/8028-3923. Fax 023/8028-3019. www.lyndhurstparkhotel.co.uk. 59 units. £120–£140 double. Rates include English breakfast. Children 13 and younger stay free in parent's room. AE, DC, MC, V. Free parking. Bus: 56. **Amenities:** Restaurant; bar; outdoor heated pool; room service; sauna; outdoor tennis court. *In room:* TV, hair dryer, Wi-Fi (free).

New Park Manor Hotel ★   This former royal hunting lodge, from the days of William the Conqueror and a favorite of Charles II, is the only hotel in the New Forest itself. Though now a modern country hotel, the original rooms have been preserved, with such features as beams and, in some rooms, open log fires. Since its purchase in 1998 by the Countess von Essen, the property has been much improved. Each room has been individually furnished, with four-poster beds in several units. Most rooms have a view overlooking the forest.

Lyndhurst Rd., Brockenhurst, Hampshire SO42 7QH. ✆ **01590/623467.** Fax 01590/622268. www. newparkmanorhotel.co.uk. 24 units. £99–£289 double; £299–£339 suite. Rates include English breakfast. AE, DC, MC, V. Head 3km (2 miles) north off A337 (Lyndhurst-Brockenhurst Rd.) toward the New Forest Show Ground. **Amenities:** Restaurant; bar; outdoor pool; small spa; Wi-Fi (free, in lobby). *In room:* TV/DVD, hair dryer.

Where to Dine

Simply ★ ANGLO/FRENCH   Some of the best food in the area is served here at the Whitley Ridge hotel just outside Brockenhurst. The menu includes an array of fish and game dishes, mainly with ingredients coming from the New Forest itself. Try individually cooked portions of pigeon, wild rabbit, hare, and the occasional venison. Tempting items include the home-raised rib-eye steak with hand-cut "chips" and a béarnaise sauce, the whole roast New Forest partridge with Jerusalem artichokes, and the seared tuna with spiced lentils and arugula.

Whitley Ridge is a mellow 18th-century country house set in secluded grounds and completely surrounded by the New Forest. If you'd like to stay over, the hotel rents 16 well-furnished and comfortably appointed bedrooms, costing £105 to £175 double.

In the Whitley Ridge hotel, Beaulieu Rd., Brockenhurst. ✆ **01590/622354.** www.whitleyridge.co.uk. Reservations required. Main courses £13–£19; fixed-price 2-course lunch £13. MC, V. Daily noon–2pm and 7:30–9:30pm.

Seeing the Sights

Beaulieu Abbey & Palace House ★★   The abbey and house, as well as the National Motor Museum, are on the property of Lord Montagu of Beaulieu (pronounced *Bew*-ley). A Cistercian abbey was founded on this spot in 1204, and you can explore its ruins. The Palace House, surrounded by gardens, was the gate-house of the abbey before it was converted into a private residence in 1538. Although much was destroyed during the reign of Henry VIII, you can still see an ancient doorway, the cloisters, and the lay brothers' refectory, housing an exhibition depicting monastic life in the abbey through a series of modern embroidered wall hangings. The cloisters are especially inviting and tranquil, planted with fragrant herbs.

The **National Motor Museum** ★★, one of the best and most comprehensive automotive museums in the world, with more than 250 vehicles, is on the grounds and is open to the public. Famous autos include four land-speed record holders, among them Donald Campbell's Bluebird. Some of the vehicles used in James Bond movies are on display, as well as those once used by everybody from Eric Clapton to Marlene Dietrich. The collection was built around Lord Montagu's family collection of vintage cars. For further information, contact the visitor reception manager at the John Montagu Building (✆ **01590/612345**).

Beaulieu, on B3056 in the New Forest (8km/5 miles southeast of Lyndhurst and 23km/14 miles west of Southampton). ✆ **01590/612345.** www.beaulieu.co.uk. Admission £16 adults, £15 seniors and students, £9.50 children 13–17, £8.50 children 5–12, £43 family ticket (2 adults, 3 children), free for children 4 and younger. May–Sept daily 10am–6pm; Oct–Apr daily 10am–5pm. Closed Dec 25. Buses run from the Lymington bus station Mon–Sat; on Sun you'll need a taxi or car.

Maritime Museum ★ Buckler's Hard, a historic 18th-century village 4km (2½ miles) from Beaulieu, on the banks of the River Beaulieu, is where ships for Nelson's fleet were built, including the admiral's favorite, *Agamemnon*, as well as *Eurylus* and *Swiftsure*. The Maritime Museum exhibits focus on the village's shipbuilding history; Henry Adams, master shipbuilder; Nelson's favorite ship; Buckler's Hard and Trafalgar; and models of Sir Francis Chichester's yachts and items of his equipment. The cottage exhibits re-create 18th-century life in Buckler's Hard—you can stroll through the New Inn of 1793 and a shipwright's cottage of the same period or look in on the family of a poor laborer.

The walk back to Beaulieu, 4km (2½ miles) on the riverbank, is well marked through the woodlands. During the summer, you can take a 30-minute cruise on the River Beaulieu in the present *Swiftsure*, an all-weather catamaran cruiser.

Buckler's Hard. ✆ **01590/616203.** www.bucklershard.co.uk. Admission to Buckler's Hard £6 adults, £5.60 seniors, £4.30 children 5–17, £18 family ticket. River cruise £4 adults, £3.50 seniors, £2.50 kids; £12 family ticket. Nov–Feb daily 10am–4:30pm; Mar–June daily 10am–5pm; July–Aug daily 10am–5:30pm; Sept–Oct daily 10am–5pm. Closed Dec 25.

THE ISLE OF WIGHT ★★

146km (91 miles) SW of London; 6.5km (4 miles) S of Southampton

The Isle of Wight is known for its sandy beaches and its ports, long favored by the yachting set. The island has attracted such literary figures as Alfred, Lord Tennyson and Charles Dickens. Tennyson wrote his beloved poem "Crossing the Bar" en route across the Solent from Lymington to Yarmouth. You may want to come just for the day. Some parts are rather tacky, especially Sandown and Shanklin, though other areas out on the island are still tranquil and quite beautiful.

To see Wight at its scenic best, you can walk at least part of a 106km (65-mile) trail called the **Coastal Path** ★★. This footpath links cross-country trails with panoramic views of sea cliffs, the ocean, and the downs. For those who don't want to walk all of it, the most scenic part of the trail is the stretch between Shanklin and Ventnor.

The Isle of Wight is compact, measuring 37km (23 miles) from east to west, 21km (13 miles) north to south. **Ryde** is the railhead for the island's transportation system. **Yarmouth** is a busy little harbor providing a mooring for yachts.

Cowes is the premier port for yachting in Britain. Henry VIII ordered the castle built here, but it's now the headquarters of the Royal Yacht Squadron. The seafront and the high cliff road are worth exploring for the scenic views. The port is divided into West Cowes and East Cowes, and separated by the narrow Medina River, which is linked only by a chain ferry called the "floating bridge." Hovercraft are built in the town, which is also the home and birthplace of the well-known maritime photographer Beken of Cowes. In winter, everyone wears oilskins and wellies (boots), leaving a wet trail behind them.

Newport, a bustling market town in the heart of the island, is the capital and has long been a favorite of British royalty. Along the southeast coast are the twin Victorian resorts of **Sandown** and **Shanklin.** Both of these family resorts have a very similar atmosphere, with cafes, shops (rather mediocre), pubs, restaurants, safe bathing, and a mild climate. The pier in Sandown dates from 1879 and provides all-weather amusements such as video games. Shanklin, at the southern end of Sandown Bay, holds the British annual sunshine record. We suggest you skip Sandown and visit at Shanklin for its old village and a glimpse of **Shanklin Cline,** a fissure in the cliff where you can walk up to see a 12m (40-ft.) waterfall. Farther along the coast, **Ventnor** is called the "Madeira of England" because it rises from the sea in a series of steep hills.

On the west coast are the many-colored sand cliffs of **Alum Bay.** The Needles, three giant chalk rocks, and the Needles Lighthouse are the features of interest at this end of the island. If you want to stay at the western end of Wight, consider **Freshwater Bay.**

Essentials

GETTING THERE   During the day, one direct train per hour departs from London's Waterloo Station to Portsmouth, depositing travelers directly at the pier for a ferry crossing to the Isle of Wight; ferries are timed to meet train arrivals. Travel time from London to the arrival point of Ryde on the Isle of Wight (including ferry-crossing time) is 2 hours. For rail information, call ✆ **0845/748-4950** or visit **www.nationalrail.co.uk**.

By car, drive to Southampton and take the ferry or leave Southampton and head west along the A35, cutting south on the A337 toward Lymington on the coast, where the ferry crossing to Yarmouth (Isle of Wight) is shorter than the trip from Southampton.

Red Funnel operates a vehicle ferry service from Terminal 1 in Southampton to East Cowes; the trip takes 55 minutes. An inclusive round-trip fare (valid for 5 days) costs £14 for adults, £9.30 for seniors, and £7 for children. More popular with train travelers from London's Waterloo Station is a high-speed passenger-only catamaran operating from the Town Quay Terminal 2 in Southampton, going to West Cowes; the trip takes 22 minutes. A round-trip fare costs £19 for adults, £14 for seniors, and £9.60 for children 5 to 15. For ferry departure times, call © **0844/8449988** or visit www.redfunnel.co.uk and www.nationalrail.co.uk.

Wightlink (© **0871/376-4342;** www.wightlink.co.uk) operates ferry service between Portsmouth and Ryde, taking 20 minutes and costing £19 for adults and £9.30 for children, round-trip standard return. Daytime departures are every 30 minutes in summer and every 60 minutes in winter.

VISITOR INFORMATION   The **Tourist Information Centre** is at 67 High St., Shanklin (© **01983/813813;** www.islandbreaks.co.uk). It's open April through October, Tuesday to Saturday from 9:30am to 5pm; and November through March, Monday, Tuesday, Friday, and Saturday from 10am to 3pm. It's best to call first, as these hours are subject to change.

There are additional information centers at Fountain Quay, Cowes; the Guildhall, High Street, Newport; 81–83 Union St., Ryde; High Street, Sandown; and the Quay, Yarmouth. Call the above number for hours.

GETTING AROUND   Visitors can explore the Isle of Wight just for the day on the Island Explorer bus service. Tickets may be purchased from the driver, and you can board or leave the bus at any stop on the island. A 1-day Rover ticket costs £10 for adults and £5 for children. It also entitles you to passage on the island's only railway, which runs from the dock at Ryde to the center of Shanklin, a distance of 13km (8 miles). For further information, contact **Southern Vectis** (© **0871/2002233;** www.islandbuses.info).

Our preferred way to get around the island is by bike or moped. Rentals are available at **1st Call,** 15 College Close, Sandown (© **01983/400055;** www.1stcallcarsales.com), costing £15 per day for a bike. Another possibility is **Tav Cycle Sport,** 140 High St., Ryde (© **01983/718068;** www.tavcycles.co.uk), where cycles rent for £15 for a day. Both outlets are open Monday to Saturday 9am to 5pm.

Where to Stay

Bourne Hall Country House Hotel   Many visitors prefer to base themselves at Shanklin. At Bourne Hall, they receive a warm welcome from the owners, who run one of the area's best-equipped hotels. It stands on nearly 1.2 hectares (3 acres), adjoining open farmland. Bedrooms are furnished in a delightful English-country-house style. Some have been redecorated, and even those that haven't are still in fine shape.

Luccombe Rd., Shanklin, Isle of Wight PO37 6RR. © **01983/862820.** Fax 01983/865138. www.bourne hallhotel.co.uk. 31 units. £40–£90 per person double; £55–£105 per person double including half-board. Rates include English breakfast. AE, DC, MC, V. Free parking. No children 17 and under. **Amenities:** Restaurant; bar; 2 pools (1 heated indoor, 1 outdoor); room service; small spa; Wi-Fi (free, in lobby). *In room:* TV, CD player, hair dryer, minibar (in some).

The George Hotel ★★   The best cuisine and most elegant lodgings are at this former governor's residence dating from the 17th century. Between the quay and the castle, overlooking the Solent, this is a tranquil oasis in the port so beloved by English yachties. The good-size bedrooms are individually decorated, each with style and an eye for comfort. The professionalism of this place is to be applauded. It's leagues ahead of some of the dowdy properties on the island, many of them looking like leftovers from Victoria's era. Even if you aren't a guest, call for a reservation at the Brasserie (see "Where to Dine," below).

Quay St., Yarmouth, Isle of Wright PO41 0PE. ✆ **01983/760331.** Fax 01983/760425. www.thegeorge. co.uk. 17 units. £190–£268 double. Rates include English breakfast. 2-night minimum Sat–Sun. AE, MC, V. Parking £6. **Amenities:** 2 restaurants; bar; room service. *In room:* A/C, TV, hair dryer.

Ryde Castle 😊   This historic seafront castle looking onto the Solent makes a fine base for exploring the island. Field Marshall Montgomery stayed here before D-day landings. The castle, dating from the 16th century, has been added to over the centuries. With its crenellated, ivy-clad exterior and its well-kept public rooms, the hotel attracts families as well as single visitors. Bedrooms, small to medium in size, have an inviting aura with traditional British styling. Comfort is key here, and some accommodations have a more romantic aura and four-poster beds. Most rooms offer sea views. Kids can hang out at the children's play area or look for the friendly ghost rumored to be a hotel resident.

The Esplanade, Ryde, Isle of Wight PO33 1JA. ✆ **01983/563755.** Fax 01983/566906. www.rydecastle. com. 18 units. £79–£185 double. Rates include English breakfast. AE, DC, MC, V. Free parking. **Amenities:** Restaurant; bar; room service. *In room:* TV, hair dryer.

St. Catherine's Hotel   This hotel lies a few minutes' walk from Sandown's sandy beach, leisure center, and pier complex, with its sun lounges, theater, and Sandown railway station. St. Catherine's was built in 1860 of creamy Purbeck stone and white trim for the dean of Winchester College. A modern extension contains streamlined and sunny bedrooms, with duvets, white furniture, and built-in headboards. The brightly redecorated lounge has wide bay windows, card tables, and a small library of books.

1 Winchester Park Rd., Sandown, Isle of Wight PO36 8HJ. ✆/fax **01983/402392.** www.stcatherines-hotel.co.uk. 19 units. £70 double. Rates include English breakfast. MC, V. **Amenities:** Restaurant; bar; babysitting; room service. *In room:* TV, Wi-Fi (free).

Wight Mouse Inn ★ 😊   The Wight Mouse is a cheerful place to stay. This old coaching inn lies on the most southerly part of the island, where the vegetation is almost tropical. From here, you can see over the Channel to the mainland coast. Though a bit small, each bedroom is prettily decorated in an English-country-house style. Children are warmly welcomed and can burn off energy in MouseWorld, an indoor play area, or at the outdoor playground.

Newport Rd. (B3399; 45m/150 ft. off Military Rd.), Chale, Isle of Wight PO38 2HA. ✆ **01983/730431.** Fax 01983/730043. www.innforanight.co.uk. 8 units. £50–£100 double. MC, V. **Amenities:** Restaurant; bar; children's center. *In room:* TV, hair dryer.

Where to Dine

The Brasserie ★ CONTINENTAL/FRENCH   Some of the most refined cuisine on the island is at the George Hotel (reviewed above). The restaurant is imbued with a rich aura of candlelight and painted panels, and the best view of the Solent is from the sunny brasserie. The place is known for its quality ingredients, deftly handled and beautifully presented in showcase fixed-price dinners. Try such delights as salmon fish cakes in a white wine sauce, butternut squash risotto with sage-laced Parmesan, slow-cooked pork with a white onion sauce, or New forest venison with a celeriac purée.

In the George Hotel, Quay St., Yarmouth. ✆ **01983/760331.** www.thegeorge.co.uk. Main courses £15–£28; fixed-price dinner £45. AE, MC, V. Daily noon–3pm and 7–10pm.

The Hambrough Restaurant ★★   In the south-coast town of Ventnor, in a stylish boutique hotel, this restaurant, among the finest on the island, opens onto panoramic views. Trained at some of the best restaurants in England, the young chef, Robert Thompson, makes clever use of the great bounty of the countryside. Fixed-price menus are offered at lunch, starting with truly superb dishes such as smoked haddock chowder with soft-boiled quail eggs, followed with Orkney salmon with a fennel confit and a saffron-laced pasta. Set menus at dinner are more elaborate, including sublime options such as roast venison or roast Anjou squab with foie gras and a licorice flavoring, pan-fried Cornish turbot with a truffle risotto, or papillote of halibut with artichokes and green olives. Vegetarian menus are available as well.

In the Hambrough hotel, Hambrough Rd., Ventnor. ✆ **01983/856333.** www.thehambrough.com. Reservations required. 2-course set lunch £22, 3-course set lunch £26; 3-course set dinner £55; tasting menu £70. DC, MC, V. Tues–Sat noon–1:30pm and 7–9:30pm.

Exploring the Isle of Wight

Carisbrooke Castle ★★   This fine medieval castle lies in the center of the Isle of Wight. In 1647, during one of the most turbulent periods of English history, Charles I was imprisoned here, far from his former seat of power in London, by Cromwell's Roundheads. On the castle premises is the 16th-century Well House, where, during periods of siege, donkeys took turns treading a large wooden wheel connected to a rope that hauled up buckets of water from a well. Accessible from the castle's courtyard is a museum (✆ **01983/523112**) with exhibits pertaining to the social history of the Isle of Wight and the history of Charles I's imprisonment.

Carisbrooke, 2km (1¼ miles) southwest of Newport. ✆ **01983/523112.** www.carisbrookecastlemuseum. org.uk. Castle and museum £6.50 adults, £5.20 seniors and students, £3.30 children, free for children under 5. Apr–Sept daily 10am–5pm; Oct–Mar daily 10am–4pm. Bus: 91A.

Osborne House ★★   Queen Victoria's most cherished residence was built at her own expense. Prince Albert, with his characteristic thoroughness, contributed to many aspects of the design of the Italian-inspired mansion, which stands amid lush gardens, right outside the village of Whippingham. The rooms remain as Victoria knew them, down to the French piano she used to play and all the cozy clutter of her sitting room. Grief-stricken at the death of Albert in 1861, she asked that Osborne House be kept as it was, and so it has been. Even the turquoise scent bottles he gave her, decorated with cupids and cherubs, are still in place. The queen died on January 22, 1901, in her bedroom at Osborne House. Within the Italianate gardens, you can visit a museum of royal mementos, a summerhouse, and a Swiss Cottage where the royal children were taught.

1.5km (1 mile) southeast of East Cowes. ✆ **01983/200022.** www.english-heritage.org.uk. House and grounds £11 adults, £9.30 seniors, £5.50 children 5–15, family ticket £27. Apr–Sept daily 10am–5pm; Oct daily 10am–4pm; Nov–Mar Wed–Sun 10am–2:30pm (by prebooked guided tour only). Closed Dec 25–26 and Jan 1. Bus: 4 or 5.

BOURNEMOUTH ★

167km (104 miles) SW of London; 24km (15 miles) W of the Isle of Wight

This south-coast resort at the doorstep of the New Forest didn't just happen: It was carefully planned and executed—a true city in a garden. Flower-filled, park-dotted Bournemouth is filled with an abundance of architecture inherited from those arbiters of taste, Victoria and her son, Edward. (The resort was discovered back in Victoria's day, when sea bathing became an institution.) Bournemouth's most distinguished feature is its chines (narrow, shrub-filled, steep-sided ravines) along the coastline. For the best view of them, walk along the waterfront promenade appropriately called the **Undercliff** ★★.

Bournemouth, along with neighboring Poole and Christchurch, forms the largest urban area in the south of England. It makes a good base for exploring a historically rich part of England; on its outskirts are the New Forest, Salisbury, Winchester, and the Isle of Wight.

Essentials

GETTING THERE   An express train from London's Victoria Station to Bournemouth takes 2 hours, with frequent service throughout the day. For schedules and information, call © **0845/748-4950** or visit **www.nationalrail.co.uk**. Arrivals are at the Bournemouth Rail Station, on Holden Surst Road.

Buses leave London's Waterloo Station every 2 hours during the day, heading for Bournemouth. The trip takes 2½ hours. For schedules and information, call © **0871/781-81-78** or visit **www.nationalexpress.com**.

If you're driving, take the M3 southwest from London to Winchester, then the A31, and then the A338 south to Bournemouth.

VISITOR INFORMATION   The **Tourist Information Centre** is at Westover Road (© **08450/511701**; www.bournemouth.co.uk). From September through May, it's open Monday to Saturday from 9:30am to 5:30pm. From June through August, it's also open Sunday from 10am to 5:30pm.

Where to Stay

EXPENSIVE

Bournemouth Highcliff Marriott ★★   This 1888 cliff-side hotel is one of the best in Bournemouth, rivaled only by Menzies Carlton, Langtry Manor, and Royal Bath. A funicular elevator takes guests from the hotel to the seaside promenade. The high-ceilinged interior has been tastefully renovated, with many bedrooms enjoying beautiful views of the sea. Each is traditionally furnished in elegant English style and is located either in the main building or in Coast Guard cottages built in 1912. Rooms are generally spacious.

105 St. Michael's Rd., West Cliff, Bournemouth, Dorset BH2 5DU. © **800/228-9290** in the U.S., or 01202/557702. Fax 01202/293155. www.marriott.co.uk. 160 units. £135–£240 double; from £215 suite. AE, DC, MC, V. Parking £10. **Amenities:** Restaurant (Highcliff Grill, p. 357); 2 bars; babysitting; concierge; exercise room; 2 pools (1 heated indoor, 1 outdoor). *In room:* A/C, TV, hair dryer, minibar.

Hotel du Vin ★★   Installed in the former landmark Mansion House, this is one of the finest hotels in the ever-popular chain. Close to Poole Harbour, it offers luxuriously furnished bedrooms and suites, with such extras as monsoon showers and

Egyptian cotton sheets. Many accommodations reflect a nautical theme, and many units have restored beams and open onto balconies with panoramic views. The on-site bistro serves a classic continental cuisine, there's an outstanding wine cellar, and cigar lovers will enjoy the Bothy Lodge. At its La Roche tasting table, wine lovers can embark on a voyage around the world, sampling vintages from some of the finest vineyards.

Thames St., The Quay, Poole, Dorset BH15 LJN38. © **01202/785570.** Fax 01202/785571. www. hotelduvin.com. 38 units. £170–£245 double, £300–£350 suite. AE, MC, V. **Amenities:** Restaurant; bar; room service. *In room:* A/C, TV/DVD, hair dryer, Wi-Fi (£10 per 24 hr.).

The Priory ★   This hotel lies 3km (2 miles) west of Bournemouth in Wareham, beside the River Frome and near the village church. It has a well-tended garden adorned by old trees. Inside, a paneled bar and a lounge filled with antiques open onto views of the lawn. Rooms are individually decorated (often with fine antiques) and offer much comfort, including such items as mineral water, fruit, and bathrobes; some feature four-poster beds. Some accommodations are in a well-crafted annex. The main building houses the standard and superior doubles, while suites are in the boathouse in the gardens by the river. Boathouse rooms also come with whirlpool tubs.

Church Green, Wareham, Dorset BH20 4ND. © **01929/551666.** Fax 01929/554519. www.thepriory hotel.co.uk. 18 units. £235–£285 double; £315–£345 suite. Rates include English breakfast. DC, MC, V. Free parking. No children under 14. **Amenities:** 2 restaurants; bar; room service. *In room:* TV, hair dryer, minibar (in some).

MODERATE

Langtry Manor ★ 🛏   A much more atmospheric choice and run with a more personal touch than Menzies Carlton and Norfolk Royale, the Red House, as this hotel was originally called, was built in 1877 for Lillie Langtry, a gift from Edward VII to his favorite mistress. The house has all sorts of reminders of its illustrious inhabitants, including initials scratched on a windowpane. The bedrooms, each a double, range from ordinary twins to the Lillie Langtry Suite, Lillie's own room, with a four-poster bed and a double heart-shaped bathtub; or you can rent the Edward VII Suite, furnished as it was when His Royal Highness lived in this spacious room.

26 Derby Rd. (north of Christchurch Rd., A35), East Cliff, Bournemouth, Dorset BH1 3QB. © **01202/553887.** Fax 01202/290115. www.langtrymanor.co.uk. 27 units. £95–£235 double; from £225 suite. Rates include English breakfast. 2-night minimum Fri–Sat. AE, MC, V. Free parking. **Amenities:** Restaurant; bar; room service. *In room:* TV/DVD, hair dryer, minibar, Wi-Fi (free).

Menzies Carlton ★   More resort than ordinary hotel, the Carlton sits atop a seaside cliff lined with private homes and other hotels. This Edwardian pile, with panoramic views, is one of the best places to stay in Bournemouth. It exudes a 1920s aura, with rather opulent public rooms. Extensively renovated, most bedrooms are spacious and open onto views of the sea. Many units have marbled wallpaper, mottled mirrors, and armchairs. On the downside, readers have complained that in some rooms, the double-glazing on the windows does little to cut down on the noise.

Meyrick Rd., East Overcliff, Bournemouth, Dorset BH1 3DN. © **01202/552011.** Fax 01202/299573. www.bookmenzies.com. 76 units. £79–£155 double; from £260 suite. AE, DC, MC, V. Free parking. **Amenities:** Restaurant; bar; exercise room; outdoor heated pool; room service; small spa. *In room:* TV, hair dryer, Wi-Fi (free).

Norfolk Royale ★★   One of the oldest and most prestigious hotels in town, a few blocks from the seafront and central shopping area, the Norfolk Royale recently underwent a major £5-million renovation program, restoring it to its former Edwardian elegance, with a two-tier, cast-iron veranda. Nevertheless, we think it still plays second fiddle to both the Carlton and the Royal Bath. It exudes the atmosphere of a country estate, with formal entrance, rear garden, and fountain shaded by trees. Rooms and suites have been luxuriously appointed with the styles of the period, blended with modern comforts.

Richmond Hill, Bournemouth, Dorset BH2 6EN. ℰ **01202/551521.** Fax 01202/229729. www.norfolk-royale.co.uk. 95 units. £143–£165 double; £207–£249 suite. Rates include English breakfast. AE, DC, MC, V. Parking £12. **Amenities:** Restaurant; bar; babysitting; exercise room; Jacuzzi; indoor heated pool; room service; sauna. *In room:* TV, hair dryer, minibar, Wi-Fi (free).

Royal Bath ★★★   This early Victorian version of a French château, with towers and bay windows looking out over the bay and Purbeck Hill, dates from June 28, 1838, the very day of Victoria's coronation. After the adolescent Prince of Wales (later Edward VII) stayed here, the hotel added "Royal" to its name. Over the years, it has attracted notables such as Oscar Wilde and Prime Minister Disraeli. Now a member of the De Vere hotel group, it is in a neck-and-neck race with the Carlton in terms of luxury and style. It's located in a 1.2-hectare (3-acre) garden where cliff-top panoramas open onto the sea. The mostly spacious bedrooms are furnished with a certain English style and grace, and the larger rooms have sitting areas.

Bath Rd., Bournemouth, Dorset BH1 2EW. ℰ **01202/555555.** Fax 01202/554158. www.devere-hotels. com. 140 units. £150–£200 double; £240–£290 suite. Rates include English breakfast. AE, DC, MC, V. Free parking. **Amenities:** 2 restaurants (including Oscars, p. 357); bar; exercise room; room service; small spa. *In room:* TV, hair dryer, minibar, Wi-Fi (free).

INEXPENSIVE

New Westcliff Hotel 🗡️   This hotel is a 5-minute walk from the town center, near Durley Chine, and was once the luxurious south-coast home of the duke of Westminster, who had it built in 1876. Now run by the Blissert family, the hotel draws lots of repeat business. As befits a former private home, bedrooms come in various shapes and sizes. All units are comfortably furnished and well maintained; some have four-posters. There's a large garden and a parking area. A special feature of the hotel is a little theater with a screening room.

27–29 Chine Crescent, West Cliff, Bournemouth, Dorset BH2 5LB. ℰ **01202/551062.** Fax 01202/315377. www.newwestcliffhotel.co.uk. 53 units. £39–£52 per person double; £49–£59 per person double including half-board; discounts for longer stays. Rates include English breakfast. MC, V. Free parking. **Amenities:** Restaurant; 2 bars; Jacuzzi; indoor heated pool; sauna. *In room:* TV, hair dryer.

Wood Lodge Hotel 🗡️   Lying a short walk from the ocean, this hotel dates from the early 20th century but has been beautifully restored and modernized to receive guests. Many of its original features remain, including stained-glass windows and an old-fashioned staircase. A Victorian presence still permeates, and there are four ground-floor rooms for those who don't like stairs. Many of the accommodations open onto views of the award-winning garden. Breakfasts are a special feature here (ever had kippers with a poached egg?).

10 Manor Rd., East Cliff, Bournemouth, Dorset BH1 3EY. ℰ **01202/290891.** Fax 01202/290892. www. woodlodgehotel.co.uk. 15 units. £35–£44 per person double. MC, V. **Amenities:** Restaurant; bar. *In room:* TV, hair dryer, Wi-Fi (free).

Where to Dine

Coriander 🌶 MEXICAN   This restaurant, located in a pedestrian-only zone, brings south-of-the-Yankee-border flair to staid Bournemouth. All menu items are prepared with fresh ingredients. Homemade soups are a feature here, based on seasonal ingredients, or you can opt for starters such as tortilla chips and salsa or crispy marinated chicken wings. Even better are the skewered tiger prawns with a sweet-chili salsa. The town's best quesadillas and burritos are served here. House specialties include a Cajun-style gumbo with chorizo and peppers and a Mexican chicken casserole called Coriander Vesuvius.

22 Richmond Hill. ✆ **01202/552202.** www.coriander-restaurant.co.uk. Reservations required Sat–Sun. Main courses £9–£13; fixed-price 2-course lunch £8.95, 3-course lunch £12. AE, MC, V. Daily noon–10pm.

Highcliff Grill ★ TRADITIONAL BRITISH/SEAFOOD   This smart brasserie-style restaurant and bar is known for the freshness and preparation of its seafood as well as its succulent chargrilled steaks. The chef makes some of the best fish soup and crab cakes in the resort area. In addition to those steaks, meat eaters will find West Country rump of lamb and an organic pork loin cutlet. Many patrons visit just for the shellfish, especially the mussels in white wine, the garlic-infused tiger prawns, or the grilled scallops in herb butter.

In the Bournemouth Highcliff Marriott, 105 St. Michael's Rd. ✆ **01202/200800.** Reservations recommended. Main courses £15–£20. AE, MC, V. Mon–Sat 6–9:30pm; Sun 1–3pm and 6–9pm.

Oscars ★ FRENCH   Sporting Oscar Wilde mementos, Bournemouth's best restaurant is located cliff-side, with panoramic sea views. The chef presents market-fresh ingredients deftly handled by a skilled staff. The excellent appetizers may include a terrine of salmon scallops or king prawns with a saffron and basil jelly. The imaginative main courses range from roasted Dorset lamb with sweet dumplings to pan-fried loin of monkfish with crab and tarragon butter.

In the Royal Bath hotel, Bath Rd. ✆ **01202/555555.** Reservations required. Main courses £17–£27. AE, DC, MC, V. Daily 12:30–2pm and 6–10pm.

Exploring the Area

The amusements here are varied, and this is a much more upmarket and tasteful resort than jazzy Brighton. It's a bit staid during the day, but at night swarms of young people flock to the bars and clubs, where loud, brassy sounds pierce the night. At the **Pavilion Theatre,** you can see West End productions from London. The **Bournemouth Symphony Orchestra** is justly famous in Europe. And there's the usual run of golf courses, band concerts, variety shows, and dancing.

And, of course, this seaside resort has a spectacular beach—11km (7 miles) of uninterrupted sand stretching from Hengistbury Head to Alum Chine. Most of it is known simply as **Bournemouth Beach,** although its western edge, when it crosses over into the municipality of Poole, is called **Sandbanks Beach.** Beach access is free, and a pair of blue flags will indicate where the water's fine for swimming. The flags also signify the highest standards of cleanliness, management, and facilities. A health-conscious, nonsmoking zone now exists at Durley Chine, East Beach, and Fisherman's Walk. Fourteen full-time lifeguards patrol the shore and the water; they are assisted by volunteers during the busiest summer months. The promenade is traffic-free during the summer. There are two piers, one at Boscombe and the other at Bournemouth.

Amenities at the beach include beach bungalows, freshwater showers, seafront bistros and cafes, boat trips, rowboats, canoes, jet skis, and Windsurfers. Cruises run in the summer from Bournemouth Pier to the Isle of Wight.

The traffic-free town center, with its wide avenues, is elegant but by no means stuffy. Entertainers perform on the corners of streets that are lined with boutiques, cafes, street furniture, and plenty of meeting places. Specialized shopping is found mainly in the suburbs—Pokesdown for antiques and collectibles, Westbourne for designer fashion and home accessories. Victorian shopping arcades can be found in both Westbourne and Boscombe.

The best golf course is at the **Club at Meyrick Park,** Central Drive (© **01202/786000;** www.theclubcompany.com), one of the south coast's most beautiful courses. It's laid out across challenging terrain. Greens fees range from £22 to £25.

Bournemouth After Dark

A choice of major venues offers great performances year-round. The **International Centre's Windsor Hall** hosts leading performers from London, the **Pavilion Theatre** puts on West End musicals as well as dancing with live music, and the **Winter Gardens,** the original home and favorite performance space of the world-famous **Bournemouth Symphony Orchestra,** offers regular concerts. Program and ticket information for all three venues is available by calling © **0870/111-3000.**

En Route to Dorchester: A 17th-Century Mansion

Kingston Lacy An imposing 17th-century mansion set on 101 hectares (250 acres) of wooded park, Kingston Lacy was the home of the Bankes family for more than 300 years. They entertained such distinguished guests as King Edward VII, Kaiser Wilhelm, Thomas Hardy, and George V. If you have an hour—better yet, 2 hours—the time could be spent exploring this attraction and its grounds. The house displays a magnificent collection of artwork by Rubens, Titian, and Van Dyck, as well as an important collection of Egyptian artifacts.

The present structure replaced Corfe Castle, the Bankes' family home that was destroyed in the civil war. During her husband's absence, while performing duties as chief justice to King Charles I, Lady Bankes led the defense of the castle, withstanding two sieges before being forced to surrender to Cromwell's forces in 1646 because of the actions of a treacherous follower. The keys to Corfe Castle hang in the library at Kingston Lacy.

At Wimborne Minster, on B3082 (Wimborne-Blandford Rd.), 2.5km (1½ miles) west of Wimborne. © **01202/883402.** www.nationaltrust.org.uk. Admission to the house, garden, and park £10 adults, £5 children, £25 family ticket; garden only £5 adults, £2.50 children, £13 family ticket. House mid-Mar to Oct Wed–Sun 11am–4pm; garden and park mid-Mar to Oct daily 10:30am–6pm, Nov to mid-Dec Fri–Sun 10:30am–4pm, Feb to mid-Mar Sat–Sun 10:30am–4pm. Closed mid-Dec to Jan.

DORCHESTER: HARDY'S HOME ★

193km (120 miles) SW of London; 43km (27 miles) W of Bournemouth

In his 1886 novel, *The Mayor of Casterbridge,* Thomas Hardy gave Dorchester literary fame. Actually, Dorchester was notable even in Roman times, when Maumbury

Rings, the best Roman amphitheater in Britain, was filled with the sounds of 12,000 spectators screaming for the blood of the gladiators. Today, it's a sleepy market town that seems to go to bed right after dinner.

Essentials

GETTING THERE   Trains run from London's Waterloo Station every hour during the day. The trip takes 2½ hours. For rail information, call ℂ **0845/748-4950** or visit **www.nationalrail.co.uk**. Dorchester has two train stations, the South Station at Station Approach and the West Station on Great Western Road.

One **National Express** coach a day departs from London's Victoria Coach Station heading for Dorchester. The trip takes 3¾ hours. For schedule information, call ℂ **0871/781-81-78** or visit **www.nationalexpress.com**.

If driving from London, take the M3 southwest, but near the end take the A30 toward Salisbury to connect with the A354 for the final approach to Dorchester.

VISITOR INFORMATION   The **Tourist Information Centre** is at Unit 11, Antelope Walk (ℂ **01305/267992;** www.visit-dorchester.co.uk). It's open April through October, Monday to Saturday 9am to 5pm (plus May–Sept Sun 10am–3pm), and November through March, Monday to Saturday 9am to 4pm.

Where to Stay & Dine in & Around Dorchester

Best Western Kings Arms   In business for more than 3 centuries, the Kings Arms offers great bow windows above the porch and a swinging sign hanging over the road, a legacy of its days as a coaching inn. It's still the best place to stay within Dorchester's center, though superior lodgings can be found on the outskirts. An archway leads to the courtyard and parking area at the back of the hotel. All rooms are comfortably furnished; most are small to medium in size and have been modernized while retaining a traditional English aura.

30 High East St., Dorchester, Dorset DT1 1HF. ℂ **01305/265353.** Fax 01305/260269. www.bestwestern. co.uk. 37 units. £90–£135 double. AE, MC, V. **Amenities:** Restaurant; bar; room service. *In room:* TV, hair dryer, Wi-Fi (free).

Summer Lodge ★★★   In this country-house hotel (a Relais & Châteaux property), located 24km (15 miles) north of Dorchester, resident owners Nigel and Margaret Corbett provide care, courtesy, and comfort. Once home to heirs of the earls of Ilchester, the house, in the village of Evershot, now stands on 1.6 hectares (4 acres) of secluded gardens. Evershot appears as Evershed in *Tess of the D'Urbervilles,* and author Thomas Hardy (that name again) designed a wing of the house. In this relaxed, informal atmosphere, bedrooms have views either of the garden or over village rooftops to fields beyond. The hotel is regularly redecorated and recarpeted, with individually decorated accommodations that come with many comforts. Rooms and suites are split among the main building, a coach house, and three cottages.

Summer Lane, Evershot, Dorset DT2 0JR. ℂ **01935/482000.** Fax 01935/482040. www.summerlodge hotel.co.uk. 24 units. £225–£360 double; £325–£445 suite; £430–£545 cottage. Rates include English breakfast, early morning tea, and newspaper. AE, DC, MC, V. Head north from Dorchester on A37. **Amenities:** Restaurant; bar; exercise room; indoor heated pool; room service; outdoor tennis court. *In room:* A/C, TV/DVD, hair dryer, Wi-Fi (free).

Yalbury Cottage ★ 🎒 This thatch-roofed cottage with inglenooks and beamed ceilings is in a small country village within walking distance of Thomas Hardy's cottage and Stinsford Church. The cottage is some 300 years old and was once home to a local shepherd and the keeper of the water meadows. About 1.6km (1 mile) to the north is Thorncombe Wood (home to badgers, deer, and many species of birds), offering a pleasant stroll and a chance to see Hardy's birthplace, which is tucked in under the edge of the woods. The bedrooms overlook the English country garden beyond, reflecting a mood of tranquillity, and have pinewood furniture in the English-cottage style.

Lower Bockhampton, near Dorchester, Dorset DT2 8PZ. *(C)* **01305/262382.** Fax 01305/266412. www. yalburycottage.com. 8 units. £110–£170 double. Rates include English breakfast. MC, V. Closed Sun–Mon Nov–Mar 20. Head 3km (2 miles) east of Dorchester (A35) and watch for signs to Lower Bockhampton. **Amenities:** Restaurant; babysitting; room service. *In room:* TV/DVD, CD player, hair dryer, Wi-Fi (free).

Seeing the Sights

To learn more about the Victorian author Thomas Hardy, you can join organized walks that follow in the footsteps of his novels in and around the Dorchester area. They are conducted April through October by the **Thomas Hardy Society** (*(C)* **01305/251501;** www.hardysociety.org). These walks and tours take up a full day and are followed by lectures on Hardy and readings of his works, both poetry and prose.

Athelhampton House & Gardens ★★ This is one of England's great medieval houses and the most beautiful and historic in the south, lying a mile east of Puddletown. Thomas Hardy mentioned it in some of his writings but called it Athelhall. It was begun during the reign of Edward IV on the legendary site of King Athelstan's palace. A family home for more than 500 years, it's noted for its 15th-century Great Hall, Tudor great chamber, state bedroom, and King's Room.

Insider's tip: Though many visitors come to see the house, the gardens are even more inspiring. Dating from 1891, they are full of vistas, and their beauty is enhanced by the River Piddle flowing through and by fountains. These walled gardens, winners of the HHA/Christie's Garden of the Year award, contain the famous topiary pyramids and two pavilions designed by Inigo Jones. You'll see fine collections of tulips and magnolias, roses, and lilies, and also a 15th-century dovecote. And yes, the gardens were often visited by Thomas Hardy.

On A35, 8km (5 miles) east of Dorchester. *(C)* **01305/848363.** www.athelhampton.co.uk. Admission £8.75 adults, £8.25 seniors, £6.75 students, free for children under 16. Feb 25–Oct Sun–Thurs 11am–4:30pm. Take the Dorchester-Bournemouth Rd. (A35) east of Dorchester for 8km (5 miles).

Dorset County Museum ★ This museum has a gallery devoted to memorabilia of Thomas Hardy's life. In addition, you'll find an archaeological gallery with displays and finds from Maiden Castle, Britain's largest Iron Age hill fort, plus exhibits on the geology, local history, and natural history of Dorset.

High West St. (next to St. Peter's Church). *(C)* **01305/262735.** www.dorsetcountymuseum.org. Admission £6.50 adults, £5 seniors and students, free for 2 accompanied children 5–15, additional children £2, free for children 4 and younger. July–Sept daily 10am–5pm; Oct–June Mon–Sat 10am–5pm. Closed Dec 25.

Hardy's Cottage Thomas Hardy was born in 1840 at Higher Bockhampton. His home, now a National Trust property, is open to the public. Approach the cottage on foot—it's a 10-minute walk—after parking your vehicle in the space provided in the woods. **Note:** At press time, the cottage was closed for renovations; check locally before heading here.

Higher Bockhampton (5km/3 miles northeast of Dorchester and 1km/½ mile south of Blandford Rd./ A35). ℂ **01297/561901.** www.nationaltrust.org.uk. Admission £4 adults. Sun–Thurs 11am–5pm. Closed Nov–Mar. Call ahead to confirm hours.

DORSET'S COASTAL TOWNS: CHARMOUTH & LYME REGIS ★★

Charmouth: 253km (157 miles) SW of London, 1.5km (1 mile) W of Bridport; Lyme Regis: 258km (160 miles) SW of London, 40km (25 miles) W of Dorchester

Situated on Lyme Bay, the village of Charmouth is a winner. With its Georgian houses and thatched cottages, it provides some of the most dramatic coastal scenery in West Dorset. The village is west of Golden Cap, which is the highest cliff along the coast of southern England.

Just to the east of Charmouth is Chideock, a charming village hamlet of thatched houses with a dairy farm in the center. About a mile from the coast, it's a gem of a place for overnight stopovers, and even better for longer stays.

Also on Lyme Bay, near the Devonshire border, the resort of Lyme Regis is one of the most attractive centers along the south coast. For those who shun big, commercial resorts, Lyme Regis is ideal—it's a true English coastal town with a mild climate. Seagulls fly overhead, the streets are steep and winding, and walks along Cobb Beach are brisk. The views, particularly of the craft in the harbor, are so photogenic that John Fowles, a longtime resident of the town, selected it as the site for the 1980 filming of his novel *The French Lieutenant's Woman*.

During its heyday, the town was a major seaport. Later, Lyme developed into a small spa, including among its visitors Jane Austen. She wrote her final novel, *Persuasion* (published posthumously and based partly on the town's life), after staying here in 1803 and 1804.

Essentials

GETTING THERE The nearest train connection to Charmouth and Chideock is Dorchester (see "Essentials" in the Dorchester section, earlier). Buses run frequently through the day, heading west from both Dorchester and Bridport.

To get to Lyme Regis, take the London-Exeter train, getting off at Axminster and continuing the rest of the way by bus. Bus no. 31 runs from Axminster to Lyme Regis, with hourly service during the day.

For rail information, call ℂ **0845/748-4950** or visit **www.nationalrail.co.uk.** For **National Express** bus information, call ℂ **0871/781-81-78** or visit **www. nationalexpress.com**.

If you're driving to Chideock or Charmouth from Bridport, continue west along the A35. To get to Lyme Regis from Bridport, continue west along the A35, cutting south to the coast at the junction with the A3070.

VISITOR INFORMATION In Lyme Regis, the **Tourist Information Centre,** at Guildhall Cottage, Church Street (ℂ **01297/442138;** www.westdorset.com), is open November through March, Monday to Saturday 10am to 3pm, and April through October, Monday to Saturday 10am to 5pm and Sunday 10am to 4pm.

Where to Stay & Dine

IN CHARMOUTH

White House Hotel ★ The White House is the best place to stay in Charmouth. This Regency home, with its period architecture and bow doors, is well preserved and tastefully furnished. Owners Ian and Liz Simpson took this place, constructed in 1827, and made it comfortable. The handsomely outfitted bedrooms range in size from small to medium and include such extras as complimentary decanters of sherry, homemade shortbread, and electric kettles.

2 Hillside, The Street, Charmouth, Dorset DT6 6PJ. ⓒ **01297/560411.** Fax 01297/560702. www.white househotel.com. 8 units. £180–£230 double. Rates include English breakfast and 5-course table d'hôte. No children 11 and under. MC, V. Closed Dec–Jan, but open for New Year's Day. Bus: 31 from Bridport. **Amenities:** Restaurant; bar; room service. *In room:* TV.

IN LYME REGIS

Alexandra Hotel ★ Built in 1735, this hotel is situated on a hill about 5 minutes from the center of Lyme Regis. Today, it has the best bedrooms and amenities of any inn in town, though it lacks the personal charm of Kersbrook (see below). The place has been discreetly modernized around its original character. In rooms once occupied by such "blue bloods" as Dowager Countess Poulett and Duc du Stacpoole, you'll sleep in grand comfort in the handsome beds. Most rooms command superb sea views over Lyme Regis and the Cobb.

Pound St., Lyme Regis, Dorset DT7 3HZ. ⓒ **01297/442010.** Fax 01297/443229. www.hotelalexandra. co.uk. 26 units. £120–£190 double. Rates include English breakfast. MC, V. **Amenities:** Restaurant; bar; room service. *In room:* TV, hair dryer.

Kersbrook ★ 🏠 Built of stone in 1790 and crowned by a thatch roof, the Kersbrook sits on a ledge above the village (which provides a panoramic view of the coast), on .6 hectare (1½ acres) of gardens landscaped according to the original 18th-century plans. The public rooms have been refurbished with antique furniture, re-creating old-world charm with modern facilities. All of the small to medium-size bedrooms have a certain 17th-century charm, with furnishings ranging from antique to contemporary. Rooms are comfortable and tidily maintained.

Pound Rd., Lyme Regis, Dorset DT7 3HX. ⓒ/fax **01297/442596.** www.kersbrook.co.uk. 10 units. £43–£48 per person double. Rates include English breakfast. AE, MC, V. **Amenities:** Bar. *In room:* TV, hair dryer, no phone.

Royal Lion Hotel ☺ This former coaching inn dates from 1610, growing throughout the years to incorporate oak-paneled bars, lounges, and comfortably up-to-date bedrooms. Situated in the center of town on a hillside climbing up from the sea, the hotel features country-inspired furnishings and venerable antiques. Accommodations are divided between the main house, where the traditionally furnished rooms have fireplaces and more character, and a modern wing, where rooms have contemporary furnishings and the added advantage of a private terrace with sea view. Children are welcomed and some of the hotel's family rooms have bunk beds.

Broad St., Lyme Regis, Dorset DT7 3QF. © **01297/445622.** Fax 01297/445859. www.royallionhotel.com. 30 units. £50–£74 per person double; £71–£96 per person double including half-board. Rates include English breakfast. AE, DC, MC, V. Free parking. **Amenities:** Restaurant; bar; exercise room; Jacuzzi; small indoor heated pool; sauna. *In room:* TV.

Exploring the Area

Charmouth and **Chideock** (about a mile inland) are the most beautiful villages in Dorset. It's fun to stroll though them to see the well-kept cottages, manicured gardens, and an occasional 18th- or 19th-century church. Charmouth, more than Chideock, also boasts a small-scale collection of unusual antiques shops. Both villages are less than a mile from the western edge of **Chesil Beach,** one of the Hampshire coast's most famous (and longest) beaches. Although it's covered with shingle (sharp rocks), and hard on your feet if you go sunbathing, the beach nonetheless provides 8km (5 miles) of sweeping views toward France. Along this stretch you'll find numerous facilities such as toilets and places to order food and drink.

The surrounding area is a fascinating place for botanists and zoologists thanks to the predominance of blue Lias, a sedimentary rock well suited to the formation of fossils. In 1810, Mary Anning (at the age of 11) discovered one of the first articulated ichthyosaur skeletons. She went on to become one of the first professional fossilists in England. Books outlining walks in the area and the regions where fossils can be studied are available at the local tourist information office.

WILTSHIRE & SOMERSET: REGAL BATH & MYSTERIOUS STONEHENGE

For our look at the "West Countree," we move into Wiltshire and Somerset, two of the most historic counties of England. Once you reach this area of pastoral woodland, London seems far removed. For a total view of the West Country, you can also visit Devon and Cornwall (see chapters 11 and 12).

Most people agree that the West Country, a loose geographical term, begins at **Salisbury,** with its Early English cathedral. Nearby is **Stonehenge,** England's oldest prehistoric monument. (Both Stonehenge and Salisbury are in Wiltshire.) When you cross into Wiltshire, you enter a country of chalky, grassy uplands and rolling plains. Much of the county is agricultural; a large part is pasture.

Somerset has some of the most beautiful scenery in England. The undulating limestone hills of **Mendip** and the irresistible **Quantocks** are especially lovely in spring and fall. Somerset opens onto the Bristol Channel, with **Minehead** serving as its chief resort. The county is rich in legend and history, possessing particularly fanciful associations with King Arthur and Queen Guinevere, Camelot, and Alfred the Great. Its villages are noted for the tall towers of its parish churches.

Somerset also encompasses the territory around the old Roman city of **Bath,** known for its abbey and spa water, lying beside the River Avon, and is adjacent to the old port of **Bristol,** a county in its own right as well as a gateway to the West Country.

The best places to base yourself while you explore the area are Salisbury, Bath, and Bristol. From Salisbury, you can visit Stonehenge and **Old Sarum,** the two most fabled ancient monuments in the West Country. Yet some say visiting the stones at **Avebury** is a much more personal

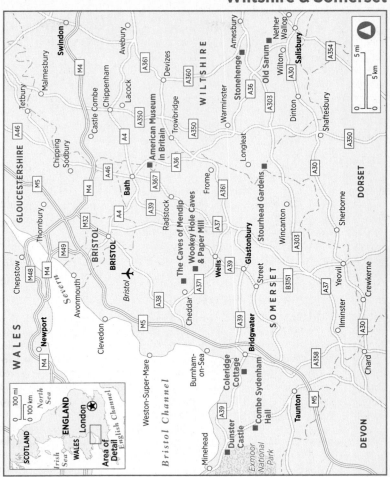

experience. And **Glastonbury,** with its once-great abbey that is now a ruined sanctuary, may be one of Britain's oldest inhabited sites. The greatest natural spectacle in the area is **Exmoor National Park,** once an English royal hunting preserve, stretching for 686 sq. km (265 sq. miles) on the north coast of Devon and Somerset. Many terrific country houses and palaces are also in this region, including **Wilton House,** the site of 17th-century staterooms designed by Inigo Jones. The other two major attractions, **Longleat House** and the fabled gardens at **Stourhead,** can be visited in a busy day while you're based in Bath or Bristol.

SALISBURY ★★

145km (90 miles) SW of London; 85km (53 miles) SE of Bristol

Long before you enter Salisbury, the spire of its cathedral comes into view—just as John Constable captured it on canvas. The 121m (404-ft.) pinnacle of the Early English and Gothic cathedral is the tallest in England.

Salisbury, or New Sarum, lies in the valley of the River Avon. Filled with Tudor inns and tearooms, it is the only true city in Wiltshire. It's an excellent base for visitors anxious to explore Stonehenge or Avebury, who, unfortunately, tend to visit the cathedral and then rush on their way. But the old market town is an interesting destination on its own, and if you choose to linger here for a day or two, you find that its pub-to-citizen ratio is perhaps the highest in the country.

Essentials

GETTING THERE   Trains for Salisbury depart hourly from Waterloo Station in London; the trip takes 1½ hours. Sprinter trains offer fast, efficient service every hour from Portsmouth, Bristol, and South Wales. Direct rail service is also available from Exeter, Plymouth, Brighton, and Reading. For rail information, call ℂ 0845/748-4950 or visit **www.nationalrail.co.uk**.

National Express (ℂ 0871/781-8178; www.nationalexpress.com) operates three daily buses that make the 3-hour run from London, costing £16 for a one-way ticket.

If you're driving from London, head west on the M3 to the end of the run, continuing the rest of the way on the A30.

VISITOR INFORMATION   The **Tourist Information Centre** is at Fish Row (ℂ 01722/334956; www.visitsalisbury.com). It's open October through April, Monday to Saturday 9:30am to 5pm; May, Monday to Saturday 9:30am to 5pm and Sunday 10am to 4pm; and June through September, Monday to Saturday 9:30am to 6pm and Sunday 10am to 4pm.

SPECIAL EVENTS   The **St. George's Spring Festival** in April is a traditional medieval celebration of the city's patron saint. You can witness St. George slaying the dragon in the Wiltshire mummers play and enjoy the acrobats and fireworks.

With spring comes the annual **Salisbury International Arts Festival** (ℂ 01722/332977; www.salisburyfestival.co.uk). The city drapes itself in banners, and street theater—traditional and unusual—is offered everywhere. There are also symphony and chamber music concerts in Salisbury Cathedral, children's events, and much more. It takes place from mid-May to the beginning of June.

Where to Stay

MODERATE

Best Western Red Lion Hotel ★ 🍴   This 1300s hotel continues to accommodate wayfarers from London on their way to the West Country. It no longer reigns supreme in town—we prefer the White Hart and the Rose and Crown—but it's still a fine choice. Cross under its arch into a courtyard with a much-photographed hanging creeper, a red lion, and a half-timbered facade, and you'll be transported back to an earlier era. The antiques-filled hotel is noted for its unique clock collection,

Salisbury

ATTRACTIONS ●
Mompesson House **9**
Old Sarum **3**
Salisbury Cathedral **12**
Wilton House **1**

ACCOMMODATIONS ■
The Beadles **2**
Best Western Red Lion
  Hotel **7**
Cricket Field House **1**
Grasmere House **14**
Legacy Rose &
  Crown Hotel **13**
Mercure White Hart **10**
Wyndham Park Lodge **4**

DINING ◆
Charter 1227
  Restaurant **6**
Curiosity **11**
Gastrobistro at the
  Pheasant Inn **5**
Haunch of Venison **8**

which includes a skeleton organ clock in the reception hall. Each small to medium-size bedroom is individually furnished and tastefully decorated. Two units are spacious enough for families, and the most expensive rooms have four-poster beds.

4 Milford St., Salisbury, Wiltshire SP1 2AN. ℂ **800/528-1234** in the U.S., or 01722/323334. Fax 01722/325756. www.the-redlion.co.uk. 51 units. £90–£125 double; £180 family room. AE, DC, MC, V. **Amenities:** Restaurant; bar; room service. *In room:* TV, hair dryer, Wi-Fi (£1.25 per hr.).

Grasmere House Hotel ★ ☺ Grasmere House stands near the confluence of the Nadder and Avon rivers on .6 hectare (1½ acres) of grounds. Constructed in 1896 for Salisbury merchants, the house still suggests a family home. The original architectural features were retained as much as possible, including a "calling box" for servants in the dining room. A conservatory restaurant and bar overlooks the cathedral, as do three luxurious rooms. Four rooms are in the original house, with the remainder in a newer wing. Each room has a distinctive character and often opens onto a scenic view. Two units are large enough for families, and the hotel welcomes young children.

70 Harnham Rd., Salisbury, Wiltshire SP2 8JN. ☎ **01722/338388.** Fax 01722/333710. www.grasmere hotel.com. 36 units. £106–£165 double; £146 family room. Rates include English breakfast. AE, DC, MC, V. Take A3094 2.5km (1½ miles) from the town center. **Amenities:** Restaurant; bar; room service. *In room:* TV, hair dryer.

Legacy Rose & Crown Hotel ★★★   This half-timbered 13th-century gem stands with its feet almost in the River Avon; beyond the water, you can see the tall spire of the cathedral. Thanks to its tranquil location, it's our top choice. From here, you can easily walk over the arched stone bridge to the center of Salisbury in 10 minutes. Old trees shade the lawns and gardens between the inn and the river, and chairs are set out so that you can enjoy the view and count the swans. The inn has both new and old wings. The new wing is modern, but the old wing is more appealing, with its sloping ceilings and antique fireplaces and furniture. Bedrooms in the main house range from small to medium in size, though those in the new wing are more spacious and better designed.

Harnham Rd., Salisbury, Wiltshire SP2 8JQ. ☎ **0870/832-9946.** Fax 0870/832-9947. www.legacy-hotels.co.uk. 29 units. £105–£160 double. Rates include continental breakfast. AE, DC, MC, V. Take A3094 2.5km (1½ miles) from the town center. **Amenities:** Restaurant; 2 bars; room service; Wi-Fi (free, in lobby). *In room:* TV, hair dryer.

Mercure White Hart Hotel ★★   Combining the best of old and new, the White Hart is a Salisbury landmark from Georgian times. Its classic facade is intact, with tall columns crowning a life-size hart (stag). The older accommodations are traditional, and a new section has been added in the rear, opening onto a large parking area. New-wing units are tastefully decorated; although rooms in the main building have more style and character, many are quite small. You can enjoy a before-dinner drink, followed by a meal of modern English fare, in the restaurant.

1 St. John's St., Salisbury, Wiltshire SP1 2SD. ☎ **800/221-4542** in U.S., or 01722/327476. Fax 01722/412761. www.mercure.com. 68 units. £100–£180 double. Rates include English breakfast. AE, DC, MC, V. Free parking. **Amenities:** Restaurant; bar; room service. *In room:* TV, hair dryer, minibar (in some), Wi-Fi (£5 per hr.).

INEXPENSIVE

The Beadles ★★ 🎁   A Georgian-style house with antique furnishings and a view of the cathedral, the Beadles offers unobstructed views of the beautiful Wiltshire countryside from its .4-hectare (1-acre) gardens. It's situated in a small, unspoiled English village, 11km (7 miles) from Salisbury, which offers excellent access to Stonehenge, Wilton House, the New Forest, and the rambling moors of Thomas Hardy country. Even the road to Winchester is an ancient Roman byway. Furnished tastefully, this household contains rooms with twins or doubles. Owners David and Anne-Marie Yuille-Baddeley delight in providing information on the area.

Middleton, Winterslow, near Salisbury, Wiltshire SP5 1QS. ☎ **01980/862922.** Fax 01980/863565. www.staywiththebeadles.com. 3 units. £70 double. Rates include English breakfast. MC, V. Free parking. Turn off A30 at Pheasant Inn to Middle Winterslow. Enter the village, make the 1st right, turn right again, and it's the 1st right after Trevano. *In room:* TV, hair dryer.

Cricket Field House ★ 🎁   This snug B&B takes its name from the cricket field it overlooks 3km (2 miles) west of Salisbury. The original structure was a gamekeeper's cottage, but it has been handsomely converted. In its own large garden, the family-run house is comfortably furnished and modernized. Rooms are in both the main house and an equally good pavilion annex. Each unit is individually decorated and furnished.

Wilton Rd., Salisbury, Wiltshire SP2 9NS. ©/fax **01722/322595.** www.cricketfieldhousehotel.co.uk. 17 units. £70–£95 double; £80–£130 family room. Rates include English breakfast. AE, MC, V. Free parking. On the A36, 3km (2 miles) west of Salisbury. **Amenities:** Restaurant (guests only); room service. *In room:* TV, hair dryer, Wi-Fi (free).

Wyndham Park Lodge   From this appealing Victorian 1880 house, it's an easy walk to the heart of Salisbury and its cathedral, and about a 5-minute walk to a swimming pool and the bus station. The small to midsize rooms are comfortably furnished with Victorian and Edwardian antiques. They have either one double or two twin beds.

51 Wyndham Rd., Salisbury, Wiltshire SP1 3AB. © **01722/416517.** Fax 01722/328851. www.wyndham parklodge.co.uk. 4 units. £55–£60 double; £70–£80 family room for 3. Rates include English breakfast. MC, V. *In room:* TV, hair dryer, Wi-Fi (free).

IN NEARBY TEFFONT EVIAS

Howard's House ★ 📖   This 17th-century dower house, which has been added to over the years, is set in a medieval hamlet. It's the most appealing small hotel and restaurant in the area. Much care is lavished on the decor, with fresh flowers in every public room and bedroom. The hotel has attractive gardens, and on chilly nights, log fires burn. Most accommodations are spacious in size, and one room is large enough for a family. Some rooms have four-poster beds.

Teffont Evias, 14km (9 miles) from Salisbury, Wiltshire SP3 5RJ. © **01722/716392.** Fax 01722/716820. www.howardshousehotel.co.uk. 9 units. £175–£195 double. Rates include English breakfast. AE, MC, V. From Salisbury, head east on the A36 until you reach a roundabout. Take the 1st left leading to the A30. On the A30, continue for 5km (3 miles) to the turnoff (B3089) for Barford Saint-Martin. Continue for 6.5km (4 miles) on this secondary road to the town of Teffont Evias, where the hotel is signposted. **Amenities:** Restaurant (see review below); bar. *In room:* TV, hair dryer.

Where to Dine

See "Salisbury After Dark," below, for a selection of pubs with affordable fare.

Charter 1227 Restaurant ENGLISH/INTERNATIONAL   The chef/owner of this place specializes in homemade and wholesome "real food." The pleasantly decorated restaurant is on the second floor of a redbrick building at the back end of Salisbury's largest parking lot, in the center of town. In the same all-purpose dining room, you can order from two different menus, one with affordable bistro-style platters. A longer menu, with items that take more time to prepare, is also available. You can try long-time British fare such as a creamy pasta with mushrooms and pesto sauce, pork and leek sausages with onion marmalade, and lamb kidneys sautéed with onions, mushrooms, and a Madeira-laced garlic cream sauce. Yes, the chef still makes that old nursery favorite, sticky toffee "pud" with toffee sauce.

6-7 Ox Row, Market Sq. © **01722/333118.** www.charter1227.co.uk. Reservations recommended. Main courses £8–£14; bistro main courses £8. AE, DC, MC, V. Mon–Sat noon–2pm and 6–9:30pm.

Curiosity ★ BRITISH   Close to the Salisbury Cathedral, this is one of the finest dining rooms within the city itself. The chefs use market-fresh ingredients to take advantage of the changing seasons. Dishes are geared to the British palate, with many favorites of the West Country, including Wiltshire mutton shoulder slowly braised for 6 hours and accompanied by root-vegetable mash and served with port and juniper berry jus; a tenderloin of Wiltshire pork accompanied by Dauphinoise potatoes, eggplant "steak," and a black pudding fritter; and the familiar Salisbury rump steak with grilled tomatoes and fries. You can also order old-fashioned picks like gilt head bream and pork belly, or perhaps steak-and-kidney pie.

In the Kings Arms Hotel, 9–3 St. John St. ℂ **01722/340000.** www.thekingsarmshotelsalisbury.com. Reservations recommended. Main courses £9–£14. AE, MC, V. Mon–Sat noon–2:30pm and 6–9:30pm. Closed Dec 24–Jan 2.

Gastrobistro at the Pheasant Inn ★★ FRENCH   With its ancient beams and cozy inglenooks, this black-and-white timbered pub in the center of Salisbury is arguably the city's finest dining spot. Owner Arnaud Rochette delivers a Gallic-inspired menu that can be served on a summer terrace. A wide range of tastes is catered to here, from the diner seeking such comfort food as a burger, to the vegetarian, to those wanting to sample delectable French dishes such as cassoulet or bouillabaisse. You can start with old favorites such as French onion soup or snails from Burgundy in garlic butter, following with stuffed peppers with zucchini and artichoke hearts, or else pan-fried sea bass flavored with a saffron sauce. Desserts are especially recommended, including the prune and Armagnac crème brûlée.

19 Salt Lane. ℂ **01722/414926.** www.restaurant-salisbury.com. Reservations required. Main courses £7–£15; fixed-price menu £17. AE, MC, V. Daily noon–2:30pm; Mon–Sat 6–9:30pm.

Haunch of Venison ENGLISH   Right in the heart of Salisbury, this creaky-timbered chophouse (dating from 1320) serves excellent dishes, especially English roasts and grills. Stick to its specialties and you'll rarely go wrong. Begin with a tasty warm salad of venison sausages with garlic croutons, and then follow with the time-honored roast haunch of venison with parsnips and juniper berries. Other tempting dishes include pan-fried orange-glazed duck breast with a beetroot salsa, or perhaps the smoked mackerel salad with roasted cherry tomatoes and a sweet chili dressing.

1 Minster St. ℂ **01722/411313.** www.haunchofvenison.uk.com. Main courses £12–£17. MC, V. Mon–Sat 11:30am–11pm; Sun noon–10:30pm.

Howard's House ★ INTERNATIONAL   If you'd like to dine in one of the loveliest places in the area and enjoy a refined cuisine at the same time, leave Salisbury and head for this previously recommended hotel (see above). It's a 14km (9-mile) drive to Teffont Evias, but well worth the trip. The village itself is one of the most beautiful in Wiltshire. The elegantly appointed restaurant showcases a finely honed cuisine prepared with first-class ingredients. The menu changes daily, but is likely to feature such starters as Cornish scallop risotto with deep-fried basil or maple-glazed pork belly. Main courses appeal with well-balanced flavors, as exemplified by seared Scottish scallops with a sweet carrot puree and black pudding, or filet of wild turbot with a goat-cheese gnocchi and a beet salad.

Teffont Evias, near Salisbury. ℂ **01722/716392.** Reservations required. Fixed-price lunch £23 for 2 courses, £27 for 3 courses; fixed-price dinner £35 for 2 courses, £45 for 3 courses. AE, MC, V. Sun–Wed 12:30–1:30pm; daily 7:30–9pm. For directions, see the Howard's House listing above.

Exploring Salisbury

You can easily see Salisbury on foot, either on your own or by taking a guided daytime or evening walk sponsored by the **Salisbury City Guides** (ℂ 01722/320349; www.salisburycityguides.co.uk). Tickets are £4 for adults and £2 for children. Check with the Tourist Information Centre about themed walks on Saturday and the Ghost Walk on Friday.

Mompesson House ★ This is one of the most distinguished houses in the area. Built by Charles Mompesson in 1701, while he was a member of Parliament for Old Sarum, it is a beautiful example of the Queen Anne style and is well known for its fine plasterwork ceilings and paneling. It also houses a collection of 18th-century drinking glasses. Visitors can wander through the garden and order a snack in the garden tearoom.

Cathedral Close. ℂ **01722/420980.** www.nationaltrust.org.uk/mompessonhouse. Admission £5.20 adults, £2.60 children 17 and younger, £13 family ticket. Mid-Mar–Oct Sat–Wed 11am–5pm. Closed Nov to early Mar.

Salisbury Cathedral ★★★ You'll find no better example of the Early English pointed architectural style than Salisbury Cathedral. Construction on this magnificent building began as early as 1220 and took only 45 years to complete. (Most of Europe's grandest cathedrals took 300 years to build.) Salisbury Cathedral is one of the most homogenous of all the great European cathedrals.

The cathedral's 13th-century octagonal chapter house possesses one of the four surviving original texts of the Magna Carta, along with treasures from the diocese of Salisbury and manuscripts and artifacts belonging to the cathedral. The cloisters enhance the cathedral's beauty, along with an exceptionally large close. At least 75 buildings are in the compound, some from the early 18th century and others from much earlier.

Insider's tip: The 121m (404-ft.) spire was one of the tallest structures in the world when completed in 1315. In its day, this was far more advanced technology than the world's tallest skyscrapers. Amazingly, the spire was not part of the original design and was conceived and added some 30 years after the rest. The name of the master mason is lost to history. In 1668, Sir Christopher Wren expressed alarm at the tilt of the spire, but no further shift has since been measured. The entire ensemble is still standing; if you trust towering architecture from 700 years ago, you can explore the tower on 1½-hour guided visits costing £8 for adults, £6 for children and seniors. Between March and October, there are two to four tours a day depending on demand. From November to February, there is only one tour a day at 2:15pm.

The Close, Salisbury. ℂ **01722/555120.** www.salisburycathedral.org.uk. Suggested donation £6 adults, £4.50 students and seniors, £4 children, £13 family. Sept to mid-June Mon–Sat 7:15am–6:15pm; late June to Aug Mon–Sat 7:15am–7:15pm; year-round Sun 7:15am–6:15pm.

Nearby Attractions

Old Sarum ★ Believed to have been an Iron Age fortification, Old Sarum was used again by the Saxons and flourished as a walled town into the Middle Ages. The Normans built a cathedral and a castle here; parts of the old cathedral were taken down to build the city of New Sarum (Salisbury).

3km (2 miles) north of Salisbury off A345 on Castle Rd. ℂ **01722/335398.** www.english-heritage.org. uk/oldsarum. Admission £3.50 adults, £3 seniors, £1.80 children. Apr–June and Sept daily 10am–5pm; July–Aug daily 9am–6pm; Mar and Oct daily 10am–4pm; Nov–Feb daily 11am–3pm. Bus: 5, 6, 7, 8, or 9, every 30 min. during the day, from the Salisbury bus station.

Wilton House ★★   This home of the earls of Pembroke is in the town of Wilton. It dates from the 16th century but has undergone numerous alterations, most recently in Victoria's day, and is noted for its 17th-century staterooms, designed by celebrated architect Inigo Jones. Shakespeare's troupe is said to have entertained here, and Eisenhower and his advisers prepared here for the D-day landings at Normandy, with only the Van Dyck paintings as silent witnesses. The house is filled with beautifully maintained furnishings and world-class art, including paintings by Rubens, Bruegel, and Reynolds. You can visit a reconstructed Tudor kitchen and Victorian laundry.

On the 8.4-hectare (21-acre) estate are giant cedars of Lebanon trees, the oldest of which were planted in 1630, as well as rose and water gardens, riverside and woodland walks, and a huge adventure playground for children.

5km (3 miles) west of Salisbury on A36. © **01722/746714.** www.wiltonhouse.co.uk. Admission (including grounds) £12 adults, £9.75 seniors, £6.50 children 5–15, £30 family ticket, free for children 4 and younger. Easter–Sept Sun–Fri 10:30am–5:30pm (last admission 4:30pm); grounds Sat only. Closed Oct to Easter Sat.

Shopping

Many shops in Salisbury are set in beautiful medieval timber-framed buildings. As you wander through the colorful market or walk the ancient streets, you'll find everything from touristy gift shops to unique specialty stores.

Hard-core shoppers and locals gravitate to the **Old George Mall Shopping Centre,** 23B High St. (© **01722/333500;** www.oldgeorgemall.co.uk), a short walk from the cathedral. With more than 40 individual shops and High Street stores, you can find the latest fashions as well as household appliances, CDs, toiletries, and greeting cards.

Salisbury After Dark

The **Salisbury Playhouse,** Malthouse Lane (© **01722/320333** for the box office; www.salisburyplayhouse.com), produces some of the finest theater in the region. Food and drink are available at the bar and restaurant to complete your evening's entertainment.

The thriving **City Hall,** Malthouse Lane (© **01722/434434** for the box office; www.cityhallsalisbury.co.uk), has a program of events to suit most tastes and ages in comfortable surroundings. It attracts many of the national touring shows in addition to local amateur events, exhibitions, and sales, thus providing good entertainment at a reasonable price.

The **Salisbury Arts Center,** Bedwin Street (© **01722/321744;** www.salisbury artscentre.co.uk), housed within the former St. Edmund's Church, features a wide range of performing and visual arts. Offerings include a broad mix of music, contemporary and classic theater, and dance performances, plus cabaret, comedy, and family shows. Regular workshops are available for all ages in arts, crafts, theater, and dance. The lively cafe/bar is a pleasant meeting place.

The **Avon Brewery Inn,** 75 Castle St. (© **01722/416184;** www.theavonbrewery inn.co.uk), is decorated like a Victorian saloon from the gay 1890s. Its idyllic garden setting overlooks the River Avon. It offers some of the tastiest and most affordable food in town.

PREHISTORIC BRITAIN: STONEHENGE ★★★ & AVEBURY ★★

On the doorstep of Salisbury you can visit two famous prehistoric monuments, all in a single day if you move fast enough. If you have time to visit only one, there is no contest: Make it Stonehenge, of course, one of the most famous prehistoric sites in the world, composed of earthworks surrounding a circular setting of large standing stones.

Stonehenge ★★★ This huge circle of lintels and megalithic pillars is considered by many to be the most important prehistoric monument in Britain.

Some visitors are disappointed when they see that Stonehenge is nothing more than concentric circles of stones. But perhaps they don't understand that Stonehenge represents an amazing engineering feat because many of the boulders, the bluestones in particular, were moved many miles (perhaps from southern Wales) to this site. If you're a romantic, come see the ruins in the early glow of dawn or else when shadows fall at sunset. The light is most dramatic at these times, the shadows longer, and the effect is often far more mesmerizing than in the glaring light of midday.

The widely held view of 18th- and 19th-century Romantics, who believed Stonehenge was the work of the Druids, is without foundation. The boulders, many weighing several tons, are believed to have predated the arrival in Britain of the Celtic culture. Controversy surrounds the prehistoric site, especially since the publication of *Stonehenge Decoded,* by Gerald S. Hawkins and John B. White, which maintains that Stonehenge was an astronomical observatory—that is, a Neolithic "computing machine" capable of predicting eclipses.

In 2008, Stonehenge made world headlines when part of its eternal mystery may have been solved. From the beginning, it was a monument to the dead, as revealed by radiocarbon dating from human cremation burials around the brooding stones. The site was used as a cemetery from 3000 B.C. until after the monuments were erected in 2500 B.C.

In yet another development, archaeologists uncovered hearths, timbers, and other remains of what was probably the village of workers who erected the monoliths on the Salisbury Plain. These ancient ruins appear to form the largest Neolithic village ever found in Britain. The trenches of this discovery, Durrington Walls, lie 3.2km (2 miles) from Stonehenge.

Your ticket permits you to go inside the fence that surrounds the site, protecting the stones from vandals and souvenir hunters. You can go all the way up to a short rope barrier, about 15m (50 ft.) from the stones.

A full circular tour around Stonehenge is possible. A modular walkway was introduced to cross the archaeologically important avenue, the area that runs between the Heel Stone and the main circle of stones. This enables visitors to complete a full circuit of the stones and to see one of the best views of a completed section of Stonehenge as they pass by, an excellent addition to the informative audio tour.

Insider's tip: From the road, if you don't mind the noise from traffic, you can get a good view of Stonehenge without paying admission for a close-up encounter. What we like to do is climb **Amesbury Hill,** clearly visible and lying 2.4km (1½ miles) up the A303. From here, you'll get a free panoramic view.

Wilts & Dorset (© 01722/336855; www.wdbus.co.uk) runs several buses daily (depending on demand) from Salisbury to Stonehenge, as well as buses from the Salisbury train station to Stonehenge. The bus trip to Stonehenge takes 40 minutes, and a round-trip ticket costs £11 for adults, £5 for children 5 to 15, £6 for seniors, and £15 for a family ticket.

At the junction of A303 and A344/A360. © **01980/623108** for information. www.stonehenge.co.uk. Admission £6.60 adults, £5.60 students and seniors, £3.30 children 5–15, £17 family ticket. June–Aug daily 9am–7pm; Mar 16–May and Sept–Oct 15 daily 9:30am–6pm; Oct 16–Mar 15 daily 9:30am–4pm. If you're driving, head north on Castle Rd. from the center of Salisbury. At the first roundabout (traffic circle), take the exit toward Amesbury (A345) and Old Sarum. Continue along this road for 13km (8 miles), and then turn left onto A303 in the direction of Exeter. You'll see signs for Stonehenge, leading you up A344 to the right. It's 3km (2 miles) west of Amesbury.

Avebury ★★   One of the largest prehistoric sites in Europe, Avebury lies on the Kennet River, 11km (7 miles) west of Marlborough and 32km (20 miles) north of Stonehenge. Some say visiting Avebury, in contrast to Stonehenge, is a more organic experience—you can walk right up and around the stones, as no fence keeps you away. Also, the site isn't mobbed with tour buses.

Visitors can walk around the 11-hectare (28-acre) site at Avebury, winding in and out of the circle of more than 100 stones, some weighing up to 50 tons. The stones are made of sarsen, a sandstone found in Wiltshire. Inside this large circle are two smaller ones, each with about 30 stones standing upright. Native Neolithic tribes are believed to have built these circles.

Wilts & Dorset (© 01722/336855; www.wdbus.co.uk) has two buses (nos. 5 and 6) that run between the Salisbury bus station and Avebury five times a day Monday through Saturday and three times a day on Sunday. The one-way trip takes 1 hour and 40 minutes. Round-trip tickets are £9 for adults, £7 for seniors, £15 for a family ticket, and £6 for children 5 to 14.

Also here is the **Alexander Keiller Museum** (© 01672/539250), which houses one of Britain's most important archaeological collections, including material from excavations at Windmill Hill and Avebury, plus artifacts from other prehistoric digs at West Kennet, Long Barrow, Silbury Hill, West Kennet Avenue, and the Sanctuary.

On A361, btw. Swindon and Devizes (1.5km/1 mile from the A4 London-Bath Rd.). © **01672/539250.** www.english-heritage.org.uk/avebury. Avebury: free admission. Alexander Keiller Museum: £4.20 adults, £2.10 children 5–14, £11 family ticket. Apr–Oct daily 10am–6pm; Nov–Mar daily 10am–4pm. The closest rail station is at Swindon, 19km (12 miles) away, which is served by the main rail line from London to Bath. For rail information, call © **0845/748-4950** or visit www.nationalrail.co.uk. A limited bus service (no. 49) runs from Swindon to Devizes through Avebury.

BATH: BRITAIN'S MOST HISTORIC SPA TOWN ★★★

185km (115 miles) W of London; 21km (13 miles) SE of Bristol

In 1702, Queen Anne made the trek from London to the mineral springs of Bath, launching a fad that was to make the city the most celebrated spa in England.

Bath

Church ✝

ATTRACTIONS ●
Bath Abbey **20**
The Circus **9**
Fashion Museum &
  Assembly Rooms **8**
Jane Austen Centre **13**
No. 1 Royal Crescent **3**
Pulteney Bridge **18**
Queen Square **12**
Roman Baths &
  Pump Room **21**
Royal Crescent **4**
Theatre Royal Bath **15**
Victoria Art Gallery **19**

ACCOMMODATIONS ■
Bath Priory **1**
Cheriton House **25**
Dukes Hotel **17**
Macdonald Bath
  Spa Hotel **17**
Mercure Francis
  Hotel **14**
One Three Nine **25**
Pratt's Hotel **24**
Queensberry **5**
Royal Crescent **2**

DINING ◆
Café Retro **22**
Casani's French
  Bistro-Restaurant **7**
Dower House **2**
Hole in the Wall **11**
Moon & Sixpence **16**
Olive Tree **5**
Pump Room at the
  Roman Baths **21**
Sally Lunn's House **23**
Woods **10**

10

WILTSHIRE & SOMERSET | Bath

The most famous name connected with Bath was the 18th-century dandy Beau Nash, who cut a striking figure as he made his way across the city, with all the plumage of a bird of paradise. This polished arbiter of taste and manners made dueling déclassé. While dispensing (at a price) trinkets to the courtiers and aspirant gentlemen of his day, Beau was carted around in a sedan chair.

The 18th-century architects John Wood the Elder and his son provided a proper backdrop for Nash's considerable social talents. These architects designed a city of stone from the nearby hills, a feat so substantial and lasting that Bath today is the most harmoniously laid-out city in England. During Georgian and Victorian times, this city, on a bend of the River Avon, attracted leading political and literary figures, such as Dickens, Thackeray, Nelson, and Pitt. Canadians may already know that General Wolfe lived on Trim Street, and Australians may want to visit the house at 19 Bennett St., where their founding father, Admiral Phillip, lived. Even Henry Fielding came this way, observing in *Tom Jones* that the ladies of Bath "endeavor to appear as ugly as possible in the morning, in order to set off that beauty which they intend to show you in the evening."

Even before its Queen Anne, Georgian, and Victorian popularity, Bath was known to the Romans as Aquae Sulis. The foreign legions founded the baths here (which you can visit today) to ease rheumatism by soaking in the curative mineral springs.

Remarkable restoration and careful planning have ensured that Bath retains its handsome look today. The city suffered devastating destruction from the infamous Baedeker air raids of 1942, when Luftwaffe pilots seemed more intent on bombing historic buildings than on hitting any military targets. After undergoing major restoration in the postwar era, Bath now has somewhat of a museum look, with the attendant gift shops. Its parks, museums, and architecture continue to draw hordes of visitors, and because of this massive tourist invasion, prices remain high. Still, it's one of the high points of the West Country and a good base for exploring Avebury.

Essentials

GETTING THERE Trains leave London's Paddington Station bound for Bath once every half-hour during the day; the trip takes about 1½ hours. The train ride from Bristol to Bath takes 11 minutes; if you're arriving at Bristol Airport, catch the airport bus to Bristol's Temple Meads station, where you can get the train to Bath. For rail information, call © 0845/748-4950 or visit **www.nationalrail.co.uk**.

National Express buses leave London's Victoria Coach Station every 90 minutes during the day. The trip takes 3½ hours. Coaches also leave Bristol bound for Bath, making the trip in 40 minutes. For schedules and information, call © 0871/781-8178 or visit **www.nationalexpress.com**.

If you're driving, head west on the M4 to the junction with the A4, and then continue west to Bath.

VISITOR INFORMATION The **Bath Tourist Information Centre** is at Abbey Chambers, Abbey Church Yard (© 09067/112000 toll call, 50p per minute; www.visitbath.co.uk), next to Bath Abbey. It's open June through September, Monday to Saturday 9:30am to 6pm and Sunday 10am to 4pm; and off-season, Monday to Saturday 9:30am to 5pm and Sunday 10am to 4pm. Closed December 25 and January 1.

GETTING AROUND   One of the best ways to explore Bath is by bike. Rentals are available at the **Bath & Dundas Canal Co.,** Brass Knocker Basin at Monkton Combe (✆ **01225/722292;** www.bathcanal.com). Daily rentals go for £14.

SPECIAL EVENTS   Bath's graceful Georgian architecture provides the setting for one of Europe's most prestigious international festivals of music and the arts, the **Bath International Music Festival.** For 15 days in late May and early June each year, the city is filled with more than 1,000 performers. The festival focuses on classical music, jazz, new music, and the contemporary visual arts, with orchestras, soloists, and artists from all over the world. In addition to the main music and art program, the festival offers walks, tours, and talks, plus free street entertainment, a free Festival Club, and opening-night celebrations with fireworks. For information, contact the **Bath Festivals Box Office,** 2 Church St., Abbey Green, Bath BA1 1NL (✆ **01225/463362;** www.bathmusicfest.org.uk).

Where to Stay
EXPENSIVE

Bath Priory ★★★   Converted from one of Bath's Georgian houses in 1969, the Priory is situated on .8 hectare (2 acres) of formal and award-winning gardens with manicured lawns and flower beds. The accommodations are furnished with antiques; our personal favorite is Clivia (all rooms are named after flowers or shrubs), a nicely appointed duplex in a circular turret. Rooms range from medium in size to spacious deluxe units, the latter with views, sitting areas, and generous dressing areas. Each has a lovely old English bed, often a half-tester.

Weston Rd., Bath, Somerset BA1 2XT. ✆ **01225/331922.** Fax 01225/448276. www.thebathpriory.co.uk. 27 units. £185–£380 standard double; from £330 junior suite; from £495 family room. Rates include English breakfast. AE, DC, MC, V. Free parking. **Amenities:** Restaurant; bar; babysitting; exercise room; 2 pools (1 heated indoor, 1 outdoor); room service; spa. *In room:* A/C, TV, hair dryer, minibar.

Macdonald Bath Spa Hotel ★★★   This stunning restored 19th-century mansion is a 10-minute walk from the center of Bath. Behind a facade of Bath stone, it lies at the end of a tree-lined drive on 2.8 hectares (7 acres) of landscaped grounds, with a Victorian grotto and a Grecian temple. In its long history, it served many purposes (once as a hostel for nurses) before being returned to its original grandeur. The hotel uses log fireplaces, elaborate moldings, and oak paneling to create country-house charm. The rooms, most of them spacious, are handsomely furnished. Most beds are doubles, and some are old-fashioned four-posters.

Sydney Rd. (east of the city, off A36), Bath, Somerset BA2 6JF. ✆ **0844/8799106.** Fax 01225/444006. www.macdonaldhotels.co.uk/bathspa. 129 units. £178–£515 double; £223–£645 suite. Rates include English breakfast. AE, MC, V. Free parking. **Amenities:** 2 restaurants; bar; exercise room; indoor heated pool; room service; spa; Wi-Fi (£5 per hr., in lobby). *In room:* A/C, TV, hair dryer, minibar.

Royal Crescent Hotel ★★★   This special place stands proudly in the center of the famed Royal Crescent. Long regarded as Bath's premier hotel (before the arrival of the even better Bath Spa Hotel), it attracts the rich and famous thanks to its location and the Bath House spa in the gardens. Accommodations, including the Jane Austen Suite, are lavishly furnished with such amenities as sumptuous four-poster beds and marble tubs. Generally quite spacious, the bedrooms are elaborately decked out with thick wool carpeting, silk wall coverings, and antiques. Each room is individually designed and offers such comforts as bottled mineral water, fruit plates, and other special touches.

15–16 Royal Crescent, Bath, Somerset BA1 2LS. © **01225/823333.** Fax 01225/339401. www.royal crescent.co.uk. 45 units. £195–£430 double; £440–£875 suite. Rates include English breakfast. AE, DC, MC, V. Parking £5. **Amenities:** Restaurant (Dower House, p. 380); bar; babysitting; exercise room; indoor heated pool; room service; sauna. *In room:* TV/DVD, hair dryer, minibar (in some), Wi-Fi (free).

MODERATE

Apsley House Hotel ★★ 🛍 This charming and stately building, just 1.5km (1 mile) west of the center of Bath, dates from 1830, during the reign of William IV. In 1994, new owners refurbished the hotel, filling it with country-house chintzes and a collection of antiques borrowed from the showrooms of an antiques store they own. (Some furniture in the hotel is for sale.) Style and comfort are the keynote here, and all the relatively spacious bedrooms are invitingly appointed with plush beds.

141 Newbridge Hill, Bath, Somerset BA1 3PT. © **01225/336966.** Fax 01225/425462. www.apsley-house. co.uk. 11 units. £70–£170 double; £90–£200 suite. Rates include English breakfast. AE, MC, V. Free parking. Take A4 to Upper Bristol Rd., fork right at the traffic signals into Newbridge Hill, and turn left at Apsley Rd. **Amenities:** Bar; room service. *In room:* TV, hair dryer.

Dukes Hotel A short walk from the heart of Bath, this 1780 building is fresher than ever following a complete restoration. Many of the original Georgian features, including cornices and moldings, have been retained. Rooms, ranging from small to medium, are exceedingly comfortable. All of the bathrooms are small but efficiently arranged and sport either tub/shower combinations or just showers. Guests can relax in a refined drawing room or patronize the cozy bar overlooking a garden. The entire setting has been called a "perfect *Masterpiece Theatre* take on Britain," with a fire burning in the grate.

53–54 Great Pulteney St., Bath, Somerset BA2 4DN. © **01225/787960.** Fax 01225/787961. www. dukesbath.co.uk. 17 units. £131–£189 double; £194–£232 4-poster room; £176–£214 suite. Rates include continental breakfast. 2-night minimum Sat–Sun. AE, MC, V. Bus: 18. **Amenities:** Restaurant; bar; room service. *In room:* TV, hair dryer, minibar (in some).

Mercure Francis Hotel ★ An integral part of Queen Square, the Francis is an example of 18th-century taste and style, but we find it too commercial and touristy. Originally consisting of six private residences dating from 1729, the Francis was opened as a private hotel by Emily Francis in 1884 and has offered guests first-class service for more than 100 years. Many of the well-furnished and traditionally styled bedrooms overlook Queen Square, named in honor of George II's consort, Caroline. Rooms range in size from rather small to medium, with either twin or double beds. Accommodations in the older building have more charm, especially the upper floor.

Queen Sq., Bath, Somerset BA1 2HH. © **888/221-4542** in the U.S. and Canada, or 01225/424105. Fax 01225/319715. www.mercure.com. 95 units. £140–£170 double; £200 suite. Rates include English breakfast. AE, DC, MC, V. Parking £12. **Amenities:** Restaurant; bar; babysitting; room service. *In room:* A/C (in some), TV, fridge, hair dryer.

Pratt's Hotel ★ Once the home of Sir Walter Scott, Pratt's dates from the heady days of Beau Nash. Functioning as a hotel since 1791, it has become part of the legend and lore of Bath. Several elegant terraced Georgian town houses were joined together to form this complex with a very traditional British atmosphere. Rooms are individually designed, and as is typical of a converted private home, they range from small to spacious (the larger ones are on the lower floors). Regardless of their dimensions, the bedrooms are furnished in a comfortable though utilitarian style.

South Parade, Bath, Somerset BA2 4AB. ℃ **01225/460441.** Fax 01225/448807. www.prattshotel.com. 46 units. £139–£149 double. Children 13 and younger stay free if sharing a room with 2 adults. Rates include English breakfast. AE, DC, MC, V. Parking £12. **Amenities:** Restaurant; bar; room service; Wi-Fi (£6 per hr., in lobby). *In room:* TV, hair dryer.

Queensberry ★   A gem of a hotel, this early Georgian-era town house has been beautifully restored. In our view, it is now among the finest places to stay in a city where the competition for restored town-house hotels is fierce. The Marquis of Queensberry commissioned John Wood the Younger to build this house in 1772. Rooms—often spacious though sometimes medium in size—are delightful, each tastefully decorated with antique furniture and such thoughtful extras as fresh flowers.

Russell St., Bath, Somerset BA1 2QF. ℃ **01225/447928.** Fax 01225/446065. www.thequeensberry. co.uk. 29 units. £125–£240 double; £240–£435 suite. AE, MC, V. Free parking. **Amenities:** Restaurant (Olive Tree, p. 381); bar; babysitting; room service; Wi-Fi (free, in lobby). *In room:* TV, CD player, hair dryer.

Tasburgh House   Set about 1.5km (1 mile) east of Bath center, amid 2.8 hectares (7 acres) of parks and gardens, this spacious Victorian country house dates from 1890. The redbrick structure contains a large glassed-in conservatory, stained-glass windows, and antiques. Bedrooms are tastefully decorated, often with half-tester beds (two with four-posters), and most have sweeping panoramic views. As there is no air-conditioning, windows have to be opened on hot summer nights, which will subject you to a lot of traffic noise. The Kennet and Avon Canal runs along the rear of the property, and guests enjoy summer walks along the adjacent towpath.

Warminster Rd., Bath, Somerset BA2 6SH. ℃ **01225/425096.** Fax 01225/463842. www.bathtasburgh. co.uk. 12 units. £115–£160 double. Rates include English breakfast. 2-night minimum Sat–Sun. MC, V. Free parking. Bus: 4. **Amenities:** Bar; room service. *In room:* TV, hair dryer, Wi-Fi (free).

INEXPENSIVE

Badminton Villa   Located about a kilometer (½ mile) south of the city center, this house dates from 1883. Constructed of honey-colored blocks of Bath stone, it lies on a hillside with sweeping views over the world-famous architecture of Bath. The owners transformed it from a villa in disrepair to one of the most charming small hotels in Bath. Furnishings are an eclectic but unpretentious mix of objects. The small to medium-size bedrooms feature double-glazed windows; there's also a three-tiered garden with patio.

10 Upper Oldfield Park, Bath, Somerset BA2 3JZ. ℃ **01225/426347.** Fax 01225/420393. www.badminton villa.co.uk. 4 units. £75–£80 double; £100 family room. Rates include English breakfast. MC, V. Free parking. Bus: 14. No children 7 and under. **Amenities:** Breakfast room. *In room:* TV, hair dryer.

Cheriton House   This elegant 1886 home still offers many of its original architectural adornments, including fireplaces. The owners work hard to make guests comfortable in their large, spotlessly clean house. Each small to midsize room is efficiently organized. This is really a house for adults, not young children. Breakfast is the only meal served.

9 Upper Oldfield Park, Bath, Somerset BA2 3IX. © **01225/429862.** Fax 01225/428403. www.cheriton house.co.uk. 13 units. £72–£110 double. Rates include English breakfast. MC, V. Free parking. Bus: 14, 14A, or 14B. No children 11 and under. *In room:* TV, hair dryer.

One Three Nine ★ 🍴   At the southern side of the city on the A367 road to Exeter (Devon), this Victorian residence from the 1870s is a 10-minute walk from the center of Bath, with minibuses passing by frequently. David and Annie Lanz offer one of the best-value accommodations in the area. Their hotel rents elegant and spacious bedrooms, individually furnished and decorated.

139 Wells Rd., Bath, Somerset BA2 3AL. © **01225/314769.** Fax 01225/443079. www.139bath.co.uk. 8 units. £65–£175 double; £85–£200 family room. Rates include English breakfast. 2-night minimum Sat–Sun. AE, MC, V. Free parking. On approaching Bath, follow A367 Exeter signs but ignore the LIGHT VEHICLES ONLY sign; turn left onto A37/A367 (Wells Rd.) and follow the black railings uphill (450m/1,500 ft.); when the railings end, turn left into Hayesfield Park; the hotel will be on the right. *In room:* A/C (in some), TV/DVD, hair dryer, Wi-Fi (free).

Where to Dine

The best place for afternoon tea is the **Pump Room** at the **Roman Baths** (p. 384). Another choice, just a 1-minute walk from the Abbey Church and Roman Baths, is **Sally Lunn's House,** 4 North Parade Passage (© **01225/461634;** www.sally lunns.co.uk), where visitors have been eating for more than 1,700 years. For £6 to £11, you can get the Fantastic Sally Lunn Cream Tea, which includes toasted and buttered scones served with strawberry jam and clotted cream, along with your choice of tea or coffee. **Café Retro,** 18 York Street (© **01225/339347;** www. caferetro.co.uk), serves a variety of teas and coffees. You can order a pot of tea for £2 or a large cappuccino for £2.50 and add a tea cake for £3.30.

EXPENSIVE

Dower House ★★ ENGLISH   The Royal Crescent contains this city's most stunning collection of Georgian architecture. An unmarked door of the discreet Royal Crescent Hotel leads to this on-site restaurant, now hailed as one of the West Country's finest dining choices. In the cozy dining room, the chef dazzles the discerning palates of Bath with a series of innovative dishes. The setting is romantic, with hand-painted wall coverings and distinctive pottery from Dartington. Through elegant French windows, tables overlook the private gardens. The contemporary British menu roams the world for inspiration, featuring everything from corn-fed guinea fowl, with foie gras and a warm truffle dressing, to wild sea bass with a smoked eel tortellini. You might finish with one of the lush desserts, such as a hazelnut chocolate teardrop autumn truffle ice cream with Marsala syrup.

In the Royal Crescent Hotel, 15–16 Royal Crescent. © **01225/823333.** www.royalcrescent.co.uk. Reservations required. Lunch main courses £19; fixed-price dinner £50 for 2 courses, £60 for 3 courses. AE, DC, MC, V. Daily noon–2pm and 7–9:30pm (until 10:30pm Sat).

Moody Goose ★★★ ENGLISH   For some of the finest food in greater Bath, you have to go outside the center to Midsomer Norton. The kitchen at the Moody Goose has an absolute passion for fresh ingredients and food cooked to order, and the chefs believe in using produce grown as close to home as possible (though the Angus beef comes in from Scotland and the fresh fish from the coasts of Cornwall and Devon). Even the breads, ice creams, and petits fours are homemade. Natural flavors are appreciated here and not smothered in sauces. The kitchen team is expert at chargrilling. Some of the best-tasting starters include crab salad with tarragon mayonnaise and tomato sorbet, or else a terrine of wood pigeon. We highly recommend the main courses of local saddle of venison with a golden beet and Jerusalem artichoke puree; steamed sea bass with River Exe mussels and a caviar butter sauce; or roast filet of beef with wild mushrooms in a Madeira sauce with roasted salsify.

In the Old Priory Hotel, Church Sq., Midsomer Norton, outside Bath. ✆ **01761/416784.** www.moody goose.co.uk. Reservations required. Main courses £18–£22; fixed-price lunch £23 for 2 courses, £29 for 3 courses; table d'hôte dinner menu £33. MC, V. Mon–Sat noon–1:30pm and 7–9:30pm.

Olive Tree ★ MODERN ENGLISH/MEDITERRANEAN The Olive Tree is one of the most sophisticated little restaurants in Bath. The chef makes use of the best local produce, with an emphasis on freshness. The menu is changed to reflect the season, with specialties of game and fish. You might begin with a tomato tart with goat-cheese fritters or a galatine of wood pigeon, duck, and rainbow chard set off with spiced gooseberry chutney. Then proceed to such good-tasting mains as pan-fried potato gnocchi with ironbark squash, Parmesan, and pumpkin seeds; filet of wild sea bass with confit fennel; or carved duck leg with bubble and squeak (cabbage and potatoes).

In the Queensberry hotel, Russell St. ✆ **01225/447928.** www.thequeensberry.co.uk. Reservations highly recommended. Main courses £15–£25. AE, MC, V. Mon–Sat noon–2pm and 7–10pm; Sun noon–2pm and 7–9:30pm.

MODERATE

A 15-minute drive from the town center is the **Wheatsheaf,** in Combe Hay (✆ **01225/833504;** www.wheatsheafcombehay.co.uk), another foodie destination that features the best seasonal products.

Casani's French Bistro-Restaurant ★ FRENCH 🍴 For authentic French cooking in Bath, foodies flock to this beautiful Georgian building on Saville Row, one of the prettiest lanes in Bath, with the Circus, Royal Crescent, and George Street just a 5-minute walk away. Chef Laurent Couvreur and his wife, Jill, offer New York efficiency and Gallic charm. Simple but stylish dishes, mostly from the south of France, are featured at both lunch and dinner. The chef's signature dishes are snails-and-garlic ravioli and confit leg of duck with fondant potatoes. Other main specialties include a rack of lamb with an herb crust and gratin Dauphinoise potatoes, or else fricassee of rabbit in a creamy mustard sauce with tarragon-seasoned gnocchi. For dessert, we recommended the lavender-flavored crème brûlée. The restaurant is on two floors, with a sheltered courtyard in back.

4 Saville Row. ✆ **01225/780055.** www.casanis.co.uk. Reservations required. Main courses £13–£24; set lunch Tues–Sat £14 for 2 courses, £17 for 3 courses; pre-theater supper (6–7pm) £17 for 2 courses, £21 for 3 courses. MC, V. Tues–Sat noon–2:30pm and 6–10:30pm.

Hole in the Wall ★ MODERN ENGLISH/FRENCH This much-renovated Georgian town house was once hailed as the best restaurant in the West Country. Due to increased competition, it no longer enjoys such a lofty position, but the food is still good. Menu choices change frequently, according to the inspiration of the chef and the availability of ingredients. Everything is made on-site and from scratch. Start with such choices as steamed River Exe mussels in sweet chili jam or locally kiln-smoked chicken on a seasonal salad bed. From here, you can order such well-crafted mains as roast filet of cod on crushed new potatoes with a champagne velouté; confit leg of duck with spicy plums and home-smoked mashed potatoes; or a whole roast partridge served on savoy cabbage with bread sauce.

16 George St. ✆ **01225/425242.** www.theholeinthewall.co.uk. Reservations recommended, especially Sat. Main courses £11–£19. MC, V. Daily noon–3pm and 6–10pm.

Moon & Sixpence BRITISH   This popular restaurant with affordable prices may not be as good as our other recommendations, but it has its devotees who come here to feed on West Country lamb, sea bass, and calf's liver, along with rib-eye steaks. There is an enclosed outside dining area. The bar offers an extensive choice of wines from around the world, as well as premium beers and lagers on tap.

27 Milsom Place ✆ **01225/320088.** www.moonandsixpence.co.uk. Reservations recommended. Main courses £11–£19. AE, MC, V. Mon–Sat noon–2:30pm and 6–10:30pm (until 11pm Fri–Sat); Sun noon–3pm and 6:30–10:30pm.

Woods MODERN ENGLISH/FRENCH/ASIAN   Named after John Wood the Younger, architect of Bath's famous Assembly Room, which lies across the street, this restaurant is run by horse-racing enthusiast David Price and his French-born wife, Claude. A fixed-price menu is printed on paper, whereas the seasonal array of a la carte items is chalked onto a frequently changing blackboard. Good bets include filet of cod with capers, anchovies, and olive butter, or else seared filet steak with oyster mushrooms and a Marsala cream sauce. Yet another winner is the roast loin of pork chop with fresh tarragon and garlic butter.

9–13 Alfred St. ✆ **01225/314812.** www.woodsrestaurant.com. Reservations recommended. Main courses £12–£20; fixed-price 2-course lunch £15, fixed-price 2-course dinner £15. MC, V. Mon–Sat noon–2:30pm and 6–10:30pm; Sun noon–2pm.

Seeing the Sights

Stroll around to see some of the buildings, crescents, and squares in town. John Wood the Elder (1704–54) laid out many of the most famous streets and buildings of Bath, including **North and South Parades** and **Queen Square.** His master-piece is the **Circus** ★★★, built on Barton Fields outside the old city walls. He showed how a row of town houses could be made to look palatial. Fellow architects have praised his "uniform facades and rhythmic proportions." Also of interest is the shop-lined **Pulteney Bridge,** designed by Robert Adam and often compared to the Ponte Vecchio of Florence.

The younger John Wood designed the **Royal Crescent** ★★★, an elegant half-moon row of town houses (copied by Astor architects for their colonnade in New York City in the 1830s). At **No. 1 Royal Crescent** (✆ **01225/428126;** www.bath-preservation-trust.org.uk), the interior has been redecorated and furnished by the Bath Preservation Trust to look as it might have toward the end of the 18th century. The house lies at one end of Bath's most magnificent crescents, west of the Circus. Admission is £6 for adults, £5 for students and seniors, and £2.50 for children 5 to 16; a family ticket is £12. The house is open from mid-February to October, Tuesday to Sunday 10:30am to 5pm, and in November, Tuesday to Sunday 10:30am to 4pm (last admission 30 min. before closing); it is closed Good Friday and from December to early February.

The **Jane Austen Centre,** 40 Gay St. (✆ **01225/443000;** www.janeausten.co.uk), is located in a Georgian town house on an elegant street where Miss Austen once lived. Exhibits and a video convey a sense of what life was like in Bath during the Regency period. The center is open mid-February to October, daily from 9:45am to 5:30pm, and November to early February, Sunday to Friday 11am to 4:30pm and Saturday 10am to 5:30pm. Admission is £7 for adults, £5.50 for students and seniors, £4 for children 6 to 15, and £18 for a family ticket.

American Museum in Britain ★★   Some 4km (2½ miles) outside Bath, get an idea of what life was like in America prior to the mid-1800s. The first American museum established outside the U.S., it sits proudly on extensive grounds high above the Somerset Valley. Among the authentic exhibits shipped over from the States are a New Mexico room, a Conestoga wagon, the dining room of a New York town house of the early 19th century, and (on the grounds) a copy of Washington's flower garden at Mount Vernon. Throughout the summer, the museum hosts various special events, from displays of Native American dancing to very realistic reenactments of the Civil War.

Claverton Manor, Bathwick Hill. ℂ **01225/460503.** www.americanmuseum.org. Admission £8 adults, £7 students and seniors, £4.50 children 5–16, £22 family ticket, free for children 4 and younger. Late Mar to Oct Tues–Sun noon–5pm for the museum. Closed Nov to mid-Mar. Bus: 18.

Bath Abbey ★   Built on the site of a much larger Norman cathedral, the present-day abbey is a fine example of the late Perpendicular style. When Queen Elizabeth I came to Bath in 1574, she ordered a national fund to be set up to restore the abbey. The west front is the sculptural embodiment of a Jacob's Ladder dream of a 15th-century bishop. When you go inside and see its many windows, you'll understand why the abbey is called the "Lantern of the West." Note the superb fan vaulting with its scalloped effect. Beau Nash was buried in the nave and is honored by a simple monument totally out of keeping with his flamboyant character. The Bath Abbey Heritage Vaults opened in 1994 on the south side of the abbey. This subterranean exhibition traces the history of Christianity at the abbey site since Saxon times.

Orange Grove. ℂ **01225/422462.** www.bathabbey.org. Suggested donation £3 adults, free for children 15 and younger. Abbey Apr–Oct Mon–Sat 9am–6pm; Nov–Mar Mon–Sat 9am–4:30pm; year-round Sun 1–2:30pm (Apr–Oct also 4:30–5:30pm). Heritage Vaults Mon–Sat 10am–3:30pm (last admission).

Fashion Museum & Assembly Rooms ★★   Operated by the National Trust and housed in an 18th-century building, the grand **Assembly Rooms** played host to dances, recitals, and tea parties. Damaged in World War II, the elegant rooms have been gloriously restored and look much as they did when Jane Austen and Thomas Gainsborough attended society events here.

Housed in the same building, the **Fashion Museum** (formerly known as the Museum of Costume) sports one of the best collections of fashion and costumes in Europe. A fascinating audio tour escorts visitors through the history of fashion—including accessories, lingerie, and shoes—from the 16th century to the present day. Highlights include a 17th-century "silver tissue" dress; an ultrarestricting whalebone corset; an original suit, once owned by Dame Margot Fonteyn, from Christian Dior's legendary "New Look" collection; and the ultrasheer Versace dress made famous—or infamous—by actress Jennifer Lopez. The museum is also known for its "Dress of the Year" collection, which highlights notable ideas in contemporary style. Some selections have been notably prescient; its choice for the 1987 dress of the year was by then-unknown designer John Galliano. Only 2,000 of the museum's 30,000 items are on display at any one time, but exhibits change frequently and special themed collections are often presented.

Bennett St. ☏ **01225/477173.** www.museumofcostume.co.uk. Admission (includes audio tour) £7 adults, £6.25 students and seniors, £5 children 6–16, £20 family ticket, free for children 5 and younger. Nov–Feb daily 10:30am–4pm; Mar–Oct daily 10:30am–5pm. Last admission 1 hr. before closing. Closed Dec 25–26.

Roman Baths ★★ & Pump Room ★

Founded in A.D. 75 by the Romans, the baths were dedicated to the goddess Sulis Minerva; in their day, they were an engineering feat. Even today, they're among the finest Roman remains in the country, and they are still fed by Britain's most famous hot-spring water. After centuries of decay, the original baths were rediscovered during Queen Victoria's reign. The site of the Temple of Sulis Minerva has been excavated and is now open to view. The museum displays many interesting objects from Victorian and recent digs (look for the head of Minerva).

Coffee, lunch, and tea, usually with music from the Pump Room Trio, can be enjoyed in the 18th-century pump room, overlooking the hot springs. You can also find a drinking fountain with hot mineral water that tastes horrible.

In the Bath Abbey churchyard, Stall St. ☏ **01225/477785.** www.romanbaths.co.uk. Admission £12 adults, £10 seniors, £7.50 children 6–16, £33 family ticket. Apr–June and Sept daily 9am–6pm; July–Aug daily 8am–10pm; Oct–Mar Mon–Sat 9:30am–5:30pm.

Theatre Royal Bath   Theatre Royal, located next to the new Seven Dials development, was restored in 1982 and refurbished with plush seats, red carpets, and a painted proscenium arch and ceiling; it is now the most beautiful theater in Britain. It has 880 seats, with a small pit and grand tiers rising to the upper circle. Despite all the work, Theatre Royal has no company, instead depending upon touring shows to fill the house during the 8-week theater season each summer. A studio theater at the rear of the main building opened in 1996. The theater publishes a list of forthcoming events; its repertoire includes West End shows, among other offerings.

Beneath the theater, reached from the back of the stalls or by a side door, are the theater vaults, where you will find a bar with stone walls in one. The next vault has a restaurant, serving an array of dishes from soup to light meals.

Sawclose. ☏ **01225/448844.** www.theatreroyal.org.uk. Tickets £10–£40. Box office Mon–Sat 10am–8pm, Sun noon–8pm; shows Mon–Wed at 7:30pm, Thurs–Sat at 8pm, Wed and Sat matinees 2:30pm.

Victoria Art Gallery   This relatively unknown gallery showcases the area's best collection of British and European art from the 15th century to the present. Most of the works are on display in the sumptuous Victorian Upper Gallery. The collection includes paintings by artists who lived and worked in the Bath area, including Gainsborough. Singled out for special attention is the art of Walter Richard Sickert (1860–1942), now that he has been "outed" as the real Jack the Ripper in Patricia Cornwell's bestseller *Portrait of a Killer: Jack the Ripper—Case Closed*. Special exhibitions are shown in the two large modern galleries downstairs; these change every 6 to 8 weeks and are likely to feature anything from cartoons to boat sculpture.

Bridge St. ☏ **01225/477782.** www.victoriagal.org.uk. Free admission. Tues–Sat 10am–5pm; Sun 1:30–5pm.

Shopping

Bath is loaded with markets and fairs, antiques centers, and small shops, with literally hundreds of opportunities to buy (and ship) anything you want (including the famous spa waters, for sale by the bottle). Prices, however, are comparable to London's.

The whole city is basically one long, slightly undulating shopping area. It's not defined by one high street, as are so many British towns. If you arrive by train, there's a new shopping center right next to the station, and within 2 blocks are several shopping streets. The single best day to visit, if you are a serious shopper intent on hitting the flea markets, is Wednesday.

The **Bartlett Street Antiques Centre,** Bartlett Street, encompasses 20 dealers and 50 showcases displaying furniture, silver, antique jewelry, paintings, toys, military items, and collectibles.

Near Bath Abbey, the **Beaux Arts Gallery,** 12–13 York St. (© **01225/464850;** www.beauxartsbath.co.uk), is the largest and most important gallery of contemporary art in Bath, specializing in well-known British artists such as Ray Richardson, John Bellany, and Nicola Bealing. Closely linked to the London art scene, the gallery occupies a pair of interconnected stone-fronted Georgian houses. Its half-dozen showrooms exhibit objects beginning at £30.

The very upscale **Rossiters,** 38–41 Broad St. (© **01225/462227;** www.rossiters ofbath.com), sells very traditional English tableware and home-decor items. It'll ship anywhere in the world. Look especially for the display of Moorcraft ginger jars, vases, and clocks, as well as the Floris perfumes.

Bath After Dark

To get a very different perspective of Bath, you may want to take the **Bizarre Bath Walking Tour** (© **01225/335124;** www.bizarrebath.co.uk), a 1½-hour improvisational tour of the streets during which the tour guides pull pranks, tell jokes, and behave in a humorously annoying manner toward tourgoers and unsuspecting residents. The tour runs nightly at 8pm from Easter to October, no reservations necessary; just show up, ready for anything, at the Huntsman Inn at North Parade Passage. Cost is £8 for adults, £5 for students and children.

After your walk, you may need a drink or want to check out the local club and music scene (though there's better nightlife in Bristol). At the **Bell,** 103 Walcot St. (© **01225/460426;** www.walcotstreet.com), music ranges from jazz and country to reggae and blues on Monday and Wednesday nights and Sunday at lunch and dinner. On music nights, the band performs in the center of the long, narrow 400-year-old room.

If you just want to relax, you can head to **Thermae Bath Spa,** Hot Bath Street (© **0844/888-0844;** www.thermaebathspa.com), and watch the sun setting over the rooftops while you soak in the warm spa waters. There's even a "Twilight Package" that includes a light meal, a glass of house wine or lager, and a 3-hour spa session.

Side Trips from Bath

LACOCK: AN 18TH-CENTURY VILLAGE ★

From Bath, take the A4 about 19km (12 miles) to the A350, and then head south to Lacock, a National Trust village showcasing English architecture from the 13th through the 18th centuries.

Unlike many villages that disappeared or were absorbed into bigger communities, Lacock remained largely unchanged because of a single family, the Talbots, who owned most of it and preferred to keep their traditional village traditional. Turned over to the National Trust in 1944, it's now one of the best-preserved villages in all of England—with many 16th-century homes, gardens, and churches—and has been used as a set for numerous films and TV series. Notable is **St. Cyriac Church,** Church Street, a Perpendicular-style church built by wealthy wool merchants between the 14th and 17th centuries.

Lacock Abbey, High Street (✆ **01249/730459;** www.nationaltrust.org.uk/lacock), founded in 1232 for Augustinian canonesses, was updated and turned into a private home in the 16th century. It fell victim to Henry VIII's Dissolution, when, upon establishing the Church of England, he seized existing church properties to bolster his own wealth. Admission for all church properties is £11 for adults and £5.30 for children; a family ticket costs £26. It is open from late March to October, Thursday through Monday from 11am to 5pm; closed on Good Friday.

While on the grounds, stop by the medieval barn, home to the **Fox Talbot Museum** (✆ **01249/730459**). This is where William Henry Fox Talbot carried out his early experiments with photography, making the first known photographic prints in 1833. In his honor, the barn is now a photography museum featuring some of those early prints. Hours are March to October, daily from 11am to 5:30pm; and November to February, Saturday and Sunday only from 11am to 4pm. Admission is included in the Lacock Abbey fee (listed above); for admission to the museum only, it's £6.30 for adults, £3.20 for children, and £16 for a family ticket.

Where to Stay

Sign of the Angel ★   The quiet rooms at this inn, built in the 14th century, are split between the main building and a 17th-century garden cottage, whose rooms we prefer because they are more spacious and have more style. Each guest room is distinctly decorated with a host of antiques. One room has a magnificently carved Spanish bed that is said to have belonged to Isambard Kingdom Brunel, the famous railway and canal builder. Some rooms in the main building are standard and rather small, while others are more spacious—no. 12, for example, has a four-poster bed, and no. 3 is a generously sized superior room with a very large bed. Bathrooms have adequate shelf space and a tub or shower.

Church St., Lacock, Chippenham, Wiltshire SN15 2LB. ✆ **01249/730230.** Fax 01249/730527. www.lacock.co.uk. 6 units. £120–£145 double. Rates include English breakfast. AE, MC, V. **Amenities:** Restaurant; room service. *In room:* TV, hair dryer.

Where to Dine

George Inn ☺ ENGLISH   Housed in a building that has been used as a pub since 1361, the George Inn has been modernized since then but still maintains many of its vestiges from the past—uneven floors, a large open fireplace with a dog-wheel once used for spit roasting—and has an extensive garden used as a dining area in the summer, as well as a children's playground. About 30 daily specials are chalked onto a blackboard in addition to a regular menu of fish, meat, and vegetarian dishes. Two of the best traditional desserts are bread-and-butter pudding and sticky toffee pudding.

4 West St. ✆ **01249/730263.** www.facebook.com/GeorgeInnLacock. Main courses £7–£17. AE, MC, V. Mon–Fri noon–2pm and 6–9pm; Sat–Sun noon–9pm.

CASTLE COMBE ★★

Castle Combe was once voted England's prettiest village (though it's also well known for its motor racing circuit on the edge of town). The financially disastrous *Dr. Doolittle* was filmed here in 1967, and the 15th-century **Upper Manor House,** used as Rex Harrison's residence in the movie, is its most famous site. Consisting of one street lined with cottages (known simply as "the Street"), it is the quintessential West Country village, easily explored in its entirety during a morning or afternoon, before moving on to your next destination.

Located 16km (10 miles) northeast of Bath, Castle Combe is reached by taking the A46 north 9.5km (6 miles) to the A420, then heading east to Ford, and following the signs north to Castle Combe. From Lacock, take the A350 north to Chippenham; then get on the A420 west and follow the signs.

Where to Stay & Dine

Manor House Hotel & Golf Club ★   This house and accompanying estate date from the 14th century and once served as the baronial seat in Castle Combe. The main building and its accompanying cottages sit regally on 19 hectares (47 acres) of gardens, with wooded trails and a lake. The trout-stocked River Bybrook flows south of the manor, and fishing is permitted. You can stay either in the main house or in a row of original stone cottages on the grounds. The latter have been upgraded to meet the standards of the main house. Bedrooms come in a variety of sizes. Some units have four-poster beds; eight are large enough for families.

Castle Combe, Wiltshire SN14 7JW. (© **01249/782206.** Fax 01249/782159. www.exclusivehotels.co.uk. 48 units. £180–£250 double; £295–£800 suite. Rates include English breakfast. AE, MC, V. Free parking. **Amenities:** Restaurant; 2 bars; babysitting; 18-hole golf course; exercise room; pool; room service; sauna; outdoor tennis court. *In room:* TV, hair dryer.

BRISTOL ★★

193km (120 miles) W of London; 21km (13 miles) NW of Bath

Bristol, the largest city in the West Country, is just across the Bristol Channel from Wales and makes a good base for touring western Britain. This historic inland port is linked to the sea by 11km (7 miles) of the navigable River Avon. Bristol has long been rich in seafaring traditions and has many links with the early colonization of America. In fact, some claim that the new continent was named after a Bristol town clerk, Richard Ameryk. In 1497, John Cabot sailed from Bristol and pioneered the discovery of the northern half of the New World. And the notorious pirate Blackbeard called Bristol home, before terrorizing his way across the oceans until he was shot in North Carolina in 1718.

Although Bath is much more famous as a tourist mecca, Bristol does have some attractions, such as a colorful harbor life, that makes it at least a good overnight stop in your exploration of the West Country. In addition, ever since British graffiti artist Banksy decided to hold a free exhibition here in his home city, Bristol has been attracting a lot of fans who come to see his graff.

Essentials

GETTING THERE   Bristol Airport (© **0871/334-4444;** www.bristolairport. co.uk) is conveniently situated beside the main A38 road, a little more than 11km

(7 miles) from the city center. The **Bristol Airport Flyer** bus service runs to town and the Temple Meads station every half hour.

Rail services to and from the area are among the fastest and most efficient in Britain. **First Great Western** runs very frequent service from London's Paddington Station to each of Bristol's two main stations: Temple Meads, in the center of Bristol, and Parkway, on the city's northern outskirts. The trip takes 1¼ hours. For rail information, call First Great Western at © **0845/000125** or visit **www.firstgreatwestern.co.uk**. You can also call © **0845/748-4950** or visit **www.nationalrail.co.uk**.

National Express buses depart every hour during the day from London's Victoria Coach Station, making the trip in 2½ hours. For more information and schedules, call © **0871/781-8178** or visit **www.nationalexpress.com**.

If you're driving, head west from London on the M4.

VISITOR INFORMATION In 2010, Bristol opened its brand-new **Tourist Information Centre,** at E Shed, 1 Canon's Rd. (© **0870/444-0654;** www.visit bristol.co.uk). It's located next to the Watershed Media Centre on the Harbourside. Hours are daily from 10am to 5pm.

Where to Stay

MODERATE TO EXPENSIVE

Bristol Marriott City Centre ★   In the heart of town, at the edge of Castle Park, this modern 11-story hotel is one of Bristol's tallest buildings and far superior to other chains in amenities, style, and comfort. Many improvements have been undertaken and the hotel now attracts business travelers as well as foreign tourists. The comfortable guest rooms are conservatively modern.

2 Lower Castle St., Bristol BS1 3AD. © **800/228-9290** in the U.S. and Canada, or 0117/929-4281. Fax 0117/927-6377. www.bristolmarriottcitycentre.co.uk. 301 units. £93–£205 double. AE, DC, MC, V. Parking £11. Bus: 9. **Amenities:** 2 restaurants; bar; babysitting; concierge; exercise room; indoor heated pool; room service; spa. *In room:* A/C, TV, hair dryer, minibar.

Hotel du Vin ★ 🛏   This stylish boutique hotel, a member of a small chain, is one of Bristol's best examples of recycling. Six 18th-century sugar-refining warehouses, lying in the vicinity of the docklands, were taken over and sensitively restored. Today, you'll find a series of "loft-style" bedrooms with superb beds covered in soft Egyptian linen. Each of the accommodations comes with a well-maintained and state-of-the-art bathroom with what management prefers to call "serious" showers (read: large). As much as possible, the original industrial features of the warehouses have been retained for dramatic effect. Even if you're not a guest, you may want to stop for a drink in the Sugar House Bar or a first-class meal in the contemporary French restaurant. For such a small hotel, the wine cellar here is most impressive, and specially staged wine tastings and dinners are frequent events throughout the year.

Narrow Lewins Mead, Bristol BS1 2NU. © **0117/925-5577.** Fax 0117/925-1199. www.hotelduvin.com. 40 units. £145–£195 double; £215–£400 suite. AE, DC, MC, V. Parking £13. **Amenities:** Restaurant; 2 bars; room service. *In room:* A/C, TV, hair dryer, minibar, Wi-Fi (£10 per 24 hr.).

Mercure Brigstow Hotel ★   In a prime position on the Welsh Back in Bristol, this contemporary hotel opens onto panoramic riverside frontage in the heart of this ancient port. Granted four stars by the government, it offers some of the city's finest bedrooms, most of which are spacious with all the extras provided. Even the bathrooms have plasma TVs, so you can bathe and watch your shows. Ellipse, the on-site restaurant, serves fresh and well-prepared food in light and airy surroundings with views of the river.

Welsh Back, Bristol BS1 4SF. © **0117/929-1030.** Fax 0117/929-2030. www.mercure.com. 116 units. £88–£165 double. AE, DC, MC, V. Parking £13. **Amenities:** Restaurant; bar; use of nearby gym; room service. *In room:* A/C, TV, hair dryer, minibar.

Ramada Bristol City ★   Situated conveniently amid the commercial bustle of the town center, this modern six-story hotel offers a good, safe haven for the night (though some readers have commented that the pealing bells of St. Mary Redcliffe next door have awakened them early in the morning). Bedrooms, furnished in a bland international style, range from small to medium and include mostly double beds.

Redcliffe Way, Bristol BS1 6NJ. © **0844/815-9100.** Fax 0117/923-0089. www.ramadajarvis.co.uk. 201 units. £81–£162 double; £160–£190 suite. AE, DC, MC, V. Parking £5. **Amenities:** Restaurant; bar; babysitting; exercise room; Jacuzzi; indoor heated pool; room service; sauna; Wi-Fi (free, in lobby). *In room:* A/C, TV, hair dryer.

INEXPENSIVE

Downlands House   This well-appointed Victorian home is on a tree-lined road on the periphery of the Durdham Downs. About 3km (2 miles) from the center of Bristol, it lies on a bus route in a residential suburb. The recently redecorated bedrooms have private, shower-only bathrooms or else adequate hallway facilities. It's basic but inviting.

33 Henleaze Gardens, Henleaze, Bristol BS9 4HH. ©/fax **0117/962-1639.** www.downlandshouse.com. 10 units, 7 with bathroom. £55–£60 double without bathroom; £68–£75 double with bathroom. Rates include English breakfast. AE, MC, V. Free parking. Bus: 1, 2, 3, or 501. *In room:* TV, hair dryer.

Tyndall's Park Hotel   This elegant early Victorian house has retained many of its original features, including a marble fireplace and ornate plasterwork. Note the fine staircase in the imposing entrance hall. The hotel still observes the old traditions of personal service. There is a Victorian aura in the bedrooms, which range from small to medium, all clean and comfortable.

4 Tyndall's Park Rd., Clifton, Bristol BS8 1PG. © **0117/973-5407.** Fax 0117/923-7965. www.tyndallspark hotel.co.uk. 15 units. £58 double. Rates include English breakfast. MC, V. Bus: 8 or 9. *In room:* TV, hair dryer.

Where to Dine

Bell's Diner ★ 🍴 MEDITERRANEAN   This little hideaway serves savory cuisine from the Mediterranean and does so exceedingly well. The bistro's hardwood floors and walls adorned with cityscapes has been installed in what used to be "the little shop on the corner." The daily offerings change frequently, based on market-fresh ingredients, but what you get is usually well prepared, fresh, and flavorful. Most of the recipes are imaginative and sometimes surprising, as in the case of honey caramelized quail with butternut squash, hazelnuts, and fresh pear. The roasted breast of chicken comes with a delightful accompaniment of black-truffle potatoes, and the grilled tuna is still moist—never dried out—and served with fresh rocket leaves and a tangy tomato confit.

1 York Rd., Montpelier. © **0117/924-0357.** www.bellsdiner.com. Reservations recommended. Main courses £15–£20; fixed-price 8-course menu Mon–Thurs £45. AE, MC, V. Tues–Fri noon–3pm; Mon–Sat 7–10:30pm. Closed 1 week in Dec. Follow A38 north (signposted STOKES CROFT), turning right on Ashley Rd. and taking the next left at Picton St. Picton leads into York Rd.

Bordeaux Quay ★ EUROPEAN Restaurants such as Bordeaux Quay, whose principles lie in creating a sustainably run environment, have been popping up all over the city lately. The food here is sourced from within the local area, the menus are printed on recycled paper, and yet the cuisine in both the upstairs restaurant and downstairs harborside brasserie are so good, it's hard for some to believe this all comes from the West Country. Starters might include Jerusalem artichoke soup with truffle oil and chives, followed by mains such as wild mushroom and black truffle risotto; filet of Glenarm salmon with beetroot, leeks, chervil, and dill butter; or roast pheasant breast with spelt-grain risotto and curly kale. The cheese selection is all British, naturally, with choices from Somerset, Devon, Wales, and Berkshire.

You can stop by the **Deli** here to pick up sandwiches to go, breads from the in-house bakery, and foodstuffs to snack on or give as gifts.

V Shed, Canon's Rd. (at the end of the waterfront, across Pero's Bridge from the Arnolfini). © **0117/943-1200.** www.bordeaux-quay.co.uk. Reservations recommended. Restaurant dinner main courses £14–£20, 2-course lunch £17, Sun lunch main courses £15; brasserie main courses £9–£11. Restaurant Tues–Fri noon–3pm and 6–10pm, Sat 5:30–10pm, Sun noon–3pm; brasserie Mon–Fri 8am–10:30pm, Sat 9–11am and noon–10:30pm, Sun 9am–4pm; bar Mon–Sat 11am–11pm, Sun 11am–5pm; deli Mon–Sat 9am–6pm, Sun 9am–4pm.

Byzantium ★ ENGLISH/FRENCH This restaurant's decor alone is stunning, with stone, crystal, wood, marble, and glass combined to create an unusual, even offbeat space with rich colors, informal corners, and subtle lighting, plus the sweep of a marble staircase. The cuisine could almost be called fusion, though it's mainly modern French. The venue is on two floors, with a cavernous bar/lounge downstairs, and entertainment ranging from tango and belly dancing to magicians. The restaurant's "Food Lantern" is unique in Bristol, consisting of a selection of elaborate nibbles served on a two-tier iron slate. For a main course, you are faced with choices such as glazed loin of pork flavored with maple syrup and served with wild mushrooms, rump of lamb marinated with rosemary, and baked filet of salmon with a beet and chive salad.

2 Portwall Lane. © **0117/922-1883.** www.byzantium.co.uk. Reservations required. Main courses £13–£19; 3-course dinner £25. DC, MC, V. Mon–Sat 6:30pm–2am.

Exploring Bristol

Bristol Harbourside ★, its rough-and-ready days of the 19th century a memory of the past, is rapidly being recycled as it moves deeper into the 21st century. Beautiful architecture, wonderful hotels, excellent restaurants, and good shopping await visitors today, along with bistros, wine bars, and art centers. The harborfront's major attractions, if you need a goal for your sightseeing, are the **SS *Great Britain*** (see below); the science center **At-Bristol,** Anchor Road (© **0845/345-1235;** www.at-bristol.org.uk); and the newly opened **Blue Reef Aquarium & IMAX 3D Cinema,** Anchor Road (© **0117/929-8929;** www.bluereefaquarium.co.uk)

Guided 2-hour **walking tours** are conducted on Saturdays at 11am from April to September. They cost £3.50 per person and depart from the Beetle sculpture at

Anchor Square. Consult the Tourist Information Centre (see above) for more information. Or you can don an eye patch and join a 1-hour walking tour led by **Pirate Pete** (© **07950/566483;** www.piratewalks.co.uk), who will tell you all about notorious Bristol residents like Blackbeard the pirate.

The **Clifton Suspension Bridge,** spanning the beautiful Avon Gorge, has become the symbol of the city of Bristol. Originally conceived in 1754, it was completed more than 100 years later, in 1864. The architect, Isambard Kingdom Brunel, died 5 years before its completion. His fellow engineers completed the bridge as a memorial to him.

Bristol Cathedral ★   Construction of the cathedral, once an Augustinian abbey, began in the 12th century; the central tower was added in 1466. The chapter house and gatehouse are good examples of late Norman architecture. In 1539, the abbey was closed, and the incomplete nave demolished. The building was turned into the Cathedral Church of the Holy and Undivided Trinity in 1542. In 1868, plans were drawn up to complete the nave to its medieval design. The architect, G. E. Street, found the original pillar bases, so the cathedral is much as it would have been when it was still the abbey church. The eastern end of the cathedral, especially the choir, gives the structure a unique place in the development of British and European architecture. The nave, choir, and aisles are all of the same height, making a large hall. Bristol Cathedral is the major example of a "hall church" in Great Britain and one of the finest anywhere in the world.

College Green. © **0117/926-4879.** www.bristol-cathedral.co.uk. Free admission; £2.50 donation requested. Mon–Fri 8am–6pm; Sat 8am–5:30pm; Sun 7:30am–5pm. Bus: 8 or 9.

SS *Great Britain*   The world's first iron steamship and luxury liner has been restored to its 1843 appearance. This vessel, which weighs 3,443 tons, was designed by Isambard Kingdom Brunel, a Victorian engineer. Incidentally, in 1831 (at the age of 25), Brunel began the Bristol landmark Clifton Suspension Bridge over the 76m-deep (250-ft.) Avon Gorge at Clifton (see above).

City Docks, Great Western Dock. © **0117/926-0680.** www.ssgreatbritain.org. Admission £11 adults, £8.50 seniors, £5.95 children 5–16, £30 family ticket. Apr–Oct daily 10am–5pm; Nov–Mar daily 10am–3:30pm. Last admission 1 hr. before closing. Bus: 500 (from city center).

St. Mary Redcliffe Church ★★   The parish church of St. Mary Redcliffe is one of the finest examples of Gothic architecture in England. Queen Elizabeth I, on her visit in 1574, is said to have described it as "the fairest, goodliest, and most famous parish church in England." Thomas Chatterton, the boy poet, called it "the pride of Bristol and the western land." The American Chapel (St. John's Chapel) houses the tomb and armor of Admiral Sir William Penn, father of Pennsylvania's founder, along with a whalebone given by John Cabot after he sailed to America in 1497.

12 Colston Parade. © **0117/929-1487.** www.stmaryredcliffe.co.uk. Free admission; donations welcome. Apr–Oct Mon–Sat 8:30am–5pm; Nov–Mar Mon–Sat 9am–4pm; Sun year-round 8am–7:30pm.

Shopping

The biggest shopping complex is **Broadmead,** mainly pedestrianized with branches of all High Street stores, plus cafes and restaurants. Many specialty shops are found at **Cabot Circus,** a huge new shopping center next to Broadmead and Quakers Friars.

At **Clifton Village,** in a Georgian setting where houses are interspaced with parks and gardens, you'll find a wide array of shops selling antiques, arts and crafts, and designer clothing. Even if you don't purchase anything, you'll enjoy strolling about the old, tree-shaded streets. Less impressive than Clifton Village, and only if you have the time, is **St. Nicholas Markets,** which opened in 1745. They are still going strong, selling antiques, memorabilia, handcrafted gifts, jewelry, and haberdashery.

The **West End** is another major shopping area, taking in Park Street, Queen's Road, and Whiteladies Road. These streets are known for clothing outlets, bookstores, and unusual gift items from around the world, as well as wine bars and restaurants. The best market for antiques is the **Bristol Antique Centre,** at Brunel Rooms, Broad Plain, which is open daily, including Sunday.

Bristol After Dark

On a cultural note, **Bristol Old Vic,** King Street (✆ **0117/987-7877;** www.bristololdvic.org.uk), is the oldest working theater company in the country, known for its performances (often Shakespeare) that were first launched in 1766. It uses different theaters for its shows; some performances are staged at other venues such as the new Vic Studio and the Basement Theatre.

Music lovers gravitate to the performances at **St. George's,** Great George Street, off Park Street (✆ **0117/929-4929;** www.stgeorgesbristol.co.uk), a converted church from the 1700s. You will hear everything from jazz concerts to classical music performances. Lunchtime concerts are a regular feature.

Bath may be more stiff and formal, but Bristol clubs and pubs are more laid-back, drawing more working-class and middle-class Brits than yuppies. Townies congregate in the city center on Saturday nights, while middle-class types tend to frequent the bars in Clifton and Whiteladies Road. One of Bristol's oldest pubs is the **Llandoger Trow,** King Street (✆ **0117/926-0783**), said to be where Robert Louis Stevenson wrote some of *Treasure Island.*

Acid jazz and other types of music rain down in **Thekla** (✆ **0117/929-3301;** www.theklabristol.co.uk), a converted freight steamer moored on the Grove. The **Old Duke,** 45 King St. (✆ **0117/927-7137;** www.theoldduke.co.uk), is popular for traditional jazz. Another leading jazz venue is the **Bebop Club** at the Bear, Hotwell Road (✆ **0117/987-7796;** www.thebebopclub.co.uk).

The leading comedy club is **Jesters,** 142 Cheltenham Rd. (✆ **0117/909-6655;** www.jesterscomedyclub.co.uk). Covers range from £14 to £15, but can vary depending on the entertainment offered.

WELLS ★★ & THE CAVES OF MENDIP ★

198km (123 miles) SW of London; 34km (21 miles) SW of Bath

To the south of the Mendip Hills, the cathedral town of Wells is a medieval gem. Wells was a vital link in the Saxon kingdom of Wessex—important long before the arrival of William the Conqueror. Once the seat of a bishopric, it was eventually toppled from its ecclesiastical hegemony by the rival city of Bath. But the subsequent loss of prestige has paid off handsomely for Wells today: After experiencing the pinnacle of prestige, it fell into a slumber—and much of its old look was preserved.

Many visitors come only for the afternoon or morning, take a look at the cathedral, and then press on to Bath for the evening. But though it's rather sleepy, Wells's old inns make for a tranquil stopover.

Essentials

GETTING THERE Wells has good bus connections with surrounding towns and cities. Take the train to Bath (see the section on Bath earlier in this chapter) and continue the rest of the way via First Bristol bus no. 173. Departures are generally every hour Monday through Saturday and every 2 hours on Sunday. Bus no. 376 runs between Bristol and Glastonbury every hour daily, with a stop at Wells each way. Call *C* **0117/955-3231** or 0845/602-0156 for schedules and information.

If you're driving, take the M4 west from London, cutting south on the A4 toward Bath and continuing along the A39 into Wells.

VISITOR INFORMATION The **Tourist Information Centre** is at the Town Hall, Market Place (*C* **01749/672552;** www.wellstourism.com). It's open November through March, Monday to Saturday 11am to 4pm, and April through October, Monday to Saturday 10am to 5pm and Sunday 10am to 4pm.

Where to Stay

Best Western Swan Hotel ★ Set behind a stucco facade on one of the town's main streets, this place was originally built in the 15th century as a coaching inn. Today, facing the west front of Wells Cathedral, it is the best of the inns within the town's central core. Rooms vary in style and size; a third of them have four-poster beds. The spacious and elegant public rooms stretch out to the left and right of the entrance. Both ends have a blazing and baronial fireplace and beamed ceilings.

11 Sadler St., Wells, Somerset BA5 2RX. *C* **800/528-1234** in the U.S. and Canada, or 01749/836300. Fax 01749/836301. www.bestwestern.co.uk. 49 units. £102–£170 double. Rates include English breakfast. AE, DC, MC, V. Free parking. **Amenities:** Restaurant; bar; room service. *In room:* TV, hair dryer, Wi-Fi (free).

The Crown ★ This is one of the oldest and most historic hotels in the area, a tradition for overnighting since medieval times. William Penn was thrown in jail here in 1695. The charge? Preaching without a license. The landmark building lies at the medieval Market Place in the heart of Wells, overlooking the splendid cathedral. The building still retains much of its 15th-century character, although the bedrooms are completely up-to-date—in fact, furnished with a Nordic contemporary style. For more tradition, ask for one of a quartet of rooms graced with four-posters.

Market Place, Wells, Somerset BA5 2RP. *C* **01749/673457.** Fax 01749/679792. www.crownatwells.co.uk. 15 units. £90 double; £110 suite. AE, MC, V. **Amenities:** Restaurant; babysitting. *In room:* TV, hair dryer, no phone.

White Hart Hotel Opposite the cathedral, this is the best-located hotel in Wells. A former coaching inn, it dates from the 15th century. The Swan is more comfortable and remarkable, but the White Hart is an enduring favorite nonetheless. The creaky old bedrooms lie in the main house, or you can stay in more modern surroundings in a converted stable block, where horses and coaches from London were housed in olden times. Each bedroom is comfortably and tastefully furnished.

Sadler St., Wells, Somerset BA5 2RR. © **01749/672056.** Fax 01749/671074. www.whitehart-wells.co.uk. 15 units. £107–£129 double. Rates include English breakfast. AE, MC, V. Free parking. **Amenities:** Restaurant; bar; room service. *In room:* TV, hair dryer, Wi-Fi (free).

Where to Dine

City Arms ENGLISH   The former city jail, 2 blocks from the bus station, is now a pub with an open courtyard furnished with tables, chairs, and umbrellas. In summer, it's a mass of flowers. Full meals may include homemade soup of the day followed by fresh salmon, lamb in burgundy sauce, or stuffed quail in Cointreau sauce. From the charcoal grill, you can order rump steak or chicken with Stilton cheese. Longtime favorites include beef Wellington and steak-kidney-and-ale pie. Vegetarian dishes are also offered. Upstairs is an Elizabethan timbered restaurant. The food is a notch above the typical pub grub.

69 High St. © **01749/673916.** www.thecityarmsatwells.com. Reservations recommended. Main courses £7–£16. AE, MC, V. Daily 9am–10pm (until 9pm Sun).

Seeing the Sights

After a visit to the Wells Cathedral, walk along its cloisters to the moat-surrounded **Bishop's Palace.** The Great Hall, built in the 13th century, is in ruins. The street known as the **Vicars' Close** is one of the most beautifully preserved in Europe.

Easily reached by heading west out of Wells, the Caves of Mendip offer two exciting natural attractions: the great caves of Cheddar and Wookey Hole (see below).

Wells Cathedral ★★★   Begun in the 12th century, this is a well-preserved example of Early English architecture. The medieval sculpture (six tiers of statues) of its west front is without equal. The western facade was completed in the mid–13th century. The landmark central tower was erected in the 14th century, with the fan vaulting attached later. A unique feature of this cathedral is the so-called **scissor arch** ★. An amazing feat of engineering, these inverted arches can be seen at the east end of the nave. The scissor arch of striking beauty was built together with similar arches at the northern and southern sides of the crossing from 1338 to 1348, when the west piers of the crossing tower began to sink. The arches strengthened the top-heavy structure and prevented the central tower from collapsing. It was the master mason, William Joy, who devised this ingenious solution, which has done the job nicely for 6½ centuries.

Much of the stained glass dates from the 14th century. The fan-vaulted Lady Chapel, also from the 14th century, is in the Decorated style. To the north is the vaulted chapter house, built in the 13th century but restored. Look also for a medieval astronomical clock in the north transept.

In the center of town, Chain Gate. © **01749/674483.** www.wellscathedral.org.uk. Free admission but donations appreciated: £5.50 adults, £4 seniors, £2.50 students and children. Apr–Sept daily 7am–7pm; Oct–Mar daily 7am–6pm.

Cheddar Caves & Gorge ★★   A short distance from Bath, Bristol, and Wells is the village of Cheddar, home of cheddar cheese. It lies at the foot of Cheddar Gorge, within which lie the Cheddar Caves, underground caverns with impressive formations. The caves, which are more than a million years old, include Gough's Cave, with its cathedral-like caverns, and Cox's Cave, with its calcite sculptures and brilliant colors. The Crystal Quest is a dark-walk "fantasy adventure" that takes you deep underground. You can also climb Jacob's Ladder for cliff-top walks and Pavey's Lookout Tower for views over Somerset—on a clear day you may even see Wales. Adults and children ages 12 to 17 can book an "Adventure Caving" expedition for £18 adults and £15 children, which includes overalls, helmets, and lamps. Other attractions include local craftspeople at work, ranging from the glass blower to the sweets maker, and a museum that contains a 9,000-year-old skeleton.

Cheddar village. ℂ **01934/742343.** www.cheddarcaves.com. Admission £17 adults, £11 children 5-15, £45 family ticket, free for children 4 and younger. July–Aug daily 10am–5:30pm; Sept–June daily 10:30am–5pm. Closed Dec 24-25. From A38 or M5, cut onto A371 to Cheddar.

Wookey Hole Caves ★   Just 3km (2 miles) west of Wells, you'll first come upon the source of the River Axe. In the first chamber of the caves, as legend has it, is the Witch of Wookey turned to stone. It is believed that these caves were inhabited by prehistoric people at least 60,000 years ago. A tunnel, opened in 1975, leads to the chambers previously unknown and, at one time, accessible only to divers.

Leaving the caves, follow a canal path to the mill, where paper was made by hand starting in the 17th century. The best-quality handmade paper is made by skilled workers according to the tradition of their ancient craft. You can purchase fine handmade stationery at an on-site shop. Also in the mill are hands-on vats, where visitors can try making a sheet of paper; an Edwardian Penny Arcade, where you can exchange new pennies for old ones to play the original machines; and a mirror maze.

Wookey Hole, near Wells. ℂ **01749/672243.** www.wookey.co.uk. Tours (allow 2 hr.) £16 adults; £11 seniors, students, and children 3-14; £45 family ticket. Apr–Oct daily 10am–5pm; Nov–Mar daily 10am–4pm. Closed Dec 20-27. Follow the signs from the center of Wells for 3km (2 miles). Bus: 172 from Wells.

GLASTONBURY ABBEY ★★

219km (136 miles) SW of London; 42km (26 miles) S of Bristol; 9.5km (6 miles) SW of Wells

Glastonbury may be one of the oldest inhabited sites in Britain. Excavations have revealed Iron Age lakeside villages on its periphery; some of the discoveries that were dug up can be seen in a little museum on High Street. After the destruction of its once-great abbey, the town lost prestige; today, it is just a market town with a rich history. The ancient gatehouse entry to the abbey is a museum, and its principal exhibit is a scale model of the abbey and its community buildings as they stood in 1539, at the time of the Dissolution.

Where Arthurian myth once held sway, now exists a subculture of mystics, spiritualists, and hippies, all drawn to the kooky legends whirling around the town. Glastonbury is England's New Age center, where Christian spirituality blends with druidic beliefs. The average visitor arrives just to see the ruins and the monuments, but the streets are often filled with people trying to track down Jesus, if not Arthur and Lancelot.

Essentials

GETTING THERE   Connections to Glastonbury are awkward when traveling by public transportation. No direct train service runs to Glastonbury. You can, however, take a train from London's Paddington Station to Bristol's Temple Meads station (trip time: 1 hr., 40 min.), where you can catch a bus into Glastonbury. Buses run twice an hour from this train station; trip time is 1¼ hours.

One **National Express** bus a day (no. 403) leaves London's Victoria Coach Station in the evening and arrives in Glastonbury nearly 4 hours later. For more information and schedules, call © **0871/781-81-78** or visit **www.nationalexpress.com**.

If you're driving, take the M4 west from London, and then cut south on the A4, via Bath, to Glastonbury.

VISITOR INFORMATION   The **Tourist Information Centre** is at the Tribunal, 9 High St. (© **01458/832954;** www.glastonburytic.co.uk). It's open October through March, Sunday to Thursday 10am to 4pm, Friday and Saturday 10am to 4:30pm; and April through September, Sunday to Thursday 10am to 5pm, Friday and Saturday till 5:30pm.

Where to Stay

George & Pilgrim ★   One of the few pre-Reformation hostelries still left in England, this inn in the center of town once offered hospitality to Glastonbury pilgrims. Its facade looks like a medieval castle, with stone-mullioned windows with leaded glass. Accommodations come in a variety of shapes and sizes, as befits a hotel of this vintage. Some rooms were formerly monks' cells; others have four-poster beds, veritable carved monuments of oak. You may be given the Henry VIII Room, from which the king watched the burning of the abbey in 1539. Some bedrooms have been refurbished.

1 High St., Glastonbury, Somerset BA6 9DP. © **01458/831146.** Fax 01458/832252. www.relaxinnz.co.uk. 14 units. £85–£120 double. Rates include English breakfast. AE, MC, V. Free parking. **Amenities:** Restaurant (Chaucer, reviewed below); bar; room service; Wi-Fi (free, in lobby). *In room:* TV, hair dryer.

Number Three Hotel   This small property, adjoining the Glastonbury ruins, is housed in a Georgian structure in which Winston Churchill once resided. The double rooms are all tastefully and individually decorated. The bathrooms are small but well organized, with adequate shelf space and tub/shower combinations.

3 Magdalene St., Glastonbury, Somerset BA6 9EW. © **01458/832129.** Fax 01458/834227. www.numberthree.co.uk. 5 units. £120–£130 double. Rates include continental breakfast. AE, DC, MC, V. Closed Nov–Feb. *In room:* TV.

Where to Dine

The Chaucer ENGLISH/CONTINENTAL   This is a solid, reliable choice in a town not known for its dining. A reasonably priced a la carte menu, with the chef's special of the day, is posted on blackboards. The food utilizes organic ingredients whenever possible and consists of brasserie-style classics such as slow-roasted belly of pork, rack of lamb, and always plenty of fresh fish, such as a duo of salmon and crab with leeks. Vegetarians can order the lasagna filled with sweet potato and spinach.

In the George & Pilgrim hotel, 1 High St. © **01458/831146.** www.relaxinnz.co.uk. Reservations recommended. Main courses £10–£15. AE, MC, V. Wed–Sun noon–2:30pm and 7–9:30pm.

Seeing the Sights

Glastonbury Abbey ★★   Though no more than a ruined sanctuary today, Glastonbury Abbey was once one of the wealthiest and most prestigious monasteries in England. It provides Glastonbury's claim to historical greatness, an assertion augmented by legendary links to such figures as Joseph of Arimathea, King Arthur, and Queen Guinevere.

Joseph of Arimathea, a biblical, perhaps mythical, figure, is said to have journeyed to what was then the Isle of Avalon with the Holy Grail in his possession. According to tradition, he buried the chalice at the foot of the conical Glastonbury Tor (a high, craggy hill), and a stream of blood burst forth. You can scale this more than 150m-high (500-ft.) hill today, on which rests a 15th-century tower.

Joseph, so it goes, erected a church of wattle in Glastonbury. (The town, in fact, may have had the oldest church in England, as excavations have shown.) At one point, the saint is said to have leaned against his staff, which was immediately transformed into a fully blossoming tree; a cutting alleged to have survived from the Holy Thorn remains on the grounds and blooms at Christmas time. Some historians trace this particular story back to Tudor times.

Another famous chapter in the story, popularized by Tennyson in the Victorian era, holds that King Arthur and Queen Guinevere were buried on the abbey grounds. In 1191, the monks dug up the skeletons of two bodies on the south side of the Lady Chapel, said to be those of the king and queen. In 1278, in the presence of Edward I, the bodies were removed and transferred to a black marble tomb in the choir. Both the burial spot and the shrine are marked today.

A large Benedictine Abbey of St. Mary grew out of the early wattle church. St. Dunstan, who was born nearby, was the abbot in the 10th century and later became archbishop of Canterbury. Edmund, Edgar, and Edmund "Ironside," three early English kings, were buried at the abbey.

In 1184, a fire destroyed most of the abbey and its vast treasures. It was eventually rebuilt, after much difficulty, only to be dissolved by Henry VIII. Its last abbot, Richard Whiting, was hanged at Glastonbury Tor. Like the Roman forum, the abbey was used as a stone quarry for years.

Today, you can visit the ruins of the chapel, linked by an Early English "Galilee" to the nave of the abbey. The best-preserved building on the grounds is a 14th-century octagonal Abbot's Kitchen, where oxen were once roasted whole to feed the wealthier pilgrims.

Magdalene St. © **01458/832267.** www.glastonburyabbey.com. Admission £5.50 adults, £5 students and seniors, £3.50 children 5-15, £16 family ticket. Dec-Jan daily 10am-4:30pm; Feb daily 10am-5pm; Mar daily 9:30am-5:30pm; Apr-May and Sept daily 9:30am-6pm; June-Aug daily 9am-6pm; Oct daily 9:30am-5pm; Nov daily 9:30am-4:30pm.

Somerset Rural Life Museum This museum chronicles the history of the Somerset countryside since the early 19th century. Its centerpiece is the abbey barn, built around 1370. The magnificent timbered room, stone tiles, and sculptural details (including the head of Edward III) make it special. Exhibits in a Victorian farmhouse illustrate farming in Somerset during the "horse age," as well as domestic and social life in Victorian times. In summer, you can watch demonstrations of butter making, weaving, basketwork, and many other traditional craft and farming activities that are rapidly disappearing.

Abbey Farm, Chilkwell St. © **01458/831197.** www.somerset.gov.uk. Free admission. Apr-Oct Tues-Fri 10am-5pm, Sat-Sun 2-6pm; Nov-Mar Tues-Sat 10am-5pm. Closed Jan 1, Good Friday, and Dec 25-28.

LONGLEAT HOUSE ★ & STOURHEAD GARDENS ★★

If you're driving, you can visit both Longleat and Stourhead in 1 busy day. Follow the directions to Longleat given below, and then drive 9.5km (6 miles) down the B3092 to Stourton, a village just off the highway, 5km (3 miles) northwest of Mere (A303), to reach Stourhead.

Longleat House & Safari Park ★   A magnificent Elizabethan house built in the early Renaissance style, Longleat House was owned by the seventh marquess of Bath. On first glimpse, it's romantic enough, but once you're inside, it's hard not to be dazzled by the lofty rooms and their exquisite paintings and furnishings. From the Elizabethan Great Hall and the library to the State Rooms and the grand staircase, Longleat is filled with all manner of beautiful things. The walls of the State Dining Room are adorned with fine tapestries and paintings. The library represents the finest private collection in the country. The Victorian kitchens offer a glimpse of life "below the stairs" in a well-ordered country home. Various exhibitions are mounted in the stable yard.

Although the house is quite grand, the attractions that have opened around it are a bit of a cheesy tourist trap. Still, thousands of visitors are fascinated by the extra amusements. Adjoining Longleat House is **Longleat Safari Park,** which hosts several species of endangered wild animals, including rhinoceroses and elephants, that are free to roam the surroundings. Here you can walk among giraffes, zebras, camels, and llamas, and view lions and tigers, as well as England's only white tiger, from your car. You can see the park by train, for a railway adventure, or ride on a safari boat around the park's lake to see gorillas and feed sea lions. The park provides plenty of theme-park amusements as well, including an Adventure Castle and a Hedge Maze.

Warminster, Wiltshire. ✆ **01985/844400.** .www.longleat.co.uk. Admission to Longleat House £12 adults, £6 children 3-14; Safari Park £12 adults, £9 seniors, £8 children; special exhibitions and rides require separate admission tickets; passport tickets for all attractions £24 adults, £19 seniors, £17 children 3-14. Longleat House Apr-Oct Mon-Fri 10am-5pm, Sat-Sun 10am-5:30pm; Nov-Mar Sat-Sun 11am-3pm. Park Apr-Oct 31 Mon-Fri 10am-4pm (last admission), Sat-Sun 10am-5pm; Sat-Sun only in Mar. From Bath or Salisbury, take the train to Warminster; then take a taxi to Longleat (about 10 min.). Driving from Bath, take A36 south to Warminster; then follow the signs. From Salisbury, take A36 north to Warminster, following the signs to Longleat House.

Stourhead ★★   In a country of superlative gardens and gardeners, Stourhead offers the most celebrated example of 18th-century English landscape gardening. More than that, it's a delightful place to wander—among its trees, flowers, and colorful shrubs are tucked bridges, grottoes, and temples. Although Stourhead is a garden for all seasons, it is at its most idyllic in summer, when the rhododendrons are in full bloom.

The art-filled house at Stourhead, designed by Colen Campbell, a leader in the neoclassical revival, was built for Henry Hoare I between 1721 and 1725. The Hoare banking family created 40 hectares (100 acres) of prime landscaped gardens. Henry Hoare II (1705–85), known as "Henry the Magnificent," contributed to the development of the landscape of this estate.

The Temple of Flora was the first building in the garden, designed by the architect Henry Flitcroft in 1744. The Grotto, constructed in 1748, is lined with tufa, a water-worn limestone deposit. The springs of the Stour flow through the cold bath, where a lead copy of the sleeping Ariadne lies. The Pantheon was built in 1753 to house Rysbrack's statues of Hercules and Flora and other classical figures. In 1765, Flitcroft built the Temple of Apollo, the route that takes the visitor over the public road via a rock-work bridge constructed in the 1760s.

Henry Hoare II's 18th-century redbrick folly, **Alfred's Tower,** is another feature at Stourhead. It sits 48m (160 ft.) above the borders of Wiltshire, Somerset, and Dorset counties and has 221 steps. The **Obelisk** was built between 1839 and 1840 of Bath stone and replaced the original of Chilmark stone, constructed by William Privet for Henry Hoare in 1746.

Stourton. ✆ **01747/841152.** www.nationaltrust.org.uk/stourhead. Mid-Mar to Oct admission house and gardens £12 adults, £6.10 children, £29 family ticket; Nov–Feb gardens only £7.40 adults, £4 children, £18 family ticket. House mid-Mar to Oct Fri–Tues 11am–4:30pm (last admission 4pm). Garden year-round daily 9am–6pm. A direct bus from Bath runs only on the 1st Sat of each month. If you don't have a car, getting to Stourhead by public transportation is very difficult. You can take the train from Bath to Frome, a 30-min. trip. From here it's still a 16km (10-mile) taxi ride away.

DUNSTER ★★ & EXMOOR NATIONAL PARK ★★

296km (184 miles) W of London; 5km (3 miles) SE of Minehead

The village of Dunster, in Somerset, lies near the eastern edge of Exmoor National Park. It grew up around the original Dunster Castle, constructed as a fortress for the de Mohun family, whose progenitor came to England with William the Conqueror. The village, about 6.5km (4 miles) from the Cistercian monastery at Cleeve, has an ancient priory church and dovecote, a 17th-century gabled yarn market, and little cobbled streets dotted with whitewashed cottages.

Essentials

GETTING THERE   The best route by rail is to travel to Minehead via Taunton, which is easily reached on the main London-Penzance line from London's Paddington Station. For rail information, call ✆ **0845/748-4950** or visit **www.national rail.co.uk**. From Minehead, a taxi or bus can take you to Dunster.

At Taunton, you can take one of the seven coaches operated by **First Somerset** (✆ **0845/606-4446;** www.firstgroup.com), leaving hourly Monday through Saturday, with only one coach on Sunday. Trip time is 1 hour and 10 minutes. Buses (no. 28 or 398) from Minehead stop in Dunster Village at the rate of one per hour.

If you're driving from London, head west along the M4, cutting south at the junction with the M5 until you reach the junction with the A39, going west to Minehead. Before your final approach to Minehead, cut south to Dunster along the A396.

VISITOR INFORMATION   Dunster doesn't have an official tourist office, but there's an **Exmoor National Park Centre** at Dunster Steep (✆ **01643/821835;** www.exmoor-nationalpark.gov.uk), 3km (2 miles) east of Minehead. It's open from Easter to October, daily 10am to 5pm, plus limited hours in winter (call ahead).

Where to Stay

Luttrell Arms ★★   A hostelry for weary travelers has been on this site for more than 600 years. Simply the best choice around, this hotel is the outgrowth of a guesthouse that the Cistercian abbots at Cleeve had built in the village of Dunster. It was named for the Luttrell lords of the manor, who bought Dunster Castle and the property attached to it in the 14th century. It has, of course, been updated with modern amenities, but from its stone porch to the 15th-century Gothic hall with hammer-beam roof, it still retains a feeling of antiquity. Bedrooms range in size and are attractively decorated in keeping with the hotel's long history; five units have four-poster beds. Rooms in a section called the "Latches" are cottagelike in style, with tight stairways and narrow corridors. One room is big enough for use by a family.

32-36 High St., Dunster, Somerset TA24 6SG. ⓒ **01643/821555.** Fax 01643/821567. www.luttrellarms. co.uk. 28 units. £104–£140 double. Rates include English breakfast. AE, MC, V. Free parking. **Amenities:** Restaurant; bar; babysitting; room service. *In room:* TV, hair dryer.

Exmoor National Park ★★

Between Somerset and Devon, along the northern coast of England's southwest peninsula, is **Exmoor National Park** (ⓒ **01398/323665;** www.exmoor-national park.gov.uk), an unspoiled plateau of lonely moors. One of the smallest but most cherished national parks in Britain, it includes the wooded valleys of the rivers Exe and Barle, the Brendon Hills, a sweeping stretch of rocky coastline, and such sleepy but charming villages as **Culbone, Selworthy, Parracombe,** and **Allerford.** Bisected by a network of heavily eroded channels for brooks and streams, the park is distinctive for its lichen-covered trees, gray-green grasses, gorse, and heather. The moors reach their highest point at Dunkery Beacon, 512m (1,707 ft.) above sea level.

Although the park boasts more than 1,127km (700 miles) of walking paths, most visitors stay on the **coastal trail** that winds around the bays and inlets of England's southwestern peninsula or along some of the shorter **riverside trails.** Of all the trails, our favorite is the **Somerset and North Devon Coast Path** ★★. It begins in the resort of Minehead in the east and goes along the coast all the way to Bude in the west. Few visitors have time to walk this entire coast, but if you leave Minehead in the morning, you will have seen the path's most beautiful scenery by nightfall. For more information, contact the **South West Coast Path Association** (ⓒ **01752/896237;** www.southwestcoastpath.com).

The park's administrative headquarters are located in a 19th-century workhouse in the village of Dulverton, in Somerset, near the park's southern edge. At the **Dulverton National Park Centre,** you can pick up a brochure that lists events, guided walks, and visitor information. A program of walking tours is offered at least five times a week; tours cost from £5 to £10 per person, depending on the length of the walk. Students and children 15 and younger go for free. Themes include Woodland Walks, Moorland Walks, Bird-Watching Excursions, and Deer Spottings. Most of the tours last from 4 to 6 hours. Wear sturdy shoes and rain gear.

Other Area Attractions

Coleridge Cottage   The hamlet of Nether Stowey is on the A39, north of Taunton, across the Quantock Hills to the east of Exmoor. At the west end of Nether

Stowey, on the south side of the A39, is the cottage where Samuel Taylor Coleridge penned "The Rime of the Ancient Mariner." During his sojourn here from 1797 to 1800, he and his friend William Wordsworth and sister Dorothy enjoyed exploring the Quantock woods. The parlor and reading room of this National Trust property are open to visitors.

35 Lime St., Nether Stowey, near Bridgwater. ✆ **01278/732662.** www.nationaltrust.org.uk/coleridge cottage. Admission £3.90 adults, £1.90 children. Apr–Sept Thurs–Sun 2–5pm. From Minehead, follow A39 east about 48km (30 miles), following signs to Bridgwater. About 13km (8 miles) from Bridgwater, turn right, following signs to Nether Stowey.

Combe Sydenham Hall & Country Park ★

This hall was the home of Elizabeth Sydenham, wife of Sir Francis Drake, and it stands on the ruins of monastic buildings that were associated with nearby Cleeve Abbey. Here you can see a cannonball that legend says halted the wedding of Lady Elizabeth to a rival suitor in 1585. The gardens include Lady Elizabeth's Walk, which circles ponds originally laid out when the knight was courting his bride-to-be. The valley ponds, fed by spring water, are full of rainbow trout (ask about fly-fishing lessons). You can take a woodland walk to Long Meadow, with its host of wildflowers. Also to be seen are a deserted hamlet, whose population reputedly was wiped out by the Black Death, and a historic corn mill. In the hall's tearoom, smoked trout and pâté are produced on oak chips, as in days of yore, and there's a shop and working bakery.

Monksilver. ✆ **01984/656284.** Admission £6 adults, £3 children. Country park Easter–Sept Sun–Fri 9am–5pm. Gardens May–Sept Mon and Wed–Thurs 1:30pm guided tours only. From Dunster, take A39, following signs pointing to Watchet and/or Bridgwater. On the right, you'll see a minor zoo, Tropiquaria, at which you turn right and follow signs to Combe Sydenham.

Dunster Castle ★★

Dunster Castle is on a tor (a high, craggy hill) from which you can see Bristol Channel. It stands on the site of a Norman castle granted to William de Mohun of Normandy by William the Conqueror shortly after the conquest of England. The 13th-century gateway, built by the de Mohuns, is all that remains of the original fortress. In 1376, the castle and its lands were bought by Lady Elizabeth Luttrell; her family owned it until it was given to the National Trust in 1976, together with 12 hectares (30 acres) of surrounding parkland.

The first castle was largely demolished during the civil war. The present Dunster Castle is a Jacobean house constructed in the lower ward of the original fortifications in 1620, then rebuilt in 1870 to look like a castle. From the terraced walks and gardens, you'll have good views of Exmoor and the Quantock Hills.

On A396 (just off A39). ✆ **01643/821314.** www.nationaltrust.org.uk/dunstercastle. Admission to castle and grounds £8.60 adults, £4.20 children, £21 family ticket; grounds only £4.80 adults, £2.20 children, £12 family ticket. Castle Mar–Oct Fri–Wed 11am–5pm; closed Nov–Feb. Grounds Jan to early Mar and Nov–Dec daily 11am–4pm; mid-Mar to Oct daily 10am–5pm; closed Jan–Feb. Bus: 28 or 38 from Minehead.

DEVON: RED CLIFFS, MOORS & PLYMOUTH PILGRIMS

The great patchwork-quilt area of southwest England, part of the "West Countree," abounds in cliffside farms, rolling hills, foreboding moors, semitropical plants, and fishing villages that provide some of the finest scenery in England. You can pony trek across moor and woodland, past streams and sheep-dotted fields; or you can soak up atmosphere and ale at a local pub. For more details on how this is accomplished, see "Exploring the Moors" (p. 414).

The British approach Devon with the same kind of excitement normally reserved for hopping over to the Continent. Especially along the coastline, the names of the seaports, villages, and resorts are synonymous with holidays in the sun: Torquay, Clovelly, and Lynton-Lynmouth. Devon is a land of jagged coasts—the red cliffs in the south face the English Channel. In South Devon, the coast from which Drake and Raleigh set sail, tranquillity prevails; and on the bay-studded coastline of North Devon, pirates and smugglers found haven.

Almost every village is geared to accommodate visitors. But many small towns and fishing villages don't allow cars; these towns have parking areas on the outskirts, with a long walk to reach the center of the harbor area. From mid-July to mid-September, the most popular villages are quite crowded, so make reservations for a place to stay well in advance.

Along the south coast, the best bases from which to explore the region are **Exeter, Plymouth,** and **Torquay.** Along the north coast, we suggest **Lynton-Lynmouth.** The area's most charming village (with very limited accommodations) is **Clovelly.** The greatest natural spectacle is

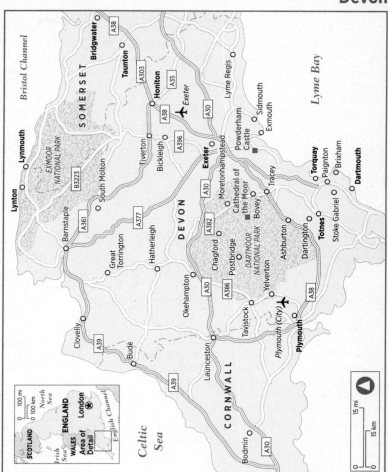

Dartmoor National Park, northeast of Plymouth, a landscape of gorges and moors filled with gorse and purple heather—home of the Dartmoor pony.

If you're taking the bus around North Devon, **First Devon & Cornwall** (✆ **0871/200-2233;** www.firstgroup.com) offers an unlimited-use ticket for specific areas. Single-day rates are £6.80 adults, £4.50 children. You can plan your journeys using the maps and timetables available at any First Devon & Cornwall office when you purchase your ticket. For information about other tours, contact **Stagecoach Devon Ltd.,** Paris Street, Exeter (✆ **01392/427711;** www.stage coachbus.com). This bus line covers a wider area of Devon, charging £6.50 for adults and £4.50 for children.

EXETER ★★

324km (201 miles) SW of London; 74km (46 miles) NE of Plymouth

Exeter was a Roman city founded in the 1st century A.D. on the banks of the River Exe. Two centuries later it was encircled by a mighty stone wall, traces of which remain today. Conquerors and would-be conquerors, especially Vikings, stormed the fortress in later centuries; none was more notable than William the Conqueror, who brought Exeter to its knees on short notice.

Under the Tudors, the city grew and prospered. Sir Walter Raleigh and Sir Francis Drake were just two of the striking figures who strolled through Exeter's streets. In May 1942, the Germans bombed Exeter, destroying many of its architectural treasures. The town was rebuilt, but the new, impersonal-looking shops and offices can't replace the Georgian crescents and the black-and-white-timbered buildings with their plastered walls. Fortunately, much was spared, and Exeter still has its Gothic cathedral, a renowned university, some museums, and several historic houses.

Exeter is a good base for exploring both Dartmoor and Exmoor national parks, two of the finest England has to offer. It's also a good place to spend a day, with a lot to do in what's left of the city's old core.

Essentials

GETTING THERE Trains from London's Paddington Station depart every hour during the day; the trip takes 2½ hours. Trains also run every 20 minutes during the day between Exeter and Plymouth; the trip takes 1 hour. For rail information, call ✆ **0845/7000125** or visit **www.firstgreatwestern.co.uk**. Trains often arrive at Exeter St. David's Station, at St. David's Hill.

A **National Express** coach departs from London's Victoria Coach Station every 2 hours during the day; the trip takes 4½ hours. For information and schedules, call ✆ **0871/781-8181** or visit **www.nationalexpress.com**. You can also take **Stagecoach** bus no. X38 or 39 between Plymouth and Exeter. During the day, two coaches depart per hour for the 1-hour trip.

If you're driving from London, take the M4 west, cutting south to Exeter on the M5 (junction near Bristol).

VISITOR INFORMATION The **Tourist Information Centre** is at the Civic Centre, Paris Street (✆ **01392/665700**). It's open from September to June, Monday to Saturday 9am to 5pm, and in July and August, Monday to Saturday 9am to 5pm and Sunday 10am to 4pm.

SPECIAL EVENTS A classical-music lover's dream, the **Exeter Summer Festival,** usually held over 2 weeks in late June and July, includes more than 150 events, ranging from concerts and opera to lectures. Festival dates and offerings vary from year to year; more information is available by contacting the Exeter Festival Office at the Civic Centre (✆ **01392/265200;** www.exeter.gov.uk/festival).

Where to Stay

EXPENSIVE

ABode Exeter at the Royal Clarence Hotel ★ ☺ Just a 2-minute walk from the rail station, the ABode Exeter, formerly the Royal Clarence Hotel, offers far more tradition and style than the sometimes better-rated and more recently built

Honiton: The World of Antique Lace

In Honiton, 26km (16 miles) northeast of Exeter, lace has been made since 1560, and many of its connoisseurs hail it as the world's highest-quality lace. Much in demand in the 17th and 18th centuries by rich families, the cottage industry is still flourishing at the **Honiton Lace Shop** ★★, 44 High St. (𝄞 **01404/42416;** www.honitonlace.

com). The shop sells and displays antique lace from the 16th to the early 20th centuries. It also carries lace-making equipment for both beginners and experienced lace makers. Demonstrations (no set times) are scheduled from June to August—always call ahead for an appointment.

Southgate at Southernhay East, or the Rougemont on Queen Street (see below). It dates back to 1769 and escaped the Nazi Blitz. Just a step away from the cathedral, it offers individually furnished rooms in categories classified as comfortable, desirable, enviable, and fabulous. Five rooms are large enough for families; some rooms have four-poster beds.

An acclaimed two-star Michelin chef (Michael Caines) and a top-notch hotelier of south England (Andrew Brownsword) have joined in partnership to run this hotel. A chic little nook, the Champagne and Cocktail Bar, has been added.

Cathedral Yard, Exeter, Devon EX1 1HD. 𝄞 **01392/319955.** Fax 01392/439423. www.abodehotels.co.uk/exeter. 53 units. £89–£175 double; £244–£260 suite. AE, DC, MC, V. Parking £8. **Amenities:** Restaurant (Michael Caines, p. 407); cafe; 2 bars (including Well House Tavern, p. 410); babysitting; exercise room; room service; spa. *In room:* A/C, TV, hair dryer, Internet (free).

Buckerell Lodge Hotel ★   This country house originated in the 12th century, but it has been altered and changed beyond recognition over the years. The latest refurbishment occurred in 2007, when the rooms were painted in neutral tones of mauve, taupe, and cream. The exterior is a symmetrical and severely dignified building with a Regency feel. Often hosting business travelers, it's also a tourist favorite, especially in summer. The bedrooms, in a range of styles and sizes, are well decorated and nicely equipped. The best rooms are the executive accommodations in the main house, though most units are in a more sterile modern addition. Two units are large enough to accommodate families.

Topsham Rd., Exeter, Devon EX2 4SQ. 𝄞 **0844/855-9112.** Fax 01392/424333. www.foliohotels.com/buckerelllodge. 54 units. £59–£125 double. AE, DC, MC, V. Free parking. Bus: S, T, or R. Take B3182 1.5km (1 mile) southeast, off Junction 30 of M5. **Amenities:** Restaurant; bar; room service. *In room:* TV, hair dryer, Wi-Fi (free).

Rougemont Hotel   Though its history is far less impressive than that of the ABode Exeter at the Royal Clarence (see above), this old-fashioned, rambling Victorian hotel is also a traditional choice for those who want to stay in the center of town. Its small to medium bedrooms are comfortably furnished in a modern style. The government-rated four-star hotel, a member of the Thistle chain, lies near the Exeter Railway Station, central to most of the town's attractions.

Queen St. (opposite the central train station), Exeter, Devon EX4 3SP. 𝄞 **0871/376-9018.** Fax 0871/376-9118. www.thistle.com. 90 units. £75–£135 double; £125–£165 suite. AE, DC, MC, V. Parking £6. **Amenities:** Restaurant; bar; room service. *In room:* TV, hair dryer, Wi-Fi (£10 per day).

MODERATE

Gipsy Hill Hotel ☺ Affiliated with Best Western, this late-Victorian country house stands on the eastern edge of the city and is close to the airport. (It's especially convenient if you're driving, as it's within easy reach of the M5.) Accommodations, ranging from small to medium, are comfortably appointed; some have four-poster beds. Rooms in the main house have more tradition and ambience; the other 17 units are located in an annex. Five rooms are large enough for families.

Gipsy Hill Lane (via Pinn Lane), Monkerton, Exeter, Devon EX1 3RN. ⓒ **01392/465252.** Fax 01392/464302. www.gipsyhillhotel.co.uk. 37 units. £70–£100 double. AE, DC, MC, V. Free parking. **Amenities:** Restaurant; bar; babysitting; room service. *In room:* TV, hair dryer, Wi-Fi (free).

St. Olaves Hotel ★ This is our favorite place to stay in town. The location is ideal, within a short walk of the cathedral—you'll hear the church bells. A Georgian mansion, it was constructed in 1827 by a rich merchant as a home. The interior has been discreetly furnished, in part with antiques, and decorated with sporting prints. Each of the bedrooms is tastefully outfitted; some have four-poster beds.

Mary Arches St. (off High St.), Exeter, Devon EX4 3AZ. ⓒ **800/544-9993** in the U.S., or 01392/217736. Fax 01392/413054. www.olaves.co.uk. 14 units. £115–£125 double; £165 family room; £155 suite. Rates include English breakfast. MC, V. Free parking. **Amenities:** Restaurant (Treasury Restaurant, p. 407); bar; room service. *In room:* TV, hair dryer.

White Hart Hotel In the center of town, the White Hart, a coaching inn in the 15th century, is one of the oldest in the city. Oliver Cromwell stabled his horses here. The hotel is a mass of polished wood, slate floors, oak beams, and gleaming brass and copper. The rooms, which combine old and new, are housed in either the old wing or a more impersonal modern one. Six rooms are large enough for families, and each comes with a bathroom equipped with a tub/shower combination.

66 South St., Exeter, Devon EX1 1EE. ⓒ **01392/279897.** Fax 01392/250159. www.whitehartpubexeter. co.uk. 55 units. £50–£130 double. Rates include English breakfast. AE, DC, MC, V. Free parking. **Amenities:** Restaurant; bar. *In room:* TV, hair dryer, Wi-Fi (free).

INEXPENSIVE

Park View Hotel This hotel lies near the heart of town and the train station. A landmark Georgian house, it offers comfortably but plainly furnished rooms, ranging in size from small to medium. The decor is regularly upgraded. The public bathrooms, available to other guests, are convenient and well maintained. Guests take their breakfast in a cozy room opening onto the hotel's garden. Although breakfast is the only meal served, the staff will prepare a packed lunch for touring.

8 Howell Rd., Exeter, Devon EX4 4LG. ⓒ **01392/271772.** Fax 01392/253047. www.parkviewexeter.co.uk. 13 units, 10 with bathroom. £58 double without bathroom; £65 double with bathroom. Rates include English breakfast. MC, V. Free parking. **Amenities:** Breakfast room; TV lounge. *In room:* TV.

Woodbine Guesthouse ★ 🍴 In the heart of Exeter, near the landmark clock tower, this is one of the cathedral city's best-run guesthouses. The hosts are friendly, the rooms are comfortable and well furnished, and the English breakfast is ample fortification for the day. The house was built in the mid-Victorian era, but is not old-fashioned—it has been completely modernized and furnished in a contemporary style. The location is an easy walk from the Exeter Coach and Bus Station, and some guest rooms open onto a city park. Rooms are named after flowers, such as Jasmine. We like the Honeysuckle, decorated in yellow, gold, and antique cream with deep-red accents. Luxuries include a power shower and under-floor heating in the bathroom.

1 Woodbine Terrace, Exeter, Devon, EX4 4LJ. ✆ **01392/203302.** Fax 01392/254162. www.woodbine guesthouse.co.uk. 5 units. £66 double. Rates include English breakfast. AE, MC, V. Free parking. **Amenities:** Breakfast room. *In room:* TV, Wi-Fi.

Where to Dine

Michael Caines Restaurant at ABode Exeter ★★ FRENCH

Exeter, at long last, offers a restaurant worthy of itself, with the aura of a smart, sophisticated brasserie. Try to get a table near one of the bay windows overlooking the cathedral. As is obvious by the establishment's name, a skilled chef is in charge of the overall operation here. Excellent, not deluxe, raw materials are purchased and turned into an impressive array of dishes beautifully prepared and served. The dishes we've sampled have been filled with flavor and perfectly spiced. For a starter, Cornish lobster appears with avocado, watermelon, and cherry tomatoes, or perhaps you can sample the foie gras with mango relish. Some enticing mains include roast partridge with a pumpkin fondant or line-caught sea bass in red-wine butter.

In the ABode Exeter at the Royal Clarence Hotel, Cathedral Yard. ✆ **01392/223638.** www.michael caines.com. Reservations required. Main courses £22–£25; fixed-price 2-course lunch £15, 3-course lunch £20; 7-course table d'hôte menu £58. AE, DC, MC, V. Mon–Sat noon–2pm and 7–10pm.

Ship Inn ★ 🍴 ENGLISH

Often visited by Sir Francis Drake, Sir Walter Raleigh, and Sir John Hawkins, this restaurant still provides tankards of real ale, lager, and stout. Real ale, as every Brit knows, means that the yeast in the drink is still present at the point of consumption—that is, it is unfiltered. A large selection of snacks is offered in the bar every day, whereas the restaurant upstairs provides more substantial English fare. At either lunch or dinner, you can order French onion soup, whole grilled lemon sole, five different steaks, and more. Portions are large, as in Elizabethan times.

St. Martin's Lane. ✆ **01392/272040.** Reservations recommended. Restaurant main courses £6–£13; pub platters £5–£9. MC, V. Daily noon–9pm.

Treasury Restaurant ★ CONTINENTAL

At one of Exeter's finest restaurants, guests enjoy before-dinner drinks in a paneled bar that overlooks a verdant garden. The menu reflects the sophisticated palate of the congenial owners. Anticipate something savory, often in unusual yet harmonious combinations of flavors. A West Country sirloin steak appears with prunes and ale sauce, while the delectable chicken breasts are served with a tarragon-laced white-wine-and-cream sauce, with a side of wild-mushroom lasagna. Vegetarians can order saffron risotto with baby vegetables and Parmesan cream.

In the St. Olaves Hotel, Mary Arches St. ✆ **01392/217736.** Reservations recommended. Main courses £16–£25. DC, MC, V. Daily noon–2pm and 7–9:30pm.

Exploring Exeter

Exeter Cathedral ★★

The Roman II Augusta Legion made its camp on the site where the Cathedral Church of Saint Peter now stands in Exeter. It has been occupied by Britons, Saxons, Danes, and Normans. The English Saint Boniface, who converted northern Germany to Christianity, was trained here in A.D. 690. The present cathedral structure was begun around 1112, and the twin Norman towers still

A Relic from William the Conqueror

Just off "the High," at the top of Castle Street, stands an impressive **Norman Gatehouse** from William the Conqueror's castle. Though only the gatehouse and walls survive, you can enjoy the panoramic view and surrounding gardens while contemplating all the invasions that have assaulted Exeter, from the Romans to the Nazi bombers of World War II.

stand. Between the towers runs the longest uninterrupted true Gothic vault in the world, at a height of 20m (66 ft.) and a length of 90m (300 ft.). It was completed in 1369 and is the finest existing example of Decorated Gothic architecture (see "Gothic Architecture [1150–1550]" in chapter 2). The Puritans destroyed the cathedral cloisters in 1655, and a German bomb finished off the twin chapels of St. James and St. Thomas in May 1942. Now restored, it's one of the prettiest churches anywhere. Its famous choir sings Evensong Monday to Friday at 5:30pm and again at 3pm on Saturday and Sunday. On school holidays, visiting choirs perform.

1 The Cloisters. ✆ **01392/285983.** www.exeter-cathedral.org.uk. Admission £5 adults, £3 children 15 and younger.

Exeter Guildhall   This colonnaded building on the main street is the oldest municipal building in the kingdom: The earliest reference to the guildhall is in a deed from 1160. The Tudor front that straddles the pavement was added in 1593. Inside you'll find a fine display of silver, plus a number of paintings. The ancient hall is paneled in oak. This is a working building, so hours of operation are not guaranteed.

High St. ✆ **01392/665500.** www.exeter.gov.uk. Free admission. Mon–Fri 10:30am–1pm and 2–4pm. It's best to call before visiting.

Powderham Castle ★   This private house is occupied by the countess and earl of Devon, who let Ismail Merchant and James Ivory use their home as a setting for *The Remains of the Day,* starring Anthony Hopkins and Emma Thompson. It was built in the late 14th century by Sir Philip Courtenay, sixth son of the second earl of Devon, and his wife, Margaret, granddaughter of Edward I. Their magnificent tomb is in the south transept of Exeter Cathedral. The castle has many family portraits and fine furniture, including a remarkable clock that plays full tunes at 4pm, 8pm, and midnight; some 17th-century tapestries; and a chair used by William III for his first council of state at Newton Abbot. The chapel dates from the 15th century, with hand-hewn roof timbers and carved pew ends.

In Powderham, Kenton. ✆ **01626/890243.** www.powderham.co.uk. Admission £9.50 adults, £8.50 seniors, £7.50 children 5–14, family ticket £27, free for children 4 and younger. Sun–Fri 10am–5:30pm. Closed Nov–Mar. Take the A379 Dawlish Rd. 13km (8 miles) south of Exeter; the castle is signposted.

Shopping

Exeter has long been famous for its silver. If you seek, ye shall find old Exeter silver, especially spoons, sold in local stores. **Brufords,** 17 Guildhall, Queen Street (✆ **01392/254901;** www.brufords.co.uk), sells modern silver and jewelry.

You can find a number of antiques dealers in Exeter, many on the Quay off Western Way. The **Quay Gallery Antiques Emporium** (✆ **01392/213283;** www.exeterquayantiques.co.uk) houses 10 dealers who sell furniture, porcelain, metalware, and other collectibles. The **Antique Centre,** on the Quay (✆ **01392/493501**), has 20 dealers.

The **Edinburgh Woollen Mill,** 23 Cathedral Yard (✆ **01392/412318;** www.ewm.co.uk), carries a large selection of woolen goods, including kilts, Aran jumpers, tartan travel rugs, quality wool suits for women, and trousers for men.

A daily **market** on Sidwell Street is Exeter's version of a flea market.

Exeter After Dark

Exeter is a lively university town offering an abundance of classical concerts and theater productions, as well as clubs and pubs.

Concerts, opera, dance, and film can be found year-round at the **Exeter Phoenix,** Bradninch Place, Gandy Street (✆ **01392/667080;** www.exeterphoenix.org.uk), and Exeter University's **Northcott Theatre,** Stocker Road (✆ **01392/493493;** www.exeternorthcott.co.uk), which is also home to a professional theater company.

The **Well House Tavern,** Cathedral Close (✆ **01392/223611;** www.michael caines.com/taverns/exeter), is part of the ABode Exeter at the Royal Clarence Hotel (p. 404). It's housed in a building believed to have been constructed in the 14th century, though the Roman well in the basement predates that estimate. The tavern is said to be haunted—though the ghost, who wears a flowing white dress and is affectionately called Alice, is said to be good-spirited when she appears. Join Alice and the other regulars for a pint or a light meal.

With a great view of the canal, **Double Locks,** Canal Banks (✆ **01392/256947;** www.doublelocks.co.uk), welcomes a varied crowd, largely students. It features live music (jazz, rock, and blues) with no cover charge, and you can get traditional pub grub to go with your pint.

DARTMOOR NATIONAL PARK ★★

343km (213 miles) SW of London; 21km (13 miles) W of Exeter

This national park lies northeast of Plymouth, stretching from Tavistock and Oke-hampton on the west to near Exeter in the east, a granite mass that sometimes rises to a height of 600m (1,968 ft.) above sea level. The landscape offers vistas of gorges with rushing water, spiny shrubs, and purple heather ranged over by Dartmoor ponies—a foreboding landscape for the experienced hiker only.

Essentials

GETTING THERE   Take the train from London to Exeter, and then use local buses to connect you with the various villages of Dartmoor. **Transmoor Link,** a public transport bus service, usually operates throughout the summer; it's an ideal way to get onto the moor. Information on the Transmoor Link and on the bus link between various towns and villages on Dartmoor is available from the **Travel Line** (✆ **0871/200-2233**).

If you're driving, Exeter is the most easily reached gateway. From here, continue west on the B3212 to such centers as Dartmoor, Chagford, Moretonhampstead, and North Bovey. From these smaller towns, tiny roads—often not really big enough for two cars—cut deeper into the moor.

VISITOR INFORMATION   The main source of information here is the **Tourist Information Centre,** Town Hall, Bedford Square, Tavistock (✆ **01822/612938**). It will book accommodations within an 80km (50-mile) radius for free. From April to October, it's open daily from 9:30am to 5pm. From November to March, it's open on Monday, Tuesday, Friday, and Saturday from 10am to 4:30pm.

Chagford ★: A Good Base for Exploring the Park

351km (218 miles) SW of London; 21km (13 miles) W of Exeter; 32km (20 miles) NW of Torquay

At 180m (590 ft.) above sea level, romantic Chagford is an ancient town. With moors all around, it's a good base for exploring the often forlorn yet enchanting north Dartmoor. You're in Sir Francis Drake country now. Chagford overlooks the River Teign and is itself overlooked by the high granite tors (high craggy hills). There's good fishing in the Teign. From Chagford, the most popular excursion is to Postbridge, a village with a prehistoric clapper bridge. This ancient form of bridge, found on the moors of Dartmoor and Exmoor, is formed by large flat slabs of granite supported on stone piers.

To get here, take a train to Exeter, and then catch a bus to Chagford (Stagecoach bus no. 173). If you're driving from Exeter, drive west on the A30, and then south on the A382 to Chagford.

WHERE TO STAY & DINE

Bovey Castle ★★★   The grandest address in Devon is an elegant 1906 estate within the national park that still offers such "gentlemanly pursuits" as trout fishing, archery, and falconry. The golf course's revamped links were first laid out in 1926. Luxury abounds at this castle, which seems to await the arrival any minute of Agatha Christie, or at least Hercule Poirot. Although the hotel has been completely restored, the halcyon Edwardian era lives on in the decor, from the Palm Court dining room to the Art Deco artwork and vintage travel posters. The spacious bedrooms are the epitome of comfort, taste, and elegance. The accommodations are virtual staterooms, the epitome of English country living. For those seeking the ultimate retreat, there is the North Lodge, with an exquisite home standing in private gardens.

North Bovey, Devon TQ13 8RE. ✆ **01647/445000.** Fax 01647/445020. www.boveycastle.com. 63 units. £179–£274 double; £359–£539 suite. AE, DC, MC, V. Rates include English breakfast. **Amenities:** Restaurant; bar; archery center; children's farm; equestrian center; exercise room; falconry; fly-fishing; 18-hole golf course; movie theater; 2 pools (1 indoor, 1 outdoor); room service; spa; 2 outdoor tennis courts. *In room:* A/C, TV, hair dryer, minibar, Wi-Fi (free).

Easton Court Bed & Breakfast ★ 🏠   Established in the 1920s, this Tudor house, standing in 1.6 hectares (4 acres) of gardens and paddocks, is a longtime favorite of the literati and theater folk. Best known as the place where Evelyn Waugh wrote *Brideshead Revisited,* the atmosphere here is very English country: an ancient stone house with thatched roof, an inglenook where log fires burn, and a high-walled flower garden. Bedrooms are snug and comfortable, ranging in size from small to medium. They're appointed with comfortable English beds where the greats of yesteryear slept; some have four-posters. Most rooms open onto views.

Easton Cross, Chagford, Devon TQ13 8JL. ✆ **01647/433469.** www.easton.co.uk. 5 units. £65–£80 double. Rates include English breakfast. MC, V. Take A382 2.5km (1½ miles) northeast of Chagford. No children 10 and under. **Amenities:** Guest lounge. *In room:* TV, CD player, hair dryer.

Gidleigh Park Hotel ★★★   This Tudor-style hotel, a Relais & Châteaux member, is country house supreme, the finest and most elegant place to stay in the Dartmoor area. On 1.8 hectares (4½ acres), the hotel lies in the Teign Valley, opening onto panoramic vistas of the Meldon and Nattadon Hills. Its owners, Andrew and Christina Brownsword, have renovated and refurnished the house with flair and imagination, often inspired by the Devon Arts and Crafts movement. They've converted the top floor into bedrooms, reached by a grand staircase; an extension also offers completely up-to-date and elegant accommodations. Rooms are spacious and furnished in the most elegant English-country-house tradition. Half-canopies often crown the sumptuous English beds. The hotel also has a two-bedroom, two-bathroom thatched cottage across the river.

Gidleigh Park (3km/2 miles outside town), Chagford, Devon TQ13 8HH. ☎ **01647/432367.** Fax 01647/432574. www.gidleigh.com. 23 units, 1 cottage. £390–£530 double; £720–£1,235 cottage (2-night minimum on weekends). Rates include English breakfast, morning tea, and dinner. AE, DC, MC, V. To get here from Chagford Sq., turn right onto Mill St. at Lloyds Bank. After 135m (450 ft.), turn right and go down the hill to the crossroads. Cross straight over onto Holy St., following the lane passing Holy St. Manor on your right and shifting into low gear to negotiate 2 sharp bends on a steep hill. Over Leigh Bridge, make a sharp right turn into Gidleigh Park. A 1km (½-mile) drive will bring you to the hotel. **Amenities:** Restaurant; bar; babysitting; bowling green; croquet lawn; putting green; spa treatments; tennis court. *In room:* TV, hair dryer, Wi-Fi (free).

EXPLORING THE AREA

Castle Drogo ★ ☺   This massive granite castle, in the hamlet of Drewsteignton, 27km (17 miles) west of Exeter, was designed and built between 1910 and 1930 by architect Sir Edwin Lutyens, then at the height of his powers, for his client, Julius Drewe, a self-made millionaire whose chain of Home & Colonial Stores enabled him to retire very rich in 1899, at the age of 33. It was the last private country house built in the United Kingdom on a grand scale. Though constructed of granite, and castellated and turreted like a medieval castle from the age of chivalry, it was never intended to be a military stronghold. The castle occupies a bleak but dramatic position high above the River Teign, with views sweeping out over the moors.

The tour covers an elegant series of formal rooms designed in the tradition of the Edwardian age. Two restaurants and a buffet-style tearoom are on premises. Serving standard English fare, these restaurants are more for convenience than any grand cuisine. But the food is at least first-class cafeteria fare, prepared with fresh ingredients.

Insider's tip: The castle is so overpowering, it's easy to forget the secluded gardens. But they are wonderful, including a sunken lawn enclosed by raised walkways, a circular croquet lawn (sets are available for rent), geometrically shaped yew hedges, and a children's playroom based on a 1930s residence.

Drewsteignton, 6.5km (4 miles) northeast of Chagford and 9.5km (6 miles) south of the Exeter-Okehampton Rd. (A30). ☎ **01647/433306.** www.nationaltrust.org.uk. Admission to castle and grounds £8.20 adults, £4.10 children, £21 family ticket; grounds only £5.25 adults, £2.90 children. House Mar–Oct Wed–Mon 11am–5pm, Dec 1–23 Sat–Sun noon–4pm; grounds Mar–Oct daily 10:30am–5:30pm, Nov–Dec 23 Fri–Sun 11am–4pm. Closed Jan–Feb. Take A30 and follow the signs.

Sir Francis Drake's House ★   Constructed in 1278, Sir Francis Drake's House was originally a Cistercian monastery. The monastery was dissolved in 1539 and became the country seat of sailors Sir Richard Grenville and, later, Sir Francis Drake. The house remained in the Drake family until 1946, when the abbey and grounds were given to the National Trust. The abbey is now a museum, with exhibits including Drake's drum, banners, and other artifacts. There is also an audiovisual presentation about the history of the house.

Buckland Abbey, Yelverton. ☎ **01822/853607.** www.nationaltrust.org.uk. Admission £9 adults, £5 children, £23 family ticket. Mid-Mar to Oct Fri–Wed 10:30am–5:30pm; Nov to early Mar Sat–Sun 2–5pm. Last admission 45 min. before closing. Go 5km (3 miles) west of Yelverton off A386.

CHAGFORD AFTER DARK

The local watering hole is **Globe Inn,** High Street (☎ **01647/433485;** www. globeinnchagford.co.uk), which puts up wayfarers the way it has done since the 16th century, when stagecoach passengers used to stop by for the night. In the center of town, it is also the most popular pub in the area, drawing locals and visitors to its

A Cuppa & an Homage to Lorna Doone

At teatime, drop in at **Whiddons,** High Street (✆ **01647/433406**), serving freshly baked scones and delectable cucumber sandwiches. After tea, visit the nearby Church of St. Michael, where a spurned lover killed Mary Whiddon on her wedding day (later fictionalized in R. D. Blackmore's classic *Lorna Doone*).

two bars and restaurants, where daily specials and traditional English dishes such as roasts are served. If you have too much of the local brew, you can stay over in a family room or one of two doubles at a cost of £75 to £90 per night.

Other Towns in & Around Dartmoor

Some 21km (13 miles) west of Exeter, the peaceful little town of **Moretonhampstead** is perched on the edge of Dartmoor. Moretonhampstead contains several 17th-century colonnaded almshouses and a Market Cross, a carved stone structure used for centuries to mark the site of the local market, which is still around.

The much-visited Dartmoor village of **Widecombe-in-the-Moor** is only 11km (7 miles) northeast of Moretonhampstead. Widecombe also has a parish church worth visiting. Called the **Cathedral of the Moor,** with a roster of vicars beginning in 1253, this house of worship in a green valley is surrounded by legends. When the building was restored, a wall plate was found bearing the badge of Richard II (1377–99), the figure of a white hart (an old word for a stag). As a personal badge of Richard II, the symbol of the hart was derived from the coat of arms of his mother, who was called Joan, the "Fair Maid of Kent." Despite its fame, the town is very disappointing, tacky, and unkempt.

Let yourself drift back in time to the days when craftspeople were the lifeblood of thriving communities. Basket weavers, wood-turners, and potters are among the traditional crafters that you can still see in the West Devon area. In the Dartmoor National Park, you'll find that the **Yelverton Paperweight Centre,** Leg O'Mutton (✆ **01822/854250;** www.paperweightcentre.co.uk), presents an impressive display of more than 800 glass paperweights for sale along with paintings of Dartmoor scenes. It's open April to October, daily 10:30am to 5pm.

WHERE TO STAY & DINE

Castle Inn   A good stopover on the road between Okehampton and Tavistock, this inn dates from the 12th century, when it was built next to Lydford Castle. With its pink facade and row of rose trellises, it is the hub of the village. The owners have maintained the character of the roomy old rustic lounge. One room, the Snug, has a group of high-backed oak benches arranged in a circle. Bedrooms are not large but are attractively furnished, often with mahogany and marble Victorian pieces.

Lydford, near Okehampton (1.5km/1 mile off A386), Devon EX20 4BH. ✆ **01822/820241.** Fax 01822/820454. www.castleinnlydford.co.uk. 8 units. £65–90 double. MC, V. **Amenities:** Restaurant; bar. *In room:* TV.

Cherrybrook Hotel   This is a small family-run hotel in the center of the Dartmoor National Park, on the high moor but within easy driving distance of Exeter and

Plymouth. It was built in the early 19th century by a prince regent's friend who received permission to enclose a large area of the Dartmoor forest for farming. The lounge and bar, with their beamed ceilings and slate floors, are reminders of those times. Ann and Roy Daniels rent small to medium-size rooms with a traditional decor, often with a granite fireplace. A different group of bedrooms is redecorated each year. Bathrooms contain a shower stall.

On B3212, btw. Postbridge and Two Bridges, Yelverton, Devon PL20 6SP. ℰ/fax **01822/880260.** www. thecherrybrook.co.uk. 7 units. £79 double; £129 double including half-board. Rates include English breakfast. MC, V. Closed Dec 22–Jan 2. **Amenities:** Restaurant; bar; lounge. *In room:* TV, hair dryer.

Horn of Plenty ★ INTERNATIONAL   As you drive from Tavistock west to Callington, a small sign points north along a leafy drive to a solid Regency house built by the duke of Bedford in the early 1800s as a private home, set on 2 hectares (5 acres) of grounds. Today's owners operate what the French call a *restaurant avec chambres;* after a day of touring the country, hotel guests enjoy well-prepared dinners at the award-winning restaurant. High-caliber starters include pan-fried scallops with king prawn and an apple-and-coriander-laced pasta, or else roast pigeon wrapped in potato and served on a foie gras salad with a port-and-red-wine dressing. For tempting mains, opt for the pan-fried sea bass on a bed of new potatoes; it's served with a saffron-laced white-wine sauce. After dining, ascend to one of the 10 spacious, warm, and elegant bedrooms that have been installed over the old stables of the house. With a full English breakfast included, doubles range from £160 to £250.

Gulworthy, Tavistock, Devon PL19 8JD. ℰ **01822/832528.** www.thehornofplenty.co.uk. Reservations recommended. Fixed-price 3-course lunch £27; fixed-price 3-course dinner £28 Mon, £47 Tues–Sun. AE, MC, V. Daily noon–2pm and 7–9pm.

Lewtrenchard Manor   On the northwest edge of Dartmoor, near the oft-visited Okehampton, this 17th-century Jacobean house has a certain charm and grace. There has been a manor of some sort on this property since 1086, when it was mentioned in the Domesday Book. It was at one time the residence of Victorian hymn writer Rev. Sabine Baring Gould (hardly a household name today). It is set in a garden open to the general public as part of the National Gardens Scheme, affording the opportunity to take several scenic walks. As was typical of its time, the house features oak paneling, leaded windows, beautifully detailed ceilings, and antiques. Accommodations come in various shapes and sizes, each exceedingly comfortable. Five bedrooms are more contemporary and stylish than the original rooms, yet are still in keeping with the Jacobean style.

Lewdown, Devon EX20 4PN. ℰ **01566/783222.** Fax 01566/783332. www.lewtrenchard.co.uk. 14 units. £135–£340 double; £280–£365 suite. Rates include English breakfast. 2-night minimum on weekends. AE, DC, MC, V. **Amenities:** Restaurant; bar; room service. *In room:* TV, hair dryer.

Exploring the Moors

This region is as rich in myth and legend as anywhere else in Britain. Crisscrossed with about 805km (500 miles) of bridle paths and hiking trails and covering about 932 sq. km (360 sq. miles)—466 sq. km (180 sq. miles) of which comprise Dartmoor National Park—the moors rest on a granite base with numerous rocky outcroppings.

The **Dartmoor National Park Authority (DNPA)** runs **guided walks** of varying difficulty, ranging from 1½ to 6 hours for a trek of some 14 to 19km (9–12 miles). All you have to do is turn up suitably clad at your selected starting point. The country is rough, and on the high moor you should always make sure you have a good map, a compass, and suitable clothing and shoes. Details are available from DNPA information centers or from the DNPA headquarters, High Moorland Visitor Centre, Tavistock Road, Princetown, near Yelverton (© **01822/890414;** www.dartmoor-npa.gov.uk). Information centers are open Easter through October, daily from 10am to 5pm; most (including the High Moorland Visitor Centre) are also open in the off-season, daily from 10am to 4pm. Guided tours cost £3 for a 2-hour walk, £5 for a 3-hour walk, £6.50 for a 4-hour walk, and £8 for a 6-hour walk. These prices are subsidized by the national park services.

Throughout the area are stables where you can arrange for a day's trek across the moors at the cost of around £25 per hour. For **horseback riding** in Dartmoor, there are too many establishments to list. All are licensed, and you are accompanied by an experienced rider/guide. (Note that the moor can be dangerous because sudden fogs descend on the treacherous marshlands without warning.) Most riding stables are listed in a useful free publication, *The Dartmoor Visitor,* which also provides details on guided walks, places to go, accommodations, local events, and articles about the national park. *The Dartmoor Visitor* is obtainable from DNPA information centers and tourist information centers.

Some of the best Dartmoor riding is provided by **Skaigh Stables,** at Belstone (© **01837/840917;** www.skaighstables.co.uk), 1.6km (1 mile) from the A30 Exeter-Okehampton road. Rides go over dramatic moorland in England's largest wilderness. Morning and afternoon rides are offered from mid-April until the end of September, with 2-hour rides beginning at £36 per person. We're also fond of the **Doone Valley Stables,** Oare, Lynton (© **01598/741234;** www.doonevalley trekking.co.uk), set in the heart of the beautiful Doone Valley and offering escorted rides, including picnic rides.

TORQUAY ★

359km (223 miles) SW of London; 37km (23 miles) S of Exeter

The resort of Torquay—the birthplace of mystery writer Agatha Christie—opens onto 35km (22 miles) of rocky coastline with 18 poor-to-fair beaches set against a backdrop of the red cliffs of Devon, with many sheltered pebbly coves. The entire area is filled with parks and gardens often planted with subtropical vegetation. At night, concerts, theatrical productions from London's West End, often-corny British vaudeville shows, and old-fashioned ballroom dancing keep the vacationers and many honeymooners entertained.

Torquay is more upscale than Brighton. Due to its easy commute from London, Brighton attracts a lot of tawdry "London-by-the-Sea" crowds, whereas Torquay, as a destination unto itself, draws a well-heeled clientele seeking a more tranquil seaside holiday.

Essentials

GETTING THERE   Frequent trains run throughout the day from London's Paddington Station to Torquay, whose station is at the town center on the seafront. The trip takes 2½ hours. For rail information, call ℂ **0845/7484950** or visit **www. nationalrail.co.uk**.

National Express coaches from London's Victoria Coach Station leave every 2 hours during the day for the 5-hour trip to Torquay. For information and schedules, call ℂ **0871/781-8181** or visit **www.nationalexpress.com**.

If you're driving from Exeter, head west on the A38, veering south at the junction with the A380.

VISITOR INFORMATION The **Tourist Information Centre** is at Vaughan Parade (ℂ **01803/2112111;** www.englishriviera.co.uk). It's open June through September, Monday to Saturday 9:30am to 5:30pm and Sunday 10am to 4pm, and October through May, Monday to Saturday 9:30am to 5pm.

Where to Stay
EXPENSIVE

Barceló Torquay Imperial Hotel ★★★   This leading government-rated five-star hotel in the West Country dates from 1866, but a major refurbishing has kept it abreast of the times and way ahead of its competition. It sits on 2.2 hectares (5½ acres) of subtropical gardens opening onto rocky cliffs, with views of the Channel. You'll follow the example of some of the characters of Agatha Christie if you check in here. She called it the Esplanade in *The Rajah's Emerald,* the Castle in *Partners in Crime,* and the Majestic in *Peril at End House.* Inside is a world of soaring ceilings, marble columns, and ornate plasterwork—enough to make a former visitor, Edward VII, feel at home. Bedrooms are studies in grand living, with beautiful reproduction pieces, striped wallpaper, and upholstered seating. Many have private balconies suspended high above the view.

Park Hill Rd., Torquay, Devon TQ1 2DG. ℂ **01803/294301.** Fax 01803/298293. www.barcelo-hotels. co.uk. 169 units. £95–£185 double; £195–£235 suite. Rates include English breakfast, use of sporting facilities, and dancing in the ballroom Mon–Sat. AE, DC, MC, V. Parking £7–£15. **Amenities:** 2 restaurants; bar; health club; 2 heated pools (indoor, outdoor); room service; sauna; solarium; spa; 2 squash courts; steam room; 2 tennis courts. *In room:* TV, hair dryer, minibar, Wi-Fi (£13 per day).

Orestone Manor ★   Sometimes the best way to enjoy a bustling seaside resort is from afar, nestled in a country home. Orestone Manor is in nearby Maidencombe, a small village north of Torquay. In one of the loveliest valleys in South Devon, this gabled manor house, constructed in the early 19th century as a private home, enjoys a tranquil rural setting, situated on .8 hectare (2 acres) of well-landscaped gardens. All of the bedrooms are handsomely furnished. The gable rooms are a bit small, but some offer sea views; all of the superior rooms have sea views and complimentary sherry. Because this was once a country lodge, all rooms have an individual character and aren't just identical square boxes.

Rockhouse Lane, Maidencombe, Torquay, Devon TQ1 4SX. ℂ **01803/328098.** Fax 01803/328336. www.orestonemanor.com. 12 units. £135–£225 double. Rates include English breakfast. AE, DC, MC, V. Free parking. Closed 2 weeks in Jan. Drive 5.5km (3½ miles) north of Torquay on A379. **Amenities:** Restaurant; bar; babysitting; outdoor pool; room service. *In room:* TV, hair dryer, Wi-Fi (free).

Palace Hotel ★   In Torquay, only the Imperial is better. This 1921 hotel was built when life was experienced on a grand scale, an attitude reflected by spacious public rooms with molded ceilings and columns. With its recent improvements, the hotel has entered the 21st century in a premier position. Luxurious through and through, the bedrooms are well furnished. The hotel occupies 10 choice hectares (25 acres) of real estate in Torquay, sweeping down to Anstey's Cove.

Babbacombe Rd., Babbacombe, Torquay, Devon TQ1 3TG. ✆ **01803/200200.** Fax 01803/299899. www.palacetorquay.com. 141 units. £130–£230 double; £270–£310 suite. Rates include English breakfast. AE, DC, MC, V. Free parking. Bus: 32. From the town center, take B3199 east. **Amenities:** Restaurant; 2 bars; babysitting; croquet; exercise room; 9-hole golf course & putting green; 2 pools (1 indoor, 1 outdoor); room service; sauna; 2 squash courts; 6 tennis courts. *In room:* TV, hair dryer, minibar.

INEXPENSIVE

Colindale This hotel is a good, centrally located choice, opening onto King's Garden, a 5-minute walk from Corbyn Beach and a 3-minute walk from the railway station. Rooms are cozily furnished, in a range of sizes and shapes, each in a Victorian style. Colindale is one of a row of attached brick Victorian houses, with gables and chimneys.

20 Rathmore Rd., Chelston, Torquay, Devon TQ2 6NY. ✆ **01803/293947.** www.colindalehotel.co.uk. 8 units. £60–£65 double; £65–£75 superior room. Rates include English breakfast. MC, V. Free parking. No children 10 and under. **Amenities:** Breakfast room; TV lounge; bar. *In room:* TV, hair dryer, Wi-Fi (free).

Fairmount House Hotel ★ 🎒 Standing on a perch overlooking the Cockington Valley, this little haven of tranquillity is far removed from the bustle of the resort, lying in the residential valley of Chelston, on the periphery of Torquay. A converted Victorian building has been turned into a winning little B&B, with its gardens facing south. Torquay Harbour is within easy reach, and the sea is less than .6km (1 mile) away. The family home, complete with cellars and servants' quarters, dates from the turn of the 20th century. The atmosphere is more that of a large family home than a hotel. A highlight is the Victorian Conservatory Bar, with French doors opening onto the sun-trap patio that is sheltered from the wind. Bedrooms are midsize and tastefully furnished. Two garden rooms have a tub and shower. An evening dinner can be arranged in advance.

Herbert Rd., Chelston, Torquay, Devon TQ2 6RW. ✆/fax **01803/605446.** www.fairmounthousehotel. co.uk. 8 units. £50–£70 double. Rates include breakfast. MC, V. Free parking. **Amenities:** Restaurant; bar. *In room:* TV, hair dryer, no phone.

Meadfoot Bay Hotel ★ 🍃 This immaculate and well-maintained hotel was created from a Victorian family residence dating from 1850. It lies just north of Torquay harbor in a fine residential area, only 200m (656 ft.) from the unspoiled beach at Meadfoot Bay. Bedrooms are furnished with taste and charm, each individually decorated. Accommodations on the second floor have direct access to the garden or a balcony. The finest and most luxuriously furnished room is the St. Andrews Suite.

Meadfoot Sea Rd., Torquay, Devon TQ1 2LQ. ✆ **01803/294722.** www.meadfoot.com. 19 units. £39–£66 double; £79 suite. Rates include breakfast. MC, V. No children under 14. **Amenities:** Restaurant; bar. *In room:* TV/DVD, Wi-Fi (free).

Where to Dine

The Elephant ★★ MODERN BRITISH At long last Torquay, once a gastronomic wasteland, has a Michelin-starred restaurant. The location is on Torquay's seafront, with two dining options: the Brasserie, on the ground floor, and the Room, the formal upstairs space. Local suppliers furnish the chefs with the best of raw

The 56km-long (35-mile) **John Musgrave Heritage Trail** ★★, launched in early 2006, starts at Maidencombe, near Torquay, and winds its way across some of the most beautiful tracts of land in South Devon. A highlight of the trip is crossing the River Dart on the Dittisham Ferry (pedestrians only) to Greenway, once home to Agatha Christie. The path continues uphill after you get off the ferry, taking in panoramic views of the river. It comes to an end at Brixham Harbour.

materials, from which are concocted imaginative dishes that are precisely cooked. At the more relaxed Brasserie, you can feast on such starters as langoustine soup with celeriac turnovers or cannelloni of squid with braised beef, followed by such mains as filet of Norwegian halibut with scallop mousse or Cornish lamb breast and rack with a thyme jus. The Room offers the resort's best fixed-price dinner: A typical one might showcase boneless thornback ray wing with verjus and a spring onion butter sauce or rump filet steak with an oxtail and lentil ragout.

3–4 Beacon Terrace. ℂ **01803/200044.** www.elephantrestaurant.co.uk. Reservations not needed for Brasserie; required for the Room. Brasserie: 2-course lunch £23, 3-course lunch £27; 2-course dinner £27, 3-course dinner £33. The Room: tasting menu £48. AE, DC, MC, V. Brasserie: Tues–Sat noon–2pm and 6:30–9pm. The Room: Tues–Sat 7–9:30pm.

Orange Tree Restaurant ★ MODERN BRITISH   Set back from the seafront near Torquay Harbour, this restaurant has character, atmosphere, and good food. The chefs create innovative dishes and change the menus based on the best produce of the season. The wine *carte* is hailed as one of the best selections in South Devon. Among the starters, we like the Brixham crab bisque with king scallops and the rondelle of confit duck with foie gras. Main-dish temptations range from a "marriage" of locally caught pheasant and partridge to grilled prime West Devon filet steak with a brandy and green peppercorn sauce.

14–16 Parkhill Rd. ℂ **01803/213936.** www.orangetreerestaurant.co.uk. Reservations required. Main courses £15–£22. MC, V. Mon–Sat 7–9:30pm.

Palm Trees & Isadora Duncan

This area is known for offering one of the balmiest climates in Britain. It's so temperate (because of its proximity to the Gulf Stream) that subtropical plants such as palm trees and succulents thrive.

Oldway Mansion   You'll see the conspicuous consumption of England's Gilded Age here. The mansion was built in 1874 by Isaac Merritt Singer, founder of the sewing-machine empire. His son, Paris, enhanced its decor, massive Ionic portico, and 6.8 hectares (17 acres) of Italianate gardens. The mansion's eclectic interior includes a scaled-down version of the Hall of Mirrors in the Palace of Versailles. During its Jazz Age heyday, Oldway served as a rehearsal space and performance venue for Isadora Duncan, who was having a not-very-discreet affair with Paris.

Torbay Rd., in Preston, near Paignton (a short drive south of the center of Torquay on the main Paignton-Torquay Rd.). ℂ **01803/207933.** Free admission. Year-round Mon–Sat 9am–5pm; also summer Sun 2–5pm.

Torquay After Dark

Seven theaters in town, all open year-round, offer everything from Gilbert and Sullivan and tributes to Sinatra and Nat King Cole to Marine Band concerts and comedy shows. Among the most active are the **Palace Theatre,** Palace Avenue, Paignton (© **01803/665800;** www.palace-theatre.org.uk), and the **Princess Theatre,** Torbay Road (© **01803/290288;** www.princesstheatre.org.uk).

Fifteen area nightclubs cater to everyone from teeny-boppers to gays, but dancing rules the town, and there's virtually nowhere to catch live club acts. Among the better dance clubs are **Bohemia,** Torwood Street (© **01803/292079;** www.claires nightclub.co.uk), attracting 20-somethings with its Thursday-to-Sunday house music. The cover varies from £3 to £20.

TOTNES ★

361km (224 miles) SW of London; 19km (12 miles) NW of Dartmouth

One of the oldest towns in the West Country, Totnes rests quietly in the past, seemingly content to let the Torquay area remain in the vanguard of the building boom. On the River Dart, upstream from Dartmouth, Totnes has several historic buildings, notably the ruins of a Norman castle, an ancient guildhall, and the 15th-century Church of St. Mary. In the Middle Ages, the town was encircled by walls; the North Gate serves as a reminder of that period.

Essentials

GETTING THERE Totnes is on the main London-Plymouth line. Trains leave London's Paddington Station once an hour throughout the day, the trip taking 2¾ hours. For rail information, call © **08457/000125** or visit **www.firstgreat western.co.uk**.

If you're driving from Torquay, head west on the A385.

Between Easter and October, many visitors approach Totnes by river steamer from Dartmouth. Contact **Dartmouth River Boats,** 5 Lower St., Dartmouth (© **01803/555872;** www.dartmouthrailriver.co.uk), for information.

VISITOR INFORMATION The **Tourist Information Centre** is at the Town Mill, Coronation Road (© **01803/863168;** www.totnesinformation.co.uk). It's open April through October, Monday to Saturday 9:30am to 5pm; in the off-season, Monday to Friday 11am to 4pm and Saturday 10am to 1pm.

Where to Stay in the Area

Cott Inn ★ 📖 Built in 1320, this hotel is the second-oldest inn in England. It's a low, rambling two-story building of stone, cob, and plaster, with a thatched roof and 1m-thick (3-ft.) walls. The owners rent low-ceilinged double rooms upstairs, with modern conveniences. The refurbished rooms come in all shapes and sizes. The Cott Inn is a gathering place for the people of Dartington, and you'll feel the pulse of English country life here.

Dartington (near Totnes, on the old Ashburton-Totnes Tpk.), Devon TQ9 6HE. © **01803/863777.** Fax 01803/866629. www.greenekinginns.co.uk/devon/inn_02/index.htm. 7 units. £65–£80 double. Rates include breakfast. MC, V. Bus: X80 travels from Totnes to Dartington, but most people take a taxi for the 2.5km (1½-mile) journey. **Amenities:** Restaurant; bar. *In room:* TV, hair dryer.

Orchard House ★ 🌶   Lying between Totnes and Kingsbridge, this is a delightful little choice. It takes its name from the location, which is within an old cider orchard. It's a real find for those who appreciate the charms of bucolic Devon. The house enjoys a tranquil setting among mature gardens. Bedrooms are beautifully furnished, and each has a private bathroom with shower. Local produce is used in the English cooked breakfasts.

Horner, Halwell (near Totnes), Devon TQ9 7LB. ✆ **01548/821448.** www.orchard-house-halwell.co.uk. 3 units. £55–£60 double. Rates include breakfast. No credit cards. Closed Nov–Feb. Get off the A38 at the Buckfastleigh Totnes junction and follow the road into Totnes. Upon entering the town, turn right for Kingsbridge (A381) and drive to Habertonford. After passing a garage, take the 2nd right for 2.5km (1½ miles), turning right at the sign marked HORNER. Take the next right. Orchard House is the 2nd house on the left. **Amenities:** Breakfast room. *In room:* TV/DVD, hair dryer, MP3 docking station, no phone, Wi-Fi (free).

Royal Seven Stars Hotel   A historic former coaching inn in the center of Totnes, this hotel largely dates from 1660. It overlooks a square in the town center, near the banks of the River Dart. The interior courtyard, once used for horses and carriages, is now enclosed in glass, with an old pine staircase. Decorated with antiques, paintings, and the hotel's own heraldic shield, the courtyard forms an inviting entrance to the inn. The bedrooms have been modernized and outfitted with built-in furniture. Two rooms have four-poster beds.

The Plains, Totnes, Devon TQ9 5DD. ✆ **01803/862125.** Fax 01803/867925. www.royalsevenstars.co.uk. 16 units. £109–£159 double. Rates include English breakfast. AE, MC, V. **Amenities:** Restaurant (TQ9, reviewed below); 2 bars; room service. *In room:* TV, hair dryer, Wi-Fi (free).

Where to Dine

When it's teatime, **Greys Dining Room,** 96 High St. (✆ **01803/866369**), sets out its fine silver and china to welcome you in an atmosphere of wood paneling and antiques. About 40 different teas, along with homemade cakes and scones, will invite you to extend the afternoon. Open Wednesday to Saturday 10am to 5pm.

TQ9 Restaurant ENGLISH   For the kind of cuisine that pleased Grandpa, this old coaching inn delivers quite well. You can order a la carte at lunch, but only a set menu is offered at night. Start perhaps with the homemade chicken liver pâté with mango- and cinnamon-flavored chutney, or else the local mussels in a sauce of white wine, herbs, and garlic. Main-dish favorites include Devon rack of lamb in a red-wine jus or pan-fried Devon duck breast with a red-currant jus. Vegetables of the day are fresh and well prepared. Finish in the British manner with blue Stilton cheese or a fruit pie with clotted cream. The adjoining Saloon bar has a wide range of ales, wine, and spirits.

In the Royal Seven Stars Hotel, The Plains. ✆ **01803/862125.** Reservations recommended. Main courses £12–£16. AE, MC, V. Daily noon–2:30pm and 6:30–9:30pm.

Exploring Totnes

You need spend no more than 2 hours or so exploring the major monuments outlined below. With any time remaining, you can visit the **Buckfast Butterflies & Dartmoor Otter Sanctuary,** Buckfastleigh (✆ **01364/642916;** www.ottersand butterflies.co.uk), which is open only from April to October, daily 10am to 5:30pm. Admission is £5 for adults, £ 5 seniors, £2.50 for children 3 to 15. On display are exotic butterflies and moths from around the world, beautiful birds in landscaped gardens, and three different species of otter, along with native British otter.

Elizabethan Museum   This 16th-century home of a wealthy merchant houses furniture, costumes, documents, and farm implements of the Elizabethan age. One room is devoted to local resident Charles Babbage (1792–1871), a mathematician and inventor. He invented a calculating machine whose memory capacity categorized it as an early version of the computer. His other inventions included the ophthalmoscope, a speedometer, and the cowcatchers later used to nudge cows off the tracks of railways around the world.

70 Fore St. ✆ **01803/863821.** www.devonmuseums.net. Admission £2 adults, £1.50 seniors, 75p children. Mon–Fri 10:30am–5pm. Closed Nov to mid-Mar.

Totnes Castle   Crowning the hilltop at the northern end of High Street, this castle was built by the Normans shortly after their conquest of England. It's one of the best examples of motte-and-bailey construction remaining in the United Kingdom. Although the outer walls survived, the interior is mostly in ruins.

Castle St. ✆ **01803/864406.** www.englishheritage.org.uk. Admission £3.20 adults, £2.70 students and seniors, £1.60 children. Apr–June and Sept daily 10am–5pm; July–Aug daily 10am–6pm; Oct daily 10am–4pm. Closed Nov–Mar.

Totnes Guildhall   This symbol of Totnes, originally built as a priory (monastery) in 1553, contains an old gaol (jail), a collection of civic memorabilia, and the table Oliver Cromwell used to sign documents during his visit to Totnes in 1646.

Ramparts Walk. ✆ **01803/862147.** www.tothestowncouncil.gov.uk. Admission £1 adults, 25p children. Mon–Fri 10:30am–1:30pm and 2–4pm. Closed Oct–Mar.

DARTMOUTH ★★

380km (236 miles) SW of London; 56km (35 miles) S of Exeter

At the mouth of the River Dart, this ancient seaport is home of the Royal Naval College. Traditionally linked to England's maritime greatness, Dartmouth sent out the young midshipmen who saw to it that "Britannia ruled the waves." The Dart is Devon's most beautiful river, and you can see for yourself by taking a river steamer up the Dart to Totnes. Dartmouth's 15th-century castle was built during the reign of Edward IV. The town's most noted architectural feature is the Butter Walk, a row of 17th-century houses standing on granite pillars. A Flemish influence, acquired through trade during the Middle Ages, is evident in some of the houses.

Essentials

GETTING THERE   Dartmouth is not easily reached by public transport. Trains run to Totnes and Paignton. Buses run hourly between Totnes and Dartmouth. Call ✆ **0870/608-2608** or visit **www.stagecoachbus.com** for schedules.

If you're driving from Exeter, take the A38 southwest, cutting southeast to Totnes on the A381; then follow the A381 to the junction with the B3207.

Riverboats make the 16km (10-mile) run from Totnes to Dartmouth, but these trips depend on the tide and operate only from Easter to the end of October. Contact **Dartmouth River Boats,** 5 Lower St., Dartmouth (✆ **01803/555872;** www.dartmouthrailriver.co.uk), for information.

VISITOR INFORMATION   The **Tourist Information Centre** is at the Engine House, Mayors Avenue (© **01803/834224;** www.discoverdartmouth.com). It's open April through October, Monday to Saturday 9:30am to 5:30pm and Sunday 10am to 2pm; in the off-season, Monday to Saturday 9:30am to 4:30pm.

Where to Stay

The inns and hotels of Dartmouth are expensive. The tourist office keeps a list of guesthouses providing affordable bed-and-breakfast rates. Our favorites include the well-run **Hill View House,** 76 Victoria Rd., Dartmouth, Devon TQ6 9DZ (© **01803/839372;** www.hillviewdartmouth.co.uk), which offers five stylishly furnished, midsize bedrooms, each with a bathroom containing a tub or a shower. The five-story restored late-Victorian house lies near the town center and waterfront. Rates start at £70 for a double, with breakfast included. Diners Club, MasterCard, and Visa are accepted.

Another good choice is the family-run **Capritia Guest House,** 69 Victoria Rd., Dartmouth, Devon TQ6 9RX (© **01803/833419;** www.capritia.co.uk), offering four small to midsize, but comfortably furnished, bedrooms ranging from £70 to £75 for a double, including breakfast. Rooms have a TV, small fridge, hair dryer, and Wi-Fi. Credit cards are not accepted.

A final possibility is **Cladda,** 88–90 Victoria Rd., Dartmouth, Devon TQ6 9EF (© **01803/835957;** www.cladda-dartmouth.co.uk), a 1km (½-mile) walk from the center. There are six units here, including two suites (with lounge and kitchen) in a building next to the main house. Rates, which include a full English breakfast, are £70 for a double, from £125 for a suite. All units have a TV, fridge, hair dryer, and Wi-Fi. American Express, Diners Club, MasterCard, and Visa are accepted.

Dart Marina Hotel & Spa ★   This hotel—the town's "second choice"—sits at the edge of its own marina, within a 3-minute walk from the center of town. Originally built as a clubhouse for local yachties late in the 19th century, it was then enlarged and transformed into a hotel just before World War II. It does not have as much charm or character as the Royal Castle, but the bar, riverside terrace, and bedrooms afford a view of yachts bobbing at anchor in the River Dart. Bedrooms on the third floor enjoy the best views and are the most contemporary, with neutral tones. Some have French windows opening onto small balconies; others have a small terrace with chaise longues and chairs. The more traditional rooms downstairs are decorated in a simpler English-country-house style, and some also have small balconies. Families will appreciate the contemporary apartments that sleep four.

Sandquay, Dartmouth, Devon TQ6 9PH. © **01803/832580.** Fax 01803/835040. www.dartmarina.com. 50 units. £135–£185 double; £225 suite for 2; £150–£325 apt for 4. Rates include English breakfast. AE, MC, V. Free parking. **Amenities:** 3 restaurants; bar; exercise room; Jacuzzi; indoor heated pool; room service; spa; steam room. *In room:* A/C (in some), TV, hair dryer, minibar (in some).

Royal Castle Hotel ★   A coaching inn on the town quay since 1639, this is the leading choice in Dartmouth. The Royal Castle has hosted Sir Francis Drake, Queen Victoria, Charles II, and Edward VII. Horse-drawn carriages (as late as 1910) dispatched passengers in a carriageway, now an enclosed reception hall. The glassed-in courtyard, with its winding wooden staircase, has the original coaching horn and a set of 20 antique spring bells connected to the bedrooms. The rambling corridors display antiques. The river-view bedrooms are the most sought after. Three rooms open off the covered courtyard; three are air-conditioned; and eight offer a Jacuzzi. Five rooms contain a four-poster bed, and each is individually decorated, although all reflect the age of the building. Four units are large enough for families.

11 The Quay, Dartmouth, Devon TQ6 9PS. © **01803/833033.** Fax 01803/835445. www.royalcastle. co.uk. 25 units. £140–£185 double. Rates include English breakfast. AE, MC, V. Free parking. **Amenities:** Restaurant; 2 bars; babysitting; room service. *In room:* A/C (in some), TV, hair dryer, Wi-Fi (free).

Where to Dine

Kendricks Restaurant 🐟 BRITISH/INTERNATIONAL   One of the most reliable local eateries, patronized by visitors and locals alike, is this restaurant set in the heart of the historic port district. Local ingredients are used whenever possible in market-fresh dishes that range from succulent ribs to sizzling fajitas. On a windy day, the homemade soup with freshly baked bread is a favorite, though you can also begin with anything from nachos to goat-cheese salad with marinated olives. Steaks from rump to filet are a West Country feature, and we like the rack of succulent pork ribs. Other specialties include blackened salmon filets and the chef's own jambalaya with chicken and prawns (based on an old New Orleans recipe).

29 Fairfax Place. © **01803/832328.** www.kendricksrestaurant.co.uk. Reservations recommended. Main courses £8–£20. MC, V. Daily 6:30–10pm.

New Angel ★★ CONTINENTAL   The best and most stylish restaurant in town stands in a half-timbered building with a heavily carved facade, rising on the harbor front. Michelin-starred chef John Burton-Race has moved into town, awakening the sleepy local taste buds. His cookery is both innovative and well executed, more akin to the creative cuisine of the Continent than the traditional food of England. Fish is brought in from the local boats and purchased from Devon fishermen. The menu also utilizes the best and freshest produce of the day. Rich, subtly intermingled flavors are featured in such dishes as roasted breast of duckling with poached white peaches or braised Dartmouth lobster with a tomato-and-basil-butter sauce.

The New Angel also rents six well-furnished and quite comfortable bedrooms, including one suite, for £95 to £125 a night.

2 South Embankment. © **01803/839425.** www.thenewangel.co.uk. Reservations required. Main courses £19–£31; fixed-price 2-course menu £29, 3-course menu £34. AE, MC, V. Wed–Sun noon–2:30pm; Tues–Sat 6:30–9:30pm.

A Favorite Local Pub

Just a 2-minute walk from Bayard's Cove is one of our favorite pubs, the **Cherub,** 13 Higher St. (© **01803/832571;** www.the-cherub.co.uk). It was originally built in 1380 as the harbor master's house. Today, this charming pub is a great place to drink and dine on simple traditional British platters and bar snacks. There's a more formal dining room upstairs that serves a number of fish dishes, steaks, lamb, and duck. Main courses range from £11 to £15.

Exploring Dartmouth

Many visitors come to Dartmouth for the bracing salt air and a chance to explore the surrounding marshlands, which are rich in bird life and natural beauty. The way to do this is to book a cruise aboard **Dartmouth River Boats,** 5 Lower St., Dartmouth (© **01803/555872;** www.dartmouthrailriver.co.uk). Schedules vary according to the seasons. For tickets and information, go to the kiosk at the Dartmouth Embankment. A combination of stream train rides and river cruises is offered, with prices ranging from £10 to £20 for adults, £7.50 to £12 for children 3 to 15.

The town's most historic and interesting church is **St. Petrox,** on Castle Road, a 17th-century Anglican monument with an ivy-draped graveyard whose tombstones evoke the sorrows of Dartmouth's maritime past. The church is open daily from 7am to dusk.

It's also worth walking through **Bayard's Cove,** a waterfront, cobbled, half-timbered neighborhood that's quite charming. Set near the end of Lower Street, it prospered during the 1600s thanks to its ship-repair services. In 1620, its quays were the site for repairs of the Pilgrims' historic ships, the *Speedwell* and the *Mayflower,* just after their departure from Plymouth.

Dartmouth Castle   Originally built during the 15th century, the castle was later outfitted with artillery and employed by the Victorians as a coastal defense station. A tour of its bulky ramparts and somber interiors provides insight into the changing nature of warfare through the centuries, and you'll see sweeping views of the surrounding coast and flatlands.

Castle Rd. (1km/½ mile south of the town center). ℰ **01803/833588.** www.english-heritage.org.uk/server/show/nav.15498. Admission £4.50 adults, £3.80 seniors, £2.30 children. Apr–June and Sept daily 10am–5pm; July–Aug daily 10am–6pm; Oct daily 10am–4pm; Nov–Mar Sat–Sun 10am–4pm.

Dartmouth Museum   This is the region's most interesting maritime museum, focusing on the British Empire's military might of the 18th century. Built between 1635 and 1640, it's set amid an interconnected row of 17th-century buildings—the Butter Walk—whose overhanging, stilt-supported facade was originally designed to provide shade for the butter, milk, and cream sold there by local milkmaids. Today, the complex houses the museum, as well as shops selling wines, baked goods, and more.

The Butterwalk. ℰ **01803/832923.** www.dartmouth.org.uk. Admission £1.50 adults, £1 seniors, 50p children. Apr–Oct Mon–Sat 11am–5pm; Nov–Mar Mon–Fri noon–5pm.

PLYMOUTH ★★

390km (242 miles) SW of London; 259km (161 miles) SW of Southampton

The historic seaport of Plymouth is more romantic in legend than in reality. But this was not always so—during World War II, greater Plymouth lost at least 75,000 buildings to Nazi bombs. The heart of present-day Plymouth, including the municipal civic center on the Royal Parade, has been entirely rebuilt; however, the way it was rebuilt is the subject of much controversy. Instead of reconstructing half-timbered Elizabethan buildings, many property owners preferred the concrete bunker approach.

For the old part of town, you must go to the Elizabethan section, known as the **Barbican,** and walk along the quay in the footsteps of Sir Francis Drake (once the mayor of Plymouth). From here, in 1577, Drake set sail on his round-the-world voyage. The Barbican also holds special interest for visitors from the United States as the final departure point of the Pilgrims in 1620. The two ships, *Mayflower* and *Speedwell,* that sailed from Southampton in August of that year put into Plymouth after suffering storm damage. The *Speedwell* was abandoned as unseaworthy; the *Mayflower* made the trip to the New World alone.

Essentials

GETTING THERE   **Plymouth Airport** (© 01752/204090; www.plymouthcity.co.uk/airport.html) lies 6.5km (4 miles) from the center of the city. **Air Southwest** (© 0870/241-8202; www.airsouthwest.com) has direct service from London's Gatwick Airport to Plymouth.

Frequent trains run from London's Paddington Station to Plymouth; the trip takes 3¼ to 4 hours. For rail information, call © 08457/000125 or visit **www.firstgreatwestern.co.uk**. In Plymouth, the rail station is on North Road, north of the center. Bus no. 83/84 (operated by Western National) runs from the rail station to the heart of Plymouth.

National Express (© 0871/781-8181; www.nationalexpress.com) has frequent daily bus service between London's Victoria Coach Station and Plymouth. The trip takes 5¼ hours.

If you're driving from London, take the M4 west to the junction with the M5 going south to Exeter. From Exeter, head southwest on the A38 to Plymouth.

VISITOR INFORMATION   The **Tourist Information Centre** is at the Mayflower, in the Barbican (© 01752/306330; www.visitplymouth.co.uk). It's open Easter through October, Monday to Saturday 9am to 5pm and Sunday 10am to 4pm; in the off-season, Monday to Friday 9am to 5pm and Saturday 10am to 4pm,

Where to Stay

Astor Hotel   This appealing and restored hotel is better than ever following massive improvements. It was once the private home of a sea captain during the Victorian era. The best rooms are the so-called executive suites, with four-poster beds, and even better are the bridal suites, with both four-posters and Jacuzzis. Of course, you don't have to be a honeymooner to book any of these. Even the mostly midsize standard rooms are exceedingly comfortable. You won't need to leave the premises at night, as there is a cozy lounge bar and a first-class restaurant serving both traditional British and international cuisine.

14–22 Elliott St., The Hoe, Plymouth, Devon PL1 2PS. © **01752/225511.** Fax 01752/251994. www.astorhotel.co.uk. 62 units. £160 double; £200 family room; £250–£400 suite. Rates include English breakfast. AE, DC, MC, V. Free parking overnight, £2.50 permit parking nearby. **Amenities:** Restaurant; 2 bars; room service. *In room:* TV.

Caledonia Guest House 🍃   This eco-friendly lodging is spread across three floors of a restored Victorian house, lying only a 2-minute walk from Plymouth Hoe, with views across Plymouth Sound. Dave and Karen Marshall run one of the best B&Bs in town, welcoming you at affordable prices. The immaculate bedrooms are individually designed and comfortably furnished.

27 Athenaeum St., The Hoe, Plymouth, Devon PL1 2RQ. © **01752/229052.** www.thecaledonia.co.uk. 7 units (6 with bathroom). £46 double without bathroom; £52–£65 double with bathroom. Rates include English breakfast. AE, MC, V. **Amenities:** Breakfast room. *In room:* TV, hair dryer, Wi-Fi (free).

Duke of Cornwall Hotel ★   This Best Western property is a Victorian Gothic building that survived World War II bombings. Constructed in 1863, it was regarded by Sir John Betjeman as the finest example of Victorian architecture in Plymouth. The refurbished bedrooms are comfortable and well maintained. Four rooms contain antique four-poster beds, and six units are large enough for families.

Millbay Rd., Plymouth, Devon PL1 3LG. (℃) **800/780-7234** in the U.S., or 01752/275850. Fax 01752/275854. www.thedukeofcornwallhotel.com. 72 units. £130–£180 double; £165–£230 suite. Rates include English breakfast. AE, DC, MC, V. Free parking. **Amenities:** Restaurant (see review below); bar; babysitting; room service. *In room:* TV, hair dryer, Internet (in some; £10), Wi-Fi (in some; £10 per day).

Holiday Inn Plymouth ★   One of the most distinguished hotels in the West Country, overlooking the harbor and the Hoe, this chain-run hotel is a midget high-rise. It is the town's finest address, superior to the long-standing Duke of Cornwall. The good-size rooms are outfitted with long double beds, wide picture windows, and compact bathrooms that have tub/shower combos. The decor is tasteful, in neutral browns and creams, and the overall atmosphere is casual and comfortable.

Armada Way, Plymouth, Devon PL1 2HJ. (℃) **888/465-4329** in the U.S., or 1752/639900. Fax 01752/673816. www.ichotelsgroup.com. 211 units. £99–£164 double. AE, DC, MC, V. Parking £3. **Amenities:** Restaurant; 2 bars; babysitting; health club; indoor pool; room service; sauna; solarium; spa. *In room:* A/C, TV, hair dryer, minibar (in executive rooms), Wi-Fi (£5 per day).

Where to Dine

The **Plymouth Arts Centre Restaurant,** 38 Looe St. ((℃) **01752/202616;** www.plymouthartscentre.org), offers one of the most filling and down-home vegetarian meals in town. Prices range from £3.50 to £12; it's also the ideal spot for a snack. You can even see a movie downstairs if you'd like. Food is served in the Green Room Tuesday through Saturday from 11am to 8:30pm.

Duke of Cornwall Restaurant ★ MODERN BRITISH   This landmark hotel dining room is one of the finest in the area. A Victorian chandelier illuminates the elegant setting. Traditional and classic favorites are included on the menu, but the taste is definitely contemporary English. High-quality ingredients are seriously and professionally prepared. Bold—but never outrageous—combinations of flavors are reflected by starters such as goat cheese with crispy pancetta and maple syrup, or smoked salmon with a halibut gâteau, cucumber "ribbons," and sweet chili vinaigrette. Among the main courses, we especially like the chargrilled rib-eye steak flavored with brandy and a peppercorn glaze, as well as the chicken breast stuffed with sun-dried tomatoes and fresh basil with an herb pesto. For dessert, finish off with a white chocolate and pistachio confection drizzled with bitter chocolate syrup. Service is first class, and there's also a good wine list.

In the Duke of Cornwall Hotel, Millbay Rd. (℃) **01752/275850.** Reservations recommended. Main courses £13–£22. AE, DC, MC, V. Daily 7–10pm.

Tanners Restaurant ★★ ENGLISH/MEDITERRANEAN   Chris and James Tanner, who welcome you to this citadel of fine cuisine, are often seen on TV food programs in Britain. Plymouth's leading restaurant lies in a character-filled 15th-century house, reputedly the oldest in town, with mullioned windows, exposed stone, antique tapestries, and even an illuminated water well. In spite of the antique surroundings near the Theatre Royal and the city's Guildhall, the cuisine is contemporary, with much use made of market-fresh ingredients. As befits a port city, you get plenty of fish. Depending on the time of year, tempting starters may include seared local mackerel with a superb lobster risotto, or else roasted wood pigeon with vanilla-flavored shallots and a sherry vinegar reduction. For a main, taste the likes of seared filet of brill with smoked salmon croquettes or roast partridge in a fresh thyme sauce.

Prysten House, Finewell St. ℂ **01752/252001.** www.tannersrestaurant.com. Reservations required. 2-course lunch £18, 3-course lunch £23; Mon–Thurs 2-course dinner £32, 3-course dinner £39; Fri–Sat 6-course dinner £48. AE, DC, MC, V. Tues–Fri noon–2:30pm; Sat noon–2pm; Tues–Sat 7–9pm.

Seeing the Sights

To commemorate the spot from which the *Mayflower* sailed for the New World, a white archway, erected in 1934 and capped with the flags of Great Britain and the United States, stands at the base of Plymouth's West Pier, on the Barbican. Incorporating a granite monument that was erected in 1891, the site is referred to as both the *Mayflower* **Steps** and the **Memorial Gateway.**

The **Barbican** is a mass of narrow streets, old houses, and quay-side shops selling antiques, brass work, old prints, and books. It's a perfect place for strolling and browsing through shops at your leisure.

Fishing boats still unload their catches at the wharves, and passenger-carrying ferryboats run short harbor cruises. The best way to view Plymouth, in our opinion, is to take one of the boat trips offered by **Tamar Cruising & Cremyll Ferry,** Cremyll Quay, Cremyll, Torpoint (ℂ **01752/822105;** www.tamarcruising.com). Not only will you get to see Plymouth from a nautical perspective, but you'll also experience an added thrill by knowing that this was the pilgrims' last view of England before departing for the New World. The trip includes views from the water of Drake's Island in the sound, the dockyards, naval vessels, and the Hoe—a greenbelt in the center of the city that opens onto Plymouth Harbour. A cruise of Plymouth Harbour is £8.50 for adults, £5 for children 5 to 15, and free for children 4 and under. Departures are April through October, with cruises leaving every half-hour from 10am to 4pm daily. Call for the latest schedule and price details.

National Marine Aquarium ★ The best aquarium in the United Kingdom stands near the center of the harbor area, displaying both freshwater and seawater fish, even a shark theater. At least three times a week, visitors can watch in awe as the sharks feed, putting on a gruesome *Jaws*-like show. You can even walk under the sharks in their holding tank. The institution, fearing many sea creatures are being destroyed, also engages in such work as a breeding program for sea horses. There are many other exhibits as well.

Rope Walk, Coxside. ℂ **01752/600301.** www.national-aquarium.co.uk. Admission £11 adults, £9 students and seniors, £6.50 children 5–16, £30 family ticket, free for children 4 and younger. Apr–Oct daily 10am–6pm; Nov–Mar daily 10am–5pm.

Plymouth Gin Distillery One of Plymouth's oldest surviving buildings, this is where the Pilgrims met before sailing for the New World. Plymouth Gin has been produced here for 200 years on a historic site that dates back to a Dominican monastery built in 1425. Public guided tours (including a tasting) are offered, and a Plymouth Gin Shop is on the premises.

Black Friars Distillery, 60 Southside St. ℂ **01752/665292.** www.plymouthgin.com. Admission £6 adults, free for children with paying adult. Nov–Easter Sat daily 9am–5pm; Easter Mon–Oct daily 9am–5:30pm. Closed Dec 25 and Easter. Bus: 54.

Prysten House Built in 1490 as a town house close to St. Andrew's Church, this is now a church house and working museum. Reconstructed in the 1930s with American help, it displays a model of Plymouth in 1620 and tapestries depicting the colonization of America. At the entrance is the gravestone of the captain of the U.S. brig *Argus,* who died on August 15, 1813, after a battle in the English Channel.

Finewell St. © **01752/661414.** Admission £1 adults, 50p children. Mon–Sat 10am–4pm.

CLOVELLY ★★

386km (240 miles) SW of London; 18km (11 miles) SW of Bideford

This is the most charming of all Devon villages and one of the main attractions of the West Country. Starting at a great height, the village cascades down the mountainside. Its narrow, cobblestone High Street makes driving impossible. You park your car at the top and make the trip on foot; supplies are carried down by donkeys. Every step of the way provides views of tiny cottages, with their terraces of flowers lining the main street. The village fleet is sheltered at the stone quay at the bottom.

The major sight of Clovelly is Clovelly itself. Victorian author Charles Kingsley once said, "It is as if the place had stood still while all the world had been rushing and rumbling past it." The price of entry to the village (see below) includes a guided tour of a fisherman's cottage as it would have been at the end of the 1800s. For the same price, you can also visit the **Kingsley Exhibition.** Author of *Westward Ho!,* Kingsley lived in Clovelly while his father was curate at the church. This exhibition traces the story of his life. He was also a social reformer, which led him to write his enduring children's classic, *The Water Babies.*

Right down below the Kingsley Exhibition—and our shopping note for the town—is a **crafts gallery** where you have a chance to see and buy a wide variety of works by local artists and craftspeople. Once you've reached the end, you can sit and relax on the quay, taking in the views and absorbing Clovelly's unique atmosphere from this tiny, beautifully restored 14th-century quay.

Once you've worked your way to the bottom, how do you get back up? You can climb back up the steep cobbled streets to the top and the parking lot. Or you can go to the rear of the Red Lion Inn and line up for a Land Rover. In summer, the line is often long.

Insider's tip: To avoid the tourist crowd, stay out of Clovelly from around 11am until teatime. When the midday congestion is at its height, visit nearby villages such as Bucks Mills (5km/3 miles to the east) and Hartland Quay (6.5km/4 miles to the west).

Essentials

GETTING THERE From London's Paddington Station, trains depart for Exeter frequently. At Exeter, transfer to a train headed for the end destination of Barnstaple. Travel time from Exeter to Barnstaple is 1¼ hours. For rail information, call © **0845/7484950** or visit **www.nationalrail.co.uk**. From Barnstaple, passengers transfer to Clovelly by bus.

From Barnstaple, about one bus per hour, operated by either the Red Bus Company or the Filers Bus Company, goes to Bideford. The trip takes 40 minutes. At Bideford, connecting buses—with no more than a 10-minute wait between arrival and departure—continue on for the 30-minute drive to Clovelly. Two Land Rovers make continuous round-trips to the Red Lion Inn from the top of the hill. The Clovelly Visitor Centre (see below) maintains up-to-the-minute transportation information about getting to Clovelly, depending on your location.

If driving from London, head west on the M4, cutting south at the junction with the M5. At the junction near Bridgewater, continue west along the A39 toward Lynton. The A39 runs all the way to the signposted turnoff for Clovelly.

VISITOR INFORMATION Go to the **Clovelly Visitor Centre** (© **01237/ 431781;** www.clovelly.co.uk), where you'll pay £5.75 for adults and £3.65 for kids 7 to 16, or £16 for a family ticket, for the cost of parking, use of facilities, entrance to the village, and admission to an audiovisual theater, offering a multiprojector show tracing the story of Clovelly from 2000 B.C. Also included in the price is a tour of a fisherman's cottage and admission to the Kingsley Exhibition (see above). The center is open July through September, daily 10am to 4pm; April through June and October, Monday to Saturday 9am to 5:30pm; and November through March, daily 9am to 4:30pm. If you're booked into one of the inns in the village, you don't have to pay the entrance fee.

Where to Stay & Dine

New Inn Hotel About halfway down High Street is the village pub, a good meeting place at sundown. It offers the best lodgings in Clovelly, in two buildings on opposite sides of the steep street (but only a 3.5m/12-ft. leap between balconies). Each room is relatively small but comfortable, and two are large enough for families. If you're driving, you can park in the lot at the entrance to the town. It's advisable to pack a smaller overnight bag because your luggage will have to be carried down (but is returned to the top by donkey).

High St., Clovelly, Devon EX39 5TQ. © **01237/431303.** Fax 01237/431636. www.clovelly.co.uk. 19 units, 8 with bathroom. £103–£113 double without bathroom, £148–£158 double with bathroom. Rates include English breakfast. AE, MC, V. **Amenities:** Restaurant; bar. *In room:* TV, Wi-Fi (free).

Red Lion Hotel At the bottom of the steep cobbled street, right on the stone seawall of the little harbor, the Red Lion occupies the prime position in the village. Rising three stories with gables and a courtyard, it's actually an unspoiled country inn where life centers on an antique pub, filled with village inhabitants (including sea captains) who gather to satisfy their thirst over pints of ale. The bedrooms have been refurbished; most look directly onto the sea with spectacular views. Many are small, but two are spacious enough for a family.

The Quay, Clovelly, Devon EX39 5TF. © **01237/431237.** Fax 01237/431044. www.clovelly.co.uk. 11 units. £124–£134 double. Rates include English breakfast. AE, MC, V. **Amenities:** Restaurant; bar. *In room:* TV, hair dryer.

En Route to Lynton-Lynmouth: A Stay on a Working Farm

Halmpstone Manor ★ 🏠 This working farm in the countryside is operated by Charles and Jane Stanbury. Originally built in the 11th century as a manor house with 22 rooms, the structure has diminished in size because of two fires that occurred in the 15th and 16th centuries. The edifice was rebuilt in 1701 in its present form, with 15th-century paneling located in the dining room and high ceilings in the four-poster bedrooms. Family heirlooms are scattered throughout, and all the

spacious bedrooms are a regal statement of English taste, luxuriously furnished with either four-poster or brass and coronet beds.

Chittlehampton Rd., Bishop's Tawton, Barnstaple, Devon EX32 0EA. (📞 **01271/830321.** Fax 01271/830826. www.halmpstonemanor.co.uk. 5 units. £100 double; £140 suite. Rates include English breakfast and afternoon tea. MC, V. From Clovelly, take A39 east for 30–45 min., turning off the A39 when you see signs for Chittlehampton. About 3km (2 miles) after the turnoff, you'll see signs pointing to Halmpstone Manor. **Amenities:** Restaurant; bar. *In room:* TV, hair dryer.

LYNTON-LYNMOUTH ★

332km (206 miles) W of London; 95km (59 miles) NW of Exeter

Our favorite places to stay along the rugged northern coast of Devon are the twin Victorian villages of Lynton and Lynmouth. The harbor town is Lynmouth, and the higher town is Lynton, rising 183m (600 ft.) over the port. The two villages are linked by a cliff railway.

Artists such as Gainsborough have long been attracted to the area for its scenic views. He called Lynmouth "the most delightful place for a landscape painter this country can boast." Other artists and writers drawn to the area include Shelley, who honeymooned here with his 16-year-old bride, Harriet Westbrook. He wrote *Queen Mab* here.

Summer visitors come here to take boat trips along the Exmoor Coast and to explore the surrounding wooded valleys with waterfalls. From the North Devon cliffs, you can see some of the greatest views in the West Country, looking across the Bristol Channel to the Welsh coast.

Essentials

GETTING THERE The town is rather remote, and the local tourist office recommends that you rent a car to get here. However, local daily trains from Exeter arrive at Barnstaple. For rail information, call (📞 **0845/7484950** or visit **www.national rail.co.uk**.

From Barnstaple, bus service is provided to Lynton at a frequency of about one per hour. Call (📞 **01598/752225** for schedules.

If you're driving, take the M4 west from London to the junction with the M5, and then head south to the junction with the A39. Continue west on the A39 to Lynton-Lynmouth.

VISITOR INFORMATION The **Tourist Information Centre** is at the Town Hall, Lee Road, Lynton (📞 **0845/660-3232;** www.lynton-lynmouth-tourism. co.uk). It's open Easter to October, Monday to Saturday 9:30am to 5pm and Sunday 10am to 4pm; and November to Easter, Monday to Saturday 10am to 4pm and Sunday 10am to 2pm.

Where to Stay & Dine

Hewitt's at the Hoe Hewitt's is named for Sir Thomas Hewitt, who helped construct the funicular railway that links the twin resorts. In the 1860s, he also built a home for himself, and today that place is one of the most successful small hotels in Lynton. Situated on some 11 hectares (27 acres), it opens onto the beautiful vistas of Lynmouth Bay (best enjoyed while seated on a sunny terrace). The old house is filled with architectural character, as exemplified by its grand staircase, time-mellowed paneling, antiques, and stained-glass windows. All bedrooms are comfortably appointed. The hotel is "for all seasons" and has a country-house atmosphere. It's a perfect Agatha Christie set, enhanced by a pianist who plays in the lobby nightly from 6:30 to 8pm.

The Hoe, North Walk, Lynton, Devon EX35 6HJ. © **01598/752293.** Fax 01598/752489. www.hewitts hotel.co.uk. 5 units. £120–£180 double; from £370 serviced apt for 3 (per week). AE, MC, V. Free parking. **Amenities:** Restaurant; bar; Jacuzzi; room service. *In room:* TV, hair dryer, minibar.

Rising Sun ★★   Bask in the wonder and warmth of an inn that has been in business for more than 600 years. Following a renovation under the direction of an international designer from London, the Rising Sun's bedrooms (and bathrooms) look more glamorous and romantic than ever, many with four-poster beds. Stylish and tasteful fabrics were used extensively to give the accommodations more elegance. Behind the inn, halfway up the cliff, a tiny garden brightens with flowers in summer. The owner also has rooms available in nearby Shelley's Cottage, where the poet honeymooned in 1812.

The Harbourside, Lynmouth, Devon EX35 6EG. © **01598/753223.** Fax 01598/753480. www.risingsun lynmouth.co.uk. 16 units, 1 cottage. £120–£150 double; £160 Shelley's Cottage for 2. Rates include English breakfast. MC, V. Parking £5. No children 6 and under. **Amenities:** Restaurant; bar; room service. *In room:* TV, hair dryer.

St. Vincent House ★   This charming house was built by a master mariner in 1834 and has since been sensitively converted to receive guests. Capt. Thomas Green fought alongside Admiral Nelson at the Battle of St. Vincent off the west coast of Portugal, hence the name of the house. All of the well-furnished and comfortable bedrooms were named after victorious battleships. Many of the original features of the seaman's home, including a beautiful Regency spiral staircase, have been retained. Belgian innkeeper Jean-Paul Saltpetier and his partner, Linda Cameron, will house and feed you well. In the traditional guest lounge, visitors can enjoy an open fire on chilly nights.

Castle Hill, Lynton, Devon EX35 6JA. © **01598/752244.** Fax 01598/752244. www.st-vincent-hotel. co.uk. 7 units. £38 per person double. No credit cards. Free parking. Closed Nov–Easter. **Amenities:** Restaurant; lounge. *In room:* TV, hair dryer, Wi-Fi (free).

Shelley's Hotel ★   Established more than 2 centuries ago, "Mrs. Hooper's Lodgings" was where the Romantic poet brought his child bride, Harriet Westbrook, in 1812. Today, it's been transformed into a remarkable little hotel of charm and grace. (Shelley left without paying his bill, incidentally.) In the center of the village, the hotel, opening onto views of Lynmouth Bay, has been tastefully restored and individually decorated, some of its handsomely furnished bedrooms with their own private conservatory and balcony. Big windows make the rooms bright when the sun is shining, and the staff is most helpful and welcoming.

8 Watersmeet Rd., Lynmouth EX35 6EP. © **01598/753219.** Fax 01598/753751. www.shelleyshotel.co. uk. 11 units. £99–£140 double. MC, V. Parking £3. **Amenities:** Breakfast room; bar. *In room:* TV, hair dryer.

Tors Hotel   Set high on a cliff, the Tors Hotel opens onto a view of the coastline and the bay. It was built in 1895 in the fashion of a Swiss château, with more than 40 gables, Tyrolean balconies jutting out to capture the sun (or the moon), and some 30 chimneys. The interior has been modernized, and much attention has been lavished on the comfortable bedrooms, five of which are large enough for families. The superior rooms all have sea views. All units contain well-maintained bathrooms with tub/shower combos.

Tors Park, Lynmouth, Lynton, Devon EX35 6NA. ⓒ **01598/753236.** Fax 01598/752544. www.tors lynmouth.co.uk. 31 units. £80–£152 double; £264 suite. Rates include English breakfast. AE, DC, MC, V. Free parking. Closed Jan–Feb. **Amenities:** Restaurant; bar; heated outdoor pool; room service. *In room:* TV, hair dryer.

Victoria Lodge This elegant hotel, west of Church Hill, is imbued with a Victorian theme throughout, following a complete refurbishing. It's known locally for its comfort and cuisine. Each centrally heated bedroom is decorated in a Victorian motif; some deluxe units have four-poster beds. The cuisine is a fairly standard blend of English and Continental; vegetarian and special diets can be accommodated.

Lee Rd., Lynton, Devon EX35 6BS. ⓒ/fax **01598/753203.** www.victorialodge.co.uk. 9 units. £70–£140 double. Rates include English breakfast. 2-night minimum Sat–Sun. MC, V. Free parking. Closed Nov–Mar. No children 11 and under. **Amenities:** Breakfast room; bar. *In room:* TV, hair dryer, no phone.

Seeing the Sights

Lynton is linked to its twin, Lynmouth, by the most celebrated railway in Devon, the **Lynton & Lynmouth Cliff Railway** (ⓒ 01598/753486; www.cliffrailwaylynton. co.uk). The century-old train uses no electricity and no power. Instead, the railway covers the differences in distance and altitude by means of a complicated network of cables and pulleys, allowing cars to travel up and down the face of the rocky cliff. The length of the track is 259m (862 ft.) with a gradient of 2.5cm (1 in.), which gives it a vertical height of approximately 150m (500 ft.). The two passenger cars are linked together with two steel cables, and the operation of the lift is on the counterbalance system, which is simply explained as a pair of scales where one side, when weighted by a water ballast, pulls the other up. The train carries about 40 passengers at a time for £2.85 adults, £1.85 children, each a round-trip ticket. Trains depart daily from March to October, at 2- to 5-minute intervals between 10am and 5pm. In peak summer season, trains often run until 8 or 9pm. From November to February, the line is shut down.

For hikers, the area abounds in trails, the most dramatic being west along North Walk, a 1.6km (1-mile) trail leading to the **Valley of the Rocks ★**. This grouping of rugged rock formations rises from a grass-covered valley to peaks of bare sandstone and shale; it's said to have been carved during the Ice Age by the harsh winds from the Bristol Channel. Locals have given names to many of these rocks, including the "Devil's Cheesewring." The centerpiece of the formation is Castle Rock, known for its resident herd of wild goats.

To learn more about the best hikes in the area, go to the tourist office (see above) and pick up a copy of *Walking in North Devon,* which outlines the best North Devon walks with the most varied scenery. Over the years, we have taken most of these walks, with our favorite being the **Lyn Gorge ★**, stretching for 8km (5 miles). This walk begins at the Hillsford Bridge on the A39 south of Lynmouth. Details of all these walks can also be downloaded at **www.devon-holiday.co.uk/walks.html**.

CORNWALL: THE ANCIENT DUCHY

The ancient duchy of Cornwall is in the extreme southwestern part of England, often called "the toe." This peninsula is a virtual island—culturally if not geographically. Encircled by coastline, it abounds in rugged cliffs, hidden bays, fishing villages, sandy beaches, and sheltered coves where smuggling was once rampant. Though many of the seaports with hillside cottages resemble towns on the Mediterranean, Cornwall retains its own distinctive flavor.

The ancient land had its own language until about 250 years ago, and some of the old words (*pol* for pool, *tre* for house) still survive. The Cornish dialect is more easily understood by the Welsh than by those who speak the queen's English.

We suggest basing yourself at one of the smaller fishing villages, such as **East Looe** or **West Looe, Polperro,** or **Mousehole,** where you'll experience the true charm of the duchy. Many of the villages, such as **St. Ives,** are artists' colonies. Except for St. Ives and **Port Isaac,** some of the best places lie on the southern coast, often hyped as the **Cornish Riviera** (though the north coast has its own peculiar charm as well). The majestic coastline is studded with fishing villages and hidden coves for swimming, which are best seen at East or West Looe and especially at Polperro, which are the most evocative. Visit these little ports even if you have to skip the rest. A little farther west is **Land's End,** where England actually comes to an end. And the **Isles of Scilly,** 43km (27 miles) off the Cornish coast, have only five islands inhabited out of more than 100. Here you'll find the **Tresco Abbey Garden,** 297 hectares (735 acres) with 5,000 species of plants. Finally, a trip to this region is incomplete without a visit to **Tintagel Castle,** linked with the legends of King Arthur, Lancelot, and Merlin.

THE FISHING VILLAGES OF LOOE & POLPERRO ★

Looe: 425km (264 miles) SW of London, 32km (20 miles) W of Plymouth; Polperro: 463km (271 miles) SW of London, 42km (26 miles) W of Plymouth, 9.5km (6 miles) SW of Looe

The ancient twin towns of **East Looe** and **West Looe** are connected by a seven-arched stone bridge that spans the River Looe. Houses on the hills are stacked one on top of the other in terrace fashion. In each fishing village are good accommodations.

The old fishing village of **Polperro,** surrounded by cliffs, is one of the handsomest settlements in Cornwall, with parts of it harkening back to the 17th century. The village is reached by a steep descent from the top of a hill from the main road. You can take the 7km (4½-mile) cliff walk from Looe to Polperro, but the less adventurous will want to drive. However, in July and August you're not allowed to take cars into town unless you have a hotel reservation, in order to prevent traffic bottlenecks. A large parking area charges according to the length of your stay. For those unable to walk, a horse-drawn bus will take visitors to the town center.

The neighboring settlements of **Lanreath** and **Pelynt** are two Cornish villages with accommodations for those seeking lodgings outside Polperro. Like many Cornish villages, they're steeped in legend—ghosts, headless horses, and the like—and actually date back to the Domesday Book of 1086. The tiny villages are relatively devoid of attractions and sustain themselves by farming and summer tourism.

Fishing and sailing are two of the major activities in the area, and the sandy coves, as well as **East Looe Beach,** are spots for sea bathing. Beyond the towns are cliff paths and chalky downs worth a ramble. Looe is noted for its shark fishing, but you may prefer simply walking the narrow, crooked medieval streets of East Looe, with its old harbor and 17th-century guildhall.

Essentials

GETTING THERE   Daily trains run from Plymouth to Looe, and rail connections can also be made from Exeter (Devon) and Bristol (Somerset). Most visitors drive to Polperro, but the nearest main-line station is at Liskeard, 3½ hours from London's Paddington Station, with a branch line to Looe. Taxis meet incoming trains to take visitors to the various little villages in the area. For rail information in the area, call ℂ 0845/748-4950 or visit **www.nationalrail.co.uk**.

Local bus companies operate various routes from Plymouth to Looe. Ask for a schedule at the Tourist Information Centre in Plymouth (p. 425). You can take a local bus to Polperro from Liskeard or Looe.

If you're driving to Looe from Plymouth, take the A38 west, and then the B3253. To get to Polperro, follow the A387 southwest from Looe.

VISITOR INFORMATION   The **Tourist Information Centre** is at the Guildhall, Fore Street (ℂ 01503/262072; www.visit-southeastcornwall.co.uk). It's open April to September, daily 10am to 5pm, and October to March, Monday to Friday 10am to noon.

Where to Stay & Dine in & Around Looe

Barclay House   This family-operated country-house hotel stands on a wooded hillside surrounded by 2.4 hectares (6 acres) of private woodlands overlooking the

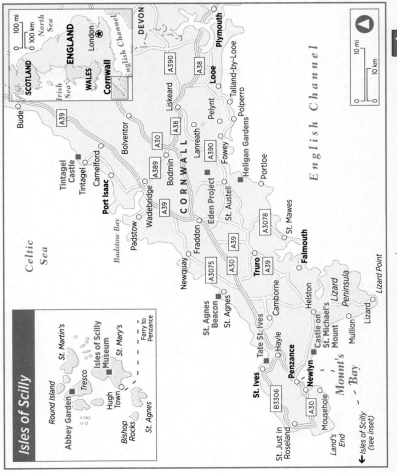

Looe River Valley, but it's also just on the edge of town at the entrance to Looe, and about a 5-minute walk from the harbor and the center of the resort. Units are spacious and fitted with soft twins or a king-size bed.

St. Martins Rd. (the main Plymouth-Looe Rd., B3253), East Looe, Cornwall PL13 1LP. ☎ **01503/262929.** www.barclayhouse.co.uk. 12 units, 8 cottages. £115–£145 double; £299–£1,399 cottage per week. Rates (except cottages) include English breakfast. AE, MC, V. **Amenities:** Restaurant; bar; babysitting; outdoor heated pool; room service. *In room:* TV, hair dryer.

Fieldhead Hotel ☺   The Fieldhead, built in 1896 as a private home, is now one of the area's best hotels. Commanding a view of the sea, it is situated on .8 hectare (2 acres) of gardens. The well-maintained rooms are warm and inviting, with a high standard of traditional furnishings; most of them open onto panoramic views of St. George's Island and the bay. *Note:* Families will like not only the kid-friendly management here, but also the location in a garden setting, where even young children can play in safety.

Portuan Rd., Hannafore, West Looe, Cornwall PL13 2DR. © **01503/262689.** Fax 01503/264114. www.fieldheadhotel.co.uk. 16 units. £96–£170 double. Rates include English breakfast. AE, MC, V. **Amenities:** Restaurant; bar; outdoor heated pool; room service. *In room:* TV, hair dryer.

Talland Bay Hotel ★   A country house dating from the 16th century, situated on 1 hectare (2½ acres), this hotel is the domain of George and Mary Granville, who will direct you to local beaches and the croquet lawn. Its rectangular swimming pool is ringed with flagstones and a semitropical garden. Views from the tastefully furnished bedrooms include the sea and rocky coastline. Some units are in a comfortable annex.

Talland-by-Looe, Porthallow, Cornwall PL13 2JB. © **01503/272667.** Fax 01503/272940. www.tallandbayhotel.co.uk. 23 units. Oct–Apr £145–£185 double; May–Sept £145–£195 double; year-round from £245–£285 suite. Rates include English breakfast and dinner. MC, V. Take A387 6.5km (4 miles) southwest of Looe. **Amenities:** Restaurant; bar; babysitting; heated outdoor pool; room service; lawn tennis. *In room:* TV, hair dryer.

Well House ★ ☺   The Well House is one of those *restaurants avec chambres* found occasionally in the West Country, and it's one of the best. Located 5km (3 miles) from Liskeard, it has 2 hectares (5 acres) of gardens opening onto vistas of the Looe Valley. It offers beautifully furnished bedrooms, with many thoughtful extras such as fresh flowers. Two lovely terrace rooms are at the garden level. Most rooms have a twin bed or else a large double. Families are welcomed into extra-large rooms; especially popular is the family suite, with one large double bedroom plus a twin-bedded unit.

St. Keyne, Liskeard, Cornwall PL14 4RN. © **01579/342001.** Fax 01579/343891. www.wellhouse.co.uk. 9 units. £155–£215 double; £255 family suite. Rates include English breakfast. MC, V. From Liskeard, take B3254 to St. Keyne, 5km (3 miles) away. **Amenities:** Restaurant; bar; heated outdoor pool; room service; tennis court. *In room:* TV, hair dryer, Internet (free).

Where to Stay & Dine in Nearby Pelynt & Lanreath

Jubilee Inn ★   Built in the 16th century, this inn takes its name from Queen Victoria's Jubilee celebration, when it underwent restoration. It's a comment on, rather than a monument to, the past. A glass-enclosed circular staircase, built to serve as a combined tower and hothouse, takes you to the bedrooms. All but the three newest rooms have excellent 19th-century furnishings. Most units are midsize, though two are large enough for families.

Jubilee Hill, Pelynt (6.5km/4 miles from Looe, 5km/3 miles from Polperro), Cornwall PL13 2JZ. © **01503/220312.** Fax 01503/220920. www.jubilee-inn.co.uk. 11 units. £50–£110 double. Rates include English breakfast. MC, V. **Amenities:** Restaurant; bar. *In room:* TV, hair dryer, Wi-Fi (£6 per 2 hr.).

Punch Bowl Inn ★   Opened in 1620, the Punch Bowl has since served as a courthouse, coaching inn, and rendezvous for smugglers. Today, its bedrooms (all with four-poster beds) provide old-fashioned comfort. Many units are quite small, though they come in various shapes and sizes, each with a compact bathroom. One of the kitchens here is among the few licensed in Britain as a bar.

CORNWALL'S GEODESIC domed eden

At first you think some spaceship filled with aliens has invaded sleepy old Cornwall. A second look reveals one of England's newest and most dramatic attractions, the **Eden Project** ★★, Bodelva, St. Austell (🕐 **01726/811911;** www.edenproject.com), a 48km (30-mile) drive west of Plymouth. This sprawling attraction presents plants from the world over. It's open late March to October, daily 10am to 6pm (last admission at 4:30pm); November to mid-March, daily 10am to 4:30pm (last admission at 3pm). Closed December 24 and 25. Admission is £16 for adults, £11 for seniors, £8 for students, £6 for children 5 to 16, and £39 for a family ticket (two adults, three children). The project lies 9.5km (6 miles) from the St. Austell train station, to which it is linked by frequent buses.

Lanreath, Cornwall PL13 2NX. 🕐 **01503/220778.** www.thefamouspunchbowlinn.co.uk. 9 units. £74–£90 double. Rates include English breakfast. MC, V. From Polperro, take B3359 north. **Amenities:** Restaurant; bar. *In room:* TV, no phone.

Where to Dine in Polperro

The Kitchen SEAFOOD   This pink cottage, halfway to the harbor from the parking area, was once a wagon-builder's shop. It's now a restaurant offering good English cooking, all homemade from fresh ingredients. The menu changes seasonally and features local fresh fish. Typical dishes include Fowey sea trout with lemon-and-herb butter or breast of duckling with blueberry-and-Drambuie sauce. Many vegetarian main courses are on offer.

The Combes. 🕐 **01503/272780.** Reservations required. Main courses £6.95–£15. MC, V. Wed–Sun 10am–4pm. Closed Jan.

Nelson's Restaurant SEAFOOD   Situated in the lower reaches of Polperro, near the spot where the local river meets the sea, this is the only structure in town specifically built as a restaurant. It features succulent preparations of regional fish and shellfish that arrive fresh from local fishing boats. The menu changes daily but usually includes fresh crab, Dover sole, lobster, and many other exotic fish. Fresh meat, poultry, and game, all from local suppliers, are also available and beautifully prepared. A lower deck features a cafe/bar and bistro. A comprehensive wine list boasts some fine vintages.

Saxon Bridge. 🕐 **01503/272366.** www.polperro.co.uk. Reservations recommended. Main courses £8–£24. MC, V. Tues–Sat noon–2pm and 6:30–10pm; Sun 10:30am–2pm. Closed mid-Jan to mid-Feb.

ST. MAWES ★

483km (300 miles) SW of London; 3km (2 miles) E of Falmouth; 29km (18 miles) S of Truro

Overlooking the mouth of the Fal River, St. Mawes is sheltered from northern winds, thus subtropical plants can grow here. From the town quay, you can take a boat to Frenchman's Creek and Helford River, as well as other places. St. Mawes is noted for its sailing, boating, fishing, and yachting, and half a dozen sandy coves lie within

DISCOVERING THE lost gardens

Seeing the **Lost Gardens of Heligan** ★★ is like traveling back in time to Victoria's day. Europe's largest garden restoration project sprawls over 32 hectares (80 acres) of pure enchantment. Near the fishing village of Mevagissey, these award-winning gardens "slept" for nearly 7 decades before they were rediscovered and restored. They're open April through September, daily 10am to 6pm (last admission at 4:30pm), and October through March, daily 10am to 5pm (last admission at 3:30pm). Closed December 24 and 25. Admission is £8.50 for adults, £7.50 for seniors, £5 for children 5 to 16, and free for kids 4 and younger. A family ticket goes for £24. For more information, call ✆ **01726/845100** or check out **www.heligan.com**.

a 15-minute drive from the port. The town, built on the Roseland Peninsula, makes for scenic walks thanks to its colorful cottages and sheltered harbor.

Getting There

Trains leave London's Paddington Station for Truro several times a day. The trip takes 4½ to 5 hours. For schedules and information, call ✆ **0845/748-4950** or visit **www.nationalrail.co.uk**. Passengers transfer at Truro to one of two buses that make the 45-minute trip from Truro to St. Mawes. It's much easier to take a taxi from Truro or, even better, from the village of St. Austell, which is the train stop before Truro.

Buses leave London's Victoria Coach Station three times a day for Truro. The trip takes 7½ hours. For schedules and information, call ✆ **0871/781-8181** or visit **www.nationalexpress.com**.

If you're driving to St. Mawes, turn left off the A390 (the main road along the southern coast of Cornwall) at a junction 6.5km (4 miles) past St. Austell, onto the Tregony road, which will take you into St. Mawes.

A ferry travels to St. Mawes from both Falmouth and Truro, but schedules are erratic, varying with the tides and the weather conditions.

Where to Stay & Dine

Hotel Tresanton ★★ ☺   Laura Ashley and the designer of an ocean liner must have joined forces to create this country-house hotel, which lies above the sea overlooking the fishing harbor. Tresanton has quickly replaced the Idle Rocks and the Rising Sun as the premier address in town. The whole place casts an aura of a chic house party, 1930s style, and even includes a movie theater where screenings are held. This glamorous hotel offers a combination of beautiful old and new furnishings in its spacious, airy bedrooms. The views from these rooms are among the most panoramic on the coast, which you'll want to explore on long walks above *Rebecca*-like cliffs. The preferred units are nos. 22 through 27, each with its own terrace overlooking the churning waters.

St. Mawes, Cornwall TR2 5DR. (C) **01326/270055.** Fax 01326/270053. www.tresanton.com. 29 units. £190–£335 double; £320–£495 suite. Rates include English breakfast. 2-night minimum Sat–Sun. AE, MC, V. Free parking. **Amenities:** Restaurant; bar; babysitting; children's playroom; room service. *In room:* TV, hair dryer.

Idle Rocks Hotel ★ ☺   The second-best place to stay in St. Mawes is this solid old building, right on the seawall, sporting gaily colored umbrellas and tables all along the terrace. Water laps at the wall, and the site opens onto views over the river and the constant traffic of sailboats and dinghies. Most rooms have sea or river views; the 17 units in the main building charge higher rates. Four rooms tout balconies and four-poster beds. Families flock here for the bustling harbor view, which kids love, and for the number of extra-large, comfortably appointed rooms.

Harbourside, St. Mawes, Cornwall TR2 5AN. (C) **01326/270771.** Fax 01326/270062. www.idlerocks.co. uk. 27 units. £156–£335 double. Rates include half-board. AE, MC, V. Parking £5. **Amenities:** Restaurant; bar; babysitting; room service. *In room:* TV, hair dryer.

The Rising Sun ★   Converted from four 17th-century fishing cottages, with a flower-draped flagstone terrace out front, this colorful seafront inn in the center of town exudes charm. Known as one of Cornwall's best inns, it offers recently refurbished bedrooms that are functional and cozy. The small to midsize rooms are graced with specially commissioned watercolors by local artists.

The Square, St. Mawes, Cornwall TR2 5DJ. (C) **01326/270233.** Fax 01326/270198. www.risingsun stmawes.co.uk. 8 units. £120–£170 double. Children 4–15 receive 50% discount. Rates include English breakfast. MC, V. Free parking. **Amenities:** Restaurant; bar; room service. *In room:* TV, hair dryer.

PENZANCE ★

451km (280 miles) SW of London; 124km (77 miles) SW of Plymouth

This little harbor town, which Gilbert and Sullivan made famous, is at the end of the so-called Cornish Riviera. It's noted for its moderate climate (it's one of the first towns in England to blossom with spring flowers) and for the summer throngs that descend for fishing, sailing, and swimming. Overlooking Mount's Bay, Penzance is graced in places with subtropical plants such as palm trees.

Those characters in *The Pirates of Penzance* were not entirely fictional. The town was raided by Barbary pirates, destroyed in part by Cromwell's troops, sacked and burned by the Spaniards, and bombed by the Germans. In spite of its turbulent past, it offers tranquil resort living today.

The most westerly town in England, Penzance is a good base for exploring Land's End; the Lizard Peninsula; St. Michael's Mount; the old fishing ports and artists' colonies of St. Ives, Newlyn, and Mousehole; and even the Isles of Scilly.

Essentials

GETTING THERE   Ten express trains leave daily from London's Paddington Station for Penzance; the trip takes 5½ hours. For information, call (C) **0845/748-4950** or visit **www.nationalrail.co.uk**.

Five buses per day, run by **National Express** ((C) **0871/781-8181;** www.national express.com), leave from London's Victoria Coach Station heading for Penzance. The trip takes 8½ to 9 hours. The buses have toilets and reclining seats.

By car, you can drive southwest across Cornwall on the A30 all the way to Penzance; the trip takes between 5 and 6 hours.

VISITOR INFORMATION   The **Tourist Information Centre** is on Station Approach (✆ **01736/362207;** www.penzance.world-guides.com/index.html). It's open Easter to September, daily 9am to 5pm; and October to Easter, Monday to Friday 9am to 5pm.

Where to Stay

Abbey Hotel   This small-scale hotel occupies a stone-sided house that was erected in 1660 on the site of a 12th-century abbey that was demolished by Henry VIII. It's situated on a narrow side street on raised terraces that overlook the panorama of Penzance Harbour. Behind the hotel is a medieval walled garden that was part of the original abbey. Bedrooms are furnished with English-country-house flair.

Abbey St., Penzance, Cornwall TR18 4AR. ✆ **01736/366906.** Fax 01736/351163. www.theabbeyonline. com. 6 units. Low season £105–£145 double; £150–£200 suite; summer £130–£200 double, £200–£250 suite. Rates include English breakfast. AE, MC, V. **Amenities:** Restaurant; bar; room service. *In room:* TV, hair dryer.

Camilla House ★   This comfortable, nicely furnished guesthouse is located near the town promenade, within walking distance of shops and restaurants. A local mariner built this house for his family in 1836. The small to midsize bedrooms will give you the feeling of being "at home," and Susan and Simon Chapman are most helpful in providing information on attractions in Penzance and surrounding areas. They're also agents for the Skybus (airplane) and *Scillonian III* (ferry), and can book day trips to the Isles of Scilly. A delicious English breakfast is served in a charming dining room.

12 Regent Terrace, Penzance, Cornwall. ✆/fax **01736/363771.** www.camillahouse.co.uk. 8 units. £70–£85 double. Rates include English breakfast. AE, MC, V. Free parking. Closed Jan 9–29. **Amenities:** Dining room; bar. *In room:* TV, hair dryer, no phone, Wi-Fi (free).

Ennys ★ 🏠   Once a flower farm, Ennys produces mainly vegetables today. Owned by Gill and Jill Charlton, this Cornish granite farmhouse has a slate roof, a front section that dates from the 17th century, and other portions thought to be much older. The bedrooms are furnished in an old-fashioned farmhouse style, with patchwork quilts and four-poster beds. The family suites are in a converted barn on the premises. The hostess prepares an afternoon Cornish-style cream tea.

Trewhella Lane, St. Hilary, Penzance, Cornwall TR20 9BZ. ✆ **01736/740262.** Fax 01736/740055. www. ennys.co.uk. 5 units. £95–£145 double; £135–£175 family suite. Rates include English breakfast and afternoon tea. MC, V. **Amenities:** Dining room; outdoor heated pool; tennis court. *In room:* TV/DVD, hair dryer, no phone, Wi-Fi (free).

Tarbert Hotel   This dignified granite-and-stucco house lies about a 2-minute walk northwest of the town center. Some of the small to midsize bedrooms retain original high ceilings and elaborate cove moldings, along with comfortable furniture. Improvements include a new reception area, a completely refurbished bar, and a patio.

11–12 Clarence St., Penzance, Cornwall TR18 2NU. ✆ **01736/363758.** Fax 01736/331336. www.tarbert-hotel.co.uk. 12 units. £75–£125 double. Rates include English breakfast. AE, MC, V. **Amenities:** Restaurant; bar. *In room:* TV, hair dryer, Wi-Fi (free).

AN escape TO AN OASIS

Just 3.2km (2 miles) west of Penzance, you'll discover **Trengwainton Garden** ★, west of Heamoor off the Penzance-Morvah Road (✆ **01736/363148;** www.nationaltrust.org.uk), a woodland garden of trees and shrubs on a 40-hectare (98-acre) plot overlooking Mount's Bay. Allow at least an hour to explore this property, with its flourishing collection of camellias, magnolias, and rhododendrons. Thanks to the mild climate, the site is famed for its series of walled gardens, with sloping beds that contain tender species not found elsewhere in the United Kingdom. You'll find feathery bamboos and Australian tree ferns along the banks of a stream, plus lilies and other water-loving plants. This National Trust property is open mid-February through October, Sunday to Thursday 10:30am to 5pm. Admission is £6.20 for adults, £3.10 for children 11 and younger, and £16 for a family pass.

Where to Dine

The **Nelson Bar,** in the Union Hotel, Chapel Street (✆ **01736/362319**), is known for its robust pub grub and collection of Nelsoniana. It's the spot where the admiral's death at Trafalgar was first revealed to the English people. Lunch and dinner are served daily.

Harris's Restaurant ★ FRENCH/ENGLISH Down a narrow cobblestone street off Market Jew Street, this warm, candlelit place has a relaxed atmosphere and is your best bet for a meal. A beacon of light against the culinary bleakness of Penzance, Harris's offers dining in two small rooms. The seasonally adjusted menu emphasizes local produce, including seafood and game. On any given night, you might enjoy such well-crafted dishes as whole steamed lobster with lime-butter sauce or steamed John Dory with a saffron sauce.

46 New St. ✆ **01736/364408.** www.harrissrestaurant.co.uk. Reservations recommended. Main courses £18–£28. AE, MC, V. Mon–Sat noon–2pm and 7–10pm. Closed 3 weeks in winter.

Turk's Head ★★ ENGLISH/INTERNATIONAL Dating from 1233, the Turk's Head, said to be the oldest inn in Penzance, serves the finest food of any pub in town. In summer, drinkers overflow into the garden. The interior is decorated in a mellow style, as befits its age, with flatirons and other artifacts hanging from the timeworn beams. Meals include fishermen's pie, local seafood, chicken curry, and prime quality steaks, including rib-eye. See the chalkboards for the daily specials.

49 Chapel St. ✆ **01736/363093.** www.turksheadpenzance.co.uk. Reservations not needed. Main courses £10–£16; bar snacks £3.75–£13. AE, MC, V. Mon–Sat 11am–2:30pm and 6–10pm; Sun noon–2:30pm and 6–9pm. From the rail station, turn left just past Lloyd's Bank.

Seeing the Sights in & Around Penzance

Unlike some tacky places along the Cornish coast, which are overrun with cheesy shops selling cheap souvenirs, Penzance maintains a bit of a regal air in spite of its hordes of summer visitors. Of course, it has a vast array of antiques stores hustling their wares, often trinkets more than genuine antiques, but it can be a lot of fun nonetheless.

A Fishing Village & Artists' Colony

From Penzance, a 3.2km (2-mile) promenade leads to **Newlyn** ★, another fishing village—second largest in the country—and a port of infinite charm on Mount's Bay. Artist Stanhope Forbes (1857–1947) founded an art school in Newlyn in 1899, and the village has been an artists' colony ever since, attracting both the serious painter and the Sunday sketcher. A bus runs throughout the day linking Penzance with Newlyn. We suggest you walk to Newlyn, and then take the bus back to Penzance if you're tired.

If you're in Newlyn at lunchtime, fish is, of course, what to order. For the tastiest fish and chips in town, head for the **Tolcarne Inn,** Tolcarne Place (℃ **01736/363074;** www.tolcarneinn. talktalk.net). Under a beamed ceiling from 1717, the main room for dining evokes a Cornish pub, with paintings by local artists on display. If you don't want fish and chips, opt for the Newlyn fish pie or, better yet, the fresh crab. Main dishes are £8 to £26 at dinner, £ 5 to £9 at lunch. MasterCard and Visa are accepted. It's open daily 10:30am to 3:30pm and 6:30 to 11:30pm.

On summer nights, young people flock to the fun-loving, often rowdy pubs to begin drinking lager in time to enjoy some of the most spectacular sunsets in the West Country.

Frankly, if you're from Miami, the waters for swimming will always be too cold for you. But for the average visitor, the best temperatures are in July and the first 2 weeks in August. Outside of that period, you can find other pastimes with which to amuse yourself.

Castle on St. Michael's Mount ★★　Rising about 75m (250 ft.) from the sea, St. Michael's Mount is topped by a part medieval, part 17th-century castle. It's 5km (3 miles) east of Penzance and is reached at low tide by a causeway. At high tide, the mount becomes an island, reached only by motor launch from Marazion. In winter, you can go over only when the causeway is dry.

A Benedictine monastery, the gift of Edward the Confessor, stood on this spot in the 11th century. The castle now has a collection of armor and antique furniture. A tea garden is on the island, as well as a National Trust restaurant, both open in summer. The steps up to the castle are steep and rough, so wear sturdy shoes. To avoid disappointment, call the number listed below to check on the tides, especially during winter. Allow 3 hours for a visit.

St. Michael's Mount, Mount's Bay. ℃ **01736/710507.** www.stmichaelsmount.co.uk. Admission £7 adults, £3.50 children, £18 family ticket. Late Mar to Oct Sun–Fri 10:30am–5pm; guided tours off-season Tues–Fri at 11am and 2pm. Bus no. 2 or 2A from Penzance to Marazion, the town opposite St. Michael's Mount. Parking £2.

Minack Theatre ★★★　One of the most unusual theaters in southern England, this open-air amphitheater was cut from the side of a rocky Cornish hill near the village of Porthcurno, 14km (9 miles) southwest of Penzance. Its legendary creator was Rowena Cade, an arts enthusiast and noted eccentric, who began work on the theater after World War I by physically carting off much of the granite from her chosen hillside. An exhibition hall on the premises showcases Cade's life and accomplishments.

Up to 750 visitors at a time can sit directly on grass- or rock-covered ledges, sometimes on cushions if they're available, within sightlines of both the actors and a sweeping view out over the ocean. Experienced theatergoers sometimes bring raincoats for protection against the occasional drizzle. Theatrical events are staged by repertory theater companies that travel throughout Britain, and performances are likely to include everything from London's visiting Royal Shakespeare Company to musical comedy. The productions staged here are the most professional and polished of any theater in the West Country; many come direct from critical acclaim in London's West End.

Porthcurno. (C) **01736/810181.** www.minack.com. Theater tickets £7–£9 adults, £4–£6 children; tour tickets £3 adults, £2.20 seniors, £1.20 children 12–15, free for kids 11 and younger. Exhibition hall Apr to mid-May daily 9:30am–5:30pm; late May to mid-Sept Sat–Tues and Thurs 9:30am–5:30pm; late Sept to Oct daily 10am–5pm; Nov to Easter daily 10am–4pm. Performances held mid-May to mid-Sept, matinees Wed and Fri at 2pm, evening shows Mon–Fri at 8pm. From Penzance, take A30 heading toward Land's End; after 5km (3 miles), bear left onto B3283 and follow the signs to Porthcurno.

THE ISLES OF SCILLY ★

43km (27 miles) SW of Land's End

Off the Cornish coast, the Isles of Scilly, a cluster of small granite masses, are warmed by the Gulf Stream to the point where semitropical plants thrive. In some winters, they never see signs of frost. The islands are the first landfall most oceangoing passengers spot on journeys from North America. Charles, the Prince of Wales (who is also the duke of Cornwall as well), makes regular visits to Scilly.

Five inhabited and more than 100 uninhabited islands are in the group. Some are only a few square miles, whereas others, such as the largest, St. Mary's, encompass some 77 sq. km (30 sq. miles). Three of these islands—**St. Mary's, Tresco,** and **St. Agnes**—attract visitors from the mainland. Early flowers are the main export here, and tourism the main industry.

The islands experience some of the harshest winds of winter, raging in from the Atlantic. Those turbulent, lashing waves played a big part in shaping the islands, creating natural "sculptures" out of the granite. The farms that still remain evoke small holdings of the late 19th century in Britain, their fields protected from the winds by hardy trees introduced here. In summer, however, these are the fairest isles in the queen's kingdom. Unlike the rest of Britain, there is subtropical vegetation here, a mass of flowers from early spring to fall. Some are cultivated, as the English do so well, but others grow wild.

The Isles of Scilly contain the best and most unspoiled beaches in Cornwall, and there are so many of them that you are likely to have a beach to yourself. We'd go just to enjoy the swarms of seabirds flying in from the Atlantic, perhaps enjoying a well-deserved rest.

On any of the islands, we'd recommend a stroll along the coastline. In fact, we've walked around many of these islands, which are small enough, and flat enough, so this can be easily accomplished.

The islands are studded with burial chambers, standing stones, and a few remains of former windmills, lighthouses, deserted cottages, and smugglers' hide-outs. Fishing is a big activity, especially for lobster, crayfish, and crabs pulled up in traditional "inkwell pots."

The Isles of Scilly figured prominently in the myths and legends of ancient Greece and Rome; in Celtic legend, they were inhabited entirely by holy men. More ancient burial mounds are on these islands than anywhere else in southern England, and artifacts have clearly established that people lived here more than 4,000 years ago.

St. Mary's is the capital, with about seven-eighths of the total population of all the islands, and it's here that the ship from the mainland docks at Hugh Town. However, if you'd like to make this a day visit, we recommend the helicopter flight from Penzance to Tresco, the neighboring island, where you can enjoy a day's walk through 297 hectares (735 acres), mostly occupied by the Abbey Garden.

Essentials

GETTING THERE   You can fly here by plane or helicopter. **Isles of Scilly Sky-bus Ltd.** (✆ **0845/7105555;** www.islesofscilly-travel.co.uk) operates 2 to 20 flights per day, depending on the season, between Penzance's Land's End Airport and Hugh Town on St. Mary's Island. Flight time on the eight-passenger fixed-wing planes is 15 minutes each way. The round-trip fare is £80 to £230 for a same-day return, £95 to £340 if you plan to stay overnight.

Weather permitting, **British International Helicopters,** Penzance Heliport Eastern Green (✆ **01736/363871** for recorded information; www.islesofscillyheli-copter.com), operates up to 26 helicopter flights, Monday through Saturday, between Penzance, St. Mary's, and Tresco. Flight time is 20 minutes from Penzance to either island. The round-trip fare is £145 for a same-day return, £170 to £185 if you stay overnight. A bus, whose timing coincides with the departure of each flight, runs to the heliport from the railway station in Penzance for £2 per person each way.

The rail line ends in Penzance (see "Getting There" in the "Penzance" section, above).

Slower, but more cadenced and contemplative, is a ship leaving from the **Isles of Scilly Travel Centre,** on Quay Street in Penzance (✆ **0845/710-5555;** www.islesofscilly-travel.co.uk). It departs at least 6 days a week between April and October, requiring 2 hours and 40 minutes for the segment between Penzance and Hugh Town, with an additional 20 or so minutes for the second leg of the trip, which is from Hugh Town to Tresco. It departs Monday to Friday at 9:15am, returning from St. Mary's at 4:30pm. Saturday departures usually follow the Monday-to-Friday timing, but not always, as the managers sometimes add a second Saturday sailing to accommodate weekend holidaymakers, depending on the season. There is no service from early November to March or early April. Depending on the time of year, a same-day round-trip ticket from Penzance to St. Mary's costs £48 for adults and £24 for children 15 and under. If you choose to spend the night, the round-trip costs £95 for adults and £48 for children.

VISITOR INFORMATION   The **Tourist Information Centre,** Hugh Street, St. Mary's (✆ **01720/422536;** www.simplyscilly.co.uk), is open November through March, Monday to Friday 9am to 5pm; and April through October, Monday to Friday 8:30am to 6pm, Saturday 8:30am to 5pm, and Sunday 9am to 2pm.

St. Mary's

St. Mary's is made for walking, biking, and exploring—casual, relaxed sightseeing, nothing too demanding. The attraction of the island is its natural beauty. It is 5km (3 miles) across at its widest point, but its coastline stretches for 15km (9 miles).

We've spent an entire day just wandering this beautiful, cove-studded coastline. If along the way you stop to chat with a local Scillonian fisherman, so much the better.

Hugh Town, the main settlement, deserves at least an hour or two of your time. It was constructed on a sandbar that lies between the principal part of St. Mary's and a hill in the west, called the **Garrison.** Constructed in the mid-1700s, a **guard gate** here gives access to the **Star Castle Hotel** (see below). We recommend a stroll inside the ramparts for one of the greatest **views** ★★ of the Scilly Islands.

From Hugh Town, you can see the island's highest point, **Telegraph Tower,** rising 48m (158 ft.). This is a memorable walk, and you can also pass on the way a stone burial chamber, **Bants Carn,** dating from the 3rd century B.C.

To get around St. Mary's, cars are available but hardly necessary. The **Island Bus Service** charges £2 for adults from one island point to another; children ride for half fare. Bicycles are one of the most practical means of transport. **St. Mary's Bicycle Hire,** the Strand (℃/fax **01720/422289**), is the only bike-rental outfit. It stocks "shopper's cycles" with 3 speeds, hybrid bikes with 6 to 12 speeds, and 18-speed mountain bikes. All are available at prices ranging from £8 to £15 daily; a £20 deposit is required.

For the best selection of island crafts, visit **Phoenix Stained Glass Studio,** Portmellon Industrial Estate (℃ **01720/422900;** www.phoenixstainedglass.co.uk). At this studio, you can watch original artifacts being made into stained glass. The shops also sell a wide assortment of gifts, including jewelry and leaded lights and souvenirs.

Isles of Scilly Perfumery, Porthloo Studios (no phone), a 10-minute walk from the center of Hugh Town, is packed with intriguing gifts, all made from plants grown on the Isles—everything from a delicate shell-shaped soap to fine fragrances, cosmetics, potpourri, and other accessories.

Isles of Scilly Museum, on Church Street (℃ **01720/422337;** www.ios museum.org), illustrates the history of the islands from 2500 B.C., with drawings, artifacts from wrecked ships, and assorted relics discovered here. A locally themed exhibit changes annually. It's open Easter through September, Monday to Saturday 10am to 4:30pm; off-season hours are Monday to Saturday 10am to noon. Admission is £3 for adults, £2 for seniors and students, and £1 for children.

WHERE TO STAY

Star Castle Hotel ★ ☺   This hotel, built as a castle in 1593 to defend the Isles of Scilly against Spanish attacks, offers views out to sea and over the town and harbor. A young prince of Wales (later King Charles II) took shelter here in 1643 when he was being hunted by Cromwell and his parliamentary forces. Eight double rooms and four single rooms are in the castle. The 18 rooms in the annex are extra-large units opening directly onto the gardens. The rooms in the castle are full of more character, with four-poster beds and beamed ceilings, but the garden apartments are more spacious and comfortable. Seventeen rooms are large enough for families.

The Garrison, St. Mary's, Isles of Scilly TR21 OTA. ℃ **01720/422317.** Fax 01720/422343. www.star-castle. co.uk. 34 units. £89–£156 per adult double; £119–£181 per adult suite. Rates include half-board. MC, V. Closed late Dec–early Feb. **Amenities:** 2 restaurants; bar; indoor pool; room service; tennis court. *In room:* TV, hair dryer.

WHERE TO DINE

Chez Michel FRENCH   The finest dining outside the hotels is found at this warm and cozy 24-seat restaurant in the heart of Hugh Town. The cooks emphasize fresh ingredients, whatever the season. Lunches are fairly light, including such standards as a Cornish crab sandwich or a fresh lobster salad made from seafood harvested right off the shores. At night, fare is more elaborate. Count on such delights as Cornish beef filet with white-mushroom sauce or baked and crusted fresh sea bass. The breast of duckling with cranberry sauce is also delicious. Beer and wine are available.

The Parade, Hugh Town, St. Mary's. ⓒ **01720/422871.** Reservation required for dinner. Lunch £6.50–£10; dinner £13–£25. No credit cards. Year-round Tues, Thurs, and Sat 10am–2pm; summer Mon–Sat 6:30–11pm; winter Sat 6:30pm–closing.

Tresco

No cars or motorbikes are allowed on Tresco, but you can rent bikes by the day; the hotels use a special wagon towed by a farm tractor to transport guests and luggage from the harbor.

Abbey Garden ★ 🎐   The most outstanding features of Tresco are the gardens, started by Augustus Smith in the mid-1830s. When he began his work, the area was a barren hillside, a fact that visitors now find hard to believe. Today, the gardens are a nature lover's dream, with more than 5,000 species of plants from 80 different countries. The old abbey, or priory, now in ruins, was allegedly founded by Benedictine monks in the 11th century, though some historians date it from A.D. 964. Of special interest in the gardens is Valhalla, a collection of nearly 60 figureheads from ships wrecked around the islands; the gaily painted figures from the past have a rather eerie quality, each one a ghost with a different story to tell.

If time remains after you visit the gardens, you can explore the meadows and coastal fields that surround them. There is no particular trail to follow: Just wander at leisure through the fields and across paths made by others who blazed these trails before you. You can walk along the dunes, which are often thick with heather, enjoying the wildflowers, the birds that fly overhead, and maybe some shell collecting. The seabirds are so fearless that they'll land within a foot or so of you, looking for a handout.

ⓒ **01720/424108.** www.tresco.co.uk. Admission £10, free for children 15 and younger. Daily 10am–4pm.

WHERE TO STAY & DINE

Island Hotel ★ ☺   This is the finest hotel in the Isles of Scilly, located at Old Grimsby Harbour near the northeastern shore of Tresco. It was established in 1960 when a late-19th-century stone cottage was enlarged with conservatory-style windows and a series of long and low extensions. Today, the plant-filled interior feels almost Caribbean. Some bedrooms overlook the sea; others face inland. All are comfortably furnished with easy chairs and storage spaces. They range in size from medium to spacious, and nearly two dozen of them are large enough for families. The hotel is noted for its subtropical garden.

Old Grimsby, Tresco, Isles of Scilly, Cornwall TR24 0PU. ⓒ **01720/422883.** Fax 01720/423008. www.tresco.co.uk. 48 units. £130–£275 per person double; £180–£360 per person suite. Rates include English breakfast and dinner. MC, V. Closed Nov–early Feb. **Amenities:** Restaurant; bar; babysitting; outdoor pool; room service; tennis court. *In room:* TV, hair dryer.

New Inn An interconnected row of 19th-century fishermen's cottages and shops, the New Inn is situated at the center of the island, beside its unnamed main road. The bedrooms are tastefully decorated in a modern style in blue and creamy yellow hues; each features matching twin or double beds. The more expensive units offer sea views.

This also serves as the island's pub, enjoying a spectacular setting overlooking the ocean, on New Grimsby Harbour some 50m (164 ft.) from the water. In summer, drinks and food can be enjoyed in the patio garden, with its direct access to the harbor. The food to order, of course, is locally caught fish, including prawns and, our favorite, white crab, but you can also enjoy John Dory, Cornish sea bass, and monkfish. The pub is open daily from 10am to 3pm and 6 to 11pm; meals are served from noon to 3pm and 6 to 9pm. Main courses cost £6 to £18.

Tresco, Isles of Scilly, Cornwall TR24 0QQ. (✆) **01720/422844.** Fax 01720/423200. www.tresco.co.uk. 15 units. £140–£230 double. Rates include English breakfast. MC, V. **Amenities:** Restaurant; pub; 2 bars; outdoor pool; tennis court. *In room:* TV, hair dryer.

St. Agnes ★

St. Agnes lies farther southwest than any other community in Britain and, luckily, remains relatively undiscovered. Many places claim to be unspoiled, but St. Agnes actually is, measuring about 1.6km (1 mile) across a somewhat flat terrain broken in parts by green hills. Little traffic moves on single-track lanes crossing the island. Much of the area is preserved by the Nature Conservancy Council.

In the western part of the island are granite outcroppings; the scenery here is much wilder than in the east, with sandy coves and rock pools. The island is known for its daffodils in the spring; its birds, butterflies, and wildflowers in the summer; and its migrant birds, including many rare species, in the fall.

Beachcombers can find beads from 17th-century shipwrecks in the sands here. The curving sandbar between St. Agnes and its neighbor, the island of Gugh, is one of the best beaches in the archipelago. The coastline is diverse and idyllic for long walks along a relatively flat, shrub-dotted landscape. A coastal trail leads to any number of sandy coves, granite outcroppings, flower-studded heaths and meadows, and even a freshwater pool. Sunsets are romantic and are followed by a brilliant showcase of the night sky.

Because the main industries are flower farming and fishing, St. Agnes has little pollution; visitors can enjoy clear waters that are ideal for snorkeling and diving. Call David Peacock of **St. Agnes Boating** (✆ **01720/422704;** www.st-agnes-boating.co.uk) to inquire about boating and snorkeling possibilities.

The widest choice of boat trips of the Isles of Scilly is offered by the **St. Mary's Boatmen's Association** (✆ **01720/423999;** www.scillyboating.co.uk). In summer, boats heading for St. Agnes leave St. Mary's at 10:15am, 11:45am, and 2pm, returning at 2:12, 4, and 4:45pm. A day trip costs £4 to £13.

THE LOCAL PUB

The **Turk's Head** (✆ **01720/422434**) dates from the 1890s, when it was constructed as a boathouse. Prominently located a few steps from the pier, it serves the best beer and ales on St. Agnes, along with other drinks. It's the second building after the arrival point of the ferryboats from St. Mary's. It's open daily 10:30am to 4:30pm and 6:30 to 11pm.

MOUSEHOLE ★ & LAND'S END ★

Mousehole: 5km (3 miles) S of Penzance; Land's End: 14km (9 miles) W of Penzance

Reached by traveling through some of Cornwall's most beautiful countryside, Land's End is literally the end of Britain. The natural grandeur of the place has been somewhat marred by theme park–type amusements, but the view of the sea crashing against rocks remains undiminished. If you want to stay in the area, you can find accommodations in Mousehole, a lovely Cornish fishing village. If you visit in July and August, you'll need reservations far in advance, as Mousehole doesn't have enough bedrooms to accommodate the summer hordes.

Getting There

From London, journey first to Penzance (see "Getting There" in the "Penzance" section, earlier in this chapter), and then take a local bus for the rest of the journey (bus no. 6 to Mousehole and bus no. 1 to Land's End). There is frequent service throughout the day.

If you're driving from Penzance, take the B3315 south for 15 minutes.

Mousehole ★

The Cornish fishing village of Mousehole (pronounced *Mou*-sel) attracts hordes of visitors, who, fortunately, haven't changed it too much. The cottages still sit close to the harbor wall, the fishermen still bring in the day's catch, the salts sit around smoking tobacco and talking about the good old days, and the lanes are as narrow as ever. About the most exciting thing to happen here was the arrival in the late 16th century of the Spanish galleons, whose sailors sacked and burned the village. In a sheltered cove of Mount's Bay, Mousehole today has developed as the nucleus of an artists' colony.

If you'd like to go fishing yourself, you can call **Tom Arnull** (© **01736/756162**), who can hook you up with rock and beach angling. Otherwise, call **S. Farley** (© **01736/731154**), who can arrange charter-boat fishing.

There is no great attraction to visit in Mousehole other than the village itself. You can spend an hour or two strolling its narrow streets and passing by its quaint, stone-built cottages. Walks always end at the quay, where you can look at the boats at harbor. Perhaps you can have lunch here and be on your way or, at the end of the day, you can walk 1.6km (1 mile) south of the village to **Spaniards' Point,** where the Iberian raiders landed to pillage the countryside, laying devastation to the Cornish landscape. It's a beautiful walk as you take in a rugged seascape and landscape.

WHERE TO STAY

Old Coastguard Hotel ★★   The best views in the area are to be enjoyed in this former lookout for the Coast Guard. It has been skillfully converted into a seacoast inn, serving some of the best food in the area. Guest rooms are split between the main building and the Lodge, a newer annex down the hill, and accommodations in both buildings are comparable in style and quality. Picture windows look out on the bay in many rooms, all of which are decorated in a modern style with beech and pine furniture. The best units open onto sea views enjoyed from a private balcony or terrace. The on-site restaurant prides itself on its use of fresh produce and fish brought into Newlyn Harbour.

The Parade, Mousehole, Penzance, Cornwall TR19 6PR. ☏ **01736/731222.** Fax 01736/731720. www. oldcoastguardhotel.co.uk. 20 units. £120–£260 double. Rates include English breakfast. AE, MC, V. **Amenities:** Restaurant; bar. *In room:* TV.

Ship Inn This charming pub and inn is located on the harbor in this fishing village. The exterior has a stone facade, while the interior has retained much of its original rustic charm, with black beams and paneling, granite floors, built-in wall benches, and the requisite nautical motif decorating its two bars. The bedrooms, offering views of the harbor and the bay, have window seats and other simple furnishings; they tend to be small but cozy.

South Cliff, Mousehole, Penzance, Cornwall TR19 6QX. ☏ **01736/731234.** www.shipmousehole.co.uk or www.staustellbrewery.co.uk. 7 units. £65–£80 double. Rates include English breakfast. MC, V. **Amenities:** Restaurant; 2 bars. *In room:* TV, hair dryer.

WHERE TO DINE

The most substantial meals are served at the restaurant of the **Ship Inn** (see above).

If you're looking for a quick bite, head for **Pam's Pantry,** 3 Mill Lane (☏ **01736/731532**), a small, cheerful cafe that specializes in locally caught fish. Accepting cash only, this hole-in-the-wall features Newlyn crab in salads, soups, and well-stuffed sandwiches. Main courses go for £5 to £12. You can also stop in for a Cornish cream tea (£5), sandwiches to go, or pizzas. Our favorite dessert is the homemade apple pie with clotted cream. Pam's is open daily 9am to 6:30pm.

Cornish Range ★ ENGLISH/MEDITERRANEAN Hidden away on a narrow street in Old Town, the Cornish Range—the finest restaurant in the area—was converted from an 18th-century cottage that processed pilchards (sardines). Filled with local paintings, this rustic, intimate eatery has a vaguely Mediterranean aura with its wooden tables and chairs. A daily changing menu is based on fresh, seasonal produce, much of it harvested from the sea by the fishermen off the coast of Newlyn. Fresh fruits and vegetables come from Cornish farms. Dishes are well balanced and enticingly prepared, including such starters as Mediterranean fish soup or potted Newlyn crab with dill crème fraîche and melted Gruyère. To follow, try Newlyn crab and pea risotto with poached salmon and a citrus crème fraîche, or else panfried wild sea bass filets with a chorizo risotto cake and king prawns.

The inn also rents out three comfortable bedrooms, each beautifully furnished with a private bathroom, costing £80 to £110 double.

6 Chapel St. ☏ **01736/731488.** www.cornishrange.co.uk. Reservations required. Main courses £13–£20. MC, V. Daily 10:45am–2:15pm and 6–9:30pm.

Land's End ★

Craggy Land's End is where England comes to an end. America's coast is 5,299km (3,291 miles) west of the rugged rocks that tumble into the sea beneath Land's End.

Once here, you'll see coastal footpaths allowing you to walk along the cliffs for dramatic **views** ★★ of the crashing sea on the rocks below. These paths are constantly being eroded and new ones built. In an attempt to prevent future erosion, the paths are protected by "hedges"—really granite walls covered with turf.

Meeting at Land's End are the northern and southern sections of the **Cornish Coastal Footpath.** This is the center of the longest continuous footpath in Britain, going from the coast at Poole Harbour to Dorset and Somerset and on to the Bristol

An Escape to Brigadoon

One of the loveliest spots in the west of England is **St. Just in Roseland** ★★, a tiny hamlet of stone cottage terraces and a church dating from the 1200s. Locals call it their Garden of Eden because of its subtropical foliage, including rhododendrons and magnolias. There are even palm trees—in England, no less.

Channel. In all, this is a walk of 804km (500 miles), but the most dramatic and spectacular scenery is found at Land's End.

WHERE TO STAY & DINE

Land's End Hotel   This hotel is situated in a complex of buildings rising from the rugged landscape at the end of the main A30 road, the very tip of England. The hotel has a panoramic cliff-top position and is exposed to the wind and sea spray. The rooms are attractively furnished and well maintained. Accommodations range from small to spacious, especially the premier or family rooms. Three contain four-poster beds and offer sea views.

Land's End, Sennen, Cornwall TR19 7AA. ℭ **01736/871844.** Fax 01736/871599. www.landsendhotel. co.uk. 33 units. £110–£170 double. Rates include breakfast. AE, MC, V. **Amenities:** Restaurant; bar; room service. *In room:* TV, hair dryer.

THE ARTISTS' COLONY OF ST. IVES ★★

514km (319 miles) SW of London; 34km (21 miles) NE of Land's End; 16km (10 miles) NE of Penzance

This north-coast fishing village, with its sandy beaches, narrow streets, and well-kept cottages, is England's most famous artists' colony. The artists settled in many years ago and have integrated with the fishermen and their families. They've been here long enough to develop several schools, or "splits," and they almost never overlap—except in the pubs. The old battle continues between the followers of the representational and the devotees of the abstract in art, with each group recruiting young artists all the time. In addition, potters, weavers, and other craftspeople all work, exhibit, and sell in this area.

St. Ives becomes virtually impossible to visit in August, when you're likely to be trampled underfoot by busloads of tourists, mostly the English themselves. However, in spring and early fall, the pace is much more relaxed.

Essentials

GETTING THERE   There is frequent service throughout the day between London's Paddington Station and the rail terminal at St. Ives. The trip takes 5½ hours. Trains are not direct; it's necessary to change at St. Erth, which is just a 10-minute ride from St. Ives. Call ℭ **0845/748-4950** or visit **www.nationalrail.co.uk** for schedules and information.

Two coaches a day run from London's Victoria Coach Station to St. Ives. The trip takes 8½ hours. Call ℭ **0871/781-8181** or visit **www.nationalexpress.com** for schedules and information.

If you're driving, take the A30 across Cornwall, heading northwest at the junction with the B3306, heading to St. Ives on the coast. During the summer, many streets in the center of town are closed to vehicles. You may want to leave your car in the **Lelant Saltings Car Park,** 5km (3 miles) from St. Ives on the A3074, and take the regular train service into town, an 11-minute journey. Departures are every half-hour. It's free to all car passengers and drivers, and the parking charge is £8 to £15 per day. You can also use the large **Trenwith Car Park,** close to the town center, for £6, and then walk down to the shops and harbor or take a bus that costs £1 per person.

VISITOR INFORMATION   The **Tourist Information Centre** is at the Guild-hall, Street-an-Pol (ⓒ **01736/796297;** www.stives-cornwall.co.uk). From October to May, hours are Monday to Friday 9am to 5pm and Saturday 10am to 1pm. From June to September, hours are Monday to Friday 9am to 5:30pm, Saturday 9am to 5pm, and Sunday 10am to 4pm.

Where to Stay

Blue Hayes Private Hotel ★   Five luxurious rooms, each a beautifully furnished suite, are rented in this villa, a 5-minute walk from the beach. An oasis of calm and tranquillity, the well-maintained house is perched on a hill just off the South West Coast Path. From the balustrade balcony, panoramic sea views unfold. The little hotel is set back on the seaward side, off the A3074, the main road into St. Ives. Rooms have special features such as four-poster beds or French doors that open onto a large private roof terrace with palms.

Trelyon Ave., St. Ives, Cornwall TR26 2AD. ⓒ **01736/797129.** Fax 01736/799098. www.bluehayes.co.uk. 5 units. £75–£105 per person double. Rates include English breakfast. MC. V. Closed Nov–Feb. **Amenities:** Bar (breakfast and light supper). *In room:* TV, hair dryer, Wi-Fi (free).

Garrack Hotel ★ 🔥   This small vine-covered hotel, once a private home, com-mands a panoramic view of St. Ives and Porthmeor Beach from its .8-hectare (2-acre) knoll at the head of a narrow lane. This is one of the friendliest and most efficiently run midprice hotels on the entire coast, and each room is furnished in a warm, homey manner. Most units are midsize, but three rooms are large enough to accommodate families.

Burthallan Lane, Higher Ayr, St. Ives, Cornwall TR26 3AA. ⓒ **01736/796199.** Fax 01736/798955. www. garrack.com. 18 units. Low season £128–£144 double; summer £142–£206 double. Rates include English breakfast. AE, DC, MC, V. Free parking. Take B3306 to the outskirts of St. Ives; after passing a gas station on the left, take the 3rd road left toward Porthmeor Beach and Ayr; after 180m (600 ft.) look for the hotel sign. **Amenities:** Restaurant (see review below); 2 bars; health club; indoor pool; room service; spa. *In room:* TV, hair dryer.

Pedn-Olva Hotel   The panoramic view of the bay afforded from its restaurant and most rooms is the outstanding feature of this establishment. It was built in the 1870s as the home of the paymaster for the local mines, before being transformed into a hotel in the 1930s. The rooms are furnished in a modern style, with comfort-able twin or double beds. Seven of the rooms are in a less desirable annex where the chambers are more sterile and lack the character of the main building. Five rooms are large enough for families. There are sun terraces with lounges, umbrellas, and a swimming pool for those who don't want to walk down the rocky path to Porthmin-ster Beach. If you crave solitude, however, scramble down the rocks to sunbathe just above the gentle rise and fall of the sea.

The Warren, St. Ives, Cornwall TR26 2EA. ✆ **01736/796222.** Fax 01736/797710. www.pednolva.co.uk. 30 units. £146–£170. Rates include English breakfast. AE, MC, V. Parking £6. **Amenities:** Restaurant; bar; outdoor pool. *In room:* TV, hair dryer.

Porthminster Hotel ★ This leading Cornish Riviera resort, the town's best address, stands on the main road into town amid a beautiful garden and within easy walking distance of Porthminster Beach. Large and imposing, the Porthminster is a traditional choice for visitors to St. Ives. With its 1894 Victorian architecture, it is warm and inviting. Over the years the bedrooms have been considerably upgraded, and the standard of comfort is high here. The spacious rooms are well furnished, although with a bland decor.

The Terrace, St. Ives, Cornwall TR26 2BN. ✆ **01736/795221.** Fax 01736/797043. www.porthminster-hotel.co.uk. 43 units. £60–£125 per person double; £125–£150 per person suite. Rates include half-board. AE, DC, MC, V. Free parking. Closed 2 weeks in Jan. **Amenities:** Restaurant; bar; gym; 2 pools (1 indoor, 1 outdoor); room service; spa; tennis court. *In room:* TV, hair dryer.

Primrose Valley Hotel ★ 📖 This Edwardian villa has been stylishly converted to receive guests from its position in a residential cul-de-sac across the railroad tracks from Porthminster Beach. The furnishings are contemporary, from the soft Italian leather chairs to the oak tables. As befits a house of its age, the bedrooms vary in size, and four of them open onto views of the sea, two from covered balconies. The owners believe that breakfast is the most important meal of the day, and they obtain quality foodstuffs from local suppliers. The morning meal is always cooked by one of the partners.

Porthminster Beach, St. Ives, Cornwall TR26 2ED. ✆ **01736/794939.** www.primroseonline.co.uk. 10 units. £100–£165 double; £190–£235 suite. Rates include breakfast. AE, MC, V. Limited free parking. No children 8 and under. **Amenities:** Restaurant; bar. *In room:* TV/DVD, Wi-Fi (free).

Where to Dine

Garrack Restaurant ENGLISH/INTERNATIONAL The restaurant at the Garrack produces excellent cuisine and, whenever possible, uses fresh ingredients from its own garden. The hotel dining room, which is open to nonguests, offers a set dinner, plus a cold buffet or snacks at the bar. The menu features some of the best English dishes, such as slow-roasted pork belly with Bramley apple purée, pan-roasted filet of hake with a pea pesto, or roast sirloin of beef in a tarragon jus. Live lobsters swim in the seawater tank—until they're removed for preparation and cooked to order. Cheese and dessert trolleys are at your service.

In the Garrack Hotel, Burthallan Lane, Higher Ayr. ✆ **01736/796199.** www.garrack.com. Reservations recommended. Main courses £8–£10; fixed-price 2-course menu £13. AE, DC, MC, V. Daily 6:30–9pm.

Sloop Inn ENGLISH/INTERNATIONAL Proud of its long history (it dates from at least 1312), this stone-and-slate building contains the busiest and most visible pub in St. Ives, located on the harborfront in the town center. Most clients come to drink at one of the three different bar areas amid comfortably battered furnishings. If you're hungry, however, place your order at one of the bars and someone will bring your food to your table. Menu items include ploughman's lunches of cheese and bread, platters of roast chicken or ham, sandwiches, chili, fish and chips, bangers and mash, and lasagna. The kitchen also offers a large selection of locally caught fish, and the eatery is known for its homemade fish pie. The seafood chowder is another excellent choice. The aim seems more to fill you up rather than tantalize your palate.

Simple yet comfortable bedrooms are also available for rent, costing £38 to £50 per person in a double.

The Wharf. ℂ **01736/965584.** www.sloop-inn.co.uk. Bar meals £6–£12. DC, MC, V. Kitchen daily noon–3pm and 5–9:30pm. Pub daily 10am–midnight.

Seeing the Sights

Barbara Hepworth Museum & Sculpture Garden ★   Dame Barbara Hepworth lived at Trewyn from 1949 until her death in 1975, at the age of 72. In her will, she asked that her working studio be turned into a museum where future visitors could see where she lived and created her world-famous sculpture. Today, the museum and garden, now an extension of London's Tate, are virtually just as she left them. On display are about 47 sculptures and drawings, covering the period from 1928 to 1974, as well as photographs, documents, and other Hepworth memorabilia. You can also visit her workshops, housing a selection of tools and some unfinished carvings.

Barnoon Hill. ℂ **01736/796226.** www.tate.org.uk/stives/hepworth. Admission £5 adults, £3 students, free for seniors and children 17 and younger. Mar–Oct daily 10am–5:20pm (last admission 5pm). Nov–Feb Tues–Sun 10am–4:20pm (last admission 4pm), with garden closing at 4:20pm or dusk, whichever is earlier.

Tate St. Ives ★★   This branch of London's famous Tate Gallery exhibits changing groups of work from the Tate's preeminent collection of St. Ives painting and sculpture, dating from about 1925 to 1975. The gallery is administered jointly with the Barbara Hepworth Museum (see above). The collection includes works by artists associated with St. Ives, such as Barbara Hepworth, Alfred Wallis, Ben Nicholson, Naum Gabo, Peter Lanyon, Terry Frost, Patrick Heron, and Roger Hilton. All artists shown here had a decisive effect on the development of painting in the United Kingdom in the second half of the 20th century. About 100 works are on display at all times.

Boasting dramatic sea views, the museum occupies a spectacular site overlooking Porthmeor Beach, close to the home of Alfred Wallis and to the studios used by many of the St. Ives artists.

Porthmeor Beach. ℂ **01736/796226.** www.tate.org.uk/stives. Admission £6 adults, £3.50 students, free for seniors and children 17 and younger. Mar–Oct daily 10am–5:20pm (last admission 5pm); Nov–Feb Tues–Sun 10am–4:20pm (last admission 4pm). Closes occasionally to change displays; call for dates.

En Route to Port Isaac

The stretch of coastline between St. Ives and Port Isaac doesn't have the charm of Cornwall's eastern coast. The fastest way to get to Port Isaac is to take the A30 northeast. However the B3301, hugging close to the Atlantic Ocean, is the more scenic route.

Heading north along the B3301, your first stop will be the estuary town of **Hayle,** once known for its tin and copper mines, but now a beach resort with miles of sand fronting the often wind-tossed Atlantic. Going north from here, the first attraction is **St. Agnes Beacon** (it's signposted). This is the most panoramic belvedere along this wild stretch of north Cornish coastline. At a height of 191m (627 ft.), you can see all the way from Trevose Head in the northeast to St. Michael's Mount in the southwest—that is, if the weather's clear. It's often rainy and cloudy.

The first town of any importance is **Newquay,** a resort with sandy beaches at the foot of the cliffs, opening onto a sheltered bay. Taking its name from a "new" quay built in 1439, it attracts everyone from young surfers to elderly ladies who check into B&Bs along the harbor for long stays. Newquay is a rather commercial town, lacking the charm of St. Ives or Port Isaac, but its beaches attract families in summer. At night, pubs fill up with surfers ready to party.

If you'd like to stay over in Newquay, we recommend the **Hotel Bristol,** Narrowcliff (© **800/528-1234** in the U.S., or 01637/875181; www.hotelbristol.co.uk). This redbrick hotel overlooking the beach has 74 well-furnished rooms that cost £99 to £129 double, including English breakfast. This friendly and inviting place is popular with families. Facilities include an indoor pool, sauna, and solarium; American Express, Diners Club, MasterCard, and Visa are accepted.

Back on the road again, the next important stop is **Padstow.** This town has a long and ancient history. It reached its heyday in the 19th century, when it was an important port. Unfortunately, ships became too big to pass the sandbar (called the "Doom Bar") at the estuary mouth. Walk along the town's quay-lined harbor and explore its narrow streets. At the end of the quay stands **St. Petroc's Church** and **Prideaux Place,** a Tudor house with 18th-century battlements.

Try to arrive in Padstow in time for lunch, because one of the restaurants here—called simply the **Seafood Restaurant** ★, at Riverside (© **01841/532700;** www.rickstein.com)—offers the best cuisine along this stretch of coastline. Here, Rick Stein selects the best "fruits of the sea," which he crafts into French-influenced dishes such as monkfish Goan curry and Dover sole with stir-fried garlic, sorrel, and asparagus. Stein also rents 16 rooms above the restaurant, bistro, and coffee shop for £135 to £235 double per night, including English breakfast; two have private balconies opening onto harbor views. The bar is open all day; lunch is served from noon to 2pm and dinner from 7 to 10pm. Main courses are £17 to £47. MasterCard and Visa are accepted.

PORT ISAAC ★

428km (265 miles) SW of London; 23km (14 miles) SW of Tintagel; 14km (9 miles) N of Wadebridge

Port Isaac remains the most unspoiled fishing village on the north Cornish coastline, in spite of large numbers of summer visitors. By all means, wander through its winding, narrow lanes, gazing at the whitewashed fishing cottages with their rainbow trims.

Essentials

GETTING THERE Bodmin is the nearest railway station. It lies on the main line from London's Paddington Station to Penzance, about a 4-hour trip. Call © **0845/748-4950** or visit www.nationalrail.co.uk for information. Many hotels will send a car to pick up guests at the Bodmin station, or you can take a taxi. If you take a bus from Bodmin, you'll have to change buses at Wadebridge, and connections are not good. Driving time from Bodmin to Port Isaac is 40 minutes.

A bus from Wadebridge goes to Port Isaac about six times a day. It's maintained by **Western Greyhound** (© **01637/871871**). Wadebridge is a local bus junction to many other places in the rest of England.

If you're driving from London, take the M4 west, and then drive south on the M5. Head west again at the junction with the A39, continuing to the junction with the B3267, which you follow until you reach the signposted cutoff for Port Isaac.

Where to Stay & Dine

Port Gaverne Hotel ★   Built in the 17th century as a coastal inn for fishermen needing a rest from their seagoing labors, Port Gaverne, 1km (½ mile) east of Port Isaac, today caters to vacationing families and couples. It's the port's best bet for food and lodgings. Its painted facade is draped with vines, and the small to midsize bedrooms are traditionally furnished. Clusters of antiques and early photographs of Cornwall add somewhat homey touches.

Port Gaverne, Port Isaac, Cornwall PL29 3SQ. ℂ **01208/880244.** Fax 01208/880151. www.chycor. co.uk/hotels/port-gaverne-inn/index.htm. 16 units. £95–£135 double. Rates include English breakfast. MC, V. Free parking. **Amenities:** Restaurant; bar. *In room:* TV, hair dryer.

Slipway Hotel ★   Built in 1527, with major additions made in the early 1700s, this waterside building has seen more uses than any other structure in town, serving as everything from fishing cottages to the headquarters of the first bank here. The building was also once a lifeboat station for rescuing sailors stranded on stormy seas. Now it's a 10-room hotel, with two family suites available. Note that the hotel's steep and narrow staircases are not suitable for young kids or persons with limited mobility.

The Slipway is also known for its restaurant, where ultrafresh seafood is the chef's specialty. Its main dining room contains a minstrel's gallery and lies adjacent to a popular bar frequented by both visitors and locals. At lunch, sandwiches, fish and chips, and seafood pancakes are served. Dinner is more elaborate, featuring fish directly from the nets of local fisherman.

Fore St., Port Isaac, Cornwall PL29 2RH. ℂ **01208/880264.** Fax 01208/880408. www.portisaachotel. com. 10 units. £90–£140 double; £130–£180 suite. Rates include English breakfast. AE, MC, V. No parking. Closed Jan to mid-Feb. **Amenities:** Restaurant; bar. *In room:* TV, hair dryer.

TINTAGEL CASTLE: KING ARTHUR'S LEGENDARY LAIR ★★

425km (264 miles) SW of London; 79km (49 miles) NW of Plymouth; 9.7km (6 miles) NW of Camelford

Even if you don't buy into the legend of King Arthur, a visit is recommended to the little village of Tintagel, which is said to have been the legendary Camelot. Once at Tintagel, signs point the way to the splendid ruins of **Tintagel Castle ★★**, allegedly the site of King Arthur's birth.

Whether or not the tales of Arthurian chivalry and the famous Round Table are true, we'd come here just for the views, which encompass some of the most dramatic coastal scenery in the West Country. Steep cliffs and a rugged sea combine to paint a powerful portrait, and it's fun climbing up and down the cliffs, though only at low tide.

The 13th-century ruins of the castle that stand here—built on the foundations of a Celtic monastery from the 6th century—are popularly known as King Arthur's Castle. They stand 90m (300 ft.) above the sea on a rocky promontory, and to get to them you must take a long, steep, tortuous walk from the parking lot. In summer, many visitors make the ascent to Arthur's Lair, up 100 rock-cut steps. You can also visit Merlin's Cave at low tide. Once you reach Merlin's Cave, the site might not be so much—after all, it's only a cave, although one of legendary status. But the climb along the steep cliffs to reach it provides the thrill.

The castle is 1km (½ mile) northwest of Tintagel. It's open April to September daily 10am to 6pm, October daily 10am to 5pm, and November to March daily 10am to 4pm. Admission is £5.20 for adults, £4.40 for students and seniors, and £2.60 for children. For information, call ℂ **01840/770328** or go to **www.english-heritage.org.uk/tintagel**.

Essentials

GETTING THERE The nearest railway station is in Bodmin, which lies on the main rail line from London to Penzance. From Bodmin, you'll have to take a 30-minute taxi ride to get to Tintagel (there's no bus service from Bodmin to Tintagel). For railway inquiries, call ℂ **0845/748-4950** or visit **www.nationalrail.co.uk**.

If you're driving, from Exeter head across Cornwall on the A30, continuing west at the junction with the A395. From this highway, various secondary roads lead to Tintagel.

VISITOR INFORMATION In Truro, the **Municipal Building,** Boscawen Street (ℂ **01872/274766;** www.truro.gov.uk), has tourist information and is open April through October, Monday to Friday 9am to 5:30pm and Saturday 9am to 5pm; and November through March, Monday through Friday 9am to 5pm.

Where to Stay & Dine

Bossiney House Hotel This comfortable hotel has an inviting location in a fairly tranquil and idyllic setting. Bedrooms have a streamlined, modern feel, accompanied by small bathrooms with either combination tub/showers or else shower stalls. The hotel's Cedar Tree Restaurant is one of the best in the area, serving excellent Cornish cuisine based on fresh regional produce and seafood caught along the coast.

Bossiney Rd., Bossiney, Tintagel, Cornwall PL34 0AX. ℂ **01840/770240.** Fax 01840/770501. www.bossineyhouse.com. 19 units. £76–£90 double. Rates include English breakfast. AE, MC, V. Closed Dec 22-28. Take B3263 1km (½ mile) northeast of Tintagel. **Amenities:** Restaurant; bar; indoor pool; sauna; solarium. *In room:* TV, hair dryer, Wi-Fi (free).

Trevigue Farm ★ ﹚ Owned by the National Trust, this working dairy farm, whose tenants are Ken and Janet Crocker, is located cliff-side, offering access to a beach called the Strangles, where swimming is best experienced during a rising tide. The hotel is housed in two stone buildings: two bedrooms in the 16th-century farmhouse and two bedrooms in a separate house with views of a wooded valley. Accommodations are cozy and tidy. Although only one bedroom contains a TV, there is a cozy sitting room with a television for all guests to enjoy, along with a log fire and a wealth of books. Meals feature English fare with a mix of international dishes.

Crackington Haven, Bude, Cornwall EX23 0LQ. ℂ/fax **01840/230418.** www.trevigue.co.uk. 4 units. £60–£72 double. Rates include English breakfast. MC, V. Closed Dec 25. No children 11 and under. **Amenities:** Restaurant (Thurs–Sat only). *In room:* TV (in 1 unit).

12

Tintagel Castle: King Arthur's Legendary Lair

CORNWALL: THE ANCIENT DUCHY

THE COTSWOLDS: HONEY STONE & "WOOL CHURCHES"

B etween Oxford and the River Severn, about a 2-hour drive west of London, the pastoral Cotswolds occupy a stretch of grassy limestone hills, deep ravines, and barren plateaus known as *wolds,* Old English for "God's high open land." Ancient villages with names such as **Stow-on-the-Wold** dot this bucolic area, most of which is in Gloucestershire, with portions in Oxfordshire, Wiltshire, and Worcestershire.

Made rich by wool from their sheep, the landowners here invested in some of the finest domestic architecture in Europe, distinctively built of honey-brown **Cotswold stone.** The gentry didn't neglect spiritual duties, either, for some of the simplest Cotswold hamlets have churches that, in style and architectural detail, seem far beyond their modest means. Because Cotswold wool was once sold all over the world and wealthy merchants used some of the money to build these churches, they are sometimes referred to as "wool churches."

You'll also see some **thatched cottages** in the Cotswolds. More common are Cotswold roof shingles fashioned from split slabs of stone, which required massive buttressing from medieval carpenters as a means of supporting the weight of the roof. Buildings erected since the 1700s, however, usually have slate roofs.

Mobbed by tourists, overrun Broadway is the most popular base for touring this area, but we suggest you instead head for **Bibury, Painswick,** or other small villages to capture the true charm of the Cotswolds. You'll find the widest range of hotels and facilities in **Cheltenham,** once one of England's most fashionable spas, with a wealth of Regency architecture. And families may want to head to **Birdland,** in Bourton-on-the-Water, where you can see some 1,200 birds of 361 different species.

Biking the country roads of the Cotswolds is one of the best ways to experience the quiet beauty of the area. For a self-guided tour (but with a lot of help), you can hook up with **Cotswold Country Cycles** (✆ 01386/438706; www.cotswold countrycycles.com), whose tours are designed to take you off the beaten track. Accommodations are arranged in advance, often at manor houses or historic homes. A typical offering is the 3-day, 2-night adventure called "Simply Cotswolds," starting at £220 per person. A simpler option is offered by **Hartwells Cycle-Hire** (✆ 01451/820405; www.hartwells.supanet.com), which rents bikes for £12 a day from its base on Bourton-on-the-Water.

The Cotswolds region is also one of the most famous in England for hiking. With such a large area in which to ramble, it's a good idea to know where you are (and aren't) welcome. The **Cotswold Voluntary Wardens Service,** Shire Hall, Gloucester (✆ 01451/862000; www.cotswoldsaonb.org.uk), offers free brochures highlighting trails and paths.

To explore on your own, you can also get info from the **Cheltenham Tourist Information Centre,** 77 The Promenade (✆ 01242/522878; www.visitcheltenham. gov.uk). Be sure to buy a copy of the Cotswold Way map.

The **Wayfarers,** 174 Bellevue Ave., Newport, RI 02840 (✆ 800/249-4620; www.thewayfarers.com), sponsors about six Cotswold walks a year from May to October. The cost of a 6-day tour is £3,695 per person, which includes all meals and snacks, first-class accommodations with private bathrooms along the route, and admission to attractions.

Offering both self-guided and guided tours, **Cotswold Walking Holidays,** Festival House, Jessop Avenue, Cheltenham (✆ 01242/518888; www.cotswoldwalks. com), is the leading purveyor of walking tours in the region. Footpaths in general are well maintained, and this outfitter can show you the way to the best of them. Each night along the way, you can stay in a good standard B&B in a Cotswold village with a wide range of pubs and restaurants. Route instructions and maps are provided. Your luggage will be transported from place to place each day. With B&B arranged, 3-night tours begin at £190 per person.

If you want to experience the Cotswolds in a nutshell and don't have a lot of vacation time, our favorite walk is "The Great Cotswold Ramble" (p. 478).

Warning to motorists: The Cotswolds in the past decades have experienced an overwhelming rise in both population and tourism. The narrow roads are sometimes impossibly overcrowded, and parking is difficult even in the smallest of villages.

TETBURY

182km (113 miles) W of London; 42km (27 miles) NE of Bristol

In the rolling Cotswolds, Tetbury was out of the tourist mainstream until the heir to the British throne and his beautiful bride, Lady Di, took up residence at the old Macmillan place, a Georgian building situated on nearly 141 hectares (350 acres). Then crowds began coming here to catch a glimpse of Prince Charles riding horses and Princess Di shopping. (Today, folks keep an eye out for Charles and his second wife, Camilla Parker Bowles.) Though it can't be seen from the road, the nine-bedroom Windsor mansion, **Highgrove,** is 2.5km (1½ miles) southwest of Tetbury on the way to Westonbirt Arboretum. If you continue out of town on the A433 toward Bath, the first big gate on the right is the entrance to Highgrove. Unlike Buckingham Palace, it can't be visited on most occasions. Actually, it can be visited, but only with

The Cotswolds

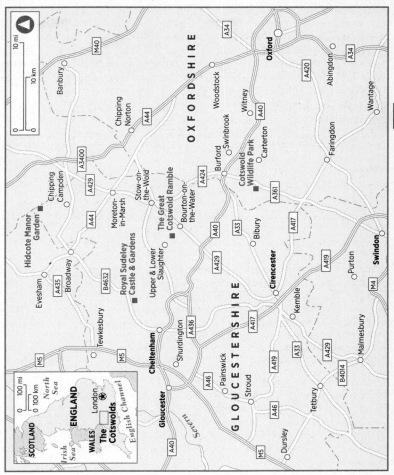

an organized group—and there is a waiting list of up to 5 years. Any interested party can apply in writing to the **Prince of Wales Office,** St. James's Palace, London SW1A 1AA.

Tetbury itself has a 17th-century market hall and a number of antiques shops and boutiques. The town's inns weren't cheap before royalty moved in, and the prices certainly have not dropped since then.

Essentials

GETTING THERE Frequent daily trains run from London's Paddington Station to Kemble, 11km (7 miles) east of Tetbury. For information and schedules, call

459

🕾 **0845/748-2950** or visit **www.nationalrail.co.uk**. You can take a bus from Kemble to Tetbury.

National Express buses leave London's Victoria Coach Station with direct service to Cirencester, 16km (10 miles) northeast of Tetbury. For information and schedules, call 🕾 **0871/781-8181** or visit **www.nationalexpress.co.uk**. Several buses a day connect Cirencester to Tetbury.

If you're driving from London, take the M40 northwest to Oxford, continuing along the A40 to the junction with the A429. Drive south to Cirencester, where you connect with the A433 southwest into Tetbury.

VISITOR INFORMATION   The **Tourist Information Centre,** 33 Church St. (🕾 **01666/503552**; www.visittetbury.co.uk or www.cotswold.info/places/tetbury. shtml), is open March through October, Monday to Saturday 9:30am to 4:30pm, and November through February, Monday to Saturday 11am to 2pm.

Where to Stay

Calcot Manor ★★ ☺   Though the Close in town has a more refined atmosphere (see below), this inn is the finest place on the outskirts. The thick stone walls of the main house shelter a flowering terrace where tea and drinks are served in good weather. The bedrooms are furnished with antiques and modern conveniences; two are equipped with whirlpool tubs, and one has a four-poster bed. Accommodations range from midsize to spacious, and some units, specially designed for families, are located in a refurbished granary near the main house. Views from many of the rooms encompass the Cotswold countryside. The building has indoor and outdoor play areas for kids in addition to child monitors in each room.

Calcot (near Tetbury), Gloucestershire GL8 8YJ. 🕾 **01666/890391.** Fax 01666/890394. www.calcot manor.co.uk. 35 units. £240–£295 double; £295–£340 family room; £416–£451 family suite. Rates include early morning tea, English breakfast, and dinner. AE, DC, MC, V. Free parking. Take A4135 5.5km (3½ miles) west of Tetbury. **Amenities:** 2 restaurants (including Gumstool Inn, below); babysitting; exercise room; indoor pool; room service; spa; tennis court. *In room:* TV, fridge (in family rooms and suites), hair dryer.

The Close Hotel ★★★   The refurbished Close, which dates from 1596 and takes its name from a Cistercian monastery that was on this site, is the town's premier inn. Once the home of a wealthy wool merchant, the house was built of Cotswold stone, with gables and stone-mullioned windows. The ecclesiastical windows in the rear overlook a garden with a reflecting pool. Most bedrooms are spacious and handsomely furnished with antiques. Three of the individually decorated rooms have four-poster beds.

8 Long St., Tetbury, Gloucestershire GL8 8AQ. 🕾 **01666/502272.** Fax 01666/504401. www.theclose-hotel.com. 15 units. £105–£240 double. Rates include English breakfast. AE, MC, V. Free parking. **Amenities:** Restaurant (see review below); bar; room service. *In room:* TV, hair dryer.

Snooty Fox ★   The Snooty Fox stands in the commercial heart of Tetbury. It was originally a 16th-century coaching inn and is today a desirable hotel choice. Despite its name, it's a lot less snooty than the Close and is a popular local rendezvous. The small to very spacious bedrooms are filled with English-country-house luxury, including sumptuous beds and fresh fruit. Two rooms have antique beds with canopies, and the rest are comfortably and tastefully furnished in a more modern style.

Market Place, Tetbury, Gloucestershire GL8 8DD. 🕾 **01666/502436.** Fax 01666/503479. www.snooty-fox.co.uk. 12 units. £80–£170 double; £165–£210 4-poster double. Rates include English breakfast. AE, DC, MC, V. Parking £2. **Amenities:** Restaurant; bar; room service. *In room:* TV, hair dryer.

Where to Dine

The Close Restaurant ★ ENGLISH   This is a dining room of distinction, set with exquisite porcelain, silver, and glass that reflects the sumptuous but discreet atmosphere and friendly service. While sipping champagne on the terrace, take time to peruse the imaginative menu, which is complemented by the town's best wine list. The a la carte menu is seasonally adjusted to take advantage of market-fresh ingredients. Main courses are likely to feature local venison, pan-fried sea bream, or filet of Scottish salmon. Braised lamb shank comes with sautéed forest mushrooms, while lobster is steamed and served with a saffron beurre blanc. Desserts sometimes reach back in England's culinary attic for inspiration, such as the parsnip-and-Cotswold-honey soufflé with whisky and lime ice.

In the Close Hotel, 8 Long St. ✆ **01666/502272.** www.theclose-hotel.com. Reservations recommended. Main courses £11–£20; fixed-price dinner £30. AE, MC, V. Daily 12:30–2:30pm and 6:30–9pm.

Gumstool Inn ★ ENGLISH   In the previously recommended Calcot Manor country hotel lies the ideal venue for traditional country pub dining. In addition to first-rate gastropub grub, you get the town's largest selection of wines and ales. Classic dishes are served under low ceilings atop a flagstone floor, creating an atmosphere of Old England. The menu is large and varied, and children under 12 can arrive for food between 5:30 and 6pm. On warm days, diners will enjoy a table on the terrace, retreating inside to a cozy fire on a chilly night. A wide selection of tasty starters includes crispy duck confit salad with pickled ginger or a ham-hock and bacon terrine. Tempting main dishes range from smoked haddock fishcakes with dill butter to half a roasted pheasant with a bacon and bread sauce.

In the Calcot Manor hotel, Calcot, near Tetbury. ✆ **01666/890391.** www.calcotmanor.co.uk. Reservations not needed. Main courses £10–£14. AE, DC, MC, V. Daily noon–2pm and 5:30–9:30pm.

Exploring Tetbury

Everything in Tetbury is conveniently located in the center of the village; you can easily spend a morning wandering in and out of the many antiques shops and gazing up at the old houses.

The **Parish Church of St. Mary the Virgin,** built between 1777 and 1781, has been hailed as the best Georgian Gothic church in the country. Extensive restoration has returned the interior to its original 18th-century appearance, and the spire is among England's tallest. For information, call ✆ **01666/502333;** it's more than likely the vicar himself will come on the line.

One of the finest examples of a Cotswold-pillared market house is the 1655 **Market House of Tetbury.** It's still in use, hosting one of the most interesting markets in the Cotswolds, in the antique stalls of its meeting hall. Try to schedule a Wednesday-morning visit here to sift through the bric-a-brac.

After the market, head for **Chipping Steps.** The Chipping (market) was for centuries the site of "mop fairs," where farmhands and domestic staff offered themselves for employment. Many surrounding buildings have medieval origins.

Another place to explore is **Gumstoll Hill,** one of Tetbury's most ancient streets and now famous for its annual Woolsack Races.

The **Tetbury Police Museum,** Old Courthouse, 63 Long St., situated in the former police station and magistrates court, is worth a peek. The old cells house a collection of relics from centuries of Cotswold law enforcement. Hours are Monday to Friday 10am to 3pm.

antiquing THE 'WOLDS

If ever there were an English fantasy, it's to drive the country back roads of the Cotswolds, stay in a manor-house hotel, and spend your days browsing the antiques shops, densely packed into these old market towns.

The **Cotswold Art & Antique Dealers' Association (CADA)** publishes a free brochure of members and will happily guide you toward shippers and even hotels. Established in the mid-1970s, and with about 45 active dealers scattered throughout the region, it offers valuable help in organizing your antiques-buying assault on a region known for its decorative treasures. Write to the Secretary, CADA, Broadwell House, Sheep Street, Stow-on-the-Wold, Gloucestershire GL54 1JS, England (✆ **07789/968319;** www.cotswolds-antiques-art.com).

Chavenage House   The drama started with Colonel Nathaniel Stephens, who owned the house during the English Civil War and met an unfortunate demise while living here. He was persuaded by Cromwell, a relative by marriage, to vote for the impeachment of King Charles. This angered Stephens's daughter to the point that she cursed him. Soon after, Stephens died, and it is rumored that his ghostly form can be seen being driven away from Chavenage by a headless coachman wearing royal vestments. The house has been a location shoot for several BBC television productions, including Agatha Christie's *Hercule Poirot*. Aside from its fine Cromwell-era tapestries, furniture, and artifacts, this Elizabethan country house is worth a visit for its rich history and legends.

3km (2 miles) northwest of Tetbury. ✆ **01666/504696.** Fax 01453/836778. www.chavenage.com. Admission (including guided tour) £7 adults, £3.50 children. May–Sept Thurs and Sun 2–5pm; also open on Easter and bank holiday Mon.

CIRENCESTER ★

143km (89 miles) W of London; 26km (16 miles) S of Cheltenham; 27km (17 miles) SE of Gloucester; 58km (36 miles) W of Oxford

Cirencester is the unofficial capital of the Cotswolds. In the Middle Ages, it flourished as the center of the great Cotswold wool industry. Dating from the 17th and 18th centuries, many well-preserved old stone houses are still intact, some having bow-fronted shops of the type familiar to Charles Dickens.

Once known as Corinium, the town had five roads converging here during the Roman occupation. In size, it ranked second only to London. Today, it is chiefly a market town and a good base for touring. We prefer to visit the **Market Place** in the center of town on Monday or Friday morning, when the people from the country flock to town to hawk their produce. (And don't worry about how to pronounce *Cirencester*. Even the English disagree. Say *Siren*-cess-ter and you'll be close enough.)

Essentials

GETTING THERE   Cirencester has no railway station, but trains depart several times a day from London's Paddington Station for the 80-minute trip to Kemble, which is 6.5km (4 miles) southwest of Cirencester. You may have to transfer trains at Swindon. For schedules and information, call ☎ **0845/748-4950** or visit **www. nationalrail.co.uk**. From Kemble, a bus travels to Cirencester four to five times a day.

National Express buses leave London's Victoria Coach Station with direct service to Cirencester. For schedules and information, call ☎ **0871/781-8181** or visit **www.nationalexpress.co.uk**.

If driving from London, take the M40 northwest to Oxford, continuing along the A40 to the junction with the A429, which you'll take south to Cirencester.

VISITOR INFORMATION The **Cirencester Visitor Information Centre** is located in the Corinium Museum, Park Street (☎ **01285/654180;** www.cirencester. gov.uk). Year-round hours are Monday to Saturday from 10am to 5pm, Sunday from 2 to 5pm.

Where to Stay & Dine in & Around Cirencester

Tatyan's, 27 Castle St., Cirencester (☎ **01285/653529;** www.tatyans.com), is a choice place to dine. It serves Beijing, Hunan, and Szechuan specialties, with nearly a dozen prawn dishes on the large menu.

For a pint, head for the town favorite, the **Crown,** 17 W. Market Place, Cirencester (☎ **01285/653206**), a friendly pub enjoyed by locals and students alike, with out-of-towners predominating in summer. The place boasts a 400-year-old tradition of serving ale and victuals on this site, and it has the most convivial nightlife in town.

Barnsley House ★★★ No place in the Cotswolds is as chic, glamorous, and trendy as the former home of garden designer Rosemary Verey. On any week, this restaurant and country house might be visited by neighbors Kate Moss, Kate Winslet, Elizabeth Hurley, or Damien Hirst. The Georgian mansion is surrounded by the best landscaped gardens in the Cotswolds. Most visitors come for the deluxe cuisine. Dishes are simple, robust, absolutely fresh, and "divine," as a patron said.

Pricey bedrooms are full of character, elegance, and individual decor, but all with a sense of whimsy. This is a classic country house with all the latest technology—you can even take a bath while watching a DVD.

Barnsley (6.4km/4 miles NE of Cirencester), Gloucestershire GL7 5EE. ☎ **01285/740000.** Fax 01285/740925. www.barnsleyhouse.com. 11 units. £295–£320 double; £355–£525 suite. Rates include continental breakfast. AE, MC, V. **Amenities:** Restaurant; bar; room service. *In room:* TV/DVD/VCR, CD player, CD library, hair dryer, minibar, MP3 docking station, Wi-Fi (free).

Fleece Hotel Charles II hid out on this site, posing as a servant to the house mistress, Jane Lane, in 1651, with Cromwell's troops in hot pursuit. The half-timbered facade here hints at origins as an Elizabethan coaching inn, but it was enlarged by the Georgians and today has had many modernizations. The comfortable, small to midsize rooms feature old-fashioned hints of yesteryear, including quilts. Two rooms are large enough for families, and two have four-poster beds.

Market Place, Cirencester, Gloucestershire GL7 2NZ. ☎ **01285/658507.** Fax 01285/651017. www.fleece hotel.co.uk. 28 units. £115–£137 double. Rates include English breakfast. Children 15 and younger stay free in same room with up to 2 paying adults. AE, MC, V. **Amenities:** Restaurant; bar; room service. *In room:* TV, hair dryer.

Pear Tree at Purton ★ 🏠 This English country hotel and restaurant, on 3 hectares (7½ acres), offers individually styled rooms in various shapes and sizes, each equipped with extras such as sherry and mineral water. All accommodations (three with four-poster beds) have views of the traditional Victorian garden and countryside;

some executive rooms have whirlpool tubs. Rooms are named for characters associated with the village of Purton—Anne Hyde, for example, mother of Queen Mary and Queen Anne. The Cotswold stone house was formerly the vicarage for the twin-towered parish Church of St. Mary.

Church End, Purton (near Swindon), Wiltshire SN5 4ED. ✆ **01793/772100.** Fax 01793/772369. www.peartreepurton.co.uk. 17 units. £110–£140 double; £140–£200 suite. Rates include English breakfast. AE, DC, MC, V. Closed Dec 26–30. Purton is 13km (8 miles) southeast of Cirencester, 5km (3 miles) from Junction 16 of M4, and 8km (5 miles) from Swindon. From Cirencester, follow B419 in the direction of Swindon. Turn left when signs point to Cricklade, and from here, follow the signs to Purton. **Amenities:** Restaurant; bar; room service. *In room:* TV, hair dryer, Wi-Fi (free).

Stratton House Hotel ★ Built in several stages throughout the 18th century, with a modern wing added in the 1990s, this inviting country house is part Jacobean and part Georgian. It is surrounded by beautiful grounds with a walled garden and herbaceous borders. Bedrooms are large and well furnished (the "cozy" rooms being the smallest of the lot); some have four-poster beds. Two-thirds of the units lie within the most modern wing—designer-decorated, with an aura evoking a traditional private English country house.

Gloucester Rd., Cirencester, Gloucestershire GL7 2LE. ✆ **01285/651761.** Fax 01285/640024. www.strattonhousehotel.co.uk. 39 units. £90–£140 double. Rates include English breakfast. AE, DC, MC, V. Take A417 2km (1¼ miles) northwest of Cirencester. **Amenities:** Restaurant; bar; room service. *In room:* TV, hair dryer.

Exploring Cirencester

Cirencester has some of the greatest walks and scenic views of any town in the Cotswolds. You don't have to go miles out of town to enjoy a stroll—they are easily reached from the center at Market Place. On the grounds of the Church of St. John the Baptist (see below), attractive trees and shrubs highlight a well-manicured landscape. You can see swans and wild fowl on the River Churn and the lake, even remnants of the town's Roman walls. For a great stroll, take the 1.6km-long (1 mile) riverside walk along the Churn from Barton Lane to the Abbey Grounds.

For more walks, head south from Market Place for 4.8km (3 miles) to **Cotswold Water Park,** a 1,214-hectare (3,000-acre) setting of parkland and woodland walks. Pedestrian access is from Cecily Hill (no vehicles). This is Britain's largest water park, with more than 133 lakes created by extracting gravel. Known for its wildlife, the park is filled with picnic tables and barbecue sites, along with a network of footpaths. Concessions here will hook you up with sailing, fishing, canoeing, cycling, kayaking, horseback riding, and water-skiing. All equipment needed is available for rent on-site. Swimming is possible June through September. The park is signposted off B4696, Shorncote (✆ **01285/861459;** www.waterpark.org). From June to August, adults pay £3 admission Monday to Friday, rising to £4 on Saturday and Sunday; the rest of the year, it's £1. Admission for children is 50p from April to September, free from October to March.

Brewery Arts Centre The living heart of this arts complex is the workshop area of 15 resident crafts workers, who produce everything from baskets to chandeliers. Other components of the center include three galleries, featuring crafts and fine-art exhibitions alike, a theater, education classes, a shop selling the best in British crafts, and a coffeehouse.

Brewery Court. ✆ **01285/657181.** www.breweryarts.org.uk. Free admission. Mon–Fri 10am–5pm; Sat 9:30am–5:30pm.

Church of St. John the Baptist   A church may have stood here in Saxon times, but the present building overlooking the Market Place in the town center dates from Norman times and Henry I. In size, it appears more like a cathedral than a mere parish church, with a variety of styles, largely Perpendicular, as in the early-15th-century tower. Among the treasures inside are a 15th-century "wineglass" pulpit and a silver-gilt cup given to Queen Anne Boleyn 2 years before her execution. In the Trinity Chapel, you can rub some great 15th-century brasses.

Market Place. ✆ **01285/654552.** www.acinc.org.uk. Free admission; donations invited. Mon–Fri 10am–1pm.

Corinium Museum ★★   This museum houses one of the finest collections of archaeological remains from the Roman occupation, found locally in and around Cirencester. Mosaic pavements excavated on Dyer Street in 1849 and other mosaics are the most important exhibits. Provincial Roman sculpture, including such figures as Minerva and Mercury, pottery, and artifacts salvaged from long-decayed buildings, provide a link with the remote civilization that once flourished here. The museum has been completely modernized to include full-scale reconstructions and special exhibitions on local history and conservation.

Park St. ✆ **01285/655611.** www.cirencester.co.uk/coriniummuseum. Admission £4.25 adults, £3.50 seniors, £2.75 students, £2 children 5–16, £12 family ticket. Mon–Sat 10am–5pm; Sun 2–5pm.

Shopping

For antiques in Cirencester, try **William H. Stokes,** the Cloisters, 6–8 Dollar St. (✆ **01285/653907;** www.williamhstokes.co.uk), which specializes in furniture, tapestries, and other items from the 16th and 17th centuries.

The arts complex known as the **Brewery Arts Centre** (see above) has 15 independent workshops of area craftspeople, ranging from jewelers and weavers to basket makers. Three galleries and a crafts shop recognized by the Crafts Council sell many of the artists' wares.

PAINSWICK ★

172km (107 miles) W of London; 16km (10 miles) SW of Cheltenham; 24km (15 miles) NW of Cirencester; 6.5km (4 miles) N of Stroud

This sleepy stone-built Cotswold wool town vies with Bibury for the title of the most beautiful in the Cotswolds. Painswick is a dream of England of long ago, the perfect escape from a string of dull market towns too often encountered. Its mellow gray stone houses and inns date from as early as the 14th century.

A visit to Painswick at any time of the year would be idyllic, in spite of the day-trippers and tourist buses, but there are two special occasions that make it an especially wonderful destination. One is the town's **Victorian Market Day** in early July; the other big occasion is the **Clipping Feast.** See "Special Events," below, for more information.

Essentials

GETTING THERE   Trains depart London's Paddington Station several times a day for Stroud, the nearest railway station, 5km (3 miles) away. The trip takes from 1½ to 2 hours, and you may have to change trains at Swindon. For rail information, call ✆ **0845/748-4950** or visit **www.nationalrail.co.uk**. From Stroud, buses run to Painswick, some as frequently as every hour. Many taxis also wait at the Stroud railway station.

If you're driving from Cirencester, continue west along the A419 to Stroud, and then head north on the A46 to Cheltenham and Painswick.

VISITOR INFORMATION The Painswick **Tourist Information Centre** is at the Painswick Library, Stroud Road (🕐 **01452/813552;** www.britainexpress.com/TIC/ gloucestershire.htm), and is open Monday to Saturday from 10am to 5pm. These hours are true at least in theory, but the volunteers manning the office don't always show up. In that case, you can visit the more reliably open **Tourist Information Centre** in Stroud, located at the Subscription Rooms, George Street (🕐 **01453/760960**).

SPECIAL EVENTS The **Clipping Feast** of Painswick, also known as the Clipping Ceremony, is an unusual, early medieval ceremony that anthropologists think may have begun in the dim Celtic prehistory of Britain. Every September, a month that coincides with the harvest ceremonies of pagans, adults and as many children as can be mustered hold hands in a circle around St. Mary's Anglican Church. The circle moves first one way, then the other, and the participants sing hymns and pray out loud in a celebration of thanksgiving. Participants and observers come from all over the region to take part in this important rite.

On **Victorian Market Day,** in early July, locals dressed in Victorian attire come into town from the neighboring villages. Shoppers meander through the streets, absorbing the festive atmosphere and purchasing handicrafts and other gifts. Food, based on old-fashioned recipes, is sold at various kiosks.

Contact the Tourist Information Centre (see above) for the exact date and schedule of these events.

Where to Stay & Dine

Cardynham House ★ 🍴 Adjacent to St. Mary's Church, this small but choice house dates from 1498. It was later enlarged thanks to beams that were salvaged from the remains of a wrecked ship from the Spanish Armada. The owner has outfitted the interior with lots of cozy accessories that fit in well with a stylish hodgepodge of cabinets, wide floorboards, and an intricate network of ceiling beams. Bedrooms are cozy, each with a different theme (Arabian Nights and Medieval Garden are good examples). All of the accommodations feature four-poster or half-tester beds. One of them is a bit larger than the others and enjoys exclusive access to a 5m (16-ft.) indoor swimming pool. The Dovecote room is good for families.

Local produce is deftly handled at the on-site restaurant, the Bistro, which is open Tuesday to Saturday for dinner and Tuesday to Sunday for lunch. Roast beef with all the trimmings is a feature at the Sunday lunch, and tender Cotswold lamb appears frequently on the menu.

The Cross/Tibbiwell St., Painswick, Gloucestershire GL6 6XX. 🕐 **01452/814006.** Fax 01452/812321. www.cardynham.co.uk. 9 units. £85–£210 double. Rates include breakfast. 2-night minimum Fri–Sun. AE, MC, V. Parking £2.50. **Amenities:** Restaurant; lounge. *In room:* TV, hair dryer.

Cotswold 88 ★★ If Henry VII or even Elizabeth I were passing through the village today, they might be horrified at what has happened to the old Painswick Hotel, a former vicarage encircled by terraces of formal gardens. This mansion behind the Painswick parish church has been completely renovated. Today, it retains its old architectural features but has been completely modernized inside, sort of what you might expect to see in a rock star's country manor. The bedrooms have been updated with a very modern and slightly crazy interior decor, decorated with works by photo artists David Hiscock and Leigh Bowery. Its restaurant and bar are the hippest in town.

Kemps Lane, Painswick, Gloucestershire GL6 6YB. © **01452/813688.** Fax 01452/814059. www. cotswolds88hotel.com. 18 units. £160–£275 double; £245–£450 suite. AE, MC, V. **Amenities:** Restaurant; bar; babysitting; room service. *In room:* TV, hair dryer, Wi-Fi (free).

Exploring Painswick

The charm of this town comes from its mellow Cotswold architecture of stone-built houses. Funded by wealthy farmers and merchants in the era when fluffy wool was called "white gold," the houses of Painswick represent a peak in English domestic architecture. It's best seen by walking around **New Street** in the center of the village. This has to be one of the most misnamed streets in England, as it dates from 1450 and there isn't anything new about it.

St. Mary's Church, the centerpiece of the village, was originally built between 1377 and 1399, and was reconstructed into its present form in 1480. Its churchyard contains 99 massive yew trees, each of which is at least 200 years old. Local legend states that no matter how hard well-meaning gardeners have tried, they've never been able to grow more than 99 of them.

Painswick Rococo Garden ★, on B4073, .8km (½ mile) north of Painswick (© **01452/813204;** www.rococogarden.co.uk), is a rare English garden and a throwback to the flamboyant English rococo period, which lasted only from 1720 to 1760. Today, the garden is best known for its spectacular display of snowdrops that appear in the early spring, sometimes when snow is still on the ground. On certain summer evenings, Shakespeare's plays are performed in the garden. Admission is £6 for adults, £5 for seniors, £3 for children 5 to 16, and £16 for a family ticket (two adults, two children); visits are possible from mid-January to October, daily 11am to 5pm.

CHELTENHAM ★

159km (99 miles) NW of London; 69km (43 miles) W of Oxford; 14km (9 miles) NE of Gloucester

Legend has it that the Cheltenham villagers discovered a mineral spring by chance when they noticed pigeons drinking from a spring and observed how healthy they were (the pigeon has been incorporated into the town's crest). King George III arrived in 1788 and launched the town's career as a spa. Today, many British look upon it as a staid, safe place for retirement, the town attracting mainly well-heeled conservatives, some of the women looking like Margaret Thatcher did in the 1980s.

Cheltenham remains one of England's most fashionable spas; many visitors come just to see its gardens. The architecture is mainly Regency, with lots of ironwork, balconies, and verandas. Attractive parks and open spaces of greenery make the town especially inviting. The main street, the Promenade, is one of the most beautiful thoroughfares in the Cotswolds. Rather similar are Lansdowne Place and Montpellier Parade (with caryatids separating the stores). Montpellier Walk contains more than 30 statues adorning its storefronts.

Essentials

GETTING THERE Twenty-one trains depart daily from London's Paddington Station for the 2¼-hour trip. You may have to change trains at Bristol or Swindon.

For information, call ✆ **0845/748-4950** or visit **www.nationalrail.co.uk**. Trains between Cheltenham and Bristol take an hour, with continuing service to Bath.

National Express offers 10 buses daily from London's Victoria Coach Station to Cheltenham. The ride takes about 2½ to 3 hours. For schedules and information, call ✆ **0871/781-8181** or visit **www.nationalexpress.co.uk**.

If you're driving from London, head northwest on the M40 to Oxford, and continue along the A40 to Cheltenham.

VISITOR INFORMATION The **Tourist Information Centre,** 77 The Promenade (✆ **01242/522878;** www.visitcheltenham.com), is open Monday to Saturday from 9:30am to 5:15pm. On Wednesday mornings, it opens at 10am.

SPECIAL EVENTS The **Cheltenham Music Festival** and the **Cheltenham Literature Festival** take place each year in July and October, respectively, and attract internationally acclaimed orchestras and performers. There are other festivals as well—a jazz festival in May, a science festival in June. For details, call ✆ **01242/774400** or visit **www.cheltenhamfestivals.co.uk**.

Where to Stay

Beaumont House ★ 🏛 One of the best-rated B&Bs in the area, this house is set in a lovely garden a short walk from the town center and convenient to local shops and restaurants. Its owners have made significant improvements and today its renovated bedrooms are among the best in the area—indeed, they've won awards. No accommodations are alike, ranging from small singles to luxurious and spacious rooms suitable for families. Comfort and style combine with a warm welcome to make this a desirable choice—and the price is right, too.

56 Shurdington Rd., Cheltenham, Gloucestershire GL53 0JE. ✆ **01242/223311.** Fax 01242/520044. www.bhhotel.co.uk. 16 units. £88–£169 double; £229 suite. Rates include breakfast. AE, MC, V. **Amenities:** Breakfast room. *In room:* TV, hair dryer, Wi-Fi (free).

Central Hotel Within easy reach of Cheltenham's range of attractions, this hotel comprises a pair of stone houses that were originally built in the 1700s and then combined. Today, it's a family-run hotel, with a street-level public house. The comfortable bedrooms are conservatively modern with everything you need, including a kitchen for self-catering.

7-9 Portland St., Cheltenham, Gloucestershire GL52 2NZ. ✆ **01242/582172.** Fax 01242/524789. www.centralhotelcheltenham.co.uk. 23 units. £46–£50 double; £59 family room. MC, V. **Amenities:** Restaurant; bar. *In room:* TV, hair dryer, kitchen, Wi-Fi (free).

The Greenway ★★ An elegant and beautifully furnished former Elizabethan manor house from the 1540s in a garden setting, this is an ivy-clad Cotswold showpiece. Restored with sensitivity, the Greenway rents rooms in both its main house and a converted coach house. Bedrooms, midsize to spacious, are sumptuously outfitted. This is the best English-country-house living in the area.

Shurdington, near Cheltenham, Gloucestershire GL51 4UG. ✆ **01242/862352.** Fax 01242/862780. www.thegreenway.co.uk. 21 units. £215–£380 double; £310–£495 suite. Rates include English breakfast and early morning tea and coffee. AE, DC, MC, V. Take A46 less than 6.5km (4 miles) southwest of Cheltenham. **Amenities:** Restaurant; bar; room service. *In room:* TV, hair dryer, Internet (free).

Hotel on the Park ★★ In what was formerly an 1830s private villa, this is one of the most talked-about hotels in town. It is located among similar terraced buildings in the once-prominent village of Pittville Spa, 1km (½ mile) north of Cheltenham's town center. Owned and operated by Darryl and Joanne Gregory, who undertook most of the Regency-inspired interior design, it has received several awards. Each bedroom is named after a prominent 19th-century visitor who came here shortly after the villa was built. Comfortable and high-ceilinged, the rooms have stylish accessories and a tasteful assortment of antique and reproduction furniture. All are beautifully appointed, with thoughtful extras such as sherry and mineral water.

Evesham Rd., Cheltenham, Gloucestershire GL52 2AH. ☎ **01242/518898.** Fax 01242/511526. www.thehoteluk.co.uk. 12 units. £155–£235 double; £395–£495 suite. AE, DC, MC, V. **Amenities:** Restaurant; bar; room service. *In room:* TV, hair dryer, Wi-Fi (free).

Lypiatt House ★ 🍴 This beautifully restored Victorian home stands in the Montpellier area, the most fashionable part of Cheltenham. A hotel of ambience and character, it offers a large elegant drawing room with a colonial-style conservatory and "honesty bar." The bedrooms are beautifully furnished and of generous size. The friendly owners are the most helpful in town.

Lypiatt Rd., Cheltenham, Gloucestershire GL50 2QW. ☎ **01242/224994.** Fax 01242/224996. www.lypiatt.co.uk. 10 units. £80–£110 double. Rates include English breakfast. AE, MC, V. **Amenities:** Bar. *In room:* TV.

Where to Dine

Brasserie Blanc ★ MODERN FRENCH   Already a bit of a dining legend in Oxford, this offspring long ago invaded Cheltenham. Under the guidance of Master Chef Raymond Blanc, a celebrity chef whose more famous, and more expensive, gastronomic restaurant is known throughout England, this is a *brasserie de luxe,* with a decor inspired by turn-of-the-20th-century Paris, modern paintings, a row of unusual sculpture that runs up the middle, and a hip and knowledgeable staff. Cuisine is beautifully presented and prepared with the freshest of the day's available ingredients. Some of the finest examples include such starters as Loch Fyne mussels with white-wine-and-cream sauce or a truffle-flavored chicken liver parfait, followed by such mains as crab and salmon fishcakes or filet of seared haddock and shellfish in a creamy wine sauce.

Next to the Queen's Hotel, the Promenade. ☎ **01242/266800.** www.brasserieblanc.com. Reservations recommended. Main courses £8.75–£17 lunch, £9.75–£18 dinner; fixed-price 2-course lunch £12, 3-course lunch £15; fixed-price 2-course dinner £15, 3-course dinner £18. AE, DC, MC, V. Mon–Fri noon–2:45pm and 5:30–10:30pm; Sat noon–11pm; Sun noon–10pm.

Le Champignon Sauvage ★★★ FRENCH   This is among the culinary highlights of the Cotswolds. David Everitt-Matthias, a chef of considerable talent, limits the selection of dishes each evening for better quality control. Some evenings his imagination roams a bit, so dining here is usually a pleasant surprise. You may begin with light cauliflower soup flavored with cumin. Main courses can include braised lamb dumplings with roasted carrots and shallots. On a more daring level, you can sample roast partridge with caramelized chicory and Puy lentils, or perhaps pumpkin risotto with pork belly and artichoke foam. Dessert choices include iced licorice parfait with damson sorbet and baked caramel cheesecake with caramelized banana.

24–26 Suffolk Rd. ☎ **01242/573449.** www.lechampignonsauvage.co.uk. Reservations required. Fixed-price 2-course meal £45, 3-course meal £55, 4-course meal £64. AE, DC, MC, V. Tues–Sat 12:30–1:30pm and 7:30–9pm. Closed 2 weeks in June, 1 week in Dec.

Exploring Cheltenham

Cheltenham Art Gallery & Museum   This gallery houses one of the foremost collections of the Arts and Crafts movement, notably the fine furniture of William Morris and his followers. One section is devoted to Edward Wilson, Cheltenham's native son, who died with Captain Scott in the Antarctic in 1912. The gallery is located near Royal Crescent and the Coach Station.

Clarence St. (✆ **01242/237431.** www.cheltenhammuseum.org.uk. Free admission; donations welcome. Mon–Sat 10am–5:20pm. Closed bank holidays.

Everyman Theatre   Cheltenham is the cultural center of the Cotswolds, a role solidified by the Everyman Theatre. Designed in the 1890s as an opera house by Frank Matcham, Victorian England's leading theater architect, it retains its ornate cornices, sculpted ceilings, and plush velvets despite extensive renovations to its stage and lighting facilities. The theater has begun to attract some of England's top dramatic companies. Shakespeare, musicals, comedies, and other genres are performed in the small (658-seat) but charming hall.

Regent St. (✆ **01242/572573.** www.everymantheatre.org.uk. Tickets £8–£45, depending on the event. Box office Mon–Sat 9:30am–8:30pm (until 6pm in Aug), and from 2 hr. before the performance on Sun.

Pittville Pump Room   Cheltenham Waters are the only natural, consumable alkaline waters in Great Britain and are still drunk at one of the spa's finest Regency buildings. The Pittville Pump Room is open Sundays from the end of May until the end of September for a host of activities, including lunch, afternoon cream teas, live classical music, landau carriage rides around the city, and brass bands playing in Pittville Park.

East Approach Dr., Pittville Park. (✆ **0844/576-2210.** www.cheltenhamtownhall.org.uk. Free admission; donations welcome. Wed–Mon 10am–4pm. From the town center, take Portland St. and Evesham Rd.

Shopping

Start in the **Montpellier quarter** for individual boutiques and craft and specialty shops. The **Courtyard,** on Montpellier Street in the heart of the quarter, has become an award-winning shopping mall that offers a fun blend of shops specializing in unique fashion, furniture, and gift items. A good mix of restaurants, cafes, and wine bars rounds out the mall.

From Montpellier, continue to the nearby **Suffolk quarter** to find most of Cheltenham's antiques stores.

An enjoyable short stroll to the **Promenade** takes you by stores featuring attractive clothing and shoes, as well as several bookstores. **Cavendish House,** the Promenade (✆ **01242/521300**), is a long-established shopping landmark.

From the Promenade, take Regent Street to **High Street,** which is mostly pedestrian-only, and you'll find several brand-name department stores in the **Beechwood Shopping Centre.**

The **weekly market** is in the Henrietta Street car park on Thursday. Weather permitting, the market is open from 9am to 2pm.

Cheltenham After Dark

The major venue for entertainment is the **Everyman Theatre** (see above), which is the premier sightseeing attraction of Cheltenham. You'll find a lot more theater at the **Playhouse,** Bath Road (✆ **01242/522852;** www.playhousecheltenham.org), which presents new local, amateur productions of drama, comedy, dance, and opera staged at the dizzying pace of every two weeks. Tickets are £6 to £32.

Otherwise, the best center for nocturnal affairs is **The Place,** 33–35 Albion St. (© **01242/570583;** www.theplacenightclub.co.uk), which is entered from High Street. It offers three floors of fun, with loud music blaring everything from R&B to hits from the Reagan era. Cover ranges from £5 to £15, but it's most often free if you enter before 10pm. The Place is open Monday and Wednesday through Saturday 9pm to 3am.

A Side Trip to Sudeley Castle ★

Royal Sudeley Castle & Gardens   This 15th-century structure is one of England's finer stately homes. It has a rich history that begins in Saxon times, when the village was the capital of the Mercian kings. Later, Catherine Parr, the sixth wife of Henry VIII, lived and died here. Her tomb is in a chapel on the grounds, which include a host of formal gardens like the Queen's Garden, now planted with old-world roses and dating from the time of Catherine Parr. While exploring the gardens, you're sure to see the waterfowl and flamboyant peacocks that call Sudeley home.

For the past 30 years, Lady Ashcombe, an American by birth, has owned the castle and welcomed visitors from the world over. The castle houses many works of art by Constable, Turner, Rubens, and Van Dyck, among others, and has several permanent exhibitions, magnificent furniture and glass, and many artifacts from the castle's past. In the area to the right of the keep, as you enter the castle, workshops are devoted to talented local artisans who continue to use traditional techniques to produce stained glass, textiles, wood and leather articles, and marbled paper. The admission prices given below are for exhibitions and the gardens. To tour the private apartments, there is an additional cost of £15 per person. These "connoisseur tours" are available Tuesday to Thursday at 11am, 1pm, and 3pm and include the stone-built drawing room, the library, and the billiard room.

In the village of Winchcombe (9.5km/6 miles northeast of Cheltenham). © **01242/602308.** www.sudeleycastle.co.uk. Admission £7.20 adults, £6.20 seniors, £4.20 children 5–15, £21 family ticket. Castle Apr–Oct daily 10:30am–5pm (last admission 4:30pm); gardens and grounds Mar–Oct daily 10:30am–5:30pm. From Cheltenham, take the regular bus to Winchcombe and get off at Abbey Terrace. Then walk the short distance along the road to the castle. If you're driving, take B4632 north out of Cheltenham, through Prestbury, and up Cleve Hill to Abbey Terrace, where you can drive right up to the castle.

BIBURY ★★

138km (86 miles) W of London; 48km (30 miles) W of Oxford; 42km (26 miles) E of Gloucester

On the road from Burford to Cirencester, Bibury is one of the loveliest spots in the Cotswolds. In fact, the utopian romancer of Victoria's day, poet William Morris, called it England's most beautiful village. In the Cotswolds, it is matched only by Painswick for its scenic village beauty and purity. Both villages are still unspoiled by modern intrusions.

Getting There

About five trains per day depart London's Paddington Station for the 1-hour, 20-minute trip to Kemble, the nearest station, 21km (13 miles) south of Bibury. Some will require an easy change of train in Swindon (the connecting train waits across the tracks). For information, call ☎ 0845/748-4950 or visit www.nationalrail.co.uk. No buses run from Kemble to Bibury, but most hotels will arrange transportation if you ask in advance.

Ten buses per day leave London's Victoria Coach Station for Cirencester, 11km (7 miles) from Bibury. For information, call ☎ 0871/781-8181 or visit www.national express.co.uk. With no connecting buses into Bibury, local hotels will send a car, otherwise taxis are available.

If driving from London, take the M4 to exit 15, head toward Cirencester, and then follow the A33 (on some maps this is still designated as the B4425) to Bibury.

Where to Stay & Dine

Bibury Court Hotel ★ 🛅   You can feel the history when you stay at this Jacobean manor house, built by Sir Thomas Sackville in 1633 (parts of it date from Tudor times). The house was a residence until it was turned into a hotel in 1968. The structure is built of Cotswold stone, with many gables, huge chimneys, and a formal graveled entryway. Many rooms have four-poster beds, original oak paneling, and antiques. They're furnished in old English style but have modern comforts.

Bibury, Gloucestershire GL7 5NT. ☎ **01285/740337.** Fax 01285/740660. www.biburycourt.co.uk. 18 units. £180–£240 double; £260 suite. Rates include continental breakfast. AE, DC, MC, V. **Amenities:** 2 restaurants; bar; room service. *In room:* TV, hair dryer.

Swan Hotel ★★   Well managed, upscale, and discreet, the Swan is the finest hotel and restaurant in the village. It originated as a riverside cottage in the 1300s, but was greatly expanded through the centuries. Much of the interior is outfitted in a traditional, warm-toned design evocative of a discreetly upscale stately home, with tartan and flowered fabrics and autumn-inspired colors. The bedrooms are outfitted with antique furniture and an individualized decor. Each contains an elegant bed— some are four-posters—with soft linens. There are three modern and luxurious suites located a short walk from the main building, each with its own landscaped garden and containing such extras as an iPod/MP3 docking station.

Bibury, Gloucestershire GL7 5NW. ☎ **01285/740695.** Fax 01285/740473. www.cotswold-inns-hotels. co.uk/property/the_swan_hotel?/swan. 18 units. £155–£275 double; £245–£285; 2-bedroom suite for 4; £255–£320 garden suite. Rates include English breakfast. AE, DC, MC, V. **Amenities:** 2 restaurants; bar; room service. *In room:* TV, hair dryer.

Exploring Bibury

On the banks of the tiny River Coln, Bibury is noted for **Arlington Row,** a group of 17th-century gabled cottages protected by the National Trust. Originally built for weavers, these houses are its biggest and most photographed attraction, but it's rude to peer into the windows, as many do, because people still live here.

To get a view of something a bit out of the ordinary for the Cotswolds, check out **St. Mary's Parish Church.** As the story goes, the wool merchants who had the power and money in the area were rebuilding the churches. However, they did not finish the restoration to St. Mary's, and, as a result, much of the original Roman-style architecture has been left intact. The 14th-century Decorated-style windows have even survived the years. This is an often-overlooked treasure. The so-called "Decorated" style was given to the second period of English Gothic architecture, mainly from the late 13th to the mid–14th centuries, when adornments became more elaborate and stone construction lighter and more spacious.

BURFORD ★

122km (76 miles) NW of London; 32km (20 miles) W of Oxford

Built of Cotswold stone and serving as a gateway to the area, the unspoiled medieval town of Burford is largely famous for its Norman church (ca. 1116) and its High Street lined with coaching inns.

Burford was one of the last of the great wool centers, the industry bleating out its last breath during Queen Victoria's day. Be sure to photograph the bridge across the River Windrush where Queen Elizabeth I once stood. As the antiques shops along High Street testify, Burford today is definitely equipped for visitors.

The River Windrush, which toward Burford is flanked by willows and meadows, passes beneath the packhorse bridge and goes around the church and away through more meadows. Strolling along its banks is one of the most delightful experiences in the Cotswolds.

Essentials

GETTING THERE   Many trains depart from London's Paddington Station to Oxford, a 1-hour trip. For information, call ✆ **0845/748-4950** or visit **www.first greatwestern.co.uk**. From Oxford, passengers walk a short distance to the entrance of the Taylor Institute, from which about three or four buses per day make the 30-minute run to Burford.

If you're driving from Oxford, head west on the A40 to Burford.

VISITOR INFORMATION   The **Tourist Information Centre** is at the Old Brewery, Sheep Street (✆ **01993/823558;** www.cotswold.info/places/burford. shtml). It's open November through February, Monday to Saturday 9:30am to 4pm, and March through October, Monday to Saturday 9:30am to 5:30pm.

Where to Stay

Bay Tree Hotel ★★   This is the best and most atmospheric of Burford's many interesting old inns. The house was built for Sir Lawrence Tanfield, the unpopular lord chief baron of the exchequer to Elizabeth I. The house has oak-paneled rooms with stone fireplaces and a high-beamed hall with a minstrel's gallery. Modern comforts have been discreetly installed in the tastefully furnished accommodations, some of which have four-poster beds. Some units are in a comfortable annex, though the chambers in the main building—nine in all—have more character. Try to get a room overlooking the terraced gardens at the rear of the house.

12–14 Sheep St., Burford, Oxfordshire OX18 4LW. ✆ **01993/822791**. Fax 01993/823008. www.broadway-cotswolds.co.uk/baytree.html. 21 units. £165–£205 double; £215–£250 suite. Rates include English breakfast. AE, DC, MC, V. **Amenities:** Restaurant; bar; babysitting; room service. *In room:* TV, hair dryer.

Golden Pheasant ★   This inn is housed in what was once the 15th-century home of a prosperous wool merchant. It began serving food and drink in the 1730s when it was used both to brew and serve beer. Today, it's one of the best places to stay in town (though it lacks the rich furnishings of the best, the Bay Tree Hotel, described above). Like many of its neighbors, the Golden Pheasant is capped with a slate roof and fronted with hand-chiseled stones. The cozy accommodations come in a range of sizes, many a bit small, and one room has a four-poster bed. Each, though, is stylishly appointed with period furniture. One room is large enough for a family.

91 High St., Burford, Oxfordshire OX18 4QA. ✆ **01993/823223.** Fax 01993/822621. www.golden pheasantburford.com. 12 units. £85–£145 double. Rates include English breakfast. MC, V. **Amenities:** Restaurant; bar. *In room:* TV, hair dryer, Wi-Fi (free).

Lamb Inn ★★ This thoroughly Cotswold house, solidly built in 1430, offers thick stone walls, mullioned and leaded windows, many chimneys and gables, and a slate roof now mossy with age. Vying with the Bay Tree in antique furnishings, it opens onto a stone-paved rear garden, with a rose-lined walk and a shaded lawn. The bedrooms are a mixture of today's comforts and antiques, and prices depend on how recently the room was furnished. Rooms vary in size, though each has a compact bathroom with a tub/shower combination (one has a shower stall). The public living rooms have heavy oak beams, stone floors, window seats, Oriental rugs, and fine antiques. An excellent restaurant (see review below) is on-site.

Sheep St., Burford, Oxfordshire OX18 4LR. ✆ **01993/823155.** Fax 01993/822228. www.cotswold-inns-hotels.co.uk. 15 units. Sun–Thurs £150–£200 double; Fri–Sat £175–£265 double. Rates include English breakfast. MC, V. **Amenities:** Restaurant; bar; room service. *In room:* TV, hair dryer.

Where to Dine

After you've browsed the antiques shops, head to **Burford House** (✆ **01993/823151**) for tea. This old Cotswold favorite serves nonresidents Monday to Saturday from 10:30am to 5pm. Freshly baked goods, including flans, scones, cakes, and muffins, will tempt you.

Lamb Restaurant MODERN A meal in this pretty pillared restaurant is the perfect way to cap off a visit to Burford. Good pub lunches dominate the agenda at midday; dinners are formal, candlelit affairs. The evening menu is beautifully cooked and served. You might begin with Jerusalem artichoke soup with a smoked bacon boudin and follow with pan-fried sea bass with an open prawn ravioli in a sun-dried tomato sauce. The pub here attracts folks from all walks of life, who seem to adore its mellow atmosphere and charm. Guinness, cider, and a carefully chosen collection of ales, including a local brew, Wadworth Hook Norton Ale, are on tap.

In the Lamb Inn, Sheep St. ✆ **01993/823155.** www.cotswold-inns-hotels.co.uk. Reservations recommended for dinner. 2-course lunch £17; 3-course lunch £20; lunch platters £9–£15; 2-course dinner £30; 3-course dinner £35; tasting menu £40. MC, V. Daily noon–2:30pm and 7–9:30pm.

Seeing the Sights

Approaching Burford from the south, you'll experience one of the finest views of any ancient market town in the country. The main street sweeps down to the River Windrush, past an extraordinary collection of houses of various styles and ages. Burford's ancient packhorse bridge still does duty at the bottom of the hill. Hills opposite provide a frame of fields, trees, and, with luck, panoramic skies.

Though the wool trade has long since vanished, most of Burford remains unchanged in appearance, with old houses in the High Street and nearby side streets. Nearly all are built of local stone. Like many Cotswold towns, Burford has a Sheep Street, with many fine stone-built houses covered with roofs of Stonesfield slate. **Burford Church** (ca. 1175) is almost cathedral-like in proportion. It was enlarged throughout succeeding centuries until the decline of the wool trade. Little has changed here since about 1500.

Traders and vendors still set up their stalls under the Tolsey on Friday, where, from the 12th century, the guild has collected tolls from anyone wishing to trade in the town. It still stands at the corner of Sheep Street. On the upper floor is the minor **Tolsey Museum,** where you can see a medieval seal bearing Burford's insignia, the "rampant cat."

On Burford's High Street, you'll find several antiques shops, including **Manfred Schotten Antiques,** the Crypt, 109 High St. (© **01993/822302;** www.schotten. com). Sporting antiques and collectibles, it also carries library and club furniture. **Gateway Antiques,** at the Burford Roundabout, on Cheltenham Road (© **01993/823678;** www.gatewayantiques.co.uk), has a variety of items displayed in large showrooms. English pottery, metalware, and 19th-century furniture dominate the inventory. Unique arts and crafts items and interesting decorative objects are fun to browse, even if you don't buy.

Three kilometers (2 miles) south of Burford on the A361 lies the **Cotswold Wildlife Park** (© **01993/823006;** www.cotswoldwildlifepark.co.uk). The 65 hectares (160 acres) of gardens and forests around this Victorian manor house have been transformed into a jungle of sorts, with a Noah's Ark consortium of animals ranging from voracious ants to rare Asiatic lions, rhinos, and leopards. Children can romp around the farmyard and the adventure playground. A narrow-gauge railway runs from April to October, and there are extensive picnic areas as well as a cafeteria. The park is open March through September, daily 10am to 4:30pm, and October through February, daily 10am to 3:30pm (last entry 1 hr. before closing). Admission is £11 for adults, £8 for seniors and children 3 to 16, and free for children 2 and younger.

Before you leave Burford, we suggest a slight detour to **Swinbrook,** a pretty village by the River Windrush immediately to the east. It's best known as the one-time home of the fabled Mitford sisters. Visit the local parish church to see the grave of writer Nancy Mitford and the impressive tiered monuments to the Fettiplace family.

BOURTON-ON-THE-WATER ★

137km (85 miles) NW of London; 58km (36 miles) NW of Oxford

This is the quintessential Cotswold village, with history dating from the Celts. Today, it's overrun with tourists in summer. Although residents fiercely protect the heritage of 15th- and 16th-century architecture, their town is singled out for nearly every bus tour that rolls through the Cotswolds.

Populated in Anglo-Saxon times, Bourton-on-the-Water developed into a strategic outpost along the ancient Roman road, Fosse Way, which traversed Britain from the North Sea to St. George's Channel. During the Middle Ages, its prosperity came from wool, which was shipped all over Europe. During the Industrial Revolution, when the greatest profits lay in finished textiles, it became a backwater as a producer of raw wool—albeit with the happy result for us that it never "modernized."

The scenic Cotswold village on the banks of the River Windrush has earned the title "Venice of the Cotswolds," with its mellow stone houses, its village greens on the banks of the water, and its bridges. Don't expect gondoliers, however. This town makes a good stopover, if not for the night, at least as a place to enjoy a lunch and a rest along the riverbanks. Afterward, you can take a peek inside St. Lawrence's Church in the center of the village. Built on the site of a Roman temple, it has a crypt from 1120 and a tower from 1784. You can also visit this lovely spot as part of a fine walking tour (see the box "The Great Cotswold Ramble," below).

Getting There

Trains go from London's Paddington Station to nearby Moreton-in-Marsh, a trip of 1½ hours. For information, call © **0845/748-4950** or visit **www.firstgreat western.co.uk**. From here, coaches operated by **Pulham's Bus Company** (© **01451/820369;** www.pulhamscoaches.com) travel the 9.5km (6 miles) to Bourton-on-the-Water. Trains also run from London to Cheltenham and Kingham; while somewhat more distant than Moreton-in-Marsh, both have bus connections to Bourton-on-the-Water.

National Express (© **0871/781-8181;** www.nationalexpress.co.uk) runs buses from London's Victoria Coach Station to both Cheltenham and Stow-on-the-Wold. **Pulham's Bus Company** operates about four buses per day from both towns to Bourton-on-the-Water.

If you're driving from Oxford, head west on the A40 to the junction with the A429 (Fosse Way). Take it northeast to Bourton-on-the-Water.

Where to Stay & Dine

Chester House Hotel   This 300-year-old Cotswold-stone house, built on the banks of the Windrush River, is conveniently located in the center of town. The main building and its adjoining row of stables have been converted into this comfortable hotel; the stables were completely renovated and turned into small to midsize bedrooms. Bathrooms are small and compact but have adequate shelf space.

Victoria St., Bourton-on-the-Water, Cheltenham, Gloucestershire GL54 2BU. © **01451/820286.** Fax 01451/820471. www.chesterhousehotel.com. 22 units. £85–£95 double; £120–£160 family room. Rates include continental or English breakfast. AE, MC, V. Closed Jan. **Amenities:** Restaurant; bar. *In room:* TV, hair dryer, Wi-Fi (free).

Dial House Hotel ★   Our top choice in town, this 1698 house is constructed from yellow Cotswold stone and stands in the heart of the village center. Mr. and Mrs. Adrian Campbell-Howard, your hosts, offer not only a nostalgic retreat but also some of the best cuisine in the area. Set on .6 hectare (1½ acres) of manicured gardens, the house overlooks the River Windrush. Each room has individual character, and some boast four-poster beds. Two of the rooms, as charming as those in the main building, are in a converted coach house. All accommodations have well-kept bathrooms with shower units and Penhaligon toiletries. Log fires burn on chilly nights, and there are two small dining rooms, one with an inglenook fireplace.

The Chestnuts, High St., Bourton-on-the-Water, Gloucestershire GL54 2AN. © **01451/822244.** Fax 01451/810126. www.dialhousehotel.com. 14 units. £130–£180 double; £195–£240 suite. Rates include English breakfast. MC, V. **Amenities:** Restaurant; bar; room service. *In room:* TV, hair dryer, Wi-Fi (free).

Old Manse Hotel ★ 👔   An architectural gem, the Old Manse sits in the center of town by the river that wanders through the village green. Built of Cotswold stone in 1748, with chimneys, dormers, and small-paned windows, it has been frequently modernized. Rooms are midsize and cozy, much like something you'd find in the home of your favorite great-aunt.

Victoria St., Bourton-on-the-Water, Cheltenham, Gloucestershire GL54 2BX. © **01451/820082.** Fax 01451/810381. www.oldmansehotel.com. 15 units. £80–£100 double. Rates include English breakfast. AE, DC, MC, V. **Amenities:** Restaurant; bar. *In room:* TV, hair dryer.

Old New Inn   The Old New Inn, originally built in 1793, is a landmark in the village. On the main street, overlooking the river, it's a good example of Queen Anne design (see the Model Village at the Old New Inn, below). Hungry and tired travelers are drawn to the old-fashioned comforts and cuisine of this most English inn. Rooms are comfortable, with homey furnishings and soft beds. Some units are spacious, especially those with a four-poster bed, but most are small and lie in a cottage annex.

High St., Bourton-on-the-Water, Cheltenham, Gloucestershire GL54 2AF. © **01451/820467.** Fax 01451/810236. www.theoldnewinn.co.uk. 9 units. £76 double. Rate includes English breakfast. MC, V. **Amenities:** Restaurant; 3 bars. *In room:* TV, hair dryer.

A Tiny Village, Birds, Vintage Cars & More

Within the town are a handful of minor museums, each of which was established from idiosyncratic collections amassed over the years by local residents. They include the **Bourton Model Railway Exhibition & Toy Shop** (© **01451/820686;** www.bourtonmodelrailway.co.uk) and the **Cotswold Motor Museum** (© **01451/821255;** www.cotswold-motor-museum.com).

Birdland ☺ This handsomely designed attraction sits on 3.4 hectares (8½ acres) of field and forests on the banks of the River Windrush, about 1.6km (1 mile) east of Bourton-on-the-Water. It houses about 500 birds, including three species of penguins. Other feathered friends include pelicans, storks, flamingos, cranes, parrots, toucans, kookaburras, and pheasants. Birdland has a picnic area and a children's playground in a wooded copse.

Rissington Rd. © **01451/820480.** www.birdland.co.uk. Admission £6 adults, £5 seniors, £3.90 children 4–14, £18 family ticket, free for children 3 and younger. Apr–Oct daily 10am–6pm; Nov–Mar daily 10am–4pm (last admission 1 hr. before closing).

Cotswold Perfumery This permanent perfume exhibition details the history of the perfume industry and also focuses on its production. Perfumes are made on the premises and sold in the shop. Flacons of these fragrances range from £2 to £35 each, depending on their size. The price of admission includes a 45-minute factory tour, but it's always best to call in advance, as the perfumery does not always have staff available to conduct such a tour.

Victoria St. © **01451/820698.** www.cotswold-perfumery.co.uk. Admission £5 adults, £3.50 children 4–16. Mon–Sat 9:30am–5pm; Sun 10:30am–5pm. Closed Dec 25–26.

Model Village at the Old New Inn ☺ Beginning in the 1930s, a local hotelier, Mr. Morris, whiled away some of the doldrums of the Great Depression by constructing a scale model (1:9) of Bourton-on-the-Water as a testimony to its architectural charms. This isn't a tiny and cramped display set behind glass—it's big enough that you can walk through this near-perfect and most realistic model village.

High St. © **01451/820467.** www.theoldnewinn.co.uk/village.htm. Admission £4 adults, £3 seniors, £2.50 children. Summer daily 10am–5:45pm; winter daily 10am–3:45pm.

UPPER & LOWER SLAUGHTER ★

3km (2 miles) N of Bourton-on-the-Water; 6.5km (4 miles) SW of Stow-on-the-Wold

Midway between Bourton-on-the-Water and Stow-on-the-Wold (see below) are two of the prettiest villages in the Cotswolds: Upper and Lower Slaughter. Don't be put off by the name—"Slaughter" is actually a corruption of *de Sclotre,* the name of the original Norman landowner. Houses here are constructed of honey-colored Cotswold stone, and a stream meanders right through the street, providing a home for free-wandering ducks, which beg scraps from kindly passersby. Upper Slaughter has a fine example of a 17th-century Cotswold manor house.

The **Old Mill,** in Lower Slaughter (*©* **01451/820052;** www.oldmill-lower slaughter.com), is a sturdy 19th-century stone structure built on the River Eye with the sole purpose of grinding out flour. The river still turns the massive water wheel that powers this Victorian flourmill today. Visitors can enjoy an ice-cream parlor and tearoom while visiting the mill. Entrance to the mill costs £1.25 for adults, 50p for children.

Getting There

Lower Slaughter and Stow-on-the-Wold are 6.5km (4 miles) apart. From Stow, take the A429 (the Main Fosse Way) and follow signs to Cirencester and Bourton-on-the-Water. Turn off the highway when you see signs to Upper and Lower Slaughter. The road will then divide, and you can pick which hamlet you want to head to.

To reach Lower Slaughter from Bourton-on-the-Water, head west along Lansdowne Road, turning right (north) onto A436; after a short distance, you'll see a signpost pointing left into Lower Slaughter along an unmarked road.

THE GREAT COTSWOLD ramble

A walking tour between the villages of Upper and Lower Slaughter, with an optional extension to Bourton-on-the-Water, is one of the most memorable in England. Between the Slaughters, it's about 1.6km (1 mile) each way, or 4km (2½ miles) from Upper Slaughter to Bourton-on-the-Water; the walk can take 2 to 4 hours.

A well-worn footpath known as **Warden's Way** meanders beside the edge of the swift-moving River Eye. From its well-marked beginning in Upper Slaughter's central parking lot, the path passes sheep grazing in meadows, antique houses crafted from local honey-colored stone, stately trees arching over ancient millponds, and footbridges that have endured centuries of pedestrian traffic and rain.

The rushing river powers a historic mill on the northwestern edge of Lower Slaughter. In quiet eddies, you'll see ample numbers of waterfowl and birds, such as wild ducks, gray wagtails, mute swans, coots, and Canada geese.

Most visitors turn around at Lower Slaughter, but Warden's Way continues another 2.5km (1½ miles) to Bourton-on-the-Water by following the Fosse Way, route of an ancient Roman footpath. Most of it, from Lower Slaughter to Bourton-on-the-Water, is covered by tarmac; it's closed to cars but ideal for walking or biking. You're legally required to close each of the several gates that stretch across the footpath.

Warden's Way will introduce you to Bourton-on-the-Water through the hamlet's northern edges. The first landmark you'll see will be the tower of St. Lawrence's Anglican Church. From the base of the church, walk south along the Avenue (one of the hamlet's main streets) and end your Cotswold ramble on the Village Green, directly in front of the War Memorial.

You can follow this route in reverse, but parking is more plentiful in Upper Slaughter than in Lower Slaughter.

Where to Stay & Dine

Lords of the Manor Hotel ★★★ A 17th-century house set on several acres of rolling fields, the Lords of the Manor offers gardens with a stream featuring brown trout. A quintessentially British hotel of great style and amenities, it's quite a show-place. It may be modernized, but it successfully maintains the quiet country-house atmosphere of 300 years ago. Half the rooms are in a converted old barn and granary, and many have lovely views. Each offers a high standard of comfort and elegant beds with sumptuous linens.

Upper Slaughter, near Bourton-on-the-Water, Gloucestershire GL54 2JD. ✆ **01451/820243.** Fax 01451/820696. www.lordsofthemanor.com. 27 units. £191–£255 double; £303–£362 suite. Rates include half-board. AE, DC, MC, V. Take A429 29km (18 miles) north of Cheltenham. **Amenities:** Restaurant; bar; room service. *In room:* TV/DVD, hair dryer, minibar, MP3 docking station.

Lower Slaughter Manor ★★★ This hotel dates from 1658, when it was owned by Sir George Whitmore, high sheriff of Gloucestershire. It remained in the same family until 1964, when it was sold as a private residence. Today, it's one of the great inns of the Cotswolds, though its charms are matched in every way by Lords of the Manor (see above). Standing on its own private grounds, it has spacious and sump-tuously furnished rooms, some with four-poster beds. Bedrooms in the main build-ing have more old English character, although those in the annex are equally comfortable and include the same luxuries.

Lower Slaughter, near Cheltenham, Gloucestershire GL54 2HP. ✆ **01451/820456.** Fax 01451/822150. www.lowerslaughter.co.uk. 19 units. £230–£420 double; £370–£880 suite. Rates include English break-fast. AE, DC, MC, V. Take A429 turnoff at the sign for the Slaughters, then drive 1km (½ mile); manor is on the right as you enter the village. No children 11 or younger. **Amenities:** Restaurant; lounge; room service; tennis court. *In room:* TV, hair dryer, Internet (free).

STOW-ON-THE-WOLD ★

34km (21 miles) S of Stratford-upon-Avon; 14km (9 miles) SE of Broadway; 16km (10 miles) S of Chip-ping Campden; 6.5km (4 miles) S of Moreton-in-Marsh

As you pass through Shakespeare's "high wild hills and rough uneven ways," you arrive at Stow-on-the-Wold, its very name evoking the elusive spirit of the Cotswolds, one of the greatest sheep-rearing districts of England. Lying 240m (800 ft.) above sea level, it stands on a plateau where "the cold winds blow," or so goes the old saying. This town prospered when Cotswold wool was demanded the world over. Stow-on-the-Wold may not be the cognoscenti's favorite—Chipping Campden takes that honor—but it's even more delightful, as it has a real Cotswold town atmosphere.

The town lies smack in the middle of the Fosse Way, one of the Roman trunk roads that cut a swath through Britain. Kings have passed through here, including Edward VI, son of Henry VIII, and they've bestowed their approval on the town. Stagecoaches stopped off here for the night on their way to Cheltenham.

A 14th-century cross stands in the large Market Square, where you can still see the stocks where past "offenders" were jeered at and punished by townspeople who threw rotten eggs at them. The final battle between the Roundheads and the Royal-ists took place outside Stow-on-the-Wold, and mean old Cromwell incarcerated 1,500 Royalist troops in St. Edward's Market Square.

The square today teems with pubs and outdoor cafes. But leave the square at some point and wander at leisure along some of the narrowest alleyways in Britain. When the summer crowds get you down, you can head in almost any direction from Stow to surrounding villages that look like sets from a Merchant Ivory film.

Essentials

GETTING THERE Several trains run daily from London's Paddington Station to Moreton-in-Marsh. For schedules and information, call *C* **0845/748-4950** or visit **www.firstgreatwestern.co.uk**. From Moreton-in-Marsh, Pulham's Bus Company makes the 10-minute ride to Stow-on-the-Wold.

If driving from Oxford, take the A40 west to the junction with the A424, near Burford. Head northwest along the A424 to Stow-on-the-Wold.

VISITOR INFORMATION The **Tourist Information Centre** is at Hollis House, the Square (*C* **01451/831082;** www.cotswold.info/places/stow-on-the-wold.shtml). It's open Easter to October, Monday to Saturday 9:30am to 5:30pm; November to mid-February, Monday to Saturday 9:30am to 4:30pm; and late February to Easter, Monday to Saturday 9:30am to 5pm.

Where to Stay & Dine

Fosse Manor Hotel Though lacking the charm of the Grapevine (see below), Fosse Manor is at least the second best in town, even more inviting than the Stow Lodge. The hotel lies near the site of an ancient Roman road that used to bisect England. Its stone walls and neo-Gothic gables are almost concealed by strands of ivy. From some of the high stone-sided windows, you can enjoy a view of a landscaped garden with a sunken lily pond and old-fashioned sundial. Inside, the interior is conservatively modern, with homey bedrooms. Some are large enough for a family; others have a four-poster bed. Six bedrooms, equal in comfort to those in the main building, are located in a converted coach house on the grounds.

Fosse Way, Stow-on-the-Wold, Cheltenham, Gloucestershire GL54 1JX. *C* **01451/830354.** Fax 01451/832486. www.fossemanor.co.uk. 22 units. Mon–Thurs £69–£194 double; Fri–Sun £95–£230 double. Rates include English breakfast. Children 9 and younger stay free in parent's room. AE, DC, MC, V. Take A429 2km (1¼ miles) south of Stow-on-the-Wold. **Amenities:** Restaurant; bar; lounge; room service. *In room:* TV, hair dryer.

Grapevine Hotel ★ 🍴 Facing the village green, the Grapevine mixes urban sophistication with reasonable prices, rural charm, and intimacy. It's the best inn in town, although it doesn't have the charm and grace of Wyck Hill House on the outskirts (see below). It was named after the ancient vine whose tendrils shade and shelter the beautiful conservatory restaurant. Many of the bedrooms have been redecorated, and each varies in size—some quite small—but comfort is the keynote here. Ten rooms are in a comfortably appointed annex and lack the character of the stone-sided walls and crooked floors in the main building.

Sheep St., Stow-on-the-Wold, Cheltenham, Gloucestershire GL54 1AU. *C* **01451/830344.** Fax 01451/832278. www.vines.co.uk. 22 units. £120–£150 double. Rates include English breakfast. AE, DC, MC, V. **Amenities:** 2 restaurants; bar; room service. *In room:* TV, hair dryer, minibar (in some).

Stow Lodge Hotel Stow Lodge dominates the marketplace but is set back far enough to avoid too much noise. Its gardens, the honeysuckle growing over the stone walls, the diamond-shaped windows, and the gables and many chimneys capture the best of country living, even though you're right in the heart of town. The ample, well-furnished rooms vary in size; one has a four-poster bed. The main building has more character, though some equally comfortable rooms are in a converted coach house (most on the ground floor). Room nos. 17 and 18—the smallest in the hotel—share a private bathroom.

The Square, Stow-on-the-Wold, Cheltenham, Gloucestershire GL54 1AB. ⓒ **01451/830485.** Fax 01451/831671. www.stowlodge.com. 20 units. £81–£142 double. Rates include English breakfast. MC, V. Closed Dec 16–Jan 25. No children 4 and under. **Amenities:** Restaurant; bar; room service. *In room:* TV, hair dryer, Wi-Fi (free).

Wyck Hill House ★★★   This is sleepy old Stow's pocket of posh. Parts of this otherwise Victorian country house, set on 40 hectares (100 acres) of grounds and gardens, date from 1720, when its stone walls were first erected. It was discovered in the course of recent restoration that one wing of the manor house rests on the foundations of a Roman villa. The interior adheres to 18th-century authenticity, with room after room leading to paneled libraries and Adam sitting rooms. The well-furnished accommodations are in the main hotel, in the coach-house annex, or in the Orangery, a building erected in the 1980s whose larger-than-usual bedrooms are outfitted in a vaguely Mediterranean theme. Some rooms offer four-poster beds and views of the surrounding countryside.

A424 Burford Rd., Stow-on-the-Wold, Cheltenham, Gloucestershire GL54 1HY. ⓒ **01451/831936.** Fax 01451/832243. www.bespokehotels.com/wyckhillhouse. 60 units. £89–£245 double; £130–£295 suite. Rates include English breakfast. AE, MC, V. Drive 4km (2½ miles) south of Stow-on-the-Wold on A424. **Amenities:** Restaurant; bar; room service; spa. *In room:* TV, hair dryer, Wi-Fi (free).

Shopping in Antiques Heaven

Don't be fooled by the village's sleepy, country setting: Stow-on-the-Wold has developed over the last 20 years into the antiques buyer's highlight of Britain, boasting at least 60 merchandisers scattered throughout the village and its environs.

Set within four showrooms inside an 18th-century building on the town's main square, **Antony Preston Antiques Ltd.,** the Square (ⓒ **01451/831586;** www. antonypreston.com), specializes in English and French furniture, including some large pieces such as bookcases, and decorative objects that include paperweights, lamps, paintings on silk, and smalls designed to add a glossy accent to carefully contrived interior decors.

Baggott Church Street Ltd., Church Street (ⓒ **01451/830370;** www.baggott antiques.com), is the smaller, and perhaps more intricately decorated, of two shops founded and maintained by a local antiques merchant, Duncan ("Jack") Baggott, a frequent denizen at estate sales of country houses throughout Britain. The shop contains four showrooms loaded with furniture and paintings from the 17th to the 19th centuries.

Covering about half a block in the heart of town, **Huntington's Antiques Ltd.,** Church Street (ⓒ **01451/830842;** www.huntington-antiques.com), contains one of the largest stocks of quality antiques in England. Wander at will through 10 ground-floor rooms, and then climb to the second floor where a long gallery and a quartet of additional showrooms bulge with refectory tables, unusual cupboards, and all kinds of finds.

SHAKESPEARE COUNTRY & THE HEART OF ENGLAND

After London, Shakespeare Country is the most popular destination in England. The main attraction is that foremost tourist town, **Stratford-upon-Avon,** birthplace of Shakespeare and one of the great meccas for writers, readers, and playgoers from around the world.

Shakespeare's hometown is the best center for touring this part of England. You'll want to take in some theater while in Stratford-upon-Avon and branch out for day trips—notably to **Warwick Castle** in nearby Warwick, to **Kenilworth Castle,** and to **Coventry Cathedral.**

And then you have the heart of England at your doorstep. The adventure can begin in nearby **Birmingham,** England's second-largest city. Though abandoned warehouses and bleak factories remain, this industrial city, like the rest of England, is being spruced up. From here, you can branch out to any number of lovely old market towns and bucolic spots. There are the scenic **Malverns,** and those who are truly passionate about porcelain flock to the fabled potteries in towns like **Stoke-on-Trent,** where factory and outlet shops sell Wedgwood, Portmeirion, and other fine brands of English tableware at a discount.

STRATFORD-UPON-AVON ★★

147km (91 miles) NW of London; 64km (40 miles) NW of Oxford; 13km (8 miles) S of Warwick

Crowds of tourists overrun this market town on the River Avon during the summer. In fact, these days, Stratford aggressively hustles its Shakespeare connection—everybody seems to be in business to make a buck off the Bard. The throngs dwindle in winter, however, when you can at least walk on the streets and seek out the places of genuine historical interest.

Aside from the historic sites, the major draw for visitors is the **Royal Shakespeare Theatre,** where Britain's foremost actors perform during

Warwickshire: Shakespeare Country

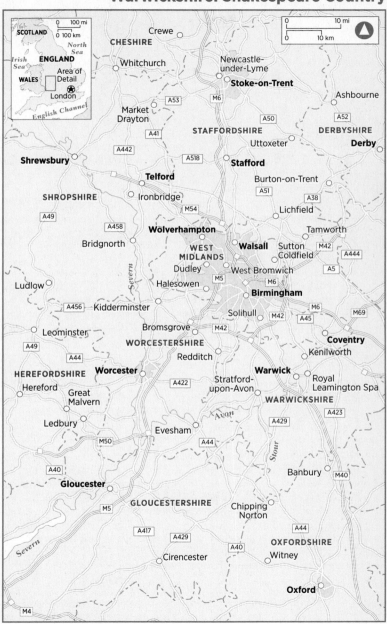

SCOTLAND

North Sea

ENGLAND

Irish Sea

WALES

Area of Detail

London

English Channel

0   100 mi
0   100 km

0   10 mi
0   10 km

Crewe

CHESHIRE

Whitchurch

Newcastle-under-Lyme

Stoke-on-Trent

Ashbourne

Market Drayton

A53

M6

A50

A52

DERBYSHIRE

STAFFORDSHIRE

Uttoxeter

Derby

A41

Shrewsbury

A442

A518

Stafford

Burton-on-Trent

Telford

A51

A38

SHROPSHIRE

Ironbridge

M54

Lichfield

A49

A458

Wolverhampton

Tamworth

Bridgnorth

WEST MIDLANDS

Walsall

Sutton Coldfield

M42

A444

Dudley

West Bromwich

A5

Ludlow

Halesowen

M5

M6

Birmingham

A456

Kidderminster

Solihull

M42

A45

M6

M69

Leominster

Bromsgrove

M42

Severn

WORCESTERSHIRE

Redditch

Coventry

A49

A44

Worcester

Kenilworth

HEREFORDSHIRE

A422

Warwick

Hereford

Great Malvern

Stratford-upon-Avon

Royal Leamington Spa

WARWICKSHIRE

Ledbury

Avon

A429

A423

Evesham

A44

M50

Stour

A40

Banbury

M40

Gloucester

M5

GLOUCESTERSHIRE

Chipping Norton

A417

A429

A44

OXFORDSHIRE

Severn

A40

Cirencester

Witney

M4

Oxford

a long season that lasts from April to November. Other than the theater, Stratford is rather devoid of any rich cultural life, and you may want to rush back to London after you've seen the literary pilgrimage sights and watched a production of *Hamlet*. But Stratford-upon-Avon is also a good center for trips to Warwick Castle, Kenilworth Castle, and Coventry Cathedral (later in this chapter).

Essentials

GETTING THERE The journey from London to Stratford-upon-Avon takes about 2¼ hours, with a round-trip ticket costing £28 to £69 depending on the train. For schedules and information, call ✆ **0845/748-4950** or go to **www.national rail.co.uk**. The train station at Stratford is on Alcester Road.

Four **National Express** buses a day leave from London's Victoria Coach Station, with a trip time of 3¼ hours. A single-day round-trip ticket costs £19. For schedules and information, call ✆ **0871/781-8181** or go to **www.nationalexpress.co.uk**.

If you're driving from London, take the M40 toward Oxford and continue to Stratford-upon-Avon on the A34.

VISITOR INFORMATION The **Tourist Information Centre,** Bridgefoot (✆ **0870/160-7930;** www.shakespeare-country.co.uk), provides any details you may wish to know about the Shakespeare houses and properties; it will also assist in booking rooms (see "Where to Stay," below). Call and ask for a copy of the free *Shakespeare Country Holiday* guide. The center also operates a Thomas Cook currency-exchange office (✆ **01789/269750**), open April through September, Monday to Saturday 9am to 5:30pm and Sunday 10am to 4pm, and October through March, Monday to Saturday 9am to 5pm and Sunday 10am to 3pm.

To contact the **Shakespeare Birthplace Trust,** which administrates many of the attractions, call the Shakespeare Centre (✆ **01789/204016;** www.shakespeare. org.uk).

Where to Stay

During the long theater season, you'll need reservations way in advance. The **Tourist Information Centre** (✆ **0870/160-7930;** www.shakespeare-country.co.uk), part of the national "Book-a-Bed-Ahead" service, will help find accommodations for you in the price range you're seeking.

VERY EXPENSIVE

Menzies Welcombe Hotel, Spa & Golf Club ★★★ For a formal, historic hotel in Stratford, there's nothing better than the Welcombe. One of England's great Jacobean country houses, this property is a 10-minute ride from the heart of Stratford-upon-Avon. Its key feature is an 18-hole golf course. The hotel is surrounded by 63 hectares (156 acres) of grounds and has a formal entrance on Warwick Road, a winding driveway leading to the main hall. Bedrooms are luxuriously outfitted in traditional Jacobean style, with fine antiques and elegant fabrics. Most rooms are seemingly big enough for tennis matches, but those in the garden wing, although comfortable, are small. Some units are sumptuously furnished with elegant four-posters.

Warwick Rd., Stratford-upon-Avon, Warwickshire CV37 0NR. ✆ **01789/295252.** Fax 01789/414666. www.menzies-hotels.co.uk. 78 units. £161–£270 double; £250–£6,000 suite. Rates include English breakfast. AE, DC, MC, V. Free parking. Take A439 2km (1¼ miles) northeast of the town center. **Amenities:** 2 restaurants; bar; golf course; gym w/aerobics studio; indoor heated pool; room service; spa; tennis court. *In room:* TV, hair dryer, Wi-Fi (£10 per day).

ATTRACTIONS ●
Anne Hathaway's Cottage 1
Courtyard Theatre 28
Hall's Croft 27
Harvard House & Museum of
British Pewter 12
Holy Trinity Church
(Shakespeare's Tomb) 29
Mary Arden's House (Glebe Farm)
& Palmer's Farm 3
Nash's House & New Place 21
Royal Shakespeare Theatre 20
Shakespeare's Birthplace 9
Stratford Brass Rubbing Centre 19
Swan Theatre 25

ACCOMMODATIONS ■
Best Western Grosvenor Hotel 6
Heron Lodge 11
Holiday Inn Stratford-upon-Avon 7
Legacy Falcon Hotel 23
Macdonald Alveston Manor Hotel 18
Menzies Welcombe Hotel,
Spa & Golf Club 5
Mercure Shakespeare Hotel 22
Moonraker Guest House 11
Penryn House 11
Salamander Guest House 24
The Stratford 2
Victoria Spa Lodge 3
White Swan 10

DINING ◆
Lambs 16
Malbec Petit Bistro 8
Marlowe's Restaurant 13
The One Elm 4
The Oppo 17
RSC Courtyard
Theatre Café Bar 19
Russons 26
Sorrento 14
Thai Boathouse 30
The Vintner 15

EXPENSIVE

Macdonald Alveston Manor Hotel ★★ This Tudor manor is perfect for the-atergoers—it's just a 5-minute walk from the theaters. The hotel has a wealth of chimneys and gables, and everything from an Elizabethan gazebo to Queen Anne windows. Mentioned in the Domesday Book, the building predates the arrival of William the Conqueror. The rooms in the manor will appeal to those who appreciate the old-world charm of slanted floors, overhead beams, and antique furnishings. Some triples or quads are available in the modern section, connected by a covered walk through the rear garden. You can live in luxury in the original rooms, with their built-in walnut furniture and a color-coordinated decor, or be assigned a rather routine standard twin that, though comfortable, will lack romance.

Clopton Bridge (off B4066), Stratford-upon-Avon, Warwickshire CV37 7HP. ℂ **0844/879-9138.** Fax 01789/414095. www.macdonaldhotels.co.uk. 113 units. £137–£153 double; £179–£239 suite. AE, MC, V. Free parking. **Amenities:** Restaurant; bar; babysitting; exercise room; indoor heated pool; room service; sauna; spa. *In room:* TV, hair dryer, minibar, Wi-Fi (£12 per day).

MODERATE

Best Western Grosvenor Hotel A pair of Georgian town houses, built in 1832 and 1843, join to form this hotel, which is one of the second-tier choices in Stratford. In the center of town, with lawns and gardens to the rear, it is a short stroll from the intersection of Bridge Street and Waterside, allowing easy access to the Avon River, Bancroft Gardens, and the Royal Shakespeare Theatre. There is a rambling ground floor that has tremendous character—it reminds us of an elegant English country house, with small intimate lounges and open fires. Bedrooms are midsize to spacious, each personally designed with a high standard of tasteful modern furnishings. Rooms are not overly adorned or stylish, but they are snug and cozy.

12–14 Warwick Rd., Stratford-upon-Avon, Warwickshire CV37 6YT. ℂ **01789/269213.** Fax 01789/266087. www.bwgh.co.uk. 73 units. £59–£114 double; £170 suite. AE, MC, V. Free parking. **Amenities:** Restaurant; bar; babysitting; room service. *In room:* TV, hair dryer, Wi-Fi (free; in most).

Holiday Inn Stratford-upon-Avon ★ This first-class hotel stands on ample landscaped lawns on the banks of the River Avon near Clopton Bridge. Although it lacks the charm of the Macdonald Alveston Manor, as far as amenities go, this modern hotel is on the same level as the Welcombe. It's one of the flagships of Queens Moat Houses, a British hotel chain, built in the early 1970s, although it's actually run by the Holiday Inn people. Every guest room has a high standard of comfort.

Bridgefoot, Stratford-upon-Avon, Warwickshire CV37 6YR. ℂ **888/465-4329** or 0871/942-9270. Fax 01789/298589. www.holidayinn.com. 259 units. £75–£170 double; £95–£215 suite. AE, DC, MC, V. Parking £5. **Amenities:** Restaurant; bar; exercise room; Jacuzzi; indoor heated pool; room service; sauna; solarium; spa. *In room:* A/C, TV, hair dryer, Wi-Fi (£10 per day).

Legacy Falcon Hotel The Falcon blends the very old and the very new. This black-and-white timbered inn was licensed a quarter of a century after Shakespeare's death; connected to its rear by a glass passageway is a more sterile extension added in 1970. In the heart of Stratford, the inn faces the Guild Chapel and the New Place Gardens. The recently upgraded rooms in the older section have oak beams, diamond leaded-glass windows, antiques, and good reproductions. In the inn's intimate Merlin Lounge, you'll find an open copper-hooded fireplace where fires are stoked under beams salvaged from old ships.

Chapel St., Stratford-upon-Avon, Warwickshire CV37 6HA. ☎ **0844/411-9005.** Fax 0844/411-9006. www.legacy-hotels.co.uk. 83 units. £75–£150 double; from £165 suite. AE, DC, MC, V. Free parking. **Amenities:** 2 restaurants; 2 bars; room service. *In room:* TV, hair dryer.

Mercure Shakespeare Hotel ★★   Filled with historical associations, the original core of this hotel, dating from the 1400s, has seen many additions in its long life. Quieter and plusher than the Falcon (see above), it is equaled in the central core of Stratford only by the Macdonald Alveston Manor (see above). Residents relax in the post-and-timber-studded public rooms, within sight of fireplaces and playbills from 19th-century productions of Shakespeare's plays. Bedrooms are named in honor of noteworthy actors, Shakespeare's plays, or Shakespearean characters. The oldest are capped with hewn timbers, and all have modern comforts. Even the newer accommodations are at least 40 to 50 years old and have rose-and-thistle patterns carved into many of their exposed timbers. Bathrooms range in size.

Chapel St., Stratford-upon-Avon, Warwickshire CV37 6ER. ☎ **01789/294997.** Fax 01789/415411. www. mercure.com. 74 units. £100–£217 double; from £150 suite. Rates include buffet breakfast. Children 12 and younger stay free in parent's room. AE, DC, MC, V. Parking £5. **Amenities:** Restaurant; bar; room service. *In room:* A/C, TV, hair dryer, minibar (in some).

The Stratford ★   This is definitely not one of the atmospheric inns of Stratford-upon-Avon. But if you prefer a modern hotel with up-to-date conveniences when paying your call on the Bard, the Stratford is for you. A member of the QHotels group, it lacks personality but has just about everything else. The location is only a short walk from the banks of the River Avon. The bedrooms are spaciously and elegantly appointed. Some of the units come with four-poster beds, as in Tudor days, but others are more geared to commercial travelers seeking streamlined conveniences—not romance. Deftly prepared market-fresh dishes change with the seasons in the on-site Quills Restaurant.

Arden St., Stratford-upon-Avon, Warwickshire CV37 6QQ. ☎ **01789/271-000.** Fax 01789/271-001. www.qhotels.co.uk. £79–£114 double. AE, DC, MC, V. Free parking. **Amenities:** Restaurant; bar; small exercise room; room service. *In room:* TV, hair dryer, Wi-Fi (2 free hr., £12 per 24 hr.).

White Swan   This cozy, intimate hotel, housed in Stratford's oldest building, is one of the most atmospheric in Stratford. In business for more than a century before Shakespeare appeared on the scene, it competes successfully with the Legacy Falcon (see above) in offering an ancient atmosphere. The gabled medieval front would present the Bard with no surprises, but the modern comforts inside would surely astonish him. Many of the bedrooms have been well preserved, despite the addition of modern conveniences, and all rooms are well appointed. Paintings dating from 1550 hang on the lounge walls.

Rother St., Stratford-upon-Avon, Warwickshire CV37 6NH. ☎ **01789/297022.** Fax 01789/268773. www.pebblehotels.com. 41 units. £95–£120 double. Rates include English breakfast. AE, DC, MC, V. Parking £5. **Amenities:** Restaurant; bar (p. 492); room service, Wi-Fi (free). *In room:* TV, hair dryer.

INEXPENSIVE

Heron Lodge ★ 🍴   Bob and Chris Heaps run one of the better B&Bs in Stratford, their lodge lying a kilometer (half mile) outside the heart of town. The midsize bedrooms have individual character, with furnishings that are both tasteful and comfortable. The Heaps still practice the old-fashioned custom of an afternoon "cuppa" served in their conservatory. Like Penryn House (see below), the Heron serve one of the town's best breakfasts, using local products when available.

260 Alcester Rd., Stratford-upon-Avon, Warwickshire CV37 9JQ. ☏ **01789/299169.** www.heronlodge. com. 5 units. £58–£88 double. Rates include English breakfast. MC, V. Free parking. *In room:* TV, hair dryer, Internet (free), no phone.

Moonraker Guest House ★ 🛍 Privately owned and personally managed by Ruth and Morris Masaaki, this is a delightful choice and a discovery, lying midway between Anne Hathaway's Cottage and Shakespeare's Birthplace. Each bedroom is comfortably and attractively furnished. A luxury suite is available, with a bedroom, lounge, and kitchenette, plus two more suites, each with two rooms. Among the amenities are four-poster beds, a lounge area, and garden patios. A hearty English breakfast includes toast and homemade marmalade and jams.

40 Alcester Rd., Stratford-upon-Avon, Warwickshire CV37 9DB. ☏/fax **01789/268774.** Fax 01789/268774. www.moonrakerhouse.com. 7 units. £70–£95 double. Rates include English breakfast. MC, V. Free parking. Located 2 min. by car from the heart of town, on A422. **Amenities:** Breakfast room. *In room:* TV, hair dryer.

Penryn House ★ 🍴 The location is convenient and the price is right at this B&B, where hosts Anne and Robert Dawkes are among the most welcoming in town. They justifiably take special pride in their breakfasts, right down to their superb "Harvest of Arden" English apple juice. Free-range Worcestershire eggs are served along with fresh seasonal fruit and locally produced bacon and sausage. They even prepare a vegetarian breakfast if requested. The bedrooms are a bit small, but well furnished and comfortable. The location is close to the rail station, Anne Hathaway's Cottage, and the heart of town.

126 Alcester Rd., Stratford-upon-Avon, Warwickshire CV37 9DP. ☏ **01789/293718.** Fax 01789/266077. www.penrynguesthouse.co.uk. 7 units. £60–£75 double. Rates include English breakfast. MC, V. Free parking. **Amenities:** Breakfast room. *In room:* TV, hair dryer, Wi-Fi (free).

Salamander Guest House This 1906 Edwardian house is a 5-minute walk from the town center, just off Evesham Road (B439). One of the better guesthouses in the area, the homelike Salamander fronts a woodsy park. The owners rent comfortable, attractive bedrooms, including one for families.

40 Grove Rd., Stratford-upon-Avon, Warwickshire CV37 6PB. ☏/fax **01789/205728.** www.salamander guesthouse.co.uk. £40–£70 double. Rates include English breakfast. MC, V. Free parking. Bus: X16. **Amenities:** Breakfast room; babysitting. *In room:* TV, hair dryer (on request), no phone, Wi-Fi (free).

Victoria Spa Lodge This B&B is old-fashioned and atmospheric. Opened in 1837, the year Queen Victoria ascended the throne, this was the first establishment to be given her name, and it is still going strong. The lodge was originally a spa frequented by the queen's eldest daughter, Princess Vicky. The accommodating hosts offer tastefully decorated, comfortable bedrooms.

Bishopton Lane (2.5km/1½ miles north of the town center, where A3400 intersects A46), Stratford-upon-Avon, Warwickshire CV37 9QY. ☏ **01789/267985.** Fax 01789/204728. www.victoriaspa.co.uk. 7 units. £60–£70 double. Rates include English breakfast. MC, V. Free parking. **Amenities:** Breakfast room. *In room:* TV, hair dryer, Wi-Fi (£10 per day).

A NEARBY PLACE TO STAY

Ettington Park Hotel ★★★ This Victorian Gothic mansion is one of the most sumptuous retreats in Shakespeare Country. It opened as a hotel in 1985, but has a history that spans 9 centuries. The land is a legacy of the Shirley family, whose 12th-century burial chapel is nearby. Like a grand private home, the hotel boasts baronial fireplaces and a conservatory. Adam ceilings, stone carvings, and ornate staircases have been beautifully restored. A modern wing, assembled with the same stone and neo-Gothic carving of the original house, stretches toward a Renaissance-style arbor entwined with vines. In the spacious and elegant bedrooms, the most up-to-date comforts are concealed behind antique facades. The best units are deluxe doubles, which are larger than the standard units and open onto garden views. Some rooms have old-fashioned four-posters.

Alderminster, Stratford-upon-Avon, Warwickshire CV37 8BU. ℂ **0845/0727454.** Fax 0845/0727455. www.handpicked.co.uk. 48 units. £125–£165 double; £235–£255 suite. Rates include English breakfast. AE, DC, MC, V. Free parking. Drive 8km (5 miles) south along A3400 just past Alderminster, and then take 2nd left (signposted) into Ettington Park. **Amenities:** Restaurant; bar; babysitting; indoor heated pool; room service; sauna; spa; tennis court; whirlpool. *In room:* TV, hair dryer, Wi-Fi (free; in main house).

Where to Dine

After visiting the birthplace of Shakespeare, pop across the street for tea at the **Brasserie,** Henley Street (ℂ **01789/262189**). This airy tearoom is tremendously popular, but the very attentive staff more than compensates for the throngs of patrons. Choose from an array of tea blends, cream teas, and freshly baked cakes, pastries, and tea cakes.

MODERATE TO EXPENSIVE

Lambs ★ CONTINENTAL/ENGLISH   Near the Royal Shakespeare Theatre, this cafe/bistro is housed in a building dating from 1547 (and with connections to Lewis Carroll). It's ideal for a quick light meal or pretheater dinner. The menu changes monthly. You might begin with such starters as an English muffin with smoked haddock and creamed leeks, or Serrano ham with fresh figs and a basil salad. Then you can tuck into such mains as filet of Scottish beef with portobello mushrooms, rack of Cornish lamb with dauphinoise potatoes, or perhaps roast Gressingham duck with Puy lentils. For dessert, why not the dark-chocolate truffle cake with white-chocolate ice cream? Look to the blackboard for daily specials. The chef takes chances (no doubt inspired by trips to the Continent), and it's a nice departure from the bland tearoom fare served for decades in Stratford.

12 Sheep St. ℂ **01789/292554.** www.lambsrestaurant.co.uk. Reservations required for dinner Fri–Sat. Main courses £10–£16; fixed-price menu £17 for 2 courses, £20 for 3 courses. MC, V. Mon 5:30–10pm; Tues–Sat noon–2pm and 5–10pm; Sun noon–2:30pm.

Malbec Petit Bistro ★★ BRITISH/FRENCH   Many savvy local foodies cite this as the best restaurant in Stratford-upon-Avon, and we're inclined to agree. The chef and owner, Simon Malin, offers market-fresh and unpretentious cuisine in fashionable surroundings. His produce is fresh, his seasonings on target, and his imagination active. On the ground floor is an intimate restaurant of character, while on the lower level is a charming cellar with vaulted ceilings and flagstone floors. You'll be impressed with such starters as sautéed lamb's kidneys with thyme-roasted onions or crispy fried squid with almond and a roasted-pepper dipping sauce. You might also savor such mains as rump of local lamb with a butternut-squash gnocchi or free-range pork belly with chorizo sausages and butter beans. Desserts are made fresh daily. How about champagne-laced rhubarb with whipped vanilla shortcake?

6 Union St. ℂ **01789/269106.** www.malbecrestaurant.co.uk. Reservations required. Main courses £10–£17. AE, MC, V. Daily noon–2pm; Mon–Sat 7–9:30pm.

Marlowe's Restaurant ENGLISH   Many famous actors appearing in Shakespeare plays have made their way here for dinner, including Paul Scofield, Vanessa Redgrave, Sir Ralph Richardson, and Sir John Gielgud. You can dine formally in the Elizabethan Room or more casually in the Bistro. The large bar, with a fireplace blazing with logs in winter, opens onto a splendid oak-paneled room. In summer, there is a spacious courtyard for alfresco dining. Starters are a harmonious blend of flavors, including terrine of guinea fowl and oyster mushrooms with sherry and a red-onion marmalade. Among the fish dishes, grilled sea bass emerges from the kitchen with roasted fennel and a tomato fondue. Or you can opt for one of the chargrilled dishes such as a filet steak with pan-fried mushrooms and grilled tomatoes. Drunken duck has been a longtime specialty here: It's marinated in gin, red wine, and juniper berries before it's roasted in the oven.

18 High St. 📞 **01789/204999.** www.marlowes.biz. Reservations recommended. Main courses £13–£43. AE, MC, V. Elizabethan Room Mon–Thurs 5:30–10pm; Fri 5:30–10:30pm; Sat 5:30–11pm. Bistro daily noon–2:15pm; Mon–Sat 5:30–11pm.

The One Elm ENGLISH   The One Elm is a convenient stopover thanks to its long hours of food service. Guests can enjoy its pub atmosphere, ground-floor restaurant, or its courtyard for dining and drinking. The cooks pride themselves on serving dishes fresh from their suppliers, including free-range chicken and eggs and high-quality Scottish beef. You can see these chefs at work in an open kitchen, so you know they are preparing everything to order. A special feature is the Deli Board, featuring all sorts of antipasti and charcuterie, such as a hot chorizo-and-butter-bean salad. Both starters and mains are an appetizing array of market freshness. Begin with shredded beef samosa or smoked Scottish salmon with horseradish blinis. Among the most enticing main dishes are salmon-and-smoked-haddock fish cakes with sautéed spinach or else whole roast black bream with kumquat potatoes. A Catalan fish stew is made from the catch of the day.

1 Guild St. 📞 **01789/404919.** www.oneelmstratford.co.uk. Main courses £10–£17. MC, V. Mon–Sat 11am–10pm; Sun noon–3pm and 6:30–9:30pm.

RSC Courtyard Theatre Café Bar ENGLISH/CONTINENTAL   This restaurant enjoys the best location in town—it's in the Royal Shakespeare Theatre itself—with glass walls providing an unobstructed view of the swans on the Avon. Consider the cafe a venue for lunch, preshow dining, or supper. You can also enjoy an intermission snack of smoked salmon or champagne. The food is prepared with market-fresh ingredients. Light meals might feature chicken liver parfait with apple chutney, the homemade soup of the day, or a sandwich. A meat-pie special is offered daily, or else you can order "shareboards," platters for two including a meze option of various appetizers ranging from hummus to zucchini and basil tapenades. For dessert, try a classic hot apple and cinnamon crumble with ice cream.

In the Royal Shakespeare Theatre, Waterside. 📞 **01789/412654.** www.rsc.org.uk. Reservations recommended. Platters for 2 £8–£10; bar snacks £2.50; light meals £4–£8. AE, MC, Mon–Sat 10:30am–8:30pm; Sun 10:30am–5pm.

Sorrento ★ ITALIAN   For a taste of Italy, visit this family-run restaurant, where Jackie and Tony de Angelis welcome you at a location only a 4-minute walk from the Shakespeare Theatre. Guests can relax on leather furniture in the lounge for a predinner aperitif before heading into the stylish yet informal restaurant itself. Everything is cooked to order using market-fresh ingredients, so allow time for each dish to be prepared. In summer, those dishes may be enjoyed alfresco on the patio. A selection of well-chosen Italian wines complements the meal, which might begin with such starters as homemade chicken liver pâté or a roast-pepper-and-artichoke salad dressed with olive oil, basil, and capers. The pastas are among the best in town. Salmon and lemon sole are united in a white-wine sauce with capers and garlic. The filet steak is flamed in brandy and served in a creamy sauce of black peppercorns, or else you can order strips of chicken breast with mixed peppers and mushrooms.

8 Ely St. ⓒ **01789/297999.** www.sorrentorestaurant.co.uk. Reservations recommended. Main courses £6–£19; 2-course lunch £13, 3-course lunch £17. MC, V. Tues–Wed 11:30am–1:45pm; Mon–Sat 5–10:30pm.

Thai Boathouse ★ THAI   Thai Boathouse, part of a group originally established 4 decades ago in Bangkok, has brought spice and zest to Stratford's lazy restaurant scene. The only restaurant set on the Avon, this charming choice is reached by crossing Clopton Bridge toward Oxford and Banbury. The second-floor dining room opens onto vistas of the river. The decor comes from Thailand itself, with elephants, wood carvings, and Buddhas adorning the place. Fresh produce, great skill in the kitchen, and exquisite presentations are the hallmarks of this restaurant. Seasonal specialties, such as wild duck and pheasant, are a special feature of the menu. Sample a selection of authentic Thai appetizers before going on to the delectable main courses, which include stir-fried mixed seafood with fresh chili and sweet Thai basil, or else chicken stir-fried with sweet peppers, pineapple, and onion in a sweet-and-sour sauce.

Swan's Nest Lane. ⓒ **01789/297733.** www.thaigroup.co.uk/restaurants/boathouse.html. Reservations recommended. Main courses £3–£16; fixed-price menus £21–£26. MC, V. Sun–Fri noon–2:30pm; daily 5:30–10:30pm.

INEXPENSIVE

The Oppo INTERNATIONAL   Located in the heart of Stratford within a 16th-century building, this refreshingly unpretentious restaurant serves good bistro cooking at reasonable prices. The Oppo's menu often includes local farm products. Salmon fish cakes are served on a bed of spinach with a sorrel sauce, while pork filet is slow roasted with fondant potatoes. The most exotic item on the menu is chicken roasted with banana in lime butter and served with basmati rice and a mild curry sauce.

13 Sheep St. ⓒ **01789/269980.** www.theoppo.co.uk. Reservations recommended. Main courses £5–£20; 2-course lunch £12, 3-course lunch £15. DC, MC, V. Daily noon–2pm; Mon–Sat 5–10pm; Sun 6–9:30pm.

Russons INTERNATIONAL   The theater is a short stroll away, making this a great place for a preshow meal. The restaurant is housed in a 400-year-old building, its two simply furnished dining rooms both featuring inglenook fireplaces. The menu changes monthly, reflecting the availability of seasonal ingredients. Fresh seafood is the specialty here, with different choices every day. Daily specials are posted on a blackboard and may include shoulder of lamb, Norfolk duck, and numerous vegetarian dishes. Finish with one of the delicious homemade desserts.

8 Church St. ⓒ **01789/268822.** www.russons.co.uk. Reservations recommended. Lunch and pretheater main courses £5–£15; dinner main courses £11–£16. AE, MC, V. Tues–Sat 11:30am–1:45pm and 5:15–9pm.

The Vintner ENGLISH/CONTINENTAL   In a timber-framed structure little altered since its construction in the late 15th century, the Vintner may very well be the place where William Shakespeare went to purchase his wine. It derives its name from John Smith, who traded as a wine merchant (vintner) during the 1600s. Close to the Shakespeare Theatre, the Vintner is both a cafe/bar and a restaurant owned by the same family for 5 centuries; its location makes it ideal for a pretheater lunch or supper. When possible, fresh local produce is used. Good-tasting mains include breast of chicken with mango and slow-roasted lamb shank with parsley mashed potatoes. Escalopes of pork filet are made more enticing by caper butter, and a rib-eye comes in a peppercorn sauce. For dessert, try that British nursery favorite, toffee pudding with vanilla ice cream.

4-5 Sheep St. ℂ **01789/297259.** www.the-vintner.co.uk. Reservations not needed. Main courses £5–£20. DC, MC, V. Mon–Sat 9:30am–10pm; Sun 9:30am–9pm.

The Best Places for a Pint

Black Swan (Dirty Duck) ★★ ENGLISH   Affectionately known as the Dirty Duck, this has been a popular hangout for Stratford players since the 18th century. The wall is lined with autographed photos of its many famous patrons. Typical English grills, among other dishes, are featured in the Dirty Duck Grill Room, though no one has ever accused it of serving the best food in Stratford. You'll have a choice of a dozen appetizers, most of which would make a meal themselves. In fair weather, you can have drinks in the front garden and watch the swans glide by on the Avon.

Waterside. ℂ **01789/297312.** Reservations required for dining. Main courses £7–£11; bar snacks £4–£10. AE, DC, MC, V (in restaurant only). Restaurant daily noon–10pm. Bar daily 11am–1am.

Garrick Inn ENGLISH   Near Harvard House, this black-and-white timbered Elizabethan pub has an unpretentious charm. The front bar is decorated with tapestry-covered settles, an old oak refectory table, and an open fireplace that attracts the locals. The back bar has a circular fireplace with a copper hood and mementos of the triumphs of the English stage. The specialty is homemade pies such as steak and kidney or chicken and mushroom. Wild boar and venison are also on offer.

25 High St. ℂ **01789/292186.** Main courses £7–£11. MC, V. Meals Mon–Sat noon–10pm; Sun noon–9:30pm. Pub Mon–Sat 11am–1pm; Sun 11am–10:30pm.

White Swan ENGLISH   In the town's oldest building is this atmospheric pub, with cushioned leather armchairs, oak paneling, and fireplaces. You're likely to meet amiable fellow drinkers who revel in a setting once enjoyed by Will Shakespeare himself, back when it was known as the Kings Head. At lunch, you can partake of hot dishes of the day, along with fresh salads and sandwiches. Typical mains include a warm brie salad with tomatoes and walnuts, salmon with savoy cabbage and potatoes, or the chef's fried chicken served with a red-wine sauce.

In the White Swan hotel, Rother St. ℂ **01789/297022.** www.pebblehotels.com. Bar snacks £2–£15; main courses £13–£17. AE, DC, MC, V. Daily noon–9pm.

The Royal Shakespeare Theatre

On the banks of the Avon, the **Royal Shakespeare Theatre (RST),** Waterside, Stratford-upon-Avon CV37 6BB (ℂ **01789/403444;** www.rsc.org.uk), seats 1,000 patrons and is a major showcase for the **Royal Shakespeare Company (RSC).** The theater's season runs from April to November and typically features five Shakespearean plays. The company has some of the finest actors on the British stage. The RSC also stages productions in the smaller **Swan Theatre,** an intimate 430-seat space next to the Royal Shakespeare Theatre.

You usually need **ticket reservations,** with two successive booking periods, each one opening about 2 months in advance. You can pick these up from a North

American or English travel agent. A small number of tickets are always held for sale on the day of a performance, but it may be too late to get a good seat if you wait until you arrive in Stratford. Tickets can be booked through **Keith Prowse** (☎ **800/669-8687** in North America, or 0870/840-1111 in England; www.keithprowse.com).

You can also call the **theater box office** (☎ **0844/800-1110**) directly and charge your tickets. The box office is open Monday to Saturday 9am to 8pm, although it closes at 6pm on days when there are no performances. Seats range in price from £5 to £45. You can make a credit card reservation and pick up your tickets on the performance day, but you must cancel at least 1 full week in advance to get a refund.

Seeing the Sights

Besides the attractions on the periphery of Stratford, many Elizabethan and Jacobean buildings are in town, a number of them administrated by the **Shakespeare Birthplace Trust** (☎ **01789/204016;** www.shakespeare.org.uk). One combination ticket—costing £19 for adults, £17 for seniors and students, and £12 for children—lets you visit the five most important sights, described below. You can also buy a family ticket, good for two adults and three children, for £49—a good deal. Pick up the ticket if you're planning to do much sightseeing; it's obtainable at your first stopover at any one of the Trust properties.

Guided tours of Stratford-upon-Avon are conducted by **City Sightseeing,** Civic Hall, Rother Street (☎ **01789/412680;** www.citysightseeing-stratford.com). In summer, open-top double-decker buses depart every 15 minutes daily from 9:30am to 6pm. You can take a 1-hour ride without stops, or you can get off at any or all of the town's five Shakespeare properties. Though the bus stops are clearly marked along the historic route, the most logical starting point is the sidewalk in front of the Pen & Parchment Pub, at the bottom of Bridge Street. Tour tickets are valid all day, so you can hop on and off the buses as many times as you want. The tours cost £11 for adults, £9 for seniors or students, and £6 for children 5 to 15 (children 4 and younger ride for free). A family ticket goes for £28. Tour frequency depends on the time of the year; call for information.

Anne Hathaway's Cottage ★ The Bard was only 18 when he married Anne Hathaway, who was much older. Before she married Shakespeare, Anne lived in this thatched wattle-and-daub cottage in the hamlet of Shottery, 1.6km (1 mile) from Stratford. It's the most interesting and the most photographed of the Trust properties. The Hathaways were yeoman farmers, and their descendants lived in the cottage until 1892. As a result, it was never renovated and provides a rare insight into the life of a family in Shakespearean times. Many original furnishings, including various kitchen utensils and the courting settle (the bench on which Shakespeare is said to have wooed Anne), are preserved inside the house. After visiting the interior, take time to linger in the garden and orchard.

Cottage Lane, Shottery. ☎ **01789/292100.** www.shakespeare.org.uk. Admission £7.50 adults, £6.50 seniors and students, £4.50 children, £20 family ticket. Combination tickets available (see above). Nov–Mar daily 10am–4pm; Apr–May and Sept–Oct Mon–Sat 9:30am–5pm, Sun 10am–5pm; June–Aug Mon–Sat 9am–5pm, Sun 9:30am–5pm. Closed Dec 23–26. Take a bus from Bridge St. or walk via a marked pathway from Evesham Place in Stratford across the meadow to Shottery.

Hall's Croft This house is on Old Town Street, not far from the parish church, Holy Trinity. It was here that Shakespeare's daughter Susanna probably lived with her husband, Dr. John Hall, who was widely respected and built up a large medical practice in the area. Hall's Croft is an outstanding Tudor house with a walled garden, furnished in the style of a middle-class home of the time. Fascinating exhibits illustrate the theory and practice of medicine in Dr. Hall's time.

Old Town St. (near Holy Trinity Church). © **01789/292107.** www.shakespeare.org.uk. Admission £13 adults, £12 seniors and students, £8 children, £33 family ticket. Combination tickets available (see above). Nov–Mar daily 11am–4pm; Apr–May daily 11am–5pm; June–Aug Mon–Sat 9:30am–5pm, Sun 10am–5pm; Sept–Oct daily 11am–5pm. Closed Dec 23–28. To reach Hall's Croft, walk west from High St., which becomes Chapel St. and Church St. At the intersection with Old Town St., go left.

Harvard House & Museum of British Pewter   The most ornate home in Stratford, Harvard House is a fine example of an Elizabethan town house. Rebuilt in 1596, it was once the home of Katherine Rogers, mother of John Harvard, founder of Harvard University. In 1909, the house was purchased by a Chicago millionaire, Edward Morris, who presented it as a gift to the famous American university. Today, following a restoration, it has reopened as the Museum of British Pewter. The museum displays trace the use of pewter from the Roman era until modern times. Pewter, as you learn, used to be the most common choice for household items. Even kiddie toys were made from pewter. Highlights include a tankard engraved with the images of William and Mary, a teapot inspired by the Portland Vase, and a rare bell-based Elizabethan candlestick. Two hands-on activities allow children to examine original items.

High St. © **01789/204507.** www.shakespeare.org.uk. Admission £3.50 adults, free for children under 16. May–June and Sept–Oct Fri–Sun noon–5pm; July–Aug Wed–Sun noon–5pm.

Holy Trinity Church (Shakespeare's Tomb)   In an attractive setting near the River Avon is the parish church where Shakespeare is buried ("and curst be he who moves my bones"). The Parish Register records his baptism in 1564 and burial in 1616; copies of the original documents are on display. The church is one of the most beautiful parish churches in England.

Shakespeare's tomb lies in the chancel, a privilege bestowed upon him when he became a lay rector in 1605. Alongside his grave are those of his widow, Anne, and other members of his family. You can also see the graves of Susanna, his daughter, and those of Thomas Nash and Dr. John Hall. Nearby on the north wall is a bust of Shakespeare that was erected approximately 7 years after his death—within the lifetime of his widow and many of his friends.

Old Town St. © **01789/290128.** Free admission to church; Shakespeare's tomb £2 adults, £1 students. Apr–Sept Mon–Sat 8:30am–6pm, Sun 12:30–5pm; Mar and Oct Mon–Sat 9am–5pm, Sun 12:30–5pm; Nov–Feb Mon–Sat 9am–4pm, Sun 12:30–5pm. Walk 4 min. past the Royal Shakespeare Theatre, with the river on your left.

Mary Arden's House (Glebe Farm) & Palmer's Farm ★   So what if millions of visitors have been tricked into thinking this timber-framed farmhouse, with its old stone dovecote and various outbuildings, was the girlhood home of Shakespeare's mother, Mary Arden? It's still one of the most intriguing sights outside Stratford, even if local historian Dr. Nat Alcock discovered in 2000 that the actual childhood home of Arden was the dull-looking brick-built farmhouse, Glebe Farm, next door. Glebe Farm has now been properly renamed Mary Arden's House. It was all the trick of an 18th-century tour guide, John Jordan, who decided Glebe Farm was too unimpressive to be the home of the Bard's mother, so he told tourists it was this farmstead instead. What was known for years as "Mary Arden's House" has been renamed Palmer's Farm. Actually, this farm wasn't constructed until the late 16th century, a little late to be Mary Arden's actual home. After the name confusion, local authorities converted Palmer's Farm into a working farm. Visitors can tour the property and see firsthand how a farming household functioned in the 1570s—yes, cows to be milked, bread to be baked, and vegetables cultivated in an authentic 16th-century manner. In the barns, stable, cowshed, and farmyard is an extensive collection of farming implements illustrating life and work in the local countryside from Shakespeare's time to the present.

Station Rd., Wilmcote. ✆ **01789/293455.** www.shakespeare.org.uk. Admission £8.50 adults, £7.50 students and seniors, £5.50 children, £23 family ticket, free for children 4 and younger. Combination tickets available (see above). Nov–Mar daily 10am–4pm; Apr–May and Sept–Oct daily 10am–5pm; June–Aug daily 9:30am–5pm. Closed Dec 23–26. Take A3400 (Birmingham) for 5.5km (3½ miles).

Nash's House & New Place   Shakespeare retired to New Place in 1610 (a prosperous man by the standards of his day) and died here 6 years later. Regrettably, the house was torn down, so only the garden remains. A mulberry tree planted by the Bard was so popular with latter-day visitors to Stratford that the garden's owner chopped it down. It is said that the mulberry tree that grows here today was planted from a cutting of the original tree. You enter the gardens through Nash's House (Thomas Nash married Elizabeth Hall, a granddaughter of the poet). Nash's House has 16th-century period rooms and an exhibition illustrating the history of Stratford. The popular Knott Garden adjoins the site and represents the style of a fashionable Elizabethan garden.

Chapel St. ✆ **01789/292325.** www.shakespeare.org.uk. Admission £13 adults, £12 seniors and students, £8 children, £34 family ticket. Combination tickets available (see above). Nov–Mar daily 11am–4pm; Apr–May and Sept–Oct daily 11am–5pm; June–Aug Mon–Sat 9:30am–5pm, Sun 10am–5pm. Closed Dec 23–26. Walk west down High St.; Chapel St. is a continuation of High St.

Shakespeare's Birthplace ★   The son of a glover and whittawer (leather worker), the Bard was born on St. George's Day, April 23, 1564, and died on the same date 52 years later. Filled with Shakespeare memorabilia, including a portrait and furnishings of the writer's time, this Trust property is a half-timbered structure, dating from the early 16th century. The house was bought by public donors in 1847 and preserved as a national shrine. You can visit the living room, the bedroom where Shakespeare was probably born, a fully equipped kitchen of the period (look for the "babyminder"), and a Shakespeare museum, illustrating his life and times. Afterward, you can walk through the garden. You won't be alone: It's estimated that some 660,000 visitors pass through the house annually.

Built next door to commemorate the 400th anniversary of the Bard's birth, the modern **Shakespeare Centre** serves both as the administrative headquarters of the Birthplace Trust and as a library and study center. An extension houses a visitor center, which acts as a reception area for those coming to the birthplace.

Henley St. (in the town center near the post office, close to Union St.). ✆ **01789/204016.** www.shakespeare.org.uk. Admission £13 adults, £12 students and seniors, £8 children, £34 family ticket. Combination tickets available (see above). Nov–Mar Mon–Sat 10am–4pm, Sun 10:30am–4pm; Apr–May and Sept–Oct daily 10am–5pm; June–Aug daily 9am–5pm. Closed Dec 23–26.

Stratford Brass Rubbing Centre   This is a brass-rubbing center, where medieval and Tudor brasses illustrate the knights and ladies, scholars, merchants, and priests of a bygone era. The Stratford collection includes a large assortment of exact replicas of brasses. Entrance is free, but visitors are charged depending on which brass they choose to rub, with prices varying according to size. They start at £2 for a small brass, up to a maximum of £20 for a rubbing of the largest brass.

Royal Shakespeare Theatre Summer House, Avon Bank Gardens. ℂ **01789/297671.** www.stratford brassrubbing.co.uk. Free admission. Mar–Oct daily 10am–6pm; Nov–Feb daily 11am–4pm.

Shopping

Among the many tacky tourist traps are some quality shops, including the ones described below.

Set within an antique house with ceiling beams, the **Shakespeare Bookshop,** 39 Henley St. (ℂ **01789/292176;** www.shakespeare.org.uk), across from the Shakespeare Birthplace Centre, is the region's premier source for textbooks and academic treatises on the Bard and his works. It specializes in books for every level of expertise on Shakespearean studies, from picture books for junior-high students to weighty tomes geared to those pursuing a Ph.D. in literature.

Everything in the **Pickwick Gallery,** 32 Henley St. (ℂ **01789/294861**), is a well-crafted work of art produced by copper or steel engraving plates, or printed by means of a carved wooden block. Hundreds of botanical prints, landscapes, and renderings of artfully arranged ruins, each suitable for framing, can be purchased. Topographical maps of regions of the United Kingdom are also available if you're planning on doing any serious hiking.

Other shopping bets include the **Antique Market,** along Ely Street, with some 50 or more stalls selling porcelain, silver, jewelry, and Shakespeare memorabilia. **Antique Arms & Armour,** Poet's Arbour on Sheep Street (ℂ **01789/293453**), has the best collection of antique swords and armor, some of it looking like old props from previous Shakespeare productions.

WARWICK: ENGLAND'S FINEST MEDIEVAL CASTLE

148km (92 miles) NW of London; 13km (8 miles) NE of Stratford-upon-Avon

Most visitors come to this town just to see Warwick Castle, the finest medieval castle in England. Some combine it with a visit to the ruins of Kenilworth Castle (see below), but the historic center of ancient Warwick has a lot more to offer.

Warwick cites Ethelfleda, daughter of Alfred the Great, as its founder. But most of its history is associated with the earls of Warwick, a title created by the son of William the Conqueror in 1088. The story of those earls—the Beaumonts and the Beauchamps (such figures as "Kingmaker" Richard Neville)—makes for an exciting episode in English history. A devastating fire swept through the heart of Warwick in 1694, but a number of Elizabethan and medieval buildings still survive, along with some fine Georgian structures from a later date.

Essentials

GETTING THERE Trains run frequently between Stratford-upon-Avon and Warwick. A one-way ticket costs around £4.50. For information, call ℂ **0845/748-4950** or go to **www.nationalrail.co.uk.**

Stagecoach bus no. 16 departs Stratford-upon-Avon every hour during the day. The trip takes roughly half an hour. Call the **tourist office** (ℂ **0870/160-7930**)

for schedules. **National Express** (📞 **0871/781-8181;** www.nationalexpress.com) runs four buses daily from the Riverside bus station in Stratford-upon-Avon to Puckerings Lane in Warwick for £1.50.

Take the A46 if you're driving from Stratford-upon-Avon.

VISITOR INFORMATION The **Tourist Information Centre** is at the Court House, Jury Street (📞 **01926/492212;** www.warwick-uk.co.uk), and is open daily from 9:30am to 4:30pm (closed Dec 24–26 and Jan 1).

Where to Stay

Many people prefer to stay in Warwick and commute to Stratford-upon-Avon, though the accommodations here are not as special as those at Stratford.

Glebe Hotel ★ 🏨 This 1820s rectory to the Church of St. Peter has been welcoming wayfarers to Stratford-upon-Avon and Warwick since it was successfully converted into a small country-house hotel in 1948. The church still stands adjacent to the hotel's grounds. Recent years have seen much redecorating and many new modern facilities, including the Cedars Conservatory Restaurant that looks out onto the gardens. A small swimming pool with hydrojets has been added as well. Each of the bedrooms has been individually designed with a tented ceiling and a four-poster or coronet-style bed. The hotel lies only a 10-minute drive from the center of Warwick.

Church St., Barford, Warwickshire CV35 8BS. 📞 **01926/624218.** Fax 01926/624625. www.glebehotel. co.uk. 39 units. £140–£150 double; £175 Shakespeare Suite (with Jacuzzi corner bathroom). Rates include full English breakfast. AE, DC, MC, V. Free parking. **Amenities:** Restaurant; bar; exercise room; hot tub; heated indoor heated pool; sauna; solarium; spa. *In room:* TV, hair dryer, Wi-Fi (£12 per day).

Hilton Warwick ★ Though outside of town, the Hilton is the best choice in the area. Lying at the junction of a network of highways, it's popular with business travelers and hosts many conferences for local companies. But tourists also find that its comfort and easy-to-find location make it a good base for touring Warwick and the surrounding regions. It's a low-rise modern design with a series of interconnected bars, lounges, and public areas. Room furnishings are bland but comfortable.

Warwick Bypass (A429 Stratford Rd.), Warwick, Warwickshire CV34 6RE. 📞 **800/445-8667** in the U.S. and Canada, or 01926/499555. Fax 01926/410020. www1.hilton.com. 181 units. £71–£150 double. AE, DC, MC, V. Parking £3. Take A429 3km (2 miles) south of Warwick or 11km (7 miles) north of Stratford-upon-Avon to the Junction 15 lying off the M40 from London. **Amenities:** Restaurant; cafe; bar; babysitting; health club; indoor heated pool; room service; sauna; steam room. *In room:* A/C (in deluxe rooms), TV, hair dryer, Internet (£15).

Lord Leycester Hotel This affordable choice lies within walking distance of the castle and the other historic buildings of Warwick. In 1726, the manor house belonged to Lord Archer of Umberslade; in 1926, it was finally turned into this modest hotel. The guest rooms are small but offer reasonable comfort for the price, with decent double or twin beds.

17 Jury St., Warwick, Warwickshire CV34 4EJ. 📞 **01926/491481.** Fax 01926/491561. www.hobyhotels. com/lordindex.php. 42 units. £87–£103 double. Rates include English breakfast. AE, DC, MC, V. **Amenities:** 2 restaurants; bar; room service. *In room:* TV, hair dryer, Wi-Fi (free).

Tudor House Inn At the edge of town, on the main road from Stratford-upon-Avon to Warwick Castle, is a 1472 timbered inn. It's one of the few buildings to escape the fire that destroyed High Street in 1694. Off the central hall are two large rooms, each of which could be the setting for an Elizabethan play. All of the simply furnished bedrooms have washbasins, and two contain doors only 1m (3 ft.) high. In the corner of the lounge is an open, turning staircase.

90–92 West St. (opposite the main Warwick Castle car park, 1km/½ mile south of town on A429), Warwick, Warwickshire CV34 6AW. ℂ **01926/495447.** Fax 01926/492948. www.thetudorhousewarwick. co.uk. 10 units, 8 with bathroom. £70–£110 double. Rates include English breakfast. DC, MC, V. **Amenities:** Restaurant; bar; Wi-Fi (free). *In room:* TV, hair dryer.

Where to Dine

For a break from sightseeing, it's hard to beat the ancient ambience of tea at **Brethren's Kitchen,** Lord Leycester Hospital (ℂ **01926/491422;** www.brethrens kitchen.co.uk). This tearoom is part of a 16th-century hospital established by the earl in the year 1571. It has cool stone floors and wonderful exposed oak beams. Indian, Chinese, and herbal teas are all available, as well as scones with fresh cream, sponge cake, and fruit cake. It's closed between November and March and on Mondays, but it is open on bank holidays.

Catalan 🗡 MEDITERRANEAN   It's the castle that draws you to Warwick, not the cuisine, but this bistro is notable for serving affordable food that is both good-tasting and prepared with fresh ingredients. If you come for lunch, you'll be greeted with a Spanish tapas menu that is both experimental and tasteful. There's also lighter fare such as sandwiches, panini, and salads. Dinner is more elaborate, with dishes such as loin of monkfish wrapped with pancetta and roasted with fresh herbs or a braised lamb shank with Spanish saffron and a rich shallot and port jus.

6 Jury St. ℂ **01926/498930.** www.cafecatalan.com. Reservations recommended. Main courses £10–£19; Mon–Fri 2-course fixed-price lunch £11. AE, MC, V. Mon–Sat noon–3pm and 6–9:30pm.

Rose & Crown BRITISH   This former coaching inn has been modernized and turned into the best city dining pub in Warwick, with large leather sofas and low tables by an open fire. Order a Wells & Youngs Bombardier ale while you peruse the carefully chosen menu. Many locals start with the homemade soup of the day with crusty bread, though you might prefer a caramelized balsamic-and-red-onion tart with goat cheese. No starter is as tasty as the crab and lime fritters with a chili dressing. For mains, try the aged Aberdeenshire rump steak with peppercorn butter or the whole roasted sea bass with shrimp and vegetable Thai broth. An old-fashioned sherry trifle is offered for dessert.

30 Market Place. ℂ **01926/411117.** www.roseandcrownwarwick.co.uk. Reservations recommended for dinner. Main courses £10–£19; lunch items £6–£19. MC, V. Daily noon–2:30pm and 6:30–10pm (until 9:30pm Sun).

Seeing the Sights

Lord Leycester Hospital   The great fire spared this group of half-timbered alms-houses at the West Gate. The buildings were erected around 1400, and the hospital was founded in 1571 by Robert Dudley, earl of Leicester, as a home for old soldiers. It's still used by ex-service personnel and their spouses. On top of the West Gate is the attractive little chapel of St. James, dating from the 12th century but renovated many times since. Nathaniel Hawthorne wrote of his visits to the gardens in 1855 and 1857; the gardens were restored based on the observations he made in his writings. If you visit in the spring, you can see some 4,000 tulips in bloom.

High St. ℂ **01926/491422.** www.lordleycester.com. Admission £4.90 adults, £4.40 seniors, £3.90 children. Easter Sat–Oct Tues–Sun 10am–5pm; Nov–Easter Tues–Sun 10am–4pm.

St. John's House Museum At Coten End, not far from the castle gates, this early-17th-century house has exhibits on Victorian domestic life. A schoolroom is furnished with original 19th-century furniture and equipment. During the school term, Warwickshire children dress in period costumes and learn Victorian-style lessons. Groups of children also use the Victorian parlor and the kitchen. Because it's impossible to display more than a small number of items at a time, a study room is available where you can see objects from the reserve collections. The costume collection is a particularly fine one; visitors can study the drawings and photos that make up the costume catalog. These facilities are available for viewing by appointment only. Upstairs is a military museum, tracing the history of the Royal Warwickshire Regiment from 1674 to the present.

St. John's, at the crossroads of the main Warwick-Leamington Rd. (A425/A429) and the Coventry Rd. (A429). ℂ **01926/412132.** www.warwickshire.gov.uk/museum. Free admission. Tues–Sat and bank holidays 10am–5pm (May–Sept also Sun 2:30–5pm).

St. Mary's Church Destroyed in part by the fire of 1694, this church, with rebuilt battlemented tower and nave, is among the finest examples of late-17th- and early-18th-century architecture. The Beauchamp Chapel, spared from the flames, encases the Purbeck marble tomb of Richard Beauchamp, a well-known earl of Warwick who died in 1439 and is commemorated by a gilded bronze effigy. Even more powerful than King Henry V, Beauchamp has a tomb that's one of the finest remaining examples of the Perpendicular Gothic style from the mid-15th century. The tomb of Robert Dudley, earl of Leicester, a favorite of Elizabeth I, is against the north wall. The Perpendicular Gothic choir dates from the 14th century; the Norman crypt and chapter house are from the 11th century.

21 Church St. ℂ **01926/403940.** www.saintmaryschurch.co.uk. Free admission; £2 donation recommended. Apr–Oct daily 10am–6pm; Nov–Mar daily 10am–4:30pm. All buses to Warwick stop at Old Sq., 2 blocks from the church.

Warwick Castle ★★★ Perched on a rocky cliff above the River Avon in the town center, a stately late-17th-century mansion is surrounded by a magnificent 14th-century fortress, the finest medieval castle in England. Surrounded by gardens, lawns, and woodland, where peacocks roam freely, and skirted by the Avon, Warwick Castle was described by Sir Walter Scott in 1828 as "that fairest monument of ancient and chivalrous splendor which yet remains uninjured by time." Even 3 hours may not be enough time to see everything here.

Ethelfleda, daughter of Alfred the Great, built the first significant fortifications here in 914. William the Conqueror ordered the construction of a motte-and-bailey castle in 1068, 2 years after the Norman Conquest. The mound is all that remains today of the Norman castle, which Simon de Montfort sacked in the Barons' War of 1264.

The Beauchamp family, the most illustrious medieval earls of Warwick, is responsible for the appearance of the castle today; much of the external structure remains unchanged from the mid–14th century. When the castle was granted to Sir Fulke Greville by James I in 1604, he spent £20,000 (an enormous sum in those days) converting the existing castle buildings into a luxurious mansion. The Grevilles have held the earl of Warwick title since 1759.

The staterooms and Great Hall house fine collections of paintings, furniture, arms, and armor. The armory, dungeon, torture chamber, ghost tower, clock tower, and Guy's tower create a vivid picture of the castle's turbulent past and its important role in the history of England.

The private apartments of Lord Brooke and his family, who in recent years sold the castle to the Tussauds Group, are open to visitors. They house a display of a carefully reconstructed Royal Weekend House Party of 1898. The major rooms contain wax portraits of important figures of the time, including a young Winston Churchill. In the Kenilworth bedroom, a likeness of the Prince of Wales, later King Edward VII, reads a letter. The duchess of Marlborough prepares for her bath in the red bedroom. Among the most lifelike of the figures is a uniformed maid bending over to test the temperature of the water running into a bathtub.

You can also see the Victorian rose garden, a re-creation of an original design from 1868 by Robert Marnock. Near the rose garden is a Victorian alpine rockery and water garden.

Warwick. © **0870/442-2000.** www.warwick-castle.co.uk. Admission £15–£21 adults, £12–£18 students and seniors, £10–£16 children 4–16, £51–£72 family ticket, free for children 3 and younger. Apr–Sept daily 10am–6pm; Oct–Mar daily 10am–5pm. Closed Dec 25.

14 KENILWORTH CASTLE ★★

164km (102 miles) NW of London; 8km (5 miles) N of Warwick; 21km (13 miles) N of Stratford-upon-Avon

The big attraction in the village of Kenilworth, an otherwise dull English market town, is Kenilworth Castle—and it's reason enough to stop here.

Essentials

GETTING THERE   **InterCity** train lines make frequent and fast connections from London's Paddington and Euston stations to either Coventry or Stratford-upon-Avon. For information, call © **0845/748-4950** or go to **www.nationalrail.co.uk.** Midland Red Line buses make regular connections from both towns to Kenilworth.

If you're driving from Warwick, take the A46 toward Coventry.

VISITOR INFORMATION   The **Tourist Information Centre** is in the village at the Kenilworth Library, 11 Smalley Place (© **01926/748900**). It's open Monday and Thursday 9:30am to 7pm; Tuesday and Friday 9am to 5:30pm; Wednesday 10:30am to 5:30pm; and Saturday 9am to 4pm. On the Web, a valuable resource is **www.kenilworthweb.com**.

Where to Stay

Milsoms Hotel Kenilworth   Located in the old part of Kenilworth, the oak tree around which the original alehouse was built in 1430 still supports the roof of the building today. The bedrooms vary greatly in size, but each is tastefully decorated with a comfortable bed—usually a double or twins, though there are two four-posters.

Clarendon House, 6–8 Old High St., Kenilworth, Warwickshire CV8 1LZ. © **01926/515450.** Fax 01926/515451. www.milsomshotel.co.uk. 31 units. £85–£105 double. Rates include English breakfast. AE, DC, MC, V. Free parking. **Amenities:** Restaurant; bar. *In room:* TV, hair dryer.

Where to Dine

Restaurant Bosquet ★ FRENCH   This narrow, stone-fronted town house from the late Victorian age is a culinary oasis. It's owned and operated by French-born Bernard Lignier, who does the cooking, and his English wife, Jane, who supervises the dining room. The a la carte menu changes every 2 months and might include such well-crafted dishes as boneless roast squab stuffed with mushrooms or wild venison on a purée of parsnips with a game sauce. The best starter is foie gras served with a sweet-wine-and-grape sauce.

97A Warwick Rd.© **01926/852463.** www.restaurantbosquet.co.uk. Reservations recommended. Main courses £20–£22; 3-course lunch or dinner £32. AE, MC, V. Tues–Fri noon–2pm; Tues–Sat 7–9:30pm. Closed 1 week for Christmas and last 3 weeks in Aug.

The Magnificent Ruins of Kenilworth Castle ★★

Kenilworth Castle (© 01926/852078; www.english-heritage.org.uk) was built by Geoffrey de Clinton, a lieutenant of Henry I. At one time, its walls enclosed an area of 4.3 hectares (7 acres), but it is now in magnificent ruins. Caesar's Tower, with its 5m-thick (16-ft.) walls, is all that remains of the original structure.

Edward II was forced to abdicate at Kenilworth in 1327 before being carried off to Berkeley Castle in Gloucestershire, where he was undoubtedly murdered. In 1563, Elizabeth I gave the castle to her favorite, Robert Dudley, earl of Leicester. He built the gatehouse, which the queen visited on several occasions. After the civil war, the Roundheads were responsible for breaching the outer walls and towers and blowing up the north wall of the keep. This was the only damage inflicted following the earl of Monmouth's plea that it be "slighted with as little spoil to the dwelling house as might be."

The castle is the subject of Sir Walter Scott's romance *Kenilworth*. In 1957, Lord Kenilworth presented the decaying castle to England, and limited restoration has since been carried out. The castle is open daily, March to August from 10am to 6pm, September and October from 10am to 5pm, and November to February from 10am to 4pm. It's closed January 1 and December 24 to December 26. Admission is £7.60 for adults, £6.50 for seniors, £3.80 for children 5 to 16, and free for children 4 and younger; a family ticket goes for £19.

COVENTRY ★

161km (100 miles) NW of London; 32km (20 miles) NE of Stratford-upon-Avon; 29km (18 miles) SE of Birmingham; 84km (52 miles) SW of Nottingham

Coventry has long been noted in legend as the ancient market town through which Lady Godiva took her famous ride in the buff. A real Lady Godiva actually existed in the 11th century and was the wife of Leofric, earl of Mercia, one of England's most powerful noblemen. She was a benefactor to the poor and urged her husband to reduce their tax burden, which he agreed to do at a price. He made her a bet: If she'd ride naked through Coventry market at midday, he would in return abolish all local taxes save those on horses. On the appointed day, she rode naked through the market, unashamed of her nudity, and the taxes were duly removed. As such, she rode into legend, and that's the naked truth. The myth goes that a Coventry tailor was struck blind after looking at Lady Godiva, giving rise to the term "Peeping Tom."

Coventry today is a Midlands industrial city. The city was partially destroyed by German bombers during World War II, but the restoration is miraculous.

Essentials

GETTING THERE   Trains run every half-hour from London's Euston Station to Coventry (trip time: 1¼ hr.). For schedules and information, call © **0845/748-4950** or go to **www.nationalrail.co.uk**.

From London's Victoria Coach Station, 12 buses run daily between 6am and 1am for the 2¼-hour trip, costing £15. From Stratford-upon-Avon, four **National Express** buses, with a trip time of 1 hour, travel to Pool Meadow bus station, at Fairfax Street in Coventry. A single-day round-trip ticket costs £3.50. For schedules and information, call ✆ **0871/781-8181** or visit **www.nationalexpress.com**.

VISITOR INFORMATION The **Coventry Tourist Information Centre,** 4 Priory Row (✆ **024/7622-5616;** www.visitcoventryandwarwickshire.co.uk is), is open from Easter to mid-October, Monday to Friday 10am to 5pm, Saturday 10am to 4:30pm, and Sunday 10am to 12:30pm and 1:30 to 4:30pm. From late October to Easter, hours are Monday to Friday 9:30am to 4:30pm, Saturday 10am to 4:30pm, and Sunday 10am to 12:30pm and 1:30 to 4:30pm.

Coventry Cathedral ★★★

Consecrated in 1962, Sir Basil Spence's controversial **Coventry Cathedral,** 7 Priory Row (✆ **024/7652-1200;** www.coventrycathedral.org.uk), is the city's main attraction. The cathedral is on the same site as the 14th-century Perpendicular building, and you can visit the original tower. Many locals maintain that the structure is more likely to be appreciated by the foreign visitor because Brits are more attached to traditional cathedral design. Some visitors consider the restored site one of the most poignant and religiously evocative modern churches in the world.

Outside is Sir Jacob Epstein's bronze masterpiece, *St. Michael Slaying the Devil.* Inside, the outstanding feature is the 21m-high (70-ft.) altar tapestry by Graham Sutherland, said to be the largest in the world. The floor-to-ceiling abstract stained-glass windows are the work of the Royal College of Art. The West Screen (an entire wall of stained glass installed during the 1950s) depicts rows of stylized saints and prophets with angels flying among them.

In the undercroft of the cathedral is a visitor center, the Walkway of Holograms, whose otherwise plain walls are accented with three-dimensional images of the Stations of the Cross, created with reflective light. One of the most evocative objects here is a charred cross wired together by local workmen from burning timbers that crashed to the cathedral's floor during the Nazi bombing. An audiovisual exhibit on the city and church includes the fact that 450 aircraft dropped 40,000 firebombs on the city in a single day.

The cathedral is open daily from 9am to 5pm; the tower is open during summer months when staff availability permits. For entrance to the cathedral, a donation of £3.50 per adult is suggested; tower admission is £3 adults, £1 children 5 to 15.

BIRMINGHAM ★

193km (120 miles) NW of London; 40km (25 miles) N of Stratford-upon-Avon

England's second-largest city may lay claim fairly to the title "Birthplace of the Industrial Revolution." It was here that James Watt first used the steam engine with success to mine the Black Country. Watt and other famous 18th-century members of the Lunar Society regularly met under a full moon in the nearby Soho mansion of manufacturer Matthew Boulton. Together, Watt, Boulton, and other "lunatics," as Joseph Priestly, Charles Darwin, and Josiah Wedgwood cheerfully called themselves, launched the revolution that thrust England and the world into the modern era.

Birmingham

Today, this brawny, unpretentious metropolis still bears some of the scars of industrial excess and the devastation of the Nazi Luftwaffe bombing during World War II. But an energetic building boom has occurred recently, and Brummies have nurtured the city's modern rebirth by fashioning Birmingham into a convention city that hosts 80% of all trade exhibitions in the country.

Birmingham has worked diligently in recent decades to overcome the blight of overindustrialization and poor urban planning. New areas of green space and the city's cultivation of a first-rate symphony and ballet company, as well as art galleries and museums, have all made Birmingham more appealing.

Though not an obvious tourist highlight, Birmingham serves as a gateway to England's north. With more than one million inhabitants, Birmingham has a vibrant nightlife and restaurant scene. Its three universities, 2,428 hectares (6,000 acres) of parks and nearby pastoral sanctuaries, and restored canal walkways also offer welcome quiet places.

Essentials

GETTING THERE

BY PLANE   Major international carriers operate transatlantic flights with direct service to **Birmingham International Airport** (**BHX; ℂ 0844/576-6000;** www. birminghamairport.co.uk).

· In the U.S., **Continental Airlines** (**ℂ 800/5233273;** www.continental.com) offers direct flights from Newark Airport to Birmingham every evening (twice a day May–Sept).

In Canada, two carriers fly direct from Toronto's Pearson Airport to Birmingham. **Air Transat** (**ℂ 866/847-1112;** www.airtransat.com) departs every Friday from March through September. **Air India** (**ℂ 800/223-7776** in the U.S., or 800/625-6424 in Canada; www.airindia.com) has flights on Monday, Wednesday, Friday, Saturday, and Sunday.

Direct air service between Birmingham and London is almost nonexistent. Many air carriers, however, maintain a virtual air-shuttle service between London airports and nearby Manchester, which is a 1½-hour trip to Birmingham via ground transport. For example, British Airways (BA) operates 12 daily flights from London's Heathrow to Manchester and seven daily flights from London's Gatwick. BA runs about the same number of return flights daily from Manchester to London.

Birmingham's airport lies about 13km (8 miles) southeast of the city center and is easily accessible by public transportation. **AirRail Link** offers a free shuttle-bus service every 10 minutes from the airport to the Birmingham International Rail Station and National Exhibition Centre (NEC). **InterCity** train services operate a shuttle from the airport to New Street Station in the city center, just a 15-minute trip.

BY TRAIN   InterCity offers train service every half-hour during the day (Mon–Fri) between London's Euston Station and Birmingham, a 90-minute rail trip. Regular service is also available from London's Euston Station, where trains depart every 2 hours for Birmingham. Birmingham is linked to the national rail network by New Street Station in the city center and the airport's International Station.

Trains leave Manchester's Piccadilly Station nearly every hour for Birmingham. The trip takes 90 minutes. Call **ℂ 0845/748-4950** or go to **www.nationalrail.co.uk** for schedules and current fares.

BY BUS   National **Express** (**ℂ 0871/781-8181;** www.nationalexpress.com) provides regular bus service, as frequent as every half-hour, between Birmingham and London (trip time: 2¾-hr.), Manchester, and regional towns.

BY CAR   From London, the best route is via the M40, which leads onto the M42, the motorway that circles south and east of Birmingham. Once on the M42, any of the roads from junctions 4 to 6 will lead into the center of Birmingham. The drive takes about 2 to 2½ hours, depending on traffic conditions. Parking is available at locations throughout Birmingham.

VISITOR INFORMATION

The **Birmingham Visitor Centre,** at the Rotunda, 150 New St., in the city center (**ℂ 0870/2250127;** www.visitbirmingham.com), is open Monday to Saturday 9:30am to 5:30pm, Sunday 10:30am to 4:30pm. It will assist travelers in arranging accommodations, obtaining theater or concert tickets, and planning itineraries.

GETTING AROUND

Birmingham's city center hosts a number of attractions within easy walking distance. **Centro** (© 0121/200-2787; www.centro.org.uk) provides information on all local bus and rail services within Birmingham and the West Midlands area. Exact change is required on one-way local bus and train trips. A **Day Saver Pass,** for bus use only, costs £3.70 for adults and is an economical way to use the Centro bus system. For both metro and buses, a weekly **Centro Card** costs from £17 to £20, depending on what zones you travel.

Taxis queue at various spots in the city center, at rail stations, and at the National Exhibition Centre. Travelers can also ring up a radio-cab operator such as **TOA Taxis** (© 0121/4278888; www.taxinumber.com).

Where to Stay

EXPENSIVE

Hotel du Vin ★★★ This celebrity hangout, a pearl in the chain of Hotel du Vin properties throughout Britain, is the most eye-catching boutique hotel in town, having been converted into a hotel from the Birmingham Eye Hospital. Behind its redbrick exterior in the revitalized Jewellery Quarter, the hotel opens onto an inner courtyard with a fountain and garden. Much of the Victorian architecture has been retained, including the magnificent sweeping staircase and granite pillars. The Bubble Lounge, decorated in the style of Venice's Café Florin, offers more than 50 champagnes. The on-site Bistro is one of the most sophisticated in the city, with such dishes as a starter of Jerusalem artichoke soup with truffle oil and a main course of wild mushroom and arugula linguine.

25 Church St., Birmingham B3 2NR. 66 units. © **0121/200-0600.** Fax 0121/236-0889. www.hotelduvin. com. 66 units. £160–£260 double; from £295 suite. AE, MC, V. Parking £18. **Amenities:** Restaurant; bar; exercise room; room service; spa. *In room:* A/C, TV, hair dryer, minibar, Wi-Fi (free).

Malmaison Birmingham ★★ 🛏 This string of oh-so-chic hotels that stretches from London to Edinburgh has now invaded Birmingham, bringing with it a touch of class. The "fab" hotel occupies part of the Mailbox complex, a converted 1960s Royal Mail Sorting Office with a panoramic canal-side setting. Bedrooms feature the latest designs and are sleekly modern and invitingly comfortable—great beds, slinky lights, bathrooms with tub and power showers, and luxe toiletries along with CD players and libraries. You can relax in Le Petit Spa, called Birmingham's "sexiest," or else work out in Gymtonic.

1 Wharfside St., Birmingham B1 1RD. © **0121/246-5000.** Fax 0121/246-5002. www.malmaison-birmingham.com. 189 units. £190–£210 double; £260–£525 suite. AE, DC, MC, V. Parking £18. **Amenities:** Restaurant; bar; gym; room service; spa. *In room:* A/C, TV, hair dryer, minibar, Wi-Fi (£10 per day).

New Hall Hotel & Spa ★★★ A 12th-century manor, reputedly the oldest in England, has been converted into a luxurious country-house hotel outside the city of Birmingham. The location is in a leafy suburb, where a tree-lined drive leads to 10 hectares (26 acres) of gardens and this moated manor at a point 11km (7 miles) northeast of the center. This is one of the best places in England for a romantic escape. Bedrooms are furnished sumptuously and luxuriously, with all the modern amenities. Most of the well-accessorized rooms are in a more contemporary addition. The public rooms are even more gracious, lit by 18th-century chandeliers and featuring a stone fireplace from the 17th century. Of particular note is the 16th-century oak-paneled dining room, where an award-winning chef serves an innovative Continental cuisine.

Walmley Rd., Sutton Coldfield, Birmingham B76 1QX. ✆ **0121/378-2442.** Fax 0121/378-4637. www.handpickedhotels.co.uk. 60 units. £107–£173 double; £167–£193 suite. AE, DC, MC, V. Free parking. **Amenities:** Restaurant; bar; exercise room; 9-hole golf course; indoor heated pool; room service; sauna; spa; tennis court. *In room:* TV, hair dryer, Wi-Fi (free).

MODERATE

Apollo Hotel A 5-minute drive from the city center, this hotel offers comfortable modern rooms, a restaurant, an Internet kiosk, and a location convenient to the convention centers and the countryside. Rooms are often a bit cramped, but all are equipped with twin or double beds. Bathrooms are small but tidily organized, though make sure to ask whether yours has a shower or tub, as the rooms vary. Double-glazed windows cut down on noise. The suites are a good value here, as they incorporate a minibar, private kitchen, and their own dining and lounge facilities.

Hagley Rd., Edgbaston, Birmingham B16 9RA. ✆ **0121/455-0271.** Fax 0121/456-2394. www.apollobirmingham.com. 126 units. £95–£105 double. AE, DC, MC, V. Free parking. Take exit 3 from M5, or exit 6 from M6. **Amenities:** Restaurant; bar; room service. *In room:* TV, hair dryer, Wi-Fi (free).

Awentsbury Hotel University and Pebble Mill Studio visitors will find this lodging—installed in a restored 1882 house—convenient and comfortable. The place is kept spick-and-span, and the rooms, while not stylish, are acceptable in every other way. Two of the units are large enough for families. Eleven units have small bathrooms with a shower stall; otherwise, there are enough corridor bathrooms so you'll rarely have to wait.

21 Serpentine Rd., Selly Park, Birmingham B29 7HU. ✆/fax **0121/472-1258.** www.awentsbury.com. 16 units, 9 with bathroom. £56 double without bathroom, £62 with bathroom; £72 family room. Rates include English breakfast. AE, DC, MC, V. Free parking. Take A38 from the city center for about 3km (2 miles), turn left at Bournebrook Rd., and then take the 1st right onto Serpentine Rd. *In room:* TV, Wi-Fi (free; in most).

City Inn ★ 🍽 A favorite of the business traveler, this is a vast hotel with a large atrium with bright rugs and blond-wood furnishings. In the heart of Brindley Place, it offers modern design. Bedrooms are midsize and a bit peas-in-the-pod, but well kept, stylish, and comfortable. An on-site restaurant is one of the best in the city for hotel dining.

1 Brunswick Sq., Brindley Place, Birmingham B1 2HW. ✆ **0121/643-1003.** Fax 0121/643-1005. www.cityinn.com. 238 units. £165–£195 double. AE, DC, MC, V. Parking £11. **Amenities:** Restaurant; bar; gym; room service. *In room:* A/C, TV, hair dryer, Wi-Fi (free).

Copperfield House Hotel This redbrick Victorian Gothic house rests on a steep slope on a residential street. Rooms are midsize for the most part, with nos. 3, 4, and 10 being the most desirable, thanks to garden views and large, well-outfitted bathrooms. Each unit is well maintained and comfortably furnished.

60 Upland Rd., Selly Park, Birmingham B29 7JS. ✆ **0121/472-8344.** Fax 0121/415-5655. www.copperfieldhousehotel.fsnet.co.uk. 17 units. £70–£90 double; £85–£105 family room. Rates include English breakfast. AE, MC, V. Free parking. The hotel is reached via the M5, Junction 4 to the A38 and the city center. Turn left at Priory Rd., then right at the 1st light on A441, and right again at Upland Rd. **Amenities:** Restaurant. *In room:* A/C, TV, hair dryer.

Novotel Birmingham Centre In the city center, this is a well-run chain hotel that offers good, comfortable rooms that have a bit of style. It's a handy choice because many of Birmingham's hotels are booked all week. Bedrooms, midsize for the most part, are in the motel style. The on-site brasserie serves affordable food made with fresh ingredients, and the bar is a popular rendezvous. All in all, especially considering the moderate prices, this isn't a bad choice.

70 Broad St., Birmingham B1 2HT. 📞 **0121/643-2000.** Fax 0121/643-9786. www.novotel.com. 148 units. £127–£146 double. Children stay free in parent's room. AE, MC, V. Free parking. **Amenities:** Restaurant; bar; exercise room; Jacuzzi; room service; sauna. *In room:* A/C, TV, hair dryer, minibar, Wi-Fi (free).

INEXPENSIVE

Elmdon Lodge 🍴   One of the most comfortable—and affordable—guesthouses lies in south Birmingham in the suburb of Acocks Green, which is linked by public transportation to the center of the city. The guesthouse is only a 5-minute walk from the Acocks Green rail station. A welcoming family-run hotel, Elmdon is filled with bedrooms that are comfortably furnished in a homelike style. Rooms come in various sizes and configurations, from single to family rooms and triples, each with a small private bathroom with shower. Guests meet fellow guests in the breakfast lounge. The hotel stands in a landscaped garden, which also has a private car park.

20–24 Elmdon Rd., Acocks Green, Birmingham B27 6LH. 📞 **0121/7066968.** Fax 0121/6285566. www. elmdonlodge.co.uk. 18 units. £59–£75 double; £75 triple; £70–£85 family room. Rates include English breakfast. AE, MC, V. Free parking. **Amenities:** Breakfast lounge. *In room:* TV, free Wi-Fi (in some).

Premier Inn Birmingham Central (East)   Lying between the M6 motorway and the city center, this is a modern, well-kept, and well-run chain hotel. It offers substantially comfortable though rather standard bedrooms. For the motorist just passing through Birmingham or spending only a night, it might be ideal. The hotel also has an affordable on-site restaurant so you don't have to drive into the center of Birmingham at night.

Richard St., Waterlinks, Birmingham B7 4AA. 📞 **0870/2383312.** Fax 0121/333-6490. www.premierinn. com. 60 units. £71 double. AE, MC, V. Free parking. **Amenities:** Restaurant; bar. *In room:* A/C, TV, hair dryer, Wi-Fi (free).

Where to Dine

Bank ★ ☺ FRENCH/BRITISH   You are likely to enjoy your finest meal at this relatively new restaurant, which is affiliated with its famous sibling in London and is now winning friends among the more discriminating palates of Birmingham. The chefs work feverishly in the open-plan kitchen on such starters as seared scallops with asparagus or a confit of duck leg with a sesame-and-honey dressing. For a main dish, you can sample such superb choices as ricotta gnocchi with roasted eggplant, zucchini, and Parma ham, or the roast marinated duck breast with potato Rösti and blueberry jus. Desserts include a classic English bread-and-butter pudding or a passion-fruit mousse. Bank features the best children's menu in town.

4 Brindley Place. 📞 **0121/633-4466.** www.bankrestaurants.com. Reservations recommended. Main courses £11–£22; children's menu £6. AE, DC, MC, V. Mon–Fri noon–11pm; Sat 11:30am–11:30pm; Sun 11:30am–10pm.

Chung Ying CANTONESE   More than 400 flavor-filled items are on this predominantly Cantonese menu (40 dim sum items alone). Samples include pancooked Shanghai dumplings, stuffed crispy duck packed with crabmeat, steamed eel in bean sauce, and a variety of tasty casseroles. Specialties include deep-fried stuffed crab claws or steamed beef dumplings. A delight is the steamed whole sea bass with ginger and spring onion. To go really authentic and sample some of the dishes popular with the local Chinese community, try fried frogs' legs with bitter melon, steamed pork pie with dried or fresh squid, or fish cakes.

Chung Ying Garden, 17 Thorpe St. (℗ **0121/666-6622**), is another restaurant owned by the same proprietor.

16-18 Wrottesley St. ℗ **0121/622-5669.** www.chungying.co.uk. Main courses £7–£18; 2-course dinner menu £29 for 2; 3-course dinner menu £45 for 3. AE, DC, MC, V. Daily noon–11:30pm.

Maharaja INDIAN   Set a few doors down from the Birmingham Hippodrome, this rather good restaurant specializes in Mughlai and north Indian dishes. Dining is on two floors, with framed fragments of Indian printed cloth on the walls. The menu features such dishes as lamb *dhansak* (cubes of lamb in thick lentil sauce), chicken *patalia* (cooked in spices, herbs, and fruit), prawn Madras, and chili Madras with tomatoes, almonds, and lemon. The most popular dish is tandoori fish marinated in yogurt, garlic, and spices. The kitchen's balanced use of spices, herbs, and other flavorings lends most dishes an aromatic but delicate taste.

23 Hurst St., near the Hippodrome. ℗ **0121/622-2641.** www.maharajarestaurant.co.uk. Main courses £8–£17. AE, DC, MC, V. Mon–Sat noon–2pm and 6–11pm.

Purnell's ★★ MODERN BRITISH   The cooking of Glyn Purnell is bold and innovative. In a redbrick Victorian building in the heart of Birmingham, you dine in a room with arched floor-to-ceiling windows, a chic, contemporary setting for fine food close to St. Phillips Cathedral. The restaurant features its own bar and lounge area for diners only, where comfortable sofas are the perfect spot for a predinner drink.

The combination of ingredients is harmonious, though they may come in flavors unfamiliar to you. Try, for example, such mains as Balmoral venison with licorice flavoring and pumpkin or else brill cooked in coconut milk with a lime-flavored and Thai-infused salsify. A delightful surprise is red mullet in vanilla-dipped potatoes and Jerusalem artichokes, or the Cornish lamb with a red pepper purée, plus toffee and cumin-flavored carrots. Only in England would you get lightly salted pork filet with sweet-and-sour parsnips, pig trotters, bacon nuggets, baby leeks, and black pudding crumble.

55 Cornwall St. ℗ **0121/2129799.** www.purnellsrestaurant.com. Reservations required. 2-course lunch £21; 3-course lunch £25; 2-course dinner £36; 3-course dinner £42; 8-course tasting menu £68. AE, MC, V. Tues–Fri noon–4:30pm; Tues–Sat 7–9:30pm. Closed 1 week at Easter, last week in July, 1st week in Aug, and 1 week at Christmas.

Simpsons ★★★ BRITISH/FRENCH   The grandest and best dining in the greater Birmingham area lies 1.6km (1 mile) south of the city center in the district of Edgbaston. In an impressive Georgian mansion, a modern British cuisine is served in an L-shaped dining room set around terraces. Many diners prefer the conservatory, with views of the garden. The menu is modern British, but with heavy French overtones. The produce is purchased fresh every day, using only the finest of seasonal produce. Specialties are forever changing, but starters might include Salcombe crabmeat with Severn & Wye salmon accompanied by an avocado mousse, or else seared hand-dived Ross-shire scallops with Indian spices and a caramelized cauliflower risotto. Move on to such mains as line-caught sea bass with a wild mushroom tart, or perhaps a pavé of Aberdeenshire beef with slow-cooked ox cheek flavored with grain mustard.

On the property is a cooking school and four luxurious bedrooms costing £160 to £225 double.

"Bucket Dining," Kashmiri Style

A growing phenomenon, which we can only call the **Birmingham Balti Experience,** may interest those who love spicy curries. *Balti* literally means bucket, but it refers to a Kashmiri style of cooking meat and vegetables over a fast, hot flame. With the city's large Kashmiri population, there are now many *baltihouses* in Birmingham, most of which are bare-bones, BYOB affairs. One of the better ones is **Celebrity Balti,** 44 Broad St. (✆ **0121/643-8969;** www.celebritybalti.co.uk), close to the Convention Centre, which is open daily from 6pm to midnight.

20 Highfield Rd., Edgbaston. ✆ **0121/454-3434.** Fax 0121/454-3399. www.simpsonsrestaurant.co.uk. Main courses £20–£27; 3-course dinner £33. AE, DC, MC, V. Mon–Fri noon–2pm; Sat–Sun noon–2:30pm; Mon–Thurs 7–9:30pm; Fri–Sat 7–10pm. Closed Dec 24–27 and Dec 31–Jan 1.

Exploring Birmingham

Stephenson Place, at the intersection of New and Corporation streets, is a good starting point for sampling the attractions of the city center. A 5-minute stroll along New Street leads to Victoria Square, where **Council House** (✆ **0121/303-2054**), the city's most impressive Victorian building, anchors the piazza. Built in 1879, it is still the meeting place for the Birmingham City Council and an impressive example of the Italian Renaissance style. It's open for viewing Monday to Thursday from 9am to 5pm and on Friday from 9am to 4pm. The chamber can be seen only by guided tour, which must be arranged in advance.

Along Broad Street is the **Gas Street Basin** (✆ **0121/236-9811**). Operated by Second City Canal Cruises, it forms the hub of the 3,220km (2,000-mile) canal network that runs in all directions from Birmingham to Liverpool, London, Nottingham, and Gloucester. From the Basin, you can take a cruise along the canals or just walk by the towpaths.

Just a 10-minute walk from the city center is the **Jewellery Quarter,** with more than 100 jewelry shops. A unique time capsule of the ancient craft of jewelry making and working with precious metals, the quarter offers bargain hunters the opportunity to arrange repairs, design a custom piece, or just browse. At the **Museum of the Jewellery Quarter,** 75–79 Vyse St. (✆ **0121/554-3598;** www.the-quarter.com), the skill of the jeweler's craft can be viewed at the restored Smith & Pepper factory displays. Admission is free; it's open April to October, Tuesday to Sunday 11:30am to 4pm, and November to March, Tuesday to Saturday 11:30am to 4pm.

Barber Institute of Fine Arts ★★   Don't be put off by the stark, stone-and-brick building that houses the Barber Institute collection. Some critics consider it the finest small art museum in England and the equal of any museum outside London. The choice selection of paintings includes works by Bellini, Botticelli, Bruegel, Canaletto, Delacroix, Gainsborough, Gauguin, Murillo, Renoir, Rubens, Turner, van Gogh, and Whistler.

University of Birmingham (just off Edgbaston Park Rd., near the University's East Gate, 4km/2½ miles south of the city center). ✆ **01214/147333.** www.barber.org.uk. Free admission. Mon–Sat 10am–5pm; Sun noon–5pm. Bus: 61, 62, or 63 from city center.

Birmingham Museum and Art Gallery ★   Known chiefly for its collection of pre-Raphaelite paintings (including works by Ford Maddox Brown, Dante Gabriel Rossetti, Edward Burne-Jones, and Holman Hunt), the gallery also houses exceptional paintings by English watercolor masters from the 18th century. In addition, there is a museum section with an Egyptian mummy, plus tools and artifacts that are 400,000 years old. The BMAG is instantly recognized by its "Big Brum" clock tower.

Chamberlain Sq. ✆ **0121/303-2834.** www.bmag.org.uk. Free admission; varying charges for special exhibitions. Mon–Thurs and Sat 10am–5pm; Fri 10:30am–5pm; Sun 12:30–5pm.

Black Country Living Museum   Much of the area immediately surrounding Birmingham is called the Black Country (after the black smoke that billowed over the area during the iron-working era). That period is best preserved at the Black Country Living Museum in Dudley, a town about 16km (10 miles) northwest of Birmingham. The museum occupies a sprawling landscape in the South Staffordshire coal fields, an early forge of the Industrial Revolution, and re-creates what it was like to work and live in the Black Country of the 1850s. An electric tramway takes visitors to a thick underground coal seam, and trolleys move through a reconstructed industrial village with a schoolhouse, anchor forge, working replica of a 1712 steam engine, and trade shops.

Tipton Rd., Dudley (5km/3 miles north of Junction 2 exit on M5). ✆ **0121/557-9643.** www.bclm.co.uk. Admission £13 adults, £10 seniors, £6.95 children 5–18, £35 family ticket. Mar–Oct daily 10am–5pm; Nov–Feb Wed–Sun 10am–4pm.

Blakesley Hall   Modern houses live outside its gates, but once inside the grounds of Blakesley Hall, you are transported back in time some 400 years. Blakesley is a restored Tudor farmhouse from 1590. The half-timbered structure is typical of buildings once common in the West Midlands. Its original architectural features, including a herringbone floor, are still intact. The Great and Little Parlours on the ground floor have been restored. Oak furnishings include carved panel-back armchairs, long refectory tables, and other period pieces. On display are many artifacts from the era, including pewter goblets and candlesticks. In the painted bedchamber, paintings on the walls from 1590 were uncovered after having been hidden for centuries.

Blakesley Rd., Yardley. ✆ **0121/464-2193.** www.bmag.org.uk. Free admission. Apr–Oct Tues–Sun 11:30am–4pm.

Sherborne Wharf Heritage Narrow Boats   One of the best ways to see Birmingham is by water, a series of artificial canals created as the "motorways" of their day during the Industrial Revolution of the 18th century. These waters, still in good shape after 2 centuries or more, cut across deep valleys on high aqueducts and embankments. Boats sailed on them, carrying finished products or raw materials. Today, departures of sightseeing boats are from the International Convention Centre Quayside, taking you on 1-hour tours of Birmingham from the water, with the city scenically passing before you.

Heritage Marina (near the junction of Macclesfield and Trent & Mersey Canals in Scholar Green). ✆ **0121/455-6163.** www.sherbornewharf.co.uk. Tickets £6.50 adults, £5.50 seniors, £5 children 5–16. Departures Easter–Oct daily at 11:30am, 1pm, 2:30pm, and 4pm. Call ahead in off-season, when tours are conducted Sat–Sun at 1 and 2:30pm, only if weather permits.

Thinktank at Millennium Point ☺   This science museum is both educational and fun, appealing to adults and kids alike. It examines the past, presents today's technology, and explores future scientific breakthroughs that may occur. Science and history meet in 10 different galleries across four floors, where children can have close encounters with the exhibits, doing everything from grabbing a handful of polar-bear blubber to taking control of a digger. Various sections focus on such subjects as "Medicine Matters," exploring surgical instruments and health in general. Nature is uncovered in the "Wild Life" section, as you learn how scientists study the wild world and how animals adapt to change. "Futures" gives you a look into a living tomorrow. An IMAX theater plays educational movies.

Curzon St. ℭ **0121/202-2222.** www.thinktank.ac. Admission £12 adults; £7.95 seniors, students, and children 3–15. Daily 10am–5pm. Call for IMAX schedule.

Shopping

In addition to the **Jewellery Quarter** (see above), Birmingham is a great town for shopping. There are more than 700 retail stores, and many people in the Midlands come here just to shop, especially along **Cannon Street** and **New Street,** with recently opened top-brand designer stores.

The city's **Mailbox** complex, at Wharfside Street (ℭ **0121/632-1000;** www.mailboxlife.com), was once used to sort the mail. It's now become a gargantuan shopping center, with such department stores as **Harvey Nichols** moving in. Emporio Armani, DKNY, Hugo Boss, Jaeger, and Crabtree & Evelyn also call the Mailbox home, along with 12 restaurants, a spa, and the upscale Malmaison hotel.

In the heart of town, the **Bullring,** near St. Martin's Square (ℭ **0121/632-1500;** www.bullring.co.uk), has been developed into Europe's largest city-center retail area, based around the historic street patterns of the city and linking New Street and High Street. It's more affordable and less classy than its cousin the Mailbox, with such mainstays as H&M, Gap, FCUK, and Foot Locker.

The reinvention of "Brum" (as Britain's much-maligned second city is nicknamed) is reflected by the opening of a grand department store at the Bullring, **Selfridges** (ℭ **0800/123400;** www.selfridges.co.uk). As a fashion emporium, its architecture was appropriately inspired by a dress: The curvaceous complex is adorned with 15,000 aluminum disks, a la Paco Rabanne's 1960 chain-mail frocks.

Birmingham After Dark
THE PERFORMING ARTS
Connected to the Convention Centre, **Symphony Hall,** Broad Street (ℭ **0121/780-3333;** www.thsh.co.uk.), has been hailed as an acoustical gem since its completion in 1990. Home to the **City of Birmingham Symphony Orchestra,** it also hosts special classical music events.

The restored **Birmingham Hippodrome,** Hurst Street (ℭ **0844/338-5000;** www.birminghamhippodrome.com), is home to the **Birmingham Royal Ballet** and visiting companies from around the world. It hosts a variety of events, from the Welsh National Opera to musicals to dance. The box office is open Monday to Saturday 9:30am to 8:30pm.

The **National Indoor Arena,** King Edward's Road (ℭ **0844/338-8000;** www.necgroup.co.uk), seats 13,000 and is a favorite site for jazz, pop, and rock concerts, as well as sporting events and conventions.

The **Birmingham Repertory Theatre,** Broad Street, at Centenary Square (ℭ **0121/236-4455;** www.birmingham-rep.co.uk), houses one of the top companies in England. Some of the world's greatest actors have performed with the repertory company over the years, including Lord Olivier, Albert Finney, Paul Scofield,

Dame Edith Evans, and Kenneth Branagh. The widely known "Rep" comprises the Main House, which seats 800 theatergoers, and the Door, a more intimate 120-seat venue that often stages new and innovative works. The box office is open Monday through Saturday 10am to 8pm on performance days, 10am to 6pm on nonperformance days. Tickets cost £10 to £30.

The **Midlands Arts Centre,** in Cannon Hill Park (*✆* **0121/446-3200;** www.macarts.co.uk), is close to the Edgbaston Cricket Ground and reached by car or bus no. 1, 45, or 47. The MAC houses three performance areas and stages a lively range of drama, dance, and musical performances, as well as films. The box office is open daily from 9am to 8:45pm.

The **Alexandra Theatre,** Station Street (*✆* **0121/643-5536;** www.alexandra theatre.org.uk), hosts national touring companies, including productions from London's West End. Contact the box office for show details.

Note: Tickets for all Birmingham theaters are available through Birmingham visitor offices.

CLUBS & PUBS

Boho Rooms, 52 Gas St., along the City Centre canal (*✆* **0121/643-2572**), is a converted warehouse with a bar and two nightclubs.

Otherwise, Broad Street has become the center of nightlife in Birmingham. Just walk up and down the street and pick your favorites. We like **Revolution,** Broad Street (*✆* **0121/665-6508;** www.revolution-bars.co.uk), a vodka bar drawing a hip collection of the under-40 crowd.

Birmingham has a thriving gay and lesbian community, most of them seemingly packed into the **Nightingale,** Kent Street (*✆* **0121/6226-1718;** www.nightingale club.co.uk), nicknamed "the Gale." With its five bars and two frenzied dance floors, it is the *Queer as Folk* choice. There's also a jazz lounge. The cover varies but is often around £5. Open Tuesday to Thursday 9pm to 2am, Friday 7pm to 4am, Saturday 7pm to 6am, and Sunday 7pm to 2am.

THE MALVERNS

195km (127 miles) NW of London; 55km (34 miles) SW of Birmingham

Once part of the ancient and formidable kingdom of Mercia, the beautiful and historic Malverns lie just west of Worcester, rising suddenly from the Severn Valley and stretching for 14km (9 miles). This tranquil area offers 13km (8 miles) of hiking trails.

Six townships cling to the Malvern Hills, making this an outstanding place to strike out for easy day hikes while in Worcester or Hereford. The towns are especially famous for their healing waters, refreshing air, and country vistas. You can wander through Great Malvern, Malvern Link, West Malvern, Weldon, Malvern Wells, Little Malvern, and several other hamlets in a day's stroll. **Great Malvern** is resplendent with Victorian grandeur, much of which was gained from its importance as a 19th-century spa resort. The town has the largest priory church in the area, dating from the 15th century and boasting some fine stained-glass windows, as well as a great Gothic tower. The monks' stalls have superb misericords and medieval titles. The greatest and most beloved singer of the 19th century—the wildly talented "Swedish Nightingale," Jenny Lind—as well as that century's greatest English composer, Sir Edward Elgar, called this area home.

The Malverns provide a breathtaking backdrop for both hiking and biking. You can take in immense views, eastward to the Cotswolds and westward to the Wye Valley and the Welsh mountains, while exploring the most beautiful countryside in England. The Malverns Tourist Information Centre (see below) can provide you with detailed maps and route descriptions.

Our favorite walk in the **Malvern Hills ★★** begins directly to the south of Great Malvern. As you leave town, you can see the ruins of an Iron Age fort high on a ridge. If you head here, you'll enjoy a magnificent vista of the countryside, with the Black Mountains looming to the west. A hike along this ridge, starting at Chase End Hill, takes about 4½ hours round-trip. The trail is well maintained and offers some of the best scenery the Malverns have to offer.

St. Wulstan's Church, 3km (2 miles) west of Great Malvern on the Ledbury Road, is where Sir Edward Elgar is buried with his wife and daughter. You'll find a bronze bust of the composer in Priory Park. He lived at Craeglea on the Malvern Wells Road and at Forli on Alexandra Road, where he composed the *Enigma Variations, Sea Pictures,* and the *Dreams of Gerontius.*

Essentials

GETTING THERE   From London's Paddington Station, trains leave every 2 hours via Worcester for the 2½-hour trip to Great Malvern. For information, call ✆ **0845/748-4950** or go to **www.nationalrail.co.uk**.

Two **National Express** buses depart daily from London's Victoria Coach Station, arriving in Great Malvern 4 hours later. One bus stops at Birmingham, making the journey 5½ hours. Call ✆ **0871/781-8181** or go to **www.nationalexpress.com** for more information.

If you're driving from London, take the M5 to the A4104 west, and then the A449 north toward Great Malvern. Depending on traffic, the drive takes about 2 hours.

VISITOR INFORMATION   The **Malvern Tourist Information Centre,** 21 Church St., Great Malvern (✆ **01684/892289;** www.malvernhills.gov.uk/cms/ leisure-and-culture/tourism.aspx), is open daily 10am to 5pm. On Sundays from December to March, it closes at 4pm.

Where to Stay

Best Western Foley Arms   Home to one of the town's most bustling pubs, this is the oldest hotel in Malvern, with a Georgian pedigree from 1810, when it welcomed the affluent and exhausted for curative sessions at the nearby spa. Princess Mary of Teck, the grandmother of Queen Elizabeth II, liked the hotel so much that she left her coat of arms, which can be seen over the rotating doors leading into this Georgian coaching hotel. Close to the town center, it rises from a very steep hillside, which makes it inconvenient for mobility-impaired guests, but also gives it glorious views over the Severn River to the edge of the Cotswolds from many of its bedroom windows. Accommodations contain old, usually antique, furniture and heavy draperies; they have all the modern conveniences but offer old-fashioned character as well.

14 Worcester Rd., Malvern, Worcestershire WR14 4QS. ✆ **01684/573397.** Fax 01684/569665. www. foleyarmshotel.com. 28 units. £114–£149 double. AE, DC, MC, V. **Amenities:** Restaurant; bar; babysitting; access to nearby gym and pool; room service. *In room:* TV, hair dryer.

Cotford Hotel ☺   A 5-minute walk east of the town center, on an acre of lawns and rock gardens, this towering and stately home dates from 1851, when it was built as the local bishop's residence. Constructed of Cotswold stone and accented with lavish gingerbread, it retains a vaguely ecclesiastical air, despite the modern-day furnishings. Views extend over the garden through elaborate windows carved from wood to resemble Gothic tracery. The main appeal of the place derives from its monumental historic premises, the warm welcome, and such Victorian touches as the tile-floored wide entrance hallway. The bedrooms, mostly midsize, have been much improved in recent years, with excellent beds. Several rooms are specifically set aside for families.

51 Graham Rd., Malvern, Worcestershire WR14 2HU. © **01684/572427.** Fax 01684/572952. www. cotfordhotel.co.uk. 15 units. £99–£115 double; £130 family room. Rates include full English breakfast. AE, DC, MC, V. Free parking. **Amenities:** Restaurant; bar; access to nearby pool and sauna; room service. *In room:* TV, hair dryer, Internet (£9.95).

Cottage in the Wood ★   There is indeed a cottage in the woods associated with this hotel—it contains four cozy bedrooms and dates from the 17th century. But most of the inn occupies a nearby Georgian house from the late 1700s. Originally built for the semiretired mother of the lord of a neighboring estate, it's referred to as the "Dower House" and is appropriately outfitted in an attractive Laura Ashley style. The bedrooms are small, but this place is so charming and offers such panoramic views that most visitors don't mind. The place is exceedingly well furnished, with thoughtfully equipped accommodations. Rooms in the Pinnacles are the most modern, though still decorated in the English-country-house style.

Holywell Rd., Malvern Wells, Worcestershire WR14 4LG. © **01684/588860.** Fax 01684/560662. www. cottageinthewood.co.uk. 31 units. £99–£189 double. Rates include full English breakfast. AE, MC, V. Free parking. After leaving Great Malvern on A449, turn right just before the B4209 turnoff on the opposite side of the road. The inn is on the right. **Amenities:** Restaurant (see review below); bar; babysitting; room service; Wi-Fi (free in lobby of main hotel). *In room:* TV, hair dryer.

Where to Dine

Cottage in the Wood MODERN BRITISH   An 18th-century Georgian-style dower's house, on a steeply sloping, wooded plot of land with panoramic views over the Herefordshire countryside, the site manages to be elegant, cozy, and nurturing at the same time, thanks to the hard work and charm of resident owners John and Sue Pattin. With the help of their son, chef Dominic Pattin, they offer modern adaptations of traditional British favorites. Featured are such imaginative appetizers as roast quail with apricot chutney, followed by tempting mains including Herefordshire beef filet served with a pearl barley risotto or braised pork belly with glazed apples. Vegetarian options are available as well. The best desserts are always the homemade ice creams. *Note:* The accommodations on the property are reviewed above.

In the Cottage of the Wood hotel, Holywell Rd., Malvern Wells. © **01684/588-860.** www.cottage inthewood.co.uk. Reservations recommended. Main courses £12–£20; fixed-price Sun lunch £23. AE, MC, V. Daily 12:30–2pm; Mon–Sat 7–9:30pm, Sun 7–9pm.

IRONBRIDGE

217km (135 miles) NW of London; 58km (36 miles) NW of Birmingham; 29km (18 miles) SE of Shrewsbury

If you're looking for pretty, bucolic England, the name of Ironbridge might turn you off. But it's a rather charming tree-lined village filled with natural beauty, even though it was one of the birthplaces of the Industrial Revolution. It is also a World Heritage Site. Today, it has a cluster of museums documenting its manufacturing history from its 19th-century heyday. There are also plenty of gift shops and other stores in town selling souvenirs to remind you of your visit.

Ironbridge, located in the Ironbridge Gorge, is famous for kicking off an early stage of the Industrial Revolution. Indeed, this stretch of the Severn Valley has been an important industrial area since the Middle Ages because of its iron and limestone deposits. But the event that clinched this area's importance came in 1709, when a Quaker ironmaster, Abraham Darby I, discovered a method for smelting iron by using coke as a fuel, rather than charcoal. This paved the way for the first iron rails, boats, wheels, aqueducts, and bridges, cast here in 1779. So momentous was this accomplishment that the area, originally called Coalbrookdale, was renamed Ironbridge. The area literally buzzed with the new transportation and engineering innovations that soon followed.

Essentials

GETTING THERE   Trains leave London's Euston Station heading for Birmingham every 30 minutes. Once at the Telford Central Station, take a taxi or bus (no. 9, 39, 76, 77, 96, or 99) into Ironbridge, a 20-minute ride. The entire journey from London takes about 2½ hours. For schedules and information, call ℂ **0845/748-4950** or go to **www.nationalrail.co.uk**.

Four daily **National Express** buses depart London's Victoria Coach Station, arriving in Telford about 4 hours later. Two of those are direct; the others make a stop in Birmingham. Call ℂ **0871/781-8181** or visit **www.nationalexpress.com** for information.

If you're driving from London, take the M1 to the M6 to the M54, which leads directly to Ironbridge.

VISITOR INFORMATION   The **Ironbridge Tourist Information Centre,** the Tollhouse (ℂ **01952/884391;** www.visitironbridge.co.uk), is open Monday to Friday 9am to 5pm, Saturday and Sunday 10am to 5pm.

Where to Stay

Best Western Valley Hotel   This hotel was originally built as a private home around 1750. The riverside inn was enlarged over the years into the sprawling, light-brown brick design you see today. The high-ceilinged interior contains hints of its original grandeur, including a worthwhile restaurant, Chez Maw (see below). Fifteen of the hotel's rooms lie within the original stable and are accessible via a glass-roofed courtyard. Although rooms in the main house usually have more panoramic views, many visitors prefer the coziness of the former stables. All units are well maintained and modern; some have four-poster beds.

Buildwas Rd., Ironbridge, Telford, Shropshire TF8 7DW. ℂ **800/528-1234** in the U.S., or 01952/432247. Fax 01952/432308. www.thevalleyhotel.co.uk. 44 units. £82–£107 double. Rates include breakfast. AE, DC, MC, V. **Amenities:** Restaurant (see review below); 2 bars; room service. *In room:* TV, hair dryer, Wi-Fi (free).

Bridge House   Set 2.5km (1½ miles) west of Ironbridge, on the outskirts of the hamlet of Buildwas, this ivy-draped, half-timbered coaching inn is from 1620. Resident proprietor Janet Hedges will tell you unusual stories about the house, such as the 365 nails (one for every day of the year) that hold together the planks of the front door, which comes from the abbey and probably dates from the 1300s. Rooms are genteel and comfortable, sometimes with touches of Edwardian drama (lavishly draped beds, in some cases). Others have exposed beams, and all have creaking floors and uneven walls that testify to the age of the building. They're small but snug, and each is individually decorated.

Buildwas Rd., near Ironbridge, Telford, Shropshire TF8 7BN. ☎ **01952/432105.** Fax 01952/432105. www.a1tourism.com/uk/bridgehs.html. 4 units. £75 double; £90 family unit. Rates include breakfast. MC, V. Closed for 2 weeks at Christmas. *In room:* TV, hair dryer.

Library House ★ 🎒 This restored landmark, parts of which date from 1752, has been used for many purposes, including a doctor's surgery and even the village library, from which the B&B takes its name. Breakfast is served in a room with a rich collection of copper. The morning meal is the best in the area, putting the house in the running for the Automobile Association's best breakfast award. The delightful bedrooms—named after such writers as Eliot, Austen, Milton, and Chaucer—are individually designed and decorated, and come complete with their own teddy bears if you want to cuddle up. There is also a pretty terraced garden.

11 Severn Bank, Ironbridge, near Telford, Shropshire TF8 7AN. ☎ **01952/432299.** Fax 01952/433967. www.libraryhouse.com. 4 units. £75–£100 double. No credit cards. **Amenities:** Breakfast room; garden. *In room:* TV, hair dryer, no phone.

Where to Dine

Chez Maw Restaurant BRITISH The name refers to Arthur Maw, long-ago owner of the house and founder of a nearby factory that produced decorative tiles during the 19th century. Prized examples of his ceramic creations line the reception area and the monumental staircase. Outfitted with crisp napery, Windsor-style chairs, and a high ceiling, the restaurant serves updated British food. The cooking is inspired by the bounty of the enveloping countryside. Try the tenderloin of pork with sage-flavored apples, the pan-seared sea trout with smoked garlic, or the breast of Gressingham duck with honey-roasted apples and pears. For dessert, nothing quite equals the dark chocolate and Bailey's torte with chocolate ice cream and a milk-chocolate sauce.

In the Best Western Valley Hotel, Buildwas Rd. ☎ **01952/432247.** www.thevalleyhotel.co.uk or www. chezmawrestaurant.co.uk. Reservations required for nonguests. Main courses £13–£20. AE, DC, MC, V. Daily noon–2pm; Mon–Sat 7–9:30pm, Sun 7–9pm.

Exploring the Area

The Ironbridge Valley plays host to seven main museums and several smaller ones, collectively called the **Ironbridge Gorge Museums ★★** (☎ **01952/433522** Mon–Fri, or 01952/432166 Sat–Sun; www.ironbridge.org.uk). Its attractions include the **Coalbrookdale Museum of Iron,** with its Darby Furnace; **Darby Houses,** the restored 19th-century homes of the Quaker ironmasters; the **Iron Bridge,** with its original tollhouse; the **Jackfield Tile Museum,** where you can see demonstrations of tile pressing, decorating, and firing; **Blists Hill Victorian Town ★★**, with its open-air re-creation of a 19th-century village; the **Coalport China Museum ★★**, with ceramics displays and demonstrations; the **Tar Tunnel,** which includes a tour of an underground mine; **Broseley Pipeworks,** a 50-year-old abandoned tobacco pipe-making factory; and **Enginuity,** an interactive exhibit that allows kids to become engineers for a day. As it is unlikely that you will have time for everything, we recommend that you visit Blists Hill Victorian Town and the Coalport China Museum, even if you have to skip all the rest. A passport ticket to all museums in Ironbridge Gorge is £22 for adults, £18 for seniors, £14 for students and children, and £60 for families of two adults and up to three children. The sites are open Monday to Friday from 9am to 5pm, Saturday and Sunday from 10am to 5pm. The Tar Tunnel, Darby Houses, and Broseley Pipeworks are closed from November to March.

You can also find some good shopping here. There's Coalport china at the **Coalport China Museum** and decorative tiles at the **Jackfield Tile Museum.** Another place worth visiting is just beyond the Jackfield Museum: **Maw's Craft Centre** (℃ **01952/883030;** www.mawscraftcentre.co.uk) is the site of 20 workshops situated in an old Victorian tile works beside the River Severn. Here you can browse for glass sculptures, dollhouses, original Celtic art, pictures with frames made while you wait, jewelry, and stained glass. There's also an on-site tearoom that's open for lunch and afternoon tea.

STOKE-ON-TRENT: THE POTTERIES

261km (162 miles) NW of London; 95km (59 miles) NW of Leicester; 74km (46 miles) N of Birmingham; 66km (41 miles) S of Manchester

Unless you have an abiding interest in pottery, you may want to skip commercial Stoke-on-Trent, one of author Arnold Bennett's famous *Five Towns* that he described so vividly. Kilns were busy here in the 14th century, long before Josiah Wedgwood (1730–95), England's most distinguished potter, arrived. Most of the great kilns have disappeared, but there is much that remains to interest tourists. The town and its architecture still reflect the dreary Victorian era, but few visitors take note as they hop from one pottery to another, seeking their favorite patterns.

Although pottery had been created in the area since 2000 B.C., it wasn't until the Romans rolled through in A.D. 46 that the first pottery kiln was set up at Trent Vale. Now it's Stoke-on-Trent, a loose confederation of six towns (Tunstall, Burslem, Stoke, Fenton, Longton, and Hanley, the most important town) covering an 11km (7-mile) area, that's the real center of the pottery trade. During the Industrial Revolution, the area known collectively as Stoke-on-Trent became the world's leading producer of pottery, and today it is a tourist attraction.

Essentials

GETTING THERE   From London's Euston Station, it's a direct train ride of 1½ hours to Stoke-on-Trent. Trains make half-hourly departures daily. For schedules and information, call ℃ **0845/748-4950** or go to **www.nationalrail.co.uk**.

Seven direct **National Express** buses leave London's Victoria Coach Station daily for the 4- to 5-hour trip to Stoke. Many others make a detour to Birmingham. For information, call ℃ **0871/781-8181** or go to **www.nationalexpress.com**.

By car from London, drive along the M1 to the M6 to the A500 at Junction 15. It will take you 2 to 3 hours.

VISITOR INFORMATION   The **Stoke-on-Trent Tourist Information Centre,** Victoria Hall, Bagnall Street, Cultural Quarter (℃ **01782/236000;** www.visit stoke.co.uk), is open Monday to Saturday 9:15am to 5:15pm. You can pick up a *China Experience* visitor map, noting most potteries, shops, and museums in the area.

Where to Stay & Dine

Best Western Stoke-on-Trent Moat House ★   This is the town's leading hotel, built in the 18th century as the home of Josiah Wedgwood. A four-story annex wing, which houses the bulk of the accommodations, has been joined to the historic core by a glass-sided corridor. The result is a modern chain hotel that retains a sense of history, which its hardworking staff strives to maintain. All of the midsize rooms have been redecorated and furnished to a comfortable standard.

Etruria Hall, Festival Way, Stoke-on-Trent, Staffordshire ST1 5BQ. ✆ **0870/225-4601.** Fax 01782/206101. www.bw-stokeontrentmoathouse.co.uk. 147 units. £129–£159 double; £169–£229 suite. Rates include breakfast and dinner. AE, DC, MC, V. Free parking. **Amenities:** Restaurant; 2 bars; health club; Jacuzzi; indoor heated pool; room service; sauna. *In room:* A/C, TV, hair dryer, Wi-Fi (free).

George Hotel   This is one of the most upscale, formal, and dignified hotels in town, the kind of place where the mayor would invite some cronies or a business-person might bring an important client. Built in 1929 of red brick, it rises three stories above the hamlet of Burslem, one of the six villages that make up the Stoke-on-Trent district. Public areas are outfitted with traditional furniture and large 19th-century oil paintings of the town and region. The conservative but comfortable bedrooms are well furnished and generally spacious.

Swan Sq., Burslem, Stoke-on-Trent, Staffordshire ST6 2AE. ✆ **01782/577544.** Fax 01782/837496. www.georgehotelstoke.co.uk. 40 units. £69–£129 double. Rates include English breakfast. AE, DC, MC, V. Free parking. **Amenities:** Restaurant; bar; room service. *In room:* TV, hair dryer, Wi-Fi (free).

Haydon House Hotel   This imposing late-Victorian house is the home of the Machin family. They've added a collection of built-in mahogany furniture to the bedrooms and reconfigured their home and their lives to welcome overnight guests. You'll find many of the original Victorian fittings, an unusual collection of clocks, and modern amenities that will make your stay comfortable in the tastefully furnished bedrooms. Suites have efficiently arranged kitchenettes and private entrances; these are usually rented for a full week.

1–9 Haydon St., Basford, Stoke-on-Trent, Staffordshire ST4 6JD. ✆ **01782/711311.** Fax 01782/717470. www.haydon-house-hotel.co.uk. 23 units. £75–£95 double; £300 suite per week. AE, DC, MC, V. Free parking. **Amenities:** Restaurant; bar; room service. *In room:* TV, hair dryer.

History First: Two Worthwhile Museums

Gladstone Pottery Museum ★   This is the only complete Victorian pottery factory that has been restored as a museum, with craftspeople providing daily demonstrations in the original workshops. Various galleries depict the rise of the Staffordshire pottery industry, tile history, and so on (check out the toilets of all shapes, sizes, colors, and decoration). There are great hands-on opportunities for plate painting, pot throwing, and ornamental-flower making.

Uttoxeter Rd., Longton. ✆ **01782/234567.** www.stokemuseums.org.uk. Admission £6 adults, £5 seniors and students, £4.50 children, £18 family ticket. Daily 10am–5pm (last admission 4pm).

Potteries Museum & Art Gallery ★   Start at the Potteries Museum for an overview of Stoke-on-Trent history. It houses departments of fine arts, decorative arts, natural history, archaeology, and social history. It also has one of the largest and finest collections of ceramics in the world. It's a great place for training your eyes before exploring the factories and shops of Stoke-on-Trent.

Bethesda St., Hanley. ✆ **01782/232323.** www.stokemuseums.org.uk. Free admission. Nov–Feb Mon–Sat 10am–4pm, Sun 1–4pm; Mar–Oct Mon–Sat 10am–5pm, Sun 2–5pm.

Touring & Shopping the Potteries

With more than 40 factories in Stoke-on-Trent—all with gift shops and seconds shops on-site—you need to be in shape for this adventure. In fact, some factories have several shops, selling everything from fine china dinner services to hand-painted tiles.

Seconds are always a great bargain. They're still high-quality pieces with imperfections that only the professional eye can detect. But don't expect bargains on top-of-the-line pieces. Shops discount their best wares once in a while, but most of the time, prices for first-quality items are the same here as they are in London, elsewhere in England, or in the United States.

During the big January sales in London, many department stores, including Harrods, truck in seconds from the factories in Stoke, so if you're in London then, you don't have to visit here to bring home a bargain.

Each factory discussed below offers shipping and can help you with the value-added tax (VAT) refund. Expect your purchases to be delivered within 1 to 3 months.

Moorcroft   Moorcroft is a welcome change from the work of the pottery world's more famous names. It was founded in 1898 by William Moorcroft, who produced his own special brand of pottery and was his own exclusive designer until his death in 1945. Decoration is part of the first firing here, giving it a higher quality of color and brilliance than, say, Spode, and creating floral designs in bright, clear colors (think of it as the Art Nouveau of the pottery world). You'll find much to admire and buy in the factory seconds shop. There is always someone around to explain the various processes and to show you around the museum, with its collections of early Moorcroft. Tours are not suitable for kids 10 and younger.

Sandbach Rd., Burslem. ✆ **01782/820500.** www.moorcroft.com. Factory tours £4.50 adults, £3.50 seniors, £2.50 children 11–16. Tours Mon and Wed–Thurs 11am and 2pm, Fri 11am; all tours must be booked 2 weeks in advance. Museum and shop Mon–Fri 10am–5pm, Sat 9:30am–4:30pm. A taxi from the Stoke-on-Trent train station will run about £10. If you're driving from London, follow M1 north to M6. Take it north to Junction 15, which becomes A500. Follow the signs.

Spode ★   The oldest English pottery company operating on the same site, since 1770, and the birthplace of fine bone china, Spode offers regular factory tours lasting about 1½ hours and connoisseur tours lasting 2½ hours. In the **Craft Centre,** visitors can see demonstrations of engraving, lithography, hand painting, printing, and clay casting. An unrivaled collection of Spode's ceramic masterpieces is on display in the **Spode Museum.** The Blue Italian Restaurant offers refreshments and lunch—all served on Spode's classic blue tableware, Blue Italian. The factory shop sells seconds at reduced prices. Tours are not suitable for kids 11 and younger.

Church St., Stoke-on-Trent. ✆ **01782/744011.** www.spode.co.uk. Free admission to Spode visitor center and museum. Basic factory tour £4.50 adults; £4 seniors, students, and children 12 and older. Connoisseur factory tour £7.50 adults; £6.50 seniors, students, and children 12 and older. Visitor center Mon–Sat 9am–5pm; Sun 10am–4pm. Tours Mon–Thurs at 10am, 1:30pm, and 3pm; Fri 10–11am; all tours must be booked weeks in advance. Spode is a 10-min. walk from the Stoke-on-Trent train station. If you're driving from London, follow M1 north until you reach M6. Take it north to Junction 15, which becomes A500. Follow the signs for Stoke.

Wedgwood ★   The **Wedgwood Museum** covers 3 centuries of design and features living displays, including Josiah Wedgwood's Etruria factory and the company's Victorian showroom. Other room settings can also be seen at the museum. The **Wedgwood Visitor Centre** includes a demonstration hall where you can watch clay pots being formed on the potter's wheel and witness plates being turned and fired, then painted. Highly skilled potters and decorators are happy to answer your questions. An art gallery and gift shop showcase samples of factory-made items that also can be purchased. (Note that the prices at this shop are the same as those found elsewhere.) The Ivy House Restaurant is the perfect place to relax with a cup of coffee or enjoy a full meal.

At press time the **Wedgwood Factory Tour** was temporarily suspended; call ahead for the latest information. Wedgwood seconds, which are available at reduced prices, are not sold at the center but are available at the **Wedgwood Group Factory Shop,** King Street, Fenton (✆ **01782/316161**).

Barlaston. ✆ **01782/371911.** www.wedgwoodmuseum.org.uk or www.wedgwoodvisitorcentre.com. Wedgwood Museum admission £6 adults, £5 seniors and students, £4.50 children 5–16, £18 family ticket, free for children 4 and younger. Wedgwood Museum and Wedgwood Visitor Centre combined admission £9.50 adults; £7 seniors, students, and children 5–16; £32 family ticket. Mon–Fri 9am–5pm; Sat–Sun 10am–5pm. Closed Dec 24–Jan 1. Take a taxi from the Stoke-on-Trent train station, a 9.5km (6-mile) trip that will cost around £11. If you're driving from London, head north along M1 until you reach M6. Continue north to Junction 14, which becomes A34. Follow A34 to Barlaston and follow the signs.

CAMBRIDGE & EAST ANGLIA: FENS & THE NORFOLK "BROADS"

T he four essentially bucolic counties of **East Anglia** (Essex, Suffolk, Norfolk, and Cambridgeshire) were once an ancient Anglo-Saxon kingdom dominated by the Danes. In part, the region is a land of heaths, fens, marshes, and inland lagoons known as "broads." Old villages and market towns abound. East Anglia is a place in which to experience the outdoors, and many walkers, cyclists, and boaters are drawn to the area. See individual towns for suggestions about how to come into a close encounter with the countryside.

Essex and Suffolk are Constable Country and boast some of England's finest landscapes. Many visitors drive through Essex, which stretches east to the English Channel, on their way to **Cambridge.** Though close to London and industrialized in places, this land of rolling fields has rural areas and villages, many on the seaside.

The easternmost county of England, Suffolk is a refuge for artists, just as it was in the day of its famous native sons, Constable and Gainsborough, who preserved its landscapes on canvas. Though a fast train can whisk visitors from London to East Suffolk in approximately 1½ hours, its fishing villages, historic homes, and national monuments remain off the beaten track for most tourists. To capture the true charm of Suffolk, you must explore its little market towns and villages. Beginning at the Essex border, we head toward the North Sea, highlighting the most scenic villages as we move eastward across the shire.

Seat of the dukes of Norfolk, **Norwich** is less popular, but those who venture toward the North Sea are rewarded with some of England's most beautiful scenery. An occasional dike or windmill will remind you of the Netherlands.

From here you can branch out and visit the **Broads,** a network of waterways. The resort town of **Wroxham,** capital of the Broads, is easily reached from Norwich, only 13km (8 miles) to the northeast. Some of the best scenery of the Broads is on the periphery, and motorboats regularly take parties on short trips from Wroxham. From Norwich you can also make a trip to **Sandringham,** the country home of four generations of British monarchs.

CAMBRIDGE: TOWN & GOWN ★★★

89km (55 miles) N of London; 129km (80 miles) NE of Oxford

The university town of Cambridge is a collage of images: the Bridge of Sighs; spires and turrets; drooping willows; dusty secondhand bookshops; carol singing on Christmas Eve in King's College Chapel; dancing until sunrise at the May balls; Elizabethan madrigals; narrow lanes upon which Darwin, Newton, and Cromwell once walked; the "Backs" where the college lawns sweep down to the River Cam; tattered black robes of hurrying upperclassmen flying in the wind.

Along with Oxford, Cambridge is one of Britain's ancient seats of learning. In many ways, their stories are similar, particularly the age-old conflict between town and gown. Cambridge can name-drop with the best of them, citing alumni such as Isaac Newton, John Milton, and Virginia Woolf. Cambridge continues to graduate many famous scientists such as physicist Stephen Hawking, author of *A Brief History of Time.*

In the 1990s, Cambridge became known as a high-tech outpost, or a "silicon fen," if you will. High-tech ventures continue to base themselves here—start-up companies produce £2 billion a year in revenues. Even Bill Gates, in 1997, financed an £80-million research center here, claiming that Cambridge was becoming a "world center of advanced technology."

Essentials

GETTING THERE   Trains depart frequently from London's Liverpool Street and Kings Cross stations, arriving an hour later. A one-way ticket costs £19 to £35. Call ✆ **0845/748-4950** or visit **www.nationalrail.co.uk** for more information.

National Express buses leave hourly from London's Victoria Coach Station for the 2-hour trip to Cambridge's Drummer Street Station. A one-way ticket costs £12. For schedules and information, call ✆ **0871/781-8181** or visit **www.national express.com**.

If you're driving from London, head north on the M11.

VISITOR INFORMATION   In back of the guildhall, the **Cambridge Tourist Information Centre,** Wheeler Street (✆ **1223/464-732;** www.visitcambridge.org), has a wide range of information, including data on public transportation and sightseeing attractions. Year-round, the office is open Monday to Friday 10am to 5:30pm and Saturday 10am to 5pm; from April to September, it's also open Sunday 11am to 4pm.

City Sightseeing, on the concourse of the Cambridge rail station (✆ **01223/561766;** www.cambridgetmtours.co.uk), sells brochures and maps. It also offers a full range of tourist services, including accommodations booking. It's open in summer daily from 8:45am to 7pm (closes at 5pm off-season). Guided tours of Cambridge leave the center daily.

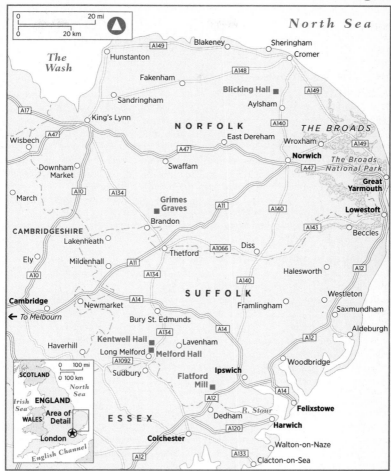

GETTING AROUND The center of Cambridge is made for pedestrians, so park your car at one of the car parks (rates increase as you approach the city center) and stroll the widely dispersed colleges. Follow the courtyards through to the Backs (the college lawns) and walk to Trinity (where Prince Charles studied) and St. John's colleges, where you'll find the Bridge of Sighs.

Another popular way of getting around is by bicycle. **Station Cycles** (☎ **01223/307125;** www.stationcycles.co.uk) has bikes for rent for £8 per half-day, £10 per day, or £20 per week. A deposit of £50 is required. Call in advance to reserve a bike; at that time you'll be told the address at which to pick up the bike. The shop is open Monday to Friday 8am to 6pm, Saturday 9am to 5pm, and Sunday 10am to 4pm.

Stagecoach, 100 Cowley Rd. (© **01223/423-578;** www.stagecoachbus.com), serves the Cambridge area with a network of buses, with fares ranging in price from 3£ to £5 for a day pass. The local tourist office has bus schedules.

SPECIAL EVENTS Cambridge's artistic bent peaks at the end of July during the **Cambridge Folk Festival** (www.cambridgefolkfestival.co.uk). Event tickets are generally £10 to £25.

Where to Stay
EXPENSIVE

De Vere University Arms ★ This 1834 hotel maintains much of its antique charm and many original architectural features despite modernization over the years. Near the city center and the university, it offers suitable accommodations. Rooms range from small to midsize, each with bedside controls; the premium units also have slippers and robes. Many of the bedrooms have been recently refurbished; eight have four-poster beds. Rooms in front are smaller but more up-to-date and have double-glazed windows. Three units are suitable for families.

Regent St., Cambridge, Cambridgeshire CB2 1AD. © **01223/273000.** Fax 01223/273037. www.devere-hotels.com. 119 units. £140–£200 double; £250 suite. Rates include English breakfast. AE, DC, MC, V. Parking £14. Bus: 1. **Amenities:** Restaurant; bar; babysitting; room service. *In room:* TV, hair dryer, minibar, Wi-Fi (free).

Doubletree by Hilton Cambridge ★ It may look a bit like a concrete bunker outside, but this Hilton warms considerably in its interior. Its location along the River Cam is one of the most desirable in Cambridge; the hotel lies in the oldest part of town, a short stroll from the major colleges. For those who want to stay in shape, it's one of the best choices thanks to its free access to an indoor pool, spa, and first-class health club. Guest rooms are spacious, contemporary, and well equipped, often opening onto views of the river from private balconies. The hotel stands on its own 3 acres of private grounds.

Granta Place, Mill Lane, Cambridge, Cambridgeshire CB2 1RT. © **01223/259988.** Fax 01223/316605. www.doubletree.hilton.co.uk. 122 units. £139–£229 double. AE, DC, MC, V. Parking £7.50. **Amenities:** Restaurant; bar; health club; Jacuzzi; indoor heated pool; room service; sauna; steam room. *In room:* A/C, TV, hair dryer, minibar, Wi-Fi (£12 per day).

Hotel du Vin ★★ This upmarket chain has taken a historic building in the heart of Cambridge and turned it into a plush hotel. Special features include some suites with private gardens and the chain's trademark bistro and champagne bar. After millions of pounds were poured into its restoration, the property is completely up to date, yet it is also a classic, as the building on this site dates from medieval times. Two wells from the Middle Ages were glassed over as a focal point for one of the larger rooms. Accommodations are elegant and beautifully furnished, some with private terraces. The hotel bar lies in the vaulted cellar. For afternoon tea, ever had a drink of hibiscus flowers, sweet blackberry leaves, apple, licorice, and poppy flowers?

Trumpington St., Cambridge, Cambridgeshire CB2 1QA. © **01223/227330.** Fax 01223/227331. www.hotelduvin.com. 41 units. £160–£190 double; £240–£390 suite. AE, DC, MC, V. **Amenities:** Restaurant; bar; room service. *In room:* A/C, TV, hair dryer, minibar, Wi-Fi (free).

Hotel Felix ★★ Although it lies about 1.6km (1 mile) from the center, this chic boutique hotel has shot up to the top of the heap as the best in Cambridge. Set in more than 1.2 hectares (3 acres) of landscaped gardens, its stylish design and tasteful

Cambridge

ACCOMMODATIONS ■
Arundel House Hotel **1**
Best Western Gonville Hotel **37**
De Vere University Arms **30**
Doubletree by Hilton Cambridge **26**
Hamilton Hotel **4**
Hotel du Vin **38**
Regent Hotel **36**

DINING ◆
Arundel House Restaurant **1**
Browns **32**
Charlie Chan **12**
Cotto **29**
Dojo Noodle Bar **27**
Mai Thai Restaurant **22**
Midsummer House **2**
Rainbow Vegetarian Café **19**
Restaurant 22 **3**

ATTRACTIONS ●
Christ's College **13**
Clare College **18**
Corpus Christi College **23**
Downing College **31**
Emmanuel College **21**
Fitzwilliam Museum **33**
Folk Museum **6**
Gonville and Caius College **15**
Great St. Mary's **16**
Jesus College **9**
King's College **17**
Magdalene College **5**
Newnham College **35**
Pembroke College **28**
Peterhouse College **34**
Punts **8**
Queens' College **24**

St. Catharine's College **20**
St. John's College **10**
Selwyn College **25**
Sidney Sussex College **11**
Trinity College **14**
Westminster College **7**

decor have brought luxury to the often staid accommodations of this university city. The Felix arises from a Victorian mansion to which two new wings were added. The *Daily Telegraph* called it "a work of art," and the *Sunday Times* hailed it as "one of the country's choicest boltholes." We like the way Cambridge's first designer hotel has harmoniously blended the old and new, all while maintaining a cozy atmosphere throughout. Imbued with specially commissioned modern art, the bedrooms have wide beds and unfussy decor.

Whitehouse Lane, Huntingdon Rd., Cambridge CB3 0LX. ✆ **01223/277977.** Fax 01223/277973. www.hotelfelix.co.uk. 52 units. £190–£235 double; from £285 suite. Rates include breakfast. AE, DC, MC, V. Free parking. **Amenities:** Restaurant; bar; access to health club, room service. *In room:* TV, CD player, hair dryer, minibar, Wi-Fi (£10 per day).

MODERATE

Arundel House Hotel   Occupying one of the most desirable sites in Cambridge, this hotel consists of six interconnected identical Victorian row houses—all fronted with dark-yellow local bricks. In 1994, after two additional houses were purchased, the hotel was enlarged, upgraded, and expanded into the well-maintained hostelry you see today. Though not as well appointed as the University Arms or the Felix (see above), it competes successfully with the Gonville (see below) and has the best cuisine of the hotels. Rooms overlooking the River Cam and Jesus Green cost more, as do those on lower floors (there's no elevator). All units are simple but comfortable, with upholstered chairs and carpeting.

53 Chesterton Rd., Cambridge, Cambridgeshire CB4 3AN. ✆ **01223/367701.** Fax 01223/367721. www.arundelhousehotels.co.uk. 103 units. £95–£150 double; £135–£160 family room. Rates include continental breakfast. AE, DC, MC, V. Free parking. Bus: 1 or 3. **Amenities:** Restaurant (see review below); bar. *In room:* A/C, TV, hair dryer, Wi-Fi (free).

Best Western Gonville Hotel   This hotel and its grounds are opposite Parker's Piece park, only a 5-minute walk from the center of town. The Gonville has been much improved in recent years and is better than ever, although not yet the equal of the Hotel Felix (see above). It's like an ivy-covered country house, with shade trees and a formal car entry. The recently refurbished bedrooms are comfortable and modern in style.

Gonville Place, Cambridge, Cambridgeshire CB1 1LY. ✆ **800/780-7234** in the U.S. and Canada, or 01223/366611. Fax 01223/315470. www.gonvillehotel.co.uk. 73 units. £95–£159 double. AE, DC, MC, V. Free parking. **Amenities:** Restaurant; bar; room service. *In room:* TV, hair dryer, Wi-Fi (free).

Holiday Inn Cambridge   Located a short walk from a small artificial lake, which the bedrooms overlook, this modern two-story hotel north of Cambridge is vaguely influenced by the designs of nearby country houses. There's a grassy courtyard partially enclosed by the hotel's wings. Public rooms with peaked ceilings are furnished with scattered clusters of sofas and chairs. The small yet comfortable bedrooms have large windows with pleasant views.

Lakeview, Bridge Rd., Lakeview Bridge, Impington, Cambridge, Cambridgeshire CB4 9PH. ✆ **888/465-4329** in the U.S. and Canada, or 08719/429015. Fax 01223/233426. www.holidayinn.co.uk. 161 units. £135–£185 double. Rates include breakfast. AE, DC, MC, V. Free parking. Bus: 104, 105, or 106. Drive 3km (2 miles) north of Cambridge on B1049 (Histon Rd.) to A45 intersection. **Amenities:** Restaurant; bar; babysitting; health club; Jacuzzi; indoor heated pool; room service; sauna; steam room; Wi-Fi in lobby (£6 per hr.). *In room:* TV, hair dryer, Internet (£15), minibar (in some).

Menzies Cambridge Hotel & Golf Club   This place offers the best sports facilities in the Cambridge area. Built around 1977, it has comfortable bedrooms with tub/shower combinations and nice views, a putting green, and an 18-hole championship golf course, where greens fees range from £45 (Mon–Fri) to £60 (Sat–Sun). There's a restaurant in the hotel, although the food is just standard stuff. Meals are also served daily in the bar.

Huntingdon Rd., Bar Hill, Cambridge, Cambridgeshire CB3 8EU. © **01954/249988.** Fax 01954/780010. www.menzies-hotels.co.uk. 136 units. £94–£205 double. Rates include breakfast. Children 15 and younger stay free in parent's room. AE, DC, MC, V. Free parking. Take A14 9km (5½ miles) northwest of the town center. **Amenities:** Restaurant; 2 bars; golf course; health club; indoor heated pool; room service; sauna; steam room; 2 tennis courts. *In room:* TV, hair dryer, Wi-Fi (£12 per day).

INEXPENSIVE

Hamilton Hotel ⚓   One of the better and more reasonably priced of the small hotels of Cambridge, this redbrick establishment lies about 1.6km (1 mile) northeast of the city center, close to the River Cam. Well run and modestly accessorized, the hotel stands on a busy highway, but there's a parking area out back. The well-furnished bedrooms contain reasonably comfortable twin or double beds. Bathrooms are compact, with shower stalls. The hotel has a small, traditionally styled licensed bar, offering standard pub food and snacks.

156 Chesterton Rd., Cambridge, Cambridgeshire CB4 1DA. © **01223/365664.** Fax 01223/314866. www.hamiltonhotelcambridge.co.uk. 20 units. £56–£105 double. Rates include English breakfast. AE, DC, MC, V. Free parking. Bus: 3 or 3A. **Amenities:** Bar. *In room:* TV, hair dryer, Wi-Fi (free).

Regent Hotel   This is one of the most desirable of Cambridge's reasonably priced small hotels. Right in the city center, overlooking Parker's Piece park, the house was built in the 1840s as the original site of Newnham College. It became a hotel when the college outgrew its quarters. Bedrooms are on the small side but are redecorated frequently in traditional Georgian style.

41 Regent St., Cambridge, Cambridgeshire CB2 1AB. © **01223/351470.** Fax 01223/464937. www.regenthotel.co.uk. 22 units. £109–£147 double. Rates include continental breakfast. AE, DC, MC, V. Parking £12. Closed Dec 22-Jan 2. Bus: 1. **Amenities:** Bar. *In room:* A/C, TV, hair dryer, Wi-Fi (£2 per day).

Where to Dine

VERY EXPENSIVE

Midsummer House ★★ 🍴 MEDITERRANEAN   Located in an Edwardian-era cottage near the River Cam, the Midsummer House is a real find. We prefer to dine in the elegant conservatory, but you can also find a smartly laid table upstairs. The fixed-price menus are wisely limited, and quality control and high standards are much in evidence here. Daniel Clifford, the master chef, has created such specialties as filet of beef Rossini, served with braised winter vegetables and sauce Perigourdine, and roast squab pigeon with *pomme* Anna, *tarte tatin* of onions, caramelized endive, and jus of morels.

Midsummer Common. © **01223/369299.** www.midsummerhouse.co.uk. Reservations required. Set lunch £30 for 2 courses, £35 for 3 courses; fixed-price 3-course dinner £65. AE, MC, V. Wed–Sat noon-1:45pm; Tues-Sat 7-9:30pm.

MODERATE

Arundel House Restaurant ★ ENGLISH/FRENCH/VEGETARIAN   One of the best and most acclaimed restaurants in Cambridge is in a hotel overlooking the River Cam and Jesus Green, a short walk from the city center. Winner of many awards, it's noted not only for its excellence and use of fresh produce, but also for its good value. The decor is warmly inviting, with Sanderson curtains, Louis

XV–upholstered chairs, and spacious tables. You can dine either a la carte or from the set menu, which changes frequently. Perhaps you'll sample such dishes as filet of plaice in lime-and-basil butter or grilled salmon wrapped in Parma ham. Medallions of pork are sautéed with sweet peppers and served in a Dijon-mustard-and-cream sauce, while supreme of chicken appears with wild mushrooms in a cream-and-brandy sauce.

In the Arundel House Hotel, 53 Chesterton Rd. © **01223/367701.** www.arundelhousehotels.co.uk. Reservations required. Main courses £12–£19; 2-course fixed-price menu £16, 3-course fixed-price menu £22. AE, DC, MC, V. Daily 7:30–10am, 12:15–1:45pm, and 6:30–9:30pm. Bus: 3 or 5.

Browns ★ 🍴 CONTINENTAL/ENGLISH After wowing them at Oxford, Browns now lures Cambridge students in equal numbers. The building lies opposite the Fitzwilliam Museum and was constructed in 1914 as the outpatient department of a hospital dedicated to Edward VII; that era's grandeur is apparent in the building's neoclassical colonnade. Today, it's the most lighthearted place for dining in the city, with wicker chairs, high ceilings, pre–World War I woodwork, and a long bar covered with bottles of wine. The extensive bill of fare includes pastas, scores of fresh salads, several selections of meat and fish (from chargrilled leg of lamb with rosemary to fresh fish in season), hot sandwiches, and the chef's daily specials. If you drop by in the afternoon, you can also order thick milkshakes or natural fruit juices. In fair weather, outdoor seats are prized possessions.

23 Trumpington St. (5 min. from King's College and opposite the Fitzwilliam Museum). © **01223/461655.** www.browns-restaurants.com. Reservations not accepted Sat–Sun. Main courses £9–£18. AE, MC, V. Mon–Sat 10am–10:30pm; Sun 11:30am–10pm. Bus: 2.

Cotto ★ BRITISH/CONTINENTAL This innovative restaurant lies above a small deli/bakery, attracting a youthful clientele to its contemporary, wood-filled interior decorated with modern paintings for sale. Its success stems from its "no frills, no choice" three-course fixed-price dinners, based on quality ingredients freshly cooked to order. Much of the produce that goes into these meals comes from local organic farms. A typical evening meal might begin with carpaccio of Cornish monkfish, followed with a soup of wood-roasted Fenland spaghetti squash with pesto. For a main, slow-roasted Suffolk partridge might appear with a beet salad, followed by a selection of cheese and poached prunes. Dessert might be a tart of Willingham pear and almond. Lunch is less elaborate, featuring such dishes as Pollock and leek fish cakes or roasted pigeon breast. You can also try Cotto for breakfast—have a slice of the sourdough bread.

183 East Rd. © **01223/302010.** www.cottocambridge.co.uk. Reservations recommended for dinner. Fixed-price dinner £35; lunch main courses £7–£17. AE, MC, V. Tues–Sat 9am–3pm; Thurs–Sat 7–10pm.

Restaurant 22 ★ CONTINENTAL/ENGLISH One of the best in Cambridge, this restaurant is located in a quiet district near Jesus Green and is a secret jealously guarded by the locals. The homelike but elegant Victorian dining room offers an ever-changing fixed-price menu based on fresh market produce. Owner David Carter uses time-tested recipes along with his own inspirations, offering creations such as white-onion soup with toasted goat cheese or sautéed breast of chicken on braised celery with thyme jus.

22 Chesterton Rd. © **01223/351880.** www.restaurant22.co.uk. Reservations required. Fixed-price menu £28. AE, MC, V. Tues–Sat 7–9:45pm.

INEXPENSIVE

Charlie Chan CHINESE   Most people say that this is the finest Chinese restaurant in Cambridge, and we agree. We've always found it reliable and capable, which is remarkable given its huge menu. Downstairs is a long corridor-like restaurant, with pristine decor. The ambience is lusher in the Blue Lagoon upstairs. Most of the dishes here are inspired by the traditional cuisine of Beijing. The specialties we've most enjoyed include an aromatic and crispy duck, lemon chicken, and prawns with garlic and ginger. Most of the dishes are affordably priced, except for the expensive shellfish specialties, especially lobster.

14 Regent St. ✆ **01223/361763.** Reservations recommended. Main courses £5–£35. AE, MC, V. Daily noon–5pm and 6–11pm.

Dojo Noodle Bar 🍴 PACIFIC RIM   It's not all noodles here. For those "anti-noodlists," a selection of rice dishes is prepared, along with many platters suitable for vegetarians. The chefs roam Asia for inspiration, with a heavy concentration on Japan, but also China, Malaysia, Taiwan, Singapore, and Vietnam. One of the most popular restaurants in Cambridge, Dojo's offers communal tables for its customers, mostly students. Portions are huge, and many of these dishes are washed down with Asahi beer.

1–2 Millers Yard, Mill Lane (off Trumpington St.). ✆ **01223/363471.** www.dojonoodlebar.co.uk. Reservations not needed. Main courses £3.85–£4.50. MC, V. Mon–Thurs noon–2:30pm and 5:30–11pm; Fri noon–4pm and 5:30–11pm; Sat–Sun noon–11pm.

Mai Thai Restaurant THAI/ASIAN   The location overlooks Parker's Piece, where 15,000 people dined alfresco to celebrate Queen Victoria's coronation in 1838. This former cricket pavilion was home to many eateries before becoming Mai Thai. The setting is minimalist, with white-tiled floors and whitewashed walls, potted palms and touches of orchid pink. Starters range from chicken satay to a mixed platter (including one for vegetarians). There's a wide range of Thai salads, from papaya with ground peanuts to green apple and prawn. Stir-fried dishes are a specialty, including squid with basil leaves, garlic, onion, beans, bamboo shoots, peppers, and chili. Vegetarian dishes, Thai curries, seafood platters, and rice and noodle plates round out the menu.

Park Terrace. ✆ **01223/367480.** www.mai-thai-restaurant.co.uk. Reservations recommended. Main courses £7–£10. AE, MC, V. Daily noon–3pm and 6–11pm.

Rainbow Vegetarian Café VEGETARIAN/VEGAN   There's often a wait to get in, but Cambridge students consider this cozy spot worth that inconvenience. Busiest times are at lunch and on weekend evenings. The location is at the end of a lily-lined path in a basement setting, with a welcoming staff eager to serve you everything from a Latvian Potato Bake to pasta marinara, or perhaps a Cuban peccadillo or one of many Mexican dishes such as tacos and enchiladas. Jamaican patties are tasty, as is the spinach lasagna, the chef's signature dish. Three-bean chili is a plate of rib-sticking fare, and Gado Gado is a specialty—that is, exotic vegetables prepared Indonesian style with citrus flavorings and such spices as turmeric, and served with sides of peanut and plum sauces. You can also drop in for just a coffee and a slice of fresh-baked cake.

9A King's Parade (across from King's College). ✆ **01223/321551.** www.rainbowcafe.co.uk. Reservations not accepted. Main courses £8–£10. No credit cards. Tues–Sat 10am–10pm; Sun–Mon 10am–4pm.

Organized Tours

The **Cambridge Tourist Information Centre** (see earlier in this chapter) sponsors 2-hour walking tours that take in the highlights of the city, costing £8 to £15 for adults, £4.50 to £7.50 for children 6 to 11, and free for children 5 and younger. Call for tour times.

City Sightseeing, on the concourse of the Cambridge rail station (✆ **01708/866000**), offers daily guided tours of Cambridge via open-top, double-decker buses. In summer, they depart every 15 minutes from 9:30am to 4pm from Silver Street. Departures are curtailed off-season, depending on demand. The tour can be a 1-hour ride, or you can get off at any of the many stops and rejoin whenever you wish. Tickets are valid all day. The fare is £13 for adults, £9 for seniors and students, £7 for children 6 to 11, and free for kids 5 and younger. A family ticket for £32 covers two adults and up to three children.

Exploring Cambridge University

Oxford University predates Cambridge, but by the early 13th century, scholars began coming here, too. Eventually, Cambridge won partial recognition from Henry III, rising or falling with the approval of subsequent English monarchs. Cambridge consists of 31 colleges for both men and women. Colleges are closed for exams from mid-April until the end of June.

The following listing is only a sample of the colleges. If you're planning to be in Cambridge a while, you may also want to visit **Magdalene College,** on Magdalene Street, founded in 1542; **Pembroke College,** on Trumpington Street, founded in 1347; **Christ's College,** on St. Andrew's Street, founded in 1505; and **Corpus Christi College,** on Trumpington Street, which dates from 1352.

KING'S COLLEGE ★★ The adolescent Henry VI founded King's College, King's Parade (✆ **01223/331100;** www.kings.cam.ac.uk), in 1441. Most of its buildings today date from the 19th century, but the construction of its crowning glory, the Perpendicular-style **King's College Chapel ★★★**, began in the Middle Ages. Owing to the whims of royalty, the chapel wasn't completed until the early 16th century.

Henry James called King's College Chapel "the most beautiful in England." Its most striking features are its magnificent fan vaulting, all in stone, and its great windows, most of which were fashioned by Flemish artisans between 1517 and 1531 (the west window dates from the late Victorian period). The chapel also boasts Rubens's *Adoration of the Magi* and an ornamental screen from the early 16th century. The chapel is famous for its choir and musical concerts. You can call the college (phone number above) for concert dates and times.

> ### Caution: Students at Work
>
> Because of disturbances caused by the influx of tourists, Cambridge limits visitors, or excludes them altogether, from various parts of the university. In some cases, a small entry fee is charged. Small groups of up to six people are generally admitted with no problem; you can inquire with the local tourist office about visiting hours. All colleges are closed during exams and graduation, on Easter and all bank holidays, and other times without notice.

Insider's tip: For a classic view of the chapel, you can admire the architectural complex from the rear, which is an ideal picnic spot along the river. E. M. Forster came here to contemplate scenes for his novel *Maurice*. To acquire the makings of a picnic, head for the vendors who peddle inexpensive food, including fresh fruit, at **Market Square** (Mon–Sat 9:30am–4:30pm). You can also get picnic fare at a major grocery store, **Sainsbury's,** 44 Sidney St. (℮ **01223/366891**), open Monday to Saturday 8am to midnight and Sunday 11am to 5pm.

The chapel is open during college term, Monday to Friday 9:30am to 3:30pm, Saturday 9:30am to 3:15pm, and Sunday 1:15 to 2:15pm. During the term, the public is welcome to attend choral services Monday to Saturday at 5:30pm and Sunday at 10:30am and 3:30pm. During school vacations, the chapel is open to visitors Monday to Saturday 9:30am to 4:30pm and Sunday 10am to 5pm; it is closed from December 23 to January 1. It may also be closed at other times for recording sessions, broadcasts, and concerts.

An exhibition in the seven northern side chapels shows why and how the chapel was built. Admission to the college and chapel, including the exhibition, is £5 for adults, £3.50 for students and seniors, and free for children 11 and younger.

 punting ON THE CAM

Punting on the **River Cam** in a wood-built, flat-bottomed boat (which looks somewhat like a Venetian gondola) is a traditional pursuit of students and visitors to Cambridge. Downstream, you pass along the ivy-covered "Backs" of the colleges, their lush gardens sweeping down to the water.

People sprawl along the banks of the Cam on a summer day to judge and tease you as you maneuver your punt with a pole about 4.5m (15 ft.) long. The river's floor is muddy, and many a student has lost his pole in the riverbed shaded by the willows. If your pole gets stuck, it's better to leave it sticking in the mud instead of risking a plunge into the river.

About 3km (2 miles) upriver lies **Grantchester,** immortalized by Rupert Brooke. Literary types flock to Grantchester, either by punting or by taking the path following the River Granta for less than an hour to Grantchester Meadows (the town lies about 1.6km/1 mile from the meadows).

When the town clock stopped for repairs in 1985, its hands were left frozen "for all time" at 10 minutes to 3, in honor of Brooke's famed sonnet "The Soldier."

After so much activity, you're bound to get hungry or thirsty, so head to the **Green Man,** 59 High St. Grantchester (℮ **01223/844669;** www.thegreenman grantchester.co.uk), a 400-year-old inn named in honor of Robin Hood, where a crackling fire warms you in cold weather and summer features a back beer garden, leading off toward the river, where your punt is waiting to take you back to Cambridge.

Scudamore's Punting Company, Granta Place (℮ **01223/359750;** www. scudamores.com), by the Anchor Pub, has been in business since 1910. Punts and rowboats rent for £14 to £18 per hour (maximum of six persons per punt). A £100 cash or credit card deposit is required. Open year-round, although March through October is the high season.

EMMANUEL COLLEGE   Emmanuel, on St. Andrew's Street (℡ **01223/334200;** www.emma.cam.ac.uk), was founded in 1584 by Sir Walter Mildmay, a chancellor of the exchequer to Elizabeth I. John Harvard, of the American university that bears his name in another city called Cambridge, studied here. You can stroll around Emmanuel's attractive gardens and visit the chapel designed by Sir Christopher Wren, consecrated in 1677. Both the chapel and college are open daily during sunlight hours.

Insider's tip: Harvard men and women, and those who love them, can look for a memorial window in Wren's chapel dedicated to John Harvard, an alumnus of Emmanuel who lent his name to that other university.

PETERHOUSE COLLEGE   Peterhouse College, on Trumpington Street (℡ **01223/338200;** www.pet.cam.ac.uk) attracts visitors because it's the oldest Cambridge college, founded in 1284 by Hugh de Balsham, the bishop of Ely. Of the original buildings, only the hall remains. It was restored in the 19th century and has stained-glass windows designed by William Morris. The chapel, called Old Court, dates from 1632 and was renovated in 1754. Ask to enter at the porter's lodge.

Insider's tip: Almost sadly neglected, the Little Church of St. Mary's next door was the college chapel until 1632. Pay it the honor of a visit.

QUEENS' COLLEGE ★★   The loveliest of Cambridge's colleges is Queens' College, on Silver Street (℡ **01223/335511;** www.quns.cam.ac.uk). Dating from 1448, it was founded by two English queens, Margaret of Anjou, the wife of Henry VI, and Elizabeth Woodville, the wife of Edward IV. Its second cloister is the most interesting, flanked by the early-16th-century half-timbered President's Lodge.

Admission is £2.50 for adults, free for children 11 and younger accompanied by an adult. A printed guide is issued. Generally, the hours are: mid-October to mid-March, daily 2 to 4pm; mid-March to mid-May, daily 10am to 4:30pm; closed late May to mid-June; late June to mid-September, daily 10am to 4:30pm; late September to October, Monday to Friday 2 to 4pm, Saturday and Sunday 10am to 4:30pm. Contact the college for specific hours, however, as these are subject to change. Entry and exit is by the old porter's lodge in Queens' Lane only. The old hall and chapel are usually open to the public when not in use.

Insider's tip: Queens' College's wide lawns lead down to the "Backs" (the backs of the colleges), where you can stroll, sit, or go punting. Take in Mathematical Bridge, best viewed from the Silver Street Bridge, dating from 1902.

ST. JOHN'S COLLEGE ★★   Wordsworth was an alumnus of this college, on St. John's Street (℡ **01223/338600;** www.joh.cam.ac.uk), which was founded in 1511 by Lady Margaret Beaufort, mother of Henry VII, who launched Christ's College a few years earlier. The impressive gateway bears the Tudor coat of arms, and the Second Court is a fine example of late Tudor brickwork. The college's best-known feature is the Bridge of Sighs crossing the Cam. Built in the 19th century, it was patterned after the covered bridge in Venice. It connects the older part of the college with New Court, a Gothic Revival on the opposite bank, where there is an outstanding view of the famous "Backs." The Bridge of Sighs is closed to visitors but can be seen from neighboring Kitchen Bridge. Visitors are admitted from March to October, Monday to Friday 10am to 5:30pm; in November and February, it is also open Saturday and Sunday 10am to 3:30pm. Contact the college for the latest hours. Admission is £3.20 for adults, £2 for seniors and children 12 to 17, and free for children 11 and younger. Visitors are welcome to attend choral services in the chapel.

Insider's tip: The Bridge of Sighs links the old college with an architectural "folly" of the 19th century, the elaborate New Court, which is a crenellated neo-Gothic fantasy. It's adorned with a riot of pinnacles and a main cupola. Students call it the "wedding cake."

TRINITY COLLEGE ★★ Trinity College, Trinity Street (*©* **01223/338400;** www.trin.cam.ac.uk)—not to be confused with Trinity Hall—is the largest college in Cambridge. It was founded in 1546 by Henry VIII, who consolidated a number of smaller colleges that had existed on the site. The courtyard is the most spacious in Cambridge, built when Thomas Neville was master. Sir Christopher Wren designed the library.

For entrance to the college, inquire at the Porter's Lodge. Trinity College is open to visitors March to November, Monday to Friday from 9am to 4pm. There's a charge of £1 adults, 50p seniors and children.

Insider's tip: It's fun to contemplate what went on here before you arrived. Pause at Neville's Court, where Isaac Newton first calculated the speed of sound. Take in the delicate fountain of the Great Court, where Lord Byron used to bathe naked with his pet bear. Why a bear? The university forbade students from having dogs, but there was no proviso for bears. Years later, Vladimir Nabokov walked through that same courtyard dreaming of the young lady he would later immortalize as *Lolita.*

Other Attractions

Fitzwilliam Museum ★★ This is one of Britain's finest museums, founded by the bequest of the seventh viscount Fitzwilliam of Merrion to the University of Cambridge in 1816. The permanent collections contain remarkable antiquities from ancient Egypt, Greece, and Rome. Galleries display Roman and Romano-Egyptian art along with Western-Asiatic exhibits. The Fitzwilliam's Applied Arts section show-cases English and European pottery and glass, as well as furniture, clocks, armor, fans, rugs and samplers, Chinese jades, and ceramics from Japan and Korea. The museum also has married a rare ancient and medieval coin collection with a host of medals created from the Renaissance onward. The Fitzwilliam is best loved for its collection of paintings, which includes masterpieces by Simone Martini, Titian, Veronese, Rubens, Van Dyck, Canaletto, Hogarth, Gainsborough, Constable, Monet, Degas, Renoir, Cézanne, and Picasso. There is also a fine collection of other 20th-century art, miniatures, drawings, watercolors, and prints. Occasional musical events, including evening concerts, are staged in Gallery III. Throughout the year, it plays host to some of the best lectures in England.

Trumpington St., near Peterhouse. *©* **01223/332900.** www.fitzmuseum.cam.ac.uk. Free admission; donations appreciated. Guided tours £3.50 per person. Tues–Sat 10am–5pm, Sun noon–5pm; tours Sat 2:45pm. Closed Jan 1, Good Friday, May Day, and Dec 24–31.

Great St. Mary's Closely associated with events of the Reformation because the leaders of the movement (Erasmus, Cranmer, Latimer, and Ridley) preached here, this university church was built mostly in 1478 on the site of an 11th-century church. The cloth that covered the hearse of King Henry VII is on display in the church. There is a fine view of Cambridge from the top of the tower.

King's Parade. *©* **01223/741716.** Admission to tower £3 adults, £1.50 children. Tower summer daily 10am–4:30pm; church daily 9am–6pm.

Shopping

Visitors will want to forage around the shops lining St. John's Street, Trinity Street, King's Parade, and Trumpington Street. Another well-defined shopping district comprises Bridge, Sidney, St. Andrew's, and Regent streets.

Primavera, 10 King's Parade (© **01223/357708;** www.primaverauk.com), is a showplace of British crafts, featuring pottery, glass, ceramics, jewelry, ironwork, and fabric crafts ranging from ties to wall hangings. Be sure to explore the basement exhibition of paintings and crafts items.

Rose Crescent is a posh area of extremely chic, small, and exclusive shops that runs between Market Square and Trinity Street. Here you can buy leather goods, smart women's clothing, and fine hats as well as jewelry and a host of very expensive gift items.

Cambridge's bookstores will truly delight book lovers. **Heffers** is a huge book, stationery, and music store with six branches, all of which can be contacted through one central phone number (© **01223/568400**). The main store, at 20 Trinity St., carries academic books; an art-and-graphics shop has an address of 15–21 King St.; and the music store at 19 Trinity St. features classical, popular, and choral college selections. Heffers also has a shop in the mall at Grafton Centre that carries new fiction and nonfiction titles.

G. David, 16 St. Edward's Passage (© **01223/354619**), hawks secondhand books, publishers' overruns at reduced prices, and antiquarian books. **Waterstone,** 22 Sydney St. (© **01223/351688**), deals exclusively in new books on a variety of subjects. The **Haunted Bookshop,** 9 St. Edward's Passage (© **01223/312913**), specializes in out-of-print children's books and first editions.

Cambridge After Dark

Nightlife in this university city revolves around the new and improved complex, **Cambridge Leisure Park,** Hills Road at Cherry Hinton Road (© **01223/212024;** www.cambridge-x.co.uk), a 10-minute walk from the rail station. The complex features a multiscreen cinema, a bowling alley, numerous chain restaurants, and bars, some of which offer live entertainment. Saturday night is the big blast here, attracting hundreds of university students. There is also a theater presenting comedy, drama, and even children's shows.

You can take in a production where Emma Thompson and other well-known thespians got their start at the **Amateur Dramatic Club,** Park Street near Jesus Lane (© **01223/359547,** or 01223/300085 for box office; www.cuadc.org). It presents two student productions nightly, Tuesday through Saturday, with the main show tending toward classic and modern drama or opera, and the late show being of a comic or experimental nature. The theater is open nearly year-round, closing in September, and tickets run from £3.50 to £10.

The most popular Cantabrigian activity is the **pub crawl** (www.cambridge-pubs. co.uk). With too many pubs in the city to list, you may as well start at Cambridge's oldest pub, the **Pickerel,** Magdalene Street (© **01223/355068**), dating from 1432. English pubs don't get more traditional than this. If the ceiling beams or floorboards groan occasionally—well, they've certainly earned the right over the years. Real ales on tap include Bulmer's Traditional Cider, Old Speckled Hen, Theakston's 6X, Old Peculiar, and Best Bitter.

The **Maypole,** Portugal Place at Park Street (© **01223/352999**), is the local hangout for actors from the nearby ADC Theatre. Known for cocktails and not ales, you can still get a Tetley's 6X or Castle Eden.

The **Eagle,** Benet Street off King's Parade (© **01223/505020**), will be forever famous as the place where Nobel Laureates Watson and Crick first announced their discovery of the DNA double helix. Real ales include Icebreaker and local brewery Greene King's Abbott, so make your order and raise a pint to the wonders of modern science.

To meet up with current Cambridge students, join the locals at the **Anchor,** Silver Street (© **01223/353554**), or the **Mill (Tap & Spile),** 14 Mill Lane, off Silver Street Bridge (© **01223/357026**), for a pint of Greene King's IPA or Abbott. The crowd at the Anchor spills out onto the bridge in fair weather, whereas the Tap & Spile's clientele lays claim to the entire riverside park.

For a gay and lesbian hangout, your best bet is **Five Bells,** 126 Newmarket St. (© **01223/314019**), especially on a Friday or Saturday night when the joint is packed. In summer, the action overflows into the garden in the rear. You might also check out **Fleur-de-Lys,** 73 Humberstone Rd. (© **01223/356095**), which features everything from drag shows to striptease, dance music, and karaoke.

For musical entertainment, you can find out who's playing by checking out fliers posted around town or by reading the *Varsity.* The **Corn Exchange,** Wheeler Street and Corn Exchange (© **01223/357851**), hosts everything from classical concerts to bigger-name rock shows. The **Graduate,** 16 Chesterton Rd. (© **01223/3118817**), is a pub located in a former movie theater.

Entertainment in some form can be found nightly at the **Junction,** Clifton Road, near the train station (© **01223/511511**), where an eclectic mix of acts takes the stage weeknights to perform all genres of music, comedy, and theater; DJs take over on the weekend. The cover varies from £5 to £25, depending on the event.

Ballare, Lion Yard (© **01223/364222;** www.ballare-nights.co.uk), a second-story club, has a huge dance floor and plays everything from house to the latest pop hits, Monday to Saturday 9pm until 2am. Sometimes it even DJs the old-fashioned way, by taking requests. The cover ranges from £3 to £10, depending on what night you're here.

ELY

113km (70 miles) NE of London; 26km (16 miles) N of Cambridge

Ely Cathedral is the top attraction in the fen country, outside of Cambridge. After you've seen the cathedral, you can be safely on your way; Ely is simply a sleepy market town that can't compete with the life and bustle found at Cambridge.

Essentials

GETTING THERE   Ely is a major railway junction served by express trains to Cambridge. Service is frequent from London's Kings Cross. For schedules and information, call © **0845/748-4950** or visit **www.nationalrail.co.uk**.

Stagecoach (© **01223/423-578;** www.stagecoachbus.com) operates frequent buses between Cambridge and Ely.

If you're driving from Cambridge, take the A10 north.

The **Tourist Information Centre** is at Oliver Cromwell's House, 29 St. Mary's St. (☎ **01353/662062;** www.ely.org.uk). It's open April through October, daily 10am to 5:30pm, and November through March, Sunday to Friday 11am to 4pm, Saturday 10am to 5pm.

Where to Stay

Lamb Hotel   Right in the center of town, this hotel is a former 14th-century coaching inn. In the 1400s, this place was known as the "Holy Lambe," a stopping-off spot for wayfarers, often pilgrims, passing through East Anglia. In the shadow of the cathedral, the Lamb today offers renovated bedrooms furnished traditionally but with modern comfort. Each contains a good English bed, usually king-size or twin. Bathrooms offer adequate shelf space and tub/shower combinations. Rather standard English meals are served.

2 Lynn Rd., Ely, Cambridgeshire CB7 4EJ. ☎ **01353/663574.** Fax 01353/662023. www.thelamb-ely. com. 31 units. £75–£110 double. Rates include English breakfast. AE, DC, MC, V. Free parking. Bus: 109. **Amenities:** Restaurant; bar; room service. *In room:* TV, hair dryer, Wi-Fi (free).

Where to Dine

An unusual choice is the **Almonry Restaurant & Tea Rooms,** in the College, Ely Cathedral, High Street (☎ **01353/666360;** www.elycathedral.org). Housed in the medieval college buildings on the north side of the cathedral, this is a comfortable tearoom with table service in a beautiful 12th-century undercroft licensed to sell drinks. You can take your tea out to a garden seat in good weather. It is open for late-morning coffee, lunch, and afternoon tea. Meals start at £7.

Boathouse ★ BRITISH/CONTINENTAL   The Boathouse is the best gastro-pub-cum-restaurant in town, housed in a converted boathouse that opens onto the Great Ouse. The cookery is generous and personal, the menus showcasing modern dishes with authentic country roots. Lunches feature dishes not usually found at midday, including pigeon with chicory and a pine-nut salad, or a snail, leek, and Gruyère gratin. At night, you can kick off with such starters as smoked loin of venison or crab cakes with ginger mayonnaise. Main courses are likely to include pork belly with honey-glazed baby onions in a cider sauce, or else sea bass with shellfish potato cakes and fried leeks. For dessert, few items equal the honey-and-hazelnut mousse.

5 Annesdale. ☎ **01353/664388.** www.cambscuisine.com. Reservations recommended. 2-course lunch £12; 3-course lunch £16; set dinner £10–£24. AE, MC, V. Daily noon–2:30pm and 6:30–9:30pm.

Old Fire Engine House ★ 🍴 ENGLISH   It's worth a special trip to this converted fire station in a walled garden, set within a building complex that includes an art gallery. Soups are served in huge bowls, accompanied by coarse-grained crusty bread. Main dishes include lamb noisettes in pastry with tomato and basil, jugged hare, casseroled pheasant, and rabbit with mustard and parsley. Two especially good dishes are the casserole of pigeon and the beef braised in both port wine and Guinness. In summer, you can dine outside in the garden and even order a cream tea for £7.30.

25 St. Mary's St. (opposite St. Mary's Church). ☎ **01353/662582.** www.theoldfireenginehouse.co.uk. Reservations required. Main courses £14–£16. MC, V. Daily noon–2pm, 3:30–5:15pm, and 7:15–9pm. Bus: 109.

Seeing the Sights

Ely Cathedral ★★   The near-legendary founder of this cathedral was Ethel-dreda, the wife of a Northumbrian king who established a monastery on the spot in

673. The present structure dates from 1081. Visible for miles around, the landmark octagonal lantern is the crowning glory of the cathedral. Erected in 1322 following the collapse of the old tower, it represents a remarkable engineering achievement. Four hundred tons of lead and wood hang in space, held there by timbers reaching to the eight pillars.

You enter the cathedral through the Galilee West Door, a good example of the Early English style of architecture. The lantern tower and the Octagon are the most notable features inside, but visit the Lady Chapel, too. Although its decor has deteriorated over the centuries, it's still a handsome example of the Perpendicular style, having been completed in the mid-14th century. The entry fee goes to help preserve the cathedral. Monday through Saturday in the off-season, guided tours gather at 11:15am and 2:15pm; in the summer, tours occur throughout the day.

At the Brass Rubbing Centre, a large selection of replica brass is available for you to rub. These can produce remarkable results for wall hangings or special gifts. It's open year-round in the North Aisle, outside the Cathedral Shop.

🕾 **01353/667735.** www.cathedral.ely.anglican.org. Admission £6 adults, £5 students and seniors, free for children 11 and younger. Apr–Oct daily 7am–7pm; Nov–Mar Mon–Sat 7:30am–6pm, Sun 7:30am–5pm.

Ely Museum A gallery presents a chronological history of Ely and the Ely Isle from the Ice Age to the present day. Displays include archaeology, social history, rural life, local industry, and military history, as well as a tableau of the debtor's cell and condemned cell, which are also on view.

Old Gaol, Market St. 🕾 **01353/666655.** www.elymuseum.org.uk. Admission £3.50 adults; £2.50 children, students, and seniors; free for children 6 and younger. Summer Mon–Sat 10:30am–5pm, Sun 1–5pm; winter Mon and Wed–Sat 10:30am–4pm, Sun 1–4pm. Closed Dec 20–Jan 2.

Grimes Graves This is the largest and best-preserved group of Neolithic flint mines in Britain; they produced the cutting edges of spears, arrows, and knives for prehistoric tribes throughout the region. Because of its isolated location within sparsely populated, fir-wooded countryside, it's easy to imagine yourself transported back through the millennia.

A guardian will meet you near the well-signposted parking lot. After determining that you are not physically impaired, he or she will open one or several of the mineshafts, each of which requires a descent down an almost-vertical 9m (30-ft.) ladder (a visit here is not recommended for very young children, elderly travelers, or those with disabilities). Because the tunnel and shaft have been restored and reinforced, it's now possible to see where work took place during Neolithic times. Although it's not essential, many archaeologists, professional and amateur, bring their own flashlights with them. The mines, incidentally, are situated close to the military bases that housed thousands of U.S. Air Force personnel during World War II.

On B1107, 4km (2¾ miles) northeast of Brandon, Norfolkshire. 🕾 **01842/810656.** www.english-heritage.org.uk. Admission £3 adults, £2.60 students and seniors, £1.50 children 5–15, £7.50 family ticket. No entry to mines for children under 5. Mar and Oct Thurs–Mon 10am–5pm; Apr–Sept daily 10am–5pm. Take A134 for 11km (7 miles) northwest of Thetford, and then transfer to B1107.

Oliver Cromwell's House This restored house was owned by the Puritan Oliver Cromwell, a name hardly beloved by the royals, even today. He rose to fame as a military and political leader during the English Civil Wars of 1642 to 1649, which led to the execution of Charles I and the replacement of the monarchy by the Commonwealth, the designation for England until the monarchy was restored. In 1653, Cromwell was declared lord protector, and the local farmer was the most powerful man in the land until his death in 1658. Exhibitions, displays, and period rooms offer insight into Cromwell's character and 17th-century domestic life. A tourist center is also located here.

29 St. Mary's St. (next to St. Mary's Church). © **01353/662062.** www.ely.org.uk/tic.htm. Admission £4.40 adults, £3.95 seniors and students, £3 children under 16, £13 family ticket. Apr–Oct daily 10am–5pm; off-season Sun–Fri 11am–4pm, Sat 10am–5pm.

NEWMARKET

100km (62 miles) NE of London; 21km (13 miles) NE of Cambridge

This old Suffolk town has been famous as a horse-racing center since the time of James I. Visitors can see Nell Gwynne's House, but mainly they come to visit Britain's first and only equestrian museum.

Getting There

Trains depart from London's Liverpool Street Station every 45 to 60 minutes for Cambridge (see earlier in this chapter). In Cambridge, passengers change trains and head in the direction of Mildenhall. Three stops later, they arrive at Newmarket. For schedules and information, call © **0845/748-4950** or visit **www.nationalrail.co.uk**.

About eight National Express buses leave London's Victoria Coach Station for Norwich every day, stopping at Stratford, Stansted, and (finally) Newmarket along the way. For schedules and information, call © **0870/580-8080** or visit **www.nationalexpress.com**.

If you're driving from Cambridge, head east on the A133.

Where to Stay & Dine

Best Western Heath Court Hotel A member of the Arlington Hotel Group, this brick-fronted hotel is near the Gallops, the exercise area for the stables at the Newmarket Heath racetrack, about a 5-minute walk from the center of town. Built in the mid-1970s, it's a favorite of the English horse-racing world and is fully booked during the racing season. Its public rooms are decorated in an appropriate country-elegant style, including, in its bar and restaurant, oil portraits of horses and souvenirs of the racing life. The bedrooms are well appointed, conservatively modern, and comfortable. Most of the units are spacious; the more expensive units, called executive rooms, also contain bathrobes and small refrigerators.

Moulton Rd., Newmarket, Suffolk CB8 8DY. © **800/780-7234** in the U.S. and Canada, or 01638/667171. Fax 01638/666533. www.heathcourt-hotel.co.uk. 43 units. £81–£153 double; £97–£195 studio; £135–£235 family room; £200–£290 suite. Extra bed £45. Rates include English breakfast. AE, DC, MC, V. Free parking. **Amenities:** Restaurant; bar; room service. *In room:* A/C, TV, hair dryer, Wi-Fi (free).

Swynford Paddocks ★ This well-appointed country house, one of the finest in the area, is situated on a 24-hectare (60-acre) stud farm surrounded by beautiful grounds. Once a retreat of Lord Byron, he wrote many of his works at the foot of a now-felled beech. The house then became the home of Lord and Lady Halifax until 1976, when it was converted into a luxury hotel. Many guests use it as a base for exploring both Newmarket and Cambridge. Each spacious bedroom, opening onto scenic views, is decorated with a special character; some have four-poster beds and are quite romantic. For extra-special occasions, try for a suite of rooms or one of the two sumptuous four-poster rooms.

London Rd., Six Mile Bottom, New Market, Cambridge CB8 0UE. © **01638/570234.** Fax 01638/570283. www.swynfordpaddocks.com. 15 units. £135–£175 double; prices double during races. Rates include English breakfast. AE, DC, MC, V. Free parking. Take A1304 9.5km (6 miles) southwest of Newmarket. **Amenities:** 2 restaurants; bar; room service. *In room:* TV, hair dryer, Wi-Fi (free).

Off to the Races

Britain's most prestigious racecourse lies at Newmarket, a small country town whose main tourist draw is the series of warm-weather horse races with origins dating from the days of James I and Charles II. Charles II was so enthusiastic about racing that he frequently ordered most of his Restoration-era court up from London to attend the races.

The headquarters of British racing, and the venue where precedents and policies are hammered out before being applied to the more formal venue of Ascot, Newmarket is the only racecourse in Britain with two separate racetracks.

The more bucolic of these is the **July Course,** where races are held during the heat and glare of June, July, and August. It's the site of the prestigious July Cup. The course is known for its rows of beech trees that shade the saddling boxes and promenade grounds, as well as the thatched roofs that add an old-English charm to ornamental entryways and some of the showcase buildings used by investors, owners, and fans. The grandstands have conventional roofs, shielding fans from the sun and the rain.

The more industrial-looking racetrack is the **Rowley Mile,** used during the season's cooler months from mid-April to late May and early September to early November. Prestigious races such as the Guineas Races, the Cesarewitch Handicap, and the Champion Stakes are run here. Dress codes are less strictly observed at the Rowley Mile than at the July Course, where men wear jackets and ties, but the venue at Rowley Mile attracts a bigger and brasher crowd.

The two courses lie within 1km (½ mile) of each other and share the same administration. For information, contact the **Newmarket Racecourses,** Westfield House, the Links, Newmarket, Suffolk CB8 0TG (© **01638/663482;** www.newmarket racecourses.co.uk).

National Horseracing Museum Visitors can see the history of horse racing over 300 years in this museum housed in the old subscription rooms, early-19th-century betting rooms. There are fine paintings of famous horses, paintings on loan from Queen Elizabeth II, and copies of old parliamentary acts governing races. A 53-minute audiovisual presentation shows races and racehorses.

To make history come alive for visitors, the museum also offers equine tours of this historic town. Guides take you to watch morning gallops on the heath, where you'll see bronzes of horses from the past.

99 High St. © **01638/667333.** www.nhrm.co.uk. Admission £6 adults, £5 seniors, £3 children, £13 family ticket (2 adults and 2 children). Mar–Oct daily 11am–4:30pm (opens 10am on race days); off-season Mon–Sat 10am–4:30pm.

National Stud Next to Newmarket's July Course, 3km (2 miles) southwest of the town, the National Stud is home to some of the world's finest horses and a renowned breeding stud operation. A tour lasting about 75 minutes lets you see many mares and foals, plus top-class stallions. Reservations for tours can be made by phoning the number below.

Next to the July Course. ☎ **01638/663464.** www.nationalstud.co.uk. Admission £7 adults, £5 seniors and children 5–15, £20 family ticket, free for children 4 and younger. Guided tours Feb–Sept daily 11:15am and 2pm; Oct daily 11:15am. Closed Nov–Jan.

BURY ST. EDMUNDS ★

127km (79 miles) NE of London; 43km (27 miles) E of Cambridge; 19km (12 miles) N of Lavenham

Bury St. Edmunds is "a handsome little town, of thriving and cleanly appearance." That's how Charles Dickens described it in *Pickwick Papers,* and it remains true today. This historic town, founded around the powerful Benedictine Abbey in 1020, derives its name from St. Edmund, king of the East Angles in the mid-9th century. The barons of England met here in the Abbey at Bury St. Edmunds and agreed to force King John to sign the Magna Carta, but the actual ceremony took place at Runnymede in 1215.

Though it's sometimes hard to tell, Bury is filled with many original medieval buildings. Although many buildings were given face-lifts in the 17th and 18th centuries, their medieval roots become clear when you step inside. During the 18th century, this market town was quite prosperous and had a thriving cloth-making industry. The large number of fine Georgian buildings bear testament to the wealth of the day.

Upon the Vikings' arrival to the area, they dubbed it the "Summer Country." And, indeed, the summer, when the town bursts into bloom, is the best time to visit. Most of the historic sites and gardens open for the season on Easter.

Essentials

GETTING THERE Trains leave regularly from London's Liverpool Street and Kings Cross stations; however, none are direct. If you depart from Liverpool Street, you will change at Ipswich. From Kings Cross, you will switch trains at Cambridge. The trip takes approximately 1½ hours. For schedules and information, call ☎ **0845/748-4950** or visit **www.nationalrail.co.uk**.

Several direct buses depart every day from London's Victoria Coach Station; they reach Bury in 2 hours. For schedules and information, call ☎ **0871/781-8181** or visit **www.nationalexpress.com**.

By car, take the M11 north out of London. As you near Cambridge, get on the A45 and continue on to Bury. The drive takes about 1½ hours.

It's also possible to get here by train or bus from Cambridge. Regular trains leave from the Cambridge rail station and arrive about 45 minutes later in Bury St. Edmunds. **Stagecoach** (☎ 01223/423578; www.stagecoachbus.com) runs five buses a day to Bury from Cambridge's Drummer Street Station; it's a 1-hour ride. By car from Cambridge, simply take the A45; it's a 45-minute drive.

VISITOR INFORMATION The **Bury St. Edmunds Tourist Information Centre,** 6 Angel Hill (☎ 01284/764667; www.stedmundsbury.gov.uk), is open November to Easter, Monday to Friday 10am to 4pm and Saturday 10am to 1pm; and from Easter to October, Monday to Saturday 9:30am to 5:30pm, Sunday 10am to 3pm.

SPECIAL EVENTS The **Bury St. Edmunds Festival** (☎ 01284/757630; www.buryfestival.co.uk) is held annually in May. The 17-day festival includes performances from leading ensembles and soloists ranging from classical to contemporary. Exhibitions, talks, walks, films, plays, and a fireworks display are integral parts of this internationally renowned festival.

Where to Stay

Angel Hotel ★   Originally a 1452 coaching inn, the Angel received an exterior face-lift during the Georgian era, and its front facade is now completely covered with lush ivy. The location is ideal for sightseeing and shopping, as both are only a short walk from the hotel. Look out the window of any of the front-facing rooms, and you'll see the romantic Abbey Gardens. Each of the rooms is individually decorated with antique furnishings and some have four-poster beds. No. 36 is one of the more popular rooms with its four-poster bed, bold peach-colored walls (a shade you can almost taste), and armchairs. Ten units have been recently refurbished.

13 Angel Hill, Bury St. Edmunds, Suffolk IP33 1LT. ℰ **01284/714000.** Fax 01284/714001. www.theangel. co.uk. 75 units. £100–£140 double; £160–£200 suite. AE, DC, MC, V. Free parking. **Amenities:** 2 restaurants; bar; babysitting; room service. *In room:* A/C (in some rooms), TV, hair dryer, Wi-Fi (free).

Ramada Bury St. Edmunds   This standard, rather ordinary hotel, built relatively recently, is located 10 minutes from Bury on the A14 motorway. The grassy grounds are landscaped, and there is a sunny patio for dining alfresco. All of the rooms are decorated in the same bland style, with landscape pictures and an armchair or two, along with an accompanying desk. Because of the proximity to the motorway, the windows are double-paned to reduce traffic noise and to help guests get a better night's rest.

Symonds Rd., Bury St. Edmunds, Suffolk IP32 7DZ. ℰ **800/2-RAMADA** (272-6232) in the U.S., or 01284/760884. Fax 01284/755476. www.ramada.com. 69 units. £50–£134 double. AE, DC, MC, V. Free parking. **Amenities:** Restaurant; bar; room service. *In room:* TV, hair dryer, Wi-Fi (free).

Ravenwood Hall ★★ 🛏   Located 5km (3 miles) outside of town, this Tudor hall dates from the 1500s and is set in a peaceful 2.8-hectare (7-acre) park with well-manicured lawns, gardens, and forest. This rustic country place has a magnificent fireplace that is the focal point of the restaurant, where diners enjoy an a la carte menu. The individually decorated guest rooms are full of atmosphere. If you're a fancier of fine beds, check out the Oak Room, with its four-poster bed, and the bridal suite, with its brass bed. Some rooms are in the main house, others in a converted stable mews; all are equally comfortable.

Rougham, Bury St. Edmunds, Suffolk IP30 9JA. ℰ **01359/270345.** Fax 01359/270788. www. ravenwoodhall.co.uk. 14 units. £157–£204 double. Rates include breakfast. AE, DC, MC, V. Free parking. **Amenities:** Restaurant; bar; babysitting; outdoor heated pool; room service; outdoor tennis court. *In room:* TV, hair dryer, Wi-Fi (free).

Where to Dine

Maison Bleue SEAFOOD   This restaurant is the town's best. The open and airy dining room has a nautical theme, in keeping with the fresh seafood that's served. The same menu is available for both lunch and dinner and changes regularly with the seasons. A sublime main course is the whole grilled sea bass marinated with lime, lemon grass, and pink peppercorns. We also revel in the layered gâteau of poached salmon and sliced king scallop, with a butter sauce flavored with parsley and fresh shallots. As another treat, the half grilled lobster and pan-fried Black Tiger prawns are topped with garlic butter.

31 Churchgate St. ℰ **01284/760623.** www.maisonbleue.co.uk. Reservations recommended for dinner. Main courses £15–£27; fixed-price lunch £17; fixed-price 3-course dinner £29. AE, MC, V. Tues–Sat noon–2:30pm and 7–9:30pm (until 10pm Fri–Sat).

Exploring the Town

For a bit of easy and always interesting sightseeing, take one of the hour-long **guided tours** around Bury St. Edmunds. Choices include theme tours with Bury's historical monk, Brother Jocelin, or with gravedigger William Hunter. Tours leave from the Tourist Information Centre (see above), where tickets can also be purchased.

The normally quiet town center is a hub of hustle and bustle on Wednesday and Saturday mornings when the **market** arrives. Weather permitting, hours are approximately from 9am to 4pm. You'll find a pleasing mix of family-run businesses and High Street names for shopping in and around town and its pedestrian zones.

Several parks are located just outside of town, including our two favorite parks—one ideal for those with kids in tow, the other perfect for romantic walks.

The **West Stow Anglo-Saxon Village** (© 01284/728718; www.stedmundsbury.gov.uk) is part of **West Stow Country Park.** This reconstructed village is built on the excavated site of an ancient Anglo-Saxon village, and period reenactments take place throughout the year. Children will prefer this park, which has more man-made attractions and is open daily from 9am to 5pm in winter, 9am to 8pm in summer. Admission to the park is free. Admission to the village, which is open year-round from 10am to 5pm, is £5 for adults, £4 for children 5 to 15, and £15 for a family ticket.

If it's unspoiled nature you seek, **Nowton Park ★** (© 01284/763666) will give you the best view of the most evocative Suffolk landscape scenery. It's located 2.5km (1½ miles) outside of Bury on 81 hectares (200 acres) of Suffolk countryside. Landscaped a century ago, the park is typically Victorian and has many country-estate features. Marked walking paths snake through the park. Depending on the path, walks take between 20 and 75 minutes. In the springtime, stroll the avenue of lime trees with its masses of bright yellow daffodils. The park is open daily from 8:30am to dusk; admission is free.

Abbey of Bury St. Edmunds ★★   The Abbey visitor center is a good starting point for a visit to the entire abbey precinct. (The abbey itself is in ruins today and sits in the middle of the Abbey Gardens.) The visitor center is housed in the west front of the abbey's remains and uses a clever series of displays to give the visitor an idea of what life was like in this powerful abbey, from its beginnings in 1020 to its dissolution in 1539.

A tour of the Abbey Gardens is led by medieval monk Brother Jocelin; book it through the town's Tourist Information Centre (© **01284/764667;** www.stedmundsbury.gov.uk).

Samson's Tower. © **01284/757490** for visitor center. Free admission. Visitor center Easter–Oct daily 10am–5pm; Abbey Gardens and ruins year-round Mon–Sat 7:30am to a half-hour before dusk, Sun 9am to a half-hour before dusk.

Ickworth House   This National Trust property was built in 1795 and contains an impressive rotunda, staterooms, and art collections of silver and paintings. An Italian garden surrounds the house, and all is set in a peaceful, landscaped park.

5km (3 miles) south of Bury at Horringer. © **01284/735270.** www.nationaltrust.org.uk. Admission £8.30 adults, £3.30 children, £20 family ticket. Mar–Sept Fri–Tues 11am–5pm; Oct–Nov Fri–Tues 11am–4:30pm. Call ahead, as hours may change.

Moyse's Hall Museum   Located in one of England's last surviving Norman stone houses, this museum has nationally important archaeological collections and local artifacts.

Cornhill. ☏ **01284/757160.** www.stedmundsbury.gov.uk/sebc/visit/moyses-hall.cfm. Admission £3 adults, £2 seniors and children. Daily 10am–4pm.

St. Edmundsbury Cathedral This 16th-century church has a magnificent font, beautiful stained-glass windows, and a display of 1,000 embroidered kneelers.

Angel Hill. ☏ **01284/748720.** www.stedscathedral.co.uk. Free admission; suggested donation of £3 adults, 50p children. Daily 8am–6pm.

St. Mary's Church St. Mary's was built on the site of a Norman church in 1427. Note its impressive roof and nave. It is also where Henry VIII's sister, Mary the "Tudor Rose," is buried.

Angel Hill. ☏ **01284/754680.** www.stmarystpeter.net. Free admission. Call the church to arrange a tour.

Bury St. Edmunds After Dark

Throughout the centuries, Bury has enjoyed a well-deserved reputation as a small center of arts and entertainment. The **Theatre Royal,** 5 Westgate St. (☏ **01284/769505;** www.theatreroyal.org), is the oldest purpose-built theater in England. Its Georgian building has been lovingly and richly restored to its original grandeur. Programs include opera, dance, music, and drama from the best touring companies. Tickets are £8.50 to £35 and can be purchased at the box office (phone number listed above).

Stop by the 17th-century pub **Dog & Partridge,** 29 Crown St. (☏ **01284/764792**), and see where the bar scenes from the BBC hit series *Lovejoy* were filmed while you sample one of the region's Greene King Ales.

Also try wiggling your way into the **Nutshell,** at the Traverse and Abbeygate Street (☏ **01284/764867**). Notoriously dubbed the smallest pub in all of England, it's a favorite tourist stop.

The **Masons Arms,** 14 Whiting St. (☏ **01284/753955**), features more of a family atmosphere and welcomes children. Home-cooked food is served along with a standard selection of ales. There's a patio garden in use in summer.

A Side Trip to Sudbury

Thirty-two kilometers (20 miles) south of Bury St. Edmunds along the A134 is Sudbury, a town that has prospered through the ages thanks to its sheep (the wool industry) and its prime location along the banks of the River Stour. A handful of medieval half-timbered buildings and Georgian homes attest to the town's ripe old age. Its most famous native son is Thomas Gainsborough, who was born in 1727 and went on to become one of England's most beloved painters.

His birthplace, **Gainsborough's House,** 46 Gainsborough St. (☏ **01787/ 372958;** www.gainsborough.org), is a museum and arts center that has many of his works of art on display. Visitors will notice that several different architectural styles make up the house; there is also a walled garden in back worth seeing. It's open Monday to Saturday from 10am to 5pm, bank holiday Sundays and Mondays from 2 to 5pm. Admission is £4.50 adults, £3.60 seniors, £2 students and children 5 to 18, but it is free to all during the month of December (and year-round for children 4 and younger).

WHERE TO STAY

Mill Hotel ★ 🛏 As its name implies, this four-story hotel, a member of the Elizabeth Hotels group, is located in the shell of an old mill. In fact, the River Stour, which runs under the hotel, still turns the mill's 5m (16-ft.) water wheel, now encased in glass and on display in the restaurant and bar. Rooms vary in size; some have heavy oak beams and massive columns, but all are outfitted with comfortable furnishings. You may even be able to watch the local cows occasionally pass by the water's edge, as many of the rooms have a river or mill-pond view. *Note:* The hotel has no elevator.

Walnut Tree Lane, Sudbury CO10 1BD. ℂ **01787/375544.** Fax 01787/373027. www.elizabethhotels. co.uk. 56 units. £51–£71 double; £91 suite. AE, DC, MC, V. Free parking. **Amenities:** Restaurant; bar; room service. *In room:* TV, hair dryer, Wi-Fi (free).

LAVENHAM ★

106km (66 miles) NE of London; 56km (35 miles) SE of Cambridge

Once a great wool center, Lavenham is the classic Suffolk village, beautifully preserved today. It features a number of half-timbered Tudor houses washed in the characteristic Suffolk pink. The town's wool-trading profits are apparent in its guildhall, on the triangular main "square." Inside, exhibits on Lavenham's textile industry show how yarn was spun and then "dyed in the wool" with woad (the plant used by ancient Picts to dye themselves blue), following on to the weaving process. Another display shows how half-timbered houses were constructed.

The Church of St. Peter and St. Paul, at the edge of Lavenham, has interesting carvings on the misericords and the chancel screen, as well as ornate tombs. This is one of the "wool churches" of the area, built by pious merchants in the Perpendicular style with a landmark tower.

Essentials

GETTING THERE   Trains depart London's Liverpool Street Station at least once an hour, sometimes more often, for Colchester, where they connect quickly to the town of Sudbury. For information, call ℂ **0845/748-4950** or visit **www.national rail.co.uk**. From Sudbury, **Chambers & Son** (ℂ **01787/227233;** www.chambers coaches.co.uk) has about nine daily buses making the short run to Lavenham. The total trip time from London is between 2 and 2½ hours.

National Express buses depart from London's Victoria Coach Station, carrying passengers to the town of Bury St. Edmunds, some 14km (9 miles) from Lavenham. For information, call ℂ **0871/781-8181** or visit **www.nationalexpress.com**. From Bury St. Edmunds, you can take another bus on to Lavenham. The trip takes about 2½ hours.

If you're driving from Bury St. Edmunds, continue south on the A134 toward Long Melford, but cut southeast to Lavenham at the junction with the A1141.

VISITOR INFORMATION   The **Lavenham Tourist Information Centre,** Lady Street (ℂ **01787/248207;** www.discoverlavenham.co.uk or www.southand heartofsuffolk.org.uk), is open mid-March through October, daily 10am to 4:45pm; November to late December, daily 11am to 3pm; and January to early March, Saturday and Sunday 11am to 3pm.

Where to Stay

Lavenham Priory ★ 🏠   The Tudor age lives again in this building dating from the 13th century and once owned by Benedictine monks. In time, the mansion became the property of the earls of Oxford before being sold to rich cloth merchants. Today, it's been restored to its appearance during its Elizabethan period. The timber-framed house has been beautifully refurbished and sensitively modernized to offer guests grand comfort. An oak Jacobean staircase leads to the bedchambers, which feature four-posters, Tudor wall paintings, and oak floors. Each room is furnished individually. You can enjoy a chair by an inglenook fireplace or order a summer breakfast in the herb garden. The hotel stands in 1.2 hectares (3 acres) of grounds in the center of the village.

Water St., Lavenham, Suffolk CO10 9SH. © **01787/247404.** Fax 01787/248472. www.lavenhampriory. co.uk. 6 units. £105–£135; £145 suite. Rates include breakfast. MC, V. **Amenities:** Breakfast lounge. *In room:* TV, Wi-Fi (free).

Swan Hotel ★★★   This lavishly timbered inn, with the best accommodations in Suffolk, is one of the oldest and best-preserved buildings in a relatively unspoiled village. The Swan has been so successful that it has expanded into an adjoining ancient wool hall, which provides a high-ceilinged guesthouse and raftered, second-story bedrooms opening onto a tiny cloistered garden. The accommodations vary in size, according to the eccentricities of the architecture. Most have beamed ceilings and a mixture of traditional pieces that blend well with the old. The more expensive rooms feature four-poster beds.

High St., Lavenham, Sudbury, Suffolk CO10 9QA. © **01787/247477.** Fax 01787/248286. www.theswan atlavenham.co.uk. 45 units. £125–£250 double; £230–£350 suite. Rates include breakfast and dinner. AE, DC, MC, V. **Amenities:** Restaurant; bar; lounge; room service. *In room:* TV, hair dryer, minibar, Wi-Fi (free).

Where to Dine

Great House Hotel ★ FRENCH   With its Georgian facade and location near the marketplace, the Great House is the town's finest place to dine, a quintessentially French hotel in a beautiful English town. The interior is attractively outfitted, with Laura Ashley prints, an inglenook fireplace, and old oak beams. Assisted by his wife, Martine, owner Régis Crépy does double duty as the *chef de cuisine*. He is an inventive, quixotic cook, as reflected by such dishes as roasted rack of English lamb with rosemary jus or grilled marinated filet of red mullet with braised chicory. Another specialty is grilled saddle of venison in red-wine-and-cranberry sauce.

The Great House also rents five elegantly decorated suites for £85 to £180 double, including an English breakfast. The units have TVs, phones, and private bathrooms.

Market Place. © **01787/247431.** Fax 01787/248007. www.greathouse.co.uk. Reservations recommended. Main courses £13–£19; Wed–Sat fixed-price lunch £17–£20; Tues–Fri fixed-price dinner and Sun lunch £32; snacks £6–£12. AE, MC, V. Wed–Sun noon–2:30pm; Tues–Sat 7–9:30pm. Closed Jan.

Shopping & Teatime

Shoppers from all over East Anglia flock to **Timbers,** 12 High St. (© **01787/247218**), a center housing 24 dealers specializing in antiques and collectibles, including books, toys, military artifacts, glass, porcelain, and much more. It's open daily.

After strolling the medieval streets of Lavenham, stop by **Tickled Pink Tearooms,** 17 High St. (© **01787/249517**). This two-story timber-frame home was built by the son of a priest in 1530 and provides an ample dose of history for patrons to absorb while sipping any one of a selection of teas that are served with English breakfast, sandwiches, or cake.

TWO STATELY HOMES IN LONG MELFORD

98km (61 miles) NE of London; 55km (34 miles) SE of Cambridge

Long Melford has been famous since the days of the early cloth makers. Like Lavenham, it attained prestige and importance during the Middle Ages. Of the old buildings remaining, the village church is often called "one of the glories of the shire." Along its 5km-long (3-mile) High Street is an array of one of the greatest concentrations of antiques shops in Europe. The Long Melford area contains many private homes erected by wealthy wool merchants, the two stateliest being Melford Hall and Kentwell Hall, recommended below.

Essentials

GETTING THERE Trains run from London's Liverpool Street Station toward Ipswich and on to Marks Tey. Here, you can take a shuttle train going back and forth between that junction and Sudbury. Call ✆ **08457/484950** or visit **www.national rail.co.uk** for information. From the town of Sudbury, it's a 5km (3-mile) taxi ride to Long Melford.

From Cambridge, buses operated by **Stagecoach** (✆ **01223/423578;** www.stagecoachbus.com) travel to Bury St. Edmunds, and then change for the final ride into Long Melford. These buses run about once an hour throughout the day and early evening.

If driving from Newmarket, continue east on the A45 to Bury St. Edmunds, but cut south on the A134 (toward Sudbury) to Long Melford.

VISITOR INFORMATION In Sudbury, there's a **Tourist Information Centre** in the Town Hall (✆ **01787/881320;** www.heritagebritain.com/county/suffolk. html or www.sudburytowncouncil.co.uk) that's open Monday to Friday 9am to 5pm and Saturday 10am to 4:45pm (until 2:45pm in winter).

Where to Stay

Black Lion Hotel The Bull (see below) has the edge, but the Black Lion is doing something right, as an inn has stood here since the 12th century. Fourteenth-century documents mention it as the spot where drinks were dispensed to revolutionaries during one of the peasants' revolts. The present building dates from the early 1800s and has been richly restored by its owners. All bedrooms are of a high standard, with antique furnishings. The hotel overlooks one of the loveliest village greens in Suffolk.

The Green, Long Melford, Suffolk CO10 9DN. ✆ **01787/312356.** Fax 01787/374557. www.blacklionhotel. net. 10 units. £157–£204 double. Rates include English breakfast. AE, MC, V. **Amenities:** Restaurant; bar; babysitting; room service. *In room:* TV, hair dryer, Wi-Fi (free).

Bull Hotel ★ Here's an opportunity to experience life in one of the great old inns of East Anglia. Built by a wool merchant in 1540, the Bull is Long Melford's finest hotel and its best-preserved building, with lots of improvements and modernizations added over the years. The interior and exterior of the hotel have been refurbished, and the bedrooms here are a mix of the old and the new; most units have king-size or twin beds. A medieval weavers' gallery and an open hearth with Elizabethan brickwork have been incorporated into the hotel's design.

Hall St., Long Melford, Suffolk CO10 9JG. (C) **01787/378494.** Fax 01787/880307. www.thebull-hotel. com. 25 units. £120–£140 double; £140–£160 suite. 2-night minimum Sat–Sun. AE, DC, MC, V. **Ameni- ties:** Restaurant; bar; room service. *In room:* TV, hair dryer, Wi-Fi (free).

Where to Dine

Scutchers Restaurant ENGLISH   This upscale bistro earns favorable recom- mendations from many locals. The building was erected in stages between the 1600s and the 1800s and was named after the workers (scutchers) who, in olden days, rendered flax into linen. As the Scutchers Arms, it was a favorite pub—until the own- ers painted its facade bright yellow and filled its heavily beamed interior with vivid Mediterranean colors. Subsequently the food here has been considerably improved and upgraded, as evoked by such dishes as filet of wild halibut, served on a prawn and chive risotto with a lobster sauce, or grilled filet of plaice with an herb crust in a lemon-butter sauce. Especially tasty is the loin filet of Suffolk lamb with mint gravy.

Westgate St. (C) **01787/310200.** www.scutchers.com. Reservations recommended. Main courses £12– £24. AE, MC, V. Tues–Sat noon–2pm and 7–9:30pm.

A Tudor Mansion & Beatrix Potter's Ancestral Home

Kentwell Hall   At the end of an avenue of linden trees, the redbrick Tudor man- sion called Kentwell Hall, surrounded by a broad moat, has been restored by its owners, Mr. and Mrs. Patrick Phillips. A 15th-century moat house, interconnecting gardens, a brick-paved maze, and a costume display are of interest. There are also rare-breed farm animals here. Two gatehouses are constructed in 16th-century style. The hall hosts regular re-creations of Tudor domestic life, including events held around mid-June to early July, when admission prices tend to escalate slightly.

Off A134, 8km (5 miles) north of Sudbury. (C) **01787/310207.** www.kentwellhall.co.uk. Admission £9.40 adults, £8.05 seniors, £6.10 children. Consult website or call ahead for opening days and hours due to special-event schedules. The entrance is north of the green in Long Melford on the west side of A134, about 1km (½ mile) north of Melford Hall.

Melford Hall   This is the ancestral home of Beatrix Potter, who often visited. Jemima Puddle-Duck still occupies a chair in one of the bedrooms upstairs, and some of her other figures are on display as well. The house, built between 1554 and 1578, has paintings, fine furniture, and Chinese porcelain. The gardens alone make a visit here worthwhile.

Off A134, 5km (3 miles) north of Sudbury. (C) **01787/379228.** www.nationaltrust.org.uk/melfordhall. Admission £6.30 adults, £3.15 children, £15 family ticket. Apr and Oct Sat–Sun 1:30–5pm; May–Sept Wed–Sun 1:30–5pm.

DEDHAM

101km (63 miles) NE of London; 13km (8 miles) NE of Colchester

Remember Constable's painting *The Vale of Dedham*? Dedham Vale lies between the towns of Colchester and Ipswich in a wide valley through which runs the River Stour, the boundary between Essex and Suffolk. It's not only the link with Constable that has made this vale so popular. It's also one of the most beautiful, unspoiled areas left in southeast England. The little Essex village on the River Stour puts you in the heart of Constable Country. Set in the midst of water meadows of the Stour,

Dedham is filled with Tudor, Georgian, and Regency houses. Constable painted its church and its tower. One of the most memorable walks in East Anglia is along a public footpath from Dedham to Flatford Mill (see below), which lies 1.5km (1 mile) farther down the river.

Getting There

Trains depart every 20 minutes from London's Liverpool Street Station for the 50-minute ride to Colchester. For schedules and information, call ☎ **0845/748-4950** or visit **www.nationalrail.co.uk**. From Colchester, it's possible to take a taxi from the rail station to the bus station, and then board an hourly bus run by Beestons for the 8km (5-mile) trip to Dedham. Most visitors, however, take a taxi from Colchester directly to Dedham.

National Express buses depart from London's Victoria Coach Station for Colchester, where you have the choice of taking either another bus or a taxi to Dedham. For bus schedules and information, call ☎ **0870/580-8080** or visit **www.national express.com**.

If you're driving from the London Ring Road, travel northeast on the A12 to Colchester, turning off at East Bergholt onto a small secondary road leading east to Dedham.

Where to Stay

If the famous, but pricey, inns of Dedham are too much for your budget, call on **May's Barn Farm,** May's Lane, off Long Road West, in Dedham (☎ **01206/323191;** www.btinternet.com/~mays.barn), which rents large, comfortable, and traditionally furnished rooms for £48 to £52 a night.

Dedham Hall & the Fountain House   A 3-minute walk east of the center of town, this well-managed hotel flourishes under the direction of Jim and Wendy Sarton. Set on 2 hectares (5 acres) of grazing land whose centerpiece is a pond favored by geese and wild swans, it consists of a 400-year-old brick-sided cottage linked to a 200-year-old home of stately proportions. The older section is reserved for the breakfast room, a bar, and a sitting room for residents of the six second-floor bedrooms. A cluster of three converted barns provides accommodations for the many artists who congregate here several times throughout the year for painting seminars and art workshops. The bedrooms are rather luxuriously furnished, often with designer pieces made of wood. Most rooms are outfitted with Asian carpets, comfortable armchairs, and subdued lighting.

Brook St., Dedham, Essex CO7 6AD. ☎ **01206/323027.** www.dedhamhall.demon.co.uk. 16 units. £110 double; £170 double with half-board. MC, V. **Amenities:** Restaurant; bar; room service; Wi-Fi (free). *In room:* TV, hair dryer, minibar.

Maison Talbooth ★★★   This small, exclusive hotel, a member of the Milsoms Group, is in a handsomely restored Victorian country house on a bluff overlooking the river valley, with views that stretch as far as the medieval Church of Stratford St. Mary. Accommodations consist of spacious suites distinctively furnished by one of England's best-known decorators. High-fashion colors abound, antiques are mixed discreetly with reproductions, and the original architectural beauty has been preserved. Fresh flowers, fruit, and a private bar are standard amenities in the suites. If accommodations are not available here, the staff can book you into neighboring hotels with which they are affiliated.

Stratford Rd., Dedham, Colchester, Essex CO7 6HN. ℂ **01206/322367.** Fax 01206/322752. www.
milsomhotels.co.uk. 12 units. £150–£400 double. Rates include continental breakfast. AE, DC, MC, V.
Take Stratford Rd. 1km (½ mile) west of the town center. **Amenities:** Restaurant; bar; babysitting; outdoor pool; room service; spa; tennis court. *In room:* TV, hair dryer, minibar, Wi-Fi (free).

Where to Dine

Le Talbooth ★★★ ENGLISH/FRENCH   Le Talbooth was featured in Constable's *Vale of Dedham.* A hand-hewn, half-timbered weaver's house is the setting for
this restaurant, part of the Milsoms Group. It stands amid beautiful gardens on the
banks of the River Stour, and to get to it you descend a sloping driveway that leads
past flowering terraces. A well-mannered staff member will usher you to a low-
ceilinged bar for an aperitif. When it's time for your meal, you'll find a high standard
of cooking in this rustically elegant place, where a well-chosen wine list complements the good food. An a la carte menu changes six times a year, and special dishes
are altered daily, reflecting the best produce available at the market. Expect elaborate creations that somehow never destroy the natural flavor. If anything, the well-
prepared sauces enhance dishes such as lobster tail and monkfish cooked in
vermouth and rosemary sauce, or farm-grown duck breast in a jasmine sauce.
Another specialty is veal-and-kidney pudding with bordelaise jus.

Gun Hill. ℂ **01206/323150.** www.milsomhotels.co.uk. Reservations recommended. Main courses £17–
£30. AE, DC, MC, V. Daily noon–2pm; Mon-Sat 7–9:30pm.

Visiting the Painters' Homes

Just 1.5km (1 mile) from the village center is the **Sir Alfred Munnings Art
Museum,** East Lane (ℂ **01206/322127;** www.siralfredmunnings.co.uk), home of
Sir Alfred Munnings, president of the Royal Academy from 1944 to 1949 and
painter extraordinaire of racehorses and other animals. The house and studio, which
have sketches and other works, are open from April to early October on Sunday,
Wednesday, and bank holidays, plus Thursdays and Saturdays in May, July, and
September, from 2 to 5pm. Admission is £5 for adults, £4 students and seniors, and
£1 for children.

The English landscape painter John Constable (1776–1837) was born at East
Bergholt, 3.2km (2 miles) northeast of Dedham. Near the village is **Flatford Mill,**
East Bergholt (ℂ **0845/3307368**), the subject of one of his most renowned works.
The mill was given to the National Trust in 1943 and has since been leased to the
Field Studies Council for use as a residential center. The center offers more than
170 short courses each year in all aspects of art and the environment. Fees start at
£140 for a weekend and £400 for a full week, which includes accommodations,
meals, and tuition. For additional information, call ℂ **01743/852100,** visit www.
field-studies-council.org/flatfordmill, or write to Field Studies Council, Flatford Mill
Field Centre, East Bergholt, Colchester, Suffolk CO7 6UL.

WOODBRIDGE & ALDEBURGH

Woodbridge: 130km (81 miles) NE of London, 29km (18 miles) NE of Dedham, 76km (47 miles) S of
Norwich; Aldeburgh: 156km (97 miles) NE of London, 66km (41 miles) SE of Norwich

The market town of Woodbridge, on the River Deben, is a yachting center. Its best-
known resident was Edward Fitzgerald, Victorian poet and translator of the *Rubaiyat*

of Omar Khayyam. You can base yourself in Woodbridge and use it to explore Aldeburgh as well. From Woodbridge, you can also explore Framlingham Castle and Sutton Hoo (see below).

Woodbridge is filled with riverside walks along quays, and you can stroll around the town in an hour or two, taking in the wide variety of architecture, including pink-washed Tudor cottages. There is also a vast array of antiques shops for browsing.

Aldeburgh, on the North Sea, 24km (15 miles) from Woodbridge, is an exclusive resort that attracts many Dutch visitors, who make the sea crossing via Harwich and Felixstowe, both major entry ports for traffic from the Continent. Aldeburgh dates from Roman times and has long been known as a small port for North Sea fisheries. The Aldeburgh Festival, held every June, is the most important arts festival in East Anglia, and one of the best attended in England.

Essentials

GETTING THERE Woodbridge is on the rail line to Lowestoft from either Victoria Station or Liverpool Street Station in London. Get off two stops after Ipswich. The nearest rail station to Aldeburgh is on the same line, at Saxmundham, six stops after Ipswich. From Saxmundham, you can take a taxi or one of six buses that run the 9.5km (6 miles) to Aldeburgh during the day. For train schedules and information, call ⓒ 0845/748-4950 or visit **www.nationalrail.co.uk**.

One **National Express** bus per day passes through Aldeburgh and Woodbridge on the way from London's Victoria Coach Station to Great Yarmouth. It stops at every country town and narrow lane along the way, so the trip to Aldeburgh takes a woeful 4½ hours. For information, call ⓒ 0871/781-8181 or visit **www.national express.com**. Many visitors reach both towns by Eastern County Bus Company's service from Ipswich. That company's no. 80/81 bus runs frequently between Woodbridge and Aldeburgh.

If driving from London's Ring Road, take the A12 northeast to Ipswich and then continue northeast on the A12 to Woodbridge. To get to Aldeburgh, stay on the A12 until you reach the junction with the A1094, and then head east to the North Sea.

VISITOR INFORMATION The **Tourist Information Centre** is at the Cinema, 152 High St., Aldeburgh (ⓒ 01728/453637; www.visit-woodbridge.co.uk). It's open year-round, Monday to Friday 9am to 5:30pm, Saturday 9am to 5pm.

SPECIAL EVENTS Aldeburgh was the home of Benjamin Britten (1913–76), renowned composer of the operas *Peter Grimes* and *Billy Budd,* as well as many orchestral works. Many of his compositions were first performed at the **Aldeburgh Festival** (ⓒ ⓒ 01728/687110; www.aldeburgh.co.uk), which he founded in 1948. The festival takes place over 2 weeks every June and features internationally known performers.

The **Snape Maltings Concert Hall** nearby is one of the more successful among the smaller British concert halls; it also houses the Britten-Pears School for Advanced Musical Studies, established in 1973.

In addition to the festival, there are other concerts and events throughout the year. Contact the tourist office for details, or check out **www.aldeburgh.co.uk**.

Where to Stay

NEAR WOODBRIDGE

Seckford Hall ★★★   This ivy-covered estate's pure Tudor, crow-stepped gables, mullioned windows, and ornate chimneys capture the spirit of the days of Henry VIII and his strong-willed daughter Elizabeth (the latter may have held court here). Today, it provides some of the finest accommodations in Suffolk. You enter through a heavy, studded Tudor door into a flagstone hallway with antiques. The butler will show you to your bedroom. Many rooms have four-poster beds, one of them a monumental 1587 specimen. Accommodations are statements in luxury and elegance. If you arrive before sundown, you may want to stroll through the 14-hectare (34-acre) gardens, which include a rose garden, herbaceous borders, and greenhouses.

On A12 (2.5km/1½ miles from the Woodbridge rail station), Woodbridge, Suffolk IP13 6NU. ⓒ **01394/385678.** Fax 01394/380610. www.seckford.co.uk. 32 units. £185–£195 double; £240–£255 suite. Rates include English breakfast and dinner. AE, DC, MC, V. Free parking. **Amenities:** 2 restaurants; 2 bars; babysitting; golf course; health club; Jacuzzi; indoor heated pool; room service. *In room:* TV, hair dryer, minibar (in some rooms), Wi-Fi (free).

IN ALDEBURGH

Brudenell Hotel   Located on the waterfront, this hotel is no match for the Wentworth (see below) but remains a good choice. It was built at the beginning of the 20th century and remodeled and redecorated to achieve a pleasant interior. Many of the bedrooms face the sea; all have comfortable beds.

The Parade, Aldeburgh, Suffolk IP15 5BU. ⓒ **01728/452071.** Fax 01728/454082. www.brudenellhotel. co.uk. 44 units. £140–£285 double. Rates include English breakfast. AE, MC, V. Free parking. **Amenities:** Restaurant; bar; babysitting; room service. *In room:* TV, hair dryer, Wi-Fi (free).

Wentworth Hotel ★   A traditional country-house hotel with tall chimneys and gables, the Wentworth overlooks the sea. Built in the early 19th century as a private residence, it was converted into a hotel around 1900. Since 1920, the Pritt family has welcomed the world, including Sir Benjamin Britten and novelist E. M. Forster. In summer, tables are placed outside so that guests can enjoy the sun; in winter, open fires in the lounges, even the cozy bar, are a welcome sight. Many guest rooms have panoramic views. A 19th-century building across the road from the main house offers a comfortable seven-room annex. The standards here match those of the main house. ***Note:*** A minimum stay of 2 nights is required.

Wentworth Rd., Aldeburgh, Suffolk IP15 5BD. ⓒ **01728/452312.** Fax 01728/454343. www.wentworth-aldeburgh.com. 35 units. £122–£174 double. Rates include English breakfast and dinner. AE, DC, MC, V. Free parking. **Amenities:** Restaurant; bar; room service. *In room:* TV, hair dryer, Wi-Fi (free).

Where to Dine in Aldeburgh

Lighthouse BRITISH/SEAFOOD   This is the showcase of a gastro center that takes in a greengrocer selling exotic products, a wine merchant, a cooking school, and a cafe/bar that is one of the most popular gathering spots in town. The highlight, though, is this bistro fish restaurant in a sort of Swedish-modern space. Its blackboard menu features seafood specials including the catch of the day, perhaps succulent Suffolk crab. Meat and poultry dishes are of a high standard, appearing in such offerings as duck confit with fresh spinach or rack of lamb seasoned with mint.

77 High St., Aldeburgh. ⓒ **01728/453377.** www.lighthouserestaurant.co.uk. Reservations recommended. Main courses £10–£17. AE, MC, V. Mon–Fri noon–2pm; Sat–Sun noon–2:30pm; daily 6:30–10pm.

Attractions Outside Woodbridge

Sixteen kilometers (10 miles) to the north of Woodbridge stands **Framlingham Castle ★** (*©* **01728/724-189;** www.english-heritage.org.uk), located along B1119 in the village of Framlingham. This is one of the best examples of a 12th-century castle still standing in East Anglia. Admission is £6 for adults, £5.10 for seniors, £3 for children 11 and younger, and £15 for a family ticket. Hours are April to October, daily 10am to 5pm (until 6pm July–Aug); and November through March, Thursday to Monday 10am to 4pm.

Sutton Hoo ★ (*©* **01394-389700;** www.nationaltrust.org.uk/suttonhoo or www.suttonhoo.org), lying 3.2km (2 miles) east of Woodbridge along B1083, is one of the great Anglo-Saxon royal burial sites of England. On a spur of land rising above the River Deben, several large burial mounds were excavated in 1939, revealing famous treasures, including gold ornaments. Admission is £6.20 for adults, £3.10 for children 11 and younger, and £16 for a family ticket. During the tourist season from mid-March to October, the property is generally open daily from 10:30am to 5pm, but call first—for 2 or 3 weeks during this period, it may be closed on Monday and Tuesday. In winter, it is typically open Saturday and Sunday from 11am to 4pm.

Attractions in & Around Aldeburgh

Constructed on a shelf of land at sea level, Aldeburgh's High Street runs parallel to the often-turbulent waterfront. A cliff face rises some 89m (55 ft.) above the main street. A major attraction is the 16th-century **Aldeburgh Museum** at Moot Hall, Market Cross Place (*©* **01728/453637;** www.aldeburghmuseum.org.uk). Moot Hall dates from the time of Henry VIII, but its tall twin chimneys are later additions. The timber-frame structure displays old maps, prints, and Anglo-Saxon burial urns, as well as other items of historical interest. It is open June through August, daily from noon to 5pm; Easter through April, Saturday and Sunday (and bank holidays) from 2:30 to 5pm; and May, September, and October, daily from 2:30 to 5pm. Admission is £1 for adults, free for children.

The seashore and the surrounding areas of Aldeburgh have been designated an Area of Outstanding Natural Beauty (AONB). The wetlands around Aldeburgh are home to the marsh harrier and booming bittern, both endangered species. If you'd like to see some of these waterfowl, you can visit the nearby bird sanctuary of **Minsmere ★**, outside Westleton (*©* **01728/648281**). Westleton lies 15km (9 miles) northwest of Aldeburgh; take B1122 northwest from Aldeburgh to the junction of B1125 north, following the signs into Westleton and the bird sanctuary.

For a game of golf in the bracing North Sea air, head for our favorite course, the **Aldeburgh Golf Club,** Saxmundham Road/A1094 (*©* **01728/452890;** www.aldeburghgolfclub.co.uk), a challenging 18-hole heathland course of dense gorge, stretching for 6,366 yards. Greens fees are £45, rising to £70 on Saturday and Sunday.

NORWICH ★★

175km (109 miles) NE of London; 32km (20 miles) W of the North Sea

Norwich still holds to its claim as the capital of East Anglia. Despite its partial industrialization, it's a charming and historic city. In addition to its cathedral, it has more than 30 medieval parish churches built of flint. It's also the most important shopping center in East Anglia and has a lot to offer in the way of entertainment and interesting hotels, many of them in its narrow streets and alleyways. A big open-air market is busy every weekday, with fruit, flowers, vegetables, and other goods sold from stalls with colored canvas roofs.

Essentials

GETTING THERE   Hourly train service from London's Liverpool Street Station takes nearly 2 hours for the journey to Norwich. For information, call ℂ **0845/748-4950** or visit **www.nationalrail.co.uk**.

National Express buses depart London's Victoria Coach Station once each hour for the 3-hour ride. For schedules and information, call ℂ **0870/580-8080** or visit **www.nationalexpress.com**.

If driving from London's Ring Road, head north toward Cambridge on the M11. Turn northeast at the junction with the A11, which takes you to Norwich.

VISITOR INFORMATION   The **Norwich Tourist Information Centre** is located in the Forum Building (ℂ **01603/213999;** www.visitnorwich.gov.uk), near the marketplace in the center of town. It's open April through October, Monday to Saturday 9:30am to 6pm and Sunday 10:30am to 4:30pm; and November through March, Monday to Saturday 9:30am to 5:30pm.

GETTING AROUND   For information on buses serving the area, go to the **Norfolk Bus Information Centre,** Castle Meadow (ℂ **0871/002233**), which can answer your transportation questions. It's open Monday to Saturday 8:30am to 5pm.

Where to Stay

EXPENSIVE

De Vere Dunston Hall ★★   Surrounded by parkland and its own golf course, this gabled house is imbued with an Elizabethan aura, even though the redbrick mansion dates from 1859. With its soaring chimneys, it has been sensitively converted and is now elegantly furnished with grand character and comfort. Many of its original 19th-century features are still intact. A wide range of bedrooms is available, including some family rooms with double sofa beds for children. You can stay in elegant four-poster comfort or try one of the attic rooms, which still boast their original beamed low ceilings. From the golf course to the indoor heated pool and aerobics studios, Dunston Hall also has the best facilities in the area.

Ipswich Rd., Norwich, Norfolk NR14 8PQ. ℂ **01508/470444.** Fax 01508/470689. www.devereonline. co.uk. 166 units. £109–£183 double; £169–£203 suite. AE, DC, MC, V. Free parking. **Amenities:** 3 restaurants; bar; exercise room w/aerobics studio; 18-hole golf course; Jacuzzi; indoor heated pool; sauna; steam room; 2 outdoor tennis courts. *In room:* TV, hair dryer, Wi-Fi (free).

Sprowston Manor Marriott Hotel & Country Club ★★★   Norfolk's premier hotel enjoys a long and illustrious history. It was once a private home before it became a hotel in the 1970s. Built in 1559 by a Protestant family prominent in the civil war of the 1640s, it was eventually sold to the lord mayor of Norwich in the late 1800s. It wasn't until 1991, however, that a comprehensive redevelopment added 87 new bedrooms and leisure and conference facilities. Now run by the Marriott chain, the hotel lies in 4 hectares (10 acres) of parkland surrounded by the 18-hole Sprowston Manor golf course. Elegance and informality are its hallmarks. The bedrooms are spacious, quiet, and filled with stylish furniture; some rooms have four-poster beds while others have fireplaces.

Sprowston Park, Wroxham Rd., Norwich, Norfolk NR7 8RP. ✆ **888/236-2427** in the U.S. and Canada, or 01603/410871. Fax 01603/423911. www.marriotthotels.com. 94 units. £110–£208 double; £150–£198 suite. Children 14 and younger stay free in parent's room. Rates include breakfast. AE, DC, MC, V. Free parking. **Amenities:** 2 restaurants; 2 bars; golf course; health club; indoor heated pool; room service; sauna; spa. *In room:* TV, hair dryer, minibar, Wi-Fi (£15 per day).

MODERATE

Holiday Inn Norwich
Situated on a sloping hillside about 3km (2 miles) from the city center, this redbrick building offers comfortable contemporary accommodations for business travelers and visitors. Although uninspired, it's a good and safe haven. Many of the bedrooms feature sitting areas with sofas and armchairs. The superior rooms offer extras such as Neutrogena toiletries and bathrobes.

Ipswich Rd., Norwich, Norfolk NR4 6EP. ✆ **888/465-4329** or 0871/9429060. Fax 01603/506400. www.holidayinn.co.uk. 119 units. £52–£144 double. Rates include breakfast. AE, DC, MC, V. Free parking. Take A140 (Ipswich Rd.) 3km (2 miles) from city center and 1.5km (1 mile) from A11 (London Rd.). **Amenities:** Restaurant; bar; health club; Jacuzzi; indoor heated pool; room service; sauna; spa; steam room. *In room:* TV, hair dryer, Wi-Fi (£15 per day).

Lansdowne Hotel & Conference Centre
The 18th-century former home of Norwich's Lord Mayor is now an affordable hotel. The refurbished bedrooms are situated in the main building and in two semidetached cottages. The cottages have bay windows and wooden beams, as well as a private garden. Most units are midsize, each with a comfortable bed; some are spacious enough for families.

116 Thorpe Rd., Norwich, Norfolk NR1 1RU. ✆ **01603/620302.** Fax 01603/761706. www.lansdowne norwich.co.uk. 40 units. £90 double. Rates include English breakfast. AE, MC, V. Free parking. Take Thorpe Rd. 1km (½ mile) east of city center. **Amenities:** Restaurant; bar; babysitting; room service. *In room:* TV, Wi-Fi (free).

Maids Head Hotel
In business since 1272, the Maids Head claims to be the oldest continuously operated hotel in the United Kingdom. Located next to Norwich Cathedral in the oldest part of the city, it has both Elizabethan and Georgian architectural styles. The Georgian section has a prim white entry and small-paned windows. Many of the bedrooms have oak beams evocative of the hotel's earlier days. Each is supplied with bowls of fresh fruit and a complimentary newspaper. The four-poster Queen Elizabeth I Suite (where the Tudor monarch allegedly once slept) is much sought after. Traditional services such as shoe cleaning, breakfast in bed, and afternoon cream teas are offered.

Palace St., Tombland, Norwich, Norfolk NR3 1LB. ✆ **0844/8559120.** Fax 01603/613688. 84 units. £69–£160 double. AE, DC, MC, V. Free parking. **Amenities:** Restaurant; bar; babysitting; room service. *In room:* TV, hair dryer, Wi-Fi (free).

Norwich Nelson Premier Inn
Set beside the River Wensum, near Thorpe Stadium and Foundry Bridge, this renovated four-story chain hotel is one of the most affordable in town. It lacks the character and atmosphere of the Maids Head (see above), but provides well-maintained and comfortably furnished accommodations, some a bit more spacious than others. Rooms open onto a view of the river or else a courtyard; a few contain four-posters.

121 Prince of Wales Rd., Norwich, Norfolk NR1 1DX. ✆ **01603/760260.** Fax 01603/620008. www. premierinn.com. 159 units. Mon–Thurs £76 double; Fri–Sun £69 double. AE, DC, MC, V. Free parking. **Amenities:** 2 restaurants; 2 bars. *In room:* A/C, TV, hair dryer, Wi-Fi (£12 per day).

Where to Dine

Belgian Monk BELGIAN   Set in the heart of Norwich, within an antique building very close to the Madderhouse Theatre, this restaurant focuses on the hearty, heady grills, stews, and shellfish of Belgium. Dig into such delights as marinated rump steak with grilled peppers and onions, breast of pork with cracklings (topped with apple fritters) and served with a Madeira sauce, or slow-roasted shank of lamb in a rich minty gravy. There's a wine list here, but most of the locals tend to favor a beer, which you can choose from a comprehensive list of dark and blond Belgian varieties. Most visitors opt for a seat beneath the massive ceiling beams of the street-level dining room, but there's additional seating upstairs if you prefer.

7 Pottergate. (C) **01603/767222.** www.thebelgianmonk.com. Reservations recommended. Main courses £10–£20. AE, MC, V. Mon–Sat noon–11pm.

Roger Hickman's Restaurant ★ BRITISH   The restaurant takes its name from a talented chef who has brought a market-fresh and imaginative cuisine to town. The stylish dining room has a clean, crisp decor, with candlelit tables and topnotch service. The chef brings his own interpretation to every dish, beginning with such starters as venison with beets or roast scallops with crispy pork belly. You might also try the chicken liver parfait with red onion jam. Mains are likely to feature roast sea bream with shallots, salsify, and onion risotto or else braised beef cheek with bacon bits.

79 Upper St. Giles St. (C) **01603/633522.** www.rogerhickmansrestaurant.com. Reservations recommended. Fixed-price lunch £16 for 2 courses, £19 for 3 courses; fixed-price dinner £30 for 2 courses, £35 for 3 courses. AE, MC, V. Tues–Sat noon–2:30pm and 7–10pm.

St. Benedict's Restaurant ENGLISH/FRENCH   This modern brasserie gives patrons a warm greeting, along with affordable and well-prepared food, in a contemporary and rather simple setting. The chef, Nigel Raffles, shops for some of the freshest market produce and fashions it into a series of tasty dishes. We recently took delight in his double-baked vegetable-and-cheese soufflé and found the slow-cooked crispy duck perfection itself. It came with a cinnamon sauce and a side of sweet-and-sour red cabbage. The filet of lemon sole is dusted in bread crumbs and pan seared, and made extra enjoyable by the Café de Paris butter and a timbale of watercress and local brown shrimp. The lip-smacking desserts include a luxurious iced praline parfait.

9 St. Benedict's St. (C) **01603/765377.** www.stbenedictsrestaurant.co.uk. Reservations recommended. Fixed-price lunch £12–£17; fixed-price dinner £19 for 2 courses, £24–£32 for 3 courses. AE, DC, MC, V. Tues–Sat noon–2pm and 7–10pm.

Seeing the Sights

Blickling Hall ★★   Massive yew hedges bordering a long drive frame your first view of Blickling Hall, a great Jacobean house built in the early 17th century, one of the finest examples of such architecture in the country. The long gallery has an elaborate 17th-century ceiling, and the Peter the Great Room, decorated later, has a fine tapestry on the wall. The house is set in ornamental parkland with a formal garden and an orangery.

Blickling, near Aylsham. (C) **01263/738030.** www.nationaltrust.org.uk. House and gardens £9.30 adults, £4.60 children; gardens only £6.30 adults, £3.50 children. Late Mar to Oct Wed–Sun and bank holiday Mon 11am–5pm. Blickling Hall lies 23km (14 miles) north of the city of Norwich, 2.5km (1½ miles) west of Aylsham on B1354; take A140 toward Cromer and follow the signs. Call ahead to confirm hours.

Mustard Shop Museum   The Victorian-style Mustard Shop displays a wealth of mahogany and shining brass. The standard of service and pace of life reflect the personality and courtesy of a bygone age. The Mustard Shop Museum features exhibits on the history of the Colman Company and the making of mustard, including its properties and origins. There are old advertisements, as well as packages and tins. You can browse in the shop, selecting whichever mustards you prefer, including the really hot English type. The shop also sells aprons, tea towels, pottery mustard pots, and mugs.

15 Royal Arcade. © **01603/627889.** www.colmansmustardshop.com. Free admission. Mon–Sat 9:30am–5pm. Closed bank holidays.

Norwich Cathedral ★★   Dating from 1096, and principally of Norman design, Norwich Cathedral is noted for its long nave with lofty columns. Built in the late Perpendicular style, the spire rises 95m (315 ft.); together with the keep of the castle, it forms a significant landmark on the Norwich skyline. More than 300 *bosses* (knoblike ornamental projections) on the ceiling depict biblical scenes. The impressive choir stalls with handsome misericords date from the 15th century. Edith Cavell, an English nurse executed by the Germans during World War I, is buried on the cathedral's Life's Green. The quadrangular cloisters, which date from the 13th century, are the largest monastic cloisters in England.

   The visitor center includes a refreshment area along with an exhibition and film room with audio slide shows about the cathedral. Guided tours run year-round, Monday to Saturday at 10:45am, noon, and 2:15pm. The tours are available in five languages—English, French, German, Italian, and Spanish. A short walk from the cathedral is Tombland, one of the most interesting old squares in Norwich.

62 The Close. © **01603/218440.** Free admission; £4 suggested donation. Oct–May daily 7:30am–6pm; June–Sept daily 7:30am–7pm.

Sainsbury Centre for Visual Arts   The center was the gift of Sir Robert and Lady Sainsbury, who, in 1973, contributed their private collection to the University of East Anglia, 5km (3 miles) west of Norwich on Earlham Road. Together with their son David, they gave an endowment to house the collection. Designed by Sir Norman Foster, the center was opened in 1978 and has since won many national and international awards. The prominent features of the structure are its flexibility, allowing solid and glass areas to be interchanged, and the superb quality of light, which permits optimum viewing of the works of art. Special exhibitions are often presented in the 1991 Crescent Wing extension. The Sainsbury Collection is one of the foremost in the country, including modern, ancient, classical, and ethnographic art. Its most prominent works are those by Francis Bacon, Alberto Giacometti, and Henry Moore.

University of East Anglia, Earlham Rd. © **01603/593199.** www.scva.org.uk. Free admission. Tues–Sun 10am–5pm (until 8pm on Wed). Bus: 25, 26, or 27 from Castle Meadow.

Second Air Division Memorial Library   A memorial room honoring the Second Air Division of the 8th U.S. Army Air Force is part of the central library here, where you can find pertinent books, audiovisual materials, and records of the various bomber groups. The library staff will assist veterans who wish to visit their old air bases in East Anglia.

The Forum, Millennium Plain. © **01603/774747.** www.2ndair.org.uk. Free admission. Mon–Sat 9am–5pm.

Exploring the Norfolk "Broads" ★★

One of the most important wetlands of Europe, the Norfolk "Broads" are part of the lush landscape of the **Broads National Park,** 18 Colegate, Norwick (✆ **01603/610734;** www.broads-authority.gov.uk), lying in both Norfolk and Suffolk counties. Long thought to be natural lakes, they are actually man-made, resulting from peat being excavated for use as fuel. Flooded by a rising water table in the 13th century, these newly formed waterways were named "Broads."

The water comes from a trio of rivers—the Bure, Waveney, and Yare—that meander across these flatlands to the east of Norwich. The rivers converge at a lake, Breydon Water, before flowing into the North Sea at the port of Great Yarmouth.

The area covers 200km (124 miles) of navigable waterways. The dominant trees are alder, sallow, and birch, but you'll also see lots of oak and ash woodland. The fen, woodland, and grazing marshes of the Broads are home to some of the rarest plants and creatures in Britain.

One of Europe's most popular waterways, the Broads attract a million visitors a year with their blend of wildlife and distinctive landscapes. On the River Bure, the town of **Wroxham** deservedly calls itself the "capital of the Broads." It lies 11km (7 miles) northeast of Norwich and is the best center for exploring the Broads, which, for the most part, are shallow lagoons linked by streams. These waterways are fun to explore by boat, of course, but some visitors prefer to ride bikes along trails in the Broads.

By public transportation, you can head to Wroxham from Norwich on bus no. 54, a 30-minute ride that costs £3 round-trip. A wealth of information about the Broads is available from the **Tourist Information Centre,** Station Road, Hoveton (✆ **01603/782281**), which is open Easter to October, daily 9am to 1pm and 2 to 5pm. At this office, you can get a list of small-boat outfitters that rent vessels for touring the Broads. Day launches generally cost £12 to £20 per hour. Among the best and most reliable boat-rental outfitters is **Barnes Brinkcraft,** River Bure, along Riverside Road in Wroxham (✆ **01603/782625**).

If you don't want to handle your own boat, you can take an organized tour. The best ones are offered by **Broads Tours,** near the Wroxham Bridge (✆ **01603/782207;** www.broads.co.uk). Its cruises last 1½ to 3½ hours, costing £6 to £16 for adults, £4.50 to £8 for children 5 to 15, and free for kids 4 and younger. In summer, most departures are at either 11:30am or 2pm.

Some areas of the Broads are reachable only by bike. The tourist office carries a pamphlet called **Broads Bike Hire,** listing the best routes and containing much useful information. The office also keeps a complete list of the many outfitters renting bikes for touring the Broads.

Shopping

For antiques, books, and crafts, shoppers can search out the historic lanes and alleys of the town center.

Tombland Antiques Centre, 14 Tombland (✆ **01603/619129**), is a three-floor house opposite the cathedral where 60-plus dealers set up shop. The selection is wide and varied and includes everything from small collectibles to antique furniture.

Norwich After Dark

From fine art to pop art, there's quite a lot happening around Norwich at night. Information on almost all of it can be found at the box office of the Theatre Royal,

Theatre Street (© **01603/630000;** www.theatreroyalnorwich.co.uk), where you can also pick up tickets to just about any event.

The **Theatre Royal** hosts touring companies performing drama, opera, ballet, and modern dance. The reduced Shakespeare Company troupe is among the regular visitors. Ticket prices run from £4 to £22, with senior and student discounts usually available for Wednesday, Thursday, and Saturday matinees. The box office is open Monday to Saturday 9:30am to 8pm on performance days, closing at 6pm on non-performance days.

The **Norwich Playhouse,** Gun Wharf, 42–58 St. George's St. (© **01603/598598;** www.norwichplayhouse.org.uk), hosts productions of classic drama on most evenings. Tickets range from £10 to £30. The box office is open Monday to Saturday 9:30am until 6pm.

An Elizabethan-style theater, **Maddermarket Theatre,** 1 St. John's Alley (© **01603/620917;** www.maddermarket.co.uk), is home to the amateur Norwich Players' productions of classical and contemporary drama. Schedules and tickets, which cost £8 to £15, are available at the box office, Monday to Saturday 10am to 7:30pm (till 5pm on nonperformance days).

Set in a converted medieval church, the **Norwich Puppet Theatre,** St. James, Whitefriars (© **01603/629921;** www.puppettheatre.co.uk), offers original puppet shows most afternoons and some mornings in an octagonal studio that holds about 50 people. Tickets are £7 for adults, £5.50 for students and seniors, and £5 for children 16 and younger; they're available at the box office Monday to Friday 10am to 7pm and on performance Saturdays 1 hour prior to the show's start.

Norwich Arts Centre, Reeves Yard, 51 St. Benedict's St. (© **01603/660352;** www.norwichartscentre.co.uk), the most versatile entertainment complex in town, hosts performances of ballet, comedy, and poetry, with an emphasis on ethnic music. Tickets are £3 to £20. The box office is open Monday to Friday 10am to 7pm (until 9pm on performance days).

For a pint, pay a call on the **Adam & Eve,** 17 Bishopgate (© **01603/667423;** www.adamandevenorwich.co.uk), the oldest pub in Norwich, founded in 1249, which serves a well-kept John Smith's or Old Peculiar.

Many beer drinkers prefer the **Fat Cat ★★**, 49 West End St. (© **01603/624364;** www.fatcatpub.co.uk). Its bartenders serve nearly three dozen real ales as well as their own beer (try Meow Mild or Top Cat). If you don't feel feline, opt for Black Dog Mild. Eight draft beers from Belgium and Germany as well as more than a dozen bottled Belgian beers and a dozen country wines are also featured, even Norfolk farm cider. In summer, tables are placed outside, and you can get a good lunch here, often meat pies, on any day except Sunday.

Finally, if you have a hankering for gay Norfolk men, dance the night away (on two floors) at the **Media Night Club,** 80 Rose Lane (© **01603/623559;** www.medianightclub.co.uk). Later you can get better acquainted with your catch of the night on one of the black leather sofas. The website lists special nights such as drag shows and the like.

THE EAST MIDLANDS: PRINCESS DI & ROBIN HOOD

This region is a mix of dreary industrial sections and incredible scenery, particularly in the **Peak District National Park,** centered in Derbyshire. Byron said that the landscapes in the Peak District rivaled those of Switzerland and Greece. He might have overstated his case just a bit, but he wasn't too far off target.

Derbyshire is noted primarily for the Peak District National Park, but it also has a number of historic homes—notably **Chatsworth,** the home of the 11th duke of Devonshire. The best places to base yourself here are in the 18th-century spa of **Buxton** and the market town of **Bakewell.**

In Nottinghamshire, the city of **Nottingham** is a good center for exploring what's left of **Sherwood Forest,** the legendary stamping grounds of Robin Hood.

If you're headed for the tulip land of Lincolnshire, the highlight is the cathedral city of **Lincoln** itself.

If you have Pilgrims in your past, you can trace your roots to the East Midlands. Over in Northamptonshire is **Sulgrave Manor,** which George Washington looked to as his ancestral home. Except for Sulgrave Manor and **Althorp House,** where Princess Di spent her girlhood, Northamptonshire is not on the tourist circuit. If you do decide to stop here, the best place to spend the night is the industrialized county town of **Leicester,** which is also a base to explore many sights in the countryside, including **Belvoir Castle,** the setting for Steven Spielberg's movie *Young Sherlock Holmes,* and **Bosworth Battlefield,** site of one of England's most important battles.

SULGRAVE MANOR: WASHINGTON'S ANCESTRAL HOME

Sulgrave Manor ★★   American visitors will be especially interested in this small mid-16th-century Tudor manor, the ancestral home of George Washington. As part of a plan to dissolve the monasteries, Henry VIII sold the priory-owned manor in 1539 to Lawrence Washington, who had been mayor of Northampton. The Washington family occupied Sulgrave for more than a century, but in 1656, Colonel John Washington left for the New World. Born in Virginia, George Washington was a direct descendant of Lawrence (seven generations removed).

A group of English people bought the manor in 1914 in honor of the friendship between Britain and the United States. Appropriate furnishings and portraits, including a Gilbert Stuart original of the first president, have been donated from both sides of the Atlantic. The Washington family coat of arms on the main doorway—two bars and a trio of mullets—is believed to have been the inspiration for the Stars and Stripes.

Manor Rd., Sulgrave. ⓒ **01295/760205.** www.sulgravemanor.org.uk. Admission £6.55 adults, £3.15 children 5–16, free for children 4 and younger. May–Oct Tues–Thurs and Sat–Sun 2–4pm; Apr Sat–Sun 2–4pm. From Northampton, drive 29km (18 miles) southwest on A43; then take B4525 to Sulgrave. From Stratford-upon-Avon, take A422 via Banbury (whose famous cross entered nursery-rhyme fame) and continue to Brackley; 9.5km (6 miles) from Brackley, leave A422 and join B4525, which goes to the tiny village of Sulgrave. Follow the signs to Sulgrave Manor.

ALTHORP: MEMORIES OF PRINCESS DI

Althorp ★   Built in 1508 by Sir John Spencer, Althorp has brought a sometimes unwelcome dose of fame to the surrounding rural area as the girlhood home of Princess Diana. It was glamorously revived by Raine Spencer, Diana's stepmother. At least part of the beauty and historical authenticity of this frequently renovated site is the result of her efforts.

Since the death of Lord Spencer, Diana's father, the house has been under the jurisdiction of Charles Spencer, Diana's older brother. Its collection includes paintings by Van Dyck, Reynolds, Gainsborough, and Rubens; an assortment of rare French and English furniture; and porcelain by Sèvres, Bow, and Chelsea.

Following the tragic death of Princess Diana in August 1997, a ticket to Althorp House became extremely difficult to obtain. More than 200 24-hour telephone lines handle orders for tickets. Althorp is open to the public only from July 1, Diana's birthday, to August 30.

Diana was buried on an island in an artificial lake on the property. Visitors do not have access to the island but have a clear view of it across the lake. A museum celebrates Diana's life, complete with schoolgirl letters, her stunning silk wedding dress, and some of her haute couture clothes.

The museum also shows poignant films of her as a carefree child dancing in the gardens and later as a mother riding with her sons, William and Harry, plus videos that include the moving footage of her funeral. The museum makes no mention of

The East Midlands

Dodi Al-Fayed, who died with her in the Paris car crash, and certainly no mention of her former lover James Hewitt. Her estranged husband is also not featured prominently in the exhibition.

On-site facilities include a restaurant and a shop selling a range of souvenirs associated with Diana. The estate states that these souvenirs do not "cheapen her memory in any way." You decide.

Althorp. © **1604/770107.** www.althorp.com. Admission £13–£15 adults, £11–£13 seniors, £6 children 5–17, £30–£35 family ticket, free for children 4 and younger. July 1–Aug 30 daily 11am–5pm (last admission 4pm). Located 9.5km (6 miles) northwest of Northampton on A428, near Harlestone.

LEICESTER

172km (107 miles) NW of London; 69km (43 miles) NE of Birmingham; 39km (24 miles) NE of Coventry; 42km (26 miles) S of Nottingham

Hang on to your hats because this county town is definitely no Sleepy Hollow. Leicester, pronounced *Les*-ter, one of the 10 largest cities in England, is by far the most cosmopolitan city in the East Midlands. Because of the scarcity of hotels in the broader area, many visitors stop in Leicester for the night on visits to Sulgrave Manor and Althorp.

Historically, Leicester was known as Ratae Coritanorum in Roman days. It was also the capital of Lear's kingdom and the seat of the East Mercian bishops back in the 8th century. Some of that past is still preserved today in Leicester's sightseeing attractions, which you can see if you have 3 or 4 hours to explore the city itself and not just its environs, which include Ashby Castle, Belvoir Castle, Bosworth Battlefield, and Melbourne Hall—all previewed below. With Di's Althorp and George's Sulgrave Manor added on, you could spend two very busy days exploring the attractions of this county, many of them A-list.

Essentials

GETTING THERE   Trains depart from London's St. Pancras Station every 25 minutes throughout the day for Leicester, a trip of about 90 minutes. The fare costs £40 each way on the day of your trip. For schedules and information, call © **0845/748-4950** or visit **www.nationalrail.co.uk**.

About 14 buses per day leave London's Victoria Coach Station for Leicester. They call at several secondary stops en route, thus taking 2 hours and 30 minutes each way. A one-way ticket from London to Leicester costs £15; a round-trip ticket goes for £19. For information, call © **08717/818181** or visit **www.nationalexpress.com**.

If you're driving from London, follow the M1 north to Junction 21 toward Leicester. The drive takes 2 hours.

VISITOR INFORMATION   The **Tourist Information Centre** is at 7–9 Every St., Town Hall Square (© **01162/994444;** www.goleicestershire.com). It's open Monday to Friday 9am to 9pm, Saturday and Sunday 9am to 5pm. It can supply a useful map and book Blue Badge guided walks.

SPECIAL EVENTS   The **Leicester Early Music Festival** (© **01162/709984;** www.earlymusicleicester.co.uk) takes place in May and June. Tickets cost £11 to £30. Also in June, the **Leicester International Music Festival** (© **01162/254916;** www.musicfestival.co.uk) attracts some of the biggest names in classical music. Ticket prices vary, but average £4 to £30.

Where to Stay

Leicester Marriott ★★   Only minutes from the city center and owned by the Royal Bank of Scotland, this was the first new hotel to be launched in the city in 14 years when it swung open its doors in 2006. It has all the amenities and features you'd expect in a first-class chain hotel. There are no surprises, but rarely any disappointments either. The bedrooms are tasteful and rather luxurious, with plenty of space and such features as duvets, fluffy pillows, and down comforters.

Smith Way, Grove Park, Leicester, Leicestershire LE19 15W. © **800/228-9290** in the U.S. and Canada, or 01162/820100. Fax 01162/820101. www.marriott.com. 227 units. £89–£169 double; £170–£209 suite. AE, DC, MC, V. Parking £6. **Amenities:** Restaurant; bar; health club; indoor heated pool; room service; sauna; spa; steam room. *In room:* A/C, TV, hair dryer, Internet (£15 per day), minibar.

Ramada Leicester ★   This is one of the finest choices in the city itself. When it was built in 1898, no expense was spared. The original oak and mahogany paneling has been retained, even though the building was enlarged in the 1970s. Bedrooms are more streamlined and contemporary than the semi-antique public areas suggest.

73 Granby St., Leicester, Leicestershire LE1 6ES. © **08448/159012.** Fax 01162/554040. www.ramada jarvis.co.uk. 104 units. Mon–Thurs £59–£110 double, £149 suite; Fri–Sun £69–£95 double, £105 suite. AE, DC, MC, V. Parking £5. **Amenities:** Restaurant; bar; room service. *In room:* TV, hair dryer, Internet, Wi-Fi (£10 per day).

Rothley Court Hotel ★ 🏨   This hotel stands on the edge of Charnwood Forest, a royal hunting ground for centuries. In 1231, Henry III granted the manor and "soke" (right to hold court under feudal law) to the Knights Templar. The chapel erected next to the existing abbey around 1240 is second only to the Temple in London as the best-preserved Templar chapel in Britain.

On 2.4 hectares (6 acres) of grounds, the hotel is surrounded by open farmland. Stone fireplaces, oak paneling, and stained-glass windows evoke its rich historical associations. The comfortable bedrooms have been handsomely restored, with modern conveniences and a number of antique furnishings. The less desirable rooms with standard furnishings are in a modern annex.

Westfield Lane, Rothley, Leicester, Leicestershire LE7 7LG. © **01162/374141.** Fax 01162/374483. www.rothleycourt.com. 30 units. £80–£130 double; £160–£210 suite. Rates include English breakfast. AE, DC, MC, V. Free parking. Head 9.5km (6 miles) north of Leicester on B5328 Rd., just off A6 between Leicester and Loughborough. **Amenities:** Restaurant (see Babington review, below); bar; babysitting; room service. *In room:* TV, hair dryer, Wi-Fi (free).

Where to Dine

Babington Restaurant ★ ENGLISH   Part of the fun of dining at the Rothley Court Hotel (see above) involves a pre- or postmeal visit to one of Britain's best-preserved strongholds of the Knights Templar, a 13th-century semi-fanatical sect that played an important role in the Crusades. Within the venerable walls of a historic manor house surrounded by parks and farmland, you can enjoy a sophisticated blend of modern and traditional English cuisine. Some of the most succulent appetizers include pan-seared foie gras with black pudding and smoked bacon or else Thai mussels topped with fresh coriander. All main courses are quite familiar—nothing experimental here—with the best dishes including duck breast stuffed with Kirsch cherries or chicken breast filled with pear and goat's cheese. Desserts are always yummy, especially the raspberry and orange cheesecake.

In the Rothley Court Hotel, Westfield Lane, Rothley. © **01162/374141.** www.rothleycourt.com. Reservations recommended. Main courses £10–£22. AE, DC, MC, V. Daily noon–2:30pm; Mon–Thurs 6:30–9:30pm, Fri–Sun 6:30–10pm.

Exploring the Town

Leicester is worth a look if you have an afternoon to spare. In addition to the Victorian-style **Shires Shopping Centre,** High Street, with its designer and collectibles stores, wide walkways, fountains, and sunny skylights, there's **St. Martins Square** in the city center, which has given new life to old restored buildings, with retailers, cafes, and teashops. A wealth of specialty shops—out .5km (¼ mile) on either side of the railway station—and several antiques stores line **Oxford Street** and **Western Boulevard.**

Venture out from the center of town to Belgrave Road, and you'll discover the **Golden Mile,** which takes its name from several jewelry shops found here, each specializing in gold. The store windows along Belgrave Road overflow with fine Indian silks, organza, and cottons. Sari shops also carry a variety of accessories including bags, jewelry, shoes, and shawls.

Jewry Wall Museum   Set near the excavation of an ancient Roman bath, this museum has nothing at all to do with Jewish history. Its name derives from a corruption of the Norman French *jurad,* which referred to the governing magistrates of an early medieval town, who used to gather in the shadow of this wall for their municipal decisions. More than 12m (40 ft.) high, the wall is higher than any other piece of ancient Roman architecture in Britain. Exhibits within the museum include a pair of ancient Roman mosaics, the Peacock Pavement and the Blackfriars Mosaic, which are the finest of their kind in the British Midlands. Each was laboriously sliced from the masonry of ancient villas within the district and set into new masonry beds here.

St. Nicholas Circle (about .5km/¼ mile from the town center). © **01162/254971.** www.leicester.gov.uk. Free admission. Sat–Sun 11am–4:30pm.

Leicester Abbey   In a verdant public park favored by joggers and picnickers, about 1km (½ mile) north of Leicester's historic core, these evocative, poetically shattered remains are all that's left of the richest Augustinian monastery in England, built in 1132. In 1530, Cardinal Wolsey came here to die, demoralized and broken after his political and religious conflicts with Henry VIII. The abbey was torn down during the Reformation, and stones were used in the construction of Cavendish House next door.

Abbey Park, Abbey Park Rd. © **01162/221000.** Free admission. Summer daily dawn–dusk; winter daily 7:30am–6pm.

Leicester Guildhall   Built in stages between the 14th and 16th centuries, the city's most prominent public building was Leicester's first town hall and contains one of the oldest libraries in Britain. Plaques commemorate its role as a die-hard last bastion of the Parliamentarians during the civil war. On its ground floor, you'll see a 19th-century police station with a pair of original prison cells, whose mournful graffiti are a powerful testimony to the horrors of the Victorian penal system. Shakespeare's troupe is said to have appeared here.

Guildhall Lane. © **01162/532569.** www.leicester.gov.uk. Free admission. Feb–Nov Sat–Wed 11am–4:30pm; Sun 1–4:30pm.

Launch Yourself into Space

The most modern attraction in Leicester is the **National Space Centre**, Exploration Drive (✆ **0870/607-7223**; www.spacecenter.co.uk), Britain's only attraction dedicated to space science and astronomy. It is crowned by a futuristic Rocket Tower. Allow 3 hours for a journey of discovery where stories, personalities, and technology of the past and present are used to explain space and how it will affect your future. You're taken through eight themed galleries, seeing space rockets, satellites, and capsules, and participating in hands-on activities. Admission is £13 for adults, £11 for children 5 to 16, £41 to £60 for a family ticket, and free for children 4 and younger. Hours year-round are Tuesday to Sunday 10am to 5pm (last admission 3:30pm).

New Walk Museum & Art Gallery This multipurpose museum has two distinctly separate features. It contains exhibits of archaeology and natural history: a dinosaur bone found in a field near Leicester; a collection of Egyptian mummies and artifacts brought back to the Midlands by Thomas Cook, the 19th-century travel mogul; and geological exhibits. There is also a collection of paintings by British and European artists (including some by Gainsborough) from the 18th through 20th centuries. The collection of early-20th-century canvasses by German expressionists is one of the largest in Europe. In 2005, the museum added three art galleries: a permanent collection of modern art including such favorites as Degas and Pissarro; a gallery devoted to German expressionism; and a third thematic gallery, highlighting diversity in art, particularly that of south Asia, China, the Caribbean, and Africa.

53 New Walk. ✆ **01162/254900.** www.leicester.gov.uk. Free admission; donations accepted. Mon–Sat 10am–5pm; Sun 11am–5pm. Closed Dec–Jan 1.

St. Martin's Cathedral (Leicester Cathedral) It may not have the soaring grandeur of the cathedrals of York or Lincoln, but this is the most venerated and historic church in Leicester. In 1086, it was one of the region's parish churches, enlarged during the 1300s and 1500s. In 1927, it was designated the cathedral of Leicester, adding considerably to its pomp and circumstance. The oak vaulting beneath the building's north porch is one of the most unusual treatments of its kind in England. For walking tours, contact the Tourist Information Centre (see above).

21 St. Martin's Lane. ✆ **01162/487400.** www.cathedral.leicester.anglican.org. Free admission. Daily 8am–6pm.

Historic Attractions near Leicester

Ashby Castle If you've read Sir Walter Scott's *Ivanhoe,* you will remember Ashby-de-la-Zouch, a town that retains a pleasant country atmosphere. The main attraction here is the ruined Norman manor house, Ashby Castle, where Mary, Queen of Scots, was imprisoned. The building was already an antique in 1464 when its thick walls were converted into a fortress.

Ashby-de-la-Zouch (29km/18 miles northwest of Leicester). ✆ **01530/413343.** www.english-heritage.org.uk. Admission £4.20 adults, £3.60 seniors and students, £2.10 children 15 and younger, £9.80 family ticket. Apr–June and Sept–Oct Thurs–Mon 10am–5pm; July–Aug daily 10am–6pm; Nov–Mar Thurs–Mon 10am–4pm.

Belvoir Castle   On the northern border of Leicestershire overlooking the Vale of Belvoir (pronounced *Beaver*), Belvoir Castle has been the seat of the dukes of Rutland since the time of Henry VII. Rebuilt by Wyatt in 1816, the castle contains paintings by Holbein, Reynolds, and Gainsborough, as well as tapestries in its magnificent staterooms. The castle was the location of the movies *Little Lord Fauntleroy* and *Young Sherlock Holmes.* In summer, it's the site of medieval jousting tournaments.

11km (7 miles) southwest of Grantham, btw. A607 to Melton Mowbray and A52 to Nottingham. ✆ **01476/871002.** www.belvoircastle.com. Admission to castle and grounds £12 adults, £10 students and seniors, £7 children 5–16, £30 family ticket. Apr–Sept Sun–Fri 11am–5pm; Sat 11am–4pm.

Bosworth Battlefield Heritage Centre and Country Park   This site commemorates the 1485 battle that ended one of England's most important conflicts. The Battle of Bosworth brought a close to the War of the Roses between the houses of York and Lancaster. When the fighting subsided, King Richard III, last of the Yorkists, lay dead, and Henry Tudor, a Welsh nobleman who had been banished to France to thwart his royal ambition, was proclaimed the victor. Henry thus became King Henry VII, and the Tudor dynasty was born.

   Today, the appropriate standards are flown where the opponents had their positions. You can see the whole scene by taking a 2km (1¼-mile) walk along the marked battle trails. In the center are exhibitions, models, book and gift shops, a cafeteria, and a theater where an audiovisual introduction, with an excerpt from the Lord Laurence Olivier film version of Shakespeare's *Richard III,* is presented.

Sutton Cheney, 29km (18 miles) southwest of Leicester btw. M1 and M6, near the town of Nuneaton. ✆ **01455/290429.** www.bosworthbattlefield.com. Admission to Heritage Centre £6 adults, £4 seniors, £3 children 3–16. Heritage Centre Apr–Oct daily 10am–5pm; Nov–Mar daily 10am–4pm (closed Jan). Country Park Apr–Sept daily 8:30am–5:30pm; Oct–Mar daily 8:30am–4:40pm

Melbourne Hall ★   Built by the bishops of Carlisle in 1133, Melbourne Hall stands in one of the most famous formal gardens in Britain. The ecclesiastical structure was restored in the 1600s by one of the cabinet ministers of Charles I and enlarged by Queen Anne's vice chamberlain. It was the home of Lord Melbourne, who was prime minister when Victoria ascended to the throne. Lady Palmerston later inherited the house, which contains an important collection of antique furniture and artwork. A special feature is the beautifully restored wrought-iron pergola by Robert Bakewell, a noted 18th-century ironsmith.

Church Sq., Melbourne, 24km (15 miles) southwest of Leicester on A50. ✆ **01332/862502.** www.melbournehall.com. Admission to house and gardens £5.50 adults, £4.50 seniors and students, £3.50 children 6–15, free for children 5 and younger; house only £3.50 adults, £3 students and seniors, £2 children; gardens only £3.50 adults, £2.50 seniors, students, and children. House Aug daily 2–4:15pm (closed the 1st 3 Mon of the month). Gardens Apr–Sept Wed, Sat–Sun, and bank holidays 1:30–5:30pm.

Leicester After Dark

Phoenix Arts Centre, Upper Brown Street (✆ **01162/422800;** www.phoenix.org.uk), hosts dance, music, and theatrical productions from around the world; local dancers, musicians, and actors also perform on its stage, and there's even an occasional film screening.

   On weekends, the area around the **Clock Tower** in the center of town is alive with bustling crowds headed out to the clubs and bars on Church Gate, Silver Street, and High Street.

As you may expect of a university town, Leicester has a variety of pubs, but the one favored most by locals is the **Pump & Tap,** 42 Duns Lane (⟨ **01162/540324**). Stop by to sample ales by Leicestershire's two home-brewers: Everards and Hoskins.

The biggest after-dark magnet is **Zanzibar,** Gravel Street (⟨ **0116/2511442;** www.zanzibar.co.uk), drawing hundreds of revelers on Friday and Saturday nights. The cover ranges from £2 to £20, depending on what's being offered. In one room you hear the sounds of pop classics, in the other hip-hop.

DERBYSHIRE & PEAK DISTRICT NATIONAL PARK

The most magnificent scenery in the Midlands is found in Derbyshire, between Nottinghamshire and Staffordshire. Some travelers avoid this part of the country because it's ringed by the industrial sprawl of Manchester, Leeds, Sheffield, and Derby. But missing this area is a pity, for Derbyshire has actually been less defaced by industry than its neighbors.

The north of the county, with Peak District National Park, contains waterfalls, hills, moors, green valleys, and dales. In the south, the land is more level, with pastoral meadows. Dovedale, Chee Dale, and Millers Dale are worth a detour. For tips on touring, see below.

Peak District National Park ★★

Peak District National Park covers some 1,404 sq. km (542 sq. miles), most of it in Derbyshire, with some spilling over into South Yorkshire and Staffordshire. It stretches from Holmfirth in the north to Ashbourne in the south, and from Sheffield in the east to Macclesfield in the west. The best central place to stay overnight is Buxton (see below).

The peak in the name is a bit misleading, because there is no actual peak—the highest point is just 630m (2,100 ft.). The park has around 4,000 walking trails that cover some of the most beautiful hill country in England.

The southern portion of the park, called **White Peak,** is filled with limestone hills, tiny villages, old stone walls, and hidden valleys. August and September are the best and most beautiful times to hike these rolling hills.

In the north, called **Dark Peak,** the scenery changes to rugged moors and deep gullies. This area is best visited in the spring when the purple heather, so beloved by Emily Brontë, comes into bloom.

If you're planning an extensive visit to the park, request details by writing to the **Peak District National Park Authority,** Aldern House, Baslow Road, Bakewell, Derbyshire DE45 1AE (⟨ **01629/816200;** www.peakdistrict.org). A list of publications will be sent to you, and you can order whichever you want.

GETTING TO THE PARK You can reach Buxton (see below) by train from Manchester. For schedules and information, call ⟨ **0845/748-4950** or visit **www. nationalrail.co.uk**.

It's also possible to travel by bus via **Transpeak** (⟨ **01773/712265;** www. transpeak.co.uk), taking 3½ hours from Manchester to Nottingham, with stops at such major centers as Buxton, Bakewell, Matlock, and Matlock Bath.

If you're planning to use public transportation, consider buying the **Derbyshire Wayfarer,** a pass sold at various rail and bus stations. For £9 for adults or £5 for students, seniors, and children, you can ride all the bus and rail lines within the peak district for a day.

If you're driving, the main route is the A515 north from Birmingham, with Buxton as the gateway. From Manchester, Route 6 heads southeast to Buxton.

GETTING AROUND THE PARK   Many visitors prefer to walk from one village to another. In our view, the best and most evocative walk in the entire park district is the **Monsal Trail,** lying between Buxton and Bakewell (see below). If you're not so hearty, you can take local buses, which connect various villages. Instead of the usual Sunday slowdown in bus service, more buses run on that day than on week-days because of increased demand, especially in summer.

Another popular way to explore the park is by bicycle. Park authorities operate three **Peak Cycle Hire Centres** (www.peakdistrict.gov.uk/cycle), renting bikes for £14 a day for adults and £10 for children 15 and younger, with a £20 deposit, helmet included. Centers are at Mapleton Lane in Ashbourne (© 01335/343156), near the Fairholmes Information Centre at Derwent (© 01433/651261), and at the junction of Tissington and High Peak Trails at Parsley Hay (© 01298/84493).

Buxton ★: A Lovely Base for Exploring the Park

277km (172 miles) NW of London; 61km (38 miles) NW of Derby; 40km (25 miles) SE of Manchester

One of the loveliest towns in Britain, Buxton rivaled the spa at Bath in the 18th century. Its waters were known to the Romans, whose settlement here was called Aquae Arnemetiae. The thermal waters were pretty much forgotten from Roman times until the reign of Queen Elizabeth I, when the baths were reactivated. Mary, Queen of Scots took the waters here, brought by her caretaker, the earl of Shrewsbury.

Buxton today is mostly the result of 18th-century development directed by the duke of Devonshire. His lordship's grandiose plan to create another Bath or Chel-tenham never came to be, but his legacy lives on in many elegant 1700s buildings. The thermal baths closed in 1972, and the town went into decay. But it's slowly being revived, with many of its aging properties restored.

Seek out, in particular, the **Crescent,** incorporating the former St. Ann's Hotel. The duke's plan to make this a model of the Royal Crescent in Bath was never real-ized, but it's worth a look anyway. At the eastern end of the Crescent rises the cast-iron and glass canopy sheltering the Cavendish Arcade Shopping Centre in the original 18th-century bathhouses of the spa.

In front of the Crescent is a beautiful park, the **Slopes,** dating from 1818. It leads up to the center of town, the **Market Place,** which is sleepy all winter but filled with heavy traffic in summer. Buxton's spa days have come and gone, but it's still the best center for exploring the peak district. The climate is amazingly mild, consider-ing that at 300m (1,000 ft.) altitude, Buxton is the second-highest town in England.

ESSENTIALS
GETTING THERE   Trains depart from Manchester at least every hour during the day. It's a 50-minute trip to Buxton. For schedules and information, call © 0845/748-4950 or visit **www.nationalrail.co.uk**.

About half a dozen buses also run between Manchester and Sheffield, stopping in Buxton en route, after a 70-minute ride.

By car, take the A6 from Manchester, heading southeast into Buxton.

VISITOR INFORMATION The **Buxton Tourist Information Centre,** Pavilion Gardens, St. John's Road (© **01298/25106;** www.visitbuxton.co.uk), is open Monday to Friday 8am to 8pm, Saturday and Sunday 10am to 4pm; off-season hours are daily from 10am to 4pm. It provides a free pamphlet, entitled *Buxton Town Trail,* that offers a map and detailed instructions for a walking tour, lasting between 75 and 90 minutes, from the town center.

SPECIAL EVENTS The town hosts the **Buxton Festival** (© **01298/70395;** www.buxtonfestival.co.uk), a well-known opera festival, during a 2½-week period in July.

WHERE TO STAY

Barceló Buxton Palace Hotel ★★ A tradition since 1868, this Victorian landmark has been restored, including its splendid exterior, the work of Henry Currey, architect to the duke of Devonshire. For service, cuisine, and comfort, this is the premier choice within the town itself. It maintains tradition but with all the modern facilities, such as a large swimming pool. In fact, the comfort is so grand you may want to make the Palace your base for touring the area. The bedrooms are well furnished, though often falling short in style. Some are equipped with half-tester beds, and all are generally spacious. You don't have to leave the premises for good food.

Palace Rd., Buxton, Derbyshire SK17 6AG. © **01298/22001.** Fax 01298/767034. www.barcelo-hotels. co.uk. 122 units. £97–£219 double. Rates include breakfast. AE, DC, MC, V. Parking £3.50. **Amenities:** Restaurant; 2 bars; exercise room; indoor heated pool; room service; sauna; steam room; solarium. *In room:* TV, hair dryer, Wi-Fi (£12 per day).

Buxton's Victorian Guest House ★ 🛍 Commissioned by the duke of Devonshire in 1860, this is one of a row of elegant terraced houses lying on a promenade overlooking a lake and the 16-hectare (40-acre) Pavilion Gardens. It is also only a 2-minute walk to the Buxton Opera House. The house is spectacularly decorated and furnished with art, prints, and antiques from both the Victorian and Edwardian eras. All of the bedchambers are individually designed with soft furnishings and bedding. The standard rooms are themed and include the Victorian Craftman's Room and the Egyptian Room. The finest of the accommodations is the premier room, decorated in a classical Victorian style and housing a four-poster bed.

3A Broad Walk, Buxton, Derbyshire SK17 6JE. © **01298/78759.** Fax 01298/74732. www.buxton victorian.co.uk. 8 units. £78–£100 double; £216–£250 family suite. Rates include English breakfast. MC, V. Free parking. **Amenities:** Breakfast room. *In room:* TV, hair dryer.

Old Hall Hotel ★ This is one of the most historic old inns of Derbyshire. Although other hostelries make the same claim, this is reputed to be the oldest hotel in England, a 16th-century building overlooking the Buxton Opera House. Mary, Queen of Scots stayed here on several occasions between 1573 and 1582. Daniel Defoe, writing as a guest in 1727, called Old Hall "indeed a very special place," and it remains so in its restored form today. Its mellowed walls and ancient rooms evoke the past, yet it is modernized inside and has kept up to date with the times. The bedrooms are generally spacious. Nostalgia buffs seek out Queen Mary's Bower in the oldest part of the hotel, still with its original moldings and a four-poster bed.

The Square, Buxton, Derbyshire SK17 6BD. ⓒ **01298/22841.** Fax 01298/72437. www.oldhallhotel
buxton.co.uk. 38 units. £85–£175 double. Rates include English breakfast. AE, DC, MC, V. Free parking.
Amenities: Restaurant; 3 bars; room service. *In room:* TV, hair dryer.

WHERE TO DINE

Columbine Restaurant ★ 🍴 CONTINENTAL/MODERN ENGLISH   Here is
Buxton's most charming restaurant, serving the town's best food. It's reasonably
priced, but still rivals some of the more formal and expensive country-house hotels
outside the center of town. Set behind a facade of gray Derbyshire stone, it was built
during the Victorian age as a private home and retains some of its oldest vestiges
within an atmospheric cellar. The place is especially popular during the town's
annual music festivals; it sometimes prepares pre- and post-theater suppers. Menu
items are straightforward and unpretentious, but fresh and flavorful, served in a
bistro-style setting. Some of the best items are likely to include baked saddle of
monkfish with a fresh crab risotto, filet of wild sea bass with stir-fried noodles, or
sautéed filets of red mullet with tiger prawns in a light basil-and-white-wine sauce,
a specialty.

7 Hall Bank. ⓒ **01298/78752.** www.buxtononline.net/columbine. Reservations recommended. Main
courses £11–£15. MC, V. May–Oct Mon–Sat 7–10pm; Nov–Apr Wed–Mon 7–10pm.

SEEING THE SIGHTS

Water from nine thermal wells is no longer available for spa treatments, but you can
visit the 9.3-hectare (23-acre) **Pavilion Gardens,** St. John's Road (ⓒ**01298/23114;**
www.paviliongardens.co.uk). The gardens themselves are open at all times (free
admission). A concert hall and ballroom under an iron-and-glass roof originally stood
here in the 1870s. They have given way today to a conservatory, boutique, restaurant,
cafe, and the Tourist Information Centre.

Another sight, **Poole's Cavern,** Buxton Country Park, Green Lane
(ⓒ **01298/26978;** www.poolescavern.co.uk), is a cave that was inhabited by Stone
Age people, who may have been the first to marvel at the natural vaulted roof
bedecked with stalactites. Visitors can walk through the spacious galleries, viewing
the incredible horizontal cave, which is electrically lighted. On a summer day, you
can get here by taking a beautiful walk: Head south of town for 1.6km (1 mile), following the boardwalk through the Pavilion Gardens and picking up the signposted
trail along Temple Road. From Easter to October, the attraction is open daily from
9:30am to 5pm; off-season hours are Saturday and Sunday from 10am to 4pm.
Admission is £8 for adults, £7 for students and seniors, £4.75 for children 5 to 16,
and free for kids 4 and younger. A family ticket costs £23.

Set about 2km (1¼ miles) south of Buxton's town center is one of the oddest
pieces of public Victorian architecture in the Midlands, **Solomon's Temple,** whose
circular design may remind you of a straight castellated Tower of Pisa as interpreted
by the neo-Gothic designers of Victorian England. Conceived as a folly in 1895 and
donated to the city by a prominent building contractor, Solomon Mycock, it sits atop
a tumulus (burial mound) from Neolithic times. Climb a small spiral staircase inside
the temple for impressive views over Buxton and the surrounding countryside, especially the hills to the west. It's open all the time, day and night, and admission is free.
Our favorite walk in the area is from Poole's Cavern (see above), strolling through
Grinlow Woods for 20 minutes until you reach Solomon's Temple.

Bakewell

258km (160 miles) NW of London; 53km (33 miles) NW of Nottingham; 42km (26 miles) N of Derby; 60km (37 miles) SE of Manchester

Lying 19km (12 miles) southeast of Buxton, Bakewell is yet another possible base for exploring the southern Peak District, especially the beautiful valleys of Ashwood Dale, Monsal Dale, and Wyedale. Since very few visitors have time to explore this vast territory, we'll let you in on a secret: You can see the park district in a nutshell by taking the **Monsal Trail ★**. First, pick up a map at the Bakewell Tourist Information Centre (see below). This trail stretches for 4.9km (3 miles) to the north, cutting through some of the county's finest limestone valleys to the bucolic village of Wyedale, which itself lies 1.8km (1 mile) east of Buxton (see above) should you decide to hit the trail from Buxton instead of Bakewell. On the River Wey, Bakewell is just a market town, but its old houses constructed from gray-brown stone and its narrow streets give it a picture-postcard look. Its most spectacular feature is a medieval bridge across the river with five graceful arches.

Still served in local tearooms is the famous **Bakewell Pudding,** which was supposedly created by accident. One day, a chef didn't put the proper proportions of ingredients into her almond sponge cake batter, and it remained gelatinous and runny. Served apologetically, as a mistake, the pudding was called wonderful, and the tradition has remained ever since. The pudding, made as it is with a rich puff pastry that lies at the bottom of the dish, and covered with a layer first of jam and then the gelatinous version of the almond sponge cake, is richer than a tart and relatively difficult to find outside of Bakewell.

The best time to be here is on Monday, **market day,** when local farmers come in to sell their produce. Entrepreneurs from throughout the Midlands also set up flea market stands in the town's main square, the Market Place. Sales are conducted from 8:30am until 5:30pm in winter and until 7:30pm in summer.

ESSENTIALS

GETTING THERE   To reach Bakewell from Derby, take the A6 north to Matlock, passing by the town and continuing on the A6 north toward Rowsley. Just past Rowsley, you'll come to a bridge. Follow the signpost across the bridge into Bakewell.

From London, take the M1 motorway north to Junction 28. Then follow the A38 for 5km (3 miles), connecting with the A615 signposted to Matlock. Once you're at Matlock, follow the A6 into Bakewell.

VISITOR INFORMATION   The **Bakewell Tourist Information Centre,** Old Market Hall, Bridge Street (✆ **01629/813227;** www.peakdistrict.gov.uk), is open from Easter through October, daily 9:30am to 5:30pm; and November through March, daily 10am to 5pm.

WHERE TO STAY & DINE

For a look at a working 19th-century flour mill, stop in at **Caudwell's Mill,** Bakewell Road (✆ **01629/734374**), where you can have afternoon tea with freshly baked cakes, breads, and pastries made right here at the mill. Afterward, stroll through a variety of shops, including a handcrafted-furniture store, glass-blowing studio, jewelry shop, and art gallery.

Cavendish Hotel ★★   Located 6.5km (4 miles) east of Bakewell, the Cavendish is one of the most stately country hotels of England. The stone-sided building was constructed in the 1780s as the Peacock Inn; it is located on the duke of Devonshire's private estate. The duke and duchess took personal charge of the hotel and its lavish restoration in 1975, furnishing its public areas and more expensive bedrooms with antiques from nearby Chatsworth, a 15-minute walk to the south. The hotel remains aristocratic and charming. Beds are sumptuous with elegant fabrics.

Baslow, Derbyshire DE45 1SP. ✆ **01246/582311.** Fax 01246/582312. www.cavendish-hotel.net. 23 units. £163–£215 double. AE, DC, MC, V. Free parking. **Amenities:** 2 restaurants; bar; room service. *In room:* TV, hair dryer, minibar.

Fischer's Baslow Hall ★★★   At the edge of the Chatsworth Estate, at the end of a winding chestnut tree-lined drive, this stately Edwardian country house is the finest choice in the area for either food or lodgings. The six bedrooms in the main house are decorated with lavish fabrics and contain ornate plasterwork ceilings, along with Egyptian cotton bedding and traditionally styled bathrooms with tub and shower. We prefer these accommodations, although you can also rent a large double in the Garden House, built of locally quarried stone with high ceilings and exposed timber joists. In contrast to the main house, the garden rooms are more modern and more minimalist.

Calver Rd., Baslow, Derbyshire DE45 1RR. ✆ **01246/583259.** Fax 01246/583818. www.fischers-baslow hall.co.uk. 11 units. £150–£220 double. Rates include breakfast. AE, DC, MC, V. Free parking. **Amenities:** Restaurant; bar. *In room:* TV.

Riber Hall Country House Hotel ★   South of Bakewell on Route 6, this symmetrically gabled structure is built of gray-toned Derbyshire stone. It's from 1450, but was enlarged and discreetly altered by the Jacobeans, and then intricately restored by the present owners to what you see today. Public areas are as richly historic and atmospheric as anything in the district. Bedrooms occupy the premises of a converted stable and are charmingly furnished, each with a four-poster bed and tasteful chintzes and antiques.

Riber, Matlock, Derbyshire DE4 5JU. ✆ **01629/582795.** Fax 01629/580475. www.riber-hall.co.uk. 14 units. £145–£190 double. Rates include English breakfast. AE, DC, MC, V. Free parking. **Amenities:** Restaurant; bar; room service; tennis court. *In room:* TV, hair dryer.

Rutland Arms Hotel   A dignified early Georgian building set behind a gray-stone facade built in 1804, this town landmark is a good base for visiting nearby Haddon Hall and Chatsworth House. Its original owner operated a prosperous livery stable; some of the bedrooms are in the old stable block in back. The renovated hotel offers cozy, well-maintained bedrooms.

The Square, Bakewell, Derbyshire DE45 1BT. ✆ **01629/812812.** Fax 01629/812309. www.rutlandarms bakewell.co.uk. 35 units. £105–£155 double. Rates include breakfast. AE, DC, MC, V. Free parking. **Amenities:** Restaurant; bar; room service. *In room:* TV, hair dryer, Wi-Fi (free).

HISTORIC HOMES NEAR BAKEWELL

The tourist office in Bakewell (see above) will provide you with a map outlining the best routes to take to reach each of the attractions below.

Chatsworth ★★★   Here stands one of the great country houses of England, the home of the 11th duke of Devonshire and his duchess, the former Deborah Mitford. With its lavishly decorated interior and a wealth of art treasures, it has 297 rooms, the most spectacular of which are open to the public. The house contains a great library and such paintings as the *Adoration of the Magi* by Veronese and *King Uzziah* by Rembrandt. On the grounds are spectacular fountains and a playground for children in the farmyard.

Dating from 1686, the present building stands on a spot where the eccentric Bess of Hardwick built the house in which Mary, Queen of Scots was held prisoner upon orders of Queen Elizabeth I. Capability Brown (who seems to have been everywhere) worked on the landscaping of the present house. But it was Joseph Paxton, the gardener to the sixth duke, who turned the garden into one of the most celebrated in Europe. Queen Victoria and Prince Albert were lavishly entertained here in 1843.

In the 2005 film adaptation of *Pride and Prejudice*, directed by Joe Wright, Chatsworth stars as Pemberley, the family home of Mr. Darcy (played by Matthew Macfadyen), whose affair with Elizabeth Bennet (Keira Knightley) is at the heart of the story.

6.5km (4 miles) east of Bakewell, beside the A6 (16km/10 miles north of Matlock). ℭ **01246/565300.** www.chatsworth.org. Admission £14–£17 adults, £10–£14 students and seniors, £8–£10 children 4–15, £42–£47 family ticket, free for children 3 and younger. Daily 11am–5:30pm (last admission 4:30pm).

Hardwick Hall   Built in 1597 for Bess of Hardwick, a woman who acquired an estate from each of her four husbands, Hardwick Hall is particularly noted for its "more glass than wall" architecture. The high great chamber and long gallery crown an unparalleled series of late-16th-century interiors, including an important collection of tapestries, needlework, and furniture. The house is surrounded by a 125-hectare (300-acre) country park, featuring walled gardens, orchards, and an herb garden.

Doe Lea, 15km (9½ miles) east of Chesterfield. ℭ **01246/850430.** www.nationaltrust.org.uk/hardwick. Admission £11 adults, £5.25 children, £26 family ticket. House Mar–Oct Wed–Thurs and Sat–Sun noon–4:30pm; gardens Mar–Oct Wed–Sun 11am–5:30pm; grounds year-round daily 8am–6pm. Take Junction 29 from M1.

NOTTINGHAMSHIRE: ROBIN HOOD COUNTRY

"Notts," as Nottinghamshire is known, lies in the heart of the East Midlands. Its towns are rich in folklore, and many have bustling markets. A number of famous people have come from Nottingham, notably those 13th-century outlaws from Sherwood Forest, Robin Hood and his Merry Men. It also was home to the Romantic poet Lord Byron; you can visit his ancestral home at **Newstead Abbey** (p. 576). D. H. Lawrence, author of *Sons and Lovers* and *Lady Chatterley's Lover,* was born in a tiny miner's cottage in Eastwood, which he later immortalized in his writings.

Nottingham

195km (121 miles) N of London; 116km (72 miles) SE of Manchester

Though an industrial center, Nottingham is a good base for exploring Sherwood Forest and the rest of the county. Nottingham is known to literary buffs for its association with author D. H. Lawrence and its medieval sheriff, who played an important role in the Robin Hood story.

It was an important pre-Norman settlement guarding the River Trent, the gateway to the north of England. Followers of William the Conqueror arrived in 1068 to erect a fort here. In a later reincarnation, the fort saw supporters of Prince John surrender to Richard the Lion-Hearted in 1194. Many other exploits occurred here—notably Edward III's capture of Roger Mortimer and Queen Isabella, the assassins of Edward II. From Nottingham, Richard III marched out with his men to face defeat and his own death at Bosworth Field in 1485.

With the arrival of the spinning jenny in 1768, Nottingham was launched into the forefront of the Industrial Revolution. It's still a center of industry and home base to many well-known British firms, turning out such products as John Player cigarettes, Boots pharmaceuticals, and Raleigh cycles.

Nottingham doesn't have many attractions, but it's a young and vital city, and is very student-oriented thanks to its two large universities. Its Hockley neighborhood is as hip as anything this side of Manchester or London. A look at one of the alternative newspapers or magazines freely distributed around town can connect you with the city's constantly changing nightlife scene.

ESSENTIALS

GETTING THERE   The best rail connection is via Lincoln, from which 28 trains arrive Monday to Saturday and about eight trains on Sunday. The trip takes about 45 minutes. Trains also leave from London's St. Pancras Station; the trip takes about 2½ hours. For information, call © **0845/748-4950** or visit **www.nationalrail. co.uk**.

Buses from London arrive at the rate of about 10 per day. For schedules and information, call © **08717/818181** or visit **www.nationalexpress.com**.

If you're driving from London, the M1 motorway runs to a few miles west of Nottingham. Feeder roads, including the A453, are well marked for the short distance into town. The drive takes about 3 to 3½ hours.

VISITOR INFORMATION   Information is available at the **Nottingham Tourism Centre,** 1–4 Smithy Row (© **08444/775678;** www.visitnottingham.com). It's open Monday to Friday 9am to 5:30pm, Saturday 9am to 5pm, and Sunday 10am to 4pm.

SPECIAL EVENTS   Nottingham still gets a lot of reflected glory from its association with Robin Hood and his gang. The **Robin Hood Festival** (© **01623/823202;** www.nottinghamshire.gov.uk/robinhoodfestival) is a family-friendly, mock-medieval festival scheduled for the first week in August every year. Diversions include food and souvenir stands, jousting and falconry exhibitions, maypole dances, crowd-pleasing jesters juggling their way through crowds, and lots of medieval costume.

WHERE TO STAY

Hart's Hotel ★   Nestled high on the ramparts of Nottingham Castle, this is a secluded and tranquil hotel, though located more or less within the city center. No other hotel in town offers such panoramic views. Although known for its restaurant (see below), it is also a lovely place at which to spend the night. Hart's offers midsize to spacious bedrooms, each furnished in a modern style with plenty of amenities. The staff is the most helpful in town, arranging everything from admission to a nearby health club to tickets to the theater.

Standard Hill, Park Row, Nottingham, Nottinghamshire NG1 6GN. © **0115/9881900.** www.harts nottingham.co.uk. 30 units. £120–£170 double; £260 suite. AE, MC, V. Parking £8. **Amenities:** Restaurant; bar; room service. *In room:* TV, minibar, Wi-Fi (£5 per day).

Lace Market Hotel ★ 📖 Opposite the Galleries of Justice, this is a boutique hotel—unusual for Nottingham—and an alternative choice for those who shun tired chain hotels for commercial travelers. In the old Lace Market district, it is a restored town house with its original architecture intact. Personal service is provided for the modernized and rather elegant bedrooms, furnished with hypoallergenic bedding and deluxe toiletries. Rooms differ in size, including studios, which are split-level and open onto views. On-site is one of the town's best restaurants, Merchants.

29–31 High Pavement, Nottingham, Nottinghamshire NG1 1HE. ⓒ **0115/8523232.** Fax 0115/8523223. www.lacemarkethotel.co.uk. 42 units. £109–£229 double; £199–£249 suite. AE, MC, V. Parking £8. **Amenities:** Restaurant; gastropub; bar; access to nearby health club; room service. *In room:* TV, Wi-Fi (free).

Park Inn Nottingham ☺ If you're driving, you'll appreciate this chain hotel's easy access from the A60 highway and its location less than 1.5km (1 mile) north of the city center. It was built in 1968 as a modern alternative to the town's B&Bs. The rooms are standardized but well maintained; most contain twin beds. Thirty of the bedrooms are suitable for families.

296 Mansfield Rd., Nottingham, Nottinghamshire NG5 2BT. ⓒ **888/285-9260** or 01159/359988. Fax 01159/924-5227. www.nottingham.parkinn.co.uk. 172 units. £81 double; £120 suite. Rates include breakfast. AE, DC, MC, V. Free parking. **Amenities:** Restaurant; bar; health club; Jacuzzi; indoor heated pool; room service; sauna; spa; steam room. *In room:* TV, hair dryer, Wi-Fi (£12 per day).

Strathdon Hotel This is a solid and unpretentious member of Peel Hotels, a nationwide chain. Built in the 1970s of gray-colored brick in the heart of town, it has seven floors, neutral public areas, and two bars. The nondescript bedrooms are equipped to a high standard, evocative of a first-class roadside motel.

44 Derby Rd., Nottingham, Nottinghamshire NG1 5FT. ⓒ **01159/418501.** Fax 01159/483725. www.peelhotels.co.uk. 68 units. £88–£112 double. AE, DC, MC, V. Free parking. **Amenities:** 2 restaurants; 2 bars; room service. *In room:* TV, hair dryer, Wi-Fi (free).

WHERE TO DINE

Hart's Restaurant ★★ MODERN ENGLISH Hart's lays claim to the best dining in the historic central core of the city, just off the main street. The location near Nottingham Castle couldn't be more convenient. A lovely interior for dining has been created in what was once part of Nottingham's general hospital. Today, it invites with its wooden floors, beautifully set tables, and abstract modern paintings on the walls. The cooking technique here is sharp and precise, culminating in a harmonious blend of flavors created from market-fresh ingredients. Excellent appetizers include the likes of leek-and-potato soup with Indian-spiced cod, followed by such well-crafted main courses as loin of venison (served pink) with peppered pineapple and braised endive, pan-fried wild sea bass with poached clams and mussels, or Gressingham duck breast with a red-onion tart.

In Hart's Hotel, 1 Standard Court, Park Row. ⓒ **0115/9110666.** www.hartsnottingham.co.uk. Main courses £15–£23; set lunch Mon–Sat £14–£17, Sun £22; set dinner £25. AE, MC, V. Daily noon–2pm and 7–9:30pm (until 9pm Sun).

Restaurant Sat Bains ★★★ CONTINENTAL The finest cuisine in the former gastronomic wasteland of Nottingham is served in this dining room installed in a hotel at the end of a quiet lane, home to a number of low-slung Victorian houses near the River Trent. The setting is elegant, with stone floors, classy black-and-white photographs, and low ceilings. The chef, Sat Bains, continues to polish his classic repertoire by using rigorous, precise cooking techniques and flawless ingredients. He's known for his intriguing "marriages" of flavors, such as roast scallops with braised oxtail or Dover sole with Hereford snails. One of our favorite dishes is poached and roasted wild duck accompanied by beans and hazelnuts with a Banyuls sauce.

Lenton Lane. 𝄾 **0115/986-6566.** www.restaurantsatbains.com. Reservations required. Fixed-price dinner £55–£150. AE, DC, MC, V. Tues–Sat 7–9:30pm. Coming into Nottingham, take the 3rd exit sign-posted BOOTS INDUSTRIAL ESTATE WEST (Thane Rd.). Then take a very sharp left onto Lenton Lane, which you follow for 450m (1,500 ft.) until you reach the restaurant.

EXPLORING THE AREA

Put on your most comfortable shoes and prepare to tackle the more than 800 shops in and around town—Nottingham boasts some of England's best shopping. Start in the city center, with its maze of pedestrian streets, and work your way out toward the two grand indoor shopping malls, the **Victoria** and the **Broad Marsh,** located to the north and to the south of the center of town. Then head over to **Derby Road** for your fill of antiques.

Fine Nottingham lace can be found in the **Lace Centre,** Castle Road, across the street from Nottingham Castle (𝄾 **01159/413539;** www.lacemarketproperties.co.uk), or in the shops around the area known as the **Lace Market,** along High Pavement.

To catch up on the hippest and latest in fashion and furnishing trends, explore the many boutiques in the **Hockley** area, the **Exchange Arcade,** and the **Flying Horse Mall,** all in the city center.

Patchings Farm Art Centre, Oxton Road, near Calverton (𝄾 **01159/653479;** www.patchingsartcentre.co.uk), is a 24-hectare (60-acre) art haven. Restored farm buildings house three galleries, working art and pottery studios, a gift shop, and art and framing shops.

Long known as Britain's first real crafts center, **Longdale Craft Centre,** Long-dale Lane, Ravenshead (𝄾 **01623/794858;** www.longdale.co.uk), is a labyrinth of re-created Victorian streets where professional craftspeople work on a range of items, including jewelry, pottery, and prints.

Newstead Abbey ★   Lord Byron once made his home at Newstead Abbey, one of eight museums administered by the city of Nottingham. Some of the original Augustinian priory, purchased by Sir John Byron in 1540, still survives. In the 19th century, the mansion was given a neo-Gothic restoration. Mementos, including first editions and manuscripts, are displayed inside. You can explore the parkland of some 121 hectares (300 acres), with waterfalls, rose gardens, Monk's Stew Pond, and a Japanese water garden.

On A60 (Mansfield Rd.), 19km (12 miles) north of Nottingham center, in Ravenshead. 𝄾 **01623/455900.** www.newsteadabbey.org.uk. Admission to house and grounds £7 adults, £4.50 students and seniors, £3 children; gardens only £3.50 adults, £3 students and seniors, £2 children. House Apr–Sept daily noon–5pm; gardens year-round daily 9am–dusk.

Nottingham Castle Museum and Art Gallery ★   Overlooking the city, Nottingham Castle was built in 1679 by the duke of Newcastle on the site of an old Norman fortress. After restoration in 1878, it opened as a provincial museum surrounded by a charmingly arranged garden. Of particular note is the History of Nottingham Gallery, re-creating the legends associated with the city, plus a rare collection of ceramics and a unique exhibition of medieval alabaster carvings, which were executed between 1350 and 1530. These delicately detailed scenes illustrate the life of Christ, the Virgin Mother, and various saints. The painting collection covers several periods but is strong on 16th-century Italian, 17th-century French and Dutch, and the richest English paintings of the past 2 centuries.

The only surviving element of the original Norman castle is a subterranean passage called Mortimer's Hole. The passage leads to **Ye Olde Trip to Jerusalem,** 1 Brewhouse Yard, at Castle Road (℗ **01159/473171;** www.triptojerusalem.com), dating from 1189 and said to be the oldest inn in England (it's now a pub and restaurant). King Edward III is said to have led a band of noblemen through these secret passages, surprising Roger Mortimer and his queen, killing Mortimer and putting his lady in prison. A statue of Robin Hood stands at the base of the castle.

Castle Rd. ℗ **01159/153700.** www.nottinghamcity.gov.uk/index.aspx?articleid=1036. Admission Sat-Sun £5.50 adults, £4 children and seniors, £15 family ticket. Mar-Oct daily 10am-5pm (last admission 4:30pm); Nov-Feb daily 10am-4pm (last admission 3:30pm).

Wollaton Hall ★   This well-preserved Elizabethan mansion, finished in 1588, is the most ornate in England and a tourist-drawing attraction itself. Today, it houses a natural history museum with lots of insects, invertebrates, British mammals, birds, reptiles, amphibians, and fish. See the camellia house, with the world's earliest cast-iron front dating from 1823. The bird dioramas here are among the best in Britain. The hall is surrounded by a deer park and garden.

In Wollaton Park, 5km (3 miles) southwest of Nottingham center. ℗ **01159/153900.** www.wollatonhall. org.uk. Free admission. Parking £ 2. Mar-Oct daily 11am-5pm; Nov-Feb daily 11am-4pm. Drive southwest along A609 (Ilkeston Rd.), which will become Wollaton Rd.

Sherwood Forest ★★

Second only to Germany's Schwarzwald in European lore and legend, **Sherwood Forest** comprises 182 hectares (450 acres) of oak and silver birch trees owned and strictly protected by a local entity, the Thoresby Estate, and maintained by the county of Nottinghamshire. Actually, very little of this area was forest even when it provided cover for Robin Hood, Friar Tuck, and Little John.

Robin Hood, the folk hero of tale and ballad, fired the imagination of a hardworking, impoverished English people, who particularly liked his adopted slogan: "Take from the rich and give to the poor."

Celebrating their freedom in verdant Sherwood Forest, Robin Hood's eternally youthful band rejoiced in "hearing the twang of the bow of yew and in watching the gray goose shaft as it cleaves the glistening willow wand or brings down the king's proud buck." Life was one long picnic beneath the splendid oaks of a primeval forest, with plenty of ale and flavorful venison poached from the forests of an oppressive king. The clever rebellion Robin Hood waged against authority (represented by the haughty, despotic, and overfed sheriff of Nottingham) was full of heroic exploits and a desire to win justice for victims of oppression.

Now, as then, the forest consists of woodland glades, farm fields, villages, and hamlets. But the surroundings are so built up that Robin Hood wouldn't recognize them today.

The **Sherwood Forest Visitor Centre** (℗ **01623/823202;** www.nottinghamshire. gov.uk) is in Sherwood Forest Country Park, part of the Sherwood Forest National Nature Reserve, at Edwinstowe, 29km (22 miles) north of Nottingham off the A614, or 13km (8 miles) east of Mansfield on the B6034. It stands near the Major Oak, popularly known as Robin Hood's tree, although analysis of its bark reveals that it wasn't around in the 13th century. Many marked walks and footpaths lead from the visitor center through the woodland. There's an exhibition of life-size models of Robin and the other well-known outlaws, as well as two shops (with books, gifts, and souvenirs) and the **Forest Table Restaurant,** with cafeteria service and meals emphasizing traditional English country recipes. The center provides as much information as is known about the Merry Men and Maid Marian, whom Robin Hood is believed to have married at Edwinstowe Church near the visitor center. Little John's grave is at Hathersage 58km (36 miles) away, and Will Scarlet's grave is at Blidworth (15km/9½ miles away). ***Note:*** Plans for a new visitor center are underway, with construction beginning in spring 2011. Check the website for the latest details.

Hours for the country park are from dawn to dusk. The visitor center is open in summer, daily from 11am to 4pm, and in winter, Saturday and Sunday from 11am to 4pm. A year-round program of events is presented, mainly on weekends and during national and school holiday periods. Parking costs £3 per day on weekends and bank holidays from April to early December, as well as daily during school summer vacation.

In the northernmost part of Sherwood Forest, **Clumber Park,** a 1,537-hectare (3,800-acre) tract of park and woodland maintained by National Trust authorities, is favored by local families for picnics and strolls. It contains a 32-hectare (80-acre) lake at its center, a monumental promenade flanked with venerable lime (linden) trees, and the Gothic Revival **Clumber Chapel.** Built between 1886 and 1889 as a site of worship for the private use of the seventh duke of Newcastle, the chapel is open early March to mid-January, daily 10am to 4pm. The park itself is open year-round during daylight hours, though its allure and services are at their lowest ebb during November and December. The gift shop and tearoom are open daily in summer 10am to 5pm (until 4pm in the off-season). Admission to the park, including the chapel, ranges from £5 to £8, depending on your vehicle.

If you're specifically interested in botany and plant life, head for the park's **Conservation Centre,** a walled garden with extensive greenhouses, open daily from April to October. For information about the park and its features, contact the **Clumber Park Estate Office,** Worksop, Nottinghamshire S80 3AZ (ⓒ **01909/544917;** www.nationaltrust.org.uk).

LINCOLN ★★

225km (140 miles) N of London; 151km (94 miles) NW of Cambridge; 132km (82 miles) SE of York

The ancient city of Lincoln was the site of a Bronze Age settlement, and later, in the 3rd century, one of four provincial capitals of Roman Britain. In the Middle Ages, it was the center of Lindsey, a famous Anglo-Saxon kingdom. After the Norman Conquest, it grew increasingly important, known for its cathedral and castle. Its merchants grew rich by shipping wool directly to Flanders.

Much of the past remains in Lincoln today to delight visitors who wander past half-timbered Tudor houses, the Norman castle, and the towering Lincoln Cathedral. Medieval streets climbing the hillsides and cobblestones re-create the past. Lincoln, unlike other East Midlands towns such as Nottingham and Leicester,

SCOTLAND

North
Sea

Irish
Sea

Lincoln

WALES ENGLAND

London

English Channel

ATTRACTIONS ●

Lincoln Castle **5**
Lincoln Cathedral **8**
Lincoln Medieval
    Bishops' Palace **9**
Museum of Lincolnshire Life **1**
Usher Gallery **11**

ACCOMMODATIONS ■

Bailhouse Hotel & Mews **3**
Castle Hotel **2**
Hillcrest Hotel **12**
Lincoln Hotel **7**
White Hart Hotel **4**

DINING ◆

Jews House Restaurant **10**
Wig & Mitre **6**

Church ✝   Information ⓘ   Post Office ✉

maintains somewhat of a country-town atmosphere, but it also extends welcoming arms to tourists, the mainstay of its economy.

Essentials

GETTING THERE   Trains arrive every hour during the day from London's Kings Cross Station, a 2-hour trip usually requiring a change of train at Newark. Trains also arrive from Cambridge, again requiring a change at Newark. For schedules and information, call ⓒ **0845/748-4950** or visit **www.nationalrail.co.uk**.

National Express buses from London's Victoria Coach Station service Lincoln, a 4-hour ride. For schedules and information, call ⓒ **08717/818181** or visit

www.nationalexpress.com. Once in Lincoln, local and regional buses service the county from the City Bus Station, off St. Mary's Street, opposite the train station.

If you're driving from London, take the M1 north to the junction with the A57; then head east to Lincoln.

VISITOR INFORMATION The **Tourist Information Centre** is at 9 Castle Hill (© **01522/545458**; www.visitnottingham.com). It's open Monday to Friday 9am to 5:30pm, Saturday 9am to 5pm, and Sunday 10am to 4pm.

Where to Stay

Bailhouse Hotel & Mews ★★ Arguably, this is the best little guesthouse in Lincoln, and it's in the very heart of town, near the castle and cathedral. It's really like a boutique hotel with a long history (ca. 1350), originally built as a medieval hall with a beamed roof and low walls that are still preserved in one of the bedrooms. Over the years, it has been substantially changed; it was a tavern for much of its life under various names such as the Blue Bell and the Falcon. When new owners took over the building, closed since 1999, they set about restoring it and preserving many of its original features. The spacious bedrooms have been decorated tastefully and comfortably, each with a view of the castle. The most dramatic rooms have luxurious four-poster beds.

34 Bailgate, Lincoln, Lincolnshire LN1 3AP. © **01522/541000.** Fax 0871/8724396. www.bailhouse.co.uk. 10 units. £99–£119 double; £149–£195 suite. MC, V. Free parking. **Amenities:** Lounge; outdoor pool. *In room:* TV, Wi-Fi (free).

Castle Hotel This redbrick, three-story, traditional English hotel is situated in old Lincoln. It has been carefully converted from what was the North District National School, dating from 1858. It boasts splendid views of the castle and cathedral, which are both just a 3-minute walk away. The bedrooms have been individually decorated—one has a four-poster bed—and all are named after British castles.

Westgate, Lincoln, Lincolnshire LN1 3AS. © **01522/538801.** Fax 01522/575457. www.castlehotel.net. 20 units. £94–£105 double; £115 suite. Rates include English breakfast. AE, DC, MC, V. Free parking. No children 7 and under. **Amenities:** Restaurant; bar; room service. *In room:* TV, hair dryer, minibar.

Hillcrest Hotel 🍴 This is a fine redbrick house, built in 1871 as the private home of a local vicar. Though converted into a small but comfortable licensed hotel, it retains many of its original features. It's on a quiet, tree-lined road overlooking 10 hectares (25 acres) of parkland, in the old high town and within easy walking distance of Lincoln Cathedral and the Roman remains. The bedrooms are well furnished and kept in shape; some units have four-poster beds. Nearly all open onto a view.

15 Lindum Terrace, Lincoln, Lincolnshire LN2 5RT. © **01522/510182.** Fax 01522/538009. www.hillcresthotel.com. 14 units. £93–£105 double. Children age 1 and younger stay free with 2 paying adults; ages 2–13 £7 per night; ages 14–18 £17 per night. Rates include English breakfast. AE, DC, MC, V. Free parking. From Wragby Rd., connect with Upper Lindum St.; continue to the bottom of this street, make a left onto Lindum Terrace, and the hotel is 180m (600 ft.) along on the right. **Amenities:** Restaurant; bar; babysitting; room service. *In room:* TV, hair dryer, Wi-Fi (free).

Lincoln Hotel Although lacking the charm of the White Hart (see below), the Lincoln is still one of the town's leading hotels. When workmen were digging the foundations here in the mid-1960s, they discovered remnants of the north tower of the East Gate of the Roman city wall, a preserved part of which is included in the hotel's rear garden. The hotel faces Lincoln Cathedral and is attached to a Victorian mansion (now the Eastgate Bar). The recently refurbished bedrooms are nicely decorated and comfortable.

Eastgate, Lincoln, Lincolnshire LN2 1PN. ✆ **01522/520348.** Fax 01522/510780. www.thelincolnhotel. com. 72 units. Mon–Thurs £105–£135 double; Fri–Sun £95–£125 double. Rates include continental breakfast. AE, DC, MC, V. Free parking. **Amenities:** Restaurant; bar; room service; spa. *In room:* TV, hair dryer.

White Hart Hotel ★★ The White Hart is named after the emblem of Richard II. The inn's facade dates from the 1700s, when it was a luxurious private home. Its life as a modern hotel began in 1913, when the live-in owners started accepting paying guests. The hotel also hosted several meetings between Churchill and Eisenhower in the darkest days of World War II. Today, the inn is still the best choice in town. You enter through a revolving mahogany door into a large and finely proportioned lounge filled with fine antiques. Each of the accommodations has some antique furniture and views of the old city. Try for a room in the older structure, where the units are more spacious and stylish than those in the lackluster annex.

Bailgate, Lincoln, Lincolnshire LN1 3AR. ✆ **01522/526222.** Fax 01522/531798. www.whitehart-lincoln. co.uk. 48 units. £110–£130 double; £155–£165 suite. 2-night minimum Sat–Sun. AE, MC, V. Free parking. Located .5km (¼ mile) from Lincoln Station. **Amenities:** Restaurant; bar; room service. *In room:* TV, hair dryer, Internet (£10 per day).

Where to Dine

Jews House Restaurant ★ CONTINENTAL Constructed around 1150, this stone-fronted building is said to be the oldest occupied house in Europe. Today, it offers the finest food in Lincoln. The dining room has a low-beamed ceiling, a cast-iron fireplace, and medieval features. Two of the massive ceiling beams date from the construction of the original house. Seating about 28 diners, the menu features stylish dishes that change every month according to market ingredients and the inspiration of the chef—perhaps roast rack of Cornish lamb with a stew of chickpeas, chorizo, and sweet peppers, or filet of cod baked with mussels and served with a mousse of basil and Parmesan. The savory dishes are prepared in a modern style without heavy saucing. *Note:* At press time, the restaurant was closed due to fire. Call ahead to find out if it has reopened at the time of your visit.

15 The Strait. ✆ **01522/524851.** www.jewshouserestaurant.co.uk. Reservations recommended. Main courses £8–£13; fixed-price 5-course dinner £75. DC, MC, V. Wed–Sat noon–2:30pm; Tues–Sat 7–9pm.

Wig & Mitre ★ ▮ INTERNATIONAL This is not only the best pub in old Lincoln, but it also serves good food. Sitting on the aptly named Steep Hill near the cathedral and loaded with an Old English atmosphere, Wig & Mitre operates somewhat like a pub/brasserie. The main restaurant, behind the bar on the second floor, has oak timbers, Victorian armchairs, and settees. If the restaurant is full, you can dine in the bar downstairs. The eager-to-please staff will tempt you with such dishes as pan-fried pork cutlet, braised beef on caramelized baby onions, roast filet of halibut with wild mushrooms, and an Aberdeen Angus filet steak with anchovy butter.

30–32 Steep Hill. ✆ **01522/535190.** www.wigandmitre.com. Reservations recommended. Main courses £10–£25; lunch items £7–£13; fixed-price 3-course menu £15 (noon–6pm). AE, DC, MC, V. Daily 8am–11pm.

Favorite Local Pubs

In addition to the **Wig & Mitre** (see above), drop by the **Adam & Eve Tavern,** 25 Lindum Rd. (✆ **01522/537108**), the oldest pub in Lincoln, dating from 1701. You can knock back a Magnet, Old Speckled Hen, or Theakston's Best Bitter in a homey cottage atmosphere complete with gas fires or else outside in the large front garden in warm weather.

The **Jolly Brewer,** 27 Broadgate (*©* **01978/261884;** www.thejollybrewer. co.uk), dates from 1850, and it's a basic wooden-floorboards place where you'll be welcomed into a friendly crowd. If you're hungry, there's pub grub at lunchtime only, and draft ales include Tiger Bitter and Robinson's, as well as rotating guests.

Exploring the City

The best lanes for strolling are those tumbling down the appropriately named Steep Hill to the Witham River.

The cathedral is a good starting point for your shopping tour of Lincoln, as the streets leading down the hill are lined with a mélange of interesting stores (and you won't be working against gravity this way). Wander in and out of these historic lanes, down Steep Hill, along Bailgate, around the Stonebow gateway and Guildhall, and then down High Street. Following this route, you'll find all sorts of clothing, books, antiques, arts and crafts, and gift items.

While walking down Steep Hill, stop in the **Harding House Gallery,** 53 Steep Hill (*©* **01522/523537;** www.hardinghousegallery.co.uk), to see some of the best local crafts: ceramics, teddy bears, textiles, wood, metal sculptures, and jewelry.

Lincoln Castle   A short walk from the cathedral, this 900-year-old fortress was once one of the most powerful strongholds in medieval England. Lincoln Castle dates from the time of William the Conqueror in 1068, though nothing remains of his original fortress. On one of the mounds where the original castle stood is the Lucy Tower, dating from the late 12th century. The East Gate also dates from the 12th century. The castle came under siege in the wars of 1135 to 1154 and again in 1216 to 1217. During the 19th century, it functioned as a prison. You can see the prison chapel with its self-locking cubicles; these cages kept prisoners from seeing one another. Inside the exhibition rooms, one of only four surviving copies of the Magna Carta is on display. Much of the appeal of a visit here involves walking along the top of the wall that surrounds the fortress, overlooking the castle's grassy court-yard, the city of Lincoln, and its cathedral.

© **01522/511068.** www.lincolnshire.gov.uk/lincolncastle. Admission £4 adults; £2.10 seniors, students, and children 15 and younger; £9.30 family ticket. Apr–Sept Mon–Sat 10am–5pm, Sun 11am–5:30pm; Oct–Mar Mon–Sat 10am–4pm.

Lincoln Cathedral ★★★   No other English cathedral dominates its surround-ings as does Lincoln's. Visible from up to 48km (30 miles) away, the central tower is 81m (271 ft.) high, which makes it the second tallest in England. The central tower once carried a huge spire, which, before heavy gale damage in 1549, made it the tallest in the world at 158m (525 ft.).

Construction on the original Norman cathedral was begun in 1072, and it was consecrated 20 years later. It sustained a major fire and, in 1185, an earthquake. Only the central portion of the West Front and lower halves of the western towers survive from this period.

The present cathedral is Gothic in style, particularly the Early English and Deco-rated periods. The nave is 13th century, but the black font of Tournai marble origi-nates from the 12th century. In the Great North Transept is a rose medallion window known as the Dean's Eye. Opposite it, in the Great South Transept, is its cousin, the Bishop's Eye. East of the high altar is the Angel Choir, consecrated in 1280, and so called after the sculpted angels high on the walls. The exquisite wood-carving in St. Hugh's Choir dates from the 14th century. Lincoln's roof bosses, dating from the 13th and 14th centuries, are handsome, and a mirror trolley assists visitors in their appreciation of these features, which are some 21m (70 ft.) above the floor. Oak bosses are in the cloister.

In the Seamen's Chapel (Great North Transept) is a window commemorating Lincolnshire-born Captain John Smith, one of the pioneers of early settlement in America and the first governor of Virginia. The library and north walk of the cloister were built in 1674 to designs by Sir Christopher Wren. In the Treasury is fine silver plate from the churches of the diocese.

C **01522/561600.** www.lincolncathedral.com. Admission £5 adults, £3.75 seniors and students, £1 children 5–16, free for children 4 and younger. June–Aug Mon–Fri 7:15am–8pm, Sat–Sun 7:15am–6pm; Sept–May Mon–Sat 7:15am–6pm, Sun 7:15am–5pm.

Lincoln Medieval Bishops' Palace   On the south side of the cathedral, this site was the headquarters of the biggest diocese in England during the Middle Ages. Launched in 1150, it held great power until it was sacked during the civil war in the 1640s. Allowed to ruin over the centuries, it has been opened to the public. Visitors can wander its grounds, taking in panoramic views of the city, and explore its ruins, including an intact entrance tower, a public hall, and a vaulted undercroft.

Minster Yard. *C* **01522/527468.** www.english-heritage.org.uk. Admission £4.20 adults, £3.60 students and seniors, £2.10 children, £11 family ticket. Apr–June daily 10am–5pm; July–Aug daily 10am–6pm; Sept–Oct daily 10am–4pm; Nov–Mar Thurs–Mon 10am–4pm.

Museum of Lincolnshire Life   This is the largest museum of social history in the Midlands. Housed in what was originally built as an army barracks in 1857, it's a short walk north of the city center. Displays here range from a Victorian schoolroom to a collection of locally built steam engines.

Burton Rd. *C* **01522/528448.** www.lincolnshire.gov.uk. Free admission. Apr–Sept daily 10am–5pm; Oct–Mar Mon–Sat 10am–5pm. Closed Dec 24–25, Dec 31, and Jan 1.

Usher Gallery   Established in 1927 at the bequest of its founder, James Ward Usher (one of the city's prominent jewelers), the gallery is a repository for paintings and an impressive collection of antique clocks, 20th-century ceramics, and artifacts and literary mementos, plus portraits of Lincolnshire-born Alfred Lord Tennyson. Most impressive are the collection of 16th- to 19th-century miniatures and an exhibition of 17th-century Dutch and Italian paintings. Our favorites are the works of Peter de Wint (1784–1849), including his moving depiction of *Lincoln Cathedral.*

Lindum Rd. *C* **01522/527980.** www.culture24.org.uk/em000027 or www.thecollection.lincoln. museum. Free admission. Daily 10am–5pm.

THE NORTHWEST: MANCHESTER, LIVERPOOL & CHESTER

17

The great industrial shadow of the 19th century cast such darkness over England's Northwest that the area has been relatively neglected by visitors. Most Americans rush through, heading for the Lake District and Scotland. But in spite of its industry and bleak commercial area, the Northwest still has a lot to offer, including some beautiful countryside that remains unspoiled.

We will concentrate, however, on only three of its more important cities—**Manchester, Liverpool,** and **Chester**—plus a side trip to **Blackpool,** a huge Coney Island–style resort. You may want to visit it not so much for its beaches as for its kitschy, old-world appeal.

MANCHESTER: GATEWAY TO THE NORTH ★★

325km (202 miles) NW of London; 138km (86 miles) N of Birmingham; 56km (35 miles) E of Liverpool

One of the largest cities in England, Manchester is becoming increasingly important, as major airlines now fly here from North America, making the city a gateway to northern England. In recent years, Manchester has made great strides to shake its image as an industrial wasteland. Though chimneys still spike the skyline, they no longer make the metropolitan sky an ash-filled canopy. Abandoned warehouses are being renovated to provide sleek new loft apartments. Rustic factory equipment turns up in museums rather than piling up in salvage yards. Even the old Victorian architecture has been given a face-lift. The overall effect is a gritty kind of charm.

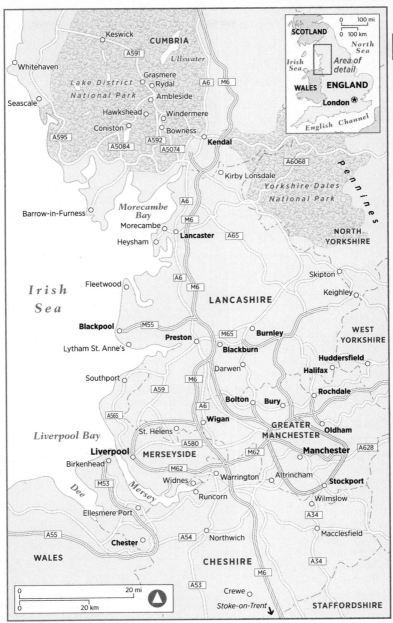

0 100 mi
0 100 km

SCOTLAND

North Sea

Irish Sea

Area of detail

WALES ENGLAND

London ✪

English Channel

Main map:

Whitehaven

Keswick

CUMBRIA

A591

Ullswater

Lake District National Park

Grasmere
Rydal

A6 M6

Seascale

Ambleside

Hawkshead

Windermere

Coniston

Bowness

A595

A5084

A592

Kendal

A5074

Kirby Lonsdale

A6068

Yorkshire Dales National Park

Pennines

Barrow-in-Furness

Morecambe Bay

A6

NORTH YORKSHIRE

Morecambe

M6

Heysham

Lancaster

A65

Irish Sea

Fleetwood

A6

M6

LANCASHIRE

Skipton

Keighley

Blackpool

M55

Preston

M65

Burnley

WEST YORKSHIRE

Lytham St. Anne's

Blackburn

Darwen

Huddersfield

Halifax

Southport

M6

A59

A6

Bolton

Bury

Rochdale

A565

Wigan

GREATER MANCHESTER

Oldham

Liverpool Bay

St. Helens

A580

Liverpool

MERSEYSIDE

M62

Manchester

A628

Birkenhead

M53

Dee

Mersey

Widnes

M62

Warrington

Altrincham

Stockport

Runcorn

Wilmslow

Ellesmere Port

A34

A55

Chester

A54

Northwich

Macclesfield

WALES

CHESTER

A34

M6

A53

Crewe

Stoke-on-Trent

STAFFORDSHIRE

0 20 mi
0 20 km

Manchester's roots date from A.D. 79, when the Romans settled here. It remained under Roman occupation until A.D. 410, when the empire began its fall. The city's west gate has since been reconstructed upon its original site.

In the mid–17th century, the city began to capitalize on the wealth of opportunity that the burgeoning textile industry offered. Manchester eventually became the Dickensian paradigm of the gritty industrial city. The railways were equally responsible for catapulting the city to the forefront of the industrial movement. England found Manchester both a convenient terminus and a refinement center through which raw goods became viable exports. Reminders from Manchester's storied role as a leader during the Industrial Revolution are literally everywhere. It is apt indeed that the **Museum of Science & Industry** (p. 597) resides here.

Many of the factory laborers were immigrants who flocked to the city for the promise of work. The atrocity of their conditions is well documented. But these immigrants had a profound effect on the city's culture. Today, Manchester's nearly 20,000 descendants of Chinese immigrants constitute England's highest Chinese population outside London. The Chinese residents have amalgamated their surroundings to fit their heritage. Falkner Street, particularly the monumental Imperial Chinese Archway, is brought to life by the murals, gardens, and vibrant decor that pay homage to the once-displaced working force.

The most recent stars of Manchester have been members of the Manchester United Football (that is, soccer) team, one of the most visible and successful in the world, with ardent legions of fans, and the rock group Oasis, best known in America for their album *(What's the Story) Morning Glory?* These rock stars haven't exactly done for Manchester what the Beatles did to put Liverpool on the map, but they certainly have made an impression. Of course, these self-styled "hard-drinking, groupie-shagging, drug-snorting geezers" make the Beatles seem like choirboys. As Manchester is increasingly cited for its hipness, Oasis, whose *Definitely Maybe* was the fastest-selling debut album in British history, helped make it so.

The once-dreary Manchester docklands, evoking a painting by local son L. S. Lowry, has a spiffy new life following a £200-million restoration. The complex, now called simply the **Lowry,** is filled with theaters, shops, galleries, and restaurants. A plaza provides space for up to 10,000 at outdoor performances.

Essentials

GETTING THERE

BY PLANE   More and more North Americans are flying directly to **Manchester International Airport** (☎ **08712/710-711;**   www.manchesterairport.co.uk), located 24km (15 miles) south of the town center, to begin their explorations of the United Kingdom.

British Airways (☎ **800/247-9297** in the U.S. and Canada, or 0844/493-0787; www.britishairways.com) has daily flights departing New York's JFK Airport for Manchester, a 7-hour journey. You can also fly nonstop from BA's many North American gateways to London, and from there take the almost shuttlelike service from either Gatwick or Heathrow airport to Manchester, a 50-minute flight.

American Airlines (☎ **800/433-7300** in the U.S. and Canada; www.aa.com) offers a daily nonstop flight to Manchester from Chicago's O'Hare. American also flies between Chicago and London's Heathrow Airport.

ATTRACTIONS ●
Bridgewater Hall 26
Lowry Galleries 21
Manchester Art Gallery 17
Manchester Cathedral 5
Manchester Jewish Museum 1
Manchester Museum 27
Manchester Town Hall 13
Museum of Science
   & Industry 20
Royal Exchange 6
Urbis 2
Whitworth Art Gallery 27

ACCOMMODATIONS ■
Castlefield Hotel 22
Hilton Manchester
   Deansgate 24
Hotel Ibis Manchester
   City Centre 19
Jurys Inn Manchester 25
Lowry Hotel 7
Malmaison Manchester 12
Manchester Marriott
   Victoria & Albert 15
Midland Hotel 16
The Ox 23

DINING ◆
Café Istanbul 9
Dimitri's 11
Lowry Restaurant 21
Market Restaurant 4
Mr. Thomas's
   Chop House 10
Olive Press 14
River Restaurant 7
TV 21 3
Yang Sing 18

BMI/British Midland (© 800/788-0555 in the U.S., or 020/8745-7321 in London; www.flybmi.com) flies from London's Heathrow to Manchester. It also has flights to Manchester from Chicago, Las Vegas, and some major cities in Canada, including Toronto.

Delta Air Lines (© 800/241-4141; www.delta.com) flies daily to Manchester from New York's JFK and from Atlanta.

US Airways (© 800/622-1015; www.usairways.com) flies once a day from Philadelphia to Manchester.

Virgin Atlantic (© 800/862-8621; www.virgin-atlantic.com) flies once a day from Orlando to Manchester.

Manchester is also served by flights from the Continent. For example, **Lufthansa** (© 800/645-3880; www.lufthansa.com) has frequent nonstop flights each week between Frankfurt and Manchester, depending on the season. Flight time is 1 hour and 45 minutes.

Trains connect the airport terminal to the Piccadilly Railway Station in the center of Manchester. These trains depart from the airport every 5 to 10 minutes for the 15- to 20-minute ride to the center. Direct rail lines link the airport to surrounding northern destinations such as Edinburgh, Liverpool, and Windermere.

Buses nos. 43 and 105 run between the airport and Piccadilly Gardens Bus Station every 15 minutes during the day, and hourly during the evening and on Sundays; the ride takes 55 minutes.

BY TRAIN Trains from London's Euston Station travel directly to Manchester; the trip takes 2½ to 3 hours. For information, call © 0845/748-4950 or go to **www.nationalrail.co.uk**.

BY BUS National Express (© 0871/781-8181; www.nationalexpress.com) operates buses that serve the Manchester region from London's Victoria Coach Station.

BY CAR If you're driving from London to Manchester, go north on the M1 and the M6. At Junction 21A, go east on the M62, which becomes the M602 as you enter Manchester. The trip from London to Manchester usually takes from 3 to 3½ hours, but it could be longer because of traffic and construction.

VISITOR INFORMATION

The **Manchester Visitor Information Centre,** Town Hall Extension, Lloyd Street (© 0871/222-8223; www.visitmanchester.com), is open Monday to Saturday 10am to 5:30pm, Sunday and bank holidays 10:30am to 4:30pm. To get here, take the Metrolink tram to St. Peter's Square. Especially useful is a series of four free pamphlets with information on accommodations, dining, city attractions, and cultural/entertainment options.

GETTING AROUND

It's not a good idea to try to hoof it in Manchester. It's better to take the bus and the Metrolink light rail. Timetables, routes, fare information, and a helpful leaflet called the *Passenger's Guide* are available from **Travelshop,** a general information booth within the Piccadilly Gardens Bus Station, Portland Street, open Monday to Saturday 7am to 6pm and Sunday 10am to 6pm. For information, call © 0161/205-2000.

Buses begin running within Manchester at 6am, operate in full force until 11pm, and then continue with limited routes until 3am. Tickets are sold at a kiosk at

Piccadilly Gardens Bus Station. A day pass, the **Wayfarer** (© **0161/205-2000**), costs £10 and is valid for a complete day of public bus travel.

Metrolink (© **0161/205-2000;** www.metrolink.co.uk) streetcars connect the bus stations and provide a useful north–south conduit. Self-service ticket machines dispense zone-based fares. The wheelchair-accessible streetcars operate Monday to Thursday from 6am to midnight, Friday and Saturday from 6am to 1am, and Sunday from 7am to 11pm.

Where to Stay

EXPENSIVE

Hilton Manchester Deansgate ★ The city's most visible and most avant-garde competitor to the also-recommended Lowry Hotel, the £150-million Hilton is housed within a reflective pencil-thin skyscraper, the Beetham Tower, which, at 47 stories and 171m (561 ft.), is the tallest residential building in Britain. "Why residential?" you might ask. It's because the lower 23 floors of the building are devoted to conventional hotel rooms and the infrastructure, while floors 24 to 47 are private condominiums. The hotel boasts a streamlined, somewhat startling design of public rooms that are spartan, minimalist, almost Zen-like in their artful simplicity. Some find it refreshing, others find it dehumanizing. But in any event, the skinny, soaring building is fast approaching—along with the Lowry Hotel and the Imperial War Museum North—status as an iconic symbol of the city itself.

303 Deansgate, Manchester M3 4LQ. © **0161/870-1600.** Fax 0161/870-1650. www.hilton.co.uk. 279 units. £84–£224 double; £256–£556 suite. AE, DC, MC, V. Parking £15. Metrolink: G-Mex or St. Peter's Sq. **Amenities:** Restaurant; 2 bars; exercise room; indoor pool; room service. *In room:* A/C, TV, hair dryer, minibar, Wi-Fi (in some; £15).

Lowry Hotel ★★★ 📷 Sexy and sinuous, the Lowry is the best hotel in the region. This government-rated five-star property (rare in this part of England) is part of the Chapel Wharf development. It rises on the banks of the River Irwell in a gentrified neighborhood of Salford, a sister city whose borders with Manchester grow blurred, and which is most often compared to New York's SoHo. The windows of the bedrooms open onto a distinctively modern footbridge linking this once blighted industrial zone to the heart of town. The steel-and-glass edifice exudes a sense of airy, spacious luxury living. Accommodations offer maximum comfort with deluxe yet minimalist furnishings and state-of-the-art marble-trimmed bathrooms. Many patrons visit just to sample the international cuisine of the hotel's River Restaurant (p. 592).

50 Dearmans Place, Chapel Wharf, Manchester M3 5LH. © **888/667-9477** or 0161/827-4000. Fax 0161/827-4001. www.thelowryhotel.com. 165 units. £385–£415 double; from £950 suite. AE, DC, MC, V. Parking £12. Metrolink: Victoria. **Amenities:** Restaurant; bar; exercise center; room service; sauna; spa; steam room. *In room:* TV, CD player (upon request), hair dryer, Internet (£15 per day), MP3 docking station.

Malmaison Manchester ★ This is one of the best examples in Manchester of combining old architectural features with the new. Behind an Edwardian facade, a dramatic and strikingly modern design reigns, enough of a statement that pop stars visiting from London often make it a point to stay here. In the heart of the city, only a minute's walk from Piccadilly Station, the individually designed and "modern-as-tomorrow" bedrooms await. These accommodations are striking, outfitted as they are in red, black, and ivory. Expect great big beds and very contemporary bathrooms with power showers. Some of the staff define the place by what it's not: "It's not baroque, it's not froufrou, and it's definitely not a Marriott," observed one of them.

Piccadilly, Manchester M1 3AQ. © **0161/278-1000.** Fax 0161/278-1002. www.malmaison-manchester. com. 167 units. £160–£190 double; from £215 suite. AE, DC, MC, V. Parking £14. Metrolink: Piccadilly Gardens. **Amenities:** Restaurant; bar; health club; sauna; spa; steam room. *In room:* TV, CD player, hair dryer, minibar, Wi-Fi (£10 per day).

Manchester Marriott Victoria & Albert Hotel ★★ 🎁

One of the most unusual hotels in Britain occupies a renovated brick-sided pair of warehouses, originally conceived in 1843 to store bales of cotton being barged along the nearby River Irwell and the Manchester Ship Canal to looms and mills throughout the Midlands. Before its present incarnation, it was owned by Granada TV as lodgings for its out-of-town media collaborators, but since its takeover by Marriott, it has become a bit more mainstream and more in keeping with the high-quality and comfortable standards of that well-respected chain. The guest rooms here drip with the authenticity and charm of the Victorian age. Each has exposed brick walls, massive ceiling beams, an individualized shape and themed decor, and, in many cases, the ornate cast-iron columns of its earlier warehouse manifestation.

Water St., Castlefield, Manchester M3 4JQ. © **800/228-9290** in U.S. and Canada, or 0161/832-1188. Fax 0161/834-2484. www.manchestermarriottva.co.uk. 148 units. £139–£174 double; from £214 suite. Rates include English breakfast. AE, DC, MC, V. Parking £14. Metrolink: G-Mex or St. Peter's Sq. **Amenities:** Restaurant; bar; exercise room; room service. *In room:* A/C, TV, hair dryer, Internet (£15), minibar.

Midland Hotel ★★★

One of the Northwest's most famous landmarks, this 1903 hotel is where Rolls first met Royce. In the heart of the city, the Midland has been restored to all its Edwardian splendor. Its major architectural features, including a vast open lobby, have been preserved. There is no better spot in Manchester to enjoy high tea than this old railway-station hotel. Guest rooms are large for the most part and decorated with wood furnishings, some in a dark purple. Atmospheric lighting, slender columns, polished marble floors, and etched glass panels bring back a bygone age, but all the modern gadgets have been installed as well. The on-site restaurant has been much improved, and still remains legendary for refusing entrance to the Beatles, who were turned away "for being inappropriately dressed."

Peter St., Manchester M60 2DS. © **0161/236-3333.** Fax 0161/932-4100. www.qhotels.co.uk. 298 units. £110–£310 double. AE, DC, MC, V. Parking £15. Metrolink: St. Peter's Sq. Bus: 3. **Amenities:** 2 restaurants; 2 bars; exercise room; indoor pool; room service. *In room:* TV, hair dryer, Wi-Fi (1st 2 hr. free, then £15).

MODERATE

Castlefield Hotel

Only minutes from the city center, this hotel lies in the historic Castlefield Canal Basin. All of the bedrooms are tastefully and comfortably decorated. They're small for the most part, but adequately equipped with such modern amenities as voicemail and beverage makers. For such a small hotel, Castlefield has a number of facilities, including a sports hall, gym, dance studio, indoor running track, and swimming pool. Prices are affordable, with many rooms at the lower end of the range (see below).

Liverpool Rd., Manchester M3 4JR. © **0161/832-7073.** Fax 0161/837-3534. www.castlefieldhotel.co.uk. 48 units. £69–£120 double. Rates include breakfast. AE, MC, V. Parking £8. Bus: 33. **Amenities:** Restaurant; bar; babysitting; concierge; exercise room; indoor pool; room service; spa. *In room:* A/C, TV, hair dryer, minibar, Wi-Fi (free).

Jurys Inn Manchester 🔑

Suitable for both commercial travelers and vacationers, this large chain hotel lies in the center of Manchester. It stands beside the Manchester Central Convention Complex, and many of the city's major attractions, including museums and galleries, lie within walking distance. Guest rooms are of the standard peas-in-a-pod variety, but they are well maintained and comfortable. The hotel is good value for the money in that the accommodations are large enough to house three adults or else two adults and two children. First-class meals in the main restaurant and delicious bar food in the pub are served here.

56 Great Bridgewater St., Manchester M1 5LE. ☎ **0161/953-8888.** Fax 0161/953-9090. www.manchester hotels.jurysinns.com. 265 units. £68–£145 double. AE, DC, MC, V. Parking £12. Metrolink: G-Mex. **Amenities:** Restaurant; bar; babysitting. *In room:* A/C, TV, hair dryer, Internet (£10).

INEXPENSIVE
Hotel Ibis Manchester City Centre   This budget chain doesn't promise more than what it is—a basic, motel-like room suitable for overnighting at an affordable price. In a modern building without soul, Ibis lies in the center of town near the Piccadilly train station. The location is convenient to a wide range of places to eat as well as some of the best pubs in Manchester. The bed is cozy, the bathroom is functional—and that's about it.

96 Portland St., Manchester M1 4GY. ☎ **0161/234-0600.** Fax 0161/234-0610. www.ibishotel.com. 127 units. £65–£75 double. MC, V. Parking £16. Metrolink: St. Peter's Sq. or Piccadilly Gardens. **Amenities:** Restaurant; bar. *In room:* A/C, TV, Wi-Fi (£10).

The Ox ⚑   This is what the British call a gastropub with rooms, meaning it offers excellent cuisine in its restaurant and guest rooms above, should you tie on a bender—or even if you don't. All accommodations have double or twin beds, are small to mid-size, and are comfortably if rather simply furnished, each with a private bathroom. In the heart of the city, the Ox offers an atmosphere that is cozy and inviting. We've crashed here a few times and found it to be one of the best bargains in town.

We're also fond of its restaurant, offering both vegetarian and Pacific Rim seafood dishes, along with a daily choice of specials. Locals pig out on the mixed grill with pork and leek sausage, rump steak, lamb chop, black pudding, smoked bacon, lamb kidneys and liver, and fried mushroom and grilled tomatoes. An individual meat pie is also a daily special.

71 Liverpool Rd., Castlefield, Manchester M3 4NQ. ☎ **0161/839-7760.** Fax 0161/839-7746. www.theox. co.uk. 10 units. £50–£65 double; £70–£80 triple. DC, MC, V. Parking £10. Metrolink: G-Mex. **Amenities:** Restaurant; bar. *In room:* TV.

Where to Dine

For some of the best-value meals in Manchester, patronize the **Ox** (see "Where to Stay," above).

EXPENSIVE
Market Restaurant ★ ENGLISH   Few other restaurants capitalize as success-fully on a sense of old-fashioned English nostalgia as this one. Set in the heart of town, it promotes itself with an allegiance to very fresh ingredients and a slightly dowdy but homelike decor that hasn't changed much since the beginning of World War II. About a third of the dishes are vegetarian. Main dishes you are likely to savor include Parmesan-crusted turkey breast with red-pepper relish or a smoked haddock pancake with a spicy cream sauce. A filet of beef comes wrapped in bacon and served in port-wine gravy with Stilton butter. A dessert delight is a chocolate pot with whipped Jersey cream and shortbread.

104 High St. ☎ **0161/834-3743.** www.market-restaurant.com. Reservations recommended. Main courses £14–£24. AE, DC, MC, V. Wed–Sat noon–2:30pm and 5:30–10pm. Metrolink: Shudehill.

River Restaurant ★★★ MODERN BRITISH/CONTINENTAL   This is the most stylish, sophisticated, and sought-after restaurant in the entire Manchester region, a culinary landmark that's on virtually everybody's list of "important" dining spots. Set one floor above lobby level of the also-recommended hotel, it's decorated in a flawlessly simple kind of postmodern minimalism, wherein a mostly white background acts as a foil for prisms of multicolored light and the superb cuisine of chef Eyck Zimmer. Great efforts are taken within the oft-changing menu to incorporate such local ingredients as Lancaster and Cheshire cheeses, cream, lamb, chicken, berries, vegetables, and fruit. What emerges from the kitchen evokes the best of Britain, as interpreted by some very savvy Continent-trained chefs and staff. Begin a meal here with pressed crabmeat served with mango, cucumber, and coriander oil, or perhaps the oyster ravioli with leeks. Main courses might include roast cod in a curry-flavored crust; a fricassee of lobster and scallops with herb-flavored gnocchi; lamb poached in olive oil with a purée of white beans; or a filet of Cheshire beef with garlic, snails, and horseradish-flavored mashed potatoes. Desserts evoke nostalgia for anyone who's ever read Charles Dickens: apple financier with clotted-cream ice cream, or an English custard tart with prunes and pear.

In the Lowry Hotel, 50 Dearmans Place, Chapel Wharf. ✆ **0161/827-4000.** www.thelowryhotel.com/dining or www.theriverrestaurant.com. Reservations recommended. Main courses £12–£40; set-price menus £20–£40. AE, DC, MC, V. Mon–Sat noon–2:30pm and 6–10:30pm; Sun 12:30–4pm and 7–10:30pm. Metrolink: Victoria.

Yang Sing ★ CANTONESE   Manchester's large population of Asian immigrants considers Yang Sing a favorite, as proven by the cacophony of languages spoken within its labyrinth of dining rooms. It's loud and spread out, but efficient with a fast turnover of tables and a big fan base that's partly due to its status as the largest and most visible Chinese restaurant in the region. The decor is inspired by colonial 1930s-era Shanghai. Delicate dim sum dumplings are served in a blissful array of choices from a pair of oversize carts in the dining room's center. Menu items cover the gamut of the Cantonese repertoire. Flavorful examples include stir-fried scallop with seasonal greens; sizzling filet of chicken in black-currant-and-blackberry sauce; braised duckling with a spicy bean casserole; and finely chopped loin of pork, stir-fried with French beans and preserved Chinese olive leaves.

34 Princess St. ✆ **0161/236-2200.** www.yang-sing.com. Reservations required. Main courses £11–£20; fixed-price menu £30 for 4 courses, £40–£45 for 5 courses. AE, MC, V. Mon–Thurs noon–11:45pm; Fri–Sat noon–12:15am; Sun 11:45am–10:45pm. Metrolink: St. Peter's Sq. or Piccadilly Gardens.

MODERATE

Café Istanbul TURKISH   Modern and appealing, with touches of exoticism that sometimes evoke an old Marlene Dietrich flick on the late, late show, this is the most savory spot in Manchester for Turkish cuisine. Decorated in a vague Mediterranean style, it draws a hip, young crowd, many who have traveled abroad and are in search of those flavors discovered on their travels. The selection of *meze* (appetizers) alone is worth the trek here, and the wine list is extensive but without price gouging. Try any of the lamb kabobs (the house specialty) or the grilled seafood.

79–81 Bridge St. ✆ **0161/833-9942.** www.cafeistanbul.co.uk. Reservations required. Main courses £10–£16. MC, V. Mon–Thurs noon–11pm; Fri–Sat 5:30–11:30pm; Sun 5:30–10pm. Metrolink: St. Peter's Sq. or Mosley St.

Lowry Restaurant ★ MODERN BRITISH   This citadel of good food is installed within an avant-garde, ultracontemporary setting in the Lowry Theatre (p. 598) in the Salford district, sometimes known as Manchester's restored dockland area. Ingredients are market fresh and served with flair by a well-trained staff. Most dishes are light and completely in step with the tenets of modern Continental cookery. Delights from the ever-changing menu include roasted pork with sage, apples, an onion tartlet, pumpkin purée, and red-wine jus; pan-fried duck breast with chestnut and parsley mash, blackberry, and pink-peppercorn jus; and Cheshire beef filet with roasted onions. The restaurant is open for dinner only when there is a theatrical performance.

Pier 8, Salford Quays. ✆ **0161/876-2121.** www.thelowry.com. Reservations recommended. Main lunch courses £6–£13; 2-course dinner £19, 3-course dinner £22. AE, DC, MC, V. Daily noon–3pm and 5–7pm (last order). Metrolink: Harbour City.

Mr. Thomas's Chop House TRADITIONAL ENGLISH   This mellow Manchester pub is also the city's oldest restaurant, established in 1872. Tall and thin, and bristling with history and a sense of Industrial Revolution nostalgia, it's the restaurant we most highly recommend for insights into the gritty cheerfulness and congenially battered charm of this region of England. The structure itself is a good example of the British Art Nouveau, and one of the first cast-iron buildings in Manchester. Under brown ceilings, within a decor that hasn't changed very much since 1901, guests dine at tables placed on the checkerboard floors. Real ales are very popular here, including Boddingtons and Timothy Taylor's. The most traditional British food served in the city center is offered here at lunch, with dishes such as steak-and-kidney pudding and braised oxtail with cabbage and dumplings. The pan-fried plaice with mushy peas is a local favorite, as is the French onion soup for a starter. Crabmeat risotto, corned beef hash cakes, fish pie, and venison and claret casserole are other always-reliable staples.

52 Cross St. ✆ **0161/832-2245.** http://tomsmanchester.thevictorianchophousecompany.com. Reservations not needed. Main courses £10–£25. AE, MC, V. Mon–Sat 11:30am–11pm; Sun noon–9pm. Metrolink: Mosley St.

Olive Press ☺ ITALIAN/PIZZA   This family favorite, a member of a small regional chain, is a good around-the-clock venue for rib-sticking Italian fare or a hot pizza from the brick oven. The pastas are handmade, and steaks and other meats are sizzling on the grill. Found right off Deansgate, the restaurant is suitable for a lunch while sightseeing in the heart of town or else for a pre-theater meal. A wide range of starters includes everything from a bowl of steamed mussels with white wine to the spicy lamb and bacon meatballs in a fresh tomato sauce. Well-stuffed sandwiches are a feature at lunch, or else you can savor one of the pastas, such as the chef's own version of lasagna. Mains feature everything from glazed cutlet of pork with honey to grilled beef with a wide selection of sauces. Pizzas are served with a vast array of toppings. Kids can order from the "Little Olives" menu.

4 Lloyd St. ✆ **0161/832-9090.** www.heathcotes.co.uk/olivepress. Reservations not needed. Main courses £12–£19; pizzas £6–£9. MC, V. Mon–Thurs 11:45am–10pm; Fri–Sat 11:45am–11pm; Sun noon–9pm. Metrolink: St. Peter's Sq.

INEXPENSIVE

Dimitri's GREEK   This bistro is a warm and friendly place in the city center. It's so popular, especially with a young crowd, that you should call a day in advance for a table. Greek delicacies are the way to go, though Spanish and Italian dishes, including tapas, are served nightly. Dimitri's also serves some of the best veggie dishes in Manchester. On weekends, sit at the bar with a savory blend of Greek coffee, and listen to a live jazz band.

1 Campfield Arcade. ☏ **0161/839-3319.** www.dimitris.co.uk. Reservations recommended. Main courses £4.85–£9. AE, MC, V. Daily 11am–midnight. Metrolink: G-Mex.

TV 21 AMERICAN   Don't come here expecting gastronomy, or even behavior that's particularly reverential or polite. It's one of the best examples of the artfully trashy, satirical hangouts, where cocktails are just as important (perhaps more so) than the platters of food that the clientele might eventually get around to ordering when they can't stave off their hunger pangs any longer. Best of all, the food is flavorful and cheap—a boon for 20-somethings looking for sociological insights and perhaps love and romance in Manchester. The decorative theme here is based on what the owners refer to as "trash TV." Menu items include sandwiches, quesadillas, spaghetti Bolognese, Thai-style curries with sticky rice, "cheeky chicken pie," sirloin steaks, lasagna, and burgers. Apple crumble and bread-and-butter pudding are uncharacteristically (for here) traditional desserts.

10 Thomas St. ☏ **0161/819-2221.** www.tv21manchester.com. Reservations not necessary. Sandwiches, salads, and platters £4.50–£7. MC, V. Sun–Tues noon–midnight; Wed–Thurs noon–1am; Fri–Sat noon–2am. Metrolink: Shudehill.

Seeing the Sights

Imperial War Museum North ★★

Usually identified as one of the most striking museums in the north of England, the Imperial War Museum North contains thousands of objects associated with 20th-century European wars, including tanks and armored motorized vehicles like your parents or grandparents drove if they were involved in the conflicts of World War II. These, set as they are into a multimedia hodgepodge of sound, light, and clips from old movies and documentaries, evoke the wrenching emotions of a world at war. Easily as interesting as the exhibits inside is the steel, concrete, and glass shell, designed by architect Daniel Libeskind, whose shape evokes a globe wrenched to pieces by international conflict. Inside, floors slope and walls careen at dizzying angles to evoke a world gone psychotic. Special exhibitions commemorate, among others, the Falklands War and other global conflicts in which Britain played a role. You'll find the place about 3.2km (2 miles) southwest of Manchester's city center, within a grimy industrial landscape crisscrossed with canals, waterways, and weirdly evocative relics of the Industrial Revolution.

The Quays, Trafford Wharf Rd., Trafford Park. ☏ **0161/836-4000.** http://north.iwm.org.uk. Free admission. Mar–Oct daily 10am–6pm; Nov–Feb daily 10am–5pm. Metrolink: Harbour City. Bus: 250.

Lowry Galleries ★

At the Lowry Galleries in the restored docklands area, the industrial city landscapes of the artist L. S. Lowry (1887–1976) are showcased as never before, within a hypermodern arts and entertainment center that in some ways symbolizes the emergence of Manchester itself as a centerpiece of avant-garde architecture. Lowry (the artist, not to be confused with the galleries, the hotel, or the theater that bears his name) depicted the horror of the England's industrial north, before it disappeared forever. His matchstick people are dwarfed by the smokestacks and viaducts in his paintings. Those paintings, as seen here, imposed a vision of a grim and gloomy urban sprawl, but he found a cohesion and lyric beauty in the industrial landscape. He was especially fond of depicting the crudeness of capitalism, forcing workers into boxlike row houses, as railroads nearby rattled across viaducts belching smoke. His best-known paintings are from 1905 to 1925.

The Lowry, Pier 8, Salford Quays. ℰ **0843/208-6000.** www.thelowry.com. Free admission. Sun–Fri 11am–5pm; Sat 10am–5pm. Metrolink: Harbour City. Bus: 25, 27, 33, 51, 52, 71, or 73.

Manchester Art Gallery ★★   Designed by Sir Charles Barry, this gallery has been a landmark since 1882. Following an extensive expansion and rejuvenation, it is now the proud owner of one of the best and most prestigious art collections in the north of England. Literally doubled in size, the gallery displays works that are wide-ranging—from the pre-Raphaelites to old Dutch masters, from the land- and sea-scapes of Turner to Lowry's industrial panoramas. Today's fine collection is also noted for its paintings by Ford Madox Brown and Holman Hunt. The decorative art is one of the finest collections outside London, especially the 17th- and 18th-century pieces, metalwork, and porcelain. The silver, in particular the Assheton Bennett collection, is especially distinguished.

If you're here between Easter and September, consider a visit to **Heaton Hall** (ℰ **0161/773-1231;** www.manchestergalleries.org), the museum's annex, 6.5km (4 miles) to the east. It's the centerpiece of 263 hectares (650 acres) of rolling parkland and accessible via the Metrolink tram (get off at Heaton Park). Built of York stone in 1772 and filled with furniture and decorative art of the 18th and 19th centuries, it is open from Easter to September, generally Thursday through Sunday from 11am to 5:30pm (call ahead to confirm hours).

Mosley St., at Princess St. ℰ **0161/235-8888.** www.manchestergalleries.org. Free admission. Tues–Sun 10am–5pm. Metrolink: St. Peter's Sq. or Mosley St. Bus 11, 16, 42, or 47.

Manchester Cathedral ★   Manchester started out as a small medieval parish in 1421 and continued to grow and expand its borders. In 1847, it was a big, bustling city, and it achieved cathedral status with the creation of a new diocese. The cathedral's nave, the widest of its kind in Britain, is formed by six bays, as is the choir. The choir stalls are beautifully carved and date from the early 16th century. The carvings depict a humorous interpretation of life in the Middle Ages. The choir screen is a wood carving from the same era. Central to the 19th-century grass-roots movement that helped abolish slavery throughout the British Empire, and frequently associated with the kinds of socialist free thinking for which Manchester itself is identified, it's one of the most resilient religious buildings in Britain, having survived vandals during the 17th-century civil wars, a direct hit by a Nazi firebomb in 1941, and damage from an IRA bombing in 1996. Of special note is the "Fire Window," a replacement for a window destroyed during World War II, whose colors evoke the infernos of the Nazi Blitz.

Victoria St. ℰ **0161/833-2220.** www.manchestercathedral.org. Free admission. Mon–Fri 8am–7pm; Sat 8am–5pm; Sun 8:30am–7:30pm. Metrolink: St. Peter's Sq. Bus: 11, 16, 41, 42, or 47.

Manchester Jewish Museum   These compact and somewhat claustrophobic premises were originally built in the Moorish Revival style in 1874 as a Sephardic synagogue. Set on the city's northern fringe, it's one of only two such museums in Britain (the other is in London). It traces the culture and history of Manchester's Jewish community, estimated today at around 27,000. Part of the emphasis is on the experiences of immigrants, many from eastern Europe, whose recorded voices describe life in Manchester's Jewish quarter in the years before World War II.

190 Cheetham Hill Rd. ℰ **0161/834-9879.** www.manchesterjewishmuseum.com. Admission £3.95 adults; £2.95 children, students, and seniors; £9.50 family ticket. Mon–Thurs 10:30am–4pm; Sun 1–5pm; Fri by appointment. Closed Jewish holidays. Metrolink: Victoria. Bus: 89 or 135.

Manchester Museum This venerable museum showcases an eclectic and some-times eccentric collection of the spoils brought back by local industrialists from their adventurous forays outside of England. It displays archaeological finds from all over the world, including England's largest collection of ancient Egyptian mummies out-side the British Museum in London.

University of Manchester, Oxford Rd., near Booth St. © **0161/275-2634.** www.museum.manchester. ac.uk. Free admission. Tues–Sat 10am–5pm; Sun–Mon 11am–4pm. Metrolink: St. Peter's Sq., then bus no. 11, 16, 41, 42, or 47.

Manchester Town Hall ★ Alfred Waterhouse designed this massive neo-Gothic structure that first opened in 1877, and extensions were added just before World War II. The tower rises nearly 90m (295 ft.) above the town. The Great Hall and its signature hammer-beam roof houses 12 pre-Raphaelite murals by Ford Madox Brown, commissioned between 1852 and 1856. The paintings chronicle the town's storied past, from the 1st-century Roman occupation to the Industrial Revolution of the 19th century.

Albert Sq. © **0161/234-5000.** www.manchester2002-uk.com/buildings/town Hall.html. Free admis-sion. Mon–Fri 9am–5pm. Closed Dec 25–26 and Jan 1. Metrolink: St. Peter's Sq. Bus: 11, 16, 41, 42, or 47.

Urbis Shimmering, glassy, avant-garde, and massive, and positioned as close to the commercial core of Manchester as a building can be, Urbis arose like a symbol of the "new Manchester" from the rubble of an IRA bomb that devastated the down-town area in 1996. It was built as an homage to the concept of "the City" as an inevitable byproduct of the human experience. The fantastic structure is clad in 2,200 handmade plates of glass with a "ski slope" copper roof. Inside, along with changing exhibits, you'll find high-tech interactive displays providing insights into Manchester life, along with various explorations of urban culture and art. Other than its core exhibit, its interior is as changeable and quixotic as its shimmering exterior. Few museums in Europe seem as deliberately undefined, or seem to change exhibits as frequently and as radically.

Cathedral Gardens. © **0161/605-8200.** www.urbis.org.uk. Free admission. Sun–Wed 10am–6pm; Thurs–Sat 10am–8pm. Metrolink: Victoria. Bus: 11, 16, 41, 42, or 47.

Whitworth Art Gallery Whitworth was originally established in 1889 with a bequest to the city from a wealthy industrialist. The gallery was opened to the pub-lic in 1908. Behind the magnificent redbrick facade lies a light and spacious interior. The gallery is one of the richest research sources in England for antique patterns of wallpaper and textiles and the weaving techniques that produced them. It also fea-tures a superb collection of 18th- and 19th-century watercolors on display, including many by Turner.

South of the University of Manchester, Whitworth Park, Oxford Rd., near the corner of Denmark Rd. © **0161/275-7450.** www.whitworth.manchester.ac.uk. Free admission. Mon–Sat 10am–5pm; Sun noon–4pm. Metrolink: St. Peter's Sq., then bus no. 41, 42, or 45.

Exploring Castlefield

Manchester had its origins in **Castlefield,** immediately southwest of the city's his-toric core, which local authorities have designated an "urban heritage park." Inter-laced with canals that helped transport building supplies during the city's late-19th-century heyday, Castlefield is known as a place to escape from more crowded venues downtown.

Long ago, it was a densely populated neighborhood that housed as many as 2,000 civilians beginning in A.D. 79, when Manchester was Mamucium, a fortified Roman camp strategically positioned between other Roman outposts, Chester and Carlisle. The roots of modern-day Manchester grew from here, providing the basic goods and services that supplied the soldiers in the nearby fort. After the Romans abandoned their fortress in A.D. 411, the settlement, by then known as Mancestra, stood alone throughout the Dark Ages.

Manchester slumbered for centuries until its heyday came in the 18th and 19th centuries. The development of the **Bridgewater Canal,** which transferred raw materials and coal to Manchester's factories from outlying regions, spurred the city's industrial growth. Warehouses arose around the wharves, their names suggesting their wares (for example, Potato Wharf). Later, Liverpool Road housed the world's first passenger railway station, today home to the Museum of Science & Industry (see below).

Though the city atrophied for decades after its reign as industrial capital of the world, an interest in urban renewal emerged in the 1970s. Many of the city's grand canals and warehouses have been restored, and Castlefield is once again a thriving, vibrant district loaded with a curious mixture of antique and ultramodern buildings randomly positioned next to one another. Such neighboring districts as the Northern Quarter seem to specialize in funky bars and shops selling all manner of used clothing and 1960s-era nostalgia.

Museum of Science & Industry   Set within five separate and antique buildings, the premises were built in 1830 as the first railway station in the world. Its many exhibits celebrate the Industrial Revolution and its myriad inventions and developments, such as printing, the railway industry, electricity, textile manufacturing, and industrial machinery, plus the history of flight and aerospace exploration.

Liverpool Rd. (1.5km/1 mile north of Manchester's center), Castlefield. © **0161/832-2244.** www.mosi. org.uk. Free admission. Daily 10am–5pm. Closed Dec 24–26 and Jan 1. Parking £5. Metrolink: G-Mex or Deansgate. Bus: 33.

Shopping

Not only does Manchester offer a vast number and variety of boutiques, shops, galleries, and crafts centers, but it's also one of the best hunting grounds for bargains in all of England.

Most of the larger shopping areas in the city are pedestrian only. These include **King Street** and **St. Ann's Square,** full of exclusive boutiques and designer stores; **Market Street,** with its major chain and department stores; **Arndale Centre,** Manchester's largest covered shopping center; and the revitalized **Piccadilly** and **Oldham Street,** for fashion, music, and plenty of bargains. **Deansgate** is not a pedestrian-only street, but does have a lot of adventure-sports shops.

For the young at heart, or anyone interested in everything from World War II RAF bomber-pilot gear to outrageous club wear, it's one-stop shopping at **Affleck Palace,** 52 Church St. This complex provides 50 of the most widely varied shops in the city, divided among four floors.

ANTIQUES & FINE ART   Those who like rooting through dusty stacks of stuff in search of treasures will find Manchester and the greater Manchester area prime hunting grounds. More pricey antiques can be found along **Bury New Road** in Prestwich village, just outside of Manchester.

ARTS & CRAFTS   You can rack up a lot of one-of-a-kind items while exploring the many shops devoted to craftspeople and their art. For ceramics, glass, textiles, jewelry, toys, dollhouses, and the like, visit the exquisite Victorian building that houses **Manchester Craft Centre,** 17 Oak St. (✆ **0161/832-4274;** www.craft anddesign.com).

DEPARTMENT STORES   For a northern outpost of London's chic department store, head for **Harvey Nichols,** 21 New Cathedral St. (✆ **0161/828-8888;** www. harveynichols.com), in the city center. The store often has sales and is always packed with the latest designer goods. For lunch, you can dine in an affordable restaurant and brasserie on the second floor. Far cheaper fashion is found at **Marks & Spencer,** 7 Market St. (✆ **0161/831-7341;** www.marksandspencer.com), the world's largest department store. Among its thousands of offerings, it is also known for its food department.

MARKETS   Here in the north, markets are a tradition and offer you a chance to jump in and barter with the locals. Tourists tend to steer clear of them, so this is a great chance for an authentic experience.

Though markets tend to sell everyday items and foodstuffs, some stalls are devoted to flea-market goods and "antiques." Market days vary throughout the city, but you're bound to find at least one in full swing each day of the workweek.

The major ones include Arndale Market and Market Hall in Manchester Arndale Centre, Grey Mare Lane Market and Beswick District Shopping Centre in Beswick, and Moss Side Market and Moss Lane East in Moss Side.

MILL SHOPS   Manchester is an industrial stronghold with lots of textile mills. Most mills used to have an on-site store, or mill shop, where customers could come to buy mill goods. Today, more and more of the mills are setting up shop in towns across the country.

Bury New Road in Cheetham Hill, near Boddingtons Brewery, has a great selection of factory shops, discount stores, warehouses, cash-and-carry outlets, and street stalls on Sunday mornings. Some of the stores along this road do not sell to the general public, and others require a minimum purchase.

NOSTALGIA   Thanks partly to its burgeoning gay and lesbian community, Manchester has functioned like a magnet or vacuum cleaner, pulling in the kind of plasticized, airport-lobby kitsch that might have been discarded in horror a dozen or more years ago. The '60s-inspired vinyl of the Carnaby Street era flourishes and thrives at **Oklahoma,** 74–76 High St. (✆ **0161/834-1136**), one of the most visible purveyors of kitsch in the city's funky Northern Quarter. Its decor is mostly constructed from recycled plastic, and the space is crammed to the rafters with things kitschier—both new and recycled—than most mainstream psyches could possibly imagine. Come here for the kind of tongue-in-cheek gag items that might have been conceived during a psychedelic fog by a dyed-in-the-wool drag queen on mescaline. There's a cafe on the premises.

Manchester After Dark

THE PERFORMING ARTS

The **Lowry Theatre ★★**, Pier 8, Salford Quays (✆ **0843/208-6000**), has become Manchester's premier center for the performing and visual arts, encompassing two main theaters, studio space, and exhibition galleries. To find out what's happening during your visit, go to www.thelowry.com. You can visit the Lowry Galleries Sunday to Friday 11am to 5pm, Saturday 10am to 5pm; admission is free. Take Metrolink to Harbour City or hop on bus no. 69, 290, or 291.

For drama with an unobstructed view, go to the nation's largest theater-in-the-round. The **Royal Exchange ★★**, St. Ann's Square (© **0161/833-9833;** www.royalexchangetheatre.org.uk), is housed in a futuristic glass-and-steel structure built within the Great Hall of Manchester's former Cotton Exchange. It offers 48 weeks of in-house dramaturgy every year.

Home of the renowned **Hallé Orchestra** (© **0161/237-7000;** www.halle.co.uk), the **Bridgewater Hall**, Lower Mosley Street (© **0161/907-9000;** www.bridgewater-hall.co.uk), is a state-of-the-art, 2,400-seat concert hall. In addition to the orchestra's season, it also presents classical performances from ensembles such as the internationally acclaimed **BBC Philharmonic,** as well as some pop and comedy, too. The calendar of performances is highly variable, so it's best to call for schedules.

The **University of Manchester's Department of Music,** Coupland Street (© **0161/275-4987;** www.arts.manchester.ac.uk), is home to one of the nation's most distinctive classical string quartets, the **Lindsay String Quartet,** which performs a series of eight evening concerts in the department's auditorium during the year. For a real bargain, check out its luncheon recital series, which is free.

THE CLUB & MUSIC SCENE

Above all else, Manchester is known for its contributions to pop music. From the Smiths and New Order to Oasis and the Stone Roses, the "Manchester sound" has been known throughout the world for more than 2 decades. Yet, surprisingly enough, live music went by the wayside in the early 1990s, and clubs were in short supply until they started making a steady comeback in the last few years.

South, 4A S. King St. (© **0161/831-7756;** www.southnightclub.com), is a small industrial-style club. A 10-minute walk north of Piccadilly Gardens, it has a sophisticated young aura, with '60s and '70s music on Friday and a hot house DJ on Saturday.

For cutting-edge music, check the stage at **Star & Garter,** Farefield Street (© **0161/273-6726;** www.starandgarter.co.uk), on Wednesday through Friday, when harder rock and hard-core acts will get in your face.

Other hot clubs include **Matt & Phred's,** 85 Oldham St. (© **0161/831-7002;** www.mattandphreds.com), which features some of the best jazz in town. It's open Monday to Saturday 5pm to 2am.

PUBS, BARS & LOUNGES

Peveril of the Peak, Great Bridgewater Street (© **0161/236-6364**), is easy enough to find—just look for a 380-year-old triangular building covered from top to bottom in antique green-glazed tiles. No one seems to know why it was designed or built that way, but you can step inside its woodsy-looking paneled interior and enjoy a pint of Theakston's Best Bitter, Yorkshire Terrier, or Webster's Best Bitter while you puzzle over it.

One of Manchester's most intriguing bars lies one floor above lobby level within the city's best-recommended and most prestigious hotel. It's the **River Bar,** in the Lowry Hotel, 50 Dearmans Place, Chapel Wharf (© **0161/827-4000;** www.thelowryhotel.com and www.theriverrestaurant.com), a rambling, contemporary citadel of understated posh that draws the young, the beautiful, and the restless from the city that surrounds it. But at least part of the attraction derives from whatever media-hungry

Loud, proud, and straight-friendly, Manchester's so-called **Gay Village** spreads across Canal Street in a once-seedy factory district that's flanked on one side by a canal with locks. The scene begins northeast of Princess Street and is active day and night. On any given day, gays and lesbians hang out at the sidewalk tables that border the canal. The bars are frequented by both young gay men and lesbians. The neighborhood contains as many as 25 different GLBT watering holes, each with their regular clienteles and niche markets, but a trio of bars that's particularly popular includes **Queer,** 4 Canal St. (✆ 0161/228-1360; www.queer-manchester.com), a gay-lifestyle cafe/bar in the heart of the village. A cruisy crowd frequents the joint, with its large booths. Entrance is free and food is served day and night. Queer is open Monday to Saturday 11am to 2am, Sunday 11am to 12:30am. On another front, **Churchills,** 37 Chorlton St. (✆ 0161/236-5181), arguably has the friendliest atmosphere. The surroundings are safe and comfortable at this pub club that features everything from drag disco to karaoke nights. Both full meals and bar snacks are offered, and there's no cover. It's open Monday to Saturday noon to 2am, Sunday noon to 12:30am. Finally, **Cruz 101,** 101 Princess St. (✆ 0161/950-0101; www.cruz101.com), is perhaps the best-attended gay venue, with music ranging from disco to funky house. It's really two clubs in one, with a large main floor and a smaller lower level. It was created from an old abandoned textile mill. Cover ranges from £4 to £6, depending on the night. It's open Monday, Thursday, and Sunday 11pm to 5am, Wednesday 11pm to 3:30am, and Friday and Saturday 11pm to 6am.

clients might be in residence at the time. In other words, don't assume that you'll be surrounded by dour business travelers here: You're more likely to meet troupes of actors, rock musicians, professional athletes (including wrestlers and kick boxers), and media folk than not, and as such, the place usually rocks and rolls. Cocktails cost £7.50 to £15 each, and platters of food, including salads, sandwiches, tapas, and upscale versions of fish and chips, go for £10 to £18.

Other hot spots for a drink include **Lammar's,** Fourways House, 57 Hilton St. (✆ 0161/237-9058; www.lammars.co.uk), in the Northern Quarter. With its kitschy decor and high camp, it was named after a fabled local drag queen, Foo Foo Lammar. To the sounds of recorded jazz, a young crowd drinks in the bar or retreats to a lounge. Out back, tapas are served.

Dukes 92, Castle Street (✆ 0161/839-3522; www.dukes92.com), lies in Castlefield, opening onto Lock 92 of the Rochdale Canal. You can sit outside and take in the view, perhaps get inspected yourself. The lounge is installed in a former stable, and it's a huge place, almost like one of the old cotton warehouses of yore. The bar passes out some free snacks, and you can also order pizzas and the like.

LIVERPOOL ★

353km (219 miles) NW of London; 166km (103 miles) NW of Birmingham; 56km (35 miles) W of Manchester

Liverpool, with its famous waterfront on the River Mersey, is a great shipping port and industrial center and is now a UNESCO World Heritage Site. It's even been called the next Barcelona. But forget about those palm trees, and carry an umbrella.

ACCOMMODATIONS ■
Aachen Hotel **13**
Atlantic Tower **3**
Britannia Adelphi Hotel **11**
Express by Holiday Inn **21**
Feathers Hotel **14**
Hard Days Night Hotel **6**
Hope Street Hotel **16**
Malmaison Liverpool **2**

DINING ◆
Alma de Cuba **18**
Bar Italia **5**
Blue Bar & Grill **19**
London Carriage Works **16**
Shangri-La **8**
Simply Heathcotes **4**
Tate Liverpool Café **22**

ATTRACTIONS ●
Albert Dock **19**
Beatles Story **20**
Cathedral Church of Christ
  (Liverpool Cathedral) **17**
Cavern Club **7**
Mendips **1**
Merseyside Maritime
  Museum **19**
Metropolitan Cathedral of
  Christ the King **12**
Philharmonic Hall **15**
Tate Liverpool **22**
20 Forthlin Road **1**
Walker Art Gallery **10**
World Museum Liverpool **9**

King John launched Liverpool on its road to glory when he granted it a charter in 1207. Before that, it had been a tiny 12th-century fishing village, but it quickly became a port for shipping men and materials to Ireland. In the 18th century, it grew to prominence because of the sugar, spice, and tobacco trade with the Americans. By the time Victoria came to the throne, Liverpool had become Britain's biggest commercial seaport.

Recent refurbishing of the Albert Dock, the establishment of a maritime museum, and the conversion of warehouses into little stores similar to those in San Francisco's Ghirardelli Square have made this an up-and-coming area once again, with many attractions for visitors. Liverpudlians are proud of their city, with its new hotels, two cathedrals, shopping and entertainment complexes, and parks. And, of course, whether they're fans of the Fab Four or not, most visitors to Liverpool want to see where Beatlemania began.

Essentials

GETTING THERE   Liverpool has its own airport, **John Lennon Airport** (© 0871/521-8484; www.liverpoolairport.com), which is served by frequent daily flights from many parts of the United Kingdom, including London, the Isle of Man, and Ireland.

Frequent express trains depart London's Euston Station for Liverpool, a 3-hour trip. There is also frequent service from Manchester, a 45-minute ride away. For schedules and information, call © 0845/748-4950 or visit **www.nationalrail.co.uk**.

National Express buses depart London's Victoria Coach Station every 3 hours for the 4½-hour trip to Liverpool. Buses also arrive every hour from Manchester, a 1-hour ride away. For schedules and information, call © 08717/81-8181 or visit **www.nationalexpress.com**.

If you're driving from London, head north on the M1, and then northwest on the M6 to the junction with the M62, which heads west to Liverpool.

VISITOR INFORMATION   The **Tourist Information Centre** is at 8 Place, Whitechapel (© 0151/233-2008; www.visitliverpool.com). It's open Monday and Wednesday to Saturday 9am to 6pm, Tuesday 10am to 6pm, and Sunday 11am to 4pm.

SPECIAL EVENTS   At the end of August and running into the beginning of September, the annual **International Beatles Week** (www.liverpooltour.com) attracts about 100,000 fans to Liverpool for a 7-day celebration. The highlights are concerts performed by bands from Argentina to Sweden (with names such as Lenny Pane, Wings Over Liverpool, and the Beats). You can hear the news today at the Sgt. Pepper concert and take in many other Beatles tributes, auctions, and tours.

Where to Stay

EXPENSIVE

Atlantic Tower ★★   Showcased in an austere high-rise evoking the bow of a great luxury liner, this first-class hotel is one of the top two big hotels in the city (the other being Britannia Adelphi; see below). It caters largely to business travelers. You check in at a spacious lobby and are shown to one of the well-furnished but fairly standard bedrooms. Many rooms, though quite small, provide views of the River Mersey, and you can request a minibar. Average—not grand—comfort can be found here. The best units are the corner bedrooms, which are triangular in shape and face the water. Accommodations are frequently renovated as the need arises.

30 Chapel St., Liverpool, Merseyside L3 9RE. ✆ **0871/376-9025.** Fax 0871/376-9125. www.thistle.com. 225 units. Mon–Fri £100–£155 double; Sat–Sun £90 double; £105–£170 suite. Rates include breakfast. AE, DC, MC, V. Parking £14. **Amenities:** 2 restaurants; bar; room service. *In room:* TV, hair dryer, Wi-Fi (£15).

Britannia Adelphi Hotel ★ This grand hotel, built in 1914, is known for its fine Edwardian rooms and good cuisine. Past the elegant entrance, you enter an over-blown world of marble corridors, molded ceilings, and dark polished wood. These traditional features are complemented by modern luxuries because the hotel has been completely refurbished. Many still view this as the best address in town, but we rank it second behind the Atlantic Tower (see above). Each recently refurbished bedroom is well furnished and comes with double-glazed windows. The mezzanine bedrooms are likely to be noisy.

Ranelagh Place, Liverpool, Merseyside L3 5UL. ✆ **866/763-4553** or 051/709-7200. Fax 0151/708-0743. www.britanniahotels.com/hotels/liverpool. 402 units. £62–£125 double; £85–£165 suite. Children 11 and younger stay free in parent's room. AE, DC, MC, V. Parking £12. **Amenities:** 4 restaurants; 2 bars; health club; Jacuzzi; heated indoor pool; room service; sauna; steam room; Wi-Fi (free; in lobby). *In room:* TV, hair dryer.

Hard Days Night Hotel ★★ If you're a devoted fan of the Rolling Stones, check in elsewhere. This government-rated four-star hotel carries out the Beatles theme with a vengeance, but with a large twist of 21st-century chic. Each area of the hotel has a different theme: The basement is dedicated to the Cavern Club, where the Beatles were discovered in 1961. The roof of the hotel commemorates their last ever performance on the roof of Apple's office in London in 1969. Every bedroom has a unique theme linked to a record or event involving the Fab Four. If you want the ultimate in luxury, check into either the Lennon Suite, with a white baby grand piano, or the McCartney Suite, with a suit of armor.

Central Buildings, N. John St., City Centre, Liverpool, Merseyside L2 6RR. ✆ **0151/236-1964.** Fax 0151/255-1263. www.harddaysnighthotel.com. 110 units. £110–£150 double; £750 Lennon or McCartney suites. AE, MC, V. **Amenities:** 2 restaurants; bar; room service. *In room:* TV, hair dryer, Wi-Fi (free).

Hope Street Hotel ★★ 🏨 This converted carriage house, constructed to evoke a palace in Venice, is Liverpool's first boutique hotel—and it's our preferred stopover. Perched on a hill with panoramic views, it stands across from the home of the Liverpool Philharmonic. Exposed brickwork and cast-iron columns from the mid-19th century, along with exposed beam ceilings and waxed oaken floors, create a warm, cozy atmosphere, evocative of Liverpool's shipbuilding past. Each room is beautifully outfitted with oversize beds, Egyptian cotton sheets, radiant heat, and natural light, along with custom-made cherrywood furniture. We love the private bathrooms' "rain dance shower heads" that are the size of dinner plates. The on-site bar is the town's most sophisticated, often a venue for visiting celebs, and the London Carriage Works restaurant is separately recommended (p. 605).

40 Hope St., Liverpool, Merseyside L1 9DA. ✆ **0151/709-3000.** Fax 0151/709-2454. www.hopestreet hotel.co.uk. 48 units. £150–£200 double; £300–£350 suite. AE, DC, MC, V. Parking £12. **Amenities:** 2 restaurants; bar; room service. *In room:* TV/DVD, CD player, hair dryer, Wi-Fi (free).

Malmaison Liverpool ★★ Lying at Princes Dock and opening onto river views, this *über*-stylish boutique hotel stands near the famous Liver Building. In homage to the Beatles, it also has a big yellow submarine installed in the middle of it, along with such decorations as rather psychedelic canvasses featuring the Fab Four in all their glory from those heady days of the 1960s. Bedrooms are midsize, even a bit small, but are decorated in trendy colors such as plum, with harmonious furnishings. For honeymooners or off-the-record weekenders, the hotel promotes "love packages," with everything from champagne on ice to aromatic oils and candles.

William Jessop Way, Princes Dock, Liverpool, Merseyside L3 1QZ. © **0151/229-5000.** Fax 0151/229-5002. www.malmaison-liverpool.com. 130 units. £170–£190 double; £195–£415 suite. AE, MC, V. **Amenities:** Restaurant; bar; exercise room; room service. *In room:* TV, hair dryer, Wi-Fi (£10 per day).

MODERATE

Feathers Hotel This brick-fronted hotel comprises four separate Georgian-style town houses. It sits in the heart of the city, adjacent to the modern Metropolitan Cathedral. The bedrooms are comfortable, with simple and traditional furniture—there are some four-poster beds—but don't expect much charm. Executive units offer additional amenities such as CD players and PlayStations. Some 40 units come with both tub and shower.

117–125 Mt. Pleasant, Liverpool, Merseyside L3 5TF. © **0151/709-9655.** Fax 0151/709-3838. www.feathers.uk.com/feathers. 66 units. £69–£99 double; £130 triple. Rates include buffet breakfast. 2-night minimum Sat–Sun. AE, MC, V. Parking £8. Bus: 80 (the airport bus). **Amenities:** Restaurant; bar; room service. *In room:* TV, Wi-Fi (free).

INEXPENSIVE

Aachen Hotel Five minutes from the city center near the Roman Catholic cathedral, this well-run establishment is a landmark building in a conservation district. The modernized bedrooms are comfortable, though a bit plain; hallway bathrooms are adequate and well maintained. Complete with an on-site bar, this efficient hotel offers a good value.

89–91 Mt. Pleasant, Liverpool, Merseyside L3 5TB. © **0151/709-3477.** Fax 0151/709-1126. www.aachenhotel.co.uk. 18 units, 12 with bathroom. £65 double without bathroom; £75 double with bathroom; £110 triple with bathroom. Rates include English breakfast. AE, MC, V. Parking £10. **Amenities:** Breakfast room; bar. *In room:* TV, hair dryer.

Express by Holiday Inn Liverpool ★ 🐾 Some of the most reasonable accommodations in Liverpool are centrally located at Albert Dock in this reconverted warehouse, where many of the original 19th-century architectural features have been preserved. There are several Holiday Inns in Liverpool, but this one is the best. The bedrooms are handsomely though modestly decorated, each spacious and well maintained. Furnishings are functional and harmonious in style. Ask for one of the units opening onto a view of the historic dock area. A continental breakfast is served daily, and many quality restaurants and bars are found outside the entrance to the hotel.

Britannia Pavillion, Albert Dock, Liverpool, Merseyside LE 4AD. © **888/444-0401** or 8448/75-75-75. Fax 0151/709-1144. www.hiexpress.co.uk. 135 units. £59–£90 double. AE, DC, MC, V. Parking £14 nearby. **Amenities:** Restaurant; bar. *In room:* TV, hair dryer, Wi-Fi (free).

Where to Dine

For such a world-famous city, Liverpool has yet to play host to a world-class restaurant, but here is the current crop of what is available.

Alma de Cuba ★ 🍴 LATIN AMERICAN It's fiesta time nightly at this hot new dining experience, installed on a back street in a former Catholic church from the 1700s. The church now simmers in the lights of thousands of candles as patrons enjoy the best mojitos this side of Havana, the kind Papa Hemingway sipped in the good ol' days. Stained-glass windows and wall-mounted antlers form the backdrop for the ground-floor bar and mezzanine restaurant. The tapas-style bar menu is a treat unto itself. Here you can order chorizo sausage and cheese or blue-fin crab croquettes, even tender cumin-laced lamb meatballs. Main dishes have spice and flair, including the slow-roasted duck with star anise and the roasted free-range chicken breast in a pistachio crust. Vegetarians delight in the roasted fig and peach tart tatin with sun-dried tomatoes and a spinach-and-fennel hummus. Serious carnivores will go for the whole, boned, and rolled roast suckling pig.

St. Peter's Church, Seel St. ℂ **0151/702-7394.** www.alma-de-cuba.com. Reservations recommended. Tapas £2.25–£5; main courses £10–£25. AE, DC, MC, V. Restaurant daily noon–2:30pm and 6–10:30pm; tapas bar Sun–Wed noon–10pm, Thurs–Sat noon–7pm.

Bar Italia ITALIAN/CONTINENTAL   In the center of the business district, this bustling little trattoria serves affordable and tasty dishes with a certain Continental flair. Roman art on the walls evokes a Mediterranean feel, and on wintry nights, the brick fireplace adds a cozy touch. The chefs here select the choicest ingredients to turn out savory dishes, such as pan-fried breast of duck with crushed black peppercorns in a cream-and-brandy sauce, or pan-fried filet steak, also with a brandy sauce. A filet of pork is served with a spicy barbecue sauce, and pasta tubes are stuffed with spicy meat and a béchamel sauce.

48A Castle St. ℂ **0151/236-3375.** www.baritalialiverpool.com. Reservations recommended. Main courses £8–£20. MC, V. Mon–Fri 11:30am–3pm; Tues–Sat 5:30–11pm.

Blue Bar & Grill ★ ENGLISH/INTERNATIONAL   This is an elegant and sophisticated contemporary restaurant and bar along the historic Liverpool waterfront. Guests come here throughout the day for items such as tasty international tapas, vegetarian specialties, fresh fish dishes, and American fusion cookery. Ingredients are market fresh and can be enjoyed informally on the downstairs level or more grandly at the upstairs gallery, where you can order fish steaks and even roast suckling pig. The cafe makes the best sandwiches in town, including the Thanksgiving, made with oven-roasted turkey and served with brambly-apple stuffing. Plates to share include a Med Platter, offering a taste of the Mediterranean. For lunch, many diners drop in for a soup and sandwich.

Edward Pavilion, Albert Dock. ℂ **0151/702-5831.** www.blue-venue.co.uk. Reservations not needed. Cafe platters and sandwiches £10–£23. MC, V. Mon–Thurs 11am–11pm; Fri–Sat 11am–11:45pm.

London Carriage Works ★ MODERN EUROPEAN   In a double-fronted Georgian carriage-house hotel, close to the Philharmonic Hall, this enticing restaurant, among the best in Liverpool, gives you a ground-floor restaurant, a basement cafe, and a bar. It's really like a brasserie you'd find on the Continent. For the most part, the food is light in texture and full of flavor, though a certain robustness permeates the cuisine. Well-crafted mains include chargrilled portobello mushrooms with a butternut squash purée, pan-seared calf's liver with pancetta and balsamic baby onions, and Colchester oysters on ice, flavored with shallots and white-wine vinegar.

In the Hope Street Hotel, 60 Hope St. ℂ **0151/705-2222.** www.hopestreethotel.co.uk. Reservations required. Main courses £11–£29. MC, V. Mon–Fri noon–2:30pm; Mon–Sat 6–10:30pm.

Shangri-La CANTONESE/SHANGHAI   One of the biggest and most consistently popular restaurants in the city center serves a wide-ranging choice of mostly Cantonese food, though there's also a special emphasis on the cuisine of Shanghai. With room for around 300 guests, it contains two separate dining rooms, each with its own bar, and a red, gold, and green decor reminiscent of a Confucian temple. Many regulars opt to begin a meal with dim sum, the delicate steamed or fried dumplings whose variations are almost infinite. Expect well-flavored treatments of virtually every succulently stir-fried vegetable that's in season at the moment and myriad preparations of fish, shellfish, duck, pork, chicken, and beef. Specialties include fried scallops and asparagus served in a "bird's nest," or sautéed king prawns and cashew nuts.

Ashcroft Buildings, 37 Victoria St. © **0151/255-0708.** Reservations not necessary. Main courses £7–£25; fixed-price lunch £9. AE, DC, MC, V. Sun–Thurs noon–midnight; Fri-Sat noon–3am.

Simply Heathcotes ENGLISH An outpost of the "chef of the north," Paul Heathcote brings his Lancashire hot pot to the center of Liverpool. It's been an enduring success since opening in 2001. The stylish decor is designed along clean, modern lines, and the freshest of ingredients is used. Try pan-fried sage gnocchi with roast squash in a blue-cheese cream sauce, or peppered filet steak, or even the char-grilled ham steak with a béarnaise sauce. Of course, those old favorites such as Heathcote's black-pudding hash browns also appear on the menu. Other temptations include roast pheasant with caramelized spiced apple, beet, and Savoy cabbage.

25 The Strand, Beetham Plaza. © **0151/236-3536.** www.heathcotes.co.uk/simply. Reservations required. Main courses £11–£26; fixed-price Sun lunch £18 for 2 courses, £20 for 3 courses. MC, V. Mon-Sat noon–2:30pm and 6-10pm; Sun noon–9pm.

Tate Liverpool Café ENGLISH When we're in Liverpool, we like to lunch at this cafe connected with its famous gallery. You can launch your day here with a late breakfast or else indulge in a hearty and delightful lunch, with as many cups of freshly brewed coffee as you wish. On summer days, try for one of the dockside seats. Freshly made salads with crisp greens and well-stuffed sandwiches are regularly featured, though you may also want to opt for more substantial fare, such as a tender lamb shank with sweet potatoes or grilled salmon with an assortment of vegetables julienne. The grilled chicken breast is another pleasing favorite. Beer, lager, and wine are served.

In the Tate Liverpool museum, Albert Dock. © **0151/702-7580.** www.tate.org.uk/liverpool. Reservations not needed. Main courses £3.25–£8; sandwiches £3–£6. AE, MC, V. Tues–Sun 10am–6pm.

Seeing the Sights

If you'd like a Beatles-related bus tour, **Cavern City Tours** (© **0151/236-9091;** www.cavernclub.org) presents a daily 2-hour Magical Mystery Tour, which covers the most famous attractions associated with the Beatles. Tickets cost £15 and are sold at the Tourist Information Centre at 8 Place, Whitechapel. Tours depart from the same center daily at 2:30pm, or from the Gower Street bus stop at Albert Dock at 2:10pm.

In the Britannia Pavilion at Albert Dock, you can visit the **Beatles Story** (© **0151/709-1963;** www.beatlesstory.com), a museum housing memorabilia of the famous group, including a yellow submarine with live fish swimming past the portholes. It's open daily from 10am to 6pm. Admission is £13 for adults, £8.50 for students, and £6.50 for children 5 to 16; a family ticket is £21 to £37.

Everyone's curious about Penny Lane and Strawberry Field. Actually, the Beatles' song about **Penny Lane** didn't refer to the small lane itself but to the area at the top of the lane called Smithdown Place. Today, this is a bustling thoroughfare for taxis and buses—hardly a place for nostalgic memories. John Lennon lived nearby and attended school in the area. When he studied at Art College, he passed here almost every day. To reach Penny Lane and the area referred to, head north of Sefton Park. From the park, Green Bank Lane leads into Penny Lane itself, and at the junction of Allerton Road and Smithdown Road stands the Penny Lane Tramsheds. This is John Lennon country—or what's left of it.

Only the most die-hard fans will want to make the journey to **Strawberry Field** along Beaconsfield Road, which is reached by taking Menlove Avenue east of the center. Today, you can stand at the iron gates and look in at a children's home run by the Salvation Army. As a child, John played on the grounds, and in 1970 he donated a large sum of money to the home.

Because these sights are hard to reach by public transport and lie outside the center, you may want to take one of the Cavern City Tours (see above) that feature both Strawberry Field and Penny Lane.

A fun thing to do is to take the famous **Mersey Ferry** that travels from the Pier Head to both Woodside and Seacombe. Service operates daily from early morning to early evening throughout the year. Special cruises run throughout the summer, including trips along the Manchester Ship Canal. For more information, call 𝄞 **0151/639-0609** or go to www.merseyferries.co.uk.

Albert Dock ★   Built of brick, stone, and cast iron, this showpiece development on Liverpool's waterfront opened in 1846, saw a long period of decline, and has now been extensively renovated and refurbished. The dockland warehouses now house shops, restaurants, cafes, an English pub, and a cellar wine bar. One pavilion encompasses the main building of the Merseyside Maritime Museum (see below) and another is the home of the Tate Liverpool (see below). Parking is available.

22 Edward Pavilion, Albert Dock. 𝄞 **0151/708-7334.** www.albertdock.com. Free admission. Shops daily 10am–6pm; bars and restaurants daily 11am–11pm. Smart Bus from city center.

Cathedral Church of Christ (Liverpool Cathedral) ★★   The great new Anglican edifice overlooking the River Mersey was begun in 1904 and was largely completed 74 years later; it was the last Gothic-style cathedral to be built worldwide. Dedicated in the presence of Queen Elizabeth II in 1978, it is the largest church in England and the fifth-largest in the world. Its vaulting under the tower is 53m (175 ft.) high, the highest in the world, and its length, 186m (619 ft.), makes it one of the longest cathedrals in the world. The organ has nearly 10,000 pipes, the most found in any church. The tower houses the highest (66m/219 ft.) and the heaviest (31 tons) bells in the world, and the Gothic arches are the highest ever built. From the tower, you can see to North Wales.

A visitor center and refectory feature an aerial sculpture of 12 huge sails, with a ship's bell, clock, and light that changes color on an hourly basis. You can enjoy full meals in the charming refectory.

St. James' Mount. 𝄞 **0151/702-7255.** www.liverpoolcathedral.org.uk. Admission to cathedral free, £3 donation suggested; tower and embroidery gallery £4.25 adults, £3 children. Cathedral daily 8am–6pm. Tower Mar–Oct daily 11am–5pm; Nov–Feb Mon–Sat 9am–4pm, Sun noon–2:30pm.

Mendips   The stucco house where John Lennon lived as a boy was purchased by his wife, Yoko Ono, and restored by the National Trust. Curators have re-created the late 1950s look of the house, right down to the posters of Rita Hayworth, Elvis Presley, and Brigitte Bardot in Lennon's bedroom. The future music great lived here with his Aunt Mimi and Uncle George, composing his early songs on the front porch

One of the World's Leading City History Museums

The big cultural news emerging from Northwest England in 2011 will be the opening of the **Museum of Liverpool** ★★★, housed in a fabulous new landmark building on the Mann Island site at Pier Head, at the core of the World Heritage Site on Liverpool's famous waterfront. More information about hours and details of the admission-free museum can be obtained at ℂ **0151/207-0001** or www.liverpool museums.org.uk.

This museum of Mersey culture tells the story of Liverpudlians and their contribution to British life, a far greater panorama than evoked by just the Fab Four. You can do everything here, from listening to Liverpool bands on a juke-box to learning how Chinese sailors created the oldest Chinese community in Liverpool in the 18th century. The richness of the city's cultural diversity is on display, and the role of the River Mersey is celebrated. There's even an exhibition of swimwear from a bygone age. The new museum tackles social, historical, and contemporary issues. If it pertains to Liverpool, it's all here, though it may be more than you really want to know.

and in his bedroom. Admission is only by guided tour, which also visits Paul McCartney's childhood home at 20 Forthlin Road. Groups are limited to 14 people at any one time, so book well in advance.

251 Menlove Ave., Woolton. ℂ **0844/800-4791.** www.nationaltrust.org.uk/beatles. Combined tour ticket for Mendips and 20 Forthlin Rd. £17 adults, £3.15 children 15 and younger. Mid-Mar to Oct, tours depart Wed–Sun 10 and 10:50am from Liverpool city center, 2:30 and 3:20pm from Speke Hall, South Liverpool. Late Feb to early Mar and Nov, tours depart Wed–Sun 10am, 12:30pm, and 3pm, all from city center.

Merseyside Maritime Museum ★   Set in the historic heart of Liverpool's waterfront, this museum provides a unique blend of floating exhibits, crafts demonstrations, working displays, and special events. In addition to restored waterfront buildings, exhibitions present the story of mass emigration through Liverpool in the last century, shipbuilding on Merseyside, the Battle of the Atlantic Gallery, and Transatlantic Slavery. There is wheelchair access.

Albert Dock. ℂ **0151/478-4499.** www.liverpoolmuseums.org.uk. Free admission. Daily 10am–5pm. Bus: Albert Dock Shuttle from city center.

Metropolitan Cathedral of Christ the King ★★   About 1km (½ mile) away from the Anglican cathedral stands this Roman Catholic cathedral—the two are joined by a road called Hope Street. The construction of the cathedral, designed by Sir Edwin Lutyens, was started in 1930, but when World War II interrupted in 1939, not even the granite-and-brick vaulting of the crypt was complete. At the end of the war, it was estimated that the cost of completing the structure as Lutyens designed it would be some £27 million. Architects throughout the world were invited to compete to design a more realistic project to cost about £1 million and to be completed in 5 years. Sir Frederick Gibberd won the competition and was commissioned to oversee the construction of the circular cathedral. Construction was completed in 1967. Today, the cathedral offers seating for more than 2,000. Above the altar rises a multicolored glass lantern weighing 2,000 tons and rising to a height of 87m (290 ft.). Called a space-age cathedral, it has a bookshop, a tearoom, and tour guides.

Mt. Pleasant. ✆ **0151/709-9222.** www.liverpoolmetrocathedral.org.uk. Free admission. Daily 8am–6pm (until 5pm on winter Sun). Bus: Albert Dock Shuttle from city center.

Tate Liverpool ★   This museum displays much of the national collection of 20th-century art, complemented by changing art exhibitions of international standing such as the prints of Joan Miró or the sculptures of the iconoclastic British sculptress Rachel Whiteread. The tourist office has full details on all special exhibitions, or you can contact the museum directly.

Albert Dock. ✆ **0151/702-7400.** www.tate.org.uk/liverpool. Free admission, except for special exhibitions. Sept–May Thurs–Sun 10am–5:50pm; June–Aug daily 10am–5:50pm. Bus: Albert Dock Shuttle from city center.

20 Forthlin Road   The house where the McCartneys lived in Liverpool before Paul's meteoric rise to superstardom has been purchased by the National Trust. Working from old photographs taken by Paul's brother Michael, the house has been restored to its original 1950s appearance, complete with patterned brown sofa and armchair with white linen antimacassars, where Paul and John scribbled out their first songs. The Chinese willow-print wallpaper doesn't reach the corners because the family was too poor to buy enough. Hardly Graceland, it does give an insight into the humble beginnings of one of the world's most famous and influential entertainers. The house is open to the public only through guided tours, which also visit Mendips, John Lennon's childhood home. Groups are limited to 14 people at any one time, so book well in advance.

20 Forthlin Rd., Allerton. ✆ **0844/800-4791.** www.nationaltrust.org.uk/beatles. Combined tour ticket for 20 Forthlin Rd. and Mendips £17 adults, £3.15 children 15 and younger. Mid-Mar to Oct, tours depart Wed–Sun 10 and 10:50am from Liverpool city center, 2:30 and 3:20pm from Speke Hall, South Liverpool. Late Feb to early Mar and Nov, tours depart Wed–Sun 10am, 12:30pm, and 3pm, all from city center.

Walker Art Gallery ★★   One of Europe's finest art galleries offers an outstanding collection of European art from 1300 to the present day. The gallery is especially rich in European Old Masters, Victorian and pre-Raphaelite works, and contemporary British art. It also has an award-winning sculpture gallery, featuring works from the 18th and 19th centuries. Seek out, in particular, Simone Martini's *Jesus Discovered in the Temple* and Salvator Rosa's *Landscape with Hermit*. Rembrandt is on show, as is an enticing *Nymph of the Fountain*, by Cranach. The work of British artists is strongest here, ranging from *Horse Frightened by a Lion,* by Stubbs, to *Snowdon from Llan Nantlle,* by Richard Wilson. Among the pre-Raphaelites are Ford Madox Brown and W. R. Yeames. The French Impressionists represented include Monet, Seurat, and Degas, among others. Modern British paintings include works by Lucian Freud and Stanley Spencer.

William Brown St. ✆ **0151/478-4199.** www.liverpoolmuseums.org.uk. Free admission. Daily 10am–5pm. Closed Dec 23–26 and Jan 1.

World Museum Liverpool ★   One of Britain's finest museums features collections from all over the world—from the earliest beginnings, with giant dinosaurs, through centuries of great art and inventions. Reopening in 2005 after a major overhaul, the galleries have doubled in space. At the Natural History Centre, you can use microscopes and video cameras to learn about the natural world. Living displays from the vivarium and aquarium form a large part of the collections, and a planetarium features daily programs covering modern space exploration—an armchair tour toward the beginning of the universe and the far-flung reaches of the cosmos. The

Wherever you turn in Liverpool today, somebody is hawking a Beatles tour. But if you'd like to see a few of the famous spots on your own, stop in at the **Cavern Club,** 8–10 Mathew St. (www.cavernclub.org), now touted as the "Most Famous Club in the World," and pick up a Cavern City Tour map to find famous Beatles locations in the city center. The Beatles played 292 gigs here between 1961 and 1963. Manager Brian Epstein first saw them here on November 9, 1961, and by December 10, he had signed a contract with the band. For tour information, call ☎ **0151/236-1965.**

latest additions are a World Cultures Gallery, with 1,500 amazing artifacts from across the globe, including Oceania, and the Weston Discovery Centre, a hands-on museum. William Brown St. ☎ **0151/478-4393.** www.liverpoolmuseums.org.uk. Free admission, except for planetarium and special exhibitions. Daily 10am–5pm.

Shopping

Pedestrian shopping areas with boutiques, specialty shops, and department stores include Church Street, Lord Street, Bold Street, Whitechapel, and Paradise Street. On the river, Albert Dock also houses a collection of small shops.

For shopping centers, go to **Cavern Walks,** 8 Mathew St. (☎ **0151/236-9082;** www.cavern-walks.co.uk), in the heart of Beatleland, or **Quiggins Centre,** 12–16 School Lane (☎ **0151/709-2462**).

If you want to buy that special piece of Beatles memorabilia, wander through the **Beatles Shop,** 31 Mathew St. (☎ **0151/236-8066;** www.thebeatleshop.co.uk).

For a huge selection of British crafts, visit **Bluecoat Display Centre,** College Lane (☎ **0151/709-4014;** ww.bluecoatdisplaycentre.com), with its gallery of metal, ceramics, glass, jewelry, and wood pieces by some 350 British craftspeople.

Frank Green's, 97 Oakfield Rd., Anfield (☎ **0151/260-3241;** www.frankgreen.co.uk), is where you'll find prints by this famous local artist who has been capturing the Liverpool scene on canvas since the 1960s. His work includes city secular buildings, churches, and street life.

A couple of other specialty shops that warrant a visit include **William Forbes,** Unit 19, Sefton Lane Industrial Estate, Maghull (☎ **0151/520-2004;** www.wmforbes.com), which has been making nautical instruments longer than anyone in the known world; and **Thorntons,** 16 Whitechapel (☎ **0151/708-6849;** www.thorntons.co.uk), where you can choose from a dizzying selection of Continental and traditional English chocolates, toffees, and mints.

Liverpool After Dark

Liverpool's nightlife is nothing if not diverse. The evening *Liverpool Echo* is a good source of daily information about larger and fine-arts events; the youth-oriented *L: Scene* magazine will provide you with a thorough calendar of club dates and gigs; and the free *City X Blag,* available in most clubs and pubs, will do the same. Available free in gay clubs and pubs, *Pulse* lists gay activities and events throughout the region.

The **Student Entertainment Office** (☎ **0151/794-4143**) at the University of Liverpool can tell you about the range of activities sponsored by the school, or you can stop by the student union on Mount Pleasant and check out the bulletin board. Another good place for finding out about the underground scene is **Quiggins Centre,** School Lane (© 0151/709-2462).

Open year-round, the **Empire Theatre,** Lime Street, hosts visiting stage productions ranging from dramas and comedies to ballets and tributes. Book through Ticketmaster at © 0151/708-3200 or online at www.liverpoolempire.org.uk.

Philharmonic Hall, Hope Street (© 0151/210-2895; www.liverpoolphil.com), is home to the **Royal Philharmonic Orchestra,** one of the best orchestras outside London, which usually performs twice weekly. When the orchestra is not on, there are often concerts by touring musicians, and films are sometimes shown as well.

Beatles fans flock to the **Cavern Club,** 8–10 Mathew St. (© 0151/236-9091; www.cavernclub.org), thinking that this is where the Fab Four appeared. Demolished years ago, the old Cavern Club has faded into history. However, locals still go to this new version to hear live bands Thursday to Sunday nights (regrettably, not as good as the dear, departed ones). The cover ranges from £1 to £8.

For a more nostalgic evening, head for the **Cavern Pub,** 5 Mathew St. (© 0151/236-4041), where many English bands got their start before going on to greater glory. The names of the groups who appeared here from 1957 to 1973 are recorded on a plaque.

Long after the mop tops' departure, the Liverpool music scene continues to thrive at various venues around town, particularly in the Ropewalks district. The best of the lot here is the **Barfly,** 90 Seel St. (© 0151/707-6171; www.barflyclub.com). The acts are constantly changing, but they're some of the best of the lot. Perhaps you'll hear the Beatles of tomorrow. Cover ranges from £3 to £15 depending on the shows, which are presented Thursday to Saturday from 10pm to 3am.

A cafe by day, **Baa Bar,** 43–45 Fleet St. (© 0151/708-8673; www.baabar.co.uk), serves an eclectic menu, and free dancing to a DJ brings in a lot of the evening's business.

At the **Zanzibar Club,** 43 Seel St. (© 0151/707-0633; www.thezanzibarclub.com), DJs spin drum-and-bass and hip-hop Wednesday to Monday nights, with the occasional rock or pop booking thrown in for good measure.

A pub with a Fab Four spin, **Ye Cracke,** 13 Rice St. (© 0151/709-4171), was a favorite watering hole of John Lennon in pre- and early Beatles days (but expect regulars to suggest you quit living in the past if you ask about it). Better just soak up the little-changed atmosphere over a pint of Oak Wobbly Bob, Cains, or Haywood Oak.

GAY BARS IN LIVERPOOL

You won't find as frenetic or as varied a nightlife scene in Liverpool as you will in, say, Manchester or Leeds. But something about the rough-and-tumble streets of this monument to the Industrial Revolution makes for hard-party times at some of the city's gay bars.

At **Masquerade,** 10 Cumberland St. (© 0151/236-7786; http://freespace.virgin.net/masquerade.bar), a gay version of a Victorian pub, the scene is the most consistently crowded and animated of the several gay bars in its neighborhood near the Moorfields railway station, off Dale Street. Come to the street-level bar to drink, talk, and watch the occasional cabaret artiste, whose acts are presented after 8pm every Friday and Saturday, 5pm on Sunday. Or head for the basement-level dance floor for a bit of boogying with the 'Pudlians.

At **G-Bar,** Eberle Street (© **0151/236-4416;** www.g-bar.com), the street level is a pseudo-Gothic piece of kitsch that only a rave party could fully appreciate. The cellar has a floor where crowds of gay and sexually neutral fans dance, dance, dance. There's even a "love lounge," where you may catch up on a bit of dialogue, or whatever, in circumstances that are highly relaxing. Cover is £5 to £15, depending on the night of the week.

The **Lisbon,** 35 Victoria St. (© **0151/231-6831**), is set close to Moorfield railway station. This is the quietest and calmest of the pubs listed in this section, luring a nicer blend of men than at some of the seedier gay dives nearby.

THE WALLED CITY OF CHESTER ★★

333km (207 miles) NW of London; 147km (91 miles) NW of Birmingham; 31km (19 miles) S of Liverpool

A Roman legion founded Chester on the River Dee in the 1st century A.D. It reached its pinnacle as a bustling port in the 13th and 14th centuries, but declined following the gradual silting up of the river. While other walls of medieval cities of England were either torn down or badly fragmented, Chester still has 3km (2 miles) of fortified city walls intact. The main entrance into Chester is Eastgate, which dates only from the 18th century. Within the walls are half-timbered houses and shops, though not all of them date from Tudor days. Chester is unusual in that some of its builders used black-and-white timbered facades even during the Georgian and Victorian eras.

Present-day Chester has aged gracefully and is now a lovely old place to visit, if you don't mind the summer crowds. It has far more charm and intimacy than either Liverpool or Manchester and is one of the most interesting medieval cities in England.

Essentials

GETTING THERE   About 21 trains depart London's Euston Station daily for the 2¼-hour trip to Chester. Trains also run every hour between Liverpool and Chester, a 45-minute ride. For schedules and information, call © **0871/781-8181** or visit **www.nationalrail.co.uk**.

Four **National Express** buses run between Birmingham and Chester; the trip takes 2½ hours. The same bus line offers service between Liverpool and Chester as well. It's also possible to catch a National Express coach from London's Victoria Coach Station to Chester. For schedules and information, call © **0870/580-8080** or visit **www.nationalexpress.com**.

If you're driving from London, head north on the M1, and then take the M6 at the junction near Coventry. Continue northwest to the junction with the A54, which leads west to Chester.

VISITOR INFORMATION   The **Tourist Information Centre** is at the Forum, Northgate Street, near Town Hall (© **01244/351609;** www.visitchester.com). It offers a hotel booking service as well as visitor information. Arrangements can also be made for coach or walking tours of Chester, including a ghost-hunter tour. It's open April to October, Monday to Saturday 9:30am to 5:30pm; off-season, Monday to Saturday 9:30am to 5pm.

SPECIAL EVENTS   July is an active time in Chester, as the 2-week **Chester Summer Music Festival** (© **01244/304618;** www.chesterfestivals.co.uk) hosts

ATTRACTIONS ●
Chester Cathedral **4**
Chester Zoo **2**
City Cross **5**
Eastgate Clock **9**
The Rows **6**

DINING ◆
La Brasserie **8**
Simon Radley **8**

ACCOMMODATIONS ■
Chester Grosvenor and Spa **8**
Crabwall Manor Hotel **1**
Green Bough Hotel &
   Olive Tree Restaurant **3**
Macdonald New Blossoms
   Hotel **10**
Mollington Banastre **1**
Ye Olde King's
   Head Hotel **7**

orchestras and other classical performers from around Britain in lunchtime concerts, with tickets averaging £6, and small indoor evening concerts, where tickets cost £6 to £30.

Where to Stay

VERY EXPENSIVE

Chester Grosvenor and Spa ★★★   This fine half-timbered, five-story building in the heart of Chester is considered one of the most luxurious hotels in northern England. Owned and named after the family of the dukes of Westminster, its origin can be traced from the reign of Queen Elizabeth I. It has hosted its share of royalty, including Prince Albert, Princess Diana, and Prince Rainier. The high-ceilinged, marble-floored foyer of the hotel, with its 200-year-old chandelier and carved wooden staircase, sets the tone. Each large, well-furnished bedroom is individually styled, with silks from France and handmade furnishings from Italy. All come with heated towel racks, Floris toiletries, and bathrobes.

Eastgate, Chester, Cheshire CH1 1LT. ⓒ **01244/324024.** Fax 01244/313246. www.chestergrosvenor. co.uk. 80 units. £205–£405 double; £395–£855 suite. 1 child 11 and younger stays free in parent's room. AE, DC, MC, V. **Amenities:** 2 restaurants (including La Brasserie and Simon Radley, p. 616); 2 bars; health club; room service; sauna; spa; steam room. *In room:* A/C, TV/DVD, CD player, hair dryer, minibar, Wi-Fi (free).

EXPENSIVE

Crabwall Manor Hotel ★★   Chester's premier country-house hotel, the imposing crenellated Crabwall Manor traces its origins from the 16th century, though most of the present building dates from the early 1800s. It has a more peaceful location than the Chester Grosvenor, though it lacks the facilities and the top-notch service of its higher-rated competitor. Standing amid 4.4 hectares (11 acres) of private grounds and gardens, the capably managed hotel offers quite large, well-furnished bedrooms. Two rooms have four-poster beds. You can relax in the full-service spa after working out in the hotel's aerobics studio.

Parkgate Rd., Mollington, Chester, Cheshire CH1 6NE. ⓒ **01244/851666.** Fax 01244/851400. www. brook-hotels.co.uk. 48 units. £109–£220 double; £200–£290 suite. Rates include breakfast. Children 15 and younger stay free when sharing room with up to 2 paying adults. AE, DC, MC, V. Take A540 3.5km (2¼ miles) northwest of Chester. **Amenities:** Restaurant; bar; health club; Jacuzzi; indoor heated pool; room service; sauna; steam room. *In room:* A/C, TV, hair dryer, Wi-Fi (£10 per day).

Green Bough Hotel ★★★   *Condé Nast* awarded this property the Johansens Award for "The Most Excellent City Hotel 2004," and it still maintains high standards. Continuing the same inn-keeping standards that won them that honor, hoteliers Janice and Philip Martin have turned this establishment into the most exclusive small luxury hotel in Chester, both for cuisine and accommodations. The bedrooms have been restored and beautifully furnished, each individually designed with elegant fabrics, beautiful wallpapers, Italian tiles, and antique cast-iron or carved wooden beds. Delightful on-site facilities include the Champagne Lounge Bar and the award-winning Olive Tree Restaurant, known for serving imaginatively conceived local produce.

60 Hoole Rd., Chester, Cheshire CH2 3NL. ⓒ **01244/326241.** Fax 01244/326265. www.chestergreen boughhotel.com. 15 units. £175–£195 double; £245–£395 suite. Rates include English breakfast. AE, DC, MC, V. **Amenities:** Restaurant; bar; room service. *In room:* TV, hair dryer.

MODERATE

Macdonald New Blossoms Hotel   This hotel enjoys an ideal location in the very heart of Chester. Blossoms Hotel has been in business since the mid–17th century, though the present structure was rebuilt late in Victoria's day. An old open staircase in the reception room helps set the tone here, but otherwise the public rooms are uninspired. Bedrooms are fitted with dark-wood pieces and firm beds— some of them four-posters or half-testers—and many units have recently been refurbished.

St. John St., Chester, Cheshire CH1 1HL. *©* **0844/879-9113.** Fax 01244/346433. www.macdonaldhotels. co.uk/blossoms. 67 units. £155–£195 double; £205 suite. AE, DC, MC, V. **Amenities:** Restaurant; bar; room service. *In room:* TV, hair dryer, Wi-Fi (£5).

Mollington Banastre ★ ☺   This Victorian mansion, a gabled house surrounded by gardens, has been successfully converted into one of the leading country-house hotels in Cheshire. Rooms have comfortable doubles or twin beds; eight are spacious enough for families and two have four-poster beds.

Parkgate Rd., Chester, Cheshire CH1 6NN. *©* **01244/851471.** Fax 01244/851165. www.brook-hotels. co.uk. 63 units. £123 double. Rates include breakfast. Children 14 and younger stay free in parent's room. AE, DC, MC, V. Take A540 3km (2 miles) northwest of the center of Chester. Or take Junction 16 of M56 and continue for 2.5km (1½ miles). **Amenities:** 2 restaurants; 2 bars; health club; Jacuzzi; indoor heated pool; room service; sauna; spa. *In room:* TV, hair dryer, Internet (£10 per day).

INEXPENSIVE

Stone Villa ★ 🍴   On the outskirts of town, just off the A56, this award-winning B&B lies in a tranquil cul-de-sac. In the post-millennium, it has twice won the coveted "Best B&B Award" in Cheshire. In fair weather, the entrance to this old stone-built villa is covered with plants, opening onto a walled floodlit car park in front. Bedrooms range from standard to executive (the most expensive rooms are larger and contain flatscreen TVs). The homemade breakfasts here are among the best of any B&B in the area, containing everything from porridge drizzled with Drambuie and local honey to vegetarian sausages.

3 Stone Place, Hoole, Chester CH2 3NR. *©* **01244/345014.** Fax 01244/345015. www.stonevillachester. co.uk. 10 units. £75–£90 double; £85 triple or family unit. MC, V. **Amenities:** Breakfast room. *In room:* TV/DVD, CD player, fridge, hair dryer, Wi-Fi (free).

Ye Olde King's Head Hotel ★   A 5-minute walk from the bus station, this place is a 16th-century museum piece of black-and-white architecture. From 1598 to 1707, it was occupied by the well-known Randle Holme family, noted heraldic painters and genealogists (some of their manuscripts have made it to the British Museum). Since 1717, the King's Head has been a licensed inn. Many of the walls and ceilings are sloped and highly pitched, with exposed beams. The host rents standard-size bedrooms, although they're nowhere near the equal of the public rooms for charm and character.

48–50 Lower Bridge St., Chester, Cheshire CH1 1RS. *©* **01244/324855.** Fax 01244/315693. 8 units. £40–£70 double; £85 family room. Rates include breakfast. AE, DC, MC, V. **Amenities:** Restaurant; bar. *In room:* TV, hair dryer.

Where to Dine

La Brasserie ENGLISH/FRENCH   For convenience and quality, this is the best all-around dining choice in Chester. Most of the main courses are priced at the lower end of the scale. In a delightful Parisian-style setting, the Brasserie has an extensive a la carte menu to suit most tastes and pocketbooks. You get robust flavors and hearty ingredients in dishes that transcend usual brasserie fare, as evoked by veal kidney with curry, smoked almonds, crispy shallots, and basmati; breast of duck with ravioli, pickled beets and sour cream; and Gloucestershire free-range chicken roasted with seasonal mushrooms.

In the Chester Grosvenor hotel, Eastgate. © **01244/324024.** Reservations recommended. Main courses £14–£27. AE, DC, MC, V. Mon–Fri 7am–10pm; Sat 7:30am–10:30pm; Sun 7:30am–10pm.

Simon Radley at the Chester Grosvenor ★★★ 🏫 ENGLISH/CONTINENTAL
Formerly known as the Arkle, and now named for the superb executive chef, this is the premier restaurant in this part of England. The 45-seat formal, gourmet restaurant has a talented 40-strong team that uses the freshest ingredients to create modern British and Continental dishes prepared with subtle touches and a certain lightness, complemented by an extensive wine cellar. Tempting main courses include grilled line-caught sea bass with a vegetable compote and shellfish vinaigrette or Lancaise duck with a hot peppercorn crust, served with ravioli and foie gras. Other temptations include breast of grouse with huckleberries. The restaurant also has a vegetarian tasting menu, an award-winning cheese selection, and a choice of at least six unique breads daily. Desserts are equally luscious and tempting. Children 11 and younger aren't permitted, and men are requested to wear a jacket—no jeans allowed.

In the Chester Grosvenor hotel, Eastgate. © **01244/324024.** www.chestergrosvenor.co.uk. Reservations required. Main courses £10–£19; tasting menu £80. AE, DC, MC, V. Tues–Sat 7:30–9:30pm (last order).

Seeing the Sights

The **Tourist Information Centre** (see above) screens a free 20-minute video presentation about Chester and offers guided walking tours of the city; tours depart daily at 10:30am in the winter and at 10:30am and 2pm in the summer.

To the accompaniment of a hand bell, the **town crier** appears at noon (Tues–Sat May–Sept) at the City Cross—the junction of Watergate, Northgate, and Bridge streets—to shout news about sales, exhibitions, and attractions in the city.

In the center of town, you'll see the much-photographed **Eastgate clock.** Climb the nearby stairs and walk along the top of the **city wall** for a view down on Chester. Passing through centuries of English history, you'll go by a cricket field, see the River Dee (formerly a major trade artery), and get a look at many 18th-century buildings. The wall also goes past some Roman ruins, and it's possible to leave the walkway to explore them. The walk is charming and free.

The **Rows** are double-decker layers of shops, one tier on the street level, the others stacked on top and connected by a footway. The upper tier is like a continuous galleried balcony—walking in the rain is never a problem here.

Chester Cathedral ★ The present building, founded in 1092 as a Benedictine abbey, was made an Anglican cathedral church in 1541. Many architectural restorations were carried out in the 19th century, but older parts have been preserved. Notable features include the fine range of monastic buildings, particularly the cloisters and refectory, the chapter house, and the superb medieval woodcarving in the choir (especially the misericords). Also worth seeing are the long south transept with its various chapels, the consistory court, and the medieval roof bosses in the Lady Chapel.

Abbey Sq. ℂ **01244/324756.** www.chestercathedral.com. Admission £5 adults, £4 seniors, £2.50 children. Mon–Sat 9am–5pm; Sun 12:30–4pm.

Chester Zoo ★ ☺   The Chester Zoo is the largest repository of animals in the north of England. It is also the site of some of the most carefully manicured gardens in the region—44 hectares (110 acres) that feature unusual shrubs, rare trees, and warm-weather displays of carpet bedding with as many as 160,000 plants timed to bloom simultaneously.

Many rare and endangered animal species breed freely here; the zoo is particularly renowned for the most successful colonies of chimpanzees and orangutans in Europe. The water bus, a popular observation aid that operates exclusively in summer, allows you to observe hundreds of water birds that make their home on the park's lake. A monorail stops at the extreme eastern and western ends of the zoo, making visits less tiring. Youngsters love the Monkey's Island exhibit.

Off A41, Upton-by-Chester, 3km (2 miles) north of the town center. ℂ **01244/380280.** www.chester zoo.org. Admission £14–£17 adults, £12–£15 seniors, £9–£13 children 3–15, £41–£55 family ticket, free for kids 2 and younger; monorail £4 adults, £3 children, free for kids 2 and younger. Reduced rates in winter. Daily from 10am; closing times vary (call for details). Closed Dec 25–26. From Chester's center, head north along Liverpool Rd.

Shopping

Chester has three main shopping areas. The **Grosvenor Precinct** is filled with classy, expensive shops and boutiques that sell trendy fashion and art items. This area is bordered on three sides by Eastgate, Bridge, and Pepper streets.

For stores with more character and lower prices, explore the **Rows,** a network of double-layered streets and sidewalks with an assortment of shops. It runs along Bridge, Watergate, Eastgate, and Northgate streets. The shopping upstairs is much more adventurous than down on the street. Among the thriving businesses operating in this traffic-free paradise are tobacco shops, restaurants, department stores, china shops, jewelers, and antiques dealers. For the best look, take a walk on arcaded Watergate Street.

Another shopping area to check out is **Cheshire Oaks,** a huge retail village of 60 shops—mainly clothing, perfume, and shoe outlet stores. Cheshire Oaks is located about 13km (8 miles) north of Chester on the M53.

Chester has a large concentration of antiques and crafts shops. Some better ones include **Lowe & Sons,** 11 Bridge St. Row (ℂ **01244/325850;** www.waltonsof chester.co.uk), with antique silver and estate jewelry; and the **Antique Shop,** 40 Watergate St. (ℂ **01244/316286**), which specializes in brass, copper, and pewter items.

 Following the Antiques Experts

To find a good deal on antiques, try a quick trip to the town of **Boughton;** every transatlantic dealer seems to go here. Along the A41, a mile from the heart of town, Boughton is filled with antiques shops along Christleden Road.

It doesn't have the charm of Chester, but shopping values are often better here than in the more historic city. Some outlets have as many as a dozen showrooms, even though they are often hidden behind rather dreary facades.

Chester After Dark

If you want to relax in a pub, grab a pint of Marston's at the **Olde Custom House,** Watergate Street (© **01244/324435**), a 17th-century customhouse with many original features still intact.

The **Pied Bull,** 57 Northgate St. (© **01244/325829**), is an 18th-century coaching inn where you can still eat, drink, or rent a room. Real ales on tap include Bitter and Traditional.

At **Ye Olde King's Head,** Lower Bridge Street (© **01244/324855**), ales are not the only spirits you may encounter. This B&B pub, built in 1622, is said to be haunted by three ghosts: a crying woman and baby in room no. 6, and a ghost whose initials, "ST," appear in steam on the bathroom mirror of room no. 4. If you prefer your spirits in a glass, stick to the pub, where you can sip on a Pedigree, or else Greenall's Original or Local.

Live Irish music and atmosphere can be sampled at the **Red Lion,** 59 Northgate St. (© **01244/321750**), where you can hear traditional music on Sunday nights for the price of a pint of Guinness. **Alexanders,** Rufus Court off Northgate Street (© **01244/340005;** http://alexanderslive.com), offers more varied entertainment.

BLACKPOOL: PLAYGROUND OF THE MIDLANDS

396km (246 miles) NW of London; 82km (51 miles) NW of Manchester; 90km (56 miles) N of Liverpool; 142km (88 miles) W of Leeds

This once-antiquated Midlands resort is struggling to make a comeback by marketing itself to a new generation of vacationers. The result may remind you of Atlantic City or even Las Vegas (with a weird Victorian twist). The city has a winter population of 125,000 that swells to three or four times that in summer.

The country's largest resort makes its living from conferences, tour groups, families, and couples looking for an affordable getaway. Its 11km (7 miles) of beaches, 9.5km (6 miles) of colored lights, and dozens of Disney-like attractions and rides make Blackpool one of the most entertaining (and least apologetic) pieces of razzle-dazzle in England.

Disadvantages include unpredictable weather that brews over the nearby Irish Channel; a sandy, flat-as-a-pancake landscape that's less than inspiring; and a (sometimes undeserved) reputation for dowdiness. But some love the brisk sea air, the architectural remnants of Britain's greatest Imperial Age, the lack of pretentiousness, and the poignant nostalgia that clings to the edges of such places, where people look back fondly on the carefree fun they had in a simpler time.

Essentials

GETTING THERE   Two trains from Manchester arrive every hour (trip time: 1½ hr.), and one from Liverpool every 2 hours (trip time: 1½ hr.). For information, call © **0845/748-4950** or visit **www.nationalrail.co.uk**.

National Express buses arrive from Chester at the rate of three per day (trip time: 4 hr.); from Liverpool at the rate of six per day (trip time: 3½ hr.); from Manchester, five per day (trip time: 2 hr.); and from London, six per day (trip time: 6½ hr.). For schedules and information, call © **0871/781-8181** or visit **www.national express.com**.

If you're driving from Manchester, take the M61 north to the M6, and then the M55 toward Blackpool. The trip takes about 1 hour.

VISITOR INFORMATION   The helpful **Tourist Information Centre,** 1 Clifton St. (✆ **01253/478222;** www.visitblackpool.com), is open November through March, Monday to Saturday 9am to 5pm; and April through October, Monday to Saturday 9am to 5pm and Sunday 10am to 4pm.

Where to Stay

EXPENSIVE

Barceló Imperial Hotel ★★   The Imperial is Blackpool's choice address. Noted as a stylish venue for group conferences, this hotel was built by the Victorians—Charles Dickens was a guest—as a massive redbrick pile, and it's still a major landmark in town. Recent renovations added vestiges of 19th-century country-house stateliness to the public areas and some of the bedrooms, along with a scattering of artwork related to such genteel pleasures as "the hunt." Accommodations are well appointed, some offering sea views.

North Promenade, Blackpool, Lancashire FY1 2HB. ✆ **01253/623971.** Fax 01253/751784. www.barcelo-hotels.co.uk. 180 units. £85–£210 double; £230–£270 suite. Rates include breakfast. AE, DC, MC, V. Parking £3. **Amenities:** 2 restaurants; bar; babysitting; health club; Jacuzzi; indoor heated pool; room service; sauna; solarium; steam room. *In room:* TV, hair dryer, Internet (£15).

De Vere Herons' Reach ★   This hotel symbolizes Blackpool's renewal. It was erected on 96 flat and sandy hectares (236 acres) in 1992, adjacent to the town's zoo and Stanley Park. Designed in a postmodern style that some visitors liken to a mansard-roofed French château, it evokes Las Vegas with a Midlands accent, partly because of the cheerful razzle-dazzle its hardworking staff throws into their jobs and partly because of the many diversions on hand. Bedrooms are traditional but modern, done with light woods; despite their relative youth, they were renovated early in 2003 and offer such extras as PlayStations. Most rooms open onto views of a golf course, and each offers the most comfortable beds in Blackpool hoteldom. Eight units are large enough for families.

East Park Dr., Blackpool, Lancashire FY3 8LL. ✆ **01253/838866.** Fax 01253/798800. www.devere.co.uk. 182 units. £70–£250 double. Rates include breakfast. AE, DC, MC, V. Free parking. **Amenities:** 2 restaurants; 3 bars; babysitting; exercise room; 18-hole golf course; Jacuzzi; indoor heated pool; room service; sauna; spa; 3 outdoor tennis courts. *In room:* TV, hair dryer, Internet (free).

Savoy Hotel ☺   The roots of this hotel stretch back to the late 19th century, when its redbrick tower and bay windows beckoned vacationers to its seaside location near the North Pier. Since then, ongoing refurbishment has kept the place well carpeted, well painted, and well upholstered. Bedrooms are conservatively up-to-date and restful. Most units are quite spacious, many offering sea views, though individual shape and size can vary considerably. Fourteen are large enough to rent to families, and each room has twin or double beds.

Queens Promenade, Blackpool, Lancashire FY2 9SJ. ✆ **01253/352561.** Fax 01253/595549. www.britanniahotels.com. 131 units. £82–£100 double; £120–£190 suite. Rates include breakfast. AE, DC, MC, V. Free parking. **Amenities:** Restaurant; bar; babysitting; room service; Wi-Fi (free). *In room:* TV, hair dryer.

INEXPENSIVE

Berwyn Hotel   The plot of land the Berwyn sits on isn't any bigger than those of most of the equivalent guesthouses in Blackpool, but you'll feel that you're in a large estate since it overlooks the city's municipal park, Gynn Gardens. There are many windows set into the ground-floor facade of this house (ca. 1910) that flood the interior with sunlight and views. The hotel was transformed in 1942 into the spacious and much-modernized establishment of today. Bedrooms are simple, even ordinary, but comfortable and restful. Rates decrease for stays of 2 nights or more, and there are senior discounts available. Evening meals, some of the best served within any comparable establishment here, cost a supplement of £10 per person.

1–2 Finchley Rd., Gynn Sq., Blackpool, Lancashire FY1 2LP. ✆ **01253/352896.** Fax 01253/594391. www. berwynhotel.co.uk. 20 units. £52–£58 double. Rates include breakfast. AE, DC, MC, V. Free parking. **Amenities:** Dining room; bar. *In room:* TV, hair dryer.

Grosvenor View   Built as halves of a brick-fronted house in the 1930s, these premises were merged by a previous owner into the free-standing guesthouse of today. Public areas are bright thanks to the large bay windows, whose leaded glass breaks the sunlight into geometric shapes. Bedrooms are well kept and comfortably furnished. A pair of TV lounges provides places to socialize.

7–9 King Edward Ave., North Shore, Blackpool, Lancashire FY2 9TD. ✆ **01253/352851.** www.grosvenor viewblackpool.com. 15 units, 11 with bathroom. £25 per person double with bathroom; £34 per person double with bathroom and dinner. Rates include breakfast. AE, MC, V. Free parking. **Amenities:** Dining room. *In room:* TV, no phone.

Where to Dine

Harry Ramsden's SEAFOOD   This is one of the most appealing of a chain of 30-some restaurants whose mission is to export British fish and chips to the world at large. Harry Ramsden's allure has resonated deeply in Blackpool, where one of the chain's most opulent locations offers a takeout counter selling a portion of haddock and chips suitable for munching during a promenade on the nearby pier. More appealing is the terra-cotta and wood-paneled interior, where the nostalgia of yesteryear is preserved with a uniformed staff, big chandeliers, and reminders of the Art Deco age. In addition to fish and chips, there's a steak-and-kidney pudding "filled with savory goodness," plain salmon with tartar sauce or lemon, meat sausages, and vegetarian selections.

60–63 Promenade. ✆ **01253/294386.** www.harryramsdens.co.uk. Reservations recommended. Main courses £6–£10. AE, DC, MC, V Sun–Thurs 11:30am–9pm; Fri–Sat 11:30am–10pm.

Twelve Restaurant ★★ ENGLISH/INTERNATIONAL   To eat well in Blackpool, you sometimes have to leave town. There is no better choice awaiting you than Twelve, which stands opposite the tallest working windmill in Europe, dating from 1794. Co-owners Caroline Upton and Paul Moss converted a former dance studio into this stellar dining spot. The minimalist space is stunningly modern, in spite of its antique backdrop. The cuisine is perfection itself, even the al dente vegetables in a land of mushy peas, and the specially prepared desserts are divine. High-quality produce is used in such dishes as Lakeland red deer or pan-fried breast of wild mallard with wild-mushroom ravioli. Baby Scottish halibut is enticingly served with mussels, and a duo of Bowland forest lamb includes both a pan-fried filet and a braised shoulder, bound together in a rosemary sauce. A winner of a dessert is the banana Betty with crème brûlée, banana ice cream, and a banana milkshake.

Marsh Mill Village, Marsh Mill in Wyre, Fleetwood Rd. S. ✆ **01253/821212.** www.twelve-restaurant. co.uk. Reservations required. Main courses £17–£27; fixed-price menu £25 Fri–Sat only. AE, MC, V. Thurs noon–2pm; Tues–Sun 6:30–10pm. Closed 2 weeks in Jan. From Blackpool, head northeast for 8.8km (5½ miles) on A584.

Seeing the Sights

The resort town is famous for the **Blackpool Illuminations** (www.visitblackpool.com/site/illuminations and www.blackpool-illuminations.net), an extravaganza of electric lights affixed to just about any stationary object along the Promenade. They feature hundreds of illuminated figures, including Diamonds Are Forever, Santa's Workshop, Lamp Lighters, and Kitchen Lites. The tradition began in 1879 with just eight electric lights; however, it has grown with time and technology to include 9.5km (6 miles) of fiber optics, low-voltage neon tubes, and traditional lamps. The Illuminations burn bright into the night from late August or September to the beginning of November. Take a tram ride down the Promenade for a great view of these tacky but festive lights.

Without a doubt, the most famous landmark in this town is the **Blackpool Tower,** along the Promenade (© **01253/622242;** www.theblackpooltower.co.uk). In 1891, during the reign of Queen Victoria, a madcap idea started floating around to construct a 155m (518-ft.) tower that resembled a half-size version of Paris's Eiffel Tower. The idea was first formally presented to the town leaders of Brighton, who laughed at the idea, thinking it was a joke. But the forward-thinking leaders of Blackpool, when presented the plan, immediately saw the advantages of having such an attraction and quickly approved the tower's construction. You be the judge.

Lighted by more than 10,000 bulbs, this landmark has become a tower of fun. The indoor-entertainment complex features the **Tower Ballroom** (one of the great Victorian ballrooms of Britain), the **Tower Circus,** the **Tower Aquarium,** the **Restaurant 1894,** and the **Jurassic Walk** through a dinosaur landscape. An elevator takes visitors to the top of the Tower for a 97km (60-mile) view. The Tower is open February through March, Saturday and Sunday 10am to 6pm and Wednesday 10am to 5pm; and April through October, daily 10am to 11pm. The circus has two to three shows daily, except on Friday evening. Tower admission is £14 to £17 for adults, £12 to £14 for seniors and children.

THE LAKE DISTRICT: HOME OF THE POETS

The Lake District, one of the most beautiful parts of Great Britain, is actually quite small, measuring about 56km (35 miles) wide. Most of the district is in Cumbria, though it begins in the northern part of Lancashire.

Bordering Scotland, the far-northwestern part of the county is generally divided geographically into three segments: the Pennines, dominating the eastern sector (loftiest point at Cross Fell, nearly 900m/3,000 ft. high); the Valley of Eden; and the lakes and secluded valleys of the west, by far the most interesting.

So beautifully described by the Romantic poets, the area enjoys literary associations with William Wordsworth, Samuel Taylor Coleridge, Charlotte Brontë, Charles Lamb, Percy Bysshe Shelley, John Keats, Alfred, Lord Tennyson, and Matthew Arnold. In Queen Victoria's day, the district was one of England's most popular summer retreats.

The largest town is Carlisle, by the Scotland border, which is a possible base for exploring Hadrian's Wall (p. 687)—but for now, we concentrate on the district's lovely lakeside villages. **Windermere** is the best base for exploring the Lake District.

KENDAL

435km (270 miles) NW of London; 116km (72 miles) NW of Leeds; 103km (64 miles) NW of Bradford; 14km (9 miles) SE of Windermere

The River Kent winds its way through a rich valley of limestone hills and cliffs, known as fells, and down through the "Auld Grey Town" of Kendal, whose moniker refers to the large number of gray stone houses found in and about the town. Many visitors to the Lake District simply pass through Kendal on their way to more attractive destinations—the town is a gateway rather than a true stopping place. It has never depended entirely on tourism. That fact should not deter you, however, from taking a bit of time to discover some of this market town's more intriguing areas.

The Lake District

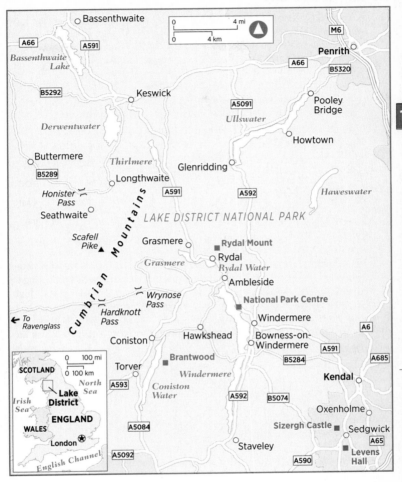

18

THE LAKE DISTRICT: HOME OF THE POETS | Kendal

Kendal contains the ruins of a castle where Catherine Parr, the last wife of Henry VIII, was allegedly born. Recent speculation about her actual birthplace has led to a clouding of the historical record. Even if she wasn't born here, it is said that she most likely lived at the castle at some time in her life. Among other historic sites, Kendal has a 13th-century parish church that merits a visit.

Today, Kendal is famous for its mint cake and its surrounding limestone fells, which offer excellent vistas of the area and make for great hikes.

Essentials

GETTING THERE Trains from London's Euston Station do not go directly to Kendal; seven daily trains arrive in Oxenholme, about 2.5km (1½ miles) away. From here, you'll be able to take a taxi or board one of the local trains that leave approximately every hour to Kendal proper (total trip time from London to Kendal: 3½ hr.). For information, call ℂ **0845/748-4950** or visit **www.nationalrail.co.uk**.

To get to Kendal from London by bus, take one of the three daily **National Express** buses (trip time: 7 hr.). For schedules and information, call ℂ **0871/781-8181** or visit **www.nationalexpress.com**.

If driving, take the M1 out of London, and then the M6 to Kendal (trip time: 5 hr.).

VISITOR INFORMATION The **Kendal Tourist Information Centre,** Town Hall, Highgate (ℂ **01539/725758;** www.golakes.co.uk), is open March through October, Monday to Saturday 10am to 5pm, and November through February, Monday to Saturday 10am to 4pm.

Where to Stay

Beech House ★ A steep walk up a hill leads to this pretty little town-house hotel situated in a tranquil area. It is one of the better B&Bs on the fringe of the Lake District National Park. Behind the walls of this ivy-clad building are modernized rooms with such extras as heated bathroom floors. Each of the boutique guest rooms is decorated differently, but in a warm and cozy style. The hearty breakfast is one reason to stay here, with dishes ranging from honey-glazed sausages to pancakes drizzled with sugar and lemon.

40 Greenside, Kendal, Cumbria LA9 4LD. ℂ **01539/720385.** Fax 01539/724082. www.beechhouse-kendal.co.uk. 6 units. £80–£100 double. Rates include breakfast. 2-night minimum on weekends. MC, V. No children. **Amenities:** Breakfast room. *In room:* TV/DVD, hair dryer, Wi-Fi (free).

Best Western Castle Green Hotel in Kendal ★ Set on 5.6 hectares (14 acres) of woodlands and gardens, the Castle Green is one of the finest hotels in the area. Though it looks like a rambling country estate, it was once a series of offices that have been cleverly converted into comfortable bedrooms. All rooms are stylish and well furnished, many opening onto panoramic views. The best, albeit most expensive, accommodations are the executive studio suites with a lot of extra space. Guests enjoy free membership in the hotel's health club. The Castle Green also has one of the best pubs, Alexander's, and one of the best restaurants, Greenhouse, in the area. On the downside, the staff could be more cordial.

Castle Green Lane, Kendal, Cumbria LA9 6BH. ℂ **01539/734000.** Fax 01539/735522. www.castlegreen.co.uk. 100 units. £97–£140 double; £175–£190 suite. Rates include English breakfast. AE, DC, MC, V. Signposted from the M6, Junction 37. **Amenities:** Restaurant; pub; fitness center; indoor heated pool; room service; solarium; steam room. *In room:* TV, hair dryer.

Where to Dine

Déjà Vu TRADITIONAL & MODERN FRENCH The interior of this small and cozy French cabaret is inspired by one of van Gogh's landscape paintings. People come for good food and a fun time. A wide range of appetizers evokes a taste of Paris, from the fresh scallops *mille-feuille,* served with a basil cream sauce, to the filet of venison with a red-wine-and-raspberry sauce. Follow with such mains as pan-fried sea bass with roasted cherry tomatoes or pan-roasted duck breast cooked pink and served with a blueberry sauce. Desserts feature many classic French favorites, including a delicious peach tartlet.

124 Strickland Gate. ⓒ **01539/724843.** www.dejavukendal.co.uk. Reservations recommended. 3-course menu £13. AE, DC, MC, V. Wed–Mon noon–2pm and 5:30–10pm. Closed Jan 4–28.

New Moon Restaurant ★ INTERNATIONAL   This bistro prepares the best food in Kendal. Set in a building that is more than 250 years old and was once a grocery store, the dining room offers patrons a close, friendly, and informal environment. The owners take pride in offering market-fresh ingredients when available, and the food is well crafted without being gimmicky. Try such dishes as braised local lamb shank with roasted root vegetables or roast turkey with chestnut stuffing. A special delight is the pan-fried duck breast in a crème de cassis jus. For dessert, try Bailey's crème brûlée with fresh fruits, or else the sticky toffee pudding with toffee sauce.

129 Highgate. ⓒ **01539/729254.** www.newmoonrestaurant.co.uk. Reservations not needed. Main courses £10–£15; early-bird dinners (before 6:30pm Tues–Fri) £10. MC, V. Tues–Fri 11:30am–2:30pm and 5:30–9:30pm; Sat 11:30am–2:30pm and 6–9:30pm.

Seeing the Sights

Abbot Hall Art Gallery   The Georgian elegance of Kendal's Abbot Hall Art Gallery has created an ideal setting for its display of fine art. Paintings by the town's famous son, 18th-century portrait painter George Romney, fill the walls of rooms furnished by Gillows of Lancaster. A major permanent display includes works by 20th-century British artists such as Graham Sutherland, John Piper, and Ben Nicholson. Visitors can see the region through the eyes of the many painters who have been inspired by the landscapes in another permanent exhibition housed in the Peter Scott Gallery.

Kirkland. ⓒ **01539/722464.** www.abbothall.org.uk. Admission £5.75 adults; free for children and students 25 and under. Mon–Sat 10:30am–5pm (until 4pm Nov–Mar). Closed Dec 22–Jan 15.

Kendal Museum   One of England's oldest museums offers a journey of discovery from Roman times to the present. A natural history section includes a nature trail from mountaintop to lakeside, bringing you face to face with many of the inhabitants of the area. The World Wildlife Gallery displays a vast collection of exotic animals. One of the exhibitions introduces visitors to the fell-tops' best-known visitor, Alfred Wainwright, who walked, talked, and wrote with a passion and flair about the region. Wainwright worked diligently until his death in 1991.

Station Rd. ⓒ **01539/815597.** www.kendalmuseum.org.uk. Admission £2.80 adults, £2.20 seniors, free for children and students. Thurs–Sat noon–5pm.

Levens Hall   This Elizabethan mansion was constructed in the 1500s by James Bellingham. Today, the house is filled with Jacobean furniture and a working model steam-train collection. The estate also has a **topiary garden** ★★ dating from 1692, with a host of yews and box hedges clipped into a variety of intriguing shapes.

8 Levens Park, Levens (6.5km/4 miles south of Kendal). ⓒ **01539/560321.** www.levenshall.co.uk. Admission house and gardens £11 adults, £4.50 children, £27 family ticket (2 adults, 3 children); gardens only £8 adults, £3.50 children, £20 family ticket. Apr to mid-Oct Sun–Thurs noon–5pm (gardens from 10am). Last admission 4:30pm.

Museum of Lakeland Life & Industry   At this re-creation of a Victorian Kendal street, complete with pharmacy and market, visitors can discover the lost crafts and trades of the region and the ways of life that accompanied them.

Abbot Hall, Kirkland. ℂ **01539/722464.** www.lakelandmuseum.org.uk. Admission £4.75 adults, £3.40 children, £14 family ticket (2 adults, 4 children). Mon–Sat 10:30am–5pm (until 4pm Nov–Mar).

Sizergh Castle Sizergh Castle has a fortified tower that dates from the 14th century. Inside, visitors can see a collection of Elizabethan carvings and paneling, fine furniture, and portraits. The complete garden, largely from the 18th century, incorporates a rock garden and a famous planting of hardy ferns and dwarf conifers. The castle is surrounded by a show of fiery colors in autumn.

Sizergh, 5.5km (3½ miles) south of Kendal (northwest of interchange A590/591). ℂ **01539/560951.** www.nationaltrust.org.uk. Admission house and gardens £7.90 adults, £4 children, £20 family ticket (2 adults, 2 children); gardens only £5.15 adults, £2.65 children. Mid-Mar to early Nov house Sun–Thurs 1–5pm; shop and gardens Sun–Thurs 11am–5pm.

Kendal After Dark

One of the best entertainment centers in the Lake District is the **Brewery Arts Centre,** Highgate (ℂ **01539/725133;** www.breweryarts.co.uk), which includes two cinemas, a theater, the Grain Store Restaurant, two cafe bars, and other venues in a converted brewery. The box office for all attractions is open Monday to Saturday 10am to 8:30pm and Sunday 11am to 8:30pm.

WINDERMERE & BOWNESS ★★

441km (274 miles) NW of London; 16km (10 miles) NW of Kendal; 89km (55 miles) N of Liverpool

The largest lake in England is Windermere, whose eastern shore washes up on the town of Bowness (or Bowness-on-Windermere), with the town of Windermere 2.5km (1½ miles) away. From either town, you can climb **Orrest Head** in less than an hour for a panoramic view of the Lakeland. From that vantage point, you can even view **Scafell Pike,** rising to a height of 963m (3,210 ft.)—it's the tallest peak in all of England.

Essentials

GETTING THERE Trains to Windermere meet the main line at Oxenholme for connections to both Scotland and London. Frequent connections are possible throughout the day. You can obtain information about rail services in the area by calling ℂ **0845/748-4950** or visiting **www.nationalrail.co.uk.** To get to Bowness and its ferry pier from Windermere, turn left from the rail terminal and cross the center of Windermere until you reach New Road, which eventually changes its name to Lake Road before it approaches the outskirts of Bowness. It's about a 20-minute walk downhill. The Lakeland Experience bus also runs from the Windermere station to Bowness every 20 minutes.

The **National Express** bus link, originating at London's Victoria Coach Station, serves Windermere, with connections also to Preston, Manchester, and Birmingham. For schedules and information, call ℂ **0871/781-8181** or visit **www.national express.com.** Local buses operated mainly by **Stagecoach** (ℂ **0871/200-2233;** www.stagecoachbus.com) go to Kendal, Ambleside, Grasmere, and Keswick. Call for information on various routings within the Lake District.

If you're driving from London, head north on the M1 and the M6 past Liverpool until you reach the A685 junction heading west to Kendal. From Kendal, the A591 continues west to Windermere.

VISITOR INFORMATION The **Windermere Tourist Information Centre** is on Victoria Street (☎ **01539/446499;** www.golakes.co.uk). It's open November through March, Monday to Saturday 9am to 5pm and Sunday 10am to 5pm, and April through October, Sunday to Thursday 9am to 6pm and Friday to Saturday until 6:30pm.

Where to Stay

EXPENSIVE

Holbeck Ghyll Country House Hotel ★★★ This is the most tranquil oasis in the area and offers the most refined cuisine. Overlooking Lake Windermere, this country-house hotel was once a 19th-century hunting lodge owned by Lord Lonsdale, one of the richest men in Britain, and has a high price tag but offers a lot for the money. An inglenook fireplace welcomes visitors. Rooms are individually designed, coming in various shapes and sizes, and most of them open onto a view of the lake. All units are fitted with a luxury bed, often crowned by a canopy or a padded headboard. The most elaborate is a honeymoon and anniversary room that has a four-poster bed and a bathroom with a spa tub for two. A separate lodge added in 1998 contains six units that are even finer than the rooms in the main building. Lodge rooms are interconnecting with panoramic lake views, individual balcony or patio areas, and fresh flowers; four units have kitchenettes. Luxurious bathrooms have separate showers and tubs. *Note:* Children 7 and younger are not welcome in the restaurant.

Holbeck Lane (on A591, 5.5km/3½ miles northwest of town center), Windermere, Cumbria LA23 1LU. ☎ **01539/432375.** Fax 01539/434743. www.holbeckghyll.com. 21 units. £119–£150 per person double; £139–£225 per person suite. Rates include English breakfast and dinner. Children 16 and younger are half-price in parent's room. AE, DC, MC, V. **Amenities:** Restaurant; bar; exercise room; room service; spa; tennis court. *In room:* TV, hair dryer, kitchenette (in 4 units).

Langdale Chase Hotel ★★ A grand old lakeside house, this hotel resembles a villa on Italy's Lake Como. It has better rooms than Miller Howe (see below), though the food is not as good. Many of the accommodations were recently refurbished and contain excellent furniture; most open onto panoramic views of the lake. A converted cottage on the grounds contains five units that are equal in comfort to those in the main building. An oft-requested bedroom lies over the boathouse on the lake. Bathrooms are tiled and come with adequate shelf space and combination tub/shower. The interior of the Victorian stone château, with its many gables, balconies, mullioned windows, and terraces, is a treasure trove of antiques. The main lounge hall looks like a setting for one of those English drawing-room comedies. On the walls are distinctive paintings, mostly Italian primitives, though one is alleged to be a Van Dyck.

On A591 (3km/2 miles north of town, toward Ambleside), Windermere, Cumbria LA23 1LW. ☎ **01539/432201.** Fax 01539/432604. www.langdalechase.co.uk. 27 units. £65–£125 per person double. Rates include breakfast and dinner. 2-night minimum Sat–Sun. AE, DC, MC, V. **Amenities:** Restaurant; bar; babysitting; room service. *In room:* TV, hair dryer.

Lindeth Fell Country House Hotel ★ High above the town is this traditional large Lakeland house, built of stone and brick in 1907. The owners, the Kennedys, run the place more like a country house than a hotel, achieving an atmosphere of comfort in pleasingly furnished surroundings. Bedrooms open onto beautiful views, especially on the lake side of the house; those on the other side face handsome gardens. Many rooms are quite spacious, others are snug, but all have comfortable beds.

Lyth Valley Rd. (on A5074, 1.5km/1 mile south of Bowness), Bowness-on-Windermere, Cumbria LA23 3JP. ✆ **01539/443286.** Fax 01539/447455. www.lindethfell.co.uk. 14 units. £184–£230 double. Rates include breakfast and dinner. MC, V. **Amenities:** Restaurant; bar; room service. *In room:* TV, hair dryer, Wi-Fi (free).

Linthwaite House Hotel ★

This hotel, built in 1900, is surrounded by woodlands and gardens, with a panoramic view of Lake Windermere, Bell Isle, and the distant mountains. As befits its former role as an Edwardian gentleman's house, this hotel has individually decorated bedrooms that come in various shapes and sizes. All are fitted with sumptuously comfortable beds and come with tub/shower combinations. The many in-room amenities include bathrobes and satellite TVs.

Crook Rd., Bowness-on-Windermere, Cumbria LA23 3JA. ✆ **01539/488600.** Fax 01539/488601. www. linthwaite.com. 27 units. £198–£300 double; £360–£495 suite. Rates include English breakfast. AE, DC, MC, V. **Amenities:** Restaurant; bar; room service; free use of nearby spa. *In room:* TV, CD player, hair dryer, Wi-Fi (free).

Miller Howe Hotel ★★

International guests come to this inn that bears the unique imprint of its creator, former actor John Tovey, who treats his guests as if they had been invited to a house party. His country estate overlooks Lake Windermere, with views of the Langdale Pikes, and offers stylish accommodations and exquisite cuisine. The house was built in 1916 in the Edwardian style, sitting on 2.2 hectares (5½ acres) of statue-dotted garden and parkland. Each of the large, graciously furnished guest rooms is supplied with binoculars to help guests fully enjoy the view; other amenities include CD players and umbrellas. Beds are sumptuous, often canopy-draped, each with colorful spreads and padded headboards. There are even copies of *Punch* from the 1890s. The chef prepares a nightly five-course menu gourmand that is one of the best in the area.

Rayrigg Rd. (on A592, btw. Windermere and Bowness), Windermere, Cumbria LA23 1EY. ✆ **01539/442536.** Fax 01539/445664. www.millerhowe.com. 16 units. £105–£155 per person double. Rates include English breakfast and 5-course dinner. AE, MC, V. **Amenities:** Restaurant; 3 lounges; conservatory room; room service. *In room:* TV, CD player, hair dryer.

The Samling ★★★ 👜

Standing on 27 hectares (67 acres) that open onto panoramic views of Lake Windermere, this hotel was fashioned from a late-18th-century stone-built manse with three gables set off with scalloped fretwork. Wordsworth used to come here to pay his rent on Dove Cottage in neighboring Grasmere. Samling bills itself as an "un-country house" hotel, free of "snooty nostalgic stuff." The tranquil hotel is becoming a secret address for the rich and famous such as soccer star David Beckham. The rooms in a converted stable block are more spacious; you'll think you're at a ski lodge. In the main building, accommodations have more of a traditional British aura. Even if you're not a guest, consider an elegant £55 set-price dinner here.

Ambleside Rd., Windermere, Cumbria LA23 1LR. ✆ **015394/31922.** www.thesamling.com. 11 units. £190–£650 suite. Rates include breakfast. AE, DC, MC, V. **Amenities:** Restaurant; bar. *In room:* TV, hair dryer, Wi-Fi (in some; free).

MODERATE

Cedar Manor Hotel ★

One of the most desirable country-house hotels in the area is Cedar Manor. Originally built in 1860, with gables and chimneys, it was the summer getaway home for a wealthy industrialist from Manchester. But since those times, it has been converted into a hotel of exceptional merit. Each well-furnished and spacious bedroom is individually designed and well maintained; some have canopied or four-poster beds. The hotel takes its name from a cedar tree, perhaps from India, which has grown in the garden for some 2 centuries.

Ambleside Rd. (A591), Windermere, Cumbria LA23 1AX. *C* **01539/443192.** Fax 01539/445970. www. cedarmanor.co.uk. 11 units. £90–£100 double; £120–£160 suite. Rates include breakfast. 2-night minimum Sat–Sun. AE, MC, V. **Amenities:** Restaurant; lounge. *In room:* TV, DVD (in some), fridge (in some), hair dryer, MP3 docking station, Wi-Fi (free).

Lindeth Howe Country House Hotel   This country house enjoys a scenic position above Lake Windermere, with 2.4 hectares (6 acres) of gardens. Part stone and part red brick, with a roof of green Westmoreland slate, the house was built for a wealthy mill owner in 1879, but its most famous owner was Beatrix Potter, who installed her mother here while she lived across the lake at Sawrey. The present owner, Norman Stoller, has furnished it in fine style. Nine of the bedrooms have lake views. Three rooms have handsome four-poster beds, some rooms have spa bathrooms, and three units are large enough for families.

Lindeth Dr., Longtail Hill, Storrs Park, Bowness-on-Windermere, Cumbria LA23 3JF. *C* **01539/445759.** Fax 01539/446368. www.lindeth-howe.co.uk. 36 units. £170–£270 double. Rates include breakfast. AE, MC, V. Take B5284 south of Bowness. **Amenities:** Restaurant; bar; health club; indoor heated pool; room service; sauna; solarium. *In room:* TV, hair dryer, Wi-Fi (free).

INEXPENSIVE

Beaumont House   This stone-sided Lakeland villa, originally built in the 1850s, is on a quiet residential street about a minute's walk from Windermere's commercial center. Mr. and Mrs. John Dixon massively upgraded what had been a rather dowdy interior. All accommodations have been refurbished, with new showers, carpets, and curtains. Each of the bedrooms is named after one of the characters in the Beatrix Potter sagas (our favorite is Jemima Puddle-Duck) and contains either an elaborate canopy bed or a four-poster, fitted with a quality mattress. No meals are served other than breakfast, so the owners keep local restaurant menus on hand for their guests to consult.

Holly Rd., Windermere, Cumbria LA23 2AF. *C* **01539/447075.** Fax 01539/488311. www.lakesbeaumont. co.uk. 10 units. £80–£130 double. Rates include English breakfast. MC, V. No children under 10. **Amenities:** Free use of nearby health club. *In room:* TV, DVD (in some), hair dryer.

Fir Trees Guest House ★   One of the finest guesthouses in Windermere, this well-run inn provides hotel-like standards at B&B prices. Opposite St. John's Church, halfway between the villages of Bowness and Windermere, Fir Trees is a Victorian house furnished with antiques. Proprietors Bob and Bea Towers offer a warm welcome and beautifully maintained bedrooms. Some units are large enough for families; a few have four-poster beds. The Towers can provide their guests with information on restaurants, country pubs, or where to go and what to see.

Lake Rd., Windermere, Cumbria LA23 2EQ. *C* **01539/442272.** Fax 01539/442512. www.fir-trees.co.uk. 9 units. £32–£48 per person double. Rates include English breakfast. MC, V. **Amenities:** Free use of nearby health club. *In room:* TV, hair dryer.

Where to Dine

Lucy4 at the Porthole BRITISH/FRENCH/ITALIAN   In a white-painted Lakeland house near the center of town, this restaurant serves French, English, and Italian cuisine. Amid a decor enhanced by rows of wine and liqueur bottles and nautical accessories, you can enjoy well-flavored specialties that change with the seasons. Try the ballottine of Lakeland lamb (lamb shoulder infused with fresh rosemary, plus a touch of anchovy and garlic, braised in red wine) or the excellent filet of beef Rossini, chargrilled to your liking and topped with a Madeira-scented chicken liver parfait. Crispy sea bass is coated with a fragrant sauce of homemade Thai red curry and cooked with coconut milk, lemon grass, and ginger, with a touch of chili.

3 Ash St. © **01539/442793.** www.lucy4.co.uk. Reservations recommended. Main courses £11–£22. AE, DC, MC, V. Mon–Fri 5–10:30pm; Sat–Sun noon–10:30pm.

Queen's Head ★ MODERN BRITISH   Once voted "Cumbria Dining Pub of the Year," and still as good, this unusual and popular 17th-century coaching inn uses a huge Elizabethan four-poster bed as its serving counter and has other eclectic antiques among its traditional wooden bar furniture. The menu, which changes every 6 weeks, also combines common items in unusual ways, making traditional dishes more exotic. Some of the best mains include slow-roasted breast of Barbary duck and confit of the leg served with a plum sauce, or else a risotto of wild mushrooms and roast salsify with a poached egg and Parmesan crisp. Finish with one of the lovely puddings, perhaps an orange-and-chocolate tart with a Grand Marnier zabaglione. There's a full bar and a good wine selection, or you can quaff a pint of Mitchell's Lancaster Bomber, Tetley's, or Boddingtons.

Looking for a place to stay? The Queen's Head has nine well-furnished rooms, with doubles priced at £100 to £130.

Off A592 in Troutbeck, about 5.6km (3½ miles) north of Windermere. © **01539/432174.** www.queens headtroutbeck.co.uk. Reservations recommended. Main courses £11–£25. MC, V. Daily noon–2pm and 6:30–9pm.

Favorite Local Pubs

Established in 1612, the **Hole in t' Wall,** Lowside (© **01539/443488**), is the oldest pub in Bowness, a real treasure for its character and friendliness. The barroom is decorated with a hodgepodge of antiquated farming tools, a large slate fireplace lends warmth on winter days, and there's a good selection of real ales on tap. The menu, determined daily, illustrates real ingenuity in its eclectic mix of vegetarian, seafood, and local game dishes. A small flagstone terrace in the front encourages lingering on warmer days and evenings.

Drive a short distance south of Windermere to Cartmel Fell, situated between the A592 and the A5074, and you'll find a pub-lover's dream. The **Mason Arms,** Strawberry Bank (© **01539/568486**), is a Jacobean pub with original oak paneling and flagstone floors. Sturdy, comfortable wooden furniture is spread through a series of five rooms in which you can wander or settle. The outside garden, attractive in its own right, offers a dramatic view of the Winster Valley beyond. The pub offers so many beers that there's a 24-page catalog to help you order, plus a creative, reasonable menu that includes several tasty vegetarian options. Beer prices start at £3.

Southeast of Windermere, off the A5074 in Crosthwaithe the **Punch Bowl,** (© **01539/568234;** www.the-punchbowl.co.uk), is a 16th-century pub whose central room features a high-beamed ceiling with upper minstrel galleries on two sides. Outdoors, a stepped terrace on the hillside offers a tranquil retreat. Theakston's Best Bitter, Jennings Cumberland, and Cocker Hoop are available on tap.

Exploring the Area

There is regular steamer service around Windermere, the largest of the lakes (about 17km/11 miles long). It's also possible to take a steamer on Coniston Water, a smaller, less heavily traveled lake that Wordsworth called "a broken spoke sticking in the rim." Launch and steamer cruises operated by **Windermere Lake Cruises Ltd.** (*𝒞* **01539/443360;** www.windermere-lakecruises.co.uk) depart from Bowness daily throughout the year. Round-trip service is available among Bowness, Ambleside, and Lakeside at rates ranging from £12 to £15 for adults, £6 to £7.25 for children, and £33 to £38 for a family ticket. A 45-minute "Islands Cruise" goes for £6.75 for adults, £3.40 for children, and £18 for a family ticket.

At Lakeside, you can ride a steam train to Haverthwaite. A combination boat/train ticket is £13 to £21 for adults, £7 to £10 for children, and £36 to £55 for a family ticket.

An attraction at Lakeside is the **Lakes Aquarium,** near Newby Bridge (*𝒞* **01539/530153;** www.lakesaquarium.co.uk), with an exhibit of fish and wildlife. The aquarium is open November to March, daily from 9am to 4pm, and April to October, daily from 9am to 5pm. Combination boat/admission tickets from Ambleside are £23 for adults, £12 for children, and £66 for a family ticket; from Bowness, tickets are £16 for adults, £9.20 for children, and £48 for a family ticket. Aquarium-only admission is £9 for adults, £6 for children 3 to 15, and £27 to £33 for a family ticket.

Directly south of Windermere, **Bowness** is an attractive old lakeside town with lots of Victorian architecture, much of it dating from Queen Victoria's day. This has been an important center for boating and fishing for a long time, and you can rent boats of all descriptions to explore the lake.

World of Beatrix Potter   This exhibit uses the latest technology to tell the story of Beatrix Potter's fascinating life. A video wall and special film describe how her tales came to be written and how she became a pioneering Lakeland farmer and conservationist. There is also a shop with a wealth of top-quality Beatrix Potter merchandise, from Wedgwood ceramics to soft toys. It's mobbed on summer weekends; try to come at any other time.

The Old Laundry, Bowness-on-Windermere. *𝒞* **01539/488444.** www.hop-skip-jump.com. Admission £6.75 adults, £3.50 children. Easter–Oct daily 10am–5:30pm; rest of year daily 10am–4:30pm. Take A591 to Lake Rd. and follow the signs.

AMBLESIDE & RYDAL

448km (278 miles) NW of London; 23km (14 miles) NW of Kendal; 6.5km (4 miles) N of Windermere

An idyllic retreat at the north end of Lake Windermere, Ambleside is just a small village, but it's one of the major places to stay in the Lake District, attracting pony trekkers, hikers, and rock climbers. It's wonderful in warm weather and even through late autumn, when it's fashionable to sport a raincoat.

Between Ambleside and Wordsworth's former retreat at Grasmere is Rydal, a small village on one of the smallest lakes, Rydal Water. The village is noted for its sheepdog trials at the end of summer. It's 2.5km (1½ miles) north of Ambleside on the A591.

Essentials

GETTING THERE   Take a train to Windermere (see "Windermere & Bowness," earlier in this chapter), and then continue the rest of the way by bus.

Stagecoach (📞 **0871/200-2233;** www.stagecoachbus.com) has hourly bus service from Grasmere and Keswick (see "Grasmere," below, and "Keswick," later in this chapter) and from Windermere. All these buses into Ambleside are labeled either no. 555 or 556.

If you're driving from Windermere, continue northwest on the A591.

VISITOR INFORMATION   The **Ambleside Tourist Information Centre** is at Market Cross Central Buildings (📞 **01539/432582;** www.golakes.co.uk). It's open daily 9am to 5:30pm.

Where to Stay

Glen Rothay Hotel   Built in the 17th century as a wayfarer's inn, this hotel adjoins Dora's Field, immortalized by Wordsworth. Set back from the highway, it has a stucco-and-flagstone facade. Inside, the place has been modernized, but original details remain, including beamed ceilings and paneling. The comfortable bedrooms upstairs are tastefully furnished. Most rooms have twin or double beds, but a couple offer four-posters. The tiled bathrooms are small and compact, each with a shower.

On A591, Rydal, Ambleside, Cumbria LA22 9LR. 📞 **01539/434500.** Fax 01539/34505. www.theglen rothay.co.uk. 8 units. £85 double; from £98 suite. Rates include English breakfast. MC, V. Located 2.5km (1½ miles) northwest of Ambleside. **Amenities:** Restaurant; bar; room service. *In room:* TV, hair dryer.

Queen's Hotel   In the heart of this area is the Queen's, an old-fashioned family-run hotel where guests are housed and fed well. It began as a private home in the Victorian era and was later transformed into a hotel. Bedrooms are a bit smallish but reasonably comfortable, and the small bathrooms have shower stalls and tubs.

Market Place, Ambleside, Cumbria LA22 9BU. 📞 **01539/432206.** Fax 01539/432721. www.queenshotel ambleside.com. 26 units. Sun–Thurs £58–£76 double; Fri–Sat £76–£94 double. AE, MC, V. **Amenities:** 2 restaurants; 2 bars. *In room:* TV, hair dryer.

Riverside Hotel ★   Secluded on a quiet lane, this is a small country hotel formed by combining three adjoining riverside houses dating from the 1820s. It has the solid slate-block walls and slate roof common to Cumbria and, despite its peaceful location, lies a few minutes' walk from the center of Ambleside. Each of the painstakingly decorated rooms is comfortably furnished—one features a four-poster bed, and two suites have a Jacuzzi. One room is large enough for families.

Near Rothay Bridge, Under Loughrigg, Ambleside, Cumbria LA22 9LJ. 📞 **01539/432395.** Fax 01539/432440. www.riverside-at-ambleside.co.uk. 6 units. £96–£108 double. Rates include English breakfast. MC, V. Closed 3 weeks in Dec. From Windermere on A591, take the left fork at Waterhead toward Coniston. Follow Coniston Rd. for about 1.5km (1 mile) until you come to the junction at Rothay Bridge. Turn left across the bridge, and then immediately make a sharp right along the small lane signposted UNDER LOUGHRIGG. **Amenities:** Access to nearby health club. *In room:* TV/DVD, hair dryer, Wi-Fi (£10 per day).

Rothay Manor Hotel ★★ ☺   At this spot, which is reminiscent of a French country inn, the stars are the cuisine, the well-chosen French and American wines, and the comfortable, centrally heated bedrooms and suites. It's our top choice in an area with stiff competition in the country-house race. Most bedrooms have shuttered

French doors opening onto a sunny balcony and a mountain view (two are wheelchair accessible). Throughout the estate, you'll find an eclectic combination of antiques (some Georgian blended harmoniously with Victorian), flowers, and enticing armchairs.

The manor is a great place for families, renting both family rooms and family suites (big enough for a brood of six), and also providing cots at no additional fee. Baby-listening devices are available, and there's a children's "high tea" served around 6 to 6:30pm, which is really a dinner, with burgers, fish sticks, pizzas, and the like. A children's playground is nearby.

Rothay Bridge, Ambleside, Cumbria LA22 0EH. © **01539/433605.** Fax 01539/433607. www.rothay manor.co.uk. 19 units. £160–£200 double; £210–£230 suite. Rates include English breakfast. AE, DC, MC, V. Take A593 1km (½ mile) south of Ambleside. **Amenities:** Restaurant; bar; babysitting; free use of nearby health club; room service; Wi-Fi (free). *In room:* TV, hair dryer.

Wateredge Inn ★ This is a winning little choice with an idyllic lakeside setting. The center of this hotel was formed long ago from two 17th-century fishing cottages. Wateredge was, in fact, listed as a lodging house as early as 1873, and further additions were made in the early 1900s. Situated in a beautiful garden overlooking Lake Windermere, the hotel also serves some of the best food in the area. Public rooms have many little nooks for reading and conversation. On sunny days, however, guests prefer to relax in the chairs on the lawn. The rooms vary in size and appointments; some are spacious, others much smaller. Furnishings are continually renewed and upgraded as the need arises. The Windermere room has a two-person tub with a separate walk-in shower.

Borrans Rd. (off A591, 1.5km/1 mile south of Ambleside), Waterhead, Ambleside, Cumbria LA22 0EP. © **01539/432332.** Fax 01539/431878. www.wateredgeinn.co.uk. 22 units. £100–£170 double. Rates include English breakfast. AE, MC, V. **Amenities:** Restaurant; bar; nearby health club. *In room:* TV, hair dryer.

Where to Dine

Glass House Restaurant ★ MODERN BRITISH/MEDITERRANEAN   In the early 1990s, the owners of this popular restaurant renovated what had originally been built in the 1400s as a water-driven mill for the crushing of wheat into flour. Today, you'll find a split-level combination of medieval and postmodern architecture, with big windows, interior views of the mill's original cogs and gears, lots of oaken interior trim and, on the buildings outside, a moss-covered, full-scale replica of the original water wheel. Menu items are more sophisticated and elegant than what's served by any of its competitors. Some of the best mains include smoked salmon in a chive-butter sauce or roast free-range Lakeland chicken stuffed with chive and cream cheese.

Rydal Rd., Ambleside. © **01539/432137.** www.theglasshouserestaurant.co.uk. Reservations recommended. Main courses £9–£18. MC, V. Wed–Mon noon–2pm and 6:30–10pm.

Lucy's on a Plate ★ 🏠 MODERN BRITISH   The most bustling cafe in town becomes one of the best and most popular restaurants after dark, when it's time for dinner by candlelight. Local farm produce is used whenever possible to create a series of well-crafted dishes. For mains in the evening, you can sample the likes of a char-grilled rib-eye with matchstick potatoes and onion marmalade, or else a bowl of fresh mussels cooked in a coconut-milk sauce. The restaurant is famous for its hot puddings, especially its sublime sticky toffee pudding or its "wicked" hot-chocolate sponge.

During the day, you can drop by the adjoining deli, **Lucy's Specialist Grocers,** to stock up on enough delights to fill a picnic basket to be enjoyed in some lakeside setting.

Church St., Ambleside. ☏ **01539/432288.** www.lucysofambleside.co.uk. Reservations not needed. Main courses £10–£21. AE, DC, MC, V. Daily 10am–9pm.

Where to Share a Pint

The friendliest pub in Ambleside is the **Golden Rule,** Smithy Brow (☏ **01539/432257;** www.ambleside.co.uk/display/goldenrule/rulemain.html), named for the brass yardstick mounted over the bar. Its country-hunt theme features comfortable leather furniture and cast-iron tables. You can step into one side room and throw darts, or go into the other for a quiet, contemplative pint. Behind the bar, a small but colorful garden provides a serene setting in warm weather. There's inexpensive pub grub if you get hungry.

Located 5km (3 miles) west of Ambleside, the **Three Shires Inn,** off the A593 in Little Langdale (☏ **01539/437215;** www.threeshiresinn.co.uk), has a stone-built pub with a stripped timber-and-flagstone interior, offering stunning views of the valley and wooded hills. You can get good pub grub here, as well as a pint of Black Sheep Bitter, Ruddles County, or Webster's Yorkshire. Malt whiskies are well represented.

A Literary Landmark

Rydal Mount ★   This was the home of William Wordsworth from 1813 until his death in 1850. Part of the house was built as a farmer's lake cottage around 1575. A descendant of Wordsworth now owns the property, which displays numerous portraits, furniture, and family possessions, as well as mementos and the poet's books. A 1.8-hectare (4½-acre) garden, landscaped by Wordsworth, is filled with rare trees, shrubs, and other features of interest.

Off A591, 2.5km (1½ miles) north of Ambleside. ☏ **01539/433002.** www.rydalmount.co.uk. Admission house and gardens £6 adults, £5 seniors and students, £2.50 children 5–15, £15 family ticket, free for kids 4 and younger. Mar–Oct daily 9:30am–5pm; Nov–Dec and Feb Wed–Mon 10am–4pm.

GRASMERE ★★

454km (282 miles) NW of London; 29km (18 miles) NW of Kendal; 69km (43 miles) S of Carlisle

On a lake of the same name, Grasmere was the home of Wordsworth from 1799 to 1808. He called this area "the loveliest spot that man hath ever known."

Getting There

Take a train to Windermere (see "Windermere & Bowness," earlier in this chapter) and continue the rest of the way by bus.

Stagecoach (☏ **0871/200-2233;** www.stagecoachbus.com) runs hourly bus service to Grasmere from Keswick (see "Keswick," later in this chapter) and Windermere. Buses in either direction are marked no. 555 or 556.

If you're driving from Windermere, continue northwest along the A591.

Where to Stay & Dine

EXPENSIVE

Swan Hotel   Sir Walter Scott used to slip in here for a secret drink early in the morning, and Wordsworth mentioned the place in "The Waggoner." In fact, the poet's wooden chair is in one of the rooms. Many bedrooms are in a modern wing, added in 1975, that fits gracefully onto the building's older core (only the shell of the original 1650 building remains). Bedrooms are comfortably furnished, each with twin or double beds; one unit has a four-poster bed.

On A591 (on the road to Keswick, 1km/½ mile outside Grasmere), Grasmere, Cumbria LA22 9RF. ✆ **0844/879-9120.** Fax 01539/435741. www.macdonaldhotels.co.uk/swan. 38 units. £153–£170 double; £189–£210 suite. Rates include breakfast. AE, DC, MC, V. **Amenities:** Restaurant; bar; room service; spa. *In room:* TV, hair dryer, Wi-Fi (£12 per day).

Wordsworth Hotel & Spa ★★   This choice in the heart of the village is situated in a 1.2-hectare (3-acre) garden next to the churchyard where Wordsworth is buried. An old stone Lakeland house that was once the hunting lodge of the earl of Cadogan, the Wordsworth Hotel has been completely refurbished to provide luxuriously appointed bedrooms with views of the fells, as well as modern bathrooms. Accommodations come with character and comfort, and the canopied beds are rather sumptuous. Three rooms have four-poster beds. The original master bedroom contains a Victorian bathroom with a brass towel rail and polished pipes and taps. Three units are spacious enough for families.

Stock Lane, Grasmere, Cumbria LA22 9SW. ✆ **01539/435592.** Fax 01539/435765. www.grasmere-hotels.co.uk. 36 units. £100–£250 double; £180–£350 suite. Rates include English breakfast and dinner. AE, DC, MC, V. Turn left on A591 at the GRASMERE VILLAGE sign, and follow the road over the bridge, past the church, and around an S-bend; the Wordsworth is on the right. **Amenities:** Restaurant; bar; exercise room; Jacuzzi; heated indoor pool; room service; sauna. *In room:* TV, hair dryer, Wi-Fi (free).

MODERATE

Best Western Grasmere Red Lion Hotel ★ ☺   This 200-year-old coaching inn is only a short stroll from Wordsworth's Dove Cottage, and it's assumed that the poet often stopped here for a meal or drink, or to warm himself by the fire. The refurbished hotel offers comfortably furnished bedrooms, half with Jacuzzis in the bathrooms. Your best bet is to ask for one of the eight modern bedrooms, which are better appointed. The older rooms are fine as well, each fitted with firm beds. Four rooms are spacious enough for families and offer bunk beds.

Red Lion Sq., Grasmere, Cumbria LA22 9SS. ✆ **800/780-7234** in the U.S. and Canada, or 01539/435456. Fax 01539/435579. www.bw-grasmereredlion.co.uk. 47 units. Sun–Thurs £105–£142 double; Fri–Sat £109–£182 double. Breakfast £9.50 per person. 2-night minimum Sat–Sun. AE, DC, MC, V. **Amenities:** Restaurant; 2 bars; exercise room; Jacuzzi; indoor heated pool; room service; sauna; steam room. *In room:* TV, hair dryer, Wi-Fi (free).

Gold Rill Hotel ★★   Paul and Cathy Jewsbury operate the best-located hotel in Grasmere, alongside the lake yet only a 2-minute walk to the center of the village. Surrounded by well-maintained gardens, the hotel stands on .8 hectare (2 acres) of land with its own heated outdoor pool and a private pier. It's really a sprawling country house of grand comfort and taste. Each midsize to spacious bedroom is individually furnished, some with a king-size bed. Those who consider themselves romantics can arrange in advance for champagne, strawberries, and fresh flowers to be placed in the room. Guests can enjoy pub lunches or a fine evening dinner here, often prepared with local produce.

Red Bank Rd., Grasmere, Cumbria LA22 9PU. ✆ **01539/435486.** www.gold-rill.com. 31 units. £136–£152 double. Rates include English breakfast. MC, V. **Amenities:** Restaurant; bar; heated outdoor pool; room service. *In room:* TV, hair dryer.

White Moss House ★ This 1730 Lakeland cottage, once owned by Wordsworth, overlooks the lake and the fells. You'll be welcomed here by Peter and Susan Dixon, who will pamper you with morning tea in bed, turn down your bedcovers at night, and cater to your culinary preferences. The rooms are individually decorated, comfortably furnished, and well heated in nippy weather. Brockstone, a cottage annex that is a 5-minute drive along the road, can accommodate two, three, or four guests comfortably in utter peace.

On A591 (2.5km/1½ miles south of town), Rydal Water, Grasmere, Cumbria LA22 9SE. *C* **01539/435295.** Fax 01539/435516. www.whitemoss.com. 6 units. £90–£110 double. Rates include breakfast and dinner. AE, MC, V. Closed Dec–Jan. **Amenities:** Restaurant; bar; access to nearby health club; room service. *In room:* TV, hair dryer.

INEXPENSIVE

Riversdale ◆ This lovely old house, built in 1830 of traditional Lakeland stone, is situated on the outskirts of the village of Grasmere along the banks of the River Rothay. The bedrooms are tastefully decorated and offer every comfort, including hospitality trays, as well as views of the surrounding fells. Most rooms are midsize and contain quality furnishings. The staff has a wealth of information on day trips, whether by car or hiking. The delightful breakfasts are served in a dining room overlooking Silver How and the fells beyond Easdale Tarn.

White Bridge, Grasmere, Cumbria LA22 9RQ. *C* **01539/435619.** www.riversdalegrasmere.co.uk. 3 units. £78–£95 double. Rates include English breakfast. MC, V. Drive 16km (10 miles) north of Windermere along A591 (signposted KESWICK), and then turn left by the Swan Hotel. In 360m (1,200 ft.), you'll find the inn on the left side of the road facing the river. No children 17 and under. **Amenities:** Breakfast room. *In room:* TV, fridge, hair dryer, no phone.

A Literary Landmark

Dove Cottage, the Wordsworth Museum & Art Gallery ★ Wordsworth lived with his writer and diarist sister, Dorothy, at Dove Cottage, which is now part of the Wordsworth Museum and administered by the Wordsworth Trust. William Wordsworth, the poet laureate, died in the spring of 1850 and was buried in the graveyard of the village church at Grasmere. Another tenant of Dove Cottage was Thomas De Quincey (*Confessions of an English Opium Eater*). The Wordsworth Museum houses manuscripts, paintings, and memorabilia. Various special exhibitions throughout the year explore the art and literature of English Romanticism.

Open to researchers who have made prior arrangements, the **Jerwood Centre Reading Room** stands next to the cottage, preserving all the major collections related to the Lake poets. More than 50,000 documents, works of art, and other general memorabilia are housed at the center.

On A591, south of the village of Grasmere on the road to Kendal. *C* **01539/435544.** www.wordsworth. org.uk. Admission to Dove Cottage and the adjoining museum £7.50 adults, £4.50 children, £17 family ticket. Daily 9:30am–5:30pm. Closed Dec 24–26 and mid-Jan to early Feb.

CONISTON & HAWKSHEAD

423km (263 miles) NW of London; 31km (19 miles) NW of Kendal; 84km (52 miles) S of Carlisle

At Coniston, you can visit the village famously associated with John Ruskin. It's also a good place for hiking and rock climbing. The Coniston Old Man towers in the background at 790m (2,633 ft.), giving mountain climbers one of the finest views of the Lake District.

THE LAKE DISTRICT: HOME OF THE POETS | Coniston & Hawkshead

Just 6.5km (4 miles) east of Coniston is the village of Hawkshead, with the 15th-century grammar school where Wordsworth studied for 8 years (he carved his name on a desk that is still there). Nearby, in the vicinity of Esthwaite Water, is the 17th-century Hill Top Farm, former home of author Beatrix Potter.

Getting There

Take a train to Windermere and proceed the rest of the way by bus. From April to September, **Mountain Goat** (ℭ **01539/445161;** www.mountain-goat.com) operates eight buses per day to Hawkshead.

By car from Windermere, proceed north on the A591 to Ambleside, cutting south-west on the B5285 to Hawkshead.

Windermere Lake Cruises Ltd. (ℭ **01539/443360;** www.windermere-lake cruises.co.uk) operates a ferry service in summer from Bowness, directly south of Windermere, to Hawkshead. It reduces driving time considerably (see "Windermere & Bowness," earlier in this chapter).

Where to Stay

Coniston Lodge Bespoke Holiday Apartments Third-generation Lakeland hoteliers Elizabeth and Anthony Robinson are converting their well-run B&B lodge into two self-catering apartments. Each apartment, named for a local mountain tarn, will contain two bedrooms (each with bathroom), a living area, a kitchen, and garden area. Laundry facilities will be available in the reception area.

Station Rd., Coniston, Cumbria LA21 8HH. ℭ **01539/441201.** Fax 015394/41201. www.coniston-lodge. com. 2 units. £345–£630 per week. AE, MC, V. **Amenities:** Foodstuffs shop. *In room:* TV, hair dryer, kitchen.

Grizedale Lodge This is one of the better B&Bs in the area. It was built in 1902 as a hunting lodge for the chairman of the Cunard Line. Today, Mr. and Mrs. Aspey offer handsomely furnished bedrooms with compact private bathrooms with showers. Some of the rooms have four-poster beds and offer panoramic views.

Grizedale, Hawkshead, Cumbria LA22 0QL. ℭ **01539/436532.** Fax 01539/436572. www.grizedale-lodge.com. 8 units. £90–£100 double. Rates include breakfast. AE, MC, V. From Hawkshead, take Newby Bridge Rd. for about 450m (1,500 ft.); turn right (signposted GRIZEDALE & FOREST PARK CENTER), and follow this road for 3km (2 miles). **Amenities:** Bar; room service. *In room:* TV, hair dryer, no phone.

Sun Hotel The Sun is the most popular, traditional, and attractive pub, restaurant, and hotel in Coniston. It's a country-house hotel of much character, dating from 1902, though the inn attached to it is from the 16th century. Situated on beautiful grounds above the village, 135m (450 ft.) from the town center, it lies at the foot of the Coniston Old Man. Each bedroom, ranging in size from small to midsize, is decorated with style and flair; one has a four-poster bed. Three are big enough for families.

Brow Hill (off A593), Coniston, Cumbria LA21 8HQ. ℭ **01539/441248.** Fax 01539/441219. www.thesun coniston.com. 10 units. £95–£120 double. Rates include English breakfast. MC, V. **Amenities:** Restaurant; bar. *In room:* TV, hair dryer.

Where to Dine

Queen's Head ENGLISH/INTERNATIONAL This is the most famous pub in town. Behind a mock black-and-white timber facade, it's a 17th-century structure of character. It serves a special brew, Robinsons Stockport, from old-fashioned wooden kegs. Temptations on the menu include a loin of tuna seared with Cajun spice and roast eggplant, filet of sea bass on a bed of watercress, and skate wing cooked in white wine, garlic butter, and cracked peppercorns.

The Queen's Head may be more inn than pub; it rents 14 bedrooms (two with four-poster beds) with private bathroom, TV, and phone. The comfortably old-fashioned rooms go for £75 to £130 double, including English breakfast.

Main St., Hawkshead. ℰ **01539/436271.** www.queensheadhotel.co.uk. Reservations recommended. Main courses £10–£18. AE, MC, V. Daily noon–2:30pm and 6:15–9:30pm.

Where to Share a Pint

A display case of fishing lures is the first tip-off, and then there's the pond itself—yes, it's true, you can fish while you drink at the **Drunken Duck,** Barngates (ℰ **01539/436347;** www.drunkenduckinn.co.uk). Or you can just sit on the front porch and gaze at Lake Windermere in the distance. Inside, you can choose from an assortment of cushioned settees, old pews, and tub or ladder-back chairs, and then order a beef filet in red-wine sauce or minted lamb casserole to go with a pint of Mitchell's Lancaster Bomber, Yates Bitter, or Yates Drunken Duck Bitter, brewed especially for the pub. If you want stronger spirits, there are more than a dozen malt whiskies to choose from. Main courses go for £13 to £25. If you wish to stay over, you can rent a comfortable double room, costing from £95 to £285.

Overlooking the central square of Hawkshead, the **Kings Arms Pub,** in the Kings Arms Hotel (ℰ **01539/436372;** www.kingsarmshawkshead.co.uk), offers a pleasant front terrace and lots of plush leather seating inside the cozy barroom. Traditional pub grub is supplemented with a few pasta dishes, burgers, and steaks. Ales include Greenall's Original, Tetley's, and Theakston's XB. Malt whiskies are also well represented.

Exploring the Area

Of the many places to go boating in the Lake District, Coniston Water, in the Lake District National Park, may be the best. It lies in a tranquil wooded valley between Grizedale Forest and the high fells of Coniston Old Man and Wetherlam. The **Coniston Boating Centre,** Lake Road, Coniston (ℰ **01539/441366;** www.lakedistrict.gov.uk), occupies a sheltered bay at the northern end of the lake. The center provides launching facilities, boat storage, and parking. You can rent rowboats that carry two to six people, sailing dinghies carrying up to six passengers, or Canadian canoes that transport two. There is a picnic area and access to the lakeshore. From the gravel beach, you may be able to spot the varied water birds and plants that make Coniston Water a valuable but fragile habitat for wildlife.

You can also cruise the lake in an original Victorian steam-powered yacht, the *Gondola* (ℰ **01539/441288;** www.nationaltrust.org.uk/gondola). Launched in 1859 and in regular service until 1937, this unique boat was rescued and completely restored by the National Trust. Since 1980, it has become a familiar sight on Coniston Water; sailings to Brantwood run throughout the summer. Service is subject to weather conditions, of course. Trips are possible from April to October, costing £8 round-trip for adults or £4 for children.

Coniston Launch (ℰ 01768/775-753; www.conistonlaunch.co.uk) is a traditional timber boat that calls at Coniston, Monk Coniston, Torver, and Brantwood. (Discounts are offered in combination with admission to Brantwood house; see

LAKE DISTRICT national park ★★★

Despite the reverence with which the English treat the Lake District, it required an act of Parliament in 1951 to protect its natural beauty. Sprawling over 2,292 sq. km (885 sq. miles) of hills, eroded mountains, forests, and lakes, the **Lake District National Park** is the largest and one of the most popular national parks in the United Kingdom, with 14 million visitors a year. Lured by descriptions from the Romantic Lake poets, visitors arrive to take in the mountains, wildlife, flora, fauna, and secluded waterfalls here. Much of the area is privately owned, but landowners work with national park officers to preserve the landscape and its 2,898km (1,800 miles) of footpaths.

Alas, the park's popularity is now one of its major drawbacks. Hordes of weekend tourists descend, especially in summertime and on bank holiday weekends. Despite the crowds, great efforts are made to maintain the trails that radiate in a network throughout the district, preserving the purity of a landscape that includes more than 100 lakes and countless numbers of grazing sheep.

Before setting out to explore the lake, stop in at the **National Park Visitor Centre** (© **01539/446601;** www.lakedistrict. gov.uk), located on the lakeshore at Brockhole, on the A591 between Windermere and Ambleside. It can be reached by bus or by one of the lake launches from Windermere. Once here, you can pick up useful information and explore 12 hectares (30 acres) of landscaped gardens and parklands; lake cruises, exhibitions, and film shows are also offered. Lunches and teas are served in the tearooms, with terrace seating.

Tourist information offices within the park are richly stocked with maps and suggestions for several dozen bracing rambles. Regardless of the itinerary you select, you'll spot frequent green-and-white signs, or their older equivalents in varnished pine with Adirondack-style routed letters, announcing FOOTPATH TO . . .

below.) This exceptional boating outfitter offers special cruises in summer; the "Swallows and Amazons" tour, for instance, was inspired by Arthur Ransome's classic story.

Summitreks operates from the lakeside at Coniston Boating Centre, offering qualified instruction in canoeing and windsurfing. You can rent a wide range of equipment from the nearby office at Lake Road (© **01539/441212;** www. summitreks.co.uk).

In Hawkshead, the **Beatrix Potter Gallery,** Main Street (© **01539/436355;** www.nationaltrust.org.uk), has an annually changing exhibition of Beatrix Potter's original illustrations from her children's storybooks. The building was once the office of her husband, solicitor William Heelis, and the interior remains largely unaltered since his day. To get here, take bus no. 505 from Ambleside and Coniston to the square in Hawkshead. Admission is £3.60 per person, or £9 for a family ticket.

Brantwood ★   John Ruskin, poet, artist, and critic, was one of the great figures of the Victorian age and a prophet of social reform, inspiring such diverse men as Proust, Frank Lloyd Wright, and Gandhi. He moved to his home, Brantwood, on the east side of Coniston Water, in 1872 and lived here until his death in 1900. Visitors today can see the house and Ruskin's memorabilia, including some 200 of his pictures.

Part of the 101-hectare (250-acre) estate is open as a nature trail. The Brantwood stables, designed by Ruskin, have been converted into a tearoom and restaurant, the Jumping Jenny. Also in the stable building is the Coach House Gallery, which follows the Ruskin tradition of encouraging contemporary craftwork of the finest quality. Literary fans may want to pay a pilgrimage to the graveyard of the village church, where Ruskin was buried; his family turned down the invitation to have him interred at Westminster Abbey.

Coniston. ☎ **01539/441396.** www.brantwood.org.uk. Admission £6.30 adults, £4.50 students, £1.35 children 5–15, £13 family ticket (2 adults, 3 children); garden walk £4. Mid-Mar to mid-Nov daily 11am–5:30pm; late Nov to early Mar Wed–Sun 11am–4:30pm. Closed Dec 25–26. Follow the signs from Coniston.

John Ruskin Museum   At this institute, in the center of the village, you can see Ruskin's personal possessions and mementos, pictures by him and his friends, letters, and his collection of mineral rocks.

Yewdale Rd., Coniston. ☎ **01539/441164.** www.ruskinmuseum.com. Admission £4.50 adults, £2 children, £12 family ticket (2 adults, 3 children). Mid-Mar to mid-Nov daily 10am–5:30pm; late Nov to early Mar Wed–Sun 10:30am–3:30pm.

KESWICK

473km (294 miles) NW of London; 50km (31 miles) NW of Kendal; 35km (22 miles) NW of Windermere

Keswick opens onto Derwentwater, one of the loveliest lakes in the region, and the town makes a good base for exploring the northern half of Lake District National Park. Keswick has two landscaped parks, and above the small town is a historic stone circle thought to be some 4,000 years old.

St. Kentigern's Church dates from A.D. 553, and a weekly market held in the center of Keswick can be traced from a charter granted in the 13th century. It's a short walk to Friar's Crag, the classic viewing point on Derwentwater. The walk will also take you past boat landings with launches that operate regular tours around the lake.

Around Derwentwater are many places with literary associations, evoking memories of Wordsworth, Robert Southey, Coleridge, and Hugh Walpole. Several of Beatrix Potter's stories were based at Keswick as well. The town also has a professional repertory theater that schedules performances in the summer, a swimming-pool complex, and an 18-hole golf course at the foot of the mountains 6.5km (4 miles) away.

Essentials

GETTING THERE   Take a train to Windermere (see "Windermere & Bowness," earlier in this chapter) and proceed the rest of the way by bus.

Stagecoach (☎ **0871/200-2233;** www.stagecoachbus.com) has regular bus service from Windermere and Grasmere (bus no. 555).

If you're driving from Windermere, drive northwest on the A591.

VISITOR INFORMATION   The **Keswick Tourist Information Centre,** at Moot Hall, Market Square (☎ **01768/772645;** www.golakes.co.uk and www.keswick.org), is open April through September, daily 9:30am to 5:30pm, and October through March, daily 9:30am to 4:30pm.

Where to Stay

Edwardene Hotel   This 1885 gray-slate house stands in a residential area, about a 3-minute walk from the town center. The three-story gabled house is well maintained with tasteful, comfortable accommodations. These rooms take their names from the Lakeland landscape—Myrtle, Bramble, Heather, Poppy, and so on. Attention to detail is paid by the hospitable owners, and guests assemble on chilly nights in the lounge by the fireplace. Cumberland sausages and free-range eggs are featured at breakfast.

26 Southey St., Keswick, Cumbria, CA12 4EF. © **01768/773586.** Fax 01768/773824. www.edwardene hotel.com. 11 units. £78–£84 double; £120 family room. MC, V. **Amenities:** Breakfast room. *In room:* TV, hair dryer.

Grange Country Guest House   A tranquil retreat, this charming hotel and gardens are situated on a hilltop. Dating from the 1840s, it is furnished in part with antiques. Guests enjoy crackling log fires in chilly weather. Many of the attractively furnished, well-kept rooms have scenic views of the Lakeland hills. There is continual upgrading of the bedrooms, which come in various shapes and sizes; each is individually decorated and most have double or twin beds.

Manor Brow, Ambleside Rd. (on the southeast side of Keswick, overlooking the town, just off A591). Keswick, Cumbria CA12 4BA. © **01768/772500.** www.grangekeswick.com. 10 units. £96–£110 double. Rates include English breakfast. MC, V. Closed Dec–Feb. **Amenities:** Breakfast room; lounge; room service. *In room:* TV, hair dryer.

Highfield Hotel ★ 🍴   Originally constructed in the late 1880s, two former private residences have been skillfully converted into this well-run hotel. The houses were built to take full advantage of mountain and lake views. A veranda, balconies, turrets, and bay windows characterize the architecture. A 5-minute walk from the center of town, the hotel is furnished in a traditional British way. All rooms are a good size and handsomely outfitted, many with bay windows where you can sit and soak up the view. The most magnificent is the spacious and elegant Woodford Room, with a four-poster bed and raised seating area. The main dining room is elegant yet informal, with daily changing menus that utilize, whenever possible, the best local products, such as Borrowdale salmon.

The Heads, Keswick, Cumbria CA12 5ER. © **01768/772508.** Fax 01768/780634. www.highfieldkeswick. co.uk. 19 units. £150–£180 double. Rates include breakfast and dinner. AE, MC, V. Closed mid-Nov to mid-Feb. **Amenities:** Restaurant; bar. *In room:* TV.

Skiddaw Hotel ☺   This hotel lies behind an impressive facade and entrance marquee built right onto the sidewalk in the heart of Keswick at the market square. The owners have refurbished the interior, retaining the best features. Bedrooms are compact and eye-catching. Seven units are large enough for families. The upgraded Summit rooms offer extras such as bathrobes and mineral water. Guests may use the pools and spa at Lodore Falls Hotel (p. 643), a 10-minute drive away, and golf at Keswick Golf Club during the week.

Main St., Market Sq., Keswick, Cumbria CA12 5BN. © **01768/772071.** Fax 01768/774850. www.lake districthotels.net/skiddawhotel. 40 units. £142–£184 double. Rates include English breakfast. MC, V. 2-night minimum Sat–Sun. **Amenities:** Restaurant; bar; access to nearby golf, pool, and spa; room service; sauna. *In room:* TV, hair dryer.

Swinside Lodge Hotel ★   Isolated on a knoll that overlooks the shores of Derwentwater, and solidly built in the 1850s as a home for the manager of the enormous estate that surrounded it at the time, this is a cozy, well-managed bed-and-breakfast hotel where evening meals are better than the norm. The venue is run by Eric and Irene Fell, with cuisine prepared by Andrew Carter. Bedrooms are outfitted with cream-painted furniture and pastel-colored fabrics that deliberately don't convey a sense of the Edwardian age. Several public rooms and lounges have shelves of books and diversionary games that take the boredom off any rainy day.

Grange Rd., Newlands, Cumbria CA12 5UE. ℂ **01768/772948.** Fax 01768/773312. www.swinsidelodge-hotel.co.uk. 7 units. £204–£272 double. Rates include breakfast and dinner for 2 occupants. MC, V. From Keswick, take A66 southwest for 5km (3 miles), following the signs to Portinscale and to Grange. No children 4 and under. **Amenities:** Restaurant; 3 lounges. *In room:* TV, hair dryer.

Where to Dine

Underscar Manor ★ ENGLISH/FRENCH The area's best cuisine is found at this Italianate manor, also a hotel, perched high in the hills with panoramic vistas over Keswick and Derwentwater. Set on 16 hectares (40 acres) in the foothills of Skiddaw, the chintzy conservatory restaurant offers formal service (men are requested to wear jackets). The ambitious menu is just as classic as the setting. Standard recipes are given modern twists, and service is impeccable. Ingredients are top quality and menus are based on the season, with everything perfectly served, from sublime breast of local pheasant wrapped in Parma ham to casserole of local venison with potato dumplings flavored with bacon and chives. Another specialty is chargrilled filets of lemon sole served with an herb-laced risotto. No children 11 or younger are accepted.

Applethwaite, near Keswick. ℂ **01768/775000.** www.keswickrestaurant.co.uk. Reservations required. Main courses £14–£25; 3-course fixed-price lunch £28; 6-course fixed-price dinner £38. AE, MC, V. Daily noon–1pm and 7–9:30pm.

Seeing the Sights

Mirehouse A tranquil Cumbrian family home that has not been sold since 1688, Mirehouse has unusually wide-ranging literary and artistic connections. The piano is played on afternoons when guests stop by to visit. The park around it stretches to Bassenthwaite Lake and has extensive gardens, plus woodland adventure play-grounds. It is in easy reach of the ancient lakeside church and the Old Sawmill Tearoom, which is known for its generous Cumbrian cooking.

On A591, 5.5km (3½ miles) north of Keswick. ℂ **01768/772287.** www.mirehouse.com. Admission to house and gardens plus a lakeside walk £6.50 adults, £3 children and seniors, £18 family ticket (2 adults, 4 kids ages 5–16); gardens only £3 adults, £1.50 children. House Apr–Oct Sun and Wed (also Fri in Aug) 2–4:30pm; tearoom and grounds Apr–Oct daily 10am–5:30pm.

Side Trips from Keswick
BORROWDALE

One of the most scenic parts of the Lake District, the valley of Borrowdale stretches south of Derwentwater to Seathwaite in the heart of the county. The valley is walled in by fell sides, and it's an excellent center for exploring, walking, and climbing. Many use it as a base for exploring Scafell, England's highest mountain, at 963m (3,210 ft.).

This resort is in the Borrowdale Valley, the southernmost settlement of which is Seatoller. The village of Seatoller, at 353m (1,176 ft.), is the terminus for buses to and from Keswick.

After leaving Seatoller, the B5289 takes you west through the Honister Pass and Buttermere Fell, one of the most dramatic drives in the Lake District. The road is lined with towering boulders. The lake village of Buttermere also merits a stopover for its lake-country scenery.

Where to Stay & Dine

Borrowdale Gates Hotel ★   The proprietors of this hotel, Terry and Christine Parkinson, welcome travelers from around the world; even former prime minister John Major has dropped in for afternoon tea. Their 1860 Victorian country house, built of Lakeland stone, received an addition of nine rooms that faithfully matches the Victorian style. All rooms range in size from medium to large and are decorated with rich Victorian colors and period reproductions. Every year some units are upgraded and refurbished. The place is warm, cozy, and inviting. The public areas, with their antiques and open-log stone fireplaces, sprawl along the ground floor and include a bar, a restaurant and dining area, and four sitting lounges. They're all airy and bright, with views of the surrounding gardens.

Grange-in-Borrowdale, Keswick, Cumbria CA12 5UQ. ℂ **0845/833-2524.** Fax 01768/777254. www. borrowdale-gates.com. 29 units. Sun–Thurs £180–£230 double; Fri–Sat £190–£240 double. Rates include English breakfast and dinner. AE, MC, V. Free parking. From Keswick, take B5289 6.5km (4 miles) south to Grange; go over the bridge, and the inn sits on the right, just beyond the curve in the road. **Amenities:** Restaurant; bar. *In room:* TV, hair dryer.

Borrowdale Hotel ★   When the weather is damp, log fires welcome guests in this Lakeland stone building, which was originally a coaching inn (ca. 1866). Each of the comfortable midsize to spacious bedrooms is well designed and furnished; many have fine views. Four rooms contain four-poster beds; several units are suitable for families. Bathrooms are well maintained and most offer a tub/shower combination.

Borrowdale Rd. (B5289), Borrowdale, Keswick, Cumbria CA12 5UY. ℂ **01768/777224.** Fax 01768/777338. www.lakedistricthotels.net/borrowdalehotel. 36 units. Sun–Thurs £144–£180 double; Fri–Sat £186–£224 double. Rates include English breakfast and dinner. MC, V. Free parking. On B5289, 5.5km (3½ miles) south of Keswick. **Amenities:** Restaurant; bar; access to nearby health club; room service. *In room:* TV, hair dryer.

Lodore Falls Hotel ★   This hotel overlooks Derwentwater from fields where cows graze. With its spike-capped mansard tower, symmetrical gables, and balcony-embellished stone facade, it seems straight out of the Swiss Alps. Ironically, the Swiss owners who built this place in the 19th century were named England. Their tradition of good rooms, food, and service continues today. The interior has been completely modernized, and the well-furnished bedrooms vary in size; it's worth opting for one of the larger ones.

Borrowdale Rd. (B5289), Borrowdale, Keswick, Cumbria CA12 5UX. ℂ **01768/777285.** Fax 01768/777343. www.lakedistricthotels.net/lodorefalls. 71 units. £156–£290 double; £342–£386 suite. Rates include breakfast. MC, V. 2-night minimum Sat–Sun. Indoor parking £5; free outdoor parking. On B5289 5.5km (3½ miles) south of Keswick. **Amenities:** Restaurant; bar; children's playground; exercise room; 2 heated pools (1 indoor, 1 outdoor); room service; sauna; spa; tennis court. *In room:* TV, hair dryer.

BASSENTHWAITE

In the Lake District National Park, 9.5km (6 miles) north of Keswick, Bassenthwaite is one of the most beautiful of Lakeland villages and makes the best center for exploring the woodlands of Thornthwaite Forest and Bassenthwaite Lake nearby. Bassenthwaite Lake is the northernmost and only true "lake" in the Lake District, and it's visited yearly by many species of migratory birds from the north of Europe.

Where to Stay & Dine

Armathwaite Hall Country House & Spa ★★   Rich in history, this hotel dates from the 1300s, when it was built as a house for Benedictine nuns. During the Middle Ages, it was plundered frequently, leaving the sisters wretchedly poor. By the

17th century, a series of wealthy landowners had completed the severe Gothic design of its stately facade, and an architecturally compatible series of wings was added in 1844. It was converted into a hotel during the 1930s. Sir Hugh Walpole, who once stayed here, found it "a house of perfect and irresistible charm." Ringed with almost 160 hectares (400 acres) of woodland (some bordering the lake), the place offers a magnificent entrance hall sheathed with expensive paneling. The bedrooms are also handsomely furnished, with padded headboards crowning comfortable beds fitted with fine linen. Four-poster and family rooms are available.

Bassenthwaite Lake (on B5291, 11km/7 miles northwest of Keswick, 2.5km/1½ miles west of Bassenthwaite), Keswick, Cumbria CA12 4RE. ✆ **01768/776551.** Fax 01768/776220. www.armathwaite-hall. com. 43 units. £240–£310 double; £350–£370 suite. Rates include English breakfast. AE, DC, MC, V. **Amenities:** Restaurant; bar; babysitting; health club; indoor heated pool; room service; sauna; steam room; tennis court. *In room:* TV, hair dryer, Wi-Fi (free).

Castle Inn Hotel   Don't expect a castle. Though this place plays up its historical importance, you'll find there is an "old" core (no one on the staff is sure of how old), with many newer additions that don't exactly merge gracefully into a unified whole. The result is a hotel that's neither whimsically antique nor strikingly modern—but it is not dowdy. Bedrooms come in various shapes and sizes, including some beautifully appointed and spacious "superior" units. Five are large enough for families. The more modern but equally comfortable rooms are in a new wing. Two of the old-fashioned rooms contain four-poster beds.

Bassenthwaite (9.5km/6 miles north of Keswick on A591), Cumbria CA12 4RG. ✆ **01768/776401.** Fax 01768/776604. www.castleinncumbria.co.uk. 48 units. £135–£175 double. Rates include half-board. AE, MC, V. From Keswick, take A591 9.5km (6 miles) north of town; the inn is on the left. **Amenities:** Restaurant; bar; bike rental; health club; Jacuzzi; indoor heated pool; room service; sauna; steam room; table tennis. *In room:* TV, hair dryer, Wi-Fi (free).

Overwater Hall ★   Built in the late 18th century, this is a Georgian mansion with battlements added to it by the Victorians. It is reminiscent of a castle and comes complete with a ghost story. All the bedrooms, though standard in size, are extremely ritzy (which may be why Overwater's phantom has chosen to stay), having been furnished with top-quality antiques. One room has an oak-paneled four-poster bed. Guests can enjoy the regal surroundings of the public rooms, with their intricate and rich cove molding and formal Victorian antiques. The drawing room is a great place for afternoon tea, and the piano bar actually has a baby grand piano.

Overwater, Ireby (3.2km/2 miles north of Bassenthwaite Lake), Cumbria CA5 1HH. ✆ **01768/776566.** Fax 01768/776921. www.overwaterhall.co.uk. 13 units. £160–£220 double. Rates include English breakfast and dinner. MC, V. 2-night minimum Sat–Sun. **Amenities:** Restaurant; bar; lounge; room service. *In room:* TV, hair dryer.

The Pheasant ★   This former 17th-century coaching inn sits near the northwestern tip of Bassenthwaite Lake. A series of extensions was later added. Everything about the place evokes old-fashioned English coziness. Fireplaces warm a moderately eccentric bar area, a mishmash of antique and merely old-fashioned furniture, and individually decorated bedrooms whose windows overlook 24 hectares (60 acres) of forest and parkland associated with the hotel. Two bedrooms offer sitting areas.

Bassenthwaite Lake, Cockermouth, Cumbria CA13 9YE. ✆ **01768/776234.** Fax 01768/776002. www. the-pheasant.co.uk. 13 units. Mon–Fri £146–£160 double, £190 suite; Sat–Sun £156–£170 double, £200 suite. Rates include breakfast. MC, V. Located midway between Keswick and Cockermouth, signposted from the A66. **Amenities:** Restaurant; bar; room service. *In room:* TV (on request), hair dryer.

ULLSWATER ★

477km (296 miles) NW of London; 42km (26 miles) SE of Keswick

Set in a region that is home to contrasting vistas of gently rolling fields and dramatic mountain rises, Ullswater is a favorite with those who enjoy spectacular natural beauty. Ullswater itself is a 14km (9-mile) expanse of water stretching from Pooley Bridge to Patterdale; it's the second-largest lake in the district. A magnet for outdoor types of all levels of ability, it offers activities that range from walks and hikes around the shore to rock climbing, mountain biking, canoeing, sailing, and even windsurfing.

This part of the Lakeland, where the majesty of nature tends to entrance and envelop, has always held a special attraction for artists and writers. The area gained most of its fame from writings by the likes of Wordsworth during the early 19th century. It was on the shores of Ullswater that Wordsworth saw his "host of golden daffodils." Aira Force waterfall, near the National Trust's Gowbarrow, inspired both Wordsworth and Coleridge with its beauty.

While using this area as a base for outdoor activities, you can also easily explore the many places of historic significance, from the times of the ancient Celts right through to modern day. Two noteworthy sites include **Long Meg and Her Daughters,** an ancient stone circle near Penrith; and **Hadrian's Wall,** marking the northern extent of the Roman Empire, east of Carlisle (p. 687).

In Ullswater, two 19th-century steamers provide the best way to see the area's panoramic mountain scenery around the lake. Weather permitting, **Ullswater "Steamers"** (✆ **01768/482229;** www.ullswater-steamers.co.uk) offers scheduled service daily between Glenridding, Howtown, and Pooley Bridge, as well as several shorter 1-hour cruises. Passengers may choose to walk back along the lakeside path or break for lunch at either end of the lake. The steamers run every day but December 24 and 25. Round-trip tickets between Glenridding, Howtown, and Pooley Bridge cost £9.45 to £12 for adults or £5.20 to £6.50 for children, with a family ticket ranging from £24 to £30. The higher prices are charged in midsummer. Glenridding is on the A592 at the southern end of Ullswater. Pooley Bridge is 8km (5 miles) from the M6 Junction 40 to Penrith.

Getting There

About three trains from London's Euston Station arrive daily in Penrith, this region's main rail junction. A change of trains isn't usually necessary. For schedules and information, call ✆ **0845/748-4950** or visit **www.nationalrail.co.uk**. Once in Penrith, passengers usually take a taxi to Ullswater.

Stagecoach (✆ **0871/200-2233;** www.stagecoachbus.com) operates two buses per day that stop at Penrith on their way between Carlisle and Keswick. Passengers must take a taxi from Penrith to Ullswater.

If you're driving from Penrith, go southeast on the B5320.

Where to Stay & Dine

Brackenrigg Inn ★ 🍴 Since the price tags at Sharrow Bay (see below) are a bit lethal, many discerning travelers instead book into this traditional inn and restaurant overlooking Ullswater. The lakeside coaching inn has kept up-to-date with the times, serving good food and offering a comfortable bed for the night. Beautiful views unfold from the bar, dining room, lounge, terrace, garden, and bedrooms.

Accommodations come in a wide range of sizes, from smaller, standard doubles to the more spacious superior rooms and the premium ground-floor suites. There's a lot of local character here, with a convivial bar, an open fire, and even a dartboard. Chefs specialize in the market-fresh food of Cumbria, "but without all the fuss." The succulent lamb dishes are some of the best in the area.

Watermillock (on A592), Cumbria CA11 OJN. © **01768/486206.** Fax 01768/486945. www.brackenrigg inn.co.uk. 17 units. £40 per person double; £60 per person double with half-board. Discount for children 3-16 staying in parent's room. Rates include breakfast. MC, V. **Amenities:** Restaurant; bar. *In room:* TV.

Sharrow Bay Country House Hotel ★★★　This was Britain's first country-house hotel, and it's the oldest British member of Relais & Châteaux. Sitting on 4.8 hectares (12 acres), it's an unusual Victorian house with a low angled roof and wide eaves. It was a private home until purchased by Francis Coulson in 1948. Realizing its potential, Coulson restored the structure, sleeping on the floor while work was in progress. Three years later, he was joined by Brian Sack, and together they turned Sharrow into one of England's finest places to dine. Today, the hotel offers 26 antiques-filled bedrooms, 17 of them in the gatehouse and cottages. Individually decorated, each is named after one or another of the glamorous (and often famous) women who have swept in and out of the lives of the articulate owners. Some of the rooms offer views of the lakes, trees, or Martindale Fells.

Howtown Rd., Ullswater, near Penrith, Cumbria CA10 2LZ. © **01768/486301.** Fax 01768/486349. www. sharrowbay.co.uk. 26 units. £200-£460 double; £350-£800 suite for 2. Rates include half-board. 2-night minimum Sat-Sun. AE, DC, MC, V. On Howtown Rd. 3km (2 miles) south of Pooley Bridge. **Amenities:** Restaurant; bar; 2 lounges; room service. *In room:* TV, hair dryer, minibar.

PENRITH

467km (290 miles) NW of London; 50km (31 miles) N of Kendal

This one-time capital of Cumbria, in the old Kingdom of Scotland and Strathclyde, takes its name, some say, from the Celts who called it "Ford by the Hill." The namesake hill is marked today by a red-sandstone beacon and tower. Because of Penrith's central location above the northern Lake District and beside the Pennines, this thriving market center was important to Scotland and England from its very beginning, eventually prompting England to take it over in 1070.

The characteristic red-sandstone town has been home to many famous and legendary figures, including Richard, duke of Gloucester; William Cookson, the grandfather of poet William Wordsworth; and Dorothy Wordsworth, William's sister. Today, Penrith remains best known as a lively market town.

Essentials

GETTING THERE　**National Express** (© **0871/781-8181;** www.national express.co.uk) operates one daily bus that leaves from London's Victoria Coach Station at 11pm, arriving in Penrith at 5:30am.

By car, take the M1 out of London, getting on the M6 to Penrith. The trip should take no more than 6 hours.

VISITOR INFORMATION　The **Penrith Tourist Information Centre,** Robinson's School, Middlegate (© **01768/867466;** www.golakes.co.uk and www.visiteden. co.uk), is open in summer, Monday to Saturday 9am to 6pm and Sunday 10am to 5pm; and in the off-season, Monday to Saturday 9am to 5pm and Sunday 10am to 4pm.

Where to Stay & Dine

George Hotel This is a 300-year-old coaching inn, built right in the heart of town. It welcomed Bonnie Prince Charlie in 1745. The front of the George looks out on a street of small specialty shops, and the guest rooms, spread among three floors, are individually decorated with light colors and up-to-date furnishings. The owners have upgraded all the bedrooms.

Devonshire St., Penrith, Cumbria CA11 7SU. (C) **01768/862696.** Fax 01768/868223. www.lakedistrict hotels.net/georgehotel. 34 units. £118–£140 double; £180 suite. Rates include full Cumbrian breakfast. MC, V. 2-night minimum Sat–Sun. **Amenities:** Restaurant; bar; free use of nearby gym and indoor pool; room service. *In room:* TV, hair dryer.

North Lakes Hotel & Spas ★ ☺ This is Penrith's finest lodging and the most family-friendly hotel in the area. The exterior may lack character, but you'll find compensation inside. A member of the Shire Hotels chain, this property is designed to meet the needs of businesspeople during the week and vacationers on weekends. Rooms are bright and spacious, decorated with classic wood furniture, large couches, and soft pastel accents. Six rooms are large enough for families, and some have bunk beds. Guests enjoy an inviting lobby sitting area with a huge stone fireplace and a grand barn-style, open ceiling with rustic beams.

Ullswater Rd., Penrith, Cumbria CA11 8QT. (C) **01768/868111.** Fax 01768/868291. www.northlakeshotel. com. 84 units. £129–£190 double; £165–£235 suite. Children 15 and younger stay free in parent's room. Rates include English breakfast. AE, DC, MC, V. **Amenities:** Restaurant; bar; babysitting; health club; 2 pools (1 indoor heated, 1 children's); room service; sauna; spa; 2 squash courts; steam room. *In room:* TV, hair dryer, Wi-Fi (free).

Queen's Head Inn ★ Lying 4km (2½ miles) south of Penrith, this is a discovery from 1719, once the property of the Wordsworths. Today, it is an inviting country pub and restaurant with overnight accommodations. It is found in the center of the village of Tirril, nestled on the edge of the Lake District National Park. Filled with bric-a-brac and memorabilia, the country inn is full of character. Expect oak beams, wooden settles, and even a roaring fire in the often chilly month of June. It's an atmosphere of hunting prints and horse brasses, along with farm tools and hunting horns. Most patrons come here to enjoy the Tirril beers on tap, although you may also enjoy wines from the family-owned vineyards. Good food has always been a tradition of the inn, and you can enjoy traditional British food like the noteworthy braised shoulder of Lakeland lamb in its own red-currant gravy. Local venison and pheasant appear in winter, locally smoked Ullswater trout in summer. The bedrooms are well maintained and most comfortable.

Tirril, near Penrith, Cumbria CA10 2JF. (C) **01768/863219.** Fax 01768/863243. www.queensheadinn. co.uk. 7 units. £80–£85 double. Rates include breakfast. MC, V. **Amenities:** Restaurant; pub; Wi-Fi (free). *In room:* No phone.

Exploring the Area

A small town of 12,500 people, Penrith still has lots of shops to explore. Major shopping areas include the covered **Devonshire Arcade,** with its name-brand stores and boutiques; the pedestrian-only **Angel Lane** and **Little Dockray,** with an abundance of family-run specialty shops; and **Angel Square,** just south of Angel Lane.

Acorn Bank Garden & Watermill For a stroll in an English garden, see the Acorn Bank Garden with its varied landscape of blooming bulbs, plants, and walled spaces. Its claim to fame is its extensive herb garden, said to be the best in all of northern England. The Acorn Bank Garden is part of an estate dating from 1228 that includes a partially restored water mill, parts of which also date from the 13th century, and a red-sandstone Tudor house (presently not open to the public).

Temple Sowerby, 9.5km (6 miles) east of Penrith on A6. © **01768/361893.** www.nationaltrust.org.uk. Admission £4.20 adults, £2.10 children, £11 family ticket (2 adults, 2 children). Wed–Sun 10am–5pm (last admission 4:30pm). Closed Nov to mid-Mar.

Penrith Castle   This park contains the massive ruins of the castle, whose construction began in 1399, as ordered by William Strickland, the bishop of Canterbury. For the next 70 years, the castle continued to grow in size and strength until it finally became the royal castle and oftentimes residence for Richard, duke of Gloucester.

Across from the train station along Ullswater Rd. www.culture24.org.uk or www.english-heritage.org.uk. Free admission. Daily 24 hr.

Penrith Museum   For perspective on Penrith and the surrounding area, a visit here isn't a bad idea. Originally constructed in the 1500s, the museum building was turned into a poor girls' school in 1670. Today, the museum surveys the archaeology and geology of Penrith and the Eden Valley, which was a desert millions of years ago.

Robinson's School, Middlegate. © **01768/212228.** Free admission. Mon–Sat 10am–4pm.

YORKSHIRE & NORTH- UMBRIA: BRONTË, MOORS & DALES

Yorkshire, known to readers of Emily Brontë's *Wuthering Heights* and James Herriot's *All Creatures Great and Small,* embraces the moors and dales of northern England.

Across this vast region came Romans, Anglo-Saxons, Vikings, monks of the Middle Ages, kings of England, lords of the manor, craftspeople, hill farmers, and wool growers, all leaving their marks. You can still see Roman roads and pavements, great abbeys and castles, stately homes, open-air museums, and crafts centers, along with parish churches, old villages, and cathedrals.

Some cities and towns still carry the taint of the Industrial Revolution, but you can also find wild and remote beauty—limestone crags, caverns along the Pennines, mountainous uplands, rolling hills, chalk land wolds, heather-covered moorlands, broad vales, and tumbling streams. Yorkshire offers not only beautiful inland scenery but also 161km (100 miles) of shoreline, with rocky headlands, cliffs, sandy bays, rock pools, sheltered coves, fishing villages, bird sanctuaries, former smugglers' dens, and yachting havens. And in the summer, the moors in **North York Moors National Park** bloom with purple heather. You can hike along the 177km (110-mile) **Cleveland Way National Trail,** which encircles the park.

The walled city of **York** is Yorkshire's most visited city. **York Minster,** part of the cathedral circuit, is noted for its 100 stained-glass windows. In West Yorkshire is the literary shrine of **Haworth,** the home of the Brontës.

Northumbria is made up of the counties of Northumberland and Durham. The Saxons, who came to northern England centuries ago, carved out this kingdom, which at the time stretched from the Firth of Forth in

Scotland to the banks of the Humber in Yorkshire. Vast tracts of that ancient king-dom remain natural and unspoiled. This slice of England has more than its share of industrial towns, but you should explore the wild hills and open spaces and cross the dales of the eastern Pennines.

The whole area evokes ancient battles and bloody border raids. Space constraints don't permit us to cover this area in great detail, and it's often overlooked by the rushed North American visitor, but we suggest at least a venture to **Hadrian's Wall,** a Roman structure that was one of the wonders of the Western world. The finest stretch of the wall lies within **Northumberland National Park,** between the stony North Tyne River and the county boundary at Gilsland. And about 64km (40 miles) of the 242km (150-mile) **Pennine Way** meanders through the park; Pennine Way is one of Britain's most challenging hiking paths.

On the way north to Hadrian's Wall, we suggest you spend the night in the ancient cathedral city of **Durham.** This great medieval city is among the most dramatically sited and most interesting in the north.

YORK ★★★

327km (203 miles) N of London; 142km (88 miles) N of Nottingham; 42km (26 miles) NE of Leeds

Few cities in England are as rich in history as York. It is still encircled by its 13th- and 14th-century city walls, about 4km (2½ miles) long, with four gates. One of these, Micklegate, once grimly greeted visitors coming from the south with the heads of traitors. To this day, you can walk on the footpath of the medieval walls.

The crowning achievement of York is its minster, or cathedral, which makes the city an ecclesiastical center equaled only by Canterbury. It's easily visible on a drive up to Edinburgh in Scotland. Or, after visiting Cambridge, you can make a swing through the great cathedral cities of Ely, Lincoln, York, and Ripon.

There was a Roman York (Hadrian came this way), then a Saxon York, a Danish York, a Norman York (William the Conqueror slept here), a medieval York, a Geor-gian York, and a Victorian York (the center of a flourishing rail business). A large amount of 18th-century York remains for visitors to explore today, including Richard Boyle's restored Assembly Rooms.

You may want to visit the Shambles; once the meat-butchering center of York, it dates from before the Norman Conquest. The messy business is gone now, but the ancient street survives, filled today with jewelry stores, cafes, and buildings that huddle so closely together that you can practically stand in the middle of the pave-ment, arms outstretched, and touch the houses on both sides of the street.

Essentials

GETTING THERE   **Leeds Bradford International Airport** (© **0871/288-2288;** www.leedsbradfordairport.co.uk) has daily flights to and from London's Heathrow and Gatwick airports and most major regional U.K., airports, with trip time from London around 1 hour. Carriers that serve Leeds from London include **Flybe** (www.flybe.com). Connecting buses at the airport take you east to York.

From London's Kings Cross Station, York-bound trains leave every 30 minutes. The trip takes 2 hours. For information, call © **0845/748-4950** or visit **www.nationalrail.co.uk.**

Yorkshire & Northumbria

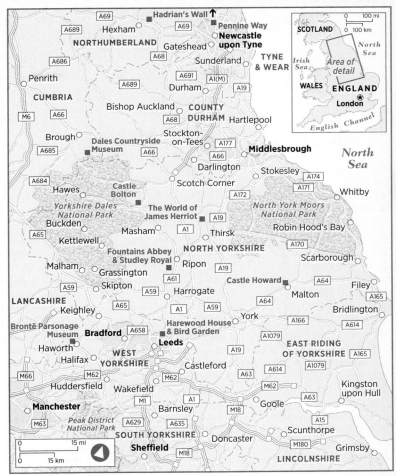

Four **National Express** buses depart daily from London's Victoria Coach Station for the 4½-hour trip to York. For schedules and information, call ✆ **0871/781-8181** or visit **www.nationalexpress.com**.

If you're driving from London, head north on the M1, cutting northeast below Leeds at the junction with the A64, heading east to York.

VISITOR INFORMATION The **Tourist Information Centre,** at De Grey Rooms, Exhibition Square (✆ **01904/550099;** www.york-tourism.co.uk), is open in winter, Monday to Saturday 9am to 5pm and Sunday 10am to 4pm; and in summer, Monday to Saturday 9am to 6pm and Sunday 10am to 5pm. Another Tourist Information Centre at the railway station keeps the same hours.

Where to Stay

EXPENSIVE

Best Western Dean Court Hotel ★   This 1850 building, today a Best Western hotel, lies right beneath the towers of the minster. It was originally constructed to provide housing for the clergy of York Minster and then converted to a hotel after World War I. It may not be the most atmospheric choice in York, but refurbishments have vastly improved the accommodations. The rooms are very comfortable, with quality linens on the beds and bathrooms equipped with tub/shower combinations. Two rooms are spacious enough for use by families.

Duncombe Place, York, North Yorkshire YO1 7EF. ✆ **800/780-7234** in the U.S. and Canada, or 01904/625082. Fax 01904/620305. www.deancourt-york.co.uk. 39 units. £140–£235 double; £200–£244 family room. Rates include English breakfast. AE, DC, MC, V. Parking £13. **Amenities:** 2 restaurants; bar; babysitting; room service. *In room:* TV, hair dryer, Wi-Fi (free).

Marmadukes Hotel ★★   Just a short walk from York Minster, this boutique hotel was created from a former "gentleman's residence" back in Queen Victoria's day. The hospitality is still old-fashioned, but the hotel was completely modernized in 2010. Its intimate atmosphere remains, including antiques, oil paintings, oriental carpeting, and public lounges with comfortable sofas. The bathrooms are some of the best in town, many with claw-foot tubs. A two-bedroom Victorian apartment is also available. The hotel's on-site restaurant, Harvilles, is known for its chargrilled Aberdeen Angus beef steaks and its fresh fish.

St. Peter's Grove, York, North Yorkshire YO30 6AQ. ✆ **01904/640101.** www.marmadukeshotels.co.uk. 20 units. £70–£175 double; £260 suite; £260 apt. AE, DC, MC, V. **Amenities:** Restaurant; bar; room service. *In room:* TV, hair dryer, Wi-Fi (free).

Middlethorpe Hall & Spa ★★★   Set in an 11-hectare (26-acre) park, this hotel is on the outskirts of York, near the racecourse and away from the traffic. It's clearly York's leading hotel. Built in 1699, the stately redbrick William and Mary country house was purchased by Historic House Hotels and beautifully restored, both inside and out. Lots of antiques create the ambience of a classic manor house. Accommodations are located in the main house and restored outbuildings. All of the bedrooms have been styled to evoke the aura of a country house, though modern comforts have been installed as well. The rooms in the annex (a converted stable block) have slightly less drama and flair.

Bishopthorpe Rd. (on A64, 2.5km/1½ miles south of town), York, North Yorkshire 4023 2GB. ✆ **800/260-8338** in the U.S. and Canada, or 01904/641241. Fax 01904/620176. www.middlethorpe. com. 30 units. £190–£350 double; £270–£450 suite. Rates include continental breakfast. AE, MC, V. Free parking. **Amenities:** 2 restaurants; bar; exercise room; indoor heated pool; room service; spa. *In room:* TV/DVD, hair dryer, Wi-Fi (£5 per 24 hr.).

Park Inn York ★   Within the ancient city walls, this modern hotel overlooks the River Ouse and is the leading hotel within the center of York. Built in the 1970s, this member of the Park Inn chain is the largest hotel in town and is conveniently located for sightseeing. Many of the well-furnished and modern bedrooms have views looking toward the minster. Ten rooms are spacious enough for families. Each comes with a well-maintained private bathroom.

North St., York, North Yorkshire YO1 6JF. ✆ **888/201-1801** or 01904/459988. Fax 01904/641793. www. york.parkinn.co.uk. 200 units. £89–£201 double. Rates include English breakfast. AE, DC, MC, V. Parking

York

ACCOMMODATIONS ■
Beechwood Close Hotel **3**
Best Western
   Dean Court Hotel **7**
Heworth Court B&B **16**
Hotel Noir **3**
Marmadukes Hotel **2**
Mount Royale Hotel **12**
Park Inn York **10**

DINING ◆
Bettys Café Tea Rooms **9**
Blue Bicycle **15**
Ivy Brasserie &
   Cellar Bar **1**
Theatre Royal Café Bar **8**
1331 Bar & Restaurant **6**

ATTRACTIONS ●
Jorvik Viking Centre **14**
National Railway
   Museum **11**
Treasurer's House **4**
York Castle Museum **13**
York Minster **5**

£12. **Amenities:** Restaurant; 2 bars; exercise room; room service; sauna. *In room:* TV, hair dryer, Wi-Fi (£15 per 24 hr.).

MODERATE

Mount Royale Hotel ★   A short walk west of York's city walls, in a neighborhood known as the Mount, this hotel is the personal statement of two generations of the Oxtaby family. They work hard to create a friendly, homey atmosphere. The main house was built as a private home in 1833, though several years ago the owners merged a neighboring house of the same era into the original core. Accommodations and public rooms are furnished with both modern pieces and antiques. Garden suites have private terraces leading to the garden.

119 The Mount, York, North Yorkshire YO2 2DA. ✆ **01904/628856.** Fax 01904/611171. www.mount
royale.co.uk. 24 units. £99–£199 double; £210 suite. Rates include English breakfast. AE, DC, MC, V. Free
parking. **Amenities:** Restaurant; bar; outdoor heated pool; room service; sauna. *In room:* TV, hair dryer,
Wi-Fi (free).

INEXPENSIVE

Alexander House ★ 🍴   Only 7 minutes from the city center, this beautifully
restored and elegantly decorated Victorian town house boasts York's most tranquil,
delightful sitting room, where porcelain and art works make it even more inviting.
Your hosts, David and Gillian Reynard, retained many of the original features of the
house while installing modern comforts. The midsize bedrooms are attractively and
comfortably furnished, with lovely bathrooms of sparkling white porcelain and elegant toiletries.

94 Bishopthorpe Rd., York, North Yorkshire YO23 1JS. ✆ **01904/625016.** www.alexanderhouseyork.
co.uk. 4 units. £79–£85 double. Rates include English breakfast. MC, V. Free parking. *In room:* TV, hair
dryer.

Beechwood Close Hotel   Beechwood is a large house that is surrounded by
trees, a garden with a putting green, and a parking area. Mr. and Mrs. Blythe run the
small hotel, which offers comfortable bedrooms with tasteful furnishings. Each
small bathroom is well maintained; most have tub/shower combinations. The hotel
is a 15-minute walk to the minster, either by road or along the river.

19 Shipton Rd. (on A19 north of the city), Clifton, York, North Yorkshire YO30 5RE. ✆ **01904/658378.**
Fax 01904/647124. www.beechwood-close.co.uk. 14 units. £80 double with breakfast; £95 double with
half-board. AE, DC, MC, V. Free parking. **Amenities:** Restaurant; bar; room service. *In room:* TV, hair dryer.

Heworth Court Bed & Breakfast   Just a 10- to 15-minute walk east of the city
center is this three-story redbrick Victorian structure. Many of its bedrooms are
located in a modern extension added during the 1980s. The rooms are agreeably
furnished, some opening onto the courtyard. Each comes with a comfortable bed
and a compact bathroom.

76 Heworth Green, York, North Yorkshire YO3 7TQ. ✆ **01904/425156.** Fax 01904/415290. www.
heworth.co.uk. 28 units. £50–£99 per person double. Rates include English breakfast. AE, DC, MC, V.
Free parking. Take the A1036 to the east side of the city. **Amenities:** Restaurant; bar; Wi-Fi (free, in
lobby). *In room:* TV, hair dryer.

Hotel Noir ★ 🍴   About a 10-minute walk north of York Minster, this hotel comprises two refurbished and extended Victorian houses overlooking the village green
of Clifton. It offers cozy, small bedrooms, some of which have undergone a lavish
restoration, emerging with a stunning "film noir" themed black-and-white decor.
Three rooms have four-poster beds. Some 400-year-old timbers, rescued from the
demolition of a medieval building in one of the city's historic streets (Micklegate),
grace the restaurant and bar, which does a thriving business in its own right.

3 Clifton Green, York, North Yorkshire YO3 6LH. ✆ **01904/643711.** Fax 01904/611230. www.hotelnoir.
co.uk. 28 units. £55–£105 double. Rates include English breakfast. MC, V. Free parking. **Amenities:**
Restaurant; bar. *In room:* TV, Wi-Fi (free).

Where to Dine

The best place for afternoon tea is **Bettys Café Tea Rooms,** 6–8 St. Helen's Sq.
(✆ **01904/659142;** www.bettys.co.uk). We also recommend the **Theatre Royal
Café Bar,** St. Leonard's Place (✆ **01904/623568;** www.yorktheatreroyal.co.uk).

Blue Bicycle ★ FRENCH/SEAFOOD   This respected restaurant with a warm ambience has been installed in a former brothel, the brass beds giving way to wooden tables for diners. The cooks earn their good reputation nightly for their fresh fish dishes, such as grilled filets of sea bass. Well-crafted mains include a sirloin of Yorkshire beef with a horseradish croquette and a red onion purée, a parsley-crusted loin of Yorkshire cod with leek purée and crispy bacon, and a seared salmon steak with a cumin purée.

34 Fossgate. ✆ **01904/673990.** www.thebluebicycle.com. Reservations required. Main courses £15–£24. AE, DC, MC, V. Mon–Wed 6–9:30pm; Thurs–Sat noon–2:30pm and 6–9:30pm; Sun noon–2:30pm and 6–9pm.

Ivy Brasserie & Cellar Bar ★ FRENCH/ENGLISH   A 10-minute walk west of York Minster, this dining complex is the most appealing in town. It lies within an ivy-covered Regency town house that's also a 36-room hotel. The less formal venue is the Cellar Bar, a crowded, paneled, candlelit hideaway in the basement. The hearty menu items here include steaks, fish, and ale. On the ground level, the more upscale Ivy Brasserie serves dishes such as a whole grilled Dover sole, skate stuffed with a crab mousse, and braised pork belly with pan-fried monkfish and roast pigs' cheeks. Meat eaters gravitate to the rump of lamb with a roast-onion salsa.

In the Grange Hotel, 1 Clifton (off Bootham Rd.). ✆ **01904/644744.** Fax 01904/612453. www.grange hotel.co.uk. Reservations recommended for Ivy; not necessary for Cellar Bar. Ivy main courses £13–£20; Cellar Bar main courses £8.50–£14. AE, DC, MC, V. Ivy Mon–Sat 6–10pm, Sun noon–2pm; Cellar Bar daily 11am–11pm.

Melton's Restaurant ★ ☺ CONTINENTAL/ENGLISH   Some local food critics claim that Michael and Lucy Hjort serve the finest food in York. Although we give that honor to the Ivy, we agree that the Hjorts have created some excitement with this family-friendly place in what has always been known as a culinary backwater town. Their small and unpretentious restaurant is approximately 1.5km (1 mile) from the heart of the city. Mr. Hjort trained with the famous Roux brothers of Le Gavroche in London, but he doesn't charge their astronomical prices. The menu here changes frequently but might include pan-fried halibut with a saffron-and-mussel risotto, leg of black-faced lamb with savoy cabbage, or breast of turkey rolled in herbs and served with cranberries and bacon noisettes.

7 Scarcroft Rd. ✆ **01904/634341.** www.meltonsrestaurant.co.uk. Reservations required. Main courses £15–£19. MC, V. Tues–Sat noon–2pm; Mon–Sat 5:30–9:30pm. Closed 1 week in early Aug and Dec 24–Jan 14.

1331 Bar & Restaurant INTERNATIONAL   About a 5-minute walk from the minster, 1331 is in the heart of York, on a small street near Stonegate (walk up a narrow staircase to the second floor). The chefs use fresh ingredients, supplied locally if possible, and turn out high-quality dishes served in an intimate and relaxed atmosphere. Vegetarians can sample such menu items as stuffed baked mushrooms topped with melted goat cheese. Meat devotees can try the braised lamb shank cooked slowly in the oven and served with rosemary and red onions. A beef-and-mushroom stroganoff is another winning dish, as are tender strips of filet of beef slow-cooked with brandy and served with a Dijon mustard sauce. There's also a modern lounge area with a comfortable bar.

13 Grape Lane. ✆ **01904/661130.** www.1331-york.co.uk. Reservations required. Main courses £11–£19. AE, DC, MC, V. Sun–Thurs 10am–1am; Fri–Sat 10am–2am.

Seeing the Sights

The best way to see York is to go to **Exhibition Square** (opposite the Tourist Information Centre), where a volunteer guide will take you on a **free 2-hour walking tour** of the city. You'll learn about history and lore through numerous intriguing stories. Tours run April to September, daily at 10:15am and 2:15pm, plus 6:45pm from June to August; from October to March, a daily tour starts at 10:15am. Groups can book by prior arrangement by contacting the **Association of Voluntary Guides,** De Grey Rooms, Exhibition Square, York YO1 2HB (✆ **01904/640780;** www.york.touristguides.btinternet.co.uk).

Jorvik Viking Centre ★   This Viking city, discovered many feet below present ground level, was reconstructed as it stood in 948, and underwent major refurbishment in 2001. In a "time car," you travel back through the ages to 1067, when Normans sacked the city, and then you ride slowly through the street market peopled by faithfully modeled Vikings. You also go through a house where a family lived and down to the river to see the ship chandlers at work and the unloading of a Norwegian cargo. At the end of the ride, you pass through the Finds Hut, where thousands of artifacts are displayed. The time car departs at regular intervals.

Coppergate. ✆ **01904/543400.** www.jorvik-viking-centre.co.uk. Admission £9–£13 adults, £7–£11 students and seniors, £6–£10 children 5–15, £26–£43 family ticket. Rates may vary depending on the event. Apr–Oct and Feb daily 10am–5pm; Nov–Jan and Mar daily 10am–4pm.

National Railway Museum ★★★   This was the first national museum to be built outside London, and it has attracted millions of train buffs. Adapted from an original steam-locomotive depot, the museum gives visitors a chance to see how Queen Victoria traveled in luxury and to look under and inside steam locomotives. In addition, there's a collection of railway memorabilia, including a penny machine for purchasing tickets on the railway platform and an early-19th-century clock. More than 40 locomotives are on display. One, the *Agenoria,* dates from 1829 and is a contemporary of Stephenson's well-known *Rocket*. Of several royal coaches, the most interesting is Queen Victoria's Royal Saloon; it's like a small hotel, with polished wood, silk, brocade, and silver accessories.

Leeman York Rd. ✆ **0844/815-3139.** www.nrm.org.uk. Free admission. Daily 10am–6pm. Closed Dec 24–26.

Treasurer's House   The Treasurer's House lies on a site where a continuous succession of buildings has stood since Roman times. The main part of the house, built in 1620, was refurbished by Yorkshire industrialist Frank Green at the turn of the 20th century; he used this elegant town house to display his collection of 17th- and 18th-century furniture, glass, and china. An audiovisual program and exhibit explain the work of the medieval treasures and the subsequent fascinating history of the house. It has an attractive small garden in the shadow of York Minster.

Minster Yard. ✆ **01904/624247.** www.nationaltrust.org.uk. Admission £5.80 adults, £2.90 children, £15 family ticket. Apr–Oct Sat–Thurs 11am–4:30pm; Nov–Mar Sat–Thurs 11am–3pm.

York Castle Museum ★   On the site of York's Castle, this is one of the finest folk museums in the country. Its unique feature is a re-creation of a Victorian cobbled street, Kirkgate, named for the museum's founder, Dr. John Kirk. He acquired his large collection while visiting his patients in rural Yorkshire at the beginning of the

20th century. The period rooms range from a neoclassical Georgian dining room to an overstuffed and heavily adorned Victorian parlor to the 1953 sitting room with a "brand-new" television set purchased to watch the coronation of Elizabeth II. In the Debtors' Prison, former prison cells display crafts workshops. There is also a superb collection of arms and armor. In the Costume Gallery, displays are changed regularly to reflect the collection's variety. Half Moon Court is an Edwardian street with a Gypsy caravan and a pub (sorry, the bar's closed!). During the summer, you can visit a water mill on the bank of the River Foss.

Eye of York, off Tower St. ⓒ **01904/687687.** www.yorkcastlemuseum.org.uk. Admission £8 adults, £7 seniors and students, free for children 15 and younger. Daily 9:30am–5pm. Closed Dec 25–26 and Jan 1.

York Minster ★★★ One of the great cathedrals of the world, York Minster traces its origins from the early 7th century; the present building, however, dates from the 13th century. Like the cathedral at Lincoln, York Minster is characterized by three towers built in the 15th century. The central tower is lantern shaped in the Perpendicular style, and on a clear day the top of the tower offers panoramic views of York and the Vale of York. The climb up a stone spiral staircase is steep and only recommended for the fit.

The outstanding characteristic of the cathedral is its **stained glass ★★★** from the Middle Ages, in glorious vibrant blues, ruby reds, forest greens, and honey-colored ambers. See especially the Great East Window, the work of a 15th-century Coventry-based glass painter. In the north transept is an architectural gem of the mid-13th century: the Five Sisters Window, with its five lancets in grisaille glass. The late-15th-century choir screen in its Octagonal Chapter House has an impressive lineup of historical figures—everybody from William the Conqueror to the overthrown Henry VI. At a reception desk near the entrance to the minster, groups can arrange for a guide, if one is available. Conducted tours are free, but donations toward the upkeep of the cathedral are requested.

At the converging point of Deangate, Duncombe Place, Minster Yard, and Petergate. ⓒ **01904/557216.** www.yorkminster.org. Chapter House £6 adults, £5 seniors and students, free for children 15 and younger; crypt, foundations, and treasury £8 adults, £7 seniors and students, free for children. Chapter House, undercroft, and tower Mon–Sat 9am–5:30pm, Sun noon–5:30pm (till 5pm in winter). Call ahead, as hours may change.

Shopping

Several of the main areas to explore include **Gillygate** for antiques dealers; **St. Mary's Square** and its **Coppergate** pedestrian mall for name brands and chain stores; and one of the best streets for shopping, **Stonegate,** with an array of independent outlets.

For ideal gift items, check out **Mulberry Hall,** 17 Stonegate (ⓒ **01904/620736;** www.mulberryhall.co.uk), a medieval house from 1436, with 16 showrooms on three floors devoted to the best in British and European porcelain, fine china, crystal, and some antiques.

For your furry friends, the **Cat Gallery,** 27 Stonegate (ⓒ **01904/413000;** www. thecatgallery.co.uk), is Britain's largest feline-themed store.

A York Pub-Crawl

One of the city's oldest inns, the **Black Swan,** Peaseholme Green (ⓒ **01904/ 679131;** www.blackswanyork.co.uk), is a fine timber-framed house that was the

York Minster

home of the lord mayor of York in 1417; the mother of General James Wolfe of Quebec also lived here. In front of a log fire in a brick inglenook, you can enjoy pub meals such as fish and chips, burgers, and steaks. This is one of York's "musical pubs," featuring live folk music on Monday and Thursday, jazz on Wednesday and Sunday, and hip-hop every second and fourth Friday, with a small cover charge starting at £4.

Situated at the base of the Ouse Bridge, a few steps from the edge of the river, the 16th-century **Kings Arms Public House,** King's Staith (© **01904/659435**), is boisterous and fun. A historic monument in its own right, it's filled with charm and character and has the ceiling beams, paneling, and weathered brickwork you'd expect. Because of its location by the river, the pub can flood if rain is heavy enough. Expect a virtually indestructible decor, the kind that can (and often does) sit under water for days at a time. In summer, rows of outdoor tables are placed beside the river. Your hosts serve a full range of draft and bottled beers, the most popular of which (Samuel Smith's) is still brewed in Tadcaster, only 16km (10 miles) away. The ghost walk we recommend leaves here every night at 7:30pm.

On a pedestrian street in Old York, **Ye Olde Starre Inne,** 40 Stonegate (© **01904/623063**), dates from 1644 and is York's oldest licensed pub. An inn (of one kind or another) has stood on this spot since A.D. 900. The pub—which is said to be haunted by an old woman, a little girl, and a cat—features cast-iron tables, an open fireplace, oak Victorian settles, and time-blackened beams. The owners added a year-round glassed-in garden so guests can enjoy the view of the minster from their tables.

LEEDS ★

328km (204 miles) NW of London; 121km (75 miles) NE of Liverpool; 119km (74 miles) N of Nottingham; 69km (43 miles) NE of Manchester

The foundations for a permanent community were laid nearly 2,000 years ago when the Romans set up a small camp here called Cambodunum, but the next step toward modern Leeds didn't come until the 7th century, when the Northumbrian King Edwin established a residence. Kirkstall Abbey was founded in 1152, and in 1207 Leeds finally obtained its charter.

During the medieval era, Leeds took the golden fleece as its coat of arms, representative of its growth and importance as a wool town. In time, it became the greatest center of cloth trade in the region. Industrial advancements have played a great role in the growth of the city, with the introduction of steam power leading to the development of the coal fields to the south. Other innovations allowed the continued expansion of its textile industry, as well as the rapid development of such upstart industries as printing, tailoring, and engineering. The Victorian era marked the city's glory days.

After languishing for years and being dismissed for its industrial blight, the city is moving progressively forward again today. It's experiencing some economic growth, and many of the great Victorian buildings in its bustling central core have been renovated: the Corn Exchange, the Grand Theatre, and the Victoria Quarter. A "24-Hour City Initiative" makes Leeds the only U.K. location that not only allows but also encourages round-the-clock work and entertainment options; it's an up-and-coming city with a lot of new energy.

Essentials

GETTING THERE Leeds Bradford International Airport (© **0871/288-2288;** www.leedsbradfordairport.co.uk), about 14km (9 miles) north of town, has daily flights to and from London's Heathrow and Gatwick airports and most major regional U.K. airports, with air transport taking an hour or so from London. Carriers that serve Leeds from London include **Flybe** (www.flybe.com). There is also a 24-hour direct rail link between Manchester Airport and Leeds. Taxi fare from the airport to the center of Leeds costs £20.

Trains from London's Kings Cross Station arrive hourly during the day, with the trip taking about 2 hours. For information, call © **0845/748-4950** or visit **www.nationalrail.co.uk**.

National Express buses from London arrive in Leeds daily. For schedules and information, call © **0871/781-8181** or visit **www.nationalexpress.com**.

Leeds lies at the crossroads of the north–south M1 and the east–west M62 routes, making it easily accessible by car from anywhere in England or Scotland.

VISITOR INFORMATION The **Gateway Yorkshire Regional Travel & Tourist Information Centre,** the Arcade, City Station (📞 **0113/242-5242;** www.yorkshire.com and www.leedsliveitloveit.com), is open Monday to Saturday 9am to 5:30pm and Sunday 10am to 4pm. The city's own website, **www.leeds.gov. uk**, offers information on transportation, lodging, dining, shopping, and entertainment in Leeds.

Information on local bus and train routes, plus timetables, is available by calling **Metroline** at 📞 **0113/245-7676.**

SPECIAL EVENTS In July, more than 40,000 opera lovers turn out at **Temple Newsam,** Temple Newsam Road, off Selby Road (📞 **0113/264-5535;** www.leeds. gov.uk/templenewsam), for the single performance of **Opera in the Park,** the largest outdoor opera concert in the United Kingdom. The gargantuan **Party in the Park** (📞 **0113/2478-222**), also held at Temple Newsam, is one of the largest free pop and rock concerts in the U.K. It's usually held the day following Opera in the Park and features some of the hottest acts in rock music.

Film buffs turn out in droves for the annual **Leeds International Film Festival** (📞 **0113/224-3801;** www.leedsfilm.com). Screened at cinemas throughout Leeds every November, it's the only theme-based film festival in the U.K. It regularly features British as well as world-premiere films and hosts film-related lectures, seminars, and workshops.

Where to Stay

If you'd like advice on local lodging, or if you'd just like to tell someone your price range and requirements and let them book you a room, contact the **Gateway Yorkshire Accommodation Booking Line** (📞 **0800/808050** or 0113/242-5242). For a £5 handling fee and a refundable deposit of 10% of your first night's stay, it will find you a bed for the night.

42 The Calls ★★★ Overlooking the River Aire in the heart of Leeds, this small but deluxe hotel is the city's most tranquil and elegant choice, created from an 18th-century grain mill in a once-dilapidated waterfront area that's all high tech and high comfort now. Accommodations range from the more traditional to units such as the Black Room, with a huge black bed and black-striped walls, or room no. 303, with an original winch hanging from the ceiling—a nod to the building's origins. Business travelers will appreciate the three phones and full-size work desk in every room, individual fax machine on request, and dictation by arrangement.

42 The Calls, Leeds, West Yorkshire LS2 7EW. 📞 **0113/244-0099.** Fax 0113/234-4100. www.theeton collection.com. 41 units. £150–£225 double; £280–£400 suite. AE, DC, MC, V. Parking £14. **Amenities:** 2 restaurants; bar; babysitting; concierge; access to nearby health club; room service. *In room:* TV, hair dryer, Wi-Fi £15 per day).

Haley's Hotel ★ 🗝 Located in a quiet, tree-lined cul-de-sac just off the main Otley-Leeds road (A660), this town-house hotel, set up in a Victorian mansion, makes it easy to forget that you're near a major metropolitan area. The hotel's rooms are comfortably laid out and opt for tasteful individuality, each with its own period-specific, polished wood antiques. Features include work desks with telephones and efficiently organized private bathrooms. As for the beds, management accurately quotes Charles Dickens: "It would make anyone go to sleep, that bedstead would, whether they wanted to or not." The staff is diligent, accommodating guests with such options as a late supper or shoe-cleaning service.

Leeds

ATTRACTIONS ●
Craft Centre &
  Design Gallery **1**
Leeds Art Gallery **1**
Henry Moore
  Institute **2**
Royal Armouries
  Museum **5**

ACCOMMODATIONS ■
42 The Calls **7**
Malmaison Leeds **5**
Quebecs **3**

DINING ◆
Anthony's Restaurant **6**
Olive Press **4**

Shire Oak Rd. (3km/2 miles from Leeds city center and 11km/7 miles from Leeds Bradford International Airport), Headingley, Leeds, West Yorkshire LS6 2DE. ℂ **0113/278-4446.** Fax 0113/275-3342. www.haleys.co.uk. 29 units. £109–£119 double. Rates include English breakfast and dinner. AE, MC, V. Free parking. **Amenities:** Restaurant (see review below); bar; babysitting; room service. *In room:* TV, hair dryer, Wi-Fi (free).

Malmaison Leeds ★ 📷 This former tram and bus garage is today a hotel of charm and character. The local newspaper hailed its rebirth as "sexy, cool, and slinky," and so it is—a stylish hotel that is intimate and cool. A great range of well-styled and individually designed bedrooms awaits you, some done up in subtle shades of taupe, with contrasting deep tones of plum, charcoal, and ocher. Downstairs is a super little bar and brasserie under a vaulted ceiling. The hotel also has a high-tech fitness suite.

1 Swinegate, Leeds, West Yorkshire LS1 4AG. ℂ **0113/398-1000.** Fax 0113/398-1002. www.malmaison-leeds.com. 100 units. £155–£175 double; from £375 suite. AE, DC, MC, V. Parking £12. **Amenities:** Restaurant; bar; exercise room; room service. *In room:* TV, CD player, hair dryer, minibar, Wi-Fi (£15 per day).

Oulton Hall ★★ A painstakingly restored 1850s Italianate mansion, this hotel offers an atmosphere of pure elegance, from the black-and-white tiled front entrance and the damask-hung walls of the public rooms with their great crystal chandeliers to the library with its mahogany wall paneling and window seat. You can enjoy butler service in the drawing room, a drink in the plush red-leather interior of the Calverley Bar, or a stroll through formal gardens re-created from the original 19th-century plans. Most of the well-furnished bedrooms are in the modern wing; the grand suites are in the original house. Accommodations enjoy views of the well-manicured grounds and championship golf course.

Rothwell Lane (9km/5½ miles east of Leeds via A61 and A639), Oulton, Leeds, West Yorkshire LS26 8HN. © **0113/282-1000.** Fax 0113/282-8066. www.devere.co.uk/our-locations/oulton-hall. 152 units. £99–£255 double; £294–£380 suite. Rates include English breakfast. AE, DC, MC, V. Free parking. **Amenities:** 2 restaurants; bar; exercise room; 9- and 18-hole golf courses and driving range; indoor heated pool; room service; spa. *In room:* TV, hair dryer, minibar, Wi-Fi (free).

Quebecs ★★ 🏨 As a sign of the renaissance of the city of Leeds, this gorgeous 1891 neo-Renaissance pile of red brick has been glamorously restored and converted into a hotel. The Victorian shell has been preserved; otherwise, the hotel is imbued with state-of-the-art amenities. The broad winding oak staircase and the ornate stained-glass windows are still there, along with handcrafted oak panels. A few minutes' walk from City Square and the main train station, the central hotel offers bedrooms that are beautifully and traditionally decorated, in chic colors such as camel brown and Wedgwood blue. The best accommodations are two mezzanine suites with spiral staircases leading to the sleeping quarters.

9 Quebec St., Leeds, West Yorkshire LS1 2HA. © **0113/244-8989.** Fax 0113/244-9090. www.theeton collection.com. 45 units. £120–£225 double; from £250 suite. AE, DC, MC, V. Parking £10. **Amenities:** Restaurant; bar; concierge; room service; Wi-Fi (free, in lobby). *In room:* A/C, TV, CD player, hair dryer, minibar.

Where to Dine

Anthony's Restaurant ★★★ MODERN BRITISH   Anthony James Flinn just may be the greatest chef in Yorkshire. He certainly is number one in Leeds. He's the most innovative, even provocative, chef around, and his creations are cutting edge— or, in his words, "molecular gastronomy," whereby physics and chemistry are applied to the kitchen. Don't you always like your baby squid with mango sherbet or your sliver of pigs' ears with cubes of honey jelly? Shredded crab comes on Jabugo ham with salted peanut foam, and fork-tender pork comes startlingly pink in the new style of preparation. For dessert? Smoked-brie ice cream—but of course.

19 Boar Lane. © **0113/245-5922.** www.anthonysrestaurant.co.uk. Reservations required. Fixed-price 2-course lunch £21; fixed-price 3-course lunch £24; 2 a la carte courses £36, 3 a la carte courses £45. AE, DC, MC, V. Tues–Sat noon–2pm and 7–9:30pm.

Haley's Restaurant ENGLISH   This hotel restaurant, in a beautifully restored Victorian mansion, is so popular among locals that even the guests overnighting here have to reserve long in advance. Chef John Vennell changes his menu monthly to take advantage of the freshest market ingredients. Starters may feature a tantalizing tasting of king prawns, marinated and grilled in lemon grass paste on a lemon risotto flavored with tamarind sauce. A heavenly tartlet is made with roast beets and goat cheese and served with a soft quail egg. Some of the best main courses include the pan-fried calf's liver in a rich red wine jus, the pan-roasted rack of lamb with a red currant and port wine jus, and the sautéed filet of salmon served on a rich lobster bisque.

In Haley's Hotel, Shire Oak Rd. (3km/2 miles from Leeds city center), Headingley. ☎ **0113/278-4446.** Reservations required well in advance. Main courses £11–£18; fixed-price menus £19–£24. AE, DC, MC, V. Mon–Sat 7:15-9:30pm; Sun 12:15-1:45pm. Closed Dec 26-30.

Olive Press ☺ ITALIAN/PIZZA   This popular restaurant, a member of a small regional chain, occupies a restored building that was a granary in the 1800s. Set beside the water in the city's revitalized canal-front district, its theatrical lighting showcases the massive beams and trusses that formed the skeleton of the building's original architecture. Menu items include a pleasing mix of comfort food and such chargrilled dishes as swordfish steak, brick-fired chump of lamb, or a whole grilled sea bream stuffed with lemon. Starters range from spicy lamb meatballs to chargrilled asparagus. The pastas and risottos are always reliable, as are the pizzas—one made with coriander-flavored crabmeat. The restaurant caters to kids, who get their own special "Little Olives" menu.

Canal Wharf, Water Lane. ☎ **0113/244-6611.** www.heathcotes.co.uk/olivepress. Reservations recommended. Main courses £10–£22. AE, MC, V. Mon–Thurs 11:30am-10pm; Fri–Sat 11:30am-11pm.

Exploring Leeds

Despite its longtime reputation as a grimy northern industrial city, Leeds will surprise you with the beauty and diversity of its city center, where £400 million has been invested during the past decade, both in new construction and renovation of warehouses and landmark Victorian structures into homes, lodgings, shops, and restaurants along the waterfront and in the central shopping district.

Henry Moore Institute   Located next door to the Leeds Art Gallery, this is one of the largest sculpture galleries in Europe. The institute is named after the greatest British sculptor of the 20th century, Henry Moore (1898–1986), who was a Yorkshireman. Three galleries of changing exhibitions display the various aspects of sculpture. The works of many of Moore's contemporaries are often on view as well. Lectures throughout the year supplement the institute's exhibitions.

74 The Headrow. ☎ **0113/246-7467.** www.henry-moore-fdn.co.uk. Free admission. Daily 10am-5:30pm (Wed until 9pm).

Leeds Art Gallery ★   Spread over three floors, this gallery, founded in 1888 as the Leeds City Art Gallery, houses England's best collection of 20th-century art outside of London, including French post-Impressionist paintings, contemporary British sculpture, prints, watercolors, and drawings. Throughout the year, it also hosts visiting exhibits, enhanced by workshops, talks, and other related events. The library reopened in 2007 following a wholesale £1.7-million restoration, including a new exhibition gallery for touring art shows and multimedia installations.

Located within the Leeds Art Gallery is the **Craft Centre & Design Gallery** (☎ **0113/247-8241;** www.craftcentreleeds.co.uk), which showcases contemporary ceramics, jewelry, prints, textiles, and applied arts from around the world. It also hosts openings and exhibits by local and regional artists.

74 The Headrow. ☎ **0113/247-8256.** www.leeds.gov.uk/artgallery. Free admission. Mon–Tues 10am-5pm; Wed noon–5pm; Thurs–Sat 10am-5pm; Sun 1-5pm.

Royal Armouries Museum ★   A notable construction along the waterfront, this £42-million facility is the home of London Tower's Royal Armouries, England's oldest museum, with exhibits that include the working arsenal of the medieval kings. It is designed to exhibit the many pieces that have been in perpetual storage because of inadequate facilities in London. The museum illustrates the development and use of arms and armor for war, sport, hunting, self-defense, and fashion.

Armouries Dr. © **0113/220-1999.** www.armouries.org.uk. Free admission. Daily 10am–5pm. Closed Dec 24–25.

Temple Newsam   This was the birthplace, in 1545, of the ill-fated Lord Darnley, husband of Mary, Queen of Scots. Construction began on this Tudor-Jacobean mansion in 1521, and substantial remodeling occurred in both the 17th and late 18th centuries. It stands as an odd but beautiful tribute to several eras of architecture. Today, it houses a splendid collection of silver and Chippendale furniture. The surrounding 480 hectares (1,200 acres) of parkland includes Home Farm, a breeding ground for rare farm animals, and the venue for Opera in the Park (p. 660).

Temple Newsam Rd. (off Selby Rd.; 6.5km/4 miles from Leeds city center off the A63). © **0113/264-5535.** www.leeds.gov.uk/templenewsam. Admission house and farm £5.75 adults, £3.50 children 5–16; house only £3.50 adults, £2.50 children 5–16. Apr–Oct Tues–Sun 10:30am–5pm (last admission 4:15pm); Nov–Mar Tues–Sun 10:30am–4pm (last admission 3:15pm).

Leeds After Dark

Thanks to a city initiative aimed at relaxing licensing restrictions and increasing late-night entertainment options, it's safe to say that Leeds now rocks 'round the clock. And it was already humming with classical concerts, opera, jazz, dance, theater, cinema, rock and dance clubs, cafes, and pubs.

THE PERFORMING ARTS   **Leeds Town Hall,** the Headrow (© **0113/247-7989**), hosts orchestras from around the globe as part of the annual **Leeds International Concert Season** (© **0113/247-8336;** www.leedsconcertseason.com); it is also home to the world-famous **Leeds International Pianoforte Competition** (© **0113/244-6586;** www.leedspiano.com), held every 3 years.

   Opera North (© **0113/243-9999;** www.operanorth.co.uk) offers three to four productions during its season from October to April at the **Leeds Grand Theatre & Opera House,** 46 New Briggate (© **0113/222-6222;** www.leedsgrandtheatre. com), featuring a well-renovated 1,500-seat auditorium behind its original 1878 Victorian facade.

   The **Yorkshire Dance Centre,** St. Peters Building, York Street (© **0113/243-8765;** www.yorkshiredance.com), houses the internationally renowned **Phoenix Dance Troupe.**

   Theatergoers are much impressed by the facilities at the £12-million **West Yorkshire Playhouse,** Playhouse Square, Quarry Hill (© **0113/213-7700;** www.wyp. org.uk), home to the "national theatre of the north." Playhouse artistic director Jude Kelly started out strong in the early inaugural seasons, with 17 productions, including eight British or world premieres. There has been no slowing down since then, and you can find a dramatic offering at most any time in either the Playhouse's Quarry Auditorium, which seats 750, or the Courtyard, which seats 350. The Playhouse, which is the cornerstone of a proposed £70-million Quarry Hill arts complex, also hosts other events throughout the year, including the annual Jazz at the Playhouse series.

THE CLUB & MUSIC SCENE   Leeds has a thriving rock scene, with recent bands, such as Sisters of Mercy and the Mission, rising out of the music world.

Today's up-and-coming music, not surprisingly, is very influenced by what's hot in Manchester (see chapter 17), but innovative bands such as Black Star Liner, Bedlam A Go Go, and Embrace show that Leeds still has a musical voice all its own.

The **Cockpit,** Bridge House, Swinegate (*©* **0113/244-1573;** www.thecockpit. co.uk), can host about 600 fans, who turn out to hear the latest indie bands in a converted railway arch setting. It's usually open Tuesday, Wednesday, Friday, and Saturday night, with a cover ranging from £3 to £5.

You'll find jazz at **Art's Café Bar,** 42 Call Lane (*©* **0113/243-8243;** www. artscafebar.co.uk), a European-style cafe/bar that offers tapas, bottled beers, and coffees.

Considering its size, Leeds has a substantial gay scene. The most popular club at the moment is **Queens Court,** Lower Briggate (*©* **0113/245-9449;** www.queens-court.co.uk), with a restaurant and bar downstairs. Queens Court is open Monday to Wednesday noon to 2am, Thursday noon to midnight, Friday and Saturday noon to 3am, and Sunday noon to 11pm. The cover ranges from £2 to £5. Another current hot spot for gay men is the **Bridge Inn,** 1–5 Bridge Inn (*©* **0113/244-4734**), which has a friendly local-pub atmosphere and becomes increasingly clubby as the night progresses (no cover).

PUBS Stop by **Whitelocks,** Turks Head Yard (*©* **0113/245-3950;** www. whitelocks.co.uk), in the alley of Briggate, next to Marks & Spencer. There's a copper-topped bar with a handmade ceramic-tile front, a marble sandwich bar, old advertising mirrors, and stained-glass windows. Locals keep the conversation flowing in a thick northern accent. If you get hungry, there's cheap traditional pub grub. Tap selections are varied and quite good, including McEwan's 80, Younger's IPA, and Theakston's Old Peculiar.

Hearkening back to Leeds's glory days, **Victoria,** Great George Street (*©* **0113/245-1386**), is every bit as Victorian as its name suggests, with ornate globe lamps, etched mirrors, and a well-adorned bar. Politicians and lawyers frequent the place. Join in the conversation or sit back and listen while you enjoy a pint of Tetley's Mild and maybe a bar snack or two.

BRADFORD ★

341km (212 miles) N of London; 52km (32 miles) NE of Manchester; 14km (9 miles) W of Leeds

This city of nearly half a million souls retains a rich ethnic heritage from the succession of immigrants who came to work the mills beginning in the mid–19th century. High-tech firms, galleries, and museums have displaced many of the textile factories of the past. But generations of Irish, German, Italian, eastern European, Asian, and African-Caribbean immigrants give this West Yorkshire town an international flavor today.

Centrally located between the Yorkshire Dales and the Pennines, Bradford provides a nice diversion and is convenient to a historic countryside where the Brontës once dwelled and armor-clad soldiers clashed in the Wars of the Roses.

Essentials

GETTING THERE Leeds Bradford International Airport (*©* **0871/288-2288;** www.leedsbradfordairport.co.uk) is located about 16km (10 miles) from Bradford. A number of scheduled flights connect it to London's Heathrow and

Gatwick airports as well as most major regional U.K. airports. Carriers that serve Leeds from London include **Flybe** (www.flybe.com). A taxi from the airport to town costs about £15.

Most rail links go through nearby Leeds (see earlier in this chapter), but at least one direct train each day connects London's Kings Cross Station with Bradford, a 3-hour trip. Train travel takes about 1 hour from Manchester, about 3 hours from Birmingham.

Bradford is reached by car via the M62 and the M606.

VISITOR INFORMATION   The **Bradford Tourist Information Centre,** City Hall, Centenary Square (© **01274/433678;** www.visitbradford.com), assists visitors in finding accommodations and provides public transit timetables and city guides. Hours are Tuesday to Saturday 9:30am to 5pm and Monday 10am to 5pm.

Where to Stay

Best Western Guide Post Hotel   Catering to both business and leisure travelers, this is a winning choice. You get a warm welcome as you're shown to your spacious, well-furnished guest room equipped with a compact bathroom with shower. The more expensive executive rooms have a spacious lounge area. The reasonable price combined with room size makes this a good choice for families as well.

Common Rd. (5km/3 miles from Junction 26 of M62), Low Moor, Bradford, West Yorkshire BD12 0ST. © **0845/409-1357.** Fax 01274/671085. www.guideposthotel.net. 43 units. £65–£108 double; £83–£120 suite. Rates include English or continental breakfast. AE, DC, MC, V. Free parking. **Amenities:** Restaurant; bar; room service. In room: TV, hair dryer, Wi-Fi (free).

Great Victoria Hotel   Built in 1875 in the city center, the Victoria has been entirely restored. Once the showpiece of the Lancashire and Yorkshire Railway, the hotel now provides stylish accommodations at affordable rates. The well-furnished and recently renovated bedrooms are comfortable and clean. Bathrooms are equipped with power showers. Four rooms are large enough for families.

Bridge St., Bradford, West Yorkshire BD1 1JX. © **01274/728706.** Fax 01274/736358. www.tomahawk hotels.co.uk. 60 units. £119–£139 double; £159 suite. Rates include English breakfast. AE, DC, MC, V. Free parking. From M62, take Junction 26 to M606, then to A6177 and A611, and exit at roundabout to Hallings; turn right at traffic light; the hotel is on the left. **Amenities:** Restaurant; bar; children's programs; room service; sauna. In room: TV/DVD, hair dryer, Wi-Fi (free).

Where to Dine

Bradford is called "the curry capital of the U.K." because it boasts a vast array of Asian restaurants featuring dishes from Kashmir, Gujarat, Punjab, and beyond. Many of the best of these curry houses are found along Morley Street near the National Media Museum. Our favorite along this street is **Kashmir,** 27 Morley St. (© **01274/726513**), which, although a very simple place, serves authentic and excellently prepared Indian food.

An even better choice is **Mumtaz,** Great Horton Road (© **01274/571861;** www.mumtaz.co.uk), Bradford's leading Kashmiri curry house, drawing large crowds of hungry diners. Meat, fish, and vegetable curries are prepared with great skill and flavor. Expat Indians prefer to accompany their meal with *masala lassi,* a yogurt drink, or perhaps sweet mango juice, as liquor isn't served.

Bradford is not a great restaurant town except for its curry houses, and some travelers prefer to dine at their hotel restaurants.

Exploring Bradford

Bradford's museums, mill shops, and restaurants provide the main attractions for tourists. The city also boasts Bradford University, one of the better regional universities in the United Kingdom.

The **Bradford Industrial Museum and Horses at Work,** Moorside Mills, Moorside Road (© 01274/435900; www.bradfordmuseums.org), depicts mill life for both worker and owner in the 1870s. It also offers Shire horse rides for kids and adults. The museum is open Tuesday to Saturday 10am to 5pm and Sunday noon to 5pm; admission is free.

Saltaire Village (www.saltairevillage.info) is the restored model factory-community developed in the mid–19th century by mill owner and philanthropist Titus Salt. The **1853 Gallery** at the former **Salts Mill** (© 01274/531163; www.saltsmill.org.uk) exhibits more than 400 works by local artist David Hockney, among others.

Visitors can travel by steam-driven train on the **Keighley & Worth Valley Railway** (© 01535/645214; www.kwvr.co.uk) for a tour of Brontë country in Haworth (see below), through Oakworth's Edwardian station and Damen's Station, billed as Britain's smallest rail station. It operates daily in summer and on Saturdays only in winter.

The National Museum of Photography, Film & Television is now known as the **National Media Museum,** Little Horton Lane (© 0870/701-0200; www.nationalmediamuseum.org.uk), which captures the history of photography, film, and television in audiovisual presentations that span 150 years. The five-story-high IMAX screen, the largest in England, explores a dazzling variety of cinematic images in a series of new and continuing exhibitions. Admission to the museum is free; the IMAX movie costs £7.75 for adults, £5.75 for children. Advance booking is recommended. The museum is open Tuesday to Sunday 10am to 8pm.

Bradford's textile industry is still represented in dozens of area **mill shops** where bargain hunters may find a great variety of mohair, pure-wool yarns, fabrics, sportswear, and other clothing and accessories. Some mill shops provide tours of factory spinning, weaving, and textile finishing.

Bradford After Dark

The **Alhambra Theatre,** Morley Street (© 01274/432000; www.bradford-theatres.co.uk), offers a variety of presentations ranging from amateur to professional. At certain times of the year, leading actors of the English stage and screen may appear here. You can also see children's theater, ballet, and musicals. Ticket prices vary depending upon the type of performance. The theater is closed for a few weeks in August.

Perhaps you're just looking for a local pub. In the city center, the **Shoulder of Mutton,** 28 Kirkgate (© 01274/726038), has a beer garden that comes complete with flower beds and hanging baskets. The oldest brewery in Yorkshire, it was originally Samuel Smith's Old Brewery. Lunch is available, as is real ale. As many as 200 drinkers can crowd in here on a summer night.

As an alternative, try the **Fighting Cock,** 21–23 Preston St. (© 01274/726907), an old-fashioned alehouse with bare floors and 12 different bitters. The best ales are Exmoor Gold, Timothy Taylor's, Black Sheep, and Green King Abbott, but foreign-bottled beers and farm ciders are also offered. On nippy nights, coal fires keep the atmosphere mellow. Bar snacks are among the most reasonable in town; the house specialty is chili (the chef guards the recipe).

HAWORTH: HOME OF THE BRONTËS ★★

72km (45 miles) SW of York; 34km (21 miles) W of Leeds

Haworth, on the moor of the Pennines, is the famed home of the Brontës, the most-visited literary shrine in England after Stratford-upon-Avon.

Essentials

GETTING THERE   To reach Haworth by rail, take the Arriva train from Leeds City Station to Keighley (it leaves approximately every 30 min.). Change trains at Keighley and take the Keighley & Worth Valley Railway to Haworth and Oxenhope. Train services operate every weekend year-round, with 7 to 12 departures per day. From late June to September, trains also run four times a day Monday through Friday. For general inquiries, call ✆ **01535/645214** or go to **www.kwvr.co.uk**; for a 24-hour timetable, dial the tourist office at ✆ **01535/642329.**

   Keighley & District offers bus service between Keighley and Haworth. Bus nos. 663, 664, and 665 will get you there. For information, call ✆ **01535/603284** or visit **www.keighleyanddistrict.co.uk**.

   Driving time from York to Haworth is about 1 hour and 15 minutes. Head west toward Leeds on the A64; this route is extremely complicated, with many different turnoffs onto various other routes, so plot your way carefully before setting out so you can avoid getting lost. It's best to start with a detailed map and downloaded driving directions.

VISITOR INFORMATION   The **Tourist Information Centre,** 2–4 West Lane, Haworth (✆ **01535/642329;** www.visitbradford.com/bronte-country), is open May through August, daily 9:30am to 5:30pm, and September through April daily 9:30am to 5pm. The center is closed December 24 to December 26.

Where to Stay

Weaver's Restaurant (see "Where to Dine," below) also offers rooms for rent.

Ashmount Country House ★★ 📖   This is the grandest B&B in this part of England, real government-rated five-star luxury living. Were they to return today, the Brontë sisters might call it decadent. The country house was the ancestral home of Dr. Amos Ingham, family physician to Charlotte and Patrick Brontë. Nestled below the evocative moors of Wuthering Heights, the home has been completely modernized with spacious, luxurious bedrooms, yet its quaint old-fashioned charm has been painstakingly preserved. Bedrooms rest under high ceilings; for the luxury-minded, there are exquisite hot-tub suites.

Mytholmes Lane, Haworth, West Yorkshire BD22 8EZ. ✆ **01535/645-726.** Fax 01535/642-550. www.ashmounthaworth.co.uk. 9 units. £85–£150 double; £165 suite. Rates include English breakfast. AE, MC, V. Free parking. **Amenities:** Room service; Wi-Fi (free, in lobby). *In room:* TV/DVD, CD player.

Old White Lion Hotel   At the top of a cobblestone street, this hotel dates from 1700, when it was built with a solid stone roof. It's almost next door to the church where the Reverend Brontë preached, as well as the parsonage where the family lived. Paul and Christopher Bradford welcome visitors to their warm, cheerful, and comfortable hotel. Though full of old-world charm, all accommodations are completely up-to-date. Room size varies considerably, but each unit is attractively furnished and has a comfortable bed and a small bathroom, most often with a tub/shower combination. Two rooms are large enough for families.

6–10 West Lane, Haworth (near Keighley), West Yorkshire BD22 8DU. (C) **01535/642313.** Fax 01535/646222. www.oldwhitelionhotel.com. 14 units. £87 double. Rates include English breakfast. AE, DC, MC, V. **Amenities:** Restaurant; bar; room service. *In room:* TV, hair dryer, Wi-Fi (free).

Where to Dine

Weaver's Restaurant ★ 🍴 MODERN BRITISH   The best restaurant in the Brontë hometown, this spot is British to the core. In an inviting, informal atmosphere, it serves excellent food made with fresh ingredients. Jane and Colin Rushworth are quite talented in the kitchen. Their dinners may include such classic dishes as slow-cooked Yorkshire lamb. If available, try one of the Gressingham ducks, which are widely praised in the United Kingdom. Other highly favored dishes include local farm chicken in a creamy green-peppercorn sauce or steamed filets of sea bass with a shallot-and-white-wine sauce. For dessert, try a British cheese or one of the homemade delicacies.

Weaver's also rents three bedrooms of high caliber that cost £99 for a double, including a full Yorkshire breakfast.

15 West Lane. (C) **01535/643822.** www.weaversmallhotel.co.uk. Reservations recommended. Main courses £13–£26. AE, DC, MC, V. Wed–Sun noon–2pm; Tues–Sat 6–9pm. Closed for a certain period each summer, so call ahead to check.

Literary Landmarks

Anne Brontë wrote two novels, *The Tenant of Wildfell Hall* and *Agnes Grey;* Charlotte wrote two masterpieces, *Jane Eyre* and *Villette,* which depicted her experiences as a teacher, as well as several other novels; and Emily is the author of *Wuthering Heights,* a novel of passion and haunting melancholy. Charlotte and Emily are buried in the family vault under the **Church of St. Michael** (Anne is buried at the **Church of St. Mary** in Scarborough). Check out **www.visitbrontecountry.com** for information.

While in Haworth, you'll want to visit the **Brontë Weaving Shed,** Townend Mill (**(C) 01535/646217**). The shop is not far from the Brontë parsonage and features the famous Brontë tweed, which combines browns, greens, and oranges to evoke the look of the local countryside. The shed is open for visitors Monday to Saturday 10am to 5:30pm and Sunday 11am to 5pm.

Brontë Parsonage Museum ★   The parsonage where the Brontë family lived has been preserved as this museum, which houses their furniture, personal treasures, pictures, books, and manuscripts. The stone-sided parsonage, built near the top of the village in 1777, was assigned for the course of his lifetime as the residence of the Brontës' father, Patrick, the perpetual curator of the Church of St. Michael and All Angels Church. (Regrettably, the church tended by the Brontës was demolished in 1870; it was rebuilt in its present form the same year.) The parsonage contains a walled garden very similar to the one cultivated by the Brontës, plus five bedrooms, a collection of family furniture (some bought with proceeds from Charlotte's literary success), and personal effects, pictures and paintings, and original manuscripts. It also contains the largest archive of Brontë family correspondence in the world.

The museum is maintained by a professional staff selected by the Brontë Society, an organization established in 1893 to perpetuate the memory and legacy of Britain's most famous literary family. Contributions to the society are welcomed. The museum tends to be extremely crowded in July and August.

Church St. ℂ **01535/642323.** www.bronte.org.uk. Admission £6.50 adults, £5 students and seniors, £3.50 children 5–16, £16 family ticket (2 adults, 3 children), free for children 4 and younger. Oct–Mar daily 11am–5pm; Apr–Sept daily 10am–5:30pm. Closed Jan and Dec 24–27.

YORKSHIRE'S COUNTRY HOUSES, CASTLES & MORE

Yorkshire's battle-scarred castles, Gothic abbeys, and great country-manor houses are unrivaled anywhere in Britain. Here are some of the highlights.

In North Yorkshire

Castle Howard ★★ In its dramatic setting of lakes, fountains, and extensive gardens, Castle Howard, the 18th-century palace designed by Sir John Vanbrugh, is undoubtedly the finest private residence in Yorkshire. This was the first major achievement of the architect who later created the lavish Blenheim Palace near Oxford. The Yorkshire palace was begun in 1699 for the third earl of Carlisle, Charles Howard. The striking facade is topped by a painted and gilded dome, which reaches more than 24m (80 ft.) into the air. The interior boasts a 58m-long (192-ft.) gallery, as well as a chapel with magnificent stained-glass windows by the 19th-century artist Sir Edward Burne-Jones. Besides the collections of antique furniture and sculpture, the castle has many important paintings, including a portrait of Henry VIII by Holbein and works by Rubens, Reynolds, and Gainsborough. The seemingly endless grounds, including two rose gardens, also feature the domed Temple of the Four Winds, by Vanbrugh, and the richly designed family mausoleum, by Hawksmoor.

Malton (24km/15 miles northeast of York, 5km/3 miles off A64). ℂ **01653/648444.** www.castlehoward. co.uk. Admission house and gardens £13 adults, £11 students and seniors, £7.50 children 5–16, £25–£33 family ticket; gardens only £8.50 adults, £8 students and seniors, £6 children, £17–£23 family ticket. Mid-Mar to Oct grounds daily 10am–4:30pm; house daily 11am–4pm (during winter, call to verify times).

Fountains Abbey & Studley Royal ★★★ On the banks of the Silver Skell, the abbey was founded by Cistercian monks in 1132 and is the largest monastic ruin in Britain. In 1987, it was awarded World Heritage Site status. The ruins provide the focal point of the 18th-century landscape garden at Studley Royal, one of the few surviving examples of a Georgian green garden. It's known for its conservation work in the water gardens, ornamental temples, follies, and vistas. The garden is bounded at its northern edge by a lake and 160 hectares (400 acres) of deer park.

At Fountains, 6.5km (4 miles) southwest of Ripon off B6265. ℂ **01765/608888.** www.fountainsabbey. org.uk. Admission £8.50 adults, £4.55 children, £22 family ticket. Oct–Mar daily 10am–4pm; Apr–Sept daily 10am–5pm. Closed Dec 24–25 and Fri in Nov–Jan. It's best to drive, though it can be reached from York by public transportation. From York, take bus no. 142 leaving from the York Hall Station to Ripon, 37km (23 miles) to the northwest (A59, A1, and B6265 lead to Ripon). From Ripon, it will be necessary to take a taxi 6.5km (4 miles) to the southwest, though some prefer to take the scenic walk.

In West Yorkshire

Harewood House & Bird Garden ★★ ☺ Thirty-five kilometers (22 miles) west of York, the home of the earl and countess of Harewood is one of England's great 18th-century houses. It has always been owned by the Lascelles family. The fine Adam interior has superb ceilings and plasterwork and furniture made especially for Harewood by Thomas Chippendale. There are also important collections of English and Italian paintings and Sèvres and Chinese porcelain.

The gardens, designed by Capability Brown, include terraces, lakeside and woodland walks, and a 1.8-hectare (4½-acre) bird garden with exotic species from all over the world, including penguins, macaws, flamingos, and snowy owls. Other facilities include an art gallery, shops, a restaurant, and a cafeteria. Parking is free, and there is a picnic area, plus an adventure playground for the children. Highest rates are charged June 28 to September 7.

At the junction of A61 and A659, midway btw. Leeds and Harrogate, at Harewood Village. © **0113/228-1010.** www.harewood.org. House, terrace gallery, grounds, bird garden £11–£14 adults, £5.50–£7.50 children, £10–£12 seniors, £35–£47 family ticket. Early Apr to Oct daily house noon–4pm, terrace gallery 10:30am–4pm, grounds and adventure playground 10am–6pm, bird garden 10am–5:30pm; Nov to mid-Dec daily grounds and playground 10am–4pm, bird garden 10am–2:30pm. From York, head west along B1224 toward Wetherby and follow the signs to Harewood.

YORKSHIRE DALES NATIONAL PARK ★

This national park consists of some 1,813 sq. km (700 sq. miles) of water-carved country. In the dales, or valleys, you'll find dramatic white-limestone crags, roads, and fields bordered by dry-stone walls, fast-running rivers, isolated sheep farms, and clusters of sandstone cottages.

Malhamdale receives more visitors annually than any dale in Yorkshire. Two of the most interesting historic attractions are the 12th-century ruins of Bolton Priory and the 14th-century Castle Bolton, to the north in Wensleydale.

Richmond, the most frequently copied town name in the world, stands at the head of the dales and, like Hawes (see below), is a good center for touring the surrounding countryside.

Exploring the Dales

For orientation purposes, head first for **Grassington,** 16km (10 miles) north of Skipton and 40km (25 miles) west of Ripon. Constructed around a cobbled marketplace, this stone-built village is ideal for exploring Upper Wharfedale, one of the most scenic parts of the dales. In fact, the **Dales Way** footpath passes right through the heart of the village.

Drop in to the **Grassington National Park Centre,** Colvend, Hebden Road (© **01756/751600;** www.yorkshiredales.org.uk), which is open April through October daily 10am to 5pm; and November through March, Friday to Sunday 10am to 4pm. Maps, bus schedules through the dales, and a choice of guidebooks are available here to help you navigate your way. If you'd like a more in-depth look than what you can do on your own, you can arrange for a qualified guide who knows the most beautiful places and can point out the most interesting geological and botanical features of the wilderness.

Sixteen kilometers (10 miles) west of Grassington (reached along the B6265), **Malham** is a great place to set out on a hike in summer. Branching out from here, you can explore some of the most remarkable limestone formations in Britain. First, it's best to stop in for maps and information at the **Malham National Park Centre** (© **01969/652380**), which is open April through October, daily 10am to 5pm; and off-season, Saturday and Sunday 10am to 4pm. Amazingly, this village of 200 or so souls receives a half-million visitors annually. May or September is the time to come; the hordes descend from June to August.

The scenery in this area has been extolled by no less an authority than Wordsworth, and it has been painted by Turner. You can explore a trio of scenic destinations—**Malham Cove, Malham Tarn,** and **Gordale Scar**—on a circular walk of 13km (8 miles) that takes most hikers 5 hours. If your time (and your stamina) is more limited, you can take a circular walk from the heart of the village to Malham Cove and Gordale Scar in about 2 hours. At least try to walk 1.5km (1 mile) north of the village to Malham Cove, a large natural rock amphitheater. Gordale Scar is a deep natural chasm between overhanging limestone cliffs, and Malham Tarn is a lake in a desolate location.

Kettlewell lies 13km (8 miles) northwest of Malham and 9.5km (6 miles) north of Grassington. This is the main village in the Upper Wharfedale and makes a good base for hiking through the local hills and valleys, which look straight out of *Wuthering Heights*. Narrow pack bridges and riverside walks characterize the region, and signs point to the **Dales Way** hiking path.

After Kettlewell, you can drive for 6.5km (4 miles) on B6160 to the hamlet of **Buckden,** the last village in the Upper Wharfedale. Once here, follow the sign to **Kidstone Pass,** still staying on B6160. At **Aysgarth** ★★, the river plummets over a series of waterfalls, one of the dramatic scenic highlights of the Yorkshire Dales.

Masham: A Room in a Castle

For luxury lovers, the little village of Masham makes the best base—certainly the most luxurious—for an overnight stay to explore the Yorkshire Dales. Swinton Park stands at the gateway to the Dales.

Swinton Park ★★★ If you weren't born in an aristocrat's vine-covered castle, you can stay here and have the experience. Mark Cunliffe-Lister, nephew of the earl and countess of Swinton, has converted this historic manor into a luxury hotel. Set in 80 hectares (200 acres) of parkland, lakes, and gardens, the family estate is a good base for exploring the Yorkshire Dales National Park, lying 52km (32 miles) northwest of York. Even with a pedigree going back to the 1500s, the castle is up-to-date, with a spa and fitness area in a conservatory. There is also a bar in the family museum, a private cinema, and even a Victorian game room. Each of the spacious and beautifully designed bedrooms is individually designed, taking the theme of a Yorkshire dale, castle, abbey, or town.

Swinton Park, Masham, North Yorkshire HG4 4JH. © **866/810-3039** or 01765/680900. Fax 01765/680901. www.swintonpark.com. 30 units. £175–£290 double; £300–£370 suite. Rates include Yorkshire breakfast. AE, DC, MC, V. **Amenities:** Restaurant; bar; babysitting; children's center; exercise room; Jacuzzi; room service; spa; Wi-Fi in lobby (free). *In room:* TV, CD player.

Hawes: A Good Base for Exploring the Park

About 105km (65 miles) northwest of York, on the A684, Hawes is the natural center of Yorkshire Dales National Park and a good place to stay. On the Pennine Way, it's England's highest market town and the capital of Wensleydale, which is famous for its cheese. Trains from York take you to Garsdale, which is 8km (5 miles) from Hawes. From Garsdale, bus connections will take you into Hawes.

While you're here, you may want to check out the **Dales Countryside Museum,** Station Yard (🕿 **01969/666210;** www.yorkshiredales.org.uk), which traces folk life in the Dales, a story of 10,000 years of human history. The museum is open April to October, daily from 10am to 5pm. Winter hours vary; you'll have to check locally. Admission is £3 for adults, £2 for students and seniors, and free for kids 11 and younger.

Cockett's Hotel & Restaurant This is an atmospheric choice, still sporting many remnants of its construction in 1668. In case you need reminding, the date of its construction is carved into one of its lintels. Set in the center of town, it's a two-story, slate-roofed, stone cottage whose front yard is almost entirely covered with flagstones. Rooms are done in an old-world style of exposed wooden beams; they're snug, cozy, and well maintained.

Market Place, Hawes, North Yorkshire DL8 3RD. 🕿 **01969/667312.** Fax 01969/667162. www.cocketts. co.uk. 8 units. £69–£92 double. Rates include English breakfast. MC, V. **Amenities:** Restaurant; bar. *In room:* TV/DVD, hair dryer.

Simonstone Hall Country House Hotel Just north of Hawes, you can stay and dine at Simonstone Hall, the former home of the earls of Wharncliffe. Constructed in 1733, this building has been converted into a comfortable, family-run country-house hotel with a helpful young staff. The public rooms and bedrooms are equally ideal for relaxation and comfort. Most bedrooms are spacious, and all are tastefully furnished with antiques. Each comes with a quality bed and an efficiently organized shower-only bathroom.

Simonstone (2.5km/1½ miles north of Hawes, on the road signposted to Muker), Hawes, North Yorkshire DL8 3RD. 🕿 **01969/667255.** Fax 01969/667741. www.simonstonehall.com. 18 units. £105–£155 double. Rates include English breakfast. AE, MC, V. **Amenities:** Restaurant; bar; room service. *In room:* TV, hair dryer.

NORTH YORK MOORS NATIONAL PARK ★

The moors, on the other side of the Vale of York, have a wild beauty all their own, quite different from that of the dales. This rather barren moorland blossoms in summer with purple heather. Bounded on the east by the North Sea, it embraces a 1,440-sq.-km (554-sq.-mile) area, which has been preserved as a national park.

The park is perfect for solitary strolls and peaceful drives. For remnants of the area's exciting days of smugglers and brave explorers, visitors can follow the Captain Cook Heritage Trail along the coast. The fishing industry is still alive in the area, though the whaling ships of yesteryear have been anchored.

If you're looking for a hot, sunny beach vacation, the North Yorkshire coast isn't for you—the climate here is cool because of the brisk waters of the North Sea. Even summer months don't get very hot. Many Britons do visit North Yorkshire for beach vacations, however, so you will find a beach-town atmosphere along the coast, with brightly colored stalls lining the seafront.

Essentials

GETTING THERE   Because the park sprawls over such a large area, you can access it from five or six different gateways. Most visitors enter it from the side closest to York, by following either the A19 north via the hamlet of **Thirsk,** or by detouring to the northeast along the A64 and entering via **Scarborough.** You can also get in through **Helmsley,** where the park's administrative headquarters are located; just follow the roads from York that are signposted HELMSLEY. Gateways along the park's northern edges, which are less convenient to York, include the villages of **Whitby** (accessible via A171) and **Stokesley** (accessible via A19).

VISITOR INFORMATION   For information on accommodations and transportation before you go, contact **North York Moors National Park,** the Old Vicarage, Bondgate, Helmsley, York YO62 5BP (© **01439/770657;** www.northyorkmoors.org. uk). You can get advice, specialized guidebooks, maps, and information at the **Sutton Bank National Park Centre,** Sutton Bank, near Thirsk (© **01845/597426**). Another well-inventoried information source, which, unlike the others, is open year-round, is the **Moors National Park Centre,** Lodge Lane, Danby, near Whitby (© **01439/772737;** www.northyorkmoors.org.uk).

Exploring the Moors

Bounded by the Cleveland and Hambleton hills, the moors are dotted with early burial grounds and ancient stone crosses. **Pickering** and **Northallerton,** both market towns, serve as gateways to the moors.

The North York Moors will always be associated with doomed trysts between unlucky lovers and ghosts who wander vengefully across the rugged plateaus of their lonely and windswept surfaces. Though the earth is relatively fertile in the river valleys, the thin, rocky soil of the heather-clad uplands has been scorned by local farmers as wasteland, suitable only for sheep grazing and healthy (but melancholy) rambles. During the 19th century, a handful of manor houses were built on their lonely promontories by moguls of the Industrial Revolution, but not until 1953 was the 1,440-sq.-km (554-sq.-mile) district designated the North York Moors National Park.

Encompassing England's largest expanse of moorland, the park is famous for the diversity of heathers, which thrive between the sandstone outcroppings of the uplands. If you visit between October and February, you'll see smoldering fires across the landscape—deliberately controlled attempts by shepherds and farmers to burn the omnipresent heather back to stubs. Repeated in age-old cycles every 15 years, the blazes encourage the heather's renewal, with new growth for the uncounted thousands of sheep that thrive in the district.

Though public bridle and footpaths take you to all corners of the moors, two noteworthy and clearly demarcated trails make up the most comprehensive moor walks in Europe. The shorter of the two is the **Lyke Wake Walk,** a 64km (40-mile) east-to-west trek that connects the hamlets of Osmotherly and Ravenscar. It traces the rugged path established by 18th-century coffin bearers. The longer trek, the **Cleveland Way,** is a 177km (110-mile) circumnavigation of the national park's perimeter. A good section skirts the edge of the Yorkshire coastline; other stretches take climbers up and down a series of steep fells in the park's interior.

Don't even consider an ambitious moor trek without good shoes, a compass, an ordinance survey map, and a detailed park guidebook. With descriptions of geologically interesting sites, safety warnings, and listings of inns and farmhouses (haunted or otherwise) offering overnight stays, the guidebooks sell for less than £4 at any local tourist office.

The isolation and the beauty of the landscape attracted the founders of **three great abbeys:** Rievaulx, near Helmsley; Byland Abbey, near the village of Wass; and Ampleforth Abbey. Nearby is **Coxwold,** one of the most beautiful villages in the moors. The Cistercian Rievaulx and Byland abbeys are in ruins, but the Benedictine Ampleforth still functions as a monastery and well-known Roman Catholic boys' school. Though many of its buildings date from the 19th and 20th centuries, they do contain earlier artifacts.

The old market town of **Thirsk,** in the Vale of Mowbray, 39km (24 miles) north of York on the A19, is near the western fringe of the park. It has a fine parish church, but what makes it such a popular stopover is its association with the late James Herriot (1916–95), author of *All Creatures Great and Small.* Mr. Herriot used to practice veterinary medicine in Thirsk. You can drop in at a visitor center, the **World of James Herriot,** 23 Kirkgate (✆ **01845/524234;** www.worldofjamesherriot.org), which is dedicated to his life and to veterinary science. The Kirkgate surgery, where he practiced from 1930 until his death in 1995, and the house next door have been transformed into *The Herriot Experience,* which allows you to view the surgery and see various exhibits and displays on veterinary science. It's open Easter to September, daily from 10am to 5pm, and October to Easter, daily from 11am to 4pm; last entrance is always an hour before closing. Admission is £6 for adults, £4.20 for children 5 to 15, £4.70 for seniors, £17 for family ticket, and free for kids 4 and younger.

Exploring the North Yorkshire Coast

Along the eastern boundary of the park, North Yorkshire's 72km (45-mile) coastline shelters such traditional seaside resorts as Filey, Whitby, and Scarborough, the latter claiming to be the oldest seaside spa in Britain, located supposedly on the site of a Roman signaling station. The spa was founded in 1622, when mineral springs with medicinal properties were discovered. In the 19th century, its Grand Hotel, a Victorian structure, was acclaimed the best in Europe. The Norman castle on the big cliffs overlooks the twin bays.

It's easy to follow the main road from Bridlington north to Scarborough and on to Robin Hood's Bay and Whitby. As you drive up the coast, you'll see small fishing ports and wide expanses of moorland.

BRIDLINGTON
29km (18 miles) SE of Scarborough; 64km (40 miles) E of York

Bridlington is a good starting point for a trip up the North Yorkshire coast. A fishing port with an ancient harbor, the wide beach and busy seafront markets draw crowds who enjoy relaxing on the sand or browsing through the gift shops and stalls that line the streets. **Flamborough Head** is one of the most distinguishable features on England's east coast. Jutting out into the North Sea, it features a 26m-tall (85-ft.)

lighthouse that stands atop a chalk cliff towering 51m (170 ft.) above the sea. A path that winds up the cliffs ends at **Bempton,** site of a bird sanctuary that is one of the finest reserves on the coast. You can enjoy watching the seabirds or simply take in the view of the sea off Flamborough, the final resting place of more than a few ships. Bridlington also has many country houses that are open for tours, in addition to Pickering and Helmsley castles and the deserted village of Wharram Percy.

Where to Stay

Flamborough Manor The current manor house of Flamborough dates from 1800. It was fully restored by local craftspeople and now boasts comfortable accommodations and a friendly atmosphere. Bedrooms are tastefully appointed and have small bathrooms equipped with showers and adequate shelf space. Many visitors come to the house to browse through the variety of antiques sold in the converted stable block or to purchase a Gansey sweater. These intricate fishermen's sweaters are handmade in the traditional way, an almost-lost process that has been revived by Lesley Berry, the house's proprietor.

Flamborough, Bridlington, East Yorkshire YO15 1PD. ✆/fax **01262/850943.** www.flamboroughmanor. co.uk. 2 units. £84–£96 double. Rates include English breakfast. AE, MC, V. No children under 8. *In room:* TV, hair dryer, no phone.

SCARBOROUGH

29km (18 miles) NW of Bridlington; 55km (34 miles) NE of York; 407km (253 miles) N of London

Scarborough, one of the first seaside resorts in Britain, has been attracting visitors for more than 3 centuries. A mineral spring discovered in the early 17th century led to the establishment of a spa that lured clients with promises of its water's healing benefits. In the 18th century, swimmers were attracted to the waters off the coast— sea bathing had come into vogue, and the beaches of England swarmed with tourists taking part in the craze.

The city of Scarborough is divided into two unique districts separated by a green headland that holds the remains of **Scarborough Castle,** which dates from Norman times. South of the headland, the town conforms to its historical molds. High cliffs and garden walks interspersed with early Victorian residences dominate the landscape. The north side is touristier; souvenir shops and fast-food stands line the promenade. Rock candy (brightly colored hard candy that can be etched with the saying of your choice) and candy floss (cotton candy) satisfy even the most die-hard sweet tooth.

For more information about what to see and do while you're in Scarborough, visit the **Tourist Information Centre,** Brunswick Shopping Centre, Westborough (✆ **01723/383636;** www.discoveryorkshirecoast.com), open May to September, daily 9am to 5:30pm; the rest of the year, it's open Monday to Saturday 9:30am to 5pm.

Trains leave London approximately every 30 minutes headed for York, where you'll have to transfer to another train. The entire trip takes just 2 hours and 10 minutes. For information on schedules and prices, call ✆ **0845/748-4950** or visit **www. nationalrail.co.uk.** Three buses a day leave London heading for York; another will take you from York to Scarborough. If you're taking the bus, plan on spending most of a day riding. For bus information, call ✆ **0871/781-8181** or visit **www.national express.com**.

Where to Stay

Crown Spa Hotel ☺   Maintained in a style that's in keeping with its "Grand Hotel" origins in 1844, this hotel overlooks South Bay and Scarborough Castle from its setting above a cliff top, just above the quieter side of the town's beachfront. In recent years, extensive renovations have brought everything up-to-date. The accommodations are comfortable, with many rooms offering pleasant views over the sea. Most of the units, ranging from midsize to spacious, have been rejuvenated. Seven rooms are large enough for families.

Esplanade, South Cliff, Scarborough, North Yorkshire YO11 2AG. ℂ **01723/357400.** Fax 01723/357404. www.crownspahotel.com. 87 units. £87–£152 double; £196–£320 suite. Rates include English breakfast. AE, MC, V. Free parking. **Amenities:** 2 restaurants; bar; exercise room; indoor heated pool; room service; spa. *In room:* TV, hair dryer, Wi-Fi (free).

Palm Court Hotel   This inn provides guests with modern amenities in an elegant, old-world atmosphere. Inviting common areas, such as the lounge and cocktail bar, provide ideal settings for sharing a drink with friends. Rooms are tastefully furnished and among the most comfortable in Scarborough. Most units are generally spacious, and six are rented to families.

St. Nicholas Cliff, Scarborough, North Yorkshire YO11 2ES. ℂ **01723/368161.** Fax 01723/371547. www. palmcourtscarborough.co.uk. 44 units. £120–£170 double. Rates include English breakfast. AE, DC, MC, V. Free parking. **Amenities:** Restaurant; bar; babysitting; indoor heated pool; room service. *In room:* TV, hair dryer, Wi-Fi (free).

Wrea Head Country House Hotel ★   This Victorian country house is situated just north of Scarborough on 5.6 hectares (14 acres) of beautifully kept grounds. Several very compelling common rooms, such as a library and comfortable bar, entice guests to sit and relax. The guest rooms vary in size and are individually styled with tasteful furnishings, including first-rate beds and well-maintained bathrooms with tub/shower combinations. Two rooms are ideal for families.

Barmoor Lane, Scalby, Scarborough, North Yorkshire YO13 0PB. ℂ **01723/378211.** Fax 01723/355936. www.wrea-head-hotel.co.uk. 20 units. £150–£195 double; from £212 suite. Rates include English breakfast. AE, MC, V. Free parking. **Amenities:** Restaurant; bar; babysitting; room service. *In room:* TV, hair dryer.

Where to Dine

Lanterna Ristorante ★ ITALIAN   Small, straightforward, and charming, this is a high-quality Italian restaurant whose owners, the Alessio family, maintain a strict allegiance to the recipes and ingredients (especially truffles) of their original home in northern Italy. Set in the center of the old town, without any view of the sea, it offers places for 30 diners at a time in a room that's ringed with art photographs of Italian wine, food products, and, of course, truffles. Menu items include lots of fresh fish (the owners make a trip to the fish market every morning), including whole sea bass roasted "on its bone" with olive oil and herbs. Pastas are made fresh almost every day and may include a succulent version of venison ravioli. A particularly unctuous starter is *tajarin* (strips of flat pasta), served with a relatively bland sauce of mushrooms and cream. The intent of this mild dish involves allowing the nutty, woodsy flavor of the truffles—added table-side at the last minute—to emerge, unencumbered by other, more strident flavors.

33 Queen St. ℂ **01723/363616.** www.lanterna-ristorante.co.uk. Reservations recommended. Main courses £13–£38. MC, V. Mon–Sat 7–9:30pm. Closed 2 weeks in Oct (dates vary).

Exploring the Town

The ruins of **Scarborough Castle,** Castle Road (© **01723/372451;** www.english-heritage.org.uk), stand on the promontory near a former Viking settlement. From the castle, you can look out over the North Bay, the beaches, and the gardens along the shore. Throughout the summer, fairs and festivals celebrate days of yore, with mock battles, pageantry, and falconry displays. The castle is open daily as follows: July and August 9:30am to 6pm; October and February 10am to 5pm; November to January 10am to 4pm; March to June and September 10am to 6pm. Admission is £4.70 for adults, £4 for seniors and persons with disabilities, £2.40 for children, and £12 for a family ticket. Children 4 and younger enter free.

Nearby is the medieval **Church of St. Mary,** Castle Road (no phone), where Anne Brontë, the youngest of the three sisters of literary fame, was buried in 1849. She died in Scarborough after being brought from her home in Haworth in hopes that the sea air would revive her health.

The permanent collection at **Scarborough Art Gallery,** the Crescent (© **01723/374753;** www.scarboroughartgallery.co.uk), features pieces ranging from 17th-century portraits to 20th-century masterworks. Many of the works relate to the Scarborough area. Changing exhibitions by young artists and local craftspeople are also displayed. If you're interested in learning how to create your own works of art, you may want to spend a while at **Crescent Arts** (© **01723/351461;** www.crescentarts.co.uk), whose studios are located in the basement of the gallery. Local artists offer courses and demonstrations in their respective mediums. Scarborough Art Gallery is open June through September, Tuesday to Sunday 10am to 5pm, and October through May, Tuesday to Sunday 11am to 4pm. Admission is £2 for adults, £1.80 for seniors and children, and free for kids 4 and younger.

Local history collections and displays of important archaeological finds can be found at the **Rotunda Museum,** Vernon Road (© **01723/374839;** www.rotundamuseum.co.uk). The museum is housed in a circular building, constructed in 1829 for William Smith, the "Father of English Geology," to display his collection; it was one of the first public buildings in England built specifically for use as a museum. The Rotunda is open June through September, Tuesday to Sunday 10am to 5pm; and October through May, Tuesday, Saturday, and Sunday 11am to 4pm. Admission is £4.50 for adults and free for children under 18.

Of course, Scarborough still has the springs that established its popularity. The **Spa Complex,** South Bay (© **01723/376774;** www.scarboroughspa.co.uk), no longer offers guests the opportunity to partake of the waters; it is now an entertainment and conference center in the midst of elegant gardens and buildings dating from several eras. In summer, there is a concert of some kind every day (usually classical and often held outdoors). Unless you just want to wander through the grounds, which is entertaining in itself, you may want to call ahead for concert times and prices.

Scarborough After Dark

Alan Ayckbourn, a popular contemporary playwright, calls Scarborough home. The **Stephen Joseph Theatre,** Westborough (© **01723/370541;** www.sjt.uk.com), performs many of his plays as well as other favorites.

Most action takes place at **Zero,** Westborough (© **01723/503170;** www.zeromusicbar.co.uk), where DJs rule the night when live bands aren't appearing. Its chief rival is **Vivaz,** Huntriss Row (© **01723/368222;** www.vivaz.co.uk). The club and its dance floor were designed to host live music. Otherwise, hot DJs dictate the music.

ROBIN HOOD'S BAY
21km (13 miles) NW of Scarborough

Though Robin Hood's Bay was once a notorious port for smugglers, it has no connection with the well-known outlaw who shares the village's name. The tiny fishing port is tucked into a deep ravine; in fact, space is so limited that cars can't enter the village center. The villagers live in cottages precariously balanced on the steep cliffs, where narrow roads curve between the dwellings.

Where to Stay
Raven Hall Hotel ☺   Many guests never leave the grounds of the hotel for entertainment, though Raven Hall makes a good base from which to venture out into Scarborough and nearby Robin Hood's Bay. Accommodations have pleasant views of the water, the moors, or the garden. Each of the traditionally furnished guest rooms is renovated and comes with a comfortable bed. Nearly half of the rooms are large enough for families. Two rooms have four-poster beds.

Ravenscar, Scarborough, North Yorkshire YO13 0ET. © **01723/870353.** Fax 01723/870072. www. ravenhall.co.uk. 53 units. £85–£168 double. Rates include English breakfast. 2-night minimum Fri–Sat. AE, DC, MC, V. **Amenities:** Restaurant; bar; exercise room; 9-hole golf course and putting green; indoor heated pool; room service; sauna; 2 outdoor tennis courts. *In room:* TV, hair dryer.

WHITBY
11km (7 miles) NW of Robin Hood's Bay; 564km (350 miles) NE of London

The resort town of Whitby, at the mouth of the River Esk, has a rich and interesting history. It began as a religious center in the 7th century, when Whitby Abbey was first founded. Whitby later became a prominent whaling port and eventually, like most coastal towns, an active participant in the smuggling trade.

Several famous explorers have pushed off from the beaches of Whitby, including Captain James Cook. As the king's surveyor, Cook circumnavigated the globe twice in ships constructed by local carpenters and craftsmen. He also claimed Australia and New Zealand for Great Britain.

Literary references to Whitby add intrigue to the town. Herman Melville paid tribute to William Scoresby, captain of some of the first ships that sailed to Greenland and inventor of the crow's nest, in his novel *Moby-Dick,* and Bram Stoker found his inspiration for *Dracula* in the quaint streets of Whitby.

The **Tourist Information Centre,** Langbourne Road (© **01723/383636;** www.discoveryorkshirecoast.com), is open May through September, daily 9:30am to 6pm, and October through April, daily 10am to 4:30pm.

One bus a day travels between London and Whitby. The trip is a direct route and takes approximately 7 hours. Call © **0871/781-8181** or visit **www.national express.com** for more details. To get to Whitby from London by train, you'll have to ride to Middlesborough or Scarborough, and then transfer to the train or bus to Whitby. The number of trains to Whitby varies, so call ahead. For rail information, call © **0845/748-4950** or go to **www.nationalrail.co.uk**.

Where to Stay

Dunsley Hall Country House Hotel ☺ Five kilometers (3 miles) north of Whitby, in the small hamlet of Dunsley, Dunsley Hall is from the turn of the 20th century, when it was built by a Hartlepool shipping magnate who lived here with his family until 1940. Some of the original carpets and furnishings remain, now adding historical charm to the well-appointed hotel. Guests can enjoy a stroll through the carefully tended gardens. Two of the spacious bedrooms are set aside for families, and bathrooms are small but well maintained; each has a shower unit (some have bathtubs as well). In 2007, a new wing opened, with eight stylish bedrooms that are more desirable than those in the main building.

Dunsley, Whitby, North Yorkshire YO21 3TL. ℂ **01947/893437.** Fax 01947/893505. www.dunsleyhall. com. 26 units. £145–£203 double; £215 family suite. Rates include English breakfast. AE, MC, V. **Amenities:** Restaurant; bar; exercise room; indoor heated pool; room service; sauna. *In room:* TV, hair dryer.

Where to Dine

Many hotels in the area offer half-board plans (with dinner) in addition to bed-and-breakfast rates; it may save time and money if you take advantage of these. If you don't, or if you're looking for lunch, try **Trenchers,** New Quay Road (ℂ **01947/603212;** www.trenchersrestaurant.co.uk), for terrific fish and chips. Fresh filets of haddock or cod are fried in a crispy batter and served with thick-cut fries.

For good food in an even better atmosphere, stop by the **White Horse & Griffin,** Church Street (ℂ **01947/604857;** www.whitehorseandgriffin.co.uk). While surrounded by the character of the 18th-century structure, you can enjoy pot-roasted pheasant with cider, crispy pork belly with a mustard sauce, or Whitby cod baked under a crust of crab and served on a bed of fresh spinach. The White Horse & Griffin also rents out 10 comfortable bedrooms, each with a private bathroom and TV, costing £65 double, including breakfast.

Seeing the Sights

The ruins of **Whitby Abbey,** Abbey Lane (ℂ **01947/603568;** www.english-heritage.org.uk), lie high on the East Cliff, where they are visible from almost anywhere in town. The abbey dates from the 12th century and adjoins the site of a Saxon Monastery that was established in A.D. 657. Caedmon, the first identifiable English-language poet, was a monk here. On this site in A.D. 664, the date for Easter was decided. The abbey is open from Easter to September, daily 10am to 6pm; October, daily 10am to 5pm; and the rest of the year, Thursday to Monday 10am to 4pm. Admission is £5.80 for adults, £4.90 for seniors, £2.90 for children 5 to 16, and £15 for a family ticket.

Another religious site is the uniquely designed **Church of St. Mary** (ℂ **01947/603421**). Stairs (199 of them) leading to the church begin at the end of Church Street. If you have the stamina to climb them, you can walk through the rather spooky churchyard; it was here that Lucy was taken as Dracula's victim in Bram Stoker's novel. The church itself is an eclectic mix of architectural styles.

Whitby Museum, Pannett Park (ℂ **01947/602908;** www.whitbymuseum.org. uk), features exhibits that highlight the city's history. Of course, ship models and details of Captain Cook's adventures are essential to the museum, but there are also displays on the archaeology and natural history of the area. The **Pannett Art Gallery,** next door, has a permanent collection featuring paintings by George Weatherill, along with constantly changing special exhibits. The museum and gallery are open Tuesday to Sunday 9:40am to 4:30pm (last entrance at 4pm). Admission to the museum is £3 for adults, £1 for children 5 to 16, and £7 for a family ticket; there is no charge for the gallery.

Captain Cook Memorial Museum, Grape Lane (✆ **01947/601900;** www. cookmuseumwhitby.co.uk), deals more specifically with the life and achievements of the famous explorer James Cook. It is open daily April through October from 9:45am to 5pm, daily in March from 11am to 3pm, and the last 2 weekends of February from 11am to 3pm. Last entrance is 30 minutes before closing. Admission is £4.50 for adults, £4 for students and seniors, £3 for children, and £11 for a family ticket.

The **Tourist Information Centre,** Langbourne Road (✆ **01723/383636;** www.discoveryorkshirecoast.com), can give anglers information about fishing along the town's coastline. Fishing is free all along the Whitby shore. If you'd rather go out to sea to reel in a big one, there are boats for hire at points throughout the city. The cost usually includes tackle and bait.

Golfers should visit the **Whitby Golf Club,** Low Straggleton (✆ **01947/600660;** www.whitbygolfclub.co.uk). The 6,134-yard course is open to visiting golfers daily. **Raven Hall Hotel Golf Course,** Ravenscar (✆ **01723/870353;** www.ravenhall. co.uk), is open to nonguests all day, every day. The 9-hole course is well tended and offers panoramic views of the moors and the sea. This is also the best place in the area for **tennis.**

DURHAM ★★★

403km (250 miles) N of London; 24km (15 miles) S of Newcastle upon Tyne

This medieval city took root in 1090 after the Normans, under William the Conqueror, took over and began construction of Durham's world-renowned cathedral and castle on a peninsula surrounded by the River Wear. The cathedral, "Half Church of God, half Castle 'gainst the Scots," was built as a shrine to protect the remains of St. Cuthbert, while also providing a sturdy fortress against the warring Scots to the north.

The cathedral castle thrust Durham into its role as a protective border post for England. For centuries, Durham Castle was the seat of the prince bishops—kings of the wild northern territories in all but name—and a pilgrimage site for Christians coming to pay tribute to St. Cuthbert, a monk on Lindisfarne. His life of contemplation and prayer led to his consecration as a bishop in 685 and his sainthood after death.

Today, Durham boasts a university (built on the cornerstone of the castle) and is a good base for exploring this stretch of the North Sea coast, as well as the unspoiled rolling hills and waterfalls of the Durham Dales in the North Pennines.

Essentials

GETTING THERE Trains from London's Kings Cross Station arrive hourly during the day, with the trip taking about 3 hours. Trains from York leave every 15 minutes, arriving approximately an hour later. Durham lies on the main London-Edinburgh rail line. For information, call ✆ **0845/748-4950** or visit **www.national rail.co.uk**.

National Express buses from London arrive twice daily, with the trip taking about 5 hours. For information, call ✆ **0871/781-8181** or visit **www.national express.com**.

If you're driving from London, follow the A1 (M) north to Durham.

VISITOR INFORMATION The **Durham Tourist Information Centre** is at 2 Millennium Place (✆ **01913/843720;** www.thisisdurham.com). It's open year-round, Monday to Saturday from 9:30am to 5:30pm and Sunday from 11am to 4pm.

SPECIAL EVENTS At the **Durham Folk Festival,** held the last weekend in July, you can sing, clog, or just cavort to music; almost every event is free. The weekend also includes free camping along the River Wear, though you'd better arrive early on Friday if you want to get a choice spot. In early June, crowds swarm along the riverbank to cheer the crew racing the **Durham Regatta.**

Where to Stay

Durham Marriott Hotel Royal County ★   This is where we prefer to stay in Durham. Though some critics consider it an anonymous chain hotel (it's part of the Marriott chain), it has many winning features in its three Georgian buildings, plus a convenient location right in the heart of Durham. Skillfully converted from a row of riverside houses, it was once the family home of the Queen Mother before being turned into one of the region's premier hotels. Many of its original details have been retained, including an oak staircase that was transported here from Loch Leven, the Scottish castle where Mary, Queen of Scots was held prisoner. Guest rooms all maintain a high standard of comfort and furnishings, though they vary in size. Most rooms are large enough for families.

Old Elvet, Durham DH1 3JN. ✆ **800/228-9290** in U.S. and Canada, or 01913/866821. Fax 01913/860704. www.durhammarriottroyalcounty.co.uk. 150 units. £99–£175 double; from £200 suite. AE, DC, MC, V. Free parking. **Amenities:** Restaurant; bar; babysitting; exercise room; Jacuzzi; heated indoor pool; room service; sauna. *In room:* TV, hair dryer, minibar, Wi-Fi (£15 per 24 hr.).

Georgian Town House ★ 🍴   This is the most desirable B&B in Durham, an unusually decorated place lying on a steep, cobbled Georgian terrace street, close to everything, including the cathedral. It is a wonder of decoration, especially the reception hallway with its stenciled pillars and leaf patterns. It's almost like entering an arbor in sunny Sicily. In the lounge, papier-mâché "stars" and "moons" twinkle on the walls. Sofas are placed around the fireplace so guests can mingle. Rooms, except for a cramped single, are light, airy, and tastefully decorated. The house has a panoramic view of the cathedral and castle.

11 Crossgate, Durham DH1 4PS. ✆/fax **01913/868070.** www.durham.bedbreakfastaccommodation. co.uk. 7 units. £75–£100 double. Rates include English breakfast. No credit cards. No children under 5. *In room:* TV.

Three Tuns Hotel   Still going strong after all these years, this hotel is the reincarnation of a 16th-century coaching inn that once housed travelers heading north into Scotland. Almost all traces of its former role are gone. Bedrooms have been completely modernized and furnished to a high, if not exciting, standard. The best and most spacious rooms are the executive units, but each room has a good comfort level. Two units are large enough for families. The public rooms have more character and are roomy and inviting.

New Elvet, Durham DH1 3AQ. 📞 **01913/864326.** Fax 01913/861406. www.swallow-hotels.com. 50 units. £51–£115 double; £175 suite. Rates include English breakfast. AE, DC, MC, V. **Amenities:** Restaurant; bar; babysitting; room service. *In room:* TV, hair dryer.

Where to Dine

Bistro 21 ★ CONTINENTAL   A big hit locally, this is a bright, farm-themed bistro. Chef Paul O'Hara's cuisine is precise and carefully prepared, with market-fresh ingredients that are allowed to keep their natural essence without being overly sauced or disguised. We especially recommend the blackboard specials, such as fish cakes with buttery spinach or pork chops with creamed cabbage and potatoes. The food is full of flavor, borrowing from all over Europe—certainly the Mediterranean—but also offering traditional British fare at times, such as deep-fried plaice and chips. You can finish with one of the rich desserts, including double chocolate truffle cake. But if you want to be terribly old-fashioned and very English, you'll ask for the toffee pudding with butterscotch sauce. It's prepared to perfection.

Aykley Heads House, Aykley Heads. 📞 **01913/844354.** www.bistrotwentyone.co.uk. Reservations recommended. Main courses £15–£25; fixed-price lunch £15–£18. AE, DC, MC, V. Mon–Sat noon–2pm and 6–10pm; Sun noon–3pm.

Seeing the Sights

Durham Castle ★   Facing the Durham Cathedral from the opposite side of the "Palace Green," this was the seat of the prince bishops of Durham for more than 800 years. In 1832, it became the first building of the fledgling local college, now Durham University; it still houses University College. During university breaks, it offers unique bed-and-breakfast accommodations to the public.

Palace Green. 📞 **01913/343800.** www.dur.ac.uk. Admission £5 adults, £3.50 children, £12 family ticket. Guided tours June–Sept daily 10am–12:30pm and 2–4:30pm; Oct–May Mon, Wed, and Sat–Sun 2–4:30pm. Closed during university Christmas breaks.

Durham Cathedral ★★★   Under construction for more than 40 years, the cathedral was completed in 1133, and today is Britain's largest, best-preserved Norman stronghold and one of its surviving Romanesque palaces. The structure is not only breathtaking to view, but also architecturally innovative, as it was the first English building with ribbed vault construction. It is also the first stone-roofed cathedral in Europe, an architectural necessity because of its role as a border fortress. The treasury houses such relics as the original 12th-century door knocker, St. Cuthbert's coffin, ancient illuminated manuscripts, and more. You can still attend daily services in the sanctuary.

Palace Green. 📞 **01913/864266.** www.durhamcathedral.co.uk. Free admission to cathedral (donation required); tower £4 adults, £2 children, £9 family ticket; treasury £2.50 adults, 70p children, £6 family ticket; monks' dormitory £1 adults, 30p children, £2 family ticket; audiovisual visitors' exhibition £1 adults, 30p children, £2 family ticket. Guided tours £4 adults, free for children 15 and under. Cathedral May–Aug daily 9:30am–8pm; Sept–Apr Mon–Sat 9:30am–6:15pm, Sun 12:30–6:15pm. Treasury Mon–Sat 10am–4:30pm; Sun 2–4:30pm. Monks' dormitory Apr–Sept Mon–Sat 10am–3:30pm, Sun 12:30–3:15pm. Audiovisual visitors' exhibition Mar–Oct Mon–Sat 10am–3pm. Guided tours July to mid-Sept Mon–Sat at 10:30am and 2pm (also 11:30am in Aug).

Oriental Museum   This is the nation's only museum devoted entirely to Eastern culture and art. The display covers all major periods of art from ancient Egypt through India, as well as relics from Tibet, China, and Japan.

Elvet Hill, off South Rd. © **01913/345694.** www.dur.ac.uk/oriental.museum. Admission £1.50 adults, 75p seniors and children 5–16, £3.50 family ticket. Mon–Fri 10am–5pm; Sat–Sun noon–5pm.

Outdoor Pursuits

Fishing is a good sport all along the rivers Tees and Wear, as well as in the several reservoirs and ponds throughout the county. Boating is also available, and **Brown's Boat House,** Elvet Bridge (© **01913/863779**), rents rowboats for pulls up or down the Wear; it also offers short cruises from April to October, at the price of £9 for adults and £6 for children.

Hikers can take the challenge provided by the 435km (270 miles) of trails (64km/40 miles of which are in the country) along the **Pennine Way;** the **Weardale Way,** a 126km (78-mile) course along the River Wear from Monkwearmouth in Sunderland to Cowshill in County Durham; or the **Teesdale Way,** running 145km (90 miles) from Middleton in Teesdale to Teesmouth in Cleveland. Rambles along the public footpaths in town are supplemented by more than 80km (50 miles) of hiking trails, which follow the tracks of a former railroad outside of town. Seven such trails make use of interlinked routes and range from the 7.5km (4.5-mile) **Auckland Walk** to the 17km (11-mile) **Derwent Walk.** If you don't feel like going it alone, there are also more than 200 guided walks throughout the county, providing background on the history, culture, and plant and animal life of the surrounding area; for details, contact the tourist office (see "Visitor Information," above).

Cyclists can opt for road biking along quiet country lanes and converted railway routes, or else mountain biking in **Hamsterley Forest.** The acclaimed **C2C Cycle Route** (www.c2c-guide.co.uk), the Coast to Coast or Sea to Sea national cycle route, passes through the Durham Dales and North Durham. The entire route covers a distance of 225km (140 miles). Both road- and mountain-bike rentals are available at several locations, including **Wood N Wheels,** Hamsterley Forest (© **01913/840319;** www.woodnwheels.co.uk), open daily 10am to 6pm. A bike rental costs £25 per day.

Durham After Dark

Most nightlife revolves around university students, who often begin the night at the **Dun Cow,** Old Elvet Street (© **0191/386-9219**), open Monday to Saturday 11am to 11pm, Sunday noon to 10:30pm. Another lively spot is the **Shakespeare Tavern,** 63 Saddler St. (© **0191/384-3261;** www.shakespearedurham.co.uk), open Monday to Saturday 11am to midnight, Sunday noon to 11pm. There are three floors to **Jimmy Allen's,** 19–21 Elvet Bridge (© **0191/357-7574**), which attracts not only students, but also a hard-drinking crowd of locals and the occasional tourist. It is especially busy on weekends, but open daily 7pm to 1am.

A Side Trip to the Durham Dales, Barnard Castle & Beamish

This densely populated county of northeast England was once pictured as a dismal place, with coal fields, ironworks, mining towns, and shipyards. Yet the **Durham Dales,** occupying the western third of the county, are a popular panorama of rolling hills, valleys of quiet charm, and wild moors. **Teesdale** is particularly notable for its several waterfalls, including **High Force,** the largest waterfall in England, which drops a thundering 21m (70 ft.) to join the River Tees. It is equally known for the rare wildflowers that grow in the sugar limestone–based soil of the region; they have helped it earn protection as a National Nature Reserve. Also notable is **Weardale,** once the hunting ground of Durham's prince bishops, with its idyllic brown-sandstone villages. For more information on the wide range of options the area has to offer, contact the **Durham Dales Centre,** Castle Garden, Stanhope, Bishop Auckland, County Durham DL13 2FJ (℗ **01388/527650;** www.durhamdalescentre. co.uk). Hours are April to October, daily 10am to 5pm, and November to March, daily 10am to 4pm.

The 12th-century **Barnard Castle** ★ (℗ **01833/690909;** www.english-heritage.co.uk) is an extensive Norman ruin overlooking the River Tees. It's open April to September, daily 10am to 6pm, and October to March, Thursday to Monday 10am to 4pm. Admission is £4.20 for adults, £3.60 for seniors, and £2.10 for students and children 15 and younger.

Barnard Castle is also home to the **Bowes Museum** ★ (℗ **01833/690606;** www.bowesmuseum.org.uk), a sprawling French-style château housing one of Britain's most important collections of European art, including paintings from Goya to El Greco, plus tapestries, ceramics, costumes, musical instruments, and French and English furniture. There is also a children's gallery. The museum is open daily from 10am to 5pm. Admission is £8 for adults; £7 for students, seniors, and children; and free for kids 15 and younger. Buses run from Durham several times daily.

Beamish, the North of England Open Air Museum   West of Chester-le-Street, 13km (8 miles) southwest of Newcastle upon Tyne, and 19km (12 miles) northwest of Durham City, this is a vivid re-creation of an early-19th-century village. Costumed interpreters go through the motions of daily life in shops, houses, pubs, a newspaper office, and garage, as well as a Methodist chapel, village school, home farm, and railway station. An average summer visit takes around 4 hours; a winter visit, including the town and railway only, takes about 2 hours.

Just off A693 in Beamish. ℗ **0191/370-4000.** www.beamish.org.uk. Admission spring and summer £16 adults, £10 children, free for children 4 and under; winter £6 adults and children, free for children 4 and under. Spring and summer daily 10am–5pm; off-season Sat–Sun and Tues–Thurs 10am–4pm.

HEXHAM, HADRIAN'S WALL ★★ & THE PENNINE WAY ★★

Hexham: 489km (304 miles) N of London; 60km (37 miles) E of Carlisle; 34km (21 miles) W of Newcastle upon Tyne

Above the River Tyne, the historic old market town of Hexham has narrow streets, an old market square, a fine abbey church, and a hall. It makes a good base for exploring Hadrian's Wall and the Roman supply base of Corstopitum at Corbridge-on-Tyne, the ancient capital of Northumberland.

Essentials

GETTING THERE   Take one of the many daily trains from London's Kings Cross Station to Newcastle upon Tyne. At Newcastle, change trains and take one in the direction of Carlisle. The fifth stop after Newcastle will be Hexham. For schedules and information, call ☎ **0845/748-4950** or visit **www.nationalrail.co.uk**.

Hexham lies 23km (14 miles) southeast of Hadrian's Wall. If you are primarily interested in the wall (rather than in Hexham), get off the Carlisle-bound train at the third stop (Haltwhistle), which is 4km (2½ miles) from the wall. At either of these hamlets, you can take a taxi to whichever part of the wall you care to visit. Taxis line up readily at the railway station in Hexham but less often at the other villages. If you get off at one of the above-mentioned villages and don't see a taxi, call ☎ **01434/321064** and a local taxi will come get you. Many visitors ask their taxi drivers to return at a prearranged time (which they gladly do) to pick them up after their excursion on the windy ridges near the wall.

Arriva coaches to Newcastle and Carlisle connect with Northumbria bus no. 685. Trip time to Hexham from Carlisle is about 1½ hours; from Newcastle, it's about 1 hour. For information, call ☎ **0871/200-2233** or visit **www.arrivabus. co.uk**. Local bus services connect Hexham with North Tynedale and the North Pennines.

If you're driving from Newcastle upon Tyne, head west on the A69 until you see the cutoff south to Hexham.

VISITOR INFORMATION   The **Hexham Tourist Information Centre** is at the Wentworth Car Park (☎ **01434/652220**). It's open from Easter through October, Monday to Saturday 9am to 6pm (Oct until 5pm) and Sunday 10am to 5pm; and November through March, Monday to Saturday 9am to 5pm.

Nearby Places to Stay & Dine

George Hotel   Standing on the banks of the Tyne, this country hotel opens onto gardens leading to the riverbank. It's a convenient base for visiting Hadrian's Wall. The hotel dates from the 18th century, when the original structure was built of Roman stone. It has been extensively refurbished to a high standard, and all bedrooms are comfortably furnished and well equipped.

Chollerford, Humshaugh, near Hexham, Northumberland NE46 4EW. ☎ **01434/681611.** Fax 01434/681727. 47 units. £98–£175 double. Rates include half-board. AE, DC, MC, V. Take A6079 8km (5 miles) north of Hexham. **Amenities:** Restaurant; bar; exercise room; indoor heated pool; room service; spa. *In room:* TV, hair dryer, Wi-Fi (free).

Hadrian Hotel   Ideal for a stopover along Hadrian's Wall, the Hadrian lies on the only street of the hamlet of Wall, 5.5km (3½ miles) north of Hexham. It's an ivy-covered 18th-century building erected of stones gathered long ago from the site of the ancient wall. The owners have carefully refurbished the place. All of the attractively renovated bedrooms have been modernized and offer comfortable double or twin beds. Three rooms have a tub only, one room has a shower only, and two rooms have a shared bathroom. The hotel has a private garden and a beer garden that serves as a warm-weather extension of its pub.

Front St. Wall, Wall, near Hexham, Northumberland NE46 4EE. ☎ **01434/681232.** Fax 01434/681512. www.hadrianhotel.co.uk. 6 units. £80 double. Rates include English breakfast. MC, V. **Amenities:** Restaurant; 2 bars. *In room:* TV, hair dryer, Wi-Fi (free).

Langley Castle Hotel ★ 🎁   This stately home is located on 4 hectares (10 acres) of woodlands at the edge of Northumberland National Park, southwest of

Haydon Bridge and about 11km (7 miles) west of Hexham. It's the only medieval fortified castle home in England that receives paying guests. The castle, built in 1350, was largely uninhabited after being damaged in 1400 during an English-and-Scottish war, until it was purchased in the late 19th century by Cadwallader Bates, a historian, who spent the rest of his life carefully restoring the property. Medieval features include the 14th-century spiral staircase, stained-glass windows, huge open fireplaces, and many turrets. The luxuriously appointed bedrooms vary in size; some have whirlpools or saunas in their well-maintained bathrooms. An adjacent building has extra rooms.

Langley-on-Tyne, Hexham, Northumberland NE47 5LU. © **01434/688888.** Fax 01434/684019. www. langleycastle.com. 18 units. £73–£93 per person double; £123–£138 per person suite. Rates include English breakfast. AE, MC, V. Free parking. From Hexham, go west on A69 to Haydon Bridge; then head south on A686 for 3km (2 miles). **Amenities:** Restaurant; bar; babysitting; room service. *In room:* TV, hair dryer, minibar, Wi-Fi (free).

Hadrian's Wall & Its Fortresses

Hadrian's Wall ★★, which extends for 118km (73 miles) across the north of England, from the North Sea to the Irish Sea, is particularly scenic for a stretch of 16km (10 miles) west of Housesteads, which lies 4km (2¾ miles) northeast of Bardon Mill on the B6318. Only the lower courses of the wall have been preserved intact; the rest were reconstructed in the 19th century using original stones. From the wall, there are incomparable views north to the Cheviot Hills along the Scottish border and south to the Durham moors.

The wall was built in A.D. 122 after the visit of the emperor Hadrian, who was inspecting far frontiers of the Roman Empire and wanted to construct a dramatic line between the empire and the barbarians. Legionnaires were ordered to build a wall across the width of the island of Britain, stretching 118km (73 miles), beginning at the North Sea and ending at the Irish Sea.

The wall is one of Europe's top Roman ruins. The western end is accessible from Carlisle, which also has an interesting museum of Roman artifacts; the eastern end can be reached from Newcastle upon Tyne, where you can see some remains on the city outskirts, as well as a nice museum at the university.

You can find more information about Hadrian's Wall online at www.hadrians-wall. org.

From early May to late September, the Tynedale Council and the Northumberland National Park run a **bus service** that visits every important site along the wall, and then turns around in the village of Haltwhistle and returns to Hexham. Buses depart from a point near the railway station in Hexham six times a day. Call © **01434/652220** for more information. The cost is £9 for adults, £6.50 for children, and £18 for a family ticket. Many visitors take one bus out and then return on a subsequent bus 2, 4, or 6 hours later. Every Sunday, a national park warden leads a 2½-hour **walking tour** of the wall, in connection with the bus service. The Hexham Tourist Information Centre (see "Visitor Information," above) can provide further details.

Housesteads Roman Fort and Museum ★★ Along the wall are several Roman forts, the largest and most well-preserved of which was called Vercovicium by the Romans. This substantially excavated fort, on a dramatic site, contains the only visible example of a Roman hospital in Britain.

5km (3 miles) northeast of Bardon Mill, on B6318. ☎ **01434/344363.** www.nationaltrust.org.uk. Admission £4.50 adults, £3.60 students and seniors, £2.30 children 5–16. Apr–Sept daily 10am–6pm; Oct–Mar daily 10am–4pm. Closed Dec 25–26 and Jan 1.

Roman Army Museum ★   Close to the village of Greenhead, the Roman Army Museum traces the influence of Rome from its early beginnings to the expansion of the empire, with emphasis on the role of the Roman army and the garrisons of Hadrian's Wall. A barracks room depicts army living conditions. Realistic life-size figures make this a strikingly visual museum experience.

Within easy walking distance of the Roman Army Museum is one of the most imposing and high-standing sections of Hadrian's Wall, **Walltown Crags;** the height of the wall and magnificent views to the north and south are impressive.

At the junction of A69 and B6318, 29km (18 miles) west of Hexham. ☎ **01697/747485.** www.vindolanda.com. Admission £4.50 adults, £4 students and seniors, £2.50 children, £13 family ticket. Mid-Mar and Oct daily 10am–5pm; Apr–Sept daily 10am–6pm. Closed Nov to early Mar.

Roman Vindolanda   This is another well-preserved fort south of the wall, the last of eight successive forts to be built on this site. An excavated civilian settlement outside the fort has an interesting museum of artifacts of everyday Roman life.

Just west of Housesteads, on a minor road 2km (1¼ miles) southeast of Twice Brewed, off B6318. ☎ **01434/344277.** www.vindolanda.com. Admission £5.90 adults, £4.90 students and seniors, £3.50 children, £16 family ticket. Mid-Feb to Mar and Oct daily 10am–5pm; Apr–Sept daily 10am–6pm. Closed Nov to early Feb.

The Pennine Way in Northumberland National Park

Northumberland National Park, established in 1956, encompasses the borderlands that were a buffer zone between the warring English and Scots during the 13th and 14th centuries. Today, the park comprises almost 1,035 sq. km (400 sq. miles) of the least populated area in England and is noted for its rugged landscape and associations with the northern frontier of the ancient Roman Empire.

Touching the border with Scotland, the park covers some of the most tortuous geology in England, the Cheviot Hills, whose surfaces have been wrinkled by volcanic pressures, inundated with seawater, scoured by glaciers, silted over by rivers, and thrust upward in a complicated series of geological events. Much of the heather-sheathed terrain here is used for sheep grazing; woolly balls of fluff adorn hillsides ravaged by high winds and frequent rain.

Northumberland National Park includes the remains of Hadrian's Wall, one of the most impressive classical ruins of northern Europe. Footpaths run alongside it, and there are a variety of walks in the country to the north and south of the monument. One of the most challenging hiking paths in Britain, the **Pennine Way ★★**, snakes up the backbone of the park. The 129km (80 miles) of the 403km (250-mile) path that are in the park are clearly marked; one of the most worthwhile (and safest) hikes is between Bellingham and the Hamlet of Riding Wood.

A SIDE TRIP TO holy island (LINDISFARNE)

This island is the cradle of Christianity in northern England, lying 10km (6 miles) east of the A1, north of Bamburgh. It's 13km (8 miles) southeast of Berwick-upon-Tweed and 97km (60 miles) north of Newcastle upon Tyne.

In 635, St. Aidan established a monastery here, which reached the zenith of its power under St. Cuthbert, who turned it into the foremost center of learning in Christendom. But in 875 Vikings destroyed the community, and only a few monks escaped. However, they did manage to remove Cuthbert's bones in time, reburying them at the cathedral at Durham.

Lindisfarne is a tidal island, and vehicles can only cross when the tide allows. Opening times vary significantly every day, so check locally before going over.

As you cross the causeway, you'll see **Lindisfarne Castle,** Lindisfarne (© 01289/389244; www.nationaltrust. org.uk), which was built around 1550 as a fort to protect the harbor. In 1903, it was converted by Sir Edwin Lutyens into a comfortable home for Edward Huson, the founder of *Country Life.* Many of the original architectural features are intact; there is also a walled garden, the work of Gertrude Jekyll, which lies nearby. Admission is £6 adults, £3 children, or £15 for a family ticket. Visits are possible

from late March through October, Tuesday to Sunday 10am to 3pm (hours are subject to change).

In the village stands **Lindisfarne Priory** (© 01289/389200; www.english-heritage.org.uk), which dates from the 11th century, when it was partially restored by monks from Durham. A museum displays ancient artifacts, including Anglo-Saxon carvings. Hours are April through September, daily 9:30am to 5pm; February, March, and October, daily 10am to 4pm; and November through January, Saturday and Sunday 10am to 2pm. Admission is £4.50 adults, £2.30 children, and £3.80 seniors.

For your base, check into the **Manor House Hotel,** Holy Island (© 01289/389207; fax 01289/389310; www.manorhouselindisfarne.co.uk), which sits beside the ruins of Lindisfarne Priory. The manor house stands in the market place in the heart of the village and opens onto panoramic views. Open February to December, the manor rents 10 comfortable and well-furnished bedrooms that enjoy sea views. Rates, which include an English breakfast, range from £95 for a standard double to £120 for a sea-view room to £150 for the deluxe master bedroom.

You can purchase a map of the trails, priced at 50p, at almost any local tourist office in the district. There are **National Park Centres** at Once Brewed (© **01434/344396**), Rothbury (© **01669/620887**), and Ingram (© **01665/ 578890**). The Head Office is at Eastburn, South Park, Hexham, Northumberland NE46 1BS (© **01434/605555;** www.nnpa.org.uk).

CARDIFF & SOUTH WALES: DYLAN THOMAS COUNTRY

20

No longer the dreary coal-exporting port it was so often depicted as in the 20th century, **Cardiff,** the capital of Wales, is hot and happening—one of the most attractive cities of Britain to visit. Cardiff (*Caerdydd* in Welsh) is a large seaport built on the tidal estuary of the River Taff.

Enriched by the Industrial Revolution, Cardiff declined after World War II with the closing of coal mines, railroads, and factories. The old industrial city is now a progressive, inviting modern port, as exemplified by the waterfront along Cardiff Bay. Here you'll find renewal at its best, with restaurants, hotels, and a hands-on exhibit called Techniquest.

Cardiff can be your launching pad for the treasures of South Wales, which has turned a bright new face to the world and is no longer known for its depressing stories of slag heaps, dreary cottages, and denuded hillsides that were once proudly forested.

In fact, South Wales is imbued with some of the great beauty spots of Britain: **Brecon Beacons National Park,** 835 sq. km (519 sq. miles) of beauty and pleasure grounds with nature reserves; the **Gower Peninsula,** an area of outstanding natural beauty stretching for 23km (14 miles) from the Mumbles to Worms Head in the West; and, finally, **Pembrokeshire Coast National Park,** one of the smallest national parks of Britain (only 362 sq. km/225 sq. miles) but an area acclaimed for its coastal scenery.

On the western side of Cardiff, the city of **Swansea,** on Swansea Bay off the Bristol Channel, seems a natural starting place for a visit to southwest Wales. After a sojourn in the vicinity of the port city, the beautiful

Gower Peninsula, Swansea's neighbor, draws you westward. You can explore where Dylan Thomas, the country's outstanding 20th-century poet, was born, and then move on to the west to Laugharne, where the poet lived, wrote, and is buried.

Swansea is on the western edge of West Glamorgan County. When the counties of Wales were realigned and consolidated in 1973, Pembrokeshire and Carmarthenshire, familiar names in Welsh history, became part of Dyfed County, an even older designation for the area they occupy. In this southwestern corner of the country, you'll be introduced to the land of St. David and Celtic crosses, of craggy coastlines, and the cromlechs marking the burial places of prehistoric humans.

In addition to Swansea, you'll find two more excellent bases outside Cardiff—**Tenby,** one of the most famous coastal resorts of Wales, its charm and character dating from the Middle Ages, plus **St. Davids,** a tiny cathedral city and birthplace of the patron saint of Wales.

Two major attractions that you may want to seek out, even on a rushed visit, are **Pembroke Castle,** oldest castle in west Wales and seat of the earls of Pembroke; and **Tintern Abbey,** in the Wye Valley, founded in 1131, once one of the richest and most important monastic houses of Wales.

CARDIFF ★

249km (155 miles) W of London; 177km (110 miles) SW of Birmingham; 64km (40 miles) SE of Swansea

If you remember Cardiff's dull, industrial reputation from yesteryear, you might be reluctant to fit the capital of Wales into your already busy schedule. But to omit it would be a shame because it has blossomed into one of the most inviting cities of Britain. It's now an ideal base for exploring its own attractions, plus the major scenic beauty spots of South Wales.

Essentials

GETTING THERE   In recent years, Cardiff has greatly expanded its air facilities, and flights now wing in from across Europe, although there are still no direct flights between London and Cardiff. Airlines that service **Cardiff International Airport** (© 01446/711111; www.tbicardiffairport.com) include **KLM** (© 0871/231-0000; www.klm.com), which offers transfers, through Amsterdam, to points around the world; **BMI Baby** (© 0905/8282828; www.bmibaby.com), which flies to Cardiff from Edinburgh; and **Aer Arann** (© 0870/8767676; www.aerarann.com), which flies between Cardiff and Dublin.

Cardiff Bus (© 0871/2002233; www.cardiffbus.com) operates bus no. X91, which travels between the airport and the bus station at hourly intervals from 8:45am to 6:40pm Monday to Friday. On Saturdays, the X91 operates from 6:25am to 6:40pm, and on Sundays, the X5 and X91 operate between 10am and 7:30pm. The cost of a one-way trip is £3.70.

Trains arrive in Cardiff at the Central Station on Wood Street, in back of the bus station. Trains from London pull in at the rate of one every half-hour during the day; the trip takes 2 hours. Trains also arrive every hour from Glasgow and Edinburgh; trip time is 7 hours. Trains from Glasgow often stop at Bristol, while trains from Edinburgh often stop at Bristol or Birmingham. For rail information and schedules, call © 0845/748-4950 or visit **www.nationalrail.co.uk.**

For bus and motor routes into Cardiff, call ℂ **0871/781-8181** or visit **www. nationalexpress.com**. The trip is about 3½ hours from London.

VISITOR INFORMATION   For information about Cardiff and its environs, the **Cardiff Tourist Information Centre** is at the Old Library, the Hayes (ℂ **029/2087-3573**; www.visitcardiff.com), in the heart of the city. Hours are Monday to Saturday 9:30am to 5:30pm and Sunday 10am to 4pm. In July and August, it is open daily 9:30am to 7pm. A branch office at Cardiff Bay, the Tube, Harbour Drive (ℂ **029/2046-3833**), lying 2.5km (1½ miles) to the south, is open daily 10am to 6pm.

GETTING AROUND   If you don't have a car, you must depend on taxis, buses, or your trusty feet to get around Cardiff.

There's fairly good bus service, even to the sights in the environs. Your hotel staff will usually be able to help you plan a day's outing. Note that prices of bus routes vary according to the number of zones you want to travel in. One-way travel within zone 1 (the commercial heart of the city) costs £1.50 for adults, £1 for children. One-way travel across all four zones of the city (a very large metropolitan area, taking in far-flung suburbs) costs £2.10 for adults, £1.40 for children.

For bus routes, go to **Cardiff Bus** (or **Bws Caerdydd** in Welsh), Wood Street, across from the bus station (ℂ **029/2066-6444**; www.cardiffbus.com), which is the office of Cardiff City Transport. It's open Monday to Friday 8:30am to 5:30pm, Saturday 9am to 4:30pm. Bus service on Sunday morning tends to be infrequent, and service stops completely every night at 11pm.

Taxis are usually easy to find, especially in the busy shopping areas, and most cab fares within Cardiff range from £5 to £15. The most prominent taxi stands are at the rail and bus station and at St. David's Hall. Or you can have your hotel or the place where you've dined call you a taxi, or contact **Capital Cabs** (ℂ **029/2077-7777**; www.taxinumber.com). Wonder of wonders, the meter starts ticking only when you get into the vehicle, not when it leaves the station, as is the case in most U.K. cities.

One of the most efficient ways to see Cardiff and the attractions within its central core involves joining up with one of the open-top bus tours conducted by **City Sightseeing** (ℂ **1708/866000** for information on its services throughout the U.K., or 029/2047-3432 for Cardiff-specific information; www.city-sightseeing. com). Tours follow a clearly signposted itinerary that begins outside Cardiff Castle (at Castle St.) and cover a route that incorporates the most visible monuments of Cardiff. Participants can get on or off the bus at any of the designated stops, returning for the next bus to carry them on to the next monument. Adults pay £9, students and seniors £7, children ages 5 to 15 £4, and a family ticket costs £22. Tour times change from month to month; call for a current schedule.

SPECIAL EVENTS   The **Cardiff Harbour Festival** in Roald Dahl Plass, outside the Millennium Stadium, is celebrated during the long bank holiday that comes at the end of summer. Tall ships and various sea craft are on display. The highlight of the festivities is a "Fish and Ships" spectacular with both aerial and water displays. Singers and entertainers from all over the country show up, while food booths entice you with their various delicacies, especially seafood.

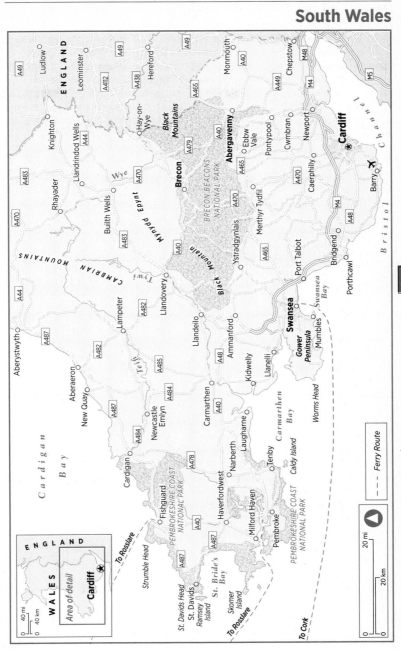

South Wales

[FastFACTS] CARDIFF

Area Code The area code for Cardiff is **029.**

Dentist For dental emergencies, contact **Parade Dental Practice,** 23 The Parade (© **029/ 2048-1486**).

Doctor For medical emergencies, dial © **999** and ask for an ambulance. Doctors are on 24-hour-call service. A full list of doctors is posted at all post offices, or else visitors can ask at their hotel desk.

Drugstores To get a prescription filled, go to **Boots the Chemist,** with outlets all over town. The main dispensing service is at 5 Wood St. (© **029/ 2037-7043;** www.boots. com), open Monday to

Friday 8am to 6:30pm, Saturday 9am to 6pm.

Emergencies To summon police or call firefighters, dial © **999,** the same number used to call an ambulance.

Hospitals The most visible and best-equipped hospital in Cardiff is the **University Hospital of Wales** (also known as the Heath Hospital), Heath Park (© **029/2074-7747**).

Internet Access If you have your own laptop, you can go to **McDonald's,** 12–14 Queen St. (© **029/ 2022-2604;** www. mcdonalds.co.uk), where Wi-Fi is free. It's open Tuesday through Thursday and Sunday from 5am to

midnight; Monday, Friday, and Saturday 24 hours.

Maps You can obtain detailed maps for free from the Cardiff Tourist Information Centre at the Old Library, the Hayes (© **029/2087-3573**).

Police In an emergency, dial © **999.** Otherwise, contact the **Central Cardiff Police Station,** King Edward VII Avenue, Cathays Park (© **029/ 2022-2111**).

Post Office The main post office is at 45–46 Queens Arcade, Queen Street (© **0845/722-3344;** www.postoffice.co.uk), open Monday to Saturday from 9am to 5:30pm.

Where to Stay
EXPENSIVE

Barceló Cardiff Angel Hotel ★   The elegant Victorian Angel Hotel, across from Cardiff Castle, was *the* place to stay in South Wales when it was first built. Over the years, it has attracted everybody from Greta Garbo to the Beatles to every prime minister of Britain. It will never regain its old supremacy, as greater hotels such as Cardiff Bay and St. Davids Hotel & Spa have long surpassed it, but the Angel is still there and still good—and it has regained some of its old prestige following a restoration. It's a world of neo-Doric decor, *trompe l'oeil* ceilings, Waterford crystal chandeliers, and hand-stippled faux-marble columns. As befits a hotel of this age, its guest rooms come in a wide variety of styles and sizes.

Castle St., Cardiff CF10 1SZ. © **029/2064-9200.** Fax 029/2039-6212. www.barcelo-hotels.co.uk. 102 units. £65–£200 double; £125–£300 suite. AE, DC, MC, V. Parking £5. **Amenities:** Restaurant; bar and lounge; babysitting; concierge; room service. *In room:* A/C, TV, hair dryer, Wi-Fi (£12 per 24 hr.).

Jolyons Hotel ★★ 🎒   This former seaman's lodge has been turned into Cardiff's most delightful boutique hotel. There are only a few bedrooms, each individually designed and furnished, so reserve early. The Georgian townhouse within Cardiff Bay's oldest terrace is modern and stylish inside, but with a rustic, slate-floored bar with a log stove and red-leather sofas. Most of the bedrooms open onto views of Cardiff Bay, and most come with king-size beds. The bathrooms are among the best in town, some with whirlpool tubs and one with a "wet room," each with extra-large fluffy towels. The Millennium Centre is just minutes away.

ATTRACTIONS ●
Bute Park **3**
Cardiff Castle **8**
Cathays Park **5**
Doctor Who Up Close Exhibition **15**
Llandaff Cathedral **7**
National Assembly for Wales **15**
National Museum Cardiff **6**
St. Fagans Castle **2**
St. Fagans: National
    History Museum **2**
Techniquest **15**

ACCOMMODATIONS ■
Abbey Hotel **2**
Barceló Cardiff
    Angel Hotel **10**
Big Sleep Hotel **13**
Jolysons Hotel **16**
Lincoln House Hotel **1**
Park Inn Cardiff
    City Centre **12**
St. Davids Hotel
    & Spa **15**
Town House **1**

DINING ◆
Armless Dragon **4**
Harry Ramsden's **14**
La Brasserie/Le Monde **11**
Laguna Kitchen & Bar **9**
Le Gallois **1**
Woods Bar & Brasserie **14**

5 Bute Crescent, Cardiff Bay, Cardiff CF10 5AN. © **029/2048-8775.** Fax 029/2048-8775. www.jolyons. co.uk. 6 units. £75–£150 double. AE, MC, V. **Amenities:** Bar; room service. *In room:* TV, hair dryer, Wi-Fi (free).

New House Country Hotel ★   On the fringe of Cardiff, this elegant Georgian mansion is our choice for a tranquil retreat from the city. Opening onto panoramic views—on a clear day you can see the North Devon coast—the hotel is imbued with an inviting country-house flavor, as evoked by open fires, exquisite furnishings, and beautifully restored bedrooms. Those individually designed rooms, many with four-poster beds, are spacious and comfortable. Although traditional, there is modern luxury here. Bathrooms are roomy and sumptuous, with deluxe toiletries. Most of the accommodations are in a large annex, whose rooms are as good as those in the main building. Three units are large enough for families.

Thornhill, Cardiff CF14 9UA. ✆ **029/2052-0280.** Fax 029/2052-0324. www.newhousehotel.com. 36 units. £96–£170 double; £190–£195 suite. AE, DC, MC, V. Free parking. **Amenities:** Restaurant; bar; exercise room; room service. *In room:* A/C (in some), TV, hair dryer, Wi-Fi (free).

St. Davids Hotel & Spa ★★★ 🎁   A strikingly contemporary structure, St. Davids dwarfs the competition, rising above the modern waterfront development. A seven-story atrium towers above the lobby, an unusual sight for a Welsh hotel. An immediate hit, it is the first five-star hotel to arrive in Wales and is the only one in South Wales that qualifies as one of the Leading Hotels of the World. Here you'll find the highest level of service in South Wales, the ultimate in comfort, and the best leisure facilities. St. Davids is especially known for its extensive spa and beauty facilities. Roomy and beautifully furnished accommodations offer floor-to-ceiling windows and open onto private balconies with panoramic sweeps of the bay.

Havannah St., Cardiff Bay, Cardiff CF10 5SD. ✆ **029/2045-4045.** Fax 029/2048-7056. www.thest davidshotel.info. 132 units. £119–£190 double; £230–£455 suite. AE, DC, MC, V. Parking £8. **Amenities:** 2 restaurants; bar; babysitting; concierge; exercise room; indoor heated pool; room service; spa. *In room:* A/C, TV/DVD/CD player (in some), fax, hair dryer, minibar.

MODERATE

Park Inn Cardiff City Centre ★ ☺   Adjacent to the Cardiff International Arena, this refurbished hotel is stylish and classic, ideal for both business travelers and vacationers. There's a vibrant spirit about the place that attracts us. Spacious and well-furnished bedrooms are grouped around a central atrium, which gives access to the hotel's fashionable public rooms. The accommodations are among the city's finest and have some of the best amenities. A few family rooms are available, and children are given a very hospitable welcome.

Mary Ann St., Cardiff CF10 2JH. ✆ **888/201-1801** or 029/2034-1441. Fax 029/2022-3742. www.cardiff-city.parkinn.co.uk. 146 units. £85–£165 double. Rates include breakfast. AE, DC, MC, V. Parking £8. **Amenities:** Restaurant; Irish-themed bar; babysitting; room service. *In room:* TV, hair dryer, Wi-Fi (£10 per day).

INEXPENSIVE

Abbey Hotel   Built in 1898 as a home for a wealthy sea captain and his family, this house retains many of its original features and is one of the better and more reasonably priced B&Bs. Richard Burton once attended elocution lessons in the public lounge back when the hotel was a private school. Bedrooms are small but comfortably and tastefully furnished; they have shower-only bathrooms. A few have four-poster beds. The on-site restaurant only occasionally serves lunch and dinner.

149-151 Cathedral Rd., Cardiff CF11 9PJ. ✆ **029/2039-0896.** Fax 029/2023-8311. www.bandb4u.co.uk. 26 units (shower only). £60–£75 double; £80–£95 triple. Rates include continental breakfast. MC, V. Free parking. **Amenities:** Restaurant; bar. *In room:* TV, hair dryer (in some).

Big Sleep Hotel ★ 🗝   What are pictures of the actor John Malkovich doing scattered throughout this hotel? The actor, who made a career out of playing "evil bastards," is one of the major shareholders. And, in 2006, his hotel was named one of *Condé Nast Traveller's* "coolest places to stay." A rather dull office tower built in the 1960s has been successfully transformed into a hotel with a certain chic minimalism but with most affordable prices. Each of the midsize bedrooms is individually decorated with contemporary pieces, a rather smart styling. The best rooms are the "New on Ninth," though they cost more. If there's a downside, it's that some of the rooms overlook the rail tracks nearby, a rather noisy location.

Bute Terrace, Cardiff CF10 2FE. ✆ **029/2063-6363.** Fax 029/2063-6364. www.thebigsleephotel.com. 81 units. Mon-Thurs £69–£100 double, Fri-Sat £65–£75 double, Sun £50–£65 double; daily £99–£135 suite. Rates include continental breakfast. AE, MC, V. Parking £6. **Amenities:** Bar. *In room:* TV, hair dryer, Wi-Fi (£7.50 per day).

Lincoln House Hotel ☺ This Victorian house provides a cozy and reasonably priced nest along popular Cathedral Road. The majestic home was created in 1900 by joining together two older residences, resulting in a superb and completely restored hotel. Surprisingly, the hotel is named for Abraham Lincoln, not the English cathedral city of Lincoln. The four-poster units exude romance, but there are also modern facilities. Accommodations are spacious, and furnishings offer both style and comfort. Several family rooms are available.

118 Cathedral Rd., Cardiff CF11 9LQ. ✆ **029/2039-5558.** Fax 029/2023-0537. www.lincolnhotel.co.uk. 18 units. £65–£110 double; £175–£300 suite. Rates include buffet breakfast. AE, MC, V. Free parking. **Amenities:** Bar; room service. *In room:* TV, hair dryer, Wi-Fi (free).

Town House ★ 🥄 This is the best B&B in Cardiff, preferable even to the neighboring Lincoln (see above). A classic Victorian town house, it lies in the shadow of the great Norman castle and has been completely restored and tastefully decorated. Its original architectural details are still here, including the mosaic-tiled floors in the elegantly decorated hallway, the stained-glass windows so beloved of Victorians, and even the original fireplaces in the public lounge and dining area. A cosmopolitan guesthouse, it attracts travelers from San Francisco to Sydney. The roomy bedrooms are immaculately furnished and have excellent bathrooms. The location is a 10-minute walk from the city center.

70 Cathedral Rd., Cardiff CF11 9LL. ✆ **029/2023-9399.** Fax 029/2022-3214. www.thetownhousecardiff. co.uk. 8 units. £70–£95 double. Rates include buffet breakfast. AE, MC, V. Free parking. **Amenities:** Wi-Fi (free, in lobby). *In room:* TV, hair dryer.

Where to Dine
EXPENSIVE

Armless Dragon WELSH About 1.6km (1 mile) north of the center in a busy suburb, this popular restaurant occupies a 19th-century stone core and is known for its unpretentious and nutritious food. The kitchen hires skilled chefs whose suppliers offer the best in Welsh produce and meats. The cooks are strong on their "Taste of Wales" dishes, as exemplified by such delights as deep-fried *laverballs* (seaweed balls) coated in sunflower and sesame seeds. Starters are divvied up among "Land," "Sea," and "Earth" platters. Try such temptations as pan-fried pigeon breasts with beetroot risotto or local mussels in a cider cream sauce. Among the mains are Welsh sirloin steak with field mushrooms and a red onion marmalade or a creamy wild mushroom and lemon thyme risotto with an herb purée.

97 Wyeverne Rd. ✆ **029/2038-2357.** www.armlessdragon.co.uk. Reservations recommended. Main courses £12–£18. MC, V. Tues-Fri noon-2pm; Tues-Thurs 7-9pm; Fri-Sat 7-9:30pm. Closed Dec 25-26.

Le Gallois ★★ FRENCH One of the most talented chefs in Wales, Grady Atkins, has cooked around the world from Paris to Hong Kong, Los Angeles to Sicily.

His basic repertoire is French-inspired, but his cuisine shows the influences of all his travels, and seasonal produce drives his menu composition. He has won many devotees since moving to Wales and setting up shop in this stylish, contemporary atmosphere. Try the grilled wild Brixham bass with blood orange or the lemon sole with razor clams and fine herbs served with a salmon ravioli. The starters are among the most creative in town, as evoked by the Jerusalem artichoke velouté with a walnut mousseline and shallot confit.

6–10 Romilly Crescent, Canton. ℰ **029/2034-1264.** www.legallois.co.uk. Reservations required. Fixed-price lunch £20–£25, fixed-price dinner £25–£30. Tues–Sat noon–2:30pm and 6:30–9:30pm.

MODERATE

Laguna Kitchen & Bar ★ WELSH/BRITISH   In a modern setting on the ground floor of the Park Plaza hotel is one of Cardiff's finest dining spots. Guests are seated either in a more formal room or in the laid-back bar, which contains private booths. The chefs secure the finest and freshest produce on the market, which they turn into an array of well-crafted dishes. These are tantalizingly flavored and served with a choice of fresh salads and vegetables. Starters are some of the best in town, especially the ham hock and parsley terrine or the carpaccio of Welsh beef filet flavored with chili, ginger, and soy sauce. A selection of rock oysters with lemon is usually available. Grills are a specialty—whole lemon sole, sirloin steak, and so on—served plain or with a choice of several sauces. Other mains include slow-cooked lamb shank or roast rabbit leg with Parma ham.

In the Park Plaza hotel, Greyfriars Rd. ℰ **029/2011-1111.** www.parkplaza.com/cardiffuk. Reservations recommended. Fixed-price 2-course lunch £12, 3-course lunch £15. Dinner main courses £8–£18. AE, MC, V. Daily noon–2:30pm and 7–10:30pm.

Woods Bar & Brasserie ★ MODERN BRITISH/CONTINENTAL   In the old Pilotage Building down by the dock, this is a haven of modernity, serving "the best of Britain," with a lot of Continental temptations as well. Food is carefully prepared using the best products in any given season. For starters, try the creamed goat cheese with poached rhubarb, candied walnuts, and truffle honey, or perhaps a pressed duck terrine with black pudding and a grape chutney. Well-crafted mains include pan-fried filet of bream with butterbeans or Loch Duart filet of salmon with herb-flavored oysters and truffled potatoes.

Pilotage Building, Stuart St., Cardiff Bay. ℰ **029/2049-2400.** www.woods-brasserie.com. Reservations required. Main courses £10–£21; fixed-price lunch £11–£17; fixed-price pretheater dinner £17–£20. AE, DC, MC, V. Mon–Sat noon–2pm and 5:30–10pm; Sun noon–3pm.

INEXPENSIVE

Harry Ramsden's SEAFOOD   This member of a chain serves the best fish and chips in Wales, at least according to its devotees. Until we finish sampling hundreds of others, we'll have to let the claim remain. Under crystal chandeliers, with nostalgic pictures displayed, this is a place for both traditional British cuisine, mainly seafood, as well as entertainment. Begin perhaps with a prawn cocktail or a smoked salmon salad. Follow with one of the fish platters, such as a 14-ounce batter-fried haddock with chips. If you finish the entire thing, you can have any dessert you want for free. You can also order such mains as New Zealand red cod or chargrilled swordfish steak, even a fish pie. Meat and poultry dishes are also served, including chicken breasts and chargrilled sirloin steaks.

Landsey House, Stuart Place. ℂ **029/2046-3334.** www.harryramsdens.co.uk. Reservations recommended. Main courses £7–£9.50. AE, DC, MC, V. Summer Mon–Thurs 11:30am–9pm; Fri–Sat 11:30am–10pm; Sun noon–8pm. Closes 1 hr. earlier off-season.

La Brasserie/Le Monde BRITISH/CONTINENTAL   A bustling informal atmosphere prevails at these two dining rooms, where the prices are virtually the same. You might prefer the Brasserie, which was originally built as a warehouse in the 19th century. You order your drinks from a wood-topped bar and food from an attendant who waits behind a well-stocked display case. The establishment serves some 50 kinds of wine. Some of the best menu items include lamb's liver on "crushed" potatoes with onion rings or bluefin tuna cooked with a mild coconut and curry sauce. Le Monde concentrates more on fresh fish, including a delectable Marseille-style fish soup or sea bass baked in rock salt.

60 St. Mary St. ℂ **029/2039-8036.** www.le-monde.co.uk. Reservations not needed. La Brasserie main courses £11–£25; Le Monde main courses £9–£32. MC, V. Mon–Sat noon–2:30pm and 7pm–midnight; Sun noon–4pm. Closed Dec 15–26.

Exploring the City

The Welsh capital has many interesting things to see, from antiquities to such modern pieces as Epstein's controversial *Christ in Majesty* sculpture at Llandaff Cathedral. If you're in Cardiff for only a short time, try to see the major sights described below.

CARDIFF BAY'S INNER HARBOR ★

Allow 2 hours to visit Cardiff Bay, the redeveloped area of the old dockland of Tiger Bay, lying about 2.5km (1½ miles) south of the town center. The salty old sea dogs of yesteryear who used to hang out here between sails wouldn't recognize the place today. No longer tawdry, it bustles with shops, restaurants, pubs, and attractions.

In the 19th century, when the area was called Tiger Bay, it became notorious among sailors around the world. The setting for many a novel, Tiger Bay meant poverty, crime, and violence. Today, the panoramic view of the harbor is worth the visit alone, as are the scenic promenades along the bay.

Drop in at the **Cardiff Bay Visitor Centre,** the Tube, Harbour Drive (ℂ **029/2046-3833;** www.visitcardiff.com), to pick up free information about the area. The center is open daily from 10am to 6pm.

Techniquest ★, Stuart Street (ℂ **029/2047-5475;** www.techniquest.org), Britain's leading science discovery center, is the chief attraction here. You can enjoy 160 hands-on exhibits and visit both the Science Theatre and the Planetarium. Some 100,000 people—both young and old—visit annually. Admission is £7 for adults, £5 for seniors or children 4 to 16 (free for children 3 and younger), and £23 for a family ticket. Techniquest is open Monday to Friday 9:30am to 4:30pm, Saturday and Sunday 10am to 5pm. Last admission is 45 minutes before closing.

The **Doctor Who Up Close Exhibition** (ℂ **029/2048-9257;** www.doctorwhoexhibitions.com) is at the Red Dragon Centre, Hemingway Road (ℂ **029/2025-6261;** www.thereddragoncentre.co.uk). It includes props, costumes, and "monsters and creatures" from the BBC hit TV series *Doctor Who*. These phenomenally popular exhibitions are found at locations throughout the U.K., but Cardiff's is the only permanent one. Props on display include "Ood Elder" from the segment called "The End of Time," as well as the fly-headed "Tritovore" and Lady Christina De Souza's costume from "The Planet of the Dead." Admission is £6.50 for adults, £5 for children 4 to 16, and £20 for a family ticket. Open daily from 10am to 6:30pm. Also see "Cardiff After Dark" for more information on the Red Dragon Centre.

In the wake of the Government of Wales Act in 2006, the 60-member **National Assembly for Wales** is now imbued with the power to govern Wales. Visitors with advance reservations (© **0845/0103300** or www.assemblywales.org for bookings) can see the *Senedd* (Senate), the debating chamber opening onto Cardiff Bay. Its members meet under a beautiful timbered ceiling. Traditional materials such as slate and Welsh oak were used in the building's construction, whose architect's goal was "to create openness and transparency."

THE TOP ATTRACTIONS

Caerphilly Castle ★★   About 13km (8 miles) north of Cardiff is this imposing moated fortress built partly on the site of a Roman fort. It was constructed by Earl Gilbert de Clare, Lord of Glamorgan, as protection against invasion by the Welsh prince Llywelyn ap Gwynedd in the 13th century. The massive water defenses of the castle form the second-largest castle area in Britain. You will note the leaning tower as you approach the castle, a result of efforts by Cromwell to blow up the towers. Perhaps you'll see the castle ghost, the Green Lady. She is supposed to be the spirit of a French princess who loved a handsome Welsh prince. When her husband, the Norman lord of Caerphilly, learned of the matter, he sent her into exile, but her ghost is still here, lamenting her lost love. There is no luxurious interior filled with fascinating paintings or antiques, but you should come mainly to see the impressive layout of the castle, with its defenses and great gatehouse, along with a fortified dam separating the outer moat from the inner moat. You can also wander into the Great Hall.

On the A469, at Caerphilly. © **029/2088-3143.** Admission £3.60 adults, £3.20 children 15 and younger. Apr–May and Oct daily 9:30am–5pm; June–Sept daily 9:30am–6pm; Nov–Mar Mon–Sat 9:30am–4pm. Bus: 26 from Cardiff leaves for Caerphilly every hour during the day (also bus no. 71 or 72). Caerphilly train with several departures daily from Central Station in Cardiff.

Cardiff Castle ★   Some 1,900 years of history are embodied in this castle located in the heart of the city. The Romans first built a forum on this site, and you can see the remains of massive 3m-thick (10-ft.) stone walls. The Normans constructed a castle on what was left of the Roman fort, and much of the Norman work still exists, added to by medieval lords. It came under assault in the Anglo-Welsh wars and was besieged during the English Civil War. The third marquis of Bute, by then the owner, had it restored in the 19th century by Victorian architect William Burges, who transformed the interior into the extravaganza of whimsy, color, and rich architectural detail you see today. The Welsh Regimental Museum and the First Queen's Dragoon Guards Regimental Museum are also here. Admission includes the full conducted tour.

Castle St. © **029/2087-8100.** www.cardiffcastle.com. Admission £11 adults, £9 students and seniors, £8 children. Mar–Oct daily 9am–6pm; Nov–Feb daily 9am–5pm. Last admission 1 hr. before closing. Closed Dec 25–26 and Jan 1. Bus: 32 or 62.

Llandaff Cathedral ★   This cathedral is in the tiny city of Llandaff, which stood just outside the western boundary of Cardiff until 1922, when it was made a part of the capital. It retains its village atmosphere, with modern shops in old half-timbered buildings. The cathedral stands in a green hollow at a place where religious history goes back 1,400 years. It began as a religious community founded by St. Teilo in the 6th century, with many churches under its aegis scattered throughout South Wales. A 10th-century Celtic cross is all that's left of the pre-Norman church. Among relics of the Norman church erected on-site is a fine arch behind the high altar. The west front, built in the 13th century, is one of the best medieval works of art in Wales. Cromwell's army used the cathedral as a beer house and post office; then, in 1941, a German bomb severely damaged the building. Postwar reconstruction gave the cathedral two fine new features: the Welsh Regiment Chapel and Sir Jacob Epstein's soaring sculpture *Christ in Majesty.* Epstein's striking work, which dominates the interior of the structure, has elicited mixed reactions from viewers. The ruin of the 800-year-old Bishop's Palace has been made into a peaceful public garden.

Cathedral Rd. © **029/2056-4554.** www.llandaffcathedral.org.uk. Free admission; donations requested. Daily 7am–7pm. Call for times of services. Bus: 25, 33, 33A, or 62.

National Museum Cardiff ★

This imposing white classic building, with a columned entrance and a large cupola, houses eclectic art and science collections. It stands at the Civic Centre along with City Hall. The diverse exhibits here focus on natural science, industry, archaeology, and geology, plus there are extensive collections of silver, china, and glass (some dating from 1250). The emphasis is on the story of Wales from the earliest of times. There are also modern and classic sculptures and works from both Old Masters and modern artists ranging from van Gogh to Kokoschka.

Much of the museum's ambience comes from the openness and light that fills the main entrance and hall below the high ceiling. From the floor of the rotunda, you can look up to the mezzanine gallery that girds the main hall. The exhibits are at the head of the impressive staircase from the main hall. Also on this level is the French Impressionist collection—our favorite part of the museum—which includes Monet's *Water Lilies,* Renoir's *Parisian Girl,* and Manet's haunting *The Rabbit.* Here you can also see Rodin's bronze *The Kiss* and paintings by Rubens, Cézanne, Augustus John, and Brangwyn. A well-stocked bookstore is situated off the main hall.

Cathays Park, in the Civic Centre. © **029/2039-7951.** www.museumwales.ac.uk. Free admission except for special exhibitions (prices vary). Tues–Sun 10am–5pm, plus bank holiday Mon. Closed some public holidays. Bus: 32 or 62.

St. Fagans: National History Museum ★★

One of the best places to visit in all of Wales is this museum, which provides a glimpse of Welsh life in centuries past. In the wooded parkland of an Elizabethan mansion, you can visit a treasury of ancient buildings that have been brought from their original sites all over the country and re-erected, in some cases even restored, to their former use. In this superb collection of traditional buildings, widely distributed over 40 hectares (100 acres), you can see a 15th-century Tudor farmhouse furnished in the fashion of its day, cottages, a tollhouse, a schoolhouse, a chapel, and a cockpit. You'll also see a woolen mill and a flour mill from long ago put back into use so that people of the present can see how such work was done in the days before electricity, steam power, and other modern conveniences. A wood-turner and a cooper (barrel maker) are also at work, using the tools and materials of another age.

Also on the grounds is **St. Fagans Castle,** the 16th-century mansion that was given to the National Museum of Wales by the earl of Plymouth. The mansion house, built inside the curtain wall of a Norman castle, with its formal gardens, has been refurbished and restored to the way it was at the end of the 18th century.

St. Fagans. (℗ **029/2057-3500.** www.museumwales.ac.uk. Free admission. Daily 10am–5pm. Bus: 32 or 320, leaving from the bus station in Cardiff every hour during the day.

Parks & Gardens

Cardiff has been called a city of parks, with some 1,092 hectares (2,700 acres) of well-designed parklands. **Bute Park,** in the heart of the city, spreads its green swath along the River Taff for the pleasure of residents and visitors alike.

Of special interest, **Roath Park,** Lake Road West (℗ **029/2068-4000;** www. cardiff.gov.uk), is east of the city center, offering facilities for boating and fishing on its 13-hectare (32-acre) lake, as well as tennis courts and bowling greens. Rose and dahlia gardens, a subtropical greenhouse, a children's play area, and an island bird sanctuary add to the pleasures found here. The lighthouse clock tower in the lake is a memorial to Captain Scott. Admission is free, and it's open daily from 10:30am to 1pm and 2 to 4:30pm (bus: 32 or 62).

Close to 5km (3 miles) from Cardiff, **Dyffryn Gardens,** St. Nicholas (℗ **029/2059-3328;** www.dyffryngardens.org.uk), stands in a secluded valley in the Vale of Glamorgan. This park of 20 hectares (50 acres) contains a landscaped botanical garden. Herbaceous borders, a rose garden, a rock garden, and the largest heather garden in Wales are found here, along with an extensive arboretum. Grass walks invite you for long, leisurely strolls through the grounds. A palm house, orchid house, cactus and succulent house, along with seasonal display houses of potted plants, are also on view. The gardens have been restored to their original design, as conceived by Thomas Mawson in 1906. From November to February, admission is £3.50 for adults, £2.50 for seniors and students, and £1.50 for children; a family ticket costs £9. From March to October, admission is £7 for adults, £5 for seniors and students, and £3 for children, with a family ticket going for £18. Dyffryn Garden is open March to October, daily 10am to 6pm, and November to February, daily 10am to 4pm.

Shopping

Whether you're looking for gifts to take home, hunting for souvenirs, or just browsing, you'll like the shops of Cardiff. They are many and varied, ranging from a multiplicity of offerings in the modern shopping precinct of St. David's Centre—a stone's throw from the castle—to the stalls of a covered market.

The main shopping streets are **St. Mary, High, Castle, Duke,** and **Queen** streets, plus the **Hayes.** Most of this area has been made into a pedestrian mall, adorned with trees, shrubs, and gracious Edwardian arcades. These arcades, a dozen in all, are the most famous shopping precincts in all of Wales. The best known is the **Castle Arcade,** constructed in 1887. The interior has a fascinating first-floor wooden gallery with a wooden second floor overhanging it. Dating from 1858, the **Royal Arcade** is the oldest of the city's shopping arcades. Look for the original Victorian storefronts at nos. 29, 30, and 32. The **Morgan Arcade,** from 1896, is the best preserved. Note the first-floor Venetian windows and the original slender wooden storefronts such as nos. 23 and 24. All in all, the arcades stretch to a length of 797m (2,655 ft.) in the city.

In **St. David's Shopping Centre** (© **029/2036-7600;** www.stdavidscardiff. com), you'll find a branch of **Marks & Spencer,** 72 Queen St. (© **029/2037-8211;** www.marksandspencer.com), one of the country's oldest branches of a major chain store, offering clothing with emphasis on British-made goods. A food section contains a range of high-quality specialty items. This is the anchor store in the enclosed center, which has shops opening off wide walkways. The best Welsh crafts shop in the center is **Castle Welsh Crafts,** 1 Castle St. (© **029/2034-3038**), opposite the castle entrance. Shipping service is available, and VAT-refund forms are available for overseas visitors. You can get to St. David's by bus no. 2, 3, 7, 8, or 9. Shops are usually open Monday to Saturday 8:30am to 6:30pm, Thursday until 9pm.

Close to St. David's Centre, **Capitol Shopping Centre,** along Queen Street, is another place to shop for bargains or special gifts. In the complex is one of Britain's best men's stores, **Austin Reed,** Unit 4 (© **029/2022-8357**). You can get here via bus no. 70, 78, 80, or 82.

Markets are held at several sites. The **Central Indoor Market,** on St. Mary Street, is open Monday to Saturday. The **Outdoor Fruit and Vegetable Market,** St. David Street and Mary Ann Street, is open Monday to Saturday. On Bessemer Road, an **open-air market** is held on Sunday morning.

For a novel shopping jaunt, visit **Jacob's Antique Centre,** West Canal Wharf (© **029/2039-0939**), to see what's for sale from Grandmother Welsh's attic: perhaps a Victorian fireplace, 19th-century jewelry, antique brass or hardware, pocket watches, and certainly furnishings from Victoria's heyday. You can get here on bus no. 2 or 3.

At the **Martin Tinney Gallery,** 18 St. Andrew's Crescent (© **029/2064-1411;** www.artwales.com), a short distance from the Cardiff rail station, you'll find the region's best commercial galleries.

Finally, **Craft in the Bay,** the Flourish, Lloyd George Avenue (© **029/2048-4611**), features the largest selection of handmade quality crafts in Wales—baskets, pottery, jewelry, handcrafted furniture, ceramics, and the like.

Cardiff After Dark

There's no Soho in Cardiff, but you can find many interesting places to go after dark.

St. David's Hall (see below) is one of Britain's leading centers of music, offering an extensive program that includes visits by international conductors, soloists, and orchestras. Top rock and pop artists also appear here. The most outstanding local troupe is the **Welsh National Opera,** which *Punch* magazine acclaimed as the "world's best opera company."

The **Red Dragon Centre,** Hemingway Road, Cardiff Bay (© **029/2025-6261;** www.thereddragoncentre.co.uk), is a lively center for shopping, entertainment, and dining. There's so much going on here in an ever-changing scene that if you drop in, you are likely to find some venue to amuse you. There's an array of amusements for children, too, so it's very much a family affair. Live entertainment takes place almost every night in one of the center's clubs.

For information about after-dark diversions, pick up the *Cardiff 2011* brochure from the Cardiff tourist office, which is revised annually. In it you'll find a selective rundown of the city's most worthwhile entertainment.

THE PERFORMING ARTS

Built at the cost of £106 million, the **Wales Millennium Centre ★★★** has made its debut at Cardiff Bay (✆ **029/2063-6400;** www.wmc.org.uk), serving as the home base for seven leading cultural organizations, including the Welsh National Opera and the Dance Company of Wales. Set against a backdrop of Welsh slate walls and a golden roof, the 1,900-seat auditorium overlooks the waterfront. Right from the beginning, it has established itself as one of the world's leading venues for the performing arts, attracting companies from all over the world, including the Australian Ballet. The center houses the Donald Gordon Theatre and the Weston Studio, plus an array of places to dine, drink, and watch free entertainment. Tickets prices vary, depending on the attraction. On our last visit, for example, prices began at £10 for the cheapest seat in the house, going up to £40.

St. David's Hall (or *Neuadd Dewi Sant* in Welsh), the Hayes (✆ **029/2087-8889;** www.newtheatrecardiff.co.uk), was designed in an octagonal format of shimmering glass and roughly textured concrete. Prince Charles laid the hall's cornerstone, and the Queen Mother officially opened the arts center in 1983. The most comprehensive forum for the arts in Wales, it hosts a number of world-class orchestras regularly, along with popular music stars—everybody from Tina Turner to Welsh-born Tom Jones. Dance, films, and classical ballet, among other events, are also presented. The top-notch acoustics are attributed to its interior arrangements of a series of interlinked sloping terraces, any of which can be opened or closed for seating depending on the size of the audience.

The hall maintains an information desk for the sale of tickets throughout the day. It also has dining facilities, plus a changing exhibition of art. Instant confirmed bookings for events are available by phone with a Visa or MasterCard, daily from 10am to 6 or 8pm, depending on the concert schedule. The box office is open Monday to Saturday 9:30am to 8pm (but only until 5:30pm on days when there's no performance). On Sunday, the box office opens an hour before the start of a scheduled performance. Ticket prices depend on the event. Take bus no. 1 or 2 to get here.

Cardiff's main repertory theater, the **Sherman Theatre,** Senghennydd Road (✆ **029/2064-6900;** www.shermantheatre.co.uk), is on the campus of the University of Wales. It has two auditoriums—the Main Theatre and the more intimate Arena Theatre. More than 600 performances a year are staged here, including drama, dance, and Welsh folkloric performances. The box office is open Monday to Saturday from 10am to 8pm (or until 5:30pm, if no performance is scheduled). The cost for most tickets is £12 to £15 for adults, £10 to £11 for students and children. Take bus no. 70, 78, 80, or 82.

Finally, **Chapter,** Market Road, in Canton (✆ **029/2030-4400;** www.chapter.org), is an arts center complete with a theater; two movie facilities; three galleries and artists' studios; video, photography, and silk-screen workshops; a dance studio; a bookshop; two bars; and a cafe. Its box office is open Monday to Saturday 11am to 8:30pm, Sunday 3 to 8:30pm.

MUSIC CLUBS

The hottest action is likely to be found at **Clwb ifor Bach** (the **Welsh Club**), 11 Womanby St. (✆ **029/2023-2199;** www.clwb.net), whose activities spread across three levels. The top floor rocks to live bands, including some of the best in Wales,

AN INFORMAL walk THROUGH CARDIFF

A good place to begin a stroll through the heart of town is at the **Hayes Island,** across from St. David's Hall. The Hayes isn't really an island; until the 18th century it was the vegetable garden of the townspeople of Cardiff, and in the city's boom days of the 19th century it became a fashionable shopping area. Head north on Trinity Street, passing the 1882 **Central Library** on your right and the 1891 **Central Market** on your left. **St. John's Church,** the oldest house of worship in Cardiff—with origins in the 12th century—is on the right at the approach to Church Street.

Turn left onto Church Street and observe the **Old Arcade** adjacent to the Old Arcade Public House; it's the oldest of the city's arcades, dating from 1835. At the end of Church Street, turn right onto High Street, the main street of medieval-era Cardiff. Follow this High Street to the main entrance to **Cardiff Castle,** which you can visit now or save for a later time. Turn left and walk along Castle Street, passing the landmark **Angel Hotel.** Continue along to Womanby Street, a Viking name that survived the Norman invasion and all subsequent government changes.

Head right at Quay Street, whose name harkens back to when the River Taff ran at its lower end. If you turn left at Westgate Street, you'll see the **Cardiff Arms Park** and the **National Rugby Football Ground.** Turn back up Quay Street to High Street. At High, turn right and walk along St. Mary Street, passing market buildings from 1885. At Guildhall Place, turn right. Notice the plaque on the southern wall of Hodge House telling the story of the **Old Town Hall,** which stood here until 1913.

Return to St. Mary Street, passing on your right the **Royal Hotel,** with its memories of Captain Scott and his South Pole explorers. At the junction with Wood Street, you'll see the Gothic facade of the **Prince of Wales Theatre,** which opened in 1878. Head across Penarth Road and walk along Custom House Street to the 1845 **Custom House.**

Return again to St. Mary Street and the **Great Western Hotel,** built in 1876 in French Gothic style. Cross St. Mary Street and pause outside the Terminus Public House. If you look up from this street, you will see an almost complete Victorian townscape.

such as Bullet for My Valentine, Lostprophets, and Super Furry Animals. There's something different happening every night the club is open. Cover ranges from £3.50 to £8, and the club rocks Wednesday to Monday, usually from 7:30pm to either 2 or 3am.

Liquid, St. Mary St. (*©* **029/2064-5464;** www.liquidclubs.com), has the best sound and lighting systems, with striking visuals. It plays all the best funk, house, electro, R&B, whatever, with the town's best DJs. Charging a £5 to £12 cover, Liquid pours over Friday and Saturday from 9:30pm to 5am.

PUBS & BARS

A traditional favorite is the **Pub at Hamon's Restaurant,** in the Thistle Hotel, Park Place (*©* **0871/3769011**), with a cozy pub and bistro format. Stained-glass windows evoke Victorian nostalgia. You can also come here for a pub dinner. Take bus no. 8 or 9.

More modern, and attracting a younger crowd, **Salt,** Stuart Street, Mermaid Quay (✆ **029/2049-4375;** www.saltcardiff.com), is a two-story bar that serves some of the best cocktails in town. Take bus no. 8.

A hangout for rugby fans, **City Arms,** 10 Quay St., at Womanby Street (✆ **029/2022-5258**), attracts sports enthusiasts and is the most likely venue for any pop star or celebrity visiting Wales. Take bus no. 50, 51, 52, 70, 71, or 72.

GAY CLUBS

Exit Club, 48 Charles St. (✆ **029/2064-0102;** www.exitclubcardiff.com), is a hot spot that is usually crowded and cruisy. Its precincts accommodate the Richard Burton or Dylan Thomas wannabes of the 21st century. Surveying the dance floor of heavy-drinking hot guys, one patron claimed, "You want to get 'em before they're too pissed." There's no cover before 9:30pm; after that, you pay from £2 to £5. The club is open Sunday to Thursday 8pm to 2am, Friday and Saturday 8pm to 3am. Sunday is cabaret night.

ABERGAVENNY

262km (163 miles) W of London; 78km (48 miles) NE of Swansea; 49km (31 miles) NE of Cardiff

This flourishing market town of nearly 10,000 people is called the "Gateway to Wales," and it's certainly the gateway to the Brecon Beacons, which lie to the west. The Welsh word *aber* means the mouth of a river, and Abergavenny lies at the mouth of the River Gavenny, where it joins the River Usk. The town is in a valley with mountains and hills spread around it. Humankind has found this a good, sometimes safe place to live for some 5,000 years, as revealed by archaeological finds from the late Neolithic Age. The Romans established one of their forts here; centuries later a Norman castle was built nearby.

The best time to visit Abergavenny is for its Tuesday **flea market** (✆ **01873/735811;** www.abergavennymarket.co.uk), held from 6am to 5pm. An **antiques market** is staged every third Sunday of the month.

Abergavenny is renowned as a center for outdoor holiday activities, including pony trekking, hill walking and climbing, golfing, hang gliding, and fishing. A Leisure Centre provides for indoor sports. The Tourist Information Centre (see below) keeps an up-to-date list of activities available at any season.

Essentials

GETTING THERE The town is linked by rail to Shrewsbury and Hereford, both in England, and to Newport, a distance of 31km (19 miles) to the southwest, in Wales. From Newport, rail connections are made to Cardiff, Bristol, and London. Travel time from London usually takes 2½ hours. For rail information and schedules, call ✆ **0845/748-4950** or visit **www.nationalrail.co.uk**. In Abergavenny, the rail station is on Station Road, off Monmouth Road.

Stagecoach bus no. X3 or X4 from Hereford arrives 10 times per day. Bus no. X43 arrives seven times per day from Brecon.

If driving from Hereford, take the A465 southwest; from Cardiff, take the M4 motorway east toward London, but cut north along the A4042 toward Abergavenny.

VISITOR INFORMATION Abergavenny's Civic Society has laid out a **Town Trail,** marking buildings and other points of interest with brass plaques. For more info about the town and its environs, get in touch with the **Tourist Information Centre,** Swan Meadow, Monmouth Road (📞 **01873/857588;** www.visit abergavenny.co.uk). It's open Easter to October, daily 10am to 1pm and 2 to 5:30pm, and November to Easter, daily 10am to 4pm.

Where to Stay in the Area

Bear Hotel ★ 🍴   This 15th-century coaching inn is hailed for its evocative atmosphere, bedrooms, and cuisine—a winning combination. About 8km (5 miles) northwest of Abergavenny in a charming little town, the Bear grew in fame back in the days when stagecoaches from London would pull in here. The place has been upgraded to keep up with modern times, but the old character has been respected—for example, some units with four-posters also have Jacuzzi tubs. In summer, a secluded outdoor garden is the place to sit and ponder a Welsh twilight. A modern addition houses a range of superior bedrooms bordering a courtyard; this annex was designed in the style of an old Tudor manse. Or you can opt for the individually furnished bedrooms in the main building, which come in a variety of styles.

High St., Crickhowell, Powys NP8 1BW. 📞 **01873/810408.** Fax 01873/811696. www.bearhotel.co.uk. 34 units. £86–£133 double; £153 suite. Rates include continental breakfast. AE, MC, V. Free parking. On A40, btw. Abergavenny and Brecon. **Amenities:** Restaurant; bar. *In room:* TV, hair dryer, Wi-Fi (free).

Llansantffraed Court ★★   You'll have to drive 16km (10 miles) from Abergavenny to reach it, but this hotel is worth the journey. As you head up the drive, an impressive redbrick country house in William and Mary style comes into view. It's set on extensive and well-kept grounds with a small lake, everything opening onto distant views of the Brecon Beacons. The midsize bedrooms are comfortably furnished, each with en-suite bathroom, and some offer panoramic views of the surrounding mountains. Some also contain four-posters. The dining room, serving Welsh and French cuisine, is decorated with oak beams and oil paintings; in good weather you can enjoy its outdoor terrace.

Llanvihangel Gobion, near Abergavenny, Monmouthshire NP7 9BA. 📞 **01873/840678.** Fax 01873/840674. www.llch.co.uk. 21 units. £125–£140 double; £175 suite. Rates include buffet breakfast. AE, DC, MC, V. At A465/A40 Abergavenny intersection, take B4598 signposted to USK. Continue toward Raglan until you see the hotel. **Amenities:** Restaurant; bar; room service. *In room:* TV, minibar, MP3 docking station, Wi-Fi (free).

Where to Dine in the Area

Walnut Tree Inn ★ WELSH   This popular restaurant wins praise all over the British Isles—and rightly so. Energetic and enthusiastic, the chefs cultivate an inventive and fresh cuisine. Come here for full-flavored dishes that may include roast partridge with chestnut stuffing or wild duck with morel mushrooms and game gravy. You might also try the local favorite: saddle of hare with celeriac and a redwine sauce. Two of the best fish dishes are Dover sole with an olive cake and anchovy sauce or turbot with scallops flavored with red pepper and served with a saffron sauce

Llandewi Skirrid, east of Abergavenny. 📞 **01873/852797.** www.thewalnuttreeinn.com. Reservations recommended. Main courses £12–£24. MC, V. Tues–Sat noon–2:30pm and 7–10pm. Closed 2 weeks at Christmas. Take the B4521 4.8km (3 miles) east of Abergavenny.

Seeing the Sights

Only fragments of the 12th-century **Abergavenny Castle,** on Castle Street, remain, but a gruesome segment of its history is remembered. An early owner of the fortress, the Norman knight William de Braose, angered at the slaying of his brother-in-law by Welsh lords of Gwent, invited a group of them to dinner and had them murdered as they sat unarmed at his table. Visitors today fare much better. Admission is free, and it's open daily from dawn to dusk.

The **Abergavenny Museum,** Castle Street (© **01873/854282;** www.abergavenny museum.co.uk), is in a house attached to the 19th-century hunting lodge on the castle grounds. The museum contains archaeological artifacts, farming tools, and a fascinating collection of old prints and pictures. A Welsh farmhouse kitchen and the contents of an old saddler's shop are on display. Admission is free. The museum is open March to October, Monday to Saturday 11am to 1pm and 2 to 5pm, Sunday 2 to 5pm; and November to February, Monday to Saturday 11am to 1pm and 2 to 4pm.

St. Mary's Parish Church, Monk Street, is all that's left of a 12th-century Benedictine priory church. Little remains of the original Norman structure, as the building was redone from the 13th to the 15th century. It is believed that Cromwell's troops, who were billeted in Abergavenny for a while during the siege of Raglan Castle, did some damage to the church and its tombs. In the Herbert Chapel are a number of sarcophagi of lords of Abergavenny and family members, with requisite effigies on top. The oldest brass memorial in the church records a death in 1587. The 15th-century Jesse Tree in the Lewis Chapel is an unusual 3.4m-long (10-ft.) wood carving portraying Christ's family tree growing out of the body of Jesse, father of David. There is also a Norman font, as well as some 14th-century oak choir stalls. In spite of vandalism that has been committed in the church throughout the centuries, the building is kept open most days for worship and inspection; official hours are daily 9am to 7pm. For information, call the vicarage (© **01873/853168;** www.stmarys-priory.org).

Side Trips from Abergavenny

TINTERN ABBEY

The famous Wye Valley winds north from Chepstow, passing by the Lancaut Peninsula at the foot of the Windcliffe, a 243m (800-ft.) hill with striking views over the Severn estuary and the English border as far as the south part of the Cotswolds. About 1.6km (1 mile) or so farther north, you come to the little village of Tintern.

Now in magnificent ruins, **Tintern Abbey ★★** (© **01291/689251;** www.cadw. wales.gov.uk) is in the exact center of this riverside village and is the focal point of the town. The Cistercian abbey is one of the greatest monastic ruins of Wales, and it was only the second Cistercian foundation in Britain and the first in Wales. The abbey was founded in 1131 and was active until the Dissolution of the Monasteries by King Henry VIII. Most of the standing structure dates from the 13th century, when the abbey was almost entirely rebuilt. It became one of the richest and most important monastic houses in Wales. Wordsworth was one of the first to appreciate the serene beauty of the abbey remains, as his poetry attests.

Admission is £3.60 for adults and £3.20 for students, seniors, and children 5 to 16; it's £10 for a family ticket. The abbey is open March to May and October, daily 9:30am to 5pm; June to September, daily 9:30am to 6pm; and November to February,

Monday to Saturday 9:30am to 4pm and Sunday 11am to 4pm. There is ample parking quite near the entrance, and refreshments are available nearby.

To get here from Abergavenny, take the A40 east to Monmouth, from which you can connect with the A466 south along the trail of Offa's Dyke to Tintern.

HAY-ON-WYE

Yet another excursion is the 40km (25-mile) drive north to Hay-on-Wye, on the Welsh-English border. Book collectors from all over the world flock to this town, as its center contains more secondhand bookstores than anywhere else in the world.

The town has only 1,300 residents—the most well read in Britain—but nearly 50 bookshops. The tradition was started in 1961 by Richard Booth, who established a secondhand bookshop here. It became so popular that other shops continued opening, until books virtually took over the town—whenever a pub or a movie theater closed, it would become yet another bookshop.

The best time to visit is during the 10-day **Hay Festival** (www.hayfestival.com), attracting authors from all over the world. It is held toward the end of May, lasting through the first week of June. Tickets to hear writers such as Tina Brown or Martin Amis range in price from £9 to £28.

To get you started on your book hunt, head for **Hay Cinema Bookshop,** Castle Street (✆ **01497/820071**; www.haycinemabookshop.co.uk), converted from the town's former movie house. From art to zoology, there are 200,000 volumes here, with prices beginning at 50p, although certain rare books can run into the thousands of pounds. You can also visit **Boz Books**, 13A Castle St. (tel. **01497/821277;** www.bozbooks.demon.co.uk), established in 1989. It carriers a wide selection of first editions by Charles Dickens and other 19th-century authors such as Thomas Hardy; there are also books by Wales's own Dylan Thomas.

For lunch, try the **Granary**, Broad Street (✆ **01497/820790**), a wood-beamed former grain store near the town's clock tower. Look for specials on the blackboard menu, a series of handmade meat pies, fresh pastas, curries, casseroles, and great salads. Main courses range from £5to £10; hours are daily 9am to 5:30pm.

The local pub is the **Old Black Lion**, Lion Street (✆ **01497/820841;** www.oldblacklion.co.uk), dating from the 1600s. It serves bar food in an oak-beamed setting. The cuisine is rather sophisticated: everything from Moroccan lamb with couscous and an apricot and fig compote to peppered venison casserole. Hours are daily noon to 2pm and 6:30 to 9pm. You can also stay overnight here in one of the country-style bedrooms, starting at £45 in a double, £58 for the Cromwell Suite.

To get to Hay-on-Wye, follow A40 north from Abergavenny, continuing north along the A479 until you see the cutoff road (B4350) into Hay-on-Wye, at the English border.

BRECON & BRECON BEACONS NATIONAL PARK

275km (171 miles) W of London; 64km (40 miles) N of Cardiff

The busy little market town of Brecon is the main base for touring Brecon Beacons National Park. Brecon, situated where the Usk and Honddu rivers meet, is the center of a farming section.

The Romans thought the area was a good place for a military encampment to discourage the Celts, and in A.D. 75 they built a fort, **Y Gaer,** about 4km (2½ miles) west of the present town. To get to Y Gaer, you walk across private farm fields. You can look around for free.

Brecon Castle, built in 1093, is practically nonexistent, but it was militarily important when Llywelyn the Great and later Owain Glyndwr were battling against outsiders who wanted sovereignty in Wales. However, at the close of the civil war after Cromwell's visitations, the people of Brecon, tired of centuries of strife, pulled the castle down. All that's left is a section of wall joined to the Castle of Brecon Hotel and the Ely Tower, named for the bishop of Ely imprisoned there by Richard III. Access to the ruins is free, and there's no time limit on when it can be viewed. Oddly, it lies on the grounds of the Castle of Brecon Hotel and requires a transit through the hotel lobby to view it.

Of special interest is the fortified red-sandstone priory church of St. John the Evangelist, with its massive tower, now the **Brecon Cathedral,** Priory Hill (© **01874/623857;** www.breconcathedral.org.uk). It stands high above the River Honddu. The oldest parts of the cathedral date from the 12th century. It's open daily 8am to 6:30pm; admission is free.

Essentials

GETTING THERE   Sixty-Sixty Coaches (© **01443/692060;** www.sixtysixty. co.uk) runs buses from Cardiff to Brecon, taking 90 minutes. Connections are also made from Merthry Tydfil, taking 40 minutes.

If you're driving from Cardiff, head north along A470.

VISITOR INFORMATION   The **Brecon Tourist Information Centre,** in the Cattle Market Car Park (© **01874/622485;** www.brecon-beacons.com), is open in summer, daily 9:30am to 5:30pm; in winter, Monday to Friday 9:30am to 5pm, Saturday and Sunday 9:30am to 4pm.

Where to Stay & Dine

All of the following establishments, with the exception of Cantre Selyf, serve lunch and dinner and are open to nonguests.

EXPENSIVE

Llangoed Hall Hotel ★★★   Sir Bernard Ashley, widower of Laura Ashley, presides over one of the great country houses of Wales. In the Wye Valley, 18km (11 miles) northeast of Brecon, the house opens onto panoramic views of the Black Mountains. A former Jacobean manor house, it was redesigned in 1912 by the celebrated architect Cloug Williams-Ellis, who wanted to evoke the aura of a great Edwardian country-house party. Sir Bernard has gone even beyond the Edwardians in this fantasy, creating grand luxury—with the help of floor-to-ceiling Laura Ashley fabrics, of course, and his own personal art collection. The individually decorated bedrooms and suites are spacious and elegant, with Laura Ashley fabrics at every turn.

Serving everything from Welsh lamb to freshly caught salmon, the restaurant at Llangoed Hall has the most refined cuisine in the area. You can make a reservation to enjoy a superb dinner for £40 per person.

Llyswen, Brecons, Powys LD3 0YP. © **01874/754525.** Fax 01874/754545. www.llangoedhall.com. 23 units. £120–£350 double; £385–£400 suite. Rates include Welsh breakfast. AE, DC, MC, V. On A470,

CARDIFF & SOUTH WALES   Brecon & Brecon Beacons National Park

3.2km (2 miles) northwest of Llyswen. **Amenities:** Restaurant; room service; 2 outdoor tennis courts. *In room:* TV, hair dryer.

Peterstone Court Hotel ★★   Your nest in the Brecons might be this pocket of luxury, with a gray-stone exterior, manicured lawns, the best spa in the area, and an outdoor heated pool. In cool weather, you might be found sipping a sherry before an open fire in the bar. In summer, you can take afternoon tea on the terrace. In the distance, the River Usk glides by. The eight rooms in the main house are spacious and handsomely furnished, and a converted stable contains four loft rooms that are larger than most London apartments. The building itself is Georgian; Charles I might have stayed at the original Peterstone Court.

Llanhamlach, Brecon, Powys LD3 7YB. ✆ **01874/665387.** Fax 01874/665376. www.peterstone-court. com. 12 units. £110–£220 double. AE, MC, V. Free parking. **Amenities:** Restaurant; bar; Jacuzzi. *In room:* TV, hair dryer.

MODERATE

Felin Fach Griffin Inn ★ ■■   This is an exceptional discovery for Wales, much of it looking as if you'd wandered back through a time portal. Old-fashioned though it may look, it is absolutely comfortable and up-to-date. Crisp white linens and soft goose-down pillows top ornate beds placed on stripped floorboards, making you want to linger in bed long into the morning. All rooms are beautifully maintained and quietly elegant, and three have four-poster beds.

Felin Fach, Brecon, Powys LD3 0UB. ✆ **01874/620111.** Fax 01874/620120. www.eatdrinksleep.ltd.uk. 7 units. £110–£155 double. Rates include full breakfast. MC, V. Free parking. On A470, directly east of Brecon. **Amenities:** Restaurant; bar; room service. *In room:* Hair dryer.

Nant Ddu Lodge ★ ☺   This is your best bet for staying in the heart of the Brecon Beacons National Park. Originally built as a shooting lodge during the 19th century for Lord Tredegar, its name translates as "Black Stream," but that is hardly meant to suggest pollution, as its situation is idyllic for walking, climbing, fishing, and escaping from urban pressures. Though unified with a common hunter's theme, each of the small to midsize bedrooms is different from its neighbor. There are panoramic views of the mountains from all units. Family rooms with sofa beds are available.

Diners can choose between the busy Bistro, the hotel's restaurant, and the intimate bar.

Cwm Taf, Brecon, Powys CF48 2HY. ✆ **01685/379111.** Fax 01685/377088. www.nant-ddu-lodge.co.uk. 31 units. £90–£100 double; £125 suite. Rates include buffet breakfast. AE, MC, V. Free parking. Beside the A470, 8km (5 miles) north of Merthyr Tydfil and 19km (12 miles) south of Brecon. **Amenities:** Bistro; bar; exercise room; indoor heated pool; room service; spa. *In room:* TV, hair dryer.

Three Cocks Hotel ★ ◢   This 15th-century inn, surrounded by the countryside of the Brecon Beacons, is one of the best-known little inns of Wales—and it deserves its fame. As you pass through the tiny hamlet of Three Cocks, don't blink, or you might miss the inn. The place is really small but has a certain charm. It's a stone building, which over the years has incorporated the trunk of a live tree into one of its walls. Downstairs is an elegant paneled drawing room, while upstairs are midsize bedrooms that have modern furnishings. Throughout the inn are rich furnishings such as antiques, Oriental rugs, and oil paintings; log fires burn on chilly nights.

The Three Cocks is known throughout the area for the high-quality fare served in both its elegant restaurant and pub.

Three Cocks, Brecon, Powys LD3 0SL. ⓒ **01497/847215.** Fax 01497/847339. www.threecockshotel.
com. 7 units. £85–£95 double. Rates include Welsh breakfast. MC, V. On A438, 18km (11 miles) northeast
of Brecon and 6.4km (4 miles) southwest of Hay-on-Wye. **Amenities:** Restaurant. *In room:* No phone.

INEXPENSIVE

Cantre Selyf ★ 🎒 One of the historic properties of Brecon, this town house
dates from the 17th century. Close to St. Mary's Church, the Georgian house is one
of the most convenient locations in town. When viewed only from the front, the
property looks rather small, but it's a nice spread, complete with a large walled garden enclosed by a Norman wall. Much of the 17th-century architecture remains
inside, although subsequent additions were made in the following century. The
bedrooms have beamed ceilings, cast-iron beds, and Georgian fireplaces. You can
meet your fellow guests in the formal sitting room.

5 Lion St., Brecon, Powys LD3 7AU. ⓒ **01874/622904.** Fax 01874/625951. www.cantreselyf.co.uk. 3
units. £72–£82 double. Rates include full breakfast. AE, MC, V. Closed Dec. **Amenities:** Bar; room service.
In room: TV, hair dryer.

Griffin Inn ★ 🎣 Though hardly in the league of Llangoed (see above), this little
oasis is infinitely more affordable. Outside Brecon, it was originally constructed in
the 15th century as a cider house. Today, it's one of the oldest inns in the Upper Wye
Valley. It's popular with fishermen hoping to get lucky while casting into the River
Wye, and lake fishing, pony trekking, and hiking are part of the summer fun in the
Brecon Beacons. Behind the inn's ivy-covered facade, four generations of the Stock-
ton family have received guests, offering them tidy bedrooms and good pub grub. We
gravitate to the small to midsize bedrooms and their somewhat cramped bathrooms,
soaking up the atmosphere of old beams and exposed stonework.

Good, unfussy food is served in both the restaurant and the Fisherman's Bar. A
few years ago, the Griffin was voted "Britain's Pub of the Year," so drinking is big
here, and the food is popular with locals.

Llyswen, Brecon, Powys LD3 0UR. ⓒ **01874/754241.** Fax 01874/754592. www.griffininnllyswen.co.uk.
7 units. £70–£90 double. MC, V. Located 16km (10 miles) northeast of Brecon, at the junction of A4079
and A470. **Amenities:** Restaurant; bar. *In room:* TV.

Exploring the Park

Brecon Beacons National Park ★★★ comprises 835 sq. km (519 sq. miles) of
land from the Black Mountains in the east to the Black Mountain in the west.
National parks in the British Isles are maintained differently from those in the
United States. Here, people own land, live, and work within the park boundaries,
though the landscape is safeguarded, and access to the park area is provided.

The national park takes its name from the Brecon Beacons mountain range in the
center of the park area. Pen y Fan, the highest peak in the range, rises to nearly
914m (3,000 ft.). The park contains sandstone moors covered with bracken and
limestone crags with wooded gorges. Vast stretches of open common land lie in
pastoral country. Farming is the main industry of the park. You can enjoy drives over
the mountains, but walking and pony trekking are the best ways to explore the area,
which encompasses nature reserves, a mountain center, and 51km (32 miles) of
canal. The limestone area contains Britain's deepest cave system. A number of
ancient monuments and historic buildings lie within the park boundaries.

For information regarding the park and its facilities, contact one of the many **National Park Information Centres** listed at www.breconbeacons.org/visit-us/information-centres-new. Information numbers include ℂ **01873/853254** in Abergavenny and ℂ **01550/720693** in Llandovery.

The **National Park Visitor Centre** (ℂ **01874/623366**; www.brecon-beacons.com), near Libanus, 8km (5 miles) southwest of Brecon, offers a good point from which to begin your tour of the park. The spacious center has displays explaining the major points of interest, talks and films, an informative staff, a picnic area, a refreshments buffet, and toilets. The entire building is wheelchair accessible.

The center is open daily, except Christmas Day, from 9:30am; the buffet is open from 10:30am (10am July–Aug). Closing times vary according to the time of year: It shuts its doors at 5pm March to June, September, and October; at 6pm July and August; and at 4:30pm November to February. Closing is a half-hour later on Saturday, Sunday, and bank holidays from April to June and in September. The buffet closing time varies, so check when you arrive.

Over the millennia, the force of flowing water has carved underground caverns through the extensive limestone regions in the southwestern portions of the park. Experienced cavers can explore many of these by making arrangements with one of the caving clubs, through the National Park Information Centres. However, only the **Dan-yr-Ogof Showcaves,** part of the **National Showcaves Centre for Wales,** Abercraf (ℂ **01639/730801**; www.showcaves.co.uk), are open to the general public, including children. Midway between Brecon and Swansea on the A4067, this is the largest commercial cave complex in Western Europe. Visitors are able to follow dry, firm walkways to see stalagmite and stalactite formations under floodlights. The **Dinosaur Park** is filled with life-size models of creatures that disappeared 65 million years ago. Children are especially awed by the massive reptiles, particularly by one of the oldest—and the most terrifying—dinosaurs, Tyrannosaurus rex.

Tours through Dan-yr-Ogof, Cathedral Cave, Bone Cave, and the Dinosaur Park last about 2½ hours. The complex is open from Easter through October, daily from 10am to 3pm (until 5pm in high season). The charge is £13 for adults, £7 for kids 3 to 16, and free for kids 2 and under. Admission also includes an open farm where people can mingle with the animals, a re-created Iron Age village, a replica of an ancient stone circle, and a horse center. Facilities include a restaurant, crafts shop, museum, dry-ski slope, and information center.

Brecon Beacons National Park's southern boundary is 40km (25 miles) from Cardiff, 23km (14 miles) from Swansea, and 16km (10 miles) from Newport. Abergavenny lies on the eastern boundary.

SWANSEA & THE GOWER PENINSULA ★

307km (190 miles) W of London; 131km (82 miles) W of Bristol; 64km (40 miles) W of Cardiff

Vikings, Normans, English, Welsh, industry, seaport activity, holiday magic, and cultural prominence—all have combined to make the Swansea of today. It's tough, bold, and fun. Parks abound, and the tender loving care bestowed on them has caused Swansea to be a winner of the "Wales in Bloom" award year after year.

Swansea entered recorded history some 800 years ago, bearing a Viking name believed to be derived from "Sweyn's ey," or Sweyn's island. The Sweyn in question may well have been Sweyn Forkbeard, king of Denmark (987–1014), known to have been active in the Bristol Channel. Normans founded the marcher lordship of Gower, with its capital at Swansea, and a small trading community grew up here, as seagoing business, including coal exportation, became important through the Middle Ages. In the early 18th century at the town at the mouth of the River Tawe (Swansea's Welsh name is Abertawe), copperworks began to be built, and soon it was the copper capital of the world, as well as a leading European center for zinc refining, tin plating, steel making, and many chemical activities.

This "ugly, lovely city," as native son Dylan Thomas described it, has today pretty well obliterated the ugliness. Devastation of the town center by German air raids during World War II led to complete rebuilding. Traditional industries in the lower Swansea Valley have vanished, leaving economic woes and an industrial wasteland. Reclamation and redevelopment, however, have long been underway. The leveling of old mine tips and slag heaps and the planting of trees in their stead points to a more attractive Swansea for both today and tomorrow. Clean industries are coming in, but they are being placed out in wooded areas and suitable industrial parks, and they do not cast a pall over the city. Nonetheless, if your time clock allows for only one of the major cities of South Wales, make it Cardiff.

Essentials

GETTING THERE   Trains arrive from both Cardiff and London every hour throughout the day. The trip takes about 1 hour from Cardiff, about 3 hours from London. For reservations and information, call © **0845/748-4950** or visit **www.nationalrail.co.uk**. The Swansea rail station is on High Street.

National Express (© **0871/781-8181;** www.nationalexpress.com) operates buses that arrive in Swansea from London, Manchester, Birmingham, and Cardiff. Many of these connections include stops with about an hour's wait.

From Cardiff, motorists can continue west along the M4.

VISITOR INFORMATION   The **Swansea Tourist Information Centre,** Plymouth Street (© **01792/468321;** www.visitswanseabay.com), is open year-round, Monday to Saturday 9:30am to 5:30pm. From Easter to September, it's also open Sunday 10am to 4pm.

GETTING AROUND   Swansea is served by a good bus network, with buses leaving from the Quadrant Bus Station, at the Quadrant Shopping Centre. Bus nos. 4, X12, X13, 25, and 404 link the train station at 35 High St. and the bus station. For bus schedules and information, call © **0870/608-2608** or visit **www.firstgroup.com**.

Because distances are usually short, you can consider calling a taxi—either **Data Cabs** (© **01792/474747;** www.datacabs.com) or **Swallow Cabs** (© **01792/895533**).

Where to Stay

Fairyhill ★   If you want to escape from the world, head to this stone-built 18th-century manor set on 10 hectares (25 acres) of wooded grounds that also hold a lake and a fishing stream. It's an ideal base for exploring not only Swansea but also the little-populated Gower Peninsula, which juts out into the British Channel west of

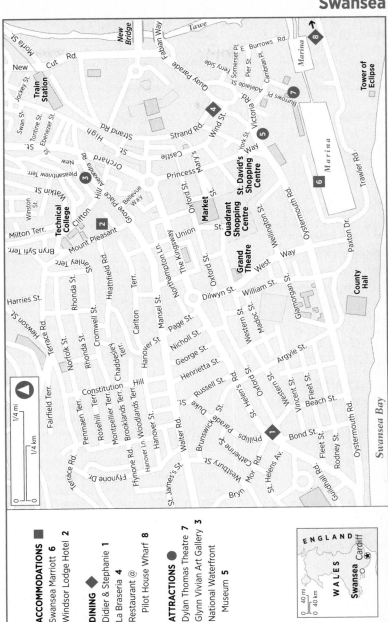

Swansea

ACCOMMODATIONS
Swansea Marriott **6**
Windsor Lodge Hotel **2**

DINING
Didier & Stephanie **1**
La Braseria **4**
Restaurant @
Pilot House Wharf **8**

ATTRACTIONS
Dylan Thomas Theatre **7**
Glynn Vivian Art Gallery **3**
National Waterfront
Museum **5**

Swansea and offers a good deal of natural beauty. After passing through a sumptu-ously appointed lounge, you are directed to one of the individually styled bed-rooms—most of them of medium size. Crackling log fires and deep-cushioned sofas create the aura of a cozy, snug country house. A real "taste of Wales" emerges from the menu.

Reynoldston, Swansea SA3 1BS. ✆ **01792/390139.** Fax 01792/391358. www.fairyhill.net. 8 units. £175–£275 double. Rates include Welsh breakfast. MC, V. Located outside Reynoldston, off the A4118 from Swansea (18km/11 miles). No children under 8. **Amenities:** Restaurant; brasserie; bar; room service. *In room:* TV/DVD, CD player, MP3 docking station.

Swansea Marriott ★★ This is the town's premier choice—with the best ameni-ties, the most dramatic location, and the most luxurious bedrooms. The four-story structure lies on the marina, opening onto panoramic views over the bay. By Swansea standards, it is large and bustling, attracting an equal mix of business clients and visitors. The hotel offers spacious bedrooms and roomy bathrooms, all immaculate and comfortable.

Maritime Quarter, Swansea SA1 3SS. ✆ **800/228-9290** in the U.S. and Canada, or 01792/642020. Fax 01792/650345. www.swanseamarriott.co.uk. 119 units. £125–£195 double. Rates include buffet breakfast. AE, DC, MC, V. Free parking. **Amenities:** Restaurant; bar; concierge; exercise room; Jacuzzi; indoor heated pool; room service; sauna. *In room:* A/C, TV, hair dryer, minibar, Wi-Fi (£7.50 per day).

Windsor Lodge Hotel Architecturally undistinguished, this is nonetheless a welcoming family-run hotel that is close to the town center and about a 5-minute walk from the train station. The building itself is 2 centuries old and has been shel-tering wayfarers to Swansea for decades. The hotel offers good value, with cozy accommodations, decent furnishings, modern decor, and tidy bathrooms. Your hosts maintain midsize bedrooms that are well cared for and provide a good night's sleep.

Mt. Pleasant, Swansea SA1 6EG. ✆ **01792/642158.** Fax 01792/648996. www.windsor-lodge.co.uk. 19 units. £60–£70 double. Rates include breakfast. AE, DC, MC, V. **Amenities:** Restaurant; bar; Internet (free, in lobby); room service. *In room:* TV.

Where to Dine

Didier & Stephanie ★ FRENCH Swansea, believe it or not, is becoming known for its fine dining, as exemplified by this sophisticated restaurant where you might see Michael Douglas and his wife, Catherine Zeta-Jones, popping in for a visit on one of their frequent visits to her hometown. Inside this little Swansea house, you'll encounter a cozy, welcoming decor and a tempting menu of Gallic-inspired recipes that often utilize Welsh-grown fresh produce. Start with the smoked duck breast or the terrine of rabbit in a Cumberland sauce, perhaps followed with such specialties as a rosemary-flavored rack of Welsh lamb or something from the local sea.

56 St. Helen's Rd. ✆ **01792/655603.** Reservations required. Main courses £17–£23. AE, DC, MC, V. Tues-Sat noon-2pm and 7-9pm.

La Braseria SPANISH No, this is not Madrid, although this Spanish bodega (in Swansea, of all places), lying only a 5-minute walk from the train station, evokes thoughts of sunny Spain. It's a marvelous change of pace after you've had too many leeks and too much Welsh lamb. The food, prepared daily from fresh ingredients, complements the list of Spanish wines and champagne; this is not the place for "lager louts." Come instead for the town's best chargrilled meats: Tossed on that grill is everything from tender suckling pig to ostrich to great chunks of beef. Flavors are straightforward here, as the cooks don't like to mess up their grills with a lot of sauces. Likewise, they prepare the catch of the day in the same manner, be it shark, bass, or snapper. In addition to items from the grill, you might opt for a savory kettle of mussels. Specific choices change according to the seasons, the availability of ingredients, and the inspirations of the kitchen.

28 Wind St. © **01792/469683.** www.labraseria.com. Reservations accepted for large parties only. Main courses £8–£22. AE, DC, MC, V. Mon–Sat noon–2:30pm and 7–11:30pm.

Restaurant @ Pilot House Wharf ★ MODERN BRITISH/SEAFOOD   In the former pilot house at the Swansea Marina, this seafood restaurant lies above a fishing tackle shop. It couldn't be more maritime, and it features some of the freshest and best seafood in Wales, each dish based on the catch of the day. The owner says that the fishermen "land their catch within a salmon's leap of my back door." That's how fresh it is. Most of the dishes are solidly British, but there are a few Mediterranean touches as well. If you don't feel like seafood, other full-flavor options include pot-roasted free-range chicken with smoked bacon, braised half shoulder of Welsh lamb, and roast breast of pheasant accompanied by black pudding and a Calvados sauce. A haunch of venison that would have pleased Henry VIII also appears on the menu, with a sauce made of plums and Jack Daniel's.

Trawler's Rd., Swansea. © **01792/466200.** Reservations recommended. Main courses £15–£24. DC, MC, V. Daily noon–2pm; Mon–Sat 6:30–9:30pm.

Seeing the Sights

In a once-dirty waterfront area, a **Maritime Quarter** has emerged. Lying between the city center and the seafront, it is centered on the historic South Dock and its Half Tide Basin and is complete with urban villages and a modern marina on the Swansea Yacht Haven. Open spaces, a promenade, and a seawall round out the scene.

The chief attraction here is the **National Waterfront Museum ★★**, Oystermouth Road (© **01792/638950;** www.waterfrontmuseum.co.uk), open daily 10am to 5pm, charging no admission. Bus no. 118 runs here from the center of town. It's altogether fitting that Swansea has a maritime museum. After all, the copper plates that sheathed the hulls of the British fleet, making Nelson's ships faster than their enemies, were cast in Swansea. The exhibits are vast, including a display of the steel rails, produced in Dowlaid, which opened up the American Midwest in the mid-1800s.

The museum explores the history of industrial Wales through a series of exhibits—Wales, incidentally, was the world's first industrial nation. Transportation is strong here, including a Cardiff-built monoplane and a full-size replica of the famous Peny-darren locomotive. The story of immigration and emigration in Wales is also told, with a focus on how the metal and coal industries created wealth, attracting workers to Wales while also making Welsh expertise an exportable commodity to other countries.

The Maritime Quarter is also home to a statue of Dylan Thomas and the nearby **Dylan Thomas Theatre,** 7 Gloucester Place (© **01792/473238;** www.dylan thomastheatre.org.uk). Many different types of plays are presented here (check the local newspapers for listings), not just works by Dylan Thomas. The poet was born in the Uplands, a residential area of Swansea, at 5 Cwmdonkin Dr., a steep street off Walter Road. You can walk in **Cwmdonkin Park** (pronounced *Quam*-don-kin) close by, which the poet made famous in his writings.

Swansea is one of the few Welsh cities to have a beach within walking distance of the center. A **promenade** leads all the way to Oystermouth, 6.4km (4 miles) away, although you can drive the route on the A4067. Along the way, you pass rugby and cricket grounds and the entrance to the city's largest park, **Singleton.** About halfway down the bay is a 9-hole golf course and a well-equipped resort beach, in an area known as **Blackpill.** It includes the entrances to the city's country park, Clyne Valley, and the Clyne Gardens. Before long, you come to the villages of Westcross and Norton, and then comes **Oystermouth,** which has a Norman castle renowned for its imposing position on a headland, commanding a view of the bay and Swansea.

Eight kilometers (5 miles) south of Swansea, across Swansea Bay, lies the **Mumbles ★**. It has been compared to the Bay of Naples because of its shape and beauty, especially after dark. This former fishing village has two faces (both pleasing): By day it has a tranquil atmosphere, but when the sun goes down, Mumbles bursts into action and becomes a nightlife center, with crowded pubs, clubs, and restaurants. Mumbles has been attracting tourists since Victorian times, when the handsome pier was built, as in most British sea towns. It protrudes 274m (900 ft.) from Mumbles Head into the bay and affords sweeping views. Away from the seafront, you can see fishermen's tiny cottages built into the limestone rock. Souvenirs and examples of local crafts are in shops that cling to the hillside. Yachting, swimming, fishing, beach games, and bowling are enjoyed here.

Glynn Vivian Art Gallery ★ 🎁   Founded in 1911, although little known, this gallery is one of the treasure-troves of art in Wales. It was created by Richard Glynn Vivian, scion of a copper industrialist family. An inveterate traveler and art collector, he wanted to pass on his treasures to the world. The special reason to visit is to see the 20th-century collection of Welsh artists, including Ceri Richards, Josef Herman, and Evan Walters. We are especially fond of Alfred Janes's penetrating portrait of Dylan Thomas, painted in 1964. There are also displays of elegant porcelain and pottery, both European and Asian. On-site is an unusual gift shop with a selection of original works by Welsh artists, including ceramics, glass, and jewelry.

Alexandra Rd. ⓒ **01792/516900.** www.swansea.gov.uk. Free admission. Tues–Sun 10am–5pm.

Swansea After Dark

Long gone are the days when Swansea's nocturnal entertainment consisted of a handful of battered pubs with a jukebox blaring out pre-Beatles tunes. Since the 1990s gentrification of many areas of Swansea's central core, there has been an explosion of nightlife options, many of them focusing on the city's nightlife-related pride and joy—**Wind Street.** (That rhymes with "wined and dined," incidentally.) The best way to explore the place involves popping in and out of the pubs, bars, and shops along this cobble-covered thoroughfare, especially on evenings when the city council has blocked off traffic, transforming it into a pedestrian-only walkway that on weekend evenings gets very crowded.

One of our favorites is the **Bank Statement,** 57–58 Wind St. (ⓒ **01792/455477;** www.jdwetherspoon.co.uk), a pub and restaurant contained within the grandly ornate premises of what was built as a bank during the Victorian age. More self-consciously trendy, evoking a hip bar in faraway London, is the **No Sign Wine Bar,**

56 Wind St. (℡ **01792/465300**), where you're likely to see off-duty members of the local TV news team, sampling whatever French, Chilean, or California vintage happens to be uncorked at the moment.

Other streets—each nearby, but none as densely packed with bars and restaurants as Wind Street—also have goodly numbers of nightlife offerings. **Exchange Bar,** 10 Strand (℡ **01792/462896**), offers glimpses of Ireland, with live music and generous amounts of Celtic *joie de vivre.* The **Potters Wheel,** 85–86 The Kingsway (℡ **01792/465113;** www.jdwetherspoon.co.uk), a member of the same chain as the above-mentioned Bank Statement, offers food and drink in a setting that's nostalgically evocative of turn-of-the-20th-century Wales.

In addition to the **Dylan Thomas Theatre** (see above), Swansea has a cultural side as well. The **Grand Theatre,** Singleton Street (℡ **01792/475715;** www.swansea.gov.uk), adjacent to the Quadrant Shopping Centre, is a Victorian theater that has been refurbished and redeveloped into a multimillion-dollar complex. The venue hosts international opera, ballet, and theater companies, plus 1-night stands that often feature internationally known entertainers. It also has its own schools of song and dance.

Side Trips from Swansea

THE GOWER PENINSULA ★

The first area in Britain designated "an area of outstanding natural beauty," Gower is a broad peninsula stretching about 22km (14 miles) from the Mumbles to Worms Head in the west. This attraction begins 6.4km (4 miles) west of Swansea on A4067. The coastline of Gower starts at Bracelet Bay, just around the corner from the Mumbles. You can drive—at least to some parts of the peninsula—but the best way to see its sometimes-rugged, sometimes-flat coast is to walk, even for short distances, if you don't have time to make the complete circuit.

There are many and varied beaches on Gower: **Caswell Bay,** with its acres of smooth, golden sand and safe swimming; **Langland,** a family attraction with facilities for golf, swimming, tennis, and surfing; and **Rotherslade,** which, at high tide, features some of the largest waves around the peninsula crashing onto the shore. Secluded **Pwll-du** is a place to sunbathe in solitude, despite the crowds elsewhere along the coast, and there are numerous other small coves tucked away beneath the cliffs. For beach devotees, **Three Cliffs Bay ★**, on the south peninsula, is hailed as one of the best beaches in Wales, if not the best. A public footpath leads down to these golden sands, although you may find the waters a bit chilly even in July. Adjoining Three Cliffs Bay is **Tor Bay** and **Crawley Wood.**

Popular with families is the beach at **Oxwich Bay,** one of the largest on the peninsula, with 4.8km (3 miles) of uninterrupted sand where you can enjoy picnics, water-skiing, sailing, and windsurfing. Oxwich village, at one end of the bay, is a typical Gower hamlet of cottages and tree-lined lanes. Tired of the beach? You can explore the coastline of rocky coves. There is also a nature reserve here that is home to some rare orchid species.

After the commercial and often-crowded Oxwich beach, you may be happy to see **Slade,** which has to be approached on foot down a steep set of steps. The spotless beach is usually wind-free. Around the next corner, you'll find the villages of **Horton** and **Port Eynon,** with a long, curving beach backed by sand dunes. Refreshments are available on the beach, and after dark you can patronize one of the pubs in either village. Sometimes live music is offered. Our favorites are the **Ship Inn** (© **01792/390204**) and the **Smuggler's Haunt** (© **01792/391257**), both at Port Eynon.

From Port Eynon, a spectacular 7.2km (4.5-mile) cliff walk leads past Culver Hole, Paviland Cave, Mewslade, and Fall Bay to Worms Head and Rhossili. The **Paviland Caves** can be explored. It is here that 100,000-year-old human remains have been found. **Worms Head** is a twisted outcrop of rock shaped into the form that sometimes, depending on the tides, looks like a prehistoric worm sticking its head up out of the water. **Rhossili** is a long, sweeping bay and a beach reached from the treeless village of Rhossili, with a church and houses perched 61m (200 ft.) up on the cliff tops. This is an international center for hang gliding. Halfway along the beach at Llangennith is the most popular surfing site on the peninsula. Rolling dunes connect it with Broughton Bay and Whitford Sands, and eventually you come to **Penclawdd,** a little village where a centuries-old cockle industry still thrives. If the tide is right, you can see the pickers with their rakes and buckets gleaning the crustaceans from the flats.

Although the coastal attractions are Gower's biggest lure, there are pleasant farms, attractive country roads, and places of interest inland. **Parc le Breos (Giant's Grave)** burial chamber, almost in the center of the peninsula, close to Parkmill on the A4118, is an ancient legacy from Stone Age people. The remains of at least four people have been found here. A central passage and four chambers are in a cairn about 21m (70 ft.) long. **Pennard Castle** has suffered under the ravages of weather and time, but from the north you can see the curtain wall almost intact; admission is free.

On North Gower, **Weobley Castle,** Llanrhidian (© **01792/390012**), is actually a fortified house rather than a castle. There was no space for a garrison, and the rooms were for domestic purposes. On the northern edge of bare upland country, it overlooks the Llanrhidian marshes and the Loughor estuary. There are still substantial remains of this 13th- and 14th-century stronghold, and the view is panoramic. Weobley is off the Llanrhidian-Cheriton road, 11km (7 miles) west of Gowerton. It is open daily 9:30am to 6pm (closes at 5pm in winter). Entrance costs £2.70 for adults, £2.30 for students and children 16 and younger.

Even though it is protected from development, Gower has been invaded by caravans (mobile homes), recreational vehicles, beach huts, retirement homes, and bungalows. Nevertheless, you can still find solitude in secluded bays and especially in the center of the peninsula, along the Cefn Bryn ridge or on Rhossili Down. From the top of **Cefn Bryn,** 185m (609 ft.) above sea level, you can see the entire peninsula and far beyond on clear days. By taking the Green Road, which runs the length of the ridge from Penmaen, you'll find a path about 1km (½ mile) east of Reynoldston that leads to **Arthur's Stone,** a circular burial chamber. The mound of earth that once covered it has been weathered away, but you can see the huge capstone that protected the burial place. From Rhossili Down, at 192m (632 ft.), the English coast comes into view. Here also are megalithic tombs, cairns, and barrows.

LAUGHARNE: MEMORIES OF DYLAN THOMAS

Laugharne (pronounced *Larne*), 24km (15 miles) east of Tenby, is a hamlet overlooking broad waters. This ancient township, on the estuary fed by the River Taf (not be confused with the River Taff in Cardiff) and the River Cywyn, was for centuries a bone of contention between Welsh, English, Cromwellians, and royal supporters. However, it did not come into the limelight of public attention until after the death of its adopted son, Swansea-born Dylan Thomas, and his acclaim as one of the great poets of the 20th century.

To get here, head west from Swansea along the A4070, which becomes the A484 signposted north to Carmarthen. Once in Carmarthen, continue west along the A40 to St. Clears, where you cut southeast along the A4066 to Laugharne.

The poet is buried in the churchyard near the **Parish Church of St. Martin,** which you pass as you drive into town. A simple wooden cross marks his grave. A visit to the church is worthwhile. It dates from the 14th century and is entered through a lych-gate (iron gate), with the entrance to the church guarded by ancient yew trees. Memorial stones and carvings are among the interesting things to see.

The **Dylan Thomas Boathouse** ★ (✆ **01994/427420;** www.dylanthomas boathouse.com), along a little path named Dylan's Walk, is the waterside house where the author lived with his wife, Caitlin, and their children until his death in 1953 during a visit to America. In the boathouse, a white-painted little three-story structure wedged between the hill and the estuary, you can see the family's rooms, photographs, interpretive panels on Thomas's life and works, an audio and audiovisual presentation that portrays him reading some of his work, a small art gallery, a book and record shop, and a little tearoom where you can have tea and Welsh cakes while you listen to the poet's voice and look out over the tranquil waters of the wide estuary. On the way along the path, before you come to the boathouse, there's a little shack where this untidy wretch of a man wrote many of his minor masterpieces. You can't enter it, but you can look through an opening and see his built-in plank desk. Wadded-up scraps of paper on the floor give the feeling that he may have just stepped out to visit a favorite pub. Admission to the boathouse is £3.75 for adults, £2.95 for seniors, £1.75 for children 7 to 16, and free for kids under 7. Hours are May to October, daily 10am to 5:30pm, and November to April, daily 10:30am to 3:30pm.

Laugharne Castle, a handsome ruin called the home of the "Last Prince of Wales," sits on the estuary at the edge of the town. A castle here, Aber Corran, was first mentioned in 1113, believed to have been built by the great Welsh leader Rhys ap Gruffydd. The present romantic ruins date from Tudor times. Dylan Thomas described the then-ivy-mantled structure as a "castle brown as owls."

National Botanic Garden of Wales ★   Lying 32km (20 miles) northwest of Swansea, this mammoth project is the first modern botanic garden in Britain dedicated to science, education, and leisure. A project costing £45 million, this 229-hectare (568-acre) Regency estate was developed by financier William Paxton in the late 18th century, with walled gardens, lakes, and cascades. Its centerpiece is a magnificent Great Glasshouse, the largest single-span greenhouse in the world, blending in naturally with the rolling and bucolic Tywi Valley. The greenhouse is dedicated to threatened Mediterranean climates of the world, and its interior includes a ravine, rock faces, bridges, and waterfalls.

Middleton Hall, Llanarthne. ✆ **01558/668768.** www.gardenofwales.org.uk. Mar–Oct admission £8 adults, £6.50 seniors, £4 children 5–16, £20 family ticket; Nov–Feb £5 adults, £3 seniors, free for children 16 and younger. Mar–Oct daily 10am–6pm (last admission at 5pm); Nov–Feb daily 10am–4:30pm (last admission at 3:30pm).

Where to Dine

Stable Door Restaurant ★ TAPAS/SPANISH   A stable block in days gone by, this is the finest dining choice in the area, serving Mediterranean-style meals with taste and flair. It operates behind walls that were originally built in the 14th century to house horses Edward I brought from England during the construction of a nearby castle. Later, Oliver Cromwell's forces shot cannon into it when the masters of the castle switched their loyalties back to the Royalist side. Today, it's the most likable and enjoyable restaurant in the area, serving a menu of fresh ingredients that is varied and artfully prepared. Chefs prepare the best tapas in the south of Wales, along with starters such as a platter of bell peppers with ricotta, feta cheese, sun-dried tomatoes, and olives. One of our favorites is fried potatoes with a chili-and-garlic sauce, given extra flavor by a homemade tomato sauce. Filet of beef skewers are marinated with cumin and served with red-onion marmalade. Skewers of chicken are marinated in spices and herbs and served with a peanut sauce.

Market Lane. © **01994/427777.** www.laugharne-restaurant.co.uk. Reservations recommended. Main courses £8–£22. MC, V. Thurs–Sun noon–2pm and 6–9pm. Closed Jan–Feb 14.

PEMBROKESHIRE

This county boasts Britain's smallest national park, Pembrokeshire Coast National Park. It's unique in that it extends over cliff and beaches, whereas most parks encompass mountains or hill country. The coastline takes in 290km (180 miles) of sheer rugged beauty, with towering cliffs and turbulent waters. **Tenby** is the chief resort for exploring the park, but **Pembroke** and **St. Davids** also make worthy stopovers.

A Word About Welsh

"Let me not understand you, then; speak it in Welsh."

—Shakespeare's *Henry IV*

Of all the Celtic languages still in use, Welsh is spoken by the greatest number of people, although most Welsh men or women also speak English. It is not a dialect of English, as commonly believed, but a distinct language with its own pedigree that is older than English.

An Indo-European language, Welsh is more allied to French, German, and the Scandinavian languages than English. The Welsh people and their language originated with the Celts who came from Britain from across central Europe, a mixture of the Germanic peoples in the north, the Slavs in the east, and the Hellenic people in the south. These tribes belonged to the Roman Empire and spoke Celtic languages most closely related to present-day Welsh.

The Welsh language, called *Cymraeg,* borrows heavily from English today, although it's based on a completely different grammatical system. Only one-eighth of Welsh people speak Welsh as a first language. The language is one of the most difficult in the world to learn. If you want to tell a Welsh girl (or boy) that you love her (or him), it's said "dw I'n dy garu di" (doo een duh *gar*-ee dee). It sounds better in French.

See chapter 23 for more information on the Welsh language.

Tenby ★

The leading resort in Pembrokeshire, Tenby is packed with vacationers during the summer months, but it has a charm and character dating from medieval times, which makes it an interesting place to visit at any time of year.

There was already a Welsh village here when the Normans built **Tenby Castle,** now in ruins. Today, the castle attracts interest because of its location on the headland overlooking the town and harbor. The town walls had four gates, one of which, the West Gate, known as Five Arches, remains. The west wall is in good condition. Tenby was also a target during the civil war.

The **Tenby Museum & Art Gallery,** Castle Hill (© **01834/842809;** www.tenbymuseum.org.uk), is housed near the ruins of Tenby Castle. Exhibits cover the geology, archaeology, and natural history of the district, as well as the history of Tenby from the 12th century. In the art gallery, you'll see works by Augustus and Gwen John, along with Charles Norris, a local artist of the early 19th century. The museum and gallery are open April to October, daily 10am to 5pm, and November to March, Monday to Friday 10am to 5pm. Admission costs £4 for adults, £3 for seniors and students, and £2 for children. A family ticket goes for £9.

Tudor Merchant's House, Quay Hill (© **01834/842279;** www.nationaltrust.org.uk), is a beautifully furnished medieval dwelling of the 15th century with a fine Flemish chimney. On three interior walls, paintings with designs similar to Flemish weaving patterns were discovered under years of whitewash. It's open April to October, Sunday to Friday 11am to 5pm. Admission costs £3 for adults and £1.50 for children 15 and younger. A family ticket costs £7.50.

Tenby's parish church, **St. Mary's,** dates from the 13th century and is the largest parish church in Wales. Giraldus Cambrensis (Gerald the Welshman), a great religious leader of the 13th century, was the first rector. Charging no admission, it is open daily from 8am to 6pm.

In the bay, just 3.2km (2 miles) south of Tenby, little **Caldy Island ★** has long been a Roman Catholic venue. A Celtic monastic cell is believed to have been here, and today it is farmed by Cistercian monks, whose abbey is the island's outstanding attraction. From the 12th century until the Dissolution of the Monasteries by Henry VIII, a Benedictine priory was here. For the next few centuries, lay people living on the island farmed and quarried limestone until, in 1906, English Benedictines established a community here.

The Benedictines left solid evidence of their occupation: the refectory, gatehouse, and priory's lodging, which is now used as a guesthouse. In 1929, the Cistercian order took over the island, and today it produces perfume, chocolate, and dairy products, all sold locally. Only male visitors are allowed to enter the monastery, but anyone can visit St. David's Church, the Old Priory, and St. Illtud's Church, with its leaning stone spire. Inside St. Illtud's is a 6th-century Ogham stone, a relic of the time when monks from Ireland came here to establish their religious house. The writing on the Ogham stones was Celtic, which was then translated into Latin by the monks.

Allow about 2 hours for a visit. Access to Caldy Island is via a boat that runs only between Easter and late October, Monday to Friday from 10am to 3pm. The vessels depart every 20 minutes; the crossing also takes 20 minutes. A round-trip passage costs £10 for adults, £5 for children 14 and younger. For information about all aspects of the island, including boat access, call ✆ **01834/844453** or go to **www. caldey-island.co.uk**.

Tenby is located 85km (53 miles) west of Swansea and 148km (92 miles) west of Cardiff. The main southern rail line through Tenby is operated by **Arriva Trains Wales** (✆ **0870/900-0773;** www.arrivatrainswales.co.uk). Trains run from Swansea seven times a day Monday to Friday and six times a day on Saturday and Sunday. For more information, call **National Rail** at ✆ **0845/748-4950.**

For visitor information, go to the **Tourist Information Centre** at Unit 2, Upper Park Road (✆ **01834/842402;** www.visitpembrokeshire.com). It is open November to March, Monday to Saturday 10am to 4pm; April and May, daily 10am to 5pm; and June to October, daily 10am to 5:30pm (until 6pm July–Aug).

WHERE TO STAY & DINE

Fourcroft Hotel ☺   This is our favorite hotel within the town itself, though we prefer the greater elegance and secluded location of Penally Abbey (see below). On the cliffs above Tenby's sheltered North Beach, the hotel lies a 5-minute walk from the medieval walled town center. Fourcroft forms part of a landmarked Georgian terrace, built more than 150 years ago as summer homes for Londoners. Accommodations, ranging from midsize to spacious, offer modern comfort, with roomy, well-kept bathrooms. The front bedrooms are generally more spacious and open onto a view of the sea. Guests can use a private garden walk leading to the beach.

North Beach, Tenby, Pembrokeshire SA70 8AP. ✆ **01834/842886.** Fax 01834/842888. www.fourcroft-hotel.co.uk. 40 units. £100–£160 double. Rates include Welsh breakfast. AE, DC, MC, V. Limited free parking (6 spaces). **Amenities:** Restaurant; bar; children's center; Jacuzzi; outdoor heated pool; room service; sauna; Wi-Fi (free). *In room:* TV, hair dryer.

Penally Abbey ★   This country-house hotel—the finest lodging in the area—opens onto a gracious, timeless world. The house is 2 centuries old, but parts of its foundation date from the 6th century, when a monastery was established here. Today, the flowering garden partially conceals the ruins of St. Deniol's Chapel and a Flemish chimney of a long-ago homestead. The wide-open sea and the still-functioning Cistercian monastery on Caldy Island contribute to the panoramic sweep from the terraces. The house is built of Pembrokeshire stone, with ogee-headed doors, large square windows, and Gothic-inspired architectural details. The spacious bedrooms are full of character, often enhanced by four-poster beds. We prefer the rooms in the family house to the newer ones in the two annexes.

Penally, Tenby, Pembrokeshire SA70 7PY. ✆ **01834/843033.** Fax 01834/844714. www.penally-abbey.com. 17 units. £150–£192 double; £245 suite. Rates include breakfast. Discounts for children sharing parent's room. AE, MC, V. Located 3.2km (2 miles) southwest of town via A4139. **Amenities:** Restaurant; bar; heated indoor pool. *In room:* TV, hair dryer, minibar.

Pembroke

At a point 92km (57 miles) west of Swansea and 156km (97 miles) west of Cardiff, the ancient borough of Pembroke is the most English town in South Wales. It was never really a typical Welsh town because the Normans and the English had such a strong hold on it. It was settled by English and Flemish people, and its first language was always English. It is visited for two reasons today—to see Pembroke Castle, one of the most impressive in South Wales, and to use it as a base for exploring the national park.

Pembroke received its charter around 1090 from King Henry I and was built around Pembroke Castle, a great fortress set on a rocky spur above the town. The town walls formed the castle's outer ward, and the entire complex, a 22km-wide (14-mile) medieval defense system, can still be viewed as a fortified town, with the castle as its hub.

Most trains coming to Pembroke require transfers in Swansea, an hour's travel away. From Swansea, there are five trains per day. For rail information, call ℂ **0870/900-0773** or visit **www.arrivatrainswales.co.uk**. You can also call ℂ **0845/748-4950** or visit **www.nationalrail.co.uk**.

Bus connections from Tenby into Pembroke run about every hour throughout the day Monday through Saturday, with limited service on Sunday. For information about bus service from Wales into Pembroke, call ℂ **0870/608-2608** or visit **www. firstgroup.com**. For information about long-distance bus transit from London or large cities of the English Midlands, contact **National Express** (ℂ **0871/781-8181**; www.nationalexpress.com).

The **Pembroke Tourist Information Centre**, Commons Road (ℂ **01437/776499**; www.visitpembrokeshire.com), is open between Easter and October, daily from 9:30am to 5pm. Off-season hours are Tuesday through Saturday from 10am to 1pm.

Pembroke Castle ★★   With its massive keep and walls, the castle still looks formidable, although little inside it remains. It is the oldest castle in west Wales, and for more than 300 years it was the seat of the earls of Pembroke. It was founded by the Montgomerys in 1093, and work began on the fine masonry a century later with the circular great tower, or keep. Dominating the castle, the tower stands 22m (75 ft.) high and is the finest of its type in Britain. Home to such great leaders as Earl William Marshal, regent to Henry III, and to the early Tudors, the castle was also the birthplace of Henry VII ("Harri Tewdwr"). During the civil war, the castle was held in turn for both Parliament and the king. Cromwell arrived in person to start the siege that led to its final surrender. A vast cavern underneath the castle, called the Wogan, is where food and water were stored. The water defenses of the fortress can still be traced in a millpond on the north and in marshes on the south, outside the walls, as well as in the River Pembroke over which it looms.

Main St. ℂ **01646/681510.** www.pembrokecastle.co.uk. Admission £4.50 for adults; £3.50 seniors, students, and children 5-15; £12 family ticket. Apr–Sept daily 9:30am–6pm; Mar and Oct daily 10am–5pm; Nov–Feb daily 10am–4pm.

WHERE TO STAY

Coach House Hotel   Built along traditional lines after World War II (though the facade dates from medieval times), the Coach House is the best place for lodgings within the town itself, although the Lamphey Court (see below) is far more elegant. Bedrooms are small to midsize, each comfortably outfitted with a private bathroom with tub or shower. Set on the main thoroughfare of Pembroke, the hotel has a classic facade of black and white. View it mainly as an overnight stopover and don't expect a lot of style.

116 Main St., Pembroke, Pembrokeshire SA71 4HN. ℂ **01646/684602.** Fax 01646/687456. www.coach househotel.uk.com. 14 units. £75–£85 double. Rates include Welsh breakfast. AE, MC, V. Free parking. **Amenities:** Restaurant; bar. *In room:* TV, Wi-Fi (free).

Lamphey Court Hotel ★ This Best Western affiliate is by far the finest place for lodging and dining around. The impressive Georgian mansion, set on several acres of landscaped gardens, adds a touch of class to the area. Both the public rooms and the bedrooms have a certain luxurious grandeur. Many units are spacious enough for family suites. Stay in the house, where the rooms are more traditional, or in an 11-room annex. Local produce is cooked to perfection in the formal restaurant. Bar food is also available.

Lamphey, Pembrokeshire SA71 5NT. ℂ **01646/672273.** Fax 01646/672480. www.lampheycourt.co.uk. 37 units. £110–£160 double. Rates include buffet breakfast. AE, DC, MC, V. Free parking. Take A477 to Pembroke, turning left at Village Milton; Lamphey is signposted from there. **Amenities:** Restaurant; bar; babysitting; exercise room; heated indoor pool; room service; spa; outdoor tennis court (lit). *In room:* TV, hair dryer, Wi-Fi (free).

WHERE TO DINE

Lamphey Court Hotel ★ WELSH/BRITISH Even if you're not a guest of this hotel (reviewed above), consider it for a fancy dinner or a more casual lunch. The Georgian Restaurant, the formal section, is open on Friday and Saturday. In summer, you can opt for a table in the Conservatory, enjoying an alfresco lunch on the patio. Ingredients are market fresh, including lobster from Freshman Bay or salmon from the River Teifi, and most definitely lamb from Pembrokeshire's green Preseli Hills. Starters range from the finest Welsh smoked salmon with a fresh dill cream to an appetizer of selected Pembrokeshire seafood. Mains are accompanied by the fresh vegetables of the day and feature oven-baked rump of Welsh lamb drizzled with honey, chili, and rosemary oil, or prime mignon of Welsh beef. A vegetarian dish is featured nightly, and a sirloin steak is always on the grill.

In the Lamphey Court Hotel, Lamphey. ℂ **01646/672272.** www.lampheycourt.co.uk. Reservations required. Main courses £15–£19. AE, DC, MC, V. Georgian Restaurant: Fri–Sat 7–9:30pm. Conservatory: daily noon–2:30pm.

St. Davids ★★

St. Davids and its environs are in a part of the Pembrokeshire Coast National Park that had inhabitants far back in Paleolithic and Mesolithic times. About 5,000 years ago, New Stone Age (Neolithic) farmers arrived and made their homes here. They didn't leave many traces, but their tombs, or cromlechs, have survived. A large number of them lie on or near St. Davids Head, on Newport Bay, and in the Preseli foothills. Many people believe that the massive blue or foreign stones at Stonehenge came from the Preseli hills more than 4,000 years ago. Bronze Age cairns have also been found in the Preseli region.

Iron Age Celts came here, bringing with them from Gaul the beginnings of the Welsh and Gaelic languages. Near St. Davids, walls built during that era are still in use around fields. The Romans ignored this part of Wales, and contacts with Ireland, where fellow Celts lived, were strong. Irish tribes settled in Dyfed in the 3rd and 4th centuries, and then the monastic movement in the early Christian church was brought by Irish and spread by Welsh missionaries, when a vigorous Christian community was established on the St. Davids Peninsula.

The coming of the Normans did not really affect this section of Wales, and Welsh is still widely spoken here. In Tudor times and later, village seafaring came in, taking the mining output of coal, silver, and lead out of small village ports. All this has changed, of course, and today the coastal area is a popular holiday territory, with beaches, boating, fishing, and other leisure pursuits taking over.

There's a tremendous allure to one of Britain's most visited surf beaches, **Whitesands ★**, located 3.2km (2 miles) northwest of St. Davids. Access to this windswept beach is free, but there's a £2 charge for parking. Whitesands is noted for some of the consistently best surf waves in Britain. As such, it's the site of surfing exhibitions, where participants arrive from as far away as Huntington Beach, California. Lifeguards are on duty from June to early September.

The tiny cathedral city of St. Davids is the birthplace of the patron saint of Wales. Dewi Sant (later St. David), son of a Welsh chieftain and a Welsh woman named Non, was a Celtic religious leader in the 6th century. He chose a grassy hollow of the River Alun as the site for a small monastic community because it was hidden from approach by attackers, yet it was conveniently only a mile from the waters of St. Bride's Bay. The little church he and his monks built was burned down in 645, rebuilt, sacked and burned by the Danes in 1078, and then burned again in 1088. After that, a Norman cathedral was built on the site, its organization changing from the Celtic monastic to diocesan type. The stone village of St. Davids grew up on the hill around the church.

Today, with its ornately carved roof and a Norman nave, **St. Davids Cathedral ★★**, Cathedral Close (© **01437/720199;** www.stdavidscathedral.org.uk), is a magnificent example of medieval religious architecture. Its reliquary contains what are supposed to be the bones of St. David. The nave, a product of 3 centuries of craftsmanship, is a place of medieval beauty. The choir stalls, from the late 15th century, have witty, even lighthearted misericord carvings. Visitors are welcome at the cathedral, open daily from 8:30am to 6:30pm. During the months of July and August, regular 90-minute tours are offered on Monday, Tuesday, Thursday, and Friday at 2:30pm. The tours cost £4 for adults, £2.50 for seniors, and £1.20 for children 6 to 16. Tickets should be purchased in the Cathedral bookshop in the nave before joining the tour. Donations are accepted to help with the upkeep of the building.

Associated with the cathedral, the ruins of the **Bishop's Palace,** Cathedral Close (© **01437/720517;** www.cadw.wales.gov.uk), stand across the meadow and river, with the gatehouse, battlements, and curtain walls showing how even such a place needed fortification in medieval days. An outstanding sight is the elegant arcaded parapet that runs along both main walls. When you visit the palace ruins, note especially the fine piscina at the east end of the chapel's south wall. The site is open April to May daily 9:30am to 5pm, June to September daily 9:30am to 6pm, October daily 9:30am to 5pm, and November to March Monday to Saturday 9:30am to 4pm and Sunday 11am to 4pm. Admission is £3 for adults; £2.60 for seniors, students, and children; and £8.60 for a family ticket.

The cathedral is no longer Roman Catholic, nor is it Church of England. It is a member of the Church of Wales. When St. David was canonized in the 12th century, the pope declared that two pilgrimages to St. Davids were worth one to Rome, and three pilgrimages equaled one to Jerusalem. You can make such a pilgrimage today; although the pope's promise may not have been honored since the days of Henry VIII, we can promise you an interesting and educational tour of St. Davids Peninsula.

About 1.6km (1 mile) south from St. Davids, **Porthclais,** at the mouth of the River Alun, was the seaport used by travelers to Ireland and elsewhere for centuries before and after the birth of Christ and then by pilgrims making their way to St. Davids. In medieval days it became a coal port, and lime kilns were used to reduce limestone to slaked lime for use on fields, in building, and for household purposes. The restored lime kilns can be seen today.

A little eastward around the bay on a headland is **St. Non's Chapel,** now in ruins, supposedly built on the spot where St. David was born. It is dedicated to his mother. St. Non's Well is here also, reportedly in full flow. Its waters were said to have healing properties in the past. The site can be viewed 24 hours a day without charge.

St. Davids is located 117km (73 miles) west of Swansea and 180km (112 miles) west of Cardiff. Haverfordwest, 24km (15 miles) away, is the nearest rail station. **Richard Brothers** (© **01239/613756;** www.richardbros.co.uk) runs buses from Haverfordwest to St. Davids every hour; a one-way ticket costs only £5.25 round-trip for adults, £3 for children. If you're driving, take the A487 from Haverfordwest.

The St. Davids tourist office is at **Oriel y Parc** (© **01437/720392;** www. orielyparc.co.uk). It's open from Easter to October, daily 9:30am to 5:30pm, and November to Easter, Monday to Saturday 10am to 4pm.

WHERE TO STAY

Ramsey House ♦ The town's best bargain lies 1km (½ mile) from the cathedral on the road to Porthclais, standing amid manicured gardens and looking very much like the private house it is. Just 1km (½ mile) from the house, you can reach the Pembrokeshire Coast Path, which takes you along some of the most panoramic coastal scenery in Wales. The owners will show you one of their immaculately kept midsize bedrooms, each with a cozy and efficient private bathroom. We prefer the second-floor rooms for their views, either of the sea, cathedral, or open country. For those who don't like stairs, there are ground-floor rooms.

Lower Moor, St. Davids, Pembrokeshire SA62 6RP. © **01437/720321.** Fax 01437/720025. www.ramsey house.co.uk. 5 units. £90–£110 double. Rates include Welsh breakfast. AE, MC, V. No children under 16. **Amenities:** Restaurant; bar. *In room:* TV, hair dryer, Wi-Fi (free).

Warpool Court Hotel ★ This hotel, a 5-minute walk from the heart of the city, is the town's premier address, far outdistancing all competitors. A country house overlooking the sea, it is privately owned and set amid secluded gardens of great natural beauty. The vine-covered structure overlooks one of the most beautiful coastal stretches in Wales. Originally the cathedral choir school, it has been success-fully transformed into a hotel with a courteous staff. Most of the rooms are midsize to spacious, and some are large enough for families. The more expensive rooms offer sea views, while the least expensive units have shower and sink but no toilet. Asa Williams, who lived here early in the 20th century, decorated some 3,000 tiles, which are positioned throughout the house.

St. Davids, Pembrokeshire SA62 6BN. © **01437/720300.** Fax 01437/720676. www.warpoolcourthotel. com. 25 units. £100–£150 double. Rates include English breakfast. AE, DC, MC, V. **Amenities:** Restaurant; bar; babysitting; covered heated pool (Easter–Oct only); outdoor tennis court (lit). *In room:* TV, hair dryer.

Pembrokeshire

CARDIFF & SOUTH WALES

WHERE TO DINE

Morgan's ★ WELSH/CONTINENTAL   Unless you dine at one of the inns, this is by far the best independent restaurant in town, and has been since it opened in 1993. Peruse the menu while admiring the art collection on the walls. The chef is known for making use of local produce and market-fresh ingredients. The fresh fish is rushed here from the Pembrokeshire coast after it lands at the nearby port of Milford Haven. Blackboard menus display the catch of the day. Meat eaters will find the most reliable Welsh spring lamb or "black steaks" from the countryside, even game in season. Well-prepared mains include pan-roasted monkfish with confit red peppers or roast guinea fowl in a wild mushroom butter. Starters might feature mussels steamed in a Thai-spiced sauce with fresh lime.

20 Nun St. © **01437/720508.** www.morgans-restaurant.co.uk. Reservations recommended. Main courses £13–£20. MC, V. Mar Fri–Sat 6:30–10:30pm; Apr–Dec Thurs–Mon 6:30–10:30pm. Closed Jan–Feb.

NORTH WALES: THE PEAKS OF SNOWDONIA

Norty Wales is a rewarding target for those willing to seek it out. Distinctly different from England, it is linguistically and culturally different from most of Britain and is known for its beauty spots, a land of mountains and lakes interspersed with castles. The most powerful of the Welsh princes held sway here, and the residents remain staunchly nationalistic. British families flock to the coastal resorts on holidays, especially in July and August, whereas others prefer to seek out the footpaths of Snowdonia National Park.

Mountain peaks and steep wooded slopes, spectacular estuaries and rugged cliffs brooding over secluded coves, lakes, little rivers, and valleys with tiny towns looking as if they were carved out of granite—all these join to make up **Snowdonia National Park.** The park, with slate mines, moors, heavy forests, mountain lakes, grain fields, pastures, swift-moving rivers, and sandy beaches, takes its name from Snowdon, at 1,085m (3,560 ft.) the highest peak in Wales and England. Most of the Snowdonia area is in the County of Gwynedd, once the ancient Welsh kingdom of that name. Its prince, Owen ap Gwynedd, never agreed to let himself be reduced to the status of baron under the English kings. Because his terrain was mountainous and wild, it helped him stave off an invasion by forces accustomed to fighting on flat land.

The rocky, majestic crags of Snowdonia National Park are rivaled by the mighty walls and soaring towers of **Caernarfon Castle,** the best example of castle building in medieval Wales. Caernarfon (formerly spelled Caernarvon) and its neighbors, Anglesey and the Lleyn Peninsula, reaching out from its northwest and west, are all part of the County of Gwynedd. Legends of holy islands and druidic mysteries flourished among the Celtic peoples who lived in this area in long-ago centuries.

Many of the native-born people of this region are of blood stock little changed over the centuries. Most are bilingual, with English as their second tongue, and signs are usually in both languages.

The County of Clwyd, in northeastern Wales, has miles of sandy beaches along its north coast; highland ranges, peat bogs, and deep valleys lush with greenery in the center; coal country to the southeast; and industry, agriculture, and sheep farming in the section nearest the estuary of the River Dee and the English border. What is now Clwyd (by order of Parliament, since 1973) used to be Denbighshire, and before that, Flintshire.

LLANBERIS

376km (233 miles) W of London; 11km (7 miles) SE of Caernarfon

The starting point for going up Snowdon by mountain railway, Llanberis nestles between Lake Padarn and Lake Peris. Views of outstanding beauty greet your eyes, both man-made sights and natural wonders.

The **Snowdon Mountain Railway ★** runs from Llanberis to within a few yards of the top of the Snowdon peak at about 1,085m (3,560 ft.). The only rack-and-pinion train in Britain, it is also the steepest train ride, and the view from the top platform, where the train stops, is one of the most panoramic in the country. It's possible to see some 160km (100 miles) away into Ireland, especially the peaks of the Wicklow Mountain chain, on the clearest and brightest of days. Another "great little train" in the region is the **Llanberis Lake Railway,** which takes you along Lake Padarn. The purpose of the trains in this area and in the Vale of Ffestiniog to the south was to bring the "gray gold" from slate caverns for shipping all over the world. For information and schedules, call © **0871/720-0033** or visit **www.snowdonrailway.co.uk**. Trains run to the summit between May and October, costing £25 round-trip for adults and £18 round-trip for children 14 and younger. *Note:* If you book by phone at least a day in advance for a 9am departure, ticket prices are cut in half.

Padarn Country Park (© 01286/870892; www.gwynedd.gov.uk), open daily until dusk, has marked footpaths that will take you past the Vivian Quarry, with its dramatic slate cliffs and deep pools, through galleries where slate was worked, and to lookouts from which the Snowdon range and the lakes can be viewed. The entrance to these 283 hectares (700 acres) of countryside is signposted from High Street and begins .8km (½ mile) north of the town center. At crafts workshops and a woodcraft center in the park, you can watch artisans work in clay, copper, slate, and wood. One workman specializes in Celtic folk harps, including miniature models and do-it-yourself kits.

The ruins of **Dolbadarn Castle** overlook Lake (Llyn) Padarn in the Llanberis pass, .8km (½ mile) east of Llanberis, a relic of the time when the pass was used by the conquering armies. It is notable for its location and a mortared masonry tower that still stands. You can take a look around the meager ruins for free.

Essentials

GETTING THERE   The nearest rail station is at Bangor, 14km (9 miles) north of Llanberis. From Monday through Saturday, buses run frequently throughout the day from Bangor to Llanberis. For information, contact **Arriva Buses Wales**

(© **0844/800-4411;** www.arriva.co.uk). Because of the many stops en route, buses take about 25 minutes each way.

Buses between Caernarfon and Llanberis run every half-hour Monday through Saturday, every 1 to 2 hours on Sunday. Timetables are available from the Llanberis Tourist Information Centre (see below) and the Caernarfon Tourist Information Centre (see "Caernarfon," later in this chapter).

If you're driving from Caernarfon, head southeast along the A4086.

VISITOR INFORMATION   The **Llanberis Tourist Information Centre,** 41B High St. (© **01286/870765;** www.llanberis.org), is open from Easter to the end of October, daily from 9:30am to 5:30pm. The rest of the year, it's open Monday, Friday, Saturday, and Sunday from 10:30am to 3pm.

Where to Stay

Legacy Royal Victoria Hotel   Although it's a venue for local weddings and social functions and is a bit stuffy, this is nonetheless the most prestigious address in town. The Royal Victoria has been long established at the foothills of Snowdon, between Padarn and Peris lakes, a bucolic setting. The bedrooms in general are spacious and recently modernized, with comfortable and endurable furniture and well-maintained private bathrooms. Four rooms are set aside for families. The place bustles with activity, often providing live entertainment at night or arranging mountain treks during the day. The restaurant has a conservatory opening onto the lakes.

Llanberis, Gwynedd LL55 4TY. © **0870/832-9903.** Fax 0870/832-9904. www.legacy-hotels.co.uk. 106 units. £110 double. Rates include Welsh breakfast. AE, DC, MC, V. Free parking. **Amenities:** Restaurant; bar; room service. *In room:* TV, hair dryer, Wi-Fi (free).

Where to Dine

Peak Restaurant ★ WELSH/BRITISH   First-class service, affordable food, and a market-fresh cuisine attract both locals and visitors to this hospitable restaurant. Chef patron Angela Dwyer worked in some of the top restaurants of Europe before setting up shop here. Her most ordered starter is goat's cheese in a walnut dressing, followed by such mains as rack of Welsh lamb in a red wine sauce, sautéed filet of halibut, or grilled Welsh sirloin with potato cake. Yet another specialty is breast of Welsh chicken in a white wine sauce.

84-86 High St. © **01286/872777.** www.peakrestaurant.co.uk. Reservations recommended. Main courses £11–£17. MC, V. Wed–Sun 7–10pm (until 8pm in winter); Sun 12:30–2pm.

Seeing the Sights

Nearly a kilometer (½ mile) north of the center of Llanberis in Padarn Country Park (see above), the **Welsh Slate Museum** (© **01286/870630;** www.museumwales. ac.uk/en/slate) is a minor museum in the workshops of Dinorwic slate quarry, one of the largest in Britain until it closed in 1969. Slate-mining communities were intensely Welsh, nonconformist in religion, and radical in politics, as films shown here reveal. The exhibitions, which should take no more than 30 minutes of your time, are mainly of interest to those who have a particular interest in this aspect of Welsh life of long ago. Admission is free. It's open from Easter to October, daily 10am to 5pm; off-season, Sunday to Friday 10am to 4pm. To get here, take the A4086 at the start of the lake railway and Padarn Country Park.

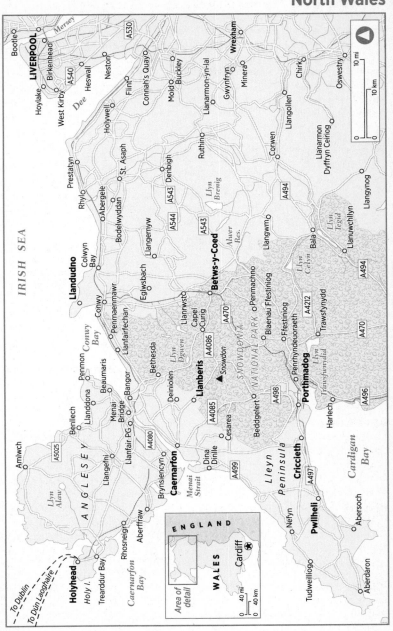

Electric Mountain Visitor Centre, along the A4086 (© **01286/870636;** www.fhc.co.uk), is a scientific-looking observation center, functioning as the meeting point between the public and one of the most technologically advanced power stations in Wales. Set about .4km (¼ mile) north of Llanberis, it incorporates a hydroelectric system harnessing the waters of a pair of nearby lakes, whose turbines and channels are concealed deep within the mountains so as not to spoil the natural beauty of the nationally protected site. Entrance to the visitor center is free. Tours run from Easter to October, daily 9:30am to 4:30pm. Reservations are advised. Once you get here, if a staff member isn't busy with other tasks, you can take a tour of the turbines for a fee of £7.50 for adults, £6 for seniors, £3.75 for children 4 to 15, and £11 to £43 for a family ticket.

BETWS-Y-COED ★

363km (226 miles) W of London; 70km (44 miles) SE of Holyhead

This idyllic Snowdonia village, with tumbling rivers, waterfalls, and mountains, is nestled in the tree-lined valley of the River Conwy. It has an antique church with a Norman font; old bridges, stone houses, and hotels on rocky outcrops; and woodland paths.

Although crowded in summer, this town is one of the best centers for exploring North Wales. It's mainly a one-street town, but you get the feel that you're in the great outdoors far removed from England's polluted cities of the Midlands. There's an alpine feeling about the place.

The town is known for its eight bridges, of which our favorite is the Waterloo Bridge at the village's southern end, the cast-iron construction of Thomas Telford in 1815. There's also a suspension bridge near St. Michael's Church. If you walk upon it, it sways in the wind but seems perfectly safe. The most regal bridge is Pont-y-Pair, "the bridge of the cauldron," bounding the Llugwy River to the north. In fact, walking across the bridges of Betws-y-Coed and taking in the views is one of the main reasons to come here.

Essentials

GETTING THERE The **Conwy Valley** line between Llandudno and Blaenau Ffestiniog passes through Betws-y-Coed with three trains daily. For rail information and schedules, call © **0845/748-4950** or visit **www.nationalrail.co.uk**.

The **Express** bus company services Betws-y-Coed from both Llandudno and Porthmadog. For schedules, call © **0844/800-4411** or visit **www.arriva.co.uk**.

Motorists from Llandudno can take A470 south.

VISITOR INFORMATION For information about the town and Snowdonia National Park, head for the local **Tourist Information Centre,** at Royal Oak Stables in the town center (© **01690/710426;** www.betws-y-coed.co.uk). It's open from Easter to October, daily 10am to 1pm and 1:30 to 6pm; and in the off-season, daily 9:30am to 1pm and 1:30 to 4:30pm.

Where to Stay & Dine

EXPENSIVE

Tan-y-Foel Country House ★★★ 🎁 A 16th-century manor house, this gem is the best hotel in the area, opening onto a panoramic sweep of Conwy Valley, with

Snowdonia looming in the background. Stay here if you can, forsaking all other places. Vibrant fabrics and modern paintings bring you into the 21st century, but the atmosphere is still yesterday. It is set on 3.2 hectares (8 acres) of woodlands and pastures 3.2km (2 miles) north of town. Charm and grace prevail in both the public and private rooms. The latter are moderate to spacious, each individually furnished with immaculate little bathrooms. Two rooms are in an annex and have less charm. We prefer one of the four bedrooms opening onto the front of the hotel, as they offer the best views.

In an intimate setting, the chef and owner, Janet Pitman, one of the best chefs in this part of Wales, takes care with her three-course dinner, which she changes daily. Dinner, which costs £45 per person, is an elegant meal featuring such specialties as Welsh black beef and catches of the day like fresh turbot or sea bass.

Capel Garmon (near Betws-y-Coed), Llanrwst, Conwy LL26 ORE. ✆ **01690/710507.** Fax 01690/710681. www.tyfhotel.co.uk. 6 units. £150–£200 double. Rates include Welsh breakfast. MC, V. Free parking. From Betws-y-Coed, take A5 onto A470, heading north to Llanrwst, turning at the signpost for Capel Garmon. No children under 12. **Amenities:** Restaurant. *In room:* TV/DVD, CD player, hair dryer, Wi-Fi (free).

MODERATE

Park Hill Hotel ★ About a 5-minute walk west of town, this small Victorian hotel is surrounded by secluded gardens and opens onto panoramic views of the Conwy and Llugwy valleys. For such a small hotel, it offers some exceptional recreational facilities and is also known for its justly praised cuisine. Your hosts, Jaap and Ghislaine Buis, run a good little inn, with moderately sized bedrooms and small but well-kept bathrooms. Three units have shower-only bathrooms and six have tub/shower combos. Front rooms are preferable to those on the side. Furnishings are traditional, and one room is graced with a four-poster.

Traditional meals are based on longtime Welsh favorites and served alongside modern dishes using local produce. Expect Welsh lamb and fresh fish from the Conwy estuary and local rivers.

Llanrwst Rd., Betws-y-Coed, Gwynedd LL24 0HD. ✆/fax **01690/710540.** www.park-hill-hotel.co.uk. 9 units. £60–£79 double. Rates include Welsh breakfast. MC, V. No children under 6. **Amenities:** Restaurant, bar; Jacuzzi; indoor heated pool; sauna. *In room:* TV, no phone.

Ty Gwyn ★ This is one of the most charming hotels and pubs in town. Laden with carved beams and local artifacts, Ty Gwyn is low slung, sitting on the opposite side of Waterloo Bridge from the rest of town. Inside, it's a world of old prints and chintz, time-darkened beams, and copper pans. Originally it was a coaching inn from the 16th century, drawing horsemen traveling between London and the ferryboats to Ireland. Bedrooms, often small, are still comfortably furnished, often with a four-poster or a half-tester bed (ca. 1800). The best unit has a "health spa" tub, small lounge, and private balcony. There are four rooms without private bathrooms.

The restaurant's menu features local Welsh dishes as well as more exotic fare from Thailand and elsewhere. There is always a homemade soup of the day and a wide selection of vegetarian dishes.

Along the A5, Betws-y-Coed, Gwynedd LL24 6SG. ✆ **01690/710383.** www.tygwynhotel.co.uk. 13 units, 9 with bathroom. £52 double without bathroom, £74 double with bathroom; £94–£120 4-poster room. Rates include Welsh breakfast. Children 11 and younger stay free in same room with up to 2 paying adults. MC, V. Free parking. **Amenities:** Restaurant; Wi-Fi (free, in lobby). *In room:* TV, no phone.

If time is short, we'd skip the minor sights of town—that is, after you've walked over those bridges—and head instead for one of the beauty spots of Wales, the **Swallow Falls** ★ and **Miners Bridge.** Take the A5 for 3.2km (2 miles) to the west of Betws-y-Coed. The Swallow Falls is one of the most mystical and evocative—also one of the most powerful—of its kind in Wales. It comprises a series of waterfalls strung together, creating a mist. Miners Bridge is a wooden footbridge impregnated with pitch for preservation and dating from the late 18th century. It's not a conventional flat bridge, but a steeply inclined staircase-style bridge, with elevation much higher on one end than on the other. The Miners Bridge doesn't charge anything to visit—and, as such, many walkers opt for a brisk half-hour riverfront walk from the center of Betws-y-Coed, with the bridge as their final destination. You'll pay £1 to see the falls, however. There's no attendant—just drop a coin into a tollbooth, and visit anytime you want, night or day.

Again, and only if you have time, there are two more evocative places to visit in the area. One is **Dolwyddelan Castle,** at the hamlet of Dolwyddelan (© **01690/750366;** www.betws-y-coed.com/castle.html). Standing lonely on a ridge, this castle was the birthplace of Llewelyn the Great, according to tradition. It was certainly his royal residence. Restored to its present condition in the 19th century, the castle's remains look out on the rugged grandeur of Moel Siabod peak. A medieval road from the Vale of Conwy ran just below the west tower, which made this a strategic site for a castle to control passage. About 1.6km (1 mile) from Dolwyddelan, the castle is accessible by a rough track off the A470 to the southwest of Betws-y-Coed, on the road to Blaenau Ffestiniog. To enter, adults pay £2.70, children ages 4 to 16 pay £2.30, and children 3 and younger get in free; a family ticket costs £7.70. It's open April to September, Monday to Saturday 10am to 6pm, Sunday from 11am to 4pm; off-season hours are Monday to Saturday 10am to 4pm, Sunday from 11am to 4pm.

One of the premier literary sights of Wales, **Ty Mawr,** Wybrnant, Penmachno (© **01690/760213;** www.nationaltrust.org.uk), lies 11km (7 miles) southeast of Betws-y-Coed. From the town, head southwest for 5.6km (3½ miles), going west of Penmachno along B4406 the rest of the way. At the head of the little valley of Gwybernant, this cottage is where Bishop William Morgan was born in the 16th century. Morgan was the first person to translate the Bible into Welsh, and his translation is viewed even today as a masterpiece and the foundation of modern Welsh literature. It's open late March through October, Thursday to Sunday noon to 5pm. Admission is £3 for adults, £1.50 for children, and £7.50 for a family ticket.

THE LLEYN PENINSULA ★★

Separating Cardigan Bay and its northern arm, Tremadog Bay, from Caernarfon Bay, the gentle western Lleyn Peninsula thrusts out alone into the Irish Sea. It's bounded by the mountains of Snowdonia on the east and by the sea. Having little communication with the outside world before the coming of railroads and highways, the peninsula has a large Welsh-speaking population, although most people also have English as a second language, made necessary by the influx of people coming here to retire, to do business, or just to take holidays.

The peninsula takes its name from an Irish tribe, the Celtic Legine, or Laigin, who didn't have very far to go from home to invade the country of fellow Celts. They were followed by missionaries and pilgrims in the Christian era. The distance from Ireland is so short that when you stand on National Trust property high on a cliff above St. Mary's Well, you can often see the Wicklow Mountains of Ireland with the naked eye.

The Lleyn Peninsula has beaches, hills, farmland, moorland, villages nestled in the hollows, trees, heather, gorse, and country lanes. There are traces of hill forts here, and you can find standing stones, monastery ruins, pilgrim trails, holy wells (four of them), and nonconformist chapels. Sporting enthusiasts enjoy fishing, golf, watersports, and rough shooting.

For information on the peninsula, get in touch with the **Tourist Information Centre,** Min Y Don, Station Square, Pwllheli (© **01758/613000;** www.wales-calling.com/guide/lleyn.htm). The two best towns on the peninsula are Porthmadog and Criccieth (see below).

Pwllheli, lying 13km (8 miles) to the west of Criccieth, is the principal transportation hub of the peninsula, with daily buses arriving from London. Buses also pull in here every hour from Bangor. You may not want to linger in Pwllheli, but instead take a connecting bus to either Porthmadog or Criccieth, which make better centers.

The **Arriva Trains Wales** line, which begins at Aberystwyth, with a change of trains at Dovey Junction, takes you to both Porthmadog and Criccieth. Call © **0845/748-4950** or visit **www.nationalrail.co.uk** for more information.

Porthmadog

The estuary of the River Glaslyn has long been the scene of shipping and fishing activity, emptying as it does into Tremadog Bay and thence into Cardigan Bay.

This is the main town east of the Lleyn Peninsula. It grew up as a slate-shipping port on the coast near the mouth of the River Glaslyn. T. E. Lawrence (Lawrence of Arabia) was born in Tremadog, close by.

Porthmadog was named after a "Celtification" of the English name of its builder, William Madocks, a mining mogul who built the town from scratch between 1808 and 1811. The harbor that later figured so prominently in the town's history was custom-built between 1821 and 1825. In the 1870s, as many as 1,000 vessels a year pulled into harbor here to haul away slate. At its peak in 1873, 116,000 tons of Blaenau slate were shipped from this harbor to points throughout the empire and the world.

The view of the mountains of Snowdonia from Porthmadog Cob, the embankment, is panoramic. Porthmadog is the coastal terminal of the Ffestiniog Railway, and a small museum may be visited at the station. The town has access to beaches at Borth-y-Gest and Black Rock Sands, where cars may be driven onto the beach. Other than the scenery, attractions are not exceptional.

The production of traditional tapestries and tweeds can be observed at the small **Brynkir Woollen Mill,** Golan, Garndolbenmaen (© **01766/530236**), in a beautiful rural setting. The products are available for sale at the mill shop. Admission is free; it is open Monday through Friday from 10am to 4pm. Head out the A487 for 5.6km (3½ miles) from Porthmadog.

The town of Porthmadog is 428km (266 miles) west of London and 32km (20 miles) south of Caernarfon. The **Tourist Information Centre,** High Street (© **01766/512981;** www.porthmadog.com), is open from Easter to October, daily 10am to 6pm. Off-season hours are Thursday to Tuesday 9:30am to 5pm.

WHERE TO STAY & DINE

Hotel Portmeirion ★★★ 🎁   Sir Clough Williams-Ellis set out to build an idyllic village on a romantic coast. Standing amid one of the finest scenic settings in Wales, this hotel existed as an early Victorian villa before it was converted into an evocative lodging in 1926. Writers such as H. G. Wells and George Bernard Shaw became habitués, Noël Coward wrote *Blithe Spirit* here in 1941, and the cult TV classic *The Prisoner* was filmed here in the late '60s. The hotel overlooks Cardigan Bay from its own private peninsula. The decor inside is exotic: fabrics from Kashmir, paintings from Rajasthan, tiles from Delft, and wallpaper from New York. Many of the rooms have half-tester or four-poster beds. About a dozen units are in the main house, the rest in a cluster of "village houses." Four accommodations are designated for families. The best sea views are from the rooms in the main house, however.

Portmeirion, Gwynedd LL48 6ET. © **01766/770000.** Fax 01766/770300. www.portmeirion-village. com. 53 units. £215–£235 double; £280–£300 suite. Rates include Welsh breakfast. AE, DC, MC, V. Free parking. Off A487, signposted from Minffordd, 3.2km (2 miles) west of Portmeirion. **Amenities:** 2 restaurants; bar; babysitting; outdoor pool; room service; outdoor tennis court. *In room:* TV, hair dryer.

Criccieth

Now in ruins, **Criccieth Castle** (© **01766/522227**), built as a native Welsh stronghold, is on a grassy headland and offers a commanding view of Tremadog Bay. During its years as an active fortress, it changed hands—Welsh to English and back and forth—until it was finally sacked and burned in 1404 by Owain Glyndwr, never to rise again as a fortification. The castle houses an interesting exhibition on the theme of the native castles of Welsh princes. On a fine day, from its heights you can see westward to the tip of the peninsula, north and east to Snowdonia, and far down the bay to the south. Admission is £3.10 for adults, £2.70 for students and children 5 to 16, and free for children 4 and younger. A family ticket goes for £8.90. It's open April through May, daily from 10am to 5pm; June through September, daily 10am to 6pm; October, daily 10am to 5pm; and November through March, Friday and Saturday 9:30am to 4pm and Sunday 11am to 4pm. Outside those hours, the castle's exhibition center is closed, but you can still enjoy the panoramic view from the site.

About 3km (2 miles) west of Criccieth in Llanystumdwy, you can visit **Highgate,** the boyhood home of David Lloyd George, prime minister of Britain in the war years of 1914 to 1918, and also the **Lloyd George Museum** (© **01766/522071;** www. gwynedd.gov.uk), designed by Sir Clough Williams-Ellis of Portmeirion resort village fame (see above). The museum outlines the statesman's life, with displays illustrating his political career. Admission is £4 for adults, £3 for children, and £10 for a family ticket. From April to June, it's open Monday to Saturday 10:30am to 5pm (closed Sat in May); July through September, daily 10:30am to 5pm; and in October, Monday to Friday 11am to 4pm. Lloyd George's grave is nearby on the banks of the swift-running River Dwyfor. The name of the hamlet, Llanystumdwy, means "the church at the bend of the River Dwyfor."

Information about the Criccieth area is available from the **Tourist Information Centre** in Porthmadog (see above).

WHERE TO STAY & DINE

Bron Eifion Country House Hotel ★★   On 2 hectares (5 acres) of well-manicured gardens, this baronial mansion is the finest and most elegant place to stay in the area. This tranquil Welsh country estate lies close to the Snowdonia National Park and makes a good base for exploring the area. The tended gardens evoke the South of France. The interior looks like it would make a good place to stage an Agatha Christie murder mystery. You'll surely be impressed by the grand stairway and the minstrels' gallery, with its lofty timbered roof. Rooms are spacious and traditionally furnished; some have four-poster beds.

The **Orangery Restaurant** offers one of the most beautiful settings for dining in the area. The set menu, which costs £30 per person, is an elegant, tasty presentation, perhaps beginning with smoked salmon and ending with a fresh dessert or (our favorite) Welsh artisan cheese with a fig-and-beet chutney and a slice of fresh walnut-and-raisin bread.

Criccieth, Gwynedd LL52 OSA. ✆ **01766/522385.** Fax 01766/523796. www.broneifion.co.uk. 19 units. £130–£180 double. Rates include full Welsh breakfast. AE, MC, V. Free parking. Located .8km (½ mile) outside Criccieth on A497, signposted PWLLHELI. **Amenities:** Restaurant; babysitting; room service. *In room:* TV, hair dryer, Wi-Fi (free).

Lion Hotel ☺   This former private home from the 18th century lies in the town's most enviable spot: beside the village green behind a painted stone facade. The lager-drinking pubbers of town head here at sundown, and it's a lively, cozy nest for an overnight stop and some good Welsh cookery. Rooms are homelike and often small but comfortably furnished, with tidy housekeeping and somewhat cramped bathrooms. Families are especially welcome here, as the hotel sets aside separate bedrooms for them and offers early dinners for children. The inn also can provide such devices as baby monitors, cots, and highchairs. In addition to rooms in the main building, the Castle Cottage offers a dozen well-furnished bedrooms.

Y Maes, Criccieth, Gwynedd LA52 OAA. ✆ **01766/522460.** Fax 01766/523075. www.lionhotelcriccieth. co.uk. 46 units. £73–£85 double. Rates include continental breakfast. AE, MC, V. **Amenities:** Restaurant; bar; babysitting; room service. *In room:* TV, hair dryer.

CAERNARFON ★★

400km (249 miles) W of London; 100km (68 miles) W of Chester; 48km (30 miles) SE of Holyhead; 14km (9 miles) SW of Bangor

In the 13th century, when King Edward I of England had defeated the Welsh after long and bitter fighting, he felt the need for a castle in this area as part of his network of fortresses in the still-rebellious country. He ordered the construction of one on the site of an old Norman castle at the western end of the Menai Strait, where the River Seiont flows into the sea, a place from which his sentinels could command a view of the land around, all the way to the mountains and far out across the bay to the Irish Sea. Based either on his firsthand observations (historians believed he might have visited Constantinople during his involvement in the Crusades) or on ancient drawings of Constantinople procured by his architect, the Savoy-born James St. George, the walls were patterned after the fortifications surrounding ancient

Byzantium. Most of the walls of the 13th-century town still stand, although growth outside the walls has been inevitable.

The main reason to come here today is to see the castle. After that, you will have seen the best of Caernarfon and can press on to another town for the night, or else stay at one of the local inns. The downside? Tourist buses overrun the place in summer. Other than the castle, there is nothing in the town that needs to take up too much of your time.

Essentials

GETTING THERE   There's no railway station in Caernarfon; the nearest connection is through Bangor, to which Caernarfon is linked by bus.

Buses run between Bangor and Caernarfon, a 25-minute ride, every 20 minutes throughout the day. Timetables are available by contacting the tourist information center (see below), calling *©* **0844/800-4411,** or visiting **www.arriva.co.uk**.

If you're driving from Bangor, head southwest along the A487; from Porthmadog, head north along the A487.

VISITOR INFORMATION   The **Caernarfon Tourist Information Centre** is at Oriel Pendeitsh, 1 Castle St. (*©* **01286/672232;** www.visitcaernarfon.com). From May through October, it's open daily 9:30am to 5:30pm; November through April, it's open Monday to Saturday 10am to 3:30pm.

Where to Stay

Celtic Royal Hotel ★   Carved out of a 19th-century grand hotel shell and massively enlarged, this is the leading choice in town. Its uniformed, well-trained staff grew accustomed long ago to groups of visitors pulling in by motor coach to see the famous castle, just a 3-minute walk away. The hotel's current look derives from a 1996 face-lift and radical enlargement of what had become a dowdy and outmoded "grand hotel" built in 1843. Today, most of the antique original vestiges lie within the hotel's lobby, with bedrooms and dining facilities placed within modern three-story wings. The midsize bedrooms are blandly uncontroversial, outfitted in pastels with comfortable furnishings.

The main restaurant, Brasserie Draco, is a chic setting for a Mediterranean-inspired cuisine. In addition, you can head to the on-site Hafana Bar & Bistro, which is much more informal and less expensive, offering an array of freshly cooked local food and a well-stocked bar.

Bangor St., Caernarfon, Gwynedd LL55 1AY. *©* **01286/674477.** Fax 01286/674139. www.celtic-royal. co.uk. 110 units. £125 double. Rates include Welsh breakfast. AE, MC, V. Free parking. **Amenities:** 2 restaurants; bar; exercise room; Jacuzzi; indoor heated pool; room service; sauna. *In room:* TV, hair dryer.

Seiont Manor Hotel ★★ ☺   Situated in the tranquil Welsh countryside, this is a great family favorite, one of the best bases for exploring Snowdonia National Park, and also makes an excellent base for visiting the Isle of Anglesey. Constructed from the original farmstead of a Georgian manor house, the hotel has been tastefully converted into a honeycomb of spacious rooms, each with a good-size bathroom, and all with views over 60 hectares (150 acres) of parkland. Come here for seclusion, a sense of style, and some of the best leisure facilities in the area. Each of the rooms has a small balcony or a terrace; several bedrooms are reserved for families.

Llanrug, Caernarfon, Gwynedd LL55 2AQ. ℂ **01286/673366.** Fax 01286/672840. www.handpicked hotels.co.uk. 28 units. £95–£115 double; from £135 suite. Rates include Welsh breakfast. AE, DC, MC, V. Free parking. From Caernarfon, head east on A4086 for 3.2km (2 miles). **Amenities:** Restaurant; bar; babysitting; exercise room; indoor heated pool; room service; sauna. *In room:* TV, hair dryer, Wi-Fi (free).

Where to Dine

Llwyn y Brain Restaurant WELSH/BRITISH   One of the town's best three-course dinners is served here in a rather formal setting. In addition to the well-crafted cuisine, you can enjoy views of the lake through the conservatory windows. The house specialty is pink-roasted rack of Snowdonia lamb with a rosemary and mustard flavor. Other mains are likely to include seared scallops enlivened with an orange-and-horseradish cream sauce. Each main dish comes with fresh vegetables such as braised red cabbage or a sweet potato puree. The chef prepares a simple but high-quality cuisine for the contemporary palate.

In the Seiont Manor Hotel, Llanrug. ℂ **01286/673-366.** www.handpickedhotels.co.uk. Reservations recommended. Fixed-price 3-course dinner £30; bar platters £8–£17; Sun brunch £13–£15. AE, DC, MC, V. Sun noon–2:30pm; daily 7–9pm.

Seeing the Sights

Every Saturday, plus Mondays from May to September, a market is held in **Castle Square,** where there's a statue of David Lloyd George, prime minister of Great Britain between 1916 and 1922, who is generally credited, along with King George V, for leading the United Kingdom through the rigors of World War I. He's also credited with introducing what's defined today as Britain's national healthcare system. Born in Manchester, he was reared on the nearby Lleyn Peninsula and was later instrumental in preserving the remnants of the town's famous castle.

The nearest thing Wales ever had to a royal palace is **Caernarfon Castle ★★★,** described by Dr. Samuel Johnson after a visit in 1774 as "an edifice of stupendous majesty and strength." Legend has it that after the birth, in 1301, of the son of Edward I in this castle, he showed the infant boy to the Welsh, calling him "the native-born prince who can speak no English." Since that time, the title "Prince of Wales" has belonged to every male heir-apparent to the English throne. The eyes of the world were on Caernarfon in 1969, when it was the scene of the investiture of Charles as prince of Wales.

Although in some places only the shell of the wall remains, some rooms and stone and wooden steps remain so that visitors can climb up into it. Eagle Tower has an exhibition on the ground floor showing the history of the fortress and of the town around it. You can also visit the **Regimental Museum of the Royal Welch Fusiliers** (the regiment retains the Old English spelling of the word *Welsh*), which occupies all three floors of Queen's Tower and contains many items of interest relating to the regiment and its military history. In 2000, millions of pounds were spent on the renovation and enlargement of this historic castle, with additional exhibition space for the museum set up within the Chamberlain Tower. But it is the castle as a whole that's of interest—not one special exhibition or hall. Allow 1½ hours for your visit. Between April and October, the castle is open daily from 9am to 5pm. From November to March, it's open Monday to Saturday 9:30am to 4pm and Sunday 11am to 4pm. Admission costs £5 for adults and £4.60 for students and children 15 and younger. For more information, call ℂ **01286/677617.**

Today, the town's quays are less animated than they were during the heyday of the region's slate mining, when boats lined up to haul roofing tiles off to points as far away as London, the United States, the mainland of Europe, and India. In the mid-1990s, a full-service marina, with about 60 slips, was built to accommodate the increasing numbers of yachts and pleasure craft that moor here when not in use.

The Romans recognized the strategic importance of northwest Wales and maintained a fort at **Segontium** for some 3 centuries. Excavations on the outskirts of Caernarfon on the A4085 have disclosed foundations of barracks, bathhouses, and other structural remains. Finds from the excavations are displayed in the **museum** (© **01286/675625;** www.nationaltrust.org.uk) on the site, open year-round Tuesday to Sunday from 12:30 to 4:30pm. Admission is free. Some archaeologists and historians think that native Britons may have been displaced from the site, which was one of their strongholds at the time of the Roman invasion. There are no outstanding relics here; allow about 30 minutes to walk around.

THE ISLE OF ANGLESEY ★★

The Welsh name of this island is Mon (the Romans called it Mona), and it is called Mon, Mam Cymru, or Anglesey, Mother of Wales. If this is true, we must say that the child doesn't much resemble the mother. The scenery differs totally from that of the mainland, with low-lying farmland interrupted here and there by rocky outcrops. The landscape is dotted with single-story whitewashed cottages, and the rolling green fields stretch down to the sea—all against a backdrop of the mountains of Snowdonia across the Menai Strait, which divides this island from the rest of Wales.

Visitors cross the strait by one of the two bridges built by celebrated engineers of the 19th century: the **Menai Suspension Bridge,** designed by Thomas Telford and completed in 1826, and the **Britannia Bridge,** originally a railroad bridge, which was the work of Robert Stephenson. The Britannia, a neighbor of the suspension bridge, had to be rebuilt after a devastating fire that destroyed its pitch and timberwork; it now carries both trains and cars on two different levels. The bridges are about 1.6km (1 mile) west of Bangor on the mainland.

Neolithic tombs of Stone Age settlers have been found on the island, as have Iron Age artifacts. The Romans left artifacts behind, as did the early Christians who settled here. The coming of steamers and then of the railroad brought Victorian-era visitors. However, if you're not really sold on antiquity, there's a lot to do on Anglesey that is totally in tune with today. Yachting, sea fishing, and leisure centers that offer swimming, squash, and other activities are within easy reach wherever you stay. Golf, tennis, nature walks, pony trekking, canoeing—and more—are offered in the daytime, and in the evening you can wine, dine, and even dance to the latest music. Many people have passed through Anglesey on the train that operates between London and Holyhead, for a ferry journey to Ireland; a stopover for a day in Anglesey is recommended.

Essentials

GETTING THERE The island has good bus service. The major route, bus no. 4, runs between Bangor and Holyhead via Llangefni. Buses operate at the rate of two per hour during the day Monday to Saturday, with limited service on Sunday. Bus no. 57 goes from Bangor to Beaumaris every 30 minutes during the day Monday to

Saturday, and about once every 2 hours on Sunday. All buses cross the Menai Bridge at the town of Menai Bridge (see below). For information, call **Arriva Buses Wales** (✆ **0844/800-4411;** www.arriva.co.uk).

VISITOR INFORMATION   To find out about activities on the island, call or write for a brochure from the **Wales Tourist Board Information Centre,** Railway Station Site, Llanfairpwllgwyngyllgogerychwyrndrobwllllantysiliogogogoch (yes, this is the real name; see below), Isle of Anglesey (✆ **01248/713177;** www. visitanglesey.co.uk). It's open November to March, daily 10am to 5pm, and April to October, daily 9:30am to 5:30pm.

Menai Bridge

The small town of Menai Bridge, 4km (2½ miles) west of Bangor, has several points of interest. Take a stroll westward along the Belgian Promenade, a walk constructed along the strait during World War II by Belgian refugees. You can go under the bridge, past some standing stones, which were recently erected, and Coed Cyrnol, a pine-wood, to **Church Island.** The island's 14th-century **Church of St. Tysilio** was originally founded in the 7th century by St. Tysilio, son of the royal house of Powys and grandson of St. Pabo. St. Pabo is believed to have been a northern British chief who sought asylum on Anglesey. Call the tourist center (see above) for information.

WHERE TO STAY & DINE

Gazelle Hotel   This former posting inn beside the Menai Strait is your top choice for a combined hotel, restaurant, and pub in the area. If you're arriving late in the day, it can be your overnight stopover and gateway to Anglesey, which you can explore the next day. Nearly 5km (3 miles) from the center of Menai Bridge, beside the road signposted to Beaumaris, the hotel's quay-side pub has panoramic views of both the waterfront and the mountains. It's the best place to meet locals and visitors, the latter of whom often have yachts moored nearby. The inn is attractively decorated; old Welsh dressers and time-blackened settles give the place character. Bedrooms are small to moderate in size, each simply decorated but comfortable. Bathrooms are just adequate for the function—nothing more—and contain showers only.

The Gazelle has the best food in the area, so try to dine here even if you're not staying as a guest.

Glyngarth, Menai Bridge, Isle of Anglesey LL59 5PD. ✆ **01248/713364.** Fax 01248/713167. www.the gazellehotel.com. 9 units. £90–£110 double. Rates include Welsh breakfast. MC, V. Located 3.2km (2 miles) northeast of Menai Bridge along A545. **Amenities:** Restaurant; bar; babysitting. *In room:* TV, hair dryer.

Beaumaris

Some 4km (2½ miles) northeast of Menai Bridge lies the tiny town of Beaumaris, the site of the largest of Edward's "iron ring" of castles. A small settlement grew up around the castle, developing into a major port and making Beaumaris a trading center until the coming of the railroad.

Today, the peaceful little town welcomes visitors who come to see **Beaumaris Castle ★** (✆ **01248/810361**), with its evocative moat and drawbridge. The unfinished castle, sitting in marshland on Menai's shore, was given the French name, meaning "beautiful marsh." It is an outstanding example of medieval military architecture, featuring concentric rings of defensive walls.

Construction on the castle began in 1295 and it was defensible by 1298. In those days the sea came up to the southern walls, and on certain tides small ships could reach the castle directly. Visitors can see the original ring where the ships were tied up.

The best way to view the castle ruins is to walk along the outer walls. You can also visit the state apartments that were once occupied by royalty. Soldiers were garrisoned in the towers, and the chapel tower contains a vaulted Gothic ceiling with five pointed windows.

Visits are possible April to October, daily from 9:30am to 5pm; and November to March, Monday to Saturday from 9:30am to 4pm, Sunday 11am to 4pm. Admission is 3.70£ for adults and 3.30£ for seniors, students, and children 16 and under; family tickets cost 10£.

WHERE TO STAY & DINE

For food and lodging in Beaumaris, consider **Ye Olde Bull's Head Inn,** Castle Street (*©* **01248/810329;** www.bullsheadinn.co.uk), a short walk from the castle. The original stagecoach entrance to the courtyard features the largest single-hinged door in Britain. During England's Civil War, Roundhead General Mytton stabled his horses in the courtyard when he laid siege to and took the castle for Cromwell in 1645. The historic inn has housed such notables as Dr. Samuel Johnson and Charles Dickens. The well-decorated bedrooms are named after Dickens characters and cost £110 and up a night. The menu features fresh seafood in summer and game dishes in the autumn and winter. American Express, MasterCard, and Visa are accepted.

Llanfair PG (Llanfairpwllgwyngyllgogerychw- yrndrobwllllantysiliogogogoch)

Practically a suburb of Menai Bridge is a village to the west that has been heard of all over the world. Its fame is its name: Llanfairpwllgwyngyllgogerychwyrndrobwllllantysiliogogogoch, or something like that. It means "St. Mary's Church in the Hollow of the White Hazel near a Rapid Whirlpool and the Church of St. Tysilio near the Red Cave." It has been suggested that perhaps the name was invented as a tourist attraction. You can get the longest train platform ticket in the world from the station here, giving the full name. On maps and most references it is usually called "Llanfair PG" to differentiate it from several other Llanfairs in Wales. The first Women's Institute in Britain was founded here in 1915.

You're sure to see the **Marquess of Anglesey Column** (www.angleseyheritage. org), standing 27m (90 ft.) high on a mount 76m (250 ft.) above sea level. It has a statue of the marquess on top, to which visitors can climb—it's 115 steps up a spiral staircase. The marquess lost a leg while he was second in command to the duke of Wellington at Waterloo and was thereafter called "One Leg" (*Ty Coch* in Welsh). The column is open year-round daily 9am to 5pm, charging £1.50 for adults, 75p for seniors and children.

About 1.6km (1 mile) southwest of the village with the long name, on the A4080, from a turn off the A5 almost opposite the Marquess of Anglesey Column, is **Plas Newydd, Llanfair PG** ★★ (*©* **01248/715272;** www.nationaltrust.org.uk), standing on the shores of the Menai Strait. It was the home of the seventh marquess of Anglesey but is now owned by the National Trust. An ancient manor house, it was converted between 1783 and 1809 into a splendid mansion in the Gothic and neoclassical styles. Its Gothic Hall features a gallery and elaborate fan vaulting. In the long dining room, see the magnificent *trompe l'oeil* mural by Rex Whistler. A military museum houses relics and uniforms of the Battle of Waterloo, where the first marquess of Anglesey lost his leg. The beautiful woodland garden and lawns are also worth visiting. The home can be visited only from Easter to early November, Saturday to Wednesday noon to 5pm. The gardens are open March to early November, Saturday to Wednesday noon to 5pm. A combined ticket for both the house and garden costs £7.80 for adults and £3.90 for children 15 and younger; it's £20 for a family ticket.

WHERE TO STAY & DINE

Carreg Môn Country Hotel   Set at the edge of the village, within a 10-minute walk from the center, this hotel dates from the late 1800s, when it was a privately owned manor house. Today, much altered and enlarged from its original design, it sports a white-painted brick facade and a modern wing that contains the simple but efficient and well-scrubbed small-to-midsize bedrooms, with little bathrooms containing shower stalls. This is the only conventional hotel in town, providing more rooms than any of its smaller and less accessorized competitors. Since the building's transformation into a hotel occurred during the mid-1970s, some of the infrastructure might seem a bit dated, but overall, it provides comfortable and safe lodgings.

Traditional Welsh cookery is always a feature at this reliable country restaurant, with local lamb, black beef, and freshly caught seafood a nightly feature. The home-cooked dishes are backed up with a fully stocked bar and a decent wine list.

Church Lane, Llanfair PG, Anglesey LL61 5YH. © **01248/714224.** Fax 01248/715983. www.carregmon hotel.co.uk. 29 units. £65–£85 double; £100–£130 family room. Rates include Welsh breakfast. AE, DC, MC, V. Free parking. **Amenities:** Restaurant; bar; cocktail lounge; room service; Wi-Fi in lobby (£5). *In room:* TV, hair dryer.

Penrhos Arms ENGLISH/WELSH   This is your best bet for pub grub for the night. It's especially inviting after you've climbed the Anglesey monument and are ready for a cold beer. You can't miss it, as it lies in the center of the village opposite the famous rail station of the village with the impossible name. The food is typical and standard, but it's made from fresh ingredients. If you like steak with mushrooms, fried seafood, or sausage and mashed potatoes, this is for you.

The pub also lets four comfortable bedrooms, each costing £55 for a double, with breakfast included. Expect a TV and a small cubicle with a shower and toilet. Rooms have a chintz-filled decor inspired by Laura Ashley, but no phones.

Holyhead Rd., Llanfair PG, Anglesey LL61 5YQ. © **01248/714892.** Reservations not needed. Main courses £8–£11. DC, MC, V. Mon–Sat 11am–11pm; Sun noon–10:30pm.

HOLYHEAD & HOLY ISLAND

550km (342 miles) NW of London; 346km (215 miles) NW of Cardiff; 305km (190 miles) N of Swansea

The largest town on Anglesey, Holyhead (it's pronounced *Holly*-head—don't ask us why) is not actually on Anglesey at all but on Holy Island. However, the two islands have long been linked. Packet boats between Holyhead and Ireland were recorded as far back as 1573. The harbor of Holyhead was reconstructed in 1880 and now serves as a terminal for container-bearing ships.

People have come to this far point of northern Wales for a long, long time by water. Celtic invaders, early Christian missionaries, Romans, Vikings—whoever—have made their way here, and in many cases stayed on for centuries.

Essentials

GETTING THERE Holyhead is the terminus of the **North Wales Coast** rail line. Trains arrive hourly during the day from Cardiff, Bangor, Llandudno, Chester, Birmingham, and London. For information and schedules, call ☎ **0845/748-4950** or visit **www.nationalrail.co.uk**.

Bus no. 4, operated by **Arriva** (☎ **0844/800-4411;** www.arriva.co.uk), pulls into Holyhead from Bangor every 30 minutes during the day. There is no station here; buses arrive along both London Road and Market Street.

A causeway carries motorists across on the A5, which comes all the way from London, and the Four Mile Bridge on B4545 also links Holy Island to Anglesey.

Two unrelated ferryboat companies operate service between Holyhead and either the Irish port of Dun Laoghaire (a railway and highway junction close to Dublin) or to Dublin harbor itself. Both companies run swift and conventional ferryboat service; transit time is 1½ hours for swift or 3½ hours for conventional each way, with three to five departures daily. On the **Stena Line** (☎ **0870/570-7070;** www.stenaline. co.uk), foot passengers are allowed on the swift ferry; passengers with cars can travel on the conventional ferries. **Irish Ferries** (☎ **0870/517-1717;** www.irishferries. com) carries both passengers and cars. Round-trip transit costs £26 by foot or £89 to £130 by car on the conventional ferryboats. Round-trip on the swift catamarans for passengers traveling or returning on the same day are £25 by foot or £75 with car.

VISITOR INFORMATION Information is available at the **Holyhead Tourist Information Centre,** Stena Line, Terminal 1 (☎ **01407/762622;** www.gonorth wales.co.uk), open year-round Monday to Saturday 8:30am to 6pm.

Where to Stay & Dine

Boathouse Hotel If you decide to overnight before taking a ferry in the morning, this hotel is just a few minutes' walk from the terminal. The town's finest inn, it lies in a stellar position looking out over the water and the Holyhead Mountains, which can be seen from your bedroom. The midsize rooms are pleasantly and comfortably furnished, and the bathrooms, though small, are spick-and-span, with shower units. One unit is large enough for families.

A widely varied selection of freshly made bar snacks is available in the hotel's bistro, along with daily specialties as noted on the blackboard. The chef specializes in freshly caught fish and lobster.

Newry Promenade, Newry Beach, Holyhead LL65 1YF. ☎ **01407/762094.** Fax 01407/764898. www. boathouse-hotel.co.uk. 19 units. £85 double; £95 family room. Rates include Welsh breakfast. AE, MC, V. Free parking. **Amenities:** Restaurant; bar; room service. *In room:* TV, hair dryer.

Bull Hotel ☺ A bustling hotel, the long-popular Bull stands right at the approach to Holyhead. We'd give its competitor, the Boathouse (see above), a slight edge, but the Bull is almost as good. We prefer the more comfortable midsize rooms in the main building, as opposed to the newer and more sterile ones in the annex, but all are comfortable, containing tidy bathrooms with showers. Four rooms are large enough for families.

Both locals and visitors meet in the restaurant to savor an array of both Welsh specialties and international dishes, including black beef, lamb, and freshly caught seafood.

London Rd., Valley, Holyhead LL65 3DP. © **01407/740351.** Fax 01407/742328. 14 units. £70 double. Rates include Welsh breakfast. DC, MC, V. **Amenities:** Restaurant; 2 bars. *In room:* TV.

Seeing the Sights

Holyhead Mountain ★ is the highest point in Anglesey, at 216m (710 ft.). From the rocky height, you can see the Isle of Man, the Mourne Mountains in Ireland, Snowdonia, and Cumbria on a clear day. The summit is the site of an ancient hill fort and the ruins of an Irish settlement from the 2nd to the 4th century A.D. The towering cliffs of North and South Stack are home to thousands of seabirds, and gray seals breed in the caves below. At the southern point of the mountain, **South Stack** is an automatic lighthouse built in 1808. It's 27m (91 ft.) high (60m/197 ft. above mean high water) and can be seen for 32km (20 miles). It's noted for its antique walls, its strategic position, and a state-of-the-art light beam. The lighthouse is open Easter to September, daily from 10:30am to 5pm, charging £4 for adults, £3 for seniors and students, and £2 for children 15 and younger. For information, call © **01407/763207.**

St. Cybi's Church, Market Street (no phone), near the town center, is on the site of a 6th-century church; a Roman fort from the 3rd century also stood here. The site is open daily from 10am to 4pm; admission is free. Services are at 9:15am and 6pm. For information, contact the tourist information center (see above).

On Friday and Saturday, general **markets** are held in Holyhead.

CONWY ★

387km (241 miles) NW of London; 59km (37 miles) E of Holyhead; 35km (22 miles) NE of Caernarfon

Unlike Llandudno, its 19th-century neighbor, Conwy is an ancient town. With its mighty medieval castle and complete town walls, this is a richly historic place.

The Conwy estuary is crossed by three bridges that lead to Conwy. The handsome suspension bridge was built in 1826 by Thomas Telford, bridge-builder extraordinaire. It looks as if it runs right into the castle, but it doesn't. It's closed to vehicular traffic now, but you can walk across it for free and marvel at how it served as the main entrance to the town for so long, with its narrow lanes and the sure bottleneck at the castle end. It replaced the ferry that was previously the only means of crossing the river. An exhibit of Telford's work is in the tollhouse. You can also see Robert Stephenson's tubular railroad bridge, built in 1848, and the modern arched road bridge, completed in 1958.

St. Mary's, the parish church, stands inside the town walls on the site of a 12th-century Cistercian abbey. In it are a Byzantine processional cross, a beautiful Tudor cross, and a 15th-century screen of fine workmanship. The churchyard contains a grave associated with William Wordsworth's poem *We Are Seven.*

Essentials

GETTING THERE   Trains run between Conwy and Llandudno, Bangor, and Holyhead, with easy connections to the rest of Wales. Llandudno is only a 3-minute ride from Conwy. For schedules and information, call © **0845/748-4950.**

Arriva buses from Bangor heading for Llandudno pass through Conwy every 15 minutes during the day Monday to Saturday, and hourly on Sunday. Call © **0844/800-4411** or visit **www.arrivabus.co.uk** for schedules and more information.

Motorists from England head west along the North Wales coastline on A548.

VISITOR INFORMATION Conwy Castle Visitor Centre, Castle Street (© **01492/592248;** www.conwy-castle.co.uk), dispenses information from Easter to May, daily 9:30am to 5pm; June to September, daily 9:30am to 6pm; October, daily 9:30am to 5pm; and November to Easter, Monday to Saturday 9:30am to 4pm and Sunday 11am to 4pm.

Where to Stay & Dine

Groes Inn ★★   Oozing with 4 centuries of atmosphere and old-fashioned charm, this inn dates from 1573 and was the first licensed house in Wales. Although it has expanded over the years, the original core is still here, evoked by log fires, antiques, and open-beamed, time-blackened ceilings. For history buffs, it's the finest choice in the area. The accommodations are in a separate house away from the pub noise, and each midsize unit is comfortably furnished. Rooms open onto bucolic views of sheep grazing in the fields and of rolling hills. The best units have balconies or private terraces; one room has a four-poster bed.

Even if you don't stay here, stop in for a lager or a hearty, home-cooked pub dinner.

Tyn-y-Groes, Conwy LL32 8TN. © **01492/650545.** Fax 01492/650855. www.groesinn.com. 14 units. £105–£190 double. Rates include Welsh breakfast. AE, DC, MC, V. Located 4.8km (3 miles) south of Conwy on B5106. **Amenities:** Restaurant; room service. *In room:* TV, hair dryer.

Old Rectory Country House ★   The Welsh motto for the house, *Hardd Hafan Hedd,* means "a beautiful haven of peace"—and so it is. From its hillside perch, with terraced gardens, the inn sweeps across the Conwy Estuary for a view of Conwy Castle and the Snowdonia mountain range. Once the Tudor home of the rectors of the parish, it is furnished with paintings and antiques. A night here is like entering a bygone era. Each good-size bedroom has its own charm and style; a few have four-poster or half-tester beds. Comfort is foremost, from the sleep-inducing bed to the well-maintained private bathroom.

Wendy Vaughan is a grand chef, producing high-quality and creative dishes that have a light touch and artistic presentation.

Llansanffraid, Glan Conwy, Conwy LL28 5LF. © **01492/580611.** Fax 01492/584555. www.oldrectory countryhouse.co.uk. 6 units. £99–£159 double. Rates include Welsh breakfast. MC, V. Take the A470 4.8km (3 miles) from Conwy; the Old Rectory is .8km (½ mile) south from A55/A470 junction on the left. No children under 5. **Amenities:** Restaurant; bar. *In room:* TV, hair dryer.

Seeing the Sights

Aberconwy House   This is the only remaining medieval merchant's house in Conwy, a town that used to have hundreds of them. Dating from the 14th century, this structure is owned by the National Trust and houses an exhibition depicting the life of Conwy from Roman times. It includes a re-created 18th-century kitchen and a mussel-fishing corner, with the traditional instruments still used by the industry.

Castle St. and High St. © **01492/592246.** www.nationaltrust.org.uk. Admission £3 adults, £1.50 children 15 and younger, £7.50 family ticket. Apr–Oct Wed–Mon 11am–5pm (last admission 4:30pm).

Conwy Castle ★★   The town centers on Conwy Castle. Edward I had this masterpiece of medieval architecture built after he conquered the last native prince of Wales, Llywelyn. The English king put up massive castles to convince the Welsh that he was the supreme authority. The castle follows the contours of a narrow strip of rock, the eight towers commanding the estuary of the River Conwy. The town wall that protected the borough, chartered by Edward in 1284, is almost intact, with 21 flanking towers and three twin-towered gateways. Visitors to the town can walk the walls. This is one castle you can't possibly miss seeing, as the road runs almost close enough for you to touch the walls in places. Allow an hour to visit.

Castle St. © **01492/592358.** Admission £4.70 adults; £4.20 seniors, students and children 15 and younger; £14 family ticket. Apr–June and Sept–Oct daily 9:30am–5pm; July–Aug daily 9:30am–6pm; Nov–Mar Mon–Sat 9:30am–4pm, Sun 11am–4pm. Closed Dec 24–26 and Jan 1.

LLANDUDNO ★

391km (243 miles) NW of London; 69km (43 miles) E of Holyhead

This Victorian seaside resort—the largest in Wales—nestles in a crescent between the giant headlands of the **Great Orme** and the **Little Orme,** which received their names from early Vikings who thought they resembled sea serpents when their bases were shrouded in mist. This premier resort of Wales has two beaches, one on the northern edge of town, flanking a boardwalk and the Irish Sea, and the other on the west side of town, opening onto the mountains of Snowdonia and the Conwy Estuary.

Llandudno was built beginning around 1850 by the Mostyn family, after whom many local roads, avenues, and sites are named. It was conceived as a means to cash in on the already-proven proclivity of the British of Queen Victoria's day—particularly the great middle classes—to go to the seashore in summer. It is built in a typically Victorian way with a promenade along the beach. The Victorian elegance and tradition of Llandudno have been maintained in the architecture of its buildings, but the days-gone-by atmosphere stops there.

Essentials

GETTING THERE **Virgin Trains** has service from London's Euston Station, frequently requiring changes of equipment in either Crewe or Chester, and in some cases, both of them. Overall, with waiting time included, it takes about 4½ hours to reach Llandudno from London by train. However, one Virgin train per day goes direct with no changes, taking 3¼ hours. For information about this or any other railway schedule in Wales, call © **0845/748-4950** or go to **www.nationalrail.co.uk**.

During the day, **Arriva** (© **0844/800-4411;** www.arriva.co.uk) maintains buses to and from neighboring Bangor. They depart every 15 to 60 minutes.

If driving from England, take the M6 to the M56, and then head across North Wales along the A55.

VISITOR INFORMATION The **Llandudno Tourist Information Centre,** Mostyn Street (© **01492/577577;** www.visitllandudno.org.uk), is open between April and October, daily from 9:30am to 5:30pm. From November to March, it's open Monday to Saturday 9:30am to 5pm.

Where to Stay

VERY EXPENSIVE

Bodysgallen Hall ★★★ This is the finest address in the north of Wales, a dramatic 17th-century country house set on 80 hectares (200 acres) of parkland and manicured gardens. It would be the only suitable address for the novelist Henry

James, were he alive today. Skillfully restored, it offers architectural merit combined with 21st-century comfort. The hall has a 13th-century tower that was a lookout post for Conwy Castle, 2.5km (1½ miles) away. You can still climb the tower for a panoramic view. Each of the spacious and elegant bedrooms evokes a certain period in their styles and colors; some have four-poster beds. Some of the units, as good as those in the main house, are in converted cottages.

3.2km (2 miles) southeast of Llandudno along A470, Llandudno LL30 IRS. ℂ **01492/584466.** Fax 01492/582519. www.bodysgallen.com. 33 units. £145–£340 double; £415 suite. Rates include Welsh breakfast. MC, V. Free parking. No children under 6. **Amenities:** Restaurant; bar; exercise room; Jacuzzi; indoor heated pool; spa; outdoor tennis court. *In room:* TV, fridge, hair dryer, Wi-Fi (£5).

EXPENSIVE

Empire Hotel ★★★   In an ocean of tacky hotels, this one is a winner, the best within the town itself. Off the Promenade, near the Great Orme cable car, it looks down on the pier and Happy Valley, about 274m (900 ft.) away. Family managed, it is furnished with antiques and fine paintings in the Victorian tradition. Bedrooms are medium-size to spacious and are luxuriously furnished. A Victorian annex, "No. 72," contains eight of the establishment's finest rooms, filled with Victorian antiques, touches of silk, and a bathtub-cum-Jacuzzi. We prefer these to the accommodations in the main building. You'll find luxury and style throughout.

Church Walks, Llandudno, Conwy LL30 2HE. ℂ **01492/860555.** Fax 01492/860791. www.empirehotel. co.uk. 58 units. £90–£120 double. AE, DC, MC, V. Free parking. **Amenities:** 2 restaurants; bar; 2 heated pools (1 indoor, 1 outdoor); room service; spa; Wi-Fi (free, in lobby). *In room:* TV, fridge, hair dryer.

St. Tudno Hotel ★★   For fans of *Alice in Wonderland*, this is the only place to stay in town. Alice Liddell, immortalized by author Lewis Carroll, checked in here at the age of 8 on her first visit to Llandudno in 1861. It's a Victorian terraced seafront hotel that escapes the tacky curse of many of its neighbors. The hotel has kept abreast of the times—you won't fall down the rabbit hole if checking in here—and is one of the top seafront hotels in North Wales. Richly decorated inside, it is opulent and luxurious, with first-class service. Martin and Janette Bland offer a beautiful experience, with individually designed bedrooms that come in a variety of sizes. Those in the rear have slightly less glamour but are more tranquil and a lot cheaper. Traditionalists prefer to check into the Alice Suite. Public rooms evoke the Victorian era.

North Parade, Promenade, Llandudno, Gwynedd LL30 2LP. ℂ **01492/874411.** Fax 01492/860407. www.st-tudno.co.uk. 18 units. £100–£210 double; £290 suite. Rates include Welsh breakfast. AE, DC, MC, V. Free parking. **Amenities:** Restaurant (Terrace, reviewed below); bar; heated indoor pool; room service. *In room:* A/C (in some), TV, hair dryer, minibar.

INEXPENSIVE

Tan Lan Hotel ★ 🪶   This is your best bet for the night if you're seeking good-value accommodations on the tranquil west shore of Llandudno. It lies under the Great Orme, and its owners offer cozy lodgings and a warm welcome. The rooms upstairs are a bit quieter, but all are medium-size, brightly decorated, and well furnished. A trio of units is big enough for families, and children get a warm welcome. The dining room, decorated in the best tradition of the English play *Separate Tables*, is known for a varied menu—nothing too experimental.

Great Ormes Rd., West Shore, Llandudno, Conwy LL30 2AR. ℂ **01492/860221.** Fax 01492/870219. www.tanlanhotel.co.uk. 17 units. £40 double. Rates include Welsh breakfast. MC, V. Free parking. Closed mid-Oct to mid-Mar. **Amenities:** Restaurant; bar. *In room:* TV, hair dryer.

1/4 mil
1/4 km

✝ Church
▪▪ Railway

Llandudno Bay

North Shore

Pier

THE GREAT ORME

Marine Dr.

Happy Valley Rd.
HAPPY VALLEY

Ty Gwyn Rd.
Wyddfyd Rd.
Llewelyn Rd.
Church Walks
Rectory Lane
Abbey Rd.
Llwynon Rd.
TY N-Y-Coed Rd.
Glodaeth Av.
Gloddaeth Av.

Aryon Av.
DeGanwy
Madoc St.
Brookes St.
Caroline Rd.
Maelgwyn Rd.
St. Mary's Rd.
St. David's Rd.
St. Seiriol Rd.
St. Andrews Av.
The Oval
Lloyd St.
Lloyd St. W.

South Parade
Glan-Y-Mor Parade
Ty Isa Rd.
St.George's Cres.
Somerset St.
Gloddaeth Cres.
Mostyn Rd.
Bodston St.
Trinity Sq.
St. Augusta St.
Jubilee St.
Argyle Rd.
Council St. W.
Builder St.
Railway Station
Oxford Rd.
Cwm Rd.
Ffrod Penmyn
Ffordd Dewi
Cwm Pl.

Promenade
Mostyn St.
Adelphi St.
Newill Cres.
Mostyn Cres.
Mostyn Broadway
Tudor Cres.
Charlotte Rd.
Conway Rd.
Penrhyn Cres.

Craig-Y-Don
Parade
East Parade
Victoria St.
Curzon Rd.
Riviere Av.
Queens Rd.
Clarence Cres.
Clarence Dr.
CRAIG-Y-DON
Clarence Rd.
Liddel Dr.
Conway Rd.

Nant-Y-Gamar Rd.
Bedford Cres.
Mostyn Av.
Carmen
Roumania Cres.
Roumania Cres.
Park Av.
Roman Dr.
Princess Dr.
Sylva Rd.
Tan-Y-Bryn Rd.
Meadow Gdns.
Fferm Bach Rd.
Balfour Rd.
N. Cymru
N. Gwalia St.
Harlech Rd.
Rhuddlan Av.
Bodnant Rd.
Maesdu Rd.
Builder St. West
Kings Rd.
Alexandra Rd.
Denness Pl.
Dinas Rd.
Winlan Av.
Brynlau Pl.
Great Ormes Rd.
Mowbra Rd.
Trinity Cres.

West Parade
Promenade
West Shore

Conwy Bay

North Shore

Church of St. Tudno **1**
Great Orme Tramway **2**
Llandudno Museum **3**
Venue Cymru
(North Wales Theatre) **4**

ENGLAND
WALES
Llandudno
Cardiff ✪
40 mil
40 km

Where to Dine

The **Cottage Loaf,** Market Square (✆ **01492/870762;** www.the-cottageloaf. co.uk), a village tavern with a summer beer garden, serves the best pub grub in town, with generous main courses (each a meal in itself) costing from £7. It's open Monday to Saturday 11am to 11pm and Sunday noon to 10:30pm.

Seahorse Restaurant ★ WELSH/CONTINENTAL   Don and Gill Hadwin run a restaurant both upstairs and in the basement. Their cuisine and friendly service have brought them a faithful list of habitués. The cooks turn out satisfying meals full of flavor. Crispy duck breast is served with a tangy plum sauce, or else you can sample chicken breast stuffed with smoked cheddar and wild mushrooms. The fish dishes are especially recommended, notably the grilled tuna steak with a lime-and-coriander butter or the grilled swordfish marinated in lemon and garlic.

7 Church Walks. ✆ **01492/875315.** www.the-seahorse.co.uk. Reservations required. 1-course menu (main only) £19, 2-course menu £25, 3-course menu £29. AE, MC. Tues–Sat 5:30–11pm.

Terrace Restaurant ★★ WELSH/BRITISH   In the previously recommended St. Tudno Hotel, this first-class restaurant enjoys a panoramic location on the promenade across from the Victorian pier. As you gaze upon blown-up photographs of Italy's Lake Como, you'll think you're in the Italian lake district. Rich fabrics and beautiful chandeliers adorn the space. The cooking is based on fine seafood and local farm products, and it is very good indeed. You might begin with slow-cooked pork belly with a tempura of vegetables or pheasant in pastry parcels with butternut coleslaw. For a main, opt for the loin of roe deer with a game pudding and a truffled Welsh honey glaze, or perhaps the roast breast of Gressingham duck. A selection of Celtic farmhouse cheese is served, or you can try the warm roast pineapple tart with "popcorn" ice cream.

In the St. Tudno Hotel, North Parade, Promenade. ✆ **01492/874-411.** www.st-tudno.co.uk. Reservations required. Main courses £16–£18. Fixed-price 2-course menu £17, 3-course menu £19. AE, DC, MC, V. Daily noon–2pm and 6:30–9:30pm.

Seeing the Sights

From the summit of the **Great Orme** ★ (206m/679 ft.), you get a panoramic view of the North Wales coast. You can walk up to the top if you're really energetic, but we advise other means. At Happy Valley, exotic sheltered gardens lie at the foot of the Great Orme, near the pier at the west end of the Llandudno Bay promenade. Take the **Great Orme Tramway** (✆ **01492/879306;** www.greatormetramway. com) to reach the top. The tramway has been carrying passengers to the summit since 1902. Between late March and October, it operates every 20 minutes, daily from 10am to 6pm. The round-trip costs £5.40 for adults, £3.70 for children 13 and younger. It is closed in winter, during which period you can drive along a spectacular cliff-edge road, the Marine Drive, which winds uphill in a circular route that reaches a point near the summit of the Great Orme. Cars pay a toll of £2.50.

Just above the Marine Drive is the ancient **Church of St. Tudno,** from which the town derives its name. The present stone building dates from the 12th century, but the church was founded 600 years earlier. Between April and October, it's open 24 hours a day, and between June and September, there are open-air worship services every Sunday at 11am. For more information about the church and its services, or to gain entrance during other times of the year, contact the rector, John Nice, at **℗ 01492/876624,** or go to **www.llandudno-parish.org.uk/sttudno.html**.

At the end of the north-shore promenade, one of Britain's finest Victorian piers was built, jutting 699m (2,295 ft.) into the bay at the base of the Great Orme, with an ornate covered pavilion at the end. You can find entertainment, food, fishing, or just relaxation on the pier. The north-shore beach is busy in summer, with traditional British seaside activities, including donkey rides, Punch-and-Judy shows, boat trips, and a children's fun land across the promenade.

The seafront's most visible public monument is the **Venue Cymru,** the Promenade (**℗ 01492/872000;** www.venuecymru.co.uk). Built in the early 1990s and previously known as the North Wales Theatre, it's the venue for everything from opera to rock concerts. Most shows begin at 8pm; tickets cost £10 to £45.

The **Llandudno Museum,** 17–19 Gloddaeth St. (**℗ 01492/876517;** www.conwy.gov.uk/doc.asp?cat=776&doc=1582), displays the development of Llandudno as a seaside resort through period rooms. It is open Easter through October, Tuesday to Saturday 10:30am to 1pm and 2 to 5pm, Sunday 2:15 to 5pm. The rest of the year, hours are Tuesday to Saturday 1:30 to 4:30pm. Admission is £3.50 for adults, £2.50 for children, and £6 for a family ticket.

FAST FACTS

FAST FACTS: ENGLAND & WALES

Area Codes   The country code for England and Wales is **44.** The area code for London is **020;** the area code for Cardiff is **029.**

Business Hours   With many, many exceptions, business hours are Monday to Friday from 9am to 5pm. In general, stores are open Monday to Saturday from 9am to 5:30pm. In country towns, there is usually an early closing day (often Wed or Thurs), when the shops close at 1pm.

Clothing Sizes   See the clothing size conversion chart, below.

Drinking Laws   The legal drinking age is 18. Children 15 and younger aren't allowed in pubs, except in certain rooms, and then only when accompanied by a parent or guardian. Don't drink and drive. Penalties are stiff.

Breaking decades of tradition, in 2005 England abandoned its strict, often draconian, liquor laws, allowing 24-hour alcohol sales in England and Wales. Many pubs no longer close at 11pm, which used to be "last call." Of course, it's up to the publican, but many, if they elect to do so, could stay open day and night. It's not total nirvana for the pub owners, however. Some counties are stationing undercover officers in pubs to fine staff members who serve liquor to visibly drunk customers, and the problems of drunk drivers on the highway, policemen fear, will only increase.

Driving Rules   See "Getting There & Getting Around," p. 55.

Drugstores   In Britain, they're called "chemists." Every police station in the country has a list of emergency chemists. Dial "0" (zero) and ask the operator for the local police, who will give you the name of one nearest you.

Electricity   Britain uses 240 volts AC (50 cycles), roughly twice the voltage in North America, which is 115 to 120 volts AC (60 cycles). American plugs don't fit British wall outlets. Always bring suitable transformers and/or adapters.

Embassies & Consulates   The **United States Embassy** is at 24 Grosvenor Sq., London, W1 (✆ **020/7499-9000;** www.usembassy.org.uk; Tube: Bond St.). Hours are Monday to Friday 8am to 5:30pm, Saturday 10am to 4pm. However, for passport and visa information, go to the **U.S. Passport and Citizenship Unit,** 55–56 Upper Grosvenor St., London, W1 (✆ **020/7894-0563;** www.london.usembassy.gov; Tube: Marble Arch or Bond St.); hours are Monday to Friday 8:30am to 12:30pm.

The **Canadian High Commission,** Macdonald House, 1 Grosvenor Sq., London, W1 (📞 **020/7258-6600;** www.canadainternational.gc.ca/united_kingdom; Tube: Bond St.), handles visas for Canada. Hours are Monday to Friday 8 to 11am for immigration services, and 9:30am to 1:30pm for passports.

The **Australian High Commission** is at Australia House, the Strand, London, WC2 (📞 **020/7379-4334;** www.australia.org.uk; Tube: Charing Cross or Aldwych). Hours are Monday to Friday 9am to 5pm; for immigration services, hours are 9 to 11am, and for passports, 9:30am to 3:30pm.

The **New Zealand High Commission** is at New Zealand House, 80 Haymarket at Pall Mall, London, SW1 (📞 **020/7930-8422;** www.nzembassy.com; Tube: Charing Cross or Piccadilly Circus). Hours are Monday to Friday 10am to 4pm.

The **Irish Embassy** is at 17 Grosvenor Place, London, SW1 (📞 **020/7235-2171;** www. ireland.embassyhomepage.com; Tube: Hyde Park Corner). Hours are Monday to Friday 9:30am to 1pm and 2 to 5pm.

Emergencies Dial **999** for police, fire, or ambulance. Give your name, address, and telephone number and state the nature of the emergency.

Gasoline (Petrol) See "Gasoline" under "Getting There & Getting Around," p. 61.

Holidays Britain observes New Year's Day, Good Friday, Easter Monday, May Day (first Mon in May), spring and summer bank holidays (the last Mon in May and Aug, respectively), Christmas Day, and Boxing Day (Dec 26).

For more information on holidays, see the "England & Wales Calendar of Events," p. 49.

Hot Lines These emergency numbers exist in London: If you're in some sort of substance abuse or legal emergency, call **Release** (📞 **020/7729-9904**), open Monday to Friday 11am to 1pm. The **Rape and Sexual Abuse Hotline** (📞 **0845/122-1331**) is open Monday to Friday noon to 2:30pm and 7 to 9:30pm, weekends and bank holidays 2:30 to 5pm. **Alcoholics Anonymous** (📞 **020/7833-0022**) answers its help line daily 10am to 10pm. Call the **Sexual Health Information Line** (📞 **0800/567-123**) for issues related to sexual health and sexually transmitted diseases.

Insurance **Medical Insurance** For travel overseas, most U.S. health plans (including Medicare and Medicaid) do not provide coverage, and the ones that do often require you to pay for services up front and reimburse you only after you return home.

As a safety net, you may want to buy travel medical insurance, particularly if you're heading to a remote or high-risk area where emergency evacuation might be necessary. If you require additional medical insurance, try **MEDEX Assistance** (📞 **800/537-2029** or 410/453-6300; www.medexassist.com) or **Travel Assistance International** (📞 **800/821-2828;** www.travelassistance.com; for general information on services, call the company's **Worldwide Assistance Services** at 📞 **800/777-8710;** www.worldwideassistance.com).

Canadians should check with their provincial health plan offices or call **Health Canada** (📞 **866/225-0709;** www.hc-sc.gc.ca) to find out the extent of their coverage and what documentation and receipts they must take home in case they are treated overseas. **Travel Insurance** The cost of travel insurance varies widely, depending on the destination, the cost and length of your trip, your age and health, and the type of trip you're taking, but expect to pay between 5% and 8% of the vacation itself. You can get estimates from various providers through **InsureMyTrip.com** (📞 **800/487-4722**). Enter your trip cost and dates, your age, and other information, for prices from more than a dozen companies.

Most big travel agencies offer their own insurance and will probably try to sell you their package when you book a holiday. Think before you sign. **Britain's Consumers' Association** recommends that you insist on seeing the policy and reading the fine print before buying travel insurance. The **Association of British Insurers** (✆ **020/ 7600-3333;** www.abi.org.uk) gives advice by phone and publishes *Holiday Insurance,* a free guide to policy provisions and prices. You might also shop around for better deals; try **Columbus Direct** (✆ **0870/033-9988;** www.columbusdirect.net).

Trip-Cancellation Insurance   Trip-cancellation insurance will help retrieve your money if you have to back out of a trip or depart early, or if your travel supplier goes bankrupt. Trip cancellation traditionally covers such events as sickness, natural disasters, and Department of State advisories. The latest news in trip-cancellation insurance is the availability of expanded hurricane coverage and "any-reason" cancellation coverage— which costs more but covers cancellations made for any reason. You won't get back 100% of your prepaid trip cost, but you'll be refunded a substantial portion.

For details, contact one of the following recommended insurers: **Access America** (✆ 800/284-8300; www.accessamerica.com), **Travel Guard International** (✆ 800/826- 4919; www.travelguard.com), **Travel Insured International** (✆ 800/243-3174; www.travel insured.com), **Travelex Insurance Services** (✆ 800/228-9792; www.travelex-insurance. com), and **TravelSafe** (✆ 888/885-7233; www.travelsafe.com).

For more information on traveler's insurance, trip-cancellation insurance, and medical insurance while traveling, please visit www.frommers.com/planning.

Internet Access   It's hard nowadays to find a city that *doesn't* have a few cybercafes. Although there's no definitive directory for cybercafes, two places to start looking are **www.cybercaptive.com** and **www.cybercafe.com**. Also see "Staying Connected" (p. 81) for more information.

Legal Aid   The American Services section of the U.S. Embassy (see above) will give you advice if you run into trouble abroad. It can advise you of your rights and will even provide a list of attorneys (for which you'll have to pay if services are used). But it cannot interfere on your behalf in the legal process of Great Britain.

For questions about American citizens who are arrested abroad, including ways of getting money to them, telephone the **Citizens Emergency Center** of the Office of Special Consulate Services, in Washington, D.C. (✆ **202/647-5225**). Citizens of other nations should go to their London-based consulate for advice.

Mail   At press time, an airmail letter to North America costs 56p for 10 grams; postcards also require a 56p stamp; letters generally take 7 to 10 days to arrive in the United States. The British postal system is among the most reliable in the world, so you don't need to depend on Federal Express or some other carrier unless you're in a great hurry.

Newspapers & Magazines   In London, the *Times, Daily Telegraph, Daily Mail,* and *Guardian* are dailies carrying the latest news. The *International Herald Tribune,* published in Paris, and an international edition of *USA Today,* beamed via satellite, are available daily (*USA Today* is printed as a newsletter). Magazines such as *Time Out* and *Where* contain useful information about the latest happenings in London.

Passports   See www.frommers.com/planning for information on how to obtain a passport. For other information, please contact the following agencies:

For Residents of Australia   Contact the **Australian Passport Information Service** at ✆ **131-232,** or visit the government website at www.passports.gov.au.

For Residents of Canada Contact the central **Passport Office,** Department of Foreign Affairs and International Trade, Ottawa, ON K1A 0G3 (☎ **800/567-6868;** www.ppt.gc.ca).

For Residents of New Zealand Contact the **Passports Office** at ☎ **0800/225-050** in New Zealand, or 04/474-8100; or log on to www.dia.govt.nz.

For Residents of the United States To find your regional passport office, either check the U.S. Department of State website or call the **National Passport Information Center** toll-free number (☎ **877/487-2778;** http://travel.state.gov) for automated information.

Police Dial ☎ **999** if the matter is serious. Losses, thefts, and other criminal matters should be reported to the police immediately.

Smoking As of July 1, 2007, a smoking ban went into effect in England. Smoking is now banned in all indoor public places such as pubs, restaurants, clubs, and hotels, although hotels can set aside some rooms for smokers.

Taxes To encourage energy conservation, the British government levies a 25% tax on gasoline (petrol). There is also a 17.5% national value-added tax (VAT) that is added to all hotel and restaurant bills and is included in the price of many items you purchase. This can be refunded if you shop at stores that participate in the Retail Export Scheme (signs are posted in the window).

Telephones See "Staying Connected," p. 81.

Time Britain follows **Greenwich Mean Time** (5 hr. ahead of Eastern Standard Time). For most of the year, including summer, Britain is 5 hours ahead of the time observed in the Eastern United States. Because of different daylight saving time practices in the two nations, there's a brief period (about a week) in autumn when Britain is only 4 hours ahead of New York and a brief period in spring when it's 6 hours ahead of New York.

Tipping In hotels, tip **porters** or **bellhops** 75p per bag, even if you have only one small suitcase. Hall porters are tipped only for special services. Tip **chamber staff** £1 per day. In top-ranking hotels, the **concierge** will often submit a separate bill showing charges for newspapers and other items; if he or she has been particularly helpful, tip extra.

 Hotels often add a service charge of 10% to 15%. In smaller **bed-and-breakfasts,** the tip is not likely to be included. Therefore, tip staff members for special services, such as the waiter who serves you breakfast. If several people have served you in a B&B, you may ask that 10% to 15% be added to the bill and divided among the staff.

 In restaurants and nightclubs, a 15% service charge is added to the bill, which is distributed among all the staff. To that, add another 3% to 5%, depending on the service. **Waiters** in deluxe restaurants and nightclubs are accustomed to the extra 5%. **Sommeliers** (wine stewards) get about £1 per bottle of wine served. Tipping in pubs isn't common, but in wine bars, the server usually gets about 75p per round of drinks.

 Tip **cab drivers** 10% to 15% of the fare on the meter. If the driver loads or unloads your luggage, add something extra. Tip **barbers** and **hairdressers** 10% to 15%. It's not mandatory, but **tour guides** expect £2.

 Gas station attendants are rarely tipped, and theater ushers don't expect tips.

Toilets The English often call toilets "loos." They're marked by PUBLIC TOILETS signs in streets, parks, and Tube stations; many are automatically sterilized after each use. You'll also find well-maintained lavatories in all larger public buildings, such as museums and galleries, large department stores, and railway stations. It's not really acceptable to use the lavatories in hotels, restaurants, and pubs if you're not a customer, but we can't say that we always stick to this rule. Public lavatories are usually free, but you may need a small coin to get in or to use a proper washroom (with a washbasin or sink).

Visitor Information Before you go, you can obtain general information from **Visit Britain** (www.visitbritain.us): In the **United States,** call ℂ 800/462-2748 or 212/986-2266; in **Canada,** ℂ 888/VISITUK (847-4885); in **Australia,** ℂ 02/1300-858589; and in **New Zealand,** ℂ 0800/700-741.

For a full information package on London, contact **Visit London** (ℂ **020/7234-5800;** www.visitlondon.co.uk).

Wales, like England, has a number of regional tourist offices. Contact the **Visit Wales Centre,** Brunel House, 2 Fitzalan Rd., Cardiff CF24 0UY (ℂ **08701/211-255;** www.visitwales.com). If you're in London, detailed information is also available from the Wales Desk at the **Britain and London Visitor Centre (BLVC),** 1 Lower Regent St., London SW1Y 4XT (ℂ **8701/566-366;** www.visitlondon.com; Tube: Piccadilly Circus).

Websites The most useful website, **www.visitbritain.us**, was created by Britain's national tourism agency. The site lets you order brochures, provides trip-planning hints, and even allows e-mail questions for prompt answers. All of Great Britain is covered.

Go to **www.baa.com** for a guide and terminal maps for Heathrow, Gatwick, Stansted, and several other airports in the U.K., including flight arrival times, duty-free shops, airport restaurants, and info on getting from the London airports to downtown London.

Getting around London can be confusing, so you may want to visit **www.tfl.gov.uk** for up-to-the-minute info on transportation.

Clothing Size Conversions

WOMEN'S CLOTHES		WOMEN'S SHOES	
U.S.	U.K.	U.S.	U.K.
8	10	4½	3
10	12	5½	4
12	14	6½	5
14	16	7½	6
16	18	8½	7
18	20	9½	8

MEN'S CLOTHES/SHIRTS	MEN'S SHOES	
Sizes are the same	U.S.	U.K.
	7	6
	8	7
	9	8
	10	9
	11	10
	12	11

At **www.britannia.com**, you'll find much more than a travel guide—it's chock-full of lively features, history, and regional profiles, including sections on Wales and King Arthur.

English Heritage (www.english-heritage.org.uk) has trip-planning information, accommodations listings, and an attractions finder that allows you to search by region. The **National Trust** (www.nationaltrust.org.uk) provides a similar service with a searchable online attractions finder, featuring castles, museums, natural wonders, and more. Many hotels and attractions that don't have their own websites can be found in one of these two directories.

For the latest on London's theater scene, consult **www.officiallondontheatre.co.uk**.

AIRLINE, HOTEL & CAR-RENTAL WEBSITES

MAJOR U.S. AIRLINES

An asterisk (*) indicates that the airline flies internationally as well.

American Airlines*
www.aa.com

Continental Airlines*
www.continental.com

Delta Air Lines*
www.delta.com

United Airlines*
www.united.com

US Airways*
www.usairways.com

MAJOR INTERNATIONAL AIRLINES

Aeroméxico
www.aeromexico.com

Air Canada
www.aircanada.com

Air France
www.airfrance.com

Air India
www.airindia.com

Air Lingus
www.aerlingus.com

Air New Zealand
www.airnewzealand.com

Alitalia
www.alitalia.com

BMI
www.flybmi.com

British Airways
www.britishairways.com

Cathay Pacific
www.cathaypacific.com

EgyptAir
www.egyptair.com

Emirates Airlines
www.emirates.com

Finnair
www.finnair.com

Iberia Airlines
www.iberia.com

Icelandair
www.icelandair.com
www.icelandair.co.uk (in the U.K.)

Korean Air
www.koreanair.com

Lufthansa
www.lufthansa.com

Olympic Airlines
www.olympicairlines.com

Qantas Airways
www.qantas.com

Swiss Air
www.swiss.com

TACA
www.taca.com

Thai Airways International
www.thaiair.com

Virgin Atlantic Airways
www.virgin-atlantic.com

BUDGET AIRLINES

Aegean Airlines
www.aegeanair.com

Aer Lingus
www.aerlingus.com

Air Berlin
www.airberlin.com
BMI Baby
www.bmibaby.com
easyJet
www.easyjet.com
Flybe
www.flybe.com
Ryanair
www.ryanair.com

MAJOR HOTEL & MOTEL CHAINS

Accor Hotels
www.accorhotels.com
Best Western International
www.bestwestern.com
Britannia Hotels
www.britanniahotels.com
Carlson Hotels
www.carlson.com
Clarion Hotels
www.choicehotels.com
Comfort Inn
www.comfortinn.com
Courtyard by Marriott
www.marriott.com/courtyard
Days Inn
www.daysinn.com
Doubletree Hotels
http://doubletree1.hilton.com
Fairfield Inn by Marriott
www.marriott.com/fairfieldinn
Firmdale Hotels
www.firmdale.com
Four Seasons
www.fourseasons.com
Grange Hotels
www.grangehotels.com
Hilton Hotels
www1.hilton.com
Holiday Inn
www.ichotelsgroup.com
Hotel Formule 1
www.hotelformule1.com
Hyatt
www.hyatt.com

InterContinental Hotels & Resorts
www.ichotelsgroup.com
Leading Hotels of the World
www.lhw.com
Marriott
www.marriott.com
Mercure Hotels
www.mercure.com
Millennium Hotels & Resorts
www.millenniumhotels.com
Novotel Hotels
www.novotel.com
Preferred Hotels
www.preferredhotels.com
Premier Inn
www.premierinn.com
Quality Inn
www.qualityinn.com
Radisson Hotels & Resorts
www.radisson.com
Ramada Worldwide
www.ramada.com
Residence Inn by Marriott
www.marriott.com/residence-inn
Roccoforte Collection
www.roccofortecollection.com
Sheraton Hotels & Resorts
www.starwoodhotels.com/sheraton
Sol Meliá Hotels
www.solmelia.com
Thistle Hotels
www.thistle.com
Westin Hotels & Resorts
www.starwoodhotels.com/westin
Wyndham Hotels & Resorts
www.wyndham.com

CAR-RENTAL AGENCIES

Alamo
www.alamo.com
Auto Europe
www.autoeurope.com
Avis
www.avis.com
Budget
www.budget.com

Dollar
www.dollar.com

Enterprise
www.enterprise.com

Hertz
www.hertz.com

Kemwel (KHA)
www.kemwel.com

National
www.nationalcar.com

Thrifty
www.thrifty.com

22

THE WELSH LANGUAGE

by Nick Dalton & Deborah Stone

23

To first-time visitors, it's quite extraordinary just how Welsh Wales is. Signs, addresses, place names, and menus are mostly in both Welsh and English, which can be baffling in itself. The road signs are in both languages, which leads the unwary to suspect there are two different towns ahead. And then sometimes there's a lone sign that's just Welsh, making you think you've missed the road to Cardiff. Because, unlike many other languages, there's rarely a translation obvious to the untrained eye, Pembrokeshire becomes Dyfed while Cardigan comes in slightly closer as Cerdigion. Llan (which seems to be the start of half the place names) means church, while aber (which seems to start the other half) is river mouth.

Several words it is handy to know are *gwesty* (hotel), *siôp* (shop), *gorsaf* (station), *traeth* (beach), *ffordd* (no, it's road) and *cawl cennin* (well, you never know when you might fancy leek soup).

And while we're on the subject we shouldn't forget the classic Llanfairpwllgwyngyllgogerychwyrndrobwllllantysiliogogogoch, the village in Anglesey, which (roughly) is The Church of St Mary by the pool with the white hazel near the rapid whirlpool by St Tysilio's church and the red cave. Although on road signs you'll see it as Llanfair PG, which isn't half as much fun. See below for a more extensive list of Welsh words.

A SMATTERING OF USEFUL WELSH WORDS

Aber river mouth

Afon river

Araf slow

bach/fach small

bont/pont bridge

bwlch gap, pass

carreg stone

cefn ridge

coed wood

croes/groes cross

cwm valley

dim mynediad no entry

dim no

dinas fort, city

dynion gentlemen

eglwys church

fawr/mawr big

felin/melin mill

ffordd road

gorsaf station

gwesty hotel

heddlu police

llan church lands

llyn lake

llwybr cyhoeddus public footpath

lôn lane

marched ladies

mynydd mountain

pen top

rhyd ford

siôp shop

Swyddfa'r Post Post Office

Toiledau toilets

Traeth beach

Ysbyty hospital

Index

See also London Accommodations and Restaurant indexes, below.

Emmanuel College (Cambridge), 532
Empire Theatre (Liverpool), 611
The End (London), 225
Enginiuty (Ironbridge), 516–517
English Heritage, 758
English Lakeland Ramblers, 78
English National Opera (London), 220
Entry requirements, 54–55
Equestrian events
Horse of the Year Show (Birmingham), 53
Royal Windsor Horse Show, 50
Equitour, 79
Escorted general-interest tours, 80–81
Essex Cycle Route, 77
Eton College, 240–241
Euro-Bike & Walking Tours, 77
Eurolines, 58
Eurostar, 57
Eurotunnel, 56–57
Everyman Theatre (Cheltenham), 470
Exchange Bar (Swansea), 719
Exeter, 402, 404–407
Exeter Cathedral, 407–408
Exeter Guildhall, 408
Exeter Phoenix, 409
Exeter Summer Festival, 51, 404
Exhibition Square (York), 656
Exit Club (Cardiff), 706
Exmoor National Park, 399, 400

F

Fabric (London), 225
Fairfax Hall (Leeds Castle), 301
Families with children, 73
London attractions, 205
suggested itinerary, 97–99
Farmhouses, 84–85
Farm Stay UK, 85
Fashion Museum (Bath), 383–384
Fat Cat (Norwich), 558
Fenton House (London), 200
Fenwick of Bond Street (London), 210
Fighting Cock (Bradford), 667
Films, 40–41
First Out Café Bar (London), 227
Fishbourne Roman Palace, 310
Fishing, 77–78
Durham, 684
Mousehole, 448
Fitzrovia (London), 106
Fitzwilliam Museum (Cambridge), 533
Five Bells (Cambridge), 535

Flamborough Head, 675–676
Flatford Mill (Dedham), 549
Flea market
Abergavenny, 706
Brighton, 321
Exeter, 409
Fleet Street (London), 108
Fleur-de-Lys (Cambridge), 535
Floris (London), 212
Flying Wheels Travel, 72
Food and cuisine, 43–47
Forthlin Road, No. 20 (Liverpool), 609
Fortnum & Mason (London), 210
Fortune of War (Brighton), 322
Fountains Abbey & Studley Royal, 670
Fox Talbot Museum (Lacock), 386
Framework (Brighton), 321
Framlingham Castle (near Woodbridge), 552
Frank Green's (Liverpool), 610
Franklin, Benjamin, House (London), 186
Freedom of Wales Flexi Pass, 64
Freshwater Bay (Isle of Wight), 350
Freud Museum (London), 200
Freud (Oxford), 266

G

Gabriel's Wharf (London), 212
Gainsborough, Thomas, 31, 430
House (Sudbury), 543
Gallico, Paul, 19
Gardens
Acorn Bank Garden & Watermill (near Penrith), 647–648
best, 8–9
Botanic Garden (Oxford), 265
Chawton Cottage (Winchester), 335
Cliveden, 245
Culpepper Garden (Leeds Castle), 301
Dyffryn Gardens (Cardiff), 702
Groombridge Place Gardens, 302
Harewood House & Bird Garden, 671
Hever Castle & Gardens, 302–303
Jubilee Gardens (Windsor), 238–239
Kensington Gardens (London), 178, 198
Levens Hall (Kendal), 625
London, 172
Lost Gardens of Heligan, 438

National Botanic Garden of Wales (Llanarthne), 721
Painswick Rococo Garden, 467
Pavilion Gardens (Buxton), 570
Royal Botanic Gardens, Kew, 202
Sissinghurst Castle Garden, 304
Studley Royal (Fountains), 670
suggested itinerary, 99–101
Trengwainton Garden, 441
Valley Gardens (Windsor), 241
Wisley Garden, 307
Gasoline (petrol), 61, 755
Gas Street Basin (Birmingham), 509
Gateway Antiques (Burford), 475
Gatwick Airport (London), 103
Gatwick Express, 103
Gay.com Travel, 71
Gays and lesbians, 71
Brighton, 322–323
Cardiff, 706
Leeds, 665
Liverpool, 611–612
Manchester, 600
Gay's the Word, 71
Gay Village (Manchester), 600
G-Bar (Liverpool), 612
G. David (Cambridge), 534
George (London), 232
Gerrards Cross, 245
Ghost tours, Oxford, 261
Giant's Grave (Parc le Breos), 720
Gilbert Collection (London), 180
Gladstone Pottery Museum (Longton), 518
Glastonbury Abbey, 395–397
Glebe Farm (Mary Arden's House), 494–495
Globe Inn (Chagford), 412–413
Globus & Cosmos Tours, 81
Glyndebourne Festival Opera, 50, 327–328
Glynn Vivian Art Gallery (Swansea), 718
Golden Cross (Oxford), 264
Golden Mile (Leicester), 564
Golden Rule (Ambleside), 634
Golf, 78
Aldeburgh, 552
Bournemouth, 358
Leeds Castle, 301
St. Albans, 273–274
Whitby, 681
Golf International, 78
Gondola **(yacht), 638**
Goodwood Motor Circuit (near Chichester), 309–310